Nineteenth-Century Literature Criticism

Topics Volume

Guide to Gale Literary Criticism Series

For criticism on	Consult these Gale series
Authors now living or who died after December 31, 1959	*CONTEMPORARY LITERARY CRITICISM (CLC)*
Authors who died between 1900 and 1959	*TWENTIETH-CENTURY LITERARY CRITICISM (TCLC)*
Authors who died between 1800 and 1899	*NINETEENTH-CENTURY LITERATURE CRITICISM (NCLC)*
Authors who died between 1400 and 1799	*LITERATURE CRITICISM FROM 1400 TO 1800 (LC)* *SHAKESPEAREAN CRITICISM (SC)*
Authors who died before 1400	*CLASSICAL AND MEDIEVAL LITERATURE CRITICISM (CMLC)*
Black writers of the past two hundred years	*BLACK LITERATURE CRITICISM (BLC)*
Authors of books for children and young adults	*CHILDREN'S LITERATURE REVIEW (CLR)*
Dramatists	*DRAMA CRITICISM (DC)*
Hispanic writers of the late nineteenth and twentieth centuries	*HISPANIC LITERATURE CRITICISM (HLC)*
Native North American writers and orators of the eighteenth, nineteenth, and twentieth centuries	*NATIVE NORTH AMERICAN LITERATURE (NNAL)*
Poets	*POETRY CRITICISM (PC)*
Short story writers	*SHORT STORY CRITICISM (SSC)*
Major authors from the Renaissance to the present	*WORLD LITERATURE CRITICISM, 1500 TO THE PRESENT (WLC)*

ISSN 0732-1864

Volume 52

Nineteenth-Century Literature Criticism

Topics Volume

Excerpts from Criticism of Various
Topics in Nineteenth-Century Literature,
including Literary and Critical Movements,
Prominent Themes and Genres, Anniversary
Celebrations, and Surveys of National Literatures

James E. Person, Jr.
Editor

Catherine C. Dominic
Denise Kasinec
Marie Lazzari
Mary L. Onorato
Contributing Editors

GALE

an International Thomson Publishing company I(T)P®

STAFF

James E. Person, Jr., *Editor*

Catherine C. Dominic, Denise Kasinec, Jelena O. Krstović, Marie Lazzari,
and Mary L. Onorato, *Contributing Editors*

Gerald R. Barterian and Ondine Le Blanc, *Assistant Editors*

Susan M. Trosky, *Managing Editor*

Marlene Hurst, *Permissions Manager*
Margaret A. Chamberlain and Maria L. Franklin, *Permissions Specialists*
Susan Brohman, Diane Cooper, Michele Lonoconus, Maureen Puhl, Shalice Shah,
Kimberly F. Smilay, and Barbara A. Wallace, *Permissions Associates*
Sarah Chesney, Edna Hedblad, Margaret McAvoy-Amato, Tyra A. Phillips,
Lori Schoenenberger, and Rita C. Velázquez, *Permissions Assistants*

Victoria B. Cariappa, *Research Manager*
Mary Beth McElmeel, Tamara C. Nott, Michele P. Pica,
and Tracie A. Richardson, *Research Associates*
Alicia Noel Biggers, Julia C. Daniel, and Michelle Lee, *Research Assistants*

Mary Beth Trimper, *Production Director*
Deborah L. Milliken, *Production Assistant*

Sherrell Hobbs, *Macintosh Artist*
Randy Bassett, *Image Database Supervisor*
Robert Duncan, *Imaging Specialist*
Pamela A. Hayes, *Photography Coordinator*

∞™ This book is printed on acid-free paper that meets the minimum requirements of American National Standard for Information Sciences—Permanence Paper for Printed Library Materials, ANSI Z39.48-1984.

Library of Congress Catalog Card Number 84-643008
ISBN 0-8103-9298-4
ISSN 0732-1864
Printed in the United States of America

I(T)P™ Gale Research, an International Thomson Publishing Company.
ITP logo is a trademark under license.

10 9 8 7 6 5 4 3 2 1

Contents

Polish Romanticism

Preface

Since its inception in 1981, *Nineteenth-Century Literature Criticism* has been a valuable resource for students and librarians seeking critical commentary on writers of this transitional period in world history. Designated an "Outstanding Reference Source" by the American Library Association with the publication of its first volume, *NCLC* has since been purchased by over 6,000 school, public, and university libraries. The series has covered more than 300 authors representing 26 nationalities and over 15,000 titles. No other reference source has surveyed the critical reaction to nineteenth-century authors and literature as thoroughly as *NCLC*.

Scope of the Series

NCLC is designed to introduce students and advanced readers to the authors of the nineteenth century, and to the most significant interpretations of these authors' works. The great poets, novelists, short story writers, playwrights, and philosophers of this period are frequently studied in high school and college literature courses. By organizing and reprinting commentary written on these authors, *NCLC* helps students develop valuable insight into literary history, promotes a better understanding of the texts, and sparks ideas for papers and assignments. Each entry in *NCLC* presents a comprehensive survey of an author's career or an individual work of literature and provides the user with a multiplicity of interpretations and assessments. Such variety allows students to pursue their own interests; furthermore, it fosters an awareness that literature is dynamic and responsive to many different opinions.

Every fourth volume of *NCLC* is devoted to literary topics that cannot be covered under the author approach used in the rest of the series. Such topics include literary movements, prominent themes in nineteenth-century literature, literary reaction to political and historical events, significant eras in literary history, prominent literary anniversaries, and the literatures of cultures that are often overlooked by English-speaking readers.

NCLC continues the survey of criticism of world literature begun by Gale's *Contemporary Literary Criticism (CLC)* and *Twentieth-Century Literary Criticism (TCLC)*, both of which excerpt and reprint commentary on authors of the twentieth century. For additional information about *TCLC*, *CLC*, and Gale's other criticism series, users should consult the Guide to Gale Literary Criticism Series preceding the title page in this volume.

Coverage

Each volume of *NCLC* is carefully compiled to present:

- criticism of authors, or literary topics, representing a variety of genres and nationalities
- both major and lesser-known writers and literary works of the period
- 6-10 authors or 4-6 topics per volume
- individual entries that survey critical response to an author's work or a topic in literary history, including early criticism to reflect initial reactions, later criticism to represent any rise or decline in reputation, and current retrospective analyses.

Organization

An author entry consists of the following elements: author heading, biographical and critical introduction, list of principal works, excerpts of criticism (each preceded by a bibliographic citation and an annotation), and a bibliography of further reading.

- The **Author Heading** consists of the name under which the author most commonly wrote, followed by birth and death dates. If an author wrote consistently under a pseudonym, the pseudonym will be listed in the author heading and the real name given in parentheses on the first line of the biographical and critical introduction. Also located at the beginning of the introduction to the author entry are any name variations under which an author wrote, including transliterated forms for an author whose language uses a nonroman alphabet.

- The **Biographical and Critical Introduction** outlines the author's life and career, as well as the critical issues surrounding his or her work. References are provided to past volumes of *NCLC* in which further information about the author may be found.

- Most *NCLC* entries include a **Portrait** of the author. Many entries also contain reproductions of materials pertinent to an author's career, including manuscript pages, title pages, dust jackets, letters, and drawings, as well as photographs of important people, places, and events in an author's life.

- The list of **Principal Works** is chronological by date of first publication and identifies the genre of each work. In the case of foreign authors with both foreign-language publications and English translations, the English-language version is given in brackets. Unless otherwise indicated, dramas are dated by first performance, not first publication.

- **Criticism** in each author entry is arranged chronologically to provide a perspective on changes in critical evaluation over the years. All titles of works by the author featured in the entry are printed in boldface type to enable the user to easily locate discussion of particular works. Also for purposes of easier identification, the critic's name and the publication date of the essay are given at the beginning of each piece of criticism. Unsigned criticism is preceded by the title of the journal in which it appeared. Publication information (such as publisher names and book prices) and parenthetical numerical references (such as footnotes or page and line references to specific editions of works) have been deleted at the editors' discretion to provide smoother reading of the text.

- A complete **Bibliographic Citation** designed to facilitate location of the original essay or book precedes each piece of criticism.

- Critical excerpts are prefaced by **Annotations** providing the reader with information about both the critic and the criticism that follows. Included are the critic's reputation, individual approach to literary criticism, and particular expertise in an author's works. Also noted are the relative importance of a work of criticism, the scope of the excerpt, and the growth of critical controversy or changes in critical trends regarding an author. In some cases, these annotations cross-reference excerpts by critics who discuss each other's commentary.

- An annotated list of **Further Reading** appearing at the end of each entry suggests secondary sources on the author. In some cases it includes essays for which the editors could not obtain reprint rights.

Cumulative Indexes

■ Each volume of *NCLC* contains a cumulative **Author Index** listing all authors who have appeared in Gale's Literary Criticism Series, along with cross-references to such biographical series as *Contemporary Authors* and *Dictionary of Literary Biography*. Useful for locating authors within the various series, this index is particularly valuable for those authors who are identified with a certain period but who, because of their death dates, are placed in another, or for those authors whose careers span two periods. For example, Fyodor Dostoevsky is found in *NCLC*, yet Leo Tolstoy, another major nineteenth-century Russian novelist, is found in *TCLC* because he died after 1899.

■ Each *NCLC* volume includes a cumulative **Nationality Index** which lists all authors who have appeared in *NCLC*, arranged alphabetically under their respective nationalities.

■ Each new volume in Gale's Literary Criticism Series includes a cumulative **Topic Index**, which lists all literary topics treated in *NCLC, TCLC, LC 1400-1800*, and the *CLC* Yearbook.

■ Each new volume of *NCLC*, with the exception of the Topics volumes, contains a **Title Index** listing the titles of all literary works discussed in the volume. In response to numerous suggestions from librarians, Gale has also produced a **Special Paperbound Edition** of the *NCLC* title index. This annual cumulation lists all titles discussed in the series since its inception. Additional copies of the index are available on request. Librarians and patrons have welcomed this separate index: it saves shelf space, is easy to use, and is recyclable upon receipt of the following year's cumulation. Titles discussed in the Topics volume entries are not included in the *NCLC* cumulative index.

Citing *Nineteenth-Century Literature Criticism*

When writing papers, students who quote directly from any volume in Gale's Literary Criticism Series may use the following general forms to footnote reprinted criticism. The first example pertains to material drawn from periodicals, the second to material reprinted from books:

[1]T.S. Eliot, "John Donne," *The Nation and Athenaeum*, 33 (9 June 1923), 321-32; excerpted and reprinted in *Literature Criticism from 1400-1800*, Vol. 10, ed. James E. Person, Jr. (Detroit: Gale Research, 1989), pp. 28-9.

[2]Clara G. Stillman, *Samuel Butler: A Mid-Victorian Modern* (Viking Press, 1932); excerpted and reprinted in *Twentieth-Century Literary Criticism*, Vol. 33, ed. Paula Kepos (Detroit: Gale Research, 1989), pp. 43-5.

Suggestions Are Welcome

In response to suggestions, several features have been added to *NCLC* since the series began, including annotations to excerpted criticism, a cumulative index to authors in all Gale literary criticism series, entries devoted to criticism on a single work by a major author, more illustrations, and a title index listing all literary works discussed in the series.

Readers who wish to suggest authors, single works, or topics to appear in future volumes, or who have other suggestions, are cordially invited to write: The Editors, *Nineteenth-Century Literature Criticism,* 835 Penobscot Bldg., 645 Griswold St., Detroit, MI 48226-4094; call toll-free at 1-800-347-GALE; or fax to 1-313-961-6599.

Acknowledgments

The editors wish to thank the copyright holders of the excerpted criticism included in this volume and the permissions managers of many book and magazine publishing companies for assisting us in securing reprint rights. We are also grateful to the staffs of the Detroit Public Library, the Library of Congress, the University of Detroit Mercy Library, Wayne State University Purdy/Kresge Library Complex, and the University of Michigan Libraries for making their resources available to us. Following is a list of the copyright holders who have granted us permission to reprint material in this volume of *NCLC*. Every effort has been made to trace copyright, but if omissions have been made, please let us know.

COPYRIGHTED EXCERPTS IN *NCLC*, VOLUME 52, WERE REPRINTED FROM THE FOLLOWING PERIODICALS:

American Studies, v. 22, Fall, 1981 for "Wit, Sentimentality and the Image of Women in the Nineteenth Century" by Nancy Walker. Copyright © Mid-America American Studies Association, 1981. Reprinted by permission of the publisher and the author.—*Children's Literature: Annual of the Modern Language Association Seminar on Children's Literature and The Children's Literature Association*, v. 21, 1993. © 1993 by Francelia Butler. All rights reserved. Reprinted by permission of Yale University Press.—*Children's Literature Association Quarterly*, v. 8, Fall, 1983; v. 13, Winter, 1988. © 1983, 1988 Children's Literature Association. Both reprinted by permission of the publisher.—*The French Review*, v. LXV, December, 1991. Copyright 1991 by the American Association of Teachers of French. Reprinted by permission of the publisher.—*Poetics Today*, v. 13, 1992. Copyright 1992 by the Porter Institute for Poetics and Semeiotics, Tel Aviv University. Reprinted with the permission of the publisher.—*Stanford French Review*, v. XI, Fall, 1987. © 1987 by Anma Libri & Co. Reprinted by permission of the publisher and the author.

COPYRIGHTED EXCERPTS IN *NCLC*, VOLUME 52, WERE REPRINTED FROM THE FOLLOWING BOOKS:

Becker, George J. From *Master European Realists of the Nineteenth Century*. Ungar, 1982. Copyright © 1982 by Frederick Ungar Publishing Co., Inc. Reprinted by permission of the publisher.—Bernbaum, Ernest. From *Guide Through the Romantic Movement*. T. Nelson and Sons, 1930. Copyright 1930, 1949, by The Ronald Press Company. All rights reserved. Reprinted by permission of John Wiley & Sons, Inc.—Bingham, Jane and Grayce Scholt. From *Fifteen Centuries of Children's Literature: An Annotated Chronology of British and American Works in Historical Context*. Greenwood Press, 1980. Copyright © 1980 by Jane Bingham and Grayce Scholt. All rights reserved. Reprinted by permission of Greenwood Publishing Group, Inc., Westport, CT.—Carnall, Geoffrey. From *Robert Southey and His Age: The Development of a Conservative Mind*. Oxford at the Clarendon Press, 1960. © Oxford University Press 1960. Reprinted by permission of Oxford University Press.—Cox, James M. From "Humor of the Old Southwest" in *The Comic Imagination in American Literature*. Edited by Louis D. Rubin, Jr. Rutgers University Press, 1973. Reprinted by permission of the author.—Eaton, Clement. From *The Mind of the Old South*. Revised edition. Louisiana State University Press, 1967. Copyright © 1964, 1967 by Louisiana State University Press. All rights reserved. Reprinted by permission of the publisher.—Fairchild, Hoxie Neale. From *The Romantic Quest*. Columbia University Press, 1931. Copyright 1931 Columbia University Press, New York. Renewed, 1959, by Hoxie Neale Fairchild. All rights reserved. Reprinted with the permission of the publisher.—Feiling, Keith Grahame. From *Sketches in Nineteenth Century Biography*. Longmans, Green and Co., 1930. Reprinted by permission of the publisher.—Habegger, Alfred. From *Gender, Fantasy, and Realism in American Literature*. Columbia University Press, 1982. Copyright © 1982 by Columbia University Press. All rights reserved. Reprinted with permission of the publisher.—Hughes-Hallett, Penelope. From *The Wordsworths and the Lakes: Home at Grasmere*. Collins & Brown, 1993. Copyright © Collins & Brown Limited 1993. Reprinted by permission of the publisher.—Hürlimann, Bettina. From *Three Centuries of Children's Books in Europe*. Edited and translated by Brian W. Alderson. Oxford

University Press, London. English translation © Oxford University Press 1967. Reprinted by permission of Oxford University Press.—Jackson, Mary V. From *Engines of Instruction, Mischief, and Magic: Children's Literature in England from Its Beginning to 1839*. University of Nebraska Press, 1989. Copyright © 1989 by the University of Nebraska Press. All rights reserved. Reprinted by permission of the publisher.—Justus, James H. From "The Underheard Reader in the Writing of the Old Southwest" in *Discovering Difference: Contemporary Essays in American Culture*. Edited by Christoph K. Lohmann. Indiana University Press, 1993. © 1993 by Indiana University Press. All rights reserved. Reprinted by permission of the publisher.—Krzyżanowski, Julian. From *A History of Polish Literature*. Translated by Doris Ronowicz. PWN-Polish Scientific Publishers, 1978. Copyright © 1978 by PWN-Polish Scientific Publishers-Warszawa. Reprinted by permission of the publisher.—Lednicki, Wacław. From *Bits of Table Talk on Pushkin, Mickiewicz, Goethe, Turgenev, and Sienkiewicz.* Martinus Nijhoff, 1956. Copyright 1956 by Martinus Nijhoff, The Hague, Netherlands. All rights reserved. Reprinted by permission of Kluwer Academic Publishers.—Levin, Harry. From *The Gates of Horn: A Study of Five French Realists*. Oxford University Press, 1963. Copyright © 1963, renewed 1991, by Harry Levin. Reprinted by permission of the publisher.—Miłosz, Czesław. From *The History of Polish Literature*. Second edition. University of California Press, 1983. Copyright © 1969, 1983 by Czesław Miłosz. Reprinted by permission of the publisher.—Modiano, Raimonda. From *Coleridge and the Concept of Nature*. Macmillan Press Ltd., 1985. © Raimonda Modiano 1985. All rights reserved. Reprinted by permission of Macmillan, London and Basingstoke.—Mylne, Vivienne. From "Social Realism in the Dialogue of Eighteenth-Century French Fiction," in *Studies in Eighteenth-Century Culture, Vol. 6*. Edited by Ronald C. Rosbottom. The University of Wisconsin Press, 1977. Copyright © 1977 American Society for Eighteenth-Century Studies. All rights reserved. Reprinted by permission of the publisher.—Pattison, Robert. From *The Child Figure in English Literature*. University of Georgia Press, 1978. Copyright © 1978 by the University of Georgia Press. All rights reserved. Reprinted by permission of the publisher.—Richardson, Alan. From "Wordsworth, Fairy Tales, and the Politics of Children's Reading," in *Romanticism and Children's Literature in Nineteenth-Century England*. Edited by James Holt McGavran, Jr. University of Georgia Press, 1991. © 1991 by the University of Georgia Press. All rights reserved. Reprinted by permission of the publisher.—Scott, Malcolm. From *The Struggle for the Soul of the French Novel: French Catholic and Realist Novelists, 1850-1970*. The Catholic University of America Press, 1990. © Malcolm Scott 1990. All rights reserved. Reprinted by permission of the publisher.—Segel, Harold B. From an introduction to *Polish Romantic Drama: Three Plays in English Translation*. Edited by Harold B. Segel. Cornell, 1977. Copyright © 1977 by Cornell University. All rights reserved. Reprinted by permission of the author.—Seldes, Gilbert. From "American Humor" in *America as Americans See It*. Edited by Fred J. Ringel. Harcourt, Brace & Company, 1932. Copyright 1932, by Harcourt Brace & Company. Renewed 1963, by James Dow McCallum. Reprinted by permission of the publisher.—Steele, H. Meili. From *Realism and the Drama of Reference: Strategies of Representation in Balzac, Flaubert, and James*. Pennsylvania State University Press, 1988. Copyright © 1988, The Pennsylvania State University Press, University Park, PA. All rights reserved. Reproduced by permission of the publisher.—Tatar, Maria. From *Off With Their Heads! Fairy Tales and the Culture of Childhood*. Princeton University Press, 1992. Copyright © 1992 by Princeton University Press. All rights reserved. Reprinted by permission of the publisher.—Treugutt, Stefan. From "Byron and Napoleon in Polish Romantic Myth," in *Lord Byron and His Contemporaries: Essays from the Sixth International Byron Seminar*. Edited by Charles E. Robinson. University of Delaware Press, 1982. © 1982 by Associated University Presses, Inc. Reprinted by permission of the publisher.—White, Hayden. From "The Problem of Style in Realistic Representation: Marx and Flaubert," in *The Concept of Style*. Edited by Berel Lang. University of Pennsylvania Press, 1979. Copyright © 1979 by Berel Lang. All rights reserved. Reprinted by permission of the publisher.—Wimsatt, W. K. From *The Verbal Icon: Studies in the Meaning of Poetry*. University of Kentucky Press, 1954. Copyright renewed 1982 by Margaret H. Wimsatt. Reprinted by permission of the University Press of Kentucky.—Zipes, Jack. From *The Complete Fairy Tales of the Brothers Grimm*. Translated by Jack Zipes. Bantam Books, 1987. Translation copyright © 1987 by Jack Zipes. All rights reserved. Used by permission of Bantam Books, a division of Bantam Doubleday Dell Publishing Group, Inc.

PHOTOGRAPHS APPEARING IN *NCLC*, VOLUME 52, WERE RECEIVED FROM THE FOLLOWING SOURCES:

Clemens, Samuel, portrait of. The Bettmann Archive. **p. 4.**

American Humor Writing

INTRODUCTION

Throughout the nineteenth century, the pages of American periodicals brimmed with humorous sketches and tall tales describing life—especially frontier or country life—in the young nation. Innumerable authors, many writing under pseudonyms, contributed to this phenomenon, the most successful frequently collecting their pieces in books and becoming national celebrities. Literary critics, however, have paid only scant attention to this part of American literary history, often relegating all but the best known and most sophisticated of the works to obscurity. In the 1930s, a few critics—particularly Constance Rourke and Walter Blair—began to argue for the importance of the lowbrow humor. Since then, the genre has received considerably more serious attention from scholars.

Almost unanimously, critics have claimed humor writing as vital to the developing nation's sense of cultural identity. Throughout the eighteenth and nineteenth centuries, in all spheres of intellectual life, colonial and post-revolutionary American writers encountered the charge—coming largely from London—that nothing "original" existed in American culture. According to this perspective, everything American philosophers, poets, and novelists produced must be second-rate imitations of European culture, since the writers were all trained in the European tradition. In the seventeenth and eighteenth centuries, England had dominated the production of wit—a specific branch of humor—in the English language, due largely to essayists such as Sir Richard Steele and Joseph Addison, who published two satirical periodicals, *The Tatler* (1709-1711) and the *Spectator* (1711-1712). In the nineteenth century, however, England's monopoly faded, giving way to the Americans who, by-and-large, abandoned the sophistication of British wit in favor of regionalism. Consequently, scholars of American literature have argued that humor writing, with its focus on the wholly American phenomena of "Yankee" New England, the "backwoods," and the Western frontier, may have been the embryo of a truly original national literature.

Critics generally attribute the first humor writing of the century to Washington Irving, who published *History of New York . . . by Diedrich Knickerbocker* and *The Sketch Book* in 1809 and 1820, respectively. Both books present their readers with exaggerated portraits of individuals bred in the immigrant mix of the colonial Northeast, and the later volume became an essential part of American folk culture as it includes "The Legend of Sleepy Hollow" and "Rip Van Winkle." The men and women who came after Irving filled newspapers and journals with their tales and sketches, introducing readers to the "Down-Easter" (or "Yankee"), the frontiersman, and other uniquely American characters. Humor writing became one of the most popular genres of the century, turning many of its creators into national celebrities and its stock characters into heroes. Consequently, even as American readers laughed at the foibles of Sut Lovingood, from George Washington Harris's *Sut Lovingood's Yarns* (1867), or the Widow Bedott, from Frances Whicher's *Widow Bedott Papers* (1852), they also developed a sense of pride over the beginnings of *American* literature. The epitome of this trajectory was Samuel Clemens—or Mark Twain—who published the *Adventures of Huckleberry Finn* in 1884.

While early critics of the genre, such as Rourke and Blair, praised the humorists for initiating this revolution in American literature, more recent critics have begun to question just how progressive much of the writing was. James Justus, for example, has argued that Southern humor belittled poor farmers and backwoodsmen for the benefit, usually, of an upper-class audience. Such debates focus particularly on the period before the Civil War, when political and economic disagreements drove the Southern states to define themselves apart from the Union in general. As the democratic politics ushered in by Andrew Jackson in the 1830s pushed for a less stratified class system, many of the Southern writers used their pens to resist. As the critical debates demonstrate, however, the conflict was more complicated than that: while Southern writers sought to preserve their culture against the apparently levelling energies of the national capitol, the movement towards secession also produced a rebellious mindset that celebrated the common man. As the Civil War and then reconstruction wrought havoc in the latter half of the century, the process only intensified.

Much critical discussion also notes that humor writing had to define itself in relation to the nineteenth-century sentimental novel, which dominated the popular book market in both England and America. Since sentimental fiction was equated with feminine virtues and opposed to base humor, humorists often presented themselves as an antidote to too much sentiment. Although female novelists produced a good deal of this fare, other female writers, many recently unearthed by feminist scholars, made it their work to satirize sentimental stereotypes of feminine virtue. Ultimately, the feminist discussion about female character in the nineteenth century pinpoints a central discussion among scholars about the era: while critics have traditionally memorialized the nineteenth century as ruled by sentiment and modesty, the study of humor writing and its tremendous popularity contributes to an understanding of the age's true complexity.

REPRESENTATIVE WORKS

Joseph G. Baldwin
   Flush Times in Alabama and Mississippi 1853
Charles Farrar Browne
   Artemus Ward; His Book 1862
Samuel L. Clemens (Mark Twain)
   *The Celebrated Jumping Frog of Calaveras
      County and Other Sketches* 1867
   The Innocents Abroad 1869
   The Gilded Age (with Charles Dudley Warner)
      1874
   Adventures of Huckleberry Finn 1884
   A Connecticut Yankee in King Arthur's Court
      1889
David Crockett
   A Narrative of the Life of David Crockett 1834
George Washington Harris
   Sut Lovingood's Yarns 1867
Bret Harte
   *The Luck of Roaring Camp and Other Sketch
      es* 1870
Marietta Holley
   My Opinions and Betsey Bobbet's 1873
Johnson James Hooper
   Some Adventures of Captain Simon Suggs 1845
Washington Irving
   *History of New York . . . by Diedrich Knick
      erbocker* 1809
   The Sketch Book 1820
Melville D. Landon (Eli Perkins)
   Eli Perkins at Large. His Sayins and Doings
      1875
Henry Clay Lewis (Madison Tensas)
   *Odd Leaves from the Life of a Louisiana
      Swamp Doctor* 1846
David Ross Locke
   *The Struggles (Social, Financial and Politi
      cal) of Petroleum Vesuvius Nasby* 1872
Augustus Baldwin Longstreet
   Georgia Scenes 1835
Edgar W. Nye (Bill Nye)
   Baled Hay 1884
Sara Willis Parton (Fanny Fern)
   Fern Leaves from Fanny's Portfolio 1853

George W. Peck
   Peck's Bad Boy and His Pa
William Trotter Porter (editor)
   The Big Bear of Arkansas and Other Sketches
      1845
John S. Robb
   Streaks from Squatter Life 1846
B. P. Shillabar
   Life and Sayins of Mrs. Partington 1854
Charles Henry Smith
   Bill Arp, So-Called 1866
Seba Smith
   The Life and Writings of Major Jack Downing
      1833
William Tappan Thompson
   Major Jones's Courtship 1843
Frances M. Whicher (also spelled Whitcher)
   Widow Bedott Papers 1852

OVERVIEWS

The London and Westminster Review

SOURCE: "Yankeeana: Slick, Crockett, Downing, Etc.," in *The London and Westminster Review*, Vol. XXXII, No. 1, December, 1838, pp. 136-45.

[*In the following excerpt from a review of several volumes of American humor writing, a commentator from* The London and Westminster Review *makes the claim that the United States has begun to create a literature of its own.*]

These books show that American literature has ceased to be exclusively imitative. A few writers have appeared in the United States, who, instead of being European and English in their styles of thought and diction, are American—who, therefore, produce original sounds instead of far-off echoes,—fresh and vigorous pictures instead of comparatively idealess copies. A portion of American literature has become national and original, and, naturally enough, this portion of it is that which in all countries is always most national and original—because made more than any other by the collective mind of the nation—the humorous.

We have many things to say on national humour, very few of which we can say on the present occasion. But two or three words we must pass on the heresies which abound in the present state of critical opinion on the subject of national humour: we say *critical*, and not *public*, opinion, for, thank God, the former has very little to do with the latter.

"Lord Byron,"—says William Hazlitt, in a very agreeable and suggestive volume of *Sketches and Essays*, now first collected by his son,—"was in the habit of railing at the spirit of our good old comedy, and of abusing Shakspeare's Clowns and Fools, which, he said, the refinement of the French and Italian stage would not endure, and which only our grossness and puerile taste could tolerate. In this I agree with him; and it is *pat* to my purpose. I flatter myself that we are almost the only people who understand and relish *nonsense.*" This is the excuse for the humour of Shakspeare, his rich and genuine English humour!

In Lord Byron the taste which the above opinion expresses is easily accounted for; it was the consequences of his having early formed himself according to the Pope and Gifford school, which was the dominant one among the Cambridge students of his time. Scottish highland scenery, and European travel, aided by the influences of the revival of a more vigorous and natural taste in the public, made his poems much better than the taste of the narrow school to which he belonged could ever have made them; but above the dicta of this school his critical judgment never rose. We thought the matter more inexplicable as regards William Hazlitt, a man superior to Byron in force and acuteness of understanding—until we found the following declaration of his views:—"In fact, I am very much of the opinion of that old Scotch gentleman who owned that 'he preferred the dullest book he had ever read to the most brilliant conversation it had ever been his lot to hear.'" A man to whom the study of books was so much and the study of men so little as this, could not possibly understand the humour of Shakspeare's Clowns and Fools, or national humour of any sort. The characters of a *Trinculo,* a *Bardolph,* a *Quickly,* or a *Silence,* are matters beyond him. That man was never born whose genuine talk, let it be as dull as it may, and whose character, if studied aright, is not pregnant with thoughts, deep and immortal thoughts, enough to fill many books. A man is a volume stored all over with thoughts and meanings, as deep and great as God. A book, even when it contains the "life's blood of an immortal spirit," still is not an immortal spirit, nor a God-created form. Wofully fast will be his growth in ignorance who prefers reading books to reading men. But the time-honoured critical journals have critics—

"The earth hath bubbles as the waters hath"—

and William Hazlitt, with his eloquent vehemence, was one of the best of them.

The public have of late, by the appreciation of the genuine English humour of Mr Dickens, shown that the days when the refinement which revises Shakespeare and ascribes the toleration of his humour to grossness and puerility of taste, or a relish for nonsense, have long gone by. The next good sign is the appreciation of the humour of the Americans, in all its peculiar and unmitigated nationality. Humour is national

when it is impregnated with the convictions, customs, and associations of a nation. What these, in the case of America, are, we thus indicated in a former number:— "The Americans are a democratic people; a people without poor; without rich; with a 'far-west' behind them; so situated as to be in no danger of aggression from without; sprung mostly from the Puritans; speaking the language of a foreign country; with no established church; with no endowments for the support of a learned class; with boundless facilities for 'raising themselves in the world;' and where a large family is a fortune. They are Englishmen who are all well off; who never were conquered; who never had feudalism on their soil; and who, instead of having the manners of society determined by a Royal court in all essentials imitative to the present hour of that of Louis the Fourteenth of France, had them formed, more or less, by the stern influences of Puritanism."

National American humour must be all this transformed into shapes which produce laughter. The humour of a people is their institutions, laws, customs, manners, habits, characters, convictions,—their scenery, whether of the sea, the city, or the hills,—expressed in the language of the ludicrous, uttering themselves in the tones of genuine and heartfelt mirth. Democracy and the 'far-west' made Colonel Crockett: he is a product of forests, freedom, universal suffrage, and bear-hunts. The Puritans and the American revolution, joined to the influence of the soil and the social manners of the time, have all contributed to the production of the character of Sam Slick. The institutions and scenery, the convictions and the habits of a people, become enwrought into their thoughts, and of course their merry as well as their serious thoughts. In America, at present, accidents of steamboats are extremely common, and have therefore a place in the mind of every American. Hence we are told that, when asked whether he was seriously injured by the explosion of the boiler of the St Leonard steamer, Major N. replied that he was so used to be blown-up by his wife that a mere steamer had no effect upon him. In another instance laughter is produced out of the very cataracts which form so noble a feature in American scenery. The Captain of a Kentucky steam-boat praises his vessel thus:—"She trots off like a horse—all boiler—full pressure—its hard work to hold her in at the wharfs and landings. *I could run her up a cataract.* She draws eight inches of water—goes at three knots a minute—and jumps all the snags and sand-banks." The Falls of Niagara themselves become redolent with humour.

> Sam Patch was a great diver, and the last dive he took was off the Falls of Niagara, and he was never heard of agin till t'other day, when Captain Enoch Wentworth, of the Susy Ann whaler, saw him in the South Sea. 'Why,' says Captain Enoch to him— 'why, Sam,' says he, 'how *on airth* did you get here, I thought you was drowned at the Canadian

Mark Twain

lines.'—'Why,' says Sam, 'I didn't get *on earth* here at all, but I came slap *through* it. In that are Niagara dive I went so everlasting deep, I thought it was just as short to come up t'other side, so out I came on these parts. If I don't take the shine off the sea-serpent, when I get back to Boston, then my name's not Sam Patch.'

The curiosity of the public regarding the peculiar nature of American humour seems to have been very easily satisfied with the application of the all-sufficing word exaggeration. We have, in a former number, sufficiently disposed of exaggeration, as an explanation of the ludicrous. Extravagance is a characteristic of American humour, though very far from being a peculiarity of it; and, when a New York paper, speaking of hot weather, says:—"We must go somewhere—we are dissolving daily—so are our neighbours.—It was rumoured yesterday that three large ridges of fat, found on the side-walk in Wall street, were caused by Thad. Phelps, Harry Ward, and Tom Van Pine, passing that way a short time before":—the humour does not consist in the exaggeration that the heat is actually dissolving people daily—a common-place at which no one would laugh—but in the representation of these respectable citizens as producing ridges of fat. It is humour, and not wit, on account of the infusion of

character and locality into it. The man who put his umbrella into bed and himself stood up in the corner, and the man who was so tall that he required to go up a ladder to shave himself, with all their brethren, are not humorous and ludicrous because their peculiarities are exaggerated, but because the umbrella and the man change places, and because a man by reason of his tallness is supposed too short to reach himself.

The cause of laughter is the ascription to objects of qualities or the representations of objects or persons with qualities the opposite of their own:—Humour is this ascription or representation when impregnated with character, whether individual or national. . . .

Henry Clay Lukens names the different "types" who populate American humor writing:

Cloud and wind wise skippers, dogmatic Solons of the quarter-deck, storm-beaten forecastle veterans, the transplanted Yankee, rough Ohio and Mississippi river boatmen, veritable loud-voiced Hoosiers, the untutored jovial frontiersman, the prairie scout, forest-hardened, weather-seamed mountaineers, the sun-basking negro, quaint and indolent pine-landers and degraded swamp-dwellers, have all supplied our literary comedians with unique characters. Requisition has been made on man and his beast, on the farm, the cross-roads tavern, the clearing, the Southern plantation, the logging camp, the backwoods settlement, the gold diggings, and even the Indian trail, for the types of animal creation, brute or human, that might surprise and amuse. In almost everything that lives and moves and has its outing, clownishness, merry sport, or latent fun is detected. The over-dressed, Thursday afternoon servant-girl on promenade, or her imminent sister, the kerosene lighter, is no longer mirth's exclusive target. In large American towns and cities newly arrived Germans, Irish, Chinamen, Italians, Turks, or Swedes take their turn (before ridicule's merciless quizzing-glass) with the travelled cockney, the "heavy swell," the painfully attired "dude," the incurable Anglomaniac, the shamelessly pilloried mother-in-law, the tailor-made girl, the snail-paced messenger-boy, and the erstwhile drowsy, now (*arrectis auribus*) sudden-heeled, emphatic, and devastating Georgia mule.

Sitting high-perched on the shoulders of eccentricity, caricature gibes at our social fabric, and finds elements of ribaldry in each layer thereof. It is far easier to scoff than to improve; much pleasanter to laugh than to be laughed at. The American paragraphic satirist is abroad in the land. His name is Swarm; his methods and merit debatable. While in squib or anecdote he is "short, sharp, and decisive," he is, nevertheless (and too often), thoughtless, abrupt, offensive, and cruel.

Henry Clay Lukens, "American Literary Comedians," Harper's New Monthly, April, 1890.

Walter Blair

SOURCE: "The Popularity of Nineteenth-Century American Humorists," in *Essays on American Humor: Blair Through the Ages,* edited by Hamlin Hill, The University of Wisconsin Press, 1993, pp. 25-39.

[*Blair is recognized as a prominent literary critic and has been identified by Hamlin Hill as "the foremost critic and analyst" of American humor writing. In this excerpt, which originally appeared in the May, 1931, issue of* American Literature, *Blair provides a comprehensive view of the genre as well as the argument that humor writing advanced the development of American literature.*]

Just how popular were the writers of American humor in the years of the last century during which they were most active (c. 1830-c. 1896)? The question seems worth considering for at least three reasons. An answer will reveal just how true is the impression, fostered by hostile critics of the period, that the great reading public existed on a diet of nothing much except the sugary fare offered by ladies' books and popular romances. Further, an answer will, perhaps, help one understand why *Innocents Abroad* [1869] found thirty-one thousand buyers within six months of its appearance and thus launched Mark Twain's remarkable career. And finally, if—as historians have recently held—American humorists were important as predecessors of the realists, data on this subject of popularity will indicate to some extent how these heralds managed to make themselves heard. For these reasons, I have attempted to discover and record some of the facts which show how the nineteenth-century literary comedians recruited an audience.

Several factors, apparently, were important in giving American humor the prominence which it achieved. An early and lasting stimulus to a wide interest in native comic creations, it is probable, was the stage presentation by many actors of humorous American characters. When *The Contrast* was performed in 1787, the stage Yankee, Jonathan, stumbled into the theater for the first time, spouting slang, parading his rustic foibles. The play was a pronounced success, and as a natural result of its popularity, dozens of other dramas portraying similarly vulgar characters followed. Not only the Yankee but also other figures important in the new humor of America were portrayed. Ralph Stackpole, frontiersman in *Nick of the Woods,* was a successful stage figure. Davy Crockett, comedian of the canebrakes, Colonel Nimrod Wildfire, and other frontiersmen pleased audiences in New York and the provinces. Minstrel troupes offered boisterous blackface jokers who used typical American humor, including some of the jests of Artemus Ward. One play, *Eli among the Cowboys,* pictured Eli Perkins captured by plainsmen during a lecture tour in Wyoming. At least two newspaper paragraphers, J. Amroy Knox and Charles H. Hoyt, became playwrights whose dramas were successful. Thus, throughout the period, humor of the salty native type found its way to the stage.

Actors made reputations as portrayers of Yankees or kindred types. Ludlow, dressed in the picturesque costume of a Western boatman, roared out the words of "The Hunters of Kentucky" while rough audiences in showhouses along the Ohio and Mississippi applauded with "a prolonged whoop, or howl. . . ." J. H. Hackett was Nimrod Wildfire, Jonathan Ploughboy, and Solon Shingle. Yankee Hill won fame in England as well as America by portraying Yankee types. Joseph Jefferson was applauded as he played the role of Asa Trenchard. Chanfrau triumphed as Mose, the tough fireboy, and John T. Raymond as Mark Twain's Colonel Mulberry Sellers in *The Gilded Age* [1874]. Some actors, in addition to playing character parts, offered monologues—Dr. W. Valentine, Sol Smith, Sol Smith Russell, and Yankee Hill. These monologues, composed by the actors or perhaps in some cases by humorists, augmented the flood of humorous books, in which monologues were often an important feature. And when J. H. Hackett went to the *New York Leader* as a journalist, writing lines similar to those which he spoke on the stage, he gave printed humor an impetus his stage career had made possible.

Thus to the theater audiences of the period the new humor became familiar. An even vaster audience, the group interested in politics, found much material in native comic writings to interest it. As Joel Chandler Harris said [in *The World's Wit and Humor*]:

> First and last, humor has played a very large part in our political campaigns; in fact, it may be said that it has played almost as large a part as principle—which is the name that politicians gave to their theories. It is a fact that . . . the happy allusion, the humorous anecdote . . . will change the whole prospects of a political struggle.

A large part of the humor between 1830 and the end of the century dealt with political themes. Major Jack Downing, from the start of his literary career, and the imitators of Jack Downing as well, constantly commented shrewdly upon political struggles. Davy Crockett, with whom Downing carried on some correspondence, was apparently exploited as a political figure; and his writings were necessarily tied up with current contests. The story of Simon Suggs was written in the guise of a campaign biography, and *Major Jones's Travels* and Bagby's *Letters of Mozis Addums* contain political comments. W. P. Trent notes [in the November 1901 issue of *Century*] the preoccupation of humorists with politics:

Lowell being put to one side, there are at least five political humorists of importance belonging to the eventful years 1830-70 . . . Seba Smith, Charles Augustus Davis (1795-1867), Robert Henry Newell (1836-1901), the "Orpheus C. Kerr" whose letters gave Lincoln needed relaxation . . . , Charles Henry Smith ("Bill Arp," born in 1826), and David R. Locke [Petroleum V. Nasby]. To these one is almost tempted to add Richard Grant White, whose *New Gospel of Peace* . . . [was] a clever and very popular parody of the style of the historical books of the Old Testament.

To the list also may be added Artemus Ward, whose political writings were, if not numerous, telling.

During the years when several of these political humorists were active, one of America's outstanding political figures did much to focus attention on contemporary humorous works. Lincoln, as Professor Pattee [*A History of American Literature Since 1870*] has pointed out, "stood in the limelight of the Presidency, transacting the nation's business with anecdotes from the frontier circuits, meeting hostile critics with shrewd border philosophy, and reading aloud with unction, while battles were raging or election returns were in doubt, from 'Artemus Ward,' or 'Petroleum Vesuvius Nasby,' or *The Flush Times of Alabama and Mississippi*—favorites of his because they too were genuine, excerpts not from books but from life itself."

Furthermore, there were few important comic journals which did not battle valiantly in the field of politics. The pages of *John Donkey* (1848), *Vanity Fair* (1859-63), *Puck* (1877-1907), and *Judge* (1888-) were full of political cartoons and satires. Newspaper comic men constantly carried on political conflicts in the period after the war as before the war: David Ross Locke, George W. Peck, Marcus M. "Brick" Pomeroy of the *LaCrosse Democrat,* James M. Bailey, Robert J. Burdette, and Eli Perkins. It was not a mere accident that one of the most vicious fictional attacks upon industrial control in politics was made by a humorist, Mark Twain, in *The Gilded Age.* The tradition of the use of political material for humorous purposes was extended through the whole period down to the jestings of Mr. Dooley and Will Rogers about statesmen and demagogues. The nation always has been interested in frank and amusing comments upon political events.

The newspapers were active in carrying this humorous material into every part of the nation. Not long after 1830, every paper that could discover a comic writer on its staff was encouraging him to provide amusement for its readers. A few comments indicate how the practice of publishing humor grew. In 1847, *Yankee Doodle* said:

After the perusal of our exchanges we could not but conclude that the demand for wit has increased of late to an alarming extent throughout the press of the country, and that as usual the supply has been equal to the demand. The whole editorial corps must have deadly designs upon the community which they propose to accomplish by making it "laugh itself to death" collectively.

In 1866, the *North American Review* remarked, with mock concern:

Our own Boston Daily Advertiser—a bulwark of resistance against needless and unauthorized innovations, a host in itself to withstand temptations of levity and trifling—has yielded so far to this demand [for humorous columns in the newspaper] that, though not yet a professedly comic paper, it has introduced a series of general paragraphs of a nature light and humorous enough to make the old issues turn in their very files for amazement. Far and wide, daily, weekly, and monthly publications issue from the press to face us with at least one feature smiling.

Six years later, a historian of American journalism [Frederick Hudson, *Journalism in the United States from 1690-1872*] said:

Our four or five thousand daily and weekly publications have columns of 'Nuts to Crack,' 'Sunbeams,' 'Sparks from the Telegraph,' 'Freshest Gleanings,' 'Odds and Ends,' 'News Sprinklings,' 'Flashes of Fun,' 'Random Readings,' 'Mere Mentions,' 'Humor of the Day,' 'Quaint Sayings,' 'Current Notes,' 'Things in General,' 'Brevities,' 'Witticisms,' 'Notes of the Day,' 'Jottings,' 'All Sorts,' 'Editor's Drawer,' 'Sparks,' 'Fun and Folly,' 'Fact and Fiction,' 'Twinklings.'

These are the daily dishes set before our sovereigns. They are the comic departments of the regular Press. We need not count the names of our wits and humorists on the ends of our fingers. . . . We are a nation full of such characters, perhaps a little thin here and there, but always in abundance and in good humor. . . . Our wit . . . goes into all the papers.

And a year later, in 1873, Edmund Clarence Stedman, one of the old school, a little frightened and somewhat disgusted, was writing to a friend: "The whole country, owing to the *contagion* of our American exchange system, is flooded, deluged, swamped, beneath a muddy tide of slang, vulgarity, inartistic bathos, impertinence and buffoonery that is not wit." He blamed John Hay and Bret Harte and particularly cited Josh Billings and "The Danbury News Man" as responsible with them for what he called "the present *horrible* degeneracy in public taste."

In 1880, when Edgar W. Nye, the last great figure of the old school, began his career, the paper which did not have a humorous column was exceptional. The *Asheville Journal, Boston Post, Oil City Derrick, Philadelphia Bulletin, Oshkosh Banner, San Francisco Post, Ouray Solid Muldoon,* and thousands of others purveyed humorous writings which were read in villages and hamlets as well as cities.

These numerous papers did not stop with the publication of the jests of their own humorists; in addition, they published material picked up from other publications. This practice was widespread, as the *Boneville Trumpet* (Bridgeport, Connecticut) pointed out at the top of a column headed "Our Grab Gag":

> everybody is informed that GOAKS found in this column never cost this establishment a cent; the Editor having adopted the *grab-game* (at present so popular with the majority of authors and editors of literary papers), not being able to pay the prices demanded for such by patentees themselves.

Giving credit sometimes, often withholding it, newspapers and periodicals all over the country passed along the best humorous sketches, anecdotes, poems, and paragraphs discovered in exchanges. And since laws allowed exchange copies to be sent without postage, and since newspapers were eager to borrow good material, exchange lists were long; each newspaper sprinkled its pages with quotations from papers of every part of the United States. I was able, with little effort, to compile a list of eighty papers which were quoted in at least two publications in 1880.

An author with a faculty for writing skits which caught the attention of editors who, scissors in hand, eagerly scanned exchanges was soon known throughout the nation. As early as 1833, at least twenty-nine and probably far more newspapers clipped and printed Seba Smith's Jack Downing letters in cities as distant from Portland, Maine, as Cincinnati, Louisville, Philadelphia, and Washington, D.C. As years passed the "contagion of our American exchange system," as Stedman called it, spread even wider. B. P. Shillaber could proudly say in his preface to *Life and Sayings of Mrs. Partington* (1854): "Mrs. Partington . . . needs no introduction. In all parts of our land, and over the sea, her name is familiar as a household word." Eli Perkins boasted that a satirical letter of 1888 was "copied into thousands of newspapers, and . . . read by 10,000,000 people within a week," and that "it brought back bushels of letters *pro* and *con* to the writer, and among them letters from so great a man as James G. Blaine and the two presidential candidates, Cleveland and Harrison."

The newspaper blessed with a witty paragrapher or amusing humorist could win national prominence. In the years before the War of the States, George D. Prentice's paragraphs, habitually copied everywhere, made the *Louisville Journal* known in every section, and when Charles G. Halpine became a humorist connected with the *New York Leader,* "the circulation of the paper increased enormously, and it became a political power." The humorist as well as the newspaper gained national prominence. In 1879, Burdette's sketch "The Brakeman at Church" was published in a paper in the little town of Burlington, Iowa. "Its popularity was immediate, and after its publication in the newspaper letter, it was republished . . . as a pamphlet, and was distributed by tens of thousands. It was copied by every newspaper of more than the slightest importance in the country . . . and few of the reading public of that generation but had an intimate knowledge of the 'Brakeman at Church.'" After a few such hits, according to the city editor of the paper, the *Burlington Hawk-Eye* "came to be read not only within the limits of Burlington and Iowa as in the past, but had its circle of readers in practically every state in the Union." While Burdette, soon known as "The Hawk-Eye Man," thus became famous, Bailey, "The Danbury News Man," built up a circulation of forty thousand for the paper employing him, though it was published in a little town in Connecticut. Other newspapers prospered. In the words of H. C. Lukens [in "American Literary Comedians"]:

> The *Danbury News* and *Detroit Free Press* became household gods that usurped the thrones of Farmers' Almanacs, and toppled them from their ivy-thatched 'high eminence'. . . . After 1876 much was heard of such special family visitors, like the *Oil City Derrick,* on which Robert Wesley Creswell . . . won his editorial, humorous spurs; of the *Burlington* (Iowa) *Hawkeye,* Robert J. Burdette's auriferous fun mine; of the Yonkers *Gazette;* Cincinnati *Breakfast Table,* long the profitable mirthy quarry of E. P. Brown; of *Peck's Sun,* a Milwaukee luminary of the *Virginia City Enterprise,* identified with "Dan De Quille" (pseudonym of W. W. Wright) and Nevada's ripples of silvered merit. . . .

Perhaps there was much logic in the belief of Frederick Hudson that one important reason why comic journals had very hard sledding lay in the fact that Americans were supplied with humor by newspapers. Yet in addition to newspapers, periodicals which published humorous materials, in spite of hardships and failures, joined other forces in lifting humor to popularity. Treating the magazines of the years between 1825 and 1850, Mr. Frank Luther Mott notes [in *A History of American Magazines, 1741-1850*]: "Humor is far more prominent in American periodical literature than it had ever been before; all except the most serious now have their 'Fun Jottings' or 'Joke Corner,' or something analogous." Lewis Gaylord Clark, the editor of the *Knickerbocker,* printed the work of Fred S. Cozzens, Charles Godfrey Leland, "Phoenix," and many another humorous writer in a comic department which, by 1853, occupied a third of the magazine. The *Southern Literary Messenger* printed the work of Joseph Glover Baldwin and George W. Bagby. *Harper's Magazine,* after 1851, in its Editor's Drawer, and *Scribner's Monthly,* after its start in 1870, used typical contemporary humor. Henry Wheeler Shaw, creator of Josh Billings, wrote humor of the type that had made him famous over the signature of Uncle Esek in the *Century.*

The whole country, owing to the *contagion* of our American exchange system, is flooded, deluged, swamped, beneath a muddy tide of slang, vulgarity, inartistic bathos, impertinence and buffoonery that is not wit.

*—Edmund Clarence Stedman
quoted by Walter Blair*

The most important periodicals, however, from the standpoint of humorists who profited by popularity, were the comic journals. To be sure many of these died at a tender age, after driving editors to despair, and there was some naturalness in the ending of Newell's burlesque novel *The Cloven Foot* (1870), which showed a comic journal editor attempting to hang himself. Nevertheless, whether they survived long or not, comic periodicals were so numerous that Newell, in the novel mentioned, could tell with some accuracy of an undertaker displaying a graveyard full of "projectors of American *Punches.*" A list of such publications, though still far from complete, shows that at least 116 such periodicals appeared between 1800 and 1900.

Most of them lived only a short time—the *Wasp,* published in New York, two years (1802-3); the *Red Book,* Baltimore, two years (1819-21); the *Galaxy of Comicalities,* Philadelphia, from October 2, 1833, to July 5, 1834; the *Picayune,* New York, eleven years (1847-58); the *City Budget,* New York, a year or less (1853-54); the *Knapsack,* Philadelphia, October 24 to November 4, 1865; *Texas Siftings,* Austin, Texas, probably no more than fifteen years (1882-97?) in spite of its popularity; the *Fat Contributor's Saturday Night,* Cincinnati, about eleven years (1872-82)—these were fairly typical. "It's a funny thing, certainly," said *Yankee Doodle,* "that a Humorous Newspaper has concluded its second volume in the United States."

But despite the high mortality rate, which, after all, was hardly higher than that of other American periodicals, humorous publications appeared during every part of the century, and there is some evidence that a number achieved rather remarkable popularity. *Yankee Doodle,* for example, published two *Pictorial Yankee Doodles* in 1847 for free distribution to subscribers, and of each of these 100,000 were printed. *John Donkey,* Philadelphia (Jan. 1, 1848-July 15, 1848), though it lived less than a year, had at one time a circulation of 12,000. This compared fairly well with the most popular magazines of the day, *Graham's* (40,000) and *Godey's* (150,000); it surpasses the *Southern Literary Messenger,* whose subscribers numbered 5,500 in its prosperous days under Poe, the *Knickerbocker* (5,000), and dozens of others. The *Picayune* had at one time a circulation of 35,000, although the number fell to 6,500 in 1853. At the same time, the *Reveille* (1853-54?) was issuing 2,800 copies of each number, and the *Pick* (1853-54?) was boasting that it sold 24,000 copies of its first number, 27,000 of its second, and 30,000 of its third. Less than a year after its start, the editor of the *Pick* was proclaiming: "We started with $5 and we have made a property that we would not sell tomorrow for $50,000." And it is probable that, in the period before the war, the *Carpet-Bag,* Boston (1851-53), and *Vanity Fair,* New York (December 31, 1859-July 4, 1863), on which definite figures are not available, surpassed most of these.

Though fewer figures are recorded, those which can be discovered indicate that in the years after the war, comic publications reached even greater numbers. *Peck's Sun,* in 1882, had a circulation of 20,000 and was "rapidly increasing." Opie Read's *Arkansas Traveler* (1883) reached a circulation of 60,000. In 1887, *Texas Siftings* had a circulation which had "long exceeded 100,000 copies each issue," and a popularity which was international. *Puck* (March 1877-September 1918), *Judge* (1881-), and *Life* (1883-) were probably even more popular. In the words of J. L. Ford "It is impossible to estimate the importance of these comic journals in the development and encouragement of American humor. They were read and widely quoted, and they popularized humor to such an extent that many other periodicals found it advisable to maintain departments consisting entirely of original humorous matter."

The writings of humorists were published in books as well as magazines, and again there is evidence of mounting popularity which prepared the way for Mark Twain and his contemporaries. *Georgia Scenes* (1835) had by 1894 passed through twelve editions, and a writer in 1874 held it had had a larger circulation than any other Southern book. According to the publisher, when Shillaber's *Life and Sayings of Mrs. Partington* appeared in 1854, at least 50,000 copies, including a first edition of 20,000 were sold. Frances M. Whitcher's *Widow Bedott Papers,* after increasing the circulation of the magazine in which they first appeared, in 1855 sold "something over 100,000 copies" [George

H. Derby, *Fifty Years Among Authors, Books, and Publishers*]. By 1855, *Major Jones's Courtship,* first issued in 1844, had run through thirteen editions in the United States. And before Ward had achieved the pinnacle of his popularity, when his first book came off the presses in 1862, "40,000 copies were sold outright, an enormous edition for the time" [Don C. Seitz, *Artemus Ward*]. Huntley's *Spoopendyke,* now completely forgotten, appeared in 1881, and "over 300,000 copies of the work were manufactured and disposed of within three months after its first appearance" [Will M. Clemens, *Famous Funny Fellows*]. Later several revised and enlarged editions were printed. Then, in 1888, Belford, Clarke & Company, in an edition of Nye's *Baled Hay,* proudly told of the following remarkable sales of the books by Peck:

How Private George W. Peck
Put Down the Rebellion . . . . .40th thousand
Peck's Bad Boy and His Pa . . . . .750th thousand
Peck's Bad Boy and His Pa, No. 2 . . . . 200th thousand
Peck's Sunshine. . . . . .125th thousand
Peck's Fun. . . . . 125th thousand
Peck's Boss Book. . . . . 50th thousand

Doubtless some allowance should be made for a publisher's enthusiasm here, but since, by now, train butchers were purveying paper editions while bookstores all over the country offered other editions, and since Peck was undoubtedly tremendously popular, the optimistic figures should not be discounted a great deal. Burdette, Bailey, and Nye were probably about as popular.

By the time this announcement was made, humorists were compiling and selling annually almanacs which, like their books, had remarkable sales. Of course, almanacs were not new things; Franklin and others had published them in colonial times; *The Crockett Almanacs* (1835-53?) had had a large sale several years after the death of Davy Crockett, and before 1842, Robert H. Elton "had gained some little notoriety for his comic almanacks . . . made up of reproductions of Cruikshank's and Seymour's designs, interspersed with humorous sketches" [L. W. Kingman in the December 1875 *American Bibliopolist*]. In the seventies, eighties, and nineties, the tradition of the comic almanac was revived. In 1870, when Josh Billings published his first *Farmer's Alminax,* it sold 90,000 copies; the following year 127,000 copies appeared, and in 1872, some 100,000 were sold. The publication ran through ten years, during each of which more than 50,000 copies were sold. Carl Pretzel of Chicago published an almanac which had "a large and ready sale" during the late seventies and early eighties, and *The Danbury News Man's Almanac* (1873), was "as successful as his volumes of sketches" [*National Cyclopedia of American Biography* 6].

In addition to the works of the humorists which they themselves published, there were humorous anthologies. As early as 1845, Porter's famous *Big Bear of Arkansas* collection appeared, to be followed by another collection by the same author. Sam Slick's two anthologies, each in three volumes, were issued in both England and America. In the sixties, three volumes of *Yankee Drolleries* were compiled by George Augustus Sala. Toward the end of the century, when Eli Perkins and Mark Twain joined the ranks of anthologists, the number increased. *American Humorists,* edited by the Rev. H. R. Haweis in 1883, had a large sale, though one of many such books. At least 32 collections or new editions of collections appeared during the years 1884-90, and at least 28 appeared between 1890 and 1894. All of these publications stimulated interest and indicated the popularity of the humor of American writers.

The literary comedians did not, however, have to depend entirely upon printed works as a medium for spreading their fame. Like motion picture actors and actresses of today, who make "appearances in person" before enthusiastic audiences, humorists went into every part of the land and appeared on lecture platforms.

Started in 1825 as a part of the lyceum system, the popular lecture, which before the war had "spread throughout the country from Boston to Detroit and Maine to Florida" and which after the war was exploited by such enterprising leaders as John H. Williams, James B. Pond, and James Redpath, proved a boon to many humorists. In 1870, an Englishman [E. P. Hingston in *The Genial Showman*] said:

America is a lecture-hall on a very extensive scale. The rostrum extends in a straight line from Boston, through New York and Philadelphia, to Washington. There are raised seats on the first tier in the Alleghenies, and gallery accommodations on the top of the Rocky Mountains. . . . The voice of the lecturer is never silent in the United States.

The Englishman, E. P. Hingston, was well acquainted with the American situation, for he had managed many of the appearances on the platform of the first important humorist of America to acquire money and fame by giving comic lectures, Artemus Ward. Ward started his career in the field in 1861, taking a hint from Barnum, who had overcome scruples of country folk visiting the theater in his museum by calling it "The Moral Lecture-Room," and advertising his speech as a "Moral Lecture." Starting modestly by appearing in a few New England towns, the lecturer traveled over widening territory. In 1861 he visited New York, Paterson, Corning, Elmira, and other towns and cities. Thereafter "dates followed in thick order," dates arranged with "bureaus and local committees" for appearances at fixed pay. In 1862 he appeared not only on Eastern platforms but also in halls in Cleveland, Milwaukee, and Memphis. The following year, on the bustling frontier of the Far West, he entertained the miners and settlers of California, Texas, Utah, and Nevada. In 1864, he appeared during a period of two months in nightly lectures in New York, had a period of two crowded weeks in Boston, and visited other cities in the United States and in Canada. After another successful season in 1865, he went, in 1866, to England, where he had a notable success which not only augmented his fortunes but also caused Americans to look more proudly upon native humorists. And through the years, there was a rather steady increase both in receipts and in the number attending his lectures.

Other lecturers followed Ward into a field which offered returns of from fifty dollars to three hundred dollars for each appearance. Josh Billings began to appear on the platform in 1863, and thereafter, for at least twenty successive seasons, he

> read the lecture in every town on this continent that has 20,000 people, and in hundreds that have not got 1,000 in them; read it in every town in Texas and California, and in all the Canadian towns, and then down South, from Baltimore to Palatka, Florida, and still across to Memphis, and then into New Orleans, reading each season from fifty to over a hundred nights [Francis Smith, *Life and Adventures of Josh Billings*].

In 1866, Locke (Nasby) began a career as a lecturer which lasted at least five years. Meanwhile A. Minor Griswold had started, in 1865, activity as a lecturer which continued through eighteen years, and which carried him as far as the Puget Sound. Other humorists who had successful lecturing careers included Richard Malcolm Johnston, George W. Peck, J. M. Bailey, Eli Perkins, Bill Arp, Benjamin P. Shillaber (Mrs. Partington), William L. Visscher, Major Burbank, Dr. George W. Bagby, Phillips Thompson, Rufus Griswold, Eugene Field, and others.

Among the others were Mark Twain, whose very popular early works were preceded and followed by almost equally popular lectures, and Robert J. Burdette. Burdette was exceedingly successful from the beginning of his career in 1876 until the end of the century. In addition to presenting "The Rise and Fall of the Moustache," his greatest success, nearly five thousand times, he gave the following comic lectures frequently: "Home," "The Pilgrimage of the Funny Man," "Advice to a Young Man," "Wild Gourds," "Woman with the Broom," "Dimity Government," "Sawing Wood," "Twice Told Tales," "Handles," and "Rainbow Chasers"; and he appeared in every corner of the nation.

Thus the humor of the stage and the humor of politics brought popularity to the American jesters of the nineteenth century, and numerous publications—newspapers, magazines, comic journals, books, almanacs—and lectures as well helped carry the native humor to a growing number of people. . . .

Gilbert Seldes

SOURCE: "American Humor," in *The College Omnibus,* edited by James Dow McCallum, revised edition, Harcourt Brace & Company, 1934, pp. 272-81.

[*In this excerpt from the essay originally published in* America as Americans See It, *Seldes describes American humor writing before the Civil War as distinctly democratic, reflecting an emphasis on the common citizen appropriate to a young democracy that was distrustful of things European.*]

There is a specific change in the direction of American humor, and this corresponds roughly to the great political change worked by the Civil War. Humor, like idealism, lags behind the facts. It desires to be familiar, so that long after the motor car has become safe and practicable, small boys cry "get a horse" and cartoonists still picture a rube with straw behind his ears a generation after the farmer has become a businessman. So it is not to be expected that the social revolution of the Civil War was instantly reflected in American humor. The change came later—the movement is slow but the direction is marked.

Early American humor is a glorification of the common sense of the common man and is directed against all pretensions of the superior. The cultivated James Russell Lowell put his political satire in the mouth of the unlettered Hosea Biglow and used the rustic New England dialect for the political satire of a Juvenal. The social satire of Artemus Ward is also written as if by one to whom spelling and the graces of style are the affectations of fops—as if the simple and uncultivated American would have none of "your airs." The misspellings of Bill Nye and Josh Billings are part of the same intention—to prove always that the average democratic man need not traffic with the delicacies and niceties of a cultured existence. This is of course a part of the violent distrust of Europe which became fixed in America shortly after the Revolutionary War and it is at the same time a salute to the hardiness of the pioneer who was creating the new frontier of America.

Nearly the last, and certainly the greatest of the humorists who used dialect, was Finley Peter Dunne who created the character of Mr. Dooley. The change of which I have spoken is beginning to be noticeable. Mr. Dooley does not pretend half so much as the others that he is inferior to the thing attacked. The dialect is more of a mask than it was before, and in fact, there is hardly a line in Mr. Dooley which would not be equally funny if written out in perfect English. (Mr. Dunne was not attempting a serious record of the Irish-American speech, as Mr. Lardner afterward recorded with a delicate ear the peculiarities of the actual American tongue.) When, in connection with the Dreyfus case, Mr. Dooley imagines a judge saying, "The witness will confine himself to forgeries" the English is as pure as that of Swift. When he advised the young and bombastic Theodore Roosevelt to call his early reminiscences *Alone in Cubia* he was departing from the American tradition of humor-by-inflation and returning to the more cultivated tradition of humor by under-statement and concentration. One looks back to the days when an American barkeeper could discuss the affairs of the world with a feeling that they were peculiarly mellow, a sort of autumn before the harsh winter of war and prohibition and millions of motor cars set in. Mr. Dooley is the transitional figure. He is skeptical about socialism and the agrarian economics of Mr. Bryan and he is also sardonic about the barons of coal and pork and the political grafters on the national government. Note that his preoccupation is always with public affairs, because this also is about to change.

Political satire in a democracy is naturally directed against the eccentric, the unique one, the pretentious one, and whoever is superior. The first hundred years of American humor are the written records of the cracker-barrel philosophy: the reduction to print of the conversations around the stove at the crossroads grocery. There is a coarseness of grain and of vitality which corresponds to the practical jokes, the tack on the chair seat and the cruel pranks of a rustic community. The fundamental attitude is a jeer at the well-spoken and the well-dressed visitor from the city, which, moving West, becomes the traditional revolver shots to make the tenderfoot dance. It is not without elaboration and it bears a striking similarly to the humor of Harlequin and Pantaloon.

Everything good or bad in American humor of the nineteenth century is summed up in the work of Mark Twain. The goodness is rich and varied and personal. But I doubt whether it was ever as popular as the badness, which is entirely traditional and which rises from Mark Twain's easy acceptance of the humorous habits of his time. The goodness lies in finding what is entertaining in actually—in such a work as *Life on the Mississippi* [1883]. The badness lies in making humor by the single process of exaggeration. When Mark Twain was a pilot on the Mississippi, or a prospector in Nevada, he was looking neither up nor down. He was neither defending the common man nor afraid of the superior man. But when he went to Europe he was defending America, and when he saw a work of art he found it necessary to belittle the artist. He called

his book *A Tramp Abroad* [1880]—a tidy pun because if he enjoyed the vagabondage he reported it as if he were a bum. The furious desire, the absolute necessity, to destroy the power of Europe becomes most marked when it is the great Europe, the Europe of the arts, that he is discussing. For the Europe of the tourist he has a kinder word and creates the figure of his Babbitt companion so that he can defend some things and save his fury for others.

The method of Mark Twain is not an easy one. The masterpieces of grotesque humor in Rabelais and Swift combine with their fantasy a sense of proportion as exquisite as that of a miniature. Everything is monstrous, but everything is monstrous to scale and with its own perfect logic. But Mark Twain is a realist and the whole humor of his exaggerations is that they are totally out of scale. It is, after all, a human being exactly like himself who is kept awake by a servant dropping one boot after another as he finishes the polishing. But when the number of boots rises to the hundreds and thousands one single item only is out of proportion. There is a wild and rather reckless imagination in Mark Twain's humor and it is associated with the fundamentally humorous folk tale of the far West, of the lumber camps and the cattle ranches. The mythical figure of Paul Bunyan is a grandson of Gargantua, and the story of the frogs in Owen Wister's *The Virginian* [1902] is a story in the Mark Twain tradition. Mark Twain is at his best when he assumes the bland air of one who expects to be believed when he seems to be telling the literal truth and soars suddenly into the wildest extravagances.

He has then the rather grand line of the men who sat about in contest to see who could tell the biggest lie. And that suggests that the critic, the literary man, may always be considerably misled as to the nature of the humor, because he so naturally concentrates his attention on humor which finds its way into print. The practical joke and the story told in the Pullman smoker are probably a better index to everything that is current and characteristic. In 1930 something of this sort began to find its way into print and typically enough the subject and the treatment both are in the style of 1860. It is perhaps a throw-back, but the fact is that the American people were so eager to read a vulgarly told description of the building of a rustic lavatory that they bought 650,000 copies of *The Specialist* in a single year, and this is some indication of the vitality of the smutty story and the lively anecdote. (Here the international difficulty becomes acute. I do not know whether outside of the Anglo-Saxon races the invented off-color funny story is at all common. My own experience is insufficient and my almost unsupported guess is that the Continental story is more likely to be the relation of an actual experience than of an imaginary one and that its object is not so specifically a roar of laughter. The contrast between *La Vie Parisienne* and the flood of "dirty magazines" of 1931-32 in America is illuminating.)

I have perhaps stressed too much the social and economic circumstances under which American humor lived in the nineteenth century, and as I am skeptical about economic interpretations in general—of any but economic phenomena—I hesitate to make a further point. But it undoubtedly has had its influence. The humorous writer before 1880 or so was not only pretending to be a provincial, but was even writing for a provincial public, or at best for a local one. The humor of Mark Twain spread from the West as the ripples in a pool may spread and in all newspapers the exchange editors who clipped the bright bits from distant contemporaries were important figures. Humor was local and had the color of its locality. . . .

Edmund Wilson stresses the harshness that could permeate American humor writing:

One of the most striking things about *Sut Lovingood* is that it is all as offensive as possible. It takes a pretty strong stomach nowadays—when so much of the disgusting in our fiction is not rural but urban or suburban—to get through it in any version. I should say that, as far as my experience goes, it is by far the most repellent book of any real literary merit in American literature. This kind of crude and brutal humor was something of an American institution all through the nineteenth century.

Edmund Wilson, Patriotic Gore, *Oxford University Press, 1962.*

THE OLD SOUTHWEST

Clement Eaton

SOURCE: "The Southern Yeoman: The Humorists' View and the Reality," in *The Mind of the Old South*, revised edition, Louisiana State University Press, 1967, pp. 130-51.

[*In this excerpt, Eaton examines the historical accuracy of antebellum humor writing, maintaining that, despite occasional distortions of truth, the works are valuable and generally accurate historical documents.*]

In studying the writings of the Southern humorists of the antebellum period the social historian has a different purpose from that of the folklorist, the student of American literature, or the investigator of the Southern vernacular. He is interested in the by-products of this type of literature—authentic details of manners, customs, amusements, and social institutions such as the militia muster, the religious revival, and the law courts.

The historian must be able to distinguish between the bias of the humorists and the facts about their subjects, for these writers were not primarily reporters but creators of literature. Nevertheless, they present through their imagination and firsthand knowledge of the plain people a kind of truth that eludes the researcher in documents.

Some of the most important humorists sought faithfully to record the mores and manners of the common people by their descriptions of frontier life, courthouse scenes, militia musters, and the uninhibited amusements of the yeomen and poor whites. After Augustus Baldwin Longstreet, the author of *Georgia Scenes* [1835], had become a preacher and a college president, he was disturbed at times by the frivolity and indelicacy of his humorous writing, but he justified his work on the ground that it was authentic social history which a later age would value. In his preface to *Major Jones's Chronicles of Pineville* [1843], William Tappan Thompson also affirmed a historical purpose—to preserve a record of the "cracker" before education had changed him

> by polishing away those peculiarities which now mark his manners and language, reduc[ing] him to the common level of commonplace people, and mak[ing] him a less curious 'specimen' for the study of the naturalist. As he now is, however, I have endeavored to catch his "manners living as they rise."

Likewise, Thomas Bangs Thorpe and Joseph M. Field seem to have purposely recorded characteristic features of frontier life and quaint customs in out-of-the-way places which were rapidly disappearing. In reporting Southern conditions the humorists had an advantage over most travelers, for they observed Southern life from within. The keen observations which they made were the fruit of a lifetime of association and understanding rather than the product of a hasty visit.

A recent student of Southwestern humor, Kenneth Lynn, has presented a thesis (which he rides hard), that these humorists were principally Whigs, who wrote with a strongly aristocratic bias. He maintains that they used their humorous writings as a weapon to combat and discredit the Jacksonian movement. Some evidence can be found, especially in the writings of Johnson J. Hooper and Joseph G. Baldwin, to support this tenuous thesis. But many of the writers wrote merely to entertain, to tell a good story, without political intent. Some of them—notably John Basil Lamar—had a genuine appreciation for the sterling virtues of the yeoman and the frontiersman—his independence, democracy, naturalness, courage, hospitality, and patriotism.

The attitude of Southern humorists toward the relatively small class of "poor whites" may have had something of aristocratic hauteur in it, but on the whole it represented the general attitude of Southern society to this debased class of people. To modern eyes the lowest class of whites of the Old South (often called "poor white trash" by the slaves) appears to be tragic figures, but to the planters and the residents of the towns they were a comic element. The upper plantation group as a class felt little sense of responsibility for the poverty, the illiteracy, the peculiar diseases of hookworm and malaria, and the drunkenness which beset the lower classes. What could be more laughable to these aristocrats than the quaint vernacular and the crude manners and dress of the "tackies" and "sand-hillers"? Even the slaves of the big house made fun of "poor white trash." In his *History of the Dividing Line* Colonel William Byrd set an example of snobbish aristocratic wit by his satire on the lubbers or backwoods people of North Carolina.

One of these aristocrats who was amused by the poor whites and collected their colloquialisms—"the piney-woods parlance"—was the Georgia doctor and poet Francis Orray Ticknor. Though Ticknor is known for his romantic poems, notably "Virginians of the Valley," his correspondence reveals that he had an earthy sense of humor. He lived on his plantation Torch Hill near Columbus, from which he made trips on his horse Kitty into the pine woods to minister to poor people. He described a learned reply that he gave to the question of a piney-woods mother: "What's the matter with my child's nose, he keeps a-picking of it?" His patients usually paid him with an X mark, but sometimes he got a cash case, "a temptation thrown in my way to reconcile me to my lot." He attended a sheriff's sale of the property of a poor white who had decamped owing him a bill. The property consisted of a cow and calf, a table, two chairs, a coffee mill without a handle, a tin pan with two holes in the bottom, and a pig of soft soap: all brought less than five dollars.

The customs and manners of the poor whites as well as of the yeomen of the South presented a rich tapestry of local material for the literary artist. This material, unsuited for use by the dominant romantic school of Southern writers, was exploited by the humorists who fluorished in the period from 1830 to 1860. Unhampered by European traditions, except for the slight influence of Addison, these writers freshly observed the life about them and reported their findings without much effort at literary finish. They found around them the racy and individualized characters of the crackers and the yeomen, whose uncouth language and provinciality afforded substance for mirth. They could therefore create a native American humor based on realistic observation and illuminated by many sidelights of local color.

The Negro, on the other hand, was seldom or only incidentally used (as in Simms's novel *Woodcraft*), as a subject for comedy by antebellum Southern writers. Not until the time of Joel Chandler Harris did the "darky" assume a prominent place in Southern humor. Perhaps the detachment essential for seeing the ludicrous side of the poor white man was lacking in the case of the Negro, who was a form of property bitterly assailed by the abolitionists. Besides, the black slave was a congruous element in the plantation regime, whereas the cracker was not.

The origin of this semirealistic literature dealing with the common man can be explained partly by the democratic upsurge of the Jacksonian movement. The rise of the Nullification movement also stirred up an intense feeling of Southernism and an interest in Southern themes. In addition, economic and social conditions were ripe for the development of a school of broad humor below the Mason-Dixon Line. Georgia was the cradle of Southern humor. In this state a remarkable contrast developed between the yeomen of the red hills and the planters of the long-settled tidewater region. Indeed, the frontier had only recently been erased in the 1830's with the removal of the Cherokees. This juxtaposition of seasoned culture and the rude frontier produced incongruities and comic situations that evoked laughter.

The school of Southern humor was founded in Georgia by Augustus Baldwin Longstreet, a graduate of Yale and of Judge Tappan Reeve's law school at Litchfield, Connecticut, and editor of the Augusta *State Rights' Sentinel*. In his *Georgia Scenes*, published in book form at Augusta in 1835, Longstreet first set forth the ludicrous aspects of the life of Southern yeomen, crackers, and poor whites. He was soon followed by others, notably William Tappan Thompson, his protegé on the *State Rights' Sentinel*; Johnson J. Hooper, who had emigrated from North Carolina to Alabama where he became an editor and politician; John Basil Lamar, a Georgia planter; Henry Clay Lewis, the "Madison Tensas" of *Odd Leaves from the Life of a Louisiana Swamp Doctor* [1858]: Joseph M. Field, editor of the St. Louis *Reveille;* and Albert Pike and Colonel C. F. M. Noland of Arkansas.

Prominent among the humorous writers from the upper South were Joseph G. Baldwin, who emigrated from Virginia to the lower South during the flush times of the 1830's; George W. Bagby, editor of the *Southern Literary Messenger* at Richmond; Hamilton C. Jones and Harden E. Taliaferro of North Carolina; and George Washington Harris, whose bold and earthy descriptions of the mountain whites of east Tennessee remind one of the pictures of Thomas Hart Benton such as "I got a Gal on Sourwood Mountain" and "In the Ozarks." The humor of the Old South found its most powerful expression in Harris's *Sut Lovingood's Yarns* [1867]. Unfortunately, the difficult dialect and the extreme realism of his work have hampered its popularity.

The creator of Sut Lovingood, after having long been neglected, has come in recent years to be regarded as the most original and imaginative of the Southern humorists. Born in Allegheny City, Pennsylvania, in 1814, he spent the formative years of his life in Knoxville and east Tennessee. Here he became a Jack-of-all-trades, never able to make much money from a succession of jobs; he was apprentice to a jeweler, farmer in the foothills of the Great Smokies, steamboat captain, railroad man, sawmill manager, and postmaster of Knoxville. Though many of the humorists were Whigs, he was a Democrat, an ardent secessionist, and a sympathizer with the common people. His writings are full of vivid pictures of the common folk—an old mountain lady with a pipe in her mouth standing by her ash hopper, a poor white riding on a bull with a saddle made with forks of dogwood, a hypocritical circuit rider who guzzled bald-face liquor, a Yankee razor-grinder cheating the gullible country folk, and mountain people dancing at a Tennessee frolic. His rich imagery is homely, almost Chaucerian in freshness, and redolent of the Southern countryside.

Some of these writers, by virtue of their background, held a position of detachment from the plantation culture. Dr. Henry Clay Lewis, who wrote *Odd Leaves from the Life of a Louisiana Swamp Doctor* under the name "Madison Tensas," was of part Jewish origin and though born in South Carolina, described himself as "a Southerner by adoption." He could make fun of the pretensions of the plantation aristocracy in such delineations as the "Man of Aristocratic Diseases." Writers such as Lewis, being outside of the aristocratic culture, could appreciate the antithesis between the folk culture and the culture of the colonnaded mansion.

A considerable number of writers who described the humorous aspects of Southern yeomen were Northerners who resided in the South. William Tappan Thompson, the creator of "Major Jones," was born in Ravenna, Ohio, and worked on Northern newspapers until he came to Georgia, where he was given a job by Longstreet on his *State Rights' Sentinel,* and later he founded the Savannah *Morning News.* Thomas Bangs Thorpe emigrated from Massachusetts in 1836 to Louisiana, where he worked as a portrait painter and journalist. John S. Robb, a journalist on the staff of the St. Louis *Reveille* who wrote *Streaks of Squatter Life* [1847], was born in Philadelphia. Albert Pike was a native of Boston and attended Harvard College before he settled in Arkansas in 1832 to become an editor, lawyer, diplomat, and commander of an Indian brigade in the Confederate Army. William T. Porter of Vermont, who founded *The Spirit of the Times,* a sporting and humorous magazine of New York City, was the great encourager of the Southern humorists by publishing their stories in his periodical. In the 1850's the connection of the Southern humorists with Porter's magazine was one of the few friendly links between North and South.

The writers who exploited the vein of Southern humor were chiefly journalists seeking to enliven the pages of their newspapers by local anecdotes, or lawyers who entertained each other on the circuit by swapping stories. They collected tales and gave them literary form, and they described comic happenings of the yeomen and crackers. These anecdotes originated in village taverns, livery stables, barrooms, or at the campfires of wagoners and hunters; they represented a different standard of stories, as Shields McIlwaine has pointed out [in *The Southern Poor-White from Lubberland to Tobacco Road*], from the type of polite and witty anecodotes told in the parlors and on the verandahs of the planters' homes. The former brand of humor bore the unmistakable stamp of the common man, having frequently evolved from the practical joking of the frontier. It had an earthy tang and was characterized by broad farce—a bull playing havoc with a quilting party, the antics of a preacher when some lizards were placed in his trousers, or the comedy arising from a horse swap in Georgia.

Despite the place of honor which romantic literature held in the estimation of Southerners, these amusing stories of low life were keenly relished. This Rabelaisian taste was indicated by the fact that ten editions of *Georgia Scenes* were printed before 1860, and *Major Jones's Courtship* [1843] appealed to such a wide circle of readers that it ran through eleven editions. Furthermore, some of the most droll personalities of the Old South—notably the plebeian Governor "Zeb" Vance of North Carolina, Judge Dooley of Georgia, and "Lean Jimmy" Jones, who defeated James K. Polk for governor in 1841—remained storytellers and wits who never committed their humor to the printed page.

From the pages of the Southern humorists we gain our most vivid descriptions of the appearance of the poor whites and of the crackers—a term often used to describe the upland farmers of Georgia as well as the poor whites. On court days they would come into the somnolent villages of the South, driving two-wheeled carts pulled by mules, bony horses, or oxen which they guided by a rope around their horns, and cracking their long whips. In the morning they seemed to be the most harmless individuals on earth; "their bilious-looking eyes, and tanney, shrivelled faces . . . wore a meek and pensive expression," according to *Major Jones's Chronicles of Pineville.* But towards noon, after they had imbibed heavily of bald-face corn liquor, a transformation occurred. "Then might be seen the cadaverous looking wiregrass boy in his glory, as he leaped out into the sand before the door, and tossing his linsey jacket into the air, proclaimed himself the best man in the country. Then, too, might be seen the torpid clay-eater, his bloated, watery countenance illuminated by the exhilarating qualities of Mr. Harley's rum, as he closed in with his antagonist," cursing, biting, and gouging.

The gregarious nature of the yeomen found an outlet in numerous social gatherings in which they combined work with pleasure. Their sports and amusements were an especially rich field for comic delineation. These diversions were mainly an outgrowth of frontier conditions. In the less developed sections of the South, as well as north of the Ohio River, wrestling matches and rude fights took place that were completely devoid of chivalry. The victor would jump up on a stump and crow like a cock, flapping his arms. Or he would boast: "I'm the yellow blossom of the forest; I'm kin to a rattlesnake on the mother's side; I'm the stepfather of the yearth; I'm a lion with a mangy tail, a bear with a sore head, a flying whale." A distinctive sport of the Southern backwoods was gander pulling, in which the contestant galloping on horseback, sought to pull off the head and neck of a well-greased gander hung high on a pole. The yeomen of Georgia indulged in a drinking game called "Bingo," in which gallons of liquor were consumed to the accompaniment of a song that began, "A farmer's dog sat on the barn-door and Bingo was his name, O!"

The tremendous vitality and optimism of Southern yeomen often found expression in tall stories with a Baron Munchausen flavor. Franklin J. Meine has collected some of these extravagant stories in his *Tall Tales of the Southwest* [1937]. This type of humor was especially prevalent on the frontier where the mysteries of an undiscovered country and the bigness of the mountains and the prairies excited the imagination. But the tall tale also fluorished in the interior regions of the South. Harden E. Taliaferro has related some of these impossible stories which he heard in the back country of North Carolina in *Fisher's River Scenes and Characters* [1859]. There were stories of marvelous snakes that took their tails in their mouths and rolled along like a hoop, of people who ate impossible quantities of peaches or watermelons, of magical trees that grew so fast that a horse who was hitched to a branch was hoisted high into the sky, of incredible fights with catamounts, and of bears that displayed human sauciness and sagacity. Finally, there were ghost stories such as those which the superstitious old hatter told Joel Chandler Harris when he was a small boy on the Joseph Turner plantation near Eatonville, Georgia.

A peculiar quality of Southern yeomen humor was its emphasis on what Professor Alphonso Smith called "the humor of discomfiture." This laughter at the painful or embarrassing predicaments of others probably arose out of the practical joking of the frontier. Good examples of such roistering humor are to be found in the Sut Lovingood tales, such as "Bart Davis's Dance"

and "Sicily Burns's Wedding," or the drover's tale related by [Frederick Law] Olmsted in his travel account *A Journey Through Texas*.

From the reports of travelers in the antebellum South we gain the impression that the poor whites, unlike the yeomen, were lacking in humor. The conditions of life were so hard for them, especially in the mountain regions, that they developed a fatalistic melancholy. James Lane Allen has described the unchanged mountaineers of Kentucky: "eyes with a slow long look of mild enquiry, or of general listlessness, or of unconcious and unaccountable melancholy; the key of life a low minor strain, losing itself in reverie, voices monotonous in intonation; movements uniformed by nervousness."

The ignorance and provincialism of these secluded people were a frequent theme of the humorist. "McAlpin's Trip to Charleston" by Hamilton C. Jones, for example contrasts the openmouthed naiveté of the country greenhorn with the sophisticated culture of the city. The countryman who had seen the wonders of "Augusty," Georgia, was looked upon as a man of the world, and a plausible Yankee with a common school education like the politician Franklin Plummer was regarded in the backwoods of Mississippi as a walking encyclopedia. The suspicion about city people entertained by the yeomen was portrayed in numerous stories, such as T. S. Lane's "The Thimble Game," and Thompson's *Major Jones's Sketches of Travel*.

One of the most valuable pictures of the rusticity of the natives is given by Johnson J. Hooper in "Taking the Census," a story based on his experience as a census enumerator in 1840. The old ladies in the rural districts of Alabama confronted the enumerators with grim countenances and with the threat of "setting the dogs on ye" for prying into such personal affairs as, "How many chickens have you?" and "How much cloth have you woven?" The government of Washington was regarded by the country people in these isolated sections of the South almost as an alien enemy.

Southern humorists presented the daughters and wives of the farmers and the poor whites in a realistic light, quite different from the romantic halo cast over the ladies of the gentry by the novelists. The humorists portrayed cracker women engaged in quite unladylike practices like fighting; they pulled out hair and scratched faces, dipped snuff, chewed tobacco, and smoked corncob pipes. The young doctor Henry Clay Lewis ("Madison Tensas") found on his first visit into the swamp country of Louisiana to attend a farmer's wife that the neighbors believed the hoot of an owl to be an omen of death. A favorite theme of the humorists was the embarassment of travelers who spent the night in a yeoman's crowded log cabin and had to go to bed in the presence of the female members of the family. The daughters of the farmers were usually modest girls, who became speechless before strangers and blushed deeply. The farmer's womenfolk were gullible patrons of Yankee peddlers, who sold them ribbons, pins, needles, nutmegs, clocks, and bustles. "Mike Hooter's" daughter in the backwoods of Mississippi did not have the money to buy a bustle—the latest in fashions—so she improvised one by tying a thick sausage under her dress. At a camp meeting when one end of the sausage came loose, she thought that the dangling object was a snake climbing up her leg; accordingly, she writhed with fear instead of with religious ecstasy.

The religion of the cracker was dramatized in the camp meeting, a method of soul-saving that gave spice to an otherwise monotonous rural life. Consequently the camp meeting holds a prominent place in Southern humor. A most realistic description of the emotional extravagance that often accompanied these religious gatherings is given in Hooper's *Some Adventures of Captain Simon Suggs, Late Captain of the Tallapoosa Volunteers* [1845]. The Captain stood on the outskirts of a great crowd of people at the Sandy Creek camp meeting in Alabama and coolly observed this mass of humanity in the throes of religious excitement. A half dozen preachers, serving in relays, were exhorting their audience, terrifying them with their somber theology and loud raucous voices. On the outer circle Negroes were singing, screaming, and praying with primitive African vehemence. Delicate women had become hysterical, so that their nerves played strange tricks known as "the jerks" or "the holy laugh"—a phenomenon that was terrifying because it resembled a maniac's chuckle. Some of the men wore a hideous grin; others were barking like dogs; while still others were shouting "Gl-o-ree!" In front of the mourner's bench the ground was covered with straw, upon which the converts were rolling in religious ecstasy or lay swooning upon each other in promiscuous heaps.

In sketching the political mores of the yeomen and crackers, the humorists emphasized their violent partisanship and their susceptibility to the arts of the demagogue. The autobiography of David Crockett tells how he won his elections by treating the voters liberally to liquor and amusing them with his folksy humor. On one occasion he defeated an opponent with a devastating smile by comparing him to a grinning coon. Crockett then boasted of his own prowess in killing coons by outgrinning them. Any sign of aristocracy exhibited by a candidate was a distinct handicap in winning the votes of the "sovereigns." John S. Robb's story of "The Standing Candidate" presents an old Missouri squatter named "Sugar" who appeared at all elections to the legislature as the standing candidate to represent Nianga County. He always came equipped with a jug of homemade whiskey and a bag of brown sugar. After one of the opposing candidates had paid him gener-

ously for his liquor supply, he would then make a speech yielding his claim to office to his patron until the next election. When a fastidious candidate refused to drink his mixture of whiskey and brown sugar (a rustic old-fashioned), he held up the unfortunate man to ridicule: "He's got an *a*-ristocracy stomach, and can't go the *native-licker*."

The Southern yeomen and poor whites, indeed, were strong advocates of democracy—a white democracy. They immediately resented any assumption of superiority of one class over another. An amusing story illustrating this trait is told in Thomas D. Clark's *The Rampaging Frontier* [1939]. John C. Breckinridge and Robert Letcher were traveling together through eastern Kentucky in 1852, stump speaking as candidates for Congress. Letcher would make a short speech to "the sovereigns," and then while his rival spoke would play his fiddle nearby. The lively music invariably drained off the auditors of Breckinridge until only a handful of followers resisted the lure. Finally the wily Breckinridge concocted a scheme that ruined his musical opponent. At the next meeting, when Letcher began to play, a lank fellow wearing a coonskin cap, yelled out, "Why don't you fiddle with that t'other hand o'yourn?"

"T'other hand!" shouted the hillbillies.

Letcher, who was left-handed, became deeply embarrassed. The man with the coonskin cap continued to roar: "T'other hand! We've heard about you! You fiddle down thar in that d———n Bluegrass country, 'mong rich folks, with your right hand and think when you git up in the hills 'mong pore folks, left-hand fiddlin's good enuf for us; you've cussedly missed it. Left-hand doin's won't run up hyar."

Indeed, the most notable trait that distinguished the Southern yeomen from European peasants was a conviction of the equality of all white men. This frontier attitude never disappeared from the great middle class of the South, a virtue that was perpetuated by the rise of Jacksonian democracy. John Basil Lamar's humorous story "Polly Peablossom's Wedding" caught the authentic spirit of this movement. At the wedding when the preacher failed to appear and a squire was asked to perform the ceremony, Mrs. Peablossom objected that "the quality" in her day in Duplin County, North Carolina, had a prejudice against being married by a magistrate. But old Mr. Peablossom remonstrated:

> None of your Duplin County aristocracy about here, now. . . . Noth Ca'lina ain't the best state in the Union nohow. . . . *Quality,* eh! Who the devil's better than we are? An't we honest? An't we raised our children decent, and learned them how to read, write, and cipher? An't I *fout* under Newman and Floyd for the country? Why, darn it! We are the *very best* sort of people.

Southern yeomen had many virtues to balance against some of the ludicrous aspects of their rural lives. William Tappan Thompson paid a high tribute to their sterling qualities when he wrote in the preface to his *Chronicles of Pineville:* "As a class they are brave, generous, honest, and withal possessed by a sturdy patriotism. The vagabond and the dissolute among them are only the exceptions to the rule, and in a few generations more, education will have made the mass a great people." This prophecy was realized within two generations. During the building of the New South, the leadership in politics, in education, and in business was often taken over by the sons and the grandsons of yeomen.

The resemblances between the Southern yeomanry and the small farmers and villagers of the North were much greater than their differences. Major Jack Downing of Maine, whom Seba Smith created for his newspaper in 1830, has much in common with Major Jones of Pineville, Georgia. They belonged approximately to the same economic level, and they had that sturdy independence and fine disregard for class distinctions that were natively American. The Yankee farmer, however, was more likely to be thrifty and enterprising, with a down-East shrewdness that was caricatured in the stock figure of Sam Slick the clockmaker, whom Haliburton popularized. The Northern humorists of the antebellum period dealt more extensively with politics than did the Southern humorists, and they drew realistic pen pictures of female comic characters. There is no character in antebellum Southern humor to correspond to Mrs. Partington or to the Widow Bedott, those garrulous old New England ladies whom Shillaber and Whitcher portrayed so skillfully.

How far does the picture of poor whites and yeomen drawn by Southern humorists correspond to reality? With respect to the relative numbers of the poor whites, they did not exaggerate, as did the abolitionists. Contrary to the abolitionist stereotype, the poor whites formed only the shabby fringe of Southern society—not the mass of whites. When Governor Henry A. Wise of Virginia addressed the legislature in 1856, he estimated that 10 per cent of the children of the state belonged to families too poor to pay for elementary schooling. In South Carolina Governor Hammond estimated that the poor whites composed 20 per cent of the whole white population.

The humorists did not realize, however, that the degraded condition of the poor whites was largely owing to their environment and the enervating diseases which beset them. Living in the isolated and infertile areas of the South—the sand hills of Carolina and Georgia, the piney woods of the coastal plain, and the mountainous areas—the poor whites were primarily hunters and fishermen; many of them were squatters like Sam Bostwick in Simms's novel *Woodcraft.* Despite their poverty,

the "crackers" and the "piney woods folk" had a striking personal pride. As the Northern traveler Frederick Law Olmsted observed in 1853, they would not deign to engage themselves to the planters to do menial work—wait on tables, carry water, bring wood, black boots, cut hair, drive a coach. Such was "nigger's work," as they phrased it.

The yeomen were often confused with the poor whites by contemporary travelers and even by native writers. They judged from appearances, for many of the independent farmers lived in log cabins that were no better than the dwellings of the poor whites. The yeomen dressed in homespun or blue jeans, and their cattle and hogs were frequently hidden in the woods where they grazed. Yet there was a real difference—not merely in material possessions, but in spirit—between the yeomen and the poor whites. The true poor white was a creature like Ransy Sniffle in Longstreet's story "The Fight" in *Georgia Scenes* or the clay eater in Hooper's *The Widow Rugby's Husband* [1851]. Such a type was comparable to the slum element in the Northern states. Besides these people, who were often scattered in the interstices of the plantations, there were the mountain whites. These secluded people preserved the ways of their ancestors, the pioneers, without the spirit and hope of the pioneers. As Rupert Vance has observed, they represented the ebb of the frontier.

In their writings the humorists described both the yeomen and the poor whites and occasionally the tradesmen in small villages. It is sometimes difficult to distinguish in their work between the yeomen, frontiersmen, and poor whites, for the classes shaded into each other. The small farmers and the villagers, in contradistinction to the poor whites, were respectable citizens forming the bulk of the population of the South. Thomas Bangs Thorpe has drawn an attractive portrait of a member of this class in "The Big Bear of Arkansas." This mighty teller of tall tales was a man in the prime of his life, enjoying perfect health and contentment: "his eyes were as sparkling as diamonds, and good-natured to simplicity. Then his perfect confidence in himself was irresistibly droll." Representative specimens of the yeomen class were sympathetically portrayed by Lamar in "Polly Peablossom's Wedding" and by Thompson in *Major Jones's Courtship.*

The humorists do not appear to have realized the importance of the middle class of small farmers. Daniel R. Hundley of Alabama, who studied at Harvard and the University of Virginia, was one of the first writers to recognize the significance of the yeoman class in the social structure of the Old South. In 1860 he published a pioneer study of Southern society entitled *Social Relations in Our Southern States,* in which he combated the abolitionist stereotype of Southern society as consisting of only three classes—planters, poor whites, and slaves. On the contrary, he maintained, its society was composed of five classes, of which the yeoman farmer constituted a large and important element.

Hundley noted some of the distinguishing characteristics of this class—their independent and democratic spirit, their industriousness, and their warmhearted hospitality. He observed that yeomen who owned slaves worked side by side with them in the fields, treating them with great kindness, almost as equals; these slaves were often allowed to call their masters by their first or Christian names and both ate the same fare.

The yeomen of the South, Hundley maintained, were much like Northern middle-class farmers, fully as intelligent though not as sophisticated as the tradesmen and mechanics in the cities. They were superior to their counterparts in the North in handling the rifle, judging the quality of liquor and brandy (for they brewed or distilled their own), and in a grasp of politics, which they acquired not from newspapers but from public speakings, barbecues, and the talk of county courthouse gatherings. In confutation of Frederick Law Olmsted's criticism of Southern hospitality, Hundley cited the testimony of a Connecticut mechanic whom he had met. This man, thrown out of work by the panic of 1857, had traveled penniless through the South seeking employment and had found a warm welcome in the homes of the farmers along his route.

The yeomen who moved into the villages and became artisans or tradesmen retained the characteristics of their former rural life with its democratic spirit and sense of equality. The Scottish wool carder William Thomson who traveled in the Southern states in 1840-42 seeking employment reported that the mechanics and tradesmen in the South, unlike their class in Great Britain, considered themselves as "men of honour"; they resented any indignity that might be shown them "even at the expense of their life, or that of those who venture to insult them."

The humorists' view of the yeomen gives no indication of the most important economic fact about them—namely, that a very large proportion of them owned their farms. According to studies made by Professor Frank L. Owsley and his students at Vanderbilt in the 1940's, approximately 80 per cent of the farmers of the South in the decade 1850-60 owned the lands they tilled. This economic stake in society, as well as the wide participation of the people in their government after the emergence of the Jacksonian movement, made the Southern yeomen one of the freest and most independent groups in the world.

The independent spirit of the Southern yeoman and his outlook on life are reflected in a rare manuscript diary kept by a small farmer of Mississippi between 1838 and 1846. The diarist, Ferdinand L. Steel, was born in 1813 in Fayetteville, North Carolina. When he was fifteen years old his family moved to western Tennessee; Steel worked on his father's farm there, helped in his father's trade as hatter, and worked on river steamboats. At the time of this diary, he was farming near Grenada, Mississippi. His silence on the subject of slavery and his slight reference to politics suggest that to the yeoman farmer these subjects were much less important than were the practical concerns of earning a living.

Steel's diary portrays the rather primitive frontier life characteristic of small farmers of the lower Mississippi Valley throughout the antebellum period. The Steel family was largely self-sufficient; Ferdinand made shoes for himself, his brother, and his sister Julia; the mother and Julia made their dresses as well as the shirts and "pantiloons" for the men. They manufactured their own lye soap, fashioned gourds into dippers, and the farmers' wives and daughters spun and wove cotton into cloth. They often concocted their medicines from herbs and roots. When Ferdinand contracted malaria, for example, he treated himself with boneset tea, although he also used quinine and calomel bought from the store in Grenada. The principal commodities the family purchased from the village store were sugar, coffee, salt, calico and domestic cloth, powder and lead. The diary records a surprising and seemingly needless expense of buying bacon from the store, but this occurred in the summer when the supply of meat from the eight or ten hogs they had killed in the fall must have been exhausted. Their accumulated store account for the year 1839 was only $73.78, which was paid after the sale of their cotton crop. Together with the sale of watermelons, their cotton crop brought a cash income of approximately $200.

Cotton was the money crop of the small Mississippi farmers, and the Steels raised five or six bales. Like most of the other small farmers, they used the gin of the near-by planter to prepare their cotton for market, paying a toll of one-eleventh; and when they took their wheat and corn to the mill, they also paid a toll. Ferdinand and his brother spent most of the fall picking cotton, on their best days picking as much as 120 pounds, an amount that was below the average of good slave hands. On several occasions Steel expressed the opinion that cotton was not a suitable crop for the yeoman farmer to raise. Cultivating cotton required such constant labor that other farm occupations had to be neglected. On June 5, 1838, in reference to his cotton crop, he wrote: "We are to [sic] weak handed. We had better raise small grain and corn and let cotton alone, raise corn and keep out of debt and we will have no necessity of raising cotton." But he was never able to abandon the crop, which indeed was his principal source of cash.

A typical day's activities in the life of Steel (and the yeomen in general) is recorded in the diary on March 22, 1839:

> I arise regularly at 5 o clock in the morning. After the rest of the family have arisen we have Prayers. I then feed 2 horses and with the assistance of my Brother milk 3 cows, from then to Breakfast I jenerally do some little job about the house. After breakfast I go to my regular work which is cultivating the soil, and work until 12 o clock at which time I come to dinner. Rest jenerally 2 hours, during which time I dine, then Pray to God and endeavor to improve my mind by some useful study. At 2 o clock I again repair to work until sun down. I then come in, feed horses milk cows, and then the days work is done. I sup and then I have a few hours for study, at 9 o clock we have prayers and then we all retire to Rest. This is the manner in which my time is spent. My Life is one of toil, but blessed be God that it is as well with me as it is.

The monotony of a life of farm toil was broken by visits to Grenada on Saturday afternoons. There he met other farmers and made small purchases. He and his brother also hunted deer and wild ducks and searched for wild bees' hives to obtain honey. He attended a celebration of the Fourth of July in Grenada, at which there was a reading of the Declaration of Independence, an oration, a "sumtious" feast, cold water toasts, and the taking of temperance pledges. He belonged to a temperance society in Grenada that had 181 members. On December 25, 1845, he left a Christmas party early because the young people were engaged in "the silly play of marching Down to New-Orleans." He had no relish, he comments, for such nonsense: "I feel thankful to God that he has, by his holy Spirit, inclined my heart to abhor that which will not tend to his glory." He enjoyed going to a singing school and concerts in the Methodist church. The principal occasions for sociability and rude amusement among the frontier farmers were log rollings, corn shuckings, and communal work on the public roads, in which Steel participated.

Steel's diary gives a remarkable view of the religion of the common man of the Old South. Steel was a devout Methodist who frequently attended various religious services—Sunday School, preaching, and especially the exciting camp meetings which often lasted a week. These meetings were held in the summer after the cultivation of the crops was completed. After coming from such a meeting, he wrote in his diary, August 13, 1841, "My Faith increases, & I enjoy much of that peace which the world cannot give; Blessed be God for the blessed hope of being free from Sin while I lived on Earth, & for the blessed anticipation of living in heaven, O Lord!" At another time after attending the quarterly meeting of the Methodist Church at Coffeeville he reported: "We had a happy time in Love feast on Sunday morning. Brother Sullivan our Itinerant preacher professed Sanctification and truly he seem'd a happy man. The people of Coffeeville were truly kind. O! how is the Religion of the Lord Jesus Calculated to make mankind sociable." He often engaged in "secret prayer" and strove to live free from sin so as to be ready to die. Untimely deaths in the community and funerals admonished him to be "ready," for "surely in the midst of life we are in death." Yet these gloomy thoughts in the diary were relieved by a note of gratitude to God for his temporal life. He displayed a strong belief in the justness of mysterious Providence, even when disasters such as a long drought came. Mingled with his unworldly religion were some folk superstitions—when a calf died after being altered, he attributed this misfortune to performing the operation in the wrong time of the moon. The religion of Ferdinand Steel was that of the common people of the Old South—full of humility, deprecating the worldly life, and believing in the literal word of the Bible as revealed religion. Tinged with the romanticism of the period, this religion of the plain people was highly emotional—Steel, for example, speaks of the Lord melting his heart to tenderness.

The most striking aspect of the diary is its revelation of Steel's ardent desire for self-improvement and his ambition to rise in the world. Forced to quit school early, he resolved to make up this deficiency by self-education. Accordingly, he procured an English grammar and a Latin grammar at the village store and devised a method of attaching his Latin grammer to his plow so that he could study it as he worked. He borrowed books from the Sunday School library and read the eight volumes of Rollins' history, the life of Martin Luther, Blackstone's *Commentaries on the Law of England,* Jones' chemistry, a Greek grammar that enabled him to translate the book of St. John in the Greek Testament, and Abercrombie's "The Intellectual Powers," which taught him rules of logic and correct thinking. It was a heroic schedule of long hours of study carried on despite adverse circumstances. Moreover, he helped his sister Julia acquire some education by paying her tuition with hog meat raised on the farm. Eventually, the serious young farmer became an itinerant Methodist preacher. The record he left in his diary contributes significantly to the opinion of the respectability of the large class of yeoman farmers of the Old South held by the modern revisionists. . . .

Kenneth S. Lynn

SOURCE: "The Politics of a Literary Movement," in *Mark Twain and Southwestern Humor,* Little, Brown and Company, 1959, pp. 46-72.

[*In the following excerpt, Lynn describes the political context in which Southern humorists wrote, and analyzes how Jacksonian politics influenced their works.*]

A passage from Samuel Clemens's *Adventures of Huckleberry Finn,* **one of the best-known works of Southwestern humor:**

The widow she cried over me, and called me a poor lost lamb, and she called me a lot of other names, too, but she never meant no harm by it. She put me in them new clothes again, and I couldn't do nothing but sweat and sweat, and felt all cramped up. Well, then, the old thing commenced again. The widow rung a bell for supper, and you had to come to time. When you got to the table you couldn't go right to eating, but you had to wait for the widow to tuck down her head and grumble a little over the victuals, though there warn't really anything the matter with them—that is, nothing only everything was cooked by itself. In a barrel of odds and ends it is different; things get mixed up, and the juice kind of swaps around, and the things go better.

After supper she got out her book and learned me about Moses and the Bulrushers, and I was in a sweat to find out all about him; but by and by she let it out that Moses had been dead a considerable long time; so then I didn't care no more about him, because I don't take no stock in dead people.

Pretty soon I wanted to smoke, and asked the widow to let me. But she wouldn't. She said it was a mean practice and wasn't clean, and I must try to not do it any more. That is just the way with some people. They get down on a thing when they don't know nothing about it. Here she was a-bothering about Moses, which was no kin to her, and no use to anybody, being gone, you see, yet finding a power of fault with me for doing a thing that had some good in it. And she took snuff, too; of course that was all right, because she done it herself.

Samuel L. Clemens, Adventures of Huckleberry Finn, *Dodd, Mead & Company, 1884.*

If one would read a noteworthy humorist of [the late eighteenth century], one must turn away from imaginative writing to the letters and speeches of John Randolph, the "wittiest man of his age." For a generation and more, Randolph defended his vision of the "Old Republic" with brilliantly sarcastic characterizations of the men who, he felt, were wrecking it. Thomas Jefferson was "that prince of projectors, St. Thomas of Cantingbury." John Quincy Adams and Henry Clay were "Blifil and Black George—the Puritan and the blackleg." The lawyer and merchant Edward Livingston was "a man of splendid abilities, but utterly corrupt. Like rotten mackerel by moonlight, he shines and stinks." Fighting with his back to the wall, lashing out in all directions, Randolph was a man whose enemies (this was his proudest boast) were legion. If he had friends, they were apt to be amongst the Jacksonians— men like Thomas Hart Benton, for instance—who respected Randolph's intransigent republicanism. In the eyes of conservative Southerners of the next generation, however, Randolph's states' rights philosophy made him the martyred hero of a sacred cause. Under attack in a hostile House of Representatives, this wealthy, brilliant man, known to be sexually impotent and rumored to be insane, arose from his seat and sneered at his enemies:

> The little dogs and all,
> Tray, Blanch and Sweetheart,
> See, they bark at me!

In the South, in days to come, that moment would be recalled and cherished.

Appropriately enough, it was in or around the year that Randolph died, 1833, that the long drought in humorous writing in the South came to an end, almost as if his death had been required to produce the literary movement that would so often invoke his name. All at once, almost in chorus, men all over the South—but most particularly in the region between the Alleghenies and the Mississippi, which was then called the Southwest— began to write comic sketches. It was a movement without a manifesto or a capital city; which had neither a recognized elder statesman nor an official journal. Yet the Southwestern humorists of the antebellum period were more cohesive in spirit, and more readily definable as a group, than the Transcendentalists, say, who were their contemporaries, and they were destined to influence later American writing in precisely definable ways. Scattered and out of touch with one another as they were, the Southwestern humorists were nevertheless bound together by all the things that counted: by a devotion to the same literary gods; by a common set of literary principles; and by the similarity of their social views. These writers were in fact so much alike that it is even possible to construct a biographical archetype that bears a fair resemblance to the lives of all of them. The ideal Southwestern humorist was a professional man—a lawyer or a newspaperman, usually, although sometimes a doctor or an actor. He was actively interested in politics, either as a party propagandist or as a candidate for office. He was well educated, relatively speaking, and well traveled, although he knew America better than Europe. He had a sense of humor, naturally enough, and in a surprising number of cases a notoriously bad temper. Wherever he had been born, and a few were of Northern origin, the ideal humorist was a Southern patriot—and this was important. Above all, he was a conservative, identified either with the aristocratic faction in state politics, or with the banker-oriented Whig party in national politics, or with both. To call the roll of the best-known Southwestern humorists in the twenty-year period from 1833 to 1853—Longstreet, Thompson, Kennedy, Noland, Pike, Cobb, Thorpe, Baldwin, Hooper—is to call in vain for a supporter of Andrew Jackson. No other fact about these writers is quite so significant.

A rendition of Huck Finn from the first edition of Clemens's novel.

In the 1820s, the men who would become humorists a decade later had fervently believed in Jackson. They yearned, as did most Southerners, for the end of the Adams administration and the accession of Jackson to the Presidency. The squire of the Hermitage would surely furnish the South a measure of relief from the unfavorably high tariff of 1828. The high tariff legislation of 1832 was thus a considerable shock; when South Carolina, under Calhoun's direction, declared the bill null and void, it was even more shocking to see Jackson push a bill through Congress empowering him to force compliance. Out of such shocks came, among other things, a new form of American literature. For it is not merely coincidental that the outpouring of Southwestern humor after 1830 began at the very moment that the Nullification crisis was reaching fever pitch, or that the most influential of all the humorists of the antebellum South, Augustus Baldwin Longstreet, idolized John C. Calhoun and was a diehard Nullifier. The fantastically bitter dispute over the tariff, beginning with Calhoun's famous Exposition of strict constructionist theories in 1828 and culminating with the Force Bill five years later, had momentous literary consequences because it inaugurated—even in those states where sympathy for South Carolina's extremism was not strong—the South's consciousness of itself as a collective entity, as a region that was apart and different from the rest of the nation. William Byrd had thought of himself as an English gentleman; Randolph had proclaimed that "When I speak of my country I mean the Commonwealth of Virginia," a sentiment in which Robert Munford would have concurred. But the flowering of Southwestern humor in the 1830s was the product of a new awareness. The humorous customs of local people in Georgia and Arkansas, and in Tennessee and Alabama and Mississippi, were to be recorded in literature because they were *Southern* customs, aspects of the life of a separate civilization, and therefore highly significant.

When to the tariff fight one adds the fact that the early 1830s saw the beginnings of a new and energetic abolitionist movement in the North, as well as a dramatic upturn in profits from slave-breeding and cotton culture, the defensive self-consciousness that inspired Southwestern humor becomes even more understandable. Many Southern writers turned, of course, to the "plantation novel" in order to justify the slavocracy, as if by pointing with pride to Greek Revival houses they hoped to make the world forget Uncle Tom's unspeakable cabin. Looting the novels of Walter Scott for a feudalistic symbolism, the plantation novelists amplified and extended the gentlemanly myth of Hugh Jones and William Byrd to gigantic proportions. Little more than a hundred years after Jones had implied that Williamsburg was another London, the plantation novelists suggested that the only proper comparison to the civilization of the cotton kingdom was the courtly life of the medieval lords. Launcelot and Guinevere, Ivanhoe and Rowena, now loomed in the Southern mind as the heroes of the Golden Age had in Don Quixote's. The humorists were equally fascinated by Scott—for they, too, were myth-makers. (Indeed, at least one Southern author, John Pendleton Kennedy, wrote both novels *and* comic stories in order to promote the Southern myth.) What the humorists learned from Scott was, first of all, the uses of history. Beginning with Longstreet, who subtitled a collection of sketches *Characters, Incidents, &c., in the First Half Century of the Republic,* the humorists attempted to foster a sense of the Southern past for the same reason that Scott had recorded Scotland's past: it was a means of asserting a national identity. Scott further taught them that "low" characters could serve their mythology as readily as could chivalrous heroes. Scott had turned to Scotch peasants and servants for his comic materials because the special flavor and peculiarity of, say, Andrew Fairservice, the gardener in *Rob Roy,* or of Jenny Dennison, Miss Bellenden's maid in *Old Mortality,* helped to define Scotland's distinctiveness; by being humorously "low," such characters also made Scott's aristocrats seem more grand by contrast. The Southwestern writers exploited the antic life of the poor white with analogous ends in view. Thanks in considerable part to the example of Scott, humor as well as romance was enlisted in the Southern cause.

As the symbol of an encroaching national power, then, Andrew Jackson came to be hated and feared by the new generation of humorists. There were other reasons, however, why Old Hickory loomed like a demon in their minds, reasons which perhaps go even further toward accounting for the startling exfoliation of Southwestern humor that began while Jackson was in the White House.

Describing, in *The Valley of Shenandoah* (1824), what life in Virginia had been like in the 1790s, the Virginia aristocrat George Tucker depicted a group of common roughnecks blocking the roads and insolently upsetting every carriage that attempts to pass. To conservative Southerners of the middle 1820s, this was not simply an isolated incident in the remote past; it was also the terrible image of what might happen to them at any moment, if they were not careful. Behind their insecurity lay certain hard facts. From the day that Jefferson had entered the White House in 1800, popular agitation had begun to build up in the Southern states for constitutional reforms to abolish religious and property qualifications for voting and holding office; to base representation on population rather than on county units; to widen popular control, in sum, over all the instruments of government. These changes could be accomplished, the reformers felt, only by means of specially summoned state conventions. For thirty years, efforts were made to call such conventions into being; and for thirty years, the conservative ruling class in the several states managed to hold the reformers at bay.

Then, quite suddenly, the reformers could no longer be denied. In 1829, a constitutional convention was called in Virginia; in 1833, a convention met in Georgia, and another in 1839; there was a convention in North Carolina in 1835, and a "Revolution of 1836" in Maryland. The democratic movement that swept Andrew Jackson into the White House in 1828 also penetrated the local defenses of the old order from Tidewater Virginia to the Gulf of Mexico. By 1860, every Southern state except South Carolina would have a democratic constitution.

The rise of Jacksonian democracy transformed Southern politics. The planter-politician who in Munford's time had condescended to the electorate now had to scramble for votes, inasmuch as in most contests the margin between victory and defeat was slim. According to one student of the subject, the vote of the Southern states was very nearly equally divided between the Whig and Democratic parties in every Presidential election from 1836 to 1852; according to another, Southern Democrats won an aggregate total of 234 seats in the five Congressional elections between 1832 and 1842, as opposed to 263 for their opponents, a difference of less than thirty seats in a ten-year period. Not until the slavery controversy reached the height of its fury in the 1850s did the South become anything like the monolithic society of legend.

In the economic sphere, life became equally competitive. Jackson's destruction of the Bank inspired other struggles against corporate privilege, until the "race for the top" had been blown wide open. Especially in the Southwest, a new breed of men emerged. Small-time stock speculators; clerks knowledgable in the mysteries of paper money and land prices; courthouse loungers with glib tongues and a smattering of law: they seemed to come out of nowhere, these men, even as Faulkner's Snopes clan would do after the Civil War. Bold, imaginative, oftentimes ruthless, sometimes unscrupulous, they were more at home in the flush-times atmosphere of Alabama or Mississippi than many a well-born *émigré* from South Carolina or Virginia, while even the cleverest and toughest *nouveau* banker or planter dared not grow soft or careless, lest he find himself no longer *riche*. The historian Richard Hildreth noted in 1836 that the poor whites in the South "are at once feared and hated by the select aristocracy of the rich planters," and these emotions were generated to a great degree by the terrific emotional cost of remaining king of the mountain in a wide-open economy devoid of rules or even precedents. Joseph G. Baldwin, one of the most accomplished of the Southwestern humorists, has left a memoir of the era which nicely captures the anxiety felt by many sons of the planter class that they simply could not compete in business with men who did not play the game the gentlemanly way. Baldwin is speaking of Mississippi and Alabama in the mid-1830s:

Superior to many of the settlers in elegance of manners and general intelligence, it was the weakness of the Virginian to imagine he was superior too in the essential art of being able to hold his hand and make his way in a new country, and especially *such* a country, and at *such* a time. What a mistake that was!. . . . All the habits of his life, his taste, his associations, his education—everything—the trustingness of his disposition—his want of business qualifications—his sanguine temper—all that was Virginian in him, made him the prey, if not of imposture, at least of unfortunate speculations. . . . If he made a bad bargain, how could he expect to get rid of it? *He* knew nothing of the elaborate machinery of ingenious chicane,—such as feigning bankruptcy—fraudulent conveyances—making over to his wife—running property—and had never heard of such tricks of trade as sending out coffins to the graveyard, with negroes inside, carried off by sudden spells of imaginary disease, to be "resurrected," in due time, grinning, on the banks of the Brazos.

To hold on to a world that seemed in danger of slipping from their grasp, Southern conservatives flocked into the newly-formed Whig party. Generally speaking, the merchants and bankers of the towns became Whigs, as did the majority of the planter class. Their allies among the professional groups, particularly the lawyers and newspaper editors who depended for their livelihood on the fees and good will of the merchants and planters, also joined the party. Inasmuch as the typical Southwestern humorist was a professional man, it is not surprising that the overwhelming percentage of those about whom political data exist were Whigs. As for the minority who were not, they might be called Whigs *manqués:* anti-Jacksonians who were too deeply committed to low tariffs and states' rights to accept the nationalist, high tariff policies fastened into the Whig platform by the Northern wing of the party. The Whiggery of the humorists is worth insisting on, for it tells us much about their entire cast of mind, including their comic imagination. In a preeminently political era, political allegiance was as important a key to American writing as religious belief once had been. About no group of American writers in the age of Jackson is this generalization more true than it is about the Southwestern humorists.

To the Whig mind, the quality of violence inherent in Jacksonianism was what made the movement so disturbing. The quality could be sensed at once in Democratic rhetoric. Taking up arms against Nicholas Biddle, the Democrats denounced his Bank as a "Monster," spewed out upon it the same sky-vaunting threats and curses, the same hyperbolic humor, that had appalled a generation of well-bred visitors to the trans-Allegheny West. The Democratic program was as violent in its effect as the oratory which put it across; wherever the Democrats touched American life, they galvanized the entire nation. There was a boldness about

Democratic ideas, a pragmatic willingness to take risks, to commit the nation to untrod paths, that the Whigs found frightening. ("They desire," cried the *American Whig Review*, "a freedom larger than the Constitution.") Hoping to avoid a repetition of the Panic of 1837, Jacksonians in the Southwest audaciously called for the abolition of all bank charters, not merely Biddle's. In the 1840s, the Democrats took up the daring theme of an American imperium that would extend southward into Mexico and as far west as the Pacific, while Whig orators timorously invoked the specter of Caesarism and the doom of all empires. The schemes of the Democrats, whatever their shortcomings, had a reckless grandeur; Whig ideas, by contrast, were prudential and cautions.

They might even be said to have been nonexistent. Henry Adams has remarked that "Of all the parties that have existed in the United States, the famous Whig party was the most feeble in ideas." To fight against economic and social mobility by means of ideas was, after all, excruciatingly difficult for a party composed largely of self-made men who agreed with Webster that "intelligence and industry ask only for fair play and an open field." Hamstrung intellectually, the Whigs counted on a series of emotional appeals to overcome the rampant Democracy. In an America made anxious, as Tocqueville observed, by the ceaseless competition of equals, the Whigs celebrated harmony and unity; denying reality, they offered the nation psychological relief in the genial vision of America as one big, happy family. In the North, the Whigs answered the class conflict analysis of a Seth Luther or an Orestes Brownson by preaching an identity of interest between merchant and mechanic (did not the Lowell mills, as Edward Everett suggested, have all the comforts of home?). In the South, the Whigs depicted gentle masters, happy yeomen, and grinning darkies living together in an atmosphere of domestic bliss. The log cabin and the white-pillared mansion were in the Whig iconology the two faces of the same charismatic image, for if the former signified democratic aspiration and the latter aristocratic pretension, both stood for the American Past, when conflicts of interest had been unknown, and both were Homes. Amidst the gathering storm of the slavery controversy, the Whigs insisted that the Union itself was a family; differences of opinion existed, of course, but as long as both North and South could go on loving the Flag and the Constitution, as long as both could look to Mount Vernon, which that fine Whig lady, Sarah Josepha Hale—author of *The Good Housekeeper,* sponsor of Thanksgiving Day, and editor of *Godey's Lady's Book*—was busily trying to have declared a national shrine, there was no sectional split that could not be healed. As for the manifold problems engendered by the headlong development of the country, the Jacksonians might agitate if they wished for political and economic reforms; the Whigs preferred to get behind the Infant School movement, do charity work, and above all, campaign for temperance. Because, to the Whig mind, the temperance movement was not simply a battle against alcoholism; it was a character ideal and a way of life. If temperance workers took George Washington as their patron saint—if somehow the Constitution crept into their discussions of juvenile drinking—if a Whig lawyer (it was Abraham Lincoln) could suddenly broaden the scope of a speech to the temperance society of Springfield, Illinois, and imagine a "Happy day, when, all appetites controlled, all passions subdued, all matters subjected, *mind,* all conquering *mind,* shall live and move the monarch of the world. Glorious consummation! Hail, fall of Fury: Reign of Reason, all hail!"—the reason was that the temperance campaign, to the political conservatives who were engaged in it, was the battle for America in microcosm. The checks and balances of the Constitution; the calm orderliness of George Washington's Virginia; the unity of the family—wild men had endangered this sacred heritage, but temperance would preserve it. Seeking to contain the violence of Jacksonian America, the Whigs spoke in praise of moderation in all things.

By now it should be clear why the literary hero developed by the Southwestern humorists was a Self-controlled Gentleman—the very model of Whiggery's ideals. His first notable appearance occurs in the comic sketches of A. B. Longstreet.

Born in Augusta, Georgia, Augustus Baldwin Longstreet had grown up in comfortable circumstances. He was educated at Moses Waddel's fashionable academy in Willington, South Carolina, where Calhoun had been a student, and then followed in the footsteps of his idol to Yale and to Tapping Reeve's law school at Litchfield, Connecticut. Like his father, William Longstreet, the graduate of Yale and Litchfield had a savage temper. When an actor in a Georgia theater sang a song one night which made light of William Longstreet's belief that he was a talented inventor, the subject of the parody, who was in the audience, got up from his seat, blind with rage, and stalked out. Angry withdrawals became one of his son's most conspicuous habits. Campaigning for Congress in 1824, he suddenly withdrew his candidacy, and eight years later he canceled his plans to run for the state legislature with equal abruptness. All during his later years as president of the Georgia temperance society and of various academic institutions, Longstreet constantly held above his trustees' heads the threat of resignation. Even as an old man, he issued warnings to his family that he was about to walk out of the house for good. That he backed Calhoun during the Nullification crisis, was a fervent supporter of states' rights, and eventually a convert to the cause of secessionism, only completes the pattern of vindictive withdrawals that shaped Longstreet's whole life.

His first sketches appeared in a newspaper in Milledgeville, Georgia, until Longstreet himself bought a paper. In 1833, the political faction in Georgia that supported Jackson and the Union had emerged more strongly than ever before. Longstreet, an aristocrat, a states' righter, and never a man to hide his opinions, decided to go into the newspaper business to defend his principles. Purchasing a paper in Augusta, he renamed it the *State Rights Sentinel*. Literary critics have often remarked the Southern vindictiveness of Poe's journalistic criticism, and Mark Twain's sketch of "Journalism in Tennessee" makes it abundantly clear that the tone of newspaper editorializing in the antebellum South was, as Twain said, "peppery and to the point," to say the least. Yet even when the journalistic temper of the times has been taken into account, one stands amazed in the furious presence of Longstreet's editorials. Corruption and filth—the words are Longstreet's—were all about him, and he attacked them with every verbal weapon he could muster, including defamation of character. One citizen who had incurred the editor's wrath found himself described in the *Sentinel* as having "two negro wives." As Longstreet's biographer has rightly observed, such editorials were the work of a fanatic.

By way of comic relief to the fury of his opinions, Longstreet supplied his newspaper with humorous sketches of Georgia life, culled mainly from his recollections of the days when, as a young lawyer, he had ridden circuit in the backwoods of Middle Georgia. As had been true of Fielding, whose vocation as Justice of the Peace for Westminster and Middlesex had taken him out of the cultivated world of Eton and Leyden where he had been educated and exposed him to what Maynard Mack has called the "vivid and barbarous life of country inns and alehouses"—an experience which formed the basis for both *Joseph Andrews* and *Tom Jones*—Longstreet the Yale man discovered in the strongly colored, highly flavored speech of the piney woods people, in their grotesque expressions and cruel sense of fun, a rich source of humor. No more than Fielding is to be equated with Black George, is Longstreet to be identified with the life he described, despite the careless confusions of numerous critics. The work of a highly self-conscious man, Longstreet's sketches were a comic version of the remorseless editorials beside which they appeared, an integral part of a continuing effort to impose the political opinions of the author and his aristocratic friends on the Georgia community, and beyond Georgia, on the whole South. Whatever its defects as a general theory, Bergson's insistence that comedy stands midway between life and the "disinterestedness" of most art in that it "accepts social life as a natural environment," and even has a "scarcely conscious intention to correct and instruct," says a good deal about Longstreet's sketches. As well as William Byrd did, Longstreet knew his Addison, the purpose of whose *Spectator* had been "to banish

vice and ignorance out of the territories of Great Britain"; destined to become a Methodist minister in later years, Longstreet in the early 1830s believed with the creator of Sir Roger de Coverley that laughter could guide the moral destiny of society as effectively as a sermon.

When George Bancroft observed in 1840 that Joseph Addison belonged by rights to the party of Daniel Webster, he was thinking not merely of the number of conservative writers in America who called the Englishman master, but of Addison's "reasonableness," which was so closely akin to the temperate ideals of American Whiggery. Certainly the Self-controlled Gentleman of Southwestern humor is the American cousin of Addison's Man of Reason, and the fact of the Gentleman's moderate nature is established by a variety of Addisonian means. The most important of them is the use of a "frame." The literary device of introducing a speaker who then tells us a story that comes to his mind was not new when Addison employed it, nor even when Boccaccio did, but Addison was the writer from whom Longstreet borrowed it. That the frame device eventually became the structural trademark of Southwestern humor is because it suited so very well the myth-making purposes of the humorists. For Longstreet and his successors found that the frame was a convenient way of keeping their first-person narrators outside and above the comic action, thereby drawing a *cordon sanitaire,* so to speak, between the morally irreproachable Gentleman and the tainted life he described. Thus the fact that the Gentleman found recollections of violence and cruelty both interesting and amusing did not imply anything ambiguous about his own life and character. However hot-tempered the author might be in private life, the literary mask of the Southwestern humorists was that of a cool and collected personality whose own emotions were thoroughly in hand.

By containing their stories within a frame, the humorists also assured their conservative readers of something they had to believe in before they could find such humor amusing, namely, that the Gentleman was as completely in control of the situation he described as he was of himself. As Maynard Mack has shrewdly observed, "even a rabbit, were it suddenly to materialize before us, . . . could be a frightening event. What makes us laugh is our secure consciousness of the magician and his hat." The frame device furnished an equivalent consciousness. When Longstreet concluded "The Fight," a particularly violent sketch, by saying, "Thanks to the Christian religion, to schools, colleges, and benevolent associations, such scenes of barbarism and cruelty as that which I have been just describing are now of rare occurrence," he reassured his readers that all was well. By asserting that barbarism was a thing of the past, the Gentleman tacitly affirmed that temperate Whig institutions were in control of the present, and in so doing released the laughter of those who might otherwise have shuddered at the comic spectacle. Finally, the frame device was a way of driving home, explicitly and directly, the social values of the author. "The peace officers," reads the last sentence of "The Fight," "who countenance . . . [barbarism and cruelty] deserve a place in the Penitentiary." To convert the entire community to the temperate values of Whiggery was the ultimate purpose of Southwestern humor, and the frame was the place where those values were most overtly insisted on.

The least successful of Longstreet's sketches are those in which his impulse to lecture the community in explicit terms carries over from the frame to the story itself. The same tendency mars much of the work of his successors as well. In "Darby, the Politician" for instance, Longstreet has barely thought through his story, or reflected on his characters; like John Pendleton Kennedy's *Quodlibet,* a dull, endless tale about good Whigs and bad Democrats, "Darby" comes closer to being a political speech than a short story. Darby Anvil is a blacksmith, "the first man who, without any qualifications for the place, was elected to the Legislature of Georgia." Instances of his ignorance and of the drunkenness of his supporters are cited with the mechanical regularity of the points in a lawyer's brief; in the end, the blacksmith is shown to be much worse off in every way than before he overreached himself by presuming to run against a Gentleman for office. One hardly needs to know that Longstreet's own political ambitions had come to naught in order to sense that "Darby" is the work of a man bent entirely on self-justification, and not at all on creating a meaningful fiction.

In his best work, however, Longstreet buries his meanings deep within the concrete action of the comedy. His finest stories are parables, not tracts. As Longstreet finally understood, the Self-controlled Gentleman was defined more convincingly by his ability to perceive eccentricity than by his habit of condemning it, and "Georgia Theatrics," "The Horse-Swap," "The Fight," and two or three other sketches which constitute the Longstreet canon, are distinguished by an intense observation of character.

In "Georgia Theatrics," the briefest of the sketches in *Georgia Scenes* (the collection of his humor that Longstreet published in 1835), the Self-controlled Gentleman is a minister of the cloth who tells us of a trip he once took through the backwoods county of Lincoln in the year 1809. Speaking in a calm and elevated tone, he remembers that the natural (although, alas, not the moral) condition of the county in those bygone days had been a thing of splendor, and he recalls his initial delight in the "undulating grounds, luxuriant woodlands . . . sportive streams . . . [and] blushing flowers." His mood of enchantment, however, had been suddenly broken by the sound coming from behind a clump of bushes of what seemed to be a terrible fight:

"You kin, kin you?"

"Yes, I kin, and am able to do it! Boo-oo-oo! Oh, wake snakes, and walk your chalks! Brimstone and—fire! Don't hold me, Nick Stoval! The fight's made up, and let's go at it.—my soul if I don't jump down his throat, and gallop every chitterling out of him before you can say 'quit!'"

The humor of the story is contained in the revelation that the commotion was not what it sounded like. Instead of the two brutes whom the minister had expected to find tearing each other apart, he had found instead a single eighteen-year-old boy, "jist seein' how I could 'a' *fout*." The story ends with the minister recollecting how he had examined the ground from which the boy had risen—"and there were the prints of his two thumbs, plunged up to the balls in the mellow earth, about the distance of a man's eyes apart; and the ground around was broken up as if two stags had been engaged upon it."

The minister's illusory contentment with the sylvan scene, his startled disillusionment, and finally his realization that his disillusionment is also an illusion, are represented with skill and economy. It is the youth, however, who makes the story. As he claws at the earth, he is a ridiculously quixotic figure, and we laugh, but the knowledge that Poe was fond of this story helps to call our attention to the darkness in the boy's life that it exposes. Victimized by the violent society of which he is a member, the boy's mind is thronged with images of violence; his fantasies of gouging out some ruffian's eyeballs with his fingernails are so real to him that he must take to the lonely woods to act them out. The subject of "Georgia Theatrics," as of Poe's "The Black Cat," is the psychology of aggression.

Did such a story have a political purpose? By its very artistry, "Georgia Theatrics" challenges the hypothesis that politics is the key to Southwestern humor. Yet the fact is that the conservative political allegory inherent in the sketch was recognized at once. Two years after the publication of *Georgia Scenes,* the Whig author of *Colonel Crockett's Exploits and Adventures in Texas* reproduced "Georgia Theatrics" as one of the episodes in the life of Whiggery's favorite backwoodsman. The author's sole adornment of Longstreet's tale was to suggest that the boy's assault on the mellow earth rather closely paralleled Andrew Jackson's ridiculous war on Biddle's Bank. The underlying political strategy of Longstreet's humor was thus clearly revealed by the more obvious literary intelligence which created *Crockett's Exploits:* if this author's allegorization reduced the richness of Longstreet's sketch, he nevertheless brought its political energies out into the open, enabling us to understand that just as the Self-controlled Gentleman who tells the story embodies a conservative political ideal, so the violent boy represents what to the Whig mind was the central quality of Jacksonism.

The moral contrast between the Gentleman and the youthful Clown is brought out in several ways. First of all, by the *cordon sanitaire* of the frame; secondly, by the superior point of view from which the story is told, a device which coerces the reader into laughing at—rather than sympathizing with—the boy; and finally—and most importantly—by the language. The language of the narrator is as urbane as Addison's; the cool elegance of the diction, the measured rhythms, the familiar yet reserved tone, are the credentials of an impeccably civilized man. Exemplifying a whole constellation of values, the narrative style speaks to us of order and rationality, of good taste, and of optimism tempered by wisdom; it is the style of "Christianity and the colleges," of sobersided and temperate adulthood—of Whiggery, in a word. The backwoods child, on the other hand, speaks in the vernacular. His idiom is not the hoked-up, synthetic mixture which the Whig propagandists represented Davy Crockett as speaking, but a barbarously authentic dialect, for Longstreet's purpose in employing the vernacular was to demonstrate the social and political incapacities of the barbarous Democracy, rather than to affirm the natural gentlemanliness of a backwoods Whig, as Crockett's ghost writers were attempting to do. By the same logic that compelled the Crockett myth-makers to be dishonest about how their pet backwoodsman talked, the mythmaking humorists were encouraged to be blisteringly accurate in their representations of popular speech. The exigencies of Southern Whig politics, which forced the writers of the Southwestern tradition to lift the ban on the vernacular, thus precipitated the linguistic revolution that led eventually to *Huckleberry Finn*. The sole consideration which restrained the Southwestern humorists in their use of the vernacular was the one which had caused William Byrd to keep the Clowns of North Carolina quiet: if the backwoodsman was too often allowed to speak out of his own grotesque nature, then perforce the language of the story would no longer present quite so clear an image of the Gentleman's values. That the vernacular menaced the moral didacticism of his style was clearly recognized by Longstreet. Trained in the classics of Roman antiquity as well as steeped in the literature of Augustan England, he did not need to be told what the reasons were for holding firm to a formal narrative mode. The formula worked out by Longstreet was to use the vernacular sparingly, and never to allow its uncouth accents to interrupt for very long the bland flow of the narrator's language. The Clown in "Georgia Theatrics," therefore, has fewer lines than the Self-controlled Gentleman, but when he does speak we hear a genuine backwoods voice. The language of the youth is a language of cruelty and violence; it tells of quixotic hallucinations and irrational fears; it is full of misspellings, bad grammar and crude expressions. In other words, it beautifully exemplifies what, to the Whig mind, were the reckless spirit and childish ignorance of Jacksonian America. Someday Mark Twain would rewrite "Georgia Theatrics" as one of the scenes in *Tom Sawyer*—which reminds us not only of how well he knew A. B. Longstreet's work, but also of how much the comic symbols of the Southwestern tradition meant to Twain's art, albeit he radically altered their moral evaluations.

Longstreet's best story is "The Fight," which Poe praised as "unsurpassed in dramatic vigor and vivid truth to nature." This sketch introduces Longstreet's most intensely observed character: first of a long line of unforgettable Southern grotesques, Ransy Sniffle anticipates—in the satiric brilliance of his name, in the comic ugliness of his appearance, and in the utter malevolence of his soul—Faulkner's Flem Snopes. He was "a sprout of Richmond," says Longstreet's narrator,

> who, in his earlier days, had fed copiously upon red clay and blackberries. This diet had given to Ransy a complexion that a corpse would have disdained to own, and an abdominal rotundity that was quite unprepossessing. Long spells of the fever and ague, too, in Ransy's youth, had conspired with clay and blackberries to throw him quite out of the order of nature. His shoulders were fleshless and elevated; his head large and flat; his neck slim and translucent; and his arms, hands, fingers, and feet were lengthened out of all proportion to the rest of his frame. His joints were large and his limbs small; and as for flesh, he could not, with propriety, be said to have any. Those parts which nature usually supplies with the most of this article—the calves of the legs, for example—presented in him the appearance of so many well-drawn blisters. His height was just five feet nothing; and his average weight in blackberry season, ninety-five.

At the end of the description comes the most telling detail of all: "He never seemed fairly alive except when he was witnessing, fomenting, or talking about a fight. Then, indeed, his deep-sunken gray eye assumed something of a living fire, and his tongue acquired a volubility that bordered upon eloquence." Infinitely more degraded than the youth of "Georgia Theatrics," Ransy Sniffle cannot set his mind at rest with mock violence; blood must flow in order to satisfy this backcountry sadist. Living only for violence, he willingly subverts the stability of society to satisfy his thirst for blood.

The figure of a sinister subversive who engineers the destruction of peaceful communities recurs often in Southwestern humor, indeed in all pre-Civil War Southern literature. As abolitionist pressure mounted, this subversive came more and more to be identified as a Yankee, and Southern variations on "The Legend of Sleepy Hollow" quickly multiplied toward infinity. As a Nullifier, Longstreet was early into the field with a story of a Yankee, called "The Village Editor." The sketch begins with a description of the "harmony" of life in Natville, the "good feeling" that prevails, the "temperate character" of all discussions, the presence in all families of "all the good things, and sweet things, and pretty things, that were found in one family." Into this Whig Utopia drifts a Connecticut Yankee named Asaph Doolittle; establishing a newspaper, he so agitates the townspeople with his editorials that soon good friends are at one another's throats. Before he is finally forced to leave Natville, "the village was completely revolutionized. The street meetings were broken up, the social parties discontinued, and many long years passed away before the citizens of Natville returned to their former friendship." The story makes its editorial point—that the North has no business interfering with the South—with awesome vigor; but as a study of character it is a failure. Doolittle derives from Longstreet's acquaintance with Ichabod Crane, rather than from his own observation. When, however, Longstreet turned from "foreign" to local subversives, he created the first memorable Clown in the Southwestern tradition. Kennedy's Flan Sucker, the "distinguished loafer"; Thompson's cadaverously ugly Sammy Stonestreet; Johnson Hooper's Simon Suggs; G. W. Harris's Sut Lovingood—these are the great Clowns of the tradition, and they all trace their ancestry back to Ransy Sniffle.

The Georgia county depicted by the gentlemanly narrator of "The Fight" is unified and peaceful—until Ransy Sniffle finds a way to tap its latent violence. Skillfully playing on hot Southern tempers, Sniffle provokes a fight between the two strongest men in the county, who previous to his machinations had had a "wonderful attachment" to one another. Soon the entire community is divided into two hostile camps. In the course of the ensuing battle, the two combatants, whose very names—Billy Stallions and Bob Durham—suggest their colossal strength, claw and tear at one another until one of the fighters has lost his left ear and a large piece of his cheek, and the other is minus a third of his nose. Ransy Sniffle is obviously well pleased by the bloodshed; but to the Self-controlled Gentleman the brawl has been a "hideous spectacle," and he concludes his story with a strong paragraph of moral condemnation. As for us, we emerge from "The Fight" as from a bad dream. Through the Gentleman's eyes, we have been witness to a vision of evil, a vision at once realistic and incredible, and made so largely by the character of the demonic Ransy Sniffle. While the clay-eater is in some basic sense a "true to life" character, as Asaph Doolittle was not, he can hardly be described as the fictionalized version of some back-

woods lout whom the author had encountered during his circuit days. His weight of ninety-five pounds, for instance, is as much of a tall tale as is the fabulous strength of Durham and Stallions. Although decked out in realistic detail, Sniffle is a creature of fantasy, like Poe's nightmarish Mob. No more than Simon Suggs would be, is Longstreet's Clown a detached and objective study of the Southern poor white; he is, rather, a projection, in outrageous caricature, of a political conservative's exacerbation. Behind the Self-controlled Gentleman's cool and collected pose was an outraged editorialist who savagely despised the new Democracy for the divisions that its upsurge had created in Southern life; and the strange story of a sadistic clay-eater who split the community in two is the product of that savage feeling. To the Whig humorists who came after Longstreet, the diabolic humor of *Georgia Scenes* would be a source of inspiration in the hard political years ahead.

James M. Cox

SOURCE: "Humor of the Old Southwest," in *The Comic Imagination in American Literature,* edited by Louis D. Rubin, Jr., Rutgers University Press, 1973, pp. 105-16.

[*In the essay that follows, Cox celebrates the unique quality of Southern humor writing, stressing its necessary intertwining of refinement and vulgarity.*]

First of all, there is the South. And the South is, as everyone must confess but very few remember to think about, beneath the North on all globes and wall maps. Even to go South in the mind is to go toward sin as well as sun. The Southerner is seen in the dominant Northern imagination as a little more poor, more ignorant, more lazy, more lawless, more violent, and more sensual than the Northerner. He is, after all, a figure of the lower regions, located, as he is, nearer to the equatorial belt which girdles the world.

If the location of the South on wall maps and globes poses one interesting possibility, the Old Southwest poses another. For what was the Southwest before the Civil War is now the Southeast. This is not at all true of the Old Northwest, which was made up of Ohio and Michigan. No one in his right mind would speak today of a Buckeye or a Wolverine as a Northeasterner. Another look at the map is instructive. Not only is the South beneath the North; it is also much to the west of it. It is well to remember that Atlanta is as far west as Detroit, just as it is well to know that Virginia's almost six-hundred-mile baseline piercing to Cumberland Gap reaches as far west as Toledo, Ohio.

There is, of course, an historical reason for our blurred sense of the original region. The Old Southwest, during the thirty years before the Civil War—the period when the Southwestern humorists flourished—was in the process of becoming the South, for the sectional strife which steadily intensified from 1830 until 1860 was reorganizing the country on a North-South rather than an East-West axis. After the Civil War, the Solid South became a decisive region in the national mind. Once that happened, Northern Americans and even many Southerners all but forgot how far west the South is of New England.

But at the beginning of the nineteenth century, the region was truly the Southwest. As West, it was wilder than the Northeast; and as South it was already involved in the whole long loss to the North which culminated in bloody Civil War. There was, then, from the beginning in the Southwest, something wild and something lost. It was bad enough to feel the cultural impoverishment of America in general. Hawthorne felt it in New England and set about recovering for his countrymen the shadow of a colonial past. Yet starkly impoverished as New England was in relation to England, Hawthorne, Emerson, Melville, Thoreau, and Whitman were making a national literature for their country between 1830 and 1860. Seen against that literature, the literature of the South is pale indeed. Poe alone—the Bostonian somehow fallen into the South—stands out. And even he stands out as writer rather than as Southerner. He is most Southern not in attaching himself to landscape as the New Englanders were doing, but in disclosing himself as displaced person. He is the Artist as Rebel; and he is most rebellious in constantly threatening to divorce truth from beauty, morality from aesthetics, and cause from effect. His perversity, his demonism, his disease, his audacious demoralization of literature all conspire to place him conspicuously against the New England tradition, causing him to seem, in the Northern imagination, something of a fraud, as if all the traditions he inherited were somehow at the point of disintegrating into his possession. Yet whatever vulgarity the practitioners of high literature might ascribe to him, his power is there. Scorn it, belittle it, lament it, exclude it, and it runs underground to be embraced as a great original imaginative current by a Baudelaire.

Aside from Poe, only the humorists of the Old Southwest are truly dominant in our early literature. Set against the Northern humorists, they are clearly more interesting. Washington Irving, the true humorist of the North, is surely a match for them, but Irving steadily moved away from his pseudonymous identity to settle at Sunnyside and become a writer of higher literature. He had left behind him "The Legend of Sleepy Hollow" and "Rip Van Winkle," both of which have about them something of the wild and humorous fantasy exposed through the elegant style of Geoffrey Crayon, *Gentleman,* and it is small wonder that "The Legend of Sleepy Hollow" was imported by Southern humor-

Washington Irving's Rip Van Winkle.

ists, disguised in one form or another, and retold along "native" lines. The process was inevitable; it was just what Irving himself had done to German stories he had read.

Aside from Irving, the greatest of the Northern humorists was Seba Smith, who graduated from Bowdoin seven years before Hawthorne received his degree there. Smith invented Jack Downing as a correspondent for his paper, and through the rural vernacular of his invention he was able to make fun of politics and politicians, particularly of the Democratic Party and Andrew Jackson. Smith's down-east vernacular was impressive; it had an acute shrewdness, a folksy plainness, and, above all, a garrulous loquaciousness which nonetheless suggested the terseness of the stage Yankee. By persistently relating Jack Downing to the subjects of politics and history, Smith directed his folk morality upon the affairs of state. Yet for all his exposure of politicians, Jack Downing's deeper social morality and essential rural quaintness remain intact. James Russell Lowell does much the same thing with Hosea Biglow. By turning to verse, Lowell gains an even greater pithiness and homely flavor for his conventional morality. James Whitcomb Riley was much later to achieve a similar effect with his poems of Hoosier life.

How different are the humorists of the Old Southwest. If Poe differs from the major Northern writers in his divorce of beauty from morality, Southwestern humor differs from Yankee humor in its threat to divorce pleasure from morality. There is of course enormous risk in such a divorce, for unless the imagination makes up in invention, surprise, and extension of language *by virtue of* the diminution of moral pressure the result is likely to be little more than joke-book and almanac humor.

The Southwestern humorists took that risk. To be sure, they did not take it abruptly or always decisively, but they took it. There were many of them—too many to discuss in detail in such brief space—but the work of Augustus Baldwin Longstreet, Johnson Jones Hooper, Joseph Glover Baldwin, Thomas Bangs Thorpe, Henry Clay Lewis, and George Washington Harris reveals the problems they encountered and the achievements they wrought. But a few more words about these writers as a group are in order.

First of all, they were determined to appear as gentlemen. Second, they tended to be professional men and political conservatives. Third, they were willing to be seen, just as they were willing to present themselves, as gentlemen first and writers second. Many of them sent their work to William T. Porter, a Vermonter, who edited a New York sporting magazine called *Spirit of the Times,* and Porter, one of the great editors of the nineteenth century, had the good sense to call for more and more of it. By and large, the writers received little or no pay for their work, and many never even collected their pieces, though Porter himself eventually made a fine anthology of them. Finally, their work generally took the form of sketches in which the polite language of the literate gentleman was made to surround and contain a frontier dialect.

Now the bifurcation between gentleman and yokel was not new; it was old as the hills and utterly inevitable in humor and comedy. The major contribution of Southwest humor lay in putting enormous imaginative pressure on both the gentleman and the bumpkin. The gentleman became more and more foppish and effete as the frontiersman threatened more and more to take over the narrative. The result was a language which, in the hands of the best of these writers, became a means of discovering a New World humor.

The problem as well as the possibility of Southwest humor is evident in the extraordinary work of Augustus Baldwin Longstreet, whose *Georgia Scenes* really ushered in the whole movement. Published in 1835, the same year in which Hawthorne's "Young Goodman Brown" and "The Haunted Mind" appeared, Longstreet made his way not into the moral wilderness of New England but into the comic and violent wilderness of the South. His "Georgia Theatrics," the brief but brilliant overture for the collection of sketches, is a refined clerical gentleman's recollection of having gone into the "Dark Corner" of Lincoln, a county which, he says, was a shade darker than the rest of the country. Moving through the green glade of Nature, he hears ahead of him the most violent and profane language of men in mortal combat.

> Yes I kin, and am able to do it! Boo-oo-oo! Oh, wake snakes, and walk your chalks! Brimstone and—fire! Don't hold me, Nick Stoval! The fight's made up, and lets go at it.—my soul if I don't jump down his throat, and gallop every chitterling out of him before you can say "quit!"

Hurrying toward the drama, the gentleman first hears one of the combatants scream in pain as his eye is torn out; then he hears the victor's cry of exultation. Appalled at the violence, he rushes through the undergrowth to the central scene, where he accosts the victor who is just rising from the fray. The youth replies to the morally vexed gentleman, "You needn't kick before you're spurr'd. There a'nt nobody there, nor ha'nt been nother. I was just seein' how I could 'a' *fout.*" So saying, the embarrassed youth leaves the refined moralist with the truth. There has been no real victim. Instead, there are only the prints of the lone actor's thumbs where they had been plunged into the earth as he imaginarily gouged out his opponent's eyes.

This opening sketch seems to me an extraordinary transcendence of the convention it employs. Although it discloses the crude and violent imagination of the uncouth swain, it just as distinctly reveals the refined narrator's impulse to disapprove of the violence. To see that far into the sketch, and it takes blindness indeed not to see that far (though anyone disposed to feel superiority to the South is likely to be so blind) is to see that the refined moralist makes his judgment on the fight before he sees that it was imaginary. If the youth is embarrassed to be "caught" in his private theatricals, the old man has wanted the drama to be real so that he can enact his superior disapproval of the violence he is hurrying to see.

That sketch alone reveals the rare superiority of Longstreet's grasp of his subject. He realizes at once that the refined moralist and the violent youth are intricately related to each other. They truly depend on and indirectly inform each other. The youth's embarrassment should be the moralist's for having leapt to a conclusion. Evading that blush, the moralist can but record the experience in language self-gratulatory and overrefined. Unless we see the joke of the sketch and see that the joke is just as much on the moralist as it is on the violent youth—just as much, but no more— we are likely to emerge with interpretations which, emphasizing how the sketch reveals the violence of the Southern mind, miss that half of the joke which exposes the moralist's need of crudity and violence in order to achieve his moral superiority.

Good though Longstreet was in that opening sketch, he was not always so good. And his weakness came from leaning too much toward refinement, politeness, and culture. At his best, as in "The Fight" and "The Horse Swap," Longstreet establishes situations in which the violence and picturesqueness recoil through the enclosing structure and expose it for the polite frame it truly is. Thus, Ransy Sniffle—the name itself is but one more stroke of Longstreet's genius—in "The Fight" is truly a progenitor of Faulkner's Snopeses. The grotesque, cowardly and depraved poor white who eggs two men into a fight, he is not so far different from the effete style which counterpoints the story, for it too needs the contrasting violence of Ransy and his fight to amuse it. Still and all, the imaginative energy, the almost gloating delight, which the frame style assumes in delineating Ransy's depraved appearance, betrays an aggression in the story which the humor in it cannot quite discharge. In "The Horse Swap," surely one of Longstreet's finest sketches, the grotesque and sensitive sore, concealed beneath the saddle blanket, enables one confidence man to edge out another, for its goading pain makes the hopeless old nag prance about like a thoroughbred. Yet the very disclosure of that raw and sensitive wound is intended to appall as much as to amuse the reader. In making this visibly shocking disclosure *as* the humorous climax of his sketch, the refined gentleman averts his eyes, as it were, in the very act of completing his joke. Though Longstreet at his best was able to show his clerical gentlemen and poor whites in a humorous act of transcendent cooperation, he nonetheless has a moral as well as an aesthetic disposition to withdraw from his humor. That is why the edge he seeks is always in danger of being outside rather than inside his world. Even so, his achievements and limitations define the possibilities of Southwestern humor. First of all, there is Longstreet's own path, following the border between refinement and vernacular yet keeping an edge of refined perspective between it and the vernacular and using that edge to barter for literary audience approval.

Longstreet's greatest successor along that path was Johnson Jones Hooper. Pursuing the essential lines of Longstreet's form, Hooper nonetheless made a significant change. He discovered for himself a central character who could make successive forays into Southwestern dialect and experience. Hooper's discovery gave his work both unity and direction, for, once committed to his character, Simon Suggs, Hooper couldn't withdraw into the weak positions of moral and aesthetic security which fatally attracted Longstreet. True, Hooper incurred risks of his own, chief among them the repetition compulsion lying at the heart of all humor. Thus, anyone reading *The Adventures of Simon Suggs* is bound to feel the author's mechanistic compulsion to send Suggs off into one more picaresque foray.

For Suggs is, after all, the old picaro reborn as the frontier confidence man. By developing a mock-eloquent and refined perspective, Hooper can, like Longstreet, release Suggs all the more forcibly as an energy and a language. By exposing frontier amorality in Suggs's central maxim, "It is good to be shifty in a new country," Hooper gains the moral edge for his humorous maneuvers. Indeed, the amorality which compels Suggs to prey upon the foolish, the ignorant and the futile releases him as a kind of fierce, predatory, wild man, whose language possesses the imaginative energy to dilate the refined language into fancier and fancier forms of mock eloquence.

In order for Suggs's repeated depredations to remain in humorous perspective, Hooper has to distort and demean his lower-class world so that it can receive Suggs's raids without offense to a civilized audience. Thus, in "The Captain Attends a Camp-Meeting" (which Mark Twain drew on so heavily in *Huckleberry Finn*), the whole evangelistic revival world is exposed as a kind of moral and sexual chaos, devoid of any redeeming intellectual or moral tone. Suggs's wildness and meanness constitute a warning for what could be released in the vernacular. Indeed, the very meanness is partly required by the moral frame which would contain him, for unless Suggs shows meanness, then the moral impulse in Hooper's enveloping frame cannot be activated.

Now one way out of the difficulty is to increase the imaginative investment in the framing literary language, thereby increasing the distance between the narration and the humorous character. Longstreet himself had managed such a maneuver in the sketches depicting Ned Brace, an irrepressible lying prankster. But it remained for Joseph Glover Baldwin in his *Flush Times of Alabama and Mississippi* to retreat almost totally into eloquent frame. If Longstreet's Ned Brace had cavorted in language as well as in act, Baldwin's Ovid Bolus, Esq., is all but completely materialized in the mock-eloquent narration. Although such a move makes any reader of *Flush Times* long for the colorful accents of Simon Suggs, Baldwin nonetheless repossesses a geniality which Longstreet and especially Hooper had been at the threshold of losing. Because he looks down on his subjects from a greater height, Baldwin can be more indulgent. As a result, *Flush Times* has a geniality of spirit which looks forward to Mark Twain's *Roughing It*. It is not really surprising that Baldwin himself made his way to California not as an outlaw, but as a judge bringing law and order into the territory.

Despite its recovery of geniality, Baldwin's refined perspective really loses more than it gains. For the future and ultimate power of Southwestern humor lay in discovering through dialect the direct experience of the frontier. The most dramatic example of that direct experience was the bear hunt. First emphasized by Davy Crockett, the bear hunt in one form or another had become the subject of innumerable stories. It remained for Thomas Bangs Thorpe, a Northerner who came to Louisiana, to realize the full possibilities of the bear hunt in one triumphant sketch, "The Big Bear of Arkansas." Retaining only the bare essentials of the frame, Thorpe practically turned over his entire sketch to the vernacular, making his bear hunter stand in the same relation to the bear that the refined gentleman stands in relation to the bear hunter. The bear embodies for the hunter the very wildness that the hunter embodies for the gentleman. If the bear hunter lives off and preys on the bear, so by economic implication does the refined frame live off and prey on the energy of the vernacular. That is why the frontiersman, once he has in effect taken over the sketch, pours his imaginative energy into releasing the bear as monster, as god of the wilderness, as sought-for mate, as dream—yet grounded in vernacular realism. This is not all; if it were, we would have no more than "poetic" vernacular and vivid metaphors. The height of Thorpe's imagination rests in embedding a joke so near the heart of his wild, free narrative that many critics have missed it. Thus, the bear hunter, after chasing the bear for years, is surprised by the bear during his morning defecation. Watch Thorpe make his frontier language all but conceal and circumlocute the "snapper" of his joke:

> I then told my neighbors, that on Monday morning—naming the day—I would start THAT BEAR, and bring him home with me, or they might divide my settlement among them, the owner having disappeared.

> Well, stranger, on the morning previous to the great day of my hunting expedition, I went into the woods near my house, taking my gun and Bowie knife along, just *from habit,* and there sitting down, also from habit, what should I see, getting over my fence, but that bear! Yes, the old varmint was within a hundred yards of me, and the way he walked over *that fence*—stranger; he loomed up like a *black mist,* he seemed so large, and he walked right towards me.

> I raised myself, took deliberate aim, and fired. Instantly the varmint wheeled, gave a yell, and *walked through* the fence, as easy as a falling tree would through a cobweb.

> I started after, but was tripped up by my inexpressibles, which, either from habit or the excitement of the moment, were about my heels, and before I had really gathered myself up, I heard the old varmint groaning, like a thousand sinners, in a thicket near by, and, by the time I reached him, he was a corpse.

There you have the most novel imagination of America linked up with the oldest joke in the world—the joke of being caught with one's britches down. Yet what ought to be embarrassment is converted into the very height of the tall tale happy ending.

That joke must have almost killed Thorpe, for in most of his work he withdrew into the moral superiority of the refined perspective. Thus he reduces Mike Fink to a kind of brutal killer as he rather tiresomely moralizes his narrative. He wants to show that he can't quite stand Mike Fink. It is not surprising that, with the approach of Civil War, he retreated North into the somber perspective of antislavery. Yet in his one sketch he had, in the form of the tall tale, achieved a reconciliation of the wild and the genial which no one before him had secured.

If Thorpe withdrew from Louisiana, young Henry Clay Lewis, who came there from South Carolina, did not. Indeed, Lewis refused to be intimidated by the meanness implicit in Southwestern humor. Whereas Longstreet, Hooper, and Thorpe attempted to keep their moral edge, Lewis threatened to drop it even as he kept the refined frame. Instead of having a lawyer or clergyman as his refined narrator, Lewis, who was himself a doctor, brought forth an older physician to recall his adventures as a young doctor. The old narrator is at once indulging and amusing himself with jokes savage enough to make many readers uncomfortable. Lewis brings Negroes as well as frontiersmen into the foreground of his sketches. His "Cupping on the Sternum" is surely one of the finest pieces of humor in all Southwestern writing, yet just as surely it could hardly be assigned to a modern college audience without embarrassment. A kind of extreme version of almanac humor, it yet has the grace and the relentlessness of high sophistication as the old doctor recalls his youthful mistake in treating a Negro woman. His mistake, though grotesque in the extreme, is inescapably funny, a final horrendous joke which many and many a civilized person could never publicly acknowledge he had privately laughed at. There would of course be many others who could not laugh at the joke even privately, but surely they would have as big a problem as those who laughed at it too easily in public.

Lewis did not stop there. His "A Tight Race Considerin'" brilliantly plots a joke in such a way as to achieve the kind of elaboration of "The Miller's Tale," without ever losing character portrayal and vernacular realism. In such a tale, all the language and style of the past are brought together to be exposed with maximum authority. Lewis also did his own version of the bear hunt; *his* bear hunter, who has lost his leg to a bear, finally conquers a bear by beating it to death with his wooden leg! The best part of it all is that he is telling his story to the doctor who had made the leg. No lover of *Moby Dick* should be without a consciousness of Lewis's humorous vision of Ahab's vengeance. Even to begin to appreciate Lewis's work is to know what American literature may have suffered with his death by drowning when he was only twenty-five.

Finally there is George Washington Harris, creator of Sut Lovingood. Harris drove himself deeper into frontier vernacular than any of his predecessors—so deep that his speaker, Sut Lovingood, embodies in their extremity all the amorality, savagery, meanness, and drunkenness of his progenitors in Southwest humor. But Sut is new. His dialect is practically a new language, for it is a deviation so remarkable that a reader must literally reconstruct his own language as well as Sut's if he is to understand it. Once the process of reconstruction begins, rich and wonderful possibilities of humor literally explode upon the page. Through it all, the figure of Sut Lovingood comes more and more to stand out as a new man himself. All but amoral, Sut seems to be the very principle of life and pleasure and chaos, all concentrated into his deviant language. He is, by his own definition, a "Nat'ral Born Durn'd Fool," and, aggressive though he is, his language reverberates with retaliation against centuries of repression. His very name, Lovingood, signifies the profundity of his relation to the world of sexual love. There is no better illustration of his potentiality as Sexual Lord of Misrule than his performance at "Sicily Burns's Wedding." There, he takes vengeance on the bride who has tricked him in an earlier sketch (Harris's whole rich world vibrates along lines of practical jokes as displacement for vengeance) by tormenting a bull with hornets ("insex" Sut calls them). The chaos which that bull visits upon the wedding party speaks worlds about the whole sexual principle so fragilely held in check by social institutions.

I could go on and on about Sut, but it is best to define Harris's master joke, which is, I take it, the pursuit of illiteracy with a language so sophisticated that only the most urbane audience could read it. That joke is, as all great humor must be, on Harris as well as on the reader. For if the reader has to be extraordinarily sensitive to the uttermost reaches of language to read the voice of the illiterate Sut, Harris himself was beginning to imagine for himself not a broad public for his jokes but an elite readership that would probably have surprised even him. Either that, or a large trained audience which he had somehow educated.

Whatever the case, the Civil War came and the humor of the Old Southwest disappeared beneath the powerful but sobering vision of *Uncle Tom's Cabin,* just as "Dixie" was to be momentarily trampled beneath the martial rhythms of "The Battle Hymn of the Republic" (that song, also written by a woman, which is to this day sung by "peace" marchers—a fact that had better be a last joke for someone).

All these humorists might have been forgotten had not Mark Twain, whose whole genius was rooted in the tradition, made his way into the dominant culture and, by placating the moral sense in an absolutely disarming way, released more humor for more people than the old "gentlemen" would have believed possible. If Mark Twain's achievement is likely to be what sends us back to them, when we get there we begin to know how strong his origins truly were.

Kenneth Lynn pinpoints the racism in Southwestern humor:

In the decade [1850s] of Dred Scott and bleeding Kansas, Southwestern jokes at the black man's expense reached an apotheosis of fury. George Washington Harris's Sut Lovingood delighted in humiliating and frightening slaves; while black men yelled with pain or terror, Sut stood by and snickered. But even Harris's vindictiveness was eclipsed by the ferocious humor of Henry Clay Lewis, a Louisiana physician. To Lewis, the female Negro was a carnal animal whom it was fun to torture under the guise of medical treatment. In a story called "Cupping the Sternum," he told of applying a "scarificator" to a slave woman's breasts and buttocks. "Click! click! went the scarificator, and amidst the shouts of the patient and my awful solicitude for fear I might cut out an artery, the 'deed was did.' But no blood flowed, nothing but grease, which trickled out slowly like molasses out of a worm hole." Elsewhere, Lewis delighted his readers with the story of his attempt to steal a Negro baby in order to dissect it; he also told, in a jocular tone, of obtaining the skull from an albino Negro cadaver—"It was the work of a few minutes to slice the face from the skull"—and then using it to frighten a superstitious widow; and he recounted in nightmarish detail how an ugly Negro dwarf tried to choke the life out of him in the middle of a swamp, and how the dwarf fell into a fire and died horribly, while the gasping author looked on. That Lewis's book, *The Swamp Doctor's Adventures in the South-West,* was considered a humorous work is amazing, but true. Published in 1858, it furnishes a significant insight into the psychology of the slavocracy on the eve of the Civil War.

Kenneth Lynn, in Mark Twain and Southwestern Humor, *Little, Brown and Company, 1959.*

James H. Justus

SOURCE: "The Underheard Reader in the Writing of the Old Southwest," in *Discovering Difference: Contemporary Essays in American Culture,* edited by Christoph K. Lohmann, Indiana University Press, 1993, pp. 48-64.

[*In the following essay, Justus examines the accuracy and politics of Southern humor writing, arguing that the fiction and the reality were far apart, and that the fiction maintained the social power of the literati who produced it.*]

What we *hear* when we read humor of the Old Southwest is funny regional dialect. What we *overhear,* especially in the 1990s, is a system of cultural values that finds great comic turns in what we now understand as sexism, racism, ageism, and xenophobia—a cluster of biases that necessarily intervenes in both the comprehension and enjoyment of the humor. What we should *underhear* when we read humor of the Old Southwest is its literariness, the substantial noise of generic forms and the casual jumble of conventions. These texts, because they are so rarely subtle in their effects, test the boundaries of the liminal for the reader who responds only to what is heard and overheard. What is underheard may not be heard at all, but even if it reaches us only subliminally, it is the last of these hearings that makes an impression.

In reading this humor, when we become aware of repetitive narrative situations and character types, we tend to process them while responding to the dominant sounds of vernacular speech, deviant language that absorbs the niceties of motivation as well as our curiosity about the relational context of characters who use it. The aural reception of this kind of text is dominant because the specialized idiom appropriates those stable constituent elements that we think of as the glory of the novel as a form—plot and character. With the possible exception of George Washington Harris' yarns about Sut Lovingood, the typical humorous sketch in this body of writing shows no interest in the creation of complex characters engaged in complicated experience. This is true partly because the vehicle of this humor is not the novel but the anecdote, the joke, the tall tale, the piece that fits into limited allotments of newspaper space, but also because they more comfortably respond to the expectations of a related body of affiliated forms: the essay, the travel letter, the sporting epistle, even the "character," that seventeenth-century form that was designed to encapsulate idealized representatives of the human species (which in the Mississippi Valley rapidly became favorite high-profile stereotypes: the half-horse half-alligator; the backwoods innocent; the sexually omniscient widow).

[Mikhail] Bakhtin told us that to understand Rabelais we should be prepared to renounce all our deeply ingrained expectations of literary taste. That is, we should be alert to the eruptive presence of "inferior" dialects, disruptive argot, the despised demotic of resolutely nonliterary groups in the shaping of texts that are otherwise written in accepted styles. I would suggest that in the writing with which I have been most recently concerned, we see almost the reverse process. To understand the writing of the Southwestern humorists—that, too, of Mark Twain which was its culmination—we should be prepared to *underhear* the eruptive hum of respectable voices even in the flamboyant orality of backwoods roustabouts whose links are not merely with their inarticulate yeoman cousins but with the very custodians of literary taste.

Southwestern humor is a refraction of one region's demographic upheaval in the second and third decades of the nineteenth century. The literary texts beginning a decade later are one version of that social instability, one in which power relations are oddly comported, an effect of rampant chicanery achieved by the simple device of wretched excess, a compositional habit articulated through obsessive recurrence, unnatural selection, and rhetorical overkill. While particular cultural traits and activities (boasting, say, or courtship rituals) are italicized—sometimes literally—others (say ordinary domestic life among all the classes) are subordinated or omitted entirely. The world of the humorists is specialized and stylized; it is also vulnerable because its cohesive familial and communal relationships are so frail. Fraternization, organization, bonding, groupings of all kinds are premised on expedience. The sketch offers us a condensed reenactment of the exercise of power in the actual geography it celebrates. The point of competition is to establish individual priority within and even despite those fragile group arrangements. There are always winners, which means that there are also losers, those who are "tuck in." From the practical joke to the swindling of widows, however, the winner's material take in all these competitions is always modest: psychological satisfaction and a few dollars to splurge on an oyster supper. The game is everything, because it is the model for the exercise of power. So pervasive is this pattern that the play of power itself becomes a convention.

What I would like to focus on here is a refinement of structure in the kind of sketch in which an educated, sophisticated, and cultivated man of the world confronts a backwoodsman who then recounts an episode out of his experience in the woods. If not exactly a gentleman, the narrator is a respectable, tolerant sort of individual willing to be amused—a stand-in for the author and, from the reader's perspective, "one of us." The backwoodsman—a yeoman farmer, a hunter, a boatman, anyone whose chosen sphere is the relative isolation beyond towns and villages—may be ignorant of some of the most basic kinds of information that the narrator takes for granted, yet he is savvy, tenacious, gregarious, and garrulous—and also willing to be amused. What adds interest to this kind of sketch is that its dynamics of winning and losing are somewhat more complex than those sketches with other structural patterns—the epistolary, say, as in Charles Noland's Pete Whetstone letters and William Tappan Thompson's Major Jones, whose letters to the editor comprise one single unmediated vernacular discourse. What we see in the sketch that features the encounter between narrator and backwoodsman is the textual representation of how the writer, committed to the values of social stability and civic order, participates in the competitive game of his time and place. As the later arrival on the scene, the narrator assumes all the conventional attitudes of the traveler in exotic newfound territory;

the native figure he encounters is seen as a cultural primitive. What is prior is Other. Though the encounter may elicit some mutual good natured scorn, it is not hostile; and indeed that narrator goes out of his way to promote this individual of such different values and habits, opening a space in his sketch for the vernacular figure to become his own hero by taking over the narrative through the sheer stylistic energy of an alternative language.

The best-loved sketch in all the writings from the Old Southwest—and the one that lent its name to what was once perceived as the "school" of Southwestern humor—is Thomas Bangs Thorpe's "The Big Bear of Arkansas," the very model of this narrative pattern. The gentlemanly narrator, on his way upriver from New Orleans on a steamboat, finds his reading interrupted by a genial and voluble backwoodsman by the name of Jim Doggett, who entertains the passengers with stories of Arkansas, a state so naturally fecund that he has found it too dangerous to be a farmer: "'I had a good-sized sow killed. . . . The old thief stole an ear of corn, and took it down to eat where she slept at night. Well, she left a grain or two on the ground, and lay down on them: before morning the corn shot up, and the percussion killed her dead.'" He has accommodated himself accordingly: "'natur intended Arkansaw for a hunting ground, and I go according to natur.'"

The narrator hears Doggett before he sees him ("we were most unexpectedly startled by a loud Indian whoop" coming from the bar); with a "confused hum" of broken sentences and a "Hurra for the Big Bear of Arkansas," he verbally propels himself into the steamboat cabin and into the company of a larger audience. His one-liners, all windy tributes to "the creation State," are received with appreciative skepticism by the "heterogeneous" passengers who seem to be from everywhere but Arkansas. The narrator approaches the hunter:

> [C]onscious that my own association with so singular a personage would probably end before morning, I asked him if he would not give me a description of some particular bear hunt; adding, that I took great interest in such things, though I was no sportsman. The desire seemed to please him, and he squared himself round towards me, saying, that he could give me an idea of a bear hunt that was never beat in this world, or in any other. His manner was so singular, that half of his story consisted in his excellent way of telling it, the great peculiarity of which was, the happy manner he had of emphasizing the prominent parts of his conversation. As near as I can recollect, I have italicized the words, and given the story in his own way.

What is to be noted is that Doggett's style is readily identified as the shrill bombast of the half-horse half-alligator figure, derived from an earlier phase of Mississippi River commercial life (that of the flatboats and

keelboats), and whose most artful reconstruction is Mark Twain's rejected raftsman chapter in *Adventures of Huckleberry Finn*; but here it is notably domesticated and humanized. The narrative focus is on the remarkable "creation bear" that the hunter declares was "an *unhuntable bear, and died when his time come*." Although Doggett typically undercuts his own predictable hyperbole—the champion hunter turns out to be a failure in his biggest challenge—that loss is compensated by the air of a mysterious supernature under whose aegis he operates, one which Doggett acknowledges by his "grave silence" when completing the tall tale and one which the narrator in turn also acknowledges by noting how the audience responds to the teller's awe with its own silence. Thorpe's variation on this pattern, reinforced by the tonal complexities arising out of it, makes "The Big Bear of Arkansas" distinctive among the other humorous sketches; but common to this family structure are (a) the accommodating relationship between the restrained, educated narrator and the garrulous backwoodsman, and (b) the ambiguous status of vernacular speech.

Although speech is a privileged mode according to certain theorists, it achieves that status *after* the advent of a text-centered culture. One of the fictions of the Southwestern sketch is the assumption that backwoods vernacular is rendered in a transparent medium meant only to reveal its spokenness. The celebration of oral culture is accomplished of course through writing. Further, it is not only second-hand (like any representation), its second-handedness comes from the same source as the blander rhythms of the narrator. The authority who complacently situates himself within a telling-and-listening context, who leisurely prepares for us a descriptive introduction to the kinetic show that is about to burst so theatrically upon us, is the same authority who stages and directs the show itself. What we are really getting from the narrator, and from the author whose mouthpiece he is, is a showy gesture of skill: *I'm talking like him, now*, which of course celebrates the *I*, not the *him* he mimics. And as "one of us," the narrator prepares for our reception of the Other, but the truth is, it is announced not by a shift in the *sounds* of English, but by a shift in the material look of the text on the page: the kinds of words or pieces of words (italicized), such as *pre-haps* and *notiony*; phrases of arcane import—*ramstugenous, slantindickler*; and clusters of odd syntax that compel attention if not understanding. Thus, the source of authority remains stable, however chaotic the local linguistic effects may appear to be or however disorderly the society depicted by those effects. There is finally no turning over of authority from a genteel narrator to a rawer, more immediately forceful storyteller.

Enfolded into the larger story of failure, Doggett's boasting mode is more perfunctory than functional, an anachronistic discharging of a debt to convention, as if this Arkansawyer must affirm his place in the Crockett/ Fink "character," only to reinterpret himself in the westward declensions of another model—perhaps Jefferson's virtuous yeoman farmer, or the chastened James of [J. Hector St. John de] Crèvecoeur's *Letters from an American Farmer*. To speculate so is not, however, to grant prior agency to the "Doggett" we see and hear but to grant some creative ambitiousness beyond the formal boundaries that contain him: the faint dissatisfaction with convention, the attempt to reformulate and reinscribe character, is Thorpe's own.

What we remember in the humorous sketch is the vernacular constructions of the narrative, not the substance. We know this in part because the authors of some of the mediocre sketches, ineptly believing that the *done* things of backwoods figures are what make them memorable, concentrate on summarized action with the said things unmemorably paraphrased. The best of the authors knew from the beginning that the *said* things—the way the backwoods men and women recounted their often less than spectacular deeds—were the primary interest. One of the great ironies of Southwestern humor is that a body of writing which purports to valorize speech only emphasizes writing itself as the originating mode. What we are expected to regard as an innocent transparency is a calculated, composed, hyper-conscious system that draws attention to itself as a vehicular agent. And the conductor of that vehicle is a writer—amateur or not—who draws upon a vast range of prior writings to render credible the illusion of a spoken English and, incidentally, the illusion of power-sharing.

The suggestion of [Claude] Lévi-Strauss—that the function of writing is to enslave—is too solemn by half, but there is no denying that in the competition to possess the Old Southwest, both the theoretical and the practical power were in the hands of the literate: those who recorded land grants, those who wrote regulatory laws in the separate legislatures, those who wrote judicial decisions in the courts at every level—and those who wrote comic versions of the confrontations between the privileged and the subordinated. It does not take great imagination to conclude that verbal authority among the Southwestern humorists is not necessarily committed to the aesthetic freedom of unending experimentation; it is a practical authority, one in which the luxury of time and tireless revision count for very little. What we know of the way so-called primitive types spoke depends almost entirely on these writers— amateur ethnologists, amateur folklorists, amateur anthropologists, but not, I think, amateur writers. They were derivative writers who relied on earlier texts to suggest the scribal means for articulating their experience of observation; their talents were synthetic, amalgamating, traditional, and (soon-to-become) conventional.

The writers of the Old Southwest were not merely literate; most of them were well read. If these preachers, doctors, lawyers, editors, actors, and planters could only incidentally parade their learning in the conduct of their primary callings, they were more than eager to exploit it when they took up their pen. Beginning with A. B. Longstreet in 1835, these writers produced a discourse that reflects less the raw, overheard, spoken language in the Old Southwest than an older turn-of-the-century written language, with its full arsenal of linguistic and rhetorical conventions. Many of the pieces retain the marks of utilitarian seriousness, as the narrating voice alerts us to the kind of information we might like to know: a geographical description (with relevant statistics about population, soil types, mineral deposits, flora and fauna); an anthropological account (with heavy emphasis on Native American culture and artifacts); a sporting episode (with personal experience of a recent hunting expedition); a sketch of a specific site (with notes on massacres, aborted settlements, pioneer trading camps, and other lore that in the 1830s pass for historical interest). But the putatively informational, which easily glides into the non-utilitarian, self-indulgent impulse toward the personal, is displaced by the expression of aesthetic needs: the topographical description, say, assumes romantic heightening according to the now-belated norms of the Sublime; the factual presentation of a hunting party is enlivened by emphatic profiles of backwoods guides and idiosyncratic hunters and trappers in the bush, an exercise in the exaggerations and summary quirks of the character out of (eventually) Webster and Overbury and (more directly) Addison and Irving.

By responding to their literary promptings through humor, these writers freed themselves from the great American cultural expectation that literature be socially responsible; yet their texts are dependent upon prior forms of respectability and prestige. Although the nature sketch, the topographical description, the essay, the public letter were all eminently flexible forms that allowed these authors individualized shaping, they also determined the gentlemanly style (allusive, balanced, complex, witty) with which the amiable amateur could maintain his authority without being an author. But the sway of convention governed not merely the "genteel" portions of the humorous sketch—those featuring the narrator as man of the world—but the depiction of the vernacular protagonist, especially the way he dressed and the way he sounded. Moreover, such convention governs the work now assigned the initiating place in this literary tradition, *Georgia Scenes* of 1835. The discoverer of the backwoods individualist is not A. B. Longstreet; the seaboard colonials in both New England and the South acknowledged his existence and described his eccentricities, and some, notably Timothy Dwight, even made an effort to render his odd speech in certain regularized linguistic forms.

Backwoods speech quickly becomes vernacular set-pieces: verbal displays of folk idioms, malapropisms, neologisms, so striking, so rhetorically revved up that they virtually become material objects. And the maker is an aural poacher, fashioning sounds into marvelous patches of wordplay. For all the editorial pieties from William T. Porter and other influential editors about cultural responsibilities to capture the flavor of natives before the natives disappear into a homogenized population, the native speakers themselves have no control over how they sound once their speech has been appropriated by the writer. What we read is a literary construct at least two removes from actual vernacular: Jim Doggett and Pete Whetstone of Arkansas sound like Jim and Chunky of Mississippi, Daddy Biggs of Alabama, and Yellow Blossom of Georgia. A few typographical tricks—the use of italic font, the apostrophe, phonetic spelling—serve equally for any of the fictionalized sites of the Old Southwest.

One of the inescapable conclusions about this process of conventionalization—which applies (with certain more discriminating provisos) to canonical writers of the nineteenth century as well—is the considerable extent to which even a third-rate contributor of funny sketches to his town's editor participates in the hegemony of social power. In the competitive games of the Old Southwest between the aggressive settlers and the less favored people whom they encountered in the drive to fill up the newly opened lands, the winners were always confident of their success. The squatters and marginalized settlers, the riverboat hustlers, the hunters poaching in Choctaw and Cherokee lands, even the reclusive and suspicious loners in the deep bush were, like their socially privileged betters, interested in their own economic survival; but unlike the settlers, they had no economic stake in seeing either the backwoods or the frontier space transformed into deep south versions of Virginia or Carolina. What these prior residents of the region were up against were determined and ambitious emigrants, the kind noted in travelers' accounts as *go-ahead* types. The term derives from Davy Crockett, that quintessential misfit whose "philosophy" was widely circulated: *Be sure you're right—then go ahead.* The final clause became a universal recipe for action, even as the first clause was a burdensome condition to be ignored. Visitors to the flush-times cross-roads and villages applied the term to middle-class artisans, displaced professionals, and shrewd, socially gifted entrepreneurs, but especially to the restless, risk-taking planters trekking in from the old seaboard states, usually with an extended family and a slave or two. The competitive spirit in the backwoods was more modest—or at least it was played in a different key. The activities of rural Georgians that first prompted Longstreet to a writing career were by and large intramural competitions—eye-gouging, ear-biting fights; horse-swaps; bouts of marksmanship; practical jokes—a tendency we see in most of the sketches that followed *Georgia Scenes.*

We can speculate, I think, that one of the reasons why Longstreet, Alexander McNutt, John S. Robb, William C. Hall, Thomas Bangs Thorpe, and many others found these activities so engaging was that they were not only largely confined to rivals within the same marginalized groups but they offered no threats to the planter and professional classes: their truculent deeds, their explosive games, their extravagant displays of independence were in fact shadow versions of the larger games ongoing among the privileged classes. There is of course no evidence that these backwoodsmen thought of their activities as a kind of surrogate, second-best version of those of the settlers—illiterates leave few records—but they were not stupid. They knew as early as the 1820s that the wielders of power were Indian agents, land commissioners, legislators, and judges—many of whom were also planters eager to expand their holdings. In the context of such larger games, mere bearhunts, fights, and courting rivalries must have been perceived by the participants as local and harmless and quaint—as they certainly were perceived by the authors. Even the backwoodsmen's hardy encroachment on and dispossession of the original inhabitants are half-hearted, frail, and desultory compared to the official program of dispossession undertaken by the shrewd moderns, the efficient and educated purveyors of governmental civilization.

The authors, who are also purveyors of that civilization, safely celebrate the games of a marginal people who will become even more marginalized in the years just before the Civil War. What these authors celebrate is the voice of the backwoods, but the celebration is on civilization's terms: writing rather than speech. The theater of the oral performance—on the decks of steamboats, in courtrooms, on village streets—has limited occupancy; the theater of the oral performance rendered in writing reaches beyond those shabby local sites into other shabby local sites, into law offices, parlors, smoking rooms, in every region of the country, into the offices of the New York *Spirit of the Times,* even into the salons of connoisseurs in England. The authority lies not with those primitives who speak with vernacular bite but with the moderns who mimic those idioms in writing.

In that writing the Southwestern author has the satisfaction of control over all the disparate elements of his world, if only in a symbolic way. He unobtrusively mimics the gentleman, even if he is only a hard-scrabbling newspaperman or an actor or a middling lawyer in a crowded field, just as he mimics all those vernacular heroes who are not as socially aspiring as he and whom he chooses to see as agents of disorder. Seeing himself in one light and the backwoods figure in another, he uses his power of literacy to assert the priority of order, measure, reason, the virtues of a civilized community, even when the text he produces is laced with irony, self-mockery, and the frequent temptation to succumb to the anarchic freedom he imagines the backwoods to be.

One of the strengths of his time and place is its *in-betweenness*. With the ejection of the native tribes by Jacksonian fiat, the Old Southwest is no longer one thing; and with the process of filling up still continuing, it is not yet what it is destined to be. In the meantime is his time, a transitional era of remaking, reformulating, repossessing; and his place, a transitional space of mobile boundaries and shifting landmarks in which making, formulating, and possessing are still provisional attempts. The Southwestern writer—himself an exile, an emigrant, committed to the party of civilization and tempted continually by the party of individualism—is defined by what historians once called the "frontier paradigm," with its "options and tensions between freedom and necessity, safety and danger, liberty and restraint, order and disorder." But these choices are never permanently made in the writing of these humorists. The *in-betweenness* is a psychic space as well as a geographical one, and within the flexible boundaries of that kind of frontier he plays out the game of his own moral amphibiousness.

The sketches from the Old Southwest are interesting to me not for their portrayal of familiar types along the swiftly changing southern frontier but for the revelation of character among the ambitious settlers, among whom the authors counted themselves. In the pieces that dramatize competition as the very linchpin of a society, the respectable authors and their narrators identify with aspiring *go-aheaders*. In passages of dialogue and in monologues that internalize and impersonate vernacular culture, the author-narrator is merely a mimic, but in the laws of rhetoric the mimic always remains superior to the speech imitated because he is both originating voice and mimicked voice. Even sympathetically generated dialect in the sketch is edged by parody, the inevitable mark of condescension, because any attempt to record a speech pattern different from one's own can never be a neutral enterprise.

But if in that process the writer most often betrays his self-consciousness, his awareness that in class and political persuasion he is superior to his marginalized hero, he also occasionally shows an often surprising capacity for unfeigned sympathy for him, a momentary suspension of judgment (ethical and political) that allows himself a kind of licensed entry into what he normally regards as the unrestraints of the Other. There is some evidence that this momentary elision of difference in the narrator functions similarly to daydream and fantasy in which transgression can be enjoyed without retribution. The very act of verbal subordination—in which the man of standard received English seemingly turns over control of his medium to one who wields a wild and deviant idiom—denotes attraction: immersing oneself in the pleasures of linguistic

deviance is to enjoy the impulse of social transgression. But there is another sense in which the stylistic opposition between narrator and vernacular hero is not as radical or cleanly defined as we often suppose. If we accept the Barthian notion that it is language that speaks, not the author, then the text that constitutes the humorous sketch is a multi-dimensional field in which many "writings" meet and compete with each other. The author behind the narrator, who is also the author behind the backwoods voice, draws upon a vast pool of writings, none of which is original, all of which preexist as convention; and his role—his "only power," in [Roland] Barthes' words—is to mix those writings, countering one with another "in such a way as never to rest in any one of them."

It is often assumed that the narrator presents himself in a standard English that even in nineteenth-century usage comes across as pretentious, too stiffly formal, and fussily accurate—the better to throw into relief the deviant idiom of his subject. It is a reasonable assumption, but one unsupported by the texts. Here, from Thorpe again, is what a narrator's introduction sounds like:

> Here may be seen, jostling together, the wealthy Southern planter and the peddler of tin-ware from New England—the Northern merchant and the Southern jockey—a venerable bishop, and a desperate gambler—the land speculator, and the honest farmer—professional men of all creeds and characters—Wolvereens, Suckers, Hoosiers, Buckeyes, and Corncrackers, beside a "plentiful sprinkling" of the half-horse and half-alligator species of men, who are peculiar to "old Mississippi," and who appear to gain a livelihood by simply going up and down the river. In the pursuit of pleasure or business, I have frequently found myself in such a crowd.

While there is a pleasing rhythm in this highly controlled and balanced prose, it is more colloquial than formal; and its self-conscious emphasis on parallel substantives contributes to its pictorial density. Here is another example, from Solomon Smith's "The Consolate Widow":

> Between Caleba Swamp and Lime Creek, in the "Nation," we saw considerable of a crowd gathered near a drinkinghouse, most of them seated and smoking. We stopped to see what was the matter. It was Sunday, and there had been a quarter race for a gallon of whisky.

This is an even more serviceable prose. The texture of such "gentlemanly" discourse is not significantly formal; it is not pretentious; indeed, it is a remarkably supple style.

I would suggest that the controlling authorial style, in its very engagement with the vernacular, loses some of the stark correctness that many mainstream writers of the time felt obliged to follow. In the juxtaposition of levels, the vernacular "degrades" the superior style. Orthographically, we do not even need the quotation marks around "plentiful sprinkling" in the first example to know that this process is underway; and in the second example, "considerable of a crowd" has neither quotation marks nor italics to proclaim its vernacular origins—it has already been effortlessly absorbed into Smith's own standard level. The reasons for this stylistic accommodation, I think, are both social and psychological. It is as if the author, while wanting to make clear the differences between his narrator and the backwoods character (a fact that is pretty obvious anyway), wants at the same time to bridge that social and cultural gap. When the narrator's style is ponderously emphatic, it functions as a blatant rhetoric of difference, satirically deflating the narrator himself. And if the purpose of a modulated standard English is to negotiate with the vernacular, to suggest a difference without grotesquerie, that function would actually reflect the situation in the communal life of the Old Southwest. The social milieu was one in which the mingling of classes and ranks was more the rule than the exception. It could hardly be otherwise in a time and place marked chiefly by demographic instability. We may imagine the young lawyer-narrator of Joseph Baldwin's *Flush Times* [1853] exclaiming to himself *what a spectacle! what odd types are these in Alabama!* But the words are usually unwritten, and the interacting levels of style are considerably less exclamatory; and what we find are the signs of mutual influence and pervasive accommodation in the heterogeneous mix of the region. In attributing motive to this stylistic accommodation, it does no harm to speculate that what the respectable man of the town wants from the unrespectable man of the margins is the sense of individual integrity and vitality behind the quaint artifice posing as self-confidence.

Despite many of the book titles (*The Flush Times of Alabama and Mississippi; Georgia Scenes; Fisher's River Scenes and Characters*), the humorous sketches only indifferently depict specific cultural customs or the topographical peculiarities of specific locales (a notable exception is Henry Clay Lewis' *Stray Leaves from a Louisiana Swamp Doctor*). Longstreet's Georgia is intended to represent the sparsely settled, raw, and morally unenlightened counties west of Augusta and Savannah; Baldwin's Alabama and Mississippi are geographically interchangeable; Cobb's Mississippi could be any of those states below the Ohio and north of Louisiana. Almost from the first the not-so-reluctant authors wrote and sent in their dispatches datelined Tuscaloosa; Greeneville, East Tennessee; Baton Rouge; Hawkins County, Kentucky; Little Rock, as if the geography mattered; but like many of the backwoods

figures that the sketches celebrated, the woods and villages in which their verbal and physical exploits are set all look the same.

For the humorists, landscape is human geography, and the space meriting their attention has in defiance of actuality already filled up: there are too many people, especially lawyers and their clients, and raw nature seems uncomfortably circumscribed. Natural features such as trails, rivers, and canebrakes are as domesticated as cabins, stables, and churches. Landscape, both natural and man-made, is crowded with frolics, courtings, quiltings, faro games, oyster suppers, camp meetings. One curious effect of this symbolic density is not that the backwoods have suddenly taken on liveliness and diversity, those advantages that towns can boast, but that the mythic backwoods have been stripped of their natural definition and function and replaced by glut and disorder, the price that boomtimes exact for more sequenced development.

The world the humorists made is neither urban nor rural; and it is neither civilized nor primitive. It is an artful construct in which everything is foregrounded, people and objects simultaneously clamoring for attention. It is a world in constant motion: greasy playing cards, hunting dogs, steamboats stopping to wood and roaring to race, mourners' benches, trading scams, disappearing fritters, disappearing oysters, disappearing turkeys, bustled girls falling in hot mush, Sut Lovingood's legs. George Washington Harris' backwoods baroque is the culmination of a composed geography that had long ignored its minimal mimetic boundaries. The worlds of the humorists may occasionally differ, but they are all stylized. Baldwin's Alabama and Mississippi seem to be populated by nothing except judges, jurors, lawyers, and clients. Longstreet's Georgia, delineated when the state had already passed its frontier stage, is neatly divided between the social competitiveness of pretentious village matrons and the physical testing of males unmediated by charming creatures or any other carriers of culture. Johnson Jones Hooper's Alabama is a moving frontier where everyone except the Indians deserves victimization at the hands of a shifty rogue. Henry Clay Lewis' Louisiana is one extended swamp of albino blacks, dwarfs, panthers, corpses, and curious landladies.

In short, the world of Southwestern humor is crowded, busy, rowdy, noisy, and filled to overflowing with specialized humanity. Figures move with dispatch over a landscape crowded with other figures. It is, in the words of Melville's Redburn, "a moving world," and it moves in a stylized way. There is no boredom, as there often is in contemporary private documents, because there is no unused time. There are no dispirited stretches of loneliness, or to put it another way, there is no privacy because people are never alone. What we see are groups: two men come together, if only to swap items of trivial value, and they are immediately joined by an audience—to observe, commit, take sides, bet. Even in the hunting stories, the hunter stalks or is stalked by bears, panthers, wildcats in a nature that is as circumscribed and domesticated as Natty Bumppo's wilderness. Houses may be to live in, but they serve mostly as magnets drawing diverse people to their premises, where getting undressed and going to bed is as public an act as fighting or storytelling. Space and time are filled up, a metaphorical congestion that therefore requires self-sufficiency and a vigilant eye trained to detect the soft spots in others. Baldwin's lawyerly sensibility sees chicanery as the spirit of the times, which he deplores even as he profits from it, and chicanery requires the successful practitioner to develop a disposition ever at the ready with a strong nose, a keen eye, and, in Baldwin's phrase, "no organs of reverence." That disposition applies not only to the litigation artists in the Flush Times but also to small-bore swappers and traders, fight contestants, hunters, preachers, quilters, and yarn-spinners.

To what extent is Southwestern humor an accurate reflection of the actual world of the Old Southwest in the three decades before the Civil War? If it is social history we want, the patterns of migration, the quality of social organization, the influence of institutions, the growth of cultural life, and much more can be understood by reading contemporaneous accounts that need no spurious justification: records of travelers both foreign and domestic, those compendia of practical advice known as emigrants' guides, and the odd amalgams of autobiography and topography that we get in such striking volumes as Timothy Flint's *Condensed Geography and Recollections of the Last Ten Years in the Valley of the Mississippi* [1826] and J. J. Audubon's *Delineations of American Scenery and Character* [1926]. Even with firm authorial biases, these works depict a society of real dimensions whose exuberance and energy emerge from its variety, not from the intensification of the same phenomena. These accounts acknowledge the rawness of the new states, but they also record a potpourri of social graces and manners with their own integrity, a wide spectrum of talents both ornamental and useful, and an urgency for establishing a society just like that which had been left behind in the Atlantic South.

This image—or, better, these images—of a more normative society are also confirmed by the writing from the Old Southwest in modes never intended to be made public: commercial daybooks, family correspondence, business journals, and private diaries. If these private documents of the antebellum Mississippi Valley seem inert and placid compared to the public writing by the humorists (or even the published memoirs and travelers' records), it is because they exude an aura relentlessly domestic and utilitarian. The writers of letters and diaries never tire of recording fevers and menus,

visits and ceremonials, texts for sermons and responses to them, weather reports and the yield of corn and cotton, the cost of muslin and lace, and laments about sickness, death, and financial failure of cousins and neighbors. But, interestingly enough, this literature of everydayness, however private its origin, also composes itself as written texts, which means that the same conventions learned from prior texts shape its articulation in much the same way as public writing.

One of the more remarkable private texts is a series of diaries by Caleb Goldsmith Forshey (1813-1881), engineer, surveyor, and amateur scientist whose time and place coincided with that of the humorists. Educated at both Kenyon and West Point (though graduating from neither), Forshey pursued his career with all the energy, ambition, and impatience of other go-aheaders who emigrated to the new lands looking for the main chance. At one time or another, he was a promoter of various railroads, a builder of a levee system for the lower Mississippi, a founder of a military institute, a designer of military defenses of the Texas coast during the Civil War, and an ardent advocate of scientific land reclamation in the Gulf South. He was both literate and literary, and he took himself seriously; and while he never relaxed long enough to write humorous sketches for the public's entertainment, he did contribute to respectable journals many technical essays for its edification. Beginning in 1845, he wrote pieces on Humboldt's Cosmos, climatology, the physics of the Mississippi River, the Indian mounds of Louisiana, the meteor showers of 1848-49, and what he calls genetic "depravity" in the children of polygamous Mormons. For obvious reasons, Forshey's extensive diaries are more interesting than his public writing: they reveal an intelligent mind that is assiduous without being innovative—just as the essays do—but they also betray a temperament that ranges with fascinating rapidity from, say, a mournful address to his dead wife to an impromptu voyeuristic letching for a sixteen-year-old backwoods girl.

We should not take at face value the humorists' own protestations that their writing was a youthful indiscretion or a hobby to pass idle hours.

—James Justus

In the 1840s Forshey settles just across the river from Natchez, in Vidalia, where Thomas Bangs Thorpe is postmaster and editor of *The Concordia Intelligencer*. As an official surveyor of public lands, Forshey lives more in the bush than the Big Bear man ever dreamed of, even when the humorist was assembling his sketches for his first book, *Mysteries of the Backwoods*. Each horseback expedition takes Forshey from ten days to two weeks; a hired guide serves as both companion and provider for campsite food, though Forshey always spends nights when possible with the semi-permanent residents in the remote areas on his route— backwoodsmen whose family, opinions, and eccentric habits provide materials for his daily entries. In towns, Forshey visits acquaintances whose collections of fossils and shells he is always eager to inspect; he sets great store by social affairs, for it is in these years that he is actively seeking another wife. The diaries offer Forshey the means for recording, for comparative purposes, the attributes of each available prospect, accompanied with meditations on each one, internalized debates about their merits and defects, and fantasized projections of what the future with each one might hold.

But Forshey's diaries are all-purpose documents. They are as necessary as his surveying tools for recording land measurements; they function as commonplace books into which he copies bad poems from the newspapers; they are a repository of his scientific observations: descriptions of geological strata, of water temperatures in wells, of wind damage at sites struck by tornadoes, of direction and frequency of meteor showers. He uses diary pages to draft official letters and to index names and dates of his correspondents. And for all personal matters, the diaries function as surrogate companion for absorbing his confidences. Their multipurpose importance is suggested by the title pages that Forshey devises for each:

> Diary & Notes
> of
> Business, Science,
> Caprice and Miscellany
>
> Diary and Notes
> of Business, fancy
> Science &
> Miscellany
>
> Journal & Diary
> of things & thoughts
> by the way
>
> Diary and Notes of
> various kinds
> Professional, scientific
> and
> Promiscuous
>
> Diary and Notes
> of Business,
> of Fancies, & Thoughts
> of Science
> and Miscellany
>
> Diary & Notes
> Scientific & Promiscuous

It is probably needless to add at this point that Caleb Forshey in his private writing shares important traits with his contemporaries among the very public humorists. His racism and sexism are not virulent or especially disfiguring over the course of several years of sustained confessions, but they tend to manifest themselves directly rather than through dramatized anecdote. He shows a Whiggish distrust of poverty and the lack of enterprise he sees as its source; but he is a spirited democrat in his distaste for foreign dandies, snobbish ladies, arrogant gentlemen, and self-serving sycophants in offices of elected officials. And while there is a rhetorical directness missing in the humorists' sketches, he has read them as well as the prior texts they all share as formative models for literary expression: Scott, Addison, Irving, Cooper, Burns, and the ever-popular Romantic poets. The pull of nostalgia and the virtues of sentiment can be triggered easily and often, in "Sweet tears of remembrance [that come] gushing." Forshey pauses often, for two years after the death of his wife, to shed regulated tears, scaled as *sobs, sighs, anguish,* and *melancholy,* in a prose carefully structured to reflect those discriminations. Even though they are thoroughly private entries, his sentences show changes in diction, with appropriate cancellations. Sentiment can overpower him in nondomestic situations, as well. His patriotic sense tells him to weep when, upon visiting Mount Vernon, he finds the grounds neglected and overgrown with noxious weeds; and when passing the tomb of William Henry Harrison on an Ohio River steamboat, he records his response: "an involuntary tear [*gushed* canceled; *dropped from my eyes* canceled] trickled my cheek, as I thought of the virtues reposing there." And he resorts to his chilliest formal prose in reprimanding "a surly & selfish John Bull" who wonders aloud what Forshey could see in William Henry Harrison.

He carries his diary wherever he goes and in whatever degree of society he finds himself, self-consciously noting that *saucy, flirty, black-eyed Sal* is watching him write and speculating about what she must be thinking as he watches her watching "the stranger" write. Forshey also carries in his head a variety of styles of appropriate range to record his diverse entries. It is a solid, reportorial prose when he fills the pages devoted to "professional" or "scientific" matters; but for those pages where he can relax in "Promiscuous" or "Random observations," he draws upon his substantial knowledge of literature, history, classical mythology, and common lore. He shows no hesitancy in thinking of himself as a writer. Literary style for him is the respectable style of an earlier generation. In a word picture of his own sylvan grounds, he notes "the shark of fresh waters . . . devouring their neighbors of the finny tribe." On a journey into Missouri he falls impeccably into the literary mood: "Dawn upon the Prairies, away to the horizon[']s verge the meadows sleep in their pearly covering, & await only the cheering smile of the glorious sun to shake off the dew drops, and wave to the morning wind a fresh salutation—onward steals the morning Light." He sings *matins* and *lays* as his *steed* bears him through the *almost pathless woods*. He is prone to draw lessons from all kinds of spectacles he comes upon—lessons of value in the vein of Longfellow and Whittier—even when the incidents themselves are reported in straightforward fashion.

Caleb Forshey is probably no more representative of the conservative Whig of the Old Southwest than any other single individual in the planter and professional ranks. That his writing shows idiosyncratic traits as richly as it does generic ones makes his case a useful one for questioning the appropriateness of "gifted amateur," the term we continue to apply to the Southwestern humorists. We should not take at face value the humorists' own protestations that their writing was a youthful indiscretion or a hobby to pass idle hours. There were simply too many in this diverse group who persisted in their trifling avocation over a number of years for us to take such claims seriously. The skilled and the clumsy, the well-known and the obscure, the ambitious who published collections of their newspaper writing and the anonymous whose sketches lie forgotten in the files of the *Spirit of the Times*: they were writers, just as Caleb Forshey was a writer. And both the published and unpublished writings are the material residue of a culture of which they were a part just as fully as was the writing of self-confessed professionals like Edgar Poe and William Gilmore Simms. Which is another way of stating that the general climate of antebellum cultural aspiration, with its alternating urgencies of restraint and transgression, touched every person who set pen to paper.

What is to be remarked about the texts from the Old Southwest is not their obvious derivation from the oral folk tradition—the strenuous attempts from Longstreet to Harris to reproduce sounds of yeomen, not sounds of gentlemen, attest to that—but their promiscuous melange of literary influence. It is my thesis that this writing is not so much an exploitation of raw, overhead spoken language as it is the residual flowering of verbal transformations of an old-fashioned written language, some of which derives from canonical writers, some from their popular imitators, and some from those quasi-professional sporting authors of both England and America who carried graceful, indolent, and witty self-consciousness to the racetrack and stables in the towns and to fishing and hunting sites in the wild.

Because it projects a specialized and dense world, stylized and conventionalized, Southwestern humor is a fiercely *made* writing, self-conscious in both its enlargements and its elisions.

Though I think the reading of private forms of discourse—letters, journals, diaries, daybooks—of the same time and place helps very little to corroborate the social reality depicted in the humorous sketches, they do provide clues to the dynamics of class relations on the southern frontier and especially to the sense of verbal propriety observed by literate and literary men and women. The writers of personal forms—creatures of piety and propriety whose *writing* presumably departs only minimally from *doing*—inscribe themselves through convention even as they live by convention.

In the hands of the humorists, piety and propriety are filtered, diluted, spiked, and queered by their opposites so intensely, so repetitiously, that impiety and impropriety become the indispensable ingredients in the recipe. Having no organs of reverence is itself a convention. But the sketches are not unbuttoned writing: what holds up even the "inexpressibles" are simply different buttons. Unlike other influential editors in antebellum America, William T. Porter decreed that politics and religion were not appropriate subjects in his paper. Most of the humorists found it easy enough to abide by Porter's prohibition. While some of them did find capital fun in Methodists, in their sketches for the *Spirit of the Times* they generally refrain from specifying party affiliation of the quaintly ridiculous subjects: preachers are just *generically* hypocritical and lecherous and corrupt; local sheriffs and judges and politicians are just *generally* hypocritical and lecherous and corrupt.

But Porter's taboo subjects are only a minor indication of conventional restraints. What importantly shaped the humorous sketch was literary convention itself; though the writers may have satirized the pompousness of the sublime used so relentlessly to describe nature, very few of them in their straightforward moments are entirely weaned from that handy nourishment—not even Mark Twain, who made the most sport of it. Though the humorists knew how to use the approved standard literary style—allusive, balanced, complex, witty—for broadly deflating certain subjects, this was their "normal" style. And in depicting the backwoods protagonist, especially the way he sounded and the way he dressed, not much was added or changed after 1835, when *Georgia Scenes* began the fashion.

All this is not to diminish the achievement of the Southwestern humorists, who until recently have been diminished quite a lot already. It is to acknowledge their achievement as complexly conceived and effectively rendered pieces of writing—not spilled folklore.

BROADER IMPACTS

Clarence Gohdes

SOURCE: "Humor," in *American Literature in Nineteenth-Century England,* Columbia University Press, 1944, pp. 71-98.

[*In the following excerpt, Gohdes documents the zeal with which British readers consumed American humor writing and speculates on the source of that popularity.*]

So impressive is the avidity with which the English consumed the products of transatlantic wits and drolls during the period immediately following the Civil War that the historian who attempts even such a superficial survey as the present one may well be asked to assign causes for the phenomenon.

Of course no explanations of quirks in public taste are really adequate. The crocuslike flowering of British enthusiasm for Artemus Ward, Mark Twain, and other American humorists of the sixties and seventies is essentially similar to the recent vogue for cross-word puzzles or for plebeian wit attributed to Confucius—something for the social-psychologists, or even the sociologists, to generalize about. The student who ponders the problem of why many men have laughed soon finds himself confronted with that unresolvable question, "Why do I laugh?" Voltaire indicated the power of his intelligence as well as his skepticism when he opined that he who probes behind laughter for its reasons soon proves himself a fool. But whether folly or not, a few reasons, all perhaps of equal weight, may be advanced.

In the first place, a number of American humorists of undeniable abilities in drollery and satire confronted the British reader within a very short period. Ward, [Charles Godfrey] Leland, [Samuel] Clemens [Mark Twain], and [Bret] Harte struck the London bookmarts in quick succession after [James Russell] Lowell and [Oliver Wendell] Holmes. Moreover, the widespread interest in the Civil War led to a perusal of and reprinting from the newspapers of the United States on a scale much greater than ever before—and the newspapers provided the peculiar shaping force as well as the chief medium through which native American humor developed, the oral yarns of the frontier notwithstanding. Reports of Lincoln's enjoyment of the "funny fellows" were circulated in England, and some of his own pronouncements were esteemed to be of the order of the tall tale, such as his statement that the Mississippi gunboats were of such light draught that they could float wherever the ground was a little damp. The British themselves recognized the influence from abroad. Consider, for example, the following statement from *Blackwood's* for October, 1867:

> Of late years, partly in consequence of the great interest excited by the Civil War, and the more than usually copious extracts made by the English newspapers from those of America, and partly in consequence of the popularity achieved by many American books—such as 'Sam Slick,' 'Uncle Tom's Cabin,' the 'Biglow Papers,' and the jests of Artemus Ward—a large number of American words and phrases, that ought not to be admitted into English literature, have been creeping into use amongst us, and exercising an influence upon the style of our popular journalists, our comic writers, and even of our ordinary conversation.

Evidently the American cinema has had predecessors in its philological suggestiveness! Hear also the opinion of a writer for *All the Year Round,* delivered in 1878:

> Everybody knows that the newspaper fun of the world is now mainly of transatlantic origin. The Americans regard drollery as an essential part of journalism—something absolutely indispensable, and to be indulged in at whatever cost; often at the sacrifice of good taste, not to mention graver considerations. . . . Over five thousand journals keep us pretty well supplied with mirth, even as the Gulfstream is said to warm our climate. They have, indeed, somewhat superseded, if not eclipsed, the native article. These facts are patent to everybody.

The quotation serves also to illustrate another important factor in the heightened zest for comedy from the United States, the recognition of its superior quality. Of course not all the critics would admit any such thing as American superiority, even in popular humor, but many did. A writer for *Temple Bar,* surveying the literary products of the year 1871, noted: "As for funny books, humorous books, and comic books, we have had none this year at all of our own. But we have had certain American books of humour, and Leland, and Mark Twain, and Bret Harte have struck out new lines of humour which are sure to be immensely popular." The *Spectator,* the following year, in a review of Mark Twain's *Screamers,* asserted that the "United States are taking a lead in the humorous literature of the day," and recognized the fact that Bret Harte, John Hay, and Artemus Ward came not as single spies. In 1873 the same journal, in a discussion of Josh Billings, reflected sadly: "the Americans are, in their way, more humorous than the English," but offered consolation in the thought that the Scotch could not enjoy Artemus Ward as keenly as their southern brethren. Samuel Waddington, considering "American Vers de Société" in *Tinsley's* for June, 1876, remarked that transatlantic authors in the field surpassed their British fellows because of the possession of a "keener sense of humour" and a "witty quaintness which seems to be indigenous to the country." Even after the peak of enthusiasm was passed one finds the *National Observer,* in 1891, gloomily wailing: "Fun we must have, of course. If we cannot import it, duty free and carriage paid, in bulk from America, it must be brought (O the pity of it!) from France."

But another reason for the concentrated fervor of the sixties and seventies is the fact that a number of the humorists came to the British as men from the wilds of the Far West. The extraordinary interest in the border settlements which had existed in England since the day of the Noble Savage, and earlier, and which had been nourished by Fenimore Cooper and a variety of other writers, had received a remarkable stimulus during the period of the gold rush. After 1849 the Golden West was a veritable stamping ground for the European imagination. Anything on California in the way of a book was likely to have a sale; even the anthology of Western poets edited by Bret Harte was brought out in London, in 1866. The only subdivision of the United States which Mudie's Select Library recognized in its catalogues was California. Speakers in Parliament referred to its wealth in their debates, and, later, the Dean of Westminster described the redwoods in his sermons. On his deathbed Charles Kingsley, who abjured democracy and all its ways, babbled of the green fields near the Pacific. Even today the most intelligent type of Englishmen who visit our shores, the Commonwealth Fellows, regularly make their pilgrimage to the West Coast. In the sixties and seventies the first literary spokesmen of the region began to be heard in Europe. Artemus Ward lectured on the Mormons; Joaquin Miller sang of the landscape; Mark Twain spun yarns from Calaveras County and discoursed on Hawaii; Bret Harte immortalized the West-Coast Chinaman and revealed the tender hearts that beat beneath the red flannels of gamblers and miners. These authors from the West were expected to be in person exuberant and eccentric; and their subject matter as well as their method was received with acclaim. Charles Warren Stoddard and Ambrose Bierce soon followed Miller and Clemens from California, Bierce publishing his first three books in London, and becoming a staff writer for the rival of *Punch* called *Fun*. Late in the century Gertrude Atherton was still able to profit from the traditional interest in Californians when she went to London to acquire a reputation, and Gelett Burgess likewise. One can explain the extraordinary praise of Joaquin Miller's early verse in England only on the grounds of his subject matter; and it is reasonable to suppose that something of the fervor with which Ward, Harte, and Clemens were greeted was due to the belief that they were spokesmen of the romantic West.

But another factor accounting for the craze for American humor during the period under discussion is the salesmanship of the publisher of the earliest books by Ambrose Bierce—again John Camden Hotten. His cheap editions of Lowell and Leland, of Clemens and Harte, and a dozen others, are as much responsible for the vogue of the "American Drolleries" as anything else. One might resist a book if it cost a good round sum, but all but the poorest could afford the sixpence or the shilling that bought from a railway stall an hilarious hour with Artemus Ward. Hotten is memorable to the student of American letters as the publisher of the first English edition of Walt Whitman, but he deserves to be remembered also as one of the chief agents

responsible for the spread of British interest in one of our most distinctive intellectual products. It is an ironic fact that Mark Twain tried to satirize him out of business.

All through the seventies and eighties the interest in American humor continued, although there seem to have been no more sudden cataracts of enthusiasm comparable to the one which has just been described. The stream of transatlantic comic writing became broader with the development of the local-color story and the tremendous expansion of journalism which increased the supply of writers like Bill Nye or Frank Stockton. Though the number of new books of humor from the United States declined later in the century and the Copyright Act of 1891 prevented the piracy of the latest offerings, the quantity of authorized editions is still very impressive. So far as books alone are concerned, very probably the early works of Artemus Ward, Mark Twain, and Bret Harte which had not been protected by copyright must have had the largest circulation, for they were constantly reprinted by several different firms. But Clemens and Harte soon acquired copyright by first publication in London, and it is doubtful whether many of their later productions had a wider sale than the books which first brought them an English reputation, in spite of the fact that the supply of readers increased by leaps and bounds throughout the eighties and nineties.

A number of the newer humorists who appeared after 1875 were protected by publisher's agreements or by prior publication in London, but many were not; and one may view an astonishing array in such a series as "Beeton's Humorous Books," issued by Ward, Lock and Company, one of the early competitors of Hotten. By 1885 this series had run to about eighty titles, three fourths of which were of American origin. The cheap libraries of Routledge, Warne, Ward and Lock, Chatto and Windus, and others offered a ready supply of transatlantic books of fun especially up to 1891; but the increasing production of anthologies of American humor in verse or prose is also deserving of mention. Compilations like Mark Twain's *Library of Humor* were of course issued also in London, and the British frequently made up their own. It was the fashion also, as indeed it had been earlier, to combine both American and English authors in an anthology or "reciter."

There were special lectures on American humor, too, such as those by Hugh R. Haweis, *mutatis mutandis,* a kind of Billy Sunday of London. In 1881 he delivered a series of discourses on transatlantic humorists for the Royal Institution, and repeated them the next year for the London Institution. They were soon gathered up into a book, published first in 1882 by Chatto and Windus under the title *American Humourists,* and reissued in the United States. Irving, Holmes, Lowell, Artemus Ward, Clemens, and Harte were the authors

The fictional Artemus Ward became a national celebrity.

upon whom he lectured, a choice which the more intelligent of his audience must have approved. Speakers who discussed humor in general or British humor in particular sometimes indulged in an excursus on the American product, for example, William S. Lilly, who found place for a few remarks in his lecture on "The Theory of the Ludicrous" delivered at the Royal Institution in 1895. Like most critics after 1870, he found the transatlantic variety to be "distinctly a thing *sui generis*"—the "only intellectual province in which the people of the United States have achieved originality." Its distinctive charm, he supposed, lay in its "homely and fresh grotesqueness"; Lowell he considered to be "one of its chief masters."

Late in the century the objections to the wholesale laudation of the more lowly types of American humor became more insistent and widespread. The freshness of the grotesquerie of the funny men seemed to be wearing out. H. D. Traill in discussing "The Future of Humour" noted significantly: "The Dickensian humour, it would seem, is 'off': the American droll, after a vogue of a good many years, is apparently ceasing to amuse; the 'inverted aphorism' had but a short popularity . . . and nothing seems growing up to take its place." Certainly *David Harum* and Mr. Dooley, though widely known, did not take England by storm, but as the old century died Mark Twain was recognized as the outstanding humorist of the English-speaking world, and penetrating observers could still find evidences of American superiority, for instance, James F. Muirhead, who denied that *Life* was equal to *Punch* or that the average of British fun was below that of its American rival. But, he maintained:

> When we reach the level of Artemus Ward, Ik Marvel, H. C. Bunner, Frank Stockton, and Mark Twain, we may find that we have no equally popular

contemporary humourists of equal excellence; and these are emphatically humourists of a pure American type. If humour of a finer point be demanded it seems to me that there are few, if any, living English writers who can rival the delicate satiric powers of a Henry James or the subtle suggestiveness of Mr. W. D. Howells' farces, for an analogy to which we have to look to the best French work of the kind.

Such an appreciation of the diffusion of the art of humor among American writers not especially professional mirth-makers was by 1890 almost a tradition. The sly touches of Hawthorne and the ethereal satire of such a work as "The Celestial Railroad" were early hailed as qualifying him; and Emerson had been found to be full of wit, capable of turning out humorous verses like those dealing with the mountain and the squirrel. Henry S. Salt lashed fiercely at Lowell for insisting that Thoreau had no humor, and Longfellow was at times credited with the virtue of funmaking. Even the stories of Poe were frequently published under the title, *Tales of Mystery, Imagination and Humour*. And when the swarm of local-colorists was unloosed, with the Stocktons, Bunners, and Aldriches besides, what could an Englishman say but that humor was almost all-pervasive in American literature—and, indeed, in American life? Occasionally the utterances on this topic pass far beyond the bounds of belief. Grant Allen, for instance, declared that "embryo Mark Twains grow in Illinois on every bush" and that the "raw material of the *Innocents Abroad* resounds nightly, like the voice of the derringer, through every saloon in Iowa and Montana. It was even asserted that English actors picked up a sharpened sense of comedy by a tour of the States, and book reviewers who wished to criticize an American novel without reading it felt pretty secure in animadverting on the general humorous tone of the work in question. All this is, of course, as unconsciously humorous in its way as the account of Rhinthon of Syracuse viewed as the father of Greek burlesque tragedy which one reviewer used as a prelude to his appraisal of Orpheus C. Kerr. But, stripped of all nonsense, the British argument that humor was more widespread in the United States was essentially sound. It is one conclusion which can be made from the "funny papers."

WOMEN HUMORISTS

The New York Times Book Review

SOURCE: "Women Among Humorists," in *The New York Times Book Review,* January 20, 1900, p. 40.

[*In the following excerpt, the anonymous writer offers an account of a conversation at a literary gathering where one male guest argued that women may be "bright conversationalists" or have "sporadic flashes of fun" but lack a genuine sense of humor.*]

At a recent gathering of what Mark Twain would call "literary persons," of both sexes, one of the men present made the sweeping assertion that most, if not all, women were entirely devoid of a sense of humor.

"I consider that an unjust assertion," remarked a well-known woman writer who was present. "I am sure that I enjoy a good joke as well as my husband or any other man."

"That may be true enough" said the man who had just spoken, "but you do not make jokes in your conversation, or write them in your books. I do not deny that there are plenty of women who are bright conversationists, but is there now, or has there ever been, a woman humorous writer?

"For instance, look at the long list of male humorists, beginning with Mr. Dooley of the present day, Mark Twain, Artemus Ward, Josh Billings, John Phoenix, Philander Doesticks, Bill Arp, Max Adler, Petroleum V. Nasby, Major Jones, Judge Neal, author of 'Charcoal Sketches'; F. C. Burnand, W. G. Gilbert, Locker, Calverley, Thackeray, Dickens, Tom Hood, and many others clear back to Rabelais. All of these men were not only bright and witty in their conversation, but their writings were permeated with fun and humor. Now, on the contrary, search the list of women writers from Mary E. Wilkins to Mrs. Aphra Behn, and you will not find a single professedly woman humorous writer. Some of them may have sporadic flashes of fun, but they soon lapse into gravity or sentimentality. I do not pretend to say why this is so, but simply state it as a fact. It may be that women are deprived of the humorous sense in the same manner that a person may be born without sight or hearing or speech. That, now-ever, is a matter for the physiologists to take up. I myself do not know of any woman humorist: do you?"

"I am afraid I do not," replied the woman addressed, "but I intend to look the matter up and see if I cannot find at least one in the long list of women writers of all ages." . . .

Alfred Habeggar

SOURCE: "Easygoing Men and Dressy Ladies," in *Gender, Fantasy, and Realism in American Literature*, Columbia University Press, 1982, pp. 115-25.

[*In this excerpt, Habeggar argues that in the 1860s, "humor . . . was a club for men only," substantiating his assertion with a study of the masculine bias in several texts.*]

The voluminous critical literature on American humor has yet to come to terms with the American habit of regarding humor as in some way masculine. Of course,

---

Marietta Holley's main characters, Betsey Bobbet and Josiah Allen's wife, argue about "woman's speah":

"I have always felt that it was woman's highest speah, her only mission to soothe, to cling, to smile, to coo. I have always felt it, and for yeah's back it has been a growin's on me. I feel that you do not feel as I do in this matter, you do not feel that it is woman's greatest privilege, her crowning blessing, to soothe lacerations, to be a sort of a poultice to the noble, manly breast when it is torn with the cares of life."

This was too much, in the agitated frame of mind I then was.
"Am I a poultice Betsey Bobbet, do I look like one?—am I in the condition to be one?" I cried turnin' my face, red and drippin' with prespiration towards her, and then attacked one of Josiah's shirt sleeves agin. "What has my sect done" says I, as I wildly rubbed his shirt sleeves, "That they have got to be lacerator soothers, when they have got everything else under the sun to do?" Here I stirred down the preserves that was a runnin' over, and turned a pail full of syrup into the sugar kettle. "Everybody says that men are stronger than women, and why should they be treated as if they was glass china, liable to break all to pieces if they haint handled careful. And if they have got to be soothed," says I in an agitated tone, caused by my emotions (and by pumpin' 6 pails of water to fill up the biler), "Why don't they get men to sooth'em? They have as much agin time as wimmen have; evenin's they don't have anything else to do, they might jest as well be a soothin' each other as to be a hangin' round grocery stores, or settin' by the fire whittlin'."

Marietta Holley, in My Opinions and Betsey Bobbet's, *American Publishing Company, 1875.*

---

one does not have to look twice to see that American humor has been basically that. Where are the women among the Southwestern humorists before the Civil War, the "literary comedians" of the 1860s, and the comedians of the silent movies? Both the hoary joke cycles and the places where they were presumably kept in circulation—saloons, smoking cars, barber-shops—were exclusively masculine. True, we have had many women humorists and comedians, some of whom, such as Marietta Holley, may have rivaled Mark Twain in popularity. But in the classic period of American humor, the 1860s, when Artemus Ward could be seen on stage, when Samuel L. Clemens turned into Mark Twain, and when we actually had an angular Western humorist for President, humor, like politics, was a club for men only. In fact, our first book about American humor, *Why We Laugh* [1876], was by a politician [Samuel S. Cox] who filled his pages with humor from the state and national legislatures, as if the government, too, was more than anything else a place where men could talk and laugh.

One can sense why humor was a gender quality by glancing at the "boy books" of the 1870s and 1880s. In *The Story of a Bad Boy* (1870), *Tom Sawyer* (1876), and *Peck's Bad Boy and His Pa* (1883), the distinguishing mark of the boy is the tireless enterprise he devotes to practical jokes. The victim of his jokes is the adult order of things, often a kind motherly woman such as Aunt Polly or Aunt Sally (and much earlier, Mrs. Partington, tormented by Ike). In Mark Twain the bad boy is likely to grow up to be a success, and in *Peck's Bad Boy* the young practical joker is the capitalist in training: "Of course all boys are not full of tricks, but the best of them are. That is, those who are the readiest to play innocent jokes, and who are continually looking for chances to make Rome howl, are the most apt to turn out to be first-class business men." The bad boy had the enterprising spirit that would bring success in business, yet he had so little stake in civilization that he could joyfully assault it—make Rome howl. He represented a juvenilizing of the rough old tricksters of Southwestern humor. But instead of belonging to a bygone Southwestern frontier, he had a promising future in the city and was destined to grow up into the capitalist, secret mover of events and the most practical joker of them all. The bad boy's adventures brought into the open the secret life of the American man. The bad boy tradition continued into the twentieth century in children's books, Sunday comics, comic books, and animated cartoons. In *Billy Whiskers' Kids* (1903) by Frances Trego Montgomery, the boy goat, Night, is black while his sister, Day, is white. Night dreams up naughty tricks, flirts with a pretty kid, and torments the Sultan in the book's climax. Day generally remains sweet and patient, except when she gets jealous. In *Little Nemo* (1906-1909), the brilliant cartoon by Winsor McCay about the dream life of a little boy, there is a bad boy named Flip, who is a natural spoiler and breaker of rules. Flip is fat and smokes a cigar; his face is ape-like. The only important girl in Little Nemo's dreams is a good and beautiful princess, who frequently reminds the dreamer to respect the fantastically elaborate procedures in her father's kingdom, Slumberland.

There was not a body of mischief-loving "girl books" in the Gilded Age, but there was *Little Women* (1868), whose theme, as the epigraph from *Pilgrim's Progress* points out, is moral discipline and serious preparation for adulthood and marriage. The practical joker in the book is a boy, Laurie, who victimizes a girl, Meg, by hoaxing her with a series of love letters purportedly from Mr. Brooke. Of course, one of the little women does have a sense of humor, but Jo is the exception that proves the rule—that humor was a masculine trait. If she makes the other girls laugh, she also whistles, uses slang, cuts her hair, has a standing quarrel with

Amy (the most feminine of the four sisters), goes by a boy's name, runs a race with Laurie, and again and again shows how much she would like to be a man.

Over a half century after the boy books and *Little Women,* the Marx Brothers developed some of their funniest routines by using a matronly woman as their straight man, so to speak. Of course there was also Zeppo but he became the romantic lead while Margaret Dumont served as the butt of humor. Dumont was the butt because she was a lady, or in other words, because she couldn't join in the fun, bend at the waist, or speak in a natural or vernacular way. Her lifted chin and stiff bosom were the outward signs of her genteel inflexibility toward life. Tall and awesome, she was always cast as a kind of comic heavy, the model of propriety, and the three madcaps who assaulted her were later versions of Tom Sawyer and the other boy practical jokers of the nineteenth century. American humor has been the literature (and cinema) of bad boys defying a civilization seen as feminine.

One of the basic explanations for the misogyny in male American humor is that women assumed control of public manners. The regrettable masculine disposition to utter oaths, for instance, led Adeline D. T. Whitney [in *The Geyworthys*] to confide an important truth about men to her gentle readers: "I am afraid that, as a general statement men are but men, too often; and that, lest they might be worse, it behooves somebody to

Mrs. Partington, a creation of Samuel P. Avery.

look after them pretty carefully." The opening chapters of the *Adventures of Huckleberry Finn* show how carefully two women try to look after Huck. These chapters give a perfect symbolic representation of the opposition in male and female roles. Huck's father takes him away to a cabin in the woods where the two males laze around all day; Huck's mothers—Widow Douglas and Miss Watson, the legally appointed guardians—try to civilize him.

It was just because women represented the approved control that Mark Twain, like many other men, both worshipped and laughed at good women. It may at first be paradoxical but it finally makes sense that the two books our best humorist was proudest of—*Adventures of Huckleberry Finn* and *Joan of Arc*—were so different: the explanation is that both were about saints. Maybe Ann Stephens was not so far off the mark after all in *Esther: A Story of the Oregon Trail* (1862) when she insisted: "It is a truth that your daring Western frontiersman makes a refined woman his idol—a creature to work for, fight for, and die for, if need be, without a murmur." This sentiment leads Kirk Waltermyer, the nature's nobleman type in the book, to affirm a sentiment so absurd that it would appear to represent the opposite pole from the sanity of humor: "All the herds on the perarer [prairie] are not worth a single curl of her har." Yet even Mark Twain entertained this sort of absolute veneration from time to time for angelic womanhood. The only painting he fell for in *Innocents Abroad* was, alas, an Immaculate Conception by Murillo—a painting that projects the virgin against the night sky, her feet resting on a crescent moon. This perfect maid, far above all sublunary contamination, was, Mark Twain wrote, "the only young and really beautiful Virgin that was ever painted by one of the old masters, some of us think." Mark Twain was not the only sucker. In [John William] De Forest's *Kate Beaumont,* at the moment when Frank proposes to Kate, she reminds him of "Murillo's Immaculate Virgin showing through hazes of aureoles." The opening scene of Henry James's novel about a practical and humorous American shows Christopher Newman gazing at another of Murillo's Immaculate Conceptions in the Louvre. And W. D. Howells' Faulkner, a " 'practical' politician" and "an unscrupulous manager of caucuses and conventions," not only worshipped Murillo's immaculate young woman but "made a complete collection of all the engravings of this Madonna." The practical man worshipped the virgin no less than he made fun of her. He couldn't help worshipping her because she had charge of the idealism, purity, and refinement to which he felt he ought to devote his life, but didn't. And he couldn't help laughing at the unearthly virgin because it was she after all who inspired so many absurdities—*St. Elmo,* the saccharine death poetry, the purification movements such as prohibition, and much much more.

The difference in clothes worn by men and women was an obvious index of their opposing social roles. Looking back on the 1850s from the early twentieth century, [William Dean] Howells wrote:

> The women dressed beautifully, to my fond young taste; they floated in airy hoops; they wore Spanish hats with drooping feathers in them, and were as silken balloons walking in the streets where men were apt to go in unblacked boots and sloven coats and trousers. The West has, of course, brushed up since, but in that easy-going day the Western man did not much trouble himself with new fashions or new clothes.

This passage suggests that some of the reasons why women dressed up had little or nothing to do with men. Frances E. Willard confirms this suspicion in her book of advice, *How to Win: A Book for Girls* (1887). Here she cites with approval a Boston lawyer "who declares that women do not dress so much to please men, but to escape the criticism or excite the envy of each other. I am afraid we must admit that this is nearer the truth than we like to confess." If Willard was right, it would explain to some extent a male tendency, generally concealed, to ridicule women's fancy clothes. In Joseph Kirkland's realistic novel about pioneer life in Illinois, *Zury, the Meanest Man in Spring County,* Anne's fine Eastern dress makes the men laugh. In Beadle's *Dime Pocket Joke Book,* we find this revealing item among the "Hints to Young Gentlemen": "Don't submit to be crowded off the pavement into a muddy gutter by two advancing balloons of silk and whalebone. Haven't your newly blacked boots as good a claim to respect as their skirts?"

Of course, one of the worst things a man could do would be to wear anything but the familiar uniform. When Zury goes into politics, his old friend Anstey takes a deep breath and reveals a horrible fact: "The' 'llaow [they allow] ye're a-puttin' on scollops." Scollops are fancy trimmings: what Anstey means is that Zury is beginning to act better than his fellow men, and Anstey says this by means of a metaphor taken from women's fashions. The clearest denunciation of a man's feminizing himself through fashionable clothes is in Ann Stephens' able satire of urban artificiality in the 1840s, *High Life in New York.* The narrator of this work is an outspoken democratic hayseed named Jonathan Slick, who hails from Weathersfield, Connecticut. When Jonathan first meets his city relative, John, he writes back to his father:

> I raly believe you wouldn't know the critter, he's altered so. . . . I tell you what, his clothes must cost him a few. . . . You could a seen your face in his boots, and his hair was parted on the top of his head, and hung down on the sides of his face and

all over his coat collar, till he looked more like a woman in men's clothes than any thing else. I thought I should a haw-hawed out a larfin, all I could do, though it made me kinder wrathy to see a feller make such an etarnal coot of himself.

All in all, there were many strong pressures that caused "the newspaper sex," as Howells once referred to men in 1870, to dress like clodhoppers and the novel-reading sex to look like a vision from an opium dream. This divergence was a central aspect of the cultural situation in force at the time the literary comedians evolved a new kind of humor in the late 1850s and early 60s. Almost to a man, these humorists began by putting on the mask of the slovenly, vernacular male. In an age when literacy was the prerequisite for gentility, characteristically male speech could not be printed, and fiction was written largely by and for women, the humorist was known for his inability to spell. The proprieties which the ladies superintended were too much for him. He was a throwback to an older, rougher ideal of masculinity. Like Bill Arp, who was modeled on an actual "unlettered countryman," he was often a homespun village philosopher. Artemus Ward, the best and most influential of the sixties' comic characters, was a traveling sideshowman from the good old days—"be4 steembotes was goin round bustin their bilers & sendin peple higher nor a kite. Them was happy days when peple was more intelligent & wax figger's & livin wild beests wasn't scoffed at." Artemus Ward could be mean to animals, as when he whipped his kangaroo for fifteen minutes after it bit the hand of a customer, and he was always full of insular, red-neck intolerance for Mormons, Shakers, women's rights, Oberlin College, and free love communities. A part-time farmer from Baldinsville, Indiana, Artemus Ward was a lazy Northern Democrat who would just as soon let the South secede.

Much rougher than Artemus Ward was Petroleum Vesuvius Nasby, created by David Ross Locke just before the Civil War. His first and middle names refer to effluents from underground that were often associated with hellfire. This man from the underground was a Copperhead during the war and a no-account spoilsman under Andrew Johnson. According to a contemporary, Nasby represented "the whisky-drinking, corner-grocery [i.e., crossroads store] statesmen who have always infested the country." His "boyhood wuz spent in the pursoot uv knollege and muskrats, mostly the latter." He once spent thirty days in jail after robbing a grocery store. On leaving jail, his vision and purpose were clear. He would always persecute niggers, he took a pledge never to drink water, and he was determined to find a profession that would allow him to steal without being hauled up for it. In due time he was appointed postmaster of Confederate X Roads in Kentucky. Thomas Nast's portrait . . . of Nasby enjoying the perquisites of office shows the archetypal slovenly

male: with his big paunch, scruffy beard, and cigar, Nasby is leaning back in his chair and resting his feet on the desk next to his bottle.

This picture was not of Nasby alone, or of the familiar office seeker who could be stopped only by civil service reform, but of the generic easygoing American man. The signature of this man was his fondness for leaning back and putting his boots up where they weren't supposed to be. A popular poem said that the American man

> Finds not in the wide world a pleasure so sweet
> As to sit near the window and tilt up his feet,
> Puff away at the Cuba, whose flavor just suits,
> And gaze at the world 'twixt the toes of his boots.

> *(Why We Laugh,)*

In Mary Jane Holmes's bestseller, *'Lena Rivers* (1859), whenever the bluff and prankish John Jr. begins "to grow crusty," he is seen "elevating his feet to the top of the mantel." In a poorly told anecdote in Beadle's *Dime Pocket Joke Book, No. I,* a group of people in Southampton try to guess the nationality of a gentleman in the coffee-room:

> "He's an Englishman," said one, "I know it by his head." "He's a Scotchman," said another, "I know it by his complexion." "He's a German," said another, "I know it by his beard." Another thought he looked like a Spaniard. Here the conversation rested, but soon one of them spoke: "I have it," said he, "he's an American; he's got his legs on the table."

Putting one's legs on the table was not merely a conspicuous way of taking one's ease. It was also a crude act of defiance. Howells probably understood this, as one senses in the contrast he draws between Venetian and American loafers: "The lasagnone is a loafer, as an Italian can be a loafer, without the admixture of ruffianism, which blemishes most loafers of northern race."

This loafing ruffianism was associated with laughing groups of men, and women's fiction often glanced in fear and disgust at such groups. In Susan Warner's second novel, *Queechy* (1852), Fleda has to travel alone on the train. She hates to hear "the muttered oath, the more than muttered jest, the various laughs that tell so much of head or heart emptiness,—the shadowy but sure tokens of that in human nature which one would not realize and which one strives to forget." In *The Wide, Wide World* the heroine goes to a store where she is waited on by a young man, a Mr. Saunders, whose bold eyes and "slovenly exterior" strike her "most unpleasantly." Before long he tries to browbeat her into making a hasty purchase. Significantly, Saunders first appears by coming out "from among a little group of clerks, with whom he had been indulging in a few jokes by way of relief from the tedium of business." For this sensitive and genteel girl, the band of jokers is the enemy. In *The Lamplighter,* the heroine similarly feels an antipathy to a lazy and humorous gentleman whose "indolent air of ease and confidence" seems "very offensive." The woman writer who took the dimmest view of joking may have been Rebecca Harding Davis. In *Margret Howth,* Huff the book-keeper tells Holmes a story he has been keeping all day:

> He liked to tell a story to Holmes; he could see into a joke; it did a man good to hear a fellow laugh like that. Holmes did laugh, for the story was a good one, and stood a moment, then went in, leaving the old fellow chuckling over his desk. Huff did not know how, lately, after every laugh, this man felt a vague scorn of himself, as if jokes and laughter belonged to a self that ought to have been dead long ago.

It is easy to understand why Warner, Cummins, and Davis felt a repugnance for male humor. And it is also easy to see that they didn't understand it. That ill-dressed, cigar-smoking man who gazed at the world through the toes of his boots was an offense in their nostrils. Part-king, but also part-tramp, crude, loafing, easygoing, insolent, he had the essential American masculinity. Walt Whitman tried to capture his spirit in "Song of Myself," and James's Christopher Newman embodies his Platonic Idea and sometimes takes on his features. But perhaps neither Whitman nor James did him as well as the actor Joseph Jefferson. According to George William Curtis, writing in 1871, Jefferson's interpretation of Rip Van Winkle was "the most familiar and famous rôle in the American theater today." Jefferson's interpretation of the "good-natured, drunken idler" who was chased by his wife from the house ("which is hers") was so popular that the actor played Rip Van Winkle for the rest of his life, offstage as well as on. At a time when being a lady sometimes meant being a corseted artificial sentimenalist, the relaxed, ill-dressed, loafing man supplied the literary comedians with the mask that formed the basis of their humor. The prevailing view of American humor is that it developed out of a kind of border warfare between two cultures, vernacular and refined. I am proposing an additional dialectic—between male and female. The social basis of American humor may have been the staggering difference in our ideal gender roles. What the humorist did was to play the ideal male type—the lazy unregenerate man who defied cultural norms perceived as feminine, not by saying "Don't tread on me" or "No" in thunder, but by relaxing, taking it easy.

Beadle's *Dime Pocket Joke Book* had an anecdote about masculine laziness that went as follows:

> THE UNIVERSAL PASSION.—A foreigner, who had mixed among many nations, was asked if he had observed any particular quality in our species that might be considered universal. He replied, "Me tink dat all men *love lazy.*"

Not only did American men love to be lazy more than they loved ladies, but they chose the former partly to spite the latter. Without knowing it, the well-traveled foreigner had identified the local passion of American men.

W. A. Jones asserts that women cannot be humor writers:

There is a body and substance in true wit, with a reflectiveness rarely found apart from a masculine intellect. . . . We know of no one writer of the other sex, that has a high character for humor—no Rabelais, no Sterne, no Swift, no Goldsmith, no Dickens, no Irving. The female character does not admit of it.

W. A. Jones, Graham's Illustrated Magazine, *December, 1842.*

Nancy Walker

SOURCE: "Wit, Sentimentality and the Image of Women in the Nineteenth Century," in *American Studies,* Vol. 22, No. 2, Fall, 1981, pp. 5-22.

[*In the following essay, Walker posits female humor writing as a challenge to the popular nineteenth-century notion of women as the frail and humorless keepers and producers of the "sentimental."*]

In two articles in *The Critic* in 1884, Alice Wellington Rollins attempted to counter the conventional notion that a sense of humor was "that rarest of qualities in woman," as Richard Grant White had written earlier in the same publication. Though she acknowledged that "as we have had no feminine Artemus Ward, so we have had no woman novelist in whose work humor has even so prominent a part as it has in Dickens," she insisted that in conversation as well as in writing women had great talent for humor. But Twain's portrait of Emmeline Grangerford in *Huck Finn* the following year seems to have solidified the image of the nineteenth-century female writer as a wan poet obsessed with morbidity. However, in the same year that *Huck Finn* was published, Kate Sanborn followed Alice Rollins' lead and published an anthology called *The Wit of Women.* Sanborn did not adhere to a rigid definition of "wit" in her comments or in her selections, which range from an eighteenth-century poem by Mercy Warren (whom Sanborn calls "a satirist quite in the strain of

Juvenal") to the dialect humor of Harriet Beecher Stowe and "Grace Greenwood," and include parodies, poems for children and bits of witty conversation overheard at dinner parties. Frances Whicher's *Widow Bedott Papers* she deems too popular to require a selection— "every one who enjoys that style of humor knows them by heart"—but she did include excerpts from Caroline Kirkland, Rose Terry Cooke, Sarah Orne Jewett and many others.

Despite the grab-bag nature of her anthology, Sanborn was both acknowledging and participating in a trend which ran counter to the prevailing sentimentality of women's literature in the 19th century. At the same time as the image of the literary woman, as well as that of the educated, middle-class woman in general, increasingly partook of the characteristics which Twain ascribed to Emmeline—frailty, emotionalism, a consummate uselessness—the female humorists of the century waged a little-recognized but persistent war against that figure. In their own work, the "witty women"—"Fanny Fern," Caroline Kirkland, Frances Whicher, "Gail Hamilton" and Marietta Holley—consistently satirized the woman who wrote pious, sentimental prose and poetry. Their efforts to demote this figure from the high status accorded her by genteel society were part of their rebellion against widely-held notions of woman's "proper" role in American culture.

In *The Feminization of American Culture,* Ann Douglas argues persuasively that an unstructured but potent coalition of Protestant ministers and middle-class, Northern women led to the sentimentalization of American popular literature between 1820 and 1880. Douglas asserts that just as liberal Protestant clergymen lost authority through the disestablishment of religion in the early 19th century and the concurrent rise to prominence of more evangelical sects such as the Methodists and the Baptists, so women lost status by virtue of the shift from a home-based to a factory-based economy. The home, "formerly an important part of a cummunal productive process under her direction, . . . had become a place where her children stayed before they began to work and where her husband rested after the strain of labor." The woman became "influence" rather than producer, and the nature of her influence was defined by the conventions of Christianity. Both ministers and women turned to literature as a means of promoting their own, strikingly similar values. "They inevitably confused theology with religiosity, religiosity with literature, and literature with self-justification." A sentimental literature, according to Douglas, was the inevitable result. "Sentimentalism is a complex phenomenon. It asserts that the values a society's activity denies are precisely the ones it cherishes; it attempts to deal with the phenomenon of cultural bifurcation by the manipulation of nostalgia. Sentimentalism provides a way to protest a power to which one has already in part capitulated."

If sentimentality in literature is a result of powerlessness, wit may be seen as its opposite: an expression of confidence and power. The word remains closely associated with its Old English origin in *wita,* "one who knows." Long before it acquired the connotation of amusement, wit was connected with knowledge, understanding, perception. Sentimentality exerts a passive, often subversive power; wit, on the other hand, is a direct and open expression of perceptions, taking for granted a position of strength and insight. It was this confident stance which both Alice Rollins and Kate Sanborn admired in the women humorists they praised in the 1880's. Humor functioned as an antidote to the pious religiosity of the sentimental novel and poem.

Among major authors of the nineteenth century, the foremost "witty woman," as Constance Rourke pointed out long ago [in *American Humor,* 1931], is Emily Dickinson, who "contrived to see a changing universe within that acceptant view which is comic in its profoundest sense, which is part reconciliation, part knowledge of eternal disparity." It is ironic that Dickinson's reclusiveness and eccentricity have caused her to remain, at least in the popular imagination, an embodiment of conventional femininity, a retiring New England spinster with her eyes fixed on the next world. In sharp contrast to this image, Dickinson's humor emerges from her lyrics precisely as moments of insight; she is the "one who knows," and her wit denies sentimentality, even—or especially—when the subject is death, that favorite subject of Emmeline Grangerford and other satiric representations of the female writer. For Emily Dickinson, wit was a natural mode; but for the more popular women writers of the 19th century, sentimentality was a constant temptation, and had to be dealt with in satire.

The recurrent satire on the sentimental female author in 19th century women's humor may therefore be seen as having a different and more pointed motive than does Twain's portrait of Emmeline. Twain's description is part of his more comprehensive attack, in *Huck Finn* and elsewhere, on Victorian tastelessness and lack of refinement. It is of a piece with his depiction of the vulgarities of household adornment and the behavior of the crowds who witness the debased versions of Shakespearean plays presented by the Duke and the Dauphin. The systematic attack on the sentimental female author— her person as well as her product—in the works in Kirkland, Whicher, Holley and other 19th century female humorists, however, is an attempt to deny the image of woman as a weak, frail vessel of Christian piety, and to posit instead an image of the "witty" woman: one who sees through sham and stereotype, for whom courage and strength of mind are positive virtues.

"Fanny Fern" (Sara Willis Parton) must figure prominently in any discussion of both witty and sentimental women writers in the 19th century because of her mastery of both styles. F. L. Pattee [*The Feminine Fifties*, 1940] calls her "the most tearful and convulsingly 'female' moralizer of the whole modern bluestocking school," and Sanborn refers to her "talent for humorous composition," and says her style "was thought very amusing." Both are correct.

Sara Willis Parton was born in 1811 and grew up in the Calvinistic atmosphere which also influenced Harriet Beecher Stowe (her father was a friend of Lyman Beecher, and she attended Catharine Beecher's Female Seminary). After two marriages, one ending in death and the other in divorce, she turned to writing to support herself. When her sketches were rejected by her brother, Nathaniel Parker Willis, editor of the *Home Journal*, her career was championed by James Parton, who became her third husband. The first series of *Fern Leaves from Fanny's Portfolio* (1853) consists of both extremely sentimental and sharply satiric pieces, and the contemporary reviewer for *Putnam's Magazine* described them quite accurately:

> They are acute, crisp, sprightly, knowing, and, though sometimes rude, evince much genuine and original talent, a keen power of observation, lively fancy, and humorous as well as pathetic sensibilities.

In Parton's own preface to the book, she announces that "some of the articles are sad, some are gay," and the first three-quarters of the book consists chiefly of the former, with titles such as "The Widow's Trial," "A Night-Watch with a Dead Infant," and "The Invalid Wife." Death and loss are the major themes, and the style is pious and overblown in the manner of the sentimental novel. Even in this section, however, Parton's wit and her objective distance from such sentimentality are apparent. The selection "A Chapter on Literary Women" consists of a dialogue between Colonel Van Zandt, who has a "perfect horror of satirical women," and Minnie, who introduces him to the woman he marries—who turns out to be a writer. The Colonel is finally forced to acknowledge that "a woman may be literary, and yet feminine and lovable."

Parton's awareness that she is merely following fashion by writing sentimental sketches is amply demonstrated in the brief essay "Borrowed Light," in which she sarcastically advises beginning authors to imitate the work of popular writers:

> Borrow whole sentences, if you like, taking care to transpose the words a little. Baptize all your heroes and heroines at the same font;—be facetious, sentimental, pathetic, terse, or diffuse, just like your leader.

And she mocks her own choice of a pseudonym when she advises:

> In choosing your signature, bear in mind that nothing goes down, now-a-days, but *alliteration.* For instance, Delia Daisy, Fanny Foxglove, Harriet Honeysuckle, Lily Laburnam, Paulena Poppy, Minnie Mignonette, Julia Jonquil, Seraphina Sunflower, etc., etc.

The selections in Part II of *Fern Leaves,* in which this essay appears, are as satiric as those in Part I are sentimental. Using a tone of ironic sarcasm, Parton comments on the vanity of women, the helplessness of men, the problems of ministers and the hypocrisy of editors. The sane, sprightly satire and the curt, pithy style are the direct opposite of the sentimental prose in the first part of the book. In "The Model Widow" she presents a husband-hunter who anticipates the Widow Bedott, and in "Bachelor Housekeeping" she satirizes the helplessness of men as Florence Guy Seabury would many years later in "The Delicatessen Husband." After quoting a scene in which a man, in answer to his servant's announcement that there is no bread for his breakfast, says, "No bread! then bring me some toast," Parton begins:

> I think I see him! Ragged dressing-gown; beard two days old; depressed dickey; scowling face; out at elbow, out of sorts, and—out of "toast!" Poor thing! Don't the sight make my heart ache? How should he be expected to know that bread was the forerunner of toast, without a wife to tell him?

The humor of this and other pieces, such as "Aunt Hetty on Matrimony," bespeaks a sincerity completely lacking in the sentimental sketches and stories. This is the real "Fanny Fern"—or rather, this is Sara Willis Parton—following no stereotypical pattern of "feminine" writing, but taking a brisk, analytical look at manners and values.

"Borrowed Light" is the closest Parton came to satirizing the sentimental female writer, but the tradition of such satire had begun some years before in Caroline Kirkland's *A New Home—Who'll Follow?* (1839). A native of New York City, Kirkland spent seven years in frontier Michigan with her husband William, a schoolteacher turned town-builder, and wrote about this experience with candor and much satiric humor in *A New Home* and the later *Forest Life* (1842). The chapter epigraphs—quotations from Rochefoucalt, Bacon, Pope, Byron and Shakespeare—testify to Kirkland's education, but are oddly at variance with her straightforward, somewhat understated style, which purports to be that of her *persona,* Mary Clavers. Mary Clavers is from the civilized East, but she is not a snob; instead she seems honestly bewildered by the actual crudeness of frontier life, and copes as well as she can with the privations of western settlement.

Into this frontier community comes the female poet, Miss Eloise Fidler, for a visit of some months, and Kirkland uses the occasion for some of her most delicate yet most barbed wit. Here, as in other female humorists' portraits of this figure, the satire is directed as much to the personality of the sentimental writer as to the quality of her writing. In fact, one of the evidences of her uselessness in society is that she produces very little. In comparison with Marietta Holley's Betsey Bobbet, later in the century, Miss Fidler is young, but "at least at mateable years; neither married, nor particularly likely to be married":

> Her age was at a stand; but I could never discover exactly where, for this point proved an exception to the general communicativeness of her disposition. I guessed it at eight-and-twenty; but perhaps she would have judged this uncharitable, so I will not insist.

Miss Fidler has an album in which she encourages her friends to write verses; Kirkland admits to having kept the book for three months without being able to think of anything to write which will match the overblown style of the entries already there. One assumes that Miss Fidler's own poetry resembles that of her friends; Kirkland is more concerned to present a picture of the artist at work:

> It was unfortunate that she could not walk out much on account of her shoes. She was obliged to make out with diluted inspiration. The nearest approach she usually made to the study of Nature, was to sit on the woodpile, under a girdled tree, and there, with her gold pencil in hand, and her "eyne, grey as glas," rolled upwards, poefy by the hour.

Miss Fidler's desire to marry comes not so much from romantic notions of marriage as from the fact that she hates her maiden name, and "the grand study of her life had been to sink this hated cognomen in one more congenial to her taste." She fixes her attention on a store clerk whose name she supposes to be Edward Dacre; when she discovers that it is actually the less euphonious "Edkins Daker," she is temporarily disenchanted, but ultimately marries him despite this fault.

It is worth noting that the occasion of Daker's entrance into the story is a debate regarding the "comparative mental capacity of the sexes," at the conclusion of which the young clerk prevails with the opinion that:

> if the natural and social disadvantages under which women labored and must ever continue to labor, could be removed; if their education could be entirely different, and their position in society the reverse of what it is at present, they would be very nearly, if not quite, equal to the nobler sex, in all but strength of mind, in which very useful quality it was his opinion that men would still have the advantage.

The "strength of mind" which Kirkland mentions here is a concomitant of wit, and a quality which Emily Dickinson possessed in abundance. The fact that Miss Fidler has neither is what qualifies her as the object of Kirkland's satire.

Shortly after Kirkland's first book was published, Frances M. Whicher began writing in the dialect of rural New York state in the "Widow Bedott" sketches and other work, published in the Albany *Argus, Neal's Saturday Gazette* and *Godey's Lady's Book.* None of her work was collected in book form until after her death in 1852. In 1856 Alice B. Neal, widow of the editor of *Neal's Saturday Gazette,* published a collection of the "Widow Bedott" and "Aunt Maguire" pieces, and in 1867 Whicher's earlier pieces were published in a volume titled *Widow Spriggins, Mary Elmer and Other Sketches.* Extremely publicity-shy, Whicher refused for a time to reveal her identity even to editor Neal, and replied to a request for information about herself with a flippant poem in which she described herself as having:

> Hands and feet
>   of respectable size
> *Mud-colored* hair,
>   And dubious eyes.

Part of her desire for anonymity seems to have come from a genuine retiring nature and a lack of confidence in her own abilities. Soon after she began writing the "Widow Bedott" sketches for Neal, she apparently considered giving up the series, which prompted a letter from Neal that testifies to the popularity of the sketches:

> All the world is full of Bedott. Our readers talk of nothing else, and almost despise "Neal" if the Widow be not there. An excellent critic in these matters, said to me the other day, that he regarded them as the best Yankee papers yet written, and such is indeed the general sentiment. I know for instance, of a lady who for several days after reading one of them, was continually, and often, at moments the most inopportune, bursting forth into fits of violent laughter, and believe me that you, gifted with such power, ought not to speak disparagingly of the gift which thus brings wholesome satire home to every reader.

Though Whicher continued to write for *Neal's* and later for *Godey's,* her shunning of the public eye was no doubt due in part to what Neal calls her "wholesome satire," but which was not so kindly regarded by some of her targets. In a letter to Alice Neal, Whicher testifies that her satiric talent was a mixed blessing from the beginning:

> I received, at my birth, the undesirable gift of a remarkably strong sense of the ridiculous. I can scarcely remember the time when the neighbors were

not afraid that I would "make fun of them." I was scolded at home, and wept over and prayed with, by certain well-meaning old maids in the neighborhood; but all to no purpose.

As the wife of a clergyman, Whicher ran particular risks as a satirist, and her husband's congregation in Elmira, New York, finally decided that they could do without his services after one parishioner threatened a lawsuit, claiming he recognized his wife in one of Whicher's comic portraits. It is probably not necessary to speculate on this gentleman's opinion of his own wife; suffice it to say that most of Whicher's portraits of women are far less than flattering.

The humor in Whicher's sketches arises in part from stock comic devices of the 1840's: humorous names for people and places (the "Rev. Sniffles," "Wiggletown," "Scrabble Hill," etc.), broadly phonetic spelling and ludicrous situations. But underlying this humorous surface is telling satire on human characteristics—in particular, vanity, foolishness and false pride. The Widow Bedott, who became a popular stage character in the 1880's, embodies several of the characteristics which are most commonly found in satiric sketches of women in the 19th century. She is a gossip, a man-chaser—and a "scribbling woman." But Whicher goes a step further than the usual satiric portrait. In Kirkland's descriptions of Miss Fidler, as well as in Holley's later characterization of Betsey Bobbet, the *persona* of the sensible, reasonable narrator provides contrast and distance to the humorous character. The character, in other words, is at two removes from the reader, eliciting laughter but little sympathy. Whicher, however, uses the technique of Josh Billings and Artemus Ward: the Widow Bedott tells her own story in her own dialect, and thus seemingly unwittingly reveals her flaws as she earnestly pursues her interests.

Whicher increases the humorous potential by having the Widow criticize the very characteristics which she herself embodies. Having set her cap for Mr. Crane the instant she hears he has been widowed, she immediately assesses the competition for his interest, one Polly Bingham Jenkins:

> Now I shouldn't wonder if she should set tew and try tew ketch Mr. Crane when he comes back, should you? I'll bet forty great apples she'll dew it, she's been ravin' distracted to git married ever since she was a widder, but I ruther guess Timothy Crane ain't a man to be took in by such a great fat, humbly, slanderin' old butter tub. She's as gray as a rat, tew, that are hair o' hern's false. . . . I think 't would be a good idear for some friendly person to warn Mr. Crane against Poll Jinkins as soon as he gits here, don't you?

The "friendly person" is, of course, the Widow herself, who writes a poem for Mr. Crane in which she pur-

ports to describe his feelings upon losing his wife. Like most of the Widow's poetry, it is a spoof of the sentimental poem, with contrived rhymes, awkward grammar, and ludicrous emotional excess. Titled "Mr. Crane's Lamentations on the Death of His Companion," the poem reads in part:

> I used to fraquently grumble at my fate
>   And be afeered I was a gwine to suffer
>   sorrer—
> But since you died my trouble is so great
>   I hain't got no occasion for to borrer.

Perhaps the best example of Whicher's satire on the sentimental poem itself is the one which the Widow writes to Rev. Sniffles during her ultimately successful pursuit of his hand in marriage. Not only does the Widow manage to rhyme "frenzy" and "influenzy," but the poem also contains the following bit of self-serving "comfort" for the widower:

> Then mourn not for yer pardner's death,
>   But to submit endevver;
> For s'posen she hadent a died so soon,
>   She couldent a lived forever.

The most direct satire on the sentimental female writer in *The Widow Bedott Papers* occurs as the Widow and Aunt Maguire discuss Sally Hugle, who writes poetry for the "Scrabble Hill Luminary," a local newspaper. Sally Hugle, a spinster, also pursues the Rev. Sniffles, and thus is a double rival of the Widow. Aunt Maguire describes her poetry:

> She generally calls 'em *"sunnets"*—Jeff [Aunt Maguire's son] says they ought to be called *moonets,* cause they're always full o' stuff about the moon and stars, and so on. She's always groanin' away about her *inward griefs,* and *unknown miseries.* I don't know what to make on't. Sally Hugle never had no partickler trouble as I know on—without 't was her not bein able to ketch a husband.

Aunt Maguire recites several stanzas of one of Sally Hugle's poems, which is almost identical to the Widow's efforts, but the Widow asserts that she could "make better poitry 'n that by throwin' an inkstand at a sheet o' paper." The composite picture of the single female—widow or spinster—who writes poetry for the local paper is one which involves extremes of vanity, petty competition and an appalling lack of sophistication. The satire, in fact, seems directed as much to low editorial standards for "literature" as to the individual perpetrators of execrable verse.

Though the Widow's nickname is "Silly" (short for "Priscilla"), she can hardly compete in silliness with her predecessor, the Widow Spriggins. Whicher wrote the Widow Spriggins letters for the Albany *Argus,* and they were later collected in the 1867 volume of her work. The humor lacks the depth and complexity of the Widow Bedott and Aunt Maguire sketches, but the Widow Spriggins letters are interesting as a different sort of satire on the "scribbling women." Sprinkled with malapropisms, the Spriggins letters tell of the courtship of Permilly Ruggles and Jabez Spriggins from the point of view of Permilly, whose romantic notions of behavior are derived from the sentimental novel. In anticipation of Tom Sawyer following the dictates of romantic fiction for setting Jim free at the end of *Huck Finn*, Permilly imitates her fictional heroine Amanda at every turn, and insists that her suitor does likewise, to the extent of requiring that he draw a small sketch of himself that she can pretend is a daguerrotype to keep when they are parted. A brief exchange between two of Permilly's sisters captures the essence of the satire. Permilly has uttered a long, derivative lament, ending by calling herself "the most onfortinate of creturs":

> "How much she talks like a book," says Ketury.
> "How much she talks like a fool," says Mirtilly, and off she went to bed.

The Widow Spriggins is even more a figure of ridicule than is the Widow Bedott, but she was undoubtedly a model for Whicher's later creation. At the conclusion of the Spriggins letters is a note to the "eddyter" saying that these sketches have been written during her widowhood after fifteen years of marriage to Spriggins, and she would be happy to tell the story of her second marriage:

> So if you ever git run ashore for stuff to put in yer paper, jest let me know, and if I ain't too much occerpied with my domestic abberations, Ile be happy to giv ye sum account of my "second love."

Despite the sincerity one detects in Whicher's satire, it seems clear that she wrote humor because of the ready market for it rather than from a commitment to the mode. Near the end of her short life she wrote to Alice Neal: "I am heartily sick of Bedotting and Maguiring, and only wish I could be as well paid for more sensible matter." She was at this point at work on *Mary Elmer*, a novel which was incomplete at the time of her death. Though serious, *Mary Elmer* lacks the flowery sentimentality of some of "Fanny Fern's" work. Whicher was afraid the writing was "too plain and homely," and in a letter to her publisher she explains both her style in the work and her attitude toward the sentimental female writer:

> I have been so anxious to avoid the grandiloquent style of many of our female story writers, that I may have gone too far the other way. I have become so entirely disgusted with that sort of composition, applied to the commonest and most trifling subjects, as well as to those more important, that I never have patience to get through an article of that description.

It is fortunate for today's readers that economic necessity forced Whicher to devote herself to humor. *Mary Elmer* is conventional; but the Widow Spriggins, the Widow Bedott and Aunt Maguire are unforgettable characters in American humor, ranking with Jack Downing and Colonel Sellers. *The Widow Bedott Papers* was a very popular book; the first edition sold more than 100,000 copies, and it remains livelier and less dated than much of the dialect humor of its era.

Far removed from the rural New York of Frances Whicher was the work of "Gail Hamilton" (Mary Abigail Dodge), whose career as a journalist and social commentator began about the time of Whicher's death and lasted until her own death in 1896. Though not a humorist in the popular mold of Whicher and Holley, Gail Hamilton was a witty observer of the political and social scenes, writing columns for the *National Era* and essays and stories for *The Atlantic Monthly*. Kate Sanborn mentions Gail Hamilton in *The Wit of Women*, though she does not include a selection from her work, and Hamilton is one of Alice Wellington Rollins' proofs that women have a sense of humor:

> In the lighter department of descriptive writing, we may fairly match against Charles Dudley Warner's "Summer in a Garden" Gail Hamilton's experience with Halicarnassus in taking a country place for the summer; and if it is objected that we have only one Gail Hamilton, we may remark that the world is not overburdened with Charles Dudley Warners.

The comparison with Warner is an apt one. Both authors use a subtle humor which sneaks out of apparently serious passages. Gail Hamilton's writing ranged over a variety of subjects, including three books on the role and status of women. Though she was sometimes equivocal about women's participation in the "male" world of politics, she ultimately rejected female suffrage on the grounds that voting would make women "aggressive, pugnacious, self-centered"; but she argued strongly that women should be self-reliant and powerful, and her writing testifies to the intellectual self-assurance which is basic to wit.

Hamilton's book *Wool-Gathering* (1867), about her travels to various parts of the country, is quite similar in style and approach to Caroline Kirkland's *A New Home*, as well as reminiscent of the journals of Sarah Kemble Knight. Hamilton writes, as do Kirkland and Knight, as an outsider who is alternately perplexed and delighted by what she encounters. Her descriptions of Minnesota recall Kirkland's more extensive ones of Michigan; but Hamilton is a traveler, not a settler, and she declares that "the worst thing about Minnesota is, that it is fifteen hundred miles from Boston!" Like Kirkland, she does not romanticize the West nor the journey to get there. There are mice in hotel rooms, unpleasant traveling companions and sometimes actual dangers. Although she holds the unusually enlightened view for her day that the violence of the Indians was the result of white injustice in dealing with them, she asserts that "the last place in the world to be sentimental over Indians is Minnesota":

> In a country where, until lately, a woman might stand frying doughnuts at her kitchen fire, and look up to see a dark, dreadful face in the gathering twilight pressed against the window-pane, watching the process, and receive for her ostensibly hospitable, but really affrighted greeting, only a noncommital grunt, it is just as well not to rhapsodize over the noble savage. When, in addition to this, the noble savage yells out a war-whoop, whips out his tomahawk, and takes off your scalp, it is all over with the poetry of the thing.

Gail Hamilton was equally unsentimental about the writing of fiction. In the middle of an otherwise straightforward and serious story published in *The Atlantic Monthly,* she pauses to comment on the romantic novel. Noting that her reader will have guessed that the couple she has introduced will eventually get married, she says, "Of course they will. Is there any reason why they should not? . . . Scoff as you may, love is the one vital principle in romance." She then protests that in comparison to the novels the "professional novel-reader" may be accustomed to, her story may seem "threadbare." However:

> Please to remember that I am not writing about a princess of the blood, nor of the days of the bold barons, but only the life of a quiet little girl in a quiet little town in the eastern part of Massachusetts; and so far as my experience and observation go, men and women in the eastern part of Massachusetts are not given to thrilling adventures, hairbreadth escapes, wonderful concatenations of circumstances, and blood and thunder generally,—but pursue the even tenor of their way, and of their love, with a sober and delightful equanimity.

In the early 1870's Marietta Holley launched the most comprehensive satire on the sentimental female poet in *My Opinions and Betsey Bobbet's* (1873) with a preface in which she declares herself unqualified to write a book:

> I don't know no underground dungeons. I haint acquainted with no haunted houses, I never see a hero suspended over a abyss by his gallusses, I never beheld a heroine swoon away, I never see a Injun tommy hawked, nor a ghost; I never had any of these advantages; I cant write a book.

In other words, she cannot write a romantic novel. But a "voice" inside her mind keeps telling her to write a book about "the great subject of Wimmen's Rites," and she has a "cast iron resolution" to do just that. The "voice" was in reality the American Publishing Company, which had published several of Twain's books and which had commissioned Holley's first book after seeing a dialect piece she had written for *Peterson's Magazine.*

My Opinions and Betsey Bobbet's, like the twenty "Samantha" books which followed it, is dialect humor of the "Widow Bedott" variety. Holley's *persona,* Samantha, makes it plain that she "never went to school much and don't know nothin' about grammer, and I never could spell worth a cent," and Holley, like Whicher, was from rural New York state, which was the basic setting for her works. By the time her last books were published on the eve of the women's suffrage amendment, the rustic style and settings were out of fashion, but her books consistently sold well, and at the turn of the century her name was as well known, some say, as that of Mark Twain. Since the vogue of dialect humor had begun to wane at this point, we must seek other reasons for her continued popularity. For some, the appeal lay in Samantha's championing of women's equality while she remained a devoted wife and homemaker; the marriage of the conventional role and the liberal philosophy would have made her views palatable to those who were threatened by more radical feminist positions. For others, the attraction was the travel format she frequently used, that of Twain's *Innocents Abroad* and Margaret Halsey's later *With Malice Toward Some;* the "wise innocent" had its greatest durability as an observer of notable places. Holley's Samantha traveled to Saratoga, the World's Fair, the St. Louis Exposition and Europe, and her commentary served to reinforce middle America's belief in traditional values of moderation and common sense (one of Samantha's favorite words is "megum" [medium]).

More importantly, Holley's work is delightfully comic. The mixture of broad caricature and delicate, ironic wit remains lively even though some of its targets have an old-fashioned ring. Like Whicher, Holley exposed human failings traditionally associated with women—vanity, nosiness, sentimentality—but her range of subjects was much wider, including racial conflict, political and social ethics and especially sexual equality. Samantha's implacable logic is the source of much of the humor, contrasted as it is with the illogicality of sentiment or prejudice, and the homely metaphor serves here, as in much of Emily Dickinson's poetry, to reinforce common sense. In *Samantha on the Race Problem* (1892), Samantha visits her son and his family in Georgia and runs head-on into a racial prejudice which rural New York has not prepared her for:

> The colored men and wimmen they [white Southerners] seemed to look upon about as Josiah

and me looked onto our dairy, though mebby not quite so favorably, for there wuz one young yearlin' heifer and one three-year-old Jersey that I always said knew enough to vote.

In London she and Josiah compare the crowded conditions in the House of Commons to those in their hen-house back home, and Samantha concludes that "there both on em kep' in too clost quarters to do well." Tied to their rural domesticity, Samantha and Josiah are to some extent stock comic characters: the nagging wife with tongue or rolling pin always at the ready, and the stubborn, somewhat lazy henpecked husband who fears neither her bark nor her bite.

But Holley's humor is more complex and delicate than this stereotypical portrait would suggest. Samantha Allen is—underneath her dialectical locutions—a woman of intelligence and wit, and this is nowhere more apparent than in her arguments about "wimmen's rites." As a committed feminist, Holley was well aware of the major arguments against female suffrage. On the one hand, women were too fragile to endure the demands of the political process; on the other, they were destined—biologically and socially—to fulfill the "higher calling" of wife and motherhood, which presumably did not place such a strain on their delicate minds and bodies. The contradiction inherent in this stance does not escape Samantha, who is capable of launching into irate, sarcastic monologues when provoked—usually by Josiah, who, after fourteen years of marriage, continues to trot out the same arguments, as when he says:

> "If wimmin know when they are well off, they will let poles and 'lections boxes alone, it is too wearin for the fair sect."

> "Josiah Allen," says I, "you think that for a woman to stand up straight on her feet, under a blazin' sun, and lift both her arms above her head, and pick seven bushels of hops, mingled with worms and spiders, into a gigantic box, day in, and day out, is awful healthy, so strenthenin' and stimulatin' to women, but when it comes to droppin' a little slip of clean paper into a small seven by nine box, once a year in a shady room, you are afraid it is goin' to break down a woman's constitution to once."

And when Samantha's friend Betsey Bobbet insists that it is woman's "greatest privilege" to be "a sort of poultice to the noble, manly breast when it is torn with the cares of life," Samantha snaps, "Am I a poultice, Betsey Bobbet, do I look like one?"

From her alliterative name—reminiscent of "Fanny Fern" and others—to her desire to be a "clinging vine," Betsey Bobbet is a full-blown caricature of the sentimental spinster who writes mournful verse. Samantha comments that "of all the sentimental creeters I ever

did see Betsey Bobbet is the sentimentalist, you couldn't squeeze a laugh out of her with a cheeze press." Betsey is pretentious about her grammar, which is often incorrect: she says "I have saw" instead of "I have seen," and thinks it vulgar to pronounce final "r" sounds, saying "deah" for "dear." As Samantha observes, "I don't know much about grammer, but common sense goes a ways."

But Betsey Bobbet is not merely a set-piece borrowed from other 19th century humorists. *My Opinions and Betsey Bobbet's* is an extended allegory, pitting common sense against sentiment, with Samantha Allen as the primary representative of the former (one of her favorite statements is "I love to see folks use reason") and Betsey as one of the embodiments of the latter. In this allegorical framework, marriage as "woman's sphere" (or "spear," as Samantha spells it, fully conscious of the pun) is part of the anti-suffrage argument, and singlehood is as unnatural as voting. Samantha several times attacks the illogicality of this stance. One of her arguments is that it takes two to make a marriage: "As our laws are at present no woman can marry unless she has a man to marry to," she says to Elder Minkly, and then challenges him:

> Which had you rather do, Elder, let Betsey Bobbet vote, or cling to you? She is fairly achin' to make a runnin' vine of herself, and says I, in slow, deep, awful tones, are you willin' to be a tree?

Elder Minkly, like other men to whom Samantha puts the same question, cannot answer, and takes the first opportunity to change the subject. If the situation provokes Samantha to logical argument, it provokes Betsey to poetry, the composition of a "song" for the "glorious cause of wimmen's only true speah," one stanza of which reads:

> Oh, do not be discouraged, when
> You find your hopes brought down;
> And when you meet unwilling men,
> Heed not their gloomy frown;
> Yield not to wild despaih;
> Press on and give no quartah,
> In battle all is faih;
> We'll win for we had orteh.

And Betsey does "win," in the sense that she eventually gets married. But it is a hollow victory, for Holley's final thrust is to have her marry a lazy drunkard with several children, and our final view of Betsey shows a woman worn with care and hard work. Her "clinging vine" has found a spindly tree which will not bear its weight, and Betsey is left defending a position which has become as pathetic as it once was ludicrous.

Marietta Holley went further than most of her fellow humorists in demolishing the image of the sentimental female writer, but the fact that so many female humorists in the 19th century satirized sentimentality argues persuasively that the popular image of the woman writer as soggy sentimentalist was considered as an insult by women of wit. The figure of the sentimental female poet was much more than a stock comic character. In the work of women humorists, it became the embodiment of all that these women knew themselves *not* to be: weak, dependent, illogical. With varying degrees of acidity, they mocked the notion that women were humorless creatures, incapable of the insight and perspective which underlay the witty utterance. Almost every nineteenth-century female humorist felt the need to create and demolish this image as if exorcising a demon which would have prevented her from writing humor.

Pointing to a deeper reality in women's humor of the 19th century is the fact that in the works of these humorists the sentimental female writer is inevitably single, and just as inevitably would rather be married. In the popular imagination the witty woman was not attractive, not feminine; she was considered too strong, too threatening, too "masculine." It is accurate, though somehow too pat, to point out that Mary Abigail Dodge ("Gail Hamilton") and Marietta Holley never married, and that Frances Whicher spoke with regret of her gift for satire. There is no necessary and simple correlation between a writer's life and her subject matter. What is clear is that these writers caricatured the sentimental female writer not on the sole basis of her style of writing, but also because of her habits and personality—her unwillingness or inability to be strong and self-reliant. They laughed at her because she was unable to laugh at herself. The issue was not that she preferred marriage to "single blessedness," but that she equated femininity with weak-minded dependence and sentimentality. For humor, as Dorothy Parker said, "There must be courage."

FURTHER READING

Blair, Walter, ed. *Native American Humor (1800-1900)*. New York: American Book Company, 1937, 573 p.

Anthologizes major short pieces from the nineteenth century and provides an informative introduction and bibliography.

Blair, Walter and Raven I. McDavid, Jr., eds. *The Mirth of a Nation*. Minneapolis: University of Minnesota Press, 1983, 302 p.

Like *Native American Humor*, anthologizes nineteenth-century American humor writing, but specifically seeks to salvage dialect humor from literary oblivion.

Cohen, Hennig and William B. Dillingham, eds. Introduction to *Humor of the Old Southwest*, pp. xiii-xxviii. Athens: The University of Georgia Press, 1964.

Describes Southwestern humor as a combination of social history and folk tale.

Cox, Samuel S. *Why We Laugh*. New York: Benjamin Blom, 1876, 448 p.

Combines a theoretical discussion of the nature of humor with a careful study of American humor writing.

Hauck, Richard Boyd. *A Cheerful Nihilism: Confidence and the Absurd in American Humorous Fiction*. Bloomington: Indiana University Press, 1971, 269 p.

Explores examples of American humor, from Benjamin Franklin to John Barth, in the context of Albert Camus's theory of the absurd.

Hubbell, Jay B. "The Humorists." In *The South in American Literature: 1607-1900*, pp. 658-83. Durham: Duke University Press, 1954.

Credits humor writers with vital social and documentary functions, applauding their ability to capture regional cultures on paper.

Lewis, Paul. *Comic Effects: Interdisciplinary Approaches to Humor in Literature*. Albany: State University of New York Press, 1989, 179 p.

Combines theories of humor from a variety of disciplines in order to offer specific analyses of particular historical moments in the production of literary humor.

Quinn, Arthur Hobson. "Mirth for the Million." In *The Literature of the American People*, pp. 701-20. New York: Appleton-Century-Crofts, Inc., 1951.

Argues that American humor writing was always either high- or low-brow; also provides a detailed history of the genre.

Rather, Lois. "Were Women Funny? Some 19th Century Humorists." *The American Book Collector* 21, No. 5 (February 1971): 5-10.

Documents the extent of women's involvement in humor writing.

Rollins, Alice Wellington. "Woman's Sense of Humor." *The Critic and Good Literature* 1, No. 13 (29 March 1884): 145-46.

Brings to bear a list of humorous characters created by women novelists in the debate with male critics who have argued that there are no women humorists because women have no sense of humor.

Rourke, Constance. "I Hear America Singing." In *American Humor: A Study of the National Character,* pp. 163-203. New York: Harcourt, Brace and Company, 1931.

Demonstrates how some major American authors—including Ralph Waldo Emerson, Henry David Thoreau, and Walt Whitman—were shaped by the presence of humor writing in the popular culture.

Schmitz, Neil. *Of Huck and Alice: Humorous Writing in American Literature.* Minneapolis: University of Minnesota Press, 1983, 268 p.

Focusing on Mark Twain and Gertrude Stein and using a psychoanalytic method, argues that humor works by revealing painful truths in situations that allow for both recognition and laughter.

——. "Tall Tale, Tall Talk: Pursuing the Lie in Jacksonian Literature." In *American Literature* 48, No. 4 (January 1977): 471-91.

Relates, in detail, the relationship between Old Southwestern humor and the economic and social impact of Jacksonian politics.

Seelye, John. "Root and Branch: Washington Irving and American Humor." In *Nineteenth-Century Fiction* 38, No. 4 (March 1984): 415-25.

Argues that Washington Irving drew on European sources, but still posits the author as the vital link translating those sources into uniquely American humor.

Sheppard, Alice. "There Were Ladies Present: American Women Cartoonists and Comic Artists in the Early Twentieth Century." In *Journal of American Culture* 7, No. 3 (Fall 1984): 38-48.

Provides extensive original research about nineteenth- and twentieth-century women cartoonists.

Children's Literature

INTRODUCTION

Nineteenth-century children's literature was dominated by two major trends, one highly didactic and the other emphasizing entertainment based in fantasy or adventure. Although the two would merge in the late Victorian era, moral tales and instructional literature defined the genre's early steps at the beginning of the century. As historians of the genre have documented, European and American cultures saw little need for children's books in the eighteenth century; when that need arose in the late 1700s, it was focused almost exclusively on education. Although some playful poems and tales did exist early in the nineteenth century, educators, writers, and publishers treated texts for pleasure with suspicion; the style would not become generally accepted as appropriate for children until the second half of the century.

Critics who study children's literature have found that what is viewed as appropriate reading for children adheres closely to a culture's notion of what a child is—a notion that may change considerably from epoch to epoch. As critic Anne Scott MacLeod has shown, the nineteenth century opened with a prevailing belief in a rational but imperfect child and moved to the Romantic idea of childish purity and innocence. When late eighteenth-century popular cultures were dominated by religion, either Catholic or Protestant, notions about the nature of children were grounded in the doctrine of Original Sin: the belief that all individuals are born with and prone to sin and must therefore battle against temptation to reach a state of grace. As a result, literature written for children—which became considerable in the first half of the nineteenth century—consisted of "moral tales" designed to instruct children in proper behavior, the most important of which was obedience to one's parents and God. The use of the moral tale had its most active adherents in various Protestant Sunday school movements, popular both in Britain and the United States, through which religious societies disseminated instruction in faith. Consequently, most of the authors were devout Protestants—especially women concerned with the instruction of children, including most notably Anna Letitia Barbauld and Maria Edgeworth. This literature made no effort to coax or please the child into learning, but instead assumed that indulgence harms children while discipline matures them.

There was also a second, secular branch of instructional literature developing at this time. The image of the rational child—the child as a miniature adult—also encouraged parents to discourage whimsy in their children, turning every activity into a lesson. The model came from French philosopher Jean-Jacques Rousseau, whose novel-cum-educational-theory *Émile* (1762) showed the boy made into an ideal rational man through this method of instruction.

A competing construction of the child, however, survived the first part of the century and gradually took precedence in the latter half. Most critics will label this the Romantic figure of the child, finding its expression and inception in the work of the Romantic poets, especially William Wordsworth and Samuel Taylor Coleridge. As imagined in Wordsworth's *The Prelude* and "Ode: Intimations of Immortality from Recollections of Early Childhood," the child is not only unfallen and beautiful, but has special perceptive powers denied corrupted adults. As this image became dominant in the more secular Victorian era, poems, fairy tales, and fantasies designed to entertain children—or to instruct them playfully—shouldered out the didactic literature of the religious societies.

When publisher John Harris printed William Roscoe's *The Butterfly's Ball* in 1807, the virtually nonsensical poem set off a wave of imitators, which Harris published at a fast pace. English audiences had fairy tales made available to them in print in 1823, when publishers issued editions of both *The Court of Oberon; or, Temple of Fairies*, which introduced Mother Goose in a print format, and an English version of the tales collected in Germany by the brothers Grimm. The books fulfilled a need that was not addressed in the didactic literature, although the heyday of fantasy was still far off. Their participation in the fantastic and often amoral met with the rejection of the leading authors of children's literature, although fairy tales did manage to make some headway even in the early part of the century when their promoters, like the Grimm brothers, refashioned the tales they transcribed into stories palatable to early nineteenth-century middle-class morality.

The gradual blending of these various currents allowed for the prevalence of a hybrid creature in the 1860s, the beginnning of the "golden age" in children's literature, when it became common for children's verse and novels to offer a "sugared pill"—a lesson imbibed through entertainment. Lewis Carroll marked the extreme in playful entertainment with the publication of *Alice's Adventures in Wonderland* in 1865. By the end of the century, fantasy and adventure novels dominated the market, defined by Carroll, Robert Louis Stevenson, Rudyard Kipling, and Louisa May Alcott, among others. Although inexpensive adventure novels known as "shilling shockers" or "penny dreadfuls" drew some fire for their sensationalism, they still served an instructional function, as contemporary critics have shown. Recently, several critics have examined in particular how this prolific genre taught children socially accepted gender roles. They encouraged boys to be ambitious, courageous, and patriotic; they encouraged girls, ultimately, to find pleasure in their families and homes. Although the package had changed considerably, children's literature maintained its educational imperative.

REPRESENTATIVE WORKS

Louisa May Alcott
> *Little Women* (novel) 1868

Lewis Carroll
> *Alice's Adventures in Wonderland* (novel) 1865
> *Through the Looking-Glass, and What Alice Found There* (novel) 1872

Charles Dickens
> *A Christmas Carol* (novel) 1843

Maria Edgeworth
> *The Parent's Assistant* (short stories) 1796
> *Early Lessons* (short stories) 1800

Juliana Horatia Ewing
> *Jackanapes* (novel) 1884

Jacob and Wilhelm Grimm
> *German Popular Stories* (stories) [first English edition] 1823

Nathaniel Hawthorne
> *A Wonder-Book For Girls and Boys* (short stories and poetry) 1852

Thomas Hughes
> *Tom Brown's School Days* (novel) 1857

Charles Kingsley
> *The Water Babies* (novel) 1863

Rudyard Kipling
> *The Jungle Books* (novel) 1894

Edward Lear
> *A Book of Nonsense* (poetry) 1846

Frederick Marryat
> *Masterman Ready* (novel) 1841-42

William Roscoe
> *The Butterfly's Ball* (poem) 1807

Mary Martha Sherwood
> *The History of the Fairchild Family* (novel) 1818

Robert Louis Stevenson
> *A Child's Garden of Verses* (poetry) 1885

Ann Taylor and Jane Taylor
> *Original Poems for Infant Minds* (poetry) 1804

Mark Twain
> *The Adventures of Tom Sawyer* (novel) 1876

OVERVIEWS

Anne Scott MacLeod

SOURCE: "From Rational to Romantic: The Children of Children's Literature in the Nineteenth Century," in *Poetics Today*, Vol. 13, No. 1, 1992, pp. 141-53.

[*In the following essay, MacLeod describes the history of nineteenth-century children's literature as a shift from rationalist concepts of the child to Romantic concepts, a shift she argues was shaped by mid-century social protest.*]

In the course of the nineteenth century, American children's literature made a momentous journey from eighteenth-century rationalism to nineteenth-century romanticism. When the journey was complete, the children of children's fiction, rational, sober, and imperfect at the beginning of the nineteenth century, had become innocent, charming, and perfect: the rational child had become the romantic child. The change in children's literature was by no means either smooth or steady, nor was it predictably linked to changes in adult literature. In fact, for the first half of the century, children's fiction was all but static in form and content. When the shift occurred around 1850, it was brought about by social change; the literature was reshaped and pressed into service as a form of social protest in a changing society. Fundamentally, the shifts in children's literature followed—although at a little distance—the nineteenth-century adult taste for romantic and sentimental literature. But the change began when and how it did for social reasons; sentiment in children's literature was borne in on a wave of social concern for the children of the urban poor.

Early nineteenth-century American fiction for children was patterned after English models, particularly the models provided by Maria Edgeworth's lively but improving stories. In writing for the young, as she said in one preface addressed to parents [*Rosamund*, 1821], Edgeworth did not try to give children knowledge of the world, "which ought not, cannot be given prematurely," but rather, "some control of their own minds . . . [which] cannot be given too early and is in the power of all to attain, even before they are called into the active scenes of life." To this end, her stories tell of mildly wayward children learning rationally from their mistakes, aided, of course, by the serene moralizing of their parents. The underlying attitude captures the essence of eighteenth-century rationalism, conceding the imperfection of human nature while endeavoring for its improvement: that is, optimism, well-laced with realism. The characteristic tone is soundly struck in one Edgeworth tale [from *The Birthday Present and the Basket Woman*, 1801?], for example, when a father tells his erring daughter, "If you have sense enough to

see your own mistakes, and can afterwards avoid them, you will never be a fool."

Edgeworth's work was much admired in America. Both before and after the turn of the nineteenth century, many children read her books with pleasure, apparently absorbing their reasonable messages without objection. It is not surprising, then, that in the second decade of the nineteenth century, when American authors began writing for American children, it was Maria Edgeworth's fiction which furnished the prototype for their work. There were hundreds of American imitations of Edgeworth's tales (less lively by half), all of them every bit as dedicated to rational modes of child nurture and the lessons of experience.

In other words, American children's fiction before 1850 told plain and sober stories of rather nice children making predictable childish errors of judgment and learning appropriately from the consequences. If they went out in hot weather against parental advice, they

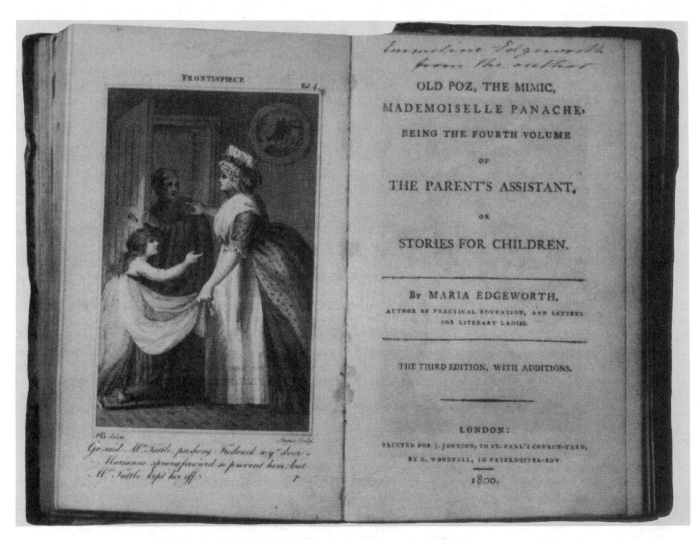

Title page for the fourth volume of Maria Edgeworth's The Parent's Assistant.

were certain to fall ill for an instructive day or two. If they teased the local dog, they were just as surely bitten, although never fatally: the point was to improve, not to die. Fictional children learned to moderate quick tempers and to restrain greediness, to consider others before themselves, to find happiness in duty and self-control. And authors saw to it that these useful lessons followed relentlessly from practical experience.

The Rational Concept of the Child

Early nineteenth-century Americans did not consider children self-sufficient; the parent's role as moral instructor was decisive. Like Emile's tireless tutor, parents in juvenile fiction were ever present, available to draw the moral and reinforce the connection between an error and its consequence. The tone of these inevitable conversations was mild and affectionate. "You see, my dear child," they typically began, going on to explain how happiness resulted from obedience and selflessness and how misery plagued the child who was self-indulgent, ill-tempered, or resistant to God's benign rule. Goodness and happiness always went hand in hand. As one little sinner [in *The Child's Portfolio,* 1823] learned, "That which we obtain by improper means, seldom contributes to our happiness; but often renders us miserable."

The structure of this early literature rested upon the concept of the child as a rational but unfinished being. By the nineteenth century, the Calvinist doctrine of innate depravity had faded from all but a few books published by sectarian presses; on the whole, the literature now showed children in a more kindly light. Most authors saw children as bundles of possibilities, some good, some evil; the young, they thought, were usually well-meaning but in need of considerable instruction. If they were not sinful by nature, neither were they naturally perfect. Although these authors expected children to have an earnest concern for their own moral development, the writers of this period regarded children as apprentices to moral perfection, not as examples of it. Early nineteenth-century adults looked on childhood almost entirely as a time of preparation for adult life. They loved and valued their children, to be sure, but they saw childishness as a condition to be outgrown and the irrational aspects of youth as qualities to be replaced by reasoned behavior as soon as possible.

Reasoned behavior, the authors believed, was best taught by rational discipline. Fictional parents were never angry with their children. A little girl [in Elizabeth Lee Foller's *The Well Spent Hour,* 1832], "spoiled . . . by her grandparents" and behaving badly to get her mother's attention, "looked into her mother's eyes and found neither anger nor pity there." Adults approached childish failings calmly, explaining rather than punishing, urging children to reflect on their behavior in order

to arrive at a better course of action on their own. When five-year-old Rollo [in Jacob Abbott's *Rollo at Play,* 1838] wants to go out to play, his mother asks if he has read his lesson for the morning. He says that he has forgotten to do so, and his mother tells him that he may not go out until he has read it.

> Rollo was sadly disappointed, and also a little displeased. He turned away, hung down his head, and began to cry.
>
> "Come here my son," said his mother.
>
> Rollo came to his mother, and she said to him kindly, "You have done wrong now twice, this morning. . . . It is my duty not to yield to such feelings as you have now, but to punish them."
>
> Rollo stood silent for a minute—he perceived that he had done wrong, and was sorry.

And so were most of these fictional children when they did wrong. Told kindly of their errors, they obligingly saw their faults in a new light and immediately set about correcting them.

To put it briefly, children's fiction in the early nineteenth century idealized children without sentimentalizing them. The tone was matter-of-fact and reasonable, the picture of children affectionate but not "enthusiastic" in the eighteenth-century sense of emotionally extravagant. These books neither praised the innate perfection of children nor waxed eloquent about their redemptive powers. Fictional children did not correct or convert their elders in this period unless by silent example, and even that was rare. Mostly, children were pupils to the wisdom of adults.

Social Protest

This picture persisted in children's fiction until about the middle of the century, when the homogeneity of the literature began to break up. New writers introduced literary extravagance into a heretofore sober literature, and sentimentality, already rampant in popular writing for adults, invaded the fiction written for children. By the 1850s, authors were harnessing children's literature to the cause of social protest, using sentimentality toward children to arouse public concern for the young victims of what they saw as a crisis in American urban society.

Poverty exploded in American cities during the 1840s and 1850s; port cities in particular were overwhelmed by the influx of thousands of increasingly destitute immigrants. Between 1845 and 1855, the percentage of the foreign-born population in New York increased from one-third to one-half. Unlike earlier immigrants, who had fanned out into the country seeking land and work, many of those who arrived at mid-century had no means to move on or to buy land and few skills that would support them. Most of the Irish who came to Boston, Oscar Handlin writes [in *Boston Immigrants, 1790-1880,* 1977], "were completely immobilized; the circumstances that brought them to Boston compelled them to remain there, to struggle on as best they could." The poorest and least skilled immigrants stayed where they landed, living in murky slums and often sending their children into the streets to earn, beg, or steal a few pennies each day with which the family might buy bread—or whiskey.

The children's desperate plight pierced the public consciousness. They were inescapable, after all, living and working as they did in the city streets.

> No one can walk the length of Broadway without meeting some hideous troop of ragged girls, from twelve years old down, brutalized already beyond redemption by premature vice, clad in filthy refuse of the rag-picker's collections, obscene of speech, the stamp of childhood gone from their faces, hurrying along with harsh laughter and foulness on their lips that some of them have learned by rote, yet too young to understand it; with thief written in their cunning eyes and whore on their depraved faces. [Louis Auchincloss, *The Hone & Strong Diaries of Old Manhattan,* 1989]

New York's chief of police in 1850 estimated that 3,000 vagrant children lived in the streets, scavenging for a living one way or another. They could be seen everywhere, "on the streets and the docks and the woodpiles," Charles Loring Brace wrote [in *The Dangerous Classes of New York and Twenty Years Among Them,* 1872], adding, "naturally enough," since their homes were too wretched to bear. In 1852 Mayor Kingsland pointed out the menace of these children: "A great majority are apt pupils in the school of vice, licentiousness and theft, who, if permitted to grow up, will constitute a large portion of the inmates of our prisons."

By the late 1840s, the children of the urban poor had begun to appear in children's stories, in books, and at times in such periodicals as different as the staid *Youth's Companion* and the lively *New York Ledger,* in its popular column written by "Fanny Fern" (Sara Parton). (*The Youth's Companion,* a weekly journal, was founded in 1827 by Nathaniel Willis to entertain and "insensibly instruct" children and also to advise parents on the moral and religious nurture of their children. It had a large circulation among middle-class American families for nearly a century. The *New York Ledger* was a weekly founded by Robert Bonner in 1851, featuring romance, simple essays, and columns by popular journalists. Its audience was adult but younger and less church-oriented than that of *The Youth's Companion.*) *The Youth's Companion* [April 19, 1855]

told its young readers about "little blue-lipped and barefooted children on the pavements" of New York, poor children "with no one to care for them, [who] spend their lives in the street, or in comfortless sheds and outbuildings, where you would think no human being could live." "Fanny Fern" told her "dear little readers" how the poor "live huddled together in garrets and cellars, half-starved, half-naked, and dirty and wretched beyond what you . . . ever could dream of."

Parton's stories described the poor children of New York as cold, hungry, and abused, driven by their parents into the streets. A little girl in one of her stories was "so filthy dirty—so ragged, that she scarcely looked like a human being," her hand "so bony it looked like a skeleton." This child was sent out each morning to beg, "or if she couldn't beg, to steal—but at any rate to bring home something unless she wanted a beating. Poor little Clara!—all alone threading her way through the great, wicked city—knocked and jostled about, *so* hungry—*so* tired—*so* frightened!" In Parton's sentimental fiction, the little sufferers were sometimes befriended or even adopted by improbably kind strangers, but more often they died in misery, a reproach to the society that could not or would not cope with their desperate needs.

As protagonists, these pitiful children shared few qualities with their rational predecessors in juvenile fiction. They were neither models for character development nor examples of rational child nurture, but only vehicles for social protest; their stories were intended to move the public. Authors dwelt on children's innocence and helplessness in order to underscore the wrongs in a social system that not only failed to help them but encouraged their corruption. Like the Mayor, Parton warned that children living in New York's slums learned vice early. Far from being protected by their parents, they were "taught to be wicked . . . whipped, and beaten for not being wicked." A street boy might be "a boy in years, but a man in vicious knowledge."

Obviously, this kind of writing was directed as much toward adults as toward children. After all, even when she addressed her pathetic tales to her "dear little readers," Parton usually published them first in her newspaper column, which was written primarily for adults. Like many a social critic, Parton knew that sentimentality would catch adult attention as chilly statistics never could. Like other children's writers, she borrowed from Dickens the weapons of sentiment with which to expose social injustice. To show both the suffering of the little victims of poverty and the wickedness they learned in the slums meant appealing to both the compassion and the fear that colored the American reaction to the urban poor. Hearts too hard to be moved by the children's misery might yet quail at Charles Loring Brace's vision of the slums as "nests in which the young fledglings of misfortune and vice begin their flight." The children of the slums, he pointed out, grow up to be "the dangerous classes." If sympathy were not forthcoming, then self-interest might be. Either way, some attention might be paid; something might be done.

The Civil War overshadowed the acute concern of the 1850s for both the problems of urban poverty and the lost children of American society. And once the war was over and a brisk economic expansionism blessed the United States everywhere but in the devastated South, most Americans were willing to enjoy the prosperity and to consign social problems to institutions. The issue all but disappeared from children's literature.

The Romantic Child

The changes introduced into the fiction of the uneasy fifties, however, endured and multiplied. Children's literature diversified rapidly in the postwar years, reflecting class lines that were becoming increasingly visible in post-Civil War society. Most authors abandoned the patterns of Edgeworthian didacticism for forms already familiar in popular adult fiction. At the genteel middle-class level, children's literature found models in the evangelical fiction and domestic novels which had constituted an enormously popular adult literature at mid-century. Less genteel publications adapted the sensational adventure tale to form a whole genre of fiction aimed at boys of the working class. The lurid, implausible "dime novel" started its long and successful career in the 1860s, as did the "rags-to-riches" theme which made Horatio Alger so famous in American popular culture. At all levels, a new sentimentality toward children increasingly colored the literature written for them.

Three well-known American children's novels, all published in the 1860s, give a sense of how quickly children's literature abandoned the formulas of the early nineteenth century and of how various were the paths taken by the authors into the new era. Closest in some ways to prewar fiction, curiously enough, was the novel that has survived longest, even in the alien culture of the twentieth century, Louisa May Alcott's *Little Women* [1868-69].

In *Little Women*—and, indeed, in all of Alcott's children's novels—the children are more rounded versions of the flat characters of earlier fiction. Like their fictional predecessors, Alcott's children are basically good and well-intentioned, but they are always less than perfect. Any reader of *Little Women* can name the March girls' characteristic faults: Jo's temper, Amy's selfishness, Meg's false pride, Beth's shyness. And every reader remembers their struggles to overcome these flaws, to learn self-control, and to acquire the strong sense of duty that was the hallmark of good

character in nineteenth-century society. The family system in which they learn these lessons is based on love and reason. Marmee is that model rational parent who believes, at least theoretically, in letting experience teach the necessary lessons of life. The well-known episode near the beginning of the novel when Marmee allows her grumbling daughters to take a holiday from their usual household chores is better told and more believable than the myriad didactic stories written earlier, but the premises are exactly the same. The girls learn that no happiness can come of neglecting the simple duties of domesticity. They find themselves bored and fretful, and they miss the orderliness of their usual home life. At the end of the experiment, they admit their mistake, but Marmee, like all earlier model parents, spells out the lesson anyway:

> I wanted you to see how the comfort of all depends on each doing her share faithfully. . . . Work is wholesome, and there is plenty for every one; it keeps us from . . . mischief, is good for health and spirits, and gives us a sense of power and independence better than money or fashion.

Alcott's protagonists were not yet those romantic children whose inborn perfection would provide them with a mission to redeem adults. Her fictional children still achieved moral character gradually, with effort and lapses, and under the careful tutelage of adults. Even Beth, whose flaw is as gentle as her nature, must try to overcome it. She is, of course, an ideal of unassuming goodness for her sisters, but she is also doomed to die before she grows up. Her role as a model is mainly an effect of her death.

In *An Old-Fashioned Girl*, Alcott (1870) allows her heroine to reform a misguided family, but she stays within the old formulas to do so. In the course of Polly's visit to the city, she transforms a "fashionable" household, although this was not her intention. She simply follows the teachings of her own wholesome, rural upbringing, which have made her happy, healthy, and "useful to others," and her unselfconscious example changes the lives of those who have lost touch with such basic values. Alcott addressed questions of child nurture in all her children's books—*Eight Cousins* is the most overt example—and left no doubt as to her opinions on the subject. Her views on children and family placed her firmly in the pre-romantic period of children's literature.

Yet, in some important ways, Alcott's work heralded the new age. Her first book for children, *Little Women,* was semiautobiographical, and her subsequent work never altogether lost the particularity of real experience. Alcott's characterizations conveyed personality and individuality rather than idealized types, and while her stories were equally as "moral" as those of earlier authors, the effort to "be good" came alive in her characters because, remembering, she made it personal and subjective. She admitted that it was hard to overcome a fault, not abstractly (as early fiction sometimes did), but concretely. She showed her major characters trying, and failing, and trying again. Marmee preached, as all good mothers did in early nineteenth-century fiction, but readers forget that. What they remember is Jo's struggle with her temper, her conscience, her overwhelming grief for Beth. They remember the passage in which Marmee tells Jo that she, too, has wrestled with a quick temper all her life. Very likely, readers also remember that even the idealized Mrs. March has never altogether defeated her own temperament, but has only learned to control it. While it is true that *Little Women,* which stayed closest to Alcott's own experience, is the best and most deeply felt of all her children's books, the less successful stories, in which the message gains the upper hand and the action is mechanical, still have personality, humor, and a specificity which set them apart from antebellum fiction for the young. Those qualities, together with Alcott's capacity for portraying children as genuine people, not just as models for her readers, went far to move children's fiction from the didactic abstractions of earlier decades toward a more romantic particularity.

At first glance, it seems odd to connect Horatio Alger's "rags-to-riches" stories with romanticism. But Alger's books, if not themselves "romantic," did contribute in their own way to the creation of a children's literature which was romantic about children. Alger's heroes were the street children who had attracted so much public attention in the 1850s. Bootblacks, match boys, newsboys, peddlers—all those youngsters who worked on the streets, on their own, living an independent, catch-as-catch-can kind of life, were his protagonists. His plots carried these boys away from their lowly occupations and on to respectability, by way of good character, hard work, luck, and the interventions of Christian businessmen. Contrary to legend, in the main it was not riches his heroes achieved but something more modest. The title of one of his books says it all: *Slow and Sure or, From the Street to the Shop.* Alger wanted his fictional characters, and the real boys they represented, to move from independent poverty to regular employment.

To make his stories attractive and persuasive, Alger had to make his characters attractive and, in doing so, to close his eyes to the worst aspect of the lives of street children: their moral corruption. Alger met this difficulty with sentimentality. He conceded the existence of some hazards of street life, admitting that boys might take to smoking or gambling or begging, but he evaded the "vicious knowledge" that Sara Parton had pointed out. *Ragged Dick,* published in 1868, was his first great success. The story of a bootblack who lived in rags and slept in a box, its protagonist, Dick, was "not a model boy in all respects," Alger admitted, but his sins were no more than bad habits. "His nature was a noble one, and had saved him from all mean faults." Alger insisted that "noble natures" were plentiful under the tattered coats of his boys, to convince readers not only that a powerful person might take an interest in a bootblack, but also that such a boy might deserve his good fortune. And Alger's tales blandly assumed that the innate goodness of his heroes would triumph over the corrupting influence of their street lives and work—a romantic notion very much at odds with the social environmentalism of the antebellum period.

Alger's sentimentality, like that of some mid-century authors, was partly an effort to create sympathy for an underclass. The effectiveness of his approach was shown by the response to his 1871 book, *Phil, the Fiddler,* which exposed the abuses of a contract-labor system then operating in New York. Boys brought from Calabria to beg in the American streets were not just exploited, but were so badly abused by their masters that many of them died. When Alger's story appeared, describing the system and the wrongs suffered by the helpless youngsters caught in it, the public responded vigorously. There were meetings, protests, and, eventually, a court case on behalf of one brutally mistreated child. In 1874, the New York legislature passed a law to prevent cruelty to children, the first of its kind in the United States. If Alger's boys were not entirely romantic children, they were nevertheless good enough, likable enough, and sometimes pathetic enough to mobilize a growing American sentimentality toward children.

Elsie Dinsmore, by Martha [Farquharson] Finley, was published in 1867. The novel owes a good deal to the Christian evangelical school of adult fiction and therefore partly belongs to the pre-Civil War tradition. But the overdrawn sentimentalism of Finley's story, together with her emphasis on her heroine's innocent purity and power to redeem others, place the book within the developing romantic strain in children's fiction.

Finley's model was surely Susan Warner's best-selling 1850 evangelical novel, *The Wide, Wide World.* In that lachrymose tale the young heroine, Ellen Montgomery, weeps and sighs and strives for Christian humility for well over 500 pages. Elsie Dinsmore does much the same, although in fewer pages. Yet the novels are fundamentally different because the relations between each child protagonist and the adults around her are fundamentally different. Where Warner's protagonist seeks out a series of adult mentors to help her understand and follow Christ's teachings, Finley's Elsie is confident that she already knows how a Christian should behave. And why not? Elsie, Finley tells us, had a "very clear and correct view on almost every subject connected with her duty to God and her neighbor." This eight year old is not only able but eager to instruct adults, including her father, on *their* duty to God.

One famous scene in the novel has Mr. Dinsmore demanding that Elsie play the piano to entertain his guests. Alas, it is Sunday, and Elsie, who knows that to play the piano on the Sabbath would be wicked, refuses. Mr. Dinsmore insists, saying that she will sit at the piano until she agrees to play. Elsie (by now becomingly bathed in the light of martyrdom) remains seated at the piano, refusing to play, until she finally slumps from the stool in a faint, banging her head and causing her father's friends to exclaim: "Dinsmore, you're a brute." In other words, Elsie shames her father, but eventually (it takes two sequels) she also redeems him, thus inverting what an earlier generation had understood to be the natural order. Adult authority now yields to the incandescent power of childhood purity; the child becomes mentor to the adult.

Elsie Dinsmore is interesting for its peculiarly radical mix of the old and the new in children's literature, although its emotionally incestuous relations between father and daughter are appalling to the post-Freudian reader. The religious intensity of the story is old-fashioned, particularly the many pages of unadorned preaching, as is Finley's insistence on Elsie's submissiveness, not so much because she is a child as because she is a Christian. Yet the overriding fact of the novel is that Elsie triumphs in every contest between herself and an adult, even (or especially) when the adult is her parent. Finley created a drama out of parent-child relations, with the child at its center, and ascendant. It was a giant step in the direction of romanticizing childhood.

If these novels of the 1860s foreshadowed the romantic child, Frances Hodgson Burnett's [1886] *Little Lord Fauntleroy* achieved the full flowering of romantic childhood in children's fiction. Burnett's enchantment with Cedric's personality dominates her story. Unlike Alcott, she will have it that her protagonist is faultless. In *Little Women,* it is the March girls' imperfections (and their efforts at self-correction) that inform the narrative; in *Little Lord Fauntleroy,* it is Cedric's perfection that moves the plot. Since he himself is without meanness of spirit, Cedric cannot see its existence in others; since his own nature is open and generous, he assumes this to be true of human nature in general. The novel's adult characters respond first by learning to love Cedric (who is, after all, irresistibly lovable) and then by reforming themselves to justify Cedric's faith in their goodness. The chief example is, of course, his noble grandfather, the selfish, embittered old Earl, who had turned away from his son after he married an American and who continues to reject his American daughter-in-law, even after she brings Cedric to him as his prospective heir. Cedric's innocent purity is proof against such ugly reality. His persistent admiration of his grandfather's nonexistent virtues soon begins to redeem the old man, reconciling him with his tenants and his daughter-in-law, and restoring his joy in life.

Like Elsie Dinsmore, Cedric is a redemptive child, although without any of her evangelical intentions.

There are parallels with Alger's characters too. Cedric has been gently but modestly raised in an unpretentious home in the United States. He is totally unaware of his aristocratic lineage. Yet, like Ragged Dick, Cedric has a "noble nature," both figuratively and literally, according to Burnett. His courage and dignity, like his manner and spirit, fit his newly exalted position with no need for adaptation. Most importantly, Cedric deserves his good fortune because he is inherently good.

Little Lord Fauntleroy is the quintessential romantic novel of childhood. Burnett folds into Cedric's character every aspect of the romantic view of children: physical beauty, innocence, personality, nobility of spirit, and the power to redeem others. The same child, with minor variations, can be found in many turn-of-the-century children's novels, from such well-known stories as *Rebecca of Sunnybrook Farm, Anne of Green Gables,* and *Sara Crewe,* to such a long-forgotten novel as Laura Richards's once very popular *Captain January.* Everything about the romantic novel of childhood conspired to create an image of youth as remote from the sober rationality of earlier children's literature as it could be. Aside from the fact that their authors approved of them, Jacob Abbott's Rollo and Frances Hodgson Burnett's Cedric had almost nothing in common.

The change was more than literary. It registered some fundamental changes in the way Americans regarded children and their place in society. While it is unlikely that late nineteenth-century American parents wholly embraced the notion that children are perfect, it is clear that their view of childhood differed fundamentally from that of earlier generations. By the last decades of the century, childhood had acquired value in and of itself. Children's innocence, emotionality, and imagination became qualities to be preserved rather than overcome; a child's sojourn in childhood was to be protected, not forcibly hastened.

It is hard to overstate how much this romantic attitude toward childhood influenced American thinking—socially, politically, and personally. It helped to extend the period of childhood generally and that of compulsory schooling specifically; it inspired a strong political movement for laws to protect children from being exploited as workers, but it also widened the social-class gap between those who could keep their children out of the labor market and those who could not. Subtly but pervasively, romanticism altered the relations between children and adults in every aspect of life. Even now, when so little romanticism survives in American attitudes toward childhood, some residue of this romantic response to children lingers, perhaps accounting for the contemporary uneasiness with today's enormous changes in children's books, in children's lives.

Bettina Hürlimann

SOURCE: An introduction to *Three Centuries of Children's Books in Europe,* edited and translated by Brian W. Alderson, 1967. Reprint by The World Publishing Company, 1968, pp. xi-xviii.

[*Hürlimann offers a brief and general history of European children's literature in the excerpt that follows, touching on the major trends and publications.*]

Almost exactly three hundred years ago, in the age of Franz Hals and Rembrandt, Velazquez and Murillo, a little book was published in Nuremberg entitled *Orbis sensualium pictus.* Its author was the Moravian bishop Jan Amos Komensky or Comenius and, like the great painters of his time, he was among the first to recognize the child as an individual. . . . [The] importance of the man lies in the effort which he made to introduce a new humanity into the idea of education at a time when Europe was still suffering from the effects of the Thirty Years War.

The *Orbis pictus* long remained a unique achievement. The age once again forgot the child or saw him only as a damned soul who must be saved from perdition by a rigorous pietism. Children were not born to live happy but to die holy and true education lay in preparing the soul to meet its maker. The result of this was a crop of seventeenth-century books zealously depicting for children the holy lives and joyous deaths of their little contemporaries. Even the first half of the eighteenth century would have been a similar blank—or rather black—page in the history of children's books, had not Rousseau discovered *Robinson Crusoe* (first edition, London, 1719), and had not the fairy stories of Charles Perrault brought in a little sweetness and light from 1700 onward.

The books which children had apart from these were little more than cunningly wrapped instruction. A French educational fanatic, Madame de Genlis, carried things particularly far in this branch of literature and became a world success. Having herself grown up almost without schooling, she saw children's books as being nothing but a means for propagating education. Her chief work, *Adèle et Théodore, ou lettres sur l'éducation* (1782) is still worth looking at today, partly for laughs and partly as a reminder of the progress which has been made in education theory.

Apart from instruction, however, the eighteenth century was a great time for morality and much good ink and paper was expended in persuading children of the profits of virtuous behaviour. Perhaps the culmination

of this movement can be seen in Mrs. Sherwood's extraordinary work *The history of the Fairchild family* (1818) with its famous afternoon outing to see the hanged man on the forest gallows.

That instruction and morality need not always be so obtrusively provided is apparent to an increasing extent in a number of books which were revolutionary for their time. Basedow's *Elementarwerk,* with Chodowiecki's masterly illustrations, and *Bertuchs Bilderbuch für Kinder,* which both appeared in the last quarter of the learned eighteenth century, are still, pictorially at any rate, handsome and enjoyable books. Campe's *Robinson der Jüngere* (1779) also appeared at this time—so the fruits of the Enlightenment were not entirely flavourless where children were concerned.

Throughout the eighteenth century the appetite of children for books was difficult to satiate. We feel something of this hunger when we read in *Dichtung und Wahrheit* how Goethe would hurry down into the street to spend his pocket-money on a little book calling itself a *Volksschrift* or a *Volksbuch,* which 'since they were printed with battered type on the foulest blotting-paper were almost illegible. . . . We children therefore had the good fortune to find daily on the little table in front of the second-hand bookseller's doorway these precious remnants of the Middle Ages: *Eulenspiegel, The four sons of Aymou, Fair Melusine, Kaiser Octavian, Fortunatus*—the whole bunch, right down to *The wandering Jew;* everything was there for us so long as we desired such things, such masterpieces, instead of some alternative delicacy.'

Not only young Wolfgang Goethe was aware of this hunger for an imaginative complement to the all too serious reading-matter of that time, when even fairy stories had only become really respectable since the turn of the century. Just as Germany had her *Volksbücher,* so France had her *Librairie bleue* whose volumes were sold in the streets by travelling pedlars and contained the same sort of legends, fairy stories, and adventures. In England they were called chapbooks, and in England for the first time a bookseller was to draw far-reaching conclusions from the fact that a great many children belonged to the readership of these little books. This was John Newbery, who moved into London from Reading in 1743 and two years later set up his famous shop at the 'Bible and Sun' in St. Paul's Churchyard. Here once again, the man is important because he took a leading part in establishing children's books not just as manuals of behaviour but as reading that was to be enjoyed.

Towards the end of the eighteenth century, and especially in Germany, the fairy story was becoming more and more respectable. In the 1780s, well before the collections of the Brothers Grimm, Musäus published his *Volksmärchen der Deutschen*—stories which even today have not lost their attractiveness. Slightly later, but still with his roots in the eighteenth century, the writer Christoph von Schmid (1786-1854) published many tales and Bible stories for Catholic children which have continued in print down to the present time. Such was his fame in his own day that he was raised to the ranks of the nobility 'for his services to literature'.

A contemporary of Schmid's who sank his roots deep in the Allemannic province of south-west Germany was Johann Peter Hebel (1760-1826). Although much of his work was written in the dialect of the area it has a poetry which has survived translation to High German. Along with such famous figures as Matthias Claudius, the Brothers Grimm, and the romantics Clemens Brentano and Achim von Arnim, Hebel saw the start of one of the great periods of German literature which was reflected in the children's books of the time by a new richness of imagination stemming directly from the revival of fairy tales and folk poetry. Even the chapbook stories were given a new literary dress in the work of Gustav Schwab (*Deutsche Volksbücher*, 1835) and Karl Simrock (*Die deutschen Volksbücher*, 1845-67).

In England, too, the foundations laid by Newbery were not being entirely neglected. While there was no reversion to folk literature comparable to that in Germany, books continued to be produced for children's enjoyment. The most notable contributions were to the small range of really successful poetry for children—an area all too often filled by the anthologized cast-offs of writers for adults. But in 1804 when Ann and Jane Taylor (with some other 'young persons') published their *Original poems for infant minds* they brought back a natural tone of voice to children's poetry in England which had not been heard since Isaac Watts issued his *Divine songs attempted in easy language* in 1715.

> No, little worm, you need not slip
> Into your hole with such a skip;
> Drawing the gravel as you glide
> On to your smooth and slimy side.

This may not be great writing, but it combines a verbal and a graphic felicity in a way particularly attractive to children. Both in their nature poems and in their cautionary verses the Taylor sisters exploited the requirements of the didactic with a sure sense of what would amuse their readers:

> 'I think I want some pies this morning,'
> Said Dick, stretching himself and yawning;
> So down he threw his slate and books
> And sauntered to the pastry cooks.

What follows is a lesson in the virtue of charity, but it is a very readable one and, given the circumstances, it is not surprising that these poems not only found favour in England and America but were also translated into Dutch, German and Russian.

Three years after their first appearance another poem was published which made no concessions at all to the demands of moral instruction. *The butterfly's ball* (1807) was written by William Roscoe for the entertainment of his own family circle, but by its very artlessness it made an immediate appeal and was followed by what Harvey Darton has called 'a crop of sequels'.

Despite this, the moralists must have continued to hold their ground for when, in 1823, the first translation of Grimm appeared as *German popular stories* the translators saw fit to lament the neglect of popular tales in England: 'They are nearly discarded from the libraries of childhood. Philosophy is made the companion of the nursery; we have lisping chemists and leading-string mathematicians; this is the age of reason, not of imagination; and the loveliest dreams of fairy innocence are considered vain and frivolous.' And indeed it was only with the arrival of Edward Lear and Lewis Carroll that frivolity gained its head, but once it had done so it brought to the English child a treasure in books possessed by no other nation of the world.

Once the principle of children's books as entertainment began to be accepted, Europe saw the emergence of more and more of them. Germany had her *Struwwelpeter* and, later, the slapstick work of Wilhelm Busch and Franz Pocci. Even France, previously poor in literature expressly for children, produced a bestseller in *Les malheurs de Sophie* by La Comtesse de Ségur (1864).

At the same time there were significant developments in the children's novel and the story of adventure—a category which in the past had relied on such adult books as *Don Quixote, Robinson Crusoe*, and *Gulliver's Travels* for its most entertaining contributions. Once again books in the English language showed the way, and such authors as James Fenimore Cooper, Harriet Beecher Stowe, and Frederick Marryat became known throughout Europe.

Jane Bingham and Grayce Scholt

SOURCE: "Nineteenth Century (1800-1899)," in *Fifteen Centuries of Children's Literature: An Annotated Chronology of British and American Works in Historical Context,* Greenwood Press, 1980, pp. 131-258.

[*In the following excerpt, Bingham and Scholt present both the British and American social contexts in which children's literature changed and developed during the nineteenth century.*]

In the early part of the [nineteenth] century, the evils of the Industrial Age were not recognized and the Age of Steam was even romanticized. The power of the mercantile classes was not yet threatening to the rich and, as in former times, the poor were largely ignored. The Georgians were in large part innocent of conditions of the world around them; the worst that wealthy children of that period were warned against was the possible sin of "false pride" in extravagant nobles.

Attitudes toward and the treatment of upper-class children of the Georgian period are clearly recognized in such children's books as Thomas Day's fictionalizing of Rousseauian theories in *Sandford and Merton*. The book also laid down methods for teaching manners and morals, which were repeated in the hordes of such books that followed in the next thirty years: the use of characters (children) with contrasting behaviors in illusive story settings; innumerable instructional facts and moral lessons on behavior dispensed by all-knowing adults; sermonizing on the evils of fashionable life, on the dignity of labor, on the importance of rational principles (that is, allowing children to learn the consequences of their actions), on kindness—especially to animals—and on the blessings of living the simple life. Like Day, Maria Edgeworth, the most gifted of these didactic writers, expounded a rational approach through the popular "instruction-through-conversation" method, but she also advocated lessons in natural science, education for girls, and "modern" rather than classical training. These books taught duty to parents and patronizing benevolence toward the poor, who by the laws of nature were "bound to their station." Sensibility was frowned upon, and self-control took precedence over all emotional states.

By the Victorian period, duty to parents had become a dominant theme in all books for children. When fairy tales as well as other allegories were allowed, they were often used to point out moral principles. While the Georgians had largely ignored religion, pointing out the physical consequence of bad behavior (the rod), the early Victorians stressed the importance of a peaceful conscience, with correction coming through mental pressure and discussion of one's duty to ultimate authority, that is, to parents (on earth) and to God (in heaven). While submission to authority was a cardinal principle, sensibility (often rhapsodic), particularly in girls, was now acclaimed. In those decades, swooning was fashionable.

The middle years of the century produced a spate of tract books which revealed the evangelistic Victorian preoccupations with the sufferings of the poor (as individuals) and the evils of drink, gambling, and bad company that brought the benighted poor (as a class) low. Death was often lingered over; fictional characters were often either near death or at least recently ill. The themes and settings of stories frequently revealed extreme intolerance of other religions, social systems, and points of view; at the same time they taught carefulness, temperance, and the importance of the fixed social caste system ("do what you are intended to do"), as well as the necessity of working hard to achieve perfection.

Not until after 1860 did changes in the treatment of children begin in earnest. Then, a new appreciation of childhood is evident in many books given to them—fantasy, history, adventure, biography—but even then these stories were often touted to keep boys away from the popular "Penny Dreadfuls," not for their intrinsic value.

By the end of the century, British children of all classes were beginning to be thought of as people with enthusiasms and emotions worth noting and encouraging. Even the lot of poor children was improving. Medical inspection and the feeding of pauper children by educational authorities in the industrial schools and workhouses where the children lived resulted in better living conditions and better education.

Important advances in education, influenced by developments on the continent, had occurred throughout the period. After visiting Switzerland in 1815, Robert Owen, for instance, had established the first British infant school for children from "as soon as they could walk" to age six. Improvements in teacher training, based on the work of Pestalozzi and Fellenberg, had also occurred. But because British democracy had long insisted that schools were outside of the sphere of government, a national system of education was slow to develop. Milestones along the way were the Factory Act of 1802 for apprentices, but it was evaded when proprietors refused to call their child laborers "apprentices." Further reforms were blocked by those who feared that education of the masses would bring about rebellion. Not until 1833 did Parliament vote any money for schools, and not until 1841 did teacher training institutions receive any government grants. Thus, education remained hard for many to achieve. In Liverpool as late as 1870 one-fourth of the children never attended school. But in that same year the Elementary Education Act was passed, providing elementary schools at public expense. For the first time school districts would have elected boards for the purpose of establishing schools where none existed. While the government continued to aid private schools, it had at last established a system of public schools for the "school-less multitudes," as Matthew Arnold called them. By 1880 England had compulsory attendance laws for all children under twelve.

In 1871 another educational reform came with the passing of the University Tests Act, which opened Oxford and Cambridge to non-Anglican students. Oxford and Cambridge had been the only universities in

England until the founding of the University of London in 1828 and the University of Durham in 1832, although Scotland had long had four universities. Near the end of the century other universities were organized in the larger provincial towns, providing higher education for a much wider spectrum of English students.

By the end of the century, British children were being raised in urban and industrial conditions unknown before: the old social order was disintegrating, and the social system was in great flux. Advice on all matters came from many quarters. One writer suggested seriously that even speaking in the proper accent, especially if accompanied with conformity to the usages of polite society, might assist one in rising from his class in order to become acceptable to "those above."

Meanwhile in America, British influences, which had been strong until about 1820, were undergoing "Americanization." Until this time, English writers with English "messages" had filled the demand for juvenile books. But experimentation, especially concerning "little Americans," was in the air. English things no longer seemed suitable or desirable, and changes occurred rapidly. Educators worked diligently at producing American spellers, dictionaries, and histories; stories of democratic American youths visiting foreign lands were popular. And books on rearing children which were aimed at American parents appeared. In them Locke's influence was obvious; they gave advice on giving children cold baths, simple foods, light clothing, and so on, but they also contained references to the importance of submitting in proper amounts to the "restraint of government," that is, American federalism, and they reflected the buoyant optimism and patriotism of the new land.

Life for country children (97 percent of the population at the beginning of the nineteenth century was rural) was still similar to pre-Revolutionary days; there was much emphasis on hard work, Bible reading, and correction by the rod. But as religious revivals became common in the rural areas, their enthusiasm and evangelical fervor, along with new political developments and economic opportunities, caused many a young farmer to grow restless under the yoke of tradition and move on to better lands and new life-styles.

The public school movement, with all of its problems of bad and often cruel schoolmasters and uncomfortable conditions, was spreading even into isolated regions. Although the public school did not teach religious doctrine, religious tracts were widely distributed by Sunday schools which often touched the lives of even the poorest children—as did chapbooks, broadsides, and cheap editions which brought inexpensive entertainment to the urban "street Arab" as well as to the lonely rural child. Families who could afford them

preferred private tutors in the home; many parents balked at the school's taking over the intellectual and moral demands made on the child. This rivalry along with complaints against the "overloaded" school-child working in crowded, unsavory conditions brought on an anti-intellectualism that plagued the public school well into the twentieth century. But more and more children of all classes went to school; the first compulsory attendance law was passed in Massachusetts in 1854.

Almost paralleling the growth of the public school was the rise of the American Sunday school. Although Sunday schools had originated in Britain, the movement in the United States was a powerful educational force throughout the century. Like the British Sunday school, the American version aimed to instruct poor children in primary education. Recognizing the declining religious zeal in the new country, Sunday school proponents also hoped to provide religious instruction through the churches for those who were no longer receiving it in their homes. The American Sunday School Union, formed in 1824, represented many denominations which attempted to provide all children with suitable oral instruction and juvenile reading material both at school and at home. The Union published hundreds of volumes as well as thousands of tracts, magazines, and journals, which generally were cheerful in tone and provided instruction about religious matters, the importance of charity to the poor, kindness to animals, the dangers of idleness, and the virtues of work. Far from being subtle, the material reflected the spirit of reform which was abroad in the land and the hope the future held for good, hardworking people.

Although the Sunday schools flourished, the public schools continued to have problems. The change to women schoolmarms about 1840 brought some hope for a more nurturing education for the young. But the idea of submitting to secular authority outside the home rankled many patriots (and their offspring) who had so recently been triumphant through self-assertion.

Traditional child-rearing methods brought from Europe held fast, but after about 1830, mothers, on whom the business of child rearing was squarely placed, were admonished by growing numbers of child-care advisors (mostly clergymen) to teach their children patriotism along with religion, hygiene, and refinement of manners. Many advisors still advocated firmness and obedience to parents, but more and more they began to plead for tenderness and diversion before resorting to whippings. Mothers, in particular, were admonished to produce sons fit to become the nation's leaders and daughters to become the mothers of suitable sons.

For the young, the colonial objectives of religious education and training for a vocation were rapidly fading as secularization, advances in transportation and communication, the growth of cities and towns—all coupled with the frontier spirit—changed the focus of education to facilitate the "rise of the common man."

Infant mortality was still high, and great numbers of Americans suffered from poor hygiene, lack of competent medical care, improper clothing, and poor diet. Throughout the nineteenth century, however, living conditions, particularly sanitation, slowly improved. Dependence on medicine, which had also improved, gradually developed, although many Americans, particularly in the rural areas, were suspicious of the new ways and clung to folk wisdom and "kitchen physick."

In general, the 1800s brought substantial changes for the better in the American child's life. Play, for example, which had been frowned upon and scorned as idleness in colonial times, was by the 1830s looked upon as a necessary part of invigorating the child's mind and body. Although not all parents accepted Rousseau's call to "look kindly on the child's play," controlled or "rational" play was gaining acceptance. The nineteenth-century child was also beginning to realize other types of emancipation: holidays were more frequently and joyously celebrated, organized sports and games were permitted and encouraged, and hygiene was improved. Bathing remained a problem in poorly heated homes in cold weather, but American parents were not as apt to follow Locke's advice to plunge children into cold baths as were their English counterparts. Although children's dress had traditionally imitated adult fashions (the first costume for a child was created in 1770), garments designed for children's special use began to appear. Although the fashions moved through high collars, ruffles, crinoline petticoats, bustles, high heels, flowered waistcoats, tight knee breeches, and the rest, the tendency ran toward simpler, looser clothing as the century progressed. Although some advisors still advocated that children wear light clothing to harden them against disease, others advised the opposite practice, that of protecting children against every draft— through the use of woolen coats, woolen drawers, flannels worn next to the skin, nightcaps, mufflers, and so on. Throughout the century, concern over every sort of child welfare grew, from toilet training to moral education. Improved management of the young had at last become a widespread interest. . . .

Books for children, both English and American, were in great favor, with children's fantasies, poetry, romances, and historical fiction especially well received. Children's periodicals were also extremely popular and were distributed to city and country children alike. . . .

Although children's books repudiated snobbishness, particularly the "sin" of the fortunate looking down on the less fortunate, the realities of life were far different from the ideals presented in stories. While merit sup-

posedly superseded money, difference in rank was acknowledged. But the only difference that "counted" was said to be in moral behavior.

In spite of such pleasant teachings, thousands of poor adults, almost always women, were legally sterilized to prevent the "filthy stream" of immigrants and former slaves from mingling with the "purer water of our communities." Under such conditions it is easy to see how far some Americans had fallen from the egalitarian ideals on which the country had been founded. Model, priggish children of the "purer water" were instilled with the notion that perfection was possible in their own persons, and that in America such perfection was possible through unswerving loyalty to stridently democratic ideals and through self-reliance. Children were taught to believe in the importance of charity toward the less fortunate, temperance, kindliness, and the possibility of reform. Both school and church preached that temptation in a hostile world of immoral nations (not America) and men (not Americans) could be overcome if democratic, Christian values were maintained, and that moral dignity commensurate with material possessions was attainable and desirable.

With such idealism, it seems clear why "right development" gradually won out over the discipline of the rod; moral instruction and Christian nurturing became the "gentle persuasion." Thus, by the end of the century, hopes for the future were high—at least among the upper classes. Although poor children, including children of minority groups, grew poorer, they were, as in former times, largely ignored.

MORAL TALES

F. J. Harvey Darton

SOURCE: "The Moral Tale: (i) Didactic" and "The Moral Tale: (ii) Persuasive; chiefly in verse," in *Children's Books in England: Five Centuries of Social Life,* Cambridge at the University Press, 1932, pp. 158-81, 182-204.

[*In the following excerpt from his seminal study of children's literature, Darton discusses in detail the history of instructional literature, listing many of its practitioners and conventions.*]

Between about 1790 and 1820 there were at least a score of writers for children whose recognition by the public was sufficient, on economic grounds, to get them into print regularly. The stronger ones . . . have escaped Time's scythe, though maybe they are only preserved for show in an old-fashioned garden. Those of less hardy growth are now little more than names, and must here have something like catalogue treatment. They were very much of a pattern. They were far better at telling a story than at constructing one. Their very themes made for feebleness of plot. They did not, till the end of the period, run to great length, a fact which upsets all comparison with modern books. Nor, except for an evidently increasing ease (fluency is the better word), did they differ greatly in their conception of what a Moral Tale should be. It should illustrate a particular platitude, and that was about all. Most of the heroes and heroines, or, if you will, villains or naughty children, were no more than those brats of the movable-head books: the same waxen face fitted into a succession of stiff bodies. Chronologically, except for a few trivial details, any year between 1790 to 1820 (with a slight bias to 1805-15) will fit most of their books, the dating of which is in fact very arbitrary.

The senior of them in order of publication may perhaps be Mrs Pilkington, who had experience as a governess to give her stories some sort of life. But she was also something of a theorist, because she translated Marmontel in 1799, and in the same year imitated Mme de Genlis's *Tales of the Castle* with her own *Tales of the Cottage.* But she was also a professional writer. In 1795 she wrote to Messrs Cadell offering them a children's book; which, as they did not wish to consider it, was probably not published. She was evidently sought after before long, because her *Marvellous Adventures; or, The Vicissitudes of a Cat* was issued in 1802 by two competitive firms, Harris, and Vernor and Hood. Harris published a fourth edition of her *Biography for Girls* in 1806 and a sixth in 1814, and Vernor and Hood an edition (the first?) of *Biography for Boys* in 1805. She was popular because of her moral sense. It is hard to find any individuality in her work, and she had none of the humour which one detects almost smothered in some of her contemporaries.

Nor can humour be attributed to a more voluminous writer, Mary Belson, afterwards Mary Elliott. She came late in this period, and reached into the 'twenties. But she was already a semi-classic by 1817, for Mrs Sherwood makes the little Fairchilds read her *Orphan Boy.* *Tales for Boys, Tales for Girls* and *Tales of Truth* were still being reprinted in Victoria's reign. Some of her works—*Truth our Best Friend,* for example—were published in French as well as English. Her titles are nearly always significant: *Precept and Example* (1812)—this contains publishers' puffs in the usual Newbery manner, but was produced by William Darton; *Ill-Temper a Bad Playmate; The Greedy Child Cured*—by eating poisonous berries, as in a famous Taylor poem; *Idle Ann, or The Dunce Reclaimed; Industry and Idleness, a Pleasing and Instructive Tale for Good Little Girls* (1814).

The most exciting sub-title used by Mrs Elliott was that of *Confidential Memoirs, or Adventures of a Par-*rot, a Greyhound, a Cat, and a Monkey* (1821). But it turns out to provide a very tame menagerie, hardly more lively than the Learned Pig. She also wrote *The Rambles of a Butterfly* (1819), and in her "original poems", *The Rose,* are some verses which are illustrated by a picture of boys carefully pulling a frog to pieces. The brute creation, in fact, receives a good deal of attention, as I have said—though it still *was* "the brute creation". Edward Augustus Kendall, in *Keeper's Travels in Search of his Master* (1798), certainly showed some dog-love, curiously in contrast with the dull solemnity of his other works (he translated Bernardin de Saint Pierre). But Elizabeth Sandham's cat, in *The Adventures of Poor Puss* (Harris, 1809; in two parts), is about as much like *felis catus* as the animal in the frontispiece to the book: which is hardly at all. (Miss Sandham was very popular. She also described, from an inverted human point of view, the careers of insects and birds, and wrote two school tales, and moral stories like *The Twin Sisters; or The Advantages of Religion* [5th ed. 1812]. In fact, as a Harris advertisement of 1812 says, she was "the author of many approved works for young persons".) Another such writer was "Arabella Argus" (the name is impossible), who specialized in donkeys, in *The Adventures of a Donkey* (1815), and *Further Adventures of Jemmy Donkey; interspersed with biographical sketches of the Horse* (1821), from which it may be learnt that donkeys were then driven tandem, whatever the difficulty most people find in driving them singly. Miss or Mrs Argus, however, was an observer as well as a moralist. In *Ostentation and Liberality: a Tale* (earliest edition undated: in print, dated, in 1821) she was the moralist. But in *The Juvenile Spectator* (1810) she was, in a small way, not unlike Mr Bickerstaff and his inventors—a commentator on juvenile humours, "tempers, manners, and foibles". Her method might have been more freely used: but the time had not yet come. Children in books were still cock-shies, good or evil qualities packed into little bodies to be praised or blamed by measure. And when animals were contrasted with them, as in these works, or in *The Dog of Knowledge* (anonymous: Harris, 1801), they too were often mere moral dummies.

But the writer of one un-natural history tale—*The Canary Bird* (Harris, 1817)—deserves mention for gifts she displayed outside the animal kingdom. Nothing seems to be known of Miss Alicia Catherine Mant except what is in her books. But in them she shows a very pleasant personality. She was didactic, but she tried with some success to be kind and amusing: Mr E. V. Lucas, quoting her in his *Old Fashioned Tales,* calls her work "Ann-and-Jane-Taylorism translated into prose". One of her stories, in *Tales for Ellen* (1825), is very similar to *The Purple Jar;* but the mother is not so cruelly logical as Rosamond's.

> When she had reached her eighth year, early as it might seem, Mrs Clavering had set aside a purse

for the use of her little girl [Agnes], which she told her was all that would be expended for her amusements during the year, and she was anxious to see how far this arrangement might be a check on the boundless wishes of the little Agnes.

She certainly saw, for Agnes happily and naturally spent her money on toys for herself instead of on a present for a loved friend. She *wanted* those toys. She suffered when there was no money left for the present. But she did not undergo that odious economic retribution of being unable to go to see a glasshouse. The mother was kind and persuasive, not Nemesis. There is a world of difference in a lesson so gently conveyed.

Miss Mant also wrote *Ellen; or The Young Godmother* (2nd ed. 1814), *The Cottage in the Chalk Pit* (1822)—both of which went into several editions—some other children's tales and one or two "grown-up" stories like *Caroline Lismore: or, The Errors of Fashion* (1815). She had a virtue not common in nursery moralists of the day—she made her incidents frequent and almost dramatic. In the passage just quoted, however, she is reproducing contemporary child-life. When Lucy Butt (afterwards Mrs Cameron, Mrs Sherwood's sister) was eight or nine, her mother made her just such an allowance as was given to Agnes—"for my clothes, as many guineas as I was years old"—and she was expected to manage and account for it.

A more prolific writer, long popular, though not always identified with her works, because they were often anonymous, was Mary Robson, afterwards Hughes (or Hughs; both spellings appear). Only by a comparison of a number of title-pages and advertisements is it possible to ascribe certainly to her many well-read books of 1815 to 1825. *The Ornaments Discovered* (1819), *The Alchemist* (1818), *The Orphan Girl* (1819), *Aunt Mary's Tales* (5th ed. 1819) are a few of them. She dedicated some to Miss Edgeworth, whose moral pattern she followed with some fidelity, but with very scant humour. I believe that so far as my own ancestors' books go, she compiled them by request, certainly with success. She wrote several juvenile pamphlets for the Christian Tract Society (founded in 1809) and in 1813 was made a life member of that undenominational body. Her works—like Mrs Barbauld's—appear in its lists and in those of several Unitarian associations. In 1818, a year after her marriage, she emigrated to the States with her husband, and, finding that the popularity of her books had preceded her, "commenced a school for young ladies" at Philadelphia, which she conducted with wide repute till her retirement in 1839. A brief record of her life, written in the best Victorian style of florid complacency, appeared in Sarah Josepha Hale's *Woman's Record* (1855).

Mrs Trimmer was of the full Establishment in religious views; Mary Robson either non-committal or Unitarian; Mary Elliott a Quaker. Priscilla Wakefield was also a Quaker, and of strong character at that, as an engraved portrait by Wageman, the theatrical artist, suggests. She wrote a dozen or more children's books between about 1795 and 1820, and also *Reflections on the Present Condition of the Female Sex* (J. Johnson, 1798). Her *Introduction to Botany* (3rd ed. Vernor and Hood, 1803; charmingly illustrated in colour) was for long an acceptable text-book. It was being reprinted as late as 1841. But her less pedagogic works were just as successful. She wrote little fiction, but strung together historical and similar stories under such titles as *Leisure Hours* (2nd ed. 1795), *Juvenile Anecdotes* (2 vols., 1798; by 1840 expanded to four); and *Domestic Recreation* (1805).

It is in *Juvenile Anecdotes* that there is recorded an illuminating piece of social usage. A parent, in her zeal for purity and reverence, was wont to examine every children's book in her nursery library very closely, and to cut bodily out of them "as many leaves as contained passages likely to give false ideas or to corrupt innocence". "Not an objectionable sentence escaped." Her offspring were

> never suffered to pronounce but in the most reverential and serious manner the sacred name of the Deity, making a solemn pause when it occurred, even in the Holy Scriptures; but, if it was ever introduced in other books, by way of exclamation, they passed it over, and mostly marked it as a word not to be repeated.

One of her sons, sent to school, was set to read "a speech in one of Madame Genlis' Dramas". He proceeded, but suddenly stopped and asked for a pencil. The master asked the reason.

> "Do you not see, Sir," said the little boy, "that there is the awful name which I dare not repeat; and my mamma used always to draw a line through those words which she did not choose we should say."

The master was so struck that he adopted this practice in all his schoolwork. The doctrine is exactly that of George Fox.

I have traced over sixty editions of twelve of Mrs Wakefield's books between 1795 and 1818. She was the wife of "an eminent merchant in flourishing circumstances" (her maiden name was Bell), so that she did not have to write for a living, like some others in this list. She was a Quaker, like her husband, though they never wore the Quaker dress. As the quotation shows, she was thoroughly Quaker in mind; but her popularity was not confined to the Society of Friends, and personally she was fond of general society and decent amusement. She has a claim on greater history than that of nursery books, however, for by her marriage she was the aunt of that extraordinary man Edward Gibbon Wakefield, and was almost entirely responsible for his early upbringing. An entry in her diary for 1807 sounds prophetic:

> My thoughts much occupied with my little Edward, whom I tenderly love, but whose inflexible pertinacious temper makes me fear for his own happiness and of those connected with him.

History was to confirm that early view of one of the makers of Australia. But at least he proves that the atmosphere of the Moral Tale was not utterly stultifying and conservative. His aunt's examples of it would not be read by any child now, but they have a characteristic sincerity and interest even yet for older readers.

Other writers of the period and manner must be passed over with the mere mention of their names and of the fact that they usually achieved more than one edition. Such are Mrs Pinchard of Taunton, who wrote *The Blind Child* (1791; 10th ed. 1814), *Dramatic Dialogues* (1792), *The Two Cousins* (1794) and *Family Affection* (1816); Mrs Marshall, author of *Henwick Tales* (6th ed. 1822); Isaac Day, *Scenes for the Young* (1807); E. Fenwick, Esther Copley (née Hewlett), Mrs Hurry (née Mitchell), Elizabeth Helme (original, but also a translator of Campe), and some whose very names are unknown, though their books sold well. Two of these shy authors wrote anti-slavery tales—*Samboe, or, The African Boy* (1823; dedicated to William Wilberforce), and *Radama, or the Enlightened African; with Sketches of Madagascar* (1824).

The enlightened African leads fitly to the most intense moralist of them all, Martha Mary Butt, afterwards Mrs Sherwood; because, apart from her more particular dogmas, she spent a great deal of her useful and indefatigable life in trying—successfully—to bring the light of Christianity into dark places; particularly into India, where she went with her husband, a Captain in the 53rd Regiment. Her earlier works nearly all had a missionary tendency; *Little Henry and his Bearer* (1814; 30th ed. 1840), *The Infants' Progress* (both written in India in 1809-10), for instance, *The Indian Pilgrim* (written in 1810, but published in 1817), and *The Ayah and the Lady* (written in 1813). These tales had an immense vogue in evangelical circles both in India, where they were translated into Hindustani, and in England.

That side of her character possibly was the best known even to her more general public. It was never much weakened. The fact, however, is that her life as a child, though strict after the fashion of the times, was by no means lacking in vivacity. But after her marriage she met and became imbued with views which tinged deeply her most popular books, and were so strongly expressed in them that no one to-day who does not feel some doctrinal faith faintly akin to what she believed from about 1812 to 1825 could read most of these works sympathetically, if at all. In India she came under the influence of the great missionary Henry Martyn. He changed her cast of mind. His evangelical zeal, passing into her, became for a time a Calvinism as rigid as any displayed by the Janeways or Whites of a century and a half before.

> All children are by nature evil, and while they have none but the natural evil principle to guide them, pious and prudent parents must check their naughty passions in any way that they have in their power, and force them into decent and proper behaviour and into what are called good habits.

was the belief she stated quite explicitly, and repeated many times, and quoted Scripture to support, throughout *The Fairchild Family*. Her doctrines, however, grew far gentler on her return to England, and in later work she used them with much less vehemence and frequency.

The Fairchild Family, a work teeming with personal force and vitality, was known to almost all English children up to about 1887, and is not yet forgotten, if alive only by strong repute. It deserved its life, for it had certain elements of greatness. It was partly written at Meerut, in 1812 to 1813, just after Martyn left India for good. The first part was published in 1818, the fourth, and last, in 1847. During its vogue, and after, it was perhaps as widely read, as completely ridiculed, and as honestly condemned by child-lovers, as any English book ever written for children. It has deserved all three fates. It contains in its mass of minatory and exegetic detail two features not surpassed elsewhere. The prose Mrs Sherwood wielded was masterly; and no one ever described very simple childish pleasures—especially those of the table—with more obvious enjoyment in them. The meals eaten by the little Fairchilds, even if they teach lessons about greed, make the mouth water to this day. The buttered toast . . . alas, so prodigally wasted.

As for the prose, I must insist on a long quotation, partly because the profoundly sombre effect is cumulative, and partly because in such versions of the book as are now provided for children, this greatest passage in it is generally omitted—for moral reasons. Lucy, Emily, and Henry (all names of Mrs Sherwood's own children) had quarrelled over a doll. Lucy bit Emily and Emily scratched Lucy. Mr Fairchild overheard them saying that they did not love one another. He whipped their hands (Henry's as well) "till they smarted again", repeated Dr Watt's views on bears and lions, and mentioned the first murder. Then he kissed them and forgave them, and they had the excellent family dinner; after which Mr Fairchild said to his wife (the italics are mine):

> "I will take the children this evening to Blackwood, and show them something there, which, I think, they will remember as long as they live; and I hope they will take warning from it, and pray more earnestly for new hearts, that they may love each other with perfect and heavenly love." . . .

> "What is there at Blackwood, papa?" cried the children.

> "Something very shocking", said Mrs Fairchild. "There is one there", said Mr Fairchild, looking very grave, "who hated his brother."

> "Will he hurt us, papa?" said Henry.

> "No", said Mr Fairchild; "*he cannot hurt you now.*"

> When the children and John were ready, Mr Fairchild set out. They went down the lane nearly as far as the village; and then, crossing over a long field, they came in front of a very thick wood.

> "This is Blackwood", said Mr Fairchild, getting over the stile; "the pathway is almost grown up; *nobody likes to come here now.*"

> "What is here, papa?" added the children; "is it very shocking? *We are afraid to go on.*"

> "There is nothing here that will hurt you, my dear children", said Mr Fairchild. "Am I not with you; and do you think I would lead my children into danger?"

> "No, papa", said the children; "*but mamma said there was something very dreadful in this wood.*"

> Then Lucy and Emily drew behind Mr Fairchild, and walked close together, and little Henry asked John to carry him. The wood was very thick and dark, and they walked on for half a mile, going down hill all the way. At last they saw, by the light through the trees, that they were come near to the end of the wood; and as they went further on, they saw an old garden wall, some parts of which being broken down they could see, beyond, a large brick house, which, from the fashion of it, seemed as if it might have stood there some hundred years, and now was fallen to ruin. The garden was overgrown with grasses and weeds, the fruit-trees wanted pruning, and it could now hardly be discovered where the walks had been. One of the old chimneys had fallen down, breaking through the roof of the house in one or two places; and the glass windows were broken near the place where the garden wall had fallen. Just between that and the wood stood a gibbet, on which the body of a man hung in chains:

it had not yet fallen to pieces, although it had hung there some years. The body had on a blue coat, a silk handkerchief round the neck, with shoes and stockings, and every other part of the dress still entire: but the face of the corpse was so shocking, that the children could not look at it.

> "Oh! papa, papa! what is that?" cried the children.

> "That is a gibbet", said Mr Fairchild; "and the man who hangs upon it is a murderer—one who first hated, and afterwards killed his brother! When people are found guilty of stealing, they are hanged upon a gallows, and taken down as soon as they are dead; but when a man commits a murder, he is hanged in iron chains upon a gibbet, till his body falls to pieces, that all who pass by may take warning by the example."

> Whilst Mr Fairchild was speaking, the wind blew strong and shook the body upon the gibbet, rattling the chains by which it hung.

> "Oh! let us go, papa!" cried the children, pulling Mr Fairchild's coat.

> *"Not yet"*, said Mr Fairchild: "I must tell you the history of that wretched man before we go from this place."

And he did, *The Fairchild Family* being "a Collection of Stories calculated to show the Importance and Effects of a Religious Education", which this murderer had neglected.

No one can fairly say nowadays that that is fit reading for children, however naughty they were. Nor was it the sort of literature usually provided for them in 1818, or even under the Puritans. But the English is little short of majestic in its economy and plainness. The picture is appallingly vivid, and that sentence "he cannot hurt you now" might, in a humbler way, come from the *Agamemnon* or *Lear*. And terrible though the episode is, Mrs Sherwood believed it to convey a holy lesson rightly needed. When the children had heard the murderer's story—how two brothers,

> when they first began to quarrel in their play, *as you did this morning,* did not think that death, and perhaps hell, would be the end of their quarrels

—they asked if they might kneel down and pray for new hearts, and did so. All hate, said Mr Fairchild, in giving his glad consent to this, must be taken from himself and all of us by the Holy Spirit of God, lest at the last, "if he took his natural heart with him to heaven, even the glory of the Almighty God would be hateful to him".

It is no use to argue with faith so completely unyielding; there is no basis of argument. Any criticism that could prevail against it would lead the victim into a black void of disbelief far more devastating than the torments of a soul that believes but knows itself short of perfection; and at that time Mrs Sherwood was unceasingly conscious of imperfection.

. . . . .

In many of her smaller booklets—little story-tracts written chiefly for Houlston, her first publisher, of Shropshire, and for my predecessors—she had been associated with her sister Lucy, afterwards Mrs Cameron. On her return to England the publishers would send proofs of illustrations which they had in stock, and round these, with great ingenuity, the sisters wove tales moral in purpose but by no means uninteresting as narratives. Mrs Cameron, though slightly overshadowed by her sister, was a voluminous and popular writer. Her life, incorporating some autobiography, was written by her son Charles. *Margaret Whyte* and *The Two Lambs* were perhaps her best-known tales. She was consistently serious. As she grew older—like most writers for children, except Maria Edgeworth—she deprecated that frivolity of her own youth which she was equally apt to deplore in the rising generation. She viewed religious changes with apprehension, but seems never to have quite reached her sister's doctrinal inflexibility. The most striking thing in her life, in fact, was its tolerant religious atmosphere. She was staunchly Church of England, and when Catholic Emancipation came wrote "Anti-Christ reigns over us". She feared Lancaster's unsectarianism. She observed the Oxford Movement with some alarm. She urged her son not "to visit the Oxford Tract People", though "many of them may mean well". She saw, none the less, that the Tractarians might "have been raised up to warn the Evangelical clergy of the danger they were likely to fall into, of mixing too much with the world". Finally, Thomas Arnold of Rugby, J. H. Shorthouse and Pusey all recommended warmly her tract-stories for young children.

These two sisters, popular and eminent in their limited sphere, focus most of the development of the Moral Tale on its less imaginative side. Mrs Sherwood abhorred fairy-tales, as her treatment of Sarah Fielding's *Governess* shows. She reverted to extreme Puritanism. She was a magnificent story-teller. She was what the Elizabethans called a "good housekeeper". Her sister would have no self-assertion in the lower orders, was a confirmed didacticist, an anti-Papist, and yet lived to half-condone as well as to be praised by the Tractarians. The average life was not taut at extremes.

One must, in judging the Moral Tale, forget what it is so easy to pick out afterwards, inaccurately, as typical—the noise made by the prophet in or near his own time. The propagandist appeared, certainly, or was heard, in the Edgeworths; and, very differently, in Mrs

Sherwood's devotion to the poor Indian and Calvinism. But for the average English middle-class writer for children—the steady purveyors for the expanding market—there was no startling voice crying in a wilderness. The Pilkingtons, the Mants, the Elliotts, never knew what a wilderness was. There were firm principles behind what they wrote, but they were acceptances, not evangels. They sought to make no conversions to a bright new gospel, and they did not think out deeply their own prepossessions or the peculiarities of their enforced audience. They started and ended with what they had always taken for granted. They lived in a kind of abstract benevolence.

It often seems, in short, as if the real child were sometimes utterly overlooked by such writers, except as a *tabula rasa* for a heavy pen. And yet they were human, and now and then suddenly saw both weakness and sheer happiness not ungently. Maria Edgeworth gave Rosamond that illuminating little hesitation about her future goodness. Mrs Sherwood recorded that as a child, after standing in an iron collar with a backboard all day to do her lessons, she "manifested her delight by taking a run for half a mile through the woods"; and she must have understood very well the fearful joy of greediness. Mrs Trimmer was willing to tread on fairies, and insisted on "really useful" toys; but she flatly refused to abolish dolls and doll's-house teathings. She pictured, with hearty sympathy, a peasant's family enjoying themselves after the day's work, while the goodwife sang at her spinning-wheel,

> and sweetened her harder labours. Her most favourite (songs) were, *The Berkshire Lady, Fair Rosamond, The Lamentations of Jane Shore,* and *Chevy Chace.* No song was ever sung by this fireside that had the least immorality in it, or that ridiculed anything that was religious: neither did anyone relate nonsensical stories about ghosts and apparitions.

But *The Guardian of Education* deplored that sort of song altogether. Many little chance touches like these hint that children were still children after all; and, what is better, that when it came down to life itself outside books, the moralists were well aware of the facts and did not try so hard as all that to get them altered.

Still, unless one reads very closely, their books cannot but give a certain impression of rigidity, of inhuman excellence, of making life not worth living in the attempt to live it worthily. Something a little different, a little more suggestive of greater changes to come, appears in the other aspect of the Moral Tale, in its expression (for the most part) in verse.

. . . . .

[Until] the early years of the nineteenth century, very little verse was written specially for children. The

Newbery scrap about "Three children sliding on the ice", whatever its origin, and the dormouse poem in *Goody Two-Shoes,* whatever *its* origin, were specks in a very small sea of adult condescensions. Nursery rhymes and rhymed alphabets, even if they were widely circulated in print, as to which the evidence is of a negative kind, were no more than traditional. Watts held a field which few people deemed worth tillage. It would be nearly true, but not quite, to say that between 1715 and 1804 no "original poems for infant minds" were uttered.

The book that awoke the nurseries of England, and those in charge of them [was] *Original Poems for Infant Minds,* "by Several Young Persons" (1804). . . . This introduction begins with a modest claim to a moral purpose, not very happily phrased:

> If a hearty affection for that interesting little race, the race of children, is any recommendation, the writers of the following pages are well recommended; and if to have studied in some degree their capacities, habits, and wants; with a wish to adapt these simple verses to their real comprehensions, and probable improvement—if this has any further claim to the indulgence of the public, it is the last and only one they attempt to make.

"Piper, pipe that song again." The several young persons heard the words, but in a different voice. The writers were Ann Taylor, aged 22 in 1804; Jane Taylor, aged 21; Isaac Taylor (third of that name in the family), aged 17—these of the younger generation; their friend—was he?—Bernard Barton, aged 20; possibly Isaac Taylor II, their father; and Adelaide O'Keefe, aged 28, who apparently was foisted into the volume by the publishers. Though "young persons", once grown-up, were fully grown-up, the backward, downward glance, by writers of years so tender, at "that interesting little race" is a trifle complacent. Were they really as mature as all that in 1804?

As a matter of fact, Ann Taylor herself had commenced [as an] author when she was only sixteen, so that perhaps there was some warrant for the adult attitude. But any fears that it would be dominant in the book are greatly allayed by the poems themselves. They were "original", as no previous poems for the young had been, in that you can see the authors, as it were, talking lovingly and naturally to real flesh-and-blood middle-class children whom they knew: almost to themselves, indeed.

> It is not to tease you, and hurt you, my sweet,
>   But only for kindness and care,
> That I wash you, and dress you, and make
>   you look neat,
>   And comb out your tanglesome hair.

I don't mind the trouble, if you would not
    cry,
    But pay me for all with a kiss;
That's right—take the towel and wipe your
    wet eye,
    I thought you'd be good after this,

wrote Ann in "Washing and Dressing"; and you feel sure that "Mrs Taylor of Ongar" had been kissing Ann herself in just that simple family way not so many years before.

That is the revolution made by *Original Poems,* and its successors *Rhymes for the Nursery* (1806) and *Hymns for Infant Minds* (1810). They rendered the "little race" natural, and the monitor's attitude to it also as natural as contemporary manners permitted. On the other hand, the *Original Poems* themselves, when they became tales in verse instead of comments on life or spontaneous little pictures of pleasant and beautiful things, as they sometimes were, lost much of their originality, and were no more than rhymed moralities. But they were that too with a difference. Miss Edgeworth had let foolishness or misconduct lead inevitably—by "Nature"—to retributive justice. The other moral fabulists in prose had done the same, less dexterously, or had brought in the tutor or schoolmistress to point out the offence. The Taylors just made things happen. Meddlesome Mattie spied the pretty snuff-box, and her idle hands mischievously opened it: "she could do nothing else but sneeze", and so she broke her grandmother's spectacles. There is no real moral in that: the box might have been Pandora's, for all Mattie knew, or a chest in King Solomon's mines, or have held a genie. The only lesson honestly conveyed is that you should never open any boxes at all. Equally untrue, didactically, is "The Little Fisherman". Harry, who *would* catch fishes (though Mrs Trimmer had given excellent reasons for proper use of the brute creation), was himself caught by the chin on a meat-hook—quite capriciously and un-morally, because he was doing what any prudent angler would have done, putting tomorrow's breakfast in the larder. The Taylors, in fact, invented the "awful warning" school of poetry, which has led to a thousand cheerful parodies very remote from the authors' intentions.

However, in spite of their moral purpose, they never lost their humanity: they were still too close to childhood, and too happy a family, to become prigs when they started writing. And they had a sense of humour surpassed, among contemporary writers for children, only by Maria Edgeworth's. "The Notorious Glutton"—

> A duck who had got such a habit of stuffing
> That all the day long she was panting and
>   puffing—

is a timeless and jolly piece, in spite of Mrs Duck's unhappy end. The awful warnings, unlike Mrs Sherwood's in prose, are really quite cheerful. They had also a gift for legitimate pathos, as in "The Last Dying Speech of Poor Puss", and for sheer unhesitating simplicity, as in "Learning to go Alone" (from *Rhymes for the Nursery*):

> Come, my darling, come away,
> Take a pretty walk to-day;
> Run along, and never fear,
> I'll take care of baby dear:
> Up and down with little feet,
> That's the way to walk, my sweet.
>
> Now it is so very near,
> Soon she'll get to mother dear.
> There she comes along at last:
> Here's my finger, hold it fast:
> Now one pretty little kiss,
> After such a walk as this.

You *must* like the Young Persons who could write in that style.

Some of their pieces, notoriously, have suffered, like Watts's, from the attrition of the school entertainment platform, or from the obloquy of easy parody. "My Mother" is one, "Twinkle, twinkle, little star" another, to meet that undeserved fate. But when it appeared, and for sixty years later, "My Mother" was admired (as it was probably meant to be) for its moral tone as much as for the honest sentiment it expresses so fluently and yet so gracefully. It was by Ann. De Morgan, the mathematician, writing of it in the *Athenaeum* in the austere 'sixties, called it "one of the most beautiful lyrics in the English language, or any other language", but thought that the "bit of religion thrust in" spoilt it. He suggested that Tennyson should be asked "in the name of all the children of England", to rewrite this verse:

> For God, who lives above the skies,
> Would look with vengeance in His eyes,
> If I should ever dare despise
> > My Mother.

He did not know that Ann—by then Mrs Gilbert—was still living, at the age of eighty-four. She at once agreed that she would no longer put the matter so straitly, and sent an alternative:

> For could our Father in the skies
> Look down with pleased or loving eyes,
> If ever I could dare despise
> > My Mother.

"*Vengeance*", she wrote, "is not a word I should now employ." But "anger" had been the word used in the first edition: it was intensified into "vengeance" at the

recollection of "a painful piece of far back family history".

That perhaps is the secret of the Taylors' freshness, which still lingers in the best of their children's verse, though the mode is nearly outworn. They were a large compact family, all alert. They wrote for and about real children—themselves—and did not press the moral issue for philosophical reasons, like Miss Edgeworth, or for theological, like Mrs Sherwood. The whole circle—in that generation Dissenters, in the next represented by Canon Isaac Taylor of *Words and Places*—could write, and most of them could also draw and engrave. They followed all these occupations in order to make a living, but they sought neither wealth nor fame. They did not go into public or literary circles to any great extent. They lived quietly in a middle-class fashion, serene and cheerful in the midst of tremendous happenings which are hardly hinted at in their writings. (But that silence is common to all domestic writers of the period.) What that meant in the way of circumscribed intercourse and mutual tolerance is best described in Ann's own words about their home at Lavenham, an old home of Pilgrim Fathers whose descendants occasionally try to transport its buildings to America to-day. The Taylors spent their early years there:

> Nurseries at Lavenham, and at that time of day, I do not remember. The parlour and the best parlour were all that was known beside the kitchens, and thus parents and children formed happily but one circle. . . . My father and mother were soon noted as good managers of their children; for little as either of them had experienced of a wise education themselves, they had formed a singularly strong resolve to train their young ones with the best judgement they could exercise, and not to suffer *humoured* children to disturb either themselves or their friends. There is scarcely an expression so fraught to my earliest recollection with ideas of disgrace and misery as that of a "humoured child", and I should have felt truly ashamed to exhibit one of my own at my father's table.

("A child should never have anything he cried for": Newbery, Rousseau. . . .) Their little world was repeated, probably, in almost every parish in England. Its difference from others lay in the fact that all its members were articulate and eager. "It was", as E. V. Lucas has excellently said, "almost impossible to be a Taylor and not write."

His centenary edition of the *Original Poems* gives a crowded little picture of the family's life and writings. Of the non-Taylor contributors to that volume, Bernard Barton is known for his friendship with Lamb, as well as by his own not very exciting work. Adelaide O'Keefe (1776-1855)—the author of one of the best and best-known poems in the collection:

The Dog will come when he is called,
  The Cat will walk away;
The Monkey's cheek is very bald;
  The Goat is fond of play.

The Parrot is a prate-a-pace.
  Yet knows not what she says;
The noble Horse will win the race,
  Or draw you in a chaise.

—deserves a few lines of comment. Her position is peculiar. She seems not to have been acquainted with the Taylors personally. There were thirty-four poems by her in the whole collection, and some of them, as compact narratives ("Idle Richard and the Goat", for instance), are among the freshest. But she was neither a Quaker—like Barton and the publishers—nor at all in the same kind of social milieu as the amiable Taylor family. Her father was John O'Keefe, the genial and for a time very successful Irish dramatist and songwriter, author of at least one song still known, "The Friar of Orders Grey". O'Keefe, in spite of help from the Regent, finally declined in wealth and popularity, and Adélaide—so she herself once spelt it—cared for him devotedly until his death in 1833. She lived with him first at Chichester, where they were "much respected and esteemed", and afterwards at Southampton. She acted as his amanuensis and wrote for him the whole of his lively but untrustworthy *Recollections* (1826): her hand was nearly incapacitated by the strain. She managed his finances, and did her best to make money by writing herself. For her children's verses she received from my ancestors £100 in all: the Taylors, by her account, got more, but she seems to have been treated not unfairly as regards actual cash. Her chief other books, all her own work, were *Original Poems calculated to Improve the Mind of Youth and Allure it to Virtue* (1808?), *National Characters* (1818: verse), *Dudley* (1819: a novel), *A Trip to the Coast* (1819), *Zenobia, Queen of Palmyra* (1814), *Patriarchal Times* (4th ed. 1826) and *Poems for Young Children* (1849?). Many of these were published by Darton and Harvey, but not all: she was therefore in some general demand. They were successful to a certain extent, but the Taylors remained in higher esteem as writers for children, while for her—as a pathetic inscription by her in one of her own copies of *Patriarchal Times* records—"the Pen burned, and no Phoenix". She is rather a melancholy and incongruous figure.

As for that lively family at Lavenham and Ongar, the Taylors themselves must here remain a representative assembly, and no more. Isaac the son wrote *The Natural History of Enthusiasm* and many other meritorious works: Isaac the father, *inter alia, Self-Cultivation Recommended; or Hints to a Youth leaving School* (1817) and *Bunyan explained to a Child* (1825): his wife, *Reciprocal Duties of Parents and Children* (1818),

The Family Mansion: a Tale (1819), and many other stories and didactic treatises, notably *Correspondence between a Mother and her Daughter at School* (1817), in which Jane collaborated as the daughter. Jane here and elsewhere showed a keen eye for kindly satire, and with a little greater freedom of circumstance might have stood near to Maria Edgeworth as a novelist for adults, if not, indeed, to Jane Austen herself. Ann wrote little independently. Another brother, Jefferys, too young to get into print in 1804, except possibly as the subject of one of the poems, produced *Aesop in Rhyme, . . . , Ralph Richards the Miser* (1821), and several other "instructive and amusing" little books.

Original Poems had an enormous success. Miss Barry records a seventh edition in the year of publication, 1804. I have not seen this, but have seen a seventh edition of 1808, and a fourth edition (Vol. 11 only) dated 1808 also. Others were, 18th, 1818; 26th, 1828; 30th, 1834. Kate Greenaway did a famous set of illustrations in 1883. In 1925 Miss Edith Sitwell "introduced" a selection under the title of one of the poems, *Meddlesome Mattie*. I do not think they have ever been wholly out of print.

Naturally, both the originality and the success bred imitations almost at once, some of them deprecating comparison with the Taylors' work, though obviously inspired by it, others simply following the fashion without admitting it. The greater number do but accentuate the virtues of Ann and Jane in respect of rhythm, ease, and the one quality their title claimed, originality. One—*Rhymes and Pictures for the Nursery and School. By a Lady* (n.d.: type and illustrations of the period)—deserves quotation for that purpose. A little girl, as in so many poems and tales of that day, *would* eat forbidden fruit:

They went on a little, but Anna complain'd
  Of pain in her stomach and head,
And very soon follow'd most terrible pains,
  She shriek'd out with anguish and
  dread. . . .
She died from not doing what Ma had desired,
  And eating the fruit of the wood.

Not all the imitations were so remote as that.

Two other workers in this trim if narrow field survive to-day in a manner they can hardly have expected. One of them might scarcely be known as a writer for children but for her illustrious surname. The other lives, it is not too much to say, through the unholy mirth she has provoked in later generations. This was the redoubtable but mysterious Elizabeth Turner, about whom nothing, outside her books, seems to be known except that she lived at Whitechurch in Shropshire and died in 1846. She wrote *The Daisy or Cautionary Stories in Verse adapted to the Ideas of Children from four to eight years old* (1807), *The Cowslip* (1811) and *The Pink* (edited, with additions, by Mary Howitt, in 1835). There were imitations by other writers.

No moralist was ever more straightforward than Elizabeth Turner. Right was right, wrong wrong, and wrong invited and received the rod, and no questions asked—or, at least, very seldom, and then only for good reason. One of her poems begins

> Mamma had ordered Ann, the maid,
>   Miss Caroline to wash.

Miss Caroline had objected. The matter did not end with a kiss, as in *Original Poems*. The last line runs "to whip her, there's no doubt". In other pieces Nature was the agent of punishment. "Jack Parker was a cruel boy", and teased animals:

> But all such boys unless they mend,
> May come to an unhappy end;
> Like Jack who got a fractur'd skull,
> Whilst bellowing at a furious bull.

The rather ludicrous sight-rhyme in the last couplet is not up to the Turner level of metrical inevitability. It would be hard to find anything more defiantly rhythmical than some of the pieces: "Truth the Best", for instance:

> Yesterday Rebecca Mason,
>   In the parlour by herself,
> Broke a handsome china basin,
>   Placed upon the mantel-shelf.
>
> Quite alarmed, she thought of going
>   Very quietly away,
> Not a single person knowing
>   Of her being there that day.
>
> But Rebecca recollected
>   She was taught deceit to shun;
> And the moment she reflected
>   Told her mother what was done;
>
> Who commended her behaviour,
> Loved her better, and forgave her.

It may be silly. It may lack humour—to such an extent that one very nearly suspects Elizabeth Turner of writing with her tongue in her cheek. But the martial beat of it is irresistible. And it could be bellowed, in the manner of Jack Parker, to half a dozen shoddy popular tunes in *Hymns Ancient and Modern:* perhaps Miss Turner even had a semiliturgical use of it in her mind, as Mrs Barbauld, more legitimately, had for her *Hymns in Prose.*

But it is also so uncommonly like W. S. Gilbert's Archibald Grosvenor poems in *Patience* that the most

sympathetic person may to-day feel uncertain about it. *Can* it be serious? Was Miss Turner in earnest? Or did she wink secretly? She also wrote this:

> "Papa", said Eugene, "is a daisy a book?
>   I thought it was only a flower;
> Just now I ran down in the meadow, and
>   look,
>   I have found one all wet with a shower.
>
> "A book would be spoil'd, you know, left in
>   the rain;
>   And could not be read for the dirt;
> But a daisy all day in the wet may remain,
>   Without in the least being hurt."
>
> "You are right", said Papa, with a smile, "but
>   you'll find
>   The Daisy a book, my boy, too,
> Containing short tales for the juvenile mind,
>   And adapted for children live [*sic*] you.
>
> "And call'd as it is by so humble a name,
>   This hint indirectly conveys;
> Like the flow'ret it spreads, unambitious of
>   fame,
>   Nor intrudes upon critical gaze."

That is the twenty-eighth blossom in *The Cowslip,* and it is nothing more or less than a recommendation of its predecessor, *The Daisy,* in a manner which John Newbery would have been proud to invent. How *could* she do it—she who had that mastery of technique, that epic "rapidity", that concentration? The sternest moralists of her tribe never leapt so swiftly and surely as she from crime to doom: her cautionary tales fascinate one almost obscenely, like a murder-trial. But she checked herself in her stride to write a puff.

The other exceptional imitator of the Taylors was Sara Coleridge, the poet's charming daughter. She too suffered from lack of humour; but there is no doubt about her being in earnest. She said:

> The *Original Poems* give too many pictures of mental depravity, bodily torture, and of adult sorrow; and I think the sentiments—the tirades, for instance, against hunting, fishing, shooting—are morbid, and partially false.

That is honestly and plainly expressed, and many would share the opinion. But Sara Coleridge went a very odd way to substitute, in her *Pretty Lessons in Verse, for Good Children* (1834), "nothing but what is bright and joyous" for the sentiments she thus deplored. A remarkable moral conclusion is reached in a poem called "Disappointment". A boy named Colin, mountaineering with old and young friends, carried with him an orange, on which he expected, rationally and even greedily, to slake his thirst in due course. He could not help playing with it, dancing about and tossing it up as he leapt over the rocks. Suddenly it jumped out of his hand and rolled far out of reach:

> For some little time he stood still as a stock, His face wore a fixed vacant stare; But soon he recover'd this terrible shock, And turning away from the edge of the rock Threw off his disconsolate air.

> With thoughts of the basket he solaced his heart, From thence real comfort might come; For he in the sandwiches still had a part, He perhaps might come in for a slice of the tart, And there was the pineapple rum.

> Since pleasure is apt through our fingers to slip, And fate we can never withstand; Whene'er the full cup is thus dashed from the lip, Before we have taken the very first sip, 'Tis well to keep temper in hand.

Pickwick did not begin to appear till three years later, so that the author cannot be accused of making Colin an amalgam of the Fat Boy and Mr Stiggins. But none of the didacticists she criticized ever thought of quite such a "pretty lesson" as is afforded by the comfort of a picnic basket and pineapple rum if you carelessly lose an orange.

Her verses were for a time popular: they reached a fourth edition in 1845. But the Taylors, mental depravity and all, have outlived her in fact. She is of some historical importance because she is on the inner fringe of great literature. She proves that the idea of the Moral Tale was at least known to the loftier minds of the day. . . .

Robert Pattison

SOURCE: "Children in Children's Literature: James Janeway to Lewis Carroll," in *The Child Figure in English Literature,* The University of Georgia Press, 1978, pp. 135-59.

[*In the following excerpt, Pattison argues that the notion of original sin—that each individual is born sinful—was fundamental to didactic children's literature; he further asserts that this belief carried into the non-didactic literature of the the latter half of the century.*]

No book could better illustrate the connection between the child figure in children's literature and the idea of a fallen universe than James Janeway's *A Token for Children: Being an exact account of the conversion, holy and exemplary lives and joyful deaths of several young children* [1972]. Janeway's book, which is perhaps the first book both for and about children (it was published sometime shortly after the Restoration), indicates in text as well as title that the highest reward to which youthful virtue can aspire in this world is to be rid of sinful life entirely. Like the bulk of writers who, in the seventeenth century, began to produce books aimed at children, Janeway was a Dissenter; Bunyan also wrote at least one children's book, *Divine Emblems* (like Janeway's *Token*, there is no certainty as to its date). William Penn is credited with another, *The Spiritual Bee* (1662).

But of the Dissenters who were interested in writing books for children, Janeway is among the very few who employ the child figure. And he makes the intention of his portraits of holy youths quite explicit: "Every Mother's Child of you are by Nature Children of Wrath," he admonishes in his introduction, and he goes on to question parents, "Are the Souls of Children of no Value? Are you willing that they should be Brands of Hell? Are you indifferent whether they be damned or saved?" Janeway's is a radical view, not so much for its strict Protestant dogmatism, which, on the question of Original Sin, is firmly rooted in Augustine, but for its insistence that the child is capable of rationally understanding and correcting his fallen condition. Later children's books either assume that the child is incapable of such understanding and hence must be persuaded by appeals to his baser instincts (the morally-instructive story developed from this view), or that the child is both too weak and too irrational to comprehend his sinful condition and hence can only be convinced of the sinful nature of the world around him. From this last view, which is Semipelagian in nature, comes that kind of children's literature which, leaving the child figure to one side, delights in exposing the follies and perversities of adults and life in general; it is neatly exemplified by an early practitioner, Nathaniel Crouch, whose *Winter Evening Entertainments* (early eighteenth century?) is advertised as "milk for children, wisdom for young men, / To teach them that they turn not babes again."

Janeway's strict connection between the child and sin was neither eccentric nor unpopular. *A Token for Children* went through dozens of editions throughout the eighteenth century and was still in print as late as 1847. His use of the child figure to instruct children in their fallen nature became a staple of children's literature. Abraham Chear's *A Looking-Glass for Children* (c. 1670) illustrates, in one of its lyrics, the way in which the child figure was employed to convey the religious dogma throughout the late seventeenth and eighteenth centuries:

> When by spectators I am told
> What beauty doth adorn me,
> Or in a glass when I behold
> How sweetly God did form me,
> Hath God such comeliness bestowed

And on me made to dwell,
What pity such a pretty maid
As I should go to Hell!

Isaac Watts's *Divine and Moral Songs for Children* continued this explicit use of the child figure to reinforce Protestant doctrine, and in the nineteenth century the tradition was still very much alive in the writings of Mrs. Sherwood (Mary Martha Butt Sherwood), whose terrifying accounts of the hell and damnation which attend the evil actions of childhood are found in her *History of the Fairchild Family* (1818). In fact, Mrs. Sherwood is, if anything, more direct in her appraisal of the nature of childhood than Janeway had been 150 years earlier; in the *Fairchild Family,* she states plainly that "All children are by nature evil, and while they have none but the natural evil principle to guide them, pious and prudent parents must check their naughty passions in any way that they have in their power." Mrs. Sherwood's books sold throughout the nineteenth century.

Of course, from the Renaissance on, many books were either written or considered suitable for children which contained none of Janeway's strictures or Mrs. Sherwood's horrors. Curiously, however, these "pleasant" books for children were often satires of adult life which once again tend to confirm that man is involved in some vast and inherent folly. *Robinson Crusoe* and *Gulliver's Travels* were, almost from their publication, considered excellent children's books, as they are today. But where the child figure was employed in children's literature, it remained, to a very late date, tied to the dogma which gives it its impetus as a literary creation.

Even the disciples of Rousseau, when writing in English, seem to fall victim to the general tendency to link childhood and Original Sin. . . . Thomas Day's *Sandford and Merton* [1783-89] [is] an example of the way in which an avowed follower of *Emile,* by a number of eccentricities extremely English, produced a work which only marginally reflects its source of inspiration. Maria Edgeworth is another example. Her *The Purple Jar* (1801), also said to be in the tradition of Rousseau, is in fact designed to illuminate the vain willfulness of childhood. In it, the child Rosamond insists upon buying a purple jar of scented water in preference to a solid pair of shoes; the result of this mad assertion of will is that the perfumed water soon becomes a useless bore while the lack of decent footwear leaves Rosamond—or at least her feet—at the mercy of the elements. Here, the *amour de soi* which Rousseau found "good and useful" is vain and foolish, and Nature, far from encouraging it, is ready to punish with rain and cold.

However, while the intention behind the use of the child figure in children's literature remains remarkably constant up to and through the nineteenth century, the tone and style of the child's depiction underwent alteration. The excessive piety and explicit dogmatism of Janeway and Chear gradually gave way to the subtler, more implicitly doctrinaire technique of telling moral stories like Maria Edgeworth's. . . . [This] was in part due to a belief that children were incapable of the kind of comprehension Janeway and Mrs. Sherwood required of them; but in part this shift of method and tone is the result of an increasing Anglicanization of children's literature. What had begun as the exclusive domain of the Dissenting factions, with whom doctrine was an ever-present concern, became progressively light in style and tone as Anglicans, at once more secure in and less overtly concerned with their dogma, began writing for children. The successful children's writers of the Victorian era who used the child figure in their work were for the most part Church of England; perhaps the two most prominent children's authors, Lewis Carroll and Charles Kingsley, were in orders.

The effect of the Anglican co-option of children's literature, which became virtually total by the end of the last century, is nicely demonstrated by a correspondence in *The Athenaeum* in the 1860s. Remembering a children's lyric from his childhood, the mathematician Augustus De Morgan remarked that it was extremely good poetry except that the "bit of religion thrust in" ruined it:

For God, who lives above the skies
Would look with vengeance in His eyes,
If I should ever dare despise
My Mother.

The coauthor of the lines, Ann Taylor, who with her brother and sister had, in the first decade of the century, produced several volumes of children's poetry (one had included the lyric "Twinkle, Twinkle, Little Star") was still living, and she agreed that the "bit of religion" no longer seemed appropriate. She accordingly altered the lines to read,

For could our Father in the skies
Look down with pleased or loving eyes,
If ever I could dare despise
My Mother.

The revision, in which vengeance is implied but not stated, manages to say the same thing as its original, only in a somewhat kinder tone, which is essentially the change which overtook Janeway's conception of children's literature during the nineteenth century.

The presence of the Original Sin dogma behind the child figure in children's literature became increasingly muted during the nineteenth century, and in several children's authors of the Victorian period, it almost disappears. Mrs. Ewing (Juliana Horatia Ewing) is perhaps the best example of this; her stories of middle-class domestic life are peopled by children who are lively, natural, and possessed of a sense of humor. Not that they are without religion. Mrs. Ewing represented the spirit of the Broad Church. The young heroine of her book *A Great Emergency* (1877) ends her narrative with the assurance that she often prays: "I often pray that if ever I am great I may be good too; and sometimes I pray that if I try hard to be good God will let me be great as well," she says with the proud kind of piety which must have marked the Broad Church in the heyday of the British Empire. Yet even in Mrs. Ewing there are traces of Janeway; her *Story of a Short Life* (1882) portrays the holy and exemplary death of young Leonard, whose dying wish is to hear the hymn, "The Son of God Goes Forth to War," on his deathbed. Similar traces of the strict doctrinaire origin of English children's literature can be found in the two most prolific children's writers of the period, Charlotte Yonge and Mrs. Molesworth (Mary Louisa Molesworth). Charlotte Younge was in her youth a neighbor of John Keble, and her books—there are over 100—are full of the spirit of the Oxford Movement. Mrs. Molesworth's children often find themselves in dark old houses or antique shops, from which they escape into a world of fantasy; her books often confront the child with people and things of great age, as Dickens had, thereby suggesting, however obliquely, the contrast between the Old and New Laws.

Christina Rossetti's poetry for children demonstrates the way in which Victorian authors were able to produce temperate and pleasant works for the young while maintaining a highly orthodox view of the relationship between the child and Original Sin. *Sing-Song* (1872), her volume of lyrics for children, seems to be free of the strictures Janeway and Watts had evoked:

> Angels at the foot
>   And angels at the head,
> And like a curly little lamb
>   My pretty babe in bed.

But Christina Rossetti's fullest use of the child figure comes in "Goblin Market" (1862), a poem which established its author as one of the chief figures of the Pre-Raphaelite movement. "Goblin Market" does not seem today like a children's poem, yet in its own day it was often included in books for the young. In it, Christina Rossetti's Anglican concept of the fallen nature of man is worked out through the child figure. Behind the poem lies the exceptional devotion to the creed and worship of the Church of England which in her later life monopolized both her poetry and her daily existence. But if "Goblin Market" is orthodox Anglican doctrine, it is also striking poetry, so much so that Swinburne greeted its publication as a lethal blow to the creed of the Philistines and regarded its author as "the Jael who led the host to victory." A closer look at the poem will help to establish the kind of religious view which was considered suitable for children to see and which was at least latently present even in some of the most cheerful works for children written in the Victorian period.

"Goblin Market" is in many respects a version of *Comus* in abbreviated and distorted form: the pentameter is reduced to a purposely halting trimeter, the Lady has shrunk to the size of a child, her tempter is replaced by the goblins, and Sabrina becomes Lizzie, the very proper child whose sacrifice breaks the spell cast over her sister. The poem is Milton as reflected in a fun-house mirror—grotesque, caught somewhere between the sinister and the amusing. In this, at least, it approaches the spirit of Swinburne's own macabre poetry.

More than this, however, "Goblin Market" achieves in its portrait of nature a passion which Swinburne attributed to Byron and Shelley, "a fierce and blind desire which exalts and impels their verse into the high places of emotion and expression. They feed upon nature with a holy hunger, follow her with a divine lust as of gods chasing the daughters of men." The natural world of "Goblin Market" is a sensual banquet, a place where spirits literally chase the daughters of men; but the divinity which presides over the realm of nature where the goblins rule is an evil one. Nature is no longer the "good cateress" of *Comus,* much less Wordsworth's source of transcendent rapture; nature is a raw, sensual power which must either be met on its own terms or must not be met at all.

Where in Wordsworth the essence of childhood is its unity with nature, for Christina Rossetti the child's purity resides in its sheltered retreat from the blandishments of nature's goblins. Laura, the fallen child of the poem, succumbs to the temptations offered "among the brookside rushes":

> You cannot think what figs
>   My teeth have met in,
> What melons icy-cold
>   Piled on a dish of gold
> Too huge for me to hold,
> What peaches with a velvet nap,
> Pellucid grapes without one seed:
> Odorous indeed must be the mead
> Whereon they grow, and pure the wave they
>   drink.

Laura is not given the Miltonic choice between moderation and indulgence; she must choose between abstinence and excess. The harmless fruits conjured up in the poem's first section invite the child to ruin, and one encounter with them is sufficient to bring Laura "knocking at Death's door."

"Goblin Market" carries this morbid concept of nature through to its logical conclusion in the martyrdom of

Lizzie, the redemption of Laura, and their final triumph. After Laura has succumbed to the goblins' invitation to buy their fruits, she is unable to hear their call or find their market again; nature is doubly cruel, not only luring innocence toward ruin, but closing off the avenues by which men might enjoy their depravity once they have fallen. As she grows weaker and weaker, her sister, Lizzie, "weighed no more / Better and worse," and determines to buy Laura the fruits she craves. Her sacrifice, however, doesn't have quite the tragic pathos of Adam's for Eve; Lizzie will buy the fruit, but won't eat it herself. "Pluck them and suck them," the goblins cry, and when she will not eat,

> They trod and hustled her,
> Elbowed and jostled her,
> Clawed with their nails,
> Barking, mewing, hissing, mocking,
> Tore her gown and soiled her stockings.
> Twitched her hair out by the roots,
> Stamped upon her tender feet,
> Held her hands and squeezed their fruits
> Against her mouth to make her eat.

The language of the poetry here becomes so graphic that it can no longer be called imagery; it is simple rape. Nature, hiding deceptively behind the seeming beauties which open the poem, is not satisfied until it has violated childhood innocence. But Lizzie escapes intact, and invites her sister to make a Communion feast of her ("Eat me, drink me, love me") for her efforts.

Laura, however, mistakes the meaning of Lizzie's sacrifice:

> "Lizzie, Lizzie, have you tasted
> For my sake the fruit forbidden?"

She does eat and drink Lizzie with kisses of "fear and pain," only to discover that the Eucharist has been a feast of poison. Having passed through these crises, Laura is restored to her former state of purity.

The God who lies behind these images and whose sacrifice is figured in them is hardly the same God who presides over Wordsworth's nature. He is a God who has been put at odds with nature; a God who, when he overcame the world, put the natural world below his feet like a vanquished foe. Insofar as man is a part of nature, he is irreconcilably God's enemy. But man can choose to emulate the state of childhood innocence embodied in Laura and Lizzie, and he does so by avoiding the world of nature entirely. A man's duty to his fellows is

> To lift one if one totters down,
> To strengthen whilst one stands.

If nature, by virtue of man's Fall, has truly become the devil's realm, as Christina Rossetti presents it in "Goblin Market," then perhaps she was right to seek and worship her God from a sickbed in Bloomsbury. Her staunch Anglicanism as expressed in her child figures and children's poems (fiercely in "Goblin Market," gently in *Sing-Song*) illustrates the religious concerns present at least implicitly in the bulk of English children's literature at a time when orthodoxy was being challenged in its letter and its spirit.

While Darwin wrote, while Huxley proclaimed that God had delivered Wilberforce into his hands, while *Essays and Reviews* (1860) questioned even the texts of faith, literature in England, insofar as it employed the child figure, continued to promulgate a nearly orthodox interpretation of the dogma of Original Sin. The generation which came to maturity in the era of the Great War would be inured to attacks on the faith and skeptical of religious tradition. Extreme religious sects such as Gosse's Plymouth Brethren were then a memory, while the Church of England, by the period between the two wars, was known chiefly as the sponsor of the English Folk Dance Society and the institution which, in 1921, tried an archdeacon for adultery in an outmoded ecclesiastical court. Many who took their dogma seriously went to Rome. Yet Englishmen exposed to the literature of the *fin-de-siècle* nursery would have had before them persuasive, if subliminal, arguments in favor of the orthodox doctrine of Original Sin. When he grew up, the same orthodoxy could be found in the child figures of his literature (always excepting Wordsworth). Who can say that this sort of belief and orthodoxy was less real than that of the dwindling number of parishioners in church and chapel?

The children's literature discussed up to this point has shared one common feature; while these poems and books were written for and about children, they were also written as diminutive versions of adult reading. Janeway's *A Token for Children* is a seventeenth-century homily in reduced form; the works of a Mrs. Sherwood or a Mrs. Ewing mimic the novel or the short story; and as already mentioned, "Goblin Market" is an elfin rendition of *Comus*. The idea of children's literature as a compressed species of adult reading naturally lends itself to Augustine's notion that the child is only a littler replica of his sinful, mature parents. Side by side with the growth of this kind of children's literature, however, another variety of children's books was developing. This variety includes those works not only written for or about children, but from their point of view. Nursery rhymes, fairy tales, and fantasies belong in this group. The distinction between works written for children and those written from the child's perspective is similar to the distinction . . . between first-and third-person narratives of childhood; like *David Copperfield* or *Father and Son*, nursery rhymes and fantasies seem unconcerned with morals and delighted by the absurd.

But what separates *David Copperfield* and *Father and Son* from the nursery rhymes, fairy tales, and fantasies written from the child's point of view is that the former have a mature narrator, either acknowledged or unacknowledged, whose function it is to render the child's perspective intelligible to adult audiences. In the work of fantasy, however, this mediating adult vanishes and the reader is brought face to face with a world which appears to him illogical, disordered, and unreal. It is the function of children's literature in its purest form to demonstrate (but only to its own satisfaction—anything less would be to compromise its integrity) that precisely the opposite is true; that the fantasy is logical and the reader absurd; that the disorder he had dismissed as childish is a parody of his own world. In *David Copperfield,* after his interview with Mr. Murdstone in the role of his new father, David wanders into the yard and is startled by the appearance in the once-empty dog house of a "great dog—deep-mouthed and black-haired like Him" (3). The true child's perspective has no time or inclination for metaphors. Let Murdstone be a black dog.

Of the types of work written from the child's point of view, nursery rhymes are the most morally neutral. In this, rhymes are exactly the opposite of fables, which are written by adults to point out a moral—usually to other adults. The rhyme which records the history of Solomon Grundy displays the simple and canny observation of facts, devoid of imperatives, which is the trademark of the nursery rhyme form:

> Born on a Monday
> Christened on Tuesday,
> Married on Wednesday,
> Took ill on Thursday,
> Worse on Friday,
> Died on Saturday,
> Buried on Sunday:
> This is the end
> Of Solomon Grundy.

The rhymes cast a very cool eye on life and death; they refuse to be pushed to a position or a conclusion, even in the case of the lady who loved a swine:

> "Wilt thou now have me,
>   Honey," quoth she;
> "Grunt, grunt, grunt," quoth he,
>   And went his way.

This particular rhyme has a wealth of astute observation about the direction of human desires and the ease with which they are frustrated, but it refuses to move beyond observation. Within the world of the rhyme,

the pig and the lady live on terms of absolute equality; whatever is grotesque or perverse in the relationship is imported into the text by the adult reader.

The nursery rhyme can seem either charming or grotesque to adults, or it can be entirely baffling and seem to be both at once:

> Here comes a candle to light you to bed,
> And here comes a chopper to chop off your
>   head.

But in fact the rhymes are meant to be neither charming nor unpleasant; they are not meant to serve any purpose other than strict observation through the eyes of the child mind:

> Around the green gravel the grass grows
>   green,
> And all the pretty maids are plain to be seen;
> Wash them with milk, and clothe them with
>   silk,
> And write their names with a pen and ink.

The final line, typical of nursery rhymes in general, halts what promises to be a soaring flight in mid-course and pulls the idyllic scene back into the realm of the dispassionate, observed fact, which is the milieu of the form.

The basic difference between the nursery rhymes and the instructive form of children's literature inaugurated by Janeway is that the Janeway type is concerned to overcome the vanity of this world while the rhymes are content merely to observe it. The distinction can be seen in a comparison of Christina Rossetti and Edward Lear. The effect of the nursery rhyme may well be the same as that of instructive children's literature, though the method and intent are different. The nonsense verses of Edward Lear, whose career ran more or less parallel to Christina Rossetti's in time, demonstrate how the nursery rhyme form may persuade us of the same facts as instructive children's literature. Lear's verses generally have exactly the same qualities as nursery rhymes: they may seem to adults to be pleasant and charming, or they may, as in the following example, appear morbid and violent:

> Suddenly Mr. Discobbolos
>   Slid from the top of the wall;
>   And beneath it he dug a dreadful trench,
>   And filled it with dynamite, gunpowder
>   gench,
>   And aloud he began to call—
>   "Let the wild bee sing,
> And the blue bird hum!
> For the end of your lives has certainly come!"
>   And Mrs. Discobbolos said,
>   "O, W! X! Y! Z!

We shall presently all be dead,
On this ancient runcible wall,
      Terrible Mr. Discobbolos."

The author of these mad lines is also the author of "The Owl and the Pussy-Cat" which is as appealing as "Mr. and Mrs. Discobbolos" is appalling. By stripping events of logic, viewing them dispassionately, and refusing to pass judgment, Lear's verses, like nursery rhymes, arrive at a self-contained world of nonsense which becomes the basis for a broad view of the world.

This broad view includes a benign fatalism which takes pleasure not in the absurdity it sees in life, but in the fact that absurdity is universal; it revels in having found a unifying principle. If the world is absurd, at least it is perfectly absurd, and both Lear and nursery rhymes make their poetry reflect this peculiar perfection.

Fairy tales also portray an absurd world, but what distinguishes them from nursery rhymes is a high sense of justice. Unlike the nursery rhyme, the fairy tale has a strong inclination built into it to deal with questions of "right" and "wrong"; it is, on the whole, a much more "grown-up" literature. Fairy tales have a plot, which naturally gives them not only a sense of mature logic, but lends them to moral interpretation as well, since any series of events leading to a logical conclusion carries an implicit or explicit message, no matter how ambiguous. The fairy tale's plot may very well stem from its heightened sense of injury done to the child figure or child surrogate. "In the little world in which children have their existence whosoever brings them up, there is nothing so finely perceived and so finely felt, as injustice," says Pip in *Great Expectations,* and the statement may serve as an introduction to fairy tales, in which the child figure or substitute is usually the passive victim of some adult injustice. Out of this sense of injustice comes the child's first participation with the system of adult values.

The two strains of children's literature—that in which the child is instructed about the folly of the world and that in which the child mind merely observes these follies—are brought together in Lewis Carroll's *Alice in Wonderland* (1865). In fact, Lewis Carroll represents the highpoint of both traditions. There is plenty of the nursery rhyme's absurdity in *Alice:* perhaps the best example of it is Alice's translation of Isaac Watts's "How doth the little busy bee" into "How doth the little crocodile." Carroll delighted in parodies of children's authors who had written in the cautionary vein. His parodies, like Lear's nonsense, are so close to the spirit of the nursery rhyme that by their presence alone *Alice* seems to belong to the class of children's literature which is content to observe rather than moralize.

But Carroll also belongs to the group of Anglican children's writers who continued to purvey Janeway's

Protestant conception of Original Sin, while modifying his tone and technique. As Charles Lutwidge Dodgson, Carroll was a deacon of the Church of England. He was so careful of his piety that in writing *Through the Looking-Glass* (1871) he changed the passion flower in "The Garden of Live Flowers" to a tiger-lily on learning that the passion flower referred to the Crucifixion. His children's books are orthodox as well as absurd. From the conclusion of *Alice,* it is clear Carroll meant his readers to derive a benefit from the book which would inform their future years; when Alice has awoken and told her sister about Wonderland, the sister

> pictured to herself how this same little sister of hers would, in the after-time, be herself a grown woman; and how she would keep, through all her riper years, the simple and loving heart of her childhood; and how she would gather about her other little children, and make their eyes bright and eager with many a strange tale, perhaps even with the dream of Wonderland of long ago; and how she would feel with all their simple sorrows, and find pleasure in all their simple joys, remembering her own child-life, and the happy summer days.

This is the end of the book, and it is remarkably similar to the final lines of "Goblin Market," which preceded it by four years. Christina Rossetti pictures Lizzie and Laura as grown-ups with children of their own:

> Laura would call the little ones
> And tell them of her early prime,
> Those pleasant days long gone
> Of not-returning time;
> Would talk about the haunted glen,
> The wicked quaint fruit-merchant men,
> Their fruits like honey to the throat
> But poison to the blood.

Nor are *Alice* and "Goblin Market" alike only in their conclusions. Much of Christina Rossetti's orthodoxy can be found in the structure of *Alice.*

The first hint that *Alice* is indeed working with the same Christian concepts which surround the child figure elsewhere in English literature comes in chapter one: "Down, down, down. Would the fall *never* come to an end? 'I wonder how many miles I've fallen by this time?' she said aloud." The Wonderland into which Alice falls is in many respects like the elfin nature which seduces Laura in "Goblin Market." In "Goblin Market," however, it is Laura who finds the goblins' world seductive while the reader sees the evil behind it; in Alice the situation is reversed: Alice consistently finds Wonderland curious, foolish, and finally "stuff and nonsense," while the reader is seduced by its attractions.

These attractions, which are presented in the absurd view of the nursery rhyme, are the allures of a fallen universe. Wonderland is a realm of Original Sin where, quite literally, everyone lies under sentence of death. This is the realm the nursery rhyme uncritically observes. Here, however, the nursery rhyme's observation has been set in a framework designed to involve the reader's critical faculties. The book is structured to have epic pretensions. Like *Through the Looking-Glass,* it has twelve books, the required Vergilian number; Alice's fall down the hole is a descent into the underworld as well as a reminder of the Original Sin theme; and Alice herself is reminiscent of Aeneas in her statuesque, Tory respectability, which is at once aloof from, and necessary to, the action of the book. The imaginative quality of *Alice* is that of the nursery rhyme, but its form is that of a mock epic and its purpose is a judgment of the fallen world through its central character, Alice. Dickens had adapted the epic and the child figure to this same end in *Dombey and Son.*

As in *Through the Looking-Glass,* the world Alice enters in *Alice in Wonderland* has reversed the true and proper meanings of things, though in Wonderland this reversal of meanings has a more obviously moral significance than in the *Looking-Glass* world. Chapter 1 offers a tantalizing vision of what appears to be a veritable Eden, "the loveliest garden you ever saw." But Alice's attempts to enter the garden are thwarted, in a parody of the Communion service, by Alice's consumption of the mysterious offerings which come complete with the mock-priestly instructions, "DRINK ME" and "EAT ME." While not quite a black mass, Alice's meal does have exactly the opposite effect of the true Communion; far from opening Eden to her, it makes her far too large to enter. As a result, there follows the deluge of tears, which amounts to Noah's flood, "crowded with the birds and animals that had fallen into it".

Next follow scenes of ever-escalating venalities: the mouse's churlishness; the White Rabbit's fastidious vexation, which threatens Alice with the loss of an arm; the caterpillar's contemptuous indifference; the savagery of the Duchess, matched only by her ugliness; the rudeness of the tea party, which almost engulfs Alice in an eternity of mad repetition reminiscent of Sisyphus's punishment. Finally, Alice enters the garden she had seen through the small door. But the supposed Eden is no paradise at all; the first thing she sees on entering it is a rosetree, which the gardeners are painting red. The idea recalls Spenser's Bower of Bliss, "That nature's work by art can imitate." The Queen's croquet ground is a place where everyone has been sentenced to death, and the story ends at precisely the moment Alice is included in this "everyone":

"Hold your tongue!" said the Queen, turning purple.

"I won't!" said Alice.

"Off with her head!" the Queen shouted at the top of her voice. Nobody moved.

"Who cares for *you*?" said Alice (she had grown to her full size by this time). "You're nothing but a pack of cards!"

At this the whole pack rose up into the air, and came flying down upon her; she gave a little scream, half of fright and half of anger, and tried to beat them off, and found herself lying on the bank, with her head in the lap of her sister, who was gently brushing away some dead leaves.

In the end, the Wonderland creatures turn out to be "some dead leaves," an image which invites us to recall Milton's own underworld creatures,

> who lay intrans't
> Thick as Autumnal Leaves that strow the
>   Brooks
> In Vallombrosa.

If *Alice in Wonderland,* like a nursery rhyme, looks at the adult world with the eyes of childhood, it also takes that vision and by framing it in a mock-epic format roundly condemns what it sees. Wonderland is the world after the Fall. The paradise behind the door is a mirror image of what it seems, a place of death where living creatures are perverted from their natural functions to suit the Queen's purposes—flamingoes as mallets, hedgehogs as balls, men as wickets. The story concludes with the monumental injustice of the trial, at which Alice realizes that to escape from the sentence of death the Queen imposes, she has but to assert her contempt for the entire proceedings.

The gradually increasing threats of Wonderland are paralleled and in a sense presented by the steady corruption of language from chapter to chapter, a process which puzzles and then infuriates Alice. Carroll himself seems to have equated the misuse of language with the perversion of the world at large, and as in the following introduction to his *Symbolic Logic* (1897), a book somewhat whimsically intended for children, regarded the correct use of words as a complete defense against worldly error:

Once master the machinery of Symbolic Logic, and you have a mental occupation always at hand, . . . and one that will be of real *use* to you in *any* subject you may take up. It will give you clearness of thought—the ability to *see your way* through a puzzle—the habit of arranging your ideas in an orderly and get-at-able form—and more valuable than all, the power to detect *fallacies,* and to tear to pieces the flimsy illogical arguments, which you will so continuously encounter in books, in newspapers, in speeches, and even in sermons, and which so easily delude those who have never taken the trouble to master this fascinating Art.

In Wonderland, the abuse of language begins with the simple lack of information in the directions "EAT ME" and "DRINK ME" and ends with the verbal mockery of justice which is the Knave's trial. In between lie various failures to impart information correctly, such as the caterpillar's, which almost results in Alice's disintegration; false syllogisms; and that lowest form of wit, the pun. Part of what makes *Alice in Wonderland* palatable, where other children's books employing the same devices are preciously trite, is the vigor with which these abuses are persecuted even as they are employed; the heroine stands resolutely above them, so that we see the corruption of language as the tool which has built the false Eden.

The underground world, as a reflection of life, seems to hold little promise of a happy destiny for Alice; in fact, her destiny depends on her "ability to see her way through a puzzle" and "tear to pieces the flimsy illogical arguments," which she continuously encounters. Aeneas had his golden bough to bring him back alive from the land of the dead; Alice likewise has a magical charm, preserving her for a glorious destiny, in her perception of events in terms of symbolic logic. She stoutly refuses to call the events she sees in Wonderland wrong—ethical distinctions are part of the structure of the underworld itself, culminating in the Knave's trial; instead, she prefers to see things as either sensible or stupid. She is allowed her share of mistakes, like any epic hero, but as the story moves along, her ability to see things in the proper absurdist perspective improves rapidly. She has an instinctive contempt for the humdrum moralizing of Isaac Watts's "How doth the little busy bee," and transforms it from religious propaganda into a nursery rhyme. The same process is repeated with Southey's didactic piece, which becomes "You are Old, Father William." These reductions to absurdity are her own invention, and not a part of Wonderland itself. The Caterpillar chastises her for not getting "Father William" "right," and the Mad Hatter stands under sentence of death for his own absurdist effort with "Twinkle, Twinkle, Little Bat."

Along with the preference for a sense-nonsense distinction over a moral system comes the detached acceptance of things as they are that marks the nursery rhyme view of events. When the Duchess's baby turns into a pig, "she felt that it would be quite absurd for her to carry it any further. So she set the little creature down and felt quite relieved to see it trot away quietly into the wood. 'If it had grown up,' she said to herself, 'it would

have made a dreadfully ugly child: but it makes rather a handsome pig, I think.'" In this genial acceptance of the bizarre, there is an almost mystical belief in the ability of life, even in its most perverse and grotesque manifestations, to come around at last to fitting conclusions. These conclusions may disturb or repel us, but to the child, they seem just and fair. The Wonderland population has no notion of this natural fitness. The Duchess is forever looking for the moral of things, the Hatter has literally killed time, and the Queen who reigns over them all gets the purpose of everything backward, from the role of king and queen, which she has reversed, to the natural order of justice: "'No, no!' said the Queen. 'Sentence first—verdict afterwards.' 'Stuff and nonsense!' said Alice loudly." Alice overturns the false order of Wonderland with the faith and assurance of the symbolic logician destroying a fallacious syllogism, and in a sense she sees the world around her as the work of a logician God. Its terms and propositions need not be "right" in the way the Queen or the Duchess would have them; they must merely conform to an inner truth, as in one of Carroll's own syllogisms (which is strictly logical):

> A prudent man shuns hyaenas;
> No banker is imprudent.
> No banker fails to shun hyaenas.

A cosmos constructed along these same lines does not lend itself to interpretation or understanding by the logic or morality of Wonderland; it must be accepted with implicit faith in the truthfulness of the great Logician to his own premises. Possessing this faith, Alice passes through Wonderland victoriously, as if with Aeneas's golden bough. Carroll is, like Aquinas and Dante before him, a Semipelagian; he cannot tolerate the idea of children as part of the world of sin, and in *Alice in Wonderland,* the heroine stands resolutely apart from the machinery of Original Sin. Yet how much hope is there in this Semipelagian view, and what threat does it represent to Augustine's dogma? Alice herself may be outside the pale of Original Sin, but the value of her observations and adventures in Wonderland is minimal for the adult world. Her dream of Wonderland is real enough to her child's mind, but its point is lost on the adult world to which it is presented. Like Aeneas's memory of the underworld, Alice's dream is destined to seem unreal to us—entertainingly absurd—even though it contains essential truths, because we are the descendants of Adam. Alice's dream has passed through the Gate of Ivory which is the fallen imagination of man:

> altera candenti perfecta nitens elephanto,
> sed falsa and caelum mittunt insomnia manes.

FAIRY TALES AND FANTASY

Jack Zipes

SOURCE: "Once There Were Two Brothers Named Grimm," in *The Complete Fairy Tales of the Brothers Grimm,* translated by Jack Zipes, Bantam Books, 1987, pp. xvii-xxxi.

[*In the following excerpt, Zipes briefly outlines the history of the Grimm brothers' famous collection of fairy tales, describing both how they collected and edited the stories and how the tales were first received in various nations.*]

Though the Grimms made important discoveries in their research on ancient German literature and customs, they were neither the founders of folklore as a study in Germany, nor were they the first to begin collecting and publishing folk and fairy tales. In fact, from the beginning their principal concern was to uncover the etymological and linguistic truths that bound the German people together and were expressed in their laws and customs. The fame of the Brothers Grimm as collectors of folk and fairy tales must be understood in this context, and even here, chance played a role in their destiny.

In 1806 Clemens Brentano, who had already published an important collection of folk songs entitled *Des Knaben Wunderhorn (The Boy's Magic Horn,* 1805) with Achim von Arnim, was advised to seek out the aid of Jacob and Wilhelm Grimm because they were known to have a vast knowledge of old German literature and folklore. They were also considered to be conscientious and indefatigable workers. Brentano hoped to use whatever tales they might send him in a future publication of folk tales, and he was able to publish some of the songs they gathered in the second and third volumes of *Des Knaben Wunderhorn* in 1808. The Grimms believed strongly in sharing their research and findings with friends and congenial scholars, and between 1807 and 1812 they began collecting tales with the express purpose of sending them to Brentano, as well as of using them as source material for gaining a greater historical understanding of the German language and customs.

Contrary to popular belief, the Grimms did not collect their tales by visiting peasants in the countryside and writing down the tales that they heard. Their primary method was to invite storytellers to their home and then have them tell the tales aloud, which the Grimms either noted down on first hearing or after a couple of hearings. Most of the storytellers during this period were educated young women from the middle class or aristocracy. For instance, in Kassel a group of young women from the Wild family (Dortchen, Gretchen, Lisette, and Marie Elisabeth), and their mother (Dorothea), and from the Hassenpflug family (Amalie, Jeanette, and Marie) used to meet regularly to relate tales they had heard from their nursemaids, governesses, and servants. In 1808 Jacob formed a friendship with Werner von Haxthausen, who came from Westphalia, and in 1811 Wilhelm visited the Haxthausen estate and became acquainted there with a circle of young men and women (Ludowine, Marianne, and August von Haxthausen, and Jenny and Annette von Droste-Hülfshoff), whose tales he noted down. Still, the majority of the storytellers came from Hessia: Dorothea Viehmann, a tailor's wife from nearby Zwehrn who used to sell fruit in Kassel, would visit the Grimms and told them a good many significant tales; and Johann Friedrich (*Wachtmeister*) Krause, an old retired soldier, gave the brothers tales in exchange for some of their old clothes. Many of the tales that the Grimms recorded had French origins because the Hassenpflugs were of Huguenot ancestry and spoke French at home. Most of the brothers' informants were familiar with both oral tradition and literary tradition and would combine motifs from both sources. In addition to the tales of these storytellers and others who came later, the Grimms took tales directly from books and journals and edited them according to their taste.

In 1810, when Brentano finally requested the Grimms' collection of tales, the brothers had copies made and sent forty-nine texts to him. They had copies made because they felt Brentano would take great poetic license and turn them into substantially different tales, whereas they were intent on using the tales to document basic truths about the customs and practices of the German people and on preserving their authentic ties to the oral tradition. Actually, the Grimms need not have worried about Brentano's use of their tales, for he never touched them but abandoned them in the Ölenberg Monastery in Alsace. Only in 1920 were the handwritten tales rediscovered, and they were published in different editions in 1924, 1927, and 1974. The last publication by Heinz Rölleke is the most scholarly and useful, for he has carefully shown how the Grimms' original handwritten manuscripts can help us to document their sources and reveal the great changes the brothers made in shaping the tales.

As it happened, after the Grimms sent their collected texts to Brentano, who was unreliable and was going through great personal difficulties, they decided to publish the tales themselves and began changing them and preparing them for publication. They also kept adding new tales to their collection. Jacob set the tone, but the brothers were very much in agreement about how they wanted to alter and stylize the tales. This last point is significant because some critics have wanted to see major differences between Jacob and Wilhelm. These critics have argued that there was a dispute between the brothers after Wilhelm assumed major

The Grimm brothers.

responsibility for the editing of the tales in 1815 and that Wilhelm transformed them against Jacob's will. There is no doubt that Wilhelm was the primary editor after 1815, but Jacob established the framework for their editing practice between 1807 and 1812 and even edited the majority of the tales for the first volume. A comparison of the way Jacob and Wilhelm worked both before and after 1815 does not reveal major differences, except that Wilhelm did take more care to refine the style and make the contents of the tales more acceptable for a children's audience, or, really, for adults who wanted the tales censored for children. Otherwise, the editing of Jacob and Wilhelm exhibits the same tendencies from the beginning to the end of their project: the endeavor to make the tales stylistically smoother; the concern for clear sequential structure; the desire to make the stories more lively and pictorial by adding adjectives, old proverbs, and direct dialogue; the reinforcement of motives for action in the plot; the infusion of psychological motifs; and the elimination of elements that might detract from a rustic tone. The model for a good many of their tales was the work of the gifted artist Philipp Otto Runge, whose two stories in dialect, *The Fisherman and His Wife* and *The Juniper Tree,* represented in tone, structure, and con-

tent the ideal narrative that the Grimms wanted to create.

And create they did. The Grimms were not merely collectors. In fact, their major accomplishment in publishing their two volumes of 156 tales in 1812 and 1815 was to *create* an ideal type for the literary fairy tale, one that sought to be as close to the oral tradition as possible, while incorporating stylistic, formal, and substantial thematic changes to appeal to a growing middle-class audience. By 1819, when the second edition of the tales, now in one volume that included 170 texts, was published and Wilhelm assumed complete charge of the revisions, the brothers had established the form and manner through which they wanted to preserve, contain, and present to the German public what they felt were profound truths about the origins of civilization. Indeed, they saw the "childhood of humankind" as embedded in customs that Germans had cultivated, and the tales were to serve as reminders of such rich, natural culture.

After 1819 there were five more editions and sixty-nine new texts added to the collection and twenty-eight omitted. By the time the seventh edition appeared in 1857, there were 211 texts in all. Most of the additions after 1819 were from literary sources, and the rest were either sent to the brothers by informants or recorded from a primary source. Indeed, the chief task after 1819 was largely one of refinement: Wilhelm often changed the original texts by comparing them to different versions that he had acquired. While he evidently tried to retain what he and Jacob considered the essential message of the tale, he tended to make the tales more proper and prudent for bourgeois audiences. Thus it is crucial to be aware of the changes both brothers made between the original handwritten manuscript and the last edition of 1857. Compare the following, for example:

"Snow White"—Ölenberg Manuscript

When Snow White awoke the next morning, they asked her how she happened to get there. And she told them everything, how her mother, the queen, had left her alone in the woods and gone away. The dwarfs took pity on her and persuaded her to remain with them and do the cooking for them when they went to the mines. However, she was to beware of the queen and not to let anyone into the house.

"Snow White"—1812 Edition

When Snow White awoke, they asked her who she was and how she happened to get into the house. Then she told them how her mother had wanted to have her put to death, but the hunter had spared her life, and how she had run the entire day and finally arrived at their house. So the dwarfs took pity on her and said, "If you keep house for us and cook, sew, make the beds, wash and knit, and keep everything tidy and clean, you may stay with us, and you will have everything you want. In the evening, when we come home, dinner must be ready. During the day we are in the mines and dig for gold, so you will be alone. Beware of the queen and let no one into the house."

"Rapunzel"—1812 Edition

At first Rapunzel was afraid, but soon she took such a liking to the young king that she made an agreement with him: he was to come every day and be pulled up. Thus they lived merrily and joyfully for a certain time, and the fairy did not discover anything until one day when Rapunzel began talking to her and said, "Tell me, Mother Gothel, why do you think my clothes have become too tight for me and no longer fit?"

"Rapunzel"—1857 Edition

When he entered the tower, Rapunzel was at first terribly afraid, for she had never laid eyes on a man before. However, the prince began to talk to her in a friendly way and told her that her song had touched his heart so deeply that he had not been able to rest until he had seen her. Rapunzel then lost her fear, and when he asked her whether she would have him for her husband, and she saw that he was young and handsome, she thought, He'll certainly love me better than old Mother Gothel. So she said yes and placed her hand in his.

"I want to go with you very much," she said, "but I don't know how I can get down. Every time you come, you must bring a skein of silk with you, and I'll weave it into a ladder. When it's finished, then I'll climb down, and you can take me away on you horse."

They agreed that until then he would come to her every evening, for the old woman came during the day. Meanwhile, the sorceress did not notice anything, until one day Rapunzel blurted out, "Mother Gothel, how is it that you're much heavier than the prince? When I pull him up, he's here in a second."

"The Three Spinners"—1812 Edition

In olden times there lived a king who loved flax spinning more than anything in the world, and his queen and daughters had to spin the entire day. If he did not hear the wheels humming, he became angry. One day he had to take a trip, and before he departed, he gave the queen a large box with flax and said, "I want this flax spun by the time I return."

"The Three Spinners"—1857 Edition

There once was a lazy maiden who did not want to spin, and no matter what her mother said, she refused to spin. Finally, her mother became so angry and impatient that she beat her, and her daughter began to cry loudly. Just then the queen happened to be driving by, and when she heard the crying, she ordered the carriage to stop, went into the house, and asked the mother why she was beating her daughter, for her screams could be heard out on the street. The woman was too ashamed to tell the queen that her daughter was lazy and said, "I can't get her to stop spinning. She does nothing but spin and spin, and I'm so poor that I can't provide the flax."

"Well," the queen replied, "there's nothing I like to hear more than the sound of spinning, and I'm never happier than when I hear the constant humming of the wheels. Let me take your daughter with me to my castle. I've got plenty of flax, and she can spin as much as she likes."

As is evident from the above examples, the Grimms made major changes while editing the tales. They eliminated erotic and sexual elements that might be offensive to middle-class morality, added numerous Christian expressions and references, emphasized specific role models for male and female protagonists according to the dominant patriarchal code of that time, and endowed many of the tales with a "homey" or *biedermeier* flavor by the use of diminutives, quaint expressions, and cute descriptions. Moreover, though the collection was not originally printed with children in mind as the primary audience—the first two volumes had scholarly annotations, which were later published separately—Wilhelm made all the editions from 1819 on more appropriate for children, or rather, to what he thought would be proper for children to learn. Indeed, some of the tales, such as *Mother Trudy* and *The Stubborn Child,* are intended to be harsh lessons for children. Such didacticism did not contradict what both the Grimms thought the collection should be, namely an *Erziehungsbuch,* an educational manual. The tendency toward attracting a virtuous middle-class audience is most evident in the so-called Kleine Ausgabe (*Small Edition*), a selection of fifty tales from the *Gross Ausgabe (Large Edition).* This *Small Edition* was first published in 1825 in an effort to popularize the larger work and to create a best-seller. There were ten editions of this book, which contained the majority of the *Zaubermärchen* (the magic fairy tales), from 1825 to 1858. With such tales as *Cinderella, Snow White, Sleeping Beauty, Little Red Riding Hood,* and *The Frog King,* all of which underline morals in keeping with the Protestant ethic and a patriarchal notion of sex roles, the book was bound to be a success.

The magic fairy tales were the ones that were the most popular and acceptable in Europe and America during the nineteenth century, but it is important to remember that the Grimms' collection also includes unusual fables, legends, anecdotes, jokes, and religious tales. The variety of their tales is often overlooked because only a handful have been selected by parents, teachers, publishers, and critics for special attention. This selective process is generally neglected when critics talk about the effects of the tales and the way they should be conveyed or not conveyed to children.

The Grimms' collection *Children's and Household Tales* was not an immediate success in Germany. In fact, Ludwig Bechstein's *Deutsches Märchenbuch (German Book of Fairy Tales,* 1845) was more popular for a time. However, by the 1870s the Grimms' tales had been incorporated into the teaching curriculum in Prussia and other German principalities, and they were also included in primers and anthologies for children throughout the western world. By the beginning of the twentieth century, the *Children's and Household Tales* was second only to the Bible as a best-seller in Germany, and it has continued to hold this position. Furthermore, there is no doubt that the Grimms' tales, published either together in a single volume or individually as illustrated books, enjoy the same popularity in the English-speaking world.

Such popularity has always intrigued critics, and advocates of various schools of thought have sought to analyze and interpret the "magic" of the Grimms' tales. Foremost among the critics are the folklorists, educators, psychologists, and literary critics of different persuasions, including structuralists, literary historians, semioticians, and Marxists. Each group has made interesting contributions to the scholarship on the Grimms' tales, although there are times when historical truths about the Grimms' work are discarded or squeezed to fit into a pet theory.

The efforts made by folklorists to categorize the Grimms' tales after the nineteenth century were complicated by the fact that numerous German folklorists used the tales to explain ancient German customs and rituals, under the assumption that the tales were authentic documents of the German people. This position, which overlooked the French and other European connections, led to an "Aryan" approach during the 1920s, 1930s, and 1940s, which allowed many German folklorists to interpret the tales along racist and elitist lines. Such an approach had always been contested by folklorists outside Germany, who viewed the tales as part of the vast historical development of the oral tradition, wherein the Grimms' collection is given special attention because of the mixture of oral and literary motifs. These motifs have been related by folklorists to motifs in other folk tales in an effort to find the origin of a particular motif or tale type and its variants. By doing this kind of research, folklorists have been able to chart distinctions in the oral traditions and customs of different countries.

Educators have not been interested in motifs so much as in the morals and the types of role models in the tales. Depending on the country and the educational standards in a particular historical period, teachers and school boards have often dictated which Grimms' tales are to be used or abused. Generally speaking, such tales as *The Wolf and the Seven Young Kids, Cinderella, Little Red Cap,* and *Snow White* have always been deemed acceptable because they instruct children through explicit warnings and lessons, even though some of the implicit messages may be harmful to children. Most of the great pedagogical debates center around the brutality and cruelty in some tales, and the tendency among publishers and adapters of the tales has been to eliminate the harsh scenes. Consequently, Cinderella's sisters will not have their eyes pecked out; Little Red Cap and her grandmother will not be gobbled up by the wolf; the witch in *Snow White* will not be forced to dance in red-hot shoes; and the witch in *Hansel and Gretel* will not be shoved into an oven.

Such changes have annoyed critics of various psychoanalytical orientations, because they believe that the violence and conflict in the tales derive from profound instinctual developments in the human psyche and hence represent symbolical modes by which children and adults deal with sexual problems. Most psychoanalytical critics take their cues from Freud, even if they have departed from his method and have joined another school of analysis. One of the first important books about the psychological impact of the Grimms' tales was Josephine Belz's *Das Märchen und die Phantasie des Kindes (The Fairy Tale and the Imagination of the Child,* 1919) in which she tried to establish important connections between children's ways of fantasizing and the symbols in the tales. Later, Carl Jung, Erich Fromm, and Gerza Roheim wrote valuable studies of fairy tales that sought to go beyond Freud's theories. In the period following World War II, Aniela Jaffé, Joseph Campbell, and Maria von Franz charted the links between archetypes, the collective unconscious, and fairy tales, while Julius Heuscher and Bruno Bettelheim focused on oedipal conflicts from neo-Freudian positions in their analyses of some Grimms' tales. Finally, André Favat published an important study, *Child and the Tale* (1977), which uses Piaget's notions of child development, interests, and stages of understanding to explore the tales and their impact. Although the various psychoanalytical approaches have shed light on the symbolical meanings of the tales from the point of view of particular schools of thought, the tales have often been taken out of context to demonstrate the value of a psychoanalytical theory rather than to render a cultural and aesthetic appreciation and evaluation of the text.

Literary critics have reacted to the psychoanalytical approach in different ways. Influenced by the theories of Vladimir Propp (*Morphology of the Folktale,* 1968) and Max Lüthi (*Once Upon a Time,* 1970), formalists, structuralists, and semioticians have analyzed individual texts to discuss the structure of the tale, its aesthetic components and functions, and the hidden meanings of the signs. Literary historians and philologists such as Ludwig Denecke and Heinz Rölleke have tried to place the Grimms' work in a greater historical context in order to show how the brothers helped develop a mixed genre, often referred to as the *Buchmärchen* (book tale), combining aspects of the oral and literary tradition. Sociological and Marxist critics such as Dieter Richter, Christa Bürger, and Bernd Wollenweber have discussed the tales in light of the social and political conditions in Germany during the nineteenth century and have drawn attention to the racist and sexist notions in the tales. In the process, they have added fuel to the debate among educators, and the use and abuse of the Grimms' tales remains a key issue even today—among educators, psychologists, folklorists, and literary critics.

Though there were debates about the value of the tales during the Grimms' own lifetime, if they were alive today, they would probably be surprised to see how vigorous and violent some of the debates are and how different the interpretations tend to be. To a certain extent, the intense interest in their tales by so many different groups of critics throughout the world is a tribute to the Grimms' uncanny sense of how folk narratives inform cultures. They were convinced that their tales possessed essential truths about the origins of civilization, and they selected and revised those tales that would best express these truths. They did this in the name of humanity and *Kultur:* the Grimms were German idealists who believed that historical knowledge of customs, mores, and laws would increase self-understanding and social enlightenment. Their book is not so much a book of magic as it is a manual for education that seeks to go beyond the irrational. It is in their impulse to educate, to pass on the experiences of a variety of people who knew the lore of survival, that we may find the reasons why we are still drawn to the tales today. Though the Grimms imbued the tales with a heavy dose of Christian morality, the Protestant work ethic, and patriarchalism, they also wanted the tales to depict social injustices and possibilities for self-determination. Their tales reflect their concerns and the contradictions of their age. Today we have inherited their concerns and contradictions, and their tales still read like innovative strategies for survival. Most of all they provide hope that there is more to life than mastering the art of survival. Their "once upon a time" keeps alive our utopian longing for a better world that can be created out of our dreams and actions.

Mary V. Jackson

SOURCE: "Oberon Leads the Counteroffensive," in *Engines of Instruction, Mischief, and Magic: Children's Literature in England from Its Beginnings to 1839,* University of Nebraska Press, 1989, pp. 191-223.

[*In the excerpt that follows, Jackson substantiates the contribution that poetry made to children's literature, crediting children's poetry with initiating in the eighteenth century the strain of fantasy literature that would ultimately seek to entertain children as much or more than it did to instruct.*]

Nonsense and Funny-sense: Comic Poetry

The real breakthrough in imaginative and humorous or adventurous books came in poetry rather than prose perhaps because the latter had been so exclusively preempted in the service of Church and State; perhaps it was mere chance. One of the things that comes through poorly in written criticism such as this is the living voice of an age. Generally in earlier times people sang more, possibly a benefit of the absence of synthetic music and canned lyrics. From what one can gather, this was true everywhere. Certainly, ballads, broadsides of songs set to well-known tunes, and even songbooks were abundant sellers in eighteenth-and nineteenth-century Britain. Moreover, this lyrical impulse was creatively wedded to homely enterprise in the street cries—of London, Glasgow, Edinburgh, or wherever a chapbook edition originated—to alert the public to the peculiar attractiveness or usefulness of small businesswomen's and -men's produce, wares, or skilled services, like rush chair mending. A considerable portion of the disreputable "Jemmy" Catnach's lucrative one-fourth-pence, one-half-pence, and one-pence business in Seven Dials (1813-39), apart from the lurid accounts of murder, mayhem, and grisly justice at Tyburn Tree, was in catches, glees, and broadside ballads, some a bit bawdy but most just comic or sentimental.

To be sure, the children chanted their street songs and game songs, many of which were printed in both shoddy and superior chapbooks and in anthologies and were thus passed along to this day. Partly out of this rich melange emerged collections of songs for the nursery. . . . [The] first such nursery collection was compiled by Mary Cooper in *Tommy Thumb's Pretty Song Book* (1744). Competing volumes were issued by Crowder and Collins, *The Top Book of All* (c. 1760), and by Newbery, *Mother Goose's Melody; or, Sonnets for the Cradle* (c. 1760). The next major work was perhaps that of the chapbook publishers Cluer Dicey and Richard Marshall, who issued the famous nursery rhyme *Simple Simon* in 1764. Imitators and reprinters of Cooper's and Newbery's songs—Isaiah Thomas in America and John Marshall and numerous other chapbook publishers in London and the provinces—busily filled the needs of patrons during the sixties, seventies, and eighties.

Inspired by Newbery's *Mother Goose's Melody,* the precise antiquarian Joseph Ritson issued a collection in 1784 that stimulated poetry in an era when prose was largely controlled by the moral utilitarians and devoted to repressing laughter and fancy. *Gammer Gurton's Garland; or, The Nursery Parnassus* contained the original (in print) of "Goosey, Goosey Gander" and "Little Bo-Peep." Many of its songs were evidently widely known and often sung in their day. *Garland* was enlarged and reissued about 1799 and was further enlarged by Francis Douce [?] in a new edition of 1810 which contained the first printed version of "Humpty Dumpty" and an imitation of *Old Mother Hubbard,* "The Surprising Old Woman." Many of our staples of Mother Goose's nursery rhymes were added to the cannon in these years. Some, like "Hot Cross Buns," originated in street cries (to sell the buns traditionally eaten on Good Friday) that had already appeared in print (this one as a "catch" by Luffman Atterbury in *A Seventh Collection of Catches, Canons & Glees,* 1768).

In the aggregate, such works reveal a yearning for the surcease of duty and moral "busy-ness" and for the resurgence of imagination and of comic amusements. This desire was perfectly fulfilled in *Old Mother Hubbard,* which seemed to open the floodgates, letting pour through a great tide of engagingly droll and occasionally witty poetry. Most of it was meant for sheer enjoyment, but its spirit infected writers of instructive books as well, and some of these soared for the first time above the dull paths their ilk usually crept on. Typically, any truly popular new book was imitated as swiftly (and deftly) as the trade could manage, often quite surprisingly successfully in these years.

Mother Hubbard was not new but was rather a stock figure from folk or nursery tales. I know of one inexpensive version of *Mother Hubbard* (c. 1770-90), put out by John Evans, publisher of farthing chapbooks and songsheets in Long Lane, West Smithfield, London; doubtless there were others. But the poetry was evidently refurbished by Sarah Catherine Martin in 1804, as were the illustrations. It was loved and recited, and imitated and followed by sequels and continuations for decades:

> Old Mother Hubbard
> Went to the cupboard
> To fetch her poor dog a bone;
> But when she came there
> The cupboard was bare
> And so the poor dog had none.
>
> She went to the baker's

> To buy him some bread;
> But when she came back
> The poor dog was dead.

Mother Hubbard appeared 1 June 1805, the 24th edition coming in 1807; *A Continuation* came out in 1805, its 12th edition in 1807; and *A Sequel,* published 1 March 1806, sold ten thousand copies in six months. "A Near Relation of Mother Hubbard" authored *Whimsical Incidents; or, The Power of Music, a Poetical Tale,* a merry bit of rhyming, on 25 October 1805. *Pug's Visit; or, The Disasters of Mr. Punch; A Poetical Tale* followed in 1806—all brought out by Harris. The "Hubbards" were all pirated in chapbooks and widely imitated.

Others joined in with their versions of the first amusing poetry for children since Mary Cooper's books in the 1740s, versions generally without moral or educational purpose. Thomas Hodgkins (i.e., William Godwin's firm) published *The King and Queen of Hearts,* Charles Lamb's anonymous but pleasant reworking of once current political jibes, in 1805; and Benjamin Tabart issued the important *Songs for the Nursery* (1805), which included "Little Miss Muffet" and "Little Bobby Shaftoe," and *Memoirs of The Little Man and the Little Maid* (1807), the first children's version of which appeared in Newbery's *Mother Goose's Melody.* Joining the trend, though in more original and ironic (and thus moral) verse, Ann Taylor wrote *Signor Topsy Turvy's Wonderful Magic Lantern* (1810), a series of comic-satiric poems that enlighteningly reverse the order of things in life, especially between men and beasts, with vivid illustrations.

In addition, Dean & Munday of Threadneedle Street, frequent copublishers with A. K. Newman (The Minerva Press), put out batches of refreshingly silly entertainments: *Dame Wiggins of Lee and Her Seven Wonderful Cats. Written Principally by a Lady of Ninety* (1823); *Deborah Dent and her Donkey* (c. 1820s), daffy doings at Brighton; *Madam Fig's Gala* (c. 1820s), the comic tussles between a greengrocer and his social-climbing wife; and *Aldiborontiphoskyphorniostikos; A Round game for Merry Parties* (c. 1822), by R. Stennet, grafting Eastern tales like *Ali Baba* to tongue twisters like "Peter Piper": "M, Muley Hassan Mufti of Moldavia put on his Barnacles to see little Tweedle gobble them up, when Kia Khan Kreuse transmogrified them into Pippins, . . . Snip's wife cried, Illikip-illiky, lass a day, 'tis too bad to titter at a body. . . ." On goes the sheer nonsense. Imagine *that* being recited speedily at a children's party.

Tongue twisting and poetry games became the rage. Some were ancient, like *The Gaping, Wide-mouthed, Waddling Frog* (Dean & Munday, E. Marshall, c. 1815-20); but many imitations appeared. E. Marshall seemed to have specialized in these, which were beautifully printed for him by David Carvalho from designs by Robert Cruikshank: *The Frisking, Barking, Lady's Lap-Dog, A Game of Forfeits; The Hopping, Prating, Chattering Magpie; The Pretty, Playful, Tortoise-Shell Cat,* and *The Noble Prancing, Cantering Horse*—all published around 1820 and all nicely hand-colored.

Most such stuff has long since been forgotten, but the rollicking comic backlash spawned at least one lasting genre, the limerick. Harris's *History of Sixteen Wonderful Old Women* (1820) led the way:

> There was an Old Woman of Harrow
> Who visited in a wheel-barrow,
>   And her servant before
>   Knock'd loud at each door;
> To announce the Old Woman of Harrow.

E. Marshall, who was proving as resourceful as his kinsman John, immediately countered with two works. *Anecdotes and Adventures of Fifteen Gentlemen* (c. 1821) and *Anecdotes and Adventures of Fifteen Young Ladies* (c. 1822), printed by Carvalho with designs by R. Cruikshank. Darton demonstrates that both text and inspiration for an illustration in Edward Lear's *Book of Nonsense* (1846) were provided by *Gentlemen:*

> There was a sick man of Tobago
> Liv'd long on rice-gruel and sago;
>   But at last, to his bliss,
>   The physician said this—
> To a roast leg of mutton you may go.

Assuredly this prolonged rash of delicious humor was a healthy reaction to years of grim earnestness. But its benefits were not limited to the healing relief of jollity; they spilt over quite wonderfully into the field of instruction. For the first time in children's literature many little works successfully combined learning and laughter. One of the earliest is the charmingly illustrated and colored *Juvenile Numerator* (London: Stevens & Co., 1810). It is the old counting rhyme "1, 2, Buckle my shoe!" that goes to "19, 20, My Belly's Empty. / So pray Dame give me some pudding."

Harris's *Peter Piper's Practical Principles of Plain and Perfect Pronunciation* appeared in 1813 and sold well through many editions, though it was attacked in 1820 for slyly bawdy innuendoes. One of its tongue twisters is widely known even today: "Peter Piper picked a peck of pickled peppers. . . ." But Harris's triumph was the 1816 *Marmaduke Multiply's Merry Method of Making Minor Mathematicians; or, The Multiplication Table,* illustrated, which went through countless editions in England and America: "3 time 10 *are* 30 / My face is very dirty. . . . 5 times 12 *are* 60 / The House is like a Pig's sty! . . . 10 times 12 *are* 120 / I laugh and sing and live in plenty" and on to "12 times 12." Marmaduke had a learned family, some

of whom rushed into print: *The Pence Table Playfully Paraphrased. By Peter Pennyless* (1818); *The Mint; or, Shillings transformed into Pounds. By Peregrine Proteus* (1819). And *Harris's Cabinet: Pence Tables* (1819?) is rhymed and illustrated, like John Wallis's *Paul Pennylove's Poetical Paraphrase of the Pence Table* (c. 1814). The impulse was clearly catching.

Publishers, naturally, were not slow to adapt these devices to language. Thomas Love Peacock's *Sir Hornbook; or, Childe Launcelot's Expedition. A Grammatico-Allegorical Ballad* (1814) was much touted in Peacock's own circle and that of the Godwins, who published it. But it is a turgid, pedantic exercise, ridiculously encumbered with footnotes to explicate nearly every line. Far more simple and pleasing is Harris's *Paths of Learning Strewed with Flowers; or, English Grammar Illustrated* (1820), which may have been influenced by Elizabeth S. Graham's *Voyage to Locuta* (Hatchard, 1818). Both are amusing and visually delightful.

Quite different in tone is Harris's *Infant's Grammar; or, A Pic-Nic Party of the Parts of Speech* (1822), a more vigorously comic mock epic influenced by the many imitations of William Roscoe's *Butterfly's Ball* (1806). It opens:

> One day, I am told, and, as it was cold,
>   I suppose it occur'd in cold weather.
> The NINE PARTS OF SPEECH, having no one to
>   teach,
>   resolv'd on a PIC-NIC together.
>
> The ARTICLE mov'd, and the PRONOUN approv'd
>   That the NOUN should preside at the feast;
> But the ADJECTIVE said, though the Noun might
>   be head,
>   The VERB should be none of the least.

And on it goes to the arrangements, the dressing up, the banqueting, and the dancing that are cleverly worked into an exposition of the rules of grammar.

Works like this competed with the duller improving and information books that descendants of the first reformers continued to publish with dreary regularity. But the old order had been restrained; and the new had made a lasting place for itself.

Flights of Butterflies—The Papillonnades

It is odd that pre-Romantic elements should have found their way into nursery and youthful libraries before neoclassical ones; but humanity often confutes mere chronology. The spiritual descendants of Alexander Pope burst into the world of children's books in late 1806 led by William Roscoe's *Butterfly's Ball and the Grasshopper's Feast,* published in book form the next year by John Harris. Before the year was out, Harris had another writer producing imitation "butterflies"—or papillonnades, as I have dubbed them after the French "Robinsonnades." Within the next year, four others had joined her in the profitable and extremely delightful enterprise of loosing more papillonnades on England's young. So polished were some that a reviewer complained they were too good for children. He was wrong, to be sure, but they were—many of them—very good indeed. In fact, an unusual phenomenon occurred in them: Whereas the first of a type is often finest and its imitations wanting, in these the imitations, especially Catherine Ann Dorset's, outshone the original.

Roscoe's cheery little poem with designs by William Mulready opens with the frontispiece showing a boy inviting a group of children to go out the open door:

> Come take up your Hats, and away let us haste.
> To the Butterfly's Ball, and the Grasshopper's feast.
> The Trumpeter Gad-Fly has summon'd the crew,
> And the Revels are now only waiting for you.
> On the smooth-shaven Grass by the side of a Wood,
> Beneath a broad oak which for ages has stood,
> See the children of earth, and the tenants of Air,
> To an evening's amusement together repair.

These are assuredly not Pope's heroic couplets, yet the happy lilt of the tetrameter dactyls does contain a regularity that brings order to this diverting account of little creatures' and little folks' versions of adult galas. Indeed, it is in this adapting of the mock epic in its gentlest form that Roscoe brought lighter neoclassical strains to nursery fare.

Catherine Dorset excelled in so precisely gauging this note in the poem and in recreating the delicate aura of the mock epic at its gentlest and airiest. Several of her nursery miniatures rival *The Rape of the Lock* in their delicious yoking of the high and the low, the regal and the ridiculous, the sublime and the showy—all held together with the merest whiff of lighthearted mockery at the very human foibles her characters display. *The Peacock "At Home"* (1807) flew from her pen:

> The Butterfly's Ball, and the Grasshopper's Feasts,
> Excited the spleen of the Birds and the Beasts:
> For their mirth and good cheer—of the Bee was the theme,
> And the Gnat blew his horn, as he danc'd in

> the beam. . . .
> The Quadrupeds listen'd with sullen displeasure.
>
> But the Tenants of Air were enrag'd beyond measure.
> The PEACOCK display'd his bright plumes to the Sun,
> And, addressing his Mates, thus indignant begun:
> "Shall we, like domestic, inelegant Fowls,
> "As unpolish'd as Geese, and as stupid as Owls,
> "Sit tamely at home, hum drum, with our Spouses,
> "While Crickets, and Butterflies, open their houses? . . .
> "If I suffer such insolent airs to prevail,
> "May Juno pluck out all the eyes in my tail;
> "So a Fete I will give, and my taste I'll display,
> "And send out my cards for Saint Valentine's Day."

Dorset's shrewd but tolerant eye for social pretensions and absurdities supplied the richly detailed vignettes of dinners, dances, card games, and the ever delectable joys of neighbor watching and fashion gauging that animate the pages of this and her other similarly successful papillonnades. In 1807 *The Lion's Masquerade: A Sequel to The Peacock "At Home"* followed. Like the creatures left out of the butterfly's grand fete, the lion takes umbrage and "vainly sought rest, / For something like envy had poison'd his breast." Naturally, the solution is to give his own ton masquerade, to which the learned Pig, a Cat in pattens, a great Hog in armor and a large wig (borrowed from Carnan's *The Lilliputian Masquerade . . . [for] Lilliputians and Tommythumbians,* 1783), the King of Siam, and many other worthies repair.

To discuss even the Harris papillonnades that appeared between 1807 and 1810 would consume more pages than can be spared. Suffice it to note that he had five known writers hot at it: Dorset was quickly joined by "W. B." with *The Elephant's Ball and Grand Fete Champetre* (1807); then A.D.M., *The Butterfly's Birthday, St. Valentine's Day, and the Whale's Ball;* Mrs. Mary Cockle, *The Fishes Grand Gala;* Dorset(?), *The Lioness's Rout;* Theresa Tyro, *The Feast of the Fishes; or, The Whale's Invitation to His Brethren of the Deep; The Lioness's Ball; Flora's Gala,* with copper plates after Maria Flaxman's designs; *The Lobster's Voyage to the Brazils; The Horse's Levee; or, The Court of Pegasus;* and two sharper satires, *Grand-Mamma; or, The Christning [sic] 'Not At Home'* and *The Rose's Breakfast*—all in 1808; in 1809, Roscoe, *The Butterfly's Birthday. By the Author of the Butterfly's Ball* and, *The Mermaid "At Home!";* Dorset, *The Peacock and Parrot on Their Search for the Author of the Peacock at Home* (1816) and *The Fancy Fair; or, Grand Gala at the Zoological Gardens* (1838).

There were certainly flocks of papillonnades uncocooned by other publishers loath to miss out on the craze. Predictably, some dwindled into mere mechanical applications of the form, used chiefly to teach botany, ornithology, or the like. But surprisingly, many were imbued with the witty vivacity that stamped the earliest. The dates are uncertain and the list by no means complete, but some that appeared from other presses are *The Water-King's Levee; or, The Gala of the Lake* (W. Lindsell, 1807?); *The Eagle's Masque. By "Tom Tit"* (J. Mawman, c. 1807; 2d ed., 1808); *The Jack Daw "At Home"* (A. K. Newman, c. 1810); *The Peahen at Home; or, The Swan's Bridal Day* (J. L. Marks, c. 1840); the exceedingly beautiful *Chrysallina; or, The Butterfly's Gala, addressed to two little girls,* by R. C. Barton (T. Boys, 1820); and, late and sadly degenerated into prose, if with good illustrations, *The Dog's Dinner Party* (George Routledge and Sons, c. 1870) and *The Cat's Tea Party* (Routledge, c. 1871). Of course there were more, for they were deservedly loved, though not by everyone it would seem: In 1808 J.L.B. wrote for John Wallis *The Butterfly's Funeral, a sequel to the Butterfly's Ball & Grasshopper's Feast,* with engravings designed by Maria Flaxman. But these poetic exequies failed to stem the flight: Reports of the death of the brave papillon were greatly exaggerated.

"When the Green Woods Laugh with the Voice of Joy"

Truly fine poetry was late coming to the nursery and even to the library of older children. For a long time, it seemed as though Anna Barbauld had been correct in her judgment that poetry could not stoop to infancy, without ceasing to be. Of course much comic poetry was written, as we have seen, some very fine indeed. And also there was a spate of moral and cautionary rhymes and jingles put out by poetasters of the More-Trimmer school. Though these were not utterly without appeal, their obsessive moralizing and grim devotion to regular meter and rhyme did snuff out imagination, as in Mary Belson Elliott's *Simple Truths, in Verse* (1812) and Elizabeth Turner's *Daisy; or, Cautionary Stories in Verse* (1807), *Cowslip; or, More . . . in Verse* (1809), and *The Crocus* (1816). Such books were cranked out through the 1840s and after.

Charles and Mary Lamb's *Poetry for Children* (1809) has bits in some poems—though rare, even in this book—that soar above the drivel around them, like "Cleanliness":

> Come my little Robert near—
> Fie! what filthy hands are here—
> Who, that e'er could understand
> The rare structure of a hand,

> With its branching fingers fine,
> Work itself of hands divine,
> Strong, yet delicately knit,
> For Ten thousand uses fit. . . .

An early serious attempt by an established poet to bend to the child's world was Christopher Smart's *Hymns, for the Amusement of Children* (1771); it was promptly pirated in two issues of a Dublin edition in 1772 (London: Carnan, 2d ed., 1773; 3rd, 1775; 4th, 1786; Philadelphia: W. Spottswood, 1791). The book was very popular. It is a religious work, but the poems depict a gentle and intimate world, like Anna Barbauld's, and they have touches of beauty and a fragile gaiety, as in "Mirth" (Hymn XXV):

> If you are merry, sing away,
>   And touch the organs sweet. . . .

> Ye little prattlers, that repair
>   For cowslips in the mead,

> Of those exulting colts beware.
> But blythe security is there
>   Where skipping lambkins feed.

> With white and crimson laughs the sky,
>   With birds the hedge-rows ring;
> To give the praise to God most High,
>   And all the sulky fiends defy,
>   Is a most joyful thing.

The second important poet to write poetry accessible to, if not precisely for, children was William Blake. It is not certain how much of his work was known, or when. Assuredly, it was not widely read; his first book, *Poetical Sketches* (1783), is extant only in printer's proofs, so far as is known. Moreover, his even more important *Songs of Innocence* (1789) and *Songs of Innocence & Experience* (1794) were engraved and colored by Blake and later by his wife, Catherine, like most of his work.

Yet he was not altogether unknown. In 1806 Benjamin Heath Malkin issued *A Father's Memoirs of his Child* in which are printed several important poems that the *boy* knew from unspecified sources: "How Sweet I Roamed," and "I Love the Jocund Dance," from *Poetical Sketches;* and "The Tiger" [*sic*], "The Divine Image," "Holy Thursday," and the incomparable "Laughing Song" from *Innocence & Experience:*

> When the green woods laugh with the voice
>   of joy
> And the dimpling stream runs laughing by,
> When air does laugh with our merry wit,
> And the green hill laughs with the noise of it,

> When the meadows laugh with the lively
>   green,

> And the grasshopper laughs in this merry
>   scene,
> When Mary and Susan and Emily,
> With their sweet round mouths, sing Ha, ha,
>   he!

Malkin had seen Blake's prophetic books, of which he said "his personifications are bold, his thoughts original, and his style of writing altogether epic in its structure." More acumen had Malkin than many who merely called Blake mad. Coleridge got hold of a copy of *Songs of Innocence & Experience* late—1818—but also thought him a "man of genius."

One can only speculate whether Ann and Jane Taylor, from a family of engravers, Blake's craft, saw some of his poems before writing *Original Poems, for Infant Minds* (1804), Pt. II (1805). They were among the earliest children's authors to offer Blake to the young. In the revised 1818 edition of *City Scenes; or, A Peep into London for Children* (1801), Ann and Jane include "Holy Thursday" in their chapter on "Charity Children." Influenced by Blake or not, they were talented and their poetry mixed the homely, the humorous, even the grimly religious, but occasionally as well true poetry, as in "Autumn":

> The sun is far risen above the old trees
>   His beams on the silver dew play;
> The gossamer tenderly waves in the breeze.
>   And the mists are fast rolling away.

Even a hasty scan of their little books, including *Rhymes for the Nursery* (1806), yields several such fragile gems.

With the best of the Taylors' art, Oberon, King of Fancy, may be said to have achieved his final triumph: To the joys of fanciful and magical tales, comic poems, funny lessons, and delicious, sheer nonsense were now added the first fruits of golden poesy.

The Court of Oberon

In 1823 John Harris published *The Court of Oberon; or, Temple of the Fairies,* with tales of Mother Goose (Perrault), Mother Bunch (d'Aulnoy), and assorted popular tales, nicely if conventionally illustrated. The same year C. Baldwin brought out *German Popular Stories. Translated from the Kinder und Haus Marchen. Collected by M. M. Grimm,* 2 vols. (1823-26), illustrated with an appropriately eccentic verve and eerieness by George Cruikshank. His illustrations of 1825 for the first English edition of Victor Hugo's *Hans of Iceland* (Paris, 1823; London: J. Robins) evince the same spirit. These years mark a watershed in children's books, chiefly because of the translations from the scholarly collections of the Grimms. Thereafter, most parents and adults interested in children's literature accepted without qualms the once dubious fairy tales.

Only the exceedingly conservative and religious extremists still rejected them.

The way to this coup had to an extent been prepared by two separate groups. The first was the numerous children's chapbook sellers who had given sanctuary not only to fairy tales but also to popular folk tales and the old English romances. It would be impossible to even list a tenth of the chapbook publications in this area in England, Ireland, and Scotland. A complete list would require many sizable volumes. It is worth noting, however, that though keeping abreast of most new developments in every sort of children's book, chapbooks regularly offered adventures, fairy tales, romances, and Eastern tales and continued to do so after respectable publishers had joined in competitively.

The second group to help prepare the way for new developments included many respectable publishers who, as we have seen, put out single volumes and collections of two or three tales. Significantly, Benjamin Tabart, with help from William and Mary Jane Godwin, also attempted a far more ambitious scheme. Until recently, however, Tabart's role in this had not been appreciated. Brain Alderson has added vital details to the picture: In 1804 Tabart began to issue his *Collection of Popular Stories for the Nursery; Newly Translated and Revised from the French, Italian and Old English Writers.* The stories were issued separately in "Lilliputian Folios," with three colored engravings, sixpence each. He also offered the set in three parts, to be sold as one or separately. There were about thirty-five booklets in all. The project continued to 1809 when the fourth volume appeared, Eastern stories and "Jack and the Beanstalk." In 1818 Tabart issued his *Popular Fairy Tales,* which contained twenty-six tales he had collected and edited.

By an amusing coincidence, John Harris published *The History of Mother Twaddle, and the Marvellous Atchievements* [sic] of her Son Jack, by *B.A.T.* (Isabella Jane Towers), a verse form of "Jack and the Beanstalk," in 1807, just before Tabart's collection. In *Mother Twaddle* Jack comes by the remarkable bean after his mother finds sixpence and sends him to the market to buy a goose. Of course, he meets the peddler and returns home with his bean, whereupon he is roundly denounced for his idiocy. But he plants the bean, climbs the stalk, and discovers the giant's castle and untold wealth. With the aid of a servant-maid enslaved by the giant, he decapitates this monster, weds the maid, sends for his mother, and lives happily ever after in luxury. Interestingly, Tabart's version, not Harris's, has prevailed. This has the cow, the hen that lays golden eggs, the fairy harp, the man-eating giant (Fe, Fi, Fo, Fum!), and the breathtaking flight down the stalk, ending with the timely dispatching of the giant with Jack's trusty axe.

Thus was the way prepared for the termination of overt hostilities between the two main factions in children's books—moral utilitarians and those tolerant of fancy. The contest never fully ceased in the century—indeed it continues to this day—but a truce was tacitly declared.

Alan Richardson

SOURCE: "Wordsworth, Fairy Tales, and the Politics of Children's Reading," in *Romanticism and Children's Literature in Nineteenth-Century England,* edited by James Holt McGavran, Jr., The University of Georgia Press, 1991, pp. 34-53.

[*In the following essay, Richardson refutes the argument, maintained by most critics of children's literature, that fairy tales were a liberal rejection of didactic literature; using Wordsworth and other Romantics as his evidence, he asserts that fairy tales could be socially conservative.*]

In his *Miscellanies* (1696) John Aubrey records a late sighting of an English fairy: "Anno 1670, not far from Cyrencester, was an Apparition: Being demanded, whether a good Spirit, or a bad? returned no answer, but disappeared with a curious Perfume and a melodious Twang. Mr. W. Lily believes it was a Fairie" (50). With this decorous exit, the fairies seem to have left England both in person and, largely, by reputation, thanks in part (as Aubrey elsewhere records) to the growth of literacy among the lower classes:

> Before Printing, Old-wives tales were ingeniose: and since Printing came in fashion, till a little before the civil-Warres, the ordinary sort of People were not taught to reade: now-a-dayes Bookes are common, and most of the poor people understand letters: and the many good Bookes, and variety of Turnes of Affaires, have put all the old Fables out of dores: and the divine art of Printing, and Gunpowder have frighted away Robin-good-fellow and the Fayries.

By the time antiquarians like Bishop Percy and Sir Walter Scott began collecting oral traditions in earnest, the "authentic" folk tale, in contrast to the popular ballad, was relatively scarce in England. In its place, however, and among a sophisticated, upper-class and predominantly adult audience, a vogue had developed for imported, modernized, and often moralized fairy tales translated from French collections—Madame d'Aulnoy in 1699, Charles Perrault in 1729, Madame Leprince de Beaumont in 1761—and from Antoine Galland's French version of the Arabic *Thousand and One Nights* first published in 1706. If a newly literate "ordinary folk" had banished Robin Goodfellow and his like from their hearths, Cinderella and Scheherazade had found a place in the libraries of their betters.

The traditional fairy tale did not readily find a place, however, in the new literature for children that emerged in the latter half of the eighteenth century. Instead, fairy tales especially and fantasy literature in general came under attack from two sides: the rationalist school of education drawing on John Locke and Jean-Jacques Rousseau, and (though significantly less so) the Christian moralist critique of children's fiction which found exponents in writers like Sarah Trimmer and M. M. Sherwood. Locke's *Some Thoughts Concerning Education* (1693) set the tone for over a century in its harsh dismissal of supernatural fictions: "I would not have children troubled whilst young with Notions of *spirits* . . . I think it inconvenient, that their yet tender Minds should receive early impressions of *Goblins, Spectres,* and *Apparitions,* wherewith their Maids, and those about them, are apt to fright them into compliance with their orders." For Locke, Aesop's *Fables* (a work tailored for children's reading well before the development of a children's literature proper) was "the only Book almost that I know fit for children."

Sharing Locke's rational and genetic approach to education but going well beyond him to criticize a pervasively irrational, "unnatural" society, Rousseau did not consider "Fables, not even those of La Fontaine" fit for Emile's education; on the contrary, "reading is the plague of childhood" and fables "contain nothing intelligible or useful for children." The rationalist tradition in education theory represented by such figures as Richard and Maria Edgeworth, John and Lucy Aikin, Anna Letitia Barbauld, and Mary Wollstonecraft followed Locke and Rousseau in rejecting any form of fantastic or supernatural reading (often including too early an exposure to Christian notions of the soul and afterlife). In his preface to his daughter's *The Parent's Assistant* (1796) Richard Edgeworth, for example, takes Samuel Johnson to task for condescending to children's fairy tales: "Why should the mind be filled with fantastic visions, instead of useful knowledge? . . . It is to be hoped that the magic of Dr. Johnson's name will not have power to restore the reign of fairies."

The objections posed by Christian moralists were on the whole gentler but ultimately no less dismissive. Although Sarah Trimmer found her own childhood reading of Perrault relatively "harmless," she nevertheless rejected fairy tales as "only fit to fill the heads of children with confused notions of wonderful and supernatural events, brought about by the agency of imaginary beings." While Trimmer dismissed Sarah Fielding's *The Governess* for its inclusion of fairy tales, Mrs. Sherwood revised them out of it (but inserted one of her own devising to give her version a period flavor): "Since fanciful productions of this sort can never be rendered generally useful, it has been thought proper to suppress the rest, substituting in their place such appropriate relations as seemed more likely to conduce to juvenile edification."

Edgeworth's emphasis on "useful knowledge" over the "fantastic," or Sherwood's on "edification" over the "fanciful," suggests the dualistic model—didacticism and imagination, instruction and delight, reason and fantasy—underlying most accounts of the development of children's literature. The latter term in each opposition is, of course, invariably privileged at the expense of the former. F. J. Harvey Darton, for whom children's literature forms a perpetual field of conflict between "instruction and amusement," nevertheless finds in the "return" of the fairy tale with such collections as Benjamin Tabart's *Popular Fairy Tales* (1818) and Edgar Taylor's translations of Grimm (1823-26) the transition to a more humane children's library dominated by delight. Samuel Pickering, who provides a detailed and fairly sympathetic account of the rationalist tradition, still celebrates the wiser Victorian age when "fairy tales would be welcomed with a more open imagination." The triumph of the fairy tale over a didactic tradition perpetrated by a "monstrous regiment" of women writers plays a similarly pivotal role in the progressive narrative informing most accounts of English children's literature.

Within this pervasive schema, the first-generation Romantic poets garner praise for their defense, in the name of the imagination, of the popular fairy tale, although this "defense" admittedly took place more in private—through letters and unpublished manuscripts—than in public. Charles Lamb, who wrote with his sister Mary a didactic children's book (*Mrs. Leicester's School*) in the tradition of Fielding and Wollstonecraft, is celebrated for his attack on Barbauld and Trimmer in a letter to Samuel Taylor Coleridge (23 October 1802): "Is there no possibility of averting this sore evil? Think what you would have been now, if instead of being fed with Tales and old wives fables in childhood, you had been crammed with Geography & Natural History? *Damn them.* I mean the cursed Barbauld crew." Coleridge had already written to Thomas Poole (16 October 1797) of his own "early reading of Faery Tales" in the same vein: "Should children be permitted to read Romances, & Relations of Giants & Magicians & Genii?—I know all that has been said against it; but I have formed my faith in the affirmative.—I know no other way of giving the mind a love of 'the Great,' & 'the Whole.'" According to Geoffrey Summerfield, whose study *Fantasy and Reason* constitutes the most recent refinement of the dichotomized, progressive history of children's literature codified by [F. J. Harvey] Darton [in *Childrens Books in England: Five centuries of Social Life,* 1932], both Lamb and Coleridge pale beside William Wordsworth's "uniquely powerful defence of freedom and of fantasy in the lives of children" in book 5 of *The Prelude*. The author of the period's "most coherent and radical critique of 'moral' literature," Wordsworth serves Summerfield's study of eighteenth-century children's literature as its hero, the Romantic champion of fantasy and fairy tale.

Such accounts, although they begin to seem inevitable, still remain attractive, appealing as they do to our own notions of the importance of fantasy in the lives and books of children. However, when placed in its historical context, a period when the rapid and unforeseen growth of popular literacy, the mass distribution of radical political pamphlets, and the reaction of established interests in the form of censorship and mass propaganda of their own produced what Richard Altick has called the literacy "crisis" of the 1790s [in *The English Common Reader,* 1957], Wordsworth's patronage of fairy tales may be interpreted as something other than disinterested libertarianism. Moreover, when read critically, Wordsworth's valorization of the fairy tale can be shown to rely on a conservative, traditionalist conception of "oral literature" which, despite its presence behind most current studies of the fairy tale as children's literature, has long been discredited. Before addressing either of these problems, however, the stock opposition of fantasy and reason, imaginative and didactic literature should itself be questioned. Especially in regard to the fairy tale, it is not always clear where the moral tale leaves off and the fantasy begins.

If one concentrates on children's literature itself rather than the ongoing polemic in reviews and prefaces, the relation of didactic writers to the fairy tale might better be described as one of appropriation than one of censorship. Fairy tales were regularly appropriated for didactic purposes in at least four ways. Children's familiarity with fairy tale personages and trappings could be exploited most simply by borrowing them for the titles, prefatory matter, and packaging of otherwise didactic works, a fairy coating over the moral pill. Eleanor Fenn, author of *The Rational Dame,* entitled one of her thoroughly didactic works *The Fairy Spectator*; John Newberry's playful but decidedly Lockean *A Little Pretty Pocket-Book* (1744) appeals to its child readers through two letters ("to little Master Tommy" and "to Pretty Miss Polly") written by Jack the Giant-Killer, returned from fairyland as an enlightened moralist. Pickering notes several such appropriations, including the disappointingly anticlimactic title *The Prettiest Book for Children; Being the History of the Enchanted Castle; Situated in one of the Fortunate Isles; and Governed by the Giant Instruction* (47). Even the "Purple Jar" of Maria Edgeworth's most celebrated moral tale has been described [by Darton] as "a property from a stage fairy-land."

More elaborately, the didactic writer could borrow fairy tale motifs, types, and settings to construct moral fairy tales of her or his own. Rousseau himself wrote (though more for adults than for children) "La Reine Fantasque," a literary fairy tale featuring "la Fée Discrète"; Samuel Johnson's fairy tale "The Fountains" illustrates the vanity of even magic wishes, and many of the "Oriental tales" in *The Idler* and *The Rambler* moralize the conventions of *The Arabian Nights*. Some of the most popular didactic story books included such moral fairy tales: "The Story of the Cruel Giant Barbarico" and "The Princess Hebe: A Fairy Tale" (an Oriental tale after Johnson) in Sarah Fielding's *Governess;* "The Transmigrations of Indur" and "Order and Disorder, A Fairy Tale" in Aikin's and Barbauld's *Evenings at Home;* "The History of Princess Rosalinda" in Sherwood's revision of Fielding, a surprisingly energetic tale which is, if anything, more imaginative than the one it replaces. Pickering describes several book-length didactic fairy tales, including a moralized Robin Goodfellow.

A didactic writer could also silently adapt fairy tale plots or patterns into the empirical world of the rational tale. The hero of Thomas Day's "The Good-Natured Little Boy" in *The History of Sandford and Merton* helps out a dog, a horse, a blind man, and a crippled sailor, who fortuitously reappear to save him from danger as night comes on; his pendant in "The Ill-Natured Little Boy" spurns a similar series of potential helpers and is later punished by them. The two tales together illustrate an extremely common fairy tale motif, the test which separates the kindly hero or heroine from unkindly (and usually older) siblings or other rivals. Day's *History of Little Jack* recounts the life of a boy abandoned in infancy and suckled by a goat. The Cinderella story was moralized as *The Renowned History of Primrose Prettyface, Who By Her Sweetness of Temper and Love of Learning, Was Raised from Being the Daughter of a Poor Cottager, to Great Riches and the Dignity of Lady of the Manor;* and Goody Two-Shoes, despite her own warning against "tales of *Ghosts, Witches* and *Fairies*" as "the Frolics of a distempered Brain," herself rises from poverty to a bourgeois establishment in Cinderella fashion.

Finally, traditional fairy tales were themselves moralized by their redactors, translators, and editors. The early fairy tale collections designed for middle-class children were cleaned up and often given didactic applications. An early (1798) children's version of *The Thousand and One Nights,* by a Rev'd. Mr. Cooper, was entitled *The Oriental Moralist;* Tabart's *Popular Fairy Tales,* the first such English collection, had a "decidedly moral slant" and was designed to meet the approval, in Tabart's words, of "every tender mother, and every intelligent tutor" [according to Gillian Avery, *Childhood's Pattern,* 1975]. As John Ellis has shown, even the Brothers Grimm, despite their claims to unvarnished folk authenticity, censored some tales, selected the most acceptable version of others, and further refined the tales both in transcribing them and in revising them for later editions; Maria Tatar has more recently argued that most of these revisions were made specifically with the burgeoning children's book market in mind. Edgar Taylor's English translations of the Grimms' tales in the 1820s, which have been described as a "point of no return" in the victory of the fairies

over didacticism, were marked by a still greater degree of what Jack Zipes has termed the "bourgeoisification" of the folk tale. Taylor assured his adult purchasers that a number of the Grimms' tales, despite their "great merit," had been passed over in deference to "the scrupulous fastidiousness of modern taste especially in works likely to attract the attention of youth." Those Taylor selected were further sanitized in the interests of middle-class morality. In Giambattista Basile's seventeenth-century Italian version, Cinderella is a determined young woman who murders her first stepmother by breaking her neck; in the Grimms' version, "Aschenputtel" is much more child-like and docile, although she does allow her attendant ravens to peck out her stepsisters' envious eyes at her wedding. In Taylor's translation, the stepsisters are spared, the better to support her character throughout as a pattern child, "always good and kind to all about her."

Contrary to what might be called the Whig version of the history of English children's reading, the opposition between moral didacticism and the imaginative fairy tale is hardly absolute. Although the fairy tales remembered by Coleridge, Lamb, and Wordsworth would have been in chapbook versions rather than the blatantly moralized collections of the early nineteenth century, the Romantic sponsorship of fairy tales can nevertheless be described as a special instance of fairy tale appropriation for moral ends; it may be less ironic than is usually supposed that Lamb begins his fulminations against the cursed Barbauld crew with a lament for the passing of *Goody Two-Shoes,* "the very foundation," as Darton writes, "of the Moral Tale." And we should not ignore entirely that, at a time when debates on children's literature were highly politicized, the Barbauld "crew" was dominated by liberal and radical figures like the Aikins, the Edgeworths, Joseph Priestley, Thomas Beddoes, Mary Wollstonecraft, and William Godwin (who produced a charming if sometimes awkward *Fables* designed to answer Rousseau's critique). The Romantic advocates of fairyland, on the other hand, had already turned from Godwin and their youthful radicalism toward the conservative social and political stances that would mark their later careers.

Aubrey, writing in the late seventeenth century, felt that the rise of literacy among the "ordinary sort of People" had driven away the fairies, but some folktales and literary fairy tales did find their way into the chapbooks that formed much of this group's reading. Although its production and distribution were almost wholly uncontrolled, the chapbook did not represent a threat to established interests. While chapbooks could be populist in tone and critical of the upper classes, Olivia Smith has argued [in *The Politics of Language 1791-1817,* 1984] against overestimating the political significance of Robin Hood or Jack the Giant Killer: "While the [lower-class] audience read chap-books and ballads, it was considered to have a distinct and subordinate province. Although such material might express ideas about political events, it was not regarded as an attempt to participate in public life." Not so the new political literature, written in a vernacular intellectual style and distributed in pamphlet form at low prices, that emerged in the late eighteenth century and found its apotheosis in Thomas Paine's vastly popular *Rights of Man* (1791-92). As T. J. Mathias noted in *Pursuits of Literature* (1794), the mass distribution of Paine's two-part tract effected a revolution in English reading habits: "We no longer look for learned authors in the usual places, in the retreats of academic erudition, and in the seats of religion. Our peasantry now read the *Rights of Man* on mountains, and on moors, and by the wayside."

Although the earlier eighteenth century apparently saw a decline in popular literacy, its sudden and unlooked-for resurgence in the 1780s and 1790s, brought out so vividly by the unprecedented sales of *The Rights of Man,* was perceived as a serious and immediate threat by the established political and religious interests. As Lawrence Stone has pointed out ["Literacy and Education in England 1640-1900," *Past and Present* 42 (1969)], the "notion that literacy is somehow good in itself, one of the natural rights of man" dates back only a hundred years or so, and [in *Tristes Tropiques,* 1977] Claude Levi-Strauss argues that literacy as a social institution has on the contrary generally "favoured the exploitation of human beings rather than their enlightenment." But in order to facilitate social control, literacy and the distribution of literature must be carefully managed by those in power. The new mass readership of the 1790s had come about almost spontaneously through a highly unregulated, disorganized, private, and largely unprofessional patchwork of educational institutions: village schools, Sunday schools supported by various (often competing) denominations, Charity schools, "dame" schools, evening and Sunday classes held by clerks or artisans. The radical writers Thomas Spence and William Cobbett were taught to read at home by their fathers, as were many others.

The English establishment's answer to the literacy crisis was to call for increased systematization and superintendence of the schools, lest they remain, as the Bishop of Rochester characterized them in 1800, "schools of Jacobinical rebellion," and to hegemonize the writing and distribution of popular reading matter. Radical tracts were prohibited in 1795 and 1798, but something was needed to fill their place. As William Hazlitt pointed out in retrospect, "when it was impossible to prevent our reading something," "the fear of the progress of knowledge and a *Reading Public* . . . made the Church and State anxious to provide us with that sort of food for our stomachs, which they thought best."

In a period when reading designed for the working classes and for children was grouped together as "class-literature," which Charlotte Yonge defined as "books . . . for children or the poor," children's literature was critically affected by the ruling interests' program for hegemonizing popular reading through such institutions as Hannah More's Cheap Repository Tracts, the Religious Tract Society, the Society for Promoting Christian Knowledge, and the early Association for Preserving Liberty and Property against Republicans and Levellers. This program included the deliberate appropriation by conservative writers of existing popular modes and styles. More, for example, who wrote fifty Cheap Repository Tracts and published one hundred between 1795 and 1797, two million copies of which had been distributed by 1796, had [according to Victor Neuberg, *Popular Literature: A History and Guide,* 1977] "made her own collection of chapbooks so that she could learn the secret of their popularity." More and other tract writers developed an "anti-intellectual" approach meant to counteract not only the message of radical pamphlets but the popular engagement with political thought which they had fostered as well. For such purposes a return to the chapbook mode helped both to insure the tracts' popularity and to restore the simpler, apolitical discursive mode temporarily displaced by Paine's intellectual vernacular. As a result, "throughout the *Cheap Repository* the characters and narrative devices of traditional chapbooks were turned to moral purposes" [in the words of Samuel Pickering, *John Locke and Children's Books in Eighteenth-Century England,* 1981].

From a historicist perspective it becomes evident that, like the chapbook tradition of which they made a part, fairy tales could represent a harmless, pacifying alternative to radical intellectualism rather than a threat to moral seriousness. And in the early nineteenth century fairyland found unexpected allies in writers who found in fantasy a happy escape from more direct assaults on conventional morality and conservative politics. If not always edifying, the fairy tale was at least, when compared with the "master pamphlets of the day" (*Prelude* [1850]), harmless. A reviewer for the *Christian Observer* (censuring, of all things, Dr. Bowdler's *Family Shakespeare*) commended fairyland for its very distance from controversial issues: "Had the creative fancy of the poets merely summoned into being elves, fairies, and other denizens of their ideal world, not the most marble-hearted moralist would have interdicted the perusal of the drama. Oberon, Puck, Titania, Cobweb and Peachblossom [sic], as far as our recollection goes, are very innoxious characters." *The London Magazine* in 1820 praised the "moral tendency" of Tabart's *Popular Fairy Tales,* while deploring the "corrupting" and "contaminating" "licentiousness" of the current vogue for social satire in children's poetry, a dangerous form undoubtedly produced by political hacks: "They are most probably the same who bring out the political caricatures, and personal lampoons of the day . . . They are evidently done by men ready to do anything."

The *London Magazine's* reviewer was further exercised by the imposition of "modern criticism" on "the solemn traditions of a people": "The nursery songs and stories, to have their proper effects, should be permitted, like the common law, to depend solely on tradition." Here the appeal to "solemn traditions," the privileging of oral over written discourse, and the analogy with English common law signal the reviewer's conceptual adherence to the Burkean conservatism which, as James Chandler has shown [in *Wordsworth's Second Nature,* 1984], had so decisive an influence on the development of Wordsworth's thought in the later 1790s. Chandler traces the increasing emphasis in Wordsworth's writing on custom, on rural traditions, and on oral tales to Burke's valorization of habit and tradition, which together constitute what Chandler terms a "second nature" for both writers. Wordsworth's Pedlar in "The Ruined Cottage" exemplifies an education guided by "second nature" rather than the suspect rational approach associated with Godwin and the Edgeworths:

> Small need had he of books; for many a tale
> Traditionary round the mountains hung,
> And many a legend peopling the dark woods
> Nourished Imagination in her growth.

> (lines 167-70).

Although Chandler does not consider the role of fairy tales in Wordsworth's attack on rational education in book 5 of *The Prelude,* his discussion of Wordsworth's "tales traditionary" and of the "ideological purport of writing that aspires to the condition of speech" helps situate the early Romantics' defense of fairy tales in terms of the contemporary politics of literacy.

Wordsworth argues in *The Prelude* for a kind of "negative education" which might seem to ally him with Rousseau. Yet his criticisms of innovatory educational schemes in book 5 are in fact directed against the rational school of educators and writers for children in a direct line of descent from *Emile.* Wordsworth opposes the literature of this movement, with its emphasis on utilitarian knowledge and rational explanations—writings fit for a "dwarf man" (*Prelude* [1805]) rather than a child—preferring the fairy tales and legends of his own childhood:

> Oh, give us once again the wishing-cap
> Of Fortunatus, and the invisible coat
> Of Jack the Giant-killer, Robin Hood,
> And Sabra in the forest with St George.

In contrast to the Satanic architecture of the rationalists—

> These mighty workmen of our later age
> Who with a broad highway have overbridged
> The froward chaos of futurity

—the traditional tales are presented as a literal "second nature," a landscape through which Wordsworth and Coleridge freely wandered as children:

> wandering as we did
> Through heights and hollows and bye-spots of
>   tales
> Rich with indigenous produce, open ground
> Of fancy, happy pastures ranged at will.

The organic "produce" of the tales is further equated with the traditionary teachings of the poet's mother, "Fetching her goodness . . . from times past," a "parent hen amid her brood" whose maxims are as natural as the "innocent milk" of "mothers' breasts." The popular ballads of children and peasants are no less natural: "Wren-like warblings made / For cottagers and spinners of the wheel . . . / Food for the hungry ears of little ones." And his childhood "slender abstract of the *Arabian Tales*" makes part of a textual landscape, "a block / Hewn from a mighty quarry." Because of their rootedness in tradition, their oral perpetuation among the folk, the "tales that charm away the wakeful night / In Araby" gain the permanence and inevitability of rocks, and stones, and trees: "These spread like day, and something of the shape / Of these will live till man should be no more."

Although the organicized text is a common trope throughout Wordsworth's poetry and criticism, his particular insistence on naturalizing fairy tales through metaphor and his Burkean emphasis on an oral tradition equivalent in its permanence to nature suggest a subtly conservative impetus behind the Romantic defense of fantasy. Wordsworth in *The Prelude* is hardly advocating increases in literacy and political awareness among the rural laboring classes. By 1805, he had firmly rejected the "master pamphlets of the day," maintaining that their effect upon him had been disastrous and barely reparable. In a letter dated a few years later, writing of the "objectionable" contents of "penny and two-penny histories," Wordsworth expressed his wish to supplant them with "indigenous produce" of his own: "I have so much felt the influence of these straggling papers, that I have many a time wished that I had talents to produce songs, poems, and little histories, that might circulate among other good things in this way, supplanting partly the bad; flowers and useful herbs to take place of weeds" (letter to Francis Wrangham, 5 June 1808). Wordsworth's advocacy of fairy tales as "innocent" food for rural folk and children—readers of "class-literature"—can be seen, like More's use of the chapbook, as yet another appropriation of the popular tale in the interests of returning the new mass readership to an apolitical, class-specific discourse.

Wordsworth's defense of fairy tales in *The Prelude* is usually viewed from a very different perspective, as

Come take up your Hats, and away let us hafte,
To the Butterfly's Ball, and the Graffhopper's feaft.

And there came the Gnat, and the Dragon-Fly too,
And all their relations, Green, Orange, and Blue.

An 1807 illustration for William Roscoe's The Butterfly's Ball.

growing out of his deep suspicion of new educational modes seeking to limit, indoctrinate, and trap the child in a "pinfold of his own conceit," constantly superintended by "some busy helper." Here fairy tales might be seen as providing an ideologically neutral "open ground" between the radical pamphlet and the reactionary tract, both symptomatic of the politicization of education in "these too industrious times." There is still much to be said for such a perspective, although it should be placed within a more fully developed account of contemporary theories of education than one based on Wordsworth's simple opposition of rationalist jailers and undisturbed natural fosterage. Wordsworth's own involvement in the educational debates of the early nineteenth century, for example, suggests a more complicated story. Within a decade of

composing the 1805 *Prelude,* Wordsworth (along with Coleridge and Robert Southey) had become an advocate of Andrew Bell's "Madras system," designed initially to facilitate the socialization of the half-Indian children of English colonial officers, and brought to England in order to provide efficient, minimal schooling, through a system of teachers and student "monitors" for poor children. In his own account of the Madras system, Bell opposed his method's inculcation of "habits of industry, morality and religion" to those "Utopian schemes for the universal diffusion of knowledge" which would "confound that distinction of ranks and classes of society, on which the general welfare hinges." Wordsworth shared Bell's distaste for the new institutions designed to provide substantial and continuing education for English laborers, like the Mechanics' Institutes, eventually characterizing them as "unnatural" schemes whose "means do not pay respect to the order of things," hotbeds of "discontented spirits and insubordinate and presumptuous workmen," (letter to Hugh James Rose, late January 1829).

Wordsworth's depiction of the fairy tale as a natural rather than a cultural product demands critical scrutiny not simply for its contemporary political implications. In assigning the fairy tale an absolute origin, and in thus claiming for it a transcendent status beyond criticism, the early Romantics set the tone for many of the literary studies of fairy tales to follow. Claims to a pure traditional status and oral, folk origins of the fairy tale inform the work of critics as diverse as Roger Sale, Bruno Bettelheim, and Jack Zipes—three of the most widely influential writers on children's literature at the present time. And yet their work relies on Romantic theories of the fairy tale which have been widely discredited by folklorists and social historians alike.

W. H. Auden's "Afterward" to George MacDonald's *The Golden Key* typifies the persistence of the Romantic idealization of fairy tales: "Most fairy tales and myths have come down to us from a prehistoric past, anonymous stories which cannot be attributed to the conscious invention of any individual author." Such an appeal to an historical, communal, and necessarily oral origin underlies the approaches of the humanist Roger Sale, the psychoanalyst Bruno Bettelheim, and the Marxist Jack Zipes, although the latter does specify a feudal, "pre-capitalist folk" origin. The Romantic myth of origin is maintained in support of the claim, in Sale and Bettelheim, that fairy tales are universal (and unassailable) expressions of human experience and, in Zipes, that European fairy tales express a utopian and thus inherently "subversive" collective folk consciousness.

There is no reason, however, to believe that most traditional fairy tales are particularly ancient, orally (or collectively) composed, or of a folk origin. As the folklorist Alan Dundes has recently pointed out [in

"Fairy Tales from a Folklorist Perspective," *Fairy Tales and Society,* 1986], "the reality of far too much of what passes for fairy tale scholarship . . . is that [unadulterated, oral] fairy tale texts are not considered." Folklorists agree that many tales in the standard repertory are not properly oral folktales at all. Stith Thompson [in *The Folktale,* 1946], for example, states: "That many of our European and Asiatic folktales go back to a literary source is as clear as any fact in scholarship can be made." Max Lüthi rejects a folk origin for fairy tales altogether [in *Once Upon a Time: On the Nature of Fairy Tales,* 1976]: "Fairy tales certainly do not originate among simple folk but with great poets, perhaps the so-called 'initiated' or religious poets"; and [in *The European Folktale: Form and Nature,* 1982] Lüthi questions the antiquity of the tales in general: "Students of the folktale have not been able to agree whether the tales still current today are many thousands of years old or only a few hundred." [In *The Classic Fairy Tales,* 1974] Iona and Peter Opie find that far from degenerating from "whole and perfect" oral originals, the "classic" fairy tales have as often gained value through literary retellings: "They are as likely to have acquired significance, or to have acquired fresh significance, as they passed through sophisticated communities, as to have lost it." And the Opies (like Ellis) point out the irony of the Grimms transcribing tales from supposedly untainted oral sources later traced to their originals in Andersen or Perrault.

Another quarrel raised by folklorists and historians with the Romantic view of fairy tales concerns the importance of context in the telling or writing of a tale. As Dundes argues in "Textures, Text, and Context," a tale cannot be accurately interpreted apart from its specific tellings, through which its message can vary considerably with the teller's audience and purpose. Robert Darnton has shown that the significance of a tale like "Little Red Riding Hood" depends on whether it is told with a cautionary or merely amusing purpose, and Ruth Bottigheimer has recently demonstrated [in *Fairy Tales and Society*] how fairy tale heroines in the Grimms' tales are "silenced" in accordance with the dominant ideology: "To the extent that these tales corroborated and codified the values of a society in which they appeared, they reinforced them powerfully, symbolizing and codifying the status quo and serving as paradigms for powerlessness." A tale can as likely be told (or published) for a repressive as for an imaginatively liberating effect. Humanists commonly complained that nurses and other paid caretakers used supernatural tales to terrify their charges into submission, a complaint we have already seen made by Locke. The folklorist Rudolf Schenda [in "Telling Tales—Spreading Tales: Change in the Communicative Forms of a Popular Genre," *Fairy Tales and Society*], after dismissing the "orality of fairy tales" and their "folk or lower-class origins," cites as early evidence that such tales were indeed told to children the author of a 1726 German dissertation who "writes about nursemaids and old women who frighten little girls in order to force their spirit and their common sense under the yoke of blind obedience."

For Schenda, the "idolatry" informing the Romantic and current literary approaches to fairy tales is not only incorrect but misguided as well, "a denial of what the folk really recounted and what the actual psycho-social requirements of the members of the lower class were." It seems ironic that a Marxist critic like Zipes, whose approach is anything but unsophisticated, should nevertheless adapt the Romantic myth of a pure origin in order to support a "subversive" reading of fairy tales as projections of the utopian strivings of an underclass. Folklorists and social historians, on the contrary, view the folk tale as a predominantly conservative form. Lüthi (whom Zipes frequently cites) cautions against reading fairy tales as expressions of wish-fulfillment in general, and as "the literature of the poverty-stricken" in particular. The Opies similarly note that "the lowly are seldom made noble. . . . Fairy tales are unlike popular romances in that they are seldom the enactments of dream wishes." Darnton explicitly rejects a "subversive" reading of fairy tales: "It would be in vain to search in such fantasies for the germ of republicanism. To dream of confounding a king by marrying a princess was hardly to challenge the moral basis of the Old Regime." Far from embodying "latent . . . radicalism," the folktale trickster validates the system by successfully exploiting its loopholes.

Whether we view the fairy tale as a safety valve for lower class aspirations, as politically neutral entertainment, or as a particularly subtle instrument of socialization, it would be naive uncritically to celebrate Wordsworth and his literary circle for liberating children's literature. When the Romantic brief for the fairy tale is set against contemporary debates on literacy and education, and when the traditionalist, conservative discourse of Wordsworth's defense has been traced to its Burkean matrix, it becomes more difficult to distance the Romantics from the common practice of fairy tale appropriation. Unlike the Grimms or the English ballad collectors, the Romantics were not motivated by the rediscovery of a national folk culture or by local antiquarianism, since the tales they mention most often and most fondly derive from a Persian literary collection by way of an Arabic recension and French translation. The "revival" of the fairy tale does fit remarkably well, however, with the call for a harmless "food" for the new mass readership recalled by Hazlitt, with the conscious attempts of More and others to reestablish the apolitical discourse of the chapbooks, and with Burke's influential valorization, in response to revolution in France and radicalism in England, of custom and tradition.

Unlike William Blake, whose *Songs of Innocence*—particularly "The Lamb," "The Chimney Sweeper," and "The Little Black Boy"—expose and deconstruct the disciplinary strategies informing contemporary children's literature, schooling, and religious instruction alike, Wordsworth responds to the politicization of childhood in the 1790s by idealizing the child and attributing to it an "ideology-proof, organic sensibility" naturally resistant to radical and conservative indoctrination alike [Richardson, "The Politics of Childhood: Wordsworth, Blake, and Catechistic Method," *ELH* 56 (1989)]. In place of Blake's subversive songs with their poetics of resistance, Wordsworth chose to advocate instead an "innocent," traditional children's reading that implicitly supported the reaction against an informed and politically engaged lower-class readership—"discontented spirits" and "presumptuous workmen."

Such a conclusion will seem harsh, and is admittedly polemical. It is meant, however, as a step toward rethinking the role of childhood in late eighteenth- and early nineteenth-century culture, a project which requires a profound revaluation of Romantic attitudes toward education and children's reading. Rather than maintain a simplistic opposition between didacticism and fantasy, indoctrination and a negative "natural" education—a model inherited from the Romantics themselves—critical studies might profitably develop more complex approaches attuned to the intricate politics of literacy and education in the Romantic period. A new history of children's literature in England, for example, could take into account such sympathetic reappraisals of didactic writers as Marilyn Butler's work on Maria Edgeworth and Mitzi Myers's on Mary Wollstonecraft, as well as the critique of fairy tales posed by feminist critics like Marcia Lieberman and Karen Rowe. The study of Romantic attitudes toward education could take greater cognizance of the Romantics' own involvement in debates on educational policy, the links between rationalist education schemes and radical politics, the conservative reaction against education for the poor, and Michel Foucault's suggestive juxtaposition of the discourses of the prison, the factory, and the school in *Discipline and Punish*. And studies of nineteenth-century childhood generally could profit from greater attention to Jacqueline Rose's analysis [in *The Case of Peter Pan or The Impossibility of Children's Fiction,* 1984] of the special "contradictions and difficulties" involved in addressing "how our culture constitutes and reproduces its image of the child." Such revaluations demand, however, that we first assess our own investment in the Romantic idealization of childhood and its fairy tales.

> **Knoepflmacher describes the challenge of Victorian fantasy literature:**
>
> Torn between the opposing demands of innocence and experience, the author who resorts to the wishful, magical thinking of the child nonetheless feels compelled, in varying degrees, to hold on to the grown-up's circumscribed notions about reality. In the better works of fantasy of the period, this dramatic tension between the outlooks of adult and childhood selves becomes rich and elastic: conflict and harmony, friction and reconciliation, realism and wonder, are allowed to interpenetrate and co-exist.
>
> *U.C. Knoepflmacher, "The Balancing of Child and Adult: An Approach to Victorian Fantasies for Children,"* Nineteenth-Century Fiction, *1983.*

Roderick McGillis

SOURCE: "Fantasy as Adventure: Nineteenth Century Children's Fiction," in *Children's Literature Association Quarterly,* Vol. 8, No. 3, Fall, 1983, pp. 18-22.

[*In the excerpt that follows, McGillis studies the ambivalence about fantasy in Victorian adventure stories, noting a simultaneous attraction to and fear of "the disruption of social reality" that fantasy promises.*]

In *The Adventurer* [1974], [Paul] Zweig suggests that in the nineteenth century, adventure, like the quest romance, became internalized; he also suggests that a "resemblance exists between the adventurer exploring the countries of the marvelous and the 'absent' one: each finds his way to the 'other' world and returns to tell the story." The "absent one" is the shaman who, through illness or some other means, transports to a mysterious world of hidden realities. As Zweig argues:

> The shaman's vocation as an ecstatic traveler resembles that of the archaic adventurer. Both forge an immunity to the perils of the demonic world by mastering them. Both return from their journey bearing stories which sustain the humanity of those who are destined to exist within the circle of domestic realities. The story itself is a way of naming the unnameable, extending the net of language into the obscure seas which defy human foresight. Telling his tale of struggles and triumphs in the demon countries, the shaman pushes back the essential ignorance in which men live, by exposing a further reach of darkness to the clarity of words.

Although fear of the shaman—or what he represents—runs through much popular Victorian children's literature, we can also recognize something of this character in the best works of the period. What makes George

MacDonald's *At the Back of the North Wind* (1871) such a strong and effective book, and Lewis Carroll's *Alice's Adventures in Wonderland* (1865) such a troublesome and complex book, is their acceptance of what the shaman in his trance-like state stands for: the disruption of social reality, the overturning of easy certainties.

Most Victorian fantasies are uneasy with their notions of adventure, whether it be adventure in this world or in some "other" world. In Mrs. Ewing's *A Great Emergency* (1874), the narrator, nine-year-old Charlie, thinks that "to begin a life of adventure is to run away." He and a friend hide on board a barge and float along a canal to London, where they intend to stow away on a ship bound for exotic shores. While on his "adventure," Charlie misses the great emergency of the title, which takes place back at his home; at the story's end he reflects: "in my vain, jealous wild-goose chase after adventures I missed the chance of distinguishing myself in the only Great Emergency which has yet occurred in our family." As Gillian Avery remarks [in her "Introduction" to the 1969 edition of *A Great Emergency*], "The story turns on this, that adventures are as likely to happen on one's own doorstep as over the other side of the fence," but more importantly she notes the "further moral," that the dullness of life is in fact "preferable to disaster." In short, for Mrs. Ewing adventure is less than respectable. Charlie, an adult at the end of *A Great Emergency,* chides himself for being "still but too apt to dream!" Indeed, for a great number of Victorian writers for children, dreams are the stuff of childhood, acceptable if poorly moral, but to be set aside when one matures.

Attitudes to fantasy in the Victorian period may have been set by a work written before the turn of the nineteenth century, Coleridge's *Rime of the Ancient Mariner*. Responding to Mrs. Barbauld's complaint that the poem lacked a moral, Coleridge asserted that it had too much moral. The pat "He prayeth best, who loveth best / All things both great and small" appeared, in retrospect, too moral to Coleridge, as if he realized that a story like the Mariner's was too rich, too haunting, too mysterious, to be captured in such aphoristic pointedness. Clearly, the wedding guest who listens to, who cannot choose but hear, the story perceives something other, something darker, which the moral conclusion the Mariner tags onto his story will not explain. The wedding guest departs a sadder and wiser man; he turns from the wedding feast, from the world of domestic relations and the celebration of the patterns of social reality. As listener to the story, he has been transported by the storyteller, the shamanistic Mariner who is periodically seized by a compulsion to retell the story of his own transport to a world where he struggled with demonic powers and confronted mysteries of the soul.

Coleridge's poem, then, exhibits two tendencies, both of which inform Victorian children's fantasies. First, there is the tendency to diminish adventure, to reduce it to moral statement, and in the process, devalue it. Once the adventure in a fantastic realm is over it is best to leave it behind, perhaps even to forget it, since it threatens to remove permanently those who experience it—like the mariner—from the duties and responsibilities of mature social activity. Second, there is the less-common (indeed, extremely rare) tendency to value the fantastic realm and those who return from it to speak of its mysteries as liberators from the inanimate cold world of duty and responsibility. The shaman's experience, which I am equating with a fictional character's or a reader's experience of fantasy, shakes those who hear it free of the lethargy of custom; it is subversive. From this perspective, Huck Finn participates in a shamanistic experience in lighting out, as he does, for the territories; he departs from the world of social contingencies to enter an "other" world. It is not difficult to understand why Twain's contemporaries were less than enthusiastic about the book.

Generally, Victorian children's books use the "other" world for both fantastic adventure and moral teaching, but they make clear their deeply felt suspicion of fantasy adventure. Examples are numerous. Jack, in Jean Ingelow's *Mopsa the Fairy* (1869), returns from Fairyland to sit on his father's knee and marvel "what a great thing a man was." Nothing so important exists in Fairyland and Jack is "glad he had come back." Mrs. Molesworth's *The Cuckoo Clock* (1877) is perhaps clearer: the heroine, Griselda, dreams at the end of the book of the cuckoo for the last time. In the morning "her pillow was wet with tears" and Mrs. Molesworth writes, "Thus many stories end. She was happy, very happy, in the thought of her kind new friends; but there were tears for the one she felt she had said farewell to, even though he was only a cuckoo in a clock."

The tone here is disquieting to a believer in fairyland, but even more disquieting is what Dinah Mulock has to say concerning belief in the wonders of fairyland in *The Little Lame Prince* (1874): "Now, I don't expect anybody to believe what I am going to relate, though a good many wise people have believed a good many sillier things. And as seeing's believing, and I never saw it, I cannot be expected implicitly to believe it myself, except in a sort of a way; and yet there is truth in it—for some people."

A tension exists here; it is as if Mulock wanted to be sure that the child reader did not take this as too seriously real. Is the fairytale real or not? Only childhood knows fantasy. In *The Adventures of a Brownie,* Mulock makes it clear that the brownie exists only for the child:

But, as Brownie was never seen, he was never suspected. And since he did no mischief—neither pinched the baby nor broke the toys, left no soap in the bath and no footmarks about the room—but was always a well-conducted Brownie in every way, he was allowed to inhabit the nursery (or supposed to do so, since, as nobody saw him, nobody could prevent him), until the children were grown up into men and women.

After that he retired into his coal cellar, and for all I know he may live there still, and have gone through hundreds of adventures since; but as I never heard them, I can't tell them. Only I think if I could be a little child again, I should exceedingly like a Brownie to play with me. Should not you?

For a writer like L. M. Montgomery—and for the most part Montgomery reflects the dominant nineteenth century attitudes—fantasy is wonderful in childhood, suggesting the child's independence of mind and his spirit of adventure. Anne of *Anne of Green Gables* (1908) and Davy Keith of *Anne of Avonlea* (1909) are refreshing counterparts to the many prim child characters in Victorian fiction, and Montgomery's attitude toward them differs markedly from, for example, Charlotte Yonge's attitude to Kate in *Countess Kate* (1862). In *Anne of Avonlea,* Anne confesses she likes Davy more than his better-behaved sister Dora because "Dora is too good." If, however, the exuberance of the child and his or her indulgence in fantasy continues into adulthood, the adult, although he or she may be wonderfully kind and likeable, must remain at a remove from real life, arrested in development like poor Miss Lavender Lewis in *Anne of Avonlea.* When Miss Lavender finally does get married at a belated forty-five years of age, Montgomery writes: "Miss Lavender drove away from the old life of dreams and make-believes to a fuller life of realities in the busy world beyond."

What makes the first Anne book—*Anne of Green Gables*—so interesting is its attempt to depict Anne as an adventurer, one who, in Zweig's terms, disrupts the pattern of social experience, one whose individualism is irrepressible, one in flight from social norms and habitual responses. But the book finally fails in this valiant attempt; Anne cannot play the shaman's role since it is she, not the people of Avonlea, who needs healing, and this healing is profoundly integrative rather than subversive. Anne, and the Cuthberts, move closer to the community and its values. In a later book, *The Story Girl* (1911), Montgomery expresses with moving intensity the conflict between conformity and the pull to fantasy, in a passage that is a precise statement of the nineteenth century attitude I have been examining:

There is such a place as fairyland—but only children can find the way to it. And they do not know that it is fairyland until they have grown so old that they forget the way. One bitter day, when they seek it and cannot find it, they realize what they have lost and that is the tragedy of life. One day the gates of Eden are shut behind them and the age of gold is over. Henceforth they must dwell in the common light of common day. Only a few, who remain children at heart, can ever find that fair, lost path again, and blessed are they above mortals. They, and only they can bring us tidings from that dear country where once we sojourned and from which we must evermore be exiles. The world calls them its singers and poets and artists and storytellers; but they are just people who have never forgotten the way to fairyland.

Fantasy has a strong tendency toward subversion, or transgression. It is *unheimlich*. At its best it shows us that our true home is elsewhere, not in the local communities in which we live day by day. Perhaps Lewis Carroll's *Alice's Adventures in Wonderland* furnishes us with the Victorian era's most compellingly ambivalent statement on fantasy. Alice's fantasy adventure is, of course, clearly a dream, her dream, and as such it is something Alice wakes from and leaves behind as she runs in to tea. Alice leaves her sister by the tree pondering Alice's dream and imagining Alice as a grownup telling tales to young children. Alice's dream, in other words, won't leave her; instead her trip to the "other" world will turn Alice into a storyteller, a shaman, who makes the eyes of children "bright and eager with many a strange tale, perhaps even with the dream of Wonderland of long ago." For these children there would not be the tedium of books "without pictures or conversations." Instead there will be Wonderland, the zany, the mad, the anarchic "other" world where aboveground certainties, social niceties, rules of decorum, and adult preoccupation with hierarchy, prestige, and justice are turned upside down. Here the rule is creative play, and survival depends on how swiftly one can turn an axis into axes or adapt to a game in which all the objects are alive. Indeed, Alice's problem is her inability to accept an overturning of the rules she has come to accept as natural: "they don't seem to have any rules in particular," she complains during the croquet game.

Here we should detect an anomaly. Alice does not enter into the madcap activity of Wonderland; she rarely, if ever, sees the fun in the antics of those she meets. When the Cheshire cat tells her she must be mad "or you wouldn't have come here," Alice doesn't think "that proved it at all." She leaves the Mad Tea Party "in great disgust." She is glad when the Lobster Quadrille is over, and in the end she rejects the whole dream, scoffing that the Queen of Hearts and her court are "nothing but a pack of cards." Why would she remember with fondness a dream in which she was bossed, bullied, threatened, and belittled? All we know is that Alice runs off to tea thinking "what a wonderful dream it had been." Then Carroll shifts the point of view to

Alice's sister, and as she contemplates Alice's dream, she domesticates it:

> So she sat on, with closed eyes, and half believed herself in Wonderland, though she knew she had but to open them again, and all would change to dull reality—the grass would be only rustling in the wind, and the pool rippling to the waving of the reeds—the rattling teacups would change to tinkling sheep bells, and the Queen's shrill cries to the voice of the shepherd boy—and the sneeze of the baby, the shriek of the Gryphon, and all the other queer noises, would change (she knew) to the confused clamor of the busy farmyard—while the lowing of the cattle in the distance would take the place of the Mock Turtle's heavy sobs.

The dream becomes a pastoral, just what Alice herself wanted in the first place when she saw through the tiny door the garden with its "bright flowers and cool fountains." But the pastoral feeling here is surely at variance with the disorder of the dream, its unsettling, nightmarish quality. Carroll refuses to decide whether the dream in all its subversive glory or the dream as filtered through a nostalgic recollection is what matters. Alice's sister only "half believes" herself in Wonderland; she knows she need only open her eyes to have all return to "dull reality." But Carroll's parenthetical remark that all would change (she knew) hints that for Carroll this dull reality might not be so dull. The tone here is elegaic, pastoral, and romantic (in a rather glib way), and it is difficult to accept that Carroll sees the rippling pool, waving reeds, tinkling sheep bells, lowing cattle, and all as dull. What has happened to the energetic play of the dream? In this, the first *Alice* book, Carroll's intense delight in adventure, his willingness to wander in wonderful seas because there is always a shore on the other side, is in the end tempered by his equally strong adherence to certitude and community. Alice will become a storyteller, and thus control the journey away from the familiar world; as adventurer she risked her life and sanity ("It's really dreadful . . . the way all the creatures argue. It's enough to drive one crazy," she says), but as storyteller she shall take on [what Zweig calls] "the truest meaning of the shaman's role as healer." But not if, as her sister projects, she tames the dream. By sliding into Alice's sister's point of view, Carroll leaves the question of the dream's subversive potential ambiguous.

Like so many nineteenth-century fantasists, Carroll might well be charged with reneging on his faith in the value of imagination. He might have something in common with those writers Anita Moss describes as having only a narrow, moralistic interest in fantasy. Speaking of Catherine Sinclair, F. E. Paget, Mark Lemon, Christina Rossetti, George MacDonald, and others [in "Crime and Punishment, or Development, in Fairy Tales," *Proceedings of the Seventh Annual Con-*ference *of the Children's Literature Association,* 1982, Anna West] Moss writes,

> While all of these writers consciously espoused the value of the imagination and its function in the lives of children and their books, none of them sustained a commitment to the pleasures of fantasy and the imagination all the way through their stories. Sooner or later they all turned their fairytales into narrow lessons. In each story the child protagonist, often a lively and spirited child, is removed from the ordinary world to a fantastic world of terror, placed under the control of a tyrannical adult figure, and transformed into the pious and saintly children to which early Victorian audiences apparently responded. One notes in these stories a deep split in the creative purposes of the writers between their avowed attitudes toward fantasy, children, and the imagination and their actual practices, a bifurcation often manifested in the split structures of the stories themselves.

Clearly, Carroll's *Alice* books escape such criticism through their sheer delight in invention, although the nuances I detect in the ending of *Alice's Adventures in Wonderland* are full-blown in *Sylvie and Bruno.* But George MacDonald is an altogether different case. Here is a writer whose commitment to imagination is fervent; for him, fantasy must inform reality at all times, not just in childhood and not merely at odd moments when we have time from the business of living to perk up our lives with a heady dose of moral fantasy. The book Moss cites as an example of MacDonald's "narrowly focused and unpleasant didacticism" is *The Lost Princess: A Double Story.* Now, only an insensitive reader would attempt to defend this book as completely successful, but it does offer a remarkably clear instance of MacDonald's belief in adventure. In Zweig's terms, MacDonald's sense of adventure may be closer to the non-adventure of *Robinson Crusoe,* since he places such emphasis on the domestic virtues of hard work and regularity, but MacDonald's insistence on constant movement, constant becoming, reminds us of the adventurer's compelling need to act and to contend.

The Lost Princess, first published as *The Wise Woman,* concerns two young girls, one a princess and one a shepherd's daughter, one who is willful and given to tantrums, and one who is conceited and self-complacent, but both of whom are selfish and unpleasant. The girls are taken in hand by a mysterious wise woman, who lives in a strange house on a wild heath. One point in this relentlessly pointless book is that whether you live in a cottage or in a castle you are still susceptible to complacency, to a settled belief in the rightness of things as perceived by the mind habituated to the familiar. The Wise Woman's function is to break up the ice of fixed ideas and expectations, for she knows that without conflict, without the piquancy of fear, there will be no progression.

But MacDonald's is not a simple moralistic vision; he does not merely offer pat goals, although at times (and many times in this book) he does speak in moralistic aphorisms reminiscent of the he-prayeth-best-who-loveth-best variety. Like his Romantic precursors, MacDonald wishes to wake his readers from a sleep of reason, and his usual method is through polysemous and paradoxical language. For example, when he speaks of Agnes, the shepherd girl, MacDonald says that she "had very fair abilities, and, were she once but made humble, would be capable not only of doing a good deal in time but of beginning at once to grow to no end." Grow to no end? This colloquial utterance means that Agnes might grow into a much better child; in other words, it reads figuratively. But MacDonald also means quite literally that Agnes's growth will be endless, that no articulation of her final identity is possible, since existence means constant, indeed eternal, movement toward identity. The word "end" contains spatial and temporal significance; MacDonald refuses to posit a goal, a point in time or space to which we set our sights. Consequently, there can be no settling complacently in the thought that an end has been achieved.

What I referred to earlier as this "relentlessly pointless book" should be clearer now. MacDonald's books, his best books anyway, deliberately avoid closure. Here is the beginning of the book's final paragraph: "And that is all my double story. How double it is, if you care to know, you must find out. If you think it is not finished—I never knew a story that was." Stories, like life and like adventures, must not end. And MacDonald's challenge to the reader to find out just how double his story is ought to remind us of MacDonald's fierce belief in two worlds coterminus with each other; for MacDonald what we might call a fantasy world can, and for some adventurous spirits does, inform mundane reality.

We can see this interplay between fantasy and reality best in *At the Back of the North Wind*, a book that Colin Manlove [*Modern Fantasy*, 1975] argues has a similar bifurcation to the kind Moss describes:

> we must feel that the supernatural episodes are so divided from the natural as to suggest that the whole book is the result of two quite separate imaginative acts. In metaphysical terms, the two worlds do interpenetrate, inasmuch as we are shown that the sorrows of this life are divinely ordained for our supernatural good; and, since North Wind exists and operates within the "real" world, they are also to some extent physically linked. The latter world, however, never becomes transfigured, as North Wind is only occasionally present to Diamond . . . Perhaps some explanation for this lies in the fact that the "real" setting of this book is largely the city, London, and MacDonald was more able to find God (through his sub-vicars) immanent in country rather than town. . . .

But such a "split" overlooks Diamond, who carries North Wind's spiritual influence to those who live "in the perfectly normal world of Victorian London." As the narrator reminds the reader on several occasions, Diamond has been to the back of the north wind, to the "other" world, and the experience has made a poet of him, or in terms of this discussion, a shaman. Diamond's shamanistic power is evident in the chapter titled, "The Drunken Cabman," which is structurally as well as thematically at the center of the book.

By this point, Diamond has been to the back of the north wind. His journey to this land of mysteries takes place during periods of illness; in short, Diamond's fever transports him the way the shaman's ecstasy transports him. Diamond's journey takes place in the first half of the book, and by the Drunken Cabman chapter he has already begun to assume a special, shamanistic status, exerting a positive influence on those he meets. At the beginning of the Drunken Cabman chapter Diamond hears a noise in the night; he rouses, realizes it is time that "somebody did something," puts on a few clothes, and goes to the drunken cabman's rooms, where he finds the cabman in a stupor, his wife sobbing, and their baby "wailing in the cradles." MacDonald refers to Diamond as "one of God's messengers," a psychopomp (or soul guide) in child's clothing. The dragon this messenger must face is Misery, and Diamond confronts it with songs, songs that put the cabman into a calming sleep. When he wakes, the cabman hears Diamond talking to the baby about the thirsty devil. Diamond's words are of little importance except as "chanting," as incantation. But the effect on the cabman is reminiscent of the effect of the Ancient Mariner on the wedding guest. The cabman, MacDonald tells us, "could not withdraw his gaze from Diamond's white face and big eyes." Rather than frightening the cabman, Diamond soothes him. The cabman, if not a sadder, is certainly a wiser man for the experience, and a transformation of his life begins.

The narrator is similarly drawn to Diamond: "It seemed to me, somehow, as if little Diamond possessed the secret of life, and was himself what he was so ready to think the lowest living thing—an angel of God with something special to say or do." The final chapters of the book recount the narrator's friendship for Diamond and his belief that Diamond has something precious to offer, but just what always remains slightly beyond understanding. What should be clear, however, is that in Diamond two worlds—fantasy and reality, dream and reality, the supernatural and the natural, the certain and the uncertain—are reconciled. Diamond subverts such categories, destroys our wrong-headed insistence on separating them, and consequently, removes the fear of the other world (some might call it Death in this instance) and inhibits us from the single vision of Nancy and Jim, who fear thunder and lightning. Diamond is an adventurer, not because he travels to the back of the north wind, but because of his intrepid faith in the rightness of things and his trust in the mystery of uncertainties. He never receives a definite answer as to whether North Wind is only a dream, yet dream or not she gives him strength and vision. Diamond, and all of MacDonald's heroes, are new kinds of adventurers, adventurers in imaginative and spiritual possibility. The monsters they face are Doubt, Misery, Fear, Death, and Self. They overcome by being, as MacDonald calls Diamond, "wise soldiers" prepared for conflict within and without, secure in the knowledge that to get to the back of the north wind is only the first stage on an endless journey.

Susan Naramore Maher

SOURCE: "Recasting Crusoe: Frederick Marryat, R. M. Ballantyne and the Nineteenth-Century Robinsonade," in *Children's Literature Association Quarterly,* Vol. 13, No. 4, Winter, 1988, pp. 169-75.

[*In the following article, Maher traces popular response to Daniel Defoe's* Robinson Crusoe *(1719) in the nineteenth century, charting both criticism of the novel and its eventual influence on Victorian adventure fiction for boys.*]

When the formidable Leslie Stephen dismissed Daniel Defoe's *Robinson Crusoe* [1719] as "a book for boys rather than men" [in "Defoe's Novels," *The Cornhill Magazine,* 1868], he was not far off the mark. By the time Stephen penned his disparaging comments in 1868, *Robinson Crusoe* had inspired numerous progeny earmarked for the young. Following the 1814 English translation of J.D.R. Wyss's *The Swiss Family Robinson,* among the most famous of the so-called Robinsonades that explore and adapt the premise of Defoe's novel, Robinsonades commanded an eager juvenile readership ready to devour the latest fiction about castaways, no matter how didactic or improbable the tale. In the nineteenth century, *Robinson Crusoe* itself became a prized nursery book, favored by children for its detail and adventure, by parents for its religious sentiment and work ethic. Indeed, Stephen's unfavorable assessment of Crusoe is anomalous. The popular nineteenth-century reading of *Robinson Crusoe* celebrates the tales of redemption and of hard work rewarded. Crusoe heroically combats madness and despair, builds himself a veritable empire on his island, transforms Friday into a loyal manservant, defends against heathen savages (native and European), and ends up with a fortune—all in all a favored son of God, an exemplary man. The words of the minor Victorian novelist, George Borrow, typify nineteenth-century admiration, as he reaches a pitch of Crusoe idolatry in *Lavengro* (1851): *Robinson Crusoe* "was a book which has exerted over the minds of Englishmen an influence certainly greater than any other of modern times . . . a book from which the most luxuriant and fertile of our modern prose writers have drunk inspiration; a book, moreover, to which from the hardy deeds which it narrates, and the spirit of strange and romantic enterprise which it tends to awaken, England owes many of her astonishing discoveries both by sea and by land, and no inconsiderable part of her naval glory."

Reviewers like Borrow omit mention of Crusoe's introspection, his inner torment and fear; instead, Crusoe, whose proportions and reputation grow increasingly sentimental, shrilly patriotic in nineteenth-century reviews, comes to signify Empire, the outer world of action, power, and expansion. His ability to subdue, to husband intractable nature into compliance; his reacceptance of both heavenly and earthly favors; his own metamorphosis into a patriarchal father of sorts prove invaluable archetypal matter to nineteenth-century writers and readers alike. Moreover, reviewers, whether praising or condemning Crusoe's vogue, agree on one thing: his tale is peculiarly suited to a boy's taste. It is significant that Stephen specifically relegates *Robinson Crusoe* to the hands of boys—for its textual mixture of adventure and enterprise, of survival and subjugation, as Mary F. Thwaite asserts [in *From Primer to Pleasure Reading,* 1963], "marks the true beginning of the adventure story for young people."

The transmutation of *Robinson Crusoe* by nineteenth-century readers into an imperialist fantasy explains its power over adventure fiction written for boys. Adventure, though read by girls, evolved into a distinctly masculine story type. By mid-century, as Patrick Brantlinger has suggested [in "Victorians and Africans: The Genealogy of the Myth of the Dark Continent," *Critical Inquiry* 12(1985)], "much imperialist discourse was . . . directed at a specifically adolescent audience, the future rulers of the world. In the works of Haggard, Captain Frederick Marryat, Mayne Reid, G.A. Henty, W.H.G. Kingston, Gordon Stables, Robert Louis Stevenson, and many others through Rudyard Kipling, Britain turned youthful as it turned outward." As *Robinson Crusoe* became codified by its Victorian audience, so, too, did its offspring, adventure books. *Crusoe*'s boys'-book imitators simplify its interplay of romance and realism in order to articulate a myth of cultural superiority. They recast their Crusoes into quintessential empire builders, create islands that signify a hierarchy of culture and race, and ultimately mirror a conquering people's mythology. The Robinsonade also suited the immediate professional aims of boys'-book writers, who sought to enlighten as well as entertain their young audience, to educate as well as exhilarate. Boys'-book writers, constrained by market forces, closely monitored by the champions of virtue, and saddled in an adventure formula, found in the Robinsonade the perfect sugared pill. Indeed, once writers for children seized upon the Robinsonade, writers of adult fiction left the genre well enough alone.

By the time the century's most memorable and influential British Robinsonades appeared, Frederick Marryat's *Masterman Ready* (1841-42) and R.M. Ballantyne's *The Coral Island* ('1857), the genre had become an institution of sorts. To isolate a character, to test his mettle and his culture's worthiness, had proven an efficacious as well as a popular concept. *Robinson Crusoe,* as Erhard Reckwitz has argued in his comprehensive survey of the genre, *Die Robinsonade* [1976], establishes a "language" that expresses crucial dialectical poles: form versus formlessness, construction versus destruction, nature versus nurture, survival versus death, the self versus the other. This dialectical structure articulates the interplay of culture and chaos, of faith and despair crucial to Defoe's narrative and to its permutations. The island setting, then, from Defoe on, serves as an archetypal laboratory for a society's ideology. Despite its undermining subtext—Crusoe continually fights his own inner fears and desires, never conclusively defeating either—Defoe's novel privileges an ideology that is protestant, middle class, and expansionist. Crusoe masters his island, his subjects, and his own waywardness, enabling him to recover an earthly Eden. It is no wonder, then, that *Robinson Crusoe* appealed to the Victorian mind and its tendency to privilege action, hard work, and material progress. Moreover, Crusoe's humbleness before God, his thanksgiving to a beneficent providence appeased those children's advocates, inspired by Maria Edgeworth, who might otherwise have denied children access to the novel.

Still, Edgeworth and others objected to the romance in Defoe's novel. Edgeworth warned in her influential *Practical Education* (1799) that "a boy, who at seven years old longs to be Robinson Crusoe, or Sinbad the Sailor, may at seventeen, retain the same taste for adventure and enterprise." Romance, adventure threaten the young mind and must be firmly collared by a practical outlook on life: in effect, readers like Edgeworth elevate Crusoe's father to the heroic level, for he rightly adheres to the middle station of life. They applaud Crusoe's minutely realized chronicle of recreation for it reclaims the middle station's dominion over his life. Evangelical writers quickly and successfully adapted the Robinsonade to quicken their young readers' religious sentiments and promote the middle station. Mary Elliott's *The English Hermit* (1822), Agnes Strickland's *The Rival Crusoes* (1826), Mrs. Hofland's (Barbara Wreaks Hoole) *The Young Crusoe* (1828), and Ann Fraser Tytler's popular *Leila; or, The Island* (1839) exploit the genre's inherent spiritual pattern to enforce duty and rightmindedness.

Significantly, Edgeworth's warning and the examples of these spiritual Robinsonades affected many writers of boys' adventure fiction throughout the nineteenth century, including writers of adventure Robinsonades, who were keenly aware of their role as socializers. *Robinson Crusoe* never synthesizes the push of culture and the pull of romance; an undertow of anarchic power disturbs the narrative of domestic achievement. Though master of acculturation on his island, Crusoe is beset by the devils of adventure and inner chaos; his obsessive wall building, as Paul Zweig suggests [in *The Adventurer,* 1974], "is almost ritualized, a psychic wall against loneliness." It is also a psychic wall against disorder, for the heart of darkness looms deep around and in him to the end. Boys'-book writers could ill afford such ambiguity. Nor were they free to imitate the license of earlier chapbook publishers, whose severely abridged editions of *Robinson Crusoe* delete the religious sections to glorify adventure. In Victorian boys' books, a highhanded morality keeps the freer hand of romance enchained. As the Robinsonade evolved into a children's genre in the eighteenth and nineteenth centuries, as *Robinson Crusoe* was increasingly relegated to children's bookshelves, a marked didacticism both sobered the young reading audience and mollified parents concerned that "adventure and enterprise" would corrupt their children. Still, the tempered romance of the nineteenth-century Robinsonade did not dissuade children from reading them. The virtually hundreds of Robinsonades that appeared in the bookstalls of the time testify to the genre's extreme popularity.

The choices that Frederick Marryat and Robert Michael Ballantyne made in recasting Crusoe tell us much about the influence of ideology on children's fiction, as well as the complex interchange between history, myth, and text. Marryat and Ballantyne had to find means to simplify the Robinsonade, to make it a mouthpiece for celebrating God and country. Their adventures must necessarily lack the subtle colorings of the prototype, *Robinson Crusoe,* a book written for adults, though beloved by children. In simplifying the Robinsonade, they produced romances that express an ambivalence to romance, novels that present a pedestrain realism. *Masterman Ready* and *The Coral Island,* the foremost Robinsonades of their day, were enthusiastically welcomed by critics. Indeed Marryat's novel rivaled the popularity of its forefather, *Robinson Crusoe.* F.J. Harvey Darton lauds it as "the most sincerely emotional of all the [Robinsonades]" [in *Children's Books in England,* 1982] and recent critical attention by J.S. Bratton, Jacqueline Rose, and Margery Fisher attest to its seminal importance in the boys'-book tradition. Ballantyne's adventure has been hailed as "perhaps the most famous of the nineteenth-century desert island tales" (*The Impact of Victorian Children's Fiction,* [by J.S. Bratton]). Translated into most European languages, *The Coral Island* has claimed such devoted, and critical, readers as Robert Louis Stevenson, J.M. Barrie, H.G. Wells, and William Golding—all creators of Robinsonades. Together their two novels present us with a fascinating look at the way mid-century romance was tempered by the braided currents of evangelical, romantic, and imperial discourse.

Frederick Marryat (1792-1848) initially earned his reputation as a novelist through the publication of sea tales for an adult readership. *Masterman Ready* marked the beginning of what Marryat affectionately called his "second harvest," his books for children. Written as a favor to his children, who requested a sequel to *The Swiss Family Robinson,* Marryat's Robinsonade is a corrective to J.D.R. Wyss's peaceable kingdom with its inaccurate assemblage of flora and fauna. More importantly, its author merges the influence of evangelical tract literature into its text, punctuating each chapter with a moral lesson and heads bowed in prayer. To this didactic end Marryat shipwrecks an aged sailor, Masterman Ready, the bizarrely named "Seagrave" family, father, mother, three sons and a daughter, and their black servant, Juno. The Seagraves are bound for Australia, emigrés of a better class who look forward to gentlemanly farming and large profits. But as the boat they are on, the ironically named *Pacific,* rounds the Cape of Good Hope, a terrible storm tosses it helplessly about, destroys its mast, and sets it afire with lightning. The crew selfishly abandons ship while the family is asleep, leaving them to a "watery death." Only one crew member, Masterman Ready, stays aboard, for he refuses to participate in a cowardly murder.

The tale of Ready's refusal to abandon the Seagraves, his newfound adoptive family, opposes the tale of his earlier abandonment of family, when, like Robinson Crusoe, he rejected the middle station of life for the lure of the sea. Part of the novel, then, chronicles the re-creation of society on an island wilderness; the other, given in bits and pieces in the form of Ready's reminiscences, chronicles the wilderness of the soul when God's love is rejected. Thus Marryat splits his narrative, balancing Ready's first-person spiritual autobiography about rebellion, folly, and ultimate salvation when he re-embraces God, against an omniscient narrator's account of the castaways' ordeal and triumph on a desert island. It is noteworthy that upon his delivery to the island with the Seagraves Ready is essentially a "saved" man. Though, as Mr. Seagrave notes, Ready analyzes himself "very minutely," his soul-searching lacks the drama of Crusoe's because there is no need for him to change.

The island story, with its emphases on affiliation and acculturation, is clearly separate from Ready's early freedom and rebellion. However romantic his flight from filial responsibility, from the French navy that impressed him, and from a South African jail, his reflections serve to teach the Seagrave children their duty to family, to homeland, and to God. In effect, his story potently enforces the claims of filiation. "When you have heard my story," Ready declares to William, Caroline, and Tommy Seagrave, "you will say that I have been very foolish in my time; and so I have; but if it proves a warning to you, it will, at all events, be of some use". Each recounted adventure lures the young Ready further away from the middle station and entangles him in offenses of pride. Ultimately, he squanders his youth, he is responsible for his mother's death (by broken heart), and he must learn that "the heart is deceitful and desperately wicked". His conversion puts an end to his wanderlust and he returns to England to find his mother in the grave and his would-be fortune dispersed to charity.

In this way, then, Marryat fences in romance for the greater good of his audience. He favors a realistic discourse that chronicles re-creation in order to instruct young minds. By transforming Crusoe's quest for selfhood into Ready's didactic oral history, Marryat dispenses with the island setting as spiritual test. Instead, the island narrative extols the social survival of the castaways and their transformation of the wilderness into an orderly settlement that exudes the imperial spirit of their homeland, England. Much of Marryat's text devotes itself to building plans and how-to-do information, furnishing its readers with a blue-print for survival. *Masterman Ready,* then, is an important milestone in the transformation of the Robinsonade. In *Robinson Crusoe,* the prototype, the hero learns that in order to survive, he, too, must be transformed. He must become the father he has rejected. This metamorphosis, which occurs after Crusoe's near fatal fever, drives the novel. As Michael Seidel has recently argued [in *Exile and the Narrative Imagination,* 1986], "Crusoe in exile is always discovering himself." But in the world of the Victorian Robinsonade, writers create characters who have already been changed for the better before their isolation, or leave out problems of self altogether. The emphasis in such Robinsonades, then, is on the outer world of action, of mastery, of domination. Ironically, Marryat, whose Robinsonade is meant to strengthen its readers' sense of religious duty, sets the stage for later juvenile Robinsonades (like those of Mayne Reid) that pay lip service to God or give up any pretense of preaching to the young. When the actions of characters become paramount, then adventure takes on increasing importance in the form of chance confrontations with wild beasts, cannibals, and pirates. However, in the sober world of *Masterman Ready,* adventure remains firmly indentured to Marryat's religious and cultural ideology.

In such a Robinsonade, as Jacqueline Rose asserts [in *The Case of Peter Pan or the Impossibility of Children's Fiction,* 1984], "the morality is the adventure." Each episode demonstrates how extraordinarily firm and plucky the Seagrave family—and by extension any British family—is. The initial storm and shipwreck force them to repress their darkest fears and learn to accept God's will cheerfully and gratefully. Sharks swim hungrily in their lagoon and indeed threaten little Tommy Seagrave, cast adrift in a rowboat, whom Ready saves. The end results of this episode are a speech on God's mysterious ways and all heads bowed in prayer. A raging typhoon smashed up their camp, but the Seagraves and Ready pick up the pieces and commence building a plantation, a home, a barnyard with outhouses, turtle and fish ponds, a salt pan, a water hole, a road system, and a harbor. Within one year the island is completely conquered. The possibility of cannibal invasion worries Ready, but he and the Seagraves are never rattled as Crusoe is rattled when faced with a single human foot print in the sand. They build a stockade, fortify themselves with arms and supplies, and then "trust in God."

Marryat's castaways are fortunate in another respect—they can retrieve much from the abandoned ship, including tools, guns and powder, clothing, books, stationery, pens, utensils, even fine china. All the comforts of home, including two servants, Juno and Ready, are available to them. In the words of Paul Elmen [in his book *William Golding,* 1967], their subjugation of the wilderness validates a nineteenth-century myth "that the white man's burden would be easily borne, that the savage corners of the earth would succumb to the attraction of the cult of the gentleman, and that in time the jungles of the world would be ridden in as safely as Regents Park." As the narrative realistically develops endless details of building plans, the savage corners of romance succumb to the safety of domesticity.

Only one thing threatens these domestic Crusoes: the unrestrained instinct of cannibals and of little Tommy Seagrave, whose sole purpose in the novel is to impress upon young readers the gravity of selfishness. Tommy, like the island, requires cultivation because untamed nature can be dangerous. His tales of misadventure, though occasionally comic, reveal the forceful stamp of evangelical literature. Tommy is ruled by his stomach, not by his mind or heart. He eats all the eggs and is locked an entire day in the chicken coop for punishment; he loses his mother's best thimble in the soup because it proves too hot a ladle; during the climactic cannibal battle, the castaways discover Tommy has squandered the water supply and the noble Ready, to save the family, sneaks out to the well only to be mortally speared by a savage. Tommy's self-abandonment proves one of the essential lessons of the novel: instinct, not reason, guides the unacculturated; with maturity and development arises the mastery of reason over instinct. Tommy's presence, then, reinforces the necessity for a code of control and discipline. If all the castaways behaved as Tommy does, *Masterman Ready* would have been the precursor of

rather than the kind of novel parodied in Golding's *Lord of the Flies.*

Luckily society is highly structured on Marryat's island. Except for instinctive Tommy, the Seagraves are exemplary. Mr. Seagrave, a benevolent master who rules with a firm but just hand, will put down axe or hoe at any moment to reflect on political economy, natural history, or God's universe. William shows promise of following his father's footsteps; he is the model boy, who has learned the importance of self-mastery and obedience to God and father. The females, Mrs. Seagrave, her black servant Juno, and "poor little Caroline," play out their roles in this benevolent paternalistic scheme. Mrs. Seagrave and Caroline fade into semi-invalidism, sewing, cooking, and nurturing one-year-old Albert. They are the least interesting of the characters because, stereotypically, gentlewomen in the wilderness are not creatures of action. Juno does much of the heavy work to protect her mistresses from exertion. She is nanny, farmhand, and construction worker. Ready, too, accepts a subservient position. "I am an old man with few wants, and whose life is of little use now," he explains. "All I wish to feel is that I am trying to do my duty in that situation into which it has pleased God to call me." He is no Admirable Crichton who inverts the master-servant relationship. Instead he works incessantly, a masterbuilder who symmetrically arranges the physical world, who accedes to an already ascribed framework, the hierarchical class system of Victorian Britain because that is God's design. Through him, through the tempered romance of his past deeds and the inspirational selflessness of his present actions, Marryat promotes the cause of continuity, of convention, of concern.

Thus Marryat's Robinsonade endorses a comforting, conservative view of life as lived in England. The castaways, Tommy excepted, act out all the graven images of Victorian iconography: they labor hard and thus prosper readily; they worship and thus behave nobly; they maintain the sanctity of family and thus survive peaceably; they accept their place and duty and thus exist happily. No cannibal invasion could ever defeat such a fortified group. The pitting of Britons against savages, then, serves to justify the necessity for emigres like the Seagraves. Every Eden may have its serpent—in this case, in the guise of cannibals—but when Eden is ruled by the right sort, by Christian Europeans, evil is soon banished and paradise regained. Though Ready dies for the cause, the Seagraves are saved by a British schooner, emigrate to Australia, and increase their flocks and herds tenfold (even Tommy we are told "grew into a very fine fellow and entered the army"). *Masterman Ready* concludes on this domestic note. The Seagraves have faced great dangers: shipwreck, typhoon, shark attack, cannibal warfare. Repeatedly their security, their blessed family circle, has been tested and found sound. Even Tommy, half savage himself, grows up, an exemplary citizen of the middle station. And to this middle station Marryat's narrative bows. What romance surfaces in *Masterman Ready* serves an instructive purpose—rebellion against parental authority is wicked, cannibals are heathen, nature must be conquered—or underscores the level-headed achievements of Ready and Mr. Seagrave. Adventure is not an end in itself but a means to glorify a "practical education." Moreso than Defoe, then, Marryat domesticates paradise and provides a safe haven for the optimistic beliefs of his time.

"There is a crude magic," writes J. S. Bratton, "in the automatic way in which the advent of a Christian Englishman is assumed to transform the lives of all he comes across: a hero has only to be present, and his superiority works wonders, without his needing to more than assert himself physically." *The Coral Island,* by Robert Michael Ballantyne, presents three such heroes, "an agreeable triumvirate," bolstered by goodness and right, qualities which are, in the boys'-book Robinsonade, invincible weapons. Ralph Rover, Jack Martin, and Peterkin Gay (those familiar with *Lord of the Flies* will recognize Ralph and Jack), are stranded on a South Sea island, unable to retrieve provisions from their ship, virtually facing nature barehanded. No adults have survived their shipwreck to supervise and guide them. Indeed, Ralph, who has neither the supremely rational mind of Jack nor the good humor of Peterkin gives

way to a Crusoe-like sense of despair: "If the ship had only stuck on the rocks we might have done pretty well, for we could have obtained provisions from her, and tools to enable us to build a shelter, but now! alas! we are lost." These words, early in the novel, are among the few that echo Crusoe's trial. For if Crusoe's wilderness contains all the tension and uncertainty of Job's in the Bible, the wilderness Ballantyne has fashioned projects all the certainty and vigor of a playing field. Thus Jack can reprove Ralph by cheerfully asserting they are all "saved," and Peterkin can proclaim, "I have made up my mind that it's capital—first rate—the best thing that ever happened to us, and the most splendid prospect that ever lay before three jolly young tars. We've got an island to ourselves. We'll take possession in the name of the king; we'll go and enter the service of its black inhabitants. Of course we'll rise, naturally, to the top of affairs. White men always do in savage countries." In a word, Peterkin has summarized the racial and colonial myths that underlie the juvenile Robinsonade, and remain the hallmark of Ballantyne's boys' books.

When the boys take inventory of their worldly goods, they discover they have but a chipped penknife, a pencil-case without any lead, a piece of whip cord, a sailmaker's needle, a broken telescope, a brass ring, and an axe. Ballantyne's ironic catalog of goods makes clear to the reader that the author, in contrast to Mar-

A depiction of Lewis Carroll's Alice.

ryat, privileges romance over realism; Ballantyne's boys do not confine time and space but are themselves free in them.

Fortunately what they lack in tools they gain in the leadership of Jack, whose good sense, cleverness, and book knowledge enable him to teach the others how to survive. "He was," in Ralph's mind, "of that disposition which *will* not be conquered. When he believed himself to be acting rightly, he overcame all obstacles." He is the kind of empire builder inspired by Crusoe. Jack introduces his companions to all the edibles on the island, he organizes their bower living quarters, leads an expedition around the island, even urges them to build a boat. Furthermore, it is Jack who initiates their hunting and fishing excursions. Not long after their untoward arrival, then, the boys have settled in as amiably as clubmen, enjoying the bounty of the island and their freedom upon it. Ballantyne's boys do not put their paradise to use in the same way Defoe's or Marryat's castaways do. Re-creation is not the order of the day in *The Coral Island:* adventure is.

Ballantyne is the first British writer to discard the conventional cataloging of achievements; a realistic examination of survival, a minute recalling of pottery making and shelter building, are not included in his tale. The boys, in their roamings, discover the remains of a former Crusoe, whose fields, houses, even his skeleton are discovered "in a state of utmost decay." All that the lone man had salvaged from his ship moulders and rusts; nothing remains to chronicle his existence, "neither a book nor a scrap of paper." A horrifying thought haunts the boys—perhaps they, too, could end up like this forlorn Crusoe. To domesticate in the boys' minds is equivalent to a slow, quiet obliteration. Thus the order they impose upon their island world is minimal. The boys themselves, not the island, come to signify their culture's ideology. The order that counts on the Coral Island is order from within. Ralph, Jack, and Peterkin follow a daily regimen that helps preserve their identity as English boys. The Sabbath Day is carefully marked each week; keeping count of the days becomes an essential means of controlling their lives. Even their hours are structured: each morning begins with a cold bath, followed by food, exercise, and exploration. By maintaining a schedule reminiscent of home, by approaching their excursions with high spirits and pluck, the boys live united, "an agreeable whole." "There was," Ralph states, "no note of discord whatever in the symphony we played together on that sweet Coral Island."

Ballantyne is interested in testing his three young Britons, in putting them face to face with danger. In this way, his Robinsonade marks a further turning away from the complexities of *Robinson Crusoe*. Defoe's narrative, Seidel points out, "does not presume a single, privileged allegorical reading for Crusoe's adven-

tures." The strata of meaning—political, psychological, spiritual—are varied, contradictory, inviting of endless exegeses. Ballantyne's juvenile odyssey, on the other hand, winds its way back to imperial Britain, and in the unfolding of the tale, it proves an unambiguous paean to the mercantile and missionary spirit of the homeland. Each confrontation with the chaotic, savage Other reinforces the inconquerable spirit of his heroes. They are impervious to evil and destructive forces.

Ballantyne builds exciting episode upon episode, ending in a resounding climax when the boys attempt to rescue a Christian native girl, Avatea, from a fate worse than death: marriage to a cannibal. Early episodes highlight the boys' brushes with natural dangers. They avert a rock slide; attacked by a shark while fishing, they ram an oar down its throat to avoid being devoured; a tidal wave also fails to swallow them up, and a typhoon forces them into a dark cave for three days. Each time the three are threatened they are delivered by their quick thinking and stalwart action. Never are they undermined by a loss of faith or a reversion to barbarism themselves. This steadfastness, then, expresses the morality of the adventure. When the narrative shifts suddenly to emphasize the depravity of heathens, to hammer home its didactic message, the reader is assured of final victory.

Ballantyne's tale borrows from quest fiction and implements a reductive morality typical of popular romance. Unfortunately, to the modern reader, the cliffhanging romance of the island setting becomes bogged down by Ballantyne's missionary zeal once his narrator, Ralph Rover, is kidnapped by pirates and forced to aid them in robbing cannibals of valuable goods. One critic has suggested that Ballantyne never understood the structure of romance. The quest his heroes undergo is [according to Bratton] no "proving ordeal" for they go forth from a "static condition of perfection" and return "meaninglessly in the ordinary world." We might add that Ballantyne never understood the power of the Robinsonade. What makes Crusoe's experience on a desert island so moving is his continual struggle against madness and despair; he is a modern-day Job whose small triumphs mark an increasingly spiritual state of being. Ballantyne merely bilks the Coral Island of whatever adventure capital he can.

The island experience is never meant to deliver the three boys' souls from darkness, for they are lightness, cheerfulness, goodness. Curiously, until cannibal canoes land on the Coral Island, Ballantyne subdues his religious message considerably. Despite Ralph's grief over the loss of his Bible and his heartfelt pledge never to omit his prayers, far fewer thanks are given to God than in *Masterman Ready*. Ralph and his two shipmates repeatedly escape harm's way, yet seldom remark upon providence. With the arrival of cannibals and pirates, however, a forceful didacticism enters the novel. Formally, then, the novel is truncated. The first part borders on secular adventure; the second part argues for further missions in the South Seas. All the romance of boys deserted on an island runs aground once Ballantyne pursues a contemporary issue, christianizing the heathen. Moreover, the boys' heraldic rescue of Avatea is deflated by propaganda. Even their quest, saving Avatea and the souls of cannibals, lacks dramatic moment because the quest reveals no inner spiritual or moral growth in Ralph, Jack, or Peterkin. Having rent asunder *Robinson Crusoe*'s crucial conflict, Ballantyne's narrative founders in two distinct but incomplete halves.

The Robinsonade section of the novel stresses the Edenic qualities of the island, and in its way touts the natural life of the boys. The amenities of civilization are not missed: "We . . . made various . . . useful articles, which added to our comfort, and once or twice spoke of building us a house, but we had so great an affection for the bower, and, withal, found it so serviceable, that we determined not to leave it, nor to attempt the building of a house, which, in such a climate, might turn out to be rather disagreeable than useful." Celebrating harmonious untouched nature, *The Coral Island* taps into the romantic myth that life nearer nature is purer, more virtuous than civilized life (a myth, incidentally, Marryat does not endorse; his castaways subdue nature). Yet as Brian Street points out, such a position was problematic for nineteenth-century novelists: "[Their] literary heritage and romantic bent inclined [them] to extol the virtues of the natural setting, but [their] cultural heritage and rational belief in progress inclined [them] to extol the 'civilized' setting." This dilemma helps explain the split nature of Ballantyne's narrative. He would have been a more gifted writer of romance had he allowed his interest in the exotic and the adventurous to prevail. But, like Marryat's *Masterman Ready, The Coral Island* exposes an underlying ambivalence toward the freer canvas of romance. To counter the lure of the natural, Ballantyne introduces "serpents" into the Eden that is the Coral Island in order to extol the civilized.

The island is invaded, first by cannibals who have come to roast their enemies and enjoy a feast, then by hardened pirates who "[care] . . . precious little for the Gospels." The cannibals, "incarnate fiends," "demons," "monsters," are obvious villains. The boys' battle with them dramatically "proves" the supposed evolutionary distance between savages and Europeans and the necessity for benevolent missionaries. The pirates, on the other hand, are able to maintain the veneer of civilization, and the Captain tries to convince Ralph his vessel trades in sandal-woods. But their souls are benighted, anarchic, savage; consistently their behavior is reminiscent of the cannibals—worse, in fact, for as Europeans they should know better than to slaughter wantonly. Missionaries have made inroads into cannibals'

hearts; but wonders Ralph of the pirate Captain, was it possible "for any missionary to tame *him*." Significantly the two forces of evil in the novel, pirates and cannibals, do battle in the night while Ralph listens from afar to their "wild shrieks" and "confusion." Evil negates evil and good escapes: a typical equation in this didactic adventure. In the end, all the pirates, save one Bloody Bill who is born again on his deathbed, are murdered and presumably roasted. Such is the fate of lawless wretches who "cannot restrain [their] wickedness."

The remainder of Ballantyne's novel continues in this vein, undermining the effect of the Coral Island adventures. Once centered on cannibals, Ralph's single-minded narrative sounds much like a missionary tract, describing a degraded, backward, immoral heathen world in need of missionary mercy. Avatea is finally rescued and married off to a Christian prince; an English gentleman, blown off course, arrives in the nick of time to convert the savages before they devour Ballantyne's heroes; and the cannibal chief, Tarraro, proves so penitent he persuades others on the island to embrace the true faith. The three boys are now free to return to England, where their descriptions of savage life will further recruiting of missionaries.

The two island worlds—the Coral Island and the cannibal Tarraro's island—represent the competing structural halves of Ballantyne's novel. Moreso than Marryat, Ballantyne turns the Robinsonade into a genre that can accommodate adventure pure and simple. In its descriptions of island life, in its exciting episodes, the novel has charm. In this way, Ballantyne anticipates the secular adventures Robert Louis Stevenson and others perfected. Ballantyne, however, re-embracing his role as educator, tacks onto the story of the Coral Island a diatribe on the evils of heathenism. Once again the light subjugates the sweet, and romance is pushed aside, enchained in heavy-handed rhetoric. A later romance writer, Rider Haggard, once remarked [in *The Secular Scripture*] "that a series of adventures was easy enough to write, but that a real story had to have 'heart,' that is, a focus or center implying a total shape with a beginning and an end." *The Coral Island,* opening up as a Robinsonade and concluding as a religious tract, lacks center; it is half wish-fulfillment, half promoter of colonial and missionary policy. Both radical and reactionary, split asunder structurally by cross purposes, it highlights the best and the worst in the juvenile Robinsonades that dominated the pages of boys' magazines and crowded the shelves of nurseries in the nineteenth century.

In a genealogy of the British Robinsonades, *Masterman Ready* and *The Coral Island* hold pivotal stations. Retaining the moral earnestness of evangelical Robinsonades, yet replacing an introspective religiosity with a delight in the material world and an emphasis on decisive action, these two works prompted the genre's transmutation into an adventure mode. Appearing after the publication of *Masterman Ready* are juvenile Robinsonades clearly intent upon adventure, Captain Mayne Reid's *The Desert Home* (1852) and Percy St John's *Arctic Crusoe* (1854). Anne Bowman's *The Castaways* (1857) and *The Boy Voyagers* (1859) owe much to both Marryat and Ballantyne, as do Reid's *The Castaways* (1870) and W.H.G. Kingston's *Rival Crusoes* (1878), to name only a few progeny. Even later writers like H.G. Wells, Joseph Conrad, J.M. Barrie, and William Golding, who subvert or parody the Robinsonade, admit their debt to Marryat and Ballantyne. In particular, the longevity of *The Coral Island,* reprinted to this day, suggests a decided fascination with a cultural mythology more assured than our own. Indeed, the language of the nineteenth-century juvenile Robinsonade continues to haunt, to influence, and to appall the twentieth-century imagination.

MAKING MEN/MAKING WOMEN

Alan Richardson

SOURCE: "Reluctant Lords and Lame Princes: Engendering the Male Child in Nineteenth-Century Juvenile Fiction," in *Children's Literature: Annual of the Modern Language Association Seminar on Children's Literature and The Children's Literature Association,* Vol. 21, 1993, pp. 3-19.

[*In the essay that follows, Richardson uses psychoanalytic theory to demonstrate that, contrary to contemporary and even late-Victorian notions of masculinity, children's literature in the mid-nineteenth century often imagined a "manliness" that was almost effeminate.*]

Wordsworth's phrase "The Child is Father of the Man," from his self-authorizing epigraph to the "Immortality" ode, could equally well introduce any number of nineteenth-century representations of childhood. What in Wordsworth's time are still relatively new-fangled notions—that childhood is a period of crucial psychic and moral development, and that adult life is largely shaped, if not quite determined, by childhood experience—grow increasingly self-evident as the nineteenth century progresses, eventually to become codified in the work of Freud. This genetic, developmental approach to childhood is as central to texts representing the child to itself as to those representing the child to adults. Nineteenth-century British children's fiction, whether didactic, fantastic, or "realistic" in character, almost invariably portrays childhood as a period of psychological and moral growth; indeed, what most differentiates Victorian literary fairy tales and fantasies from traditional fairy tales is this very insistence on development as opposed to the static, "flat" characterizations of the folktale.

It is no accident, then, that works as otherwise disparate as Charles Kingsley's *Water Babies* (1863) and Thomas Hughes's *Tom Brown's Schooldays* (1857) both place their hero's "schooling" at the center of their narratives and draw authority for their fictional projects by reference to Wordsworth, "that venerable and learned poet," as Hughes writes, who "most truly says, 'the child is father to the man'; *a fortiori,* therefore, he must be father to the boy." And yet, as Geoffrey Hartman has remarked [in "Words, Wish, Worth: Wordsworth," *Deconstruction and Criticism,* 1979], if Wordsworth's phrase eventually "becomes an axiom for modern developmental psychology," it nevertheless "remains as scandalous a paradox as ever founded a poetry of experience," disordering as it does the expected temporal, genealogical, and disciplinary relations of parent and child. Taking Hughes's seemingly vague but in fact critical distinction between "child" and "boy" as a starting point, we can locate yet another scandal within Wordsworth's proposition, which oddly defers assigning gender to the child, who, in the subject, is neuter and who is sex-typed as male retroactively in the predicate. Only from the standpoint of the "man" it will become can the "child" be differentiated as a potential "father." This retrospective or backwards process of gendering also anticipates Freud, for whom the "pregenital erotic stages" of the pre-Oedipal period are "sexually undifferentiated" yet reconfigured in terms of male (or female) development from the later perspective of the Oedipus complex, which "casts its mark back over their whole meaning" [in the words of Juliet Mitchell, *Psychoanalysis and Feminism,* 1975]. It simultaneously imposes an imagined family romance on the young boy's memories or fantasies of an earlier, "bisexual" psychic era. The child who suffers the father's prohibition knows itself in retrospect as man.

This disjunction—however temporary or however obscured by "infantile amnesia"—between the "child" and the male child brings out a crucial problem for any developmental portrayal of childhood in juvenile fiction. That boys will be boys we know from Kingsley, Hughes, and many other Victorian writers for children; but how do they *become* boys? What, to resort again to the suggestive difficulties of Freud's developmental paradigm, facilitates the (male) child's abandonment of the mother's warm, affectionate sphere for the harsh world of the father; what motivates (his) exchange of "polymorphously perverse" bisexuality for an exclusive, prohibited romance with the mother—the mother with whom (he) so recently and intimately identified?

From the perspective of Freud's writings, even as re-read by a Lacanian feminist like Juliet Mitchell, the answer is fairly direct: the boy assumes his "phallic heritage" because the "male position" is the only place where "anyone really wants to be . . . within the patriarchal order." But other, more frankly revisionist psychoanalytic approaches, such as that of Nancy Chodorow, describe taking the male position as an ambivalent, even somewhat dubious act. Departing [in her essay "Gender, Relation, and Difference in Psychoanalytic Perspective," *The Future of Difference,* 1980] explicitly from the traditional Freudian assumption that the boy child "instantly knows that a penis is better," Chodorow emphasizes instead the "conflictual" aspect of assuming a male identity, a process that for her is not less but more problematic than the girl child's accession to femininity. Underlying the child's male identity, Chodorow argues, is the "early, nonverbal, unconscious, almost somatic sense of primary oneness with the mother"—arising from the indistinct boundaries between mother and child characteristic of the pre-oedipal stage—which persists in an "underlying sense of femaleness that continually, usually unnoticeably, but sometimes insistently, challenges and undermines the sense of maleness." What Chodorow terms the boy's "primary femaleness" entails that the production and maintenance of a male identity is and remains problematic, difficult, and in an important sense negative: "learning what it is to be masculine means learning to be not-feminine, or not-womanly." The boy's ongoing repression of his pre-oedipal femininity can entail, in turn, an aggressive, self-conscious maleness, a valorization of sexual difference as difference, a denial of feelings experienced as (because culturally encoded as) feminine: "feelings of dependence, relational needs, emotions generally."

The advantage of Chodorow's theory of gendering for studies of nineteenth-century juvenile fiction is that it brings to the fore two distinct and apparently contradictory modes of representing the development of masculinity to the child—and more particularly, to the boy—reader. Her description of the boy's "negative definition" of masculine identity, and its "assumption by denial" of his primary femininity, helps account for the aggressive masculinity of a boy's book like *Tom Brown's Schooldays,* in which the worst insult is to be called "Molly, or Jenny, or some derogatory feminine nickname." It helps explain the gusto and desperate haste with which Tom leaves the maternal sphere to plunge into a man's world of boxing and bird-nesting, cricket and beer-drinking, and a particularly violent form of football—a world in which desire takes almost exclusively that direction which Eve Sedgwick identifies [in *Between Men,* 1985] as "homosocial." We can discuss more critically the virtual cult of masculinity developed not only throughout boys' school stories but also in adventure novels (which almost invariably displace the boy hero into a world no less masculine and aggressive than that of the public school) and even in such fantasies as *The Water Babies,* which teaches its addressee, Grenville Arthur Kingsley (and "all other good little boys" with him), how to take a beating like a "little man."

We can, at the same time, begin to account for children's books that portray instead a distinctly feminized boy hero and undercut the development of masculinity in ways that seem to register the power of what Robert Stoller (in an essay [in *Women and Analysis*] cited by Chodorow) calls the "tidal pull" of the "original, primal symbiosis" experienced by the male infant and his mother. The problematic status of the feminized boy hero in nineteenth-century British children's fiction has been noted by U.C. Knoepflmacher [in "Resisting Growth through Fairy Tale in Ruskin's *The King of the Golden River,*" *Children's Literature* 13 (1985)], who identifies John Ruskin's Gluck, in *The King of the Golden River,* as a "boy-Cinderella" whose very appearance is "decidedly girlish" and curiously anticipates Sir John Tenniel's drawings of Alice. For Knoepflmacher, Ruskin's "feminized" hero embodies Ruskin's own "regressive" fantasy of childhood innocence, his "defense" against confronting "potentially disabling childhood conflicts he had never fully resolved in the process of growing up." But it is possible to see the program of psychic defense associated with the "feminized boy" hero of Victorian juvenile fiction as expressing a cultural rather than a personal fantasy, as the imaginative resolution of a widely experienced social conflict not limited to the biographies of a few children's authors. If there was a Victorian cult of sorts built around the "manly" public school experience as defined by Hughes and his imitators, there was also a cult—one marked by an intensity and extent that may seem bewildering today—centered on the figure of Frances Hodgson Burnett's Little Lord Fauntleroy, that veritable icon of boyish effeminacy, the definitive mama's boy. Nor were such feminized boy heroes limited to the fictions of Ruskin and Burnett: they can be found as well, to cite a few instances, in George MacDonald's *Back of the North Wind* (1871), in Jean Ingelow's *Mopsa the Fairy* (1869), in Mark Lemon's *Tinykin's Transformations* (1869), and in Dinah Maria Craik's *Little Lame Prince and His Travelling-Cloak* (1875).

Jacqueline Rose has argued persuasively [in *The Case of Peter Pan, or The Impossibility of Children's Fiction,* 1984] that the repression of sexuality characteristic of almost all children's fiction, and the "refusal of sexual difference" that marks some children's books, reflect adult fantasies of a pristine, innocent, asexual past rather than the rich and fluid sexual life of the child—again, "bisexual, polymorphous, perverse." Yet we should keep in mind that children's books, although written and selected by adults, are nevertheless frequently (if not exclusively or ever solely) aimed at children. And the developmental narratives they unfold not only speak to the needs of the adult reading, as it were, over the child's head but also embody the adult's wish to shape the child reader in certain modes, directing its growth in the very act of representing it. These narratives may not simply prescribe one-dimensional patterns of feminine or masculine behavior and identity—as *Tom Brown's Schooldays* so transparently offers its boy reader a boisterously "manly" ideal—but may, more subtly, attempt to guide the child reader through the dilemmas implicit in the maturational paradigm they encode. If the transition from child to boy involves a critical moment when the (male) child hesitates to abandon his feminine identity and side instead with the father, if the "pull toward merging again into the mother's femaleness" [as Stoller asserts] persists in the psychic life of the young boy, we might well expect to find fictional representations and imaginary resolutions of this ambivalence in the developmental tales written for children. It is from this perspective that I propose reading *The Little Lame Prince* and *Little Lord Fauntleroy,* both immensely popular works that feature a "little" boy hero who temporarily rejects his "patriarchal heritage," who continues to identify with his mother and is portrayed in decidedly effeminate terms, and who in the end takes on a significantly qualified masculine identity and a social role at once paternal and maternal.

Craik's *Little Lame Prince* was one of the best-selling children's fantasies of the later nineteenth century. Set in the kingdom of "Nomansland," it features a child hero, Prince Dolor, who would not be king: when placed (still an infant) on his deceased father's throne and invested with his crown, Prince Dolor "shook it off again, it was so heavy and uncomfortable." Refusing to take on his father's identity, Dolor instead takes after his mother, Queen Dolorez, who dies when Dolor is only six weeks but leaves him, in addition to her name, her looks (in both senses): Dolor grows into a "pretty little boy" with "just his mother's face" and "his mother's eyes." When Dolor meets his fairy godmother, a "dear friend" of Queen Dolorez and her effective substitute, she finds him altogether "as like [his mother] as ever" he could be. If he is like his mother, however, Dolor is "not like other little boys." Thanks to a "slight disaster" on the day of his christening (a lady in waiting drops him on the marble stairs), Dolor's body remains undeveloped from the waist down: "his limbs were useless appendages to his body," decidedly "not like those of other little boys." Effectively castrated, Dolor is no more wanted for the throne than he himself wishes it, and his uncle, Claudius to Dolor's Hamlet, has no trouble spiriting the prince off to exile and announcing his death.

Dolor's exile takes place in a "round tower," which, for all its phallic prominence on the desert plain from which it rises, is curiously womblike and domestic—a "perfect little house"—within. Tended only by a woman servant (and, on occasion, the fairy godmother), Dolor is afforded an extended period in which to remain like his mother and as unlike his uncle, archetype of the "great, strong, wicked man," as possible. His life in the tower, though ostensibly one of depri-

vation, affords the boy-child reader a fantasy not so much of eternal childhood (never growing up like Peter Pan) as of growing older without having to give up his identification with the mother. Even Dolor's magic carpet rides, which seem fantasies of power, are enabled by a decidedly maternal cloak (a "circular" poncho with a "split cut to the center" where there is an accommodating "round hole" for his head, and introduce him to a feminized nature: "There was the glorious arch of the sky, with a little young moon sitting in the west like a baby queen. And the evening breeze was so sweet and fresh—it kissed him like his godmother's kisses."

As Dolor grows into a kind of maturity, he takes on a complicated, ambivalent gender identity; his sexuality is at once dysfunctional and overdetermined.

> Prince Dolor was now quite a big boy. Not tall—alas! he never could be that, with his poor little shrunken legs, which were of no use. . . . But he was stout and strong, with great sturdy shoulders, and muscular arms. . . . As if in compensation for his useless lower limbs, Nature had given to these extra strength and activity. His face, too, was very handsome. It was thinner, firmer, more manly; but still the sweet face of his childhood—his mother's face.

Below the waist Dolor remains neuter, while above the waist he seems to have become hyper-masculine, until the femininity of "his mother's face" reasserts itself. His gender identity is not so much androgynous (although it could be easily mistaken for such) as fragmented, his masculine and feminine aspects disjointed and ill-fitting rather than harmoniously blended. Neither quite manly nor altogether womanly, and no longer childlike, Dolor inhabits a "nomansland" of his own in which gender remains in flux, chaotic and indefinite.

At last Dolor elects to assume the throne after all, in order to prevent a political anarchy ("no government at all!") that seems to mirror the anarchic identity of the reluctant prince. But the fantasy's closure is tentative at best. The narrator asks, "Was he . . . 'the father of his people,' as all kings ought to be?", and refuses to answer the question. Instead we learn that Dolor's lameness was "never cured," that, a favorite of his people in other ways, he "never gave them a queen," and that he eventually abdicates in favor of a "tall and straight" cousin. Dolor, that is, may take on a version of the patriarchal role, but he never becomes a father, or even a husband, and he passes on the phallic heritage as early as possible to a successor as "erect" as a king should be. In Dolor's story, the young boy reader can imagine a version of growing up without ever growing into a "great, bad, clever man" like the more conventionally masculine uncle, without ever growing away from the mother within (and without ever entirely giving up the mother without, as the ageless fairy godmother remains Dolor's confidant throughout his reign). Dolor is a curious figure of wishful projection, suggesting at once omnipotence (the flying cloak) and impotence, appealing to readers for whom potency—the male power and privilege that come only at the expense of repressing the feminine—remains a dubious inheritance.

Although formally a realistic children's novel, Burnett's *Little Lord Fauntleroy* is no less concerned than Craik's fantasy to provide wishful resolutions to the dilemma of the growing boy. Published serially (in *St Nicholas*) in 1885 and in book form in 1886, the novel sold quickly and extremely well, and the Fauntleroy "craze" (which swept through Britain as well as America) followed the successful production of stage versions in London and New York a few years later. Irving Cobb, who published a fictionalized account of his childhood in 1924, described the Fauntleroy cult in a chapter called "Little Short Pantsleroy": "A mania was laying hold on the mothers of the nation. . . . *Little Lord Fauntleroy* infected thousands of worthy matrons of America with a catching lunacy, which raged like sedge fire and left enduring scars upon the seared memories of its chief sufferers—their sons, notably between the ages of seven and eleven." Compton Mackenzie was one of many British victims of what he recalled as "that confounded Little Lord Fauntleroy craze"; he was forced to wear a Fauntleroy costume (black velvet suit, lacy Vandyke collar) to dancing class while the other boys wore sailor suits. These accounts, and others like them (the story, for example, of the eight-year-old boy in Iowa who burned down the family barn when forced to wear the Fauntleroy regalia) suggest that the Fauntleroy ideal appealed to parents (particularly mothers) more than children and aggravated rather than allayed boys' anxieties about gender identity. And yet the novel itself, which regularly applies the reassuring adjective "manly" to its little hero, seems to have aimed at a quite different effect.

Cedric Errol, the future Lord Fauntleroy, is initially presented as being "like both [his mother] and his father"—a puerile androgyne. But, as his notoriously feminized appearance ("gold-colored hair" in "loose rings," "big brown eyes and long eyelashes and a darling little face") suggests, his feminine aspect is dominant. In fact, Ceddie's father is himself described in androgynous terms: "He had a beautiful face and a fine, strong, graceful figure; he had a bright smile and a sweet, gay voice; he was brave and generous, and had the kindest heart in the world, and seemed to have the power to make everyone love him." With his beautiful face, graceful figure, sweet voice, kind heart, and loveable demeanor, Errol *père* recalls not so much the Romantic androgyne as the feminine conduct book ideal of the same period—Fanny Price with a moustache.

He turns out to have been, like Ruskin's Gluck, a boy-Cinderella: the youngest and gentlest of three, suppressed in favor of his older, duller, brutes of brothers.

Cedric junior thus doubly inherits, not only a girlish demeanor, but a feminized character as well, replete with what Chodorow calls "relational" qualities: "quick to understand the feelings of those about him," with a "kind little heart that sympathized with everyone" and a "childish soul . . . full of kindness and innocent warm feeling." He calls his mother "Dearest" and when his father dies becomes her all but constant companion (a young democrat, he saves some time for the neighborhood grocer and a friendly bootblack). At age seven, he still appears girlish (strikingly so in the book's original illustrations); he grows out of his "short white kilt skirt" and into a "black velvet skirt"—cut from the material of his mother's gown. When it develops that his two boorish uncles have, like his father, died young, and Ceddie has, suddenly, become Lord Fauntleroy, his response is couched in democratic tones: "I should rather not be an earl. None of the boys are earls. Can't I *not* be one?" But, according to the book's representational logic, refusing to accept the patriarchal inheritance also means (as in *The Little Lame Prince*) refusing to give up what are coded as feminine qualities for those presented as exclusively masculine.

The masculine/feminine oppositions that seem reconciled in the characters of both Cedric and his father become separate and discordant on Ceddie's arrival in England. From the start, Cedric must endure having his mother, "Dearest," banished to an outhouse on the paternal estate, while he is assigned to the great house or "Castle," securely within the masculine orbit of the misogynistic old Earl. The Earl is portrayed as entirely bereft of the relational qualities exemplified by Cedric and his parents. Vicious, savage, ill-tempered, and violent, he has neglected his wife as well as his children; the deaths of all of them are more or less directly attributed to his self-enclosed sterility. A tacit contest takes place over the course of the novel, as Ceddie seeks (quite disingenuously) to humanize, or rather, feminize the old man through his "kindly" and "affectionate" approaches, while the Earl struggles unsuccessfully to detach the boy from Dearest: "Do you *never* forget about your mother?" Eventually, Ceddie wins: the old heart thaws, Dearest moves into the Castle, and a new model of nobility—"simple and loving," "kind and gentle"—is asserted.

With his "strong . . . back" and "splendid sturdy legs" Cedric is no lame prince. And yet his effeminate hair and clothing, his refusal to give up Dearest, and his distinctly feminized character ally him much more nearly to Craik's hero than to the rowdy Tom Brown set, for whom to be called "mammy-sick" is almost as damning as to be given a feminine nickname. Both Cedric and Dolor are separated from their mothers only to discover maternal qualities within themselves; both insist on redefining the patriarchal role in relational terms. Burnett's fiction, like Craik's, seems addressed to the younger boy reader who is not ready to enter into the homosocial world of the public school or adventure story, whose resistance is disarmed by tales that valorize the boy's feminine characteristics and promise—however fraudulently—an androgynous adult role. These stories engender the fantasy that the child is mother to the man, that to become manly can mean remaining womanly, and that the patriarch may be mother as well as father to his people.

If the ideal of the womanly boy indeed embodies a cultural as well as a personal fantasy—as the transatlantic Fauntleroy cult suggests—it remains to be asked why this fantasy would find expression in the later nineteenth century, a period widely perceived as marked by an intensification, rather than qualifying, of gender differences. [In *The Reproduction of Mothering*, 1978] Chodorow has suggested that the development of modern "capitalist relations of production" entails both the progressive isolation of the nuclear family and the exaggeration and rigidification of masculine gender roles. Just such a firming of the prescribed masculine character is delineated by Claudia Nelson in her study ["Sex and the Single Boy: Ideals of Manliness and Sexuality in Victoria Literature for Boys," *Victorian Studies* 32 (1989)] of ideals of manliness in Victorian boys' fiction and treatises on "sexology" alike, both genres demonstrating a "gradual reclassification of the attitudes and behavioral patterns considered appropriate to men, often combined with a rejection of qualities associated with femininity" over the second half of the nineteenth century. In an essay on the socializing function of nineteenth-century school stories ["Breaking in the Colt: Socialization in Nineteenth-Century School Stories," *Children's Literature Association Quarterly* 15 (1990)], Dieter Petzold relates the growing emphasis on an aggressive, even pugnacious masculinity over the same period to the human requirements of both industrial capitalism and British imperialism: "The new age of economic and imperialistic expansion demanded new virtues, such as ambition and initiative, discipline and team spirit, readiness to take up responsibility, and a talent for leadership." Hughes suggests the association between the playing fields of Rugby and the needs of a military-industrial empire in envisioning the schoolboys buried in "many a grave in the Crimea or distant India" or surviving to manage, as Tom Brown more crudely puts it, "Cherokees or Patagonians, or some such wild niggers."

What role does the feminized boy of Victorian children's fiction play in an increasingly masculinized culture? Why do books like *The Little Lame Prince* and *Little Lord Fauntleroy* find such wide popularity during a period that witnesses the hardening of male roles in boys' books generally? It would be tempting to argue that, as women authors, Craik and Burnett are consciously writing against the grain of Victorian conceptions of gender, drawing on the conventions of Romantic "androgyny" in a manner that critically challenges Victorian patriarchy and enjoins a counter-ideal: the "Governor" who (to quote Wordsworth again ["1801"]) "must be wise and good, / And temper with the sternness of the brain / Thoughts motherly, and meek as womanhood." The conclusions of both stories gesture toward a feminized vision of society, marked by consensual rather than coercive modes of governing a kingdom or estate, by a progressive concern with the condition of the poor and dispossessed, and by relational rather than authoritative methods of social discipline—the power of love displacing the love of power.

It would be naive, however, to overemphasize the feminist, subversive aspect of children's books that, ultimately, redefine the patriarchal role only to reassert it; Dolor assumes the throne, after all, to quell a popular rebellion evocative of the revolutions of 1848. Nor does Cedric, in spite of his democratic fervor, finally refuse to accept his preferred role as future lord of his uncle's quasi-feudal estate. Rather, the effeminate boy hero of Victorian children's fiction can be viewed as a strategic concession to the male child who, in response to the very intensification of aggressive masculinity and the concurrent devaluation of feminine characteristics in the culture around him, resists taking on his prescribed role. Temporarily releasing him from this cultural pressure, disingenuously promising him an androgynous future, such fictions allay the younger boy reader's resistance in order to coax him into accepting the phallic heritage he may prove otherwise unwilling to assume. Fantasies like *The Little Lame Prince* and *Little Lord Fauntleroy* function, that is, not to subvert the masculine role within patriarchy but to soften it, encouraging "little" boy readers to identify imaginatively with a patriarchal position made (in response to the ambivalence of a critical developmental stage) to *seem* more motherly and subject to qualification and deferral.

Burnett's account of "How Fauntleroy Occurred," subtitled "And a Very Real Little Boy Became an Ideal One," suggests that her fiction is indeed both modeled on and addressed to a younger boy whose eventual assumption of a masculine identity is in no way threatened or undermined by his temporary loitering in the precincts of the maternal sphere. Burnett's son, Vivian, is seven years old when he "becomes" Fauntleroy. Burnett's retrospective essay seems at first to cry out for a psychobiographical reading. She confesses that until his birth Vivian "had always been thought of as a little girl" (to be named Vivien): "It was the old story of 'Your sister, Betsey Trotwood'; and when he presented himself, with an unflinching firmness, in the unexpected character of a little boy, serious remonstrance was addressed to him." But Burnett's very openness and self-irony on this point disarms analysis (or at least renders it superfluous). Although she gives her son an effeminate appearance (we learn a great deal about hair-brushing in the essay) up to, and perhaps a little beyond, the age of seven, she stresses that now, at sixteen, Vivian "plays foot-ball and tennis, and battles sternly with Greek. He is anxious not to 'flunk' in geometry, and his hair is exceedingly short and brown." That is, he now conforms to another ideal: Tom Brown at school.

For Burnett, then, the adjective "little" is key. Only as a "little boy" is Vivian feminized, only at a young age does he suggest—in a double sense—the effeminate Fauntleroy, both as model for its hero and as the story's original addressee (according to Vivian's own retrospective account): "Why don't you write some books that *little* boys would like to read?" That Burnett did see Fauntleroy as effeminate is readily apparent, both from the notorious illustrations by Reginald Birch, which she approved, and from the casting, in the London and New York stage versions of Fauntleroy, which she supervised, of girls (one aged nine, one "about" seven) in the title role. (A film version, produced by Mary Pickford, emphasizes both Fauntleroy's femininity and his identification with Dearest: Pickford herself played both roles.) But it is equally clear that for Burnett the effeminate phase had its period and facilitated (rather than simply delayed) the boy's later assumption of a thoroughly masculine character. In the photograph Burnett sent to Birch as a model for the illustrations to *Little Lord Fauntleroy,* Vivian's lace and flowing locks are coyly offset by a small decorative sword, an earnest of his eventual masculinity.

The children's text has sometimes been seen as uniquely tinged by its historical matrix, a "kind of cultural barometer" [Ruth K. MacDonald, *Literature for Children in England and America from 1646 to 1774,* 1982] in its ideological transparency. Even if we were to accept the view of juvenile fiction as merely reflecting a pre-existent social reality, the inadequacies of such a position should seem clear. But children's books are concerned not only with reproducing ideology but with producing certain kinds of subjects as well; the "ideal" children they represent are intended to help shape the characters of "real" boys and girls. Chodorow's revision of Freudian psychoanalytic theory—which remains one of the most compelling accounts we have of the development of modern subjectivity—suggests that, if ultimately geared toward the functioning of male-dominated industrial capitalism, the boy's maturation within an isolated nuclear family and with the mother as primary socializer entails detours, disruptions, or gaps in the production of masculine subjects. In their recognition of such developmental crises and the ingenuity of their fictional strategies for meeting them, *The Little Lame Prince* and *Little Lord Fauntleroy* attest to the flexibility, the sophistication, and the cultural power of nineteenth-century fiction for children.

Vallone defines how fiction treated adolescent boys and girls differently:

This fundamental difference between the boy's adventure and the girl's learning experience, is reflected in the function of humor in these texts. Humor serves, in *Tom Sawyer,* to help us laugh at the "boy" in each of us, at caricatures of people we all recognize, and at Mark Twain's wry tales of childhood. In an adolescent girl's world, by contrast, humor teaches us the necessity of exorcising the evil in ourselves and becoming selfless little women.

> *Lynne M. Vallone, "Laughing with the Boys and Learning With the Girls: Humor in Nineteenth-Century American Juvenile Fiction,"* Children's Literature Association Quarterly, *1990.*

Maria Tatar

SOURCE: "Daughters of Eve: Fairy-Tale Heroines and Their Seven Sins," in *Off With Their Heads! Fairy Tales and the Culture of Childhood,* Princeton University Press, 1992, 94-119.

[*Tatar presents a feminist reading of fairy tales in the following chapter from her book; she elucidates not only that the tales were largely didactic, but that they were particularly designed to encourage their female readers to grow into submissive women.*]

The numbers of children who go up in flames in nineteenth-century storybooks is nothing short of extraordinary. *Little Truths, for the Instruction of Children* (1802) begins its second volume with the illustrated story of Polly Rust—"*Yes: she was one day left alone, and, I think, playing with the fire; her clothes were burnt off her back, and she so scorched as to die the next morning in great pain.*" Little Pauline, we recall, perishes in Dr. Heinrich Hoffmann's *Struwwelpeter* because she played with matches. A pair of shoes, "so pretty and fine," along with a pile of ashes, are all that are left of her. Then there is poor Augusta Noble, who is found "in a blaze, from head to foot" after carrying a lighted candle into her bedroom in *The History of the Fairchild Family* (1828). Even those who survive the conflagrations they have set off must endure months of torment, as does a little girl featured in *Select Rhymes for the Nursery* (1808):

> For many months, before 'twas cur'd,
> Most shocking torments she endur'd;

And even now, in passing by her,
You see what 'tis to play with fire!

As cruel as these nursery rhymes and stories may seem, they are not completely devoid of merit, for they offered children a program for survival in an age where ubiquitous open fires and flames made the dangers of being burned to death far more acute than they are today. Some of the cautionary tales and verse may dwell too long on the consequences of playing with fire, and others may try to exploit the prohibition against playing with fire by enlarging on the evils of disobedience, but most have at least a kernel of wisdom to them. The same could be said for the many cautionary tales designed for women, young and old. In harping on the evils of pride, disobedience, stubbornness, and curiosity, these tales indulge in the same need to promote a safe docility while also participating in the cultural project of stabilizing gender roles. As folktales dropped contestatory stances and adopted the conciliatory mode of cautionary tales, they sought to provide (in however misguided and coercive a fashion) models of successful acculturation while supplying women with what conventional wisdom perceived as the correct program for making and preserving a good marriage. Women who did not accommodate themselves to these patterns would indeed be playing with fire.

The numbers of children who go up in flames in nineteenth-century storybooks is nothing short of extraordinary.

—*Maria Tatar*

Moving from the culture of childhood to the world of women and their marriages does not require a giant step. Fairy tales with children as heroes and heroines often culminate in marriage, and the gap between the behavior expected from children and the conduct demanded of wives is not, as we shall see, as great as one might expect. Like children, women—by nature volatile and unruly—were positioned as targets of disciplinary intervention that would mold them for subservient roles, making more visible forms of coercion superfluous.

Many [traditional children's stories] can be seen as replayings of one biblical masterplot: the Genesis account of the Fall. For several centuries now, standard interpretations have identified Eve as the principal agent of transgression and have infused her act of disobedience with strong sexual overtones. Eve not only "disobeys" commands but also "tempts" and "seduces" Adam. She has become the real serpent in the garden. Kierkegaard, as Margaret Miles has pointed out, re-

vealed the missing link between what goes on in the biblical text and what critics have made of it. "Eve is a derived creature," Kierkegaard writes. "To be sure, she is created like Adam, but she is created out of a previous creature. To be sure, she is innocent like Adam, but there is, as it were, a presentiment or a disposition that indeed is not sinfulness but may seem like a hint of sinfulness that is posited by propagation." Eve's body indelibly marks her (despite Kierkegaard's hedging about "a hint of sinfulness") as a creature of transgressive sensuality. That Kierkegaard locates Eve's insubordination in her role as agent of propagation, in her ability to reproduce, is especially striking in light of his insistence that Eve is also "a derived creature." What seems to irritate him more than anything else is that, while Eve must suffer the pains of childbirth, she also receives the reward of giving life.

What orthodox readings of the episode from Genesis make clear is that a predominantly male interpretive community has relentlessly projected onto women a kind of innate hypersensuality and seditiousness that must be contained to prevent the human race from falling into a state of deeper sin. The biblical punishment for Eve's act of defiance takes the form of pain in childbearing along with perpetual subordination to her husband. Woman must henceforth live under the sign of labor and obedience—her untamed, unstable nature must be held in check through physical degradation and the demand for blind submission. The biblical authority that established Eve as subservient to Adam was gradually converted to natural law that admitted no contestation; it was "a hidden law of nature" or man's privilege "by nature" that fixed male superiority in the hierarchy of gender.

It is one of the lesser-known facts of folkloric life that women are rarely as virtuous as they are beautiful. Cinderella and Snow White may combine good behavior with good looks, but they are exceptional in that respect. Wherever we look in folklore, we can find disagreeable heroines. There are princesses who cannot bring themselves to crack a smile, undutiful daughters, lazy peasant women, gluttonous girls, and unfaithful wives. Among the many sins of folkloric heroines, vanity and pride—traits that breed a willful self-sufficiency—figure especially prominently. Oddly enough, these traits rarely discourage suitors; quite to the contrary, they seem to send a powerfully attractive message, in the form of a challenge, to men. Often, however, we read that beauty overrides all other considerations. In a Norwegian tale, a king's daughter "puts on airs," but suitors nonetheless flock to the manor, for the "hateful shrew" is "very pretty." Beauty breeds a sense of superiority that spells disaster for suitors— think of the countless princes who line up one after another to lose their heads at the castles of proud beauties who spurn alliances. It is left to heroes to design prenuptial rites of passage that will turn these arrogant girls into marriageable women—women who are as humble and deferential as they are beautiful.

No condition is better designed to put a woman in her "proper" place than pregnancy. What better way to humble a patronizing princess than by turning her body into a visible sign of her sexual condescension, particularly when she is unmarried. An entire set of folktales shows us women subjected to physical and social mortification in order to prepare them for a life of meek subordination.

Like many a humbled heroine, Cinziella, in Basile's "Pride Punished," learns her lesson so well that she considers herself the basest of creatures and welcomes all manner of insults. She is the first to admit that she has gotten exactly what she deserves: "The miserable Cinziella, agonised at what had befallen her, held it to be the punishment of Heaven for her former arrogance and pride, that she who had treated so many kings and princes as doormats should now be treated like the vilest slut." Her fall, engineered by the King of Belpaese, is a dramatic one. Scorned by the haughty Cinziella, whose every "dram of beauty" is counterbalanced by "a full pound of pride," the king swears revenge. He masquerades as a gardener in order to make his way into the service of Cinziella's father, then, by appealing to Cinziella's vanity with offers of magnificent jewelry and apparel, succeeds in installing himself first in her apartments, then in her antechamber, and finally in her bedroom. There the wily gardener labors in the "fields of love" and gathers the "fruits of his love." Sexual conquest and attendant impregnation do not, however, satisfy the King of Belpaese's appetite for revenge. He continues to keep his identity secret, installs Cinziella in his stables, and encourages her to engage in petty thievery, always ensuring that she will be caught so she may be mocked and jeered at by her social inferiors. The pain of her humiliation becomes so unbearable that Cinziella goes into labor and delivers twin boys. Only after the King has seen his two sons does he finally declare a truce, largely because there is no need for further abasement. From that time on, his wife never forgets "to keep her sails low, bearing in mind that *Ruin is the daughter of Pride.*"

"The Crumb in the Beard," recorded in Bologna, tells a similar story of seduction and humiliation as the disciplinary route leading to marital accord. A princess named Stelle calls the hero a dirty fellow because a crumb remains in his beard after he has dined. Wounded vanity leads the young man to vow "vengeance" and to conspire with his own father and the father of the princess to "punish Stelle for her pride." Disguising himself as a baker's helper, the prince enchants the girl with his music, elopes with her, and subjects her to a life of poverty and other humiliations. When Stelle finally faints dead away from shame at one particular-

ly mortifying moment, her mother-in-law intervenes, proclaiming that her son has avenged himself sufficiently. From that day on, Stelle was "never haughty, and had learned to her cost that pride is the greatest fault."

Seduction is the quickest way to conquer proud Italian heroines. Peruonto, "the greatest idiot and the most perfect boor that nature had ever produced," works faster than most men. All he must do to avenge himself when a princess named Vastolla laughs at him is to shout "Oh, Vastolla, may you become pregnant by me!" and the princess first misses her periods, then experiences "certain attacks of nausea and palpitations," as Basile pointedly states. The princess is not only publicly humiliated, but also socially humbled, and therefore becomes a suitable match for a handsome young prince imprisoned in the body of a boor. This is also the case in the Grimms' "Hans Dumm," a story that was deleted from the first edition of the *Nursery and Household Tales* because of its bawdy plot. Hans Dumm can team up with the princess of the story only after he has impregnated her by wishing her with child. He then lifts her back to her former social station by turning himself into a clever young prince.

The tales of Peruonto and Hans Dumm are both lighthearted in tone, in part because both stories elevate the power of the word over the deed. These are racy stories, but their actors remain innocent, since mere words function as causal agents for physical transformations normally requiring sexual contact. This contrasts starkly with what happens in a darker version of the tale type—one that attributes the pregnancy of the female protagonist to rape. This is no laughing matter. The humiliated suitor in an Arabic story, for example, gets even with the tale's proud heroine by violating her. Whatever the technique—seduction, curse, or rape—the result is always the physical, emotional, and social degradation of the heroine.

The Grimms may have found "Hans Dumm" inappropriate for a collection of children's stories, but they did include in the *Nursery and Household Tales* the story of a proud princess's humiliation at the hands of her husband. Side by side with adult tales detailing the seduction and humiliation of a haughty heroine (with special attention to a woman's public mortification through her pregnancy) exists a second tradition depicting proud women coerced into carrying out demeaning acts of physical labor. The princess of the Grimms' "King Thrushbeard" is a case in point. She makes a habit of mocking every one of her many suitors, especially King Thrushbeard, who has a crooked chin. Forced by her father to marry the first beggar to appear at the door (who happens to be King Thrushbeard in disguise), she lives with him in a wretched hut, where she must tend fires, cook, and clean. When she fails miserably in carrying out these domestic tasks, and shows herself equally inept at weaving baskets, spinning, and selling crockery, she finally lands in the palace kitchen where she is obliged to do utterly disagreeable work. Like Cinziella, she is quick to recognize her failings and to reproach herself: "She thought about her sad fate and cursed the pride and arrogance that had brought her so low and made her so poor." After being treated to a scene of public disgrace, with courtiers laughing and jeering as scraps stolen from the kitchen come tumbling out of her pockets, she is rescued from further obloquy by King Thrushbeard, who has removed his beggar disguise. But demeaning physical labor and public humiliation have operated in tandem to produce just what King Thrushbeard wants: a deferential wife. In the end, the tamed heroine regains her dignity, but only by renouncing any claims to self-esteem: "I've done a great wrong and I don't deserve to be your wife." The scandal of the wife's public humiliation along with a self-proclaimed acknowledgement of her inferiority becomes a *rite de passage* in the ceremony of courtship and marriage.

The not-so-hidden agenda of "King Thrushbeard" remains remarkably stable from one telling to the next. Yet the tale could also quickly be transformed from a gender-oriented to a class-oriented cautionary tale. One version of the tale begins by emphasizing the heroine's beauty and pride, but ends by teaching her a lesson about the hardships faced by the poor. "I did all this to you," King Drosselbart declares, "because you were so proud. I wanted you to know how the poor have to work to get their bread, how hard it is for them to work for their bread." The same narrator turns "The Frog King, or Iron Heinrich" into a story about a princess who is so proud that she does not even deign to look at her servants. After the transformation of the prince, she casts off her arrogant manner, "and from then on she liked her servants and the poor and helped them as much as she could." These versions of the two tales highlight the ideological instability of folk narratives by demonstrating the way in which a few quick strokes can reorient a story to produce a message consonant with an audience's need to correct everyday life.

Hans Christian Andersen seems to have understood more keenly than anyone else the innate contradictions of "King Thrushbeard." That the tale's relentless abasement and trivialization of its heroine might put her on a collision course with her future husband rather than turn her into the ideal marriage partner seems to have escaped the attention of most rewriters. Andersen's literary version of the tale type, however, frankly admits the possibility that a woman who has humiliated herself by revealing her frivolously false sense of values may be beneath contempt rather than desirable. As in a number of Scandinavian folktales, a passion for material possessions gets the heroine of Andersen's "Swineherd" in trouble. But while popular versions of

the tale show the heroine trading her chastity for objects made of gold, Andersen eliminated the bawdy element in one quick stroke by turning the exchange into kisses for magical toys. More importantly, however, his princess, despite her remorse, is in the end deserted by the prince/swineherd, who states with a depth of acerbic vehemence unparalleled in folktales: "I've come to despise you. An honest prince you rejected. The rose and the nightingale were not to your taste. But the swineherd—you could kiss him for the sake of a musical box. Now you can have what you asked for!" The tale ends with the deserted princess sitting in the rain, regretting her foolish pride and mourning her desolate state. Andersen's ending demystifies the message that degradation can spell happiness for a woman.

In many tales women themselves conspire to create a balance of power tilted in favor of their husbands, thus revealing the degree to which social codes could become internalized and self-regulated. The Grimms' "Little Hamster from the Water" tells of a princess who is "proud," refuses to "subject herself" to anyone, and rules her kingdom "singlehandedly." The test that ninety nine of her hundred suitors fail requires them to hide so well that she cannot find them. The hundredth suitor outwits her and never reveals how he did it. "That way she looked up to him, for she thought he had done it all on his own and said to herself: 'He's smarter than I am.'" Here, instead of a husband who has to prove his physical or moral superiority, we have a bride who deliberately seeks out a husband who has earned the badge of intellectual superiority and is thus entitled to have the upper hand in the marriage. The autonomous female subject who resists subordination to men at the start of this tale ends by mobilizing her intelligence to devise a plan designed to subject her to domination.

The folktale's tenacious emphasis on the evils of female pride becomes evident when we see that virtually every inflection of female frailty contains within it an element of arrogance. Take, for example, the sad predicament of the many folkloric princesses who cannot laugh. Interestingly, the solemnness of these young women, which stands in sharp contrast to the derisive style of proud princesses who belittle and make sport of their suitors, is often traced to arrogance. In the Norwegian "Taper-Tom Who Made the Princess Laugh," the princess takes herself "so seriously" that she can never laugh. She is also "so haughty" that she rejects all suitors. "She would not have anyone, no matter how fine, whether he was prince or gentleman." The challenge facing her suitors, as the Norwegian folktale makes clear, is to make her laugh—an act that will function as a sign that she has ceased to consider herself above-it-all.

Vanity and pride stand, then, as the cardinal sins of women in folktales. These vices make for the strong will (familiar enough to us from fairy tales about children) that must be broken before a woman is sufficiently obedient to qualify for matrimony. That the horrors of haughtiness can be inscribed on virtually any tale is amply documented by Ludwig Bechstein's "Proud Bride." Bechstein takes a tale that, in its oral renditions, celebrates female ingenuity in the face of chilling dangers and turns it into a moral lesson on the hazards of female vanity. "The Robber Bridegroom" gives us a heroine who discovers that her betrothed leads a band of ruthless criminals. She witnesses the murder of a girl and watches in horror from her hiding place while one of the robbers chops off the girl's finger in order to release a ring on it. When the robbers leave, the heroine takes the severed finger and uses it as evidence to convict her betrothed and his accomplices.

Most variants of this tale type celebrate the courage and craft of a heroine who singlehandedly gets the better of a team of murderers. Bechstein, in his *Book of German Fairy Tales* (1845), would have none of that. The heroine of his "Proud Bride" is beautiful, but vain and disobedient. While most of her counterparts in the tale type "The Robber Bridegroom" are depicted as innocent victims who come face-to-face with unspeakable atrocities, the protagonist of Bechstein's tale is held responsible for the perils she faces. "You are going to die," the robber groom tells the girl whose murder the heroine witnesses. "And soon you'll have company. A pastor's daughter, a proud young thing like you, will follow you." From her hiding place, the heroine silently swears to herself that, if she survives this hideous ordeal, she will never again act arrogantly. In the end, she is indeed "cured" and settles down to become the "good wife" of a clergyman.

When Bechstein points out in this tale that it is "a well known fact that by telling a woman not to do something that she ought to do, you can get her to do it," it becomes clear that no female figure of his, no matter how heroic, could possibly escape the charge of disobedience: woman is by nature a transgressor. More importantly, by enunciating a "general truth" about the way in which women have to be treated like children in order to get them to "behave," Bechstein reveals that tales like his are out to belittle the women who read the story as much as the heroine whose story is told. The degree to which this holds true becomes evident as one teller after another of cautionary tales about proud women engages in an emphatic denial that the specific case related has anything to do with women in general. This is all too reminiscent of seventeenth-century marriage satires which, after regaling the reader with pictures and texts about shrewish wives oppressing their husbands, routinely end with hollow disclaimers emphasizing that few women are really like this, least of all "the gentle female reader." One broadsheet, for example, ends with a "Protestation to all

honest, pious and gentle wives": "The above verses refer only to shrewish wives, not good ones. So I beg that no female reader should imagine that she is intended." This formulaic ending only fully affirms and underscores the extent to which the entire sex comes under fire.

Bawdy tales of proud women brought to a fall by spurned suitors focus on the problem of getting even and restoring the "natural" order in the hierarchy of gender. From an initial position of social inferiority, the heroes succeed in recovering their social status while at the same time putting brides in their proper places—somewhere beneath them. Cleaned-up literary versions of these tales also show old scores being settled, but they so sharpen the didactic point in these narratives of revenge that the characters themselves teach and preach. Heroines ceaselessly blame themselves for their degradation and are forever declaring their own worthlessness. By the time they reach the altar, they have learned their lessons so well that they recite them, often in detail, for the reader. The proud heroines of this tale type are always taught lessons in humility, but the lessons are spelled out with increasing clarity as one moves from the earliest narratives—whether oral or literary—to later stylized literary texts.

Arrogance, haughtiness, and pride—whatever the name, it runs in the blood of most royal fairy-tale women and motivates a plot that relentlessly degrades women and declares them to be social misfits until they have positioned themselves as wives in subordinate roles to husbands. That King Thrushbeard and other folkloric monarchs succeed in driving out those gender-inappropriate traits is consistently presented as a credit to their ingenuity and as a happy ending that stabilizes the "natural" asymmetry of gender relationships. Husbands in folktales of an earthier quality have a different but equally formidable task—one that has aptly been captured in the tale type index by the Shakespearian formulation "The Taming of the Shrew." Humble folk must work just as hard as their royal counterparts to reform their brides who, though commoners, can be just as uppity as princesses.

A Danish version of "The Taming of the Shrew"—a folktale that is widely disseminated across the American and European folklore map and that existed in both oral and literary forms well before Shakespeare's play—gives us the essentials of the tale type and reminds us of the degree to which these stories authorize men to restore the divinely ordained hierarchy of gender relationships by adopting the very traits that they so ardently wish to banish in women. In "The Most Obedient Wife," a wealthy farmer marries off two of his daughters, but hesitates with the third and oldest, a girl who is described as "stubborn," "quarrelsome," "obstinate," "violent," and "ill-tempered." One suitor insists on the match despite the girl's reputation, marries, and returns home on horseback with his new wife. When the pet dog accompanying the couple ignores a command, the husband shoots him outright. (Some versions show the husband giving the dog two chances before shooting him for a third show of disobedience.) The same fate befalls the horse, and the wife cannot but get the message that she had better shape up. In the versions that show the animals shot after three acts of misconduct, the husband frightens his wife into submission by declaring "That's once!" after she has stepped out of line in one way or another. The Danish tale ends with the once recalcitrant woman becoming "gentle" and "obedient" even as her husband has become the double of the "obstinate," "violent," and "ill-tempered" woman he has now tamed.

Some versions of the tale type further celebrate obedience by adding a coda in which a woman wins a prize from her father by being the fastest to respond to a call from her husband, thus offering both a program for instilling blind obedience and a tableau displaying the desired results. This relentless foregrounding of women's vices and virtues successfully suppresses consideration of the way in which men are viewed as admirably reasonable and responsible at the very moment when they adopt the traits seen as untoward in the "shrews" they are taming.

American versions of "The Taming of the Shrew" generally take the form of a pointed anecdote that, by making fun of a woman's fall from notorious willfulness to abject subservience, is doubly invested in a move that degrades women. As Jan Harold Brunvand has shown, these stories have entered and flourished in the sphere of jokelore rather than folklore. As abbreviated forms of their fuller European counterparts, and with a snappy punchline ("That's once!"), they have become so popular a form of entertainment that they recently found their way into a "bedside book" for guests at Hilton hotels. Like their European counterparts, American versions of the tale usually make a point of underscoring the wife's obedience ("Went home, and she made him a good wife") or of emphasizing that henceforth the husband will be in charge ("There was only one pair of britches in the family, and it was Creekmore that wore 'em"). But they often also add a scene that goes beyond the idea of enforced psychological submission by displaying a woman's physical degradation as part of her permanent married condition. One recorded version illustrates a wife's physical subservience by showing her with the saddle from the dead horse on her back and with reins around her neck. A literary version inspired by popular accounts also ends with the wife literally (and voluntarily) in harness: the wife "trotted to the fallen horse, stripped the traces off, and pulled the buggy to the church steps by holding to the ends of the shafts. Leaping up and standing in the buggy, Ezra cracked the whip above his wife's head, and they drove out of

the churchyard." The real point of this tale seems to be that once a woman is treated like an animal, she will work like a horse. While the American "jokes" focus on physical degradation as the mark of a successful taming, the European tales tend to limit themselves to a less spectacular and less corporal form of coercion. Neither inflection of the tale type is especially subtle in its reproduction of grotesquely bullying variants of sanctioned social practices.

The coercive tactics dramatized in "The Taming of the Shrew" thrive on exaggeration for the production of a humorous effect. But hyperbole can also be placed in the service of pathos—a woman can, for example, take obedience to such an extreme that she becomes positioned as a martyr whose suffering stirs our emotions even as her moral superiority sets impossibly high standards for all women. Take the case of that female Job known in Western literature by the name Griselda. Her story does not, strictly speaking, belong to the fairy-tale canon, but it is firmly rooted in traditional literature. Of the many versions of "Griselda," those by Boccaccio, Petrarch, and Chaucer are probably the best known. But Perrault, who was more profoundly under the influence of fairy-tale traditions than the other three authors, has the version that provides the most legitimate grounds for comparison with the tales under discussion here.

In announcing that Griselda stands as a "perfect model" for women everywhere, Perrault not only declares self-effacing masochism to be woman's most noble project, but also shifts the target of disciplinary intervention from his heroine (for whom lessons are superfluous) to his female readers. "Patient Griselda" tells of a prince who believes that happy marriages are based on the dominance of one partner over the other. "If you wish to see me wed," he declares, "find me a young beauty without pride or vanity, obedient, with tried and proven patience, and, above all, without a domineering will of her own." A young shepherdess catches his fancy and, once she agrees to comply with his every wish, he marries her. With time, Griselda's devotion begins to rankle him, and he decides to test her love by first separating her from her child, then communicating to her a false report about the child's death. As if this were not enough, he dispatches Griselda back to her humble cottage where she resumes her duties tending sheep. Finally, to deepen her humiliation and display his complete mastery of her will, he recalls her from exile so that she may attend his new betrothed. "I must obey," Griselda tells herself. "Nothing is nearer to my heart than to obey you completely," she says to her husband in a gesture of subordination so extravagant as to effect her own mastery of the situation. Griselda's long-suffering patience has been celebrated as the virtue that wins back her husband (this may seem more punishment than reward), but there is a way in which her patience can also be seen as a powerful social currency that buys for her a form of grim satisfaction through suffering. That message, more forcefully than the manifest lesson that blind obedience and slavish devotion pay off in the end, is probably what has reached most readers of the tale.

In its repeated disavowals of any sort of didactic agenda, the story of Griselda denies its disciplinary intent and aims to enlist the consciousness of its readers in the effort to foster patient suffering as the preferred modality of power for women. Boccaccio's narrator asserts that the deeds of Griselda's husband represent a "mad piece of stupidity." Chaucer's version of "Patient Griselda" concludes with a strong disclaimer about the heroine's value as a role model: "This story does not mean it would be good/For wives to ape Griselda's humility,/It would be unendurable they should." Instead of offering a model for husband/wife relations, the tale symbolically dramatizes the relationship of man to God: " . . . everybody in his own degree / Should be as perfect in his constancy / As was Griselda."

It may well be that for Chaucer's Oxford student narrator, life on earth was nothing more than an allegory rich in implications about man's relationship to his maker. But it is also interesting that he shuttles with such evident ease from a story about husband and wife to a lesson about God and man. Christian theology clearly organizes the two sets of relationships in analogous fashion. As if this covert declaration of woman's ordained subordination to her husband were not enough, Chaucer's envoy adds a tongue-in-cheek exhortation to all women to "take the helm" and "trim the sail" even if their husbands "weep" and "wail." Here is his mock advice about husbands:

> Never revere them, never be in dread,
> For though your husband wears a coat of mail
> Your shafts of crabbed eloquence will thread
> His armour through and drub him like a flail.
> Voice your suspicions of him! Guilt will bind
> Him down, he'll couch as quiet as a quail.

The pervasive irony of the passage subverts the earlier critique of Griselda as a model for women, for what comes under the heaviest fire here is not the transgressing husband but the shrewish wife who is forever abridging her spouse's freedom and coercing him into silent submission.

In Boccaccio's tale, Griselda's husband justifies his actions by explaining that all along he has had an end in view: "namely to teach you to be a wife"—as if Griselda ever needed lessons in deference and obedience. Katherina, the "tamed shrew" of Shakespeare's play, tells us (not without an undercurrent of irony) exactly what being a wife implied in the age of Boccaccio and Shakespeare. After Petruchio has provided evidence of Katherina's "new-built virtue and obedi-ence," he charges her to tell the assembled women "what duty they do owe their lords and husbands." In her speech, Katherina recites the lessons she has learned and preaches submission to husbands:

> Thy husband is thy lord, thy life, thy keeper,
> Thy head, thy sovereign; . . .
> And craves no other tribute at thy hands
> But love, fair looks, and true obedience—
> Too little payment for so great a debt.
> Such duty as the subject owes the prince,
> Even such a woman oweth to her husband.
> And when she is froward, peevish, sullen, sour,
> And not obedient to his honest will,
> What is she but a foul contending rebel
> And graceless traitor to her loving lord?
> I am ashamed that women are so simple
> To offer war where they should kneel for peace,
> Or seek for rule, supremacy, and sway,
> When they are bound to serve, love, and obey.
>
> *(The Taming of the Shrew)*

Disobedience can stand on its own as a vice, but it can also be seen as the effect of deeper causes, among them stubbornness and curiosity (as was the case in fairy tales about children). Russian folklore is especially rich in tales about stubborn women. "The Bad Wife" tells of a woman who makes life "impossible" for her husband because of her perverse ways: "She disobeys him in everything." There is also "The Mayoress," in which a woman is cured of ambition, gives up her aspirations to public office, and ends by "obeying her husband." Tales about pig-headed women, even more than tales about disobedient wives, took special hold in Russian folklore. "The Stubborn Wife," like many Russian tales, boldly illustrates the lengths to which a woman will go to have the last word:

> Once a peasant shaved his beard and said to his wife: "Look how well I have shaved." "But you haven't shaved, you have only clipped your beard!" "You're lying, you wretch, I have shaved." "No, it's clipped." The husband thrashed his wife and insisted: "Say it's shaved, or I'll drown you!" "Do what you will, it's still clipped." He took her to the river to drown her. "Say it's shaved?" "No it's clipped." He led her into the water up to her neck and shoved her head in. "Say it's shaved!" The wife could no longer speak, but she raised her hand from the water and showed by moving two fingers like a pair of scissors that his beard was clipped.

Exaggeration in the service of a comic effect makes it impossible to take this traditional tale too seriously without looking like a fool, but it is telling that capital punishment is represented as the natural penalty for female stubbornness, just as it is repeatedly depicted as the appropriate form of retaliation for disobedience. As in many other tales, the woman's vice is foregrounded, exaggerated, and mocked, even as the husband's behavior is neutralized—here, by virtue of the contrast with a willingness to die rather than give in on a wholly trivial point. This is, after all, the story of the "stubborn wife," not the "stubborn husband who first beats then drowns his wife."

Charles Perrault's "Bluebeard" makes the point, more forcefully than any other tale, that female curiosity can lead to no good. It is important, however, to bear in mind that "Bluebeard" began to impart that lesson only in its latter-day versions, when it fell into the hands of those who saw it as a platform for preaching and teaching. Perrault, who decried frivolous stories and insisted on including a "useful moral" in every tale, launched the tradition with his judgmental pronouncements on the tale's characters. Bluebeard's wife, who cannot resist the temptation to disobey her husband, becomes the transgressor, even when the man she "betrays" turns out to be a serial murderer. Here, female curiosity becomes implicated (notwithstanding Perrault's oversimplifying commentary) in a knot of productive contradictions, for Bluebeard's wives would be engaging in a self-effacing gesture tantamount to suicide were they to suppress their curiosity to know what lies behind the door to the forbidden chamber. Yet by opening the door, they willfully insert themselves into an infamous genealogy that can be traced to Eve, even as they play into the hands of a husband who is ready to execute them for discovering his secrets.

"Bloody key as sign of disobedience"—this is the motif that folklorists customarily and insistently refer to in their explications of "Bluebeard." But for many critics, the bloodstained key takes on a momentous relevance for the way in which it points to a double conjugal transgression—one that is both moral and sexual. It becomes a sign of "martial infidelity"; it marks the heroine's "irreversible loss of her virginity"; it stands as a sign of "defloration." For one critic, the forbidden chamber is "clearly the vaginal area," while the bloody key is a "symbol of the loss of chastity." If one recalls that the bloody chamber is strewn with the corpses of Bluebeard's previous wives, this reading becomes willfully idiosyncratic in its attempt to produce a stable ideology. The story itself offers no grounds for connecting the heroine's act of opening a door with sexual betrayal.

Curiosity, along with stubbornness, occupies a privileged position in the pantheon of female sins. Since female curiosity is so often tainted with evil, while male curiosity is enshrined as a virtue, it is not surprising to find many more daughters of Eve than sons of Adam in fairy tales. Joseph Jacobs' "Son of Adam" in his *English Fairy Tales* is exceptional in this respect. The story tells of a worker who learns from his master

that Adam, the man whom the worker holds responsible for the curse of labor, was not unique in his susceptibility to curiosity. The master gives his servant the following instructions: "Now you can eat as much as ever you like from any of the dishes on the table; but don't touch the covered dish in the middle till I come back." Like Bluebeard's wife, who gets similar instructions about the rooms in her husband's castle, the servant can't resist the temptation to take a peek at the forbidden dish. When he lifts its lid, a mouse pops out. "Never you blame Adam again, my man!" his master proclaims. Oddly enough, a failing usually attributed to the daughters of Eve is in this text assigned to their male counterparts. This British son of Adam would seem to be a striking exception to the rule that in folklore curiosity becomes infused with negative connotations only when associated with women and children. Yet if we consider that Adam is a *servant* and that, like women and children, he has been schooled in the art of submission, it becomes clear just why his curiosity gets him in trouble rather than getting him ahead.

In one folktale collection after another female disobedience is condemned in terms so harsh that it is reassuring to find at least one story that celebrates disobedience. Basile's "She-Bear" commences with a brief sermon on the merits of refusing to carry out commands:

> The wise man spoke well when he said that one cannot obey gall with obedience sweet as sugar. Man must only give well-measured commands if he expects well-weighed obedience, and resistance springs from wrongful orders, as happened *in the case of the King of Roccaspra,* who, by asking for what was unseemly from his daughter, caused her to run away at the peril of her life and honour.

That the king asks for something "unseemly" figures here as an understatement—what he demands is the hand of his own daughter in marriage. Here at last is one case in which a women is deemed undeniably right to protest an order and to resist obeying it. The narrator thus validates female disobedience, though under circumstances so extreme that it would cause a public scandal to comply with the command (hence, perhaps, the term "unseemly"). Furthermore, his praise of disobedience is embedded in a context that reviles women for their cunning and deceit. Only a few lines before female disobedience is given a small degree of validity, female trickery and manipulative skill are described in baroque detail:

> Woman is full of artful tricks strung like beads by the hundred on every hair of her head: fraud is her mother, lying her nurse, flattery her tutor, dissimulation her councillor and deceit her companion, so that she twists and turns man to her whim.

What initially appears to be a discourse on the legitimacy of disobedience and a woman's right to resist coercion gradually becomes part of a successful effort to condemn women in general.

The narrator's terms are instructive, for they forcefully remind us that, ever since Eve, woman has been seen as the chief agent of dissimulation and deceit. It is she who introduced evil into the world by tricking Adam into taking the apple, and she who continues to control and coerce despite the biblical words about being under her husband's rule. To wax on about woman's teachery in a tale describing a man's premeditated attempt to seduce his daughter and her spontaneous resistance invites some skepticism about the narrator's declarations, though few signs point to the presence of ironic inversions.

While Basile's tale of female disobedience makes a point of associating woman with artifice and art, Perrault's monument to female obedience sees in its female heroine the incarnation of "Nature in all its simplicity and naiveté." Disobedience is the mark of woman's defection from nature; once a woman repeats Eve's sin, she enters the realm of culture, where she relentlessly employs deception and artifice to secure an "unnatural" superior position in the gender hierarchy. In folktales, women's roles are so starkly polarized that we have either dutifully obedient figures aligned with nature, or foul, contending rebels whose every act is tainted with corrupt and corrupting deceit.

The vices highlighted thus far—pride, disobedience, curiosity, stubbornness, and infidelity—are all constructed as shading into each other and can be seen as symptomatic of impudently unbecoming behavior. These brazen marks of self-assertion are supplemented by a cluster of sins that stand under the sign of self-indulgence: licentiousness, sloth, and gluttony. As with the sins of self-assertion, here too there is no clear line of demarcation separating one vice from the other. The licentious woman, for example, indulges her appetite for food and drink even as she evades her household chores. Stories illustrating these vices belong, for the most part, to the earthy variety of comic folktales that give license to licentiousness. Rather than serving as solemn cautionary narratives warning of the evils of various forms of behavior, they give us the facts of life in crude, ribald strokes. Rarely do they pass judgment on the tale's actors, preferring instead to display and celebrate the failures of productive discipline and repressive social codes.

The pleasures of the flesh are obviously not a subject for children's books, but this did not prevent the Grimms from including one toned-down version of a popular bawdy story in the *Nursery and Household Tales.* "Old Hildebrand" gives us the familiar folkloric triangle of a simple peasant, his hot-blooded wife, and a philandering village priest. The wife and priest want to spend "a whole day" together—"having a good time," as the Grimms discreetly put it. The two conspire to trick the peasant into taking a journey, but halfway to his destination, the man learns of their deception. He returns to witness the following scene: "The woman had already slaughtered whatever she could find in the barnyard and had also baked a lot of pancakes. The priest had also arrived and was strumming on his fiddle." This good clean fun is interrupted by the peasant, who has returned home on the advice of a wiser and worldlier neighbor. He gives the priest a "good beating" and presumably cures his wife of her "generosity."

Not all folktale collections present the weaknesses of the flesh in so subtle and tame a fashion. Thanks to the efforts of Friedrich Krauss, who opened the pages of his journal *Anthropophyteia* (1904-1913) to all manner of bawdy folklore, we have ten substantial volumes of off-color items from various regions and cultures. *Kryptadia* (1883-1911), the French counterpart to this Viennese journal, offers twelve, more compact volumes of "obscene" tales from Italy, France, Great Britain, Russia, Germany, and the Scandinavian countries. On the basis of the tales in these collections, we can often reconstruct motifs suppressed in the Aarne-Thompson tale type index. Tale type 1420G (*Anser Venalis—Goose as Gift*), for example, remains cryptic in its details ("the lover regains his gift by a ruse [obscene]") until we discover an entire set of tales in which lusty young peasants bribe women for sexual favors, then mercilessly tease them until the women are prepared to return the original bribes in exchange for sexual satisfaction.

The *Kryptadia* gave its readers a privileged look at documents that had never before reached print in the Western world. It was the first to publish *Russian Secret Tales,* collected by Alexander Afanasev as a supplement to his *Popular Russian Tales.* Womanizing priests, priapic peasants, and lascivious women fill the pages of Afanasev's collection, which contains stories explicit in their sexual detail. In these most unexpurgated of all folktales, adulterous wives are rarely judged and condemned, but shown to be especially resourceful when it comes to outwitting their husbands or getting the better of their lovers. In "The Blind Man's Wife," a woman takes advantage of her husband's infirmity to deceive him with a lawyer's clerk. A miracle occurs, and the blind husband recovers his sight just in time to catch the guilty parties in flagrante. The wife does not, for a moment, lose her composure: "How glad I am, my dear," she tells him gleefully, claiming that, in a dream the night before, a voice had told her: "If you commit adultery with such and such a lawyer's clerk, the Lord will open your husband's eyes." Not one to miss an opportunity, she immediately takes credit for the miracle. "Thanks to me, God has restored your sight."

While a number of Russian tales celebrate female inventiveness and its power to turn virtues into vices, others glorify adultery as a strategem for getting ahead in life. In "The Cunning Woman," a "pretty wife" conspires with her husband to entrap her suitors (the local priest, deacon, clerk, and sexton). One by one, she lures them into the house, persuades them to undress, then tells them to hide in a chest of soot when her husband "unexpectedly" returns home. The story concludes with the husband earning five hundred roubles for displaying to a wealthy lord the devils hiding in his chest. In another version of the tale, the wife collects twenty roubles from the priest, the churchwarden, and a gypsy in exchange for an evening rendezvous. As each of the three suitors descends into the house through the chimney, the woman's husband, a blacksmith, awaits them "with red hot pincers" applied to their private parts. A second rendezvous results in similar tortures. In the end, the blacksmith and his wife make bets and take bribes that net them enough roubles to live "a little more comfortably."

Bawdy folktales typically show women indulging with great zest in promiscuous behavior and adulterous relationships. Their heroines relish the prospect of the sexual act itself and use sexual liaisons to turn one kind of profit or another. The presentation of female sexuality in these tales, which rarely reached print and which circulate today in the form of dirty jokes (oriented toward a male audience), stands in stark contrast to the picture of sexuality in stories about female infidelity. Cautionary tales rarely concern themselves directly with adultery, in part because they engage in a form of self-censorship that blocks representations of cuckolded husbands. As in marriage satires, the wife's "besetting sin" is pride rather than lust, and the tales are designed more or less to secure a woman's obedience before she gets into any real trouble. This did not, however, prevent listeners and readers from implicating willful women—Bluebeard's wife is the most obvious example—in sexual transgression, thus creating stern cautionary texts against infidelity as a corollary of disobedience.

Gluttony and sloth, the final two items in our catalog of sins, are closely allied. Where there is a well-fed heroine, you can be sure that there will also be a lazy one. The belief that plenty goes hand in hand with laziness—even breeds it—is one that permeates the folklore of virtually every culture. The Italian tale "Jump into My Sack" succinctly formulates the relationship between the two. In it, the hero uses a magical sack to feed the inhabitants of a village struck by famine: "He did this for as long as the famine lasted. But he stopped, once times of plenty returned, so as not to encourage laziness." At the time that these tales were being told, life for the great majority was an unending struggle for survival. "To eat one's fill . . . was the principal pleasure that the peasants dangled before their imaginations, and one that they rarely realized in their lives," Robert Darnton has asserted. If a full stomach signaled the fulfillment of dreams, it also marked an end to struggling for advancement, and the consequent onset of sloth. Hence the constant equation in folktales between hunger and hard work on the one hand, gluttony and idleness on the other.

Nowhere is the equation between gluttony and idleness worked out in greater detail than in stories about marriageable women. In "And Seven!" (an Italian version of "Rumpelstiltskin"), the heroine is "big and fat and so gluttonous that when her mother brought the soup to the table she would eat one bowl, then a second, then a third, and keep on calling for more." By the time the girl has downed six bowls, the mother gets fed up and responds to the request for a seventh by whacking her daughter over the head and shouting "And seven!" A handsome young man hears the phrase and, after asking its meaning, learns that it refers to the seven spindles of hemp spun in one morning by the woman's daughter. The girl seems to be so "crazy about work" that the young man has no reservations about taking her as his bride.

In one version of "Rumpelstiltskin" after another, we find a heroine who succeeds in getting married because an expression of astonishment at her greed is taken as praise for her industry. Just as "The Brave Little Tailor" succeeds in getting ahead because the world misreads the declaration of his accomplishments ("Seven at one blow!"), so too the heroines of various versions of "Rumpelstiltskin" climb the ladder to social success when the description of their deeds is misinterpreted. In this context, it is interesting to note that brave little tailors become desirable matches for the daughters of kings once the world sees them as men of courage rather than as weaklings, while the heroines of "Rumpelstiltskin" become attractive marriage partners as soon as they are perceived to be hard workers rather than big eaters.

The vices that folktales attribute to women are not entirely without a referential relation to real life. To be sure they are often exaggerated, as in the case of the Russian wife who insists with her last dying gasp that her husband's beard has been clipped rather than shaved. But many vices, in particular the sins of self-indulgence, are ordinary human traits that women seem to share equally with their male counterparts in folktales. When it comes to sins of self-assertion, however, women come out far worse than men. Women are the ones who suffer from pride, curiosity, disobedience, stubbornness, and infidelity—traits to be driven out, not cultivated or enjoyed for the pleasurable gains they can produce.

Far more troubling than the negative valorization of pride, curiosity, disobedience, stubbornness, and infidelity, whenever they are attached to female characters, is the consistency with which women are punished with death, threats of murder, and cruel physical abuse for displaying those traits. Time and again, brute strength is used to tame shrews, as in Ludwig Bechstein's "Rage Roast," in which a woman who is not tamed after being beaten every day for a week is finally subjected to a surgery in which the "rage" is sliced off her hips. The hero of the Italian "Animal Talk and the Nosy Wife" takes his cue from the animal kingdom when it comes to dealing with his wife. Once he magically acquires the ability to understand the speech of animals, he compares notes with them on how to manage women. From a rooster, who rules his roost with an iron claw, he learns that "the hens must do as I say, even if there are great numbers of them. I'm not like you who have only one wife. You let her rule you." Like the rooster, who drives his hens away whenever they want anything, the husband discovers the advantages of resorting to physical violence, especially when his wife becomes too curious: "The husband took his belt and lashed the daylights out of her." In folktales and fairy tales, physical coercion becomes a legitimate, even pleasurable, form of disciplinary action.

For pride, curiosity, disobedience, and stubbornness, a good lashing usually does the trick, though there are many occasions on which death threats are required for good measure. Adulterous wives in a small number of tales that do not conform to the contours of the bawdy tales described earlier call for more extreme measures, not so much for their sexual indiscretion as for their defiant and deviant behavior. In the Italian folktale "Solomon's Advice," a man lodges for one night at a house where a blind woman is kept in the cellar. In the evening, the woman emerges from her underground abode to have a bowl of soup, then returns to the cellar. The master of the house explains: "That is my wife. When I used to go away, she would receive another man. Once I came back and found them together. The bowl she eats out of is the man's head; the spoon is the reed I used to gouge out her eyes." In the Grimms' collection, a treacherous wife is put to death by her father when she betrays her husband—she is sent out to sea with her accomplice in a boat filled with holes. At the end of another story, a king declares the appropriate punishment for a deceitful wife, without realizing that he is pronouncing the death sentence for his own unfaithful spouse. "Hang her first," he insists, "then burn her, then throw her ashes to the wind."

In folktales and fairy tales, laziness, gluttony, and licentiousness are taken to such comic extremes that they are less vices than subversive negations of a regime that requires continuous productive exertions to sustain life. The plots of stories recounting the consequences of these attributes may move in a realistic mode, but they take advantage of hyperbole to slide into the surreal. When it comes to depicting sins of self-assertion, however, we find an entirely different set of laws at work. Women who display arrogance, curiosity, disobedience, and stubbornness, along with those who engage in adulterous behavior that is less good, clean fun than a flagrant sign of defiance, are the protagonists of tales that take a tragic turn. Here it is not so much the vices that are shown taking an extreme form as the punishments for the vices—the act of transgression that authorizes the presentation of the punishment is, in fact, often trivial. Even the harshest penalties remain unchallenged when women begin breaking all the rules in the book of feminine behavior by taking steps in the direction of acquiring knowledge and power.

FURTHER READING

Avery, Gillian. "Death." In *Nineteenth Century Children: Heroes and Heroines in English Children's Stories 1780-1900*, pp. 212-25. London: Hodder & Stoughton Ltd., 1965.

> Examines the presence of death in nineteenth-century children's literature, characterizing it as a form of punishment in early didactic stories and as a sign of innocence in later Victorian writing.

Bingham, Jane, and Grayce Scholt, eds. "Nineteenth Century (1800-1899)." In *Fifteen Centuries of Children's Literature: An Annotated Chronology of British and American Works in Historical Context*, pp. 131-256. Westport, Conn.: Greenwood Press, 1980.

> Places children's literature of the period in social, national, and historical contexts; prefaces a chronologically arranged annotated list of published children's books. The essay is excerpted in the entry above.

Bottigheimer, Ruth B., ed. *Fairy Tales and Society: Illusion, Allusion, and Paradigm*. Philadelphia: University of Pennsylvania Press, 1986, 317 p.

> A collection of critical essays, all of which consider the various social functions that fairy tales serve in different cultures.

Bratton, J. S. *The Impact of Victorian Children's Fiction*. London: Croom Helm, 1981, 230 p.

> Combines historical documentation of nineteenth-century children's literature in England with critical inquiry into the basic concepts and cultural effects of the genre.

Carpenter, Humphrey. *Secret Gardens: A Study of the Golden Age of Children's Literature*. Boston: Houghton Mifflin Co., 1985, 235 p.

> Studies late Victorian fiction for children as the era in which didacticism and entertainment combined to produce a major literary trend and market force.

Hotchkiss, Jeanette. *European Historical Fiction and Biography for Children and Young People*. Second edition. Metuchen, N.J.: Scarecrow Press, 1972, 272 p.

Geographically arranged primary bibliography. Each chapter is further divided into chronological periods, with sections devoted to nineteenth-century children's literature in the British Isles, central Europe, France and the lowlands, Greece and the Balkans, Italy and Switzerland, Russia and Poland, Scandinavia, and Spain and Portugal.

Muir, Percy. *English Children's Books, 1600-1900*. London: B. T. Batsford, 1954, 256 p.

Presents detailed chronology of literature for children in England, providing synopses of works most important to each period and trend.

Nelson, Claudia. "Sex and the Single Boy: Ideals of Manliness and Sexuality in Victorian Literature for Boys." *Victorian Studies*, 32 (Summer, 1989): 525-50.

Describes masculinity as defined by Victorian literature for boys, demonstrating how that image fit into contemporary sexual practices, male gender roles, and social ideals.

Patterson, Sylvia W. *Rousseau's Emile and Early Children's Literature*. Metuchen, N.J.: The Scarecrow Press, 1971, 185 p.

Focusing on the late eighteenth century, argues that Rousseau's 1762 volume shaped the development of children's literature.

Rahn, Suzanne. *Children's Literature: An Annotated Bibliography of the History and Criticism*. New York: Garland, 1981, 451 p.

Focuses on the "Golden Age" of children's books, from 1860 to 1911.

Rose, Jacqueline. *The Case of Peter Pan, or The Impossibility of Children's Fiction*. London: Macmillan Press, 1984, 181 p.

Drawing on psychoanalytic method and exemplary texts from the late nineteenth and early twentieth centuries, argues that children's literature represents adult efforts to imagine and "secure the child who is outside the book."

Sutherland, Zena, and Mary Hill Arbuthnot. "The History of Children's Books." In *Children and Books*, pp. 53-74. New York: HarperCollins, 1991.

Includes discussion of developments in nineteenth-century children's literature, a chronologically arranged list of "Milestones in the History of Children's Literature" spanning 1484-1908, and a bibliography of secondary sources.

Thwaite, Mary F. *From Primer to Pleasure in Reading*. Boston: Horn Book, 1972, 340 p.

Details five centuries of children's literature, approaching its development through epochs and major trends.

Townsend, John Rowe. *Written for Children: An Outline of English-language Children's Literature*. Boston: Horn Book, 1974, 368 p.

History of children's literature in English known for its accessiblity.

Zipes, Jack. *Fairy Tales and the Art of Subversion*. New York: Wildman Press, 1983, 214 p.

Combines a detailed history of the genre with a critical investigation of how, in different ways, fairy tales have participated in the development of Western civilization through its children.

French Realism

INTRODUCTION

By the mid-nineteenth century, Realism had become the dominant mode of literary production in France, and for the next half-century, until the mid 1890s, the movement maintained its hegemony. The basic goals and tenets of the Realist movement were stated by many, and thus a large diversity of opinion existed as to its definition. Essentially, though, the Realists wanted to remove some of the distinctions between literature and science, thereby allowing themselves to attain truth by the simple observation and recording of reality. To achieve this end, the early theorists of Realism advocated a plain writing style, devoid of moral intention or authorial interpretation, that was primarily concerned with character and represented common people engaged in everyday activities. These thoughts were adopted and later manipulated by the great figures of French Realism; among them are Gustave Flaubert, author of *Madame Bovary* (1857) and widely considered the father of the realistic novel; Guy de Maupassant, Flaubert's disciple and the acknowledged master of the realistic short story; and Emile Zola, principal theorist of Naturalism, a later development in Realism, and the author of the twenty-novel *Les Rougon-Macquart* series.

While not a formal member of the Realist school, Honoré de Balzac is generally considered the chief precursor of French Realism. He is the author of *La Comédie humaine*, a series of novels published between 1842 and 1855 that examine French society between the years 1789 and 1848; his works, however, are said to evince a strongly romantic sensibility, to which many later writers reacted. Among the early writers, Edmond Duranty formally emphasized the use of an unadorned style of writing that took as its subject lower- and middle-class people in his periodical *Le Réalisme* (first published in 1856). Jules-François-Felix Husson (called Champfleury), a novelist and art critic, also stressed the importance of careful research and factual documentation in the modern novel. Champfleury is also remembered for another significant theoretical innovation, his 1856 declaration "that every serious novelist was an impersonal being who did not judge, condemn, or absolve." The Realists embraced this stance of total impartiality and sought a complete elimination of the artist from the work in much the same way that the contemporary painter Gustave Courbet had. Courbet, whose essentially disinterested and almost photographic renderings of ordinary people in

the 1850s had initially conjured the word "realism," was, like the literary artists of his time, attacked by harsh criticism. Among the flaws that commentators noted were an excessive emphasis on "trivial" detail. Likewise, accusations of representing "commonness" and "ugliness" were levelled at the Realists, as was a general disparagement of the newly "unartistic" arrangement of material. This negative response by critics was typical, as in the case of immorality charges brought against Flaubert for his novel *Madame Bovary*. The work, which is commonly considered the seminal piece of Realist literature, details the life of Emma Bovary, a bored, middle-class housewife whose attempts to fulfill her romantic dreams prove untenable and lead to her financial ruin and eventual suicide. In the novel, Flaubert attempted to portray contemporary, bourgeois French society not simply as he saw it, but with an objective and impersonal tone. Despite early detractors (a trial was held, and Flaubert was eventually cleared of immorality charges), the work launched the then-obscure Flaubert to the forefront of the French literary scene, a position that was reluctantly shared with him by Edmond and Jules de Goncourt.

Little read in the twentieth century, the Goncourt brothers were, like Duranty and Champfleury, theorists as well as novelists, whose writings again emphasized the new direction for the French novel based on the exploitation and extensive research into what they called "human documents." In 1864 they wrote, "the novel of today is composed from documents, received by word of mouth or taken direct from nature, just as history is composed from written documents. Historians write narratives of the past, novelists narratives of the present." Their results, considered by some to be the first works of Naturalism, included writings dealing with the minutiae of character, such as *Renée Mauperin* (1864), one of the first novels to analyze its protagonist as a psychological "case study."

In 1880, the publication of a collection of short stories under the title *Les Soirées de Médan* by Emile Zola, Guy de Maupassant, Joris-Karl Huysmans, Paul Alexis, Henry Céard, and Léon Hennique, formally initiated the movement of Naturalism. Zola, who had already published *L'Assommoir* (1877) and written his essay "Le Roman expérimental" (1880), took his place as head of the new movement, claiming a greater emphasis on the scientific and analytical than in its predecessor, Realism. Since both the terms *réalisme* and *natu-*

ralisme had been in use since mid-century with varying definitions and significances, however, critics have acknowledged that the distinctions between the two are somewhat hazy. As a movement, therefore, Naturalism is discrete from Realism more in name than in fact, although scholars have generally characterized it as distinguished by Zola's heightened sense of determinism and more complete rejection of literary idealism. Among the other Naturalists only Maupassant, whose novel *Une Vie* (1883) is reminiscent of *Madame Bovary*, has approached Flaubert and Zola in terms of overall importance. In addition, Maupassant is typically remembered for his short stories, which often lack the emotional detachment that the theorists of both Realism and Naturalism demanded. Likewise, commentators have since observed that Zola failed to maintain impartiality in his novels, which display a tendency toward symbolism and a highly personalized and moralistic vision.

These fissures between Realism in theory and practice have become a primary focus of criticism in the twentieth century. While "realistic" literature continues to be produced, as a movement Realism has long since been replaced. J. K. Huysmans, one of the original members of the *Médan* circle, is now more commonly associated with the French Decadent movement in literature, his *A rebours* (1884) being something of an early manifesto of Decadence that shares little with Naturalism except in its highly deterministic bent. Likewise, critics in the second half of the twentieth century have observed that the goals of the Realists were often subverted by the problematic nature of realistic representation. Contemporary commentators find in the works of Flaubert, Zola, and Maupassant a failure to efface the personal biases of the author or to eliminate ideological and allegorical aspects from their works in favor of a truly objective tone. Still, the prevalent influence of the Realists in the twentieth century is consistently acknowledged by critics, who have elevated Flaubert, Zola, and some of their precursors (such as Stendhal and Balzac) into the most important figures in nineteenth-century French literature and have seen in their works the roots of the great novels of the twentieth century.

REPRESENTATIVE WORKS

Honoré de Balzac
Le Père Goriot 1835
La Comédie humaine 1842-1855

Henry Céard
Une Belle Journée 1881

Champfleury (Jules-François-Felix Husson)
Chien-Caillou 1847

Alphonse Daudet
Les Contes du lundi 1873

Edmond Duranty
La Cause du Beau Guillaume 1862

Gustave Flaubert
Madame Bovary 1857
L'Education sentimentale: Histoire d'un jeune homme 1870

Edmond and Jules de Goncourt
Germinie Lacerteux 1864
Renée Mauperin 1864

Guy de Maupassant
Les Soirées de Médan 1880 [with Zola and others]
Une Vie 1883

Emile Zola
L'Assommoir 1877
Nana 1880
Germinal 1885

ORIGINS AND DEFINITIONS

Lafcadio Hearn

SOURCE: "Realism and Idealism," in *Essays in European and Oriental Literature,* edited by Albert Mordell, Dodd, Mead and Company, 1923, pp. 16-18.

[*In the following essay, originally published in 1886, Hearn decries the "revolting realism" prevalent among the works of his contemporary writers in France.*]

We have frequently drawn attention to the increasing tendency toward a revolting realism which is manifested by the leading authors of France. Indeed, the methods of the dissecting-room are growing in favor with the *literateurs* of the world. French authors have been the chief sinners in this regard, because they have to cater to a peculiar public taste, and because the French language is peculiarly adapted to embalming with exquisite literary art the most awful forms of human depravity. No English writer dares to treat the topics which give life and color to the masterpieces of Emile Zola, Alphonse Daudet and Guy de Maupassant. With us, this realism takes the form of a most exhaustive and exhausting analysis, which extends to the most inane and commonplace people. First, these people tell you what they think, then the author proceeds to tell you why they think so, and then somebody else expatiates on what they might have thought in different circumstances. This is, in the main, the method of James and Howells. It lacks the coarseness of vice which belongs to the French school, but it also lacks the deep interest which the works of the French masters possess for the student of morbid anatomy.

What our age really needs is not more realism, but more of that pure idealism which is founded on a perfect knowledge of the essential facts of human life. There is so much misery visible on every hand that the youngest of us stands in but slight danger of taking too roseate a view of the new world. The most imminent danger to every man and woman lies in the loss of the idealism which is the basis of the loftiest relations and the holiest duties of our lot. To believe that all men and women are, in reality, morally rotten is but preliminary to floating with the tide. When once a man comes to believe in the general depravity of his fellow men, he is far beyond the saving power of such maxims as "Honesty is the Best Policy," and the like. Realism should be the means, not the absolute end, of the writer of fiction.

In truth this debauching realism tends to make fiction miss its highest purpose—the recreation of minds that are weary of the toil and strife of the world. The average man sees enough of human depravity; he knows too many absolutely commonplace people; he is too often at the mercy of bores; therefore, when he turns to fiction for rest, he wants and expects something different from the routine of his daily life. Fiction has perhaps become more scientific than it was in the hands of Thackeray and Dickens, but it has lost the restfulness and the brawny, moral tone which it then possessed. This is a real loss, for the novel reader wants neither a medical treatise nor an essay on political and social economy. So long as the world endures there will be no lack of heartrending realism; so long as human nature remains unchanged there will be an unappeasable yearning for the idealism without which men have neither the courage to struggle nor the power to enjoy.

Ernest Boyd

SOURCE: "Flaubert and French Realism," in *Studies from Ten Literatures,* Charles Scribner's Sons, 1925, pp. 3-20.

[*In the following essay, Boyd surveys the history of French Realism from the writings of Balzac to those of his contemporaries in the 1920s.*]

The connotations of the word "realism" in French literature are varied. In its later developments realistic literature presented a considerable problem, and a constant source of irritation to the guardians of the academic portals to Fame. Wherefore, these gentlemen exercised a remarkable ingenuity in the art of evasion

and denial, which is responsible very largely for the diversity of opinion as to what realism is, and when it made its appearance in France. When challenged by modern realism they evaded the issue by asserting that it was not modern, and by denying that it was realistic. Thus, as every text-book will show, it was seriously argued that "the real French realists" were Racine, Molière, Boileau, La Bruyère, and Lesage. The rise of the Classical School in 1660 was described as a reaction against the Romantic period of the preceding half-century. Then followed a didactic era, when theses and theories were the essential, and finally, after an interval of sterility, there came, with Chateaubriand, a renaissance of the imagination. The Romantic movement was born, and it dominated the literary scene until about the middle of the nineteenth century.

It is at this point that we encounter realism as it is understood to-day. Balzac, who died in 1850, is accepted by all parties to the controversy as the precursor of the movement which was to crystallize in the work of Flaubert, the Goncourt brothers, Emile Zola, and the Naturalists. Balzac has been called "a realist in the observation of material facts," but "a Romanticist in his invention of plot and incident," and this dualism in his work accounts, I think, for the strange unanimity of such irreconcilable adversaries as Brunetière and Zola in greeting him as the founder of the Realistic movement. The mandarins claimed him joyfully, because he served admirably to becloud the issue which the Goncourts, Flaubert, and Zola were trying to force to a decision. Zola and his disciples were glad to invoke a venerable name when fighting for their literary lives against a criticism which never ceased to decry them until they died or renounced their heresies.

Balzac, therefore, is the first name associated in modern French literature with realism, and his work provided material for the species of argument which, as I have said, involves the whole subject in a maze of qualified statements and contradictions. His successor Flaubert, after his death in 1880, was also drawn into the debate for the same purpose; namely, to support the thesis of the conservative critics that the modern realists were neither realistic nor modern. Both writers were powerfully influenced by the Romantic movement, and thus lent themselves to such interpretations as were placed upon them by the conflicting groups of their admirers. Flaubert, however, seemed more definitely to belong to the new school, for several reasons. In the first place, he did set himself deliberately to repress and finally to dominate that exuberant Romantic imagination which he shared with his age. He conceived *Madame Bovary* in a thoroughly realistic fashion and accomplished his task in strenuous obedience to a theory which was to become the dogma of Naturalism a generation later. In the second place, unlike Balzac, he enjoyed a clash with the official moralists, and at the outset of his career he acquired the halo without which, I suspect, no modern realist is authentic in the eyes of the average reader. When Flaubert was indicted for the immorality of *Madame Bovary* he was irrevocably committed to the company—since so numerous—of those writers euphemistically called in English "unpleasant."

Although the term "realism" does not, as is often supposed, date from the publication of that work, Flaubert is generally accepted as the father of the realistic novel. It was after a dinner given in his honor by Maupassant, Zola, Huysmans, and Octave Mirbeau, in 1877, that the "Naturalistic" school was created by the French press. The fame of Flaubert is definitely associated with Realism and Naturalism, and, as these are precisely the elements in contemporary American literature which are cultivated by the younger novelists, it is interesting to glance back at the chapter in French literature which began with *Madame Bovary* in 1857.

It was a year in which the unsuspecting Flaubert had every reason to believe that he could go on quietly writing for himself, as he had been doing ever since his return from the East. Labiche's comedies and the melodramas of Dumas *fils,* kept the theatre public busy; at the opera the first performance of Weber's *Oberon* occupied the attention of music-lovers, while the reception of Augier at the French Academy and the death of Alfred de Musset provided the literary world with excitement, varied by the thrills of legal scandals, the trial of Baudelaire for *Les Fleurs du Mal,* and Victor Hugo's attempted injunction against *Rigoletto,* on the ground that it was stolen from *Le Roi s'amuse.* Paris had obviously plenty of things to attend to without troubling over the first novel of Gustave Flaubert, whose name was utterly unknown to more than a small circle when he began to issue *Madame Bovary* as a serial in *La Revue de Paris.*

Unfortunately, that review was in bad odor politically with the authorities, and they made the novel a pretext for harassing the editors. Flaubert was, however, more fortunate than Baudelaire, a few months later, for he was acquitted, in consideration of the serious artistic purpose which clearly inspired his work. The trial, as is the custom in these affairs, merely served as an enormous advertisement for the new author, of which his publisher reaped the immediate benefit, for Flaubert had received only five hundred francs for the rights to the book during five years. So great was the success of the scandal that a newspaper at once offered him fifty centimes a line for his next novel, clearly a substantial advance upon the terms he had received for his first work. All the interests of the crowd were driven into the background by *Madame Bovary;* no vaudeville show was complete without its song on the subject, and burlesque playlets were written with Emma

Bovary as the central figure. The reviewers had naturally jumped into the fray and the furious and eternal battle was waged with great vigor, only Sainte-Beuve, Barbey d'Aurevilly, Baudelaire, and a few of the more discriminating realizing the true value and the literary significance of *Madame Bovary.* The press as a whole gave preference to Ernest Feydeau's *Fanny,* a novel which appeared about the same time and presented a certain superficial resemblance to Flaubert's in its treatment of a similar theme, but is long since forgotten.

All the circumstances were propitious for a further exploitation of public curiosity, but Flaubert returned to his home near Rouen and gave no heed to popular clamor for five years, when he published *Salammbô.* In the interval all sorts of rumors had been in circulation; the author's first book was flying backward and forward like a shuttle-cock between the camps of the Realists and their opponents, and the general expectation was that Flaubert would either aggravate his former offenses, or offer some sort of *amende honorable.* Flaubert did neither; he simply flabber-gasted both his friends and his enemies by publishing this lengthy novel of Carthaginian life. Sainte-Beuve, even, called for a lexicon with which to decipher this mass of exotic words and archæological terms; the learned experts denounced the pretensions of this novelist turned historian, and the inaccuracies of detail were solemnly exposed. In the main there was agreement on one point: the book was dull, though some suspected, and tried to prove, that indecencies were concealed beneath its soporific weight. The dulness and latent obscenity of *Salammbô* were the leading counts in the popular indictment of the book, for Flaubert was now a public personage and had to pay the penalty. Once more his name and his work were bandied about in the couplets of vaudeville singers, and an elaborate burlesque, *Folammbô, ou les Cocasseries carthaginoises,* was produced at the Palais-Royal Theatre, in which Hamilcar became Arriv'tar, and by dint of much punning of this type the whole story was turned into ridicule, precisely in such a manner as to preserve the legend of the author's manifold indecencies. It is remarkable how the cheap humor of this parody summed up the general tendency of contemporary criticism toward *Salammbô,* into which Flaubert had poured all his romanticism, his love of the fabulous Orient, of color and sound and primitive passion.

The author himself considered this book to be an even more definite manifestation of his theory of art than *Madame Bovary,* and it was upon his theory, the doctrine of "impersonal" literature, that the whole reaction against the Romantic Movement took its stand. The Romanticists were entirely personal and subjective; the Realists sought for an objective, dispassionate notation of life, from which the author's personality and his sentiments are eliminated. What is the explanation of this misunderstanding between the master and his disciples? To ask this is to raise the whole problem of Flaubert's realism, for, it has often been pointed out, his works are apparently realistic and romantic alternately. After *Madame Bovary* came *Salammbô,* and then *L'Education sentimentale,* which was followed by *La Tentation de Saint-Antoine;* after which came the unfinished *Bouvard et Pécuchet.* If the author of these works was hailed and denounced as the begetter of the realistic novel, if the Goncourts and Maupassant and Zola elected him as master, later criticism is disposed to regard him rather differently, and to refuse to allow him to be claimed either by the Realists or the Romanticists. He seems at bottom to have belonged to the latter rather than the former, but his romanticism was not based upon that horror of reality which is the true mark of the French Romantic school.

Thus in his works of sheer imagination, *Salammbô* and *La Tentation,* the desire for reality, for verisimilitude, for the suppression of his own personality, leads him to write his romance as Zola documented himself for his records of the Second Empire. In his realistic novels, on the other hand, he took refuge from the despotism of facts by transferring his romanticism to his characters, to Frédéric in *L'Education sentimentale,* to Emma in *Madame Bovary,* and, above all, by allowing himself the freest play in the beauty of his words, in the wonderful rhythm of his phrases, so that a story of provincial adultery, the most hackneyed theme in fiction, takes on the glamour of Chateaubriand's adventures in mythical regions of tropical beauty. As his correspondence reveals, Flaubert's romantic imagination was never more powerfully stimulated than when he was engaged upon a work of realism, but when he turned to a work of imagination, then his scrupulous concern for reality insisted upon satisfaction.

This Romanticist who had no fear of reality was destined to live just long enough to see the rise of a literary generation which cultivated that fearlessness to a point where the Realist dominated everything else. In 1877 he was the guest at a dinner-party from which came the six authors, Emile Zola, Guy de Maupassant, J. K. Huysmans, Henry Céard, Léon Hennique, and Paul Alexis, who launched the Naturalistic movement with *Les Soirées de Médan,* which was published the year of Flaubert's death. Looking over the work of this group, not to mention the deservedly forgotten host of their imitators, it is difficult to connect them with Flaubert. That scrupulous artist, who could spend five days over the writing of one page, whose style is one of the delights of French literature, was surely the strangest progenitor for that brood of Naturalists. The Goncourts still preserved their cult of the "exact word," of the "rare epithet," but these writers cultivated the commonplace in both style and matter. Their virtues are seen in the work of

Maupassant and in that sardonic little masterpiece of Henry Céard's, *Une Belle Journée,* but who even remembers Léon Hennique and Paul Alexis, "the shadow of Zola," as he was called?

With the exception of Baudelaire, no other French writer in modern times has exercised so powerful an influence as Flaubert with so small a volume of published work.

—Ernest Boyd

In the pleasant process of progressing backward, in which the younger American novelists are just now engaged, the oblivion which has descended upon Flaubert's succession seems to be ignored, or, at least, to suggest no disquieting reflections. There is a drift in contemporary fiction which takes the novel back to France of the eighties and late seventies, but not to the fifties, when Flaubert expressed the only durable reaction against Romanticism. All literature is the history of the reaction of one generation against the idols of another, and *Madame Bovary* marked the end of the Romantic movement. It was the work of the transition and is therefore characterized by that hesitation between two schools which is the essence of Flaubert. The modern Realists, like his immediate successors, have emphasized only one element in the movement of which he was the leader, and their preoccupation with the mere details of actuality will as surely condemn them to neglect as it has condemned the voluminous literature of the Naturalistic school. With the exception of Baudelaire, no other French writer in modern times has exercised so powerful an influence as Flaubert with so small a volume of published work. During his lifetime only five books of his were published, yet they endure, while the twenty volumes of Zola's Rougon-Macquart series and the sixteen other volumes of his miscellaneous fiction have fallen into increasing disrepute, together with most of the "polygraphy" of that period. *Madame Bovary* shocked the bourgeoisie in accordance with all the rules of Naturalistic procedure; it evoked and reconstructed the life of a provincial town with the superb skill of the creative genius who is master of detail, in a fashion which only makes the labored piling up of facts seem intolerable in his successors. Yet it lives, after all these years, as photographic realism never lives after the external circumstances of the time have changed. It lives because of that dual element in the genius of Gustave Flaubert, which enabled him to see the dream and the reality which together make up the sum of human existence, and to express both with the sensitive beauty of a great artist.

Flaubert having been acquitted, in due course his sins were forgiven, and he became a respectable figure, to be cited by the orthodox, together with Balzac, as an example of what decent realism should be. In this country, where French literature is simultaneously suspected by the moralists of outrageous licentiousness and credited by ingenuous youths with an ideal tolerance of the freedom of the artist, the fortunes of the realistic school from this point onward are instructive. Balzac having been canonized, and Flaubert being accepted for his romanticism tempered by realism, it might be imagined that the course of true literature ran smooth. It did not, however, for there continued an extraordinary confusion as to what a Realist really was. Brunetière actually discussed Rhoda Broughton in the same category as Flaubert, Zola, and Maupassant, while Dickens, George Eliot, and George Sand were—and still are—cited in every well-behaved French literary manual in discussions of realism.

In the circumstances, it is not surprising that, when a generation arose with a literature corresponding exactly to what the outside world now understands by French realism, the battle of *Madame Bovary* was resumed with intense vigor. The protagonist of this struggle was, of course, Emile Zola, whose name and influence have loomed larger in America, England, and Germany than those of any of his predecessors or contemporaries in the Realistic movement. Nevertheless, amongst both will be found men who never wrote worse than he, and several whose craftsmanship was vastly superior to his.

Let us begin with his own avatars. As early as 1847 there was Champfleury's *Chien-Caillou,* which was the first stone to be thrown at Romanticism by the actual pioneers in the campaign subsequently led by Zola. These pioneers were three gentlemen, of whom I need name only one, since his fame in this connection has survived him, Edmond Duranty, whose best novel, *La Cause du Beau Guillaume,* has been republished in Paris. During the early years of the Second Empire Duranty and his friends published a periodical whose title, *Le Réalisme,* was in itself a manifesto. When the first of its six numbers appeared, in 1856, Flaubert had not yet published *Madame Bovary,* and the very name of realism was something challenging, heretical, diabolical. Duranty had little to offer except his belief that a new literary epoch was imminent, that Champfleury was its precursor, and that romanticism was anathema.

When Zola was a young and unknown employee at the publisher Hachette's he came in contact with Duranty, who published *La Cause du Beau Guillaume* with that firm in 1862, at a time when Zola himself had not even issued his *Contes à Ninon.* Later Zola paid a brief tribute to this interesting and neglected figure in the history of modern French fiction, citing from *Le Réalisme* the formula which so largely anticipated the programme of the Naturalists: "Realism aims at an exact, complete, and honest reproduction of the social environment, of the age in which the author lives, because such studies are justified by reason, by the demands made by public interest and understanding, and because they are free from falsehood and deception. This reproduction should be as simple as possible so that all may understand it." Zola accepts this definition of purpose, merely extending it to include all classes of society, for he contends that Duranty's realism was too much restricted to the middle classes. Champfleury, however, was not a writer of sufficient stature to bear the brunt of such a programme, and by one of those ironies of literary history which are so delightful, Flaubert's *Madame Bovary* received only a brief and not very appreciatory notice in *Le Réalisme,* which thus died without being aware that it had witnessed the first serious breach in the ramparts it had attempted to storm.

Although Zola's earliest fiction was too unorthodox for Hachette, who refused one of the stories in the *Contes à Ninon,* and although his first novel, *La Confession de Claude,* in 1865, outraged the pruderies of the Empire, he had not yet produced the great work which was to place him at the head of the Realists, now christened Naturalists, in accordance with his scientific theories. That work was *L'Assommoir,* published in 1877, and the first big success of the twenty volumes of the Rougon-Macquart series. This is a date in Zola's evolution, but in the history of French realism that date was anticipated by Edmond and Jules de Goncourt in 1865, when their *Germinie Lacerteux* appeared. They were the real successors of Flaubert, and they had actually formulated the whole doctrine of Naturalism when they wrote, in 1864: "The novel of to-day is composed from documents, received by word of mouth or taken direct from nature, just as history is composed from written documents. Historians write narratives of the past, novelists narratives of the present."

Germinie Lacerteux contained a preface which is regarded as a document of historic importance, not only because it emphasizes the revolutionary character of the novel itself, but also because it lays down the theory of Naturalism. "The public like novels that are untrue. This is a true novel. They like books which seem to take them into society: this work comes from the streets. This is a clinical study of love. The public like harmless and comforting stories, adventures that end happily, ideas which disturb neither their digestion nor their peace of mind. Nowadays, when the novel has assumed the studies and the duties of science, it may claim the liberty and frankness of science." When this manifesto appeared Zola was an obscure journalist, and in a provincial paper he wrote one of the earliest of the few favorable reviews which the book received. The comments were, in the main, exceedingly violent in their hostility. "Putrid literature," cried one pundit, while a notorious pornographer described the book as "sculptured slime." Flaubert, however, was enthusiastic, and declared that "the great question of realism was never so frankly propounded." Sainte-Beuve realized that a new æsthetic was needed to criticise the new literature.

However, he kept this opinion and his appreciation of the book for the private consumption of his friends, following the precedent he had set for himself in the more delicate affair of *Les Fleurs du Mal*. The result is that, to this day, the Goncourts are viewed with a cold eye in academic circles. Even in Professor Saintsbury's enormous and catholic survey of the French novel they receive a few intolerant paragraphs, in which indignation takes the place of criticism and historical perspective. Zola himself, for some reason, escapes with milder censure, although his debt to the Goncourt brothers is obvious, the difference between the authors of *Germinie Lacerteux* and the author of *L'Assommoir* being that the former were artists, whereas the latter was a reporter. The Goncourts had a style and an æsthetic. Zola's style consisted in his having none, and for an æsthetic he substituted a scientific superstition.

Needless to say, it was Zola, not Edmond de Goncourt, who enjoyed the popular fame which for some years was the reward of the realistic novelists. To the end Goncourt, who outlived his brother Jules by a whole generation, was the object of an incredible vendetta. It seemed as if neither the mob nor its masters could pardon him for being a perfect man of letters, happily independent of the exigencies of his critics or his potential patrons. Zola, on the other hand, threw himself into the struggle which the Goncourts disdained. The critics wildly denounced each book of the Rougon-Macquart series as it appeared, as they had begun, in 1868, by fulminating against his earliest novel of importance, *Thérèse Raquin*. Alphonse Daudet was kindly treated, as the tame Realist who managed to be so much more gentlemanlike than his terrible friends and literary confrères, Zola, Huysmans, Paul Alexis, Henry Céard, and the Goncourts. But the strange fact remained that Zola's readers surpassed those of Daudet in number, and the sales of such books as *Nana* and *La Débâcle* were rivalled only by those of the estimable George Ohnet.

Everything tended to constitute Zola the leader and spokesman of what was now known as Naturalism. He came forward with his flock around him in 1880, when the celebrated collection of stories, *Les Soirées de Médan,* was published under the ægis of the master. In addition to that of Zola, some of the five other names in that volume are still remembered, such as Huysmans and Maupassant; Léon Hennique and Paul Alexis are forgotten, though George Moore retold the one story of Alexis, *La Fin de Lucie Pellegrin,* which deserves to survive. Henry Céard, who was a member

of the Academy Goncourt, and until his death on August 16, 1924, one of the few remaining members of the original Goncourt circle, has never had the fame outside his own country to which that sardonic little masterpiece, *Une Belle Journée,* entitles him. It was issued here in an English translation just as he died, leaving Léon Hennique as the last survivor of the Médan group.

If only because, with *Boule de Suif,* it introduced Maupassant, *Les Soirées de Médan* contained enough to justify its existence, and to impose the new generation of Realists upon the attention of public and critics alike. It presented six writers who were to play a considerable part in current French literature for a decade or more, and of whom two, Maupassant and Huysmans, outlived the merely transient fame attaching to the work of a challenging school. Moreover, the arrival of recruits was not delayed, and soon to those names were added Camille Lemonnier, Octave Mirbeau, J. H. Rosny, Paul Adam, Lucien Descaves, and the brothers Margueritte, to mention a few which will be familiar to the general reader of to-day. These writers all gravitated around Zola, and the formula of the experimental novel, with its scientific observation of facts, its exact documentation, its objective study of social environment, seemed to be assured of success.

England and Germany were translating Zola, George Moore in London, and Michael Georg Conrad in Munich were imitating him, and the upholders of morals and traditions at home and abroad were up in arms against this literary Antichrist. Not only did the professors like Brunetière recoil in terror, but critics as urbane as Lemaître and Anatole France were troubled. France, in particular, was desperately aggrieved by the lack of patriotism in Abel Hermant (now repentant and in turn the censor of that venerable radical), and deeply offended by the salaciousness and indecencies of such works as *La Terre*. All that suburban moralists abhor in the younger generation in America to-day was duly abhorred and castigated in Zola and his followers during the last quarter of the nineteenth century. With a virtuous indignation worthy of a contemporary Society of Authors holding its skirts aloof from a Dreiser or a Cabell, a group of schismatics in the ranks of Naturalism turned upon Zola, and provided us with one of the best jokes in the history of French literature.

In *Le Figaro* of the 18th August, 1887, shortly after the publication of *La Terre,* there appeared "The Manifesto of the Five." The signatories were Paul Bonnetain, J. H. Rosny, Lucien Descaves, Paul Margueritte, and Gustave Guiches, and they solemnly recorded their sternest disapproval of the master, whom they had weighed in the balance both of morals and æsthetics and found wanting. In order to appreciate the charm of their virtuous censure of Zola, one must know that Bonnetain had acquired fame as the author of a novel whose theme was onanism, J. H. Rosny had in that very year published *L'Immolation,* a novel of incest, Paul Margueritte was the author of a Lesbian master-piece, entitled *Tous Quatre,* while neither Guiches nor Descaves could have been translated without consider-able bowdlerization. However, they proceeded to a formal indictment of their literary progenitor, accusing him of having lowered the standard of Naturalism, of catering to large sales by deliberate obscenities, of being a morbid and impotent hypochondriac, incapable of taking a sane and healthy view of mankind. They free-ly referred to Zola's physiological weaknesses and expressed the utmost horror at the crudeness of *La Terre.*

At the same time they did not ignore the literary side of their brief for the prosecution. His experimental novels based on documentation are described as the work of a man "armed with faked documents picked up at third hand, full of Hugoesque bombast . . . and lapsing into perpetual repetition and stereo-typed phras-es." The observation in *La Terre* is "superficial, its technic old-fashioned, and the narrative is vulgar and commonplace, while the filthiness is exaggerated . . . the Master has descended to the lowest depths of dirt-iness." Therefore, they conclude, "we energetically repudiate this imposture on real literature . . . we re-pudiate these rhetorical mouthpieces, these gigantic, superhuman, and incredible figures, devoid of all sub-tlety, projected brutally, in heavy masses, upon scenes viewed in chance glimpses from the windows of ex-press-trains . . . we refuse to be parties to a shameful degeneration."

Thus ended a glorious adventure in realism, perhaps the greatest deliberate effort of the school in any coun-try to impose its æsthetic and to alter the course of literary evolution by violent effort. The Five formulat-ed in their literary criticism the substance of our judg-ment to-day on the work of Zola and his disciples. The scientific notation of life is an illusion, and when an illusory theory is added to an execrable style, the re-sult is a foregone conclusion. It was left, however, to writers not one whit less improper, in the moralists' sense, than those they attacked, to break the spell of Naturalism, not by producing "realistic" novels in the manner of Rhoda Broughton, but by throwing over the preposterous convention which was the real offense of Zola against literature. The names that will survive from that period, between the death of Balzac and the decline of Zola in the last years of the 'nineties, are those of writers like Flaubert, the Goncourts, and Maupassant, whose genius transcended the limitations of the realistic dogma.

Yet, it is still on moral and not upon æsthetic grounds that realism is impugned. In English-speaking coun-tries the term is synonymous, in the popular mind, with literature that is unpleasant and more or less ob-

scene. To such an extent is this convention accepted, even unconsciously, by those who theoretically know better, that a French work which is not avowedly re-alistic, which treats of psychological and spiritual rath-er than physical and material conditions, may with impunity emulate the strangest aberrations of the much-decried Naturalists. Marcel Proust's astonish-ing epic of sexual inversion, though not lacking in the crudest details, receives tributes of admiration from English and American critics who indorsed the pure-ly political vendetta which resulted in the condemna-tion of Victor Margueritte's *La Garçonne.* The latter is nothing more than a typical volume amongst many which have recently far exceeded its frankness in describing the sexual life of a certain type of woman. Let us recall that time, more than thirty years ago, when Paul Margueritte was seized with a moral fer-vor ostensibly as genuine, and inherently as ridicu-lous, as that of which the surviving brother is now the victim. These incidents have only the remotest concern with literature.

At the present time realism in French literature is in abeyance. Its exponents are chiefly the survivors of the Naturalistic period: Céard, Victor Margueritte, Lucien Descaves, and Paul Adam, to whom must be added the isolated creator of *Jean Christophe.* The younger men who may be counted as the continuators of the realistic tradition are not numerous, for they are separated from their literary forebears by the Symbol-ist generation, whose fiction cannot be called realistic, although Anglo-Saxon virtue would blush at the charm-ing impudicity of Henri de Régnier's novels, were he not protected by that unwritten law in favor of those who have no specific purpose in exhibiting "human documents." A few names deserve mention among the contemporary Realists, Gaston Chérau, with his *Cham-pi-Tortu;* Léon Werth with *La Maison Blanche;* Roger Martin du Gard with *Les Thibault.*

Realism, as it has thus evolved, more closely approx-imates to the English variety; it has shed its exuber-ances and modified its crudities, for it is no longer bemused by the pseudo-science of Zola. Such excesses as used to interrupt the easy flow of French fiction are disappearing, to make way for the very different ex-periments of impressionists like Jean Giraudoux and the fantastic adventures of Francis Carco, André Salm-on, and Pierre MacOrlan. Such incidents as the expul-sion of Victor Margueritte from the order of the Le-gion of Honor have no literary significance. Only ex-treme innocence of the character of the works which have simultaneously passed unnoticed can account for the foreign comment upon *La Garçonne.* No legal proceedings, it will be noticed, were instituted. We are far from the heroic period of Flaubert or even Zola. Realism, in that peculiar Anglo-Saxon connotation of the word, is a dead issue in France. That is why French critics who are aware of the real import of Proust's *A la Recherche du Temps Perdu* have wasted no inappropriate zeal in repudiating Victor Margueritte. *Ils en ont vu bien d'autres!*

Bernard Weinberg

SOURCE: "Theory and Opposition (1840-1870)," in *French Realism: The Critical Reaction, 1830-1870,* Modern Language Association of America, 1937, pp. 117-44.

[*In the following excerpt, Weinberg reviews the basic tenets of, and the vehement reaction against, French Realism of the mid-nineteenth century.*]

To state adequately the history of realistic theory, one would have to go back at least as far as the eighteenth century, to the formulations of Diderot. It would then be necessary to trace in romantic credos and manifestoes the development of certain contentions which eventually formed the basis of the realistic gospel. Special attention would need to be paid, for example, to the prefaces and critical pronouncements of Stendhal and Balzac, and to minor novels and novelists of the '20's and '30's. Such a study, however, is beyond the scope of my investigation. In the present [essay] . . . I shall consider the situation only as it affected the critics and the press during the period indicated. For statements of realistic doctrine, I shall use only such articles as were accessible to contemporaries (thus eliminating private correspondences and unpublished treatises), and I shall attempt an analysis of that doctrine only to show what it was that critics were opposing when they opposed realism. In the second place, I shall try to state the nature of the critical reaction to the new movement, as this reaction affected the movement in general rather than any specific author. I have chosen 1840 as a *terminus a quo,* since before that date there was no realistic school and no doctrine recognizable by contemporaries as such.

As a prelude to this study, it will be well to examine the history of the words *réalisme* and *réaliste* in their literary connections. As philosophical terms, both had long been known; but it was only during the nineteenth century that they were transferred to the vocabulary of aesthetics, and applied especially to painting and literature. It is impossible to say how early the transfer took place, for not all the relevant documents have been studied. Whatever statements I shall make with regard to this early history must therefore be taken as tentative, and as valid only for the materials examined. As early as 1834, Hippolyte Fortoul uses "réalisme" in a review of Antony Thouret's *Toussaint-le-Mulâtre;* after speaking of the "souffrances réelles" and the "passions actuelles" depicted in the work, he goes on to say:

M. Thouret a écrit son livre avec une exagération de réalisme, qu'il a empruntée à la manière de M. Hugo. Lorsqu'il l'applique purement à des descriptions extérieures, aux révélations des ténèbres de la police, aux réminiscences du cachot, aux souvenirs du jour-nalisme, il donne vraiment à son matérialisme une verve et une chaleur originales.

In 1835 and 1837, Gustave Planche uses the words in a number of articles appearing in the *Revue des deux mondes;* for a time, indeed, they seem to be the property of this writer and this journal. Planche conceives of realism as an exact reproduction or imitation of nature, limited strictly to the physical aspects of observable things; he regards it as incompatible with beauty, with the ideal, with art. "Envisagé comme une réaction accidentelle et passagère contre la dégénérescence des formes convenues, il peut avoir son utilité; mais ce n'est tout au plus qu'un moyen; et s'en tenir au réalisme, c'est méconnaître d'emblée le véritable but de l'invention." During the same period (1836), Hains speaks of Balzac as "quittant le sentier mystérieux qui sépare le réalisme du monde fantastique"; but this is probably only a misuse of the philosophical term, taken as meaning *réalité.* Again, in 1840, an anonymous critic of *Le Semeur* reviews Eugène Villard's *Idéalisme et réalité,* and asks: "Ce romancier avait-il à coeur de combattre le *réalisme* ou le *positivisme,* termes barbares qu'il faut employer pourtant, parce qu'ils expriment des idées pour lesquelles il n'y a pas de mots dans notre vieille langue française?" Here, too, the meaning is philosophical rather than literary. But more distinctly literary uses of the words come in 1846. Then, in June, Marc Fournier applies *réalisme* to Charles de Bernard:

Il semble, à première vue, que ce grand cachet de réalisme, dont M. de Bernard a le mérite d'empreindre ses ouvrages, doive leur donner un certain tour pittoresque et original. Oui, si c'était le véritable cachet d'un véritable réalisme.

In October, Hippolyte Castille speaks of Balzac and Mérimée as belonging to the *école réaliste,* of Balzac as losing *la physionomie réaliste* when he portrays exceptional rather than typical characters. In connection with these early specific uses, several facts are significant: first, that the words are for a time used almost exclusively by the *Revue des deux mondes,* and that they then 'disappear' for almost ten years; second, that when they reappear, it is to become the property of writers in *L'Artiste.* For Fournier's article appeared in that journal, edited by Arsène Houssaye, and it was Houssaye's *Histoire de la peinture flamande et hollandaise* (published in January, 1846) that first gave the words any real prominence. . . . *L'Artiste* was instrumental in supporting the realists and in formulating their doctrine; its whole connection with the movement deserves careful and detailed study.

After 1846, the words *réalisme* and *réaliste* become increasingly prominent. Houssaye in 1847 and Thomas in 1848 (both writing in *L'Artiste*) are the next authors to use them. It is not until 1851, however, that they gain any real currency, both in criticism of literature and of painting. In 1856, they attain a sort of consecration when Duranty founds his review called *Réalisme;* in 1857, Champfleury publishes his volume of essays called *Le Réalisme.* From that time onward, they appear in almost every literary discussion, applied—and misapplied—to the most diverse writers, definitely a part of current critical vocabulary. For a long time, however, writers continue to italicize the term, which remains for them a neologism; cf. Janin in 1852, Champfleury in 1853, Pontmartin in 1855, Claude Vignon in 1858, Barthet in 1859, Reymond in 1860, Lefrançais as late as 1867, Laprade as late as 1868, and many others too numerous to list. It is important to remark, too, that in this period *naturalisme* is used only rarely as a literary term equivalent to *réalisme,* and that even in these few cases its meaning is not demonstrably literary. *Naturalisme* had long been an accepted term in painting, where *réalisme* was merely adopted as a new synonym; it had not previously been used in regard to literature, however, and had to await a later school to be adopted as a literary by-word.

How, we may now ask, did realism present itself to its contemporaries?

(1) In 1843, before the days of a realistic school, Hippolyte Babou gave a definition of the "roman d'analyse" which merits a place as our first statement of realistic doctrine. Speaking of Balzac and his school, and especially of Charles de Bernard, Babou outlined the conditions of what Bernard himself had called "la chimie morale." His terms, in some passages, are remarkably similar to those of Taine a number of years later.

> C'est par l'énumération des détails que les analystes réussissent à donner une idée de l'ensemble. Ils saisissent sur les objets extérieurs et matériels les reflets des sentiments et du caractère de leurs personnages. A leurs yeux, une existence humaine n'est pas concentrée tout entière au foyer de la pensée. Elle se compose de milliers d'atomes épars autour d'elle; la forme et la disposition des meubles, la couleur du vêtement, les particularités de l'habitation, le degré de lumière qui entre par la croisée, mille autres petites choses imperceptibles, révèlent les moeurs et les instincts d'un individu, d'une famille. L'analyste consciencieux pousse la religion du détail aussi loin que l'antiquaire.

> L'analyse avait été jusque-là [before Balzac] une action réglée par un talent spontané; elle devint alors une science: de là le mal. Toute science qui se constitue a besoin d'une nomenclature; la chimie morale eut la sienne. Les passions et les caractères furent désormais traités comme l'oxygène et

l'hydrogène. Une technologie barbare, pédantesque, obscure, remplaça le langage ordinaire. Peu s'en fallut que la chimie morale ne nous donnât des oxides d'amour et des sulfures de haine, correspondants aux oxides de fer et aux sulfures de plomb de la chimie proprement dite . . . Ces manipulations qui avaient, il faut en convenir, un certain air de nouveauté, tendaient de plus en plus à changer en laboratoire le cabinet de l'écrivain. Le roman de moeurs échappait à la littérature pour entrer dans le domaine des sciences physiques et naturelles. Aprés avoir été chimiste, le romancier se faisait médecin. Il tâtait le pouls de ses personnages, au lieu d'interpréter les secrets mouvements du coeur. Les passions se transformaient en maladies, et les caractères en tics. Le monde matériel, que l'intelligence humaine avait semblé d'abord élever jusqu'à elle, réagissait à son tour et envahissait l'intelligence.

These same ideas, as we shall see, appear often in later statements of realistic theory.

(2) Ten years later, 1853. Champfleury voices a *confession de foi* and a complaint in his "Lettre à M. Ampère touchant la poésie populaire":

> L'art vrai, ce qu'on pourchasse aujourd'hui sous le nom de réalisme . . . , l'art simple, l'art qui consiste à rendre des idées sans "les faire danser sur la phrase" comme disait Jean-Paul Richter, l'art qui se fait modeste, l'art qui dédaigne de vains ornements de style, l'art qui creuse et qui cherche la nature comme les ouvriers cherchent l'eau dans un puits artésien, cet art qui est une utile réaction contre les faiseurs de ronsardisme, de gongorisme, cet art trouve partout dans les gazettes, les revues, parmi les beaux-esprits, les délicats, les maniérés, les faiseurs de mots, les chercheurs d'épithèles, les architectes en antithèse, des adversaires aussi obstiés que les bourgeois dont je vous ai donné un portrait.

(3) April, 1854. Elme-Marie Caro, professed adversary of the realist group, states what he considers to be its point of view:

> Nos jeunes réalistes du théâtre . . . annoncent hautement la prétention de donner à notre siècle la représentation du siècle lui-même exactement copié dans tous ses traits même les plus difformes, dans tous les éléments même les plus vulgaires de sa physionomie, dans les réalités les plus honteuses de son existence. Ils font de l'art, et ils s'en vantent, un trompe l'oeil; leur but n'est plus l'expression de l'idéal, c'est l'illusion du réel. Leur poétique a pour règle unique l'imitation; l'art véritable sera pour eux le plus exact plagiat de la nature. Produire sur la scène des hommes et des femmes comme ceux que vous rencontrez chaque jour dans les ateliers, dans les estaminets, dans la rue ou ailleurs, et jeter tous ces personnages de bas aloi dans le moule d'une action vulgaire, en leur donnant des moeurs de

hasard et un langage brutalement vrai, c'est là une pratique destinée à remplacer les théories discréditées des romantiques et des classiques, la théorie d'*Hernani* aussi bien que celle d'*Athalie.* C'est ce qu'on appelle briser les formes usées de la vieille tragédie et renouveler l'aspect du romantisme épuisé.

(4) May, 1854. Champfleury, in the *Revue de Paris,* publishes two articles on the "Aventurier Challes," an early eighteenth-century novelist whom Champfleury hailed as a precursor of realism. From the mass of anecdotic and biographical materials, we may isolate the following critical theories. (a) The novel should proceed by the observation of minute details, not by "invention" or "imagination"; (b) limiting itself thus to reality and to truth, it is absolutely sincere; (c) at the same time, it must be contemporary, giving *peintures de moeurs* and *scènes de la vie habituelle;* (d) but this does not mean photography, for the author's personality everywhere prevents him from giving a mechanical reproduction; (e) choice, indeed, is necessary, and the artist must arrange and distribute his materials to make of them a work of art; (f) the style of the novel should be simple.

(5) In December, 1855, in *L'Artiste,* the poet Fernand Desnoyers published the first deliberate manifesto of the school, entitled "Du réalisme," and beginning with "Cet article n'est ni la défense d'un client ni le plaidoyer pour un individu, il est un manifeste, une profession de foi." I quote the most important passages:

Le Réalisme est la peinture vraie des objects.

Il n'y a pas de peinture *vraie* sans couleur, sans esprit, sans vie ou animation, sans physionomie ou sentiment. Il serait donc vulgaire d'appliquer la définition qui précède à un art mécanique. . . .

Le mot réaliste n'a été employé que pour distinguer l'artiste qui est sincère et clairvoyant, d'avec l'être qui s'obstine, de bonne ou de mauvaise foi, à regarder les choses à travers des verres de couleur.

Comme le mot vérité met tout le monde d'accord et que tout le monde aime ce mot, même les menteurs, il faut bien admettre que le réalisme, sans être l'apologie du laid et du mal, a le droit de représenter ce qui existe et ce qu'on voit.

On ne conteste à personne le droit d'aimer ce qui est faux, ridicule ou déteint, et de l'appeler idéal et poésie; mais il est permis de contester que cette mythologie soit notre monde, dans lequel il serait peut-être temps de faire un tour.

D'ailleurs, on abuse de la poésie. . . . La poésie pousse comme l'herbe entre les pavés de Paris. Elle est rare . . . Quant à moi, je crois que cette poésie que chacun pense avoir dans sa poche, se trouve aussi bien dans le laid que dans le beau, dans le fantastique que dans le réel, pourvu que la poésie soit naïve et convaincue et que la forme soit sincère. Le laid ou le beau est l'affaire du peintre ou du poète: c'est à lui de choisir et de décider; mais à coup sûr la poésie, comme le Réalisme, ne peut se rencontrer que dans ce qui existe, dans ce qui se voit, se sent, s'entend, se rêve, à la condition de ne pas faire exprès de rêver. Il est singulier à ce propos qu'on se soit spécialement suspendu aux pans de l'habit du Réalisme, comme s'il avait inventé la peinture du laid. [All the great artists of the past have depicted evil and the ugly.] Que les réalistes jouissent de la même liberté! si les gens en paletot qui passent devant nos yeux ne sont pas beaux; tant pis! ce n'est pas une raison de mettre une redingote à Narcisse ou à Apollon. Je réclame le droit qu'ont les miroirs, pour la peinture comme pour la littérature.

[Mockery of the classicists and the romanticists.]

Enfin, le Réalisme *vient!*

C'est à travers ces broussailles, cette bataille des Cimbres, ce Pandémonium de temples grecs, de lyres et de guimbardes, d'alhambras et de chênes phtisiques, de boléros, de sonnets ridicules, d'odes en or, de dagues, de rapières et de feuilletons rouillés, d'hamadryades au clair de la lune et d'attendrissements vénériens, de mariages de M. Scribe, de caricatures spirituelles et de photographies sans retouche, de cannes, de faux cols d'amateurs, de discussions et critiques édentées, de traditions branlantes, de coutumes crochues et couplets au public, que le Réalisme a fait une trouée.

[The noisy objections to its advent.]

Et tout cela pourquoi? parce que le Réalisme dit aux gens: Nous avons toujours été Grecs, Latins, Anglais, Allemands, Espagnols, etc., soyons un peu nous, fussions-nous laids. N'écrivons, ne peignons que ce qui est, ou du moins, ce que nous voyons, ce que nous savons, ce que nous avons vécu. N'ayons ni maîtres ni élèves! Singulière école, n'est-ce-pas? que celle où il n'y a ni maître ni élève, et dont les seuls principes sont l'indépendance, la sincérité, l'individualisme.

(6) The first number of *Réalisme* (July, 1856) included, besides [an] article of Duranty . . . , one other item of interest for realistic theory. This was a review, by Jules Assézat, of Auguste Vacquerie's *Profiles et grimaces,* attacking Vacquerie's romanticism:

Pour les romantiques, le but de la littérature était une chose fantastique: l'art; pour nous, c'est une chose réelle, existante, compréhensible, visible, palpable: l'imitation scrupuleuse de la nature.

Pour nous, nous admettons le laid, parce qu'il est vrai; nous admettons le beau, parce qu'il est vrai aussi; nous admettons le vulgaire comme l'extraordinaire, parce que tous deux sont vrais; mais ce que nous n'admettons pas, et ce qui a tué le romantisme, c'est la manie exclusive du laid-horrible et de l'extraordinaire-monstrueux.

(7) August, 1856. Champfleury publishes, in *Figaro*, a letter from one of his readers criticizing *M. de Bois-dhyver;* to it he appends a reply, which he terms "ma poétique":

Tout romancier sérieux est un être impersonnel qui, par une sorte de métempsycose, passe de son vivant dans le corps de ses personnages.

Il serait dangereux de présumer de son tempérament, de ses vices ou de ses vertus, de son caractère, par les personnages qu'il met en scène.

Tout homme qui ne se sentira pas assez de courage pour devenir une sorte d'encyclopédiste, pour ne rien ignorer des tendances scientifiques et morales de son époque, devra renoncer à faire du roman. Joignez à ces études une attention profonde, une indifférence pour les actualités politiques, artistiques et religieuses, une oreille fine, un regard profond, une intelligence native, un travail absorbant, une volonté de fer dans un corps robuste ou maladif, et vous aurez un type de romancier auquel il est donné à bien peu d'atteindre.

Au-dessous de ces fortes intelligences se place le romancier personnel, qui n'a qu'à se regarder au dedans, pour, à un certain âge, retrouver au fond d'un tiroir les bouquets séchés de sa jeunesse, et, grâce, à la réalité, laisser un livre curieux, quelquefois plus longuement vivace que les oeuvres de cerveaux puissants. [e.g. *Adolphe, Manon Lescaut.*]

L'idéal, pour le romancier impersonnel, est d'être un protée souple, changeant, multiforme, tout à la fois victime et bourreau, juge et accusé, qui sait tour à tour prendre la robe du prêtre, du magistrat, le sabre du militaire, la charrue du laboureur, la naïveté du peuple, la sottise du petit bourgeois.

Par ses incarnations si diverses, l'auteur est obligé d'étudier en même temps le physique et le moral de ses héros; s'il endosse divers habits, il connaît diverses consciences.

Le romancier ne juge pas, ne condamne pas, n'absout pas.

Il expose des faits.

(8) November, 1856. Xavier Aubryet, in *L'Artiste,* discusses Champfleury; incidentally, he states his own concept of the realist:

Qu'est-ce en effet et que doit être un réaliste? Un homme qui n'est d'aucum parti, qui n'a pas de préférence, qui réfléchit les êtres et les choses, sinon avec sévérité, du moins avec une exactitude impartiale; il peint l'humanité dans tous ses milieux et dans toutes ses sphères, il ne la parque pas dans un coin obscur. De l'homme du peuple au patricien, de la beauté à la laideur, de la détresse à l'opulence, de l'infirmité à la toute puissance, il passe sans indifférence, mais sans élection déterminée; au point de vue de l'art, il choisit,—car c'est là la condition de l'art,—mais au point de vue humain, il ne choisit pas; car sa nature de *réaliste* le force à reproduire la réalité telle qu'elle est; or, la *réalité* est aussi charmante qu'horrible, aussi délicate que grossière, aussi naïve que raffinée. [Balzac and Shakespeare are true realists.] Ils n'ont ni haine ni engouement; il y aurait là deux périls d'aveuglement; ils sont surtout *impersonnels, objectifs.—Le moi, ce moi humain* qui est le secret de tant d'oeuvres, ne joue aucun rôle dans leurs créations; ils ont le don de ne *pas rester* eux-mêmes, non pas comme écrivains, mais comme observateurs.

(9) December, 1856. Duranty, in the second number of *Réalisme,* summarizes—"pour ceux qui ne comprennent jamais"—the content of the first issue:

. . . il a été très-nettement établi:

Que le Réalisme proscrivait l'*historique* dans la peinture, dans le roman et dans le théâtre, afin qu'il ne s'y trouvât aucun mensonge, et que l'artiste ne pût pas emprunter son intelligence aux autres;

Que le Réalisme ne voulait, des artistes, que l'étude de leur époque;

Que dans cette étude de leur époque, il leur demandait de ne rien déformer, mais bien de conserver à chaque chose son exacte proportion;

Que la meilleure manière de ne pas errer dans cette étude, était de toujours songer à l'idée de représenter le côté *social* de l'homme, qui est le plus visible, le plus compréhensible et le plus varié, et de songer ainsi à l'idée de reproduire les choses qui touchent à la vie du plus grand nombre, qui se passent souvent, dans l'ordre des instincts, des désirs, des passions;

Que le Réalisme attribue par là à l'artiste un but philosophique pratique, utile, et non un but divertissant, et par conséquent le relève;

Que, demandant à l'artiste *le vrai* utile, il lui demande surtout le sentiment, l'observation intelligente qui *voit* un enseignement, une émotion dans un spectacle de quelque ordre qu'il soit, bas ou noble, selon la convention, et qui tire toujours cet enseignement, cette émotion, de ce spectacle en sachant le représenter *complet* et le rattacher à l'ensemble social, de sorte que par exemple les reproductions à la Henry Monnier, isolées, fragmentaires, doivent être rejetées de l'art et du réalisme bien qu'on ait voulu les y rattacher;

Que le public était juge définitif de la valeur *des sentiments* étudiés dans une oeuvre, parce que la foule est tout aussi accessible à la pitié, au malheur, à la colère, etc., que l'écrivain qui s'adresse à elle . . .

(10) In Numbers 2, 3, 5, and 6 of *Réalisme,* from December, 1856 to May, 1857, Henri Thulié published four articles on the novel, treating respectively character, description, action, and style. These constitute the most important body of theoretical materials in the journal. We may summarize them briefly thus: (a) The character—the most important element in the novel—must be depicted as an individual, not as a type, and with all of the special traits springing from his rank and his environment; he must be typical only in the sense that he represents all the traits of his class; naturally, he must be contemporary, and drawn from any social level. (b) Description is valid only as a means to characterization: landscape and setting as influences on character, together with interiors, physiques and clothing as expressions of character, must be fully described as seen by the artist. (c) Action, too, is subsidiary to character; it arises from differences between the characters of the various actors, and exists only as a further explanation of these characters; hence it must be as simple as possible. (d) Style must be simple, clear, using only as many words as are necessary to express the idea, cultivating the *mot propre* always in preference to the periphrasis.

(11) August, 1857. Antonio Watripon writes, in *Le Présent,* an article called "De la moralité en matière d'art et de littérature," in which he insists on the necessity of truthful depiction:

Au fond, ce prétendu idéal de beauté, ce type primitif, n'est qu'une chose de convention et n'aboutit presque toujours qu'au *maniérisme*. . . . Aussi, les moeurs contemporaines ne tentent-elles que les écrivains vraiment observateurs et les artistes sérieux.

Ce sont précisément ces gardiens antédiluviens de la beauté primitive qui ont toujours à la bouche le *rappel au sens moral.*

. . . une littérature ne peut pas plus se passer d'observation que les rayons lumineux ne peuvent se passer de demi-teintes et d'oppositions. Or,

l'observation n'est pas autre chose que la science; c'est la somme acquise des investigations d'une époque, aussi bien du laid que du beau, de ses croyances que de ses négations. Donc, littérature et science ne peuvent vivre, c'est-à-dire s'élever, qu'autant qu'elles expriment d'une façon générale les besoins, les aspirations et les moeurs, QUELLES QU'ELLES SOIENT, du temps qu'elles prétendent guider et éclairer.

L'oeuvre du romancier est donc de peindre la vie comme elle est; il serait souverainement immoral et dangereux de la peindre autrement; ce serait induire en erreur une masse de lecteurs et conseiller implicitement l'hypocrisie.

Etre vrai avant tout! La vérité ne peut effrayer qui que ce soit; elle ne peut égarer personne.

(12) Francisque Sarcey, in an attack on Champfleury (*Figaro,* February, 1859), defines "Réalisme et champfleurisme." For each statement on realism, he gives a parallel remark about Champfleury; I quote only the former here:

"Il ne faut peindre que ce que l'on a vu, et le peindre comme on l'a vu; en d'autres termes: il n'y a de véritablement bon dans les lettres, que ce qui est absolument vrai, et les romantiques ne sont pas vrais."

Le Réalisme peint des caractères: sous la variété infinie et toujours changeante des traits qui distinguent chaque individu et lui donnent sa physionomie propre, il cherche les traits immuables de l'espèce où rentre cet individu; il les fixe en un portrait, qui vit et ne doit plus périr.

Le réalisme jette ses personnages dans une action, qui a son commencement, ses progrès et sa fin. Il prend la peine de former ses drames, comme il a pris la peine de les ouvrir.

Le réalisme étudie les passions et les étale à nos yeux dans un relief puissant. C'est ainsi que le peintre fait jaillir, sous la surface unie de la peau, des muscles qui èchappent à la vue courte et inattentive du vulgaire.

Le monde est mêlé de bien et de mal; c'est ainsi que le réalisme l'a toujours représenté. Il met des vertus sublimes à côté de vices hideux, d'héroïques dévouements près depassions égoïstes ou furieuses.

Le réalisme ne remue ces misères que du bout du doigt et pour en inspirer l'horreur . . .

Le réalisme ne mourra point: au moment même où le faux, le convenu, le boursouflé, le grotesque triomphaient sous le couvert du romantisme, les trois grands maîtres du roman contemporain, Stendhal, Balzac et Mérimée, maintenaient avec des fortunes diverses les fortes traditions du réalisme. Ils ont laissé leur succession à de jeunes écrivains, qui la transmettront à d'autres.

(13) 1863. Ernest Feydeau, in a "Préface" to *Un Début à l'Opéra,* reopened the discussion of realism, especially in its relation to the moot question of morality; the preface excited much comment and controversy. Feydeau pointed out that the contemporary, materialistic public no longer demanded in fiction the *pittoresque,* but rather an exact representation of itself; hence realism was the only possible form of literature for the second half of the nineteenth century. Realism he defined as "le système qui consiste à peindre la nature (ou l'humanité) telle qu'on la voit." This portrayal involves choice, arrangement, and interpretation of the materials, it includes the ideal as well as the real. If it represents corrupt manners, it is because society itself is corrupt; the novel derives from society, rather than being responsible for social corruption. Hence the reproach of immorality is nonsense.

These are the documents. They extend (if we exclude the first) over a period of ten years. They are the work of ardent realists, of no less ardent adversaries of realism, of critics and novelists, poets and journalists. They appear in the most conventional and in the most progressive of Parisian reviews. Nevertheless, they show a striking unity of conception: realism stating its case in "la bataille réaliste," stated it in approximately these terms. Romanticism and classicism, striving for an ideal beauty and seeking it mainly in the historical subject, arrive only at affectation and falseness. Realism, on the contrary, aims to attain truth. Now truth is attainable only by the observation (scientific and impersonal) of reality—and hence of contemporary life—and by the unadulterated representation of that reality in the work of art. Therefore, in his observations, the artist must be sincere, unprejudiced, encyclopedic. Whatever is real, whatever exists is a proper subject for art; this means that the beautiful and the ugly, the physical and the spiritual, are susceptible of artistic treatment; it does not imply that the artist refrains from choosing his subject and his detail, for choice is fundamental in art. The principal object of imitation is always man; description of the material world, construction of plot, are thus subsidiary and contributory to character portrayal. In setting down his observations, the artist must of course arrange and dispose his materials; but he avoids all possible falsification of them by practicing the utmost simplicity of style and form. The product of this method is moral in the highest sense—truth being the highest morality—and is eminently adapted to the needs of a materialistic, 'realistic' society.

Realism in literature, so conceived, differs in certain respects from realism in painting; these divergences are to be explained largely by the difference in the media of the two arts. The desire for truth, contemporaneity, and completeness, the insistence upon observation and impersonality, the reaction against romantic and classical convention, are common to both. But literary realism goes farther in proclaiming the priority of man and human character among the objects to be imitated, and in declaring that character must be approached by a scientific, analytical method of observation. Again, and unlike pictorial realism, it insists that the artist must choose and arrange his materials. This insistence, in all probability, was merely an answer on the part of the theorists to the attacks levelled previously at the practices of the painters and at the early manifestations of realism in literature. In spite of these differences, however, the doctrine of the realists is essentially the same in both arts.

This similarity is borne out more strikingly still when we consult the definitions of realism which appear in the criticisms of these years. "Calque de la réalité," "copie fidèle de la nature," "peinture exacte," "vérité dans l'art," these and similar phrases recur in practically all of the seventy odd definitions given by the critics. As in the definitions of realism in painting, *réalisme* is again contrasted with *fantaisie, idéalisme, spiritualisme.* These formulations, indeed, are almost monotonous in their similarity; very few of them go beyond some phrase such as those quoted, and it would hardly be profitable to list them all here. I cite only a few of the most representative:

[1846]

Fournier: "donner à tous ses récits comme à tous ses personnages les solides contours de la réalité." "rendre la société telle qu'il la voit."

[1847]

Houssaye: "ceux-là qui violent la vérité toute ruisselante encore sur la margelle de son puits."

[1851]

Poincelot: "culte de la vulgarité." "la reproduction infime et systématique de la réalité, sans élévation, sans aspiration vers l'idéal." "l'antithèse de l'*Idéalisme.*"

[1852]

Baschet: "le côté magnifique du Réalisme dans le roman. La vie réelle, la société telle quelle, le monde avec ses accessoires, la représentation des sentiments et des désirs."

[1853]

Mazade: "la minutieuse anatomie des choses qu'il entreprend de peindre et de décrire." "il suffit d'observer, quelle que soit la chose qu'on observe, pourvu qu'elle ait un caractère réel." "la reproduction minutieuse des vulgarités les plus crues."

Villedeuil: "la vie réelle avec ses drames mesquins et ses catastrophes exiguës; . . . avec ses grandeurs et ses petitesses, ses misères et ses ridicules."

Rouquette: "[copier] la nature ligne pour ligne, contour pour contour." "la nature telle qu'elle est, mais non pas telle qu'elle paraît être."

[1854]

Caro: "sensualistes de la forme et de la couleur." "l'imitation brutale de nos moeurs, une sorte de contr'épreuve daguerrienne de la vie de chaque jour."

[1855]

Pontmartin: "le sentiment vrai ou excessif de la réalité se passant de toute poésie ou ne la cherchant qu'en lui-même."

Janin: "tout ce qu'il entend, il le répète; tout ce qu'il voit, il le raconte; il n'arrange rien, il ne déguise rien."

[1859]

Monpont: "peindre de préférence, avec le pinceau ou la plume, les scènes et les objects les plus grossiers, les plus vulgaires, dans ce qu'ils ont de plus vrai, de plus naturel, de plus saisissant, et même de plus repoussant, et ne pas sortir de là."

[1864]

Delaplace: "copier simplement la nature, et mettre son ambition suprême dans l'exactitude de la peinture, dans la perfection des détails."

[1868]

Laprade: "l'art sans idéal." "la reproduction aussi exacte, aussi directe que possible des qualités matérielles d'un objet, . . . la représentation de ce qui tombe sous les sens, de manière à tromper les sens eux-mêmes." "photographier en quelque sorte la nature, . . . reproduire le monde matériel avec toutes les qualités les plus saisissantes de la matière."

From the earliest years, realists and critics alike cast about for ancestors of the new school, for prototypes and examples in the past. Balzac, of course, was the most obvious choice. He had, since 1830, practiced in his works most of the teachings of the new group; in fact, his example had been a major factor in the development of the theory of realism. Others sought farther afield. André Thomas, for instance, went back to Brantôme, Lesage, Prévost, Sterne, and Voltaire. Jules Janin saw sources for the new Bohemian school, including Champfleury and Murger, in Diderot, Prévost, Restif de la Bretonne, and Musset. Champfleury himself would include Challes, Lesage, Prévost, Diderot, Sorel, Furetière, and Vigny, while Auguste de Belloy would elect Voltaire. For Paul Boiteau, Rabelais, Pascal, and Molière are *réalistes*. Even Homer was claimed by Sarcey, and Goethe by Saint-René Taillandier. Among nineteenth-century authors, Pontmartin traces a filiation from Hugo, through Balzac, Gautier, Musset and Karr, to Murger; others see Eugène Sue and Paul de Kock as forerunners of the new school. In considering the sources, it is interesting to note that many critics regarded realism as having derived rather from a new materialistic spirit in society, following upon the Revolution of 1848, than from any literary tradition. Camille de Chancel's attitude is typical:

> Au moment où nous sommes du temps et de l'histoire, il n'est point étonnant que la réalité ait en littérature le dessus sur l'idéal. Dans l'ordre économique, les applications ont le pas sur les théories. La société que 1830 et 1848 ont couverte de philosophies, d'utopies, de religions, est en train, aujourd'hui que les grandes eaux fécondantes se sont abaissées, de s'assimiler petit à petit, par un travail silencieux et intime, mais actif et incessant, les débris de doctrines, les fragments de projects, les amas d'idées accumulés autour d'elles. Pour l'instant, l'attention est plus particulièrement aux améliorations immédiatement réalisables, aux aspirations qui peuvent se traduire en affaires, aux réformes qui peuvent se mettre en actions, aux progrès qui donnent des dividendes. Entre la tendance sociale aux choses pratiques et la tendance littéraire aux héros réels, il y a un certain parallélisme assez exact qui saute aux yeux.

No less curious and varied than the sources suggested for the realists were the authors considered as belonging to the new movement. A mere listing of the names (with the dates when they first appeared in association with the movement) will indicate how carelessly and indiscriminately writers were attached to the group; it will indicate, too, how vacillating was the concept of the term *réalisme* for about a decade. Hugo, Thouret, and Dumas *père* were early called realists by Planche. Novelists such as Stendhal, Mérimée, and Balzac were, from the earliest years, considered as having similar literary practices, and were promptly identified with realism when the new movement came into existence. Henri Monnier was regarded as embodying the same principles both in writing and in acting. With them, too, was linked Balzac's 'disciple,' Charles de Bernard. Then, beginning with 1848, the following French authors were connected by the critics with the new realistic school: Champfleury (1848), Murger (1849), Dumas *fils* (1852), Dupont and Büchon (1852), Reybaud (1852), Barthet (1853), Sand (1853), Souvestre, Gautier, and Gozlan (1854), Augier (1854), About (1855), Desnoyers (1855), Barrière (1856), Flaubert (1857), Taine (1857), Baudelaire and Renan (1858), Feydeau (1858), Thierry and Thiers (1859), Malot and Gourdon (1859), Perret and Deltuf (1860), Vermorel, Kéraniou, and Scholl (1861), Achard and Roux-Ferrand (1861), Charles Bataille (1863).

Returning now to the realistic doctrine as we have stated it, we may attempt to discover the reaction of the critics to the various constituent elements of that doctrine. First, the open opposition of the realists to the classical and the romantic approaches in literature. For most critics, realism was anti-romantic rather than anti-classical; surprisingly enough, for many of them this departure from the romantic was a welcome step. That is evident from statements such as Thomas's:

> . . . ils [le cénacle qui se moque des bavards et des lyres éoliennes] rient au nez des ciselures, des guillochages, des arabesques, des contours, des mignardises, des crevés de satin, de l'oiseau Rock, du lapis-lazzuli et des fanfreluches de toute sorte que la flamme de l'oubli a brûlés d'un clin d'oeil.

We might compare Pontmartin's remark that "quand le réalisme se prend au sérieux, quand il se propose de ramener au réel et au vrai l'art que nous avions égaré sur les vagues hauteurs du romantisme, il mérite que l'on compte avec lui." Only rarely do we find a critic who, longing nostalgically for the glitter and tinkle of romanticism, attacks the banishment of these ornaments by the realists. A few critics see in realism an attempt to overthrow classical convention—similar in that respect to romanticism—and they, too, approve the effort. Witness the remark of Léon Gautier:

> . . . nous n'avons pas été trop indignes de notre châtiment [le Réalisme]. Pendant plusieurs siècles, la périphrase a régné parmi nous; pendant plusieurs siècles, on s'est pudiquement efforcé de ne jamais écrire ou prononcer le mot propre.

In this sharp turn from romanticism and classicism, the realists naturally proscribed what they considered to be the essential aim of those schools—the quest for the beautiful and the ideal. But on this point the critics were in violent opposition to the theorists. For the former, like their colleagues in the field of painting, conceived of art as an idealization of nature. . . . For example, that of Charles de Mazade: "le but essentiel de l'art, c'est de rechercher et de reproduire une certaine vérité générale dans la nature physique comme dans la nature morale, dans la combinaison des lignes comme dans la combinaison des sentiments et des caractères." Likewise, Caro contends that art must be an aspiration of the intelligence towards immaterial beauty, that it must use nature only as a point of departure, that it must cultivate the ideal which is superior in every respect to the real. Critics so disposed were apt to exaggerate the realists' disdain for the ideal, and to condemn their product as lacking in that ideal. This is one of the most persistent objections to the new tendency; indeed, there are so many good statements of this reproach that it is difficult to choose among them. Albert Aubert's is one of the most typical:

> Le roman, quoi qu'en dise Stendhal, n'est pas "une suite de petits faits vrais"; l'idéal y doit bien aussi avoir sa part, l'idéal . . . un grand mot, difficile à définir, et dont on a trop abusé! . . . Il faut . . . que le roman, comme la poésie dont il est frère, nous arrache aux étroites limites du réel, et nous emporte à quelque distance du pauvre *moi,* l'hôte fastidieux du matin et du soir; il faut qu'il caresse la chimère que chacun de nous au-dedans de lui nourrit amoureusement, qu'il nous console de la vérité présente par une autre vérité plus haute et plus belle.

Without the ideal, says another, a work of art is incomprehensible, for the real and the particular may never be understood by the reader. Without the ideal, declares a third, people and things have no meaning, they are merely matter. And a host of other reasons are given.

Instead of this ideal, the realists would seek and incarnate in their art only the true, the observable, the verifiable. This, for the critics, is the salient feature of the doctrine; the Goncourts, for example, in their burlesque of a realist, make him declare: "je pense que le vrai, le vrai tout cru et tout nu est l'art." Almost all the critical discussions of realism point to this as its *sine qua non;* but none is as explicit as the celebrated passage of Sainte-Beuve on "la réalité":

> . . . si, en ressouvenir de toutes ces questions de réalité et de réalisme qui se rattachent à son nom [Champfleury], on voulait absolument de moi une conclusion plus générale et d'une portée plus étendue, je ne me refuserais pas à produire toute ma pensée, et je dirais encore:

> Réalité, tu es le fond de la vie, et comme telle, même dans tes aspérités, même dans tes rudesses, tu attaches les esprits curieux, et tu as pour eux un charme. Et pourtant, à la longue et toute seule, tu finirais par rebuter insensiblement, par rassasier; tu es trop souvent plate, vulgaire et lassante. C'est bien assez de te rencontrer à chaque pas dans la vie; on veut du moins dans l'art, en te retrouvant et en te sentant présente ou voisine toujours, avoir affaire encore à autre chose que toi. Oui, tu as besoin, à tout instant, d'être relevée par quelque endroit, sous

peine d'accabler et peut-être d'ennuyer comme trop ordinaire. Il te faut, pour le moins, posséder et joindre à tes mérites ce génie d'imitation si parfait, si animé, si fin, qu'il devient comme une création et une magie à son tour, cet emploi merveilleux des moyens et des procédés de l'art qui, sans étaler et sans faire montre, respire ou brille dans chaque détail comme dans l'ensemble. Il te faut le *style,* en un mot.

Il te faut encore, s'il se peut, le *sentiment,* un coin de sympathie, un rayon moral qui te traverse et qui te vienne éclairer . . .

Il te faut encore, et c'est là le plus beau triomphe, il te faut, tout en étant observée et respectée, je ne sais quoi qui t'accomplisse et qui t'achève, qui te rectifie sans te fausser, qui t'élève sans te faire perdre terre, qui te donne tout l'esprit que tu peux avoir sans cesser un moment de paraître naturelle, qui te laisse reconnaissable à tous, mais plus lumineuse que dans l'ordinaire de la vie, plus adorable et plus belle—ce qu'on appelle l'*idéal* enfin.

Que si tout cela te manque et que tu te bornes strictement à ce que tu es, sans presque nul choix et selon le hasard de la rencontre, si tu te tiens à tes pauvretés, à tes sécheresses, à tes inégalités et à tes rugosités de toutes sortes, eh bien! je t'accepterai encore, et s'il fallait opter, je te préférerais même ainsi, pauvre et médiocre, mais prise sur le fait, mais sincère, à toutes les chimères brillantes, aux fantaisies, aux imaginations les plus folles ou les plus fines . . . parce qu'il y a en toi la source, le fond humain et naturel duquel tout jaillit à son heure, et un attrait de vérité, parfois un inattendu touchant, que rien ne vaut et ne rachète.

If Sainte-Beuve's enthusiasm for reality was shared by but few critics, his objections to the pursuit of this goal in art were reiterated by many. Some of these arguments we shall consider under the discussion of specific realistic tenets, other we may now examine briefly. In the first place, this "truth" was unsatisfactory because it excluded the ideal: truth was taken as meaning, in its strictest sense, reality, also taken as meaning, in its strictest sense, the material and the factual. Hence there was no room for the ideal. I have already cited the objections of the critics to the lack of idealism. In the second place, it was denied that truth was identical with reality. For "truth," metaphysically speaking, is something greater and more far-reaching than the world as we see it—even if we see it completely. "La réalité," says Barbey d'Aurevilly, "est complexe; c'est une implication qu'il faut fouiller pour en démêler les mélanges et les profondeurs." "La vérité," says Arnould, "n'est pas la réalité: la vérité est éternelle, la réalité change comme la mode." "La réalité," according to Montégut, "n'est vraie pour [le spectateur] que lorsqu'il la rencontre dans sa propre expérience." And so on down the line. In the third

place, truth so conceived was regarded as unattainable; as A. de Belloy phrases it:

. . . le réalisme a cela contre lui, que son principe, étant absolu, est par cela même absolument inapplicable. . . . Dans l'art, tout est plus ou moins de convention. Le trompe-l'oeil même ne trompe que les yeux qui consentent à l'être. Si simple que soit, en apparence, le programme des réalistes, ils ne peuvent s'y conformer . . . [The necessary omission of vulgar language, for example.] L'auteur répugne, je veux le croire, à ce douloureux sacrifice; mais il faut bien qu'il s'y résigne, et, dès lors, il n'est plus réel; il cherche un compromis, un moyen terme, un procédé; il fait de l'art, je suis fâché de le lui dire.

To attain the truth they desired, the realists advocated a careful observation of nature, an impersonal and scientific approach on the part of the artist. The response to this demand for observation was complex. The critics would admit of it in principle, but they found that in application it led to a multitude of vices. They would welcome it as an antidote to the riot of romantic imagination, but at the same time they would condemn it as leading inevitably to an accumulation of meaningless, minute details, and as tending to replace the study of man by that of inanimate objects. As to minute details, preoccupation with them was regarded by many as being the basis of realism. Baudelaire, for example, points out that "*réalisme . . . signifie, pour le vulgaire, non pas une méthode nouvelle de création, mais description minutieuse des accessoires.*" And George Sand, unwittingly placing herself in the "vulgaire," defines realism as "le simple nom de science des détails." So defined, realism cannot but dethrone man and exalt things. As Jules Levallois says:

Le brin d'herbe, le moucheron, l'arbre, le chat, le chien, le perroquet, la batterie de cuisine, les fauteuils, le canapé, la couleur des rideaux, l'étoffe de la jupe et les rubans du corsage, voilà les éléments qui suffisent aux prétendus héritiers de Balzac pour construire aujourd'hui un roman de longueur raisonnable. Ils y mettent bien de temps en temps, par un reste d'habitude, quelques hommes et quelques femmes . . . , mais de l'âme humaine aucune nouvelle.

Even when man is the object of study, it is his external rather than his psychological aspects that attract the attention of the novelist. Vapereau exclaimed against this practice: "Il est si commode de substituer la description des formes à l'analyse des sentiments, les scènes matérielles de la débauche aux orages intérieurs de la passion, les impressions brutales des sens aux charmes mystérieux de l'amour, en un mot, le corps à l'âme!" Of the numerous other passages offering a similar complaint, I quote only that of Merlet in his definition of realism: "Le monde moral n'offrant à

Emile Zola, known as the principal theorist of the Naturalist movement in nineteenth-century France.

l'imitation ni la figure ni la couleur, l'imagination, qui n'a pas charge d'âmes, doit se renfermer dans le monde physique, comme dans un immense atelier peuplé de modèles qui tous ont la même valeur à ses yeux." This amounts to saying that the realists are frankly materialistic. Their disdain for idealism pointed immediately to this conclusion, their desire for "reality" contributed to it, their method of observation now confirms it. *Réalisme, matérialisme:* the words are synonymous. The new school is an *école matérialiste;* it answers the "tendance toute *matérialiste* de notre époque."

Realistic observation, as I have already said, must be impersonal and scientific in so far as possible. . . . [Literary critics] demanded that art be a reflection of reality against the temperament of the artist, and the definite program of realism to suppress such a reflection could not but be rejected. Few critics, in fact, pointed to impersonality as a plank in the realistic platform; but many of them revolted against what seemed to them, in one realistic novel after another, the suppression of the artist. Among them, none was more eloquent than Clément de Ris:

En vertu même de la dénomination sous laquelle ils sont connus et qu'ils ont acceptée, ils semblent repousser non-seulement l'intervention de l'imagination, mais celle du goût, de la réflexion, du caractère. Copiez la réalité, transcrivez-la littéralement, telles sont les suprêmes conditions de l'art, tout le reste n'est qu'erreur; c'est-à-dire ne sentez pas, ne pensez pas, ne réfléchissez pas, comprimez votre coeur, éteignez votre intelligence, étouffez votre goût, faites de votre cerveau un objectif de daguerréotype, et tout ira bien.

Arnould is equally angry in his repudiation of realism on these grounds:

. . . le réalisme n'étant point de l'art, est simplement un procédé. Comme il ne demande ni goût, ni style, ni imagination, ni pensées neuves ou idées fortes, ni études préalables, comme c'est un travail mécanique exigeant de l'exactitude et de la patience, tout homme qui en connaît un autre peut devenir auteur. On regarde, on écoute, on transcrit. Au besoin, on se peut servir de modèle à soi-même, à condition toutefois qu'on ait une glace où se mirer.

Of the many others who scoffed at realism for its elimination of the artist, there were of course some who found a simple reason for this state of affairs: the realists had no talent, and were forced to invent an art which could dispense with genius. Many critics, too, compared the artist so reduced and so minimized to a photographic apparatus. For what difference is there between a writer who copies nature exactly as it is, without interpretation, and a sensitized plaque exposed momentarily to the light? Many critics saw none whatsoever. Hence article after article equates realism with photography, with a purely mechanical rendition of the object imitated, with the consequent absence of anything recognizable as 'art.'

Along with impersonality, a scientific approach. An attempt at classification of the people studied, at discovering the motives and causes of their actions, at indicating influences of heredity, environment, circumstance on their personalities. This technique, applicable essentially to the study of character, was often commented upon by the critics; Babou's article of 1843 is the most striking example. Another is Auguste de Belloy's summary which, in 1857, foreshadows Zola's theory of the novel:

. . . si, à l'instar de la science actuelle, la littérature s'est faite expérimentale, empirique, si vous le voulez, il n'en pouvait arriver autrement, car tout s'enchaîne et se déduit plus rigoureusement qu'on ne le pense dans le cerveau d'un peuple bien organisé. Petit ou grand, chacun a son laboratoire, et là fait des expériences dont il publie les résultats sans s'occuper en aucune façon de les relier à un système, à une théorie quelconque. Tout le monde en agit plus ou moins ainsi.

By 1860 the tendency towards the experimental and medical novel was so widespread that Ernest Bersot was moved to write, in the *Débats,* two articles called "De l'application de la médecine à la littérature." Of the numerous references to this method, most were disapproving; critics believed such scientific analysis incompatible with art, they saw it as rapidly leading to the description of the rare bird and the exceptional case, they feared that it would replace the normal by the pathological.

These various realistic techniques were applicable only to the contemporary world; indeed, they arose as means to the adequate study and portrayal of that world. The demand for contemporaneity, so important a part of the realists' doctrine, was only rarely discussed by the critics, and in those rare discussions it was heartily welcomed. For critics and public alike were surfeited with the exotic in time and in space, they were eager for a literature treating their own times. The objections raised to the banal nineteenth-century costume by the critics of painting did not appear in the case of the novel: again a difference to be explained by the difference in the artistic medium.

Similarly, and for almost the same reasons, the insistence upon 'sincerity' met with no opposition. Who would not applaud a return from the forced lyricism, the artificial passion, the counterfeit heroics of the preceding period? Jules Levallois, for one, was delighted at such a return: 'L'école sincère nous a débarrassés de la sentimentalité factice, de la hâblerie nuageuse, de l'exaltation à froid, de l'imagination déréglée."

But on the broader question of the subject-matter of literature, the outburst of censure was violent, and the point of view of the realists was entirely repudiated. It will be remembered that the realists had declared all subjects proper for literary treatment; that is, they believed that all levels of society, all classes of people, might supply heroes for the novel. In the later years, largely in rebuttal of insistent criticism, they had maintained that a choice of people was to be made within each class, a choice of details within each object. But this secondary, *ex post facto* affirmation was never accepted by the critics, who persisted in blaming realism for its failure to select. The reasons for so blaming it will be obvious when we recall the definitions they gave of art. These reasons will be obvious, again, from such a statement as the following by Peytel:

> Ce qui fait l'erreur de l'école réaliste actuelle, c'est qu'elle a pris pour axiome, qu'il suffit qu'une chose soit vraie pour qu'elle soit bonne à peindre ou à raconter; c'est que, dans l'intention d'affirmer plus

énergiquement son principe, elle a choisi des sujets dépourvus de toute autre qualité que leur vérité, et qu'ainsi par une pente naturelle l'amour du réel est devenu le culte du laid. Les réalistes ont oublié que la copie, si elle est exacte, ne peut pas être plus intéressante que l'original. . . . c'est précisément la difficulté de trouver dans ce qui est sous nos yeux des sujets intéressants qui a introduit ce qu'on nomme l'idéal dans l'art et la littérature.

The attitude is epitomized by Fournel: "qui dit art, dit choix, et le réalisme ne se croit pas libre de faire un choix." On the other hand if the realists, theoretically, aimed at being all-inclusive, practically they did make a choice. But whereas the romanticists and the classicists had chosen the beautiful, the ideal, the grandiose, the realists—if we are to believe the critics—chose only the low, the trivial, the ugly. Commonness, triviality, ugliness: these three combine to make what is by far the most sweeping and the most vigorous denunciation of the realistic movement.

By 'lowness' and 'commonness' the critics meant the tendency of realistic writers to seek their subjects in the very lowest spheres of society. Say Gustave Merlet: "à les entendre, il n'y a dans le monde que des filles de joie plus ou moins déguisées; tous les coeurs ne battent que pour le vice; la société serait un lieu mal famé dont leur plume tient le registre." Says Louis de Cormenin:

> Lisez ses oeuvres, voyez dans quels repairs il entre, quelles effronteries sociales il coudoie, quel cloaque de sentiments il remue,—des voleurs, des filles de joie, des consciences douteuses, des êtres avilis. Au lieu de faire lever de généreuses semences dans le coeur de l'homme, il en agite les souillures, et tenant à la main, non la lancette qui sonde les plaies pour les guérir, mais le scalpel qui les fouille pour les étaler, il se promène de l'amphithéâtre au charnier.

Again, in a poem entitled *Réalisme* and purporting to exemplify realistic literature, Henri Dubellay presents a horrible "bouge" and the encounter of a man with a prostitute. Charles Monselet, too, writes his *Poème réaliste,* dedicated to "Gustave Courbet, maître peintre":

> Mon tailleur me pressait pour un billet échu.
> Je n'avais pas les fonds. Grande était ma
>   torture.
> Mon concierge railleur me donnait tablature,
> Vers mon seuil s'avançait l'huissier au pied
>   fourchu.
>
> Un long voile timbré pesait sur la nature
> Et dans l'opinion je me voyais déchu.
> Donc, n'aimant pas à voir traîner ma
>   signature,
> Afin qu'il m'obligeât j'allai voir Barbanchu.

Il n'était pas chez lui. Ce n'était plus tenable.
Je rêvais je ne sais quel fatal dénouement.
Enfin, pour terminer ce drame à l'amiable,
Je fis à mon tailleur un renouvellement.

These and other passages show conclusively that the critics saw in realism an abasement of art through the choice of inferior objects of imitation; that they objected in each case to this abasement need hardly be indicated.

By "triviality' the critics designated the readiness of the realists to select as objects of imitation persons and things eminently unworthy of artistic treatment. This reproach is related to the preceding, but it is not identical. For here it envisages, first, things so insignificant in themselves as not to merit attention in a work of art; then, language and actions which by their vulgarity or even their obscenity rank as unfit for art; finally, people and problems entirely uninteresting in life, and hence all the more so in literature. A passage in which Aurélien Scholl parodies the method of the realists (with special reference to Champfleury) will demonstrate the current conception of realistic triviality:

Jean Chouyou, souffrances domestiques des porteurs d'eau

Chapitre premier.—Les personnes qui passent à huit heures du matin par la rue Grégoire de Tours, ont pu remarquer au pied d'un mur humide et lézardé qui se trouve sur la droite, un peu avant d'arriver à la rue de Buci, un bourrier dont l'observation ne manque pas d'intérêt. C'est un amas pittoresque de bouts de carottes, de cosses de pois, de feuilles de salade, d'arêtes de poissons et autres rebuts. A de certaines saisons, les côtes odorantes du melon et la peau fine et rouge de la tomate viennent augmenter l'attrait du coup d'oeil. Les os y sont rares. On les vend jusqu'à trois sols la livre pour fabriquer du *noir animal,* denrée

qui sert à raffiner le sucre. . . .
Un homme sale et mal mis, appartenant à la lie du peuple, s'arrêta devant le bourrier.

Cet homme, c'était Jean Chouyou, notre héros.

Il considéra le bourrier avec une attention pleine d'amour; puis, tout à coup, il pâlit horriblement.

—Mon Dieu, murmura-t-il sourdement, elle ne m'aime plus.

Cet homme aux larges épaules, aux cheveux roux, aux mains noires et velues, aimait éperdument une femme de journée qui faisait le ménage de M. Nourrichet, employé du Mont-de-Piété. Cette femme, nommée mademoiselle Porquin, avait coutume d'indiquer des rendez-vous à son amoureux par la disposition des morceaux de navets et par l'arrangement des cosses de pois.

C'est ce que les Orientaux appellent selam. . . .

Mademoiselle Porquin était une femme de quarante ans. Une petite moustache brune ombrageait sa lèvre, et un énorme bouquet de poils jaillissait d'une tache foncée placée sur sa joue droite. Elle portait un bonnet tuyauté, une espèce de bonnet acariâtre et grincheux qui lui avait été donné pour sa fête par M. Nourrichet.

Hippolyte Babou uses a different image to express the same notion; desirous of discovering "What is realism?" he turns to the works of Champfleury:

Je me trouvais transporté dès la première ligne dans une société de Lilliputiens. Il me fallut regarder presque à terre pour examiner de près le monde microscopique où j'avais mis le pied. Tous ces êtres de convention étaient uniformément petits, maigres, mesquins, plats, secs, décolorés. Je les considérai à la loupe, afin de savoir si, dans leur petitesse, ils gardaient du moins forme humaine. Je m'aperçus très-vite qu'on avait bridé des oisons, habillé des poupées, suspendu des marionnettes, mais qu'en fait de créature humaine il n'y avait pas même un nain de Laponie dans cette collection de jouets d'enfants.

He finally decides that *réalisme* should properly be called *rachitisme.* Again, we might consult the opinion of Fournel, who says: "il [le réalisme] choisit de préférence . . . ce qui justement ne vaut pas la peine d'être peint, les petits caractères, les petits hommes, les petites choses, les côtés bas et vils, vulgaires et mesquins de la nature humaine." A multitude of other passages contain the same reproach, which is the most prominent of these three prominent censures.

By 'ugliness' (in the third place) the critics obviously refer to the realists' preference for the repulsive and their disdain for the beautiful. The same charge appears, we remember, in the case of painting; there, however, it is much more prominent than in the case of the novel. 'Ugliness' itself is a term more applicable to the pictorial than to the literary, and for the latter the equivalent terms 'lowness' and 'triviality' are more apt to be used. Nevertheless, the realistic school in literature is called "l'école du laid," it is described as "celle qui outre le principe et qui recherche seulement la vérité dans la laideur." Léon Gautier maintains that:

Le Réaliste est épris de la réalité laide, et enlaidit le beau pour le rendre réel. C'est la première fois peut-être que l'on voit toute une foule se passionner pour le laid, marcher, courir, voler à sa recherche, pousser des cris de joie à sa découverte, se prosterner devant lui et l'adorer.

In an article entitled "Du laid dans les arts," Edouard L'Hôte characterizes the realistic method: "Introduire dans la pratique et l'exécution des oeuvres d'art la représentation des choses vulgaires ou dépourvues d'élégance et de beauté, se passionner pour le commun, consacrer son ciseau, son pinceau ou sa plume à l'exaltation du laid . . ." Thus we find a group of critics who insist on the realists' emphasis on the ugly; but it should be noted that they are comparatively few in number and that their reproach comes relatively late, appearing with frequency only after 1857.

One clause of the realistic credo, that which established the primacy of character among the components of the novel, was entirely ignored by the critics. They made no comment upon it. Rather did they indicate constantly, as we have seen, that the realists were preoccupied chiefly with external and accessory detail, with things, with the physical side of reality, and that they neglected what was essentially human.

The realists' attitude towards form, however, did elicit considerable comment. They held that arrangement and disposition of the materials was necessary, but that it must be guided always by the severest principle of simplicity. A few critics recognized this demand for simplicity as a part of realistic theory, and in general they approved of it heartily. "Les grandes inventions d'autrefois," said Charles de Mazade, "ont fait leur temps. Il y a un effort pour ressaisir un certain naturel, une certaine simplicité de conception et de style." Pontmartin, wondering what was meant by "réalisme," asked: "Est-ce une bonne et franche haine contre la convention, la manière, la sensibilité factice, l'artificiel et le guindé? Alors nous ne pouvons qu'applaudir." Similarly, Granier de Cassagnac declared: "Exprimer simplement une idée claire semble un secret perdu. Retrouver ce secret et protester, en le pratiquant, contre le verbiage et la boursouflure, est un dessein digne d'éloges." Many more writers distinguished in realism a reaction against the conventional in form and in vocabulary; to this they raised no objection, although there are few statements of definite approval.

But when the critics read the works of the new school, they discovered that those works were in direct contradiction to their own aesthetic notions. The realistic novels lacked beauty of form; "faisant fi du style, de la forme et de la couleur," says Cormenin, "les réalistes se rabattent sur les idées." The various authors of the groups are similar in "la négligence du style"; a realist may even be defined as a *"contempteur de la grammaire et du beau langage."* The realistic novels failed to arrange their materials; they tended to present objects in their natural juxtapositions—necessarily an unartistic arrangement. Worst of all, the realistic writings neglected all principles of subordination, of perspective, of ensemble. Important and insignificant details were given the same attention—when the insignificant ones did not entirely outbalance the others—to such an extent that the work was confused and dis-

proportionate. This was a fault. "Les réalistes manquent à cette loi de la perspective," says Rouquette. "Il est certains détails dont l'effet doit être amoindri, qui ne doivent paraître que dans l'enfoncement, avec les proportions que leur place demande." According to Lataye, "Le grand défaut de cette école est de sacrifier l'ensemble au détail, et de là résulte une cause d'impuissance non moins grave que le culte exagéré de la forme." I might cite, finally, the opinion of Arnould: "Ils se perdent dans le détail, et l'ensemble leur échappe. Or le détail est un fait brutal, sans portée et sans moralité, dès qu'on cesse de le rattacher à un ensemble qui lui donne sa signification vraie." It should be noted, in conclusion, that while this reproach on the basis of form was varied and well represented, it was nevertheless a minor reproach as compared with others outlined above.

The claim of the realists to a moral function for their art was essentially an *ex post facto* manifestation; it came late and only after the reproach of immorality had been frequently voiced. But this reproach itself was of much later appearance than many others. To be sure, it was very early applied to specific authors—especially Stendhal and Balzac—but as a censure directed at the realistic school as a whole and at the doctrine of that school, it does not occur with any regularity until the publication of *Madame Bovary*. Before 1857, we find only isolated assaults on realism as immoral—especially Caro's article (1854) on "Le Sensualisme dans la littératue." With the prosecution of *Madame Bovary,* however, the cry of immorality enters definitely into the arsenal of the adversaries. Pinard's accusation contains the elements:

> Cette morale [la morale chrétienne] stigmatise la littérature réaliste, non pas parce qu'elle peint des passions: la haine, la vengeance, l'amour; le monde ne vit que là-dessus, et l'art doit les peindre; mais quand elle les peint sans frein, sans mesure.

Subsequently, the cry of immorality finds various expressions. The critics blame realism for treating the "mauvais monde," that of the prostitute, the "demi-monde"; for neglecting wholly "la vérité morale" in its search for "la vérité toute matérielle"; for concentrating its attention on the sensual. They see realism as seeking always the scandalous subject, in the desire to "taquiner les bourgeois," and as exposing aspects of life which should remain private and hidden:

> Il y a des détails de notre existence qui se passent derrière la scène; je demande par pure convenance qu'ils les laissent là, qu'ils ne retournent pas cette arrière scène de la vie et ne la donnent pas pour le spectacle. Il y a des séductions naturelles: qu'elles restent séductions; il y a des entraînements terribles:

que ces entraînements restent entraînements, et qu'on les regarde passer comme on regarde passer la tempête.

Several writers, on the contrary, do not admit that given subjects are in themselves immoral; rather it is the manner in which the novelist handles them that makes them immoral. Nor is a work moral because it has a moral ending: it may indeed bear throughout the stamp of an unmistakable immorality. Everything depends on the attitude of the artist, on his possession of the "moral sense." Rigault and Vapereau give the best statements of this point of view.

These various types of immorality were, for the critics, inevitable consequences of the realistic doctrine. The reasons adduced are the same as those given for the inevitable appearance of the ugly: the realist, seeking truth, soon discovers that common, everyday life is uninteresting; but he has a prejudice against depicting men as better than they are; hence he is obliged to treat exclusively of men as worse than they generally are. He becomes an apostle of the ugly and the immoral; and the farther he pushes his system, the more deeply he sinks into the distasteful and the repulsive.

The realists, in rebuttal, asserted that there could be no immorality in truth, that the only immorality was in falsification of the real by the ideal, by the fantastic, by the impossible. But this was a feeble answer indeed, and was immediately rejected by the critics. The more closely we approach the end of the period, the more vigorous and constant becomes the assertion that realism is an immoral system of art.

For realistic doctrine as a whole, then, the critics had little sympathy. They were ready to accept a literature which would correct the excesses of romanticism and replace the dead conventions of classicism. But realism, either because it erred in its theory or because it failed to apply properly the acceptable parts of that theory, did not supply the desired corrective. It neglected the ideal and the immaterial, and hence it did not attain truth. It replaced the study of man by the study of things, and hence it did not achieve an adequate representation of human action. It chose, among the objects of imitation, those which were undesirable for art, and hence it did not achieve the universality of subject to which it pretended. It disdained form, style, proportion, and hence it did not attain artistic beauty. In a word, as reflected against the preconceived aesthetic notions of the critics, realism could not fail to be regarded as an affront to artistic principles, as a diminution of the artist's function, as a vicious step towards the complete annihilation of art. Thus it was rejected as a doctrine, rejected as a general practice, rejected as a method for the individual novelist. . . .

Harry Levin

SOURCE: "Romance and Realism," in *The Gates of Horn: A Study of Five French Realists,* Oxford University Press, Inc., 1963, pp. 24-83.

[*In the following excerpt, Levin outlines the historical contexts of Realism and discusses its predominance in the French literary tradition.*]

The Context of Realism

We are dealing with a general tendency, and not a specific doctrine. Since no hard and fast definition of realism will cover all the manifestations occurring under its name, we must examine them for its pertinent meaning in each case. "'Realism,'" says Karl Mannheim, "means different things in different contexts." The same word, Benedetto Croce points out, is applied by some critics in praise and by others in blame. Zola's meat was Brunetière's poison. "Men and women as they are," as they are for Howells, barely exist for his successors. *Jane Eyre,* which preserves a schoolgirlish innocence for us, so shocked its reviewers that they could not believe it had been written by a respectable woman. Charlotte Brontë, for her part, found Jane Austen's fiction "more *real* than *true.*" Diderot praised Richardson for achieving "toute la réalité possible." Fielding would not have agreed. The history of taste, by lending its comparative standards, may resolve these conflicts of opinion. It suggests a sense in which Racine, though we do not ordinarily classify him as a realist, could be more realistic than Corneille. But, as between two contemporaries, one refining the analysis and the other broadening the scope of literature, which is the realist? Is it Trollope, with his accurate notations of provincial or parliamentary life, or Dickens, with his exaggerated efforts to delve in dust heaps which Trollope so quietly ignored? Is the penetrating self-portrait of *Adolphe* less realistic than the panoramic irreality of *Les Misérables?* Some novelists, evidently, go as far as they can within a restricted sphere; others, in enlarging those restrictions, overstep the borderline of romance. Every novel is realistic in some respects and unrealistic in others. Criticism can but try to estimate the proportions by comparing what the writer endeavors to show with what the reader is able to see.

When realism appeals neither to ontological argument nor to scientific experiment but to human experience, philosophers consider it "naïve." This is the kind of everyday realism that interests us most, but it would be naïve indeed if we expected reality to be the same for everyone. And we should be disappointed, like the princess in the fairy tale, if we supposed that nature could be perfectly reproduced by any artifice. Even the purely visual reproduction of the painter or the sculptor is admittedly angled, heightened, foreshortened. The brand of realism that has had the widest application in recent years is the politician's, which, instead of committing itself to a set of principles, rather implies the rejection of principle. The political objective of bourgcois society, freedom, seems to be undefinable in positive terms. "Freedom from what?" is the question that liberalism undertakes to answer, and its answers constitute a negative catalogue of our age's problems. Absolute liberty is as meaningless as realism in a vacuum. Both are relative terms, referring us back to a definite series of restraints from which we have managed to secure some degree of release. When we call a book realistic, we mean that it is relatively free from bookish artificialities; it convinces us, where more conventional books do not. It offers us *realiora,* if not *realia,* as Eugene Zamyatin succinctly put it: not quite the real things, but things that seem more real than those offered by others. By rereading those other books too and reconstructing their conventions, we can relate them to our comparatively realistic book and specify its new departures more precisely. We can define realism by its context.

Our excuse for studying literary history is that the mediocre works help us to place the masterpieces. By establishing the rules we learn to recognize the exceptions. It is the exceptional writer who changes the context of literature, and who—from generation to generation—readjusts it to the vicissitudes of life. Among such writers, Rabelais is doubly exceptional, one of the most original of originals, and he should be saluted in passing as a realist by any criterion, historical or otherwise. Though he preached a naturalistic ethic, he adorned it with an extravagant learning which could scarcely have belonged to a child of nature. Such an attitude is never primordial or spontaneous; it is always a stringent revision of more complicated views. When Schiller ascribed *Realism*—his word was not *Realismus*—to the Greeks, he meant that their outlook was not as idealistic as that of himself and his romantic contemporaries; but this was premised upon his nostalgic contrast between the self-consciousness of the moderns and the simplicity of the ancients. It remained for the twentieth century to perceive, with Léon-Paul Fargue: "There is no genuine simplicity; there are only simplifications. The natural in literature presupposes the utmost effort, or else mannerism." Insofar as realism presupposes an idealism to be corrected, a convention to be superseded, or an orthodoxy to be criticized, George Moore is right: "No more literary school than the realists has ever existed." No writers have been more intensely conscious of what was already written. We can measure their contributions by a sliding scale which moves from literature toward life, but which likewise gravitates in the opposite direction under the counter-influence of romance.

Any work of imagination is likely to exhibit both tendencies, romantic and realistic; they are by no means confined to those historical movements which we re-spectively associate with the première of *Hernani* in 1830 and the prosecution of *Madame Bovary* in 1857. "Realism had existed long before this great controversy," Baudelaire had written in 1846, under the caption "What is Romanticism?" Nor can we assume, without considerable qualification, that romanticism and realism are historically opposed. "Romanticism is the most recent, the most up-to-date expression of the beautiful . . . To say romanticism is to say modern art." In their eagerness to garner local color, to tackle forbidding subjects, and to break down classical genres, the romanticists anticipated the realists; while the realists, we must bear in mind, took over a considerable residue of romance. These intermixtures are strikingly evident in the romantic realism of Dickens, the "fantastic" realism of Dostoevsky, and the "poetic" realism of Otto Ludwig and Adalbert Stifter. In France there was Victor Hugo; but, on the whole, the transition was more homogeneous. Yet, when Georges Pellissier stressed the continuities in a suggestive study, *Le Réalisme du romantisme,* Emile Faguet repeated the usual textbook distinctions by way of review. Mario Praz does not avoid this verbal impasse by applying the term Biedermeier to the bourgeois romanticism of the mid-Victorians or by illustrating from Dutch genre-paintings. More precise definition should clarify both the extent to which the elder generation paved the way for the younger and the extent to which the younger generation reacted against the elder.

Of the successive generations that have been shaken by literary revolution, only one—the middle generation of the nineteenth century—claims the explicit label of realism. Like most critical categories, the term comes after the fact, and comes later to other languages than to French. English seems to have borrowed it, in 1853, through an article on Balzac in the *Westminster Review.* The first independently relevant instance cited by the *New English Dictionary* came in 1857, when Ruskin criticized the "base grotesque" of Bronzino, the attempt to compensate for lack of imagination by "startling realism." The context here, as in so many early instances, refers to painting and expresses hostility. The previous year Emerson had employed the adjective "realistic," as a synonym for "materialistic" and an antonym for "idealistic," in characterizing Swift. Here the word betrays its ultimately philosophical origin, and its long association with the dualistic arguments of the metaphysicians. In France, though Littré still classifies *réalisme* as a neologism in 1872, the word had been utilized by literary criticism as early as 1826. Through the 'thirties it was used occasionally to designate some of the same things that romanticism stood for; it was consistently attacked, in the *Revue des deux mondes* and other conservative periodicals, as an artistic symptom of the growing radicalism of the epoch. It was usually mentioned in a disparaging sense, until some of the younger bohemians, protesting against the outmoded pomp of the academic tradition, began to pride themselves on the designation. Arsène Houssaye's history of Flemish painting, published in 1846, proved that there was also a realistic tradition. Théophile Gautier and other friendly critics defended the new esthetic by invoking the ancient concept of the imitation of nature.

It was "the landscape-painter of humanity," as Gustave Courbet was known to his admirers, who first proclaimed himself a realist—or rather, accepted the epithet thrust upon him. When the Salons objected to his literal treatment of peasants and laborers and the middle classes, he retorted by issuing manifestoes in the name of realism. When the Paris exposition of 1855 refused to hang his pictures, he erected his own *Pavillon du Réalisme,* and began to publicize the movement on an international scale. Later years brought out the socialistic and anticlerical implications of his work, and he was finally exiled for the part he had taken in the Commune. Whenever his critics complained that he had caricatured his models, he would insist, as Balzac did: "Les bourgeois sont ainsi!" Meanwhile realism was being widely popularized by the quasi-photographic genre-painting of the Barbizon school. The technique of photography, which had been invented by Niepce de Saint-Victor in 1824 and subsequently developed by Jacques Daguerre, had been acquired by the state and divulged to the public in 1839. Neither painters nor writers welcomed the new invention, for it drew them into a competition which they were both destined to lose. Nothing short of the *Comédie humaine* could compete with the daguerreotype; Balzac's ingenuity and facility, in reproducing characters and exhibiting scenes, was hardly less inventive; and Daguerre's other novelty, the diorama, echoes across the dinner-table in *Le Père Goriot.* Once perfected, photography served to demonstrate the difference between artistic means and mechanical processes of reproduction. Its ultimate effect was to discourage photographic realism. Painters became impressionists, writers rediscovered the personality of the observer, and even photographers called art to the aid of technology.

Though Balzac won retrospective recognition as the arch-realist, chronologically he belonged to the romantic generation. And though *Madame Bovary* was the most notable and the most notorious book of the realistic generation, Flaubert cultivated an aloofness from his contemporaries. The fanfares were sounded by a pair of journalists whose own novels stirred up less excitement than their articles on contemporary art and literature. Jules Fleury-Husson, under the pseudonym of Champfleury, collected some of his criticism into a volume, *Le Réalisme,* which came out in 1857. Edmond Duranty edited seven numbers of a little magazine, *Réalisme,* at monthly intervals between November 1856 and May 1857. Both men were acute enough to sense that the trend, which they followed rather than led, was far too fundamental to be identified with the special program of a single group. "That terrible word 'realism' is the reverse of the word 'school,'" announced Duranty. "To say 'realistic school' is nonsense. Realism signifies the frank and complete expression of individualities; it is actually an attack upon convention, imitation, every sort of school." More affirmatively, he went on to describe the envisaged result as "the exact, complete, sincere reproduction of the social milieu and the epoch in which one lives." But this was merely to make the description vary with the individual consciousness of one's place and time. As the slogan of a school, announced Champfleury, realism was only "a transitional term which will last no longer than thirty years."

While it lasted, Balzac and Courbet were avenging gods, and Champfleury was their publicist and prophet. He was also the historian of French caricature, which was even then reaching its height and leaving its incisive mark upon fiction. In an embittered tale of bohemian life, *Chien-Caillou,* he schematized the formula of Cervantes by printing side by side in parallel columns the idealistic expectations of his readers and the disappointments that reality would hold for them. His own laconic definition of realism, "sincerity in art," was based upon one of the most elusive words in the critical vocabulary; but it meant something against a context of artistic affectation, and against the constant enthymeme that the lower classes were more rewarding than upper-class subjects because they were more sincere. Here critical logic is overtaken by revolutionary zeal. Champfleury reminds us that realism is the insurrection of a minority, one of those "religions in -ism" like socialism that gained headway with the Revolution of 1848. Even then, while Marx and Engels were framing *The Communist Manifesto,* Champfleury and Baudelaire were conducting a republican paper. Champfleury's distrust of form, and his attempt to judge works of art by their content, foreshadowed the Marxist critics. Disliking poetry, he distinguished the friends and enemies of realism as *sincéristes* and *formistes*—a distinction which left little room for the ironic interplay of Baudelaire or of Flaubert. Political expression, submerged with the failure of the socialist Republic, came to the surface in controversies over realism. Both *Madame Bovary* and *Les Fleurs du mal* were prosecuted by the imperial regime.

Literature was taking stranger and more sensational shapes, artists were making private gestures of opposition to the Empire, while the realists were expressing, in Champfleury's terms, "a latent and unconscious aspiration toward democracy." These impulses converge in the rejected picture, *L'Atelier du peintre: allégorie réelle,* where Courbet has depicted himself, his easel and canvas, a number of cast-off romantic properties, a nude woman, a group of working-class models, and several friends, including Champfleury, Baudelaire, the folk-poet Büchon, and the socialist Proudhon. Here the real allegory is that of the self-portraying artist, whose world is the studio and whose studio is the world, whose symbols are actualities and whose ideology is his art. Even more paradoxically, the distance between Flaubert's material and his style illustrates the ambivalence of realism, as a characteristic product of middle-class society and an unsparing commentary upon it. "As an expression of manners and social conditions, the school seems to correspond in art with the bourgeois element that has become predominant in the new society, reproducing its spirit and image as the novel does in literature," wrote a hostile critic, Louis Peisse, in 1851, the year that witnessed the enthronement of Napoleon III. In 1857, M. Prudhomme himself, succumbing to the vogue, subscribed a letter with assurances of his "distinguished consideration and realism."

With the predominance of the bourgeoisie, with the grandeur and decadence of Birotteau, it was certainly time to explore fresh fields. In 1864, the year of Claude Bernard's *Introduction à l'étude de la médecine expérimentale,* the Goncourts prefaced their *Germinie Lacerteux* with the usual declaration outdating all previous fiction: "The public likes false novels; this is a true novel." They were now proposing a further extension of the literary franchise, *le droit au roman:* "Living in the nineteenth century, in a time of universal suffrage, of democracy, of liberalism, we have asked ourselves whether those we call 'the lower classes' have not their right to the novel." French literature, in all its critical awareness and circumstantial candor, was ready to investigate the servant problem. "Today, when the novel undertakes the investigations and obligations of science, it may also claim the privileges and freedoms." Realism had fully crystallized by 1858, when Taine's essay on Balzac appeared. After the appearance of Darwin's *Origin of Species* in the following year, every mode of interpreting human experience had to be gradually revised. A younger generation, children of the realists and grandchildren of the romanticists, demanded still another readjustment. During the 'seventies Zola sought to consolidate Taine's critical position with Bernard's experimental method, within the widening—or was it the narrowing?—orientation of Darwin's naturalism.

Heretofore "naturalism" had occasionally figured in the critical vocabulary; on occasion it was loosely synonymous with impressionism; but it had never been sharply differentiated from the connotations of realism, the more inclusive term. Zola, the literary executor of Duranty, sought to reinvigorate the realistic novel by substituting a naturalistic slogan. Just as the realists had adopted Balzac, so the naturalists adopted Flaubert, though Flaubert had never accepted the label, and Zola admitted in cynical moments that it was mere publicity. In serious moments, his naturalism looked beyond Flaubert's hatred of the bourgeoisie to an interest in the proletariat, and beyond the conventions of art to the investigations of science. A novel, though it might be impeded by political barriers, was free to lose itself in the uncharted contexts of nature. But the naturalistic novel also involved certain deterministic premises that realism ignored, that inhibited freedom of action and relieved the characters from responsibility for the degrading condition in which the novelist found them. The novelist himself was now a passive observer, a rigorous compiler of what Edmond de Goncourt first termed "human documents." Observation, it was presumed, would eliminate imagination and convert the art of fiction into a branch of scientific research. For Zola the realism of the Empire had been "too exclusively bourgeois." He in turn, with greater success than his forerunners, founded a school. He virtually established naturalism as an official doctrine of the Third Republic, a hardening orthodoxy from which the divergent movements of the twentieth century still take their departure.

Neither Stendhal nor Balzac nor Flaubert nor Zola nor Proust belonged to the French Academy—a sequence of omissions which throws light on the relationship of the novel to the establishment. Novelists less distinguished have been admitted, since the immortalization of the bland Octave Feuillet in 1863. Through one of the most carefully managed ironies of literary history, plus a bequest from Edmond de Goncourt, naturalism established its own academy in 1903. The issue is internationally reflected in the terms by which the Nobel Prize has been awarded, from 1901, to an author of idealistic tendency. Nonetheless most of its laureates, like the winners of the Prix Goncourt, have written in what became the naturalistic tradition. Now that the naturalists, the realists, and the romanticists are venerated alike by literary historians, we must not forget how often—during the nineteenth century—they were damned by critics, ignored by professors, turned down by publishers, opposed by the academies and the Salons, and censored and suppressed by the state. Whatever creed of realism they professed, their work was regarded as a form of subversion, and all the forces of convention were arrayed against them. While art propagandized against the middle class, the middle class invoked morality as a weapon against art. Literature had come too close to life for comfort. Brunetière, who led the counter-attack against the naturalists, accused them of overstressing the grosser aspects of reality, and pleaded for a revival of idealism. The naturalists hinted, by way of reply, that the traditionalists preferred the timeless to the timely because they were out of touch with their own time.

We have something to learn from their objections to specific details; traditionalism, however, objected in principle to the use of detail, and predisposed its critics to find realism tedious or trivial, ugly or obscene, decadent or improbable. On the other hand, the realists, in their revolt against tradition, felt impelled to exaggerate "the true in the horrible and the horrible in the true." Jules Janin's horrendous parody, *L'Ane mort et la femme guillotinée,* is worth remembering, if only because it proves that the popular novelists of *le bas romantisme* had scarcely been less sensational than Zola. Incidentally, it characterizes the bourgeois idealist who prefers romance to realism as "a Don Quixote in a cotton nightcap," surmounting his shop with battlements and surrounding it with a moat. Thus realism, as Georg Lukács puts it, moves in cycles. Proust, who used the word pejoratively, put his finger on the impetus: "From age to age a certain realism is reborn, by way of reaction against the art that has been theretofore admired." Consequently Erich Auerbach could range across many ages, cultures, and languages, from the *Odyssey* to Virginia Woolf, in order to show us "the representation of reality in western literature." His *Mimesis* is a magistral explication of a rich and eclectic series of texts. It illustrates the stylistic interplay between the grandiose and the plain-spoken, demonstrates the way symbolic conceptions yield to more materialistic approaches, and indicates the realistic component in the formal artistry of Dante and Shakespeare. *A fortiori* the weight of authority must be accorded to Auerbach's considered opinion that historic realism, fully conscious of socio-politico-economic circumstance, is a strictly modern phenomenon beginning with Stendhal.

The Dynasty of Realism

Not every age, unfortunately, can be a great age of poetry; and a flourishing drama seems to require a rare conjunction of time and place. If any literary form has flourished in the modern epoch of the western world, it has been prose fiction. And surely, if this form has any nucleus of tradition, it has been the parallel and interconnected development of the novel in England and France. The Occidental novel harks back to brilliant beginnings in Italy and Spain; perhaps it registers its highest degree of imaginative intensity in Russia and America; and it has some interesting later offshoots in the Scandinavian countries and elsewhere. But it was England which led the way in the eighteenth century, and France in the nineteenth century seems to have taken the lead. The fact that Germany has had so few novelists of distinction is clarified by a remark of André Gide's: "The fatherlands of the novel are the lands of individualism." Admitting that German fiction lacks European significance, a sociological study has concluded that it identified itself too uncritically with the interests of the middle class. No land has been more self-critical or more individualistic than France, and no literature has spoken for all of Europe with more authority. Recognizing this authority, Tolstoy advised Maxim Gorky to read the French realists;

Henry James wrote Howells that they were the only contemporaries whose work he respected; and George Moore never ceased to tell English novelists how much they could learn from Balzac, Flaubert, and Zola. "Yes, when I read a novel I mostly read a French one," says one of James's heroines, "for I seem with it to get hold of more of the real thing—to get more life for my money."

Circulating in foreign translations or between its original yellow covers, the French novel has acquired an international notoriety, which is based not merely on its pioneer frankness in the matter of sex but on its intransigent refusal to take any human relationship for granted. Its abiding preoccupation might be summed up in the single word *moeurs,* which must be translated by two different English words, "manners" and "morals," but which retains the impersonality of the Latin *mores.* In English literature, ever since the debate between Congreve and Collier, there seems to have been a gradual divorce between manners and morals. Novels of manners, like Meredith's, have been rather eccentric and superficial; novels of morals, like George Eliot's, have been more earnest and didactic. There has been an irresistible temptation, indelibly exemplified in the happy endings of Dickens, to sacrifice the real to the ideal. Too often, when the novelist has not arranged for the triumph of virtue, or modified the conduct of his characters to suit the ethical prepossessions of his readers, they have held him responsible for immoralities which he has simply attempted to describe. Mrs. Grundy equated "realistic" with "pornographic." Guizot, who was an Anglophile as well as an official spokesman for middle-class morality, publicly regretted that French novels were not as respectable as *The Heir of Redclyffe.* Brunetière—that exponent of universality—preferred George Eliot, and even Rhoda Broughton, to Flaubert and Zola. For Flaubert and Zola there could be no compromise with domesticated taste. Morals were the criteria of manners, and manners the test of morals; and, where the practice failed to live up to the theory, nothing less than an uncompromising realism could deal with the situation.

"French novelists are very lucky in having the French to write about," Stephen Spender has remarked. Supremely articulate and gesticulative, their consistent reactions to concrete situations invite such aphoristic remarks; but an almost proverbial example may prove more illuminating, particularly when it is borrowed from Molière. The very title of his comedy, *L'Amour médecin,* characteristically inclines toward a clinical view of an emotional theme. Sganarelle's daughter, having secretly fallen in love, displays symptoms of melancholia, and the father consults his neighbors in the opening scene. M. Josse recommends some gift to cheer her spirits, a diamond necklace or some piece of jewelry, and the others make various other recommendations. Sganarelle listens patiently until they all have spoken, and then tells them off one by one, pointing out that M. Josse happens to be a jeweler—who would profit by the occasion to sell his wares—and that the advice of the others is no more disinterested. "Vous êtes orfêvre, M. Josse!" The line is more than a gag; it is a flash of revelation. Another writer, taken in by the show of pathos and benevolence, might have taken M. Josse at his neighborly word; or, having detected the ulterior economic motive, might have cried out in righteous indignation. Molière, in a mood which is seldom too far from detached amusement, sees through the characters, grasps the situation, and lays bare the *moeurs*. Now there is nothing about a lovesick girl or a worried parent or a merchant with his eye on the main chance that could not be encountered anywhere else. What is characteristic is not the pattern of behavior but the exposure of motivation: the dissembled emotions and calculations of the personalities, the conflicting interests and responsibilities of the group.

French literature has been preoccupied, not so much with the individual in isolation or with society in the mass, as with the problem of keeping the balance between them. Psychology and sociology have contributed in equal measure to whet the analysis. Long before those twin sciences in -ology had been professionally exploited, their potentialities had been explored by the self-knowledge of Montaigne and the introspection of Pascal, by the maxims of La Rochefoucauld and the memoirs of Saint-Simon. The method of Descartes had located the ego against its context. La Bruyère had subtitled his character-sketches *Les Moeurs de ce siècle*. Voltaire had condensed the history of civilization into an *Essai sur les moeurs*. Even Rousseau, in probing the subjective, had retained a quantum of objectivity. We often hear that the French language is better accommodated to prose than to poetry, that the Gallic genius rises to greater heights in comedy than in tragedy, or that the most creative achievements of this particular culture are the most critical. Though these generalizations are far too sweeping to pass unqualified, they are borne out by the achievements of French fiction. The comparatively short distance between fiction and criticism is due, in Harold Laski's phrase, to "the great French tradition of making criticism a commentary on life." In other countries literature and society are two distinct things, said Renan. "In our country . . . they interpenetrate." Hence the novelist is *ex officio* a social critic. Theory without practice or practice without theory might subsist elsewhere, fostered by German metaphysics or British empiricism. French philosophy, under the aspect of Cartesian dualism, has insisted upon a clear-cut distinction and a running parallel between material reality and the realm of ideas. Realism, as we define it, is therefore implicit in the traditional structure of French thought.

An incomparable control of the instruments of culture has made France's experience available to the rest of the world, but it is the experience itself that has made France, and has made it the second fatherland of educated foreigners. Its explicative talents have reinforced its diagrammatic position. Geographically and historically France has played the typical role of *l'homme sensuel moyen,* as Matthew Arnold was so acutely aware, for Arnold faced the thankless task of upholding a critical tradition in a more decentralized culture. The centrality of France among nations strengthened the centripetal position of Paris among cities, making it the geographical and historical capital of bourgeois democracy. "France is at the heart, and is the heart, of Europe; if it beats too hard or too fast, fever and disorder may spread through the whole body," warned Bonald, fearful lest cultural continuities had been destroyed by the Revolution of 1789. The Revolution of 1830 brought to Michelet, at the other extreme of political opinion, a sense of France's mission: to reveal the social Word, as Judea and Greece had revealed the moral Word. "All social and intellectual solutions are fruitless for Europe until France has interpreted, translated, and popularized them." Bonald's organic metaphor differs significantly from Michelet's conception of the French people, piloting the ship of humanity. "But today this ship is navigating in a hurricane; it goes so fast, so fast that dizziness overcomes the sturdiest, and every breast is troubled. What can I do in this beautiful and terrible movement? One thing—understand it. I shall try, at least."

> **French literature has been preoccupied, not so much with the individual in isolation or with society in the mass, as with the problem of keeping the balance between them.**
>
> *— Harry Levin*

Why should French writers, with such unflinching effort, have dedicated themselves to that comprehensive task? The reason is the salient circumstance of modern history. It was revolution that inspired both the reactionary Bonald and the radical Michelet. Not less than ten times during the hundred and fifty years that divide the *ancien régime* from the Vichy government, Frenchmen were called upon to overthrow their leaders and to establish a new order. Alas, these overturns have since continued, and Michelet's trepidations would be even stronger today. The record, repeating itself with cumulative emphasis, testifies to a high degree of social consciousness, and to an equally high degree of individualism. Revolutionary movements end in Napoleonic careers, and the cult of Napoleon ends in the Commune.

Napoleon introduces the need for success, unbridled emulation, unscrupulous ambition—crass egoism, in short, primarily his own egoism—as the central motive and the universal spring. This spring breaks, stretched too far, and ruins his machine. After him, under his successors, the same mechanism will operate in the same way, and will break down in the same way after a more or less protected period. Up to the present day, the longest of these periods has lasted less than twenty years.

When Taine was writing this passage in 1889, just a century after the first revolution, he was expecting another man on horseback, General Boulanger, to trample down the Third Republic. But the democratic regime, having already lasted nineteen years, and having proved more durable than its predecessors, was to live fifty years longer. The statue of Liberty Enlightening the World, its gift to a sister republic, retains an undimmed image in a poem by Marianne Moore, written upon the dark days of collapse and capitulation under Marshal Pétain:

> . . . we with re-
> enforced Bartholdi's
> Liberty holding up her
> torch beside the port, hear France
> demand, "Tell me the truth,
> especially when it is
>   unpleasant." And we
> cannot but reply,
> "The word France means
> enfranchisement . . ."

Enfranchisement prompted mingled reverberations of despair and hope in 1941. "French writers, the freest in the universe"—so began a pamphlet published that year by Kléber Haedens, *Paradoxe sur le roman,* which terminated with the imprimatur of the Vichy censorship. The calculated irony was a bid for independence in the very teeth of disheartening odds.

Fanny Burney, who as Madame d'Arblay had lived under the Napoleonic Empire, declared upon her return to England that it would henceforth be impossible to delineate "any picture of actual human life without reference to the French Revolution." Yet it never occurred to Jane Austen that the young officers, who figure as dancing partners for the heroines of her novels, were on furlough from Trafalgar and Waterloo. One had then to breathe the air of France to be fully conscious of the difference between the eighteenth and nineteenth centuries. The new issues were quite as urgent in England, but not so desperately clear; the French were tearing down and building up institutions, while the English were preserving and adapting them. The English novel was free to go its own way, if it chose, and to be content with domestic life; the French novel, for lack of answerable government, assumed

certain quasi-public obligations. In the absence of regular institutions, literature became one, whose leadership was conceded in Europe, if not in France. Since the breakdown of the old Latin republic of letters, French books had kept up a kind of International among the intellectuals. Elsewhere, when modern ideas penetrated, they were recognized and ticketed as overtly French. It was the French Revolution of July 1830, according to the historian of materialism, Friedrich Lange, that subverted German idealism. "It was toward France—'realistic' France—that men loved to look even from a political point of view. But what so specially endeared the July Monarchy and French constitutionalism to the men who now gave the tone in Germany was their relation to the material interests of the moneyed classes."

Revolution secured, not the realization of its own slogans, but the enthronement of the middle class. Writers thereafter could only express their doubts and disappointments, and hope for another revolution. The hopes of the first revolutionists had been dashed by the Terror; the grand illusion of Napoleon's Empire had been lost at Waterloo. The monumental past, with its legend of conquest and its rhetoric of freedom, could only reduce the present to mock-heroic dimensions. Alfred de Musset, in his *Confession d'un enfant du siècle,* gave a first-hand diagnosis of the disillusioned state of mind that was inciting his contemporaries to realism. "All the sickness of the present century comes from two causes: the people who have gone through '93 and 1814 bear two wounds in their hearts. Everything that was is no more; everything that will be is not yet. Look no farther for the secret of our troubles." Though the nobleman had been deprived of his prerogatives, it was not the common man who profited. M. Prudhomme, rushing into the breach, was the man of the hour. Eulogizing himself, he parodied Musset. "No matter what you do or say, everything today is bourgeois. Aristocracy exists no more, democracy does not yet exist, there is nothing but bourgeoisie. Your ideas, your opinions, your manners [*moeurs*], your literature, your arts, your instincts are transitional; then hail to Joseph Prudhomme, the man of transition—that is to say, of the bourgeoisie!" Perhaps Musset, as he himself had confessed, had been born too late. Stendhal, who was old enough to be a child of the previous century, liked to think that he had been born too early. But Prudhomme, emerging between revolutions, was the personification of self-conscious modernity, immune to the disenchantments and undeceptions of the *maladie du siècle.*

When the Goncourts portrayed the generic man of letters in *Charles Demailly,* they confronted him with the generic theme. His novel, *La Bourgeoisie,* would apparently have been a French equivalent of *The Way of All Flesh* or *Buddenbrooks.* But, since it was French, it would also have been a "social synthesis"; it would have traced, through three generations of a single family, the evolution of society and behavior (*moeurs*); it would have depicted "the plutocracy of the nineteenth century in its full expansion." The grandfather would have been "the incarnation of the sense of property," the son an ardent believer in "the religions of human and national solidarity," and the grandson a degenerate embodiment of "all the practical skepticisms of modern youth." And, since Charles Demailly depended on observation rather than imagination, like a dutiful disciple of the Goncourts, his characterizations would have been historically sound. At any rate, other observers confirm the story. They show how, through political agitation and dynastic change, the bourgeois dynasties continued to enrich themselves; how the French nation as a whole enacted, in the ambivalent phrase of the intellectual historian, Bernhard Groethuysen, "a virtual epos of the bourgeoisie." The development of capitalism has been divided by the economic historian, Werner Sombart, into two phases. During the first phase, from the Renaissance to the latter part of the eighteenth century, manners and morals were restricted by the sanctions of orthodox Christianity. The second phase, the period of individual competition in a dynamic society, has been unrestricted and expansive. If we accept Sombart's criteria, the presence or the absence of restrictions, it requires no prophet to point out that, since the second World War, this phase has been moving toward a cyclical ending.

This period of bourgeois capitalism, roughly from 1789 to 1939, happens by no accident to be the heyday of the realistic novel. With due allowance for lag and experiment, we are concerned with exactly a hundred years—from Stendhal's first novel, *Armance,* published in 1827, to Proust's last volume, *Le Temps retrouvé,* published in 1927. Our five novelists, posted at intervals, chronicle the intervening century and bear witness for their interconnected generations. Thus in 1842, when Stendhal died and Flaubert came of age, the foreword to the *Comédie humaine* marked Balzac's prime, and Zola's birth had just occurred. If we consider the symbolist overtones of Proust as an epilogue and the classical origins of Stendhal as a prologue, there is a consistent and continuous tendency from romanticism through realism proper to naturalism, which we can follow through the work of Balzac, Flaubert, and Zola. All five, realists according to their respective lights, explicitly render an account of their day, and address themselves directly to posterity—a title which seems for the moment to have devolved upon ourselves. Looking back upon the total configuration of their work, we can hardly fail to notice its chronological links with politics, and with comparable revolutions in the advancing sciences and the plastic arts. We notice that their respective accounts are soon corroborated: Mérimée refines upon Stendhal, Charles de Bernard emulates Balzac, Maupassant sits at the feet of Flaubert, Zola's disciples from the school of

Médan, and the influence of Proust is still with us. The imitators lead us back to the innovators. They are the dynasts of realism, and their authority has outlasted the Bourbons and the Bonapartes. Their books, not less than Vigny's, may be read as successive cantos in an epic poem of disillusionment.

By a series of approximations, we arrive at our subject. Novels are such bulky, opaque, and many-faceted items, so easy to conjure with and so much harder to analyze. We have not analyzed a novel until we have discovered its place in the mind of the novelist, in the movement of the age, and in the tradition of literature. Every great novelist has his own solutions to the technical and historical problems that I have been too summarily reviewing. In touching upon some ancestors of the French realists, some of their rivals in English and other literatures, and some of the efforts to formulate their genre, I have tried to test the generality of certain definitions before applying them to these specific examples. The question remains . . . whether I have chosen the best examples. It can only be hoped that the choice of this sequence of novelists is not arbitrary, but would agree with the consensus of readers and critics and other novelists over the years. The reasons for literary survival, depending as they do upon a peculiar combination of powers and circumstances, are never single or simple. If popular appeal were our criterion, we should have to discuss Eugène Sue and Georges Ohnet. If every author lived up to his literary pretensions, none would be greater than Edmond de Goncourt or Anatole France. If we wanted skillful story-tellers, and did not want them to tell us very much more, we should find them in Alexandre Dumas and Guy de Maupassant. If we rated authors by their humanitarian sympathies, rather than by their comprehension of human beings, we should rate George Sand and Victor Hugo above the authors on our list.

If all books belonged to their period like furniture and bric-a-brac, Octave Feuillet would be the novelist of the Second Empire. His novels fit as neatly into Louis Bonaparte's world as the boulevards of Haussmann, the opera-house of Garnier, the music of Offenbach, the drama of Meilhac and Halévy, or the painting of Meissonier and Winterhalter. But that world, though self-satisfied, was not self-sustaining. The Salon des Refusés opened more spacious vistas with the art of Manet and Pissarro; the suppressed poems of Baudelaire uncovered gulfs beneath the very pavements of Paris; and the exile of Hugo held out to later writers the alternatives of intransigence and conformity. Convention dried up Mérimée's inspiration and weakened Daudet's talents, but realism stiffened Flaubert's opposition. Where Feuillet belonged, Flaubert detached himself; and *Madame Bovary* is still alive, where *Le Roman d'un jeune homme pauvre* is as dead as the Empress Eugénie. But Flaubert's detachment, which has kept his work from fading into the debris of his period, is not to be confused with indifference, nor is it an empty gesture; rather it indicates broken attachments, and asserts stronger allegiances to higher standards of integrity. No lack of conviction but too many convictions troubled him, he told George Sand. To conclude that Flaubert and [the] other realists were misanthropic and negativistic would be to accept the short-sighted view of their contemporaries. Taking advantage of an enlarged perspective, we shall see them—without exception—as men of generous enthusiasms, positive values, and fruitful ideas. They belong, as I would interpret them, to that world which is inhabited by the greatest writers of all time; for all great writers, in so far as they are committed to a searching and scrupulous critique of life as they know it, may be reckoned among the realists.

Jill Kelly

SOURCE: "Photographic Reality and French Literary Realism: Nineteenth-Century Synchronism and Symbiosis," in *The French Review,* Vol. LXV, No. 2, December, 1991, pp. 195-205.

[*In the following essay, Kelly examines the critical reaction to the rise of both photography and the Realist aesthetic in mid-nineteenth century France.*]

In May 1841, two years after François Arago's public announcement in Paris of the invention of photography, an anonymous critic compared Balzac's descriptive technique to the daguerreotype ("Les Lecamus"). Contemporary critics were more than reluctant to acknowledge photography as an artistic medium; they perceived it as a threat to aesthetics in general. Their reticence to accept realism as a valid literary form was equally strong. Negative comparisons between photography and the realist novel became an offensive tactic for conservative critics who sensed a battle looming between objective and subjective realities, a battle that would threaten the established order of art and aesthetics.

The early technical progress of the new graphic medium paralleled in chronology the transition from romanticism to the major period of production of the realist novel (1839 to the mid-1890s). Yet traditional literary historians of the nineteenth century in France, and most especially those who have focused on realism, have, for the most part, ignored any connections between literary realism and photography's rapid rise as an artistic and social phenomenon. At best, respected historians have seen the connection between photography and literary realism as nothing more than a "synchronisme douteux." But information about photography was widely available from the very beginning through the scientific, artistic, and journalistic circles that were so closely intertwined in mid-nine-

teenth-century Paris, circles in which the realist writers had an integral part. Writers were photographers, and photographers, writers. Contemporary literary critics quickly recognized the corollaries between the capabilities of the new graphic medium and the professed goals of the literary realists, so much so that those critics adopted and used the terms of the new graphic medium in their lexicon, assuming an influence on literary realism by photography, albeit a negative one.

The nineteenth century was increasingly a world of the real, *real* in its most basic etymological sense: the production, accumulation, and consumption of things. Auguste Comte's philosophy of positivism, of man's need to organize and explain his world by investigating what was accessible and by developing an objective knowledge of external phenomena was crucial to the philosophy of the realists. What man could sense, and primarily what he could see, isolate, and capture was all-important. Contemporaries believed that the surface of things, their external and primarily visible aspects, could convey to the beholder an understanding and appreciation of what lay beneath. Nature could be reproduced, objective reality captured. Truth was becoming tangible and conservable. Collecting evidence, documenting reality, recording and observing, the realists were part of a mindset that believed in induction, that patiently collecting one instance after another will gradually produce a correct image of nature, provided that such observations are not colored by subjective bias. Recording . . . observation . . . factual evidence—these obvious traits of the camera were traits that realist writers emulated, whether consciously or unconsciously.

In the realist novel as in photography, the subject itself is of primary importance, for each medium seems to reassure its audience that art is not hard; each medium seems to be more about its subject than about art, to paraphrase Susan Sontag. Each tends to focus our attention on that subject itself and not on the way the subject is rendered; the manipulations and transformations of the subject by the artist are not meant to be apparent. Photographs seem to be the reality we see with our eyes; the straightforward language of the novel seems to be the way we ourselves speak; and the lives portrayed in both seem to be recognizably like our own.

Contemporary reality is, of course, the only possible subject for a photograph; our belief in the photo's truthfulness is integrally tied to our acceptance of the fact that at the time the picture was taken, the subject actually existed in that place. The realist writers were not confined to such a narrow view of time by the fundamental characteristics of their medium, but they were similarly confined by the tenets of realism which dictated a preference for concrete observable reality. Instead of chronicling what they had experienced before or what they imagined had happened or could happen, the realist novelists concentrated on a scrutiny and a description of the world around them.

A primary task of early photography was to conserve the memory of grandiose events in a simple existence. The new graphic medium first did this through its presence at the rituals of christenings, first communions, weddings, and funerals. Then, as travel between the cities and the provinces as well as between countries and continents became easier, travelers became tourists wanting to preserve the memory of the occasion with tangible proof. As access to photography increased, more and more photos were taken of more and more events until as Paul Valéry remarked in 1939 at the Centenaire de la Photographie, "Chaque événement de l'existence se marque par quelque cliché," an idea we take for granted.

Chronicling the events of the lives of ordinary people was also a main thrust of realist fiction. For the arch-realist Duranty, the most important goal of literature was to represent "le côté social de l'homme, ce qui est le plus visible." The significant happenings—birth, marriage, death—of common people were as important to record as those of the rich and famous. In that age of inductive reasoning, of serious scientific experimentation, and of a new fascination with history, these detailed recountings of the very ordinariness of daily life were a contribution to the new documentation. Champfleury and Flaubert took very seriously their efforts to enumerate the high and low points of provincial existence, while others like the Goncourts and the young Zola described city life. No event was too insignificant, no person too menial, no object too lowly to be included in the portrayal of reality. "Avec la photographie, tout ce qui se passe dans le monde devient spectacle." The same was true for the realist novel.

The camera captures reality in successive instants and in minute detail. Contemporaries were astounded by the perfection of the image, by the magic fidelity with which even the smallest details were rendered. (In fact, as an accurate representation of reality, the glass daguerreotype with its more difficult and expensive process was preferred over the calotype, or paper print, because the former demonstrated a much greater clarity and intricacy of detail.)

Details served a similar function in realist fiction. Descriptive details were used to convince the reader that the picture being verbally painted was true to life. Such detailing helped anchor the writing to a specific time and place—local color, if you will—and was pushed to almost astonishing limits by the realists. The more details about the physical objects in a character's environment, for example, the more complete the picture; the more complete the picture, the easier for the mind's eye to see and accept it. Details were intended to persuade the reader that the object could be rendered in words in a way that would rival reality.

The realist writers chose as their technique the most direct presentation possible, relying on a heavy use of external, visual details in description in order to transfer the reality they saw to the page; these writers hoped to get everything down on paper, to approximate [according to Harry Levin in *The Gates of Horn,* 1963], a "one-to-one correspondence between language and reality." For the most part, this approximation of reality was done through descriptive passages in which the writer evoked images of detailed visual objects and environments for the mind's eye. Of course, this one-to-one correspondence between art and reality that the realist writers were seeking had already been accomplished by photography. Since the very beginning, we have seen photographs as the truth since we can intellectually equate that small paper image of an object with the tiny retinal image that our eyes communicate to our brain.

A further association with the truth stemmed from the seeming impersonality of the photographic process. Early practitioners [according to Edward Lucie-Smith in *The Invented Eye: Masterpieces of Photography, 1839-1914,* 1975] thought of photography as a kind of "collaboration with nature . . . a means whereby natural forces could be allowed to speak for themselves, instead of having to filter their message through an individual temperament." To contemporaries, early photography appeared to produce immediate copies of the real world, copies distorted only by the rapidly decreasing mechanical flaws of the apparatus, copies uninfluenced, as were other visual forms, by the mind or hand of the artist. For realist writers, a similar idea was clear. Zola described it thus: "L'Ecran réaliste est un simple verre à vitre, très mince, très clair, et qui a la prétention d'être si parfaitement transparent que les images le traversent et se reproduisent ensuite dans leur réalité."

Photography was born into the same world in which the French realist novel grew up, a world that wished to see reality as though in a mirror, a world where much of science and most of history were descriptive, a world where radical artists were reacting against an art that seemed to them excessively personal. Realist writers sought a direct reflection of reality, a reflection evident not only in the transparency of Zola's screen but also in the frequent use of mirror analogies in describing both media. The nineteenth-century writer and critic Edmond About declared that the camera was a "miroir qui se souvient" and Stendhal had already declared at the beginning of *Le Rouge et le noir* that "(u)n roman: c'est un miroir qu'on promène le long d'un chemin." The author's impartiality and rigor of observation were imperative; these traits, of course, were built into the photographic process.

Jules Champfleury declared in 1856 that every serious novelist was an impersonal being who did not judge, condemn, or absolve; all he did was expose the truth. This is the essence of the truthfulness of photographic representation. The reality of photography lies in its visual depiction of the exterior of contemporaneous objects in all their detail: this seemed to be the professed goal of the realist writer. The camera was an accurate and seemingly completely objective observer: this was what the realist writer seemed to want to be. Literary critics of the time were not slow to see these connections.

Comparisons between literature and the visual arts had, of course, long been an effective tool for the literary critic. Such comparisons were particularly widespread during the height of romanticism, when artists and writers deliberately grouped together to articulate an aesthetic theory. Comraderie among the realists was not uncommon either, perhaps more common than many realize, as artists and writers sought each other out as often to exchange technical information as to exchange aesthetic theories.

For the critic to move from discussions of literature in terms of visual art to discussions of literature in terms of photography was a small step, not only because photography and painting were visual media but also because the framed pictorialness and realism of detail in both were things sought after in realist painting and in the *trompe-l'œil* art of the establishment. (Rather ironically, the technique of some of the more accepted painters was more photographic in its precise clarity of form and tone than the more impressionistic work of the realists.) But this mattered little, for "photographic" was becoming an increasingly loaded word.

In the beginning, literary critics commonly confused the terminology in their allusions to the various media. Such seemingly disparate processes as stenography and photography became interchangeable terms for describing the transcription of reality in realist literature, just as photograph and daguerreotype were interchangeable terms for the product of the new graphic medium. What became important to the literary critic was not the definition of a particular term but its possible association with a mechanical, objective, materialist philosophy, so much so that strict distinctions would eventually be made between descriptive "painterly" techniques and those that were photographic. This, I shall show, was not surprising because for the conservative critic a painterly description in literature could be acceptable since it retained at least a little bit of the author's own personality and therefore held at least a faint glimmer of a personal, subjective ideal. Photographic descriptions, on the other hand, were not acceptable because they represented only the grossly material, the surface reality; they represented the objective philosophy of writers who, the critics staunchly

maintained, denied the ideal. As realism moved into a more demanding position in artistic considerations, photography and the realist novel found themselves allied on the wrong side of a realist/idealist debate. The use of photographic comparisons when speaking of a novel lay at the heart of a fundamental clash in values and mirrored the threat that critics felt realism posed to aesthetics.

In the beginning "photographic" was not a pejorative term. It meant real, true-to-life accuracy, and few of the critics denied the importance of a truthful depiction of the real world. Nor did they deny the importance of the study of contemporary life and mores that this depiction implied or the helpful use of observation. Indeed, most of them applauded a return to the concrete, contemporary world as subject because it meant a return from the lyrical, imaginative, and exotic intemperances of the late romantic period. An early cautious evaluation in 1860 [by Armand de Pontmartin in *Union,* 18-19 May, 1860] summed it up thus: "quand le réalisme se prend au sérieux, quand il se propose de ramener au réel et au vrai l'art que nous avions égaré sur les vagues hauteurs du romantisme, il mérite que l'on compte avec lui."

Skill at visual observation was a good thing, as various journalists of the day pointed out. Hippolyte Castille in 1846 appluaded Balzac's ability to describe: "Chez M. de Balzac, la réalité occupe une grande place au point de vue matériel; il décrit un intérieur avec autant d'exactitude que le daguerréotype." Louis Enault wrote some years later of Prosper Mérimée: "un de ses plus vrais mérites, c'est la sagacité de l'observation. Nul ne voit plus finement et ne dit mieux comme il a vu. Il daguerréotype ses personnages." The camera could reproduce exactly what it saw; as a tool, photography could provide a more accurate and impersonal rendering of some of the essential external reality needed to make physical descriptions believable. By using his powers of observation as a comparable tool, an author could give verisimilitude to his descriptions of the external world; he could obtain or retain factual information. As Baudelaire had commented in his "Le Public moderne et la photographie" in the *Salon of 1859,* the use of photography as a "servant" was acceptable because keen visual perceptions of external reality were valuable to art and keen visual perceptions of external reality were what the camera did best.

But for Baudelaire photography was not content to remain a servant. Nor, according to the critics, were realist writers content to use photographic tools as a technique. Most of the critics echoed Baudelaire's fears about photography's encroachment on art and they gave those fears a literary interpretation. Photography as a part of literary realism was becoming an end in itself. Armand Barthet lamented that same year: "Il faut, en vérité, que l'art soit en décadence, pour que l'on prenne au sérieux et que l'on discute une littérature qui ne vit que de procédés.—Et quels procédés! la loupe qui grossit l'objet, mais qui rapetisse le cadre; le détail, toujours le détail, et le détail mal choisi." Arthur Arnould stated the case even more bluntly: "le réalisme n'étant point de l'art, est simplement un procédé . . . c'est un travail mécanique exigeant de l'exactitude et de la patience." There was process but no substance.

Although the critics could not agree as to what realism was, they could agree as to what it was not. At the center of their negative definition, and their subsequent increasingly pejorative use of photographic terminology, was an author's idealism, or rather lack thereof. What Bernard Weinberg said about Balzac and his relationship to his contemporary critics [in *French Realism: The Critical Reaction, 1830-1870,* 1936] was generally applicable to realist writers of the period: "It was a critic's estimate of Balzac's idealism which determined, usually, his opinion on Balzac as a realist. If he regarded the novelist as lacking in idealism or even in imagination, he was apt to classify him as a realist." In a split between *forme* and *fond, forme* was winning and the *forme* of literary realism bore a strong resemblance to photography.

Because of its inherent limitations, the camera could not cross the all-important border between the visible and the invisible, the real and the spiritual; it could only reproduce the exterior aspect of things; it was an eye with no intelligence. Writers bent wholeheartedly on using this technique were no better. Like a photographer, a realist writer needed only skill and patience, not talent or genius. Anyone could become a realist.

The worst offense was a blatant lack of concern for a balance between objective and subjective realities, between the real and the ideal. Since photography could only reveal external reality, it could not participate in the true purpose of Art as the critics saw it. Photography, or a literary technique derived from it, could perhaps reproduce reality with exact detail and precision; critics did not see how either medium could reveal the Ideal. Art that did not do so was not art but a debasement of traditional values. Photographic allusions thus served to define all that was wrong with a realist's writing and with literary realism in general. The realists lacked soul; they were as mechanical as the photographic device.

For this reason, Barbey d'Aurevilly was very much against *l'école du daguerréotype,* as he called it, and the man he saw as its leader, Flaubert:

> Si l'on forgeait à Birmingham ou à Manchester des machines à raconter ou à analyser en bon acier anglais, qui fonctionnent toutes seules par des procédés inconnus de dynamique, elles

fonctionneraient absolument comme M. Flaubert. On sentirait dans ces machines autant de vie, d'âme, d'entrailles humaines que dans l'homme de marbre qui a écrit *Madame Bovary* avec une plume de pierre.

Gustave Merlet, one of the chief anti-realist critics, felt much the same way. In a satirical review of the novels of Champfleury, the self-proclaimed head of the literary realism school, Merlet put these words into the mouth of the novelist: "J'ai vu ceci, j'ai entendu cela. Je suis le secrétaire du premier venu: mon imagination est une chambre obscure. Et Dieu me garde de retoucher les épreuves que je tire . . . je suis M. Champfleury, homme d'esprit et réaliste."

The realist writers were not only as mechanical as the camera. In their concentration on physical reality as truth, they focused on the visible surface just as the camera did. The camera as machine could be excused for this limitation; flesh-and-blood writers could not. Ferdinand Brunetière complained in *Le Roman naturaliste* that Flaubert and Balzac were both "peintres vigoureux de la réalité palpable, mais explorateurs moins que médiocres de la réalité qui ne se voit pas."

In another seeming imitation of the camera, realist writers tried to include as many details as possible since these details were essential for reproducing a complete reality. But realism's detractors saw those details as a smokescreen, a device that caused a loss of perception of any whole. Baudelaire called this anarchy, the loss of any hierarchy or subordination. Merlet remarked of Flaubert that each time any semblance of an ideal tried to express itself in *Madame Bovary,* it was shot down by a barrage of pointless trivial details.

For the critics, this use of excessive detail was itself a by-product of the realists' inability to make a choice. These so-called "democratic" authors included everything and anything in their writing. Just as the camera photographed everything within its visual range, so the realist writers were undiscriminating. Armand de Pontmartin criticized Flaubert in 1860:

> J'assiste au progrès du réalisme ou de la démocratie dans l'art et [que] je me demande avec inquiétude où ces progrès s'arrêteront. . . . L'école dont *Madame Bovary* nous donne le dernier mot . . . décrit sans amour, sans préférence, uniquement parce que les objects matériels sont là, que l'appareil photographique est dressé, et qu'il faut tout reproduire.

Truth to the realists seemed to lie in the bringing forth of physical evidence: more was better, everything was best. Merlet satirically commented on the passage describing Dr. Bovary's arrival at the Rouault farm:

Le voilà qui arrive à la ferme dès le point du jour.
Vous vous imaginez qu'il va sauter lestement en
bas du cheval et aller droit au lit du blessé qui se
morfond d'impatience, en jurant, criant, geignant et
buvant des petits verres pour se donner du cœur?
Non, le réalisme ordonne qu'on mesure la hauteur
de la grange, la longueur de la bergerie, qu'on profite
du lever de l'aurore pour photographier les paons,
les dindons, les poules qui picorent sur le fumier,
les oies qui battent des ailes près de la mare, les
vaches qui ruminent nonchalamment de labour,
jusqu'aux fouets, aux colliers et aux toisons de laine
bleue que salit la poussière fine des greniers. . . .
La jambe du bonhomme attendra.

Le démon du pittoresque possède tellement M. Flaubert,
que parfois ses personnages ne paraissent plus que
des machines à description.

The critics could find no reasoned choice for the details the realists used; anything seemed to be fair game
to the novelists as long as it was objectively verifiable.
The critics could find no logic to their decisions; there
seemed to be no basis for their selections. Victor Fournel summed it up in his review of the novels of 1860:
"Qui dit art, dit choix, et le réalisme ne se croit pas
libre de faire un choix." Critics believed that the realist
writer, like the camera, gave an equal emphasis to
whatever came across his field of vision.

Like the camera as well, the realist writer tried to
maintain a strict impersonality by reproducing exactly
what he observed and by imparting as little of his own
self to the work as possible. This was in strict keeping
with his belief in his participation in documentation, in
seeking the truth. Yet this was not a virtue in the eyes
of the critics. Choice and decision-making were essential to art; so was an obvious personal involvement on
the part of the artist. The impartial, mechanical ob-
server/camera did not make those choices or decisions.
As A. A. Cuvillier-Fleury said in 1857: "Dans le roman tel qu'on l'écrit aujourd'hui, avec les procédés de
la reproduction photographique, l'homme disparaît dans
le peintre: il ne reste qu'une plaque d'acier."

Because there seemed to be no part of his own self
reflected in his work and because he seemed to limit
himself to the visual surface of external reality, to what
his "camera" could record, the realist was dealing only
with what was material and therefore crude and base.
For the critics, the use of such subjects meant that the
realist writer had again lost sight of the true goal of
art: to uplift and enlighten the soul. Realism instead
appealed to all the grosser instincts of humanity. In
1868 Victor de Laprade decried the materialism that
he saw as the goal of realism: "photographier en
quelque sorte la nature . . . reproduire le monde matériel avec toutes les qualités saisissantes de la matière."
For his contemporary, Elme-Marie Caro, this technique
could only lead to an immoral sensualism; realism

dictated "l'imitation brutale de nos mœurs, une sorte
de contr'épreuve daguérrienne de la vie de chaque jour."
For Xavier Aubryet, it was "la fidélité goguenarde du
procédé Daguerre appliquée à la reproduction du ridicule et de l'odieux."

This democracy of subject matter, when combined with
the vulgarity of the photographic technique, led inevitably to a wider and cruder audience, one that would
find such base subjects interesting but, of course, not
edifying. Specific details of external reality could not
by themselves educate or morally enrich the reader;
moral implications had to be drawn and applied by the
author. A vulgar audience was incapable of drawing
the right conclusions from such details, a point much
belabored by the prosecution in the morality trials of
writers of the period, like Flaubert and Baudelaire,
writers who revealed but did not appear to comment
and who certainly did not overtly condemn what they
revealed.

L'Art, le Beau, l'Idéal . . . these were the things consciously or unconsciously ignored by the realist writers who had set their sights too low, if they had set
them at all. For the critics, the realist's desire to find
the truth in physical nature alone had little to do with
true art or with being a true artist. True art was not
the sad flat realism of black and white and grey of a
Flaubert or a Jules Champfleury. True Art had a sense
of illusion, not an insistent focus on the base and the
crude.

And just as truth was found not in ugliness but in
beauty, so it was not found in the here and now, in the
reality capturable by the camera. Truth was eternal,
not temporal. Only a sordid, dirty, shameful half-truth
came from realism; this was nothing compared to the
lofty, consoling, poetic truth of idealism. The ugly side
of reality was to be ignored, not exalted to the status
of art; hence, nothing symbolized the sad and sordid
truth of the realists better than the mechanical, concrete products of technology.

The fundamental clash between the realists and their
critics centered on definitions of beauty, truth and art.
For the idealist, art was the expression of external truth
and the beauty found in the sum of the outer and, more
importantly, inner perceptions of the self. The external
world was only a springboard to the ideal world that
waited beyond. Truth and beauty were inexorably en-
twined, inseparable in artistic creation. By relying
completely on a mechanical process, by focusing only
on external reality, by eliminating the eternal and the
internal, the personal and the subjective, the realists
were denying art. They were reducing their brains to
daguerreotype lenses, as Clément de Ris noted in 1862.

The daguerreotype, the photograph, were not art. Writing which stressed the concrete and the factual and

which purposefully eliminated the moral and the ideal was not art. Authors who based their work on these negative, non-artistic tenets, filtering everything through an impersonal, objective process, were no better than machines. The camera objectified for the conservative critic all the sins of the realists: all the excesses of observation, of the use of the details of physical reality, of the indiscriminate cataloguing of the visible, of mechanical impersonality, of the immoral use of base materialism as subject. The dominance of a mechanical process was incompatible with true artistic goals; therefore, these literary "daguérreotypeurs" were not true artists.

While photography played a less ubiquitous role in mid-nineteenth-century French life than it does in ours, it was a dynamic part of the artistic and aesthetic world in which the realist writers lived and worked. Martino's "synchronisme" is not at all "douteux": photography developed in France in the mid nineteenth century and literary realism flourished then; the two were natural and inevitable products of their age. The many instances of photographic allusion in critical texts demonstrate that for literary critics of the time there was an equally natural and inevitable symbiosis.

ISSUES AND INFLUENCE

Vivienne Mylne

SOURCE: "Social Realism in the Dialogue of Eighteenth-Century French Fiction," in *Studies in Eighteenth-Century Culture, Vol. 6,* edited by Ronald C. Rosbottom, The University of Wisconsin Press, 1977, pp. 265-84.

[*In the following essay, Mylne explores the trend toward increased use of realistic dialogue in French fiction of the eighteenth century.*]

One element of French novels which shows a marked change during the eighteenth century is that of dialogue. The simplest and most obvious way of describing the change is to say that, in a significant number of novels, dialogue becomes more "realistic" in manner and presentation: the style of conversations in a work by Balzac is more like the way people talk in real life than is, say, the dialogue style of *La Princesse de Clèves.* However, once we try to go beyond simplistic statements of this kind, the criterion of "realism" becomes less satisfactory. There are problems in applying the criterion (some of which involve conflicts between different types of "realism"); and in any case, "realism" alone cannot serve as a criterion of literary excellence.

In this essay we shall consider the theoretical problems as they arise in the course of discussing our examples, while the question of the evaluation of literary merit will be left until the end.

In order to keep the discussion within manageable limits, I shall concentrate here on the kinds of realism which can be most easily identified. These are the cases where a novelist indicates—by grammar, vocabulary and even spelling—that the character in question does not use the language of well-educated Parisians. Such divergences from standard French thus carry implicit information about the character's social class, level of education, and place of origin.

Before considering eighteenth-century developments, however, we need to look briefly at some of the conventions concerning dialogue which were in force toward the end of the seventeenth century. There are two main points which should be mentioned here. The first is merely one aspect of the more general question of levels of style: the concept of literary genres, and of maintaining a style consonant with each genre or type of work. This "rule" was followed in fiction as well as in drama and poetry, and it covered not only passages where the voice is that of the narrator, but dialogue too. Thus, in France, it was only in comic fiction, and more especially in burlesque novels or *anti-romans,* that one found common characters talking in a low style. Far more frequent were novels in which the protagonists were noble and the dialogue was presented in correct and fairly formal language. Commenting on the style of such works, Henri Coulet says [in *Le Roman jusqu'à la Révolution,* 1967]:

> Sa politesse amortit toute violence, toute crudité, son absence d'élan est propre à insinuer la tristesse; les conversations sont très souvent rapportées au style indirect, dans le même but d'atténuation, et quand elles sont transcrites au style direct, toujours très éloignées de la phraséologie baroque, elles ne sont pas moins éloignées du dialogue familier.

This regular correlation between certain identifiable kinds of fiction and their corresponding stylistic registers is one that begins to break down in the eighteenth century; and dialogue, as we shall see, is one of the elements which contributes to the breakdown.

Coulet's remark about the frequency of reported speech brings me to my second point concerning conventions. In this case we are dealing with a specific device or technique. Besides using indirect speech liberally, seventeenth-century writers also had frequent recourse to what one might call narrated speech, which presents the gist of what was said—sometimes fully, sometimes in a compressed form—but without supplying the actual words of the speaker. Narrated speech is often combined with reported speech, and this mode of presentation continued throughout the eighteenth century. In the hands of a skillful writer the technique can be quite lively and effective. The following passage, by Louvet de Couvray, relates a scene in which the Count is teasing the Marquise, in her husband's presence, about her guilty secret ("Mlle Duportail" is in reality young Faublas himself, disguised as a girl):

> Préludant avec la Marquise par de légeres épigrammes, il protestoit qu'elle seule, jusqu'à présent, savoit précisément combien Mademoiselle Duportail méritoit d'être aimée. La Marquise, également adroite et prompte, répondoit vîte et toujours bien; mesurant la défense à l'attaque, elle éludoit sans affectation ou se défendoit sans aigreur; déterminée à ménager un ennemi qu'elle ne pouvoit espérer de vaincre, aux questions pressantes elle opposoit les aveux équivoques, elle atténuoit les allégations fortes par les négations mitigées; et repoussoit les sarcasmes plus amers qu'embarrassans, par des récriminations plus fines que méchantes.

Narrated speech offers several advantages: it can convey the sense of a long conversation economically; and it can save the novelist the trouble of trying to invent witty or subtle remarks. It may also be used to outline utterances which would, in direct speech, be out of keeping with the context. Thus when the young Dupuis, in *Les Illustres Françoises,* asks a prostitute if trade is brisk, the reply is, "Toujours de pis en pis, me dit-elle." The narrator then continues:

> Elle invectiva ensuite contre le Lieutenant de Police et contre le Lieutenant Criminel, et contre les Commissaires, et contre le bon ordre qu'ils établissoient dans Paris.

Her exact words would, presumably, have gone beyond even the fairly ribald tone of Dupuis's reminiscences.

Reported and narrated speech serve a further purpose, which is connected with the status of direct speech. It seems to me that for the majority of novelists in the seventeenth and eighteenth centuries, direct speech was felt to be a privileged and peculiarly forceful kind of discourse. As such, it was not a feature to be used indiscriminately. Instead, these early novelists frequently proceed as though direct speech can be introduced only after the way has been duly prepared. The transition between narrated actions and dialogue is made by means of reported and/or narrated speech. And once the conversation has begun it is quite usual, after a few exchanges in direct speech, to find reported or narrated speech brought in again. In this way certain remarks, those in direct speech, are highlighted. The modern reader, accustomed to long stretches of direct speech at any and every juncture, may well fail to perceive these effects of added immediacy and vigor.

Some writers seem also to have related the importance of direct speech to the social importance of certain characters; the words of a servant or peasant are narrated or put into reported speech, while the utterances of nobles are given in the direct form. A case in point is the episode in *Manon Lescaut* where Des Grieux is helping Manon to escape. His command to the coach driver and his promise of a *louis d'or* are given in direct speech; but it is in reported speech that the driver's doubts are expressed, as also his final threat: "Celui-ci . . . s'enfuit de peur, . . . en criant que je l'avais trompé, mais que j'aurais de ses nouvelles."

What emerges from all this is that even when a novelist does introduce characters who are uneducated or of humble social rank, he can still, if he chooses, avoid the "realism" of low or vulgar expressions by transmitting all their remarks in the form of reported or narrated speech. With this in mind, let us turn to our eighteenth-century examples.

Les Illustres Françoises is clearly worth discussing from the point of view of dialogue. Apart from the third-person narrator who provides the framework passages, the book consists entirely of conversations and of stories supposedly told in direct speech. Chasle's handling of dialogue is very skilled, and much could be said about the way he controls the various levels and types of conversation. The first six tales are largely serious in tone, and the protagonists are aristocrats or prosperous bourgeois. Their usage is of course correct and cultivated, though Chasles can also descend to a register of familiar speech which now seems wholly "natural."

With the last tale, that of the younger Dupuis, we move into a different world, one of youthful follies, escapades, and sexual intrigues. The earliest detailed review of the book expressed the opinion that this story was "fort inférieur à toutes les autres," adding: "On ne trouve pas ce récit trop bien à la suite du précédent." The grounds for complaint are thus that Chasles has sinned by juxtaposing different genres. We should note, however, that he has not allowed himself the full range of comic effects which a tale of this kind could, according to the conventions, include. He does not make the many low-life characters who come into these pages express themselves in low language. We have already seen how the prostitute's invective is attenuated. Similarly, when a *savetier* protests over being asked to carry out an unwelcome errand, we are simply told: "Cet homme fit quelque difficulté." The most noticeable instance of uneducated speech is a piece of mockery from Dupuis's brother. World had got around that Dupuis meant to marry Célénie, and over dinner he was teased about this:

> J'avois soutenu en homme qui entendoit raillerie toutes celles qu'on m'avoit faites; mais je fus assommé de celle que mon frère fit mal à propos. Comme il ne regardoit Célénie que du haut de sa

fortune, & qu'en effet ce n'étoit pas un bon parti pour moi, elle lui paroissoit tout à fait au-dessous de lui. Il la traita comme une gueuse & une misérable. Je lui répondis d'une manière à lui imposer silence, s'il avoit eu quelque égard pour moi; mais il continua ses airs de mépris qu'il finit par me dire, en prenant un ton de village: Palsangué, puisque j'allons entrer dans son alliance, faut que j'allions lui faire la révérence.

I have supplied the whole of the passage leading up to this remark, because it makes clear the extent of the insult and the attitude of contempt implied by the imitation of countrified speech. Chasles does not attempt to create comic effects by making his uneducated Parisians use their equivalent "jargon," and to this extent he keeps within the norms of a correct, if sometimes familiar, style.

There are no grounds for supposing that he ever contemplated taking a more "realistic" approach in this story. But had he done so, we can see an objection which might have restrained him. This involves realism of a different order: Dupuis is supposedly an educated man, telling his story to a group of well-bred people, including some ladies. In such a setting a real-life storyteller might be expected not to utter vulgarisms or incorrect French. Thus we can see that realism about the narrator's situation could sometimes, in theory at least, inhibit realism in the dialogue which he or she quotes.

Turning now to *Gil Blas,* we find that Lesage is somewhat more generous in the quantity of direct speech he attributes to characters of humble origins. In the episode of the brigands' cave (Book I, chapters IV-X), the old Negro hostler, Domingo, and the cook, Léonarde, both have quite a lot to say. They have in common the use of familiar forms of address when talking to Gil Blas, and an otherwise "polite" style, with overtones of irony. Léonarde shows Gil Blas the cemetery-cum-cellar where he is to sleep:

Voilà votre chambre, mon petit poulet, me dit-elle en me passant doucement la main sous le menton: le garçon dont vous avez le bonheur d'occuper la place y a couché tant qu'il a vécu parmi nous, et il y repose encore après sa mort. Il s'est laissé mourir à la fleur de son âge; ne soyez pas assez simple pour suivre son exemple.

And when Gil Blas tries to escape, only to be caught by Domingo:

Ah! ah! dit-il, petit drôle, vous voulez vous sauver! oh! ne pensez pas que vous puissiez me surprendre; je vous ai bien entendu. Vous avez cru trouver la grille ouverte, n'est-ce pas? Apprenez, mon ami, que vous la trouverez désormais toujours fermée. Quand

nous retenons quelqu'un malgré lui, il faut qu'il soit plus fin que vous pour nous échapper.

These and other remarks by Domingo and Léonarde create an effect which is closer to sophistication than to naïveté. It is almost as though Lesage were writing with double satire, or antiburlesque, intentions. Instead of parodying an inflated serious style by using exaggeratedly vulgar dialogue, he turns the joke around and makes his vulgar characters talk with a neat correctness and even elegance.

In the last volume of the novel, which appeared in 1735, Gil Blas seeks the hand of Antonia, a farmer's daughter. The conversation between Gil Blas and this farmer does suggest a more straightforwardly realistic approach to uneducated speech. When Gil Blas says he wants to be quite sure that Antonia is willing to marry him:

Oh dame! dit Basile, je n'entends pas toutes ces philosophies: parlez vous-même à Antonia, et vous verrez, ou je me trompe fort, qu'elle ne demande pas mieux que d'être votre femme.

Here the interjection, and the phrase "Je n'entends pas toutes ces philosophies," do have an air of simple rustic speech; and Basile's sentences are markedly simpler in construction and vocabulary than those of Gil Blas. There is also a fresh tone in the context: Lesage has now dropped the ironic detachment with which the narrator spoke of his early adventures. Gil Blas is sincerely attached to Antonia—his first sight of her leaves him "étonné, troublé, interdit." And it is appropriate to this atmosphere of frankness and sentiment that the simple approach of Basile should be reflected in his turns of speech. If we laugh over the style of these remarks, it is as much with Basile as at him.

Lesage's "realism" in this last quotation is in any case a slight and not very noticeable effort. The reverse is true of our next example, probably the best-known single instance of vulgar dialogue in eighteenth-century French fiction. It is of course the dispute between Mme. Dutour and the cab driver in *La Vie de Marianne.*

Frédéric Deloffre has already provided an authoritative discussion of the linguistic aspects of this scene [in *Une préciosité nouvelle: Marivaux et le marivaudage,* 1967]. Among the points he makes is one that creates yet more difficulties with the notion of "realism": although Marivaux's presentation of this quarrel is doubtless more like real life than, say, the speech habits of Léonarde in *Gil Blas,* yet the language of Mme. Dutour and the cab driver is also highly conventional, even stylized. Patterns of demotic speech, as used by dramatists such as Cyrano de Bergerac, Molière, and Dancourt, had established a repertoire of typical vocabulary and grammatical forms. So a writer did not need to go out and listen to street quarrels in Paris. The educated man would have, in his mind's ear, an accepted model of vulgar speech, much as an English-speaking man of our own day knows the turns of speech associated with the stage Irishman.

Even within these limits, Marivaux's practice here is quite restrained. The cab driver is made to use "Palsambleu!" rather than "Palsangué!" or "Palsanguienne!," the coarser forms. And Marivaux does not indicate any lapses from received pronunciation; some writers would have put, for instance, "Faut-y pas" or "Faut-i pas" for "Faut-il pas."

Yet this limited excursion into realism attracted, as we know, the blame of several critics. As Deloffre remarks, "Ce qui était permis au théâtre dans une pièce comique ne l'était pas dans un roman"—or at least, not in a novel which is supposedly written by a countess, and which begins in the tone of the sentimental life story. What displeased the complaining critics was the shock of flouted expectations. Jacob, in *Le Paysan parvenu,* would not provoke the same protests over his occasional slips into countrified speech, because he *was* of peasant stock and because, from its opening pages, the book offers an atmosphere much closer to that of the conventional comic novel, in which vulgarisms are tolerated.

The adverse criticisms of the demotic dialogue in *La Vie de Marianne* rest on assumptions not only about the correlation of genre and style but also about the inherently comic or ridiculous nature of uneducated speech. This latter assumption had never, of course, been as widely accepted in England; and many English novelists of the eighteenth century introduce into more-or-less serious fiction a range of stylistic effects, including familiar and even low turns of speech, which would have offended French standards of literary *bienséance.* The difference of attitudes can be aptly seen in the English translations of *La Vie de Marianne.* Take the following sentences:

> Jarnibleu! ne me frappez pas, lui dit le cocher qui lui retenait le bras; ne soyez pas si osée! je me donne au diable, ne badinons point! Voyez-vous! je suis un gaillard qui n'aime pas les coups, ou la peste m'étouffe! Je ne demande que mon dû, entendez-vous? il n'y a point de mal à ça.

The first translator, generally thought to be John Lockman, produced the following:

> Damn you! don't strike me, said the Coachman, laying hold of her arm:—Don't be so pert as that comes to! For—the Devil take me!—if you won't be quiet—I will shew you a Fellow that won't be beat. Pox take you! I don't ask a Farthing more

than my due, you rotten Jade. And is there any Thing wrong in that?

In Mrs. Collyer's version, which appeared in 1743, we find the euphemistic spelling, "D—n you," but the rest of the paragraph follows Lockman fairly faithfully. The final gratuitous insult, however, is intensified to become: "You stinking good-for-nothing jade." A desire for vigor and liveliness, at the expense of refinement, appears in both translations.

Once the language of dialogue moves away from standard correct usage, it is of course notoriously difficult for a translator to strike and maintain the exact corresponding level. The eighteenth-century translator's free approach to his task is apt to produce further variations. So it is perhaps not surprising that, after comparing about fifty French versions of English novels with the original texts, I should feel obliged to admit that, at least until a more comprehensive review is carried out, it is impossible to discern any clear trends or tendencies in the handling of dialogue in this domain. It is perhaps slightly more common for the translator to tone down vulgarisms, as Prévost did on occasion, than to attempt a faithful equivalence. But there are also cases where the French writer has exaggerated, in his translation, some merely familiar English turn of phrase. In *Zoriada,* by Mrs. Hughes, we find: "Lo and behold, after a hasty rap at the door, in comes a gentleman in blue and gold, and advances towards me." This is conveyed as: "Voilà-t-il pas qu'on frappe à enfoncer la porte, et voyez-vous, vlà que j'vois entrer un Monsieur vêtu de bleu et d'or, qui avance à moi." Willingness to use "incorrect" forms in French seems to vary according to the individual translator's whim. And since other factors are involved, such as the degree to which the translator grasps the nuances of English usage, one would be rash to generalize about the way in which dialogue is translated.

Returning to novels by French authors, we can find an obvious parallel to *La Vie de Marianne* in Mouhy's *La Paysanne parvenue* (1735-37). To judge by the number of re-editions, these two works were equally popular: *Marianne* went into nineteen re-editions before the Revolution, and *La Paysanne* had seventeen for the same period. (These figures suggest, incidentally, that the public did not concur with the disapproving critics of *La Vie de Marianne.*) Like Marivaux, Mouhy has mixed his styles and tones; but he is far less competent in maintaining the various levels at which he appears to aim. This is apparent, as one might expect, in the dialogue. By the time she writes her memoirs, Jeannette has become a Marquise, though she started life as a woodcutter's daughter. Mouhy does allude to her naïve country speech when she was a girl: "Ce que ce brave monsieur m'avoit dit (car c'étoit mon expression dans ce tems) me revenoit souvent." However, when the royal hunting party passes, and she gets one of the riders to point out the King, her exclamations are less convincing: "Oui, oui, c'est le roi; repris-je avec transport; mon Dieu, qu'il est beau! Ah! s'il n'alloit pas si vîte, que je serois heureuse! O ciel! il est déjà bien loin." Is this the talk of a Fontainebleu *paysanne* of thirteen? We might suppose that Mouhy had decided not to attempt any realistic speech effects. But when Jeannette talks to Colin, her village suitor, we can see how, in successive conversations, the young man's remarks become more and more "rustic." Here is part of his first contribution:

> Tenez, Jeannette, je vous aime, et je vois bien que vous commencez à me rendre le réciproque; mordienne! si cela étoit, je ne sais ce qu'il en arriveroit. Je sais bien que vous n'avez rien; mais n'importe, ce n'est pas là l'histoire pour vivre contens: vous êtes gentille et blanche comme neige, vous avez des yeux comme une souris, vous êtes droite comme un cierge, et cela vaut bien quelques écus de plus. Mon père ne pense peut-être pas comme moi: comment faire? Il faudra bien cependant qu'il se mette à la raison; autrement, jarni, j'irai m'engager.

Apart from the interjections (and this part of speech is a universal resource for cheap-and-easy local color in dialogue), the *paysan* quality of this passage seems to depend rather more on content than on manner.

A few pages later, Colin discusses how a village girl should answer a courting letter from a nobleman (he does not know that the letter in question was actually addressed to Jeannette):

> Non, sans doute, reprit Colin, qui refuse, muse; s'il parle à bon escient, it faut tout droit l'accepter, et ne faire point tant de raisonnemens; c'est ce qui perd la plus grande partie de nos filles. Elles font les réservées; chipotons, lanternons, qu'en arrive-t-il? le gaillard prend parti ailleurs, il en trouve de moins difficultueuses; elles en enrageons, zeste, l'oiseau est déniché; ils n'en voulons plus, et dame, ce sont les regrets, n'est-il pas vrai, Jeannette?

For the reader who notices this progressive countrification of Colin, the effect is the reverse of that which realism should ideally produce. One can no longer be absorbed in the world of the story, since one is reminded of the author's role, as an artist touching up his picture.

The plot of *La Paysanne parvenue* continues in a fairly sombre and sentimental vein: Jeannette and the young Marquis are in love, but are kept apart by family opposition and the machinations of various malicious characters. However, occasional touches of the comic, or even the grotesque, do break in. One of these is the irruption, when Jeannette is leading a secluded life in Paris, of a blind army officer who believes, because of the false name she has adopted, that she must be his wife. The officer is accompanied by a valet who remarks "dans un langage allemand: *Nous ferons, nous ferons si fou mocque long-tems de fotre mari; men Goth! men Goth!* ajouta-t-il, . . . *que les femmes sont toubles, et qu'on est malhéré de se laisser bercer par sté chienne d'enchance"* (the italics are in the text).

Now during the second half of the century, peasants and working-class folk in general ceased to be automatic subjects for laughter when they appeared in literature. But up to and beyond the Revolution, some touch of comedy appears to be intended whenever a foreign accent is indicated by an attempt at phonetic spelling. The inability of anyone from outside France to converse adequately in the language of civilization is bound to seem ridiculous. Conversely, any foreign character in French fiction who is *not* meant to be ridiculous will have a perfect command of French, however unrealistic this may seem. For example, Mme. de Grafigny's Peruvian princess, after only a few months in France, can speak fluently and correctly (the "je" of this dialogue is the princess herself):

> —Vous m'étonnez, repris-je; d'où naît votre défiance? Depuis que je vous connais, si je n'ai pu me fair entendre par des paroles, toutes mes actions n'ont-elles pas dû vous prouver que je vous aime?

> —Non, répliqua-t-il, je ne puis encore me flatter: vous ne parlez pas assez bien le francais pour détruire mes justes craintes; vous ne cherchez point à me tromper, je le sais: mais expliquez-moi quel sens vous attachez à ces mots adorables, "je vous aime." . . . —Ces mots, lui dis-je, . . . doivent, je crois, vous faire entendre que vous m'êtes cher, que votre sort m'intéresse, que l'amitié et la reconnaissance m'attachent à vous; ces sentimens plaisent à mon coeur, et doivent satisfaire le vôtre.

It seems on the face of it unlikely that anyone could define some senses of "aimer" in this way without being aware of the further sense, that of a "love" which goes beyond friendship.

Perhaps we may find it more realistic for foreign characters like Wolmar in *La Nouvelle Héloïse,* or the Polish nobles in *Les Amours du chevalier de Faublas,* to speak perfect French. After all, history books tell us that French was the language of the upper classes in Russia and Poland. But one may still wonder whether, in real life, all these people spoke such pure, fluent, unaccented French as the novels of the time would suggest. It would not, I think, be difficult to assemble enough evidence to support the notion that, in literature, noble birth was assumed to carry with it the ability to speak elegantly in any language. (Theodore, in Walpole's *The Castle of Otranto,* would certainly be a case in point.)

The earliest novel in which I have found any practical comments on the problems and advantages of speaking in a foreign language is *Adolphe*. The hero says of Ellénore:

> Elle parlait plusieurs langues, imparfaitement à la vérité, mais toujours avec vivacité, quelquefois avec grâce. Ses idées semblaient se faire jour à travers les obstacles, et sortir de cette lutte, plus agréables, plus naïves et plus neuves: car les idiomes étrangers rajeunissent les pensées, et les débarrassent de ces tournures qui les font paraître tour-à-tour communes et affectées.

But however imperfectly Ellénore spoke other languages, there is never any suggestion in the dialogue of *Adolphe* that her command of French is limited. It is only later in the nineteenth century that we find a foreign accent brought into novels to contribute to the sinister effect of some characters, or the charm of others.

Before we return to our virtuous peasants, we should perhaps spend a moment on a less reputable type of fiction. From the 1740s onwards, there is a small but steady flow of stories about girls who have become prostitutes or courtesans. Such novels are often narrated in the first person, and the "heroine" is always of humble origins. The titles of a few of these works (which tend to be omitted from histories of literature) will indicate their scope: Antoine Bret, *La Belle Allemande ou les galanteries de Thérèse* (1745); Paul Baret, *Mademoiselle Javotte, ouvrage peu moral écrit par elle-même* (1757); *La Belle Cauchoise, ou mémoires d'une jolie Normande devenue courtisane célèbre* (1783). Stylistically, they range from the merely suggestive to the pornographically precise. Although gaiety often prevails during much of the narrative, these works generally offer an edifying conclusion, sometimes with a somber turn of events in which the woman suffers for her sins. Thus they cannot all be classed, in any simple sense, as "comic" novels. In certain cases the narrator maintains a level of correct language. In others, the dialogue presents linguistic forms which may recall the heroine's social origins. Thus Mademoiselle Javotte, a Parisian, revisits her "quartier natal" and is greeted by remarks such as, "Eh quoi donc, est-ce que j'ai la barlue? c'est-y là Javotte Godeau?" and, "Parguienne oui, c'est elle; et comme te v'là brave, Mameselle Javotte." Refusing to put a crude name to Javotte's new way of life, one of her friends adds, "Tu m'entends. Je n'ons pas la manigance du parlement-age; mais je savons minager un queuquesun."

These *poissard* turns of speech had become familiar to many members of the reading public through works by Caylus, Vadé, and others. *Poissard* was generally exploited only for crude comic effects. We may admit that, for all its conventions, it does entail some effort to convey the sounds produced by the proletariat of Paris. But it also illustrates another of the pitfalls of "realism," on the aesthetic level: even apart from the triviality of content, most *poissard* writing is manifestly tedious to read.

Tedium of another kind, from works aspiring to greater value as literature, awaits the twentieth-century reader who pursues the lower classes into the *conte moral*. Marmontel, whose set of *Contes moraux* can be said to have launched the vogue, plumed himself on the naturalness of his dialogue:

> Quand je fais parler mes personnages, tout l'art que j'y emploie est d'être présent à leur entretien, et d'écrire ce que je crois entendre. En général, la plus naïve imitation de la nature dans les moeurs et dans le langage, est ce que j'ai recherché dans ces *Contes*. S'ils n'ont pas ce mérite, ils n'en ont aucun.

The condition of this last sentence is all to unfortunately fulfilled, and more particularly so of Marmontel's rustic characters. We can see, from what they say, that literary attitudes have changed, to the extent that peasant naïveté is now meant to be admirable rather than ridiculous. But a story such as *La Bergère des Alpes* is still likely to provoke laughter, unintentionally.

Some travellers passing through the mountains of Savoy hear a shepherdess talking to herself: "Que le soleil couchant brille d'une douce lumière! C'est ainsi (disoit-elle) qu'au terme d'une carrière pénible, l'âme épuisée va se rajeunir dans la source pure de l'immortalité." When this young woman leads the travellers to her humble abode, they find there an old couple (compared, inevitably, to Baucis and Philemon), who explain that she is not their daughter, but that she arrived four years ago "enhabit de paysanne," and offered to look after their flocks. "Nous nous doutâmes qu'elle n'étoit pas une villageoise," the old woman goes on, "mais nos questions l'affligeoient et nous crûmes devoir en abstenir." After some more dialogue of this sort, we the readers do more than suspect that the old couple do not sound like villagers either. As Marmontel was brought up in a small hamlet until the age of about eleven, he must have had some notion of how country people might talk. But obviously he assumed that naturalness of this kind would impair our respect for these characters. In any case, they remain subsidiary personages. The *bergère* of the title turns out, to no one's surprise, to be of noble birth. As for Marmontel's other tale about shepherds, *Annette et Lubin,* this is a modern version of *Daphnis and Chloé.* Here the protagonists speak a French which is self-consciously simple, but is also clearly literary rather than naturalistic.

In *Jacques le fataliste,* Diderot too refrains from the cruder and more obvious ways of indicating how speech reflects social levels, though his portrayal of lower-class speakers does of course have the convincing quality so markedly lacking in Marmontel's *contes.* I shall not make any further comments on *Jacques,* partly because its general tone is comic, so that some realism of dialogue is not unexpected, and partly because Diderot's handling of direct speech is too varied, complex, and idiosyncratic to be adequately discussed in a few paragraphs.

We have now reached the period when Restif de la Bretonne's works began to appear. Restif, of course, was an author who deliberately advocated the use of dialect words as one way of enriching French, and who lived up to his own advice. There is no need to engage here in a detailed discussion of his range of styles in dialogue, as various critics have already covered the ground. We may merely note some general points in order to relate Restif to his contemporaries. The main fact to keep in mind is perhaps that much of Restif's handling of lower-class dialogue is still influenced either by a tendency to idealize (in the case of *paysans*), or by the convention that vulgarisms are laughable (as regards town dwellers). However, in any discussion of the development of a realistic dialogue manner in French, Restif must always occupy, and deservedly, a place of honor. It is also a place apart, for no major author can be said to have adopted him as a model, and the minor writers who might be thought to have followed in his tracks are the palest of imitators in this respect.

(As a brief parenthesis on the fiction of the 1790s, we may observe that some of these imitators now treated the poor of Paris seriously as characters, and indicated their vulgarisms of speech without scorn. Gorgy's *Blançay* provides some examples. But as we might expect, such portrayal has swung towards an unrealistically favorable view of the lower classes in towns.)

In spite of his interest in regional differences, Restif never achieved a work which could properly be called a regional novel. The honor of writing "the first regional novel in English, and perhaps in all Europe" has been attributed to Maria Edgeworth, for *Castle Rackrent* (1800). In French, if not in France, Mme. de Charrière may be said to have been breaking the same ground when she brought out her *Lettres neuchâteloises* in 1784. And this work owed something to a Dutch novel, *Histoire van Mejuffrow Sara Burgerhart* (1782), by Betje Wolff and Aagje Deken. Discussing the composition of the *Lettres neuchâteloises,* Mme. de Charrière said:

> Je venais de voir dans *Sara Burgerhart* . . . qu'en peignant des lieux et des moeurs qu'on connaît bien, l'on donne à des personnages fictifs une réalité précieuse. . . . Ne peignant personne, on peint tout le monde.

In spite of its relative shortness, this novel builds up a surprisingly complete and coherent picture of life in Neuchâtel. And in the letters from Julianne C——, the little seamstress, we have a persuasive sketch of a working-class girl. Although shown as a victim of social conditions, she is not sentimentalized and does not accept uncritically her own unfavorable situation. Comparing herself with the ladies of Nauchâtel society, she says:

> —et peut-être ne sont-elles seulement pas aussi braves qu'une pauvre fille qu'on laisse pleurer en faisant son ouvrage, et qui n'a pas été à toutes leurs écoles et leurs pensions, et n'a pas appris à lire sur leurs beaux livres; et elles ont des bonnets, et des rubans, et des robes avec des garnitures de gaze, qu'il faut que nous travaillions toute la nuit et quelquefois les dimanches.

Elsewhere Julianne uses various local words—*jaublâmes, un pierrot*—which accentuate her social origins.

Thus she expresses herself in a convincingly colloquial way. But these turns of speech come to us in letters she wrote, rather than as her spoken words. It is no easy matter to decide whether, and if so how far, the style of a given character's letters can be equated with a spoken style; for this reason I have refrained from discussing here the question of what the characters say in letters.

If we now look onwards to Balzac, as the first great exponent of "realistic" dialogue in the nineteenth century, we find that his approach stems from the kind of work foreshadowed by Mme. de Charrière rather than from the rich confusion of Restif. Balzac's vivid impressions of the speech habits of the poorer classes first appear as an element in the local color of an historical novel, *Les Chouans.* Apart from a few attempts at medieval pastiche, the eighteenth-century historical novel generally produces correct and colorless speech for its largely aristocratic characters. It was not, of course, from works like these that Balzac learnt social realism in dialogue, but from the historical novels of Sir Walter Scott. And the first such work, *Waverley* (1814), was written according to Scott, "so as in some distant degree to emulate the admirable Irish portraits drawn by Miss Edgeworth." However, even if we see Scott and Edgeworth as Balzac's immediate literary forebears in this aspect of his work, it is also true to say that the general tendencies of eighteenth-century French practice would in all probability have led him in the same direction.

What has emerged from this review of the development of dialogue is that we can indeed observe an increase in realism in the practice of a number of novelists, but that it is impossible to define the nature and degree of this realism with any accuracy. Moreover, realism can, in any case, provide no more than a descriptive standard. If we wish to evaluate the literary effectiveness of a given author's dialogue, mere faithfulness to real-life speech habits is an inadequate criterion. Instead we must consider the congruence of the dialogue style with a range of elements inside the novel, and notably with the tone and the mode of literary expression which the novelist has established right from the beginning of the novel in question. Such factors may be extremely complex, and the critical verdict will inevitably depend in part on subjective reactions. But it is more satisfactory, and more honest, to recognize this personal factor in our judgments than to suppose that "realism" constitutes a yardstick which will allow us to measure objectively the novelist's skill in presenting his dialogue.

George J. Becker

SOURCE: "Edmond and Jules de Goncourt," in *Master European Realists of the Nineteenth Century,* Frederick Ungar Publishing Co., 1982, pp. 58-92.

[*In the following essay, Becker investigates the works of the Goncourt brothers, highlighting their innovations in the techniques of realism and overall importance to the Realist movement.*]

Of all the major realists of the nineteenth century the Goncourt brothers, Edmond and Jules, have had the least success in maintaining their renown as novelists. Today it is the Académie Goncourt and its annual prize that keep their name alive. Some twenty years ago there was a brief flurry over the publication of the integral text of their *Journal,* an event that had been delayed for forty years. But the excitement quickly subsided when it became apparent that nothing of importance had been suppressed in the incomplete edition, and this monument, interesting as it is, has not led to widespread fame for the Goncourts. Among connoisseurs Edmond Goncourt has a certain reputation for his part in introducing Japanese art to Western eyes, and both brothers are known in such circles for their lively interest in the art, life, and manners of eighteenth-century France. Although there is in the world of letters a vague awareness that the Goncourts wrote, together or singly, some eleven novels, it is rare to find a general reader who is acquainted with these works, and outside of libraries it is difficult even to find the works themselves in French, let alone in English.

Diminished literary reputations must usually be left to their fate. In this case, however, since the Goncourt brothers were a major force in the development of French realism, their contribution to that literary current must be assessed. *Germinie Lacerteux* and its famous manifesto-preface published in 1865 are of pri-

mary importance, bridging the span between *Madame Bovary* and Zola's Rougon-Macquart series. To this work should be added at least *Renée Mauperin, Manette Salomon,* and Edmond's *La Fille Elisa* as important examples of realism in fiction. Beyond what these of their works offered as examples is the fact of the brothers' *literary presence* in Paris at the very center of critical discussion and novelistic and dramatic experimentation from the early 1850s until Edmond's death in July 1896—a period of artistic and literary ferment faithfully, if chaotically, chronicled in the famous *Journal.* None of the other realists, major or minor, has as much to say about their art as did the Goncourts. Even the vociferous Zola confined his critical utterances to a relatively short period of time.

Finally, though this is a matter of less importance, the Goncourts were acquainted with all the French realists as well as with writers from other countries. Through the various regular dinners—Brébant, Magny, and others—in which they participated, and later through Edmond's Sunday gatherings in his *Grenier,* there came within range of the Goncourt talk, and the Goncourt recording pen, such intimates as Flaubert, Zola, Daudet, and Turgenev; such intellectual leaders as Taine, Renan, and Berthelot; and a whole host of lesser writers and writers who would become famous but were then still in formation, among them Henry James, George Moore, J.-K. Huysmans, and Guy de Maupassant, to mention only those with an obvious affiliation with the realist-naturalist school. There was, in short, some truth in Edmond's irritating reiteration in his later years that he and his brother had been the chief catalytic agent in the creation of the new literature.

A belated formal recognition of this role was accorded to Edmond by his literary brethren on March 1, 1895, at a dinner attended by 310 persons at which eulogies were read from such foreigners as Georg Brandes, who wrote: "All Scandinavian writers will join with me today as I shout: *'Glory to the innovating master!'"* Raymond Poincaré, at that time Minister of Public Instruction, gave an address in which he conferred on Edmond the grade of officer of the Legion of Honor. There was also a toast by J. M. Hérédia, a discourse by Georges Clemenceau, and tributes by Henri Céard, Henri de Regnier, Zola, and Daudet. Many of those in attendance must have recalled the memories of Flaubert, dead in 1880, of Turgenev, dead in 1883, and of Maupassant, dead in 1893, who in sympathy and brotherhood belonged to that living assembly.

Before we examine the works of the two Goncourt brothers for what they contained that was new to the novel, it will be useful to follow in some detail the critical utterances they made *seriatim* over the years in the prefaces and entries in the *Journal.* What we discern from these entries after the inception of the *Journal* on December 2, 1851, is that these brothers did not begin as realists. Their dreams were typical: They offered a play, *La Nuit de Saint-Sylvestre,* to the Comédie Francaise because Jules Janin had told them that the way to achieve success was to conquer the theater. When the play was refused, they wrote in the *Journal* on December 21, 1851: "That was the end of that. Our soap bubble had burst. And actually our little piece was no more than that. That's the way of first dreams in literature." Their next enthusiasm was the publication *Paris,* which they called "the first literary daily paper since the beginning of the world." For some years they were typical young men enamored of literature, seeking fame rather than any specific literary accomplishment, modeling themselves after writers who were then in vogue.

As it turned out, the Goncourts' way to realism came not through literary efforts but through research for, and writing of, a kind of social history. Their interest in objects d'art of the eighteenth century led them from collector's mania to study of the period and a resultant cultivation of a talent for observation. The *Journal* for June 9, 1856, records the brothers' visit to Montalembert, who praised their *Histoire de la Société Francaise pendant le Directoire* for its catalogue of Paris sights and buildings (the first chapter was a hundred-page promenade through the Paris of sixty years before). The brothers have left us abundant evidence of their avidity for research, telling of the thousands of drawings, prints, paintings—*documents* in short—that they had examined before writing their various social histories and intimate biographies. Like Stendhal they became enamored of *le petit fait vrai,* though they did seek in it an element of color and the picturesque. Of their originality in this kind of writing Pierre Sabatier says [in *Germinie Lacerteux des Goncourts,* 1948]: "They brought to history a conception completely different from that of the writers who before them had attempted this genre. If to them, in Michelet's words, history was to be 'a resurrection,' that resurrection was to be brought about above all by the most exact and most documented evocation of milieu and décor in which the human beings of the past had lived." This critic suggests that such a taste led the Goncourts straight to the novel, i.e., "history that might have been," since their desire to make historical characters live in an authentic background would be one of the necessary elements of the modern novel.

A subsidiary enthusiasm also led the brothers in this direction. They were for many years closely allied by friendship and interests with Gavarni, an important artist whose forte was subjects from everyday life. On November 25, 1856, they wrote in the *Journal:* "To think that, except for Gavarni, there is absolutely nobody who has made himself the painter of nineteenth-century life and costume. A whole world is there, and the brush has not touched it." A month before (October

30) they had commented, "Realism is born and breaks out at the time when the daguerreotype and photograph show how much art differs from reality"—so far as I have been able to discover, their first use of the term *realism* in print. A few years later (November 12, 1861) they recede a bit from a realistic position: "The future of modern art, will it not be in a combination of Gavarni and Rembrandt, the reality of man and his costume transfigured by the magic of shadows and light, by the sun, a poetry of the colors that fall from the hand of the painter?"

There is early recognition by the brothers of the importance of *Madame Bovary* and of Sainte-Beuve's famous article in *Lundi* about it. Also in the September 3-21, 1857, entry they make an interesting contrast between Balzac's *Les Paysans* and George Sand's *La Mare au Diable,* assailing the false tradition of the latter that bedecks peasants with ribbons, a convention that has come down from *Paul et Virginie.* Yet on October 6, 1861, the brothers express reservations about Balzac, who is "perhaps less a great physiological anatomist than a great painter of interiors. It seems to me sometimes that he has observed furniture much more than people." A notation on October 24, 1864, brings Diderot and Balzac together in a way that helps to define the Goncourts' emerging conception of the novel: "Dramatic movement, gesture, and life did not begin in the novel until Diderot. Up to then there were dialogues but no novels. The novel, since Balzac, no longer has anything in common with what our ancestors understood by a novel. The novel of today is made from *documents,* recounted or copied from nature, as history is made from written documents." Given this position, it is not surprising that the Goncourts think that the best education for a writer would be, from the time he leaves school until he is twenty-five or thirty, to set down without action all that he sees and feels, at the same time forgetting what he has read as completely as possible.

The critical comments made by Edmond during the quarter century after Jules' death are less spontaneous and often seem to be motivated by fraternal piety, by a desire to see justice done to the memory of Jules and therefore to the living Edmond, and also by a gnawing jealousy of Zola's preeminence. During those years Edmond thought of himself increasingly as *chef d'école,* and conceived of that school in terms much less dogmatic and restrictive than did the militant naturalists. He came to see realism, as some modern critics do, more as an extension of the renovating force of romanticism than as the product of scientific thought. He wrote on January 25, 1876, that "the literature inaugurated by Flaubert and the Goncourts could, I think, be defined as follows: a rigorous study of nature in a prose speaking the language of poetry." He did concede, however, that the value of romanticism was to infuse blood and color into the French language, which was dying of anemia; as for the human beings it created, they were not of this world (April 13, 1879).

The outspoken, and often niggling, depreciation of Zola is the least happy part of Edmond de Goncourt's critical writing. As early as 1876, months before the success of *L'Assommoir*, Edmond was proclaiming that he and his brother were the great literary revolutionists of the century, something that had not been noticed because they did not shout it to the heavens. A couple of months later, in a better mood, Edmond complacently recorded a dinner at which "the young people of realist-naturalist letters" officially consecrated Flaubert, Zola, and himself as "the three masters of the present hour." Yet again a few days later Edmond denied Zola's right to an equal place, asking what Zola had written before Edmond's *Germinie Lacerteux,* which came to Zola as a revelation and on which he immediately modeled *Thérèse Raquin.*

The culmination of jealousy and charges of plagiarism came in October 1885 over similarities that Goncourt saw in Zola's *L'Oeuvre* to his own *Manette Salomon.* He burst out against Zola's "thefts, his plagiarisms, his piracies, his scarcely honest behavior toward me in leading people to believe that the phrase *human documents* and many other expressions and ideas came from him and, in his critical statements, pretending a benevolent attitude, even representing my literature as a small chapel which the young should refrain from entering." A few months later Edmond accused Zola's play *Renée* (drawn from the novel *La Curée*) of being a plagiarism of the Goncourts' *Renée Mauperin.*

On June 1, 1891, commenting on the interview he had given Jules Huret for the latter's *Enquête sur l'Evolution Littéraire,* Edmond pointed out that he might have said to the reporter: "I provided the complete formula for naturalism in *Germinie Lacerteux,* and *L'Assommoir* was made absolutely according to the method shown in the former. Now I have been the first one to emerge from naturalism—and not the way Zola did it in servile imitation, when the success of *L'Abbé Constantin* caused him to write *Le Rêve*—but because I found the genre in its original form worn out. Yes, I was the first to move out of it by using the new materials with which the young of today wish to replace it—by *dreams, symbolism, satanism,* etc., etc.—by writing *Les Frères Zemganno* and *La Faustin,* I, the inventor of naturalism, sought to dematerialize it before anyone else thought of doing so."

Whereas Edmond de Goncourt declared himself on the side of the moderns on many occasions, his acceptance of the new literature was nonetheless considerably qualified, and rather temperamentally so. He expressed agreement with Daudet in depreciating psychological novels in the manner of Stendhal, works in which

An etching of Flaubert made from a drawing by Caroline, his niece.

thought is more important than action. He was generally hostile to the new writing in Russia and Scandinavia, largely because of the growing reputation of foreign writers. The vogue for the Russians in the 1880s he saw as a reaction of right-thinking people who were looking for something with which to counter the success of the French "naturist" novel: "For incontestably it is the same kind of literature: the reality of things human seen from the sad human side, not the poetic. And neither Tolstoy nor Dosteovsky nor the others invented this literature! They took it from Flaubert, from me, from Zola, at the same time crossing it strongly with a strain of Poe" (*Journal,* October 1887). In 1895 Edmond gave an interview to *Le Rappel* in which he inveighed against the Russians and Scandinavians, who, he said, owed everything to the French school and particularly to the Goncourts: "Strindberg admitted to me the other day that he was aware that he owed me the secret of his analytical theater; and Ibsen and the others have also had to recognize that they derived from me."

From these sporadic and often biased outbursts, and from the more carefully considered prefaces, we can discern certain more or less firmly held positions:

The Goncourts considered themselves *realists,* though they often used the term *naturiste.* On many occasions Edmond equated realism and naturalism; on others he shrank from the sordidness and vulgarity often ascribed to naturalism.

They preached the right and the necessity of the novelist to open up the subject of the poor and the outcast in a "spirit of intellectual curiosity and out of pity for human misery." However, this was not normally their chosen subject matter and they insisted that for those who were well acquainted with higher social levels a realism of the drawing room was equally possible.

They placed great emphasis on the use of *human documents*.

Although they did not make a cult of authorial objectivity, they practiced it with fair consistency.

They saw themselves as using an analytical method in fiction.

They placed great stress on the use of a natural language, not a literary one; yet at the same time they were exponents of what they called *l'écriture artiste*.

The Goncourts' claims to innovation in doctrine and technique are sometimes overstressed for polemic purposes. They must yield primacy to Flaubert's *Madame Bovary* in showing the way to a new prose fiction, but it cannot be denied that after Flaubert they are the next in line among the innovators of the French novel. Moreover, the Goncourts developed a type of realistic novel that is different from that produced by either Flaubert or Zola, a type that had some influence on those two writers as well as on the younger members of the realist-naturalist group. Writing in collaboration, the brothers published seven novels before Jules's death on June 20, 1870: *En 18. .* (1851), *Charles Demailly* (made over from a play, *Les Hommes de Lettres*) (1860), *Soeur Philomène* (1861), *Renée Mauperin* (1864), *Germinie Lacerteux* (1865), *Manette Salomon* (1867), and *Madame Gervaisais* (1869). Edmond, the surviving brother, published four more novels: *La Fille Elisa* (1877), *Les Frères Zemganno* (1879), *La Faustin* (1882), and *Chérie* (1884). In addition, there was the early play *Henriette Maréchal,* not to mention the dramatic vehicles drawn from the novels in later years.

When we ask ourselves what world these novels depict, what new territory is opened up by the Goncourts, we get a somewhat ambiguous answer. The world which they appropriated to themselves is less definitive than that of their rivals and contemporaries. The reason for this is simple enough. The Goncourts were actually less interested in details of physical and social setting than they were in analysis of character. The range of milieus in their novels is therefore as wide and as varied as their works: the lower levels of society for *Germinie Lacerteux* and *La Fille Elisa;* the world of the arts in *Charles Demailly, Manette*

Salomon, and *La Faustin;* the upper levels of society in *Renée Mauperin* and *Chérie;* and three very special milieus in *Les Frères Zemganno, Madame Gervaisais,* and *Soeur Philomène*. Even where the general background is the same, as in *Renée Mauperin* and *Chérie,* the individuals and the specific environment studied are distinct. Whatever the merits of the Goncourt novels, they have as catholic a range as Zola provided in the Rougon-Macquart, and the milieus are consistently well studied. The Goncourts' claim that there could and should be a realism of the drawing room, of the Faubourg St. Germain, was put to the test in some of the novels, though for the time in which they wrote, their most original investigations were of the lower world of servants and prostitutes.

The preface to *Germinie Lacerteux* is deservedly famous for its scorn of "alcove confessions," "vapid and consolatory reading," and for its insistence that the novel should be "the great, serious, impassioned, living form of literary study and social examination," that it should become a form of social history. This position is restated thirteen years later in the preface to *La Fille Elisa,* which the author said was "written with the same feeling of intellectual curiosity and pity for human misery" as the earlier book and which he had consciously made "austere and chaste," seeking to do nothing more than move the reader to a sad meditation. "But it has been impossible for me at times not to speak as a doctor, as a scientist, as an historian. It would be truly harmful to us, the young and serious school of the modern novel, to forbid us to think, to analyze, to describe all that it is permitted to others to put in a volume which on its cover is inscribed STUDY or some such serious title. At this point in time it is not possible to condemn the genre to be the amusement of young ladies on railway journeys."

The great innovation of the Goncourts is less in the precise corner of reality chosen than in the idea of the case study, of the psychological analysis of a single character, usually a woman. Even in their genesis these works bear the mark of the case study. *La Fille Elisa* had its beginning as early as 1855, when a note appeared in the *Journal* about a dinner at a brothel and an inmate who is enamored of a traveling salesman, to which a number of years later is added a statement about the outrage felt on a visit to a women's penitentiary because of the imposition of the rule of silence on the prisoners. *Germinie Lacerteux* grew out of the shocking discovery of the debauched life led for many years by their own servant Rose, revelations that shook the brothers to the roots of their moral being but which they speedily translated into literature. *Madame Gervaisais* was patterned closely on the life of an aunt who became a *dévotée* and died in Rome. In only one novel, *Manette Salomon,* might it be said that these authors began with a world into which characters gradually found their way.

What we have here, considerably before Zola thought of the term, is a series of *experiments,* where an individual is placed in a situation and his or her actions are traced to their logical end. In nearly every instance we have a case of breakdown brought about by nervosity (with the clear exception of *Les Frères Zemganno,* where the breakdown is physical and for the most part by reason of external causes). If it were not for the fact that seven of the Goncourts' novels were written before the illness and death of Jules, we might look upon them as a repeated morbid statement of his fate. At any rate, the brothers seize upon a basic fact of their observation, the tendency of the human organism to run off the track, not necessarily by reason of some exceptional or overwhelming strain. They observe this nervosity chiefly in women, and for the most part in women who occupy a physically comfortable place in the world, though the two representatives of *le bas monde,* Germinie and Elisa, degenerate the most dramatically. These, however, are not psychological novels as we understand the term today. There is virtually no effort to probe the mind or to represent its interior states. These novelists are generally content to look on from the outside, to chronicle the process of degeneration without attempting to explain it in any but general terms. These case histories are perhaps too simplified, too monolithic for our contemporary taste, but they are written with authority, and in their way are as portentous for the future of fiction as are Dostovesky's studies of driven personalities.

Balzacian prolixity of detail is not for the Goncourts. As they were working on *Manette Salomon,* the most dense of their novels in background, they declared: "Material description of things and places is not, in the novel as we understand it, description for description's sake." Their insistence on the relative unimportance of detail does not imply that they scanted their research. Rather they performed it faithfully, though complainingly, and attempted, like Flaubert, to keep their spadework from showing. *Soeur Philomène* was preceded by a careful examination of the hospital milieu. They read books of medicine in profusion to get exact information on the maladies from which their characters suffered. As they prepared to write *Madame Gervaisais* the Goncourts shuffled through their notes on Rome, and they hung a plan of that city on their door so as to be almost physically there and able to pass their eyes over it as they wrote their novel. They went to trials at the Cour d'Assises to gather material for *La Fille Elisa,* and when Edmond took that book up again six years later, his immediate complaint was against his need to be a "conscientious policeman" as he, now alone, went on the prowl for human documents in the area around the Ecole Militaire.

When we turn to the technical devices and innovations of the Goncourts, we are on ground that is of great interest today, because, as has been suggested, they stand for a procedure somewhat counter to the massive, saturated cross section of society which we generally associate with the realist-naturalists. If *Soeur Philomène,* their first real novel, is slight, scarcely more than a suggestive, tantalizing anecdote, *Renée Mauperin* is a work of substance and must be examined carefully. Pierre Sabatier states that the brothers wrote this novel "with the idea of showing the faults of the young bourgeoisie, its egoism, its hypocrisy, its conventions, the web of ordinary intrigues which make up its life, and its thirst for honor and riches and its scorn for the individual aspirations of the soul." It is hard to see this novel as so overtly programmatic, but it does provide a broad cross section of the bourgeoisie: M. Mauperin, a former officer and now a successful manufacturer, who is very indulgent to Renée, his third child; Madame Mauperin, the usual mother eager for advantageous marriage and worldly success for her children, conveniently forgetful of her own ordinary origins but caustic about those of others; Henri Mauperin, the essence of calculation, seeking the most advantageous marriage possible while sowing his wild oats with what he considers distinction; a daughter older than Renée who is exactly like all other right-thinking young matrons; a suitor who is like all other young men of his class, and who succeeds in being "mediocre with éclat." There is also the Bourjot family representing a higher level of the middle class and able to offer a dowry of a million francs for their daughter Noémi, who is an anemic contrast with the vital Renée. They are a family of *arrivistes* on a superior scale, the father a turncoat from liberalism who worries about the threat of new ideas to his property and money; the mother achieving a calculated social success of chill grandeur, dominated by a passion for Henri Mauperin, whose mistress she is, and going mad after his death. Finally, there is a peripheral figure, Denoisel, a friend of the Mauperin family, who contrives on a limited income to play the game of bourgeois values without believing in them.

Whereas this collection of middle-class figures is drawn carefully from life, the action of the novel is not, for it abounds in excessively romanesque elements: Henri's liaison and Noémi's knowledge of her mother's guilt; the fatal duel with its ironic significance; the surprise revelation that Renée has alerted Villacourt as to her brother's assumption of his family name. There is also a difficulty in the handling of exposition. Biographical information about the various characters is introduced at intervals in an evident effort to avoid the dense expository beginning of the typical Balzac novel, but sporadic introduction is also awkward, particularly when as late as Chapter 35 we encounter eight pages of history of the Villacourt family from 1803 to the present.

What is most arresting about this novel is its reliance on dramatic scene—to an extent not equalled in the later works of the Goncourts. There is an opening conversation between Renée and her current suitor as they swim lazily in the Seine. This is continued by a scene in the Mauperin salon that evening in which Renée, by her outrageous behavior, disposes of the suitor permanently. In all some fifty pages are almost entirely in dialogue, interrupted only by a block of biographical information about M. Mauperin. These scenes are followed by a dialogue between Madame Mauperin and the Abbé Blampoix, a society priest, which is perfect in its urbanity and unction, then by one between Renée and her father alone at lunch. In short, the first hundred pages of the novel are devoted to events of two days in a scenic manner that is vivid and dramatic.

The remainder of the work is not so tight-knit in organization or so direct in presentation, though there are excellent scenes, such as the call the Mauperins make on the Bourjots, or the at home given by the elder Mauperin daughter, which is presented in eight pages of dialogue. It is this kind of scene plus a considerable amount of narrated material that gives us the substance of the bourgeois world of Paris. The rest of the novel suffers from having to exist in time so as to permit a series of plot developments to take place. The Mauperin son receives consent to his marriage with Noémi on condition that he provide her with a noble name. Over a year must elapse before he can bring this about, and the sudden irruption of the farouche Villacourt on scene to provoke a duel is a radical change of tone. Similarly, Renée's fatal illness is prepared for in the most perfunctory way, by a brief indication of faintness and palpitation early in the novel. Her collapse after her brother's death and her inescapable decline seem out of key with the other events. The ending of the work is flawed by a page of sentimental writing showing the Mauperin parents wandering disconsolately over Europe in a kind of shadow existence during their last years, for we suddenly learn that not only have they lost Renée and Henri but also their other daughter has catastrophically died in childbirth.

We find, then, in this work a somewhat dubious success, in that manner and expedients are not all of a piece. If the novel is to be basically scenic in treatment, as it promises in the beginning, then it must give up a good deal of narrated material and move more closely toward a dramatic presentation. If it is to be a picture of a young woman in revolt against the conventions and values of her society and who therefore shows a certain recalcitrance of social behavior, then it would be better not to bring in physiological decline. If the tone is to be one of clinical detachment in the presentation of characters and mores, then we cannot tolerate the descent into sentimentality at the end. In spite of these qualifications, however, it is a fresh and lively work; above all it has a wonderful vigor of language, especially in the dialogue. This does not strike

today's reader as in any way unusual, but the authors themselves were aware of their audacity, writing in the *Journal* for April 13, 1864; "People are protesting a good deal right now against the language of our *Renée Mauperin*—especially the men of the world of the brasserie. Yet the tonality we gave it was far short of actuality."

Whether Sabatier is correct in seeing *Germinie Lacerteux* as the high point in the Goncourts' career, as *Madame Bovary* was for Flaubert and *L'Assommoir* was for Zola, we must agree that this is an important work: "Whether one considers the subject treated, or the way in which they treated it, bearing in mind the date when it was written, one is obliged to salute *Germinie Lacerteux* as the arrival of naturalism." What strikes Sabatier as particularly original about the work is its clinical detachment:

> The Goncourts renewed in literature the experiment of Vesalius in the field of medicine when he decided to plunge his scalpel into a corpse in order to seek there a lesson of life. Certainly above everything else the authors of *Germinie Lacerteux* were interested in explaining physiologically the reactions of their characters. They were drawn by the clinical "side" of their subjects; that is why, in spite of their repugnance, they forced themselves to visits to the hospital, forced themselves to look at the sick, to have cases explained to them by technicians and even to be present at operations. No novelist before them had felt such scruples and such desire for scientific documentation.

Structurally this novel marks an advance over its predecessor in certain respects, and a retrogression so far as dramatic presentation is concerned. A whole life is to be summed up and illuminated here; thus dramatic scene may well have struck the authors as uneconomical. Although there are bits of dialogue, there are only two main occasions when it strikes the reader's attention. The first occurs in Chapter 14, where there is a conversation in argot with Adèle, the servant of a kept woman. It is not until Chapter 48 that speech again comes to the fore in a conversation between Adèle and Gautruche, whom Germinie meets at a picnic in the Bois de Vincennes. Otherwise this work uses dialogue sparingly, at most giving it as a culmination to a narrative passage.

The initial expository information is presented with some ingenuity. The novel begins with a conversation between Germinie and her ailing employer, Mlle de Varandeuil, which quickly becomes a monologue account by Germinie of her past life. Then there are thirty pages of summary narrative of the life of the listener, who is not paying much attention to her servant. After this there are ten more pages of narration of Germinie's experiences after her arrival in Paris. Thereafter the novel proceeds in short chapters, rarely given any dramatic organization, in which we follow Germinie in the ups and downs of her life in the capital. We learn that she has gone through a period of intense religious devotion, which is followed by an equally intense devotion to a niece until that is brought to an end by the removal of the niece's family to Algeria. A new phase begins with her acquaintance with Madame Jupillon, the proprietor of a neighborhood creamery. Germinie takes the latter's schoolboy son under her wing, visiting him at his pension with his mother and then alone when the mother is ill, generally coming to treat him as if he were her own child.

After several years Germinie finds that she is in love with the rapidly developing adolescent, though she is able to contain her passion for a time: "That happy and unsatisfied love produced in Germinie's physical being a singular physiological phenomenon. One would have said that the passion that flowed in her renewed and transformed her lymphatic personality. . . . A marvelous animation had come to her." She now gives herself completely to the life of the creamery, spending every spare moment from her service there. We are flatly told by the narrator that "In all this by-play the creamery proprietor wanted only one thing, to attach and keep a servant who cost her nothing." We are even told that young Jupillon is no good: "This man, emerging from childhood, brought to his first liaison as his entire ardor and flame the cold instincts of swinishness that are awakened in childhood by bad books, by the whisperings of comrades, by conversations at boarding school—the first breath of impurity which deflowers desire." This is editorializing of a very overt sort, a sin of which the Goncourts were, fortunately, not often guilty.

The central portion, a graphic account of Germinie's besotted passion for Jupillon, by its tone and subject makes an important contribution to the vividness of the novel. We see her humiliated at a dance hall. We are told that she has lost the respect of the inhabitants of the quartier as soon as her relations with the young man are known. She takes all her savings and even borrows money in order to set him up in a glove shop. She becomes pregnant by him, and in one of the most moving scenes of the novel manages to prepare and serve Mlle de Varandeuil's annual Twelfth Night dinner for the children of relatives and friends in spite of the onset of labor. As she leaves the building to take a taxi to the hospital, Germinie is accosted by Jupillon, who succeeds in extorting from her forty francs that she needs for her accouchement. The daughter is born and put with a wet nurse in the country. Germinie is ecstatic over being a mother and makes regular visits to see the child on her days off. Her joy is destroyed when the child suddenly dies, and she undergoes a severe crisis that is described in close physical detail. This is followed by months of "brutish sorrow." She takes to drink with Adèle and others as she is increas-

ingly neglected by Jupillon, whose mother casts her off in a burst of virtuous indignation when she learns, or pretends to learn, for the first time that Germinie has had a child. However, after some months when Jupillon finds that he has drawn an unlucky number in the draft lottery, he and his mother play up to Germinie and she is cajoled into finding the twenty-three hundred francs needed to buy a substitute. By this time she is so deeply in debt that she can never recover; her debts are her master and will possess her forever.

Though she has no illusions about her lover, Germinie is devoured by jealousy. She spies on him; she becomes a solitary drinker; she steals from her mistress when Jupillon demands money. Her whole demeanor changes; she seems to become again the stupid peasant who arrived in Paris years before. Sexual need torments her, though she resists the frightful temptation for months before giving in. Then comes the picnic at Vincennes and an affair with Gautruche, whose indignities she suffers without complaint. She beats the pavement when he is not available and finds her lovers "between a hospital, a slaughterhouse, and a cemetery." (Compare the boundaries in Zola's *L'Assommoir*.) When Gautruche, like the Jupillons, thinks of acquiring a servant by marriage, she turns on him, particularly outraged at the suggestion that she desert Mlle de Varandeuil. At last, having spent a whole night night in the rain spying on Jupillon, Germinie is attacked by pleurisy, refuses to go to bed, and soon reaches the point where tuberculosis has destroyed one lung and is making inroads on the other. Her peasant stubbornness finally gives way, and she consents to go to Lariboisière Hospital, where she dies at the age of forty-one. The novel ends with the discovery by Mlle de Varandeuil of her servant's hidden debauched life in a powerful scene with the concierge. Mlle de Varandeuil's revulsion and rejection—she says a common grave is good enough for Germinie—is followed by repentance. She goes to the cemetery, looks for the grave, and we leave her kneeling in the snow at the approximate place where Germinie lies. Again the authors mar the ending by two or three pages of sentimental effusion: "Oh, Paris, thou art the heart of the world, the great humane city, the great city of love and brotherhood. . . . The poor are thy citizens like the rich."

The details of this work, which probes to the very center of human depravity, are handled with restraint. The novel manages to convey an atmosphere of debauchery in terms that are nonspecific. Perhaps such modesty in approach was a necessity: We learn from the *Journal* for October 12, 1864, that the publisher, Charpentier, objected to a passage at the end of Chapter 1 in which Germinie recounts that upon her arrival in Paris she was covered with lice. The publisher thought that "vermin" was as far as the authors could be allowed to go in affronting the public. They burst out against that public, asking why they should conceal the existence of lice on the bodies of the poor and be forced to "lie to the public and conceal all the ugly side of life."

Whereas *Germinie Lacerteux* is one of those novels that concentrates on the life of a single individual, it has a framework that goes beyond limited scope. It is built from beginning to end, though with somewhat uneven emphasis, on a contrast between the peasant woman and her aristocratic mistress. The stoic, austere rectitude of the latter is established at the beginning, and her shocked rejection and ultimate acceptance of Germinie provide the dramatic ending. Though in the body of the novel there is little about Mlle de Varandeuil, she is always present, and Germinie's varying modes of behavior take on meaning and proportion as they are set beside the unvarying goodness, simplicity, and naive blindness of her employer. Yet at the same time devotion is the one constant in Germinie's life. She is ennobled by this stubborn adherence to duty, even though she steals, just as her mistress is ennobled by affection, trust, and final acceptance of her erring servant. This device of contrast works exceptionally well, for it helps us to keep the protagonist in perspective without depreciating her.

Though much less famous than the article about *Madame Bovary,* Sainte-Beuve's letter about *Germinie Lacerteux* shows a strong sense of the originality of this work: " . . . already I have been struck by one thing, that to judge this work properly and talk about it, we need a poetics quite different from the old, a poetics suited to the production of a nervous art and a new kind of research. And that in itself is great praise for a work: that it should raise a question of this importance forces one out of the old attitudes and onto new tracks. I hope your daring will be understood; I should like to find means to help bring this about." There is considerable irony in the fact that when Flaubert came to write *Un Coeur Simple* some years later, he drew on *Germinie Lacerteux* both for the relationship of servant and mistress and for the psychological pattern of Félicité's life, though he reduced the erotic element to a minimum. On the other hand, Zola, who confessed that his direction was changed by reading this book, immediately conceived *Thérèse Raquin,* in which the erotic content and sensationalism in general dominate the work.

The next Goncourt novel, *Manette Salomon,* is quite different from the other works of these writers, both for its scope and for its detail. The title is a misnomer, for Manette Salomon figures almost incidentally (except by obvious contrivance at the end), and the proper title is the one which the authors discarded, *L'Atelier Langibout.* This is an unusually long novel for the Goncourts, running to 472 pages, which attests to the density of description. Only in this work do they attempt to present a milieu extensively, perhaps because here the background is primary and the characters emerge naturally from it in a manner not unlike that of Zola as he developed the Rougon-Macquart.

Manette Salomon contains a good deal of authorial commentary about the development of the arts, which is interesting in itself and necessary to the statement of the work, though it is presented somewhat less than spontaneously. For example, as early as Chapter 3 there is a discussion of the cultural climate, of the fall of romanticism, and of the disastrous effect of literature on painting, which is polarized between Ingres and Delacroix: "One saw nowhere any attempt, any effort, any audacity which sought truth, which came to grips with modern life, which showed to the ambitious young on their way up that great despised side of art, contemporaneity." Such commentaries frequently come from the characters themselves, as when Chassagnol suggests: "It may be that the Beautiful today is enveloped, interred, concentrated. Perhaps in order to find it there must be analysis, a microscope, myopic eyes, the methods of the new psychology. . . . Did not Balzac find greatness in money, housekeeping, and the dirtiness of modern things, in a heap of things in which past centuries did not see two cents' worth of art?" In spite of numerous statements of this sort the novel does not preach to any disconcerting extent. Rather it exhibits the awkwardness and self-consciousness frequently found among realists when they need to supply special technical backgrounds to make their actions intelligible.

The work opens with a dramatic scene of a very mixed crowd going into the Botanical Gardens and with a highly impressionistic description of the view down on Paris from that slight elevation. This leads to several pages of dialogue, pretty much in argot, introducing various young painters who are to figure later in the novel. A bit later we have a detailed description of the Langibout studio, of the artists, and of their workaday routine, a scene that is summed up in conventional literary terms as "atelier of misery and of youth, a real garret of hope." Numerous other artistic interiors are rather briefly sketched, and there are accounts of the Salons of various years, the intrigues involved in the acceptance of paintings for the Salons, and the philistine reactions of the public. The most impressive part of the novel from the standpoint of documentation is an eighty-page passage beginning with Chapter 71 that describes, without any particular narrative continuity except what the presence of Coriolis and his mistress provides, the life of the artists of the so-called Barbizon group at a time when Barbizon represented Bohemia and not the sacred groves of hallowed genius.

This general background is supported, perhaps too mechanically, by a developed cross section. The artist whom we follow most closely is Naz de Coriolis, a Creole from Mauritius, who has a real ability to see in a new way. He is contrasted with Garnotelle, a canny opportunist without a shred of originality who nonetheless wins all the prizes, from the Prix de Rome to riches and popular acclaim. On the sidelines is Chassagnol, a kind of self-taught theoretician of art, who becomes a useful, if obvious, mouthpiece for opinions about art. Finally, there is Anatole, essentially an adventurer in life, who never gives much continuous application to his modest talents as artist, but whose presence in the novel does endow it with a lively reality. Through his precarious existence we get a sense of the poverty and gaiety traditional among artists, and also a sense of the waste that comes from their hit-or-miss effort to see and create in an original way. For a time Anatole seems to be the central figure, but once he is rescued from destitution in Marseilles by Coriolis, who is returning from the Middle East, his position becomes secondary as he provides a kind of foil to both Garnotelle's conventionality and Coriolis' nervewracking attempts at originality. Manette Salomon also has a place in this cross section as model and inevitable mistress of painters, until an intrusive critical note is struck by the narrative voice and she is made the target of ungracious antifeminine, anti-Semitic attack.

About a third of the way through the novel Coriolis becomes the central figure and the major action seems to be his attempts to break through into a new kind of painting. From his sojourn in the Orient he has gained a new feeling for color, but the three pictures accepted by the 1852 Salon are not well received, partly because of the machinations of Garnotelle. At the 1853 Salon his *Bain Turc* is a success, but two pictures in the 1855 Salon, *A Draft Board* and *A Church Wedding*—done in the manner of Courbet—are failures because of the public's firm antipathy to the modern in painting, an attitude encouraged by the scandals attending Courbet's efforts. Not willing to accept the "new realism which he brought, a realism outside the stupidity of the daguerreotype and the charlatanism of the ugly," the public blocks Coriolis' development. His worldly failure causes his mistress, Manette, to ally herself with Garnotelle. In time her lover finds her so tyrannical that he attempts to escape, but he fails as the novel ends with a return to the Botanical Gardens where it began. There is a vision of nature, of animals, of vibrant life in a lyrical vein as "the former bohemian revisited the joys of Eden, and there arose in him, in almost heavenly fashion, a bit of the happiness of the first man before virgin nature."

In spite of the misleading title this novel is only incidentally a study of the breakdown of a single individual. Critics customarily speak of it as a demonstration of the havoc brought about by women, by domesticity, and by fixed affections in the domain of artistic creation. It is true that Coriolis does go down hill, that he

is tamed by Manette's implacable desire for security and respectability. Yet the reader, though irritated by the occasional repetition of this theme, is not convinced and feels that there is a fatal weakness in Coriolis himself which is never uncovered. Because of this incomplete analysis, as well as the overt argument, the novel errs in placing too much emphasis upon Coriolis. It is with actual relief that we come back with Anatole to the normal life of artists, for we feel that the novel has at last returned to its true subject, a general picture of artist life. In short, this is a case where the materials of the novel do not permit the typical Goncourt analysis; the milieu is more important than the individuals, though the authors do not realize it.

The last of the Goncourt works under joint authorship is *Madame Gervaisais,* published in 1868. The brothers' trip to Rome in 1867 had as part of its purpose a study of the milieu in which the action of their novel would take place, a careful preparation that Edmond, with biting scorn, later compared to the quick way in which Zola worked up his massive *Rome.* The Goncourt novel is based on events that occurred in the life of an aunt, Nephtalie de Courmont, an account of which is given in *La Maison d'un Artiste,* and is repeated in the *Journal* for August 30, 1890. This is by far the most specialized of the Goncourt studies, one best described in Zola's words in an article in *Le Gaulois* for March 9, 1869: "I am going to consider this book as a simple psychological problem: How did Madame Gervaisais, taking the negations of philosophy as her starting point, arrive at the ecstasy of Saint Teresa? That is what I want to study with the Goncourts step by step. Enough of the critics will speak of the exquisite art of these authors. It will be a good thing also to show that these artists know where they are going and that a supreme logic presides over their delicately worked compositions." Armand de Pontmartin in *La Gazette de France* for March 14 of the same year gives a parallel description: "It is purely and simply (even though it be neither pure nor simple) a pathological study, applied this time to the effects of religious devotion—a moral or physical illness which is to be ranged alongside those of Renée Mauperin and Germinie Lacerteux."

In no other novel of the Goncourts do we get a better demonstration of the strength and weakness of the Goncourt approach. *Madame Gervaisais* is conducted on a line of absolute and incontrovertible logic in a style that is lucid and completely unmannered, yet evocative where evocation is needed. We see the protagonist first on her arrival in Rome, a woman somewhat ailing, somewhat ill at ease in a foreign city, chiefly concerned for the well-being of her beautiful son, who is not quite right. Her withdrawal from the world seems normal for the circumstances. Then as she gets better and becomes accustomed to Rome, she gives herself to the city, enjoys its special qualities, shares it in a simple way with her child, Pierre-Charles, and condones the thefts and incivilities of her Roman servant.

In no other novel of the Goncourts do we get a better demonstration of the strength and weakness of the Goncourt approach. *Madame Gervaisais* **is conducted on a line of absolute and incontrovertible logic in a style that is lucid and completely unmannered. . . .**

—*George J. Becker*

We learn that the special circumstances of her childhood association with her father and her withdrawal into herself during an unhappy marriage have made her into a bluestocking for whom the banal content of Catholicism has no attraction. At first her residence in Rome only strengthens this antipathy, for the sight of "certain gross idolatries had wounded the natural and delicate religiosity of her spiritual nature." Yet as she is drawn, almost in self-protection, to the beauty of pagan art and monuments, she at the same time finds them inadequate, and so "pagan art drew her back toward the beliefs rejected by the vigorous masculine reflections of her youth, beliefs to which the woman thought herself completely dead." The precipitant to change, however, comes through her situation as mother. Her son is near death when, at the suggestion of her landladies, she prays at San Agostino and a miracle occurs. A little later, at Castel Gandolfo, she meets a Polish countess who scorns her free-thinking and gives her the name of a Jesuit confessor. From the moment she enters the Gesù to confess to this priest, she is lost. Her decline is a descent that is almost a paradigm of saintly renunciation of the world: "Covertly a metamorphosis was taking place within Madame Gervaisais. The pride of her intelligence, her spirit of analysis, of research, of criticism; her personality based on judgment and energy, rare in her sex; her own ideas seemed bit by bit to decline in her through a revolution in her moral being, a sort of reversal of her nature." Finding the Jesuit confessor too mild, too indulgent, she has recourse to Father Sibilla, a kind of spiritual brute, whose sole design is to reduce her to absolute denial of the world, even including her child, with the result that finally "in her the earthly being ceased to exist," and she sinks to a perfect imitation of death in life. This spiritual denuding is accompanied by a rapid development of tuberculosis, so that even though she is roused to the world for a moment by the visit of her brother and to a realization of what she has done to

herself and others, she dies, actually at the moment when she is about to be received in audience by the Pope.

This downward progress is logical, relentless, and completely comprehensible. But the weakness of the novel is that it is too geometrical and proceeds almost as an abstraction. It yields very little of revelatory action, even though there are brief dialogue passages that have the breath of life in them. Moreover, since other people, including the unfortunate Pierre-Charles, are of little importance in the novel, we must rely on what we are told about the protagonist, whose situation we do not come to feel because of the paucity of life-giving circumstances. At any rate, the novel is pure: it does not sentimentalize; it does not approve or condemn. It merely places before our eyes a case of intense religious disintegration. It is a preliminary sketch, a scenario, from which another novelist might have built a work filled with the substance of actuality. It is the essence of realism, with too little of its existential content, of the close engagement with actuality that gives life to other works in this mode.

Of the novels written by Edmond alone only two need more than casual examination. *Les Frères Zemganno* has a kind of sweetness because of its nostalgic tone. Except for some elements describing the milieu of the traveling circus it cannot be said to be realistic or to aim at being so. *La Faustin* can be considered to be a complete failure. Granted the trite subject of life in the theater, one might still expect from the author an accurate examination of that life. Instead the book is intensely, almost grotesquely, romantic, and it is hard to conceive of an action further removed from ordinary reality than it provides. Of the other two works *La Fille Elisa* is the one to which Edmond turned four years after his brother's death, since the brothers had had this work in mind for years and had done some preparation for it—going to the Cour d'Assises in March 1869 to get the background for the court scenes. The publication of this novel was preceded by the appearance of Huysmans' *Marthe; l'Histoire d'une Fille,* which immediately fell afoul of censorship. Edmond in the *Journal* professed to be worried over the fate of his novel, stating on December 30, 1876:

> I had planned to go farther in it and to spice up the manuscript with a lot of little discoveries that I could make in the worlds of prostitution and prison; but perhaps that would have been going too far. Also the thought that the book might be brought into court makes me lazy about doing anything more. I don't have the courage to do any more work on a book that is in danger of being suppressed.

As things turned out, this was the most successful of the Goncourt books, no doubt because of its subject, with a first printing of six thousand copies being sold out immediately, followed by a second printing of four thousand.

This work is more intricate in structure than those that preceded it. Like *Germinie Lacerteux,* to which it is closely related in subject, it gives a full-length treatment of the protagonist's life, but since the portions of that life which are under examination are of two sharply different kinds, a new approach is used. The opening scene is in a courtroom where the spectators are waiting for the jury to bring in a verdict after Elisa's trial for the murder of a young soldier. She is found guilty, and the emotion of the reader is heightened by the reading from the penal code of the requirement that all persons condemned to death be decapitated.

The first part of the novel then recapitulates in detail Elisa's life up to this point in a running narrative rather than by dramatic presentation of the life of a prostitute. There is no development, only a dipping into the events of her life from time to time for significant samples. Of all the Goncourt works this is the one with the most insistence on physiological and psychological causality. As Robert Ricatte says of it [in *La Genèse de 'La Fille Elisa,'* 1960]: "Edmond never enjoyed playing the realistic game so clearly." We get a picture of Elisa's childhood with her mother, a midwife of brutal and uncertain temper. The child, who has typhoid twice in six years, is also given to violent outbursts of anger: "A refractory character, a disordered being with whom nothing could be done, whom there was no way of controlling. At the same time a flighty and changeable nature. . . ." From the clients whom her mother kept in the house Elisa learned "almost from the cradle everything that children do not know about love." In her early teens this obstinate creature ran away from her mother to a brothel in Lorraine, not out of desire for sensual pleasure but because she thought she would have an easy life. "She gave herself to the firstcomer. Elisa became a prostitute simply, naturally, almost without a tremor of consciousness . . . she had come to consider the sale and provision of love as a profession, a little less laborious than others, a profession where there was no off-season." "There was in Elisa neither erotic ardor nor desire for debauchery, nor turbulence of the senses." We follow her all over France with a traveling salesman lover. When she tires of his exploitation, she takes up the life of a Paris prostitute, frequently changing houses for the sake of variety. We learn about the brothels that serve the soldiers of the Ecole Militaire. For the first time we get an extended account of the interior of one of these establishments during working hours and a fair amount of information about Elisa's colleagues, though a quick cross sectioning of this kind was also done for the brothel in Lorraine. A very exceptional circumstance occurs when Elisa falls in love with a young soldier and has the joy of walking out with him on her days off.

The narrative continuity breaks off here, and we return to Elisa's later life, watching her arrival at the prison (the death sentence has been commuted), an arrival curiously similar to her arrival at the brothel years before. There is a vivid account of the prison regime of silence and its deleterious effects as well as of the general routine of the prison, symbolically called *Noir-lieu.* Elisa's recalcitrant nature is aroused; she goes on a kind of strike against authority and is subjected to harsh punishment, but she cannot bend her will even though she would like to do so. At last the prison doctor intervenes, insisting that she has no normal sense of guilt or of free will. Thereafter she is kept in special wards but in a deepening condition of hebetude as she regresses to childhood and its recollections. At the very end she receives permission to speak to a visitor, but it is too late. She is dead.

This section is interspersed with sentimental elements. Elisa has kept a letter from the little soldier, and it is from her ruminations over it that we belatedly get an account of how she murdered him in the Bois de Boulogne when she thought he was treating her merely as a sex object. Her mother and sister come to visit her, and she is terribly let down to discover that their motive is money, not affection. To make the death scene more poignant and the point of the book more explicit, there is a drastic shift in point of view in the final chapters. The narrator now becomes a person and recounts his visit to the prison, his horror at the regime of silence, and his attempt to give Elisa a chance to speak—which comes too late.

It is difficult to find a basis for unity in the two sections of the novel; their being yoked together is a kind of tour de force. However, the work is direct, precise, and balanced in the choice of detail. There is no inclination toward the picturesque, though there is a limited use of argot, which is printed in italics. There is careful attention to motivation and behavior patterns, even if this errs in the direction of generality. All of this is admirable for the kind of work it is. Yet most readers will conclude that the dramatic dislocation that comes from giving primacy to the trial warps the novel out of its desired focus of impersonal observation. From the very start it can be read as a plea, not as an analysis.

Chérie recalls *Renée Mauperin* written some twenty years before, and is a more convincing, more clinically presented book than the earlier one. In the preface to *La Faustin* in 1881, Goncourt alerted his readers that he wanted to write a novel that would simply be a psychological and physiological study of a young girl "reared and educated in the hot-house of the capital, a novel built on *human documents.*" (In a footnote Edmond defended the phrase as one that "most meaningfully defines the new method of the school which followed romanticism. . . .") Edmond went on to solicit the collaboration of women to write him details about the life of little girls, about the awakening of their minds and coquetry, about the essential qualities of "the new being created at adolescence." The preface to *Chérie* characterizes the novel as "a monograph on the young girl, observed in the elegant setting of Riches, Power, and the best people, a study of the young girl in the official circles of the Second Empire." For this work, the author tells us, he has done research to a depth that might be expected for a work of history. His aim is to render "the pretty and distinguished aspects of my subject, and I have worked to recreate the reality of elegance . . . I could not bring myself to make my young girl the nonhuman individual, the sexless, abstract, and lyingly ideal creature of the *chic* novels of today and yesterday."

> It will certainly be found that the narration of *Chérie* lacks indent, peripeties, intrigue. For my part, I find that there is still too much of this. If I might become younger by a few years, I would like to write novels with no more complication than exists in most of the intimate dramas of existence, with love affairs ending without any more suicides than the affairs through which we have all passed; and as for death, death which I employ deliberately as the denouement of my novels, of this one as well as the others, although it is a little more *comme il faut* than marriage, I would reject it also from my books as a theatrical means that should be scorned in serious literature. . . . I believe that adventure, *bookish* machination, has been worn out by Soulié and Sue and the great imaginative writers of the beginning of the century, and my idea is that the final evolution of the novel, in order for it to succeed completely in becoming the great vehicle of modern times, is to make it a work of pure analysis.

For this kind of writing Edmond believes that some other label than *novel* will have to be found. He makes an interesting protest against those who do not believe in making an effort to write well, asserting the necessity of "a personal language, a language that bears our signature." He expresses approval of neologisms and presumably of vernacular and slang as well. Language must be well handled, for a failure to write well would allow vulgar reportage to take over.

Considering the preface to this, his last book, as "a sort of literary testament," Edmond recalls a statement made by Jules on a walk in the Bois de Boulogne a few months before his death: "Some day people will have to recognize that we wrote *Germinie Lacerteux* . . . and that *Germinie Lacerteux* is the paradigm of all that has been written since under the name of realism, naturalism, etc." This is a somewhat portentous preface for what J. H. Rosny called a minor work, but it does reflect the "temperament, the tastes, and the doctrines of Edmond de Goncourt." Certainly the novel proceeds in a straight line, never losing sight of its intention to present the development of a young girl of the upper classes. The heroine is the granddaughter of a Marshal of France, who has been recalled to public life as Minister of War. Her mother had become mad with grief after the death of her soldier husband at Sevastopol. The child is serious, usually sad, extraordinarily impressionable, and subject to disquieting outbursts of anger, examples of which are given in the form of a case study.

Nothing happens in the novel, which begins pictorially with a scene in which Chérie presides over a dinner party for eight little friends on her ninth birthday. There is an elaborate account of her preparation for her First Communion, which is accompanied by a temporary state of religious exaltation. This religious enthusiasm subsides; she goes through puberty torn between a sense of pride and a feeling of disgust over menstruation. We learn of her crushes and her first love by means of eleven pages of a diary covering a year. There is a ten-page disquisition on her friends, one of whom is described rather too emphatically by the narrator as *une possédée, une détraquée,* a perfect example of the moral illness of the nineteenth century as embodied in some of the women of the official world of the Second Empire. A chapter describes a visit to the office of Siesmeyer, a famous horticulturist at Versailles, which consists of a detailed inventory and no action whatever. Another chapter is given over to fourteen pages about taking tea in the salon; the next is about balls that Chérie attends, though in less detail. Thus we have a fairly complete picture of the young woman as she reaches adulthood.

Given her background, it is not surprising that Chérie may be psychologically unbalanced, but the novel gives little evidence of this and we are not prepared for the sudden and spectacular change of personality that she undergoes. A doctor comments that "ovulation demands fecundation" and says that in the exciting atmosphere of Paris young women sometimes die as a result of this nervous state. Chérie at any rate does die. Instead of death agonies we are given a powerful account of her erratic behavior toward the end of her life. The novel concludes documentarily with a *faire-part* announcing her death at the age of nineteen on June 20, 1870 (an unwarranted indulgence in private sentiment on the part of the author, since it is the day of Jules' death). What is remarkable about this last novel is that the author is still trying out new techniques. He abandons sustained action completely and tries to fill out his subject by means of literal documentation. It is not a successful experiment, but it does indicate one of the main lines of development that realists have tried to follow in this century, toward a fusion of factual data and fictional framework.

We cannot conclude an examination of the *opus* of the Goncourt brothers without recognizing their addiction to the theater. Their joint disappointment was the failure of a very mediocre play, *Henriette Maréchal,* which was staged in December 1865. The performance created such a tumult that virtually nothing of the play could be heard, and the diarist wrote on the morning after with a certain pride: "The head of the claque told me this morning that the theater has not seen such an uproar since [Victor Hugo's] *Hernani* and *Les Burgaves.*" Interest in the theater continued to be one of Edmond's chief preoccupations in his later years, partly in deference to his brother's memory but also out of rivalry with the more successful Daudet and Zola. All of the Goncourt novels were dramatized during Edmond's last years, but none of them achieved any great success on the stage. The great event for Edmond was the reprise of *Henriette Maréchal* in March 1885. Only *Le Figaro* did it justice; the rest of the press was rather niggling. The critics did not recognize the play's originality in language and depiction of humanity. A few months later, on December 19, 1885, still smarting from critical condescension, Edmond declares: "When you get right down to it, up to now I know of only two plays which belong to the modern theater: *Henriette Maréchal,* which has the misfortune to be a forerunner, *Henriette Maréchal* and *Saphô.* You can't count the *Busnached* plays of Zola, and as for *Thérèse Raquin,* the play does indeed contain the novel but it does not have the least scenic modernity."

In November 1886, *Renée Mauperin* was put on. As usual, Edmond had high expectations and hoped for a run of 100 performances. Though these hopes were not realized, he was consoled when the play was bought for American production. In October 1887, it was the turn of *Soeur Philomène,* which had its premiere at Antoine's Théâtre-Libre. During the next season Antoine undertook to do Goncourt's original play, *La Patrie en Danger,* without any overwhelming success. In December 1888, Edmond confided to his *Journal* that war had been declared on *Germinie Lacerteux* while the play was still in rehearsal by means of the canard that the leading actress, Réjane, had been forced against her will to utter the word *putain* (whore). The first performance is described on December 19 as "a real battle." *Le Figaro* for December 25, in an article entitled "Le Mot Sale" ("Dirty Words"), attacked the crudities of language in the novel, which, it said, were compounded in the play. (During this time the author took what comfort he could from the news that *Henriette Maréchal* had been performed with success in St. Petersburg.) Two years later, in December 1890, it was the turn of *La Fille Elisa,* and finally on February 29, 1896, *Manette Salomon* was put on and panned as usual. Edmond could not contain his amazement when two months later he went to pick up his share of the receipts from this play and found that it came to 7600 francs.

These various attempts, by Zola and even by Daudet as well, show the difficulty with which the citadel of conventional drama was to be reduced, and the deepseated antagonism that existed on the part of theatergoers toward anything that sought to do more than entertain. But the obdurate response of the public should not lead us to overlook the inadequacies of these plays. They were essentially static; they lacked any sort of forward motion. Their power, if they had any, was the power of a real-life situation to speak for itself in language that rang true. Scenically, the plays seem to have been little more than a series of tableaus, like the children's party in *Germinie Lacerteux,* the brothel scene in *La Fille Elisa,* or, indeed, the fight at the washhouse in Zola's *L'Assommoir.* For the most respectful audience in the world these would still have failed to be absorbing dramas.

Although Edmond de Goncourt frequently spoke in the scientific idiom of Taine, Flaubert, and Zola, it is hard to believe that he had any particular grounding in the new materialistic science and philosophy. Indeed, his role of aristocrat and conservative militated against his assimilation of the new currents of thought. The *Journal* for April 7, 1869, contains an entry that is typical of his attitude (in this case of both brothers, since Jules was still alive):

> They were saying that Berthelot had predicted that in a hundred years of science man would know the secret of the atom and would be able at will to extinguish or relight the sun; that Claude Bernard for his part was asserting that after a hundred years of physiological science it would be possible to know the laws of organic life, of human creation. We raised no objections, but we firmly believe that at that point in the history of the world the good Lord with his white beard will arrive on earth with his bundle of keys and say to humankind, as they say at the Salon: "Gentlemen, it's closing time!"

Edmond clearly does not believe that the millennium will come through science, and he does not share in Zola's messianism for the novel as a branch of science. Yet it is equally clear that for the most part the characters whose lives he studies in his novels are subject to the unwavering force of determinism. He associates himself with this current of thought almost casually in a footnote to a *Journal* entry of May 24, 1885: "It is true that Taine marked Zola's thought rather early and readily: Taine's literary determinism, which was received with reticence in 1864, was accepted by Zola by September 1866. But determination of character by milieus is something that Zola verified among the novelists who influenced him directly, in Balzac and in a novel like *Germinie Lacerteux,* which he saluted as a revelation in 1865 twelve years before *L'Assommoir* and one year before his adherence to Taine." Sabatier says of the brothers that "They too were determinists, or rather fatalists, and in their pessimism and their distaste for surrounding vulgarity we must discover, as in Flaubert, the principal motive for their retreat into art."

Retreat it no doubt was, but a retreat remarkable for its forward-looking aesthetic outlook. The Goncourts, especially Edmond, did accept the power of materiality and were disdainful of efforts to seek refuge in daydreams masquerading as novels. They methodically presented a gallery of modern characters, showing lives that they attempted to make authentic by massive research and cumulative observation. In a late *Journal* entry for August 30, 1893, Edmond wrote with disdain of the unwillingness of younger writers to do studies after nature and their penchant for creating what he called *metaphysical beings*. On the other hand, he had some reservations lest the prevailing materiality of the novel stifle the characters, lest milieu stand in such high relief around the feelings and passions that it almost stifle them. On July 24, 1885, Edmond set down the observation that "Perfection in art is the mixing in proper proportion of the real and *the imagined*. At the beginning of my literary career I had a predilection for the imagined. Later I became enamored exclusively of reality and that which is studied after nature. Now I remain faithful to reality but sometimes present it under a special light, which modifies it, poetizes it, tints it with fantasy."

This remark is not an accurate statement of Edmond's general practice, though it is applicable to the two offbeat last works. It represents the path that he might well have been expected to take in view of his repugnance for vulgarity, his connoisseurship of eighteenth-century and Japanese art, and in the years after Jules's death his stoic acceptance of an emotionally empty existence. Instead Edmond remained faithful to reality and to realism as he understood it and was able to embody it in his own works of fiction. The presence of the Goncourts' clinically examined and presented case studies was a valuable addition to French realism, which might otherwise have been smothered in the accessory. It is with justice that Paul Bourget said that no one since Balzac had modified the art of the novel to as great an extent as the Goncourts.

Malcolm Scott

SOURCE: "The Sceptical Mode," in *The Struggle for the Soul of the French Novel: French Catholic and Realist Novelists, 1850-1970,* The Catholic University of America Press, 1990, pp. 11-51.

[*In the following excerpt, Scott discusses the importance of religion, primarily as an object of ridicule and derision, in several French Realist novels.*]

An aim common to most novelists during the second half of the nineteenth century was to depict as fully as

possible the physical appearance and social structures of the modern world. Thus churches as buildings and the Church as institution were necessary ingredients of their novels on a purely documentary level. The grander the scale of the social panorama, the truer this was, and it is in the novels of Zola that churches and church ceremonial, as an important aspect of life at all social levels, are the most fully and frequently depicted. Some of Zola's most memorable set-piece descriptions are of church interiors, like that of Notre-Dame-des-Grâces in Passy, decked with flowers for the *mois de Marie (Une page d'amour)* or Saint-Roch with its sculpted Christ flanked by Virgin and Magdalene *(Pot-Bouille)*. It would be an inhibiting theory of literature that would deny the value of these descriptions for their own sake, providing as they do a concrete link between reality and fiction, between Zola's age and ours. Similarly, the accounts of baptism, first communion, weddings and funerals, as they appeared to nineteenth-century writers, are essential parts of their achievement as social historians, which is how they often defined themselves. The same function is fulfilled by the depiction of the Church's social role, or of popular attitudes towards it, and in such material the novels of Zola are uniquely rich.

The documentary aspect of fiction, although an important one, is not sustained for long in a state of innocence. Zola's famous definition of art reminds us that these particular 'corners of creation' are always seen 'through a temperament'. The novelist's angle of vision asserts itself, satirical intention meets rhetorical device. Underfunded country churches falling on the heads of priests already tortured enough by the attentions of misnamed 'filles de la Vierge', working-class folk turning to the Church only on the occasion of their daughter's wedding—such details, in *La Terre* or *L'Assommoir,* reveal as much of the author's viewpoint as they do of historical realities. Maupassant's cameo of the blessing of the boats ceremony in *Une vie* moves swiftly from *reportage* to unflattering portraits of provincial clerics:

> Les trois vieux chantres, crasseux dans leur blanche vêture, le menton poileux, l'air grave, l'œil sur le livre de plain-chant, détonnaient à pleine gueule dans la claire matinée. [. . .] Le prêtre, d'une voix empâteé, gloussa quelques mots latins dont on ne distinguait que les terminaisons sonores.

Such mild irreverence, but escalating from dirty cassocks to incomprehensible and socially irrelevant Latin chants, is typical of Maupassant's presentation of the clergy. His short stories are full of insalubrious priests, or negligent ones, arriving late for their duties or hurrying quickly through them in half-swallowed utterances for which his favourite term, like Flaubert's for the same thing, was 'un marmottement'.

The satire is light and superficial here, but the irony cuts more deeply when religious practice is given a more developed social setting. The Goncourts explore the relationship between the wealthy middle-class world of Renée Mauperin and a certain type of clergy through the character of the abbé Blampoix, 'le prêtre du monde, du beau monde et du grand monde,' self-appointed saviour of the faubourgs Saint-Germain and Saint-Honoré, and especially prized in such circles for his talent as marriage-broker. The type is alive nearly two decades later in the form of Zola's abbé Mauduit, who has graced every death-bed in the quartier Saint-Roch and has mastered the art of closing his eyes to the moral bankruptcy of the bourgeoisie *(Pot-Bouille)*. That religion existed merely for the convenience and protection of the middle class is an idea expressed with increasing acerbity from the mocking sketches of Monnier's *La Religion des Imbéciles* (1846) to the harsher denuciations of Maupassant and Zola, in whose work religious attitudes are often the banners of class warfare. The *bien-pensants* who accompany Boule-de-Suif on the coach from Rouen to Le Havre and who persuade her to sleep with a Prussian officer in order to ensure their swift passage boast of possessing 'de la Religion et des Principes.' The same facade cloaks middle-class turpitude in Zola's novels, whereas the poor regard religion as an irrelevance in the daily struggle for bread. 'Est-ce que vous avez besoin d'un bon Dieu et de son paradis pour être heureux?' Étienne Lantier asks his fellow miners in *Germinal*. Empty churches, to Count Muffat's father-in-law in *Nana* signify imminent revolution; he would have readily agreed with the Goncourts' Monsieur Bourjot that 'il faudrait que toutes ces canailles allassent à la messe.' The brothers, whose interest in the working class was a notoriously dilettante one and who could never have been suspected of harbouring any sympathies for the political left, nevertheless expose through Bourjot the complicity between Catholicism and reaction: 'Il se précipitait vers les doctrines d'ordre, il se retournait vers l'Église comme vers une gendarmerie, vers le droit divin comme vers l'absolu de l'autorité et la garantie providentielle de ses valeurs.' The same alliance is evoked by Maupassant's fanatical abbé Tolbiac, who tells the young châtelaine: 'Il faut que nous soyons unis pour être puissants et respectés. L'église et le château se donnant la main, la chaumière nous craindra et nous obéira.' One of the most powerful images of the exploitation of religion in the interests of repressive authority appears in *La Fille Élisa,* written by Edmond de Goncourt after Jules' death. In the prison cell where the former prostitute Élisa serves her sentence for the killing of her lover, a crucifix hangs above a sign saying DIEU ME VOIT—'et au-dessous de l'œil divin [. . .] il y avait, au trou imperceptible fait par un clou dans la porte, l'œil d'un inspecteur en tournée dans les corridors.' The eye of God and the eye of the law become indistinguishable from each other, and the nail used to drill the spy-hole seems a mocking image of the nails of the Crucifixion.

In *Madame Bovary* too there are reflections of the same contract between Church and political regime. One of the newest buildings in Yonville is the church, renovated under Charles X, a symbol of the clericalism of the Restoration period. Above its altar hangs a painting of the Holy Family, a gift from the Minister of the Interior; in exchange, the *tricolore* flies from the steeple. Flaubert's eye for such detail was matched by Zola's, and it is in the Rougon-Macquart cycle that the Church is most provocatively identified as the accomplice of state power. In the first novel of the series, *La Fortune des Rougon,* it is the clergy which plots and leads the insurrection in Plassans and wins power for Louis-Napoleon Bonaparte. In *La Conquête de Plassans,* the abbé Faujas' usurpation of power in the Mouret household represents in miniature the rape of France by the Emperor; but under the surface, a more fundamental takeover is in process, embodied in the gradual expulsion of the Mourets and the priest from their bourgeois home by Faujas' working-class sister and her husband. Thus does Zola express his view of the Church as a sinister force but, like the regime it supports, an ultimately doomed one.

. . . . .

In the forefront of Realism's presentation of the Catholic Church is a character type of which all the leading novelists create memorable individual examples: the priest; and the manner in which he is depicted is crucial for the interpretation of many a text. Not all Realist priests are negative figures. One can cite to the contrary Maupassant's abbé Picot, 'gai, vrai prêtre campagnard, tolérant, bavard et brave homme' (*Une vie*), and Zola's well-meaning pro-worker priest Ranvier in *Germinal*. But the majority of them are shallow and incompetent, figures of fun at best, callous and sinister at their worst. One of the best known examples of clerical *bêtise* is Flaubert's Bournisien, whose failure to recognise Emma Bovary's problems aggravates her self-induced despair. Maupassant's priests, in their altogether different encounters with the fair sex, rejoin the traditions of the *fabliaux,* as in the tale of the cleric who visits his supposedly chaste nephew and inadvertently climbs into bed alongside the young man's girlfriend—this in a tale appropriately entitled 'Une Surprise'. The confrontation of religion with sexuality, treated here as farce, has more serious overtones in other Maupassant stories. In 'Clair de lune' (one of two *contes* bearing this title) the abbé Marignan is shaken to learn that his niece, whom he had hoped to see become a nun, has a lover, but the sight of the couple walking happily in the moonlight causes the priest to question his former mistrust of human love. Perhaps God, he reflects, has made the night specially as a setting for lovers; perhaps love is legitimised, even sanctified. The abbé feels an obscure shame, 'comme s'il eût pénétré dans un temple où il n'avait pas le droit d'entrer,' a shame that recalls that of Adam and Eve though the story implies that human love is a greater paradise than the biblical one. The abbé stops on the brink of denying God and tries instead to reconcile his discovery with his faith in Providence, but the experience has changed for ever his notion of life's priorities. The story is typical of Realist and Naturalist concern with the man beneath the priest's vestments and with the sexual urges which these writers see, much more than religious aspirations, as constituting the prime nature of human beings. Another Maupassant priest, in 'Le Baptême' (again, two stories share this title), holds in his arms a newly baptised infant and sobs in unspoken frustration at his own eternal separation from the joys of paternity. Yet another, in 'Le Champ des oliviers', is so overcome to find that he has a son that he murders the latter and then kills himself: the roles of priest and father are tragically incompatible. A similar fascination with the priest's encounter with sex is shown by Paul Alexis in his story 'Après la bataille', which he contributed to the Naturalist volume *Les Soirées de Médan*. Here a priest, wounded by the invading Prussians, is picked up by a young widow travelling home with her husband's corpse, and through the mutual comfort they offer each other he recognises his true nature as a sexual being.

The central text on this theme is Zola's novel *La Faute de l'abbé Mouret,* in which a priest has a love affair with a girl, only to reject her and their unborn child on resuming his priestly function. Although this novel predated the stories by Maupassant and Alexis described above, Zola did not invent the character of the *prêtre amoureux,* of which there is no shortage of examples in Romantic literature. Lamartine's narrative poem *Jocelyn,* especially, invites comparison, for it too relates the abandonment of a girl by a priest who has been her lover. *Jocelyn* is an obvious source of *Mouret,* but what Zola adds to the original melodrama is a sharpness of anticlerical satire, a questioning of the nature of the man within the priest, a probing of the neuroses common to both sexual and religious experience. No text in the whole of the Rougon-Macquart cycle challenges Christian attitudes and values more radically than this one, although this has not always been recognised. F. W. J. Hemmings sees a neutral Zola at work here, on the grounds that his preparatory notes for the novel reveal no ironical intention, and he supports his judgment by referring to a review by Zola of Ernest Daudet's *Le Missionnaire* (a novel on a similar theme) in which he objects to the use of novels as weapons for or against Catholicism. Other reviews, however, give different impressions. Writing of Lavalley's novel *Aurélieu* Zola, as was his custom in incidental writing, pleads his freedom from *parti pris,* but supports nonetheless the author's opposition to priestly celibacy. The priest, he goes on, is rightly less venerated than of old, acceptable as a human brother but not as the spokesman of the divine. His pretension to chastity denies nature in a way that Zola finds 'repugnant.' This review prefigures very accurately Zola's ironical stance towards the central character of his novel. Serge Mouret is sexually neutered by his priestly calling, and this offence against nature is temporarily righted by his making love to Albine in the overgrown park called Le Paradou, after which 'il se sentait complet.'

Despite the absolute clarity of what the novel conveys here, its coherence has been questioned. Hemmings objects that because Serge is suffering from amnesia, 'he must be exonerated at least from the fault of consciously rejecting the demands of the religious life he had embraced,' and he implies that this is a flaw in the novel's logic. But this is to take the 'faute' of the title in its conventional moral sense, or even in its special Catholic sense: that is, a sin. The priest's loss of memory, far from being an error on Zola's part, is a deliberate narrative device, used to obliterate Serge's sense of sin and to invalidate Christian interpretation from the outset. A further comparison with *Jocelyn* is useful here. Lamartine's priest does not set out to seduce the girl Laurence; his love is not premeditated. He believes her to be a boy, left in his care by a dying father, and the relationship that develops only gradually reveals itself as a sexual one. Jocelyn cannot be blamed for his love, but only for abandoning the girl who needs him. Exactly the same is true of Zola's priest. Whereas Hemmings seems to identify Mouret's fault as loving Albine, for Zola, in ironical reversal of Christian morality, it is in not loving her enough. It is in his betrayal of her, in his rejection of life in favour of what is specifically identified as a religion of death.

The novel's challenge to Catholic values is thus undeniable, even though the forces that constitute the other side of the conflict—nature and sex—are not depicted in glorified and unproblematic terms. What Valerie Minogue [in *Forum for Modern Language Studies* XIV (July 1978)] calls Zola's 'characteristic ambivalence' towards sex is certainly evident in the lovers' post-coital shame; and if nature is supposed to be Man's guiding light, then the fact that only Serge's half-witted sister Désirée relates easily to it (in her relationship with animals) creates an immediate difficulty. Zola here reveals, not confusion, but rather artistic integrity. To depict the discovery of sex as the path to eternal happiness, to pretend that human beings have no difficulty in accepting their condition and earthly environment would have been obvious distortions of the truth he sought to portray. If Le Paradou is the site of conflict between the two lovers, if it is wild and disturbing and tainted with the memories of the tragic love of its former owners, it is because Zola did not want to create a paradise on earth. There are no earthly paradises. Yet earth and life constitute for Zola the only sure reality, and his hope is founded on their eventual improvement. That is why the fault of the abbé Mouret is a crime against life.

Zola also implies that sex, far from belonging to a world remote from religious experience, is part and parcel of it. Serge's special devotion to the Holy Virgin contains unmistakable sexual elements, and Frère Archangias, the lay brother who embodies Catholic misogyny at its fiercest, is not wrong in suspecting this. Serge hides pictures of the Virgin under his pillow. Alternately erotic symbol and mother figure (replacing his own mother, burned alive in her Plassans home), the Virgin is a compound of all that he seeks from the female sex. He imagines himself 'buvant le lait d'amour infini qui tombait goutte à goutte de ce sein virginal.' As he recites his countless *Aves* he is voicing a declaration of love, 'cette parole sans cesse la même qui revenait, pareille au "Je t'aime" des amants.' His eyes fix on her bodice, on her heart pierced by a sword, and he feels the urge to kiss her breast. As he recites the litany, each appelation is a step towards obscure sexual union, and the end of his prayer leaves Serge 'les genoux cassés, la tête vide, comme après une grande chute,' in anticipation of the pleasurable fatigue he will discover with Albine. Zola's pre-Freudian conviction of the sexual element within Man's spiritual aspirations produces a parody of the cult of the Virgin, which was so strong in Second Empire France.

La Faute de l'abbé Mouret directly influenced Maupassant's treatment of the priest figure, especially in his attitudes to sex and procreation. Frère Archangias' terror at the spectacle of farmyard reproduction, and his killing of a nestful of baby birds, are echoed in the story 'Le Saut du berger' and also in *Une vie*. In both texts, a priest destroys a litter of puppies, whose birth has been innocently attended by a group of peasant children. The abbé Tolbiac in *Une vie* is given an ideological opponent in the shape of Baron le Perthuis, father of the heroine Jeanne and direct fictional descendant of Albine's father, the old libertarian Jean-bernat. Seeing nothing but beauty in sex and procreation, he rejects Catholic prudery as an exacerbation of middle-class taste; and of priests he declares: 'Il faut combattre ces hommes-là, c'est notre droit et notre devoir. Ils ne sont pas humains' (*Une vie*). Less rigorous a thinker than Zola, less reluctant to pronounce a naïve faith in life-giving sex (which ironically, was to kill him, through syphilis), Maupassant's talents were those, not of a creator of philosophies, but of a denouncer of hypocrisy and falsehood. Through the mouth of the Baron, he produces a sort of Realist's Ecce Homo: 'Le voilà, le voilà, l'homme en soutane! L'as-tu vu maintenant?' This is not just the voice of one character, a cranky and profligate anti-clerical. The entire narrative structure of *Une vie* maroons the abbé Tolbiac at its negative pole. Increasingly fanatical, he

delights in assuring Jeanne that all her troubles have been sent as deserved punishment from God, and refuses to consecrate her father's burial. He is the prime embodiment of an anti-life viewpoint, a foil for the text's humanitarian affirmations. The novel is not quite anti-religious, for the conflicts at its heart are not between religious belief and unbelief, but between a wide-ranging liberal religion and a perverted clerical fanaticism. But there can be no mistaking the view of the Catholic Church which it projects. Jeanne's young son, misunderstanding his great aunt's inarticulate reply to his question: 'Where is God?', tells his grandfather: 'Le bon Dieu, il est partout, mais il n'est pas dans l'Église.' The child's naïve comment carries more than a grain of Maupassant's truth.

．．．．．

It is implied in *La Faute de l'abbé Mouret* that priestly devotion and even, by extension, all Christian faith betray essentially feminine aspects of character. Albine's view of her former lover in his priestly vestments makes this clear: 'Toute sa virilité séchait sous cette robe de femme qui le laissait sans sexe.' The association between religion and femininity is one of the constants of Realist characterisation, and religious experience one of the principal channels by which it explores female psychology. Misogynism and sexism combine with religious scepticism to produce some of the most markedly ironic portraits of character in the Realist corpus. 'La religion,' quip the Goncourts, 'est une partie du sexe de la femme,' and they add to their own *bon mot* one of Gavarni's: 'Savez-vous de quoi me fait l'effet une femme qui n'a pas de religion? D'une sorte d'hermaphrodite.' The diary is full of comments on the dubious sensuality of women's religion. Convent girls are described as having their heads stuffed with 'tout ce vaporeux mystique,' which will make them ill suited as wives of brutish husbands. Religion is seen as 'cette grande machine de la femme,' church-going as a chance to show off new dresses; to a woman, 'Dieu lui semble *chic*.' The sanctification of Marie Alacoque, foundress of the cult of the Sacred Heart, is regarded by the brothers as no less than the glorification of 'le paganisme féminin.' Such views abound in their novels too. The attitude of middle-class ladies to religion is summed up simply: 'Les femmes en raffolaient.' The Goncourts are echoed nearly two decades later by Maupassant, whose heroine Jeanne 'était toute de sentiment; elle avait cette foi rêveuse que garde toujours une femme' (*Une vie*). She shares with another of his female characters, Madame Walter, 'ces idées superstitieuses qui sont souvent toute la raison des femmes.'

The unavowed sexuality of Serge Mouret's love of the Virgin has its counterpart in women's attachment to the masculinity of Christ. 'Les femmes,' says Flaubert's Hilarion as part of his subtle undermining of the hapless Saint-Antoine, 'sont toujours pour Jésus, même les idolâtres.' Passion for the person of Christ, expressed in the language of human love—Jesus as 'l'Époux de son âme, le Roi de son amour, le Bienaimé de son coeur'—underlies the vocation of the Goncourts' soeur Philomène. Sexual and religious awakening, the second as the by-product of the first, are explored in the account of her adolescence; without heavy irony, and indeed with compassion for their character, the Goncourts nevertheless suggest that religious yearnings are the product of imminent puberty. The account of Philomène's first communion, the moment of 'receiving God', is expressed in a blend of the diffuse—'un ineffable sentiment de défaillance'—and of the more suggestively precise—'ravissement,' 'évanouissement'—that hints at sexual initiation, sharply and intimately felt but indescribably unfamiliar. However mildly and undogmatically, the text contrasts that which is undeniably real—the emotion and its unspoken physiological causes—with what is fondly imagined: the encounter with the divine. The former exists not only in Philomène's flesh but also in the authoritative testimony of the narrator; the latter is a strand in the imagination of a simple girl.

Of all the examples of the type to which Philomène belongs, the convent girl unable to disentangle spiritual and amorous impulses, the best known is Emma Bovary. Like Philomène, 'les comparaisons de fiancé, d'époux, d'amant céleste et de mariage éternel qui reviennent dans les sermons lui soulevaient au fond de l'âme des douceurs inattendues.' 'La religion' and 'les délicatesses de coeur' are interlaced in her imagination through the figure of Mademoiselle de la Vallière, royal mistress turned Carmelite, to whose legend her thirteen-year-old eyes are opened by illustrations on dinner plates in the inn next door to the convent. Menacing reality intrudes in the shape of the 'égragnitures' left by past diners' knives, but Emma is sublimely oblivious to reality, preferring instead distorted romantic images which are often the product of religious reverie. Religion itself is not the prime target of Flaubert's irony, but it provides another level on which the portrait of the muddled, self-deceiving woman can be sharpened. It merges with the broader theme of romantic delusion when Emma reads *Le Génie du christianisme* and when her brain swims with Lamartinian clichés of falling leaves, dying swans and the voice of the Eternal 'discourant dans les vallons.' Emma's direct descendant is Angélique in Zola's *Le Rêve,* to whom the saints and martyrs of Voragine's Golden Legend are more real than the flesh and blood people around her, and whose adolescent fantasies of handsome young lovers are interchangeable with her longing for Christ. Another Zola heroine, Hélène in *Une page d'amour,* recognises more clearly that even prayer, far from being a refuge from the temptations of adulterous love, can be a sublimation of erotic yearnings,

'toujours la même passion, traduite par le même mot ou le même signe.'

To less innocent women, churches, in the words of Bel-Ami, 'sont bonnes à tous les usages [. . .] Il leur semble tout simple de filer l'amour au pied des autels.' Fewer places are more convenient as sites for amorous rendezvous, away from prying eyes, or more stimulating, the senses quickening as candles flicker in incense-laden darkness. The church of the Trinity is the haunt of Bel-Ami and Madame Walter, he pretending to pray while muttering words of seduction into her ear, she hypocritically imploring heaven's protection from his charms. For Emma and Léon, Rouen cathedral is the preferred meeting-place, and it is here, in the 'boudoir gigantesque' of the church, that takes place the final apotheosis of Emma as perfume-laden sexobject, her face resplendent in the reflections of stained glass.

Often the object of the female's pursuit need not be imported, but is already inside the church: namely, the priest himself. The Goncourts' Germinie Lacerteux falls in love with her young confessor, follows him from confessional to vestry and back. When prudently diverted to a less seductive minister of God, she simply stops going to church, and when asked what the priests have done to her to cool her ardour, she answers: 'Rien.' This is clearly meant as a complaint.

Germinie's working-class sisters in Zola's *Le Ventre de Paris* have more success with priests, at least in the eyes of the malicious gossips who see the *charcutière* Lisa Quenu going to church with suspicious regularity: 'La grosse donne dans le curés, maintenant. Ça la calmera, cette femme, de se tremper le derrière dans l'eau bénite.' The eroticism of confession is suggested as Lisa, awaiting her turn, sees, under the door of the confessional, the hem of a blue dress lying suggestively at the feet of the priest; the chapel of the Virgin is 'toute moite de silence et d'obscurité'; women recline 'pâmées sur des chaises retournées, abîmées dans cette volupté noire'; stained glass images burn 'comme des flammes d'amour mystique'; Lisa feels 'une indécence dans cette ombre, un jour et un souffle d'alcôve.' The wife of her cousin Mouret, in *La Conquête de Plassans,* knows no such inhibitions. Confessing to the priest whom she loves is an undisguised sexual experience; it is 'extase,' 'évanouissement,' marked by attraction to the very odour of the priestly garb, rising to the crisis of 'sanglots nerveux' and climaxing in overwhelming fatigue.

Another female character whose slide into religious belief is a preordained hazard of her sex is Madame Gervaisais, the eponymous heroine of the Goncourts' last joint novel. A reader of philosophical works which have led her to reject the supernatural and an aesthete subscribing to 'une religion du Beau, du Vrai, du Bien,'

Madame Gervaisais stands aloof from Christian belief when she arrives in Rome with her mentally retarded son Pierre-Charles. What she seeks in visiting churches is not 'l'approche de Dieu dans sa maison,' but simply peace. She possesses nevertheless 'un respect de femme pour la personne du Christ,' and gradually comes to regard him as '[le] patron de son sexe.' When her son falls ill, her identification with the Virgin as the archetype of the suffering mother further erodes her scepticism, and fosters the growth of the religious sensibility which is 'caché [. . .] au fond de la femme.' This process is represented as one of decline, as the regression of a sharply intelligent woman to the banality of female religiosity. Under the influence of the atmosphere of Rome, or what the narrator calls '[la] contagion sainte,' and believing her prayers to be responsible for her son's recovery, she becomes a fanatical convert, abandoning friends and artistic pursuits for the company of her austere confessor. Her vision darkens, she sees sin all around, and her devotion takes on the sinisterly sexual overtones of so many other women in the Realist corpus, her thoughts full of lurid images of penetration by God and by Christ. Her son, whose illness had led her to religion in the first place, is now seen as the rival to her divine consort, an obstacle to union with him. In their description of the 'haine sainte' directed by mother against son, of 'cette monstrueuse victoire dénaturée sur le sang, la dernière et suprême victoire de la religion,' the Goncourts express more overtly than in any other of their novels their dismay at the effects of Christian belief on human behaviour. Like Zola and Maupassant they espouse the cause of nature in its eternal struggle with grace: 'La Grâce finissait d'assassiner la Nature. En elle, la femme, l'être terrestre, n'existait plus. [. . .] L'humanité s'en était allée d'elle.'

Like Zola too, they identify this life-denying Catholicism as a religion of death. Madame Gervaisais, in her final phase, is 'amoureuse de la mort,' obsessively visiting the Catacombs to stare at the skulls and skeletons, 'prête à dire, avec Job, à la pourriture: "Vous êtes ma mère!" à dire aux vers: "Vous êtes mes frères et mes sœurs!"' Though the novel has its formal ending in Madame Gervaisais' death as she awaits an audience at the door of the Pope, these scenes of horror constitute its real conclusion. It is to this corruption that religious conversion has led the woman, the chosen bride of Christ.

. . . . .

In the portraits of priests and penitents which abound in Realist novels, religious belief is used as a means to artistic ends. Such all-consuming emotions, such fiercely held convictions, are effective delineators of personality, producing psychological types that, with particular colouring and different sets of circumstances, can be turned into sharply etched individual charac-

ters. With the added pathos of self-delusion, the vulnerability of the credulous pilgrim embarked on a false track, the novelist has the ingredients of a rich emotional mix as well as a source of powerful irony. Flaubert exploits these possibilities as well as anyone in his account of Emma Bovary's reading. Depicting Emma as she contemplates a pile of pious works supplied by Bournisien, the narrator tells us: 'Madame Bovary n'avait pas encore l'intelligence assez nette pour s'appliquer sérieusement à n'importe quoi . . .' He is caught here in a rare moment of overt judgment of Emma, for this can only be *his* opinion; it is certainly not hers, and no other witness to her thoughts is present. But despite what he has just said, Emma seems after all to apply a critical sense to this material, seeing it as betraying ignorance of the world. Then comes a further switch: she reads the books despite her low evaluation of them: 'Elle persista pourtant, et, lorsque le volume lui tombait des mains, elle se croyait prise par la plus fine mélancolie catholique qu'une âme éthérée pût concevoir.' Shafts of irony fly in all directions here: against Emma and against the religious literature which she scorns but nevertheless reads, and which she turns into a means of reaching the lofty heights of romantic melancholia where her ego can flourish. It is a strange passage, with apparent contradictions: Emma is unintelligent, yet has critical judgement; she is unable to apply herself seriously to anything, yet she persists in her reading. Such contradictions are deliberate, designed to create a series of disconnected views of this fickle and inconsistent character, unable to make use of what meagre intellectual strength she might possess. A central aspect of Emma's character is illuminated here, and the religious element in her nature has supplied the necessary lighting.

Religion does not emerge unscathed from its role as an ironic reflector of character. The cumulative effect of novel after novel in which religion is disguised sexuality, or a prop to establishment values, or a sentimental stimulus, undermines not just the integrity of the character concerned, but the status of religion itself. It appears a purely subjective phenomenon with no external referent. The very concentration of novelists on what is happening within their characters detaches religious emotion from the transcendental world to which it is supposed to relate. The contrast between the imagined world of a character who believes in God and the enveloping world of the novel itself, in which God does not and cannot appear, is a further source of ironic distance between protagonist and narrator which the best of the Realists exploit to great advantage. It is instructive to compare at this point Maupassant's novel *Fort comme la mort* with the much earlier, pioneering Realist text of Duranty, *Le Malheur d'Henriette Gérard*. Duranty's universe is ontologically and metaphysically neutral. He describes the surface of social life with no reference to a spiritual dimension. A mildly acerbic anti-clericalism is conveyed through priest characters whose significance is wholly social, involved as they are in the marital schemes of the Gérard family. But on the truth or falsehood of the spiritual beliefs that these priests represent, the text implies no particular view. In Maupassant's novel, however, through a series of apparently trivial references, the philosophical ground rules for the interpretation of the fictional universe are firmly established. The Baron de Corbelle, seeking to justify his taste in social companions, 'le fit avec des arguments inconsistants et irréfutables, de ces arguments qui fondent devant la raison comme la neige au feu, et qu'on ne peut saisir, des arguments absurdes et triomphants de curé de campagne qui démontre Dieu.' In other words, the baselessness of believing in God is taken here as proverbial, as a yardstick of the absurd and the unprovable, not by a character, but by the narrator himself, and it conditions what may or may not happen in the text. Thus, when the reader sees the comtesse de Guilleroy pray for the soul of her dead mother, he knows he has been forewarned of the narrator's detachment from such impulses. When the countess calls for divine intervention, implores 'un secours surnaturel contre les dangers prochains,' he knows that such aid is not only logically but aesthetically impossible in a tale told by this particular teller. Our mode of reading, our strategies for interpreting the text, are thus effectively manipulated.

There are Realist novels in which prayers *are* answered, in which miracles happen and God manifests his presence in the most visible and audible ways. When this happens, we know that the novelist is displaying his conjuring tricks, enjoying his own ironic devices. At the end of *Bel-Ami,* for example, Christ arrives in person at the wedding of the caddish hero to the wealthy Suzanne Walter. This is given as a piece of straight narrative: 'L'encens répandait une odeur finie de benjoin, et sur l'autel le sacrifice divin s'accomplissait; l'Homme-Dieu, à l'appel de son prêtre, descendait sur la terre pour consacrer le triomphe du baron Georges Du Roy.' Even more spectacularly, in *La Faute de l'abbé Mouret,* Jesus converses in familiar fashion with Serge in the young priest's moment of decision:

> L'abbé Mouret disait tout à Jésus, comme à un Dieu venu dans l'intimité de sa tendresse et qui peut tout entendre. [. . .] Et Jésus répondait que cela ne devait pas l'étonner. [. . .] Jésus se montrait tolérant; il expliquait que la faiblesse de l'homme est la continuelle occupation de Dieu. [. . .] Là, Jésus avait un léger rire de bienveillance.

Jesus' laugh probably had nothing on Zola's while these words were being written. Neither this passage nor Maupassant's needs much comment, so obviously do both novelists' tongues protrude into their cheeks. The ironic adoption of the character's false standpoint—triumphant in the case of Bel-Ami and his cohorts,

hallucinatory in the case of Serge—is kept at a distance by the use of the imperfect tense, placing the 'events' outside the current chronological sequences of the novel, and outside the ontological assumptions on which the narrator bases his story. There are narratives written wholly from within a perspective alien to the novelist. Flaubert's *Légende de Saint-Julien l'Hospitalier* is one. In it the supernatural events are presented straightforwardly, as the tale requires. Reader and author share the same suspension of disbelief. Of Julien's mother, the narrator simply tells us: 'A force de prier Dieu, il lui vint un fils,' but in a story in which stages speak and old men appear out of moonbeams to predict Julien's saintly future, this can hardly be taken as a Flaubertian conversion to belief in Providence. In any event, the final sentence of the text gives the whole work its necessary frame and isolates it from contemporary modes of judgement: 'Et voilà l'histoire de saint Julien l'Hospitalier, telle à peu près qu'on la trouve, sur un vitrail d'église, dans mon pays.' Here—in mediaeval stained glass—are such miraculous events possible. Modern novels have different conventions, but it is a delightful paradox that no Christian novelist would dare depict the intervention of the divine into human lives as freely and as cheerfully as do Maupassant, Zola and Flaubert!

In most Realist texts, God, when he is invoked, suffers from acute deafness. In a famous scene in *L'Assommoir,* Gervaise, having prayed for fine weather, is submerged in a snow storm. There are more serious examples than this. Emma Bovary on her death-bed suddenly seems better following the last rites—'comme si le sacrement l'eût guérie.' Charles' hopes of a miraculous recovery are raised . . . and dashed, for this calm is merely the prelude to a horrific death agony. This cruel failure of the miracle in its moment of promise is echoed in Angélique's death scene at the end of *Le Rêve.* She too has just received extreme unction, and has lapsed into the appearance of death, which moves the bishop to kiss her on the lips. At once she comes to life: has God's mercy restored the girl who has devoted her life to him? No, for this is a temporary reprieve; Angélique dies shortly after. Complaints of God's cruelty abound in these texts, ironic or grave according to the circumstances. 'Il y a un bon Dieu contre moi!' cries Anatole in the Goncourts' *Manette Salomon,* seeking a scapegoat for his failure as a painter. Emma too 'exécrait l'injustice de Dieu' as a way of cloaking from herself her own inadequacies. Charles' reaction to Bournisien when Emma dies—'Je l'exécre, votre Dieu!'—is more profoundly moving, except that, because the reader knows that God has played no part in Emma's banal demise, it falls short of the tragic. Flaubert's denial of tragic status to his heroine, his creation of an ironic and anti-tragic novel, depends on the relegation of the metaphysical to the role of just one more delusion in the mind of a hapless character. The Goncourts, by contrast, seeking to raise the lowly to tragic level, allow Germinie to see the lucklessness of her life as a modern equivalent of fate, in which Christian notions of providence are cleverly manipulated:

> Elle se sentait dans le courant de quelque chose allant toujours, qu'il était inutile, *presque impie,* de vouloir arrêter. Cette grande force du monde qui fait souffrir, la puissance mauvaise qui porte le nom d'un dieu sur le marbre des tragédies antiques, et qui s'appelle Pas-de-chance sur le front tatoué des bagnes, la Fatalité l'écrasait, et Germinie baissait le tête sous son pied. [. . .] Cette file de douleurs qui avait suivi ses années et grandi avec elles, tout ce qui s'était succédé dans son existence comme une rencontre et un arrangement de misère, sans que jamais elle y eût vu apparaître la main de cette Providence dont on lui avait tant parlé, elle se disait qu'elle était une de ces malheureuses vouées en naissant à une éternité de misères. . . .

Though Germinie invests the adverse currents of life with a religious aura—that is, she feels a sense of impiety because she resents them—it is clear that, whereas Greek tragedy depends on the malice of the gods, nineteenth-century Realist tragedy, as conceived by the Goncourts, depends on God's absence: there is no trace of Providence. The brothers' masterly *trompe-l'œil* has it both ways: fate, always a useful *literary* device, exists, but God, traditional source of solace, remains invisible. Germinie is dwarfed by a force larger than herself, raising her plight to a grander plane, but the force is without spiritual substance, thus protecting the Goncourts' philosophical position.

The accusation of God's wickedness is expressed most forcefully of all by Maupassant.

—*Malcolm Scott*

God's failure to protect men from suffering is a common theme in Realist fiction. It is expressed through the mouth of the young doctor Barnier, who falls in love with sœur Philomène and who spends his days combating disease and pain. 'Vous trouvez,' he asks the nun, 'un père à remercier au bout de tout cela?' Barnier is a sceptic, whose question is a rhetorical device in his argument with Philomène. In Zola's *Thérèse Raquin,* it is, on the contrary, a life-long believer who rejects God for his non-intervention on behalf of the victims of violence. Madame Raquin, Thérèse's mother-in-law, learns from the mouth of Thérèse that she and Laurent have conspired to drown Thérèse's first husband, the old woman's son Camille; but mute and paralysed, her only recourse is to implore God which she does in vain. What is revealed to

her is not God's mercy but the inescapable brutality of human beings, which her faith in heaven's redemptive powers had cloaked from her all through life. Only one conclusion is possible: 'Dieu était mauvais; il aurait dû lui dire la vérité plus tôt, ou la laisser s'en aller avec ses innocences et son aveuglement. Maintenant, il ne lui restait qu'à mourir en niant l'amitié, en niant le dévouement. Rien n'existait que le meurtre et la luxure.' Zola uses here the misguided optimism of a blissful Christian view of life as the revealed untruth on which to found his portrayal of human bestiality. Edmond de Goncourt employs a similar strategy in *La Fille Élisa,* but adds a further factor. The young soldier who forces his brutal sexual attentions on Élisa, leading her to the act of killing which in turn causes her imprisonment, is a Christian, through whom the text weaves a series of associations between religious ecstasy, eroticism and violence. The fact that the soldier had been, in civilian life, a shepherd, is also significant, allowing the image of the Good Shepherd himself to emerge in sinister light, while Élisa is left echoing the words of the crucified Christ: why has God abandoned her?

The accusation of God's wickedness is expressed most forcefully of all by Maupassant. His tale 'Moiron' is about a child murderer whose career of killing has been triggered by the deaths of his own children. God, he reasons, could have saved his children; for him murder is simply protest by emulation. 'Je compris que Dieu est méchant,' Moiron tells the narrator. 'Pourquoi avait-il tué mes enfants? J'ouvris les yeux, et je vis qu'il aime tuer. Il n'aime que ça, monsieur. Il ne fait vivre que pour détruire! Dieu, monsieur, c'est un massacreur.' Maupassant's last work, a literary testament which was barely begun before his final decline into madness and death, was designed as an elaboration of this theme of divine cruelty. It was to be called *L'Angélus.* Although only fragments of it were written, Maupassant's verbal testimony to the poet Auguste Dorchain shows that his aim was to create a bitter parody of the Nativity, the story of a crippled boy born in a stable to a life of unrelenting pain. The first extant fragment introduces the pregnant comtesse de Brémontal, who has prayed to the Virgin Mary, patroness of mothers, for the birth of a daughter. Prussian officers arrive at the house (for Maupassant has returned to the period of his first great success *Boule de suif*) and eject the young countess into the night. . . . A second brief fragment introduces a young doctor, Paturel; the third is a dialogue between him and a priest, the abbé Marvaux. In this fragment, Paturel says that all gods are monsters, that his experience as a doctor has given him evidence of the crimes of so-called Providence that he could write up in a legal 'dossier de Dieu.' The priest replies that the concept of God is hard to grasp, but that Christ, whom he adores, makes God accessible. But to this exemplary Christian thought he adds that Christ too was a victim of God, that his love of mankind was a reflection of his human, not his divine, self; and that this is why Christ had to be punished more severely than any man has ever been. The fourth and final fragment is a speech by this same troubled priest, and, echoing the words of the killer Moiron, it is perhaps the most ferocious onslaught on the Christian God in the whole of the Realist canon. God is presented as an unrelenting sadist, giving life merely to extinguish it, inventing cholera and typhus as instruments of torture, creating animals whose beauty and vitality cloak with cruel mockery the physical corruption into which they are doomed to fall. This was the final passage Maupassant was ever to write, his message to posterity. The career that had begun with satire of religious bigotry ends in an explosion of fury against God himself.

. . . . .

The spectacle of nature, and especially of animals, links Maupassant's first novel *Une vie* to this last unfinished text. In both, the opposition of innocent nature to divine cruelty reverses the Christian message of grace redeeming a fallen physical universe. Horses running free in meadows, birds singing in their nests, all unaware of their inevitable fate at the hands of the great destroyer that men call God, are manifestations of life's flawed beauty; despite their inherent pathos, they occupy the positive pole in Maupassant's view of the world, against the stern and life-denying dictates of so-called Providence. Other Realist novelists use animals, especially birds, as emblems of innocent freshness and vitality and as representatives of an eternal natural order, in contrast to which the Christian church appears a mere fleeting expression of one cultural phase in the earth's long history. In the Rome visited by Madame Gervaisais, the lesson of the transience of all civilisations, embodied in the monuments of antiquity and extending by implication to the Church of Rome itself, is underpinned by the encroachment of nature into the ruins, and by the flight of birds around the crumbling stones. 'Des oiseaux volaient familièrement dans le monstrueux nid de pierre,' runs the text; '[. . .] La ruine revenait à la nature [. . .]—toutes les revendications et toutes les reprises de la nature éternelle sur la Ville éternelle.' In the authors' earlier novel *Renée Mauperin,* a description of a country church visited by the dying heroine includes the same contrast between nature's animation and dead ecclesiastical stone:

> L'église avait comme un murmure de voix éteintes, l'azur jouait dans les vitraux. Des envolées de pigeons partaient à tout instant et couraient se nicher dans le creux des sculptures et les trous des vieilles pierres. La rivière qu'on voyait bruissait; un poulain blanc courait à l'eau fou et tout bondissant.

Was Zola thinking of this passage when describing Serge Mouret's dilapidated church? The elements of the picture are the same, but as usual it is Zola who

hones them into the most intense degree of polemical sharpness. As Serge says mass, a veritable invasion is taking place, nature forcing its way into the church, interrupting, deriding, challenging the supremacy of the priest's religion. The sun does not simply play on the stained glass windows as in the Goncourt text; it bursts in, illuminates the previous bleakness of the nave, seems to bring a smile to the face of the plaster Virgin, but leaves in shade the corner where 'le grand christ [. . .] mettait la mort.' Birds enter the church via the broken windows, their songs drowning the voice of the priest and the ringing of the bells of the mass; at the supreme moment when 'le corps et le sang d'un Dieu allaient descendre sur l'autel,' Mouret's housekeeper is chasing sparrows from the altar. As Christ comes to redeem 'la nature damnée,' damned nature asserts itself, healthy, free and joyful, needing no redemption. Serge's sister Désirée arrives with a bevy of chicks. The sun beams more brightly, the gold of the holy vessels paling in its rays. 'L'astre demeura seul maître de l'église,' writes Zola; 'les murailles badigeonnées, la grande vierge, le grand christ lui-même, prenaient un frisson de sève, comme si la mort était vaincue par l'éternelle jeunesse de la terre.' Seldom can an allegedly objective Naturalist have written so ambiguously partial an opening scene. When we follow Serge Mouret out of his church, see it from outside, the same testimony to nature's force goes on. The exterior walls are eaten by vegetation. The implacable opposition of nature and church is even expressed in the hostile contact between thistles and the hem of Frère Archangias' robes as he walks across the fields. The natural world has declared war on the usurping Christian deity; and when the priest, lying with Albine in the shade of the Tree of Life, finally follows nature's laws, this is identified as the triumph for which the opening scene of the book was the preparation: 'Et c'était une victoire pour les bêtes, les plantes, les choses, qui avaient voulu l'entrée de ces deux enfants dans l'éternité de la vie. Le parc applaudissait formidablement.' Animals, plants, *things*. It is matter itself, 'les atomes de la matière', the substance of the physical world, in opposition to the spiritual, that has won the day.

REALISM AND REPRESENTATION

Hayden White

SOURCE: "The Problem of Style in Realistic Representation: Marx and Flaubert," in *The Concept of Style,* edited by Berel Lang, University of Pennsylvania Press, 1979, pp. 213-29.

[*In the following essay, originally delivered as a lecture in 1977, White examines affinities between the realistic style of Flaubert's* Sentimental Education *and*

Marx's historical and ideological rendering of nineteenth-century French history in The Eighteenth Brumaire of Louis Bonaparte.]

Prior to the nineteenth century, the problem of style in literature turned upon discussion of techniques of rhetorical composition and especially techniques of figuration by which to generate a secondary or allegorical meaning in the text beyond the literal meaning displayed on its surface. But the advent of realism meant, among other things, the rejection of allegory, the search for a perfect literality of expression, and the achievement of a style from which every element of rhetorical artifice had been expunged. For Flaubert, for example, style was conceived to be the antithesis of rhetoric; in fact, he identified style with what he called "the soul of thought," its very "content," to be distinguished from "form," which was merely thought's "body." Realism in the novel, like its counterpart in historiography, strove for a manner of representation in which the *interpretation* of the phenomena dealt with in the discourse would be indistinguishable from its *description;* or, to put it another way, in which *mimesis* and *diegesis* would be reduced to the same thing. Instead of mediating between two or more levels of meaning within the text, which "style" had been conceived to do during the time when "literature" was identified with "allegory," style now became a manner of translating phenomena into structures of discourse, transforming "things" into "words" without residue or conceptual superaddition.

The aim of realism, then, was literalness as against figurative expression, so much so that the difference between the style of Balzac and his successor Flaubert can be marked by the relative paucity of metaphors in the latter as compared with the former. Nonetheless, writers continued to seek to cultivate distinctive styles of representation. There was no thought, as far as I can determine, that the perfection of a realistic mimesis would result in a uniform mode of expression, with every discourse resembling every other. But the criterion for determining stylistic achievement had changed; it was no longer the manner or form of utterance that constituted style, but rather the matter or content of the discourse, as Flaubert had insisted. This meant that style had to do with cognitive perspicuity, the insight which the writer had into "the nature of things." To *see* clearly was to *understand* aright, and understanding was nothing other than the clear perception of the "way things are."

But this conflation of understanding with perception meant, obviously, that if allegory had been barred from entering the house of art by the front door, it had found entry at the back. It entered in the form of "history," no longer considered as a construction of the historian's powers of composition, as it had been considered in earlier times when historiography itself was regarded as a branch of rhetoric, but as a domain of "facts" which offered itself to perception in much the same way that "nature" did to the unclouded eye of the physical scientist. The "truth" of the realistic novel, then, was measurable by the extent to which it permitted one to see clearly the "historical world" of which it was a representation. Certain characters and events in the realistic novel were manifestly "invented," rather than "found" in the historical record, to be sure, but these figures moved against and realized their destinies in a world which was "real" because it was "historical," which was to say, given to perception in the way that "nature" was.

Now, arguably, history does not exist except insofar as a certain body of phenomena are organized in terms of the categories that we have come to associate with a specifically "historical consciousness." History does not consist of all of the events that ever happened, as the distinction between merely natural and specifically human events itself suggests. But neither do all human events belong to history, not even all human events that have been recorded and therefore can be known to a later consciousness. For if history consisted of all of the human events that ever happened, it would make as little sense, be as little cognizable, as a nature conceived to consist of all of the natural events that ever happened. History, like nature, is cognizable only insofar as it is perceived selectively, insofar as it is divided up into domains of happening, their elements discriminated, and these elements unified in structures of relationships, which structures, in turn, are conceived to manifest specifiable rules, principles, or laws which give to them their determinate forms.

The dominant view underlying early nineteenth-century historiography was that the structures and processes of history were self-revealing to the consciousness unclouded by preconceptions or ideological prejudices, that one had only to "look at the facts" or let the facts "speak for themselves" in order for their inherent meaning or significance as historical phenomena to come clear. And this view was shared by novelists and historians alike, with the former grounding their "realism" in their willingness to view history "objectively" and the latter distinguishing their work from that of the novelist by their exclusion of every "fictional" element from their discourse. Few commentators (Hegel, Droysen, and Nietzsche are notable exceptions) perceived that there were as many possible conceptualizations of history as there were ways of fashioning novelistic fictions; that there were as many styles of historical discourse as there were styles of realistic representation: that if realism in the novel could have its Constant, its Balzac, its Stendhal, and its Flaubert, realism in historical representation had its Michelet, its Tocqueville, its Ranke, its Droysen, and its Mommsen, each of whom felt himself to be representing history realistically, letting the facts "speak for themselves," and aspiring to a discourse from which every element of allegory had been expunged. In supposing that history constituted a kind of "zero degree" of reality, against which the fictive elements of a novelistic discourse could be measured, the realistic novelists of the nineteenth-century both begged the question of the metaphysical base of their realism and effected an identification of style with content with which modern critical theory continues to have to contend. But this supposition, when examined critically, gives insight into the hidden allegorical elements in every realistic representation and raises the question of the problem of style in a way different from that which takes the form-content distinction for granted.

I propose to examine the problem of style which the project of realism in the novel raises by comparing a novelistic and a historical text produced at about the same time, both of which deal with the same general set of historical events and lay claims to a realistic representation of the events in question, but which are generally recognized as representing virtually antithetical ideological positions and different stylistic attributes. These texts are Flaubert's novel, *The Sentimental Education,* and Marx's history, *The Eighteenth Brumaire of Louis Bonaparte.* No two texts could be more dissimilar when viewed from the conventional standpoint of stylistic analysis that turns upon the distinction between form and content and identifies style with the former. Flaubert's discourse is cool, detached, leisurely to the point of shapelessness in its depiction of what Lukacs calls the fragmented world of its protagonist. Marx's discourse, by contrast, is shot through with an irony bordering on open sarcasm and contempt for the personalities, situations, and events he depicts; it manifestly originates in a preconceived judgment, ideological in nature, of the Second Republic, the bourgeoisie which created it, and the "charlatan," Louis Bonaparte, who overturned it. Whereas Flaubert forebears to intervene, in his function as author, in the narrative, permitting his narrator's voice only a few laconic observations on the folly of human desire in a world devoid of heroism, Marx intervenes continually, alternating between the manner of the clear-eyed analyst of events, on the one side, and the ranting ideologue, on the other. If we conceive style, then, as manner of utterance, we would have to mark down Marx as a representative of the ornate and Flaubert of the plain or mixed style, so different are the rhetorics of these discourses, so opposed the attitudes revealed on the level of language alone.

But if we conceive style as a perceivable strategy for fusing a certain form with a certain content, then there are remarkable similarities to be discerned between the two texts. The manifest form of both works is the mock *Bildungsroman,* in the one case, of a young French provincial seeking love and self-realization in Parisian society in the 1840s, in other, of the French bourgeoi-sie itself, seeking to deal with the vicissitudes of its rise to power in a society fatally divided between contending classes, groups, and factions. This means that the content of both works is the drama of a development of a kind of consciousness—personal on the one side, and class on the other. The *Eighteenth Brumaire* is, we might say, "the sentimental education" of the French bourgeoisie, just as *The Sentimental Education* is "the eighteenth Brumaire" of a personification of a typical member of the French *haute bourgeoisie.* As thus envisaged, the respective plot-structures of the two works describe the same patterns of development: what begins as an epic or heroic effort at the implementation of values—personal on the one side, class on the other (although these reduce to the same thing ultimately, inasmuch as Frédéric Moreau, the protagonist of Flaubert's novel, has no values other than those given him by his historical situation)—progresses through a series of delusory triumphs and real defeats, to an ironic acceptance of the necessity of abandoning ideals to the accommodation to realities in the end.

At the end of Flaubert's novel, Frédéric Moreau exists in precisely the same condition that the French bourgeoisie is depicted as having come to at the end of Marx's history, that is to say, as the very incarnation of a cynical acceptance of comfort at the expense of ideals. Even more strikingly, both authors insist—the one indirectly, the other directly—that the final condition in which their protagonists find themselves was already implicitly present in the structure of consciousness with which each embarked upon its "sentimental education." This structure of consciousness is shown to have been fractured from the beginning, fractured as a result of a fundamental contradiction between ideals consciously held at the outset and the conditions of existence in a dehumanizing society, one in which no *human* value can be distinguished from its commodity status. Frédéric Moreau's final rejection of his ideal love, Madame Arnoux, and his recognition that his life had failed at all crucial points correspond precisely with the French bourgeoisie's rejection of the ideals of "liberty, equality, and fraternity" which it had defended since the French Revolution and its acceptance of the card-sharp Bonaparte as the custodian of "order, family, property, and religion."

What is most remarkable, however, is yet a fourth resemblance between the two discourses, what I wish to name as their shared style, considered as a transformational model for marking off the phases in the development of the consciousnesses being depicted and for integrating them across a time series so as to demonstrate their progressive transumption. This model I call *tropological,* since it consists of a pattern of figurations which follows the sequence: metaphoric, metonymic, synecdochic, and ironic; and I identify this tropological model with the style of the discourses being analyzed since it constitutes a virtual "logic" of narration which, once perceived, permits us to understand why these discourses are organized in the way they are both on their surfaces and in their depths. The tropes of figuration, in other words, constitute a model for tracking processes of consciousness by defining the possible modes through which a given consciousness must pass from an original, metaphoric apprehension of reality to a terminal, ironic comprehension of the relationship between consciousness itself on the one side and its possible objects on the other. The tropes of metonymy and synecdoche function as models of transitional phases in this procession of modes of comprehending reality, the former governing the arrangement of phenomena into temporal series or spatial sets, the latter governing its integration into hierarchies of genera and species. The deployment and elaboration of experience under these modes of figuration is what I mean by style, a usage which permits us to pay tribute simultaneously to the conception of style as form and style as content, of style as the union of the two in a discourse, of style as both group and individual signature, of style as the process of composing a discourse, and of style as an attribute of the finished composition. Style as process, thus conceived, is the movement through the possibilities of figuration offered by the tropes of language; style as structure is the achieved union of form and content which the completed discourse represents.

Let us begin with a consideration of Flaubert's *Sentimental Education*. Tropological criticism directs us to look, first, not at plot, character development, or manifest ideological content (for this would presuppose that we already had an understanding of these phenomena at least as subtle as that of the author, or a better understanding of them, or that these were not problems for the author but solutions to problems), but rather at the principal *turns* in the protagonist's relationship to his milieux. Flaubert's narrative is divided into four chronological segments, three covering the years 1840-51 and ending with the coup d'état of Louis Bonaparte, and a fourth, comprising chapters 6 and 7 of part 3, which is separated by fifteen years from the last event recorded in chapter 5 of this part. In the last segment, the protagonist, Frédéric Moreau, and the woman he had loved, Madame Arnoux, meet after a fifteen-year separation in order to realize how ill-fated their love had been from the beginning; and Frédéric and his best friend, Deslauriers, meet in order to reflect on how and why their lives had gone wrong from first to last. We have no difficulty recognizing the ironic tone of these two chapters. The three characters in it display themselves the attainment of an ironic distance on their earlier passions, beliefs, ideals, follies, pride, and actions; and as Jonathan Culler points out in his reading of this passage, Flaubert himself reaches sublime heights of ironic sympathy for the attempts of the actors to ironize their own lives.

Having specified the ironic nature of the conclusion, we might be inclined retrospectively to cast the shadow of irony back over the sections preceding it. And this is legitimate enough, since we must suppose that irony (or what Freud called secondary revision) is the dominant trope of any consciously wrought fiction—and the governing, even if unacknowledged trope of all "realistic" discourse, insofar as its author supposes that he sees clearer or understands better what was "really happening" than did the agents whose actions he is describing or retailing. But here we must distinguish between the irony of the author and the consciousness he ascribes to his agents; and discriminate among the changing modes of relationship, between the protagonist and his milieux, which mark off the significant turns in the narrative. And we may say, following a Hegelian reading of the text, that here we have an allegory of desire, personified in all of the figures but condensed especially in that of Frédéric Moreau, projected into a world in which everything appears in the opaque form of a commodity, to be bought, exchanged, and consumed or destroyed without any awareness of what might be its true, its human value. It is the commoditization of reality that accounts for the melancholy tone of the whole novel, even in those moments of *hysterica passio* that constitute the most sensual scenes in the story. Flaubert has no need to set forth explicitly a theory of the true value of things; the absence of that value or its absence in the consciousness of the agents in his story is sufficiently suggested by the succession of frustrations which he recounts in the efforts of every one of them to achieve a deep union with its ideal object of desire. It is the absence of this human value, we may say, in the face of the oppressive presence of the dehumanizing uses made of others, which is the true subject of the discourse.

But that being given, what are the stages supposed to have been passed through by Frédéric Moreau in the process of realizing the discrepancy between aspiration and possibility of achievement which he comes to in the conclusion? When we ask this question in the light of tropology, the structure of and relationships among the first three sections of the book become clearly discernible.

We may say that the first part, which covers the period 1840-45, presents us with an image of desire personified in Frédéric projected in the mode of metaphor, desire seeking an object but unaware of anything but practical obstacles to its gratification. Here the object of desire is first presented to Frédéric in the mystery of Mme. Arnoux's *appearance* only, as mere image rather than as image grounded in substantial reality, desire not yet individualized, and sensed to be painfully unattainable—in Frédéric's mind, simply because he is not wealthy enough to pursue it. This is the period of Frédéric's reluctant exile from Paris to the dull life of

Nogent which, in retrospect, will have turned out to be no more dull, no more dispiriting than Paris itself. While there, he encounters another potential object of desire, in the figure of the girl-child, half provincial bourgeoise, half savage peasant, Louise Rocque, the ambiguity of whose nature is signalled in her illegitimate birth no less than in the precociousness of the passion she feels for Frédéric from the start. But Frédéric's desire for her is still unfocused, still sublimated in the unconsummated Paolo and Francesa relationship they have and limited to caresses and fraternal kisses in Frédéric's part. This part of the novel, which opened with a leisurely journey by water from Paris to Nogent, ends with Frédéric's inheritance, by pure chance, of the fortune that will permit him to imagine that by returning to Paris, he will be able to possess whatever he wishes and achieve whatever he likes, spiritual as well as carnal.

Part 2 begins with a journey, not by paque boat, but by coach, the rapidity of the sensations of which already signals the disjunctions and discontinuities of the relationships figured in this section. Permit me to call the dominant mode of relationships figured in this section, between Frédéric and his world as well as between the objects inhabiting that world, *metonymic,* not only because the literal meaning of the word, "name change," suggests the shifting, evanescent nature of the play of appearances rather than an apprehension of any putative reality, but also because the mode of relationship supposed to exist between things in the use of this trope is that of mere contiguity. Here desire becomes specified, fixed upon particular objects, all of which are equally desirable but found to be in the possession of them equally unsatisfying, frustrating, finally unpossessable in their essence. Kierkegaard would call this *desire* "desiring" (insect-like), as against *desire* "sleeping" (plant-like); desire carnal, but desire conscious of itself as desire, and rising to the level of technical competence and cunning in pursuit of objects—like Don Juan in Mozart's opera, seeking the universal in the particular. Which means that all particulars become possible objects of desire, irrespective of any considerations of intrinsic value. The image of desire is now endowed with material substance, is apprehended as merely material in its very consumption, is totally consumable thereby, hence in need of endless replacement, substitution, repetition.

Frédéric now has money and a desire for women, pursues Mme. Arnoux and cunningly contrives her seduction, fights a duel for her honor, tries his hand at law, painting, writing a novel, and finds them all equally unsatisfying. And when Mme. Arnoux fails to meet him at the room he had taken (because of the illness of one of her children which she, stupidly, takes to be a sign from heaven warning her of sin), Frédéric substitutes in her place, in the same room and same bed he had reserved for Mme. Arnoux, the mistress of M. Arnoux, the dissembling and opaque, and utterly sensual, Rosanette. The last scene of the last chapter of this section has Frédéric in bed with Rosanette, in a state of post-coital depression, weeping for his loss of Mme. Arnoux, but telling Rosanette that he is weeping because "I am too happy. . . . I have wanted you for such a long time."

The evanescent quality of Frédéric's desire for Mme. Arnoux is suggested by his inability to fix her image in its specifically human incarnation. At times, his lust for her is concretized in a fascination with some part of her body, her foot, the inner side of her arm, some object that she possesses but which, magically, seems to have taken on her essency by its physical proximity to her. At times, her essence dissolves and spreads over the whole of the city of Paris, in such a way that she and the city become identified in Frédéric's enfevered imagination. She remains unspecified as an individual, however, unlocatable between the universal which she represents and the particulars which characterize her as image. In this respect, the alternate feelings of lust and repulsion that Frédéric feels for her, when she returns after 15 years, in the penultimate chapter, are perfectly consistent with the relationship which he bears to her in the second section of the book. Things fall apart because their essence is indiscernible. In the end, there are only things, and the relationships they sustain with one another are nothing but their placement side by side, nearer or further, from one another in a universe of objects. Whence the seeming ease of the displacements of desire from one object to another, the slippage of desire across a series of objects, all of which turn out to be exactly the same, however the imagination, in the service of desire, construes them.

Part 3 begins with the sound of gunshots in the streets. It signals the opening phase of the Revolution of 25 February 1848, the events of which—down to the coup by Louis Bonaparte (Napoleon III), of December 1851—form alternatively the foreground and background of Frédéric's life during that time. Frédéric has much to do in these three and a half years. He must participate in the February Revolution; attempt a political career; take care of his business affairs; squander his fortune in the process; keep Rosanette as his official mistress; continue to pursue Mme. Arnoux; seduce Mme. Dambreuse, the wife of a wealthy banker; witness the death of the child born to Rosanette; be betrayed by his best friend, Deslauriers; reject and then seek to win Louise Rocque; and witness the death of the only true political idealist among his friends, Dussardier, shot by another of his friends, Sénécal, a socialist in principle who, in pursuit of *his* ideals, has become a policeman. Things not only fall apart, they come apart at the seams in the process, and reveal the counteressence—the nothingness—which is the real substance behind all seemingly ideal forms.

Guy de Maupassant, whose greatest influence was probably Flaubert.

Such, admittedly, is the moral of the story. And yet it is not the whole story. Flaubert's decision to place this grotesque series of events against the backdrop of the 1848 Revolution reflects—arguably—the despairing idealism of his vision. The absurdity of Dussardier's death is apparent enough, but so too is his goodness, decency, and humaneness. The absurdity which Flaubert finds in the events of 1848-51 does not fully hide the bitterness which he must have felt while witnessing France's last effort to construct a society on principles of social justice. To be sure, we know that he did not confuse justice with a belief in the equality of individuals, but neither did Marx. That confusion lies at the heart of Social Democratic sentimentalism and feeds the Utopian brand of socialism. True, he did not, like Marx, present the proletariat as the martyred heroes of the Revolution, but nor did he see them as more misguided and victimized by their own stupidity than Marx did. And he has his hero, Frédéric, participate in the events of February-March 1848 with the same enthusiasm, the same hopes, even the same bravery and idealism with which Marx credits the Parisian populace during that same period. He participates, that is, until, like the bourgeoisie itself, he becomes dis-

tracted by his own self-interest. Moreau, it is important to recall, is not a proletarian; he is a bourgeois through and through; and his life during the period 1848-51 mirrors perfectly, in microcosm, as it were, the career and betrayals, of itself and others, of the French bourgeoisie.

In part 3 of the novel, Frédéric displays a higher degree of consciousness, both social and psychological, and of conscience than he does in the rest of the book. It is as if Flaubert wished us to perceive Frédéric at this stage as one who grasps fully, even if in the end despairingly, the nature of his class, its strengths as well as its weaknesses, the disparity between its ideals and its actions, and the disillusionment which that disparity caused in that class as a result of the events of 1848-51. In this section, Frédéric's desire is—if only for a moment—generalized and idealized; it reaches out in a spirit of service and even sacrifice to the people, to the nation. He feels genuine anger when a citizen standing next to him on the barricades is shot by the soldiery, although he is as much angered by the thought that the shot might have been aimed at him as he is by the realization that it has killed a fellow citizen. He enthusiastically joins the mob in the sacking of the Tuileries and insists that "The people are sublime." Flaubert's characterization of the "carnival" mood of the days following the deposition of Louis Phillippe, when "People dressed in a careless way that blurred the distinctions between classes, hatreds were concealed, and hopes blossomed . . ." and "pride" shone in the face of the people "at having won their rights," has no irony in it at all. "Paris," he writes, was, during those days "the most delightful place."

But this pride is soon smothered in the realization, by the bourgeoisie especially, that social justice threatened private property, and the tone of the account shifts perceptibly with the narrator's remark:

> Now Property was raised in men's eyes to the level of Religion and became confused with God. The attacks made on it seemed sacrilegious, almost cannibalistic. In spite of the most humane laws that had ever been enacted, the spectre of '93 reappeared, and the knife of the guillotine vibrated in every syllable of the word "Republic"—which in no way prevented the government being despised for its weakness. France, realizing that she was without a master, started crying with fright like a blind man deprived of his stick, or a child who has lost his nurse.

The fragility of the alliance between the bourgeoisie and the people is symbolized by the pregnancy of Rosanette, the sickness of the child born of the union of a proletarian and a bourgeois, and, finally, by Frédéric's growing disgust for his mistress and his decision to take a new mistress, the aristocratic wife of the banker, M. Dambreuse. This decision is as cynical on Frédéric's part as it is calculated on Mme. Dambreuse's part to accept him as a lover.

The narrator tells us that, as of June 1848, the time of the infamous June Days, when the proletariat was ruthlessly suppressed, "The mind of the nation was unbalanced," a condition reflected in Frédéric's recognition that his "morality" had become "flabby" but also reflected in his choice of an antidote: "A mistress like Mme. Dambreuse," he muses, "would establish his position." We are not left with any doubts as to the nature of his attraction to her: "He coveted her because she was noble, rich, pious," and this recognition coincides with Frédéric's growing conviction that perhaps "progress is attainable only through an aristocracy," a conviction that is revealed to be as absurd as his earlier belief that "the people are sublime."

His deception of Rosanette now gives him infinite pleasure: "What a bastard I am!" he says; "Glorying in his own perversity," the narrator adds. His political interests fade, and with them his intention to stand as a candidate for the Assembly. He now luxuriates in "a feeling of gratification, of deep satisfaction. His joy of possessing a rich woman was unspoilt by any contrast; his feelings harmonized with their setting. His whole life, nowadays, was filled with pleasures." And the greatest, "perhaps, was to watch Madame Dambreuse surrounded by a group" of admirers: " . . . all the respect shown to her virtue delighted him as an indirect homage to himself, and he sometimes longed to cry: 'But I know her better than you do. She's mine!'"

Not quite, of course. Mme. Dambreuse is Frédéric's equal in venality and cunning self-servitude. The limits of his desire for her are set by his distaste for her "skinny chest": "At that moment, he admitted what he had hitherto concealed from himself; the disillusionment of his senses. This did not prevent him from feigning great ardor, but to feel it he had to evoke the image of Rosanette or Madame Arnoux. This atrophy of the heart," however, "left his head entirely free; and his ambition for a great position in society was stronger than ever." The death of M. Dambreuse, the subsequent revelation of the hatred and contempt underlying the Dambreuse's marriage, and Frédéric's growing disillusionment with Madame Dambreuse foreshadow the deterioration of the political situation, a situation laconically summed up by the narrator in a two-word paragraph: "Hatred flourished."

The death of Rosanette's child provides an occasion for the depiction of the total depravity of Frédéric's nature, his narcissism and emotional self-indulgence, his disinterest even in desire itself, along with a correlation of the death of realism in art (Pellerin's portrait of the dead child) and the death of idealism in politics. Frédéric's tears at the death-watch of his child are for himself. He had forgotten the child while it was gestating in Rosanette's womb. His tears are caused by the news that Mme. Arnoux has left Paris forever.

His break with both Rosanette and Mme. Dambreuse is followed by a decision to marry Louise, his "savage" and "peasant" girl-child; and he flees to her, but this too is frustrated when he arrives to find her marrying his best friend Deslauriers. He returns to Paris just in time to witness the coup of Napoleon III and the murder of the communist Dussardier by the former socialist, now policeman of reaction, Sénécal.

The interweaving of political events with the events in the life of Frédéric in this section of the novel is highly complex and invites a host of different interpretations. I call the mode of the whole section *synecdochic,* inasmuch as, here, it is borne in upon Frédéric's consciousness and upon that of the reader, the author's conviction that in the society depicted, the object of all desire is commodity possession. Desire is generalized and universalized by the equation of the value of every object with its value as commodity. This generalized and universalized form of value appears, however, in **two** guises: as a desire for human unity, in the first **instance**, reflected in the celebration of political liberation; and in the absurd form of the commodity fetishized. Mme. Dambreuse is indistinguishable from her wealth and social position.

The melancholy tone of the last two chapters, the retrospective summing up of this epic of disillusionment and frustration, can only derive from the juxtaposition of the way things are in modern society and the way they ought to be. The absent ideal is present as tacit antithesis to the painful reality. The irony of the last two chapters is melancholic because, whether he knew it or not, Flaubert had succeeded in representing more vividly than Hegel himself the path of development of consciousness's encounter with reality which leads to the condition of "the unhappy consciousness,"—that consciousness which is not only in and for itself, but also *by* itself, *beside* itself in its simultaneous dissemblance and awareness of this dissemblance. The melancholy of the last section is precisely similar to that which Marx depicts as a mode of bourgeois life in France under the absurd Napoleon III. And his analysis of the etiology of this symptom follows the same outline as that given to us figuratively in Flaubert's novel.

You will recall that Marx opens the *Eighteenth Brumaire* with a signal that he is about to unfold a "farce." The farcical nature of the events to be depicted is manifested in their outcome: the elevation of the charlatan "Crapulinski," the roué, opportunist, and fool— the original Napoleon the Great's nephew—Louis Bonaparte, to the imperial purple by a coalition of criminals, lumpenproletariat, peasants, and high bourgeois property owners. But, Marx reminds us a number of times throughout the discourse, this grotesque or absurd outcome of events—in which the least admirable man in France is hailed as the representative and defender of the interests of all classes of French society—was already implicitly present in the first, or February, phase of the Revolution of 1848, which had swept Louis Philippe from the throne and proclaimed the Second Republic.

How had this transformation, so remarkable and unforeseen by most of the actors in the spectacle, come about? Marx's answer to this question consists of an explication of the relationship between what he calls the true content of the "modern revolution" and the forms which specific revolutions take as a result of the conflict of interests which a class-divided society engenders.

The relation between the form and the content of any social phenomenon in any specific historical situation, Marx argues here and elsewhere, is a product of a conflict between specific class interests as these are envisaged and lived by a given class, on the one side, and general or universal human interests, which derive from the system of needs, primary and secondary, that are peculiar to mankind, on the other. Ideals are always formulated in terms of putatively universal human values, but since social perceptions are limited to the range of experiences of a given social class, the universally shared common interests of living men everywhere are always interpreted in a situation in which goods and political power are unevenly distributed in terms of the immediately envisaged *material* interests of the dominant class. This is why the political program of 1848, designed to establish a republic, quickly got transformed into a program designed to undermine this republic in the interest of protecting private property. The bourgeoisie in power says "Republic," against the old regime of inherited privilege and despotism, but it means "aristocracy of wealth." It says: "Justice," when it seeks to enlist the lower classes in its struggle against the old regime; but it means "Law and Order" when the aristocracy of wealth is established. It says, "Liberty, Equality, and Fraternity," when it is at the barricades or sending the lower classes to them; but it invokes "infantry, cavalry, and artillery," when the lower classes try to claim these rights in concrete terms. It comports itself on the historical stage like a tragic hero in its early phases of development, but its avarice and fetishism of commodities soon force it to abandon in practice every ideal it continues to preach in theory, and to reveal itself as the "monster" which any human being who conceives of life as an epic of production for profit alone must become.

So much is commonplace for Marxists, but exists only as a judgment still to be demonstrated. Part of the demonstration must be historical, since the process being analyzed is construed as a historical process. Marx chooses the events in France between 1848 and 1852 as a microcosm of the plot which every bourgeoisie must ultimately play out. And his demonstration of the adequacy of this judgment to the events themselves consists of a dialectical explication of those events as products of an interplay between forms and their actual contents, on the one side, and the form of the whole and its obscured universal meaning, on the other.

On the surface of the events, Marx discerns a succession of four formal incarnations of the revolutionary impulse. Each of these incarnations is simultaneously a response to socioeconomic reality (here construed as class interests) and an attempt to deny the universal meaning of the revolution in relation to ideal human aspiration. He divides the drama into four phases, each of which is signalled by a change in the form of government established on the political level. But the form of government established is itself a projection of a form of political consciousness, itself a product of either a coalition of classes, more or less self-consciously contrived, or of a specific class.

The real protagonist of Marx's narrative is neither the proletariat (its Dussardier) nor Louis Bonaparte (its Sénécal), but rather the bourgeoisie as it lives through the longings, sufferings, and contradictions of its existence that constitute its own "Sentimental Education." Its *Bildung,* like that of Moreau, consists of a progressive evacuation of ideals in order to become reconciled to a reality conceived as the melancholy consumption of commodities whose real value remains indiscernible.

Like Frédéric, the bourgeoisie and the revolution in which it will achieve its "absurd" triumph, passes through four stages of consciousness: February 1848 is metaphoric; political aspiration and social ideals are entertained in the euphoric spirit of unspecified desires and glimpsed in the image of "a social republic." Marx says of this period: "Nothing and nobody ventured to lay claim to the right of existence and of real action. All the elements that had prepared or determined the Revolution, the dynastic opposition, the republican bourgeoisie, the democratic-republican petty bourgeoisie and the social-democratic workers, provisionally found their place in the February *government*." "It could not be otherwise," Marx continues; "Every party construed [the republic] in its own sense." Although the proletariat proclaimed a "social republic," and thereby "indicated the general content of the modern revolution," the proclamation was both naive and premature, given the interests and powers of other social groups. And this accounts for the "confused mixture of high-flown phrases and actual uncertainty and clumsiness, of more enthusiastic striving for innovation and more deeply rooted domination of the old routine, of more apparent harmony of the whole society and more profound estrangement of its elements," which characterized this phase of the whole revolutionary process.

Phase two of the Revolution, the period of the Constituent National Assembly, 4 May 1848 to 29 May 1849, represents the period of dispersion of the revolutionary impulse across a series of contending parties and groups, a period of strife and specification of contents, emblematized by the bloody street warfare of the June Days (23-26 June 1848) and the progressive betrayal of one group by another until the bourgeois republicans accede to dictatorial power in the Legislative National Assembly, an accession which demonstrated to every observer of the event that "in Europe there are other questions involved than that of 'republic or monarchy.' It had revealed," Marx says, "that here [in Europe] *bourgeois republic* signifies the unlimited despotism of one class over other classes." Under the sign of the motto, "property, family, religion, order," every alternative party is crushed. "Society is saved just as often as the circle of its rulers contracts, as a more exclusive interest is maintained against a wider one. Every demand of the simplest bourgeois social reform, of the most ordinary liberalism, of the most formal republicanism, of the most insipid democracy, is simultaneously castigated as an 'attempt on society' and stigmatised as 'socialism'."

With the dictatorship of the bourgeoisie, we have passed into the third phrase of the Revolution, the synecdochic phase in which the interests of a specific segment of society is identified with the interest of society as a whole. This pseudo-universalization of the interests of the bourgeoisie, this incarnation of the universal in the particular, this fetishism by a class of itself, is a preparation for the absurdity represented by Bonaparte's claims to be "the savior of society" and the irony of his use of the motto "property, family, religion, order" to justify his suppression of the *political* power of the bourgeoisie.

In this, the last phase of the Revolution, bourgeois 'high priests' of 'religion and order' themselves are driven with kicks from their Pythian tripods, hauled out of their beds in the darkness of night, put in prison vans, thrown into dungeons or sent into exile; their temple is razed to the ground, their mouths are sealed, their pens broken, their law torn to pieces in the name of religion, of property, of family, of order. Bourgeois fanatics for order are shot down on their balconies by mobs of drunken soldiers, their domestic sanctuaries profaned, their houses bombarded for amusement—in the name of property, of family, of religion, and of order. Finally the scum of bourgeois society forms the *holy phalanx of order* and the hero Crapulinski [from Fr. *crapule* 'gluttony'] installs himself in the Tuileries as the 'savior of society'."

What justification do I have for calling the modes of relationship among the elements of society represented in Marx's characterization of the phases of the Revolution by the names of the tropes of figurative language? The best reason is that Marx himself provides us with schematic representations of the modes of figuration by which to characterize the relation between the forms of value and their contents in his analysis of the "language of commodities" in chapter 1 of *Capital*. Most of this chapter consists of an adaptation of the traditional conception of the rhetorical tropes to the method of dialectical analysis. Here the problem, Marx says, is to understand the Money Form of Value, the "absurd" notion that the value of a commodity is equivalent to the amount of money it is worth in a given system of exchange. And just as the explanation of the "absurd" spectacle of Bonaparte's posing as the "savior of society"—while unleashing all of the criminal elements of society to an orgy of a consumption ungoverned by any respect for human values or the persons who produced by their labor the commodities being consumed—is contained in the understanding of the first phase of the Revolution which brought him to power, the February phase; so too the absurd form of value is explained by reference to the structure of the Elementary or Original Form of value, the form contained in the simple metaphorical *identification* of "x amount of Commodity A" with "y amount of Commodity B." Once the purely figurative nature of this statement of equivalency is grasped, once it is seen that, like any metaphor, it both contains a deep truth (regarding the similarity of any two commodities by virtue of their nature as products of human labor) and at the same time masks this truth (by remaining on the superficial level of an apprehension of their manifest similarity as commodities), the secret of men's capacity to bewitch themselves into believing that the value of anything equals its exchange, rather than its use, value is revealed for everyone to see. Just as irony is implicitly present in any original, primitive or naive characterization of reality in a metaphor, so too the absurdity of equating the value of a product of human labor with its money value is contained implicitly in the equating of any given commodity with any other as a basis of exchange. And so too with the other two forms of value, the Extended and the Generalized forms, which Marx analyzes in this chapter of *Capital*. They are to *metonymy* and *synecdoche,* the relationships by contiguity and putative essential identity, respectively, as the second and third phases of the Revolution are to the same tropes.

To be sure, Marx's analysis of the forms of social phenomena, whether of commodity values or of political systems, is carried forth on the assumption that he has perceived their true contents, which the forms simultaneously figure forth and conceal from clear view. The true value-content of all commodities is for him the amount of human labor expended in their production, which is precisely equivalent to their use value, whatever their apparent value in a given system of exchange. The true content of all political and social forms, similarly, is the universal human needs which they at once manifest and obscure. Marx's aim as a writer was to clarify this relation of content to form in a way which he thought, correctly I believe, was consistent with Hegel's dialectical method of analysis, although—in his view—Hegel had got the form-content distinction wrong way about. But he carried forward the method of Hegel's *Phenomenology* and *Logic* by divining the element of consciousness which was the basis and bane of humanity's efforts to grasp reality and turn it to its service. This element was man's capacity for what Vico called "creative error," a capacity of the figurative imagination without which reason itself would be inconceivable, just as prose without poetry would be unthinkable. More: he divined clearly what Hegel only in passing glimpses and in his pursuit of the secret of Being-in-General too quickly passes over; namely, that the secret of human consciousness is to be found in its most original product, which is not reason, but figurative language, without which reason could never have arisen.

What does the discernment of a common pattern of tropological representations of the modes of consciousness imply with respect to the project of "realistic representation," on the one side, and the problem of style, on the other? With respect to the former, I would suggest, it permits us to identify the "allegorical" element in realistic discourse, the secondary meaning of the events depicted on the surface of the narrative which mediates between those events and the judgment rendered on them, launched from the consciously held ideological position of the writer. The progression of these structures of consciousness permits the encodation of the process through which the protagonist is passing in his/its "education," in terms which allow the writer a judgment on its end phase as a stage of cognitive awareness. This quite apart from whatever archetypal schema may be revealed in the literary encodation of the events in generic terms, i.e., as comedy, tragedy, romance, satire or farce. The discourses of Marx and Flaubert can thus be construed as correlations of events with their mythic archetypes, on the one side, and with types of cognition, on the other. And it is the twofold encodation of these events, as satires and as reductions of consciousness to a condition of "ironic" self-reflexivity, which tacitly justifies the ideological judgment rendered on them, in the narrator's voice on the diegetic level of the discourse. To be sure, the revelation of the "farcical" nature of a given set of events constitutes a judgment on their "meaning" in itself. But merely to have emplotted a given set of events as a "farce" testifies only to the literary skill of the narrator; every set of events can be emplotted in any number of ways without doing violence to their "factuality." Every specific emplotment

of a set of events, then, requires at least tacit appeal to some cognitive criterion, some notion of the way things really are, in order to establish that the emplotment in question is both plausible and illuminative of the true structure of the events in question. The theory of consciousness, which construes it as a process of passage from a metaphoric, through metonymic and synecdochic phases of development, to the condition of self-consciousness represented by irony, serves this cognitive purpose in Marx's and Flaubert's discourses. Their "realism" is thus revealed to be triply allegorical, possessing levels of elaboration corresponding to the figurative, moral, and anagogical levels discriminated in the Augustinian hermeneutic tradition. The meaning of the processes depicted on the literal level of the texts is revealed by the transcoding of the processes in generic, ideological, and cognitive terms.

With respect to the problem of style, our analysis of the discourses of Marx and Flaubert suggests that we should regard style, at least in realistic discourse, as the process of this transcoding operation. When we speak of the style of a discourse, we should not feel compelled to limit ourselves to a consideration of either the linguistic-rhetorical features of a text or to its discernible ideological posture, but should seek rather to characterize the moves made, on the axes of both selection and combination, by which a form is identified with a content and the reverse. Flaubert was certainly right when he sought to identify "style" with the "content" of the discourse, but specified that the content in question had to do with "thought" rather than with the manifest referent of the discourse, the characters, situations, and events depicted in the narrative. What he may have been pointing to here was the inexpungable element of "construct" contained in every discourse, however "realistic," however perfectly "mimetic," it might strive to be. If the linguistic sign is to be identified neither with the signifier nor the signified, but with their conjunction, then every representation of reality in language must possess, as an element of its content, the "form" of the signifier itself. Discourse turns the union of signifier and signified in the sign into the problem with which it must deal. Its aim is less to match up a group of signifiers with their signifieds, in a relationship of perfect equivalency, than to create a system of signs that are their own signifieds. To put it this way is no doubt to muddy the waters, but it at least helps to explain why every "realism" in the end fails and is supplanted by yet another "realism" which, although claiming at last to be a pure *mimesis,* is soon revealed by a vigilant criticism to be only another perspective on the ever shifting relationship between words and the things they are supposed to signify.

Finally, this approach to the problem of style, considered within the context of mid-nineteenth-century realism, as represented by Marx and Flaubert, helps us to comprehend better the seemingly substantive "modernity" of their discourses. Their embedding of the tropes of figurative language within their discourse as a model of the processes of consciousness allows them to appear to be the very types of a certain *kind* of realism, on the one side, and heralds of "modernism" in both writing and criticism, on the other. For modernism, whatever else it may be, is characterized by a hyper-selfconsciousness with respect to the opacity of language, by language's demonic capacity to intrude itself into discourse as a content alongside of whatever referent may be signalled on the surface of the text. Marx's and Flaubert's identification of the stages of consciousness with tropological structures, the structures of language in its prefigurative aspect, amnestied them against the perils of literalism, on the one side, and of symbolization, on the other. Their discourses are not reducible either to the manifest forms in which they appear or to the specific ideological positions they held. On the contrary, their discourses remain eternally fresh and enduringly "realistic" precisely to the degree that their "contents" were identified as the process of their own production.

Jefferson Humphries

SOURCE: "Flaubert's Parrot and Huysmans's Cricket: The Decadence of Realism and the Realism of Decadence," in *Stanford French Review* XI, No. 3, Fall, 1987, pp. 323-30.

[*In the following essay, Humphries questions the ability of realistic fiction faithfully to reproduce reality without evoking an allegorical significance.*]

It has become almost a cliché of modern literary theory that realism—the school and practice of fiction most closely associated with certain French writers of the nineteenth century (Balzac, Stendhal, Flaubert)—finally embraces the failure of its own project, indeed that the failure of mimesis—of art as imitation of reality—is the ultimate subject of every so-called realistic text. Ross Chambers has written [in *Story and Situation: Narrative Seduction and the Power of Fiction,* 1984] that the famous parrot of Flaubert's story, "A Simple Heart," "represents less the mimesis of everyday life and speech in repetitive time and more the perils of identification, the product of mimetic duplicity." Frederic Jameson has argued [in *The Political Unconscious,* 1981] that in fact the "realistic" novel produces the referent which it claims to reflect (the real), as fiction, and so as absence, as failure. Both Lucien Dällenbach, reading Balzac, and Roland Barthes, reading Flaubert, have made the point that "realistic" texts are grounded not in a positively conceived, stable relation between art and life, but rather in a sense of profound discrepancy between them, and therefore within each. The realistic text—and so the

real itself, as well as its representation—are grounded in fragmentariness, contingency, what Dällenbach has called the world (literary and real) as *chaosmos.* In this context, it is easy to understand why Flaubert aspired, as he put it, to "write a book about nothing." No self-conscious practitioner of realism could aspire to anything else than to write about the gap in which the realistic text hovers between the reader and the real, across which literary experience (reading) and knowledge of the real must occur.

Recent studies of decadence, however, have not reassessed its relationship with such a newly conceived realism, which preceded it directly in France. In a recent study, Richard Gilman does not even bother to quarrel with the canonical view of decadence, but rather suggests we stop using the term for lack of an adequate and consistent definition. Suzanne Nalbantian still describes decadence [in *Seeds of Decadence in the Nineteenth-Century Novel,* 1985] as a "decline in values," if not in literary quality, and a turning away from "referentiality" (realism) toward "symbolization." As surely as the word comes from the Latin *de-cadere* (to fall from), a fall is implied, but one which I believe *began* with realism. Flaubert, in this view, was the first fully fledged decadent writer, because he was first to fall *into* the theoretical implications of realism.

He fell into them by pursuing with relentless rigor the theoretical ramifications of realism (as *truquage*—the manipulation of the reader's senses, desire, through language, aiming momentarily to sustain the "hallucination" of no difference between the text and the real). His fascination for ironic desire—desire which turns on itself, which is its own object—is clear in every one of his novels, but perhaps most obviously in *L'éducation sentimentale,* whose hero, Frédéric Moreau, is remarkable only for his impotence, his ineffectuality, his devotion to an unrequitable desire which sustains itself precisely because it is unrequited, because its "real" object, Marie Arnoux, is not its object at all in fact, but merely its pretext. The real object is the desire itself, with all its concomitant emotions and sensations, which the presence or absence of Madame Arnoux allows Frédéric to modulate his desire very much as the hero of Huysmans's *A rebours,* Des Esseintes, would later seek to "create" the illusion of various realities in order to modulate his sensations. The object of realism is thus not reality—the real is rather the simulation in the reader of certain sensations associated with certain kinds of reality—but sensual hallucination, artificial stimulation of cerebral cathexes. The ostensible desire of Bouvard and Pécuchet in Flaubert's novel of that name is, through scientific, positivistic (therefore "realistic") procedure, to discover an objective knowledge of the real. Their efforts fail, persistently and ludicrously, yet they continue, demonstrating again that the object of realistic desire is not the real, and for that matter is not objective. It is rather the sensation, the delusion of realistic desire itself, and this means that desire directed toward the real is ultimately *textual,* literary—at the end of *Bouvard and Pécuchet* the two would-be scientists begin writing, "copying." Madame Bovary's desire is in the same sense, and very evidently, literary. Each of these works reflects Flaubert's ambition "to write a book about nothing," to transcribe the absence and alterity of the "real."

This theoretical aspect of realism is nowhere more clearly elaborated than in *Trois contes.* The unity of the *Trois contes,* so often overlooked or misunderstood by critics of Flaubert's work, is grounded in the representation of three kinds of religious experience, all of which may be read as allegories of the process of reading (understood as a sort of "religious" suspension of disbelief, a "rational" hallucination) and as statements of profound disbelief and disinterest in the project of a simply mimetic realism. *Un coeur simple* deals with the way in which a *naif* reads texts and reality, without making any distinction between the two, between figures and their various levels of reference. When Félicité hears the Gospel read aloud, she "sees" all the events described as though they were transpiring before her. Confronted with the signifier of a map, she expects it to coincide so perfectly with the topography it represents that her nephew, Victor, should be visible on it. The parrot Loulou represents this collapse of difference between signifier and signified, between visual, sensual signifiers (bright color) and textual, linguistic signifiers. He is also the figure of Félicité's hallucinatory vision at the end of the story, in which he—as representing precisely the collapse of distinction between text and sensual reality, figure and proper meaning—becomes deified. The parrot—as is so often the case with birds, especially talking ones—is a figure for figural language, a trope of troping. What he signifies, as a figure, is the logic of literary representation, by which words are not distinct from the experience of a fictive sensual, visual reality. This logic is the premise of mimetic realism, and yet it leads inevitably to anti-realism, to hallucinatory perception, on the part of the reader and here the principal character as well.

In "Saint Julien," the narration represents the pursuit of sensual pleasure through the hunt, through blood-lust. Such lust would appear to be identical with a desire to end things, for closure, which can never be requited. That desire is turned into a sort of madness by another animal who speaks, and is endowed, like the parrot, with spiritual significance: the stag who damns Julien three times and foretells his murder of his parents. The remainder of the narration recounts Julien's coming to terms with the non-distinction of the sensual (the hunt) and the verbal, the textual (*script-*ure). This story, like the first one, ends with a representation of hallucinatory experience in which the dif-

ference between religious ecstasy and "real" perception is exploded. The stag is another trope of troping.

In the final story, "Herodias," there is a violent clash between the *script-*ural, the textual or religious (the prophetic words of John the Baptist), and the *sensual* (Herod's desire for Salomé). Salomé is described very overtly as a trope of a trope, an object of desire because she signifies Herod's past desire for her mother—she signifies the game of displacement and deferment which desire is, desire itself being a figure, as in Proust, of literary troping. The Baptist is described as beast-like, and comprising for the most part nothing but a *voice* which "roars" prophetic words. Salomé, like Loulou the parrot a crazyquilt of violent colors, enveloped in diaphanous, iridescent fabric and wearing slippers of *hummingbird* feathers, is characterized mainly by her dance, by movement and color which are extra-human, and says only one thing, her request for the Baptist's head which *she repeats like a parrot after her mother's instructions*. Both she and the Baptist are figures for figuration as were the stag (John the Baptist, the Prophet, the "Voice Crying Out in the Wilderness": "Je crierai comme un ours, comme un âne sauvage, . . . ") and the parrot (loud, sensuous, seductive color coupled with a talent for mimicry). The Baptist is executed, "concluded," "definitively read," and yet he isn't: in the story's final vignette, his decapitated head, described in gory detail as just one object among others in the debris of the festivities, characterized by its heaviness (which makes John the Baptist's disciples take turns carrying it), still bears its textual, *script-*ural inflection; what it meant before, it still means to the religious: the words of the Baptist that "Pour qu'il croisse, il faut que je diminue." The significance of this object as an object is not altered by death—it did not, and still does not at the end of the story, take its significance from the palpably real, any more than Flaubert's story, or any of his books, does. The ultimate object of Flaubert's realism is to represent its own logic, its own rhetoric, and thus to embrace its own bankruptcy as mimetic realism. These stories represent the failure of distinction, the play of *différance,* between the sensual (the real) and the verbal or textual, as a sort of religious experience encompassing hallucination, virtual madness, and simple overpowering lust (as in Herod's case).

To recapitulate briefly, in the naiveté of Félicité, there is no difference between the text of the Bible and reality, between a map and the terrain which it signifies, between a parrot and God—the real and the text are one in her ecstatic hallucination:

> Une vapeur d'azur monta dans la chambre de Félicité. Elle avança les narines, en la humant avec une sensualité mystique; puis ferma les paupières. Ses lèvres souriaient. Les mouvements de son coeur se ralentirent un à un, plus vagues chaque fois, plus

doux, comme une fontaine s'épuise, comme un écho disparaît; et, quand elle exhala son dernier souffle, elle crut voir, dans les cieux entr'ouverts, un perroquet gigantesque, planant au-dessus de sa tête.

In the second story, another animal—the stag, which speaks a prophesy to Julien—becomes the same sort of figure of figuration as the parrot—representing the way in which the mute, brute, objectively real depends on language, on representation, on literary experience, to embody, to represent all these qualities of the "real." His encounter with the stag causes Julien to suffer a kind of madness of uncertainty. He is no longer sure of the difference between the real and the text (of the real), between bloodlust (material desire) and another, spiritual, *script*-ural desire. This discrepancy is collapsed in his final hallucinatory experience of God.

> Alors le Lépreux l'étreignit; et ses yeux tout à coup prirent une clarté d'étoiles; ses cheveux s'allongèrent comme les rais du soleil; le souffle de ses narines avait la douceur des roses; un nuage d'encens s'éleva du foyer; les flots chantaient. Cependant une abondance de délices, une joie surhumaine descendait comme une inondation dans l'âme de Julien pâmé; et celui dont le bras le serraient toujours grandissait, grandissait, touchant de sa tête et de ses pieds les deux murs de la cabane. Le toit s'envola, le firmament se déployait—et Julien monta vers les espaces bleus, face à face avec Notre-Seigneur Jésus, qui l'emportait dans le ciel.

In *Hérodias,* Herod's erotic, material desire is similarly contrasted with the scriptural, religious desire of the Baptist. Salomé is mute movement; the Baptist is nothing but a voice crying in the wilderness, housed like the stag's and the parrot's voices in a "brutish" body:

> Un être humain était couché par terre sous de longs cheveux se confondant avec les poils de bête qui garnissaient son dos. Il se leva. Son front touchait à une grille horizontalement scellée; et, de temps à autre, il disparaissait dans les profondeurs de son antre.

Both are grounded in hallucinatory experience, not reality but the achievement of a certain *truquage* or illusion of reality—which may be "true." The contrast at the end of the story between the Baptist's head as material object, just one more among the detritus of the night's festivities, and religious object, is one more representation of the aporia in the very concept of the real, on which our day-to-day experience is nevertheless based.

> A l'instant où se levait le soleil, deux hommes, expédiés autrefois par Iaokanann, survinrent, avec la réponse si longtemps espérée.

> Ils la confièrent à Phanuel, qui en eut un ravissement.

> Puis il leur montra l'objet lugubre, sur le plateau, entre les débris du festin. Un des hommes lui dit:

> —Console-toi! Il est descendu chez les morts annoncer le Christ!

> "Pour qu'il croisse, il faut que je diminue."

> Et tous les trois, ayant pris la tête de Iaokanann, s'en allèrent du côté de la Galilée.

> Comme elle était très lourde, ils la portèrent alternativement.

Des Esseintes keeps a cricket rather than a parrot, which however plays the same role as Félicité's Loulou: just as the bird served to manipulate Félicité's experience of the real, subsuming all sorts of referents and signifieds such as her nephew's whereabouts, the Holy Spirit, the New World, etc., Des Esseintes's cricket serves to manipulate his perceptions, memories, emotions, sensations. This, indeed, is the governing principle behind his careful orchestration of all the physical sensations to which he is subject, all of his surroundings. That manipulation, which occurs here on the mimetic plane of the text, perfectly duplicates Flaubert's project as a realist: to *truquer* the real, to manipulate the reader's imagination so as to—hallucinatorily—collapse the gap between the text and the real, to bring both within that "nothing." This makes Des Esseintes into a realist even more zealous than Flaubert—he practices, in his life, the very stylistic principles of *truquage* which caused Flaubert to try to allude to at least three of the senses (touch, sight, and hearing, for instance) in his descriptive passages.

Des Esseintes's cricket is the figure of a logic implicit in the parrot Loulou, in the stag that prophesies to Julien, in the head of John the Baptist and the dance of Salomé, but the cricket is more explicitly a figure of the *truquage* of realistic style, the manipulation of imaginary sensation. At the same time that Des Esseintes "hallucinates" in the signifier of the cricket's voice all sorts of signifieds and referents which are not there, precisely as Félicité did with the parrot, he (Des Esseintes) knows perfectly well what he is doing:

> Ainsi, par haine, par mépris de son enfance, il avait pendu au plafond de cette pièce une petite cage en fil d'argent où un grillon enfermé chantait comme dans les cendres des cheminées du chateau de Lourps; quand il écoutait ce cri tant de fois entendu, toutes les soirées contraintes et muettes chez sa mère, tout l'abandon d'une jeunesse souffrante et refoulée, se bousculaient devant lui, et alors, aux secousses de la femme qu'il caressait machinalement dont les paroles ou le rire rompaient sa vision et le

ramenaient brusquement dans la réalité, dans le boudoir, à terre, un tumulte se levait en son âme, un besoin de vengeance des tristesses endurées, une rage de salir par des turpitudes des souvenirs de famille, un désir furieux de panteler sur des coussins de chair, d'épuiser jusqu'à leurs dernières gouttes, les plus véhémentes et les plus acres des folies charnelles.

Flaubert and Huysmans are finally *theorists* of realism inasmuch as what they practice in their writing is the pursuit and representation of the theoretical implications of realism. Huysmans goes one step further in showing how the principles of realistic style, and the implications of realistic theory, apply not just to literature but to life, to our real perception of the real. In the fictional character of Des Esseintes it becomes more evident than ever before that the theoretical implications of realism, and the realistic implications of theory, are decadent—that is to say, anti-realistic. Perhaps it would make more sense to say that decadence is nothing but the theoretical development of mimetic realism to its logical end. This may in fact be the best answer available to the question of what decadence is.

Poe entered the French canon via the translations of Mallarmé and Baudelaire, and his paradoxical insistence on the mechanical nature of literature feeds directly into the idea, already suggested by Huysmans, of literature as a machine which produces the real, and of the real as a "mechanical" process of self-generation involving all sorts of essentially literary techniques. This notion of the machine as a metaphor for literature and for reality, and so for the discontinuity and contingency of art and the real, would be developed by Alfred Jarry. The machine, in Jarry's earliest work and in *Le surmâle,* was the possibility, the potentiality, of a reversal of polarities. It was the point of distinction, and the dissolution of distinction. Jarry's machines (his *"pompe à merdre,"* for instance) evacuate and fill, empty and penetrate, desecrate and consecrate. Machine and trope are figures for each other as part of a process of production which always produces only more production, further substitutions. In this way, as a reader like Frederic Jameson might point out, the realist/decadent text "produces" the reality of capitalist consumerism.

Ultimately such a literary machine must subsume and deconstruct the authority (sic) of a coherent writing and reading subjectivity, and this is what happens in Lautréamont's *Les chants de Maldoror.* The distinction between author and text, and between textual content and the reader's affective response to the text, are reduced as much as possible. Inasmuch as his text produces more violent responses—of revulsion, moral indignation, or morbid fascination—in the reader than *Madame Bovary,* Lautréamont might claim to be a more accomplished realist than Flaubert. He does succeed in

forcing the text and the reader's experience, the reader's intellectual and affective "reality," to coincide. What occurred within the pages of Huysmans's text—the conflation in Des Esseintes of writer, reader, and character—is carried one step further, to engulf the actual reader in the illusory "reality" of the text. It is "Maldoror," Lautréamont's text—*and* authorial identity—who is the cricket (*grillon*) here, and we who are in the place of Des Esseintes: "N'avez-vous pas remarqué la gracilité d'un joli grillon, aux mouvements alertes, dans les égouts de Paris? Il n'y a que celui-là: c'était Maldoror!"

H. Meili Steele

SOURCE: "Setting: Reference Beyond Signification," in *Realism and the Drama of Reference: Strategies of Representation in Balzac, Flaubert, and James,* The Pennsylvania State University Press, 1988, pp. 13-22.

[*In the following excerpt, Steele analyzes the setting of* L'Education sentimentale *in order to examine the problematic nature of representation in this Realist text.*]

The setting of *L'Education sentimentale* has all the features of the realistic novel. It is set in a historical place (Paris), in a defined historical period (1840-51, with an epilogue in 1867), and there are many details about the social environment without the suggestion of a transcendent realm beyond the positivistic world of sensations and facts. For the most part, the narrator generates the setting without reference to the narrative instance (e.g., use of first or second person or adverbs that refer to time of narration) and thus emphasizes the forces of disengagement, of reference. Neither the sense nor the reference of the words seems problematic. The text's setting could therefore be read as simply a refined version of the representation of Parisian society in *Les Illusions perdues,* a representation that is purged of needless commentary and metaphoric extravagance in Balzac's text.

Nonetheless, this apparently unproblematic setting has been read in a variety of ways, and the center of the controversy is description. For Flaubert's contemporaries, the text's description violates the norms of the novel. Barbey d'Aurevilly says, "This novel's style is description, an infinite, eternal, atomistic and blind description that takes up the entire book and replaces all the faculties of the mind." Indeed, these early critics find that the novel breaks almost all textual norms of the day. [In *L'Education sentimentale de Gustave Flaubert,* 1963] René Dumesnil summarizes their reaction: "The same complaints, the same arguments are repeated from one article to the next as if all the critics had agreed about what they were going to say and decided to crush Flaubert under the weight of their censure." Though I cannot go into the fascinating reception of the text, a brief look at two opposing modern traditions of reading will help to locate my own analysis on the map of criticism and to clear a path for the discussion. . . .

One of the traditions reads the description according to realistic and New Critical criteria (e.g., Victor Brombert and Robert Sherrington); another tradition, the structuralist readings of Jonathan Culler and Roland Barthes, finds that the text explodes the institution of the realistic novel. The issue revolves on whether some of the novel's descriptions are gratuitous. The New Critical reading recuperates all descriptions by assigning them to a function—e.g., they reveal the psychology of the character who views them—or by finding thematic analogies that unify the work. The other tradition maintains that some descriptions cannot be recuperated into the literary tradition and that the text thus breaks with the institution of the novel. "Recuperability" joins the question of reference since understanding reference depends on the discourse situation, the speaker and the context. If these factors become ambiguous, then the referential effect will change. Since my reading follows Culler's to a certain extent, I shall begin with an example that violates the discourse of realism. The following description appears in Part II when Frédéric returns to Paris after his inheritance:

> The plain had changed beyond recognition and looked like a town in ruins. The fortifications crossed it in a horizontal ridge, and on the unpaved paths edging the road stood small branchless trees protected by battens bristling with nails. Chemical factories alternated with timber-merchants' yards. Tall gateways, like those of farms, revealed between their half-open doors sordid yards full of refuse, with pools of dirty water in the middle. Long-fronted, dull red taverns displayed a pair of crossed billiard cues in a wreath of painted flowers between their first-floor windows; here and there a little stucco shanty had been left half-finished.

The most important feature of the passage is that the language of representation is the language of perception, not whether the description is reported from the narrator's or Frédéric's point of view. (The scene opens a new paragraph, and the last sentence of the preceding paragraph includes a perceptual verb: "all of a sudden he caught sight of the dome of the Pantheon.") The passage does not seem to emphasize a thematic point nor insert itself into plot-functions (e.g., expositions) or character-functions. One could index these details with a category such as "the horror of industrialization," but this category does not account for the passage's independence from literary functions or from social purposes in the represented world. The referential power of the language gives the objects a hallucinatory quality, as if they were contemplated without regard to their practical uses, as if matter were assert-

ing its autonomy from humanity. The eye of observation does not master reference.

This autonomy of the representation of objects is even more striking in the description of interior social settings than of the external environment. In the former, the reader expects not only the articulation of physical space but also of thematic space through redundancy or a general comment. The reader can accept purposelessness in natural objects more easily than in cultural artifacts supposedly informed by human intentions. In *L'Education* objects appear that can be grouped thematically—e.g., "eroticism," "bourgeois tastelessness"—however, the heterogeneity and the quantity of the objects overwhelm these thematic categories and the characters. A good example of this kind of description appears in Frédéric's introduction to Rosanette's salon at the beginning of Part II. This scene is typical of the *Bildungsroman:* the young provincial confronts a world that he does not understand but that the reader comprehends through his (the reader's) cultural knowledge, through the redundancy or symbolism of the description, through dialogue, or through the explanations of the narrator or initiator. In *Les Illusions perdues,* for example, Balzac's narrator sets up Lucien de Rubempré's first evening out in Paris as follows: "It was a memorable evening for him, thanks to his unvoiced repudiation of a great number of his ideas about life in the provinces. His little world was broadening out and society was assuming vaster proportions. The proximity of several beautiful Parisian women, so elegantly and so daintily attired, made him aware that Madame de Bargeton's *toilette,* though passably ambitious, was behind the times." In the scene at Rosanette's, however, there is no explanatory dialogue, little reflection by the hero, and almost no action. Balzacian description is inserted into the plot so that the objects participate in the action even if they do not assume an actantial function themselves. Objects are not just phenomena but actors whose meaning emerges through their history. Since action and social discourse in *L'Education* are displaced by description—with regard to Balzacian text—what is traditionally "background" takes on a great semantic burden. (The scene occupies fifteen pages.) The following passage appears at its beginning:

> At first Frédéric was dazzled by the lights; he could see nothing but silk, velvet, bare shoulders, a mass of colours swaying to the strains of an orchestra hidden by some foliage, between walls hung with yellow silk, and adorned here and there with pastel portraits and crystal sconces in the Louis Seize style. Tall lamps, whose frosted globes looked like snow-balls, rose above baskets of flowers which stood on little tables in the corners; and opposite, beyond a second smaller room, a third could be seen, containing a bed with twisted posts and a Venetian mirror behind it.

Victor Brombert's reading of the scene illustrates how the passage can be integrated with other elements of the text and how Flaubert's differences from Balzac can be naturalized. First, Brombert compares the scene with the Taillefer orgy in *La Peau de chagrin* and dismisses the flatness of the description in *L'Education* by praising Flaubert. The critic finds "the same display of available carnality, the same specter of disease and death, the same garish couplings of the lascivious and the macabre. Only Flaubert is not concerned with sheer pyrotechnics." Finding a unifying bordello motif, he then relates this scene to one at Dambreuse's and to one at the café Alhambra. Brombert sees the menacing heterogeneity of the objects in the last of these scenes; however, he naturalizes heterogeneity by making the bordello motif a metaphor: "This shocking combination is not merely a sign of vulgarity. It represents the particular attempt at facile poetry. . . . In this light, the bordello becomes the convenient metaphor for any catering to the thirst for illusion." Invested with the power of metaphor, the bordello gathers fragmented meanings and unifies the text: "This aspect of the metaphorical unity of *L'Education sentimentale* is further strengthened by the presence of key characters who, in one form or another, are for sale."

Culler shows [in *Flaubert: The Uses of Uncertainty,* 1974] how the description in the scene at Rosanette's resists Brombert's thematic and symbolic recuperation, and his discussion is worth summarizing here. He supports his contention by following Brombert's suggestion and comparing the description in *La Peau de chagrin* with that in *L'Education.* Even though both passages include many similar objects, they are not presented in the same way. Balzac's objects are framed by an englobing proposition that links the objects to human interests and makes them illustrations of this interest: "The whole company remained for a moment immobile and charmed on the threshold. The excessive pleasures of the feast paled before the tempting spectacle that the host offered to the most voluptuous of their senses." Diversity in the scene is contained by the sentence that generalizes the force of the objects and associates them with known desires: "This harem offered visual seductions, voluptuous pleasures for all caprices." These suggestions for reading the objects are reinforced by what Culler calls "synoptic movements," a panorama that contains the scene visually and semantically: "The salons at this moment presented an advance view of Milton's Pandemonium." In the passage from *L'Education,* the objects are not offered as knowledge. Frédéric perceives these objects, but perception of their existence is not followed by synthetic statements about the meaning of these objects nor is the reader given clues that escape Frédéric. Here and elsewhere in the novel, the hero's response is stunned silence or a reverie that is independent of the objects that stimulate it. Balzac's text moves easily between the language of designation and the language of explanation so that the milieu, the individual characters, and the society are interconnected. Balzac's narrator often makes those connections allegorical as well as causal. In *Les Illusions perdues,* we read: "The outside of the Séchard premises was in keeping with the squalor reigning inside." After a description of Lousteau's room, the narrator says: "This room, at once dirty and dreary, gave evidence of a life lacking both repose and dignity." Objects in the text are always placed in systems of signification that act on the characters, and the narrator of *Les Illusions* makes explicit what is implicit in most realistic novels: "It is all the more necessary at this point to make some remarks on Angouleme because they will help us to understand Madame de Bargeton, one of the most important characters of this story."

To this point, my analysis is consistent with Culler's; I disagree, however, with the limits imposed by his conclusion that we should read for "the ways in which . . . it is written against the novel as institution." Culler's analysis is thus intended not only to show the difference between Balzac's text and Flaubert's but to show how *L'Education* resists all attempts to read it. This attempt differs from my reading in several ways. First, it equates the Balzacian novel with the "institution of the novel"—with the reader's intertexts in the genre. Second, it makes no distinction between the interpretative strategy and the text. For Culler, texts are either intelligible or unintelligible, recuperable or nonrecuperable. That is, texts and commentary "fit" in recuperable texts, while unreadable texts are not appropriate for commentary. In brief, he uses a structuralist model of genre in which Balzac's texts are the norm. My reading invokes modern intertexts (specifically Beckett), rejects the opposition intelligible/unintelligible for Balzac and Flaubert and attempts to separate text and reading, though such a separation is not "objective" but defined by my own hermeneutic position that sets up a dialogue between "text" and critical language. The difference between Balzac and Flaubert's texts does not mean that all interpretations are inappropriate except the antinovelistic one; nor does it mean that reference must serve the interests of realism. Instead, *L'Education* opens possibilities at the same time that it questions the presuppositions of Balzacian realism. An examination of Roland Barthes's important article "L'Effet de réel" will show how this possibility is opened.

In this article Barthes examines a short description from "Un Coeur simple" and assigns those details that do not have a thematic function to a new function that he calls "the real," a category that appears in the nineteenth century. The innovative nature of this feature of the novel can be seen in the comments of Balzac's narrator who wants to assure the reader that the details in his work are both real and necessary to the story. After Balzac, the "real" entered into the system of verisimilitude that is available to the reader and the justification for such "superfluous" material was no longer necessary. In most novels during this period "the real" is just such an innocuous category that does not raise the problematic nature of the representation nor the relationship of the characters to these objects. The description in *L'Education,* however, breaks this category by overloading it with objects that hover outside the discourse of the characters.

Flaubert's text thus brings into conflict two models of understanding that dominate the nineteenth century—observation and narrative. In "Narrate or Describe?" Georg Lukács condemns Flaubert and Zola for replacing narration with description so that objects do not become part of the actions of the characters, as in Balzac and Tolstoy: "The description of things no longer has anything to do with the lives of the characters." The result is that "description merely levels" and "contemporizes everything," whereas "narration recounts the past." Although I do not follow Lukács's call for a centered narrative, his analysis brings Flaubert's text to crisis. That is, by interrogating the text in terms of narrative, Lukács asks us to consider the way the text's description presents unrepresentable social and economic forces through these objects, objects that cannot be represented in narrative. Listing objects calls up their tangled histories and opens a fissure between observation and mastery. However, the importance of this fissure cannot be reduced to the modernist reading, in which Flaubert violates the generic patterns of the classic realist text. Rather, the text's description—as well as other features—also makes the novel available to a postmodern reading, in which representability and narration are thematized.

The simple naming of objects in the language of perception is called into question. In these evocations of matter, the reference to things opens a hole in signification. Barthes describes this power of reference: "The best way for a language to be indirect is to refer as constantly as possible to objects and not to their concepts." In these passages the language of perception is not just relativized through the point of view, but is given an ontological force that overwhelms the characters and their language. In his essay "Wittgenstein's Problem," Maurice Blanchot discusses Flaubert's struggle with language, with "l'Autre de la parole":

> Now, ever since Mallarmé we have felt that the other of language is always posed by the language itself as that in which it looks for a way out, in order to disappear into it, or for an Outside, in which to be reflected. Which means not simply that the Other is already part of *this* language, but that as soon as this language turns around to respond to its Other, it is turning towards another language, and we must be aware that this other language is other, and also that it, too, has its Other. At this point we come very close to Wittgenstein's problem, as

corrected by Bertrand Russell: that every language has a structure about which one can say nothing *in* that language, but that there must be another language dealing with the structure of the first and possessing a new structure about which one cannot say anything except in a third language—and so forth. Several consequences follow from this, among them these: 1) what is inexpressible is inexpressible in relation to a certain system of expression; 2) although there may be reason to regard the group of things and values as constituting a whole (for example, in a given scientific conception . . .), the virtual group of the different possibilities of speech could not constitute a totality; 3) the Other of all speech is never anything but the Other of a given speech or else the *infinite movement* through which one mode of expression—always prepared to extend itself in the multiple requirements of simultaneous series—fights itself, exalts itself, challenges itself or obliterates itself in some other mode.

These evocations of things in *L'Education* do not indicate the triumph of the designative power of language to fix the world but the presence of the unknown in language, objects, and consciousness. Physical objects resemble the space of Beckett's plays (particularly *Krapp's Last Tape* and *Happy Days*), where the staging solicits and crushes human speech and desire. Moreover, in Flaubert's text as in these plays, matter is not securely outside the subject; rather, it invades consciousness and speech.

The setting is not just composed of objects that are named by a subjectless text. It is also composed of historical names. The originality of the role of these names in *L'Education* emerges clearly against the use of these names in *Les Illusions perdues*. Historical names appear extensively in Balzac's novel, and they serve to link the narrator's discourse to the historical world outside. Authors' names are sometimes used in the narrator's address to the reader, in which reference to this common known entity helps the reader to understand the representation. For example, in the description of Nicolas Séchard, we read: "His cranium, completely bald on top, though it was still fringed with greying curls, called to mind the Franciscan friars in La Fontaine's *Tales*." To help us grasp Lucien's disillusionment, the narrator invokes our knowledge of Rousseau and then secures the link between history, verisimilitude, and the text by asking us to assent to the probability and the naturalness of the feeling: "Losing his illusions about Madame de Bargeton while Madame de Bargeton was losing hers about him, the unhappy youth, whose destiny was a little like that of Jean-Jacques Rousseau, imitated him in this respect: he was fascinated by Madame d'Espard and fell in love with her immediately. Men who are young or who remember the emotions of their youth will understand that this passion was extremely likely and natural."

This kind of reference between narrator and reader, which almost never appears in *L'Education,* helps establish the appropriation of history by the text. The narrator speaks of historical figures in the same way as he does of characters. In addition, historical names play a prominent role in the story itself, both in the narrator's exposition and in the characters' own speech, not just in the extradiegetic language of the narrator. In the portrait of Meyraux, one of the members of the Cénacle, the narrator tells us that this character "died after initiating the famous discussion between Cuvier and Saint-Hilaire over a momentous question which was to divide the world of scientists into equal camps behind these two men of genius. He died some months before the former, who stood out for a narrow, analytical science as against the pantheistic Saint-Hilaire who is still alive and is revered in Germany." The narrator takes up historical authors and their ideas, masters them by his own language, and connects the time of their lives to the narrative instance. Moreover, the presence of historical authors is reinforced by their appearance in dialogue. Lucien and David discuss André Chénier and one of the lines that they read together appears in the text. Daniel d'Arthez criticizes Lucien for his imitation of Walter Scott: "If you don't want to ape Walter Scott you must invent a different manner for yourself, whereas you have imitated him." Thus, when the narrator describes Mme de Bargeton's hazy uncritical reading of romantic authors, a background that resembles that of Frédéric or Emma Bovary, he (the narrator) also assures us of the system of the "real" that surrounds her infection with these authors: "She worshipped Lord Byron, Jean-Jacques Rousseau and those who led poetic and dramatic lives."

In *L'Education sentimentale* historical names do not participate in the creation of an authoritarian language that englobes the text and absorbs history. On the contrary, these names participate in irrealization of history. One of the ways that this process operates is through listing and intermingling of authors so that their specific ideas are not only never articulated but are designated by a language that makes no differences among them: "he [Frédéric] prized passion above all else; Werther, René, Franck, Lara, Lelia, and other less distinguished writers roused him to almost equal enthusiasm." (This is also the case in *Madame Bovary,* where Emma's dreams are a mixture of various sources.) In the fascinating portrait of Sénécal, we learn that "he was familiar with Mably, Morelly, Fourier, Saint-Simon, Comte, Cabet, Louis Blanc," but what appears in his speech is indistinct: "out of this mixture he had evolved an ideal of virtuous democracy. . . ." In the dialogues, proper names are bandied about with little comprehension. At Frédéric's apartment, the talk turns to Malthus, but Cisy does not know who he is and the topic is dropped. Of the conversation at the café Alhambra, we read the following narration: "an argument followed which

touched on [*mêla*] Shakespeare, the censorship, style, the lower classes, the takings at the Porte-Saint-Martin, Alexandre Dumas, Victor Hugo, and Dumersan." (The French verb "mêler" indicates a confusion that Baldick's translation does not capture.) In all of these cases, historical names, like historical facts, are an eruption of the real in the text, and these allusions engage the reader's cultural knowledge only to dissipate the coherence of this knowledge in a cacophony of conflicting voices. The significations that these allusions bear are not ordered by an englobing voice as in *Les Illusions.* In Flaubert's text, historical allusions and objects are not part of a referentially secure discourse. The ideas that appear in the text do not "belong" to any authors, for these ideas are an anonymous melange of *lieux communs.* As Sartre says of Flaubert's *Dictionnaire des idées reçues:* "More than a thousand articles, and who feels attacked? No one." History's power to guarantee meaning, to serve as a referent for fiction, is shaken and reinscribed, so that both are deconstructed. Derrida describes the deconstructive project as a challenge to our assumptions about the relationship between text and reference, not as an assertion of the autoreferentiality of all texts: "What is produced in the current trembling is a reevaluation of the relationship between the general text and what was believed to be, in the form of reality (history, politics, economics, sexuality, etc.), the simple referable exterior of language or writing . . ." (*Positions*).

FURTHER READING

Cogny, Pierre. "Realism and Naturalism: Roots of the Twentieth Century," translated by Leslie Brittman and Will L. McLendon with Michel Bodin. In *L'Hénaurme Siècle: A Miscellany of Essays on Nineteenth-Century French Literature,* edited by Will L. McLendon, pp. 135-43. Heidelberg: Carl Winter Universitätsverlag, 1984.

> Traces the importance of the nineteeth-century French Realists to twentieth-century literature.

Cook, Malcolm. *Fictional France: Social Reality in the French Novel, 1775-1800.* Providence, R.I.: Berg, 1993, 169 p.

> Surveys the fictional representation of French society during the period immediately preceding and following the French Revolution.

Gaillard, Françoise. "The Great Illusion of Realism, or the Real as Representation." *Poetics Today: International Journal for the Theory and Analysis of Literature and Communication* 5, No. 4 (1984): 753-66.

> Questions the possibility that the real is "intrinsically capable of being known" or "mimetically representable" using examples from Flaubert's *Bouvard and Pécuchet.*

Griffin, Robert. *Rape of the Lock: Flaubert's Mythic Realism.* Lexington, Ky.: French Forum, Publishers, 1988, 391 p.

> Examines mythological substructures in the novels of Flaubert.

Jefferson, Ann. "Realism Reconsidered: Bakhtin's Dialogism and the 'Will to Reference.'" *Australian Journal of French Studies* XXIII, No. 2 (May-August 1986): 169-84.

> Argues that realism and self-consciousness are complementary, rather than contradictory, aspects of the novel.

Petrey, Sandy. *Realism and Revolution: Balzac, Stendhal, Zola, and the Performances of History.* Ithaca, N.Y.: Cornell University Press, 1988, 211 p.

> Argues that "the dilemmas of representation, far from being realism's blind spot, figure among its major narrative subjects."

Reid, James H. *Narration and Description in the French Realist Novel: The Temporality of Lying and Forgetting.* Cambridge: Cambridge University Press, 1993, 219 p.

> Studies "the difference, and fundamental incompatibility, between the narrative and descriptive modes of discourse" in nineteenth-century French fiction.

Schehr, Lawrence R. *Flaubert and Sons: Readings of Flaubert, Zola and Proust.* New York: Peter Lang, 1986, 268 p.

> Offers Post-structuralist interpretations of *Madame Bovary*, *Thérèse Raquin*, and *A la recherche du temps perdu*, dealing with the problem of representation in the realistic novel.

Schor, Naomi. *Breaking the Chain: Women, Theory, and French Realist Fiction.* New York: Columbia University Press, 1985, 203 p.

> Applies Feminist and Structuralist theories to an analysis of the representation of women in nineteenth-century French fiction.

The Lake Poets

INTRODUCTION

William Wordsworth, Samuel Taylor Coleridge, and Robert Southey became known as the Lake Poets in the early years of the nineteenth century when critic Francis Jeffrey conferred this designation on them. In an 1817 article published in *The Edinburgh Review*, Jeffrey referred to the three poets as belonging to the "Lake School." The term refers to the Lake District of England, where all three poets resided for a time.

Jeffrey began writing about the group of poets as early as 1802. In a review of Southey's *Thalaba* (1801), Jeffrey began his harsh criticism of a "sect" of poets that included Southey, Coleridge, and Wordsworth. Attributing a number of characteristics to the writings of the Lake Poets, Jeffrey argued that their work was based on anti-social principles and that while it reflected the simplicity and energy inspired by nature, it was also both harsh and quaint in its use of "ordinary" language and themes. Other critics, including Thomas De Quincey, have argued that there existed no such "school" of poetry. According to these critics, the Lake Poets shared only friendship and brief periods of collaboration, not similar philosophies or poetic styles.

Southey and Coleridge met in 1794, at Balliol College in Oxford. There they hatched a plan to create a Utopian community in America called "Pantisocracy." They collaborated on works that reflected their radical political beliefs, such as the drama *The Fall of Robespierre* (1794). Southey soon gave up on their political agenda, and Coleridge terminated the friendship. The two were married to sisters, however, and these familial bonds soon encouraged the poets to reconcile.

By 1797, Coleridge had begun a close friendship with Wordsworth. They worked together closely in and near both the Lake District home that Wordsworth shared with his sister Dorothy and Coleridge's nearby residence. Together they wrote *Lyrical Ballads* (1798), a collection of poetry that was prefaced by a statement of Wordsworth's poetic theory and that helped define the Romantic Movement. During this period, the two poets influenced each other greatly, with Coleridge encouraging Wordsworth to explore philosophic poetry and Wordsworth offering Coleridge his insights and perspectives on nature.

As Coleridge's relationship with Wordsworth continued to develop, Southey's and Coleridge's friendship cooled. Even so, Southey and his wife took up residence with Coleridge and his family in Keswick, a part of the Lake District, in 1803. This was a time of increasing marital discord for Coleridge. During this period, Coleridge traveled extensively and lived with the Wordsworths for several years. Meanwhile, Southey helped raise Coleridge's children, frequently admonishing Coleridge to stop using opium and to write with some regularity in order to provide for his family.

Despite their distinctly different styles and philosophies, Coleridge, Southey, and Wordsworth are all considered Romantic poets. The Romantic fascination with the unusual and the supernatural is reflected in many of the works of Coleridge and Southey, most notably in Coleridge's *The Rime of the Ancient Mariner* (1798). Wordsworth and Coleridge both possessed an active imagination as well as a strong sense of perception. While Wordsworth used his imaginative powers to idealize the familiar, Coleridge explored the philosophical aspects of poetry. Southey's Romantic efforts centered on travel and adventure. He used exotic historical settings, such as Spain and the Orient, in his examination of the mythic and supernatural, but on the whole he was regarded more for his prose and literary criticism than for his poetry.

The connection of the Lake Poets to Romanticism also encompassed a love of liberty and radical political convictions. The poets had, to varying degrees, sympathized with the French Revolution, believing that France was Europe's champion of liberty. Immersed in their love and worship of nature, the Lake Poets also believed in the spirit of reform through revolution, while maintaining that the union of the soul with nature was of primary importance. During the end of the eighteenth century and the early years of the nineteenth century, they were sheltered from the affairs of the world in their Lake Country homes. But in the aftermath of the French Revolution they began to regain interest in worldly events, and their attitudes became increasingly conservative. Their early revolutionary fervor was severely diminished and their hopes for France dashed as the nation, under Napoleon's rule, began conquering other countries. Their love of liberty was transformed into nationalism as they became convinced that England's constitutional monarchy and the guiding force of the Protestant Church were the only guarantors of freedom.

This transition of the Lake Poets to conservatism has been a major focus of study by twentieth century critics. Hoxie Neal Fairchild and others have attributed the change primarily to the Lake Poets' reaction to the French Revolution and its aftermath. Fairchild has also suggested that the transition was part of a greater maturation process and that personal events in each of the poets' lives may have influenced their growing conservatism. These incidents include the death of Wordsworth's brother and Coleridge's immersion in German philosophy as well as his battle with opium addiction. While nineteenth-century critics such as George Brandes have condemned the Lake Poets as traitors to liberty, most recent critics have found a number of justifications for the shift from liberalism to conservatism.

Another area of interest for recent scholars has been the relationship of the Lake Poets to each other and to their contemporaries. Critics such as Earl Leslie Griggs, Malcolm Elwin, and Raimonda Modiano have focused their attention on the Lake Poets' opinions of each other, and on the intense collaboration between Wordsworth and Coleridge. The debate centering on Wordsworth's and Coleridge's relationship continues, with scholars questioning which poet more strongly influenced the other.

REPRESENTATIVE WORKS

Samuel Taylor Coleridge
  †"This Lime-Tree Bower My Prison" (poem) 1798
  †*The Rime of the Ancient Mariner* (poem) 1798

Robert Southey
  ‡*The Fall of Robespierre* (drama) 1794
  Thalaba (poem) 1801

William Wordsworth
  ‡*Lyrical Ballads* (poetry) 1798
  †"Lines composed a few miles above Tintern Abbey" (poem) 1798

†First appeared in *Lyrical Ballads*
‡Collaboration with Coleridge

CHARACTERISTICS OF THE LAKE POETS AND THEIR WORKS

Francis Jeffrey

SOURCE: A review of *Thalaba, the Destroyer,* in *The Edinburgh Review,* Vol. I, No. I, October, 1802, pp. 63-83.

[In the following excerpt, Jeffrey identifies Southey as one of a "sect of poets" that included Wordsworth and Coleridge, and offers a harsh assessment of this group and its aim to focus on "ordinary" language and themes.]

Poetry has this much, at least, in common with religion, that its standards were fixed long ago, by certain inspired writers, whose authority it is no longer lawful to call in question; and that many profess to be entirely devoted to it, who have no *good works* to produce in support of their pretensions. The catholic poetical church, too, has worked but few miracles since the first ages of its establishment; and has been more prolific, for a long time, of doctors than of saints: it has had its corruptions, and reformation also, and has given birth to an infinite variety of heresies and errors, the followers of which have hated and persecuted each other as cordially as other bigots.

The author who is now before us, [Robert Southey] belongs to a *sect* of poets, that has established itself in this country within these ten or twelve years and is looked upon, we believe, as one of its chief champions and apostles. The peculiar doctrines of this sect, it would not, perhaps, be very easy to explain; but, that they are *dissenters* from the established systems in poetry and criticism, is admitted, and proved indeed, by the whole tenor of their compositions. Though they lay claim, we believe, to a creed and a revelation of their own, there can be little doubt, that their doctrines are of *German* origin, and have been derived from some of the great modern reformers in that country. Some of their leading principles, indeed, are probably of an earlier date, and seem to have been borrowed from the great apostle of Geneva. As Mr. Southey is the first author of this persuasion, that has yet been brought before us for judgment, we cannot discharge our inquisitorial office conscientiously, without premising a few words upon the nature and tendency of the tenets he has helped to promulgate.

The disciples of this school boast much of its originality, and seem to value themselves very highly, for having broken loose from the bondage of ancient authority, and re-asserted the independence of genius. Originality, however, we are persuaded, is rarer than mere alteration; and a man may change a good master for a bad one, without finding himself at all nearer to independence. That our new poets have abandoned the old models, may certainly be admitted; but we have not been able to discover that they have yet created any models of their own; and are very much inclined to call in question the worthiness of those to which they have transferred their admiration. The productions of this school, we conceive, are so far from being entitled to the praise of originality, that they cannot be better characterised, than by an enumeration of the sources from which their materials have been derived.

The greatest part of them, we apprehend, will be found to be composed of the following elements: 1. The antisocial principles, and distempered sensibility of Rousseau—his discontent with the present constitution of society—his paradoxical morality, and his perpetual hankerings after some unattainable state of voluptuous virtue and perfection. 2. The simplicity and energy (*horresco referens*) of Kotzebue and Schiller. 3. The homeliness and harshness of some of Cowper's language and versification, interchanged occasionally with the *innocence* of Ambrose Philips, or the quaintness of Quarles and Dr. Donne. From the diligent study of these few originals, we have no doubt that an entire art of poetry may be collected, by the assistance of which the very *gentlest* of our readers may soon be qualified to compose a poem as correctly versified as *Thalaba,* and to deal out sentiment and description, with all the sweetness of Lambe, and all the magnificence of Coleridge.

The authors of whom we are now speaking, have, among them, unquestionably, a very considerable portion of poetical talent, and have, consequently, been enabled to seduce many into an admiration of the false taste (as it appears to us) in which most of these productions are composed. They constitute, at present, the most formidable conspiracy that has lately been formed against sound judgment in matters poetical; and are entitled to a larger share of our censorial notice, than could be spared for an individual delinquent. We shall hope for the indulgence of our readers, therefore, in taking this opportunity to inquire a little more particularly into their merits, and to make a few remarks upon those peculiarities which seem to be regarded by their admirers as the surest proofs of their excellence.

Their most distinguishing symbol, is undoubtedly an affectation of great simplicity and familiarity of language. They disdain to make use of the common poetical phraseology, or to ennoble their diction by a selection of fine or dignified expressions. There would be too much *art* in this, for that great love of nature with which they are all of them inspired; and their sentiments, they are determined shall be indebted, for their effect, to nothing but their intrinsic tenderness or elevation. There is something very noble and conscientious, we will confess, in this plan of composition; but the misfortune is, that there are passages in all poems that can neither be pathetic nor sublime; and that, on these occasions, a neglect of the establishments of language is very apt to produce absolute meanness and insipidity. The language of passion, indeed, can scarcely be deficient in elevation; and when an author is wanting in that particular, he may commonly be presumed to have failed in the truth, as well as in the dignity of his expression. The case, however, is extremely different with the subordinate parts of a composition; with the narrative and description, that are necessary to preserve its connexion; and the explanation, that must frequently prepare us for the great scenes and splendid passages. In these, all the requisite ideas may be conveyed, with sufficient clearness, by the meanest and most negligent expressions; and, if magnificence or beauty is ever to be observed in them, it must have been introduced from some other motive than that of adapting the style to the subject. It is in such passages, accordingly, that we are most frequently offended with low and inelegant expressions; and that the language, which was intended to be simple and natural, is found oftenest to degenerate into mere slovenliness and vulgarity. It is in vain, too, to expect that the meanness of those parts may be redeemed by the excellence of others. A poet who aims at all at sublimity or pathos, is like an actor in a high tragic character, and must sustain his dignity throughout, or become altogether ridiculous. We are apt enough to laugh at the mock-majesty of those whom we know to be but common mortals in private; and cannot permit Hamlet to make use of a single provincial intonation, although it should only be in his conversation with the grave-diggers.

The followers of simplicity are, therefore, at all times in danger of occasional degradation; but the simplicity of this new school seems intended to ensure it. *Their* simplicity does not consist, by any means, in the rejection of glaring or superfluous ornament,—in the substitution of elegance to splendour,—or in that refinement of art which seeks concealment in its own perfection. It consists, on the contrary, in a very great degree, in the positive and *bona fide* rejection of art altogether, and in the bold use of those rude and negligent expressions, which would be banished by a little discrimination. One of their own authors, indeed, has very ingeniously set forth, (in a kind of manifesto, that preceded one of their most flagrant acts of hostility), that it was their capital object 'to adapt to the uses of poetry, the ordinary language of conversation among the middling and lower orders of the people' [William Wordsworth, in the Preface to *Lyrical Ballads*]. What advantages are to be gained by the success of this project, we confess ourselves unable to conjecture. The language of the higher and more cultivated orders may fairly be presumed to be better than that of their inferiors; at any rate, it has all those associations in its favour, by means of which a style can ever appear beautiful or exalted, and is adapted to the purposes of poetry, by having been long consecrated to its use. The language of the vulgar, on the other hand, has all the opposite associations to contend with; and must seem unfit for poetry, (if there were no other reason), merely because it has scarcely ever been employed in it. A great genius may indeed overcome these disadvantages; but we scarcely conceive that he should court them. We may excuse a certain homeliness of language in the productions of a ploughman or a milkwoman; but we cannot bring ourselves to admire it in an author, who has had occasion to indite odes to his college-bell, and inscribe hymns to the Penates.

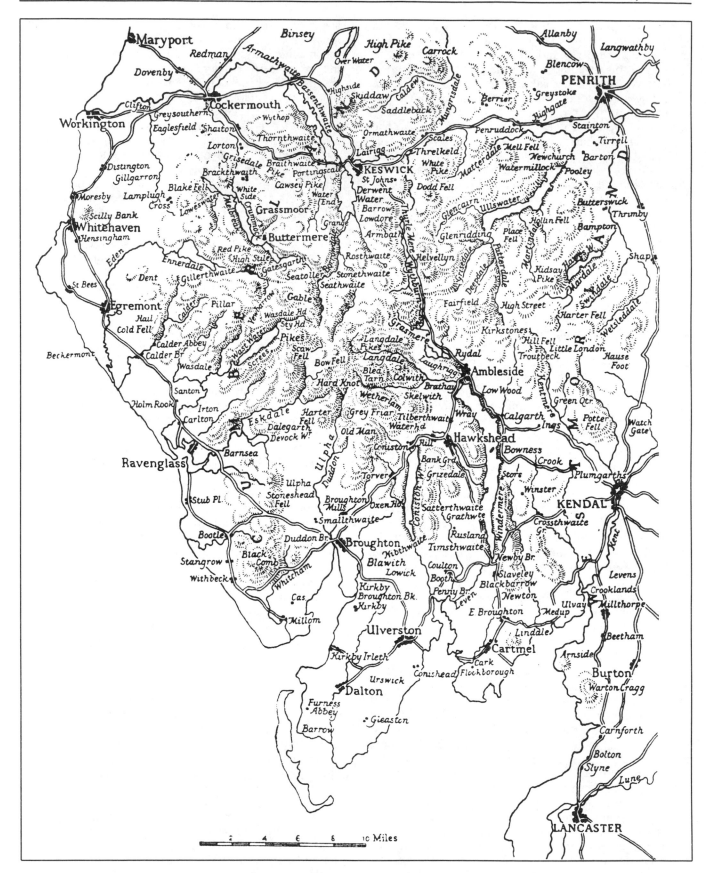

Map of England's Lake District, by K. C. Jordan.

But the mischief of this new system is not confined to the depravation of language only; it extends to the sentiments and emotions; and leads to the debasement of all those feelings which poetry is designed to communicate. It is absurd to suppose, that an author should make use of the language of the vulgar to express the sentiments of the refined. His professed object, in employing that language, is to bring his compositions nearer to the true standard of nature; and his intention to copy the sentiments of the lower orders, is implied in his resolution to make use of their style. Now, the different classes of society have each of them a distinct character, as well as a separate idiom; and the names of the various passions to which they are subject respectively, have a signification that varies essentially, according to the condition of the persons to whom they are applied. The love, or grief, or indignation of an enlightened and refined character, is not only expressed in a different language, but is in itself a different emotion from the love, or grief, or anger of a clown, a tradesman, or a market-wench. The things themselves are radically and obviously distinct; and the representation of them is calculated to convey a very different train of sympathies and sensations to the mind. The question, therefore, comes simply to be—Which of them is the most proper object for poetical imitation? It is needless for us to answer a question, which the practice of all the world has long ago decided irrevocably. The poor and vulgar may interest us, in poetry, by their *situation;* but never, we apprehend, by any sentiments that are peculiar to their condition, and still less by any language that is characteristic of it. The truth is, that it is impossible to copy their diction or their sentiments correctly, in a serious composition; and this, not merely because poverty makes men ridiculous, but because just taste and refined sentiment are rarely to be met with among the uncultivated part of mankind; and a language fitted for their expression, can still more rarely form any part of their 'ordinary conversation.'

The low-bred heroes, and interesting rustics of poetry, have no sort of affinity to the real vulgar of this world; they are imaginary beings, whose characters and language are in contrast with their situation; and please those who can be pleased with them, by the marvellous, and not by the nature of such a combination. In serious poetry, a man of the middling or lower order *must necessarily* lay aside a great deal of his ordinary language; he must avoid errors in grammar and orthography; and steer clear of the cant of particular professions, and of every impropriety that is ludicrous or disgusting: nay, he must speak in good verse, and observe all the graces in prosody and collocation. After all this, it may not be very easy to say how we are to find him out to be a low man, or what marks can remain of the ordinary language of conversation in the inferior orders of society. If there be any phrases that are not used in good society, they will appear as blem-

ishes in the composition, no less palpably than errors in syntax or quantity; and if there be no such phrases, the style cannot be characteristic of that condition of life, the language of which it professes to have adopted. All approximation to that language, in the same manner, implies a deviation from that purity and precision, which no one, we believe, ever violated spontaneously.

It has been argued, indeed, (for men will argue in support of what they do not venture to practise), that, as the middling and lower orders of society constitute by far the greater part of mankind, so, their feelings and expressions should interest more extensively, and may be taken, more fairly than any other, for the standards of what is natural and true. To this, it seems obvious to answer, that the arts that aim at exciting admiration and delight, do not take their models from what is ordinary, but from what is excellent; and that our interest in the representation of any event, does not depend upon our familiarity with the original, but on its intrinsic importance, and the celebrity of the parties it concerns. The sculptor employs his art in delineating the graces of Antinous or Apollo, and not in the representation of those ordinary forms that belong to the crowd of his admirers. When a chieftain perishes in battle, his followers mourn more for him than for thousands of their equals that may have fallen around him.

After all, it must be admitted, that there is a class of persons (we are afraid they cannot be called *readers*), to whom the representation of vulgar manners, in vulgar language, will afford much entertainment. We are afraid, however, that the ingenious writers who supply the hawkers and ballad-singers, have very nearly monopolized that department, and are probably better qualified to hit the taste of their customers, than Mr. Southey, or any of his brethren, can yet pretend to be. To fit them for the higher task of original composition, it would not be amiss if they were to undertake a translation of Pope or Milton into the vulgar tongue, for the benefit of those children of nature.

There is another disagreeable effect of this affected simplicity, which, though of less importance than those which have been already noticed, it may yet be worth while to mention: This is, the extreme difficulty of supporting the same low tone of expression throughout, and the inequality that is consequently introduced into the texture of the composition. To an author of reading and education, it is a style that must always be assumed and unnatural, and one from which he will be perpetually tempted to deviate. He will rise, therefore, every now and then, above the level to which he has professedly degraded himself; and make amends for that transgression by a fresh effort of descension. His composition, in short, will be like that of a person who is attempting to speak in an obsolete or provincial dialect; he will betray himself by expressions of occasional purity and elegance, and exert himself to efface that impression, by passages of unnatural meanness or absurdity. . . .

Thomas De Quincey

SOURCE: "Southey, Wordsworth, and Coleridge: From 1807 to 1830," in *Reminiscences of the English Lake Poets,* 1839. Reprint by J. M. Dent & Sons, Ltd., 1907, pp. 189-201.

[*In this essay De Quincey offers his reflections on the personalities of Southey, Wordsworth, and Coleridge, and compares their poetic styles and philosophical views.*]

A circumstance which, as much as anything, expounded to the very eye the characteristic distinctions between Wordsworth and Southey, and would not suffer a stranger to forget it for a moment, was the insignificant place and consideration allowed to the small book-collection of the former, contrasted with the splendid library of the latter. The two or three hundred volumes of Wordsworth occupied a little, homely, painted book-case, fixed into one of two shallow recesses, formed on each side of the fireplace by the projection of the chimney in the little sitting-room up-stairs, which he had already described as his half kitchen and half parlour. They were ill bound, or not bound at all—in boards, sometimes in tatters; many were imperfect as to the number of volumes, mutilated as to the number of pages; sometimes, where it seemed worth while, the defects being supplied by manuscript; sometimes not: in short, everything showed that the books were for use, and not for show; and their limited amount showed that their possessor must have independent sources of enjoyment to fill up the major part of his time. In reality, when the weather was tolerable, I believe that Wordsworth rarely resorted to his books, (unless, perhaps, to some little pocket edition of a poet, which accompanied him in his rambles,) except in the evenings, or after he had tired himself by walking. On the other hand, Southey's collection occupied a separate room, the largest, and, every way, the most agreeable in the house; and this room was styled, and not ostentatiously, (for it really merited that name,) the library. The house itself, Greta Hall, stood upon a little eminence, (as I have before mentioned,) overhanging the river Greta. There was nothing remarkable in its internal arrangements: in all respects, it was a very plain unadorned family dwelling; large enough, by a little contrivance, to accommodate two or, in some sense, three families, viz. Mr. Southey, and *his* family; Mr. Coleridge, and *his;* together with Mrs. Lovell, who, when her son was with her, might be said to compose a third. Mrs. Coleridge, Mrs. Southey, and Mrs. Lovell were sisters; all having come originally from Bristol; and, as the different sets of children in this one house

had each three several aunts, all the ladies, by turns, assuming that relation twice over, it was one of Southey's many amusing jests, to call the hill on which Greta Hall was placed, the *ant-hill.* Mrs. Lovell was the widow of Mr. Robert Lovell, who had published a volume of poems, in conjunction with Southey, somewhere about the year 1797, under the signatures of Bion and Moschus. This lady, having only one son, did not require any large suite of rooms; and the less so, as her son quitted her, at an early age, to pursue a professional education. The house had therefore been divided (not by absolute partition, into two distinct apartments, but by an amicable distribution of rooms) between the two families of Mr. Coleridge and Mr. Southey; Mr. Coleridge had a separate study, which was distinguished by nothing except by an organ amongst its furniture, and by a magnificent view from its window, (or windows,) if that could be considered a distinction, in a situation whose local necessities presented you with magnificent objects in whatever direction you might happen to turn your eyes. In the morning, the two families might live apart; but they met at dinner, and in a common drawing-room; and Southey's library, in both senses of the word, was placed at the service of all the ladies alike. However, they did not intrude upon him, except in cases where they wished for a larger reception room, or a more interesting place for suggesting the topics of conversation. Interesting this room was, indeed, and in a degree not often rivalled. The library—the collection of books, I mean, which formed the most conspicuous part of its furniture within—was in all senses a good one. The books were chiefly English, Spanish, and Portuguese; well selected, being the great cardinal classics of the three literatures; fine copies, and decorated externally with a reasonable elegance, so as to make them in harmony with the other embellishments of the room. This effect was aided by the horizontal arrangement upon brackets, of many rare manuscripts—Spanish or Portuguese. Made thus gay within, this room stood in little need of attractions from without. Yet, even upon the gloomiest day of winter, the landscape from the different windows was too permanently commanding in its grandeur, too essentially independent of the seasons or the pomp of woods, to fail in fascinating the gaze of the coldest and dullest of spectators. The lake of Derwent Water in one direction, with its lovely islands—a lake about ten miles in circuit, and shaped pretty much like a boy's kite; the lake of Bassinthwaite in another; the mountains of Newlands arranging themselves like pavilions; the gorgeous confusion of Borrowdale just revealing its sublime chaos through the narrow vista of its gorge; all these objects lay in different angles to the front; whilst the sullen rear, not fully visible on this side of the house, was closed for many a league by the vast and towering masses of Skiddaw and Blencathara—mountains which are rather to be considered as frontier barriers, and chains of hilly ground, cutting the county of Cumberland into great chambers and different climates, than as insulated eminences; so vast is the area which they occupy; though there *are* also such separate and insulated heights, and nearly amongst the highest in the country. Southey's lot had therefore fallen, locally considered, into a goodly heritage. This grand panorama of mountain scenery, so varied, so expansive, and yet having the delightful feeling about it of a deep seclusion and dell-like sequestration from the world—a feeling which, in the midst of so expansive an area, spread out below his windows, could not have been sustained by any barriers less elevated than Glaramara, Skiddaw, or (which could be also described) "the mighty Helvellyn and Catchedicam;" this congregation of hill and lake, so wide, and yet so prison-like, in its separation from all beyond it, lay for ever under the eyes of Southey. His position locally and, in some respects, intellectually reminded one of Gibbon: but with great advantage in the comparison to Southey. The little town of Keswick and its adjacent lake bore something of the same relation to mighty London that Geneva and its lake may be thought to bear towards brilliant Paris. Southey, like Gibbon, was a miscellaneous scholar; he, like Gibbon, of vast historical research; he, like Gibbon, signally industrious, and patient, and elaborate in collecting the materials for his historical works. Like Gibbon, he had dedicated a life of competent ease, in a pecuniary sense, to literature; like Gibbon, he had gathered to the shores of a beautiful lake, remote from great capitals, a large, or, at least, sufficient library; (in each case, I believe, the library ranged, as to numerical amount, between seven and ten thousand;) and, like Gibbon, he was the most accomplished litterateur amongst the erudite scholars of his time, and the most of an erudite scholar amongst the accomplished litterateurs. After all these points of agreement known, it remains as a pure advantage on the side of Southey— a mere *lucro ponatur*—that he was a poet; and, by all men's confession, a respectable poet, brilliant in his descriptive powers, and fascinating in his narration, however much he might want of

"The vision and the faculty divine."

It is remarkable amongst the series of parallelisms that have been or might be pursued between two men, both had the honour of retreating from a parliamentary life; Gibbon, after some silent and inert experience of that warfare; Southey, with a prudent foresight of the ruin to his health and literary usefulness, won from the experience of his nearest friends.

I took leave of Southey in 1807, at the descent into the vale of Legbesthwaite, as I have already noticed. One year afterwards, I became a permanent resident in his neighbourhood; and, although, on various accounts, my intercourse with him was at no time very strict, partly from the very uncongenial constitution of my own mind, and the different direction of my studies, partly from

my reluctance to levy any tax on time so precious and so fully employed, I was yet on such terms for the next ten or eleven years, that I might, in a qualified sense, call myself his friend.

[The Lake Poets] were obstinately bent upon learning nothing; they were all alike too proud to acknowledge that any man knew better than they, unless it were upon some purely professional subject, or some art remote from all intellectual bearings, such as conferred no honour in its possession.

—Thomas De Quincey

Yes! there were long years through which Southey might respect me, I *him*. But the years came—for I have lived too long, reader, in relation to many things! and the report of me would have been better, or more uniform at least, had I died some twenty years ago— the years came in which circumstances made me an Opium-Eater; years through which a shadow as of sad eclipse sate and rested upon my faculties; years through which I was careless of all but those who lived within *my* inner circle, within "my hearts of hearts"; years— ah! heavenly years!—through which I lived, beloved, *with* thee, *to* thee, *for* thee, *by* thee! Ah! happy, happy years! in which I was a mere football of reproach, but in which every wind and sounding hurricane of wrath or contempt flew by like chasing enemies past some defying gates of adamant, and left me too blessed in thy smiles—angel of life!—to heed the curses or the mocking which sometimes I heard raving outside of our impregnable Eden. What any man said of me in those days, what he thought, did I ask? did I care? Then it was, or nearly then, that I ceased to see, ceased to hear of Southey; as much abstracted from all which concerned the world outside, and from the Southeys, or even the Coleridges, in its van, as though I had lived with the darlings of my heart in the centre of Canadian forests, and all men else in the centre of Hindostan.

But, before I part from Greta Hall and its distinguished master, one word let me say, to protect myself from the imputation of sharing in some peculiar opinions of Southey with respect to political economy, which have been but too familiar to the world; and some opinions of the world, hardly less familiar, with respect to Southey himself and his accomplishments. Probably, with respect to the first, before this paper will be made public, I shall have sufficiently vindicated my own opinions in these matters by a distinct treatment of some great questions which lie at the base of all sound political economy; above all, the radical question of value, upon which no man has ever seen the full truth except Mr. Ricardo; and, unfortunately, he had but little of the *polemic* skill which is required to meet the errors of his opponents. For it is noticeable, that the most conspicuous of those opponents, viz. Mr. Malthus, though too much, I fear, actuated by a spirit of jealousy, and, therefore, likely enough to have scattered sophistry and disingenuous quibbling over the subject, had no need whatever of any further confusion for darkening and perplexing his themes than what inevitably belonged to his own most chaotic understanding. He and Say, the Frenchman, were both plagued by understandings of the same quality—having a clear vision in shallow waters, and this misleading them into the belief that they saw with equal clearness through the remote and the obscure; whereas, universally, their acuteness is like that of Hobbes—the gift of shallowness, and the result of *not* being subtle or profound enough to apprehend the true *locus* of the difficulty; and the barriers, which to them limit the view, and give to it, together with the contraction, all the distinctness and definite outline of limitation, are, in nine cases out of ten, the product of their own defective and aberrating vision, and not real barriers at all. Meantime, until I write fully and deliberately upon this subject, I shall observe simply, that all "the Lake Poets," as they are called, were not only in error, but most presumptuously in error, upon these subjects. They were ignorant of every principle belonging to every question alike in political economy, and they were obstinately bent upon learning nothing; they were all alike too proud to acknowledge that any man knew better than they, unless it were upon some purely professional subject, or some art remote from all intellectual bearings, such as conferred no honour in its possession. Wordsworth was the least tainted with error upon political economy; and that because he rarely applied his thoughts to any question of that nature, and, in fact, despised every study of a moral or political aspect unless it drew its materials from such revelations of truth as could be won from the *prima philosophia* of human nature approached with the poet's eye. Coleridge was the one whom Nature and his own multifarious studies had the best qualified for thinking justly on a theme such as this; but he also was shut out from the possibility of knowledge by presumption, and the habit of despising all the analytic studies of his own day—a habit for which he certainly had some warrant in the peculiar feebleness of all that has offered itself for *philosophy* in modern England. In particular, the religious discussions of the age, which touch inevitably at every point upon the profounder philosophy of man and his constitution, had laid bare the weakness of his own age to Coleridge's eye; and, because all was hollow and trivial in this direction, he chose to think that it was so in every other. And hence he has laid himself open to the just scoffs of persons far inferior to himself. In a foot-note in some late

number of *The Westminster Review,* it is most truly asserted, (not in these words, but to this effect,) that Coleridge's *Table Talk* exhibits a superannuation of error fit only for two centuries before. And what gave peculiar point to this display of ignorance was, that Coleridge did not, like Wordsworth, dismiss political economy from his notice, disdainfully, as a puerile tissue of truisms, or of falsehoods not less obvious, but actually addressed himself to the subject; fancied he had made discoveries in the science; and even promised us a systematic work on its whole compass.

To give a sample of this new and reformed political economy, it cannot well be necessary to trouble the reader with more than one chimera culled from those which Mr. Coleridge first brought forward in his early model of *The Friend.* He there propounds, as an original hypothesis of his own, that taxation never burthens a people, or, as a mere possibility, *can* burthen a people, simply by its amount. And why? Surely it draws from the purse of him who pays the quota a sum which it may be very difficult or even ruinous for him to pay, were it no more important in a public point of view than as so much deducted from his own unproductive expenditure, and which may happen to have even a national importance if it should chance to be deducted from the funds destined to productive industry. What is Mr. Coleridge's answer to these little objections? Why, thus: the latter case he evades entirely, apparently not adverting to it as a case in any respect distinguished from the other; and this other— how is *that* answered? Doubtless, says Mr. Coleridge, it may be inconvenient to John or Samuel that a sum of money, otherwise disposable for their own separate uses, should be abstracted for the purchase of bayonets or grapeshot; but with this the public, the commonwealth, have nothing to do, any more than with the losses at a gaming-table, where A's loss is B's gain— the total funds of the nation remaining exactly the same. It is, in fact, nothing but the accidental distribution of the funds which is affected—possibly for the worse, (no other "worse," however, is contemplated than shifting it into hands less deserving,) but, also, by possibility, for the better: and the better and the worse may be well supposed, in the long run, to balance each other. And that this is Mr. Coleridge's meaning cannot be doubted, upon looking into his illustrative image in support of it: he says that money raised by Government in the shape of taxes is like moisture exhaled from the earth—doubtless, for the moment, injurious to the crops, but re-acting abundantly for their final benefit when returning in the shape of showers. So natural, so obvious, so inevitable, by the way, is this conceit, (or, to speak less harshly, this hypothesis,) and so equally natural, obvious, and inevitable is the illustration from the abstraction and restoration of moisture, the exhalations and rains which affect this earth of ours, like the systole and the diastole of the heart, the flux and reflux of the ocean, that precisely the same doctrine, and precisely the same exemplification of the doctrine, is to be found in a Parliamentary speech, of some orator in the famous Long Parliament, about the year 1642. And to my mind it was a bitter humiliation, to find, about 150 years afterwards, in a shallow French work, the famous *"Compte Rendu"* of the French Chancellor of the Exchequer (Comptroller of the Finances)—Neckar—in that work, most humiliating it was to me, on a certain day, that I found this idle Coleridgian fantasy, not merely repeated, as it had been by scores—not merely anticipated by full twenty and two years, so that these French people had been beforehand with him, and had made Coleridge, to all appearance, their plagiarist, but also (hear it, ye gods!) answered, satisfactorily refuted, by this very feeble old sentimentalist, Neckar. Yes; positively Neckar, the slip-shod old system-fancier and political driveller, had been so much above falling into the shallow snare, that he had, on sound principles, exposed its specious delusions. Coleridge, the subtlest of men, in his proper walk, had brought forward, as a novel hypothesis of his own, in 1810, what Neckar, the rickety old Charlatan, had scarcely condescended, in a hurried foot-note, to expose as a vulgar error and the shallowest of sophisms, in 1787-88. There was another enormous blunder which Coleridge was constantly authorizing, both in his writings and his conversation. Quoting a passage from Sir James Stuart, in which he speaks of a vine-dresser as adding nothing to the public wealth, unless his labour did something more than replace his own consumption—that is, unless it reproduced it together with a profit; he asks contemptuously, whether the happiness and moral dignity that may have been exhibited in the vine-dresser's family are to pass for nothing? And then he proceeds to abuse the economists, because they take no account of such important considerations. Doubtless these are invaluable elements of social grandeur, in a *total* estimate of those elements. But what has political economy to do with them, a science openly professing to insulate and to treat apart from all other constituents of national well-being, those which concern the production and circulation of wealth? So far from gaining anything by enlarging its field in the way demanded by Coleridge's critic, political economy would be as idly travelling out of the limits indicated and held forth in its very name, as if logic were to teach ethics, or ethics to teach diplomacy. With respect to the Malthusian doctrine of population, it is difficult to know who was the true proprietor of the arguments urged against it sometimes by Southey sometimes by Coleridge. Those used by Southey are chiefly to be found up and down *The Quarterly Review*. But a more elaborate attack was published by Hazlitt; and this must be supposed to speak the peculiar objections of Coleridge, for he was in the habit of charging Hazlitt with having pillaged his conversation, and occasionally garbled it throughout the whole of this book. One single argument there was, undoubtedly just, and it was one which others

Portrait of Thomas De Quincey.

stumbled upon no less than Coleridge, exposing the fallacy of the supposed different laws of increase for vegetable and animal life. But though this frail prop withdrawn took away from Mr. Malthus's theory all its scientific rigour, the main *practical* conclusions were still valid as respected any argument from the lakers; for the strongest of these arguments that ever came to my knowledge was a mere appeal—not *ad verecundiam,* in the ordinary sense of the phrase, but *ad honestatem,* as if it were shocking to the *honestum* of Roman ethics (the *honnêteté* of French minor ethics,) that the check derived from self-restraint should not be supposed amply competent to redress all the dangers from a redundant population, under any certain knowledge generally diffused that such dangers existed. But these are topics which it is sufficient in this place to have noticed, *currente calamo.* I was anxious however to protest against the probable imputation, that I, because generally so intense an admirer of these men, adopted their blind and hasty reveries in political economy.

There were (and perhaps more justly I might say there *are*) two other notions currently received about Southey, one of which is altogether erroneous, and the other true only in a limited sense. The first is, the belief that he belonged to what is known as the lake school in poetry; with respect to which all that I need say in this place, is involved in his own declaration frankly made to myself in Easedale, during the summer of 1812; that he considered Wordsworth's theory of poetic diction, and still more his principles as to the selection of subjects, and as to what constituted a poetic treatment, as founded on error. There is certainly some community of phraseology between Southey and the other lakers, naturally arising out of their joint reverence for Scriptural language: this was a field in which they met in common: else it shews but little discernment and power of valuing the essences of things, to have classed Southey in the same school with Wordsworth and Coleridge. The other popular notion about Southey, which I conceive to be expressed with much too little limitation, regards his style. He has been praised, and justly, for his plain, manly, unaffected English, until the parrot echoers of other men's judgments, who adopt all they relish with undistinguishing blindness, have begun to hold him up as a great master of his own language, and a classical model of fine composition. Now, if the error were only in the degree, it would not be worth while to notice it; but the truth is, that Southey's defects in this particular power, are as striking as his characteristic graces. Let a subject arise— and almost in any path, there is a ready possibility that it should—in which a higher tone is required, of splendid declamation, or of impassionate fervour, and Southey's style will immediately betray its want of the loftier qualities as flagrantly as it now asserts its powers in that unpretending form which is best suited to his level character of writing and his humbler choice of themes. It is to mistake the character of Southey's mind, which is elevated but not sustained by the higher modes of enthusiasm, to think otherwise. Were a magnificent dedication required, moving with a stately and measured solemnity, and putting forward some majestic pretensions, arising out of a long and laborious life; were a pleading required against some capital abuse of the earth—war, slavery, oppression in its thousand forms; were a *Defensio pro Populo Anglicano* required; Southey's is not the mind, and, by a necessary consequence, Southey's is not the style, for carrying such purposes into full and memorable effect. His style is *therefore* good, because it has been suited to his themes; and those themes have hitherto been either narrative, which usually imposes a modest diction, and a modest structure of sentences, or argumentative in that class which is too overburthened with details, with replies, with interruption, and every mode of discontinuity, to allow a thought of eloquence, or of the periodic style which a perfect eloquence instinctively seeks.

I here close my separate notice of the Lake Poets— meaning those three who were originally so denominated—three men upon whom posterity, in every age, will look back with interest as profound as, perhaps, belongs to any other names of our era; for it happens, not unfrequently, that the *personal* interest in the author is not in the direct ratio of that which belongs to his works: and the character of an author, better qualified to command a vast popularity for the creations of his pen, is oftentimes more of a universal character, less peculiar, less fitted to stimulate the curiosity, or to sustain the sympathy of the intellectual, than the profounder and more ascetic solemnity of a Wordsworth, or the prodigal and magnificent eccentricities of a Coleridge. . . .

John Carne describes a visit to the Lake District:

The next morning after breakfast, Mr. Wordsworth and I set out at ten o'clock and did not return till eight at night. . . . We came to a fine waterfall amidst a naked and rugged scene. Wordsworth suddenly became silent, and he walked for some time along the rushing stream: its sound amidst the savageness of nature was no doubt inspiring him with some poetic imagery. We had reached a most interesting point of view, when he said he wished to repeat to me a passage of his poetry. We sat down on a part of the rock; before us was Helvellyn, and the sun shone vividly on the low land on the right while the mountains above were still covered with gloom. It was impossible not to be struck with such a scene, and so well suited to the character of the man; and the lines he repeated with energy were on 'Enterprise' inciting to visit the far and the savage scene; the path of the Euphrates, the burning wild, the storm-lashed and dreary shore. At last we arrived at the summit of the mountain, and enjoyed a very extensive prospect. . . . Next morning after breakfast I took coach for Keswick, near which Mr. Southey lives. Mr. W. gave me an introduction to him; it was impossible to have a better, as they are bosom friends. The Poet of the Lakes (Wordsworth) is very retired in his habits, and extremely amiable in his domestic circle. . . . I drank tea and spent Thursday evening with Mr. Southey. His house is at the end of the town, but quite detached, and stands on a rising ground. His family is a very charming one— Mrs. S., a genteel and well looking woman; Miss S., a handsome and interesting girl, and two lovely younger daughters, about the ages of 11 or 13. Mrs. Coleridge resides there; Mr. C., you know, is a very erratic genius, fond of his family, but, oddly enough, always living away from them. He ruins himself by taking opium, and quite destroys his talents, so that his family are left dependent. The pleasing and accomplished Miss Coleridge now resides here. She understands several languages, and has lately wrote a translation from the Latin.

John Carne, quoted in "The Lake Poets in 1823," The Bookworm, Vol. 3, 1890.

Penelope Hughes-Hallett

SOURCE: An introduction to *The Wordsworths and the Lakes: Home at Grasmere,* Collins & Brown Limited, 1993, pp. 7-9.

[*In the following excerpt, Hughes-Hallett comments on the beginnings of the friendship between Wordsworth, Coleridge, Southey, and De Quincey.*]

Soon after reaching Grasmere in Christmas week 1799 the young William Wordsworth expressed his feelings of joy in the poem 'Home at Grasmere.' . . . At Dove Cottage he and his sister Dorothy settled together into their small home, to them a paradise after years of separation from each other and of exile from the Lakes. 'Home' implied a return to their roots, to the countryside of their birth.

Here William was to compose the major body of his work. Surrounded by the lakes and valleys of his childhood, and cherished and encouraged by his beloved Dorothy, he could pursue that life of the imagination, the key to spiritual awareness, in which state, he said, 'We see into the life of things.'

Although solitude was always precious to William and Dorothy, they did not live the lives of hermits. They became, rather, the centre of an ardent and loving circle that included Thomas De Quincey, Robert Southey and, pre-eminently, Samuel Taylor Coleridge. William married Mary Hutchinson in 1802 and in the following years they had five children. Sara, Mary's sister and the adored of Coleridge, also joined the Wordsworth household. This little company of extraordinarily gifted men and women lived their lives with an eager intensity, whether they were loving, quarrelling, laughing, mourning or striding over enormous tracts of mountainous country, glorying as they went in the beauties of the Lakes about which they felt so proprietorial.

Above all, they wrote and wrote: poems, diaries, notebooks and long letters. As their fame grew, others outside their charmed circle wrote about them too. The happy result for posterity is that they can tell their own story, speaking directly and spontaneously to the reader of today. . . . Life was full of extremes of ecstasy and grief; but all the while there was also a steady flow of mundane happenings, vivid in their simplicity. We hear of Coleridge in bed eating a mutton chop; Wordsworth sitting at breakfast in his open shirt, neglecting his basin of broth and writing a poem to a butterfly; Dorothy making a mattress or copying out her brother's nearly indecipherable verse. In this way of life, with its combination of the visionary and the everyday, William could achieve the sought-after harmony with the natural world that formed the bedrock of his poetry.

No other landscape provided so potent an inspiration for his imagination as did these lakes and hills, hallowed by the memory of his childhood dreams, so that he could feel

A presence that disturbs me with the joy
Of elevated thoughts; a sense sublime
Of something far more deeply interfused,
Whose dwelling is the light of setting suns,
And the round ocean and the living air,
And the blue sky, and in the mind of man;

The works that emerged from this fortunate confluence of poetic genius and natural beauty have become a part of the furniture of all our minds.

LITERARY INFLUENCES AND COLLABORATIONS

C. H. Herford

SOURCE: "Poetry," in *The Age of Wordsworth*, 1897. Reprint by G. Bell and Sons Ltd., 1930, pp. 146-284.

[*In the following excerpt, Herford discusses the poetic styles of Wordsworth, Coleridge, and Southey and comments on the influence that the three poets had on each other.*]

[Wordsworth and Coleridge] were at once profoundly akin and strikingly different, and both their points of kinship and their points of divergence go to the heart of English Romanticism. It is therefore necessary to define these with some care. On a first glance the two men seem, physically and psychologically, of wholly different make. Wordsworth, a rugged North-countryman, somewhat ascetic and austere, constant in all relations, with a rigid framework of character behind which intellectual passion 'burnt like an unconsuming fire of light;' Coleridge, a Devonian, of softer, but more richly sensitive, fibre, every vibration of which stirred or shattered purpose, or started imagination on some new evolution of phantasmal shapes and sounds. Hazlitt admirably noted their different habits of composition. Coleridge 'liked to compose in walking over uneven ground, or breaking through the straggling branches of a copse-wood' where the physical obstacle incessantly deflected the current of thought; while Wordsworth 'always wrote walking up and down a straight gravel path.' These traits of the workshop illustrate several differences in their work. Coleridge loved broken surfaces, picturesque interruptions,—maythorn amid yew, purple islands amid bright sea: Wordsworth painted with a broader touch, treating detail with even prosaic fidelity, but rarely lingering over its bright play. And Coleridge was, as we have seen, peculiarly fascinated by the 'interruptions' of the spiritual world, the straggling branches of marvel which startle and waylay the observer. Wordsworth, on the other hand, found the marvels in the familiar and normal, and only there, and could not be persuaded to concern himself with the fairy-lore of Stowey.

These diversities sufficiently imply the affinities which underlay them. Both surpassed all other poets of their generation, both in delicacy of sense-perception and in that kind of imaginative power which acts not by arbitrary recombinations of the facts of sense, but by a peculiar subtle scrutiny of them. For both, the universe was alive and mysteriously divine. But they differed alike in the direction of their sensibility, in the regions of experience to which their imagination attached itself, and in the character of that imagination itself. To the beauty of landscape they were equally sensitive; Coleridge with a more delicate voluptuousness, Wordsworth with more penetrating veracity. In painting strange mystic effects upon mountains or water they become at moments almost indistinguishable. But human nature attracted them at widely different points. Both indeed were 'made glad' by the beauty of children, and had an equal share in the poetry of childhood. Neither again was in any special sense a poet of love—love that was 'denied' to the one who was 'made for it,' and so serenely and securely given to the other. But simple human nature, 'the common growth of Mother Earth,' consecrated by 'her humblest mirth and tears,' and devoid of any charm of virtue or wit, appealed only to Wordsworth; while Coleridge was allured to rarer and remoter tracts of humanity, lurking places of strange dreams and fantastic anomalies of belief. 'Facts of the mind' were for Wordsworth the elementary passions; for Coleridge, as we have seen, they meant those curiosities of superstition which Wordsworth disdained. Horace Walpole and others had amused themselves by loose agglomerations of these curiosities. It was not by outbidding his predecessors in invention of wonders, but by the extraordinary delicacy with which he painted the passions they excite, that the 'subtle-souled psychologist' made an epoch in the poetry of the supernatural. And, finally, they differed in character of imagination. Wordsworth was more penetrating, Coleridge more dreamlike. Wordsworth transfigured the little domain he lived in, but hardly or rarely found poetry where he had not set his eye; Coleridge, feeding with yet more ravishment upon his sensations, had also the mystic's impatience and disbelief of them, and with all his exquisite power of poetic realism, was yet more himself when he abandoned himself to dreams like *Kubla Khan,* in which all the elements of experience are flung up, 'like chaffy grain beneath the mower's flail,' under the sole yet absolute control of an imperial instinct for beauty.

These diversities would, however, have been more palpable had the two poets never met. Each has impressively recorded his gratitude to the other. Wordsworth, as we have seen, owed to Coleridge something both of human tenderness and of speculative and critical thought (*Prelude,* Book XIV.). Coleridge, though even more fervid, is less explicit. 'William, my teacher and friend,' 'William, my head and my heart,'—his verse epistles to the brother and sister at Goslar (1798-

99) abound with affectionate outbursts like these. What Wordsworth had 'taught' him was, we cannot doubt, in the first place, a more strong and confident acceptance of the faith in the joyousness and joy-evoking power of Nature which was part of the being of William and Dorothy. It is in his Stowey poems that it first distinctly emerges. It is now that he indignantly rebukes the conventional 'melancholy' of the nightingale of literature—'in Nature there is nothing melancholy' (*Nightingale*); now that he promises his sleeping babe an upbringing 'by lakes' and 'ancient mountains' (*Frost at Midnight*), as Shelley vowed for his, Italy and Greece; now that he seems to owe all his own intellectual life to those 'lakes and mountain-hills and quiet dales' of England, among which so very few of his days had been passed (*Fears in Solitude*). After the return from Germany it gives way, and the *Dejection* sadly puts by the belief that joy has any other source than the soul itself.

Further, Coleridge's subtler supernaturalism itself, alien as it was from Wordsworth, yet owed much to him. If we compare the supernaturalism of the monads, even of the pixies, with that of *Christabel* or the *Ancient Mariner,* we shall feel little hesitation in connecting the change with the impression confessedly made upon Coleridge by Wordsworth's 'unique faculty' of idealizing familiar things. To give the world of marvel the convincing power of the familiar, was but to translate that Wordsworthian formula as it were into Coleridgean terms.

Both poets were thus, as Wordsworth said, 'prophets of Nature,' though Coleridge's prophecy was far less continuous, many-sided, and serene; and both were Romantic poets, though Wordsworth's Romance, elicited as it was from the immediate neighbourhood of prose, and little controlled by self-criticism, was liable in its loftiest moments, to relapse. Both are the great English masters, as Goethe, who unites and transcends their spheres, is the great European master, of poetic realism; both possess, though not with equal security, the region in which Romance and Nature meet, though Coleridge reaches it by 'the ladder of the impossible.' Wordsworth by the steeper and more treacherous ladder of the commonplace. . . .

Robert Southey was, as a schoolboy, already a scribbler of epics, and an eager reader of history and romantic poetry—Gibbon and Ariosto, Josephus and Spenser, and the *Arabian Nights*. At Westminster his truant hours were spent over old folios, one of which, Picart's *Religious Ceremonies,* sowed the seed of most of his future work in verse. 'Before I left school I had formed the intention of exhibiting all the more prominent and poetical forms of mythology which have at any time obtained among mankind, by making each the groundwork of an heroic poem.' At Oxford (1792-94) he became a notorious democrat; but the naturalism of Rousseau was, in him, tinged with the more austere naturalism of Lucan and Epictetus, with whose book 'my very heart was ingrained.' These heterogeneous enthusiasms found vent, in the summer of 1793, in his epic, *Joan of Arc,* where the heroine champions republicanism, in the vein of Lucan, amid scenery full of visionary romance; as well as in a slighter and cruder piece, *Wat Tyler,* the surreptitious revival of which embarrassed the Tory laureate of 1817. In the spring of 1794 he first met Coleridge. *Pantisocracy* and the *Fall of Robespierre,* a piece of poetic bravado in keeping with it, by Southey, Coleridge, and Lovell, followed, and when *Joan* was at length published (1796), its heterogeneity was heightened by 400 lines of mysticism and science from Coleridge. His first journey to Spain and Portugal (1795-96) ended his pantisocratic dream by plunging him into the romance of the past. New epic projects began to occupy him, and the rich material gathered in explorations of remote and forgotten mythologies arranged itself round heroic types no longer borrowed from the country of Rousseau. He thought of Wales and America no longer as places of refuge for ideal communities, but as the scene of the wanderings of the mediaeval prince Madoc. A visit to Norwich (1798) brought him into touch with German influence. From Dr. Sayers he learned the irregular verse which became the garb of *Thalaba* and *Kehama,* and caught the fine ear of the author of *Queen Mab.* He thought Kotzebue 'of unsurpassed and unsurpassable genius' (*to Wynn,* April 5th, 1799), hoped that his *Thalaba* would stand above Wieland's *Oberon* and next to Ariosto (*ib.*), and meant not to rest satisfied till he had a ballad as good as *Lenore* (*ib.,* January 5th). To this time belong his ballads, *Rudiger, Lord William,* and the *Maid of the Inn.* Here, and elsewhere, his inspirations were thoroughly bookish. His eye, quick and alert, but not brooding, won poetic harvests only from books, and from books in proportion as they were remote from the life he knew. His ardently loved home and the beautiful Somerset country around it left his imagination cold; but the thought of an epic on the prehistoric Zoroaster or the antediluvian Noah kindled him at once. *Thalaba,* the epic of Islam, was finished in 1801. In 1803 he made his final home at Greta Hall, Keswick, where Coleridge's family were already settled, and where Coleridge himself, during 1802-3, was a flitting inmate. The days of intimacy with Coleridge were over for Southey; but he found a stauncher, if less stimulating, friend in Wordsworth at Grasmere. Here *Madoc* was completed (1805), and here, five years later, a Brahman epic followed the epic of Islam. The *Curse of Kehama* and *Thalaba* are the results of precisely the same principles and method, save that the irregular blank verse of the earlier became irregular rhymed verse in the later. *Thalaba* tells the adventures of a young Arabian in the effort to avenge his father; *Kehama,* the sufferings of a young Hindoo whom a father has 'cursed' for the death of his son. Upon these threads are hung the fruits of busy toils in books of

oriental travel and legend. Thalaba's progress is assisted by a magic ring, thwarted by genii, beguiled by allurements forbidden to the Mussulman; and in the woof of the tale of Kehama's wrath are interwoven Suttee and Juggernaut, Siva and Yamen, the ship of heaven in which the heroine is wafted aloft, and the oriental Inferno, Padalon, into which she is plunged down. In all this there is much rich and beautiful description. The fluent verse bears us easily along, like a great eastern river, by torrid desert and perfumed garden, magical mountains, subterranean chasms. Scott thought he had read nothing more impressive than the description of the approach to Padalon in *Kehama;* Shelley modelled the opening of *Queen Mab* upon the beautiful verses on night at the opening of *Thalaba.* The general public did not refuse a certain mild applause. Southey was in fact exploiting two sources of interest, one long neglected, the other almost new, in poetry: the interest of story and the interest of the Eastern world. Before Scott, and in a sense rather than he, Southey earned the right to be called 'the Ariosto of the north,' by re-introducing the poetic romance of adventure: and his *Thalaba* struck, with Landor's *Gebir,* the first note in English poetry of the orientalism revived a little later by Oehlenschläger's *Aladdin* and Goethe's *Westöstlicher Divan,* by Moore's *Lalla Rookh,* and (faintly) by Shelley's *Revolt of Islam.*

But Southey's epics lack imaginative wholeness. Through all the phantasmagoria of oriental adventure we detect the decorous English Protestant, Southey, animating his hero with ideals of virtue and good sense caught from Epictetus and the Age of Reason. Thalaba, as he owned, is but Joan in a new disguise. He was too 'enlightened' to penetrate into the inner genius of the faiths whose picturesque beauty he admired. He stood on the verge of the two centuries between rationalism and Romanticism, participating in both, possessed by neither. He toiled before the threshold of Romanticism, while Coleridge stood already at its inner shrine.

There was, indeed, one region in which Southey fairly crossed this limit. No Englishman had penetrated so far as he into the genius of the poetry of Spain and Portugal. For the religious doctrines of Catholic and Saracen he roundly expressed his scorn, but he found in the brilliant ballads of their chivalry an untheological religion of honour, valour, and purity altogether his own. While Scott was busy with the Border lay of *Sir Tristrem,* Southey translated the last faded flower of Spanish romance, *Amadis of Gaul* (1803). When Scott advanced to *Marmion,* Southey was weaving out a cycle of Spanish song, the *Chronicle of the Cid* (1808). The French invasion of the Peninsula, in the same year, fired all England with enthusiasm for Spain. Wordsworth denounced the Convention of Cintra in noble prose, and joined with Byron in celebrating Saragoza. And three other writers of high distinction took up, within a few years, the old Spanish legend of

Roderick the Goth. Scott's *Vision of Roderick* appeared in 1811. Landor, after equipping a force of volunteers at his own expense, and marching into Spain at their head, sat down to carve the marble iambics of his *Count Julian;* and the early copy which he sent to Southey found his friend already deep in his own tale of *Don Roderick,* the last and most human of his romantic epics. The Gothic king, hurled from his throne at a stroke by the invading Arabs, in league with a deeply injured subject of his own, and then, through countless hardships and rebuffs, organizing his broken people into an irresistible host, was as fine an epic hero as Bruce, Alfred, or his own Joan of Arc. The actual passion of the analogous crisis before his eyes kindled in him as he wrote, and bore down the bookish demon who might have turned the poem into an exhibition of Gothic mythology. And his rich memories of Spanish scenery and customs furnished him with descriptions agreeably unlike the laborious mosaics of his oriental epics. *Roderick* is not a great poem, but it is a brilliant tale, written in verse which has all the excellences of good prose, and in fact illustrates Wordsworth's theory of poetic language far better than his own practice.

In 1813 Southey succeeded Pye as laureate; ominously, for his verse in future rarely did more than merit the laurel of Pye. But his worst work had the excuse of compulsion; his annual New Year odes to the king, and the unlucky *Vision of Judgment* itself, were distasteful task work. To describe the celestial adventures of George III was to subject the scheme of exhibiting the mythologies of the world in verse to a disastrous strain. This abortion of his own art Southey chose to introduce (1821) with an outspoken attack on the art of others. *Don Juan* had been launched forth in 1819, with a defiant dedication, reluctantly suppressed in print, to the laureate. Between Byron and Southey there could be no accommodation, and neither could judge the other. Byron thought Southey a political turncoat because he demanded that freedom should be limited by order and hallowed by home-sanctities. Southey thought Byron the founder of a 'Satanic school' because his poetry ignored all moral impulses but the passion to be free. Of the two, Byron's criticism was the less just. In genius, however, there could be no rivalry. Byron's masterpiece, the *Vision of Judgment,* published in the *Liberal,* 1822, extorted the admiration of a public which execrated it, and Southey's concern in it was remembered with a persistence which helped to make his better work forgotten.

For twenty years longer Southey continued busy in his vast and ever-growing library, but now chiefly with *prose*. Prose, clear, buoyant, vigorous, was in fact his true speech. 'This desire [to make money]' he naïvely confessed as a young man, 'has already led me to write sometimes in poetry what would perhaps otherwise have been in prose' (*Letter,* January 15th, 1798)—a significant fact in the annals of popular taste. He had al-

ready poured immense stores of learning into the *History of Brazil* (1810); and his later life was largely occupied with a series of excellent and popular biographies, some of men already famous (Nelson, Wesley); others, of men who, like Kirke White, owe to his generous and sympathetic labour almost all such fame as they possess. It is the prose of the historian, of the critic, of the letter-writer; but of a historian who describes more than he analyses, of a critic who points out beauties more than he penetrates or divines, of a letter-writer who touches with ease and charm all the notes of everyday life, boisterously jocose to Grosvenor Bedford, wise and practical to a hundred others, the large-hearted friend and the 'funny papa,' but who never approaches the subtle emotion of Shelley's letters, or the exquisite fun of Lamb's.

Earl Leslie Griggs

SOURCE: "Robert Southey's Estimate of Samuel Taylor Coleridge: A Study in Human Relations," in *The Huntington Library Quarterly,* Vol. IX, No. 1, November, 1945, pp. 61-94.

[*In the following essay, Griggs details the association between Southey and Coleridge, commenting on the impact the two poets had on one another's work.*]

"O Southey," wrote Coleridge just before his departure for Malta in the spring of 1804, "from Oxford to Greta Hall—a spiritual map with our tracks as if two ships had left Port in company." The lives of these two men, indeed, from their first meeting in 1794, were destined to be so inextricably interwoven that any consideration of the one necessarily involves a study of the other; and it would seem advantageous, therefore, to draw together Southey's many comments upon Coleridge. The remarks run the gamut from adulation to downright condemnation, representing as they do judgments based upon "the ups and downs" of a long association, but their total effect offers considerable information about Coleridge. While Southey's passing remarks are not often free from personal prejudice—perhaps they are mainly the result of it—they do show the impact of Coleridge's personality and genius upon a contemporary writer. Likewise, out of these comments arises a self-portrait of Southey, not always flattering it is true, but all the more real because it was presented unconsciously.

In order to understand the changing and at times contradictory comments upon Coleridge which follow, one ought to glance briefly at Southey's character. Gifted with powers of application and perseverance, he was intolerant of their lack in other persons. Self-disciplined, he not only deplored want of self-management in others but also offered active interference. Inclined to be meddlesome, he often seems no better than a busybody. When he was thwarted in his desires to regulate others, he quite naturally became bitter, even to pointing an accusing finger. Perhaps one might overlook this tendency in Southey, for it emanated from good intentions, but unfortunately there was combined with it an inability to rise above personal prejudice. In many ways Southey was an admirable man, but he was capable of petty jealousy and intolerance.

It should be remarked, too, that Coleridge and Southey were not especially suited to one another. Although their early revolutionary enthusiasm first drew them together and their marriage to sisters led to an intimacy not wholly compatible to either, almost from the first their diversity of temperament caused friction. Coleridge soon recognized this; Southey was slower to do so. It was Southey, far more than Coleridge, who sought intimacy and who spoke of congeniality. For Southey never truly understood Coleridge. Though he had more opportunities than most men for judging Coleridge, his own habits of mind, sense of propriety, and rigid morality led him to condemn what he did not understand. For a while he was caught by the dazzle of Coleridge's personality but was neither wise nor tolerant enough to forgive Coleridge's aberrations. Southey recognized Coleridge's genius, but personal considerations often modified and sometimes distorted his judgment. Perhaps, then, the orderly mind of a man of talent tried to evaluate the disorderly one of a man of genius.

In June 1794 Coleridge and Southey met in the latter's rooms in Balliol College, Oxford. Both were enthusiastic young revolutionaries, and both were embryonic poets. Each immediately conceived a warm affection for the other. Coleridge, Southey wrote to a friend on June 12, 1794, "is of most uncommon merit,—of the strongest genius, the clearest judgment, the best heart. My friend he already is, and must hereafter be yours." Together he and Coleridge proposed a scheme for forming an ideal community in America, where a practical experiment in human relations might be undertaken. This Utopian plan, which they called Pantisocracy, was a source of mutual enthusiasm and dominated their thoughts for many months. They talked and dreamed at Oxford; then after Coleridge's tour of Wales, they were reunited and stayed all summer in or near Bristol. Thus was Coleridge introduced to Sara Fricker, a sister of Southey's fiancee, to whom in a moment of Pantisocratic ardor he immediately proposed marriage. Another mutual enterprise of this summer was a tragedy entitled the *Fall of Robespierre,* of which Coleridge wrote the first act.

At the end of the summer Coleridge left Bristol and stayed in London for about a month on his way to Cambridge, but a few weeks later he abandoned the University and settled in London, Southey remaining in the West. Coleridge turned to other friends, partic-

ularly to Charles Lamb. He wrote only infrequently to Southey, who already had begun to complain of the neglect of himself and Sara Fricker. Coleridge, however, remained an ardent Pantisocrat, refusing advantageous employment with the Earl of Buchan and rejecting a liberal proposal from his family. Southey, probably spurred on by the Fricker sisters and already beginning his interference in Coleridge's affairs, went to London for the express purpose of seeking him out and returning him to Bristol. "Coleridge," he wrote to Joseph Cottle after Coleridge's death, "did not come back to Bristol till January, 1795, *nor would he, I believe, have come back at all,* if I had not gone to London to look for him. For having got there from Cambridge at the beginning of winter, there he remained without writing to Miss F[ricker] or to me." Southey's mission was successful, and early in 1795 the two men took up lodgings together in Bristol.

They now tried to earn enough for their emigration to America, though they later compromised on a settlement in Wales to try out their scheme. They were constantly together. "Coleridge," Southey wrote on February 8, 1795, "is writing at the same table; our names are written in the book of destiny, on the same page." They gave lectures. They wrote poetry. They planned a magazine. But for all their efforts they earned barely enough to support themselves.

Southey began to take stock of the situation, his examination of his affairs undoubtedly being induced by the promise of an annuity of £160 from his friend Wynn and the insistence on the part of his uncle that he go into the church or the legal profession. Southey wavered. Although responsible for Coleridge's return from Bristol, he was anxious to marry Edith Fricker as soon as possible, and he saw that their Pantisocratic plans were no nearer achievement than they had been a year before. He determined, therefore, to abandon Pantisocracy; and he made good his decision, when in November 1795, immediately after a secret marriage, he left for Portugal under his uncle's auspices.

From the beginning of Southey's defection Coleridge was profoundly moved. At first he sought to reconvert Southey, but when he saw that all efforts were hopeless, he penned a letter of bitter reproach, declaring that Southey had selfishly abandoned both his friends and Pantisocracy and that their friendship was at an end. Coleridge detailed his own sacrifices for the sake of principles and with irrefragable arguments proved the treachery of Southey's conduct. Thus the golden dream of Pantisocracy died. The only tangible result was Coleridge's marriage to Sara Fricker, soon to be the source of unending turmoil.

When Southey returned from Portugal in May 1796 he found Coleridge among new friends. He and his wife settled in Bristol across the street from the Coleridges, but the alienation continued. Southey took the first step towards a reconciliation when he sent over to Coleridge a slip of paper containing a sentence from Schiller: "Fiesco! Fiesco! thou leavest a void in my bosom, which the human race, thrice told, will never fill up." Southey's overtures produced only a temporary understanding. Coleridge was unmistakably clear on the subject. "We are now reconciled," he wrote to John Thelwall on December 31, 1796, "but the cause of the difference was solemn, and 'the blasted oak puts not forth its buds anew.' We are *acquaintances,* and feel *kindliness* towards each other, but I do not *esteem* or *love* Southey, . . . and vice versâ Southey of me."

Two further matters caused a renewed breach between the brothers-in-law. In November 1797 Coleridge published three sonnets in the *Monthly Magazine.* They were signed Nehemiah Higginbottom and were intended as satires upon the poems of Lamb, Lloyd, and Coleridge himself. For some reason Southey assumed that the sonnet, "Simplicity," was a parody upon his early poems and took offense. Then, too, he became intimate with Charles Lloyd, an erstwhile housemate of the Coleridges, and like Lamb was turned against Coleridge by Lloyd's gossip and tale-bearing. Undoubtedly stung by Coleridge's aloofness, he was ready to quarrel anew, and these two reasons gave him an excuse.

There may have been a deeper cause for Southey's growing resentment, however. By the summer of 1797 Coleridge's acquaintance with William and Dorothy Wordsworth had ripened into a warm friendship. Wordsworth, now the repository of Coleridge's inmost feelings, had supplanted Southey. This may partly explain Southey's attack on the *Lyrical Ballads.* "Have you," he wrote to William Taylor on September 5, 1798,

> seen a volume of Lyrical Ballads &c.? They are by Coleridge & Wordsworth but their names are not affixed. Coleridge's ballad of The Auncient Marinere is I think the clumsiest attempt at German sublimity I ever saw. Many of the others are very fine, & some I shall re-read, upon the same principle that led me thro Trissino, whenever I am afraid of writing like a child or an old woman.

Had Southey confined himself to criticism in a private letter, for undoubtedly he was incapable of appreciating the subtle merits of *The Ancient Mariner,* one could condone his conduct, but he saw fit to repeat his opinions in an unsigned article in the *Critical Review,* one of the leading reviews of the day. He must have known what injury such a review of the poems would inflict, not only upon the sale of the volume but upon the feelings of the authors; but apparently personal animosity determined his course of action. It would seem evident, too, that he expressed his opinion of the *Lyr-*

ical Ballads to Mrs. Coleridge, for during Coleridge's absence in Germany, when she was with the Southeys a good deal, she twice wrote slightingly of that volume to Thomas Poole. "The Lyrical Ballads are laughed at and disliked by all with very few excepted," she wrote in March 1799; and a little later she was even more emphatic—"The Lyrical Ballads are not liked at all by any."

Southey's review appeared while Coleridge was in Germany, and in pleasant contrast to his treatment of the *Lyrical Ballads,* Southey ministered to Mrs. Coleridge during her husband's absence. When Berkeley, the Coleridges' second child, died, he saw to its interment. Thus, soon after Coleridge returned to England in July 1799 the two men resumed at least amicable relations. Coleridge, undoubtedly appreciative of Southey's kindness to Mrs. Coleridge and recognizing the affection of his three-year-old son for Southey—"little Hartley prattles about you"—made the first overtures. Southey, still resentful, accused Coleridge of having slandered him. Coleridge replied that he had "never charged Southey with 'aught but deep and implacable enmity towards himself'," and appealed to both Poole and Wordsworth as witnesses. Finally Poole wrote to Southey to allay his suspicions—"In the many conversations I have had with Coleridge concerning yourself, he has never discovered the least personal enmity against, but, on the contrary, the strongest affection for you stifled only by the untoward events of your separation." Thus on August 20, 1799, Southey wrote to Charles Danvers:

> I write to you from Stowey, and at the same table with Coleridge: this will surprise you. . . . However, here I am, and have been some days wholly immersed in conversation. In one point of view Coleridge and I are bad companions for each other. Without being talkative I am conversational, and the hours slip away, and the ink dries upon the pen in my hand.

On February 5, 1800, apropos of a poem in hexameters on Mohammed upon which he and Coleridge planned to collaborate, he remarked to William Taylor:

> From Coleridge I am promised the half, & we divided the books according as their subjects suited us—but I expect to have nearly the whole work. His ardour is not lasting, & the only inconvenience that his dereliction can occasion will be that I shall write the poem in fragments & have to seam them together at last.

In the late summer of 1799 the Southeys accompanied the Coleridges to Ottery St. Mary to meet Coleridge's family. Afterwards Coleridge went off to London, and a number of friendly letters passed between him and

Sketch of Greta Hall, where Coleridge and his family made their home in 1800. Later, Southey and his family shared the home with the Coleridges.

Southey. Then, in April 1800, Southey departed for Portugal in search of health, but before leaving he made Coleridge his literary executor. "A man," the punctilious Southey wrote to Coleridge,

> when he goes abroad should make his will; and this [*Madoc* and the completed portions of *Thalaba*] is all my wealth: be my executor, in case I am summoned upon the grand tour of the universe, and do with them, and with whatever you may find of mine, what may be most advantageous for Edith, for my brothers . . . and for my mother.

Southey also told Coleridge that he would take along a few books, and he specified, as if in atonement for his review, "your poems, the Lyrics, the Lyrical Ballads, and Gebir; . . . these make all my library." While in Portugal he begged Coleridge for "some long letters," and "your Christabell and your Three Graves, and finish them on purpose to send them." Nevertheless, he still had misgivings: "Coleridge ought to be upon the Life of Lessing: he ought also to write to me, and I have my fears lest the more important business should be neglected like the other." Elsewhere he was more critical. "Coleridge," he said, "has never written to me: where no expectation existed there can be no disappointment." It is, however, in a letter to Humphry Davy that Southey betrays what was, perhaps, the main cause of his adverse view of Coleridge—the intimacy with the Wordsworths. When Coleridge renounced Southey's friendship in November 1795 he meant to make a complete break. Later family considerations forced a renewal of association with Southey, but new friendships had displaced the old. Southey knew that Coleridge had transferred his affection to Wordsworth,

and he resented it. On July 26, 1800, having heard of the migration of Coleridge to the North, he wrote almost spitefully to Davy:

> Coleridge's translation [of *Wallenstein*] is admirable; but Coleridge, who can write as well as Schiller, ought not to have translated. He has done wrong, I think, in removing so far from his other friends, and wholly giving himself to Wordsworth; it is wrong on his own account, and more so on his wife's, who is now at an unreachable distance from all her sisters. What of the life of Lessing? the [proposed] essay on the "Genius of Schiller" amused me, it is not the first nor the second time that he had advertised what has not been written.

To Coleridge, however, Southey continued cordial as ever. On March 28, 1801, he wrote from Lisbon, as if to wean Coleridge away from Wordsworth, that he wished they could settle together at Alfoxden; "there was a house big enough: and you would talk me into healthy indolence, and I should spur you to profitable industry." He suggested that they might undertake "some joint journeyman works, which might keep up winter fires and Christmas tables"; thus beginning a series of fruitless plans for collaboration and money-making.

Immediately upon Southey's return to England in July 1801 he and Coleridge began to talk of living together, but except for brief visits at Greta Hall, Keswick, where the Coleridges were domesticated, no plans materialized until later. Southey wrote frequently to his friends about Coleridge. "I am going to Keswick," he wrote to William Taylor on July 27, 1801,

> to pass the Autumn with Coleridge—to work like a negro—& to arrange his future plans with my own. He is miserably ill, & must quit England for a warmer climate or perish. I found letters announcing his determination to ship himself & family for the Azores, the only spot his finances could reach. This I have stopt; & the probability is that he will accompany me abroad. Thus Edith will have one sister with her to reconcile her to an abandonment of the rest—& I shall have with me the man, to whom, in all the ups & downs of six years, my heart has clung with most affection, despite even of its own efforts.

By this time Southey has revealed the most important aspect of his own relationship to Coleridge. He found his friend irresistible. Like almost everyone else, he was spellbound by Coleridge's scintillating personality. He saw Coleridge's faults with unvarnished clarity and he wrote of them with relentless frankness; but when all was said and done, he knew he was in the presence of genius.

"Lamb I hear has been at Keswick this summer," Southey wrote to Rickman on October 18, 1802.

Conjugal vexation of which he speaks would not have affected me—indeed my presence would have greatly repressed it—for I am the only man among his acquaintance to whom Coleridge does not complain of his wife—& that I think implies some merit on my part. It is all from his want of *calculation,* from that constant sacrifice to present impulse which marks his character & blasts the brightest talents that I have ever witnessed. I very much wished you to have seen him once. Lamb knows him better than most men—& I thoroughly know him—you would have given a fair first-sight opinion—because you would have looked thro the dazzle of conversation. Lamb says "the rogue has given me philtres to make me love him"—I never feel so little satisfied with myself as upon recollecting that my inclination to like him has always got the better of a judgement—felt at first sight—& deliberately & perpetually strengthened by every experience.

By 1803 Coleridge's health had become so bad that his friends began to despair of his life, and Southey was ready to sympathize with him. To William Taylor he wrote on June 23, 1803:

Coleridge & I have often talked of making a great work upon English Literature—but Coleridge only talking—& poor fellow he will not do that long I fear— . . . by God it provokes me when I see a set of puppies yelping at him, upon whom he—a great good-natured mastiff, if he came up to them, would just lift up his leg & pass on . . . It vexes & grieves me to the heart that when he is gone, as go he will, nobody will believe what a mind goes with him, how infinitely & ten-thousand-thousand-fold—the mightiest of his generation!

In August 1803 the Southeys lost their only child, and, seeking solace, they went almost at once to join the Coleridges at Greta Hall, Keswick, on a visit which ended only with their deaths. Coleridge, trudging about Scotland in a desperate endeavor to regain his health, hurried home. Fate had again united his destiny to Southey's.

For a time Southey becomes a little more generous in his judgment. "Coleridge," he remarks in a letter of November 19, 1803, "is now in bed with the lumbago. Never was poor fellow so tormented with such pantomimic complaints." Then after details of the illness, he continues:

He is arranging materials for what, if it be made, will be a most valuable work, under the title of "Consolations and Comforts," which will be the very essential oil of metaphysics, fragrant as otto of roses, and useful as wheat, rice, port wine, or any other necessary of human life.

Three weeks later Southey is even more eulogistic:

I know not when any of his works will appear—& tremble lest an untimely death should leave me the task of putting together the fragments of his materials—when in sober truth I do believe [his death] would be a more serious loss to the world of literature than it ever suffered from the wreck of antient science.

Among Southey's correspondents the one most severe in his judgment of Coleridge was John Rickman. "He is very unwell in body," Rickman wrote to Southey on March 26, 1804, " . . . and his Mind is very depressed, & very excitable by objects to other Men scarce visible or feelable . . . If he dies, it will be from a sulky imagination, produced from the general cause of such things: i.e. Want of regular Work or Application: which is a great pity." In his answer to Rickman, Southey is less sympathetic than usual.

You are in great measure right about Coleridge. He is worse in body than you seem to believe, but the main cause lies in his own management of himself—or rather want of management. His mind is in a perpetual St. Vitus's dance—eternal activity without action. At times he feels mortified that he should have done so little, but this feeling never produces any exertion—I will begin tomorrow—he says—& thus has all his life long been letting today slip. He has had no calamities in life—& so contrives to be miserable about trifles—picking every pimple into a wound. Poor fellow there is no one thing which gives me so much pain as the witnessing such a waste of unequalled powers. . . . Having so much to do, so many errors to weed out of the world which he is capable of eradicating—if he does die without doing his work—it will half break my heart, & he will deserve a damnation by the parable to a heavy amount! for no human being has had more talents allotted.

Though Coleridge had been talking of a stay in a warmer climate for two or three years, it was not until 1804 that he finally fixed upon Malta as his destination. Southey seems to have wished him well, and the series of friendly letters between them during the early months of this year suggests a continuation of their friendship. Southey's letter of February 1804, however, deserves special mention, for it shows an unquenchable desire to interfere in matters really none of his concern. He regrets to find Coleridge "so lavish of the outward and visible signs of friendship" with "a set of fellows whom you do not care for and ought not to care for." He warns Coleridge:

You have accustomed yourself to talk affectionately, and write affectionately, to your friends, till the expressions of affection flow by habit in your conversation, and in your letters, and pass for more than they are worth; the worst of all this is, that your letters will one day rise up in judgment against you . . . and you will be convicted of a double dealing, which, though you do not design, you certainly do practise.

Southey goes on to be more specific:

> You say in yours to Sara, that you love and honour me; upon my soul I believe you: but if I did not thoroughly believe it before, your saying so is the thing of all things that would make me open my eyes and look about me to see if I were not deceived. . . . Your feelings go naked, I cover mine with a bear-skin; I will not say that you harden yours by your mode, but I am sure that mine are the warmer for their clothing.

Southey, nevertheless, sincerely regretted Coleridge's departure. "Coleridge and I are the best companions possible," he wrote in early 1804, "in almost all moods of mind, for all kinds of wisdom, and all kinds of nonsense, to the very heights and depths thereof"; and to William Taylor he remarked that he had delayed reviewing the work of Malthus "in expectation that Coleridge would put his Samson gripe upon that wretched Philistine." To Coleridge he was equally pointed: "Your departure hangs upon me with something the same effect that the heavy atmosphere presses upon you." But the best commentary on Coleridge, and one which sums up the attitude of Southey, occurs in a letter to Miss Barker, dated April 3, 1804.

> Coleridge is gone for Malta, and his departure affects me more than I let be seen. Let what will trouble me, I bear a calm face . . . It is now almost ten years since he and I first met, in my rooms at Oxford, which meeting decided the destiny of both; and now when, after so many ups and downs, I am, for a time, settled under his roof, he is driven abroad in search of health. Ill he is, certainly and sorely ill; yet I believe if his mind was as well regulated as mine, the body would be quite as manageable. I am perpetually pained and mortified by thinking what he ought to be, for mine is an eye of microscopic discernment to the faults of my friends; but the tidings of his death would come upon me more like a stroke of lightning than any evil I have ever yet endured; almost it would make me superstitious, for we were two ships that left port in company.

During the first part of Coleridge's long absence, which lasted until August 1806, Southey was genuinely concerned. Since Coleridge had left in wretched health, so bad, indeed, that his death seemed almost inevitable to his friends, Southey waited expectantly for letters; but when the absence lengthened into months, and Coleridge took on the private and then the public secretaryship to the Military Governor of Malta, his neglect of letter-writing caused irritation rather than solicitude. "I am more angry at his silence than I choose to express," Southey burst forth in a letter of May 13, 1806, on hearing indirectly of Coleridge's removal to Rome,

"because I have no doubt whatever that the reason why we receive no letters is, that he writes none; when he comes he will probably tell a different story, and it will be proper to admit his excuse without believing it."

This marks a definite change in Southey's estimate of Coleridge. Henceforth there is less toleration and more condemnation. Disappointed by Coleridge's failure to perform, impatient at delay and excuse-making, he was coming to recognize that Coleridge would not be molded into a practical man. As long as they were in close association Southey could not for long withstand the spell of Coleridge's personality; now a long absence emphasized the utter diversity of their temperaments, characters, and minds. A greater man than Southey might have risen above petty irritations, but Southey, whatever his merits may have been, was unable to do so, and his fault-finding continued for many years.

The first unmitigated condemnation of Coleridge was written in April 1807, eight months after his return from Malta. Southey deals particularly with Coleridge's domestic disaster, but it should be noted, too, that he still looks upon the Wordsworths with bitter enmity. The letter is addressed to John Rickman.

> What you have heard of Coleridge is true, he is about to seperate from his wife, & as he chuses to do every thing in a way different from the rest of the world, is first going with her to visit his relations where however she has long since been introduced. The seperation is a good thing,—his habits are so murderous of all domestic comfort that I am only surprized Mrs. C. is not rejoiced at being rid of him. He besots himself with opium, or with spirits, till his eyes look like a Turks who is half reduced to idiotcy by the practise;—he calls up the servants at all hours of the night to prepare food for him,— he does in short all things, at all times except the proper time,—does nothing which he ought to do, & every thing which he ought not. His present scheme is to live with Wordsworth—it is from his idolatry of that family that this has begun,—they have always humoured him in all his follies,— listened to his complaints of his wife,—& when he has complained of the itch, helped him to scratch, instead of covering him with brimstone ointment, & shutting him up by himself. Wordsworth & his sister who pride themselves upon having no selfishness, are of all human beings whom I have ever known the most intensely selfish. The one thing to which W. would sacrifice all others is his own reputation, concerning which his anxiety is perfectly childish—like a woman of her beauty: & so he can get Coleridge to talk his own writings over with him, & criticise them & (without amending them) teach him how to do it,—to be in fact the very rain & air & sunshine of his intellect, he thinks C. is very well employed & this arrangement a very good one. I myself, as I have told Coleridge, think it

highly fit that the seperation should take place, but by no means that it should ever have been necessary.

For a time, however, Coleridge may have redeemed himself in the eyes of Southey by successfully completing a series of lectures at the Royal Institution, though Southey, with his usual propensity to meddle in Coleridge's life, had attempted to dissuade him from delivering them. Southey argued that the lectures would keep Coleridge "from what is of greater immediate importance; because he will never be ready, and therefore always on the fret; and because I think his prospects such that it is not prudent to give lectures to ladies and gentlemen in Albemarle St.—Sidney Smith is good enough for them." Southey was gratified to find Coleridge in agreement with him about the Roman Catholic Bill, and out of admiration for Coleridge's philosophical ability, remarked concerning Wordsworth's "Intimations" ode: "The Ode upon Pre-existence is a dark subject darkly handled. Coleridge is the only man who could make such a subject luminous." It is worth noting, however, that Southey thought him guilty of chameleon-like changes in his philosophical opinions:

> [Coleridge] is at present with Mrs. Clarkson at Bury. . . . Dr. Sayers would not find him now the warm Hartleian that he has been. Hartley was ousted by Berkeley, Berkeley by Spinoza, & Spinoza by Plato. When last I saw him Jacob Behmen had some chance of coming in. The truth is that he plays with systems, & any nonsense will serve him for a text from which he can deduce something new & surprizing.

The circumstances surrounding Coleridge's periodical, *The Friend,* were such as to give Southey unlimited opportunities for advice and censure. Beginning with a prospectus in December 1808 Coleridge spent six months in feverish preparation. Since he had undertaken to publish *The Friend* himself, all the business problems, such as printing, circulation, and financial responsibility, fell upon his shoulders; and were the story of his mismanagement and ill-fortune not so tragic to him, it would be a comedy of errors.

When Coleridge issued the prospectus, Southey was skeptical. "Coleridge," he wrote to William Taylor on December 6, 1808, "I understand has ordered some of his Prospectuses to be sent to you, relying upon me to write to you on the subject. He manages things badly . . . a few advertisements in newspapers & magazines would have done better than any prospectus at all." In a letter to Rickman, Southey regretted Coleridge's precipitancy in issuing the prospectus "wet from the pen to the printer, without consulting any body, or giving himself time for consideration," and he expressed displeasure with its tone:

> The prospectus looks too much like what it pretends to be, talks confidentially to the Public about what the Public cares not a curse for—& has about it a sort of unmanly *humblefication,* which is not sincere, which the very object of the paper gives the lie to, which may provoke some people, & can conciliate nobody. Yet such as it is I should augur best of those persons who expected most from it, such a habit of thinking & such a train of thinking is manifested there.

Southey was not sanguine concerning the appearance of *The Friend*—"For the Friend itself you may whistle these three months, & God knows how much longer," he wrote to Rickman, and he answered his own query, "Will he carry the thing on?" with *"Dios es que sabe"*; but he had no doubt of Coleridge's intellectual powers. Writing to William Taylor he says:

> Assuredly if he carries it into effect great things will be done;—sounder criticism and sounder philosophy established as well as advanced, than modern ages have seen; great truths upholden, & the axe laid at the root of those great errors which have been for the last century held to be the very nine & thirty articles of philosophical faith.

On June 1, 1809, despite the fears of his friends, Coleridge issued the first number of *The Friend*. Southey, beyond his irritation over the irregular appearance of a paper which had been promised as a weekly periodical, confined his adverse criticism to Coleridge's style. "Coleridge," he wrote to William Taylor on September 7, 1809,

> has sent out a fourth number today. I have always expected every number to be the last. He may however possibly go on in this intermitting way till subscribers enough withdraw their names (partly in anger at its irregularity, more because they find it Heathen Greek)—to give him an ostensible reason for stopping short. Both he & Wordsworth powerfully as they can write & profoundly as they usually think, have been betrayed into the same fault,—that of making things easy of comprehension in themselves, difficult to be comprehended by their way of stating them.—Instead of going to the natural spring for water they seem to like the labour of dipping wells.

Southey best expressed his judgment of Coleridge at this time in a letter written to Miss Barker on January 29, 1809. The letter is especially interesting because Southey offers an analysis of himself as well as one of Coleridge:

> It is not a little extraordinary that Coleridge, who is fond of logic, and who has an actual love and passion for close, hard thinking, should write in so rambling and inconclusive a manner; while I, who

am utterly incapable of that toil of thought in which he delights, never fail to express myself perspicuously, and to the point. I owe, perhaps, something of this to the circumstance of having lived with him during that year in my life which was most likely to give my mind its lasting character. Disliking his inordinate love of talking, I was naturally led to avoid the same fault; when we were alone, and he talked his best (which was always at those times), I was pleased to listen; and when we were in company, and I heard the same things repeated,—repeated to every fresh company, seven times in the week if we were in seven parties,—still I was silent, in great measure from depression of spirits at perceiving those vices in his nature which soon appeared to be incurable. When he provoked me into an argument, I made the most of my time; and, as it was not easy to get in more than a few words, took care to make up in weight for what they wanted in measure. His habits have continued, and so have mine. Coleridge requested me to write him such a letter upon the faults of the "Friend" as he might insert and reply to. I did so; but it was not inserted. . . . It described the fault you have remarked as existing in Burke. . . . So it is with C.; he goes to work like a hound, nosing his way, turning, and twisting, and winding, and doubling, till you get weary with following the mazy movements. My way is, when I see my object, to dart at it like a greyhound.

The Friend ceased unceremoniously *in medius res* with the twenty-seventh number on March 15, 1810. After its demise, Coleridge returned to Keswick from the Wordsworths, with whom he had been domesticated for about two years. He remained for six months at Greta Hall under the watchful eyes of his wife and Southey, but before long he was determined to escape to London. Southey, who opposed such a plan, wrote pointedly to Rickman on August 1, 1810:

Coleridge who has been quartered here since the beginning of May, talks of a journey to London! God help him!—He has been in better health than usual, & excellent spirits,—reading very hard, & to no purpose,—for nothing comes of it, except an accumulation of knowledge equal to that of any man living & a body of sound philosophy superior to what any man either of this or any former age has possessed,—all which will perish with him. I do not know any other motive that he has for going to London, than that he becomes daily more & more uneasy at having done nothing for so long, & therefore flies away to avoid the sight of persons, who he knows must be grieved by his misconduct, tho they refrain from all remonstrances.

Undeterred, Coleridge left for London in October, and Southey, not without rancor, wrote to Charles Danvers on November 13:

Coleridge is in London—gone *professedly* to be cured of taking opium & drinking spirits by

Carlisle—*really* because he was tired of being here, & wanted to do both more at his ease elsewhere. I have a dismal letter about him from Carlisle. The case is utterly hopeless—that is the *moral* case; for as for his body, it is yet sound if he would let it be so,—but the will is so thoroughly & radically diseased, that in this instance there is an actual fall of man, from which little short of a miraculous interposition can redeem him.

Four months later Southey repeats this estimate, a little more kindly perhaps, in a letter to Sir George Beaumont:

The more necessary it becomes for Coleridge to exert himself in providing means for meeting the growing demands of his children, the more incapable, by some strange and fatal infirmity, does he become of exertion. Knowing his prodigious powers, and that there is no bodily disease which incapacitates him, so that the mere effort of his own will would at any moment render him all that his friends and family wish him to be, it is impossible not to feel a hope that that effort will one day be made; yet this is hoping for an intellectual and moral conversion, a new birth produced by an operation of grace, of which there is no example to encourage us to hope for it.

Before Coleridge left for London, Southey made another effort to stir him to activity, in a series of articles to be drawn from their notebooks—a work eventually entitled *Omniana*. Most of the contributions were Southey's. "I urged Coleridge," Southey wrote,

to double the number of "Omniana" volumes, merely for the sake of making him do something for his family; this requiring, literally, no other trouble than either cutting out of his common-place books what has for years been accumulating there, or marking the passage off for a transcriber. He promised to add two volumes, and has contributed about one sheet, which, I dare say, unless he soon returns to Cumberland, will be all.

Southey, however, still reverenced Coleridge's intellectual powers. "If you talk to him about your theological theories," he wrote to William Taylor in November 1810, "you will find a man thoroughly versed in the subject,—bringing to it all that can brought from erudition & meditation"; and late in 1811 he made arrangements to have Coleridge's lectures taken down in shorthand: "I am very anxious that Coleridge should complete this course of lectures, because whatever comes from him now will not be lost as it was at the Royal Institution. I have taken care that they shall be taken down in shorthand."

From the time of his arrival in Keswick, Coleridge had been only a fitful occupant of Greta Hall, spending much of his time elsewhere. Then in 1812, after returning home for a stay of two months, a visit destined to be his last in the North, he departed for London, leaving his family to share the house with the Southeys; and with his departure the personal relations between himself and Southey, save for a few subsequent meetings in London, came to an end. Southey had hardened his heart against Coleridge. When *Remorse* appeared on the Drury Lane stage in January 1813 he did, indeed, wish "Coleridge *joy* of his *Remorse;*" but not without a sneer he went on to note that had Sheridan and Kemble

> brought it out when it was written [1797], C. might probably (yea probably,—for the applause of pit, box & gallery are the best stimulants for him)—have produced a dozen other such plays, or better, in the years which have intervened since they rejected this. Better however late than [n]ever,—& it is a most seasonable prize in the lottery for his family.

In the autumn of 1813 Coleridge made his way to Bristol. Here he remained about a year and delivered several successful courses of lectures. His opium habit, however, had almost wholly possessed him, and this period (1813 to 1815) is the darkest of his life. In the spring of 1814 Joseph Cottle learned, apparently for the first time, of Coleridge's indulgence in opium. When confronted by Cottle, Coleridge frankly admitted his weakness. Cottle determined to procure among Coleridge's friends an annuity of £150 as the best means of helping him, but before proceeding in the matter, he sought Southey's advice. Southey replied on April 17, 1814, utterly disapproving of any such financial assistance and pointing out that Coleridge had long enjoyed an annuity from the Wedgwoods, though it had been reduced to £75 less taxes. He admitted that since the annuity was being paid directly to Mrs. Coleridge, Coleridge was not embarrassed by his family, "except that he has insured his life for a thousand pounds, and pays the annual premium." It would seem that Southey would sanction no plan for Coleridge save his own:

> There are but two grounds on which a subscription of this nature can proceed: either when the object is disabled from exerting himself; or when his exertions are unproductive. Coleridge is in neither of these predicaments. . . . He is at this moment as capable of exertion as I am, and would be paid as well for whatever he might be pleased to do. There are two Reviews,—the 'Quarterly,' and the 'Eclectic,' in both of which he might have employment at ten guineas a sheet. As to the former I could obtain it for him. . . .

Southey went on to suggest that Coleridge return to Keswick, collecting money on the way by lecturing at Birmingham and Liverpool. He said he would be unwilling to contribute anything should Cottle persist in his plan for an annuity.

Not satisfied with this letter to Cottle, Southey wrote again the next day. Adverting to the Wedgwood annuity, he said Coleridge had long since enjoyed its benefits, though the previous day he had noted its payment to Mrs. Coleridge. Southey was determined to have his way:

> You will probably write to Poole on this subject. In that case, state to him distinctly what my opinion is: that Coleridge should return home to Keswick, raising a supply for his present exigencies, by lecturing at Birmingham and Liverpool, and then, if there be a necessity, as I fear there *will be* (arising solely and wholly from his own most culpable habits of sloth and self-indulgence) of calling on his friends to do that which *he can* and *ought to do,*—for *that* time the humiliating solicitation should be reserved.

On receipt of the letters from Southey, Cottle accordingly dropped the plan of raising an annuity for Coleridge. Instead he wrote a long letter of advice and remonstrance to Coleridge on April 25th, suggesting that he would gladly defray Coleridge's expenses to Keswick, and assuring him that "with better habits, you would be hailed by your family . . . as an angel from heaven." Nor did Cottle conclude without bringing up the name of Southey, who, he said, "has a family of his own, which by his literary labour, he supports, to his great honour."

On April 26th, Coleridge replied to Cottle: "I but barely glanced at the middle of the first page of your letter, and have seen no more of it—not from resentment . . . but from the state of my bodily and mental sufferings." He went on to say that had he "but a few hundred pounds, but £200,—half to send to Mrs. Coleridge, and half to place myself in a private mad house . . . how willingly would I place myself under Dr. Fox, in his establishment." In another letter Coleridge wrote to Cottle that he was resolved to place himself in an establishment for a month or two, but had no money. He asked Cottle to confer with two or three friends in Bristol and see what could be done.

Again Cottle wrote to Southey for advice, this time forwarding all of his correspondence with Coleridge. Southey's answer shows how utterly incapable he was of understanding Coleridge, much less sympathizing with him in his hour of trial. "You may imagine," Southey replied,

> with what feelings I have read your correspondence with Coleridge. Shocking as his letters are, perhaps the most mournful thing they discover is, that while acknowledging the guilt of the habit, he imputes it still to morbid bodily causes, whereas after every possible allowance is made for these, every person who has witnessed his habits, knows that for the

greater, infinitely the greater part, inclination and indulgence are its motives. . . .

The Morgans, with great difficulty and perseverance, *did* break him of the habit, at a time when his ordinary consumption of laudanum was, from *two quarts a week,* to *a pint a day!* He suffered dreadfully during the first abstinence, so much so, as to say it was better for him to die than to endure his present feelings. . . .

Unquestionably, restraint would do as much for him as it did when the Morgans tried it, but I do not see the slightest reason for believing it would be more permanent. . . . Could he be compelled to a certain quantity of labour every day, *for his family,* the pleasure of having done it would make his heart glad, and the sane mind would make the body whole.

I see nothing so advisable for him, as that he should come here to Greta Hall. My advice is, that he should visit T. Poole for two or three weeks, to freshen himself and recover spirits. . . . When there, he may consult his friends at Birmingham and Liverpool, on the fitness of lecturing at those two places. . . . Here it is that he ought to be. He knows in what manner he would be received;—by his children with joy; by his wife, not with tears, if she can control them—certainly not with reproaches;— by myself only with encouragement.

He has sources of direct emolument open to him in the *'Courier,'* and in the *'Eclectic Review.'*—These for his immediate wants, and for everything else, his pen is more rapid than mine, and would be paid as well. . . . His great object should be, to get out a play, and appropriate the whole produce to the support of his son Hartley, at College. Three months' pleasurable exertion would effect this. Of some such fit of industry I by no means despair; of any thing more than fits, I am afraid I do. But this of course I shall never say to him. From me he shall never hear ought but cheerful encouragement, and the language of hope.

Coleridge, of course, would have none of this advice. Domestication with Southey, who now wished to regulate his every movement, no less than with Mrs. Coleridge, was utterly repugnant to him. It is worth remarking, however, that Coleridge's Bristol friends did not abandon him, and he was able to rouse himself far more than Southey predicted. Though the years 1814 and 1815 present a tragic spectacle in his abject slavery to opium and the evils attendant upon that habit, nevertheless the year 1815 saw the creation of his most sustained critical writing, the *Biographia Literaria.* His powers of thinking were unimpaired, and his almost complete emancipation from the drug after 1816 shows that his will was not so "radically diseased" as Southey had imagined.

In the autumn of 1814, however, Southey renewed his attacks. Since Coleridge did not reply to his letters about the entrance of Hartley Coleridge into college, Southey got in touch with Coleridge's brothers at Ottery and, with their financial assistance and that of friends, arranged for Hartley to attend Merton College, Oxford. The following extracts from two of his unpublished letters to George Coleridge show the nature of his resentment. On October 12, 1814, he wrote:

The task of addressing you upon this subject Sir is a painful one. It would be more so if I did not verily believe that your brother labours under a species of insanity. His intellect is as powerful as it ever was, and perfectly unclouded—but all moral strength is paralysed in him; and when any thing comes before him in the form of duty, it seems to take away from him not merely the inclination but even the power of performing it. It would scarcely be speaking too strongly were I to say that he has abandoned his family to chance and charity.

In his letter of November 14 Southey tried to be more generous in his estimate:

Impossible as it is to depend upon him, [Coleridge] I never have wholly given up the hope that in some fit of exertion he may produce some thing worthy of the powers with which he has been gifted— powers which considering their variety as well as their extent, exceed that of any person whom it has ever been my fortune to meet with. I do not mean to extenuate his total disregard of all duties,—but it must be some consolation to you to know that those persons who have been most intimately connected with him during the last twenty years, who best know his conduct and have most cause to deplore and to condemn it, retain for him thro' all a degree of affection which it is not easy to express.

On October 17, 1814, Southey wrote to Cottle:

Can you tell us anything of Coleridge? A few lines of introduction to a son of Mr. Biddulph . . . are all that we have received from him since I saw him last September twelvemonth in town. The children being thus entirely left to chance, I have applied to his brothers at Ottery. . . . Lady Beaumont has promised £30 annually for this purpose, Poole £10. . . . The brothers, as I expected, promise their concurrence, and I daily expect a letter stating to what amount they will contribute. What is to become of Coleridge himself! He may continue to find men who will give him board and lodging for the sake of his conversation, but who will pay his other expenses? I cannot but apprehend some shameful and dreadful end to this deplorable course.

Southey's personal animosity, indeed, knew no bounds, for a year later he began to fear lest Coleridge become a bad influence upon his son. Nowhere is his meddling interference more flagrant. Hartley's "greatest danger," he wrote to J. N. White on May 8, 1815,

> arises from a mournful cause, against which it is impossible to protect, or even to caution him,—it arises from his father. . . . If Coleridge should take it in his head to send for the boy to pass any of his vacations with him, there is the most imminent danger of his unsettling his mind upon the most important subjects, and the end would be utter and irremediable ruin. For Coleridge, totally regardless of all consequences, will lead him into all the depths and mazes of metaphysics: he would root up from his mind, without intending it, all established principles; and if he should succeed in establishing others in their place, with one of Hartley's ardour and sincerity, they would never serve for the practical purposes of society, and he would be thrown out from the only profession or way of life for which he is qualified.

Southey, too, may have been responsible for Mrs. Coleridge's remarks about the publication of *Christabel* in 1816: "Oh! when will he ever give his friends anything but pain? he has been so unwise as to publish his fragments of 'Christabel' & 'Koula-Khan' Murray is the publisher, & the price is 4*s* 6*d*—we were all sadly vexed when we read the advertizment of these things." Southey's neglect of the poems seems deplorable. In 1808, he had written, "Puff me, Coleridge! if you love me, puff me! Puff a couple of hundred into my pocket!" for he knew how much reviewing did for the sale of a publication; but now, when he had become a mainstay of the *Quarterly Review,* he never lifted a finger, either in that publication or elsewhere.

When Southey's *Wat Tyler,* his youthful outburst written in the fervor of Republicanism in 1794, was published in a pirated edition, Coleridge loyally defended him in two letters to the *Courier.* Southey was stirred by Coleridge's vindication of him:

> I am glad to see . . . that this business has called forth Coleridge, and with the recollections of old times, brought back something like old feelings. He wrote a very excellent paper on the subject in the 'Courier,' and I hope it will be the means of his joining us ere long; so good will come out of evil, and the devil can do nothing but what he is permitted.

Moved to temporary friendliness by Coleridge's defense, Southey wrote favorably to Humphrey Senhouse of Coleridge's second *Lay Sermon* a few days later:

> There are some excellent remarks in Coleridge's second lay sermon upon the over-balance of the commercial spirit, that greediness of gain among all ranks to which I have more than once alluded in the Quarterly. If Coleridge could but learn how to

deliver his opinions in a way to make them read, and to separate that which would be profitable for all, from that which scarcely half a dozen men in England can understand (I certainly am not one of the number), he would be the most useful man of the age, as I verily believe him in acquirements and in powers of mind to be very far the greatest.

In August 1817, Southey apparently paid a visit to Coleridge at Highgate. Writing to his wife on August 13, he speaks most unkindly of Coleridge and protests bitterly against Coleridge's suggestion, probably made only casually, of settling in Keswick. Southey's remarks seem quite contradictory to his positive recommendations to Cottle three years earlier. At that time the only solution for Coleridge had been to return to Keswick and work under Southey's surveillance:

> I shall go to Highgate to-morrow. I gather from his [Coleridge's] note which I received this morning that he looks toward Keswick as if he meant to live there. At present this cannot be for want of room— the Rickmans being our guests—if he meant to live with his family it must be upon a separate establishment. I shall neither speak harshly nor unkindly, but at my time of life, with my occupations [the thing is impossible]. This is a hateful visit and I wish it were over. He will begin as he did when last I saw him, about Animal Magnetism or some equally congruous subject, and go on from Dan to Beersheba in his endless loquacity.

With Southey's visit to Highgate we come to the end of his comments on Coleridge during the latter's lifetime, save for a few passing references. Southey took no notice of Coleridge's *Biographia Literaria,* nor did he see fit to review it, even though Coleridge had made so generous an estimate of him in that publication. Southey might have remembered Coleridge's defense of *Wat Tyler* in the *Courier,* but he remained ungraciously silent. With the publication of the *Biographia Literaria* and *Sibylline Leaves* in 1817, Coleridge had admirably fulfilled Southey's constant urgings to carry something through to completion. As Sir E. K. Chambers points out, the years 1815-1817 "represent Coleridge's most continuous period of literary activity." *The Friend,* reissued in 1818, the *Aids to Reflection* of 1825, the *Poetical Works* of 1828, and the *Constitution of the Church and State* of 1830 were further evidence of Coleridge's industry. Southey, though in a prominent and influential position, preferred to let Coleridge's works make their way without encouragement from his pen. Had he shown the same utter indifference to Coleridge during the early years of their association—had he, for example, refrained from active interference in the marriage—the whole pattern of Coleridge's life might have been different. Examined in the light of all the facts, the friendship between the two men handicapped rather than benefited Coleridge almost from the beginning.

Coleridge died on July 25, 1834. To Wynn, Southey merely noted the event—"Poor Coleridge has just died at sixty-two, of old age"—and to Mrs. Hughes he wrote:

> It is just forty years since I became acquainted with Coleridge; he had long been dead to me, but his decease has naturally wakened up old recollections. . . . All who are of his blood were in the highest degree proud of his reputation, but this was their only feeling concerning him.

In two sentences from an unpublished letter to Rickman, Southey displays more feeling: "The day's letters bring the news of S.T.C.'s death.—It will not intrude much upon my waking thoughts, but I expect to feel it for some time to come in my dreams."

Unfortunately, this is not all. On February 20, 1835, Wordsworth and Tom Moore were guests at Samuel Rogers'. Coleridge came up for discussion. The report in Tom Moore's diary affords an unpleasant comment upon Southey:

> [Wordsworth] talked of Coleridge, and praised him, not merely as a poet, but as a man, to a degree which I could not listen to without putting in my protest. . . . [I] hinted something of this in reply to Wordsworth's praises, and adverted to Southey's opinion of him, as expressed in a letter to Bowles, (saying, if I recollect right, that he was "lamented by few, and regretted by none,") but Wordsworth continued his eulogium. Defended Coleridge's desertion of his family on the grounds of incompatibility, &c. between him and Mrs. Coleridge: said that Southey took a "rigid view" of the whole matter.

Southey let his antagonism to Coleridge reach beyond the grave. In his will, Coleridge had left to the discretion of Joseph Henry Green, his literary executor, the publication of his remains, including letters, and accordingly applications for manuscripts were made to Coleridge's former intimates. Most of them willingly complied. Southey, however, refused. Writing to Coleridge's nephew on November 7, 1834, he said:

> I have all the letters that I ever received from S.T.C. To make any selection from them is what I have not heart to do; & it is not a task that could be delegated to any one. A time will come when the whole may be published without offending the feelings, or gratifying the malice of any one; & they will lose none of their value by keeping.— Indeed as I hear nothing of any intended collection of his letters, I conclude that those who are most concerned agree with me in their opinion upon this point.

In 1835, Cottle determined to prepare a memoir of Coleridge. When the Coleridge family learned of his projected work, they succeeded, through the good offices of Thomas Poole, in persuading him to abandon plans for publication. Henry Nelson Coleridge discussed the matter in a letter to Poole on September 21, 1835:

> Between ourselves, and without any undue disparagement of Mr. C[ottle] I think you have done us all a great service in extinguishing his publication. His materials, in any shape, must be most valuable of course; . . . I hope Mr. Cottle will not refuse to let Mr. Green have either the originals or copies of the letters. . . . I think it might be mentioned to him that my Uncle . . . has in his very solemn will committed the care of collecting letters to Mr. Green.

Again on April 16, 1836, he wrote to Poole: "Mr. Cottle's memoir will be most highly valuable in whatever shape he may think fit to compose it, and I wish you would express to him, as I believe Mr. Green will himself do, how grateful we shall be for his communication when he considers it finished."

As his memoir took shape, Cottle planned to send it as a contribution to James Gillman, who was writing a biography of Coleridge, with the approbation of Mr. Green. Since he had unbounded faith in Southey's judgment, however, Cottle first sent him the manuscript early in 1836. On March 5, Southey wrote a long letter in reply:

> You will see that I have drawn my pen across several passages in your MSS. The easiest way of showing you the incorrectness of these passages will be by giving you a slight summary of the facts. Let me however premise that this is only for your satisfaction and for your own use, if you should like to draw up your own Reminiscences, and leave them for publication at some proper time. . . . But with regard to Mr. Green's intended publication without intending the slightest disrespect to him, my desire is that as little as possible concerning me may be communicated to it. Reserve for my own memoirs (whenever they may be wanted) such materials in your possession as belong to them, and do not send them to S.T.C.'s executors, for a work of which it is desirable that I should be kept as clear as possible. Whatever shew of respect may be made in it, I very well know that it will be composed in no spirit of good will to me.

Southey went on to tell Cottle of a letter he had just received from Edward Moxon, stating that at his "earnest solicitation, many objectionable passages" respecting Southey and Wordsworth had been expunged from Allsop's *Letters, Conversations and Recollections of S. T. Coleridge,* which he had published. Southey remarked that "there is nothing in this work relating to myself of the slightest consequence" and that "Mr. Green certainly will not be guilty of any such indiscretions; but beyond a doubt he has been imbued with the same feelings toward me."

Not satisfied with this outburst and determined to exert his influence over Cottle, Southey wrote again on April 14, 1836, emphatically declaring that "it is my wish that nothing of mine may go into the hands of any persons who are concerned in bringing forward his [Coleridge's] papers," and pointing out that "If you were drawing up your 'Recollections of Coleridge,' for separate publication, you should be most welcome to insert anything of mine which you thought proper." Southey added a very significant warning: "If you send what you have written, upon this subject, [Coleridge's opium habit] it will not be made use of, and . . . Coleridge's biographer will seek to find excuses for his abuse of that drug." Nor could Southey refrain from an acrimonious attack on Coleridge:

> I know that Coleridge at different times of his life never let pass an opportunity of speaking ill of me. Both Wordsworth and myself have often lamented the exposure of duplicity that must result from the publication of his letters, and of what he has delivered by word of mouth to the worshippers by whom he was always surrounded. To Wordsworth and to me, it matters little. When our lives come to be written there will be nothing that needs either concealment or varnishing.

Southey's letter apparently led Cottle "to stipulate [to Coleridge's biographer, Gillman] that, whatever else was omitted, the opium letters should be printed verbatim. But this being promptly refused, I determined to throw my materials into a separate work."

Realizing that they would be unable to stop Cottle's book, both Mr. Green and the Coleridge family now tried to induce him to delete two parts of it: the reference to DeQuincey's gift of £300 to Coleridge in 1807, DeQuincey having attacked him so bitterly in *Tait's Magazine,* and allusions to the opium habit, including a letter to Wade, in which Coleridge solemnly requested the publication of the full opium story after his death. John Taylor Coleridge, the poet's nephew, being in the Lake Country in the autumn of 1836 and wholly unsuspecting Southey's disloyalty, requested him to influence Cottle to make these omissions. Southey claimed ignorance of Wade's letter but said that Cottle had told him the circumstances of DeQuincey's gift. He assured John Taylor Coleridge that he would write to Cottle and induce him, if possible, "to forego—or modify his intention."

Southey's letter to Cottle of September 30, 1836 advised that "Coleridge's relations are uneasy at what they hear of your intention to publish," and declared: "They cannot say that any one of themselves will bring out a full and authentic account of C. because they know how much there is, which all who have any regard for Coleridge's memory, would wish to be buried with him." In this letter Southey noticeably fails to write anything to induce Cottle to give up or modify his plan.

On October 10, 1836, he wrote again to Cottle, apparently in consequence of a letter he had just received from John Taylor Coleridge on the subject of Cottle's proposed memoir. Unable to resist a criticism of Coleridge, he remarked: "I have long foreseen that poor S. T. Coleridge would leave a large inheritance of uneasiness to his surviving friends, and those who were the most nearly connected with him." He still makes no attempt to persuade Cottle to give up the publication, but he suggests that

> A few omissions (one letter in particular, respecting the habit of taking opium,) would spare them great pain. . . . You have enough to tell that is harmless as well as interesting, and not only harmless, but valuable and instructive, and that *ought* to be told, and which *no one but yourself can tell*. . . . I will read over the Memoir when we meet.

On receipt of this letter Cottle says "his first impression" was "wholly to *withdraw the work*," but he resolved to suspend his decision until he had talked to Southey. In November, Southey visited him, and having re-read the whole manuscript urged him to publish the work. Southey also changed his opinion in regard to any omissions in deference to the wishes of the Coleridge family. He objected alone to "a few trifles, which were expunged" and gave his "unqualified approval" to the publication of the opium letters.

Accordingly, in 1837, Cottle issued his *Early Recollections* with its revelations. Southey, it will be seen, not only refused to cooperate with Coleridge's executor, but was actually responsible for the publication of a work whose contents brought suffering and humiliation to all bearing the name of Coleridge.

After so much ado, one might expect Southey to have approved of *Early Recollections* when it appeared. On the contrary, he was most displeased with the book. Nowhere is his duplicity more blatant. In an unpublished letter to Mrs. Septimus Hodson he wrote on August 7, 1837:

> Cottle's book would have been much more disagreeable to Coleridge's friends than it is, if I had not prevailed on him to strike out many parts. Painful enough the book still is to those who have any regard for his memory: & never surely was there any book that would so completely mislead any one who should use it as materials either for Coleridge's biography or mine, the confusion of dates & circumstances being such as I never saw elsewhere.

The foregoing judgments of Coleridge, albeit they are often harsh and dictated by personal resentment, are among the fullest of contemporary accounts. Perhaps the animosity was increased by Coleridge's well-intentioned but often forthright criticism of Southey's poetry. Coleridge's daughter sums up the matter rather well:

> My father had a strong impression that Southey took a dislike to him from his free & friendly criticism of his verses—& I know that my Uncle did not take this sort of thing genially & frankly. . . . The severity, the bitterness, of my Uncle's censures of my Father arose from the ill offices of tale bearers, & from a suspicion in my Uncle that my father despised & disparaged openly his productions & joined with his disparagers & enemies. . . . My Uncle would have been lenient enough to such shortcomings as my Father's—*was* lenient to misconduct of a worse kind, had not resentment taken the form of disapprobation & given it an edge.

The forty-year association of Coleridge and Southey is, with the exception of that with Charles Lamb, the longest of Coleridge's career. At first Southey loved Coleridge, then pitied him, came to condemn him, and finally, as far as he was able, tried to forget him.

C. H. Herford on Southey's status as a Lake Poet:

Southey belongs only by residence and friendship to that misbirth of criticism the 'Lake School.' Between his industrious and learned explorations of the myth and the mystic supernaturalism of Wordsworth and Coleridge there is no affinity. They approach the wonderful as mystics, he as a historian. They are prophets of the 'Renascence of Marvel,' he a picturesque exploiter of marvellous beliefs.

C. H. Herford, in The Age of Wordsworth, *G. Bell and Sons, 1930.*

Malcolm Elwin

SOURCE: "Partners in Poetry," in *The First Romantics,* Longmans, Green and Co., 1948, pp. 159-194.

[*In the following essay, Elwin examines the work of Wordsworth and Coleridge in the context of their personal and literary relationships with each other and with their circle of relatives and acquaintances, including Southey, Dorothy Wordsworth, and Charles Lamb.*]

1. SUSPECTS AT ALFOXDEN

Wordsworth left Coleridge at Stowey with an invitation to visit him at Racedown. As soon as Coleridge had finally corrected his poems to his satisfaction, and sent them with Lamb's and Lloyd's to Cottle for the

printer, he set off. On Sundays he frequently preached in the Unitarian chapels at Bridgwater and Taunton, usually walking and never accepting a fee for his sermons. On Sunday 4th June 1797 he preached at Bridgwater, breakfasted next morning at Taunton, and then walked the twenty miles to Racedown. The distance was nothing to him. Later in the summer he walked to Bristol and back, a distance of forty miles, in a single day—to make the personal acquaintance of "that great and excellent woman," Mrs. Barbauld, to whom he had sent a copy of his poems. He found Wordsworth and Dorothy alone, Mary Hutchinson having left only that morning for London. In old age they both remembered how Coleridge, eager to meet them and unfatigued by his long walk, "did not keep to the highway, but leapt over a gate and bounded down the pathless field, by which he cut off an angle." That evening Wordsworth read his latest poem, *The Ruined Cottage,* and Coleridge then recited two and a half acts of his tragedy *Osorio;* next morning Wordsworth read *The Borderers.*

The Ruined Cottage, afterwards included in the first book of *The Excursion,* was the story of the simple cottage couple, whose happiness is withered by the poverty and famine induced by the country's going to war, impelling the husband to enlist, while the lonely wife loses first her growing boy as a farmer's apprentice and then her younger child by death. The simplicity of its telling, in unadorned blank verse, confirmed Coleridge's impression of Wordsworth's powers from his reading of *Guilt and Sorrow.* With wonderful fidelity he remembered his impressions in *Biographia Literaria.* Some harshness of versification, to his unfailing musical ear, remained—and always did remain—but "the occasional obscurities, which had risen from an imperfect control over the resources of his native language, had almost wholly disappeared, together with that worse defect of arbitrary and illogical phrases, at once hackneyed and fantastic, which hold so distinguished a place in the *technique* of ordinary poetry, and will, more or less, alloy the earlier poems of the truest genius." He saw that he and Southey, though led by Bowles and Akenside to seek their inspiration directly from nature, had pursued the shadow of the substance in valuing their manipulation of difficult metres, their hard-sought metaphors and similes, their artful allegories and brightly polished phrases. Here was "no mark of strained thought, or forced diction, no crowd or turbulence of imagery," such as had been held again his *Religious Musings,* and he was impressed by "the union of deep feeling with profound thought; the fine balance of truth in observing, with the imaginative faculty in modifying, the objects observed; and above all the original gift of spreading the tone, the atmosphere, and with it the depth and height of the ideal world around forms, incidents, and situations, of which, for the common view, custom had bedimmed all the lustre, had dried up the sparkle and the dew drops." Though he had before confessed that his critical vice was "a precipitance in praise," his admiration was spontaneous and unstinted. After three weeks at Racedown he wrote, "Wordsworth is a very great man, the only man to whom *at all times* and *in all modes of excellence* I feel myself inferior."

Aside from his personal attractions, his admiration of her beloved brother won Dorothy's heart, for she knew that such admiration was what Wordsworth most needed to dispel his despondency and encourage him to fresh efforts. In her adoration she extravagantly applauded his work—as her most fervent admirer, Professor de Selincourt, admitted, she became "a dangerously undiscriminating critic"—but Wordsworth knew that her praise was neither unprejudiced nor endowed with critical experience. Coleridge, however, was a poet whose gifts he recognised however unwillingly, and also the possessor of intellectual attainments compelling the admiration of all who knew him.

Ten years later Southey shrewdly diagnosed the vice of Wordsworth's intellect as being "always upon the stretch and strain," looking "at pileworts and daffy-downdillies through the same telescope which he applies to the moon and the stars." For want of wider experience and of the moderating influence of taste and discrimination deriving from intellectual culture—a want intensified by narrowness of life and the habit of self-absorption—Wordsworth increasingly tended to magnify the trivial, and Dorothy, intent on sharing his impressions, lost her sense of proportion and likewise saw with distortion. To this tendency Coleridge was a corrective; his quick selective sense seized on the significant, and his eloquence as rapidly translated its meaning. The speed of his perception must have been a breathtaking revelation to Wordsworth and Dorothy. While Wordsworth mused over an idea, his mental energies labouring exhaustingly to move his sluggish imagination, Coleridge had only to take up the trend of his thought to provide the clue to the solution. His leaping imagination was a hare to Wordsworth's tortoise; he understood, and painted in a few swift strokes, the notion which Wordsworth would have sweated hours to sketch.

Probably Wordsworth never fully grasped the implications of the poetic theory that Coleridge eloquently expounded and of which he declared his poetry to be the purest practical example. He said with truth in old age that he "never cared a straw about the theory." But he did immediately realise that Coleridge's endless conversation enabled him to see with clarity where before he had groped unsteadily in baffling fog. Both he and Dorothy recognised, as the latter confessed, that Coleridge's conversation was necessary to his artistic development.

So when Coleridge at length tore himself away on 28th June, it was only to return from Stowey four days later with Poole's one-horse chaise, in which he was to drive Dorothy "over forty miles of execrable roads," while Wordsworth walked. Though he retained rueful recollections of his charger in dragooning days, and when he borrowed a mount from Poole to ride between Stowey and Bridgewater, he begged for a steed "of tolerable meekness," he was delighted after his venture to reckon himself "now no inexpert whip."

The Wordsworths were guests for a fortnight at Coleridge's cottage, which must have been overcrowded when Charles Lamb arrived for his long-promised visit on 7th July. Coleridge was laid up throughout his week's stay, for two days after the Wordsworths' arrival, "dear Sara accidentally emptied a skiller of boiling milk" over his foot. One evening, when all had gone for a walk, leaving him alone in Poole's arbour, he wrote the first of his poems under Wordsworth's influence, *This Lime-Tree Bower My Prison.*

> Well, they are gone, and here must I remain,
> This lime-tree bower my prison! I have lost
> Beauties and feelings, such as would have
>   been
> Most sweet to my remembrance even when
>   age
> Had dimm'd mine eyes to blindness! They,
>   meanwhile,
> Friends, whom I never more may meet again,
> On springy heath, along the hill-top edge,
> Wander in gladness, and wind down,
>   perchance,
> To that still roaring dell of which I told.

In imagination he accompanied their walk, seeing their delight in the beautiful scenery he had described to them, and especially he felt pleasure in picturing the gladness of his "gentle-hearted Charles," who had pined

> And hunger'd after Nature, many a year,
> In the great City pent, winning thy way
> With sad yet patient soul, through evil and
>   pain
> And strange calamity!

In the last year of his life, with a full heart, he re-read the poem and wrote in the margin, "Ch. and Mary Lamb—dear to my heart, yea, as it were my Heart—S.T.C. Aet. 63; 1834-1797-1834-37 years!"

The simplicity of thought and diction, the preference of blank verse to a complicated form, the complete absence of "manchineel" ornament, indicates the fresh influence of Wordsworth and the speed with which Coleridge had learned his lesson. A few days later, replying to Southey's request for a contribution to a volume to be published for the benefit of Chatterton's sister, he promised a preliminary essay and possibly a poem, but prohibited the reprinting of his "Monody."

"On a life and death so full of heart-going *realities* as poor Chatterton's," he wrote, "to find such shadowy nobodies as cherub-winged *Death*, trees of *Hope*, bare-bosomed *Affection*, and simpering *Peace*, makes one's blood circulate like ipecacuanha." The second edition of his poems was in the press and published in the course of the current month. They could not be altered; but he was so out of love with his own compositions, so conscious of their defects, that he felt irritated at the praise of reviewers. Unable to express his self-criticism in a review of his own work, he published in the *Monthly Magazine* the three sonnets under the pseudonym of "Nehemiah Higginbottom," which he reprinted in *Biographia Literaria*. The first sonnet was "to excite a good-natured laugh at the spirit of doleful egotism, and at the recurrence of favourite phrases, with the double defect of being at once trite and licentious"; the second on "low creeping language and thoughts, under the pretence of simplicity"; the third, "the phrases of which were borrowed entirely from my own poems, on the indiscriminate use of elaborate and swelling language and imagery."

Though in later years professing a contempt for the country as an inveterate Londoner, Charles Lamb valued every minute of brief escape from the office-stool into the little intellectual society gathered in the rural peace of the Quantocks. He felt "improvement in the recollection of many a casual conversation," and "the names of Tom Poole, of Wordsworth and his good sister, with thine and Sara's are become 'familiar in my mouth as household words.'" On leaving, he forgot his greatcoat, and writing for its return, expressed envy of "that greatcoat lingering so cunningly behind." As he travelled alone from Bridgwater to Bristol, heart-full at parting, he looked out for John Thelwall, who was daily expected at Stowey, but felt that if he had met him, going to the happy scene he was himself leaving, "it would have moved me almost to tears."

Thelwall was a notorious enthusiast for the French Revolution and opponent of the war and the government. At the age of thirty, in November 1794, he had stood in the dock with the veterans Horne Tooke, Hardy and Holcroft on a charge of high treason. If the accused had been found guilty, said the banker-poet, Samuel Rogers, they would certainly have been hanged, for "we lived in a reign of terror then." After his acquittal, he had campaigned courageously against Pitt's government, and when he held a mass-meeting in Marylebone Fields, his paper, the *Tribune,* was suppressed. Banned from holding meetings in London, he wandered about the country, lecturing on historical subjects, drawing pointed parallels with current politics. Often he was mobbed at lectures, and magistrates refused him the law's protection. Coleridge had opened correspondence with him in the spring of 1796 by sending him a copy of his poems. Thelwall returned the compliment with a present of his latest book, and

they exchanged in friendly argument their views on religion and politics in an interesting series of letters. Months before, Coleridge had invited him to visit him at Bristol, but now for the first time Thelwall had the opportunity to meet in the flesh the man whose reputation and writings so much interested him. He arrived at Stowey on 17th July, at nine in the evening, and found Sara alone, as Coleridge was staying with the Wordsworths at Alfoxden, about three miles away.

The Wordsworths were enchanted with the Quantocks. "There is everything here," wrote Dorothy, for while she found the brooks and woods as attractive as those of Cumberland, there was also the sea at hand and many "romantic" villages. Especially they liked the park of Alfoxden House, and indulging "dreams of happiness in a little cottage" near there, they made inquiries for such a place. Then came the news that Bartholomew, the farm bailiff of the St. Albyn family, was empowered to let Alfoxden House furnished, with immediate possession, for the astonishingly small rent of twenty-three pounds a year. Wordsworth immediately took the house on an annual tenancy, signing the agreement with Bartholomew on 14th July, Poole witnessing.

Coleridge was assisting in his friends' installation when Thelwall arrived, while Sara remained at home to deal with the accumulated laundry of her husband and guests. Thelwall slept the night at Stowey, and was next morning conducted by Sara to Alfoxden for breakfast. For three days the whole party remained at Alfoxden, wandering about the beautiful gardens, discussing poetry, the "moral character" of democrats and aristocrats, and "pursuits proper for literary men" who were "unfit for management of pecuniary affairs," like Rousseau, Bacon, and Arthur Young. They were "a most philosophical party," and Thelwall desired only the company of his wife to complete his pleasure in a "delightful spot." Since his paper had been suppressed and he seemed well advised to leave London to escape the probability of another government prosecution, Thelwall was looking for a small farm, and Poole and Coleridge undertook to find something suitable for him in the neighbourhood.

But "Citizen" Thelwall was a marked man, and his presence in the district excited suspicion of a seditious plot in the war-fearful minds of neighbouring gentry. Though, as Coleridge remarked, the coast from Clevedon to Minehead scarcely permitted the approach of a fishing-boat, it was suspected that this convocation of "suspects" might indicate the proposed landing of a French invasion. So, owing to "the grave alarm of a titled Dogberry of our neighbourhood," Coleridge related in *Biographia Literaria,* "a spy was actually sent down from the government *pour surveillance* of myself and friends." Coleridge was actually interviewed by the disguised Bow Street runner, who, readily drawing the friendly and talkative philosopher into conversation, affected extreme democratic opinions, and was so impressed by Coleridge's eloquent exposition of his familiar arguments against Jacobinism that he shamefacedly confessed "he had only *put it on*." The landlord of the inn at Stowey also confided to Coleridge how he was questioned by the spy about him and his mysterious friend at Alfoxden, and how finally he declared, "Why, folks do say, your Honour! as how that he is a *Poet,* and that he is going to put Quantocks and all about here in print; and as they be so much together, I suppose that the strange gentleman has some *consarn* in the business."

But the "strange gentleman," in his old age as Poet Laureate and the respected friend of all the Tory gentry, titled or untitled, lay or clerical, in the Lake district, felt that the story of his being once the quarry of a government spy, derogated from his dignity and respectability. He did not definitely deny its truth; he implied a doubt of its truth by stating that the facts related by Coleridge only came to his knowledge after he had left Alfoxden. Victorian biographers naturally supposed that no spy could enter the gossipping confines of a remote country village without every child's mother chattering of the phenomenon, and as Wordsworth was eminently respectable while Coleridge had certain regrettable foibles unhappily too often coincident with genius, respectability accepted, as always, the testimony of respectability. Even Coleridge's grandson, confronted with his grandfather's letters to Thelwall, referred to "apocryphal anecdotes about the spy" in *Biographia Literaria.*

Researches by Mr. A. J. Eagleston revealed records in the Home Office archives of a spy having been sent to Stowey, on representations from Lord Somerville, of Fitzhead Court, Taunton (curiously, a distant relative of Southey's), a landowner near Bridgwater named Sir Philip Hale, and a Bath physician named Lysons, who acted on the gossip of his cook, who had been formerly employed at Alfoxden. The spy lodged at Stowey during August, and reported that Poole protected "a mischievous gang of disaffected Englishmen," who had been visited by the notorious Thelwall. Ironically for respectability, Wordsworth was the chief object of suspicion, as he had no wife with him, but only a woman who "posed for his sister!" Coleridge, as he relates, was planning a poem to be called "The Brook," and made many excursions with pencil and notebook to the stream running from Holford to Kilve; the following spy duly noted that he was "apparently taking observations" on the "river" in his "portfolio." On such momentous information some excited clerk in the Home Office must have had visions of the French fleet sailing into the bowels of Somerset, with dire consequences to the minnows and greyling! "Coldridge" was reported as "a man of superior ability," who kept a press in his house and was believed to print his own compositions. But the fact that Coleridge often preached sermons on Sundays must have weighed in his favour, and the spy regretfully decided that he was "respectable." And when Basil Montagu, described as "a great counsellor from London," came to see his son at Alfoxden, and such an eminently respectable Bristol citizen as Cottle visited Coleridge, the spy packed up in disgust.

In the nineteen-twenties, when a man with a beard appeared on a Labour platform during an election in a cathedral town, he was popularly reckoned a Russian in disguise. So, in country villages, young men in beards and corduroy trousers are labelled "a rum lot," and if they show no visible signs of making money by selling something for more than they bought it for, they will be objects of suspicion. Poole was locally notorious for revolutionary opinions, Coleridge was his friend, and now came a dark, gaunt young man, with a woman supposed to be his sister, but obviously showing to him more than a normal sisterly affection. They kept unconventional hours, and used each other's houses as their own. In Stowey Coleridge's friendliness and willingness to talk with anybody had won him the villagers' tolerant affection, but in the neighbouring villages his name was a subject for dark gossip. He once encountered a woman from George Burnett's village, who talked of him as "that vile iacobin villain" who had seduced "a young man of our parish"; he listened patiently, exclaiming at appropriate intervals, and so won her heart by his "civilities" that he "had not courage enough to undeceive her." As for Wordsworth, after half a century's residence in Cumberland, he was still regarded with dubious glances by the dalesmen; striding along, often muttering to himself, he was too lost in thought to notice their tentative greetings. As a stranger of unknown antecedents, he was big game for gossip in a country village.

Poole, as a man of important standing locally, suffered from his association with these eccentrics. "We are shocked to hear that Mr. Thelwall has spent some time at Stowey this week with Mr. Coleridge, and consequently with Tom Poole," wrote one of his orthodox cousins on 23rd July. "Alfoxden house is taken by one of the fraternity. . . . To what are we coming?" These virtuous relatives made representations to his aging invalid mother, who was alarmed at the possibility of her son's ostracism by neighbours with whom she had been friendly for fifty years. His work as organiser of the village benefit club and book society faced probable frustration, and even his business and credit were likely to be affected. He was therefore compelled to tell Coleridge that he could not risk the consequences of finding a farm for Thelwall.

Coleridge did not immediately abandon his efforts. His favourable impression of Thelwall in correspondence was confirmed by personal contact. "Thelwall," he said,, "is a very warm hearted honest man—and disagreeing, as we do, on almost every point of religion, of morals, of politics, and of philosophy, we like each other uncommonly well." He believed him to be "perhaps the only *acting* Democrat, that *is* honest—for the *Patriots* are ragged cattle—a most execrable herd—arrogant because they are ignorant, and boastful of the strength of reason, because they have never tried it enough to know its *weakness*." Writing to Thelwall that "the aristocrats seem to persecute *even Wordsworth*," he assured him that "we will at least not yield without a struggle; and if I cannot get you near me, it shall not be for want of a trial on my part."

Though he had been ill the day before, he walked one day in September to Bridgwater to sound two of the principal land-agents. One was "powerless"; the other, a Mr. Chubb, was unable to see him on account of the assizes. Returning home, he wrote to Chubb, praising Thelwall's personality and even arguing as a reason for his settlement near Stowey, that, in the event of revolution, Thelwall might have great influence on the lower classes, in which case it would "prove of no mean utility to the cause of Truth and Humanity that he had spent some years in a society, where his natural impetuosity had been disciplined into patience, and salutary scepticism, and the slow energies of a *Calculating* spirit." But Chubb replied that he would find Thelwall a farm if Poole and Coleridge were agreed on the advisability of his settling there. As this again reposed responsibility on Poole, Coleridge had to inform Thelwall of his inability to serve him.

In excusing Poole's unwillingness and his own helplessness, he explained to Thelwall the local atmosphere of antagonism and suspicion. "Very great odium T. Poole incurred by bringing *me* here. My peaceable manners and known attachment to Christianity had almost worn it away when Wordsworth came, and he, likewise by T. Poole's agency, settled here. You cannot conceive the tumult, calumnies, and apparatus of threatened persecutions which this event has occasioned round about us. If *you,* too, should come, I am afraid that even riots, and dangerous riots, might be the consequence. Either of us separately would perhaps be tolerable, but *all three* together, what can it be less than plot and damned conspiracy—a school for the propagation of Demagogy and Atheism?" Yet the aged and respectable Poet Laureate could assert that at Alfoxden "annoyances I had none," and expressed himself so decisively that the restrained, though whimsically satirical, account in *Biographia Literaria* was for a century fancied a fiction of Coleridge's picturesque imagination!

Truly Wordsworth suffered no personal "annoyances." Poole suffered the annoyances and Coleridge the vexation of having implicated him by introducing Words-worth. It was characteristic of Wordsworth that, unaffected by the village gossip in the seclusion of Alfoxden, he should be unperturbed by the inconvenience and discomfort endured by his friends on his account. He had a furnished mansion, with beautiful grounds, for at least a year at a nominal rent; he had an assured income from the annuity purchased with Raisley Calvert's legacy, supplemented by Montagu's fee for allowing his boy to educate himself. He had even discovered salve for his conscience in the decision of Coleridge and Thelwall to snap their "squeaking baby-trumpet of sedition" and retire from the unsavoury business of politics to the peace of rural seclusion. Former fretfulness over his impotence to combat the rising tide of war hysteria was now forgotten, and though he had not blown his trumpet-blast, like Coleridge and Thelwall, before retirement, but had removed his trumpet from his lips by leaving his letter to the Bishop of Llandaff in manuscript, he was capable of assuming virtue to himself in forbearance from futility. He was free to cultivate his fresh confidence in his poetic powers in Coleridge's society, which, as Dorothy wrote, was their "principal inducement" to taking Alfoxden.

Coleridge was easily distracted from worry over local politics by the delight of discussing poetry with a fellow artist; in fact, Alfoxden became for him a refuge from domestic and financial anxiety. As he told Thelwall, "I get nothing by literature." The second edition of his poems, including those of Lamb and Lloyd, was published in July or August, but he had probably forestalled its small profits in advances from Cottle. He had no means of subsistence apart from the fund organised by Poole and Estlin, and his hopes now rested on the possibility of Sheridan's accepting his tragedy for performance at Drury Lane. On completing and dispatching the manuscript of the tragedy on 16th October, feeling "no hope of its success, or even of its being acted," he wrote, "I suppose that at last I must become a Unitarian minister, as a less evil than starvation."

It may be supposed that Sara became eventually jealous and resentful of his habitual absences at Alfoxden. Coleridge did not conceal his delight in Dorothy's company. Wordsworth's "exquisite sister" was "a woman indeed!—in mind, I mean, and heart—for her person is such, that if you expected to see a pretty woman, you would think her ordinary—if you expected to find an ordinary woman, you would think her pretty!—But her manners are simple, ardent, impressive—

In every motion her most innocent soul
Outbeams so brightly, that who saw would say,
Guilt was a thing impossible in her.

Her information various—her eye watchful in minutest observation of nature—and her taste a perfect electrometer—it bends, protrudes, and draws in, at subtlest beauties and most recondite faults." Such praise must have brought petulant frowns to Sara's pretty brow, for Coleridge's letters to her show that he never discussed his intellectual acrobatics with her. She was interested only in things and people, and Coleridge would make frivolous references to some woman's evident admiration of him, pointing the playfulness by immediately mentioning his ever-present visions of her with his "sweet babe."

Later, Dorothy made no secret of her opinion that Sara was an unworthy mate for Coleridge and that his unhappiness was due to lack of a wife's sympathetic understanding. From the first there can have been no love lost between the two women, the one resenting her husband's delight in the other's company, the other resenting the wife's possession of her husband. Dorothy's fanatical devotion to her brother is generally supposed to have been so exorbitant as to have excluded any natural feminine passion for another man, but such supposition ignores the growth and gradation of her devotion. Before she met Coleridge, her fervent attachment to her brother was extravagant, but only after she left Alfoxden, after she ceased to be daily in Coleridge's company, did it become neurotic, disturbing and even dangerous. Her early Grasmere journals show that she loved Coleridge, and frustration of this natural passion excited her hysterically emotional temperament to vent her feelings in unnatural adoration of her brother. If Coleridge had been free, she would undoubtedly have married him. Practically it would have been a perfect arrangement, since both she and Wordsworth so eagerly desired his society that they gave up a house which cost them nothing; she would have retained her brother and secured for him the daily companionship of the one man whose intellectual stimulus was necessary to his development. As certainly, Coleridge would have married her; he admired her, felt tenderness for her, and his sentimentalising would soon have been construed by the emotional Dorothy into an avowal of passion.

Her middle-class upbringing prohibited the mere idea of her becoming his mistress, nor could she have consciously contemplated the possibility of falling in love with a married man. Her enthusiasm and admiration for Coleridge's attainments and her delight in his beneficial effect on her brother, developed a seemingly sisterly affection, which she only recognised as love after prolonged separation. On his side, the puritan in Coleridge combined with an under-sexed nature to preclude temptation to adultery. He craved sympathy, encouragement and maternal tenderness from women—not passion.

Nor had Dorothy's understanding yet awakened dissatisfaction in Sara's lack of it. He was still making the best of a bad job. Sara was a devoted mother, a tolerably efficient housekeeper, if inclined to muddle and bustle, and her admiration for her brilliant husband, amounting to astonishment at her possession of him, was not yet blurred by disappointment in his want of worldly success. While her plump prettiness was of the type that quickly develops middle age in commonplace dumpiness, as yet she retained her freshness and a superficial charm. She liked Thelwall and contributed to the success of his visit. Another visitor, Richard Reynell, thought her "indeed a pretty woman," saw at the cottage "domestic life in all its beauty and simplicity," and declared it "a treat, a luxury, to see Coleridge hanging over his infant and talking to it, and fancying what he will be in future days."

But domesticity could not compete with intellectual excitement, any more than could Tom Poole's ponderous praise and affectionate encouragement. Poole's arbour more rarely echoed Coleridge's chanting of his poetry, which he now preferred to repeat in the woods of Alfoxden. The garden grew neglected; weeds flourished during his absence at Racedown, and Coleridge had neither time nor inclination to clear them. Four and five days a week he spent at Alfoxden, frequently spending the night, and in the wooded groves expounded splendid plans for poetic achievement.

2. THE ANCIENT MARINER

The idea of an epic, first suggested by Lamb, recurred to Coleridge in his ambitious enthusiasm. His subject, *The Brook,* was to afford opportunities for "description, incident, and impassioned reflections on men, nature, and society" by tracing a stream from its source, past barns, sheepfolds, hamlet, town and factory, to the sea. To Wordsworth he recommended a similar theme, with the title of *The Recluse.* But wishing to collaborate with Wordsworth as closely as formerly with Southey, he planned the scheme and contents of a poem in three cantos on *The Wanderings of Cain,* of which he was to write the second while Wordsworth wrote the first canto, "and which ever had *done first,* was to set about the third." He completed a rough draft of his canto, but hastening to Alfoxden with the manuscript, found Wordsworth with a "look of humourous despondency fixed on his almost blank sheet of paper." Wordsworth had none of Southey's application or fluency. He could write only what and when he was in the mood to write, and his two long poems, *The Prelude* and *The Excursion,* both only parts of the original scheme of *The Recluse,* were the result of forced labour over many years, which explains their unevenness of quality. Later he was to condemn in Coleridge the inability to write to order—because Coleridge needed money from his writings, while he himself successfully evaded the necessity.

After this failure, their collaboration became limited to exchange of ideas and the joint-publication of their poems. The plan of the proposed volume, as explained by Coleridge, indicates the source of his fascination for Wordsworth and Dorothy. Their conversations "turned frequently on the two cardinal points of poetry, the power of exciting the sympathy of the reader by a faithful adherence to the truth of nature, and the power of giving the interest of novelty by the modifying colours of the imagination." Coleridge pointed out that "the sudden charm which accidents of light and shade, which moonlight or sunset diffused over a known and familiar landscape, appeared to represent the practicability of combining both." Such deductive interpretation of natural phenomena was new to the Wordsworths, who were accustomed to purely objective observation. Wordsworth felt on safer ground by persevering with the line he had already adopted. It was therefore left to Coleridge to attempt "the interesting of the affections" in incidents and characters "supernatural, or at least romantic," "by the dramatic truth of such emotions as would naturally accompany such situations, supposing them real."

The occasion for a first experiment occurred when Coleridge and the Wordsworths decided in November 1797 to walk to Lynton by Porlock, and see the wonderful wild moorland scenery of the seaboard and the celebrated Valley of Rocks—or Valley of Stones, as it was then frequently called. As their "united funds were very scarce," they proposed to defray the expenses of the trip by writing a poem for a magazine. Coleridge related a dream of his friend Cruikshank about a skeleton ship with a skeleton crew, and proceeded to discuss stories of superstition remembered from various books of travel he had read. One such story he recalled from Shelvocke's *Voyages* about a ship's mate who, persuaded that a long spell of adverse weather was due to the persistent pursuit of the ship by an albatross, shot the bird in hope of relieving their misfortune. According to Wordsworth, he then suggested that Coleridge should write a poem about the ghostly navigator of the phantom ship, who was doomed to his fate for the crime of killing an albatross.

That same "memorable evening" they began the poem together. But Coleridge's falcon imagination left the pedestrian Wordsworth's plodding hopelessly behind. After suggesting two or three lines, to which he afterwards pompously laid claim, Wordsworth decided that "our respective manners proved so widely different that it would have been quite presumptuous in me to do anything but separate from an undertaking upon which I could only have been a clog," and he left Coleridge to follow the flights of his imagination alone.

Thirteen years later, when he was living at Dove Cottage and reading books of travel, De Quincey came on the passage in Shelvocke and recognised the germ of *The Ancient Mariner*. He mentioned it to Coleridge, who, having forgotten that he had remembered the albatross incident from a previous reading of Shelvocke, denied that he had received the idea directly from reading the book. Wordsworth, however, remembered that Coleridge had derived the idea from some travel book, and now with curiosity noted the book, which De Quincey probably left at Grasmere and came to repose in Wordsworth's library at Rydal. After Coleridge's death, Wordsworth decided to appropriate to himself the albatross idea, and he told his adoring Miss Fenwick, "I had been reading in Shelvocke's *Voyages,* a day or two before, that while doubling Cape Horn they frequently saw albatrosses in that latitude, the largest sort of sea-fowl, some extending their wings twelve or thirteen feet."

Dutifully Victorian biographers accepted Wordsworth's word. But unluckily for Wordsworth's reputation as "a man of stern veracity," Professor Livingstone Lowes, in that extraordinary study of the mechanics of a poet's mind, *The Road to Xanadu,* discovered that his words to Miss Fenwick were almost precisely quoted from Shelvocke, produced proof that there was a copy of Shelvocke in the Rydal library, and fairly deduced that Wordsworth looked up the passage for Miss Fenwick's benefit. On another occasion, after the appearance of De Quincey's reminiscences of Coleridge,

Portrait of Samuel Taylor Coleridge.

Wordsworth told Alexander Dyce that the "idea of 'shooting an albatross' was mine; for I had been reading Shelvocke's *Voyages,* which probably Coleridge never saw."

The notion of Wordsworth's having ever read anything which Coleridge never saw is comic. He was never in his life a reader; after leaving Cambridge he lamented to Mathews his poverty of reading; at Racedown he read the *Gentleman's Magazine;* in a few years he devised the excuse from his eye trouble for his little reading as for leaving his correspondence to his women-folk. Coleridge, by contrast, read insatiably, and he had moreover dipped into many books of travel while contemplating emigration to America. From these facts Professor Lowes fairly deduced that Coleridge had the idea himself from Shelvocke; that his copy of the book was at Dove Cottage and was found there by De Quincey; that Wordsworth first heard definitely of the derivation from De Quincey, and retaining it in his mind, he informed Dyce and Miss Fenwick, after Coleridge's death, that he had read Shelvocke and suggested the subject to Coleridge!

Professor Lowes also produced circumstantial evidence that Coleridge derived other ideas from Shelvocke in the course of the poem, proving that he had first-hand knowledge of the book. But these details, Wordsworth, of course, did not "remember." Obviously Coleridge, who had never at that time experienced a sea trip, had gathered vivid impressions from reading books of maritime adventure. The greatest marvel of *The Ancient Mariner* is the vividness of its imagery, the versimilitude of atmosphere, the accumulated effect of awful eeriness:

> Are those *her* ribs through which the Sun
> Did peer, as through a grate?
> And is that Woman all her crew?
> Is that a Death? and are there two?
> Is Death that woman's mate?

Critics have been content to accept *The Ancient Mariner* as a masterpiece in the fantastic, and biographers have hesitated to seek autobiography in its apparent unreality, though latterly some have ventured to read in the Mariner's haunted conscience a reflection of the discord in Coleridge's own mind. But the sense of discord, to find final agonised expression in *Dejection* had not yet stricken Coleridge. He was still happy, unafflicted by consciousness of frustration, of inability to apply his powers and to appease his friends' hopes for him. He was content in a sense of achievement by having finished his tragedy.

The theme of *Osorio*—which had occupied his mind for more than six months past, and which probably first occurred to him from reading *Guilt and Sorrow*—

was its later title, *Remorse,* which supplied the motive of the Mariner's hallucinations. Lately, too, he had been converted from his satisfaction in Hartley's philosophy of the association of ideas by reading Bishop Berkeley, whose doctrines derive from the axiom that the act of seeing is in fact an act of interpretation, involving a rational process, and that ideas are to be interpreted through sensations. For some months while Lloyd lived with him, he had witnessed—and striven to comprehend and combat—the morbid hallucinations of an unbalanced mind. He had realised how the act of interpretations, when governed by an irrational instead of a rational mind, created distorted visions incredible to rational sight. So, in his Mariner, he visualised a mind unbalanced by remorse and fear, fanned to frenzy by the awful circumstances of men dying of thirst on a ship becalmed. The reality of its unreality, the incredibility of its horror, and the conviction of its possibility prove the success of the poem in achieving its creator's design of treating the supernatural, "so as to transfer from our inward nature a human interest and a semblance of truth sufficient to procure for these shadows of imagination that willing suspension of disbelief for the moment, which constitutes poetic faith." It is the supreme masterpiece in successful projection of metaphysical speculation into narrative poetry.

The last lines, often condemned as superfluous moralising, contain a statement of Coleridge's faith.

> Farewell, farewell! But this I tell
> To thee, thou Wedding-Guest!
> He prayeth well, who loveth well
> Both man and bird and beast.
> He prayeth best, who loveth best
> All things both great and small;
> For the dear God who loveth us,
> He made and loveth all.

This is the faith of the pacifist, the convinced and literal Christian who declines to differentiate between individual murder, punishable by the laws of society, and wholesale murder, encouraged and embellished with the trumpery of glory by governments and peoples at war. It was likewise the faith of the true lover of nature, whose tenderness forbade him to set traps for the mice which plagued his household. It was a completer faith than the idolatry of beauty, which, as Mr. Herbert Read has pointed out, was seized upon by young men like John Stuart Mill, whose religious beliefs were shaped by the materialism of the Industrial Revolution and whose emotional senses found a substitute for religion in Wordsworth's poetry, and again by young men even more spiritually derelict in consequence of direct contact with war. This idolatry was a form of intellectual escape, available only to the trained mind; Coleridge's was the simple doctrine of Jesus Christ, realisable alike by the illiterate and the intellectual.

3. THE INSPIRED PREACHER

Soon after returning from Lynton, while *The Ancient Mariner* was advancing and expanding far beyond the bounds of the originally intended magazine poem, Coleridge heard at the beginning of December 1797 that Sheridan had rejected *Osorio* on account of the obscurity of the last three acts. The news confirmed his conviction that he could not live by literature, and he faced the choice between a journalistic job and accepting a post as a Unitarian minister.

Through Poole or Dr. Beddoes, he had become acquainted with Thomas and Josiah Wedgwood, wealthy sons of the famous potter. Thomas, an incurable invalid and an enthusiast for chemical research, was a patient of Dr. Beddoes; Josiah lived at Cole House, Westbury, near Bristol, and had country estates in the management of which he accepted advice from Poole. During the autumn Thomas came to Stowey and visited the Wordsworths, whose spacious accommodation at Alfoxden was more suited to hospitality than Coleridge's modest cottage. Coleridge, on a visit to Cole House, met James Mackintosh, eminent as a political journalist and champion of democracy since his able reply to Burke's *Reflections on the French Revolution,* and Mackintosh's brother-in-law, Daniel Stuart, proprietor of the *Morning Post,* offered him a guinea a week for verses. His first contribution under this arrangement, the lines "To an Unfortunate Woman at the Theatre," appeared on 7th December.

But this newspaper engagement revived memories of his difficulties on the *Watchman,* and reminded him of Poole's remark that he was "not born to be a compiler." The mere consciousness of being under an obligation to write punctually to order froze his faculties. "Something must be written and written immediately—if any important Truth, any striking beauty, occur to my mind, I feel a repugnance at sending it garbled to a newspaper: and if any idea of ludicrous personality, or apt anti-ministerial joke, crosses me, I feel a repugnance at rejecting it, because *something must be written,* and nothing else suitable occurs." He felt that the longer he continued "a hired paragraph-scribbler," the more powerful he would find these temptations. Besides, "of all things I most dislike party-politics," and his employer especially welcomed contributions with "a *tang* of personality or *vindictive* feeling."

There were moral and intellectual objections to his becoming a Unitarian minister. Though he had regularly preached in the chapels at Taunton and Bridgwater, he had declined payment for his services, and he disliked the idea of "becoming an hired Teacher in any sect" because "it makes one's livelihood hang upon the profession of *particular opinions:* and tends therefore to warp the intellectual faculty." Also, he had observed that a minister depending for revenue on collections from the congregation inclined "to adapt his moral exhortations to their wishes rather than to their needs." A minister at Derby had been compelled to resign "on account of his sermons respecting Riches and Rich Men." On the other hand, there were compensations. As a Unitarian minister, he had only to retain his belief that "Jesus Christ was the Messiah—in all other points I may play off my Intellect *ad libitum.*" Further, "by law I shall be excepted from military service—to which, Heaven only knows how soon we may be dragged," for he thought it likely "that in case of an invasion our government will serve all, whom they choose to suspect of disaffection, in the same way that good King David served Uriah—'set ye Uriah in the forefront of the hottest Battle, and retire ye from him, that he may be smitten and die.'"

All things considered, the pulpit seemed preferable to the press, and when Estlin advised him that he might have the place of the retiring Unitarian minister at Shrewsbury, where the living was endowed and not dependent on the congregation's approval, he decided to accept. A temptation to revoke his decision was immediately inspired by a cheque for a hundred pounds sent by the Wedgwoods to relieve his present necessities and to prevent his deciding hastily under duress. At first he gladly accepted the prospect of "tranquillity and leisure of independence for the next two years," but after a week's "fluctuations of mind" and sleepless nights, he decided that acceptance would only temporarily postpone the evil of financial anxiety. "A permanent income not inconsistent with my religious or political creeds, I find necessary to my quietness—without it I should be a prey to anxiety, and anxiety with me always induces Sickliness, and too often Sloth." So he returned the cheque, and in the second week of January set off for Shrewsbury.

On Sunday 14th January 1798 Coleridge preached in Shrewsbury's Unitarian Chapel, and among the congregation was William Hazlitt, the nineteen-year-old son of the Unitarian minister in the neighbouring town of Wem. Cottle once heard Coleridge preach at Bath to a meagre congregation, which yawned through a sermon amounting to little more than a lecture on the Corn Laws. But either Coleridge was depressed by his small and unresponsive audience or Cottle was no great connoisseur of sermons. Young Hazlitt was so intrigued by the romantic notion of a poet and philosopher as a preacher of the gospel that he walked ten miles through mud to hear him, but his impression is consistent with Coleridge's reputation for eloquence and with the eager invitations to preach he received from ministers. As he gave out his text—"And he went up into the mountain to pray, himself, alone,"—"his voice rose like a stream of rich distilled perfumes, and when he came to the two last words, which he pronounced, loud, deep, and distinct," it seemed to young Hazlitt "as if the sounds had echoed from the bottom of the human heart, and as if that prayer might have floated in solemn silence through the universe," so that the idea of St. John, "crying in the wilderness," came to his mind. "The sermon was upon peace and war; upon church and state—not their alliance, but their separation—on the spirit of the world and the spirit of Christianity, not as the same, but as opposed to one another." He inveighed against those who "inscribed the cross of Christ on banners dripping with human gore," and "to show the fatal effects of war, drew a striking contrast between the simple shepherd boy, driving his team afield, or sitting under the hawthorn, piping to his flock," and "the same poor country-lad, crimped, kidnapped, brought into town, made drunk at an ale-house, turned into a wretched drummer-boy . . . and tricked out in the loathsome finery of the profession of blood." It was more than Hazlitt had hoped for—"Poetry and Philosophy had met together, Truth and Genius had embraced, under the eye and with the sanction of Religion"—and he went home satisfied.

The following Tuesday Coleridge went to Wem to dine and stay the night with Hazlitt's father. For two hours he conversed "with William Hazlitt's forehead," for Hazlitt, shy, diffident, tongue-tied, was "shoe-contemplative," as Coleridge afterwards described his habitual demeanour when entering a room full of people. But while Coleridge talked, Hazlitt noted his appearance. "His forehead was broad and high, light as if built of ivory, with large projecting eyebrows, and his eyes rolling beneath them, like a sea with darkened lustre." His face had a faintly purple tinge, as in the pale thoughtful complexions of Murillo and Velasquez. "His mouth was gross, voluptuous, open, eloquent; his chin good-humoured and round; but his nose, the rudder of the face, the index of the will, was small, feeble, nothing." His hair, "black and glossy as the raven's . . . fell in smooth masses over his forehead." The impression tallies with Coleridge's self-description in a letter to Thelwall of a year before, but Hazlitt's memory failed in describing his person as "rather above the common size, inclining to the corpulent." He was picturing Coleridge's figure as it became in middle age; when Dorothy Wordsworth first saw him, he was "pale and thin."

Coleridge talked familiarly and agreeably on a variety of subjects, mentioning Godwin and Mary Wollstonecraft, Burke and Mackintosh, Holcroft, Wordsworth, and Tom Wedgwood. He flattered Hazlitt by seeming to take much notice of him, and eventually drew him out on the subject of Burke.

When Hazlitt came down to breakfast next morning, he found Coleridge with a letter from Josiah Wedgwood, saying that he and his brother had "a considerable superfluity of fortune," of which they regarded themselves "rather as Trustees than Proprietors," and having "canvassed" Coleridge's past life, his present situation and prospects, and his character and abilities, they asked him to "accept an annuity for life of £150," to be regularly paid by them, "no condition whatever being annexed to it." It was a princely offer, even in those days when wealthy men still retained a just sense of the responsibility of riches, and it is not surprising that Coleridge, as Hazlitt said, "seemed to make up his mind to close with this proposal in the act of tying on one of his shoes."

Hazlitt "felt very little gratitude for Mr. Wedgwood's bounty," for he had looked forward to having a pastor so gifted only ten miles away. But he was more than appeased, even overwhelmed, by an invitation from Coleridge to visit Stowey. He walked with him six miles of the distance to Shrewsbury, and noticed—as did Carlyle long afterwards—that Coleridge continually crossed him "by shifting from one side of the footpath to the other," as if "unable to keep on in a straight line." It struck Hazlitt only as an odd movement; he did not then "connect it with any instability of purpose or involuntary change of principle," as he did twenty-five years later. All the way Coleridge talked of English philosophers. He drew the difference between a subtle and an acute mind, the one characteristic of a philosopher, the other a mere shop-boy's quality. Significantly, he "dwelt particularly" on Berkeley's *Essay on Vision* "as a masterpiece of analytical reasoning."

Hazlitt's habitual reserve was so far overcome that he talked of his own proposed thesis on "The Natural Disinterestedness of the Human Mind." Coleridge "listened with great willingness," and Hazlitt returned home with renewed zeal for his work. For, "till the light of his genius shone into my soul," he had been "dumb, inarticulate, helpless," and "that my understanding . . . did not remain dumb and brutish, or at length found a language to express itself, I owe to Coleridge. . . . He was the first poet I had known, and he certainly answered to that inspired name. I had heard a great deal of his powers of conversation, and was not disappointed. In fact, I never met with anything at all like them, either before or since." Thus another man of genius—following Southey, Lamb, Lloyd, and Wordsworth—fell under the spell of the archangel, not yet "a little damaged."

Josiah Wedgwood's letter was accompanied by one from Poole, showing that his influence had weighed with the brothers in inspiring their offer and urging Coleridge to accept. In Poole's opinion, he could accept the annuity and still enter the ministry if he wished. But Coleridge, despite appeals from his Unitarian admirers and exhortations from Estlin that "the cause of Christianity and practical Religion demands your exertions," felt that he could not accept both the annuity and a minister's living, since the Wedgwoods would not have made the offer if he had already had other means of subsistence. He argued fairly that he could serve the cause of Christianity as effectively outside as inside the ministry, and that, while he had preferred—"as more *innocent* in the first place, and more *useful* in the second place"—the ministry to the press as a trade, the necessity for bondage to either was now removed. Thelwall's comment, on receiving a letter in which Coleridge did not make clear that he had decided against entering the ministry, had shrewdness and humour: "I suppose he did not . . . accept the cure of Unitarian souls . . . for I know his aversion to preaching God's holy word for hire, which is seconded not a little, I expect, by his repugnance to all regular routine and application. I also hope he did not, for I know he cannot preach very often without travelling from the pulpit to the Tower. Mount him but upon his darling hobby-horse, 'the republic of God's own making,' and away he goes like hey-go-mad, spattering and splashing through thick and thin and scattering more *levelling* sedition and constructive treason than poor Gilly or myself ever dreamt of."

Another reason for Coleridge's rejection of the ministry appeared in a letter written from Shrewsbury to Wordsworth: "But dismissing severer thoughts, believe me, my dear fellow! that of the pleasant ideas which accompanied this unexpected event, it was not the least pleasant, nor did it pass through my mind the last in the procession, that I should at least be able to trace the spring and early summer at Alfoxden with you, and that wherever your after residence may be, it is probable that you will be within the reach of my tether, lengthened as it now is."

4. POETS IN CONTRAST

Coleridge stayed three weeks at Shrewsbury. He was "talking at a great rate to his fellow-passengers" when he arrived, "he did not cease while he stayed," and, added Hazlitt, "nor has he since, that I know of." He was certainly an unqualified success and would have received the living if he had wanted it. Even some of the Anglican clergy were "eminently courteous" and went to hear him preach. He had reason to think that he would have "doubled the congregation almost immediately," though he may have been deceived by the many who came from curiosity to hear the unusual young preacher and would have stayed at home when lure of novelty lapsed. Though he declined even payment of his travelling expenses, the Shrewsbury Unitarians begged his acceptance of "a small compensation," for while they expressed disappointment at the deprivation "of that pleasure and edification we had so much reason to promise" themselves, they were "not so selfish as not to feel also the most lively satisfaction" in the good fortune that placed him in "a situation more conformable to your inclinations and Views."

He arrived at Bristol on 30th January, full of eager joy at the prospect of returning to Stowey and determined

"to settle and persevere in some mode of repaying the Wedgwoods thro' the medium of Mankind." On 3rd February he walked with Dorothy Wordsworth over the hills and watched the mist drifting over the sea. During his absence at Shrewsbury Dorothy had begun to keep a journal, in which she recorded impressions of scenery and weather effects. Her object was the preservation of these impressions for future use by Wordsworth and Coleridge. In later years Wordsworth depended more and more on her journals, and of their tours together he used at home the notes she had written in the freshness of the moment. The impressions were not necessarily Dorothy's own, but those she derived in company with Coleridge or Wordsworth, mutually compounded and clarified; a specially happy descriptive phrase would be noted. Walking with Coleridge, she noticed how "the withered leaves danced with the hailstones"; the notion was probably his, and was not improved in Wordsworth's lines:

> But see! where'er the hailstones drop
> The withered leaves all skip and hop.

So, on 27th February, when Coleridge walked with her from Stowey to Alfoxden on "a very bright moonlight night," they saw how "the sea big and white, swelled to the very shores," and Coleridge wrote in *The Ancient Mariner:*

> The harbour-bay was clear as glass,
> So smoothly it was strewn!
> And on the bay the moonlight lay,
> And the shadow of the Moon.
>
>   . . . . .
>
> And the bay was white with silent light,
> Till rising from the same
> Full many shapes, that shadows were,
> In crimson colours came.

Together, too, they saw the "horned moon," "stardogged," and on 24th March, "a duller night than last night," they noticed "a sort of white shade over the blue sky," and Coleridge wrote in *Christabel:*

> The night is chilly, but not dark.
> The thin gray cloud is spread on high,
> It covers but not hides the sky.

From February to April few days passed without Dorothy's walking with Coleridge, and all the time he was buoyed on the full tide of imaginative creation. To Cottle he wrote cryptically on 18th February: "I have finished my ballad—it is 340 lines. I am going on with the Visions. . . ." The "ballad" cannot have been *The Ancient Mariner,* which ran to 658 lines. Those who suppose *Kubla Khan* to have been written in the summer or autumn of the previous year may read here a vain determination to finish that "vision," but the "visions" were more likely those of the Mariner. The first part of *Christabel* comprised 331 lines, but it seems improbable that he had progressed so far with that poem, and the "ballad" may have been a first draft of *The Three Graves*. On 23rd March Dorothy noted that Coleridge "brought his ballad finished," and this may have been *The Ancient Mariner*.

"I gave him the subject of his *Three Graves*," said the oracular Wordsworth after Coleridge's death, "but he made it too shocking and painful, and not sufficiently softened by any healing views." The criticism is just; into the story of a mother's passion for her daughter's lover Coleridge instilled the dramatic horror of Webster and Tourneur. The simple fireside story, based on material of village gossip, was used by Wordsworth in the ballads he was writing at this time—*We are Seven, The Thorn, The Last of the Flock, Goody Blake and Harry Gill, The Idiot Boy,* and *Simon Lee*. The form and treatment is that of the modern short story, and it may be fairly argued that the subjects are better suited to prose than verse. In *The Thorn,* for instance, as Coleridge pointed out, Wordsworth falls into bathos by putting the telling of the tale into the mouth of a dull and garrulous narrator. Prosaic narrative was outside Coleridge's conception of poetry. To him it was instinctive to seek beneath the surface; his treatment was subjective where Wordsworth's was objective. It is doubtful if Wordsworth ever grasped Coleridge's application to poetry of Berkeley's theory that vision is individual interpretation. His own earthbound imagination being incapable of accompanying Coleridge's metaphysical flights, he conceived the intangible as "supernatural," and as an attempt at practical proof of his argument against Coleridge, he wrote *Peter Bell* to show "that the Imagination not only does not require for its exercise the intervention of supernatural agency, but that, though such agency be excluded, the faculty may be called forth as imperiously and for kindred results of pleasure, by incidents within the compass of poetic probability, in the humblest departments of daily life."

Very soon Coleridge was to realise that Wordsworth had "hurtfully segregated and isolated his being." Beginning with an escapist's desire to deaden his conscience about Annette [Vallon, with whom Wordsworth became involved in France, shortly after he finished his university career], about his motiveless inactivity, and about his failure to serve the political cause in which he fervently believed, he had acquired a detachment almost inhuman, which, while it enabled him to live entirely with his thoughts and so to concentrate on creative work, gradually deadened his faculty of sympathy. Because he knew that great thoughts depended upon subtle and sensitive perception, and because he saw that Wordsworth was imaginatively incapable of projecting himself into the minds and senses of others,

Coleridge encouraged him to write an autobiographical poem, as the only medium through which he could describe the metaphysical experience regarded by Coleridge as the richest matter for poetic expression. So, while writing his ballads on rustic subjects according to his own inclination, Wordsworth also in these months began *The Prelude* at the instigation of Coleridge, who informed Cottle on 8th March that Wordsworth had written "more than 1,200 lines of a blank verse, superior . . . to anything in our language which in any way resembles it," quoting Poole's opinion as confirming his own that it was "likely to benefit mankind much more than anything Wordsworth had yet written."

To everybody Coleridge sang Wordsworth's praises. He was "a great man," "a tried good man," a poet "the latchet of whose shoes I am unworthy to unloose." When Tom Wedgwood and Mackintosh ventured to aver that they saw nothing in Wordsworth's conversation to justify such applause, Coleridge told them, "He strides on so far before you that he dwindles in the distance!" After this objection by Wedgwood and Mackintosh, he forestalled the adverse impression of Wordsworth's awkward manners and stilted speech. "His genius is most *apparent* in poetry," he warned Estlin, "and rarely, except to me in *tête-à-tête,* breaks forth in conversational eloquence." By belittling himself in comparison, he created among his friends, who recognised him as the greatest genius of their acquaintance, a legend about Wordsworth's genius, which in time became rooted in their minds, and in the course of a decade or so, without any praise in the press, Wordsworth became accepted by an influential minority at Coleridge's valuation.

While at first intimate communion with Wordsworth stimulated Coleridge to poetic achievement, his extravagant admiration unsettled the always unstable foundations of his self-confidence. Wordsworth's obstinate preference for his rustic ballads and his confusion of the metaphysical with the "supernatural," which he regarded as inferior to the realistic, caused him to imagine in himself a deficiency from which Wordsworth was immune. Wordsworth must have expressed to him freely in conversation the disparaging opinion he afterwards avowed: "Not being able to dwell on natural woes, he took to the supernatural, and hence his *Ancient Mariner* and *Christabel,* in which he shows great poetical power; but these have not the hold on the heart which Nature gives, and will never be popular poems, like those of Goldsmith or Burns." Coleridge could not withstand the disapproval of his idol, and more than a year before he had arrived at the depths of despair that found expression in *Dejection,* he told Francis Wrangham that Wordsworth "is a great, a true Poet—I am only a kind of a Metaphysician."

Yet in those fruitful early months of 1798 Coleridge's poetic achievement outweighed Wordsworth's. This fact is rarely recognised, largely because the joint volume of *Lyrical Ballads* contained nineteen poems by Wordsworth and only four by Coleridge, and because Coleridge, as usual, pushed Wordsworth into prominence at his own expense. "I wrote *The Ancient Mariner,* and was preparing, among other poems, the *Dark Ladie* and the *Christabel,* in which I should have more nearly realised my ideal than I had done in my first attempt," he related. "But Mr. Wordsworth's industry had proved so much more successful, and the number of the poems so much greater, that my compositions, instead of forming a balance, appeared rather an interpolation of heterogeneous matter." Wordsworth's "industry" was more successful because he concentrated—with a single-minded intensity of purpose of which Coleridge was inherently incapable and which he consequently admired as a symptom of Wordsworth's superiority—on his chosen function of giving "the charm of novelty to things of everyday," while Coleridge was distracted by the multiplicity of ideas crowding upon his more fertile imagination. The conceptions of *Christabel* or the *Dark Ladie* were each more ambitious in length and scope than anything attempted by Wordsworth, but they were unfinished and therefore excluded from the volume. *The Three Graves* required little addition for completeness, but it was thrown aside probably because Coleridge had no heart to finish it after Wordsworth's adverse criticism. The composition of these ballads was interrupted by a number of completed poems, none of which fell within the scope of Coleridge's function of lending human interest to the supernatural or romantic. *Frost at Midnight,* in which Coleridge, musing over the cradle of his infant son, fondly pictures for him a happier boyhood than his own, was written in February: *The Old Man of the Alps, Lewti,* and *The Recantation,* afterwards called *France: An Ode,* were published in the *Morning Post* during March and April, while *Fears in Solitude* was written in the latter month. All these were extraneous from the scheme and therefore excluded from the volume, though they had claims for inclusion at least equal to Wordsworth's *Expostulation and Reply* and *Lines written in Early Spring.*

"It was dear Coleridge's constant infelicity that prevented him from being the poet that Nature had given him the power to be," said Wordsworth. "He had always too much personal and domestic discontent to paint the sorrows of mankind," he could not—

>   afford to suffer
> With those whom he saw suffer.

As Wordsworth well knew, Coleridge's subsequent unhappiness dried up the fount of his poetry. But he was never capable of the egotistic detachment that enabled Wordsworth to wrestle with harrowing emotions in imagination and then retire to bed to relax and be read to sleep by Dorothy—a detachment eventually

deepening to an insensibility fatal to his poetry in its turn. Coleridge could not "afford to suffer," and so suffered the more acutely. While Wordsworth was now content in his own pursuits, Coleridge, despite his contempt for politics and politicians, felt anguish at the unnecessary sufferings inflicted by materialistic and amoral governments upon their people. His fading faith in France as the European pioneers of liberty finally vanished when the French invaded the Swiss cantons and instituted military dictatorship under the thin disguise of democracy.

In the five stanzas of the ode originally called *The Recantation* he traced the transition of his political faith. He told how he had loved the spirit of liberty, had welcomed the French Revolution and abhorred England's joining "the dire army" against it, had regarded the atrocities of the Terror as inevitable excesses of violent revolution and retained the hope that France would eventually establish the ideal government; but how he now saw their government competing with the corrupt monarchies for dominion over lesser nations, and was forced to the conclusion that the ideal of freedom was attainable by no community under any form of government, but only by the individual, "so far as he is pure, and inflamed with the love and adoration of God in Nature." He was now confirmed in the belief with which he had retired to Stowey sixteen months before. Witnessing with disgust the jealous dissension among democratic leaders, the want of principle preventing their unity in common endeavour, he concluded that men of principle and enlightenment had no place in politics. He now recognised in "the *Rulers of* France . . . nothing that distinguishes them to their advantage from other animals of the same species." Landor, his junior by over two years, who had declined political employment and likewise retired to rural contemplation, exclaimed in his violent way, "As to the cause of liberty, this cursed nation has ruined it for ever." But, though he never forgave the French, he continued throughout his long life to regard hopefully every revolutionary movement as potentially pregnant with the betrayed ideals of the French Revolution. Coleridge, however, while he too felt lasting bitterness against the French for their betrayal, no longer believed in the ability of popular movements to promote the people's improvement. Contrasting the disinterested integrity of men like Grey and Stanhope with the unscrupulous careerism of intriguing demagogues, he inclined to regard aristocrats as more likely to govern for the general benefit.

Godwin justly argued that "government, even in its best state, is an evil," and therefore it is desirable to "have as little of it, as the general peace of human society will permit." But this was among the arguments instanced by Coleridge when he convinced Southey that Godwin was dogmatising for a future state of civilisation. In his Bristol lectures he had plainly expressed the opinion that the people were not ripe even for representative government. "I regard governments," he now wrote, "as I regard the abcesses produced by certain fevers—they are necessary consequences of the disease, and by their pain they increase the disease; but . . . not only are they physically necessary as effects but also as causes they are morally necessary in order to prevent the utter dissolution of the patient."

Though "no Whig, no Reformist, no Republican," he remained a bitter opponent of Pitt's government, whose policy he condemned for having coerced the French into military aggression and created democratic unrest at home. In *Fears in Solitude,* written in April 1798, when invasion was considered imminent, he regarded the threatened calamity as just retribution for imperialist ambition and for the war against France:

> We have offended, Oh! my countrymen!
> We have offended very grievously,
> And been most tyrannous. From east to west
> A groan of accusation pierces Heaven!
> The wretched plead against us; multitudes
> Countless and vehement, the sons of God,
> Our brethren!

When Sheridan and Tierney were accused of "recanting" because, after originally supporting the French Revolution, they now condemned the revolutionists for betrayal of its principles, he published in the *Morning Post* on 30th July *Recantation Illustrated in the Story of the Mad Ox.* The French Revolution is represented as an ox, which being released from work in "yoke and chain," frisked gladly in the field, till the stupid rustics, seeing its gambols, declared in a panic that it had gone mad, and started to hound it down.

> The frighted beast scamper'd about—
>   Plunge! through the hedge he drove:
> The mob pursue with hideous rout,
> A bull-dog fastens on his snout;
> 'He gores the dog! his tongue hangs out!
>   He's mad, he's mad, by Jove!'

A "man that kept his senses" sought to stop the hunt, but the mob cursed him—"What? would you have him toss us all?"—till he withdrew protesting. Goaded and terrified, the ox at last turns on his pursuers and plays havoc among them, whereupon the wise man joins in organising its capture, to the indignation of the mob.

> 'A lying dog! just now he said
>   The Ox was only glad—
> Let's break his Presbyterian head!'
> 'Hush!' quoth the sage, 'you've been misled;
> No quarrels now! let's all make head,
>   *You drove the poor Ox mad!'*

So Coleridge defended the apostasy of himself and others, but he could not reconcile his conscience with the revised policy admitted by his reason. He described himself as

> The humble man, who, in his youthful years,
> Knew just so much of folly, as had made
> His early manhood more securely wise!

who, in the peace of rural retreat, had

>   With many feelings, many thoughts,
> Made up a meditative joy, and found
>   Religious meanings in the forms of Nature!

And the anguish of his soul cried out:

> My God! it is a melancholy thing
> For such a man, who would full fain preserve
> His soul in calmness, yet perforce must feel
> For all his human brethren—O my God!
> It weighs upon the heart, that he must think
> What uproar and what strife may now be
>   stirring
> This way or that way o'er these silent hills.

In imagination he suffered the agonies of the maimed and wounded, the bereaved wife and mother, the frightened or starving child. As Wordsworth said, with his temperament and circumstances, he could not afford so to suffer. Wordsworth was untroubled by such sufferings at second hand; having determined on detachment in rural seclusion, he banished the world and its troubles as outside his perspective. He allowed Coleridge to argue him out of respect for Godwin's doctrines, because he no longer needed the moral support of Godwinism. From Coleridge, too, he absorbed a smattering of Hartley's philosophy of association, as appeared in his prefaces and part of *The Prelude,* but idleness reinforced his inclination to avoid philosophical speculation. What might be deemed deficiency in others became, as always, virtue in Wordsworth. "It is his practice and almost his nature," lauded Coleridge, "to convey all the truth he knows without any attack on what he supposes falsehood, if that falsehood be interwoven with virtues or happiness." When he first met Coleridge, he was "a republican, and, at least, a *semi*-atheist," but by the spring of 1798 Coleridge could declare, "He loves and venerates Christ and Christianity. I wish he did more." But this was the "one subject" on which "we are habitually silent; we found our data dissimilar, and never renewed the subject." Wordsworth's "data" remains unrevealed, but doubtless differed little from that assembled by many a materialist. Christianity well suited Coleridge's expansive nature, which excited him to friendliness with all and sundry and to unrewarded and often uncomfortable exertions on their behalf, as when he tried to find a farm for Thelwall. But Christianity would have been an embarrassment to Wordsworth, who cultivated only such friends as could practically serve him. Morally weak, Coleridge needed some supporting faith; but Wordsworth was a man of moral strength, whose masculinity despised weakness as feminine.

The time was soon to come when Wordsworth became a steadfast and respected supporter of the established Church. His health or occupation often prevented his own attendance at Sunday observance, but he was always careful to be represented by his women folk. But the Church had no closer affiliation to Christianity than the Pharisees to Jesus Christ; it was a respectable British institution, to which Wordsworth necessarily subscribed when he became articled to respectability. When Coleridge declared his belief in religion as the only "universally *efficient*" cure for social ills, Wordsworth might have retorted with his own argument against Godwin— that he was dogmatising "for a future state," as eighteen hundred years after Christ the prospect of a Christian world seemed as remote as ever.

But Wordsworth had no desire to expose his data to Coleridge's scrutiny. Instead, he absorbed from Coleridge's conversation a smattering of philosophy sufficient to disguise his devout study of Nature as a substitute religion, of which he became the prophet accepted by materialists, like himself, whose faith required to rest in the tangible and external. As a poet, Wordsworth became Nature's apostle; in his preface of 1815 he explained how poetry emerged from exact observation and description, coloured by sensibility, reflection and imagination. He gathered from Coleridge enough of Berkeley's theories to understand that vision was interpretation; but with him interpretation was a decisively rational process, originating from impressions of photographic exactitude. Imagination began its function only after conception of the impression; he could not grasp Coleridge's notion of actually seeing with imagination—of a subjective as opposed to an objective process. His art, therefore, was realistic where Coleridge's was romantic and symbolic, and his realism, with its basis in the tangible, recommended itself to the materialist mind in search of a faith unmisted by mysticism. It is not remarkable that a purely aesthetic attitude of mind—which was actually Wordsworth's only religion—should be accepted by his disciples as a substitute religion. For the aesthetic sense has always played a potent part in the externals of religious observance; the severe simplicity of recalcitrant nonconformity is a reaction against the obscuring of religion by elaborate ritual, and the superstitious awe excited by aesthetic window-dressing in cathedrals was exposed in Hugh Walpole's *The Cathedral* and *The Inquisitor*.

But Coleridge's intellectual vision could not be hypnotised nor his spiritual requirements satisfied by an aesthetic attitude. Suffering the more because he could not afford to suffer, he was now about to embark on a long pilgrimage in search of spiritual and mental peace.

Raimonda Modiano

SOURCE: "Chivalry or Contest? Coleridge, Wordsworth, and 'The Goddess Nature'," in *Coleridge and the Concept of Nature,* The Macmillan Press Ltd., 1985, pp. 33-50.

[*In the following excerpt, Modiano traces the gradual process of alienation that occurred between Wordsworth and Coleridge, focusing on the role of the poets' attitudes regarding nature in the disintegration of their literary and personal relationship.*]

It is well known that Coleridge's opinion of himself depended excessively on how others viewed him and that he continuously regarded himself through the eyes of powerful men on whom he bestowed more affection than he would or could hope to get in return. He was given to idolizing his friends and easily disappointed when he sensed the slightest breach of loyalty. He was also easily persuaded of his own worthlessness by comparison with the creative stamina and successful lives he attributed to his friends, while at the same time he knew that he possessed extraordinary powers that, potentially at least, far exceeded those of his rivals. Of all the men Coleridge successively chose as his idols, none engaged his admiration more and none caused him as much anguish and perilous self-doubt as Wordsworth. From the early stages of their collaboration on the *Lyrical Ballads* and even after their quarrel in 1810, 'The Giant Wordsworth' remained for Coleridge an intimidating example of personal success that far outweighed anything Coleridge thought he had accomplished. While Wordsworth's poetic star was rising, his was setting, and Coleridge saw himself increasingly pushed into the inferior role of a metaphysician. While Wordsworth's private life, after the turbulent episode with Annette Vallon, was finally settling into a peaceful marriage, Coleridge's was disintegrating due to his aggravated opium addiction, increasing marital tensions, and his passionate but hopeless love for Sara Hutchinson. While the women of the Wordsworth household all flocked around his friend, obviously attracted by his masculinity, Coleridge had to struggle for their attention, and he even suspected, to his utmost despair, that Sara Hutchinson was in love with Wordsworth. Wordsworth was constantly in the way, conquering and appropriating more of the territory Coleridge felt should have been his but which he had no power to withhold.

It is apparent that among their friends Wordsworth enjoyed the reputation of being best acquainted with 'Lady Nature' and that Coleridge would have liked to have some recognition on this score. Thus, Coleridge often engaged in competition with Wordsworth—directly, by claiming to perceive more clearly the identity of some misty phenomenon in a landscape they were both observing, or to understand more profoundly the impact of natural forms upon the soul; and indirectly, by trying to impress upon his friends the extent of his passion for nature. To Sara Hutchinson, for instance, he described in great detail his adventurous second tour of the Lakes (1802) and his nearly fatal descent from Scafell, which left him with shaking limbs but a 'fearless' spirit and an even greater confidence in the safe abode of nature, provided one's 'powers of Reason & the Will' were in order. Two years earlier Coleridge wrote to Francis Wrangham about a less risky, though still slightly sacrificial activity stirred by his great attraction to nature: 'I seldom shave without cutting myself. Some Mountain or Peak is rising out of the Mist, or some slanting Column of misty Sunlight is sailing cross me / so that I offer soap & blood daily, as an Eye-servant of the Goddess Nature'.

This light and somewhat jocular remark should not mislead us. It is not a casual remark but reflects Coleridge's acute anxieties, voiced earlier in the letter, that in relationship to Wordsworth he was no more than an inferior sort of metaphysician: 'As to our literary occupations they are still more distant than our residences—He [Wordsworth] is a great, a true Poet—I am only a kind of Metaphysician.—He has even now sent off the last sheet of a second volume of his *Lyrical Ballads*'. In his subsequent confession of his daily sacrifice to nature, Coleridge is clearly trying to subvert the validity of his self-portrait as a metaphysician. He is not, as Charles Lamb fondly remembered him at Christ's Hospital, a man removed from reality by his metaphysical pursuits, but, on the contrary, irresistibly drawn to nature to the point of becoming oblivious to his daily occupations. Coleridge's confession is by no means inauthentic. As his passionate explorations of picturesque scenery attest, he had every right to present himself as a devotee of nature. But the confession betrays a sense of embarrassment. Coleridge, it appears, cannot speak to Francis Wrangham, a friend of Wordsworth, about his interest in nature, except by way of a joke. No doubt Coleridge was sufficiently wary of the mind's surrender to sense objects to resist a complete identification with nature. But the irony injected into his declaration of subservience to 'the Goddess Nature' has more complex sources. At this time Coleridge wanted very much to assert his passion for nature as a testimony that he was not exclusively preoccupied with metaphysics, and by implication, still capable of becoming a 'true Poet'. Coleridge perceived a direct link between one's communion with natural objects and poetic power, a link fully and somewhat painfully confirmed by Wordsworth's fortunes as a poet. Wordsworth was at once completely integrated in his

natural environment at Grasmere—a place, Coleridge wrote to Wrangham, 'worthy of him, & of which he is worthy'—and happily productive completing the second volume of the *Lyrical Ballads*.

The cooperation with Wordsworth on the *Lyrical Ballads* left Coleridge with a huge complex of poetic inferiority, fostered to a great extent by Wordsworth's insinuation that the supernatural strangeness of 'The Rime of the Ancient Mariner' was largely responsible for the poor reception of the volume as a whole. It is significant that in the letter to Wrangham Coleridge referred to the *Lyrical Ballads* as Wordsworth's sole property, even though the volume contained some of Coleridge's own poems and was conceived as a joint literary endeavour. But the letter to Wrangham is suggestive in another respect: it shows that Coleridge's feelings of poetic inferiority in relationship to Wordsworth also affected his self-image as a lover of nature. It is as if, having failed to prove himself as a great poet, Coleridge could not seriously claim a great attraction to nature, but only a fated passion for metaphysics. Coleridge's confession of loyalty towards nature has a double edge to it. It serves as a protection against a full surrender to the natural world, which Coleridge found dangerous to the life of the mind. It also allows Coleridge to express his passion for nature by way of self-mockery, thus saving himself from possible ridicule for striking the pose of a devotee of nature, a pose as improbable for Coleridge as that of a successful poet.

The link between Coleridge's sense of poetic failure *vis-à-vis* Wordsworth and his conflicting desire to attach himself to nature and yet to remain detached from it is not incidental and bears further scrutiny. When Coleridge left for Germany after the publication of the *Lyrical Ballads,* he had, supposedly, also left behind his career as a poet, returning fully dressed in the garb of a philosopher. This view, to which Coleridge himself gave currency, cannot be taken at face value, though the psychological toll it took of Coleridge cannot be underestimated either. Furthermore, his reputation as a poet had been severely wounded by the publication of 'The Rime of the Ancient Mariner', a work which one reviewer characterized as a 'rhapsody of unintelligible wildness and incoherence' and about which Wordsworth himself had expressed serious reservations. In Wordsworth's eyes Coleridge's experiment in the species of poetry 'directed to persons and characters supernatural' had failed, and Wordsworth was hardly diplomatic in conveying his dissatisfaction with the contribution of his partner, as shown by the apologetic note to the poem he included in the second edition of the *Lyrical Ballads*. Wordsworth also refused to include 'Christabel' in the second edition of the *Lyrical Ballads* on the grounds that it was 'disproportionate both in size & merit, & as discordant in it's [*sic*] character'.

Sketch from an engraving of the vale of Grasmere, where Words-
worth and his wife came to live in 1802.

The impact on Coleridge of Wordsworth's disappointment with his supernatural poems was devastating and long-lasting. It virtually maimed the poet in him, as I. A. Richards put it. Wordsworth's rejection of 'Christabel', a poem in which Coleridge was nearer to realizing his ideal, at least in his own estimate, brought him to the verge of a physical breakdown. Coleridge did not publish 'Christabel' until sixteen years after he had begun it, and then only perhaps because Byron urged him to do so. It was also not until 1817 that Coleridge included the revised version of 'The Rime of the Ancient Mariner' in a volume of his own poetry (*Sibylline Leaves*). That after the *Lyrical Ballads* Coleridge no longer wrote 'Christabels and Ancient Mariners', as Charles Lamb deplored, is not, therefore, surprising. Coleridge could not bring himself to repeat the creative effort which, in Wordsworth's opinion, resulted in a poetry of questionable quality and taste. Already the composition of 'Christabel' proved to be extremely difficult, and Coleridge left the poem unfinished.

In the period following the publication of the *Lyrical Ballads*, Coleridge, despite his protestations to the contrary, was still very much concerned with his prospects as a poet and planned to write a good number of poems and collections of poetry. Many of these projects, interestingly enough, mark a complete break from the supernatural poetry Coleridge undertook to write as part of the *Lyrical Ballads* experiment. The plans Coleridge frequently announced after 1800 concern topographic poems, poems celebrating the daily performance of nature in the vale of Keswick, or transcriptions of landscape drawings in the form of a 'moral Descriptive poem', 'an Inscription' or 'a Tale'. Consistently, Coleridge's privileged subject for future poetry turned on 'the virtues connected with the Love of Nature', a choice less peculiar than it may seem when we take into account Coleridge's extreme vulnerability to Wordsworth's opinions and his instinct to emulate his influential friend.

When 'Christabel' was dropped from the *Lyrical Ballads,* Coleridge was to replace it with a group of poems on 'the Naming of Places'—a project that Wordsworth seemed to encourage, making a special trip to Keswick in mid-October 1800 to acquire the poems for the *Lyrical Ballads*. Coleridge never produced the promised poems, but the plan is itself symptomatic of his willingness to substitute naturalistic poems for a supernatural tale and to produce the kind of poetry that he thought Wordsworth would approve. The poems on 'the Naming of Places' fit in with the characteristic projects on topographic or moral—descriptive subjects Coleridge envisioned writing after 1800. One other project, perhaps the most ambitious of all, should be mentioned here, as it reveals poignantly the extent to which Coleridge felt compelled to imitate the Wordsworthian canon. The plan was conceived during a walk Coleridge took through Borrodale in October 1803 and appears to be no less than an intended replica of *The Prelude,* which Wordsworth was working on at the time. The immediate occasion that prompted Coleridge to devise this plan was his discovery in Borrodale of a magnificent spot that deserved to be marked with a 'Cross or Heap of Stones' and honoured in verse. Just before announcing his projected poem in his entry, Coleridge drops a casual reference to an argument he and Wordsworth had about the size of 'Bowder Stone' compared to two other rocks in Borrodale. This trivial argument introduces a far more serious battle with Wordsworth that Coleridge does not openly acknowledge—the battle of a dispossessed poet trying to regain his status by borrowing his rival's own means of success. Here is how Coleridge conceives of *his* autobiographical poem:

> Go & build up a pile of three [stones], by that Coppice—measure the Strides from the Bridge where the water rushes down a rock in no mean cataract if the Rains should have swoln the River . . . from this Bridge measure the Strides to the Place, build the Stone heap, & write a Poem, thus beginning—From the Bridge &c repeat such a Song, of Milton, or Homer—so many Lines I ~~will~~ must find out, may be distinctly recited during a moderate healthy man's walk from the Bridge thither—or better perhaps from the other Bridge—so to this Heap of Stones—there turn in—& then describe the Scene.—O surely I might make a noble Poem of all my Youth nay *of all my Life*—One section on plants & flowers, my passion for them, always deadened by their learned names.

As much as we can infer from this brief description, it appears that Coleridge's 'noble Poem' was to be written in the high style of an epic or perhaps an ode and grafted onto the Wordsworthian topos of adherence to natural spots. It was to be a poem celebrating Coleridge's passion for nature and, possibly, tracing the history of his relationship with nature throughout his life. Coleridge would have found a model for such a poem in 'Tintern Abbey', and from talks with William and Dorothy he might have also anticipated the kind of project Wordsworth was engaged in at the time. There is, however, something altogether peculiar about the way Coleridge proceeds to lay out his poem. It is as if Coleridge is trying not just to evoke a certain place in a poem, but virtually to tailor his composition according to the physical pattern provided by the place. There

is a deliberate binding of poem to place or, borrowing one of Coleridge's own phrases in another context, what I would like to call spot fixation 'with a vengeance'. Thus, Coleridge's preliminary concern is to count the number of strides from the bridge to the discovered spot and to schedule the length of his poem accordingly. The writing of the poem is presented as an activity that is continuous with and undifferentiated from the purely mechanical parts of the project: 'measure the Strides to the Place, build the Stone heap, & write a Poem'.

It is to be expected that no *Prelude* ever emerged from such tight measurements. Coleridge's 'noble Poem', so far as we know, was never written, just as the other projects in the naturalistic mode never materialized. This evidence seems to corroborate the opinion of some critics that Coleridge is not concerned with external objects and incapable of writing good nature poetry because for him the main source of inspiration came from 'the life within', from fantasy and dream. Wordsworth summarized this view best when he told Henry Crabb Robinson in 1812 that Coleridge was addicted to 'his own extraordinary powers summoning up an image or series of images in his own mind' and thus given to 'a sort of dreaminess which would not let him see things as they were' or experience the 'influence of external objects'. But surely this view, while capturing a certain direction in the later Coleridge of which he was himself most critical, is an inadequate description both of his poetry and of his personality as a whole. To say that Coleridge could not write nature poetry or that he was perpetually sleep-walking in an imaginary realm closed to nature's 'living images' is to ignore his having composed a poem like 'This Lime-tree Bower my Prison', and the fastidiously precise observations of various sensory phenomena in his journals. In fact, comparing Coleridge's description of a spot in the hills of Alfoxden in 'This Lime-tree Bower my Prison' with Wordsworth's own account of this place in 'Lines Written in Early Spring', Stephen Maxfield Parrish concludes that 'Coleridge traces the surfaces of Nature with close attention to realistic detail, only unobtrusively committing the pathetic fallacy, while Wordsworth glances at but moves beyond the surfaces, boldly investing Nature with life and feeling, then turns from Nature to man. In the end, Coleridge's poem is more an outright celebration of nature than Wordsworth's, and closer to the matter-of-fact world of eye and ear'.

If we accept the premise that Coleridge could—and did—write nature poetry, then his failure to turn out the projected topographic and autobiographic poems cannot be attributed to some constitutional handicap of his temperament or to his reputation as a poet of trance. I would like to advance a speculation here that may shed some light on this matter. The history of Coleridge's early collaboration with Wordsworth shows that the two poets could not engage successfully in the same project and that they wrote some of their best work when dealing with completely different subjects and methods of exploration. Coleridge's and Wordsworth's attempts to collaborate on a single poem, which was the earliest plan for the *Lyrical Ballads,* resulted instead in a more voluminous output of 'two sorts' of poems, one adhering to 'the truth of nature' and lending 'the charm of novelty to things of every day', the other proposing to show 'the dramatic truth' of emotions experienced by 'every human being who, from whatever source of delusion, has at any time believed himself under supernatural agency'. This account given by Coleridge in *Biographia Literaria* is an accurate description of what came out of the *Lyrical Ballads* venture, but, as Shawcross pointed out, it is not a reliable testimony of how the volume was originally conceived. In a letter to Humphry Davy written in October 1800, Coleridge presents the *Lyrical Ballads* as 'an experiment to see how far those passions which alone give any value to extraordinary Incidents, were capable of interesting, in & for themselves, in the incidents of common Life'. This version of the project, which approximates the way Wordsworth himself recalled it in his Fenwick note to 'We Are Seven', makes no provision for 'persons and characters supernatural' or 'the willing suspension of disbelief'. From the written evidence we have and from what we know about Wordsworth's sensibility, it is safe to assume that Wordsworth had in mind a homogeneous volume of poetry by theme and purpose, and not a Coleridgean meeting of extremes, or a synthesis of opposite artistic modes, as his partner presented the case in *Biographia Literaria.*

If we take into account the fact that Wordsworth was by nature averse to the merging of discordant elements, then his decision to exclude 'Christabel' on the grounds that the poem was 'in direct opposition to the very purpose for which the Lyrical Ballads were published' is understandable, particularly if his expectations of the volume were those conveyed by Coleridge's letter to Davy. When Wordsworth, for the purpose of minimizing the discrepancies in the projected second edition of the *Lyrical Ballads,* encouraged Coleridge to produce his poems of 'the Naming of Places', he in effect invited Coleridge to surrender his sovereign territory and join in a truly communal enterprise. But in so doing Wordsworth presented Coleridge with a dangerous challenge that Coleridge accepted with determination, though not without some foreboding. Wordsworth held out for Coleridge the attractive prospect of becoming a successful poet, acceptable to his partner, if he abandoned the supernatural ideal and concerned himself instead with the feelings which grow from 'little Incidents' among 'rural Objects'. The extent to which Coleridge accepted the Wordsworthian challenge is evident from the number of naturalistic poems he kept on devising. As much as one might sympathize

with Charles Lamb's regret that Coleridge stopped writing 'Christabels and Ancient Mariners', it is important to realize that after 1800 Coleridge tried very hard to do just that, to move away from a supernatural poetry that had incurred Wordsworth's opprobrium. But by giving in to the pressure of becoming a naturalistic poet, Coleridge was forced into an impossible competition on his rival's home ground. In this context, his inability to complete his topographic poems and the obvious self-defeating mechanism ingrained in his formula for a *Prelude* of his own become increasingly comprehensible.

It was not uncharacteristic of Coleridge to take on unsuitable projects of various magnitude and kinds, especially during times of personal unhappiness, which would usually deepen his feelings of inadequacy, guilt and self-reproach. His failure, therefore, to write poems in the naturalistic vein cannot be seen simply as externally induced by Wordsworth's demands, but as related to Coleridge's personality as well as his fluctuating views regarding the value of nature poetry. In this respect one may recall that Coleridge vigorously encouraged Wordsworth to write philosophical poetry, and was most critical of his friend's unwise devotion to small projects of the kind he produced for the *Lyrical Ballads*. If this reflects at all Coleridge's ideal of high poetry, then his attitude towards poems set in a rural setting and dealing with commonplace incidents could only be unenthusiastic if not downright disparaging. It is as if Coleridge were willing to assume the burden of writing minor poetry in order to allow Wordsworth to devote himself to the great task of becoming 'the first & greatest philosophical Poet'. The fact that Coleridge did not go ahead with his projected naturalistic poems reveals the limits of such self-sacrificial generosity in this literary relationship and of Coleridge's own capacity for self-denial.

In a later notebook entry, recalling the painful, humiliating reception that his supernatural poems received from the Wordsworths, Coleridge reflected on their 'cold praise and effective discouragement of every attempt of mine to roll onward in a distinct current of my own'. Although this statement may be more indicative of Coleridge's excessive need for approval than of the total disapproval he met with in his relationship with the Wordsworths, it offers, none the less, a valuable insight into the nature of the crisis of poetic power Coleridge encountered during the years of his literary association with Wordsworth on the *Lyrical Ballads*. Coleridge's supernatural poems, which clearly signalled a 'distinct current' of his own, were not appreciated by the Wordsworths. On the other hand, naturalistic poems of the kind Wordsworth seemed to like did not fully satisfy Coleridge's standards for good poetry. Coleridge's disorientation as to what should be his own direction in poetry accounts to a large extent for the feelings of creative paralysis he experienced especially in 1802 and dramatized in 'Dejection: An Ode'. Though this perspective does not offer a full explanation of how Coleridge lost his poetic momentum after 1800, it provides a useful corrective to the view enunciated by Coleridge in 'Dejection' that metaphysics killed the 'shaping spirit' of his imagination, and with it, his sensitivity to nature.

Coleridge's relationship with Wordsworth thus had a direct influence on his ambivalent response to nature and his damaged confidence regarding his prospects as a poet. In the early stages of their association, while mutual admiration and love were still the overriding sentiments between them, Coleridge's interest in nature was undoubtedly stimulated by the spirited nature talk they conducted during their walks and travels. His successful composition of 'This Lime-tree Bower my Prison' might owe something to a more relaxed attitude towards nature that Coleridge derived from his communication with the Wordsworths and that helped him to overcome the feelings of guilt fostered by earlier encounters with the natural world, as conveyed in 'Reflections on having left a Place of Retirement' or 'The Eolian Harp'. By March 1798, in a letter to his brother George, Coleridge already presents himself as a poet of nature, inspired by 'fields & woods & mountains with almost a visionary fondness' and seeking to 'elevate the imagination & set the affections in right tune by the beauty of the inanimate impregnated, as with a living soul, by the presence of Life'. Coleridge illustrates his position by quoting some lines from 'The Ruined Cottage', thus showing his eagerness to align his poetic goals with those of Wordsworth, though, of course, the sentiment and theme of 'the one Life' were indigenous to Coleridge. It is worth remembering that at the time Coleridge assumed the identity of a poet of nature, 'The Rime of the Ancient Mariner' was for the most part written. This, as well as the close proximity between the composition of 'This Lime-tree Bower my Prison' and 'The Rime of the Ancient Mariner', indicates that before his relationship with Wordsworth deteriorated, Coleridge could function successfully as a poet both of nature and of the supernatural, just as prior to 1800 he was tormented neither by his identity as a metaphysician nor by the conviction that metaphysics was detrimental to poetry.

While the relationship with Wordsworth in its early, benevolent phase greatly spurred Coleridge's passion for nature, it also had the opposite effect of turning Coleridge's rapport with nature into a highly complicated affair. Two related matters show how a weakening of Coleridge's ties with nature can be linked to the increasing tensions caused by his collaboration with Wordsworth. The first pertains to Coleridge's tormented struggle for poetic survival after Wordsworth assumed sole authorship of the *Lyrical Ballads*. We have already seen that Coleridge, despite frequent announcements to friends that he had surrendered poetry to

Wordsworth, tried to keep a low profile as a naturalistic poet. Moreover, he continued to look on nature as a revitalizing source of creative energy. In a sense, as the relationship with Wordsworth became less reassuring, Coleridge transferred his dependency from his friend to nature, from a stern father-figure to a more forgiving, motherly guardian. This transference is most clearly seen in a notebook entry written around the time of Coleridge's severe rift with Wordsworth in 1810. Here, adapting a consoling passage from Richter's *Geist,* Coleridge speaks of nature as a steadfast and loyal companion, lulling one's grief and extending generous protection and sympathy 'even when all men have seemed to desert us'. While the 'Love of Nature is ever returned double to us', the love of man appears to Coleridge as a one-way, inconstant and disappointing affair. In his rift with Wordsworth, Coleridge experienced the reversal of the Wordsworthian mythos 'love of Nature leads to love of Man'. Instead, love of man leads, *via negativa,* to an appreciation of nature.

The transference of dependency from Wordsworth to nature took place much earlier than the time of the quarrel in 1810 and caused, as relationships of dependency normally do, a disquieting awareness of an imperfect guardianship. When his prospects as a poet became uncertain after his banishment from the *Lyrical Ballads,* Coleridge often turned to nature with hopes of finding an immediate stimulus for poetic productivity. His expectations of the bountiful gifts nature held in store for him and his mode of gaining possession of such gifts are best represented by a few lines from Coleridge's free translation of Stolberg's 'Hymne an die Erde':

> Thrilled with thy beauty and love in the
>   wooded slope of the mountain
> Here, great mother, I lie, thy child, with his
>   head on thy bosom!
> Playful the spirits of noon, that rushing soft
>   through thy tresses,
> Green-haired goddess! refresh me; and hark!
>   as they hurry or linger,
> Fill the pause of my harp, or sustain it with
>   musical murmurs.

(ll. 7-11)

What Coleridge found, however, is that while nature might perform miraculous acts of benevolence for a loving and needy child, it does not fill those pauses of the poetic lyre with a steady voice 'but half its own'. Consistently, Coleridge discovered that the strategy of courting nature to gain instant poetic recovery did not succeed. As his notebooks show, Coleridge's repeated efforts to provoke inspiration by dwelling on 'outward forms' finally convinced him that, while his sensitivity to nature was ample and visitations of 'poetic feeling' *did* occur in the midst of natural objects, without 'the combining Power, the power to do, the manly effective *Will*', such visitations finally dissipated into nothingness. This experience differs from the crisis Coleridge dramatizes in 'Dejection: An Ode'. It is not the failure of responding to the natural world, but the very amplitude of this response that makes the absence of the 'genial spirits' so much more evident and painful to endure. While Coleridge could persuade himself (as he tried to persuade Francis Wrangham) that his love of metaphysics by no means overshadowed his devotion to the 'Goddess Nature', he could not thereby also prove that he was, like Wordsworth, a great poet. In the decline of a poetic career, Coleridge recognized that encounters with the natural world that merely tease but do not satisfy the 'genial spirits' were hopelessly defective and self-defeating.

Coleridge's growing alienation from nature also originated from his need, contrary to the dependency drive, to dissociate himself from Wordsworth's values. Several small incidents show that Coleridge found Wordsworth's nature worship irritating, just as he began to find fault with his friend's self-involuted personality and artistic principles. In a letter of August 1801, Coleridge invited Francis Wrangham for a visit to the Lakes, mentioning in a tone of light mockery that Wordsworth would undoubtedly introduce him to nature's 'best things in all her mollissima tempora—for few men can boast, I believe, of so intimate an acquaintance with her Ladyship'. There is here a covert criticism of Wordsworth's engagement with the transitory 'superficies of Objects', an activity which, as Coleridge remarked, is bound to weaken 'the Health and manhood of Intellect'. We find again that during their tour through Scotland Coleridge conducted a silent battle with the Wordsworths on an issue most likely pertaining to the picturesque, referring specifically to the authority of the mind in its dealings with nature:

> Those who hold it undignified to illustrate Nature by Art—how little would the truly dignified say so—how else can we bring the forms of Nature within our voluntary memory!—The first Business is to subjugate them to our Intellect & voluntary memory—then comes their Dignity by Sensation of Magnitude, Forms & Passions connected therewith.

We are familiar with Wordsworth's aversion to applying the 'rules of mimic art' to nature and can infer from Coleridge's note that he must have spoken vehemently against a standard presupposition about the picturesque. Coleridge privately replies to Wordsworth that the dignity of nature depends upon man's intellectual mastery, and that the function of art is therefore to provide the medium through which the mind can assimilate, control and retain the forms of nature, thereby endowing them with the 'life and passion' they do not by themselves possess. The view that the mind must be granted dominion over the world of the senses is not unusual in Coleridge, but the recommendation that nature must be 'subjugated' by the mind, which would undoubtedly have irritated Wordsworth, has a more extreme edge to it that comes from the controversial dispute with Wordsworth. Such origins are important to bear in mind. As a way of asserting his independence from Wordsworth, Coleridge is likely to make radical claims that are not fully representative of his view of nature at a given time.

During the years of growing disaffection with Wordsworth, Coleridge identified an area of difference between himself and his friend where he could, comfortably, prove Wordsworth to be in the wrong. It concerned Wordsworth's tendency to place the mind in a relationship of servitude to the great 'Green-haired goddess'. (This is not, of course, the Wordsworth we know, though Coleridge's interpretation of Wordsworth's cult of nature is not different from the view of other contemporaries, such as Blake or Shelley.) It concerned, moreover, Wordsworth's taste for the accidental and transitory aspects of nature, his stubborn matter-of-factness and unwillingness to devote himself to 'great objects & elevated Conceptions'. Coleridge used this line of criticism in *Biographia Literaria,* where he adopted in opposition to Wordsworth's views the Aristotelian notion that 'poetry is essentially *ideal,* that it avoids and excludes all *accident*'. Earlier, before he could turn his disagreement with Wordsworth into a fully-fledged literary theory, he charted out a private region of sensibility in which he took great pride. But in sorting out his differences from his partner, Coleridge found himself in an ambivalent position as to how prominent a place he should allot to nature. A good example of Coleridge's dilemma in this regard is provided by a notebook entry written during his Malta journey in April 1804.

The entry commemorates Coleridge's first sight of the coast of Africa and his discovery that the continents of Europe and Africa, so distinct by names, are in nature nothing but two undivided 'Mountain Banks, that make a noble River of the interfluent Sea'. The discovery prompted Coleridge to meditate on the 'Power of Names to give Interest' to certain objects or places and on his inability to derive more than light amusement from contingent associations such names might carry. 'Of all men, I ever knew', Coleridge writes, 'Wordsworth himself not expected, I have the faintest pleasure in things contingent & transitory. I never, except as a forced Courtesy of Conversation, ask in a ~~Coach~~ Stage, whose House is that . . . I am not certain, whether I should have seen with any Emotion the Mulberry Tree of Shakespeare.' The knowledge that Shakespeare planted the tree would in effect intrude upon any 'unity of Feeling' he might have experienced otherwise, preventing him from losing himself 'in the flexures of its Branches & interweaving of its Roots'. There are, however, 'conceivable circumstances', Coleridge adds, where 'the contrary would be true', where the knowledge that Giordano Bruno or Milton inhabited a certain 'Rock by this Sea' or 'Bank' would greatly enhance one's experience of the place. Coleridge explains the difference as follows:

> At certain times, uncalled and sudden, subject to no bidding of my own or others, these Thoughts would come upon me, like a Storm, & fill the Place with something more than Nature.—But these are not contingent or transitory / they are Nature, even as the Elements are Nature / yea, more to the human mind / for the mind has the power of abstracting all agency from the former, & considering as mere effects & instruments, but a Shakespere, a Milton, a Bruno, exist in the mind as *pure Action,* defecated of all that is material & passive / .—And the great moments, that formed them—it is hard & an impiety against a Voice within us, not to regard as predestined, & therefore things of Now & For Ever and which were Always. But it degrades this sacred Feeling; & is to it what stupid Superstition is to enthusiastic Religion, when a man makes a Pilgrimage to see a great man's Shin Bone found unmouldered in his Coffin . . .

On the surface Coleridge's argument is fairly clear and consistent. Coleridge distinguishes between an artificially programmed association of a place with a famous person or incident in history and a completely spontaneous train of thought that transcends the immediate material object or circumstantial event which provoked it. His point is that by trying to induce some heightened thrill through linking Shakespeare to the mulberry tree he planted, one does neither the tree nor Shakespeare any service. On the one hand, one could not immerse oneself in a fully empathic experience of the tree due to the expectations of what an experience of Shakespeare's tree should be, along with the ensuing disappointment when the actual feelings were found to be ordinary. On the other hand, to link Shakespeare to his tree is in effect to confuse a spiritual presence, a thing of the mind existing as *'pure Action'* in the mind, with a material object. The failure to distinguish between 'things of Now & For Ever' and 'contingent or transitory' things is at the root of all idolatry and superstition. So far Coleridge's argument proceeds evenly and seems sure-footed. But it is by no means completed. Towards the end of his entry Coleridge's tone becomes more vehement as he launches an attack against the 'mass of mankind' who 'whether from Nature or . . . Error of Rearing & the Worldliness of their after Pursuits, are rarely susceptible of any other Pleasures than those of *amusement,* gratifications of curiosity, Novelty, Surprize, Wonderment from the Glaring, the harshly Contrasted, the Odd, the Accidental: and find in the reading of Paradise Lost a task, somewhat alleviated by a few entertaining Incidents'. Next follows an attack on Johnson, both for his lack of interest in nature and his view of Milton, and finally,

a brief memorandum on the subject of 'the virtues connected with the Love of Nature' for Coleridge's projected volume of poetry 'Comforts and Consolations'.

There is something intriguing about the closure of Coleridge's entry. The last three steps in Coleridge's line of argument have a distinctly Wordsworthian genealogy. Wordsworth himself had severely chastised the public for its 'craving for extraordinary incident' and 'degrading thirst after outrageous stimulation' to the extent that the 'works of Shakespeare and Milton, are driven into neglect'. It is unclear whether Coleridge had Wordsworth's Preface to the *Lyrical Ballads* in mind towards the end of his entry. If, however, we assume (and this must remain a tentative speculation) that the reference to Wordsworth at the beginning of the entry is not a casual one but a stimulus for the whole entry, then the final part of Coleridge's argument acquires added significance. By suggesting that Wordsworth was not free from the love of the 'contingent' and by linking such habits with the vulgar taste for novelty, Coleridge has in effect included Wordsworth in the very category of people he criticized in the Preface to the *Lyrical Ballads*. At the same time, Coleridge has located himself within the sacred circle of those who respect the pure act of the mind—a circle which excludes 'all that is material and passive'. The nice Wordsworthian touch at the end of the entry concerning the 'virtues connected with the Love of Nature' does not cancel the fact that midstream in his argument Coleridge identified certain forms of nature worship as superstitious idolatry and circumscribed the area of the sacred as that which contains 'something more than Nature', the spirituality of the human mind itself.

Characteristically, Coleridge's ambivalent feelings of dependence on and rejection of the Wordsworthian canon were not confined to private utterances in his journals but left their mark on his published works as well. I shall refer here to one example from Coleridge's poetry, namely 'Dejection: An Ode', and deal briefly with only a few moments in the dramatic development of the poem. It need hardly be emphasized that the relationship with Wordsworth was at the heart of the crisis of imaginative inhibition that Coleridge analysed in 'Dejection'. As de Selincourt pointed out, 'the root idea of "Dejection" ' was 'a conscious and deliberate contrast' between Coleridge and his more fortunate friend. Predictably, in Coleridge's case such comparison led to a painful and debilitating complex of inferiority. By following the textual variants of the poem we can almost follow chronologically the effects of Coleridge's subordination to and gradual liberation from Wordsworth's commanding authority.

An examination of the several versions of 'Dejection' clearly reveals Coleridge's uncertainty in deciding whom he wanted to address in the ode. Coleridge successively changes the form of address from Sara ('Letter—',) to William (Letter to William Sotheby of 19 July 1802 and to Sir George Beaumont of 13 August 1803), to 'Edmund' (the *Morning Post* text published on 4 October 1802), and finally to the anonymous 'Lady' of the 1817 *Sibylline Leaves* version. Beverly Fields attributes this uncertainty to Oedipal tensions that made it difficult for Coleridge 'to separate his feelings for men from his feelings for women'. This is why the 'object of his emotions' in the poem can be interchangeably a male or a female. But there is a significant difference in the ending of the various versions of the poem, depending on whether a man or a woman is the intended love object. As the closing lines in the following four versions indicate, Coleridge assumes a much more subordinate role towards his friend when he addresses Wordsworth or Edmund (a 'transparent sobriquet for Wordsworth', as de Selincourt puts it), than towards Sara or the anonymous 'Lady':

1. 'Calm stedfast Spirit guided from above, / O Wordsworth! friend of my devoutest choice, / Great Son of Genius! full of Light & Love / Thus, thus *dost thou rejoice.* / To thee *do* all things *live* from pole to pole . . .' (Letter to Sotheby)

2. 'O EDMUND, friend of my devoutest choice . . . Joy *lifts* thy spirit, joy *attunes* thy voice, / To thee *do* all things *live* from pole to pole . . .' (*Morning Post*)

3. 'By the Immenseness of the Good & Fair / Which thou see'st every where— / Thus, thus *should'st* thou rejoice! To thee *would* all Things live from Pole to Pole . . .' (Letter to Sara)

4. 'Joy *lift* her spirit, joy *attune* her voice; / To her *may* all things *live,* from pole to pole . . .' (*Sibylline Leaves*) [my italics]

In the first two versions, the poet-friend is presented as positively possessing the joy that ensures poetic creativity and, therefore, hardly needing protective prayers from the speaker. The *Morning Post* version makes clear that the friend is capable not only of maintaining his 'genial spirits', but also of teaching the speaker how 'to rejoice' with 'his lofty song'. The speaker's prayer in the end that his friend be visited by 'gentle Sleep, with wings of healing' seems incongruous, because there is no indication that things are other than 'good and fair' for the friend. In the early versions where Coleridge unfolds his doleful tale under the imagined scrutiny of Wordsworth, he virtually pushes himself into a position of complete uselessness. Years later when Coleridge revised the poem for his collection *Sibylline Leaves,* at a time when he experienced a period of significant productivity and, through the writing of *Biographia Literaria,* defined more clearly his differences with Wordsworth, he replaced Words-

worth with the anonymous 'lady' and at the same time granted the speaker a much more meaningful role in the end. This change is marked by a subtle shift from the present indicative of the letter to Sotheby and *Morning Post* versions to the optative mood that was present in the original letter to Sara. Thus, it no longer appears that the friend is in full possession of joy as a *fait accompli,* and by implication more dependent on the speaker's selfless guidance and prayers.

There is in 'Dejection' another Wordsworthian moment that also reveals Coleridge in the typically helpless role he assumed towards his friend: the story of the little lost child in Part VII, which alludes to Wordsworth's 'Lucy Gray'. As Irene Chayes notes, 'partly seeking a similar lyric inspiration from without and partly coming on it unexpectedly during his impromptu literary survey, the poet of "Dejection" begins in his reverie to re-compose another man's poem and for the moment become a poet again'. As we have seen, Coleridge was in the habit of imitating Wordsworth in a desperate attempt at poetic survival, and such attempts usually failed. In a similar fashion, in 'Dejection' the very act of reformulating another man's work points to the absence of radical creativity on the part of the speaker, confirming his worst fears about the state of his 'genial spirits'. The one revision Coleridge introduced in his version of 'Lucy Gray', namely the change of focus from the parents' to the child's despair, indicates Coleridge's own self-projection as a dependent and helpless being, rather than an actual rebirth of poetic vigour at the heels of his poet-master.

But dependency is not the only mood voiced in 'Dejection'. We have seen previously that Coleridge's sense of inferiority towards Wordsworth was invariably accompanied by a strong drive towards self-assertion. The speaker of 'Dejection' repeatedly slips in and out of two roles that closely parallel Coleridge's divided reactions to Wordsworth: one is the role of a defeated poet, opening his wounds, so to speak, to dwell on his despair and to invite the pity and protection due to the defenceless; the other is that of a man who finds considerable power in speculative insights and the benediction of a friend. It is certainly not from a position of a defenceless and injured poet that Coleridge formulates the doctrine of creative joy in stanzas IV and V. The tone here is as assertive as it is confident, and as Suther sensed, it is even a little overly insistent. The speaker is aware that he is in possession of a precious gift, the knowledge of nature's complete dependence on the life of the mind, a knowledge that is not given to the 'sensual and the proud' and, evidently, needs to be preached even to the 'pure of Heart'. In effect, Coleridge holds before Wordsworth the bright torch of higher knowledge, which he is willing to pass on to his friend in order to protect him from the dark passage of dejection where Coleridge remains imprisoned and alone. Coleridge thus achieves a double victory on both intellectual and moral grounds. He becomes the enlightened philosopher-poet, teaching, as he had hoped Wordsworth would, that the mind rules over and is not ruled by the senses. At the same time Coleridge presents himself in the flattering posture of a disinterested poet, seeking nothing for himself and keeping nothing to himself, but caring only for the well-being of another.

The partial record I have reconstructed here of the progressive alienation of Coleridge and Wordsworth shows all the conflicting attitudes and desires that are at the heart of such separations. Coleridge's inclination to surrender both poetry and nature to Wordsworth often brought him into the arena where courteous chivalry gave way to contest, just as his desire to subordinate his artistic goals to those of his partner merely intensified his need for independence. In his effort to locate a 'distinct current' of his own, Coleridge found it imperative to reject Wordsworth's cult of nature and isolate himself in the magic sphere of the mind which contained '*pure Action,* defecated of all that is material & passive'. It is difficult to tell whether Coleridge's existing ambivalence towards nature led to his disagreement with Wordsworth, or whether the Wordsworthian challenge provoked a much more radical denial of nature than would otherwise have occurred. But the difficulty itself suggests that much of the text of Coleridge's love song and breach of loyalty to the 'Goddess Nature' is buried in the psychic history of a most extraordinary literary friendship.

DEFINING AND DEVELOPING ROMANTIC IDEALS

David Watson Rannie

SOURCE: An introduction to *Wordsworth and His Circle,* G. P. Putnam's Sons, 1907, pp. 1-17.

[*In the following excerpt, Rannie discusses the Romantic characteristics and influences of Wordsworth's work and the poet's association with Coleridge, Southey, De Quincey, and Charles Lamb.*]

In one sense it seems a dubious use of metaphor to regard Wordsworth as the centre of any circle. For, if we think of a body of men as a circle, we must think of the centre as one of a group who shares its qualities; one who gives and takes, who lives in intellectual community and not alone. Yet no fact about Wordsworth is more certain and more striking than his essential solitariness. To him, even more than to Milton, his own words belong: *his soul was like a star and dwelt apart.* The Puritanism of his age, the culture of his age, are much more perceptible in Milton, than are any sympathies of the eighteenth or nineteenth century in

the work of Wordsworth. Milton, for all his mighty originality, was a *classicist*; he was proud to work on traditional lines; his form was as great as his matter, and is inseparable from it. But Wordsworth had the daring, defiant individuality of the true Romantic. He thought of himself, and he thought rightly, as a reformer, an innovator, in poetry; and he neither had, nor believed himself to have, much essential kinship with any of his contemporaries. He always had enthusiastic admirers, and always friends whose cordial admiration fell short of enthusiasm; but there was not one of them, who was wholly without perplexity and disappointment about the master, not one who could wholly abandon the attitude of apology.

While disciples and admirers were not without uncertainty and occasional dissent, Wordsworth himself habitually felt a serene self-complacency which enclosed him as a constant envelope, but which must not be confounded with any kind of vulgar egotism. Traces of such egotism there undoubtedly were in Wordsworth; but they have really nothing to do with that consciousness of mission and certainty of ultimate success which gave to this poet the prophet's high self-regard and solitary outlook.

Wordsworth wrote to Lady Beaumont in 1807 that he was "easy-hearted" with respect to his poems. "Trouble not yourself," he wrote, "upon their present reception; of what moment is that compared with what I trust in their destiny?—to console the afflicted; to add sunshine to daylight by making the happy happier; to teach the young and the gracious of every age to see, to think, and feel, and therefore to become more actively and securely virtuous; this is their office." Such self-criticism is nearly as impersonal as the words which immediately precede it—

> It is an awful truth, that there neither is nor can be, any genuine enjoyment of poetry among nineteen out of twenty of those persons who live, or wish to live, in the broad light of the world—among those who either are, or are striving to make themselves, people of consideration in society. This is a truth, and an awful one, because to be incapable of a feeling of poetry, in my sense of the word, is to be without love of human nature and reverence for God.

One who thus thinks of poetry and of his own effort in its service, must feel and speak as if alone in a wilderness; and perhaps no British man of letters was ever in this sense so unrelated, so original, as Wordsworth. His detachment is only made more obvious by the recognition of his debt to forerunners, and of his disciples' debt to him. In two very important respects, the way was prepared for Wordsworth, not in Britain only, but in Europe: men's affections were turning from purely human interests to interests in which landscape had a large share; and from the attractions of elaborate civilization to those of extreme simplicity. No two men ever moved further apart than Rousseau and Wordsworth; yet their common ground and the identity of some of their presuppositions are notorious. Nor, among his British contemporaries, is it only Wordsworth who reminds us of Rousseau. Goldsmith and Cowper, not less than the ballad-restorers or such a Romantic mediævalist as Chatterton, felt, each in his own way, that disapproval of things as they were, that discontent with civilized man, which Rousseau indulged with such startling results. Goldsmith expressed them with a somewhat conventional pensiveness; in Cowper they were made to subserve the Evangelicalism of the age; but the burden, in both, was a praise of rusticity and simplicity, an appreciation of man as man, without any lendings or trappings, which are not far from Rousseau's central thought. And if Rousseau's thought became revolutionary, it must be remembered that Wordsworth's sympathies, in some of his strongest hours, were on the side of the Revolution. He hailed the great French upheaval as a resuscitation of man; and the passion of his maturity, his hatred of Napoleon, was passion for the freedom which the tyrant had overthrown. So he read the events.

But none of this makes Wordsworth's originality less complete. The Nature to which he preached and led a return, had a very different complexion from the Nature of Rousseau's worship; and in the rare atmosphere of its high places we may be sure that Goldsmith and Cowper would have found it hard to breathe. Even in his earliest work, in the *Evening Walk* and *Descriptive Sketches* (in the latter of which, indeed, Coleridge saw "the emergence of an original poetic genius above the horizon," but which are only remotely Wordsworthian), we find a treatment of landscape very different from Cowper's. Cowper's feeling for landscape leaves little to be desired in genuineness; but his method of description has nothing of the intimacy of Wordsworth's. And when, in and after *Lyrical Ballads,* Wordsworth became Wordsworthian, he thought and spoke of Nature, whether as revealed in man, or in that world of the open air in which man lives and moves, as no one, either in or out of Britain, had thought and spoken of it before. Some of his predecessors had observed Nature with affectionate care and truly and beautifully rendered her details; many had personified her; but it was left for Wordsworth to realize her as a living unity, and to love her as the saints love God.

Nor is Wordsworth's isolation less striking if we think of the history of his influence. Immediately and remotely, by repulsion as well as by attraction, his influence has been immense; but it has never been of the kind which leads to imitation. Wordsworth founded no school. His words ran over the length and breadth of the land; his thought has sunk deep into one generation after another; but hardly any one has borrowed his accents or attempted to complete his message. Nor can

Portrait of William Wordsworth, drawn by Robert Hancock in 1798.

it be said of him, as it can be said of, *e.g.* Byron, Scott, or Tennyson, that he was the spokesman of an age, that he ministered to prevalent taste, that he made articulate the thoughts and feelings which were striving for expression in younger as well as lesser men. What in this sense we call *popularity* could never be affirmed of Wordsworth. He sang of "things common" indeed; but there are many ways of "touching" such things, and Wordsworth's way was not the world's.

To find Wordsworth's circle, then, we must think partly of his many contemporary literary and artistic friends and admirers, cordial always, but always critical; partly of that opulent cluster of Romantic poets with their attendant and like-minded critics, among whom Wordsworth, in spite of his singularity, must be ranked. In the latter sense, the circle must be held to include Burns and Blake, Shelley and Keats, as much as Coleridge and Southey, De Quincey and Charles Lamb.

About the great literary outburst which marked the close of the eighteenth, and the first quarter of the nineteenth century, so much has been said that, probably, the less one now says the better. All that one may hope, or need attempt, to do, is to rehearse some generally recognized conclusions and point out some special aspects and distinctions. If we ignore these we shall miss Wordsworth's place in literary history.

The Romantic Revival, as it is the fashion to call the outburst, was a unity in diversity. It was a unity, as the springtime is a unity, inasmuch as it brought new life into the world, the world of verse and prose, of feeling and thought. It was a unity inasmuch as it depended upon novelty; as it worked on men's minds by way of surprise, excitement, sense of change. It was a unity inasmuch as it came to be associated, often loosely and rhetorically, with the French Revolution, as if it were a kind of literary and artistic counterpart of that great social and political movement. But its diversity is more apparent than its unity. Even if we could bring ourselves to believe that one impulse, or a small number of kindred impulses, produced the Romantic Revival, we should have to acknowledge that the Revival included a great many very different things, of which the interconnection is by no means obvious. It has been called—not without good reason—the "Renascence of Wonder." It has been called, with equally good reason, the restoration of English poetry to Nature, or of Nature to English poetry. It was certainly the revival of various and beautiful lyrical measures; it was a new birth of lyrical passion; it was the revival of delight in love; it was the recovery of power to recognize and render the beautiful. It was a reaction against a long monopoly in poetry of the satire of society. It included, as we have seen, a recovered sense of the beauty and significance of landscape; and with this must be conjoined a recovered sense of the attractiveness of animals, and of their claim on human interest and affection. It was an assertion of the rights of individuality in genius against the obligation of literary tradition. It was the discovery of light in the "Dark Ages," in that mediæval world which had seemed the mere ruin and negation of classical culture. Last, but not least, in the Romantic Revival poetry became essentially and truly "metaphysical." It asserted its kinship with theology and philosophy; it assumed prophetic garments and mystical accents; it became the interpreter of symbols, the revealer of realities beyond the phantasmagoria of the senses.

One feature was, on the whole, common to the many aspects of the movement, and the recognition of it will bring us back to Wordsworth. Romance is the cult of the extraordinary, the unusual; its presupposition is that in the world of art a refuge is to be found from the tyranny of what is common, under which daily experience groans. Very different were the presuppositions of the poetry and fiction dominant in Britain for more than a hundred years before the Romantic Revival can be said to have begun. The poetry of Dryden and Pope assumed the all-sufficiency as poetic themes of contemporary society, manners, and politics. The so-called "comedy of manners," which culminated in Congreve, found its subject-matter and inspiration in the same quarters. The English novel renounced all connection with the preposterous romance of the seventeenth century, and nourished its mighty youth on the most home-

ly, sometimes the most sordid, realities of British life. The poetry which intervened between Pope on the one hand, and Coleridge and Wordsworth on the other, was a poetry of transition, which foreshadowed the future as well as recalled the past. But in the prose romance of awe and supernatural terror which Horace Walpole handed on to Mrs. Radcliffe, and in the old-world opulence of Chatterton and Ossian and the ballad-restorers, literature turned its face resolutely from the temporary and the ordinary towards the extraordinary and the remote. And this conversion was of the very essence of the Romanticism which glowed like a bright star on the opening of the nineteenth century.

"But what," the reader may ask, "has it got to do with Wordsworth?" Was not Wordsworth's battle for the homely, the ordinary; was it not his boast, his reproach, and his glory, that he found "a tale in everything"; that "the moving accident" was not his trade; and that in humble, everyday life, its peasantry, its flowers, its speech, its "nameless unregarded acts," the best stuff of poetry was to be found? The Romanticism of Coleridge, of Byron, of Scott, of Southey, of Keats, is evident; but, if the cult of the extraordinary and remote is essential to Romanticism, is it consistent, is it reasonable, to call Wordsworth a Romantic?

The answer is that Romanticism claims Wordsworth by virtue of his *imagination*. In the following pages we shall have to hear much about imagination. It is enough to say now that Wordsworth regarded that faculty very seriously; that he conceived himself to possess it in large measure; and that he thought of it as the poet's chief warrant. And while he gloried in choosing lowly themes for poetry, he utterly repudiated the judgment that his poetry itself was lowly. He believed that his imaginative faculty transformed the themes, and transformed them creatively, as we may believe that Divine Power transforms the raw material or primordial protoplasm of the physical universe. The result, according to Wordsworth, was that the common lost its commonness, and gained what Romanticism of the more ordinary type sought in the preternatural, the remote, the unusual.

When Wordsworth and Coleridge made the famous compact out of which *Lyrical Ballads* sprang in 1798, they agreed upon a division of labour in a joint enterprise. How they did it cannot be better told than in Coleridge's words:

> It was agreed that my endeavours should be directed to persons and characters supernatural, or at least romantic; yet so as to transfer from our inward nature a human interest and a semblance of truth sufficient to procure for these shadows of imagination that willing suspension of disbelief for the moment, which constitutes poetic faith. Mr. Wordsworth, on the other hand, was to propose to himself as his object, to give the charm of novelty to things of

every day, and to excite a feeling analogous to the supernatural, by awakening the mind's attention from the lethargy of custom, and directing it to the loveliness and the wonders of the world before us; an inexhaustible treasure, but for which, in consequence of the film of familiarity and selfish solicitude, we have eyes, yet see not, ears that hear not, and hearts that neither feel nor understand.

"To excite a feeling analogous to the supernatural;" that was the end which Wordsworth proposed to himself in his poetic operations. It was to be reached by the exercise of imagination, and, by virtue of imagination, he was a fellow-worker with the author of the *Rime of the Ancient Mariner.*

Perhaps we best understand Wordsworth's literary relationships and his place in literary history when we realize his differences from one or two of his predecessors on the one hand, and from some of his famous contemporaries on the other.

Among the predecessors none are more eminent and none more characteristic of the eighteenth century than Pope and Gray. With both Wordsworth thought of himself as in antagonism; against both, at least in certain respects, he led a revolt. Against Pope, indeed, the revolt had begun long before Wordsworth's day, when, in 1756, Joseph Warton published the first volume of his *Essay on the Writings and Genius of Pope.* The reputation of Pope's successors, of Gray and Ossian and the ballad-editors, was itself a testimony to reaction against the Popian despotism. But Wordsworth was more than ten years old when Dr. Johnson published his *Lives of the Poets,* in which Pope, though treated with searching critical discrimination, was held up as a genuine and great poet. "Let us look round upon the present time," cried the Doctor, "and back upon the past; let us inquire to whom the voice of mankind has decreed the wreath of poetry; let their productions be examined and their claims stated; and the pretensions of Pope will be no more disputed. Had he given the world only his version [of Homer] the name of poet must have been allowed him." Wordsworth's view of Pope was very different. He admits that he had "melody" and "a polished style," but he considered his great reputation a false one. He hated personal satire, which plays such a large part in the poetry of Dryden and Pope; and he found Pope wanting in the three essentials of poetry—passion, imagination, and truth to Nature. It was chiefly because of his lack of the last-named quality that Wordsworth was in antagonism to Pope. In an admirable sentence he says that Pope "having wandered from humanity [in his *Pastorals*] with boyish inexperience, the praise which these compositions obtained tempted him into a belief that Nature was not to be trusted, at least in pastoral poetry." Pope, like Dryden before him, wrote about Nature as a man born blind might

write. And Wordsworth's mission was to show that Nature might be trusted.

"Nature never did betray the heart that loved her."

Wordsworth's revolt against Gray was part of his revolt against "poetic diction." He tried, in practice and in criticism, to break down distinctions between expression in prose and expression in verse; and, rightly or wrongly, he held that Gray did all he could to raise and confirm such distinctions. In other words, he thought Gray an *artificial* poet, and as such, he, the Poet of Nature, felt obliged to treat him as a foe.

Towards the more Romantic of his predecessors, the author of the Ossian poems, and the ballad-writers, and even towards such true landscape lovers as Thomson and Cowper, Wordsworth was very critical. He frankly admits Thomson's inspiration; but he says that he has a vicious style with false ornaments, and that he utters sentimental commonplaces. He mocks at Cowper for his apologetic admiration of "that coarse object, a furze-bush." For Percy's *Reliques,* indeed, he has nothing but praise. But Ossian! Gray, whose work it is not easy to regard as in any sense Romantic, Gray, the most fastidious of classicists, was delighted with Ossian. When the first instalment appeared, he wrote to Horace Walpole: "Is there any more to be had of equal beauty, or at all approaching to it?" And on a further acquaintance with the poems, he describes himself as "struck, *extasié,* with their infinite beauty."

Wordsworth, for his part, mercilessly tears the unhappy imposture to tatters; he spurs on his somewhat sluggish rhetoric, and decides that the book "is essentially unnatural . . . a forgery audacious as worthless."

As the world knows, Wordsworth's unsympathetic critics tried to fix him in a circle of their own drawing. "The Lake School," the "Lakists," such was the circle of Francis Jeffrey's devising: it was a triangle rather, and denoted Wordsworth, Coleridge, and Southey, while it connoted "lakishness," that is to say, poetical incompetence and triviality, parading as affected simplicity, and pretentious philosophy.

—*David Watson Rannie*

With the rank and file of Germano-British Romanticism in prose fiction and in verse, Wordsworth had no sympathy. Reformer among reformers as he was, he took a pessimistic view of the efforts of those who were in some respects his fellow-workers. Like all the reformers, he wished literature to be exciting and stimulating rather than formal and dull; but he held that the ruck of the Romanticists used "gross and violent stimulants" to attain their end. He aimed at passion and emotion, they at sentimentalism and sensationalism; and the result was a degradation of literature. "The invaluable works of our elder writers," he wrote in 1800, "I had almost said the works of Shakespeare and Milton, are driven into neglect by frantic novels, sickly and stupid German tragedies, and deluges of idle and extravagant stories in verse."

Such being Wordsworth's temper, it is a matter of interest to observe his relation to his great poetic contemporaries, and to the younger men who came after them. Coleridge was his dear and life-long friend; and, in *Lyrical Ballads,* one of the landmarks of Romanticism, the *Ancient Mariner* appeared side by side with the *Idiot Boy* and the *Tintern Abbey* lines. Was not the *Ancient Mariner* an "idle and extravagant story in verse," or was it redeemed only by Wordsworth's contributions to it, the tale of the shot albatross and a line or two here and there, and by the moral about cruelty to animals? There is no evidence to show that critical questions greatly disturbed Wordsworth's admiration of and loyalty to his "marvellous" colleague and friend. But we do know that Wordsworth had his doubts about the rank of Coleridge's most distinctively Romantic poetry. We know that he considered that Coleridge's poetic achievement fell short of his poetic gifts; that the infelicity of his lot had shut him from that sympathy with others, which is granted only to long and tranquil experience, and without which the best poetry, which is a poetry of human nature, cannot be made. And we know, finally, that he regarded the preternatural, which counts for so much in Coleridge, as the *pis aller* of a poet who could not reach the natural.

If Wordsworth thought thus of Coleridge's most famous efforts in poetry, we must be prepared to find him somewhat cold to others of his contemporaries. We should hardly expect him to find spiritual kinship in Byron, whose satirical treatment of him was hardly relieved by even a passing expression of admiration. But what of him who was in R. L. Stevenson's phrase, "far and away the King of the Romantics," what of Walter Scott? Deep was the respect, and genuine the love which the two men had for one another; and much of their work, surely, was done in the same field. Scott was more of a narrative poet than Wordsworth; he had the externalism to which the narrative poet is prone, and his love of pomp and circumstance; and Wordsworth recognized this. In the introduction to *The White Doe of Rylstone* he points out that it was the *inwardness* of historical events that interested him; and that whereas Scott made events march in the orthodox

manner towards a catastrophe, he, for his part, was content with an external pageantry of mere failure, so long as it might be made the exponent of some hidden moral victory. But surely in their rendering of Nature, in the loving portraiture of mountain and sky and flower, the two poets were in fullest sympathy and co-operation. Yet Wordsworth does not seem to have felt the sympathy. His criticism of Scott is always depreciatory, and he does not seem to have even dreamed of placing him in a high rank. He recognized Southey's great cleverness and power of narrative in verse; but denied him imagination and inspiration. Burns he loved and reverenced; but could never forget his moral shortcomings, and was curiously insensible of his lyrical merit.

Keats and Shelley were a generation younger than Wordsworth; yet they were as truly reformers and restorers of English poetry as he was. In spite of occasional scoffings, they regarded him as a *doyen;* and the three were linked together against all artificiality and Philistinism in their art. Yet it does not appear that Wordsworth took any real interest in the work of his two great junior contemporaries.

As the world knows, Wordsworth's unsympathetic critics tried to fix him in a circle of their own drawing. "The Lake School," the "Lakists," such was the circle of Francis Jeffrey's devising: it was a triangle rather, and denoted Wordsworth, Coleridge, and Southey, while it connoted "lakishness," that is to say, poetical incompetence and triviality, parading as affected simplicity, and pretentious philosophy. The *animus* which Jeffrey breathed into others is dead, and the criticism which it moved is obsolete; but the Lake School will live for ever, not as a sect, but as a noble band of pioneers, or say rather as a cluster of satellites about a star, whose brightness, like that in the prophet's vision, shines "out of the North." Nowhere else in Britain, save in the wizard-held borderland, has any limited area of soil been so definitely and solemnly set apart for, and consecrated to, the Muses, as that region of mountain, lake, and gushing streams which is shared by the three counties of Cumberland, Westmorland, and Lancaster. Grasmere Vale, with its sweet lake and engirdling hills; Windermere, with its islands, reaching away to the south; the shores of Derwentwater under the stately bulk of Skiddaw; these are the spots where the ghostly presences are thickest. It was a great moment in British literary annals when Wordsworth, a wanderer on the face of the earth, resolved to return to the place of his birth, and live and die there.

> Many were the thoughts
> Encouraged and dismissed, till choice was
> made,
> Of a known Vale, whither my feet should
> turn,
> Nor rest till they had reached the very door
> Of the one cottage which methought I saw.

Nearly as memorable was the July day, six months after the Wordsworths settled at Grasmere, when Coleridge tried to become a respectable householder at Greta Hall, near Keswick. For to Greta Hall, three years later, came Southey; and there he remained for half a century, a centre of strenuous intellectual life long after poor Coleridge had drifted away on his dreary and discreditable course. Wordsworth and Southey were the two fixed points in the Lake Country to which admirers and settlers resorted. Coleridge was sometimes to be seen. Thomas de Quincey, like Coleridge an opium-eater, one of Wordsworth's sympathetic exponents in the ears of an unbelieving generation, came to be his neighbour for about twenty years. Shelley took his first wife to Keswick and tried, though in vain, to become something of a Lakist. To the shores of Windermere, came "Christopher North" and Mrs. Hemans, both well within Wordsworth's circle. Hardly could that be said of Harriet Martineau, who nevertheless was Wordsworth's fairly intimate neighbour for a few years. But it might surely be said of Thomas Arnold, the great headmaster of Rugby, who was lord of Fox How and Wordsworth's true friend from 1832 to his sudden death ten years later. Whatever share Wordsworth's influence may have had in bringing John Ruskin to spend the afternoon and evening of his days on Coniston Water, it is legitimate to remark on the fitting juxtaposition of the two men who, more than any age, were the interpreters of Nature's message to mankind.

The poet who dwelt in so imperial a solitude and in so royal a company remains, after the criticism of a hundred years has done its worst and best on him, somewhat of an enigmatical figure. That which the blunt insensibility of the early critics scorned as "lakishness," was undoubtedly there, in the man, his genius and his work; and, though we no longer scorn it, we are sometimes daunted and sometimes perplexed by it. In the climate of poetry we expect sunshine and balmy airs; in Wordsworth we feel, now and again, a chill and blight which spoil one's pleasure. Whence come this east wind and these dull skies? Why does Wordsworth's poetry seem so unequal in value, so apt to fail in charm? How can one who sometimes, who often, rises so high, sink at times so low? How should so transcendent and so inartificial a poet fail to know when he is writing mere dull prose in conventional form of verse? Or is it we, his readers, who are at fault, and not Wordsworth? Is it only that we are but partially initiated, and that, with more perfectly purged ears, we should hear nothing but music?

These questions are put only that they may be deprecated and dismissed. It is best to take Wordsworth as he took himself, quite seriously, and to dwell with him for a season, not so much that we may reconsider him critically, not that we may make a new attempt to "place" him, not that we may sift what we like in his poetry from what we dislike, but that we may know him as he was, and try to be worthy of his friendship.

Some things we shall do well to grasp firmly at the outset. There were certain features in Wordsworth which give a kind of gnarled structure to his character and his poetry. He insisted on reconciling and combining certain things which are often kept apart, and which some people think should always be kept apart. Imagination and morality are two such things. In Wordsworth's estimation, imagination was the mainspring of poetry. When he speaks about imagination in prose, Wordsworth tries to be logical and precise; but when he speaks of it in poetry, he uses language of that vaguely adumbrative kind which one has to be content with in presence of transcendent religious ideas. And, indeed, Wordsworth's feeling about imagination was *quasi*-religious. Imagination was *creative* energy, in using which the poet was transmitting Divine power. And so has many another poet thought of it—so far, at least, as its prerogatives go. Many poets and many critics have claimed for genius the absolutism of a Divine right, as though it could make its own rules or dispense with rules of any kind; as if it had its own atmosphere and independent *criteria*. But no such claim did Wordsworth make. For him imagination had rules as stringent as its power was divine. Not for one instant did he conceive of his art as exercised in a non-moral way, representing, without any preference that was not purely æsthetic, the facts of life for pleasure's sake only. Wordsworth's morality makes him enigmatic and hard to approach. There would be no enigma in the matter if we could class him as a didactic poet, as one who simply sought to recommend religion and morality in good verse. From some of his writing about his own work, some of the letters in which he spoke with least formality about his own purposes, we might almost conclude that he aimed at nothing but the crudest didacticism. But, if his achievement had been of this kind, his name might have been conspicuous in the annals of morality and religion, but could not have stood where all men now find it, in the front rank of English poetry. When Wordsworth thought carefully about his poetry, he made it plain that its object was *artistic;* he spoke of pleasure as his end, with a frankness which might satisfy the most ardent devotee of art for art's sake. And indeed his practice speaks as eloquently as his theory. In all his central poetic work he sings of the human and the Divine at their meeting-points with the vagueness of the poet, not the definiteness of the moralist or theologian. Yet it is not always so; occasions are frequent when he seems to lapse into the didactic; when the mood which he creates is too serious to be called pleasure, and the truth which he enforces is too austere to be called beauty. And the reader of Wordsworth will often be embarrassed by the apparently conflicting efforts of such imagination as Shakespeare might have done obeisance to, and such mere moral reflectiveness as seems anything but imaginative. He is troubled by an uncomfortable antithesis between philosophy and profit; and he is surprised that the poet seems to have felt so little the discomfort that is so irksome to him. He wonders whether Wordsworth's imagination acted intermittently; whether his genius was a kind of mechanical mixture of gold and clay; or whether a more patient and intense study may not show some higher unity in which the contradiction is resolved.

Another knot in the Wordsworthian structure which forces the reader to exert himself, is the political element in his genius and poetry. He has to realize, in fact, that the two cardinal things in Wordsworth are his passion for Nature and his passion for public liberty, and that the latter passion is as strong as the former. He once told an American visitor, the Rev. Orville Dewey, that he had given twelve hours' thought to the condition and prospects of society for one to poetry; and we can believe it. We find that, strictly speaking, even Wordsworth's best poetry of Nature has a social and political source; that not until the impulses of his boyhood had been chastened by social experience and political shocks, was he able to *interpret* Nature at all. The whole of his early manhood was determined by England's active hostility to France; by the shock and the shame of finding his country at war—so it seemed to him—with the struggle for liberty of a neighbouring land. His best poetry was made as the result of, and in reaction from, that shock; through it mainly he heard "the still, sad music of humanity;" and he first truly knew Nature as the healer of a soul thus suffering. Not less true is it, though perhaps less widely known, that the main bent of his genius in middle life was determined by another political shock, the revelation of the aims of Napoleon. A common, and not wholly erroneous, way of putting this matter is to represent Wordsworth as having changed his political opinions from something not far short of republicanism to a Toryism that would admit no thought of compromise. But the change was more dramatic. No reader of the *Sonnets Dedicated to National Independence and Liberty* can miss the wonderful ring of their passionate patriotism, or will be surprised to learn that such passion had a powerful and very definite cause. It was in 1793 that Wordsworth's love of England was shocked by her hostility to the French Revolution; it was in 1807, when he knew that Swiss liberty had been destroyed by Napoleon, that his sympathies forsook a nation which could suffer its destinies to be moulded by such a tyrant. Even as late as September, 1806, the solemn hymn on the dying of Charles James Fox shows that Wordsworth was not alienated from the statesman whose sympathy with the French had been so constant. When the Genius of Liberty, the "High-souled Maid," was driven from the sound of her Alpine torrent, the poet's patriotism became less anxious and more passionate; but it was none the less a passion for freedom and the impartial sway of righteous law.

Then, when the tyrant was overthrown, the passion fell, and the poet passed into that mood of undisturbed tranquillity with which we most easily associate him. In theory he had always insisted on tranquillity as the necessary solvent of poetic emotion; he defined poetry as *emotion recollected in tranquillity,* and he had always, in some measure, realized the theory. For the last twenty-five or thirty years of his life, the pulse of emotion was feeble, and there seemed little but tranquil reflection left. These uncertain relations between emotion and tranquillity make a difficulty for the student of Wordsworth. The idea of Browning's *Lost Leader* haunts him; and though he may have no word of political blame for the eager revolutionist who became so stern a Conservative, he can hardly help feeling that the poet whom he hailed as the herald of a new age seemed to become a mere holder of forlorn hopes, a timid and obstinate opponent of essays towards freedom in almost all directions.

It is, indeed, at once Wordsworth's weakness and his glory that the tranquillity of his genius put him to some extent out of sympathy with the adventurous temper of the nineteenth century. For if it is part of the business of a great poet to lead the van in the conflict of his age, it is surely not alien from his office to proclaim the peace which passeth all understanding apart from which the stress of battle would be unendurable; to sing in the ears of a generation much given to change of "a repose which ever is the same." Wordsworth lived long enough to witness many reactions; and perhaps, when we know him better, we shall come to feel that both flow and ebb were less marked in him than in the periods in which he lived. Perhaps, as in fancy we grow with his growth, share his companionship and compare our poet with contemporary leaders of thought and action as they speak for themselves, we shall learn to rate higher that perfect self-control, those "sober certainties," that philosophic mind which were the conquest of Wordsworth's years. We may find that the conquest was won earlier than we knew or he realized, and that the thought which underlies his work from first to last was more timeless and less dependent upon either external events or changes of mood than at first sight appears. Wordsworth was, after all, a philosopher; and it is a poor philosophy which does not transcend the changing appearances of the time in which it utters itself.

One thing the associate of Wordsworth is sure to feel as a mere drawback, and that is his lack of humour. Probably this lack, so common yet always so lamentable, apparently so unimportant but really so far-reaching in its power of hindrance and harm, is one of the chief sources of what is unpleasant in the "lakishness" of Wordsworth. It makes it possible to feel his poetry *old-fashioned:* an epithet complimentary to furniture and landscape-gardening, but hardly to poetry. For poetry, at all events of the rank of Wordsworth's, should always be fresh, fresh with the eternal freshness of the spring or the morning. And if this freshness, this unmistakable, inexpressible, irresistible gusto is sometimes lacking in Wordsworth, is it not very often because humour is weak? For humour is much more than the parent of wit, though this is not to be despised in poetry. It is a phase of intelligence, an exercise of sympathy; and the lack of it involves, possibly earnestness, but certainly dulness, and some insensitiveness, both of the understanding and the affections. Such insensitiveness was undoubtedly present in Wordsworth; and it prevented the man, as it prevents his poetry, from being wholly and unfailingly fresh and charming. It explains also the occasional lapses into individual self-satisfaction which flaw the noble self-consciousness of the great poet. For humour, even better than humility, makes a man immune from the possibility of conceit.

Wordsworth's fame, like his genius, suffered great vicissitudes. "Forty and seven years it is," wrote De Quincey in 1845, "since William Wordsworth first appeared as an author (*i.e.* since the publication of *Lyrical Ballads*). Twenty of those years he was the scoff of the world, and his poetry a by-word of scorn. Since then, and more than once, Senates have rung with acclamations to the echo of his name."

Ernest Bernbaum

SOURCE: "The Romantic Movement and Selected General Bibliography," in *Guide Through the Romantic Movement,* revised edition, The Ronald Press Company, 1949, pp. 300-22.

[*In the following essay, originally published in the 1930 edition of* Guide Through the Romantic Movement, *Bernbaum offers an overview of the Romantic Movement and discusses the differences in the beliefs of Romantic poets, including Wordsworth, Southey, and Coleridge.*]

Differences Among the Romantics.—The chief Romantics differed from one another in origin, schooling, personality, conduct, and many other respects. Some, like Landor and Shelley, were of aristocratic birth; others, like Blake and Keats, of the humblest. Some had next to no formal schooling, others were forced to end theirs at an early age, and only about one half of their number attended a university. Some of them acquired sufficiently extensive knowledge to be considered scholars, e.g., Coleridge, Wordsworth, Lamb, Scott, Southey, De Quincey, and Carlyle; others died too young to amass much learning; and some, like Blake and Byron, were not scholars in the usual sense of the term. In their character and conduct, there were likewise great differences among them, from Byron at one extreme to Lamb, Blake, or Keats at the other. To some of them verse was the only or the chief medium of literary expression (Blake, Wordsworth, Byron, and

Keats); others were mainly prosemen (Lamb, Hazlitt, De Quincey, and Carlyle); and a few found both forms congenial (Coleridge, Scott, Landor, and Shelley). In politics, they represented almost every shade of contemporaneous opinion, from the Toryism of Coleridge, Wordsworth, Scott, and De Quincey, to the Liberalism of Byron, Hazlitt, and Shelley.

Perhaps after their deaths, dwelling in Elysium under the aspects of Eternity, they may have reconciled their differences; but while they lived their disagreements and dislikes were more conspicuous than their congeniality. For longer or shorter periods two or three of them formed friendly alliances—e.g., Wordsworth, Coleridge, Southey, and Lamb—and Byron, Shelley, and Hunt—but even such groups were subject to disagreements or dissolution; and some Romantics, notably Blake, Hazlitt, and Landor, were solitary rather than companionable. Nearly all at some time uttered derogatory opinions about the views or writings of some of the others. Most of them—including Lamb, Southey, and Keats—disliked Byron's poetry, particularly *Don Juan.* Byron returned the dislike with interest; he respected only Scott and Shelley, and he ranked Wordsworth and Coleridge lower than the third-rate versifier, Rogers. Hazlitt thought Wordsworth a time-server and place-hunter; Shelley deplored his supposed apostasy; and even Keats, who loved his poetry, at times censured him for rudeness. Wordsworth was once heard to mutter something about Keats's "paganism"; he found the young Carlyle "an enthusiast and nothing more"; and he detested *Don Juan.* These hostilities cannot be explained wholly on the ground that two generations of Romantics (those active before c. 1815, and those whose careers began thereafter) would naturally be at odds; for the young Carlyle spoke contemptuously of Keats's "maudlin sensibility," and scorned Shelley as one "filling the earth with inarticulate wail." . . .

Inability to Define, No Proof of Unreality.—Prosaic logicians have analyzed Romanticism into fragments, some of which do not neatly fit into one another; and they suppose that thereby they have proved the meaninglessness of the term. What they actually have shown is that the varieties, and the aberrations, of Romanticism are many; but not that among the varieties there is no basic unity at all. There are other vitally important concepts, such as Democracy and Christianity, that are too comprehensive and complex to be satisfactorily summed up in the oversimple brevity of a dictionary definition; nevertheless such concepts correspond to realities which can be set forth in ampler forms of discourse. The unity amid the variety of romantic works has been felt for generations by readers with literary and imaginative sensibility. Those who in the preceding chapters have studied the sixteen leading Romantics will have observed that there was much similarity among their views, despite surface differences; and that their attitudes toward God, Man, and Nature were essentially in harmony, as well as their principles of art and literature.

Romanticism and Classicism.—The main characteristics of a literary movement are best discerned in its historical development, and in the hostile forces that arise to attack it. The dominance of Romanticism was assailed by the middle of the nineteenth century; its Everlasting Yeas were called into question. Matthew Arnold, for example, occasionally raised doubts about the romantic faith in Nature, and wrote:

> Nature is cruel, man is sick of blood . . .
> Nature and Man can never be fast friends.

But, as we shall see, the chief opposition which Romanticism was to encounter did not arise from any form of feeling, taste, or thought that can fairly be termed classical. For that reason, among others, it seems doubtful whether there is any *essential* difference (whatever differences of relative emphasis may exist) between the spirit of great classical literature and that of great romantic literature. Even as Christianity stands toward the "paganism" of Plato and Aristotle not in a relation of opposition so much as in one of fulfillment, so Shakspeare, Milton, and the Romantics stand in relation to Homer, Pindar, Aeschylus, and Virgil. In this opinion, "Grecians" like Coleridge, Shelley, and De Quincey, would agree.

Romantic Beliefs.—The Romantics were keenly conscious of the difference between two worlds. One was the world of ideal truth, goodness, and beauty: this was eternal, infinite, and absolutely real. The other was the world of actual appearances, which to common sense was the only world, and which to the idealist was so obviously full of untruth, ignorance, evil, ugliness, and wretchedness, as to compel him to dejection or indignation. This state of the romantic mind was brilliantly expressed by Byron, and all the Romantics passed through it at times. Most of them, however, passed onward to a faith that the ideal world and the actual world were not so dissevered as mere common sense or an abstract and escapist kind of idealism assumed. Man was gifted with a higher reason, called the imagination, which enabled him to see that the good, the true, and the beautiful were not removed to a sphere unattainable to him in this life, but were interwoven with his human existence and earthly environment. It was the highest function of literature and art to portray man and his world in such a way that the presence of the infinite within the finite, of the ideal within the actual, would be revealed in all its beauty. Hence, although a smug acceptance of things as they were was fatuous, we should overcome despair, and by sympathizing with certain aspects of nature, and with certain characteristics of man, achieve fortitude and wisdom. In short, most of the Romantics, after

passing through the Slough of Despond, found somewhere the possibility of happiness. Wordsworth found it in nature and in the moral nobility of the simple life; Lamb, in the delightful variety of individual characters and in the amenities of urban existence; Scott and Landor, in historical epochs and traditional types of character; Coleridge, in the revelation of the Eternal in literature; Keats, in Universal Love as manifested in nature, friendship, and art; Carlyle, in the working out of one's individual ideal for one's fellowmen; and Shelley, in contemplating the glorious future of humanity. Different as these means of seeking happiness were (it is their endless diversity that frustrates definition), all rested on the assumption that our universe is rich in ideal blessings and therefore not inhospitable to the better nature of man.

The Opposition.—The real opposition and distinction is between Romanticism on the one hand, and, on the other, materialism, mechanistic science, secularism, and "common sense" in the baser meaning of the term. The most hostile anti-romantic writers, including the "Humanists" and the "New Critics," have assumed that modern science made it rationally impossible to maintain the romantic beliefs about Nature and Man. Romanticism, said Paul Elmer More, is "the illusion of beholding the infinite within the stream of nature itself, instead of apart from that stream." He and the other anti-romantics assumed without question that this was an "illusion," because they supposed that science had failed to find any indications of a spiritual or ideal purpose in the flux of natural phenomena. In the second half of the nineteenth century that assumption seemed to rationalists an inevitable one.

The Doubts Raised by Darwinism.—The first serious threat against fundamental romantic beliefs arose out of interpretations of Darwin's *Origin of Species* (1859). His theory of evolution was misrepresented by its adherents, and misunderstood by its opponents. It was supposed to prove that the processes of nature did not manifest anything that indicated purposiveness. All that happened was by chance; there was no directive tendency, no foresight, nothing like moral governance or an ultimate tendency towards righteousness. The widespread, though ill-founded, notion that Darwin had refuted all evidence of design in the universe is at the bottom of that modern doubt which presently grew into the tragic conviction of the utter meaninglessness of human life. The Darwinians emphasized everything that showed Nature wasteful and cruelly savage. Huxley, their champion, declared: "The animal world is on about the same level as a gladiator's show." Those who survived in the brutish struggle for existence were the fittest only in the sense that they were the most selfish, aggressive, rapacious, physically strong, and mentally keen.

Philosophers of this school accumulated more and more data which seemed to them to prove that the universe is nothing but colorless, soundless, scentless masses, wholly unbeautiful, describing aimless orbits through infinite space and time in obedience to mechanical laws and indifferent to all human aspirations. "Man," said Bertrand Russell as recently as 1925, "is the product of causes which had no prevision of the end they were achieving; his origin, his growth, his hopes and fears, his loves and beliefs, are but the outcome of accidental collocations of atoms." Man is merely a product of matter. Psychology is wholly a branch of physiology. Man has no free will. He is a prisoner under a life sentence in a horrible prison house. His art and literature and religion are merely pleasant narcotics enabling him to escape from the brutal facts into false dreaming. He learns the truth only when he studies natural and human history by strictly scientific methods, i.e., on mechanistic and deterministic assumptions. The only real knower is the scientist, and his imitator in the humanities. The Romantics were dreamers: the beauty of Nature was an illusion; its moral value was nothingness. In such a modern world the Romantic became, like Keats's lover.

> a wretched wight,
> Alone and palely loitering;
> The sedge is withered from the lake,
> And no birds sing.

The triumph of this materialistic philosophy was followed, in the field of action, by two devastating world wars; and in the field of imagination by the dominance of pessimistic literature, frenetic art, and cacophonous music. It seemed as if Man, having been scientifically assured that his cosmos was an infernal Chaos, had tried to make his own little world as nearly hell-like and inhuman as his limited powers of deviltry would permit.

The Rehabilitation of Romanticism.—During the 1920's and even earlier, in physics, zoology, biology, psychology, and other sciences, many phenomena attracted attention that could not be satisfactorily explained on the materialistic hypotheses. The progress of knowledge imperatively called for a radical revision in the philosophy of nature. In works of the highest scientific or philosophical importance—by Lloyd Morgan, A. N. Whitehead, Sir Arthur Eddington, J. D. Haldane, John Oman, Jan Christian Smuts, and many others—there was no longer that contempt for romantic ideas about Nature and Man which has ruled for two generations. Since the rise of Einstein, Rutherford, and Heisenberg, the notion that Science (and Science only) would be able to reduce all nature to the definitely knowable and fully predictable has been abandoned. The new school admits that there are limits to what can be ascertained through scientific methods; and henceforth those other fields of human experience and other methods of inquiry which the Romantics believed in are reassuming their former dignity. To continue to talk of the sciences as alone giving real truths, and of the humanities, art, and literature, as giving only imperfect truths or mere dreams, has in the twentieth century again become indefensible. For the guidance of human life, humane culture, as the Romantics insisted, is at least as important as scientific knowledge.

When the evolution of nature and man was re-examined by the science of today, truths emerged which were neglected by the Pseudo-Darwinians. The process appears far less revolting. Struggle, agony, and death have played their grim roles; but not, as was formerly implied, the chief ones. There is no special amorality, or cruelty, in nature that is not found on the human level, though on the latter the possibilities of high moral achievements are present. Of great significance are the abundant manifestations of mutual helpfulness, or symbiosis, in flora and fauna; it is a vast system of beneficent interrelationships. As for survival, it has not usually been the lone wolves, the savage, the predatory, who have been most successful; but rather the adaptable, the responsive, the cooperative, and those who have developed enough imagination and intelligence to learn by experience.

The emergence of new life phenomena in evolution (what we call progress) has not been the result only of savage struggle. Struggle educates some needed traits; but it does not inaugurate creative originality; to talk, like the Fascists or Communists, about "creative strife," whether on the physical or psychic level, is to talk in ignorance of evolutionary history. The emergence of new life phenomena is the consequence of freedom, of liberty for fuller and more complex development.

Phenomena which the Pseudo-Darwinians either did not explain at all or assumed to be due to mere chance—phenomena like the structure of the eye, or the intricate mechanism of flight, or symbiotic cooperation among plants and animals—cannot have developed step by step accidentally; their appearance required simultaneous and correlated modifications of many factors. Modern science and philosophy recognize in such natural processes a coordinating "holistic" principle or design, as Smuts calls it; or, in Bergson's phrase, an *élan vital,* a creative evolution. The Gestalt psychology, insisting that "perceptual wholes are more than the sum of their parts," exhibits similar tendencies of thought, and, militating against mechanization and fragmentation, lays new foundations for the romantic philosophy.

Nineteenth-century materialism drew man's attention to his base origin; twentieth-century science and philosophy point to the advances that all living creatures have made. They dwell upon the upward gradations in the evolution of beings from their lowest forms—from rudimentary reflexes through more and more amazing development of instincts toward the gradual achievement of real intelligence and imaginative foresight. At the lowest stages of life there was between existences a bare relatedness; subsequently came a progressive development of sexual and social life from instinctively formed communities up to higher stages where fully developed individuals, having increased in sensitiveness and having developed through the discipline of suffering the beginnings of imaginative sympathy, consciously and voluntarily form social groups which in the course of time enter into wider and wider relationships. Crescent throughout the evolution of man have been freedom, reason, imagination, and love. Each has been intermittent and imperfect, but has nevertheless groped and stumbled toward perfection. The capacity to improve, and the will to aspire, have been manifested again and again. Evolution has always shown an urge toward the prolific creation of freer and freer and more highly individual personalities, and toward their voluntary association in societies with the intention of protecting and fostering the progress of such free individuals. The advance has often been retarded by convulsions of nature, or by man's own follies and crimes. But it is manifestly a process which Man, the vanguard of evolution, can partly direct and accelerate toward higher stages of individual and social well-being. The account which modern science gives of evolution is not so preoccupied as it was in the nineteenth century with the *descent* of man from the ape. It gives at least equal importance to man's occasional *ascent* into the genius, the hero, or the saint.

As W. Macneile Dixon says in *The Human Situation* a scholarly and eloquent work undeservedly neglected by students of Romanticism:

> By her own methods nature has brought us into being, raised us above the organic world, and conferred upon us a primacy in the organic. By her own methods she has elevated us to intellectual heights whence at least other heights can be discerned . . . The astonishing and least comprehensible thing about Man is his range of vision; his lonely passion for ideas and ideals far removed from his material surroundings and animal activities, and in no way suggested by them, yet for which, such is his affection, he is willing to endure toils and privations, to sacrifice pleasures, to disdain griefs and frustrations, for which, rating them in value above his own life, he will stand until he dies, the profound conviction he entertains being that if nothing be worth dying for nothing is worth living for.

Those are the words of a man of letters and philosopher; but the conviction that in Man Nature comes into consciousness of its possibilities, and of its freedom to attain them, is shared by as strictly scientific a mind as that of Julian Huxley, who writes:

> The new history has a basis of hope. Biological evolution has been appallingly slow and wasteful. . . . It has led life up innumerable blind alleys. But in

spite of this it has achieved progress. . . . The evolution of the human brain at one bound altered the perspective of evolution. Experience could now be handed down from generation to generation. . . . In man evolution could become conscious.

> Past human history represents but the tiniest portion of the time man has before him . . . His setbacks are as natural as the tumbles of a child learning to walk. . . . The potentialities of progress which are revealed, once his eyes have opened to the evolutionary vista, are unlimited. . . . At last we have an optimistic instead of a pessimistic theory of this world and our life upon it. . . . Perhaps we had better call it a melioristic rather than optimistic view; but at least it preaches hope and inspires to action.

Such is the attitude of science today. It is an almost complete reversal of the nineteenth-century attitude, and it destroys the supposedly scientific foundations for that materialistic philosophy which temporarily had made Romanticism seem an unbelievable faith.

The Effect of the Scientific Revolution upon the Status of Romanticism.—Romanticism is a faith, or system of beliefs, expressible only through a symbolical and emotional art such as literature. Its truths are chiefly discerned by the imagination, and it is chiefly to the imagination that they appeal for acceptance. The truths of Romanticism are neither "proved" nor "disproved" by the methods of science. What the revolution in scientific opinion in our day has done is, so to speak, to make Romanticism an intellectually respectable faith, which for a time it had ceased to be. Coleridge always maintained that the genuine Imagination did not contradict Reason, although it was an independent pathway to higher truths. The Romantic believes in "the evidence of things not seen"; and the modern scientist does not deny the possibility that such visions may be revelatory. Says Albert Einstein:

> The most beautiful thing we can experience is the mysterious. It is the source of all true art and science. He to whom the emotion is a stranger, who can no longer pause to wonder and stand wrapped in awe, is as good as dead; his eyes are closed. The insight into the mystery of life, coupled though it be with fear has also given rise to religion. To know that what is impenetrable to us really exists, manifesting itself as the highest wisdom and the most radiant beauty, which our dull faculties can comprehend only in their most primitive forms, this feeling is at the center of true religiousness. . . . It is enough for me to contemplate the mystery of conscious life perpetuating itself through all eternity, to reflect upon the marvelous structure of the universe we can dimly perceive, and to try humbly to comprehend even an infinitesimal part of the intelligence manifested in Nature.

Thus today the scientist and the Romantic pursue their different paths in the same spirit toward the same goal.

Joseph Warren Beach

SOURCE: "Wordsworth's Naturalism," in *The Concept of Nature in Nineteenth-Century English Poetry,* The Macmillan Publishing Company, 1936, pp. 110-57.

[In the following excerpt, Beach compares Coleridge's beliefs regarding nature and "spirit" with Wordsworth's stance regarding nature and religion.]

There was a moment, in [Coleridge's] own verse, when he was disposed to express himself in vaguely pantheistic terms. But there was relatively little of "naturalism" in this phase, and it was soon over. In his prose writings Coleridge took particular pains to deny the validity of the current conceptions of nature—which, he says, should be regarded as the direct antithesis of spirit.

> I have attempted to fix the meaning of the words, Nature and Spirit, the one being the *antithesis* to the other: so that the most general and *negative* definition of Nature is, Whatever is not Spirit; and *vice versa* of Spirit, That which is not comprehended in Nature; or in the language of our elder divines, that which *transcends* Nature.

There are several distinct philosophical reasons for making this sharp division between nature and spirit. One of these is the inadequacy of nature (cause and effect) to explain the *origin* of existence. The word origin, Coleridge declares,

> . . . can never be applied to a mere *link* in a chain of effects, where each, indeed, stands in the relation of a *cause* to those that follow, but is at the same time the *effect* of all that precede. For in these cases the cause amounts to little more than an antecedent. At the utmost it means only a *conductor* of the causative influence; and the old axiom, *causa causae causa causati,* applies, with never-ending regress to each several link, up the whole chain of nature. But this *is* Nature; and no natural thing or act can be called originant, or be truly said to have an *origin* in any other. The moment we assume an origin in nature, a true *beginning,* an actual first—that moment we rise *above* nature, and are compelled to assume a *supernatural* power.

Another reason for this sharp distinction between nature and spirit is the inadequacy of the conception of cause and effect to explain the autonomous character of spirit (involving will)—its independence of time and space. This involves considerations of both metaphysics and ethics.

> I have already given one definition of Nature. Another, and differing from the former in words only, is this: Whatever is representable in the forms of Time and Space, is Nature. But whatever is comprehended in Time and Space, is included in the mechanism of Cause and Effect. And conversely, whatever, by whatever means, has its principle in itself, so far as to *originate* its actions, cannot be contemplated in any of the forms of Space and Time; it must, therefore, be considered as *Spirit* or *Spiritual* by a mind in that stage of its development which is here supposed, and which we have agreed to understand under the name of Morality, or the Moral State: for in this stage we are concerned only with the forming of *negative* conceptions, *negative* convictions; and by spiritual I do not pretend to determine *what* the WILL *is,* but what is is *not*— namely, that it is not Nature. And as no man who admits a Will at all (for we may safely presume that no man not meaning to speak figuratively, would call the shifting current of a stream the WILL of the river), will suppose it *below* Nature, we may safely add, that it is super-natural. . . .

Coleridge is here reacting vehemently against the necessitarianism of writers like Godwin and Priestley. The concept of nature, being bound up with the mere ideal forms of space and time, and the merely mechanical "enchaînement des causes secondes," cannot account for its own origin, which must be outside the chain of cause and effect. It cannot account for the self-originating activities of spirit and will, and give a basis for morality, which implies freedom and responsibility in action.

Still further, Coleridge indicates—allying himself with the idealism of Berkeley and the Germans—the very nature which we behold with the bodily eye is in some sense the creation of our own minds, and dependent upon them for the character it bears. Thus in his famous ode, "Dejection" (1802), in speaking of the loss of his power for finding nature beautiful and joyous, he declares that this beauty and joyousness which, as a young man, he found in nature, was an emanation from his own soul.

> O Lady! we receive but what we give,
> And in our life alone does Nature live:
> Ours is her wedding garment, ours her shroud!
>   And would we ought behold of higher worth
> Than that inanimate cold world allowed
> To the poor loveless ever-anxious crowd,
>   Ah! from the soul itself must issue forth
> A light, a glory, a fair luminous cloud
>   Enveloping the Earth—
> And from the soul itself must there be sent
>   A sweet and potent voice, of its own birth,
> Of all sweet sounds the life and element.

Wordsworth was never so greatly disturbed, it seems, by these metaphysical scruples. He may never have held a purely mechanical view of nature; he may have naturally shared the traditional English craving for a spiritual or "dynamic" interpretation. But he does not seem to have taken so hard as Coleridge either the necessary sequence of cause and effect, nor the difficulty of reconciling our moral freedom with this hard and fast necessity. Time and space he would accept more simply as the natural forms for the manifestation of eternal law. He was temperamentally inclined to dwell not on the distinctness of "objective" and "subjective," of natural and supernatural, but on the oneness of the impulse in things which makes itself felt equally in the outward and the inward reality.

Moreover, at the time when he wrote "Tintern Abbey," he was, so far as we can make out, much less far advanced than Coleridge on the road of religious orthodoxy. M. Legouis points out that the French officer Beaupuy, under whose influence Wordsworth had fallen so deeply during his French sojourn, regarded religion as the enemy of liberty and progress, and that the same thing was true of William Matthews, "who, since Wordsworth's return to England, had been his most intimate friend and most regular correspondent." M. Legouis reminds us further that for some years Wordsworth was one of Godwin's most fervent disciples, and that occasionally he sat under the preaching of the dissenting minister Joseph Fawcett, who "readily turned to Christian doctrine for arguments in defence of revolutionary ideas," but abandoned it "the moment he found himself in conflict with it, whether he desired to make a profession of determinism, or to glorify the intelligence, which he regarded as the source of virtue." In 1796 Coleridge, in a letter to John Thelwall, described his friend Wordsworth as "a republican, and, at least, a semi-atheist." This same John Thelwall was of the society at Alfoxden in 1797-98, engaged in many disputes with Coleridge on subjects political and religious. Thelwall was a dyed-in-the-wool democrat. "His ruling passion was a hatred of prejudices, amongst which he included religion. He seldom mentioned them without some sarcastic allusion."

It is probable, as M. Legouis suggests, that Wordsworth, at this time, occupied a position somewhere between Coleridge and Thelwall. He was no doubt beginning to be influenced by Coleridge's mysticism. M. Legouis even suggests, with great plausibility, that Wordsworth was strongly influenced, in his own nature-philosophy, by the notions expressed by Coleridge in poems like "The Eolian Harp" and "Religious Musings." But the naturalistic strain was strong in his thought and feeling. For him, accordingly, there was no difficulty in seeking within nature herself for clues to the ultimate motive-power of the universe. It was from the contemplation of external nature, from "nature and the language of the sense," that he received his "sense sublime of something far more deeply interfused."

There is a most interesting passage in *Aids to Reflection* in which Coleridge betrays a certain nervousness

he felt in reading this passage in "Tintern Abbey." He has been giving a review of the development of the mechanical philosophy in modern thought. When, he says, the Cartesian vortices had been expelled by Newton:

> Then the necessity of an active power, of positive forces present in the material universe, forced itself on the conviction. For a Law without a Lawgiver is a mere abstraction. . . . And what was the result? How was this necessity provided for? God himself— my hand trembles as I write! Rather, then, let me employ the word, which the religious feeling, in its perplexity, suggested as the substitute—the *Deity itself* was declared to be the real agent, the actual gravitating power! The law and the law-giver were identified. God (says Dr. Priestley) not only does, but *is* every thing. *Jupiter est quodcunque vides.* And thus a system, which commenced by excluding all life and immanent activity from the visible universe and evacuating the natural world of all nature, ended by substituting the Deity, and reducing the Creator to a mere anima mundi: a scheme which has no advantage over Spinosism but its inconsistency. . . . And what has been the consequence? An increasing unwillingness to contemplate the Supreme Being in his personal attributes: and thence a distaste to all the peculiar doctrines of the Christian Faith, the Trinity, the Incarnation of the Son of God, and Redemption. . . . Many do I know, and yearly meet with, in whom a false and sickly *taste* co-operates with the prevailing fashion: many, who find the God of Abraham, Isaac, and Jacob, far too *real,* too substantial; who feel it more in harmony with their indefinite sensations

> To worship Nature in the hill and valley,
> Not knowing what they love;—

> and (to use the language, but not the sense or purpose of the great poet of our age) would fain substitute for the Jehovah of their Bible

>   A sense sublime
> Of something far more deeply interfused . . .

Where there is smoke there is fire. If Coleridge in 1825 repudiates the notion that Wordsworth had succumbed to the prevailing taste, and would fain substitute a depersonalized "principle" for the personal God as the animating power in nature, it is doubtless because, in 1798, he greatly feared that this is what Wordsworth had done. And it seems fairly probable that this is just what, at that period, he was inclined to do.

Coleridge counted passionately on Wordsworth as the great philosophical poet of the age, and was able to interpret the poetic expressions of "Tintern Abbey" in the light of his own dualism. But Wordsworth's poems of this period do indicate, I believe, a fundamental opposition between his and Coleridge's approach to the world. They indicate a disposition to take one's start with natural phenomena, to read everything in the moral world in their light, and while admitting, of course, the paramount importance of the spirit, to regard this as forming a part of "nature." In short, they show a tendency to rule out of consideration the concept of the supernatural. Wordsworth's imagination was steeped in eighteenth-century natural theology, which was the nurseling of seventeenth- and eighteenth-century science. He had been as deeply impressed as any other natural philosopher with the synthesis of physical laws made possible by Newton's formula. In "The Prelude" he mentions Newton with awed reverence. And even so late as the "Ode to Duty" he suggests the essential identity of law in the physical world with law in the moral world.

In "The Prelude" he lays great stress on nature as the seat of lawful order, and consequently suited to give moral instruction to man.

> . . . not in vain
> I had been taught to reverence a Power
> That is the very quality and shape
> And image of right reason, that matures
> Her processes by steadfast laws, gives birth
> To no impatient or fallacious hopes,
> No heat of passion or excessive zeal,
> No vain conceits, provokes to no quick turns
> Of self-applauding intellect, but lifts
> The Being into magnanimity;
> Holds up before the mind intoxicate
> With present objects and the busy dance
> Of things that pass away, a temperate show
> Of objects that endure . . .

In another most interesting passage of "The Prelude," Wordsworth signalizes the difference between himself and Coleridge, underlining Coleridge's want of realism. This, he suggests, was caused partly by his friend's enforced exile from nature in his childhood.

> I have thought
> Of Thee, thy learning, gorgeous eloquence,
> And all the strength and plumage of thy
>   Youth,
> Thy subtle speculations, toils abstruse
> Among the Schoolmen, and platonic forms
> Of wild ideal pageantry, shap'd out
> From things well-match'd, or ill, and words
>   for things,
> The self-created sustenance of a mind
> Debarr'd from Nature's living images,
> Compell'd to be a life unto itself,
> And unrelentingly possess'd by thirst
> Of greatness, love, and beauty.

Thus, with the greatest admiration for the nobility of his friend's spirit, Wordsworth considers that he has been led astray by the *verbalism* of scholastic and "platonic" speculation, to the point of substituting metaphysical notions for actual things.

The fundamental difference of mental habit between the two poets is brought into striking relief by a remark of Coleridge's set down in "Table Talk." Coleridge has been expressing his regret that Wordsworth did not publish "The Prelude" before the inferior "Excursion." In "the plan laid out, and, I believe, partly suggested by me," Wordsworth "was to treat man as man,—a subject of eye, ear, touch, and taste, in contact with external nature, and *informing the senses from the mind, and not compounding a mind out of the senses.*" Now Coleridge's statement exactly reverses the order of things as carried out by Wordsworth. What he mainly did in "The Prelude" was to compound a mind out of the senses, not inform the senses from the mind.

"Informing the senses from the mind" represents the idealism of Coleridge, which was radical, consistent and thorough-going. Derived first perhaps from Plato and the neoplatonists, nourished on the seventeenth-century English divines and upon Berkeley, it was triumphantly confirmed in his later years by Kant (as he understood him), by Fichte, Schelling and Hegel. Wordsworth's idealism was partial and intermittent. In metaphysics, he was more or less of an idealist, instructed no doubt by Coleridge, by Plato and the seventeenth-century divines. That is, he seems to suggest that the universe is at bottom spiritual or rational, and that the process of nature must be interpreted as dynamic rather than mechanical. But in psychology he draws his inspiration, in his most representative period, from the school of English philosophy that derives from Locke, and that lays its stress on sensations as the basis of experience and so of the intellectual and spiritual life of man. As Mr. Beatty says, "There can be no manner of doubt that he approaches the problem of mind from the angle of Locke, basing his whole theory on the assumption that thought originates inexperience, and that out of the product of sensation, or experience, ideas and the more complex forms of mentality are developed." The only exception that I take to Mr. Beatty's statement is that he oversimplifies the situation—ignoring the elements of confusion or ambiguity in Wordsworth's theory, and the gradual shift of position that makes the doctrine of the "Intimations" ode so different (at least in emphasis) from that of "Tintern Abbey."

W. K. Wimsatt

SOURCE: "The Structure of Romantic Nature Imagery," in *English Romantic Poets: Modern Essays in Criticism,* edited by M. H. Abrams, Oxford University Press, Inc., 1960, pp. 25-36.

[In the following essay, originally published in 1954 in
The Verbal Icon, *Wimsatt examines the various poetic
structures used by Romantic poets, including Wordsworth
and Coleridge, in works with naturalistic themes.]*

Students of romantic nature poetry have had a great
deal to tell us about the philosophic components of
this poetry: the specific blend of deistic theology,
Newtonian physics, and pantheistic naturalism which
pervades the Wordsworthian landscape in the period
of 'Tintern Abbey,' the theism which sounds in the
'Eolian Harp' of Coleridge, the conflict between French
atheism and Platonic idealism which even in
'Prometheus Unbound' Shelley was not able to resolve.
We have been instructed in some of the more purely
scientific coloring of the poetry—the images derived
from geology, astronomy, and magnetism, and the
coruscant green mystery which the electricians contributed to such phenomena as Shelley's Spirit of Earth.
We have considered also the 'sensibility' of romantic
readers, distinct, according to one persuasive interpretation, from that of neoclassic readers. What was exciting to the age of Pope, 'Puffs, Powders, Patches,
Bibles, Billet-doux' (even about these the age might
be loath to admit its excitement), was not, we are told,
what was so manifestly exciting to the age of Wordsworth. 'High mountains are a feeling, but the hum of
cities torture.' Lastly, recent critical history has rein-
vited attention to the romantic theory of imagination,
and especially to the version of that theory which
Coleridge derived from the German metaphysicians,
the view of poetic imagination as the *esemplastic* power which reshapes our primary awareness of the world
into symbolic avenues to the theological.

We have, in short, a *subject*—simply considered, the
nature of birds and trees and streams—a *metaphysics*
of an animating principle, a special *sensibility,* and a
theory of poetic imagination—the value of the last a
matter of debate. Romantic poetry itself has recently
suffered some disfavor among advanced critics. One
interesting question, however, seems still to want discussion; that is, whether romantic poetry (or more
specifically romantic nature poetry) exhibits any
imaginative *structure* which may be considered a special counterpart of the subject, the philosophy, the
sensibility, and the theory—and hence perhaps an explanation of the last. Something like an answer to such
a question is what I would sketch.

For the purpose of providing an antithetic point of
departure, I quote here a part of one of the best known
and most toughly reasonable of all metaphysical images:

> If they be two, they are two so
>   As stiff twin compasses are two,
> Thy soul the fixed foot, makes no show
>   To move, but doth, if th' other do.

It will be relevant if we remark that this similitude,
rather farfetched as some might think, is yet unmistakable to interpretation because quite overtly stated, but
again is not, by being stated, precisely defined or limited in its poetic value. The kind of similarity and the
kind of disparity that ordinarily obtain between a drawing compass and a pair of parting lovers are things to
be attentively considered in reading this image. And
the disparity between living lovers and stiff metal is
not least important to the tone of precision, restraint,
and conviction which it is the triumph of the poem to
convey. Though the similitude is cast in the form of
statement, its mood is actually a kind of subimpera-
tive. In the next age the tension of such a severe disparity was relaxed, yet the overtness and crispness of
statement remained, and a wit of its own sort.

> 'Tis with our judgments as our watches, none
> Go just alike, yet each believes his own.

We may take this as typical, I believe, of the metaphoric structure in which Pope achieves perfection and
which survives a few years later in the couplets of
Samuel Johnson or the more agile Churchill. The difference between our judgments and our watches, if
noted at all, may be a pleasant epistemological joke
for a person who questions the existence of a judgment
which is taken out like a watch and consulted by another judgment.

But the 'sensibility,' as we know, had begun to shift
even in the age of Pope. Examples of a new sensibility, and of a different structure, having something to
do with Miltonic verse and a 'physico-theological
nomenclature,' are to be found in Thomson's *Seasons*.
Both a new sensibility and a new structure appear in
the 'hamlets brown and dim-discovered spires' of
Collins' early example of the full romantic dream. In
several poets of the mid century, in the Wartons, in
Grainger, or in Cunningham, one may feel, or rather
see stated, a new sensibility, but at the same time one
may lament an absence of poetic quality—that is, of a
poetic structure adequate to embody or objectify the
new feeling. It is as if these harbingers of another era
had felt but had not felt strongly enough to work upon
the objects of their feelings a pattern of meaning which
would speak for itself—and which would hence endure as a poetic monument.

As a central exhibit I shall take two sonnets, that of
William Lisle Bowles 'To the River Itchin' (1789) and
for contrast that of Coleridge 'To the River Otter'
(1796)—written in confessed imitation of Bowles.
Coleridge owed his first poetic inspiration to Bowles
(the 'father' of English romantic poetry) and continued
to express unlimited admiration for him as late as 1796.
That is, they shared the same sensibility—as for that
matter did Wordsworth and Southey, who too were
deeply impressed by the sonnets of Bowles. As a

schoolboy Coleridge read eagerly in Bowles' second edition of 1789 (among other sonnets not much superior):

> Itchin, when I behold thy banks again,
> Thy crumbling margin, and thy silver breast,
> On which the self-same tints still seem to rest,
> Why feels my heart the shiv'ring sense of
>   pain?
> Is it—that many a summer's day has past
> Since, in life's morn, I carol'd on thy side?
> Is it—that oft, since then, my heart has sigh'd,
> As Youth, and Hope's delusive gleams, flew
>   fast?
> Is it—that those, who circled on thy shore,
> Companions of my youth, now meet no more?
> Whate'er the cause, upon thy banks I bend
> Sorrowing, yet feel such solace at my heart,
> As at the meeting of some long-lost friend,
> From whom, in happier hours, we wept to
>   part.

Here is an emotive expression which once appealed to the sensibility of its author and of his more cultivated contemporaries, but which has with the lapse of time gone flat. The speaker was happy as a boy by the banks of the river. Age has brought disillusion and the dispersal of his friends. So a return to the river, in reminding him of the past, brings both sorrow and consolation. The facts are stated in four rhetorical questions and a concluding declaration. There is also something about how the river looks and how its looks might contribute to his feelings—in the metaphoric suggestion of the 'crumbling' margin and in the almost illusory tints on the surface of the stream which surprisingly have outlasted the 'delusive gleams' of his own hopes. Yet the total impression is one of simple association (by contiguity in time) simply asserted— what might be described in the theory of Hume or Hartley or what Hazlitt talks about in his essay 'On the Love of the Country.' 'It is because natural objects have been associated with the sports of our childhood, . . . with our feelings in solitude . . . that we love them as we do ourselves.'

Coleridge himself in his 'Lines Written at Elbingerode in 1799' was to speak of a 'spot with which the heart associates Holy remembrances of child or friend.' His enthusiasm for Hartley in this period is well known. But later, in the *Biographia Literaria* and in the third of his essays on 'Genial Criticism,' he was to repudiate explicitly the Hartleyan and mechanistic way of shifting back burdens of meaning. And already, in 1796, Coleridge as poet was concerned with the more complex ontological grounds of association (the various levels of sameness, of correspondence and analogy), where mental activity transcends mere 'associative response'—where it is in fact the unifying activity known both to later eighteenth century associationists

and to romantic poets as 'imagination.' The 'sweet and indissoluble union between the intellectual and the material world' of which Coleridge speaks in the introduction to his pamphlet anthology of sonnets in 1796 must be applied by us in one sense to the sonnets of Bowles, but in another to the best romantic poetry and even to Coleridge's imitation of Bowles. There is an important difference between the kinds of unity. In a letter to Sotheby of 1802 Coleridge was to say more emphatically: 'The poet's heart and intellect should be *combined,* intimately combined and unified with the great appearances of nature, and not merely held in solution and loose mixture with them.' In the same paragraph he says of Bowles' later poetry: 'Bowles has indeed the *sensibility* of a poet, but he has not the *passion* of a great poet . . . he has no native passion because he is not a thinker.'

The sententious melancholy of Bowles' sonnets and the asserted connection between this mood and the appearances of nature are enough to explain the hold of the sonnets upon Coleridge. Doubtless the metaphoric coloring, faint but nonetheless real, which we have remarked in Bowles' descriptive details had also something to do with it. What is of great importance to note is that Coleridge's own sonnet 'To the River Otter' (while not a completely successful poem) shows a remarkable intensification of such color.

> Dear native Brook! wild Streamlet of the
>   West!
> How many various-fated years have past,
> What happy and what mournful hours, since
>   last
> I skimmed the smooth thin stone along thy
>   breast,
> Numbering its light leaps! yet so deep imprest
> Sink the sweet scenes of childhood, that mine
>   eyes
> I never shut amid the sunny ray,
> But straight with all their tints thy waters rise,
> Thy crossing plank, thy marge with willows
>   grey,
> And bedded sand that veined with various
>   dyes
> Gleamed through thy bright transparence! On
>   my way,
> Visions of Childhood! oft have ye beguiled
> Lone manhood's cares, yet waking fondest
>   sighs:
> Ah! that once more I were a careless Child!

Almost the same statement as that of Bowles' sonnet—the sweet scenes of childhood by the river have only to be remembered to bring both beguilement and melancholy. One notices immediately, however, that the speaker has kept his eye more closely on the object. There are more details. The picture is more vivid, a fact which according to one school of poetics would in itself make the sonnet superior. But a more analytic theory will find it worth remarking also that certain ideas, latent or involved in the description, have much to do with its vividness. As a child, careless and free, wild like the streamlet, the speaker amused himself with one of the most carefree motions of youth—skimming smooth thin stones which leapt lightly on the breast of the water. One might have thought such experiences would sink no deeper in the child's breast than the stones in the water—'yet so deep imprest'—the very antithesis (though it refers overtly only to the many hours which have intervened) defines imaginatively the depth of the impressions. When he closes his eyes, they *rise* again (the word *rise* may be taken as a trope which hints the whole unstated similitude); they rise like the tinted waters of the stream; they gleam up through the depths of memory—the 'various-fated years'—like the 'various dyes' which vein the sand of the river bed. In short, there is a rich ground of meaning in Coleridge's sonnet beyond what is overtly stated. The descriptive details of his sonnet gleam brightly because (consciously or unconsciously—it would be fruitless to inquire how deliberately he wrote these meanings into his lines) he has invested them with significance. Here is a special perception, 'invention' if one prefers, 'imagination,' or even 'wit.' It can be explored and tested by the wit of the reader. In this way it differs from the mere flat announcement of a Hartleian association, which is not open to challenge and hence not susceptible of confirmation. If this romantic wit differs from that of the metaphysicals, it differs for one thing in making less use of the central overt statement of similitude which is so important in all rhetoric stemming from Aristotle and the Renaissance. The metaphor in fact is scarcely noticed by the main statement of the poem. Both tenor and vehicle, furthermore, are wrought in a parallel process out of the same material. The river landscape is both the occasion of reminiscence and the source of the metaphors by which reminiscence is described. A poem of this structure is a signal instance of that kind of fallacy (or strategy) by which death in poetry occurs so often in winter or at night, and sweethearts meet in the spring countryside. The tenor of such a similitude is likely to be subjective—reminiscence or sorrow or beguilement—not an object distinct from the vehicle, as lovers or their souls are distinct from twin compasses. Hence the emphasis of Bowles, Coleridge, and all other romantics on spontaneous feelings and sincerity. Hence the recurrent themes of One Being and Eolian Influence and Wordsworth's 'ennobling interchange of action from within and from without.' In such a structure again the element of tension in disparity is not so important as for metaphysical wit. The interest derives not from our being aware of disparity where likeness is firmly insisted on, but in an opposite activity of discerning the design which is latent in the multiform sensuous picture.

Let us notice for a moment the 'crossing plank' of Coleridge's sonnet, a minor symbol in the poem, a sign of shadowy presences, the lads who had once been there. The technique of this symbol is the same as that which Keats was to employ in a far more brilliant romantic instance, the second stanza of his 'Ode to Autumn,' where the very seasonal spirit is conjured into reality out of such haunted spots—in which a gesture lingers—the half-reaped furrow, the oozing cider press, the brook where the gleaners have crossed with laden heads. To return to our metaphysics—of an animate, plastic Nature, not transcending but immanent in and breathing through all things—and to discount for the moment such differences as may relate to Wordsworth's naturalism, Coleridge's theology, Shelley's Platonism, or Blake's visions: we may observe that the common feat of the romantic nature poets was to read meanings into the landscape. 'A puddle,' says Hazlitt, 'is filled with preternatural faces.' The meaning might be such as we have seen in Coleridge's sonnet, but it might more characteristically be more profound, concerning the spirit or soul of things—'the one life within us and abroad.' And that meaning especially was summoned out of the very surface of nature itself. It was embodied imaginatively and without the explicit religious or philosophic statements which one will find in classical or Christian instances—for example in Pope's 'Essay on Man':

> Here then we rest: 'The Universal Cause
> Acts to one end, but acts by various laws,'

or in the teleological divines, More, Cudworth, Bentley, and others of the seventeenth and eighteenth centuries, or in Paley during the same era as the romantics. The romantic poets want to have it and not have it too—a spirit which the poet himself as superidealist creates by his own higher reason or esemplastic imagination. Here one may recall Ruskin's chapter of *Modern Painters* on the difference between the Greek gods of rivers and trees and the vaguer suffusions of the romantic vista—'the curious web of hesitating sentiment, pathetic fallacy, and wandering fancy, which form a great part of our modern view of nature.' Wordsworth's 'Prelude,' from the cliff that 'upreared its head' in the night above Ullswater to the 'blue chasm' that was the 'soul' of the moonlit cloudscape beneath his feet on Snowdon, is the archpoet's testament, both theory and demonstration of this way of reading nature. His 'Tintern Abbey' is another classic instance, a whole pantheistic poem woven of the landscape, where God is not once mentioned. After the 'soft inland murmur,' the 'one green hue,' the 'wreaths of smoke . . . as . . . Of vagrant dwellers in the houseless woods' (always something just out of sight or beyond definition), it is an easy leap to the 'still, sad music of humanity,' and

> a sense sublime
> Of something far more deeply interfused,
> Whose dwelling is the light of setting suns.

This poem, written as Wordsworth revisited the banks of a familiar stream, the 'Sylvan Wye,' is the full realization of a poem for which Coleridge and Bowles had drawn slight sketches. In Shelley's 'Hymn to Intellectual Beauty' the 'awful shadow' of the 'unseen Power' is substantiated of 'moonbeam' showers of light behind the 'piny mountain,' of 'mist o'er mountains driven.' On the Lake of Geneva in the summer of 1816 Byron, with Shelley the evangelist of Wordsworth at his side, spoke of 'a living fragrance from the shore,' a 'floating whisper on the hill.' We remark in each of these examples a dramatization of the spiritual through the use of the faint, the shifting, the least tangible and most mysterious parts of nature—a poetic counterpart of the several theories of spirit as subtle matter current in the eighteenth century, Newton's 'electric and elastic' active principle, Hartley's 'infinitesimal elementary body.' The application of this philosophy to poetry by way of direct statement had been made as early as 1735 in Henry Brooke's 'Universal Beauty,' where an 'elastick Flue of fluctuating Air' pervades the universe as 'animating Soul.' In the high romantic period the most scientific version to appear in poetry was the now well recognized imagery which Shelley drew from the electricians.

In such a view of spirituality the landscape itself is kept in focus as a literal object of attention. Without it Wordsworth and Byron in the examples just cited would not get a start. And one effect of such a use of natural imagery—an effect implicit in the very philosophy of a World Spirit—is a tendency in the landscape imagery to a curious split. If we have not only the landscape but the spirit which either informs or visits it, and if both of these must be rendered for the sensible imagination, a certain parceling of the landscape may be the result. The most curious illustrations which I know are in two of Blake's early quartet of poems to the seasons. Thus, 'To Spring':

> O Thou with dewy locks, who lookest down
> Thro' the clear windows of the morning, turn
> Thine angel eyes upon our western isle,
> Which in full choir hails thy approach, O
>   Spring!
>
> The hills tell each other, and the list'ning
> Vallies hear; all our longing eyes are turned
> Up to thy bright pavillions; issue forth,
> And let thy holy feet visit our clime.
>
> Come o'er the eastern hills, and let our winds
> Kiss thy perfumed garments; let us taste
> Thy morn and evening breath; scatter thy
>   pearls
> Upon our love-sick land that mourns for thee.

And 'To Summer':

> O Thou, who passest' thro' our vallies in
> Thy strength, curb thy fierce steeds, allay the
>   heat
> That flames from their large nostrils! thou, O
>   Summer,
> Oft pitched'st here thy golden tent, and oft
> Beneath our oaks hast slept, while we beheld
> With joy thy ruddy limbs and flourishing hair.
>
> Beneath our thickest shades we oft have heard
> Thy voice, when noon upon his fervid ear
> Rode o'er the deep of heaven; beside our
>   springs
> Sit down, and in our mossy vallies, on
> Some bank beside a river clear, throw thy
> Silk draperies off, and rush into the stream.

Blake's starting point, it is true, is the opposite of Wordsworth's or Byron's, not the landscape but a spirit personified or allegorized. Nevertheless, this spirit as it approaches the 'western isle' takes on certain distinctly terrestrial hues. Spring, an oriental bridegroom, lives behind the 'clear windows of the morning' and is invited to issue from 'bright pavillions,' doubtless the sky at dawn. He has 'perfumed garments' which when kissed by the winds will smell much like the flowers and leaves of the season. At the same time, his *own* morn and evening breaths are most convincing in their likeness to morning and evening breezes. The pearls scattered by the hand of Spring are, we must suppose, no other than the flowers and buds which literally appear in the landscape at this season. They function as landscape details and simultaneously as properties of the bridegroom and—we note here a further complication—as properties of the land taken as lovesick maiden. We have in fact a double personification conjured from one nature, one landscape, in a wedding which approximates fusion. Even more curious is the case of King Summer, a divided tyrant and victim, who first appears as the source and spirit of heat, his steeds with flaming nostrils, his limbs ruddy, his tent golden, but who arrives in our valleys only to sleep in the shade of the oaks and be invited to rush into the river for a swim. These early romantic poems are examples of the Biblical, classical, and Renaissance tradition of allegory as it approaches the romantic condition of landscape naturalism—as Spring and Summer descend into the landscape and are fused with it. Shelley's Alastor is a spirit of this kind, making the 'wild his home,' a spectral 'Spirit of wind,' expiring 'Like some frail exhalation; which the dawn Robes in its golden beams.' Byron's Childe Harold desired that he himself might become a 'portion' of that around him, of the tempest and the night. 'Be thou, Spirit fierce,' said Shelley to the West Wind, 'My spirit! Be thou me.'

An English student of the arts in the Jacobean era, Henry Peacham, wrote a book on painting in which he gave allegorical prescriptions for representing the months, quoted under the names of months by Dr. Johnson in his *Dictionary:*

April is represented by a young man in green, with a garland of myrtle and hawthorn buds; in one hand primroses and violets, in the other the sign Taurus.

July I would have drawn in a jacket of light yellow, eating cherries, with his face and bosom sunburnt.

But that would have been the end of it. April would not have been painted into a puzzle picture where hawthorn buds and primroses were arranged to shadow forth the form of a person. There were probably deep enough reasons why the latter nineteenth century went so far in the development of so trivial a thing as the actual landscape puzzle picture.

In his Preface of 1815 Wordsworth spoke of the *abstracting* and *'modifying* powers of the imagination.' He gave as example a passage from his own poem, 'Resolution and Independence,' where an old leech gatherer is likened to a stone which in turn is likened to a sea beast crawled forth to sun itself. The poems which we have just considered, those of Coleridge, Wordsworth, and Blake especially, with their blurring of literal and figurative, might also be taken, I believe, as excellent examples. In another of his best poems Wordsworth produced an image which shows so strange yet artistic a warping, or modification, of vehicle by tenor that, though not strictly a nature image, it may be quoted here with close relevance. In the ode 'Intimations of Immortality':

Hence, in a season of calm weather,
Though inland far we be,
Our souls have sight of that immortal sea
Which brought us hither;
Can in a moment travel thither—
And see the children sport upon the shore,
And hear the mighty waters rolling evermore.

Or, as one might drably paraphrase, our souls in a calm mood look back to the infinity from which they came, as persons inland on clear days can look back to the sea by which they have voyaged to the land. The tenor concerns souls and age and time. The vehicle concerns travelers and space. The question for the analyst of structure is: Why are the children found on the seashore? In what way do they add to the solemnity or mystery of the sea? Or do they at all? The answer is that they are not strictly parts of the traveler-space vehicle, but of the soul-age-time tenor, attracted over, from tenor to vehicle. The travelers looking back in both space and time see themselves as children on the shore, as if just born like Venus from the foam. This is a sleight of words, an imposition of image upon image, by the *modifying* power of imagination.

Poetic structure is always a fusion of ideas with material, a statement in which the solidity of symbol and the sensory verbal qualities are somehow not washed out by the abstraction. For this effect the iconic or directly imitative powers of language are important— and of these the well known onomatopoeia or imitation of sound is only one, and one of the simplest. The 'stiff twin compasses' of Donne have a kind of iconicity in the very stiffness and odd emphasis of the metrical situation. Neoclassic iconicity is on the whole of a highly ordered, formal, or intellectual sort, that of the 'figures of speech' such as antithesis, isocolon, homoeoteleuton, or chiasmus. But romantic nature poetry tends to achieve iconicity by a more direct sensory imitation of something headlong and impassioned, less ordered, nearer perhaps to the subrational. Thus: in Shelley's 'Ode to the West Wind' the shifts in imagery of the second stanza, the pell-mell raggedness and confusion of loose clouds, decaying leaves, angels and Maenads with hair uplifted, the dirge, the dome, the vapors, and the enjambment from tercet to tercet combine to give an impression beyond statement of the very wildness, the breath and power which is the vehicle of the poem's radical metaphor. If we think of a scale of structures having at one end logic, the completely reasoned and abstracted, and at the other some form of madness or surrealism, matter or impression unformed and undisciplined (the imitation of disorder by the idiom of disorder), we may see metaphysical and neoclassical poetry as near the extreme of logic (though by no means reduced to that status) and romantic poetry as a step toward the directness of sensory presentation (though by no means sunk into subrationality). As a structure which favors implication rather than overt statement, the romantic is far closer than the metaphysical to symbolist poetry and the varieties of postsymbolist most in vogue today. Both types of structure, the metaphysical and the romantic, are valid. Each has gorgeously enriched the history of English poetry.

EMBRACING CONSERVATISM

George Brandes

SOURCE: "The Lake School's Conception of Liberty," in *Main Currents in Nineteenth Century Literature: Naturalism in England, Vol. IV,* translated by Mary Morison, William Heinemann, 1905, pp. 85-89.

[*In the following essay, originally published in 1875, Brandes compares the views of liberty held by the Lake Poets with those of the later Romantic poets Lord Byron and Percy Shelley.*]

Coleridge and the other members of the Lake School would never have dreamt of calling themselves anything but warm friends of liberty; the days were past when the reactionaries called themselves by another name. Coleridge wrote one of his most beautiful poems, the *Ode to France,* in the form of a hymn to liberty, to his constant love for which he calls clouds, waves, and forests to testify; and Wordsworth, who dedicated two long series of his poems to liberty, regarded himself as her acknowledged champion. A cursory glance at the works of these poets might well leave us with the impression that they were as true lovers of liberty as Moore, or Shelley, or Byron. But the word liberty in their mouths meant something different from what it did in Moore's, or Shelley's, or Byron's. To understand this we must dissect the word by means of two simple questions: freedom, from what?—liberty, to do what?

To these conservative poets freedom is a perfectly definite thing, a right which England has and the other countries of Europe have not—the right of a country to govern itself, untyrannised over by an autocratic ruler of foreign extraction. The country which has this privilege is free. By liberty, then, the men in question understood freedom from foreign political tyranny; there is no thought of liberty of action in their conception at all. Look through Wordsworth's *Sonnets Dedicated to Liberty,* and see what it is they celebrate. It is the struggle of the different nations against Napoleon, who is described as a species of Antichrist. (Scott calls him "the Devil on his burning throne.")

The poet mourns the conquest of Spain, Switzerland, Venice, the Tyrol, by the French; he chants the praises of Hofer, the undaunted, of brave Schill, and daring Toussaint L'Ouverture, the men who ventured to face the fierce conquerors; and he sings with quite as great admiration of the King of Sweden, who with romantically chivalrous folly threw down the gauntlet to Napoleon, and proclaimed his longing for the restoration of the Bourbons. (Ere long Victor Hugo and Lamartine, in their character of supporters of the Legitimist monarchy, followed suit in singing the praises of the Swedish king and his son, Prince Gustavus Vasa.) Hatred of Napoleon becomes aversion for France. In one of the sonnets ("Inland, within a hollow vale, I stood") Wordsworth tells how the "barrier flood" between England and France for a moment seemed to him to have dwindled to the dimensions of a river, and how he shrank from the thought of "the frightful neighbourhood"; in another he rejoices in the remembrance of the great men and great books England has produced, and remarks that France has brought forth "no single volume paramount . . . no master spirit," that with her there is "equally a want of books and men."

He always comes back to England. His sonnets are one long declaration of love to the country for which he feels "as a lover or a child," the country of which he writes: "Earth's best hopes are all with thee." He follows her through her long war, celebrating, like Southey, each of her victories; and it is significant of his attitude that, appended to the *Sonnets Dedicated to Liberty,* we find the great, pompous thanksgiving ode for the battle of Waterloo. We of to-day ask what kind of liberty it was that Waterloo gained; but we know full well that the group of poets whose heroes were the national heroes—Pitt, Nelson, and Wellington, and who sang the praises of the English constitution as being in itself liberty, and lauded England as the model nation, won a degree of favour with the majority of their countrymen to which their great poetic antagonists have not even yet attained. Wordsworth and his school considered the nation ideal as it was, whereas the others tried to compel it to turn its eyes towards an ideal, not only unattained, but as yet unrecognised; the former flattered it, and were rewarded with laurels; the latter educated and castigated it, and were spurned by it. Scott was offered the post of Poet Laureate, and Southey and Wordsworth in turn occupied it; but to this day the English nation has shown no public recognition of what it owes to Shelley and Byron. And the reason is, that these men's conception of liberty was utterly different from that of the Lake School. To them it was not realised in a nation or a constitution— for it was no accomplished, finished thing; neither was their idea of the struggle for liberty realised in a highly egoistic war against a revolutionary conqueror. They felt strongly what an absence of liberty, political as well as intellectual, religious as well as social, there might be under a so-called *free* constitution. They had no inclination to write poems in honour of the glorious attainments of the human race, and more especially of their own countrymen; for in the so-called land of freedom they felt a terrible, oppressive want of freedom— of liberty to think without consideration of recognised dogmas, to write without paying homage to public opinion, to act as it was natural to men to their character to act, without injury from the verdict of those who, because they had no particular character of their own, were the most clamorous and unmerciful condemners of the faults which accompanied independence, originality, and genius. They saw that in this "free" country the ruling caste canted and lied, extorted and plundered, curbed and constrained quite as much as did the one great autocrat with his absolute power— and without his excuse, the authority of intellect and of genius.

To the poets of the Lake School, coercion was not coercion when it was *English,* tyranny was not tyranny when it was practised under a *constitutional monarchy,* hostility to enlightenment was not hostility to enlightenment when it was displayed by a *Protestant* church. The Radical poets called coercion coercion, even when it proceeded to action with the English flag flying and the arms of England as its policemen's badge; they cherished towards monarchs generally, the objection of the Lake School poets to absolute monarchs; they desired to free the world not only from the dominion of the Roman Catholic priesthood, but from priestly tutelage of every description. When they heard poets of the other school, who in the ardour of youth had been as progressive as themselves, extolling the Tory Government of England with the fervour which distinguishes renegades, they could not but regard them as enemies of liberty. Therefore it is that Shelley, in his sonnet to Wordsworth, writes:—

> In honoured poverty thy voice did weave
> Songs consecrate to truth and liberty.
> Deserting these, thou leavest me to grieve,
> Thus having been, that thou shouldst cease to
>   be.

Therefore it is that Byron is tempted again and again "to cut up Southey like a gourd." And therefore it is that the love of liberty of the Radical poets is a divine frenzy, a sacred fire, of which not a spark is to be found in the Platonic love of the Lake School. When Shelley sings to liberty:—

> But keener thy gaze than the lightning's glare,
> And swifter thy step than the earthquake's
>   tramp;
> Thou deafenest the rage of the ocean; thy
>   stare
> Makes blind the volcanoes; the sun's bright
>   lamp
>
>   To thine is a fen-fire damp;

we feel that this liberty is not a thing which we can grasp with our hands, or confer as a gift in a constitution, or inscribe among the articles of a state-church. It is the eternal cry of the human spirit, its never-ending requirement of itself; it is the spark of heavenly fire which Prometheus placed in the human heart when he formed it, and which it has been the work of the greatest among men to fan into the flame that is the source of all light and all warmth in those who feel that life would be dark as the grave and cold as stone without it. This liberty makes its appearance in each new century with a new name. In the Middle Ages it was persecuted and stamped out under the name of heresy; in the sixteenth century it was championed and opposed under the name of the Reformation; in the seventeenth it was sentenced to the stake as witchcraft and atheism; in the eighteenth it became first a philosophical gospel, and then, through the Revolution, a political power; in the nineteenth it receives from the champions of the past the new nickname of Radicalism.

What the poets of the Lake School extolled was a definite, actually existing *sum of liberties*—not liberty. What the revolutionary poets extolled was undoubtedly true liberty; but their conception was so extremely ideal, that in practical matters they too often shot beyond the mark. In the weakening of all established

government they saw only the weakening of bad government; in the half-barbaric revolts of oppressed races they saw the dawn of perfect liberty. Shelley had so little knowledge of his fellow-men that he thought the great victory would be won if he could exterminate kings and priests at a blow; and Byron's life was almost over before he learned by experience how few republican virtues the European revolutionists leagued together in the name of liberty possessed. The poets of the Lake School were safeguarded against the generous delusions and overhastiness of the Radical poets; but posterity has derived more pleasure and profit from the aberrations due to the love of liberty in the latter than from the carefully hedged in and limited Liberalism of the former.

William Wordsworth describes the lakes of the Lake District:

I shall now speak of the lakes of this country. The form of the lake is most perfect when, like Derwent-water, and some of the smaller lakes, it least resembles that of a river;—I mean, when being looked at from any given point where the whole may be seen at once, the width of it bears such proportion to the length, that, however the outline may be diversified by far-receding bays, it never assumes the shape of a river, and is contemplated with that placid and quiet feeling which belongs peculiarly to the lake—as a body of still water under the influence of no current; reflecting therefore the clouds, the light, and all the imagery of the sky and surrounding hills; expressing also and making visible the changes of the atmosphere, and motions of the lightest breeze, and subject to agitation only from the winds—

>   The visible scene
> Would enter unawares into his mind
> With all its solemn imagery, its rocks,
> Its woods, and that uncertain heaven received
> Into the bosom of the *steady* lake!

It must be notified, as a favourable characteristic of the lakes of this country, that, though several of the largest, such as Winandermere, Ullswater, Haweswater, do, when the whole length of them is commanded from an elevated point, lose somewhat of the peculiar form of the lake, and assume the resemblance of a magnificent river; yet, as their shape is winding (particularly that of Ullswater and Haweswater), when the view of the whole is obstructed by those barriers which determine the windings, and the spectator is confined to one reach, the appropriate feeling is revived; and one lake may thus in succession present to the eye the essential characteristic of many.

William Wordsworth, in A Guide through the District of the Lakes in the North of England, *Rupert Hart-Davis, 1951.*

Keith Grahame Feiling

SOURCE: "Southey and Wordsworth," in *Sketches in Nineteenth Century Biography,* 1930. Reprint by Books for Libraries Press, 1970, pp. 71-84.

[*In the following essay, Feiling presents Southey's and Wordsworth's often criticized transformation from liberalism to conservatism as a shift based on the two poets' desire to safeguard democracy for future generations.*]

When George the Magnificent was Regent and King, Southey as Poet Laureate was official head of English letters, and in common, even in uncommon opinion, best represented the Lake school. To the Disraeli of 1833 he seemed "the greatest man of the age," to Byron or Hazlitt he was the arch-apostate; high and dry Anglicanism reckoned him as chief pillar of the Church. Except for a few duty Odes, produced not without assistance from doses of magnesia, he had abandoned poetry, but his achievement in prose was ceaseless, omniscient, and formally almost perfect. It would be hard to find purer models of narrative than his lives of Nelson (for which he received thanks in person from the *ingénue* Princess Victoria), of Cowper and of Wesley—than the *Colloquies,* or *The Book of the Church,* while his *Quarterly* essays, broad in sweep, dogmatic and pointed, justly appealed for twenty-five years to the gentlemen of England. A pension, remuneration of £100 an article, the offers of a baronetcy and of the editorial chair of *The Times,* measure his political services to the Tories.

A quarter of a century had gone by since young Southey, already a Stoic and a republican, had been ejected from Westminster, rejected at Christ Church and received at Balliol; since he and Coleridge (gently removed from the 15th Light Dragoons) had planned to transport themselves and the two Misses Fricker to the Susquehanna, there to energise an agricultural colony on principles of fraternity; since the young Wordsworth had been dogged by Pittite spies and had found love in Girondin France. By the 'thirties these fiery furnaces were out. Southey at Keswick was annotating from 14,000 volumes the inevitable doom of revolution; the owner of Rydal had become successively a militiaman, a revenue official, and a justice of the peace; from the cloud-encompassed hill of Highgate, Coleridge was conversing upon the timeless conservatism of the Deity. Yet it would be fallacious to ascribe their disillusionment wholly to senility, love of place, or power of common opinion, and far more so to ignore its political instruction. For the Lake poets, unlike Burke, learned their revolution by experience; they had ascended into its high places, and seen the kingdoms of the world fouled by anarchs. If conservatism survived to keep democracy partially safe for the next century, all three "Lakers" share in the achievement.

Southey, the one ordinary mortal of this extraordinary band, can be dissected in bald prose. One of those thin, energetic, noisy men who love cats, puns, and controversial writings, there is something parched and unkind about his virtue. The quiet conviction of immortal fame, which Dante or Milton could wear as a toga, sits rather absurdly on him, and we are naturally unimpressed by the boasted blows he promises to deal the Satanic Byron. His exhausting cheerfulness in early life, like his later gloom, seems to expose a purely physical basis of vitality, which expired after years of mechanical literary toil, leaving a dim light in the socket. Few who have held so high a place have had so little intrinsic wisdom. No one who has reached middle age will upbraid a public man for the mere changing his mind, but Southey passed violently from one pole or extremity to the other, never relating his revisions to the facts as a whole. His prejudices, once acquired, became physical obsessions; from some particular evil he must always generalize to universal calamity; he is a master of the *post hoc propter hoc* method, that worst vice of argumentation. On major issues he was ever in the wrong; he was an anti-bullionist, an anti-Catholic, an anti-Reformer; he wished the repeal of Fox's Libel Act, and he thought in 1814 that France should lose more territory. He was one of those unhappy publicists who can find no public man to their liking, save one who is irretrievably dead. Pouring scorn on the administration and the memory of Pitt, he was dissatisfied with Fox and disappointed in Canning; only the admirable but assassinated Percival reached his standard. There are too many femininities of epithet about his political criticism—"the Futilitarians," "the Noddles," and the like, and too many surpassing perversities, as that only the missionaries would save India for Britain. The dedication of his collected essays to Sir Robert Inglis (the chosen representative of Protestant Oxford to replace the renegade Robert Peel) shows with what difficulty the pious recluse can escape becoming a pious prig; "we who know in Whom we believe"—such effusions are akin to his view, which was almost a hope, of a cholera epidemic about to smite an apostate nation. In sum, Southey lived for forty years in a wilderness with an adoring community of cats and mortals, a library, and commonplace books; his rare visits to London or the Continent, and his prolific correspondence with friends and relations (from which filial piety has selected for us ten volumes) were no substitute for the full tide of human existence.

But enough of detraction. A patient reading must always end in affection for this man of real virtue, while the very average vicissitudes of his character make him in some ways a figure of more political significance than the two men of genius whose glory surrounds him. That regular pen brought bread not to his own children only, but to those of Coleridge; his hand was ever open to help men of letters who needed it; he can be acquitted, in an age of literary savagery, of private rancour or seeking strife. He was by temperament the only man of action of his school; his love of country bore the wear of daily life better than Wordsworth's—the historian of Nelson and the Peninsular War felt with what majesty the men in the ranks could fight. A photographic power of mind marked from his first days the actual woes of society, and while Coleridge was distilling ecstasy or abasement from opium, Southey was trying to heal poverty in correspondence with Owen and Sadler.

Given a compound of Southey's intense purity, sensitiveness, and mercurial conviction, some sharp reaction from the Revolution was certain. Bonaparte, not Burke, turned the Lake poets into conservatives. France had played traitor to liberty, and nowhere more so than in the lands Southey of all Englishmen knew best— Spain and Portugal. On this matter above all, he fell foul of the Whigs; "when Bonaparte would persuade the French that the conquest of Spain and Portugal is easy, and the ruin of England certain, his surest policy is to fill the *Moniteur* with the speeches of a party leader, the cowardly sophistry of a party critic, and the fallacies and falsehoods of an Opposition paper."

He derived two further conclusions from the revolutionary era. Two years of travel in Portugal and ten years of the Irish question embued him with a hatred of the Papacy. If he had been born a century earlier or later, he must surely have become an Anglican prelate. As it was, a child of the late eighteenth century, he had refused to take orders and passed through pantheism to a sort of Christian quietude; if Rome offended his reason and the Revolution his heart, what form of institutionalism was elastic enough to include this exacting idealistic patriot? Stamped still deeper into his consciousness was the association of cruelty and violence with "the mob," and he believed now that sheer anarchy must follow any public recognition of the rights of man. The real Terror at Paris had obliterated his hopes of France; a pinchbeck Pittite terror at home had maimed his ideals for England. "Whether the fiend," he wrote later, "who bestrides it and spurs it on, have Jacobin or Anti-Jacobin written in his forehead, the many-headed beast is the same." By a more prosaic route than his friends, Southey at this stage had come to the same conclusion, that the statesman must substitute morals for rights, obedience for will, and character for expediency.

Till 1811, and at heart perhaps even beyond that date, he clung to many reforming views. "The political system of Christianity," which he had meant to realize in America, he still hoped to find, though on a changed plan. In 1808, he declares himself to be of "the school of Sydney, and Hutchinson, and Milton"; in 1814, he hoped against the Bourbons' restoration, and would be a republican, were England fit for such liberty. He had

spoken of "the ineffaceable infamy of bombarding Copenhagen," and called for the liberalizing of South America. He saw no alternatives for England, but ruin or constitutional reform.

But by 1812 the combination of menace from foreign enemies and from the English Radical Left had worked its usual havoc in consolidating the English Right; Cobbett, Burdett, and Orator Hunt had completed the work of Bonaparte. Southey was convinced that Press licence would make possible the revolution which the democrats desired, and that drastic reform of the franchise would mean a Convention. Up to 1816 at least he was ready to grant some concession to freeholders and copyholders, and some representation to the great towns, but he began to argue that such legislation, even if innocuous, was of very secondary importance to moral and administrative energy. With advancing age and mental inbreeding, a half-light of pessimism darkened his eyes, that once had seen man and his future in such sanguine colours. He demanded more repression and transportation, discovered in Anglicanism the only city of refuge, and sank at last into something indistinguishable from timorous other-worldliness.

If pre-Reform England had listened to all that Southey wrote, and not only to the meaner part of it, enormous evil would have been spared to their own age and to ours. For though those who see politics, not through reason but the heart, may end in apparent reaction as a means to save what they love, anything they do see is real and poignant. It was Southey's achievement to perceive that nothing could perpetuate England as she stood between 1815 and 1830, and that nothing ought to. He saw that the condition of the people cried to heaven; that "there can be no safety with a population half Luddite, half Lazzaroni." In an image of frightful truth he compared the submerged classes of the new industrialism to the dogs of Constantinople, "a nuisance to the community while they live, and dying miserably at last." With the teachers of his youth, he thought that man was by nature virtuous, and good principle native within us, and therefore attributed responsibility for revolutions to bad government. Refusing to swallow the iron draughts of Malthus, he found the root of the trouble in the quack remedies, the accumulated sins and omissions, of the ruling class.

The "morbid change" in England was immediately due, in his opinion, to industrialism; to Adam Smith, and his "tedious and hard-hearted book"—to that negation of government which had deprived the poor of their hope, the essential salt of a commonwealth. From the moment of the peace in 1815, he implored the legislators not to be drowned under the false cry of retrenchment, but to discharge their debt to those who had fought by giving them work. The State should assist emigration, colonize the empty spaces of England, check enclosure, and set up Savings banks. He hoped, vainly as it happened, that Canning would rouse himself to remodel the Poor-law, and pleaded for public work as against doles. He examined with candour and sympathy the activities of Spence, the land nationalizer, and of Robert Owen, and approved the first rudiments of the co-operative movement. No man better illustrates the reality of that never-yet wholly severed link between one sort of Tory and one sort of Socialist. Prison reform, law reform, licensing, the game-laws, adulteration, limitation of entail, heavier income-tax, restoration of parish government, a federal Empire—for twenty years Southey preached these things, in and out of season, to a generation of Tories worn by war and hag-ridden by economics. But it is not unusual for that party to stop their ears against their prophets.

Laissez-faire was to him principally the sin against society, and he was not prepared to compromise, like Peel or Russell, with "the cool calculating inhumanity" of the cotton kings. As he saw it, both cause and remedy lay far deeper than economics. If the cause of pauperism were "misfortune in one instance, misconduct in fifty," a true government (not one of "Noddles" like Liverpool's, which he thought "deficient in everything except good intentions") would bulwark by reform the native goodness of the English people. They would even go beyond the practical remedies Southey had urged, and recognise by their action that virtue and happiness are the ingredients of States. It is immaterial, for us at least, that Southey was speaking rather as an Anglican than a sociologist. It is enough that he saw that gain, "the principle of our social system," was "awfully opposed to the spirit of Christianity." Only by education, and that on Christian principle, could he see a chance of reconciling the two things which he desired to unite, "Conservation and Improvement."

Macaulay, the young master of false antithesis and contemporary optimism, pounced upon Southey's *Colloquies,* and scarified his supposed ideal of an "omniscient and omnipotent State"; those who reflect upon our social history during the next century may judge between them.

> All that the world's coarse thumb
> And finger failed to plumb

in the heyday of Macaulay and Bright, all this may rise up and call Southey blessed. Embedded in tracts of aridity or gloom, the oases stand out in the huge area of his writing—not all mirage, but with here and there a tree for healing, here and there water at which posterity may quench its thirst.

"I have no respect whatever for Whigs," said Wordsworth in old age, "but I have a great deal of the Chartist in me." Making the due allowances, the greater man did pass through much the same political cycle as

Southey, and though the Chartist element needs research to find it, something of the sort is there. At least it is permissible to question the worth of some modern criticism, which bifurcates the poet's life and ascribes some poetic decline of later years to a loss of ideal, proved by acceptance of government pay or the patronage of Lord Lonsdale. Actually, the "beastly and pitiful wretch" pilloried by Shelley never, I think, turned apostate to his vow of 1811:

> That an accursed thing it is to gaze
> On prosperous tyrants with a dazzled eye.

But whatever the consistency of the teaching, it was always of higher calibre and more resonant depth than that we have gathered from Southey.

Far more than any of his friends, Wordsworth had staked his soul on the truth of the Revolution, and the nemesis of his faith was a process infinitely more torturing and intolerable. He had traversed France in the first flush of fraternity; he had thought of dedicating his life to that cause; his first earthly child, his first spiritual visions, were born in France. The decline of France into butchery and imperialism broke for ten years the thread of his life; between that, and what he viewed as Pitt's despotism, he wandered like an outcast, finding nothing on earth except "the noble living and the noble dead." Even *The Prelude,* written between 1799 and 1805, shows that his reaction owed nothing substantial to events after Waterloo; compressed and agonizing, it was also complete. He had been too early a child of Nature to endure a gross loss of identity between Nature and plain morals, or the dominion of men who claimed by bare reason to verify Nature's rights. An unspanned gulf lay between the executioners on the Seine or the Loire, and his Cumberland "statesmen," armed in their primitive excellence and "pure religion breathing household laws." France had cast herself down the steep places with many swine. "The life in the soul," as the memorable Cintra essay puts it, "has been directly and mortally warred against"; reason "had abominations to endure in her inmost sanctuary."

The poet, crowning himself like Dante, had early attained conviction of his high calling. No "unreasoning herd" could lay laws upon him, for "the poet binds together by passion and knowledge the vast empire of human society." All the deeper fundamentals of his teaching, all the germs of *Prelude* and *Excursion,* are in the preface of 1800 to *Lyrical Ballads.* He desired to record "the primary laws of our nature," "the great and simple affections of our nature," and to do this with permanence of speech which was impossible in the artificiality of great cities. Amid all contradictions of reason and fluctuating opinion, he was seeking the permanent—"the central peace subsisting at the heart of endless agitation."

Formerly, in France, he had followed nature unreflectingly, and filled his eyes with genial pleasure, "as if life's business were a summer mood." Tragedy and suffering had taught him that human reason, if abstracted from love, duty, and circumstance, determined no right and provided no happiness. The riddle of the universe was not to be read by a faculty dealing in "minute and speculative pains"; the constancy of the imaginative will alone could bear with, and master, the facts of life. A philosophy of sensual experience,

> One that would peep and botanize
> Upon his mother's grave;

the rationalist—

> One to whose smooth-rubbed soul can cling
> Nor form, nor feeling, great nor small;
> A reasoning self-sufficient thing,
> An intellectual all in all;

neither of these could make harmony of "the still sad music of humanity." God had never abandoned man "to feel the weight of his own reason"; "nature's gradual processes" were not caught in a sudden glory by one short generation; yet it was impossible, on the other hand, that truth and virtue had been made

> Hard to be won, and only by a few,

and denied for ever to the lowly, the oppressed, the inexorably deprived.

Not so—and here Wordsworth re-echoes a vital doctrine of the greatest mystic conservative of the seventeenth century, Henry Vaughan—

> The primal duties shine aloft, like stars;
> The charities that soothe, and heal, and bless,
> Are scattered at the feet of man, like flowers.

Duty for men, children of God, will be found in the common road; duties and rights must be fixed in the lasting scheme of things, open to the humble, but concealed from the arrogance of reason. The poet thus approaches the conclusion of Oliver Cromwell, the Calvinist; "we have found the cause of God by the works of God, which are the testimony of God."

Live then, he says, according to nature, but nature as read in her lasting works. Go close to her, in places where she is easily to be found; you will find the child is father to the man, and all generations bound close by natural piety. Men may pass, but

> The form remains, the function never dies.

Nature "matures her processes by steadfast laws," and the mass of creation springs in articulated progress from creeping things up to the moralized man. Variety and degree are of her ordaining; as "similitude in dissimilitude" is the test of moral aesthetic, so

> The shifting aims,
> The moral interests, the creative might,
> The varied functions and high attributes
> Of civil action

cannot be smothered, or down-levelled, by tyranny and mobs. The poet shares, then, in that anti-intellectuality, that scepticism as to the merit of unaided mind, which is found in all transcended conservatives, in Vaughan, in Newman, or in Burke. He found in reason too much "power and energy detached from moral purpose"; book knowledge would always "neglect the universal heart"—it must be brought to its proper and final test,

> Life, human life, with all its sacred claims
> Of sex and age, and heaven-descended rights.

Nature, so passive, so majestical, is falsified, he tells us, and her code distorted by the critical intellect. Moral judgment, and "this alone is genuine liberty," has something of resignation in it. Those who have attained it accept their place in a great scheme;

> Willing to work and to be wrought upon,

they maintain in themselves the law of existence, and poise the balance "of action from without and from within." But the teaching of this pure transcendentalist can never finally lead to passive obedience. His very revolt, alike from eighteenth-century convention and revolutionary abstraction, sprang from their suppression of individual worth; human personality is the base to his philosophy of right, which rests on a God-given equality of soul and a moral liberty to which all may ascend. His virtue is an active principle; you must give something to Nature, or you can never receive; the Happy Warrior and the old Leech-gatherer go hard to their work. Logically, Wordsworth could, therefore, denounce the new manufacturing system, which deprived the poor of self-subsistence and the joy of mutual help. Man was not born to be "a tool or implement"; any "discipline of virtue" made it incumbent on the State to educate all her members.

It is easy enough to frame an indictment against the Lake poets' politics—to depict this mystic in old age manufacturing freeholders for the Lonsdales, evolving his *Ecclesiastical Sonnets,* and sharing at large in the shovel-hatted politics of Southey. But compare their teaching, in hope for the future, with the Conservatism of Eldon, of Scott, even of Canning, or even of Burke, and the superiority of their basis, in the scale of enduringness, is surely manifest. The lawyer may become sterile, the historian static, even the empirical genius mistake prejudice for principle, but those who, with all mistakes, stand on the moral law are never far removed from the principle of growth. Their fire is never extinct, a strong wind may set the embers glowing.

Hoxie Neale Fairchild

SOURCE: "At Length the Man Perceives It Die Away," in *The Romantic Quest,* Columbia University Press, 1931, pp. 189-217.

[*In the following essay, Fairchild traces the passage of the Lake Poets from liberalism and naturalistic Romanticism to conservatism and Burkian Romanticism.*]

The Lake poets gradually cease to find in nature the guide of all their moral being. This change, sympathetically regarded, is rather tragic. Somewhere in his letters Coleridge tells how he and his children went out one day and shouted "Dr. Dodd!" in order to enjoy the echo. At first I failed to understand why the name of a famous forger of Dr. Johnson's time should have been chosen for this purpose; but remembering the childish custom of shouting "Board of Health" in order that the echo may say something that sounds like "Go to Hell," I decided that Coleridge shouted "Dr. Dodd" in order that the echo might say something that sounded like "God." This may stand as a symbol of romantic naturalism. It was not long before the Lakists perceived that the tones of the echo had originated in their own vocal chords; and this discovery, while it could be interpreted in a way flattering to their imaginative powers, diminished their sense of the objective significance of nature.

Here is perhaps the best place to offer the unorthodox thesis that Wordsworth began to lose his spontaneous enjoyment of nature almost as soon as he knew its value, and that his philosophy is in part a subconscious attempt to find a compensation for that loss. This idea does not conflict with what has been said heretofore. Wordsworth's philosophy of nature was sincere, and it gave him deep spiritual satisfaction. I would merely suggest that this philosophy is tinged with an anxious and defensive element, as if he hoped by means of it to preserve something even more precious that was slipping from his grasp. He so frequently says that he is glad that he does not feel toward nature as he did in his youth; then almost in the same breath says wistfully that he *does* feel *almost* as he did in his youth; then in the next breath, or the next poem, says that he hopes he will die if he ever *stops* feeling as he did in his youth.

In *Tintern Abbey,* for example, Wordsworth distinguishes the stages in his attitude toward nature up to 1798, when the poem was written. Brushing aside "the coarser pleasures of my boyish days, and their glad animal

movements," he tells how he felt when, a youth of twenty-three, he visited this spot five years before:

> I cannot paint
> What then I was. The sounding cataract
> Haunted me like a passion: the tall rock,
> The mountain, and the deep and gloomy wood,
> Their colours and their forms, were then to me
> An appetite; a feeling and a love,
> That had no need of a remoter charm,
> By thought supplied, nor any interest
> Unborrowed from the eye.—That time is past,
> And all its aching joys are now no more,
> And all its dizzy raptures. Not for this
> Faint I, nor mourn nor murmur; other gifts
> Have followed; for such loss, I would believe,
> Abundant recompense.

Then comes the great passage which was quoted in the preceding lecture, expressing the poet's mature attitude toward nature—one of more or less mystical pantheism. But if Wordsworth were completely resigned to the loss of the old aching joys and dizzy raptures, would he now turn to his sister and ask her to keep alive before him his own earlier feelings?

> Oh! yet a little while
> May I behold in thee what I was once,
> My dear, dear Sister! and this prayer I make,
> Knowing that Nature never did betray
> The heart that loved her . . .
> Therefore let the moon
> Shine on thee in thy solitary walk;
> And let the misty mountain-winds be free
> To blow against thee: and, in after years,
> When these wild ecstasies shall be matured
> Into a sober pleasure; . . .
> Oh! then,
> If solitude, or fear, or pain, or grief,
> Should be thy portion, with what healing thoughts
> Of tender joy wilt thou remember me,
> And these my exhortations!

The time will come, says Wordsworth, when Dorothy will have the complete philosophy of nature; but he hopes that the substitution of sober pleasure for wild ecstasies will not be unduly hastened. "She gave me eyes, she gave me ears." He knows that she has the sensuousness indispensible to poetry, and he trusts that she may keep it "yet a little while" as a living reminder of what he "was once." We recall the almost desperate "or let me die" of *My heart leaps up.*

The *Ode on Intimations of Immortality,* which uses the last three lines of *My heart leaps up* as a heading or motto, definitely expresses Wordsworth's tragedy:

There was a time when meadow, grove and
  stream,
The earth, and every common sight,
    To me did seem
    Apparelled in celestial light,
The glory and the freshness of a dream.
It is not now as it hath been of yore;—
    Turn wheresoe'er I may,
      By night or day,
The things which I have seen I now can see
  no more.

      The Rainbow comes and goes,
      And lovely is the Rose,
      The Moon doth with delight
    Look round her when the heavens are bare,
      Waters on a starry night
      Are beautiful and fair;
    The sunshine is a glorious birth;
    But yet I know, where'er I go,
  That there hath passed away a glory from the
    earth.

· · · · ·

Whither is fled the visionary gleam?
Where is it now, the glory and the dream?

This is not merely Wordsworth's tragedy, but mankind's:

Heaven lies about us in our infancy!
Shades of the prison-house begin to close
    Upon the growing Boy,
But He beholds the light, and whence it
  flows,
    He sees it in his joy;
The Youth, who daily farther from the east
    Must travel, still is Nature's Priest,
    And by the vision splendid
    Is on his way attended;
At length the Man perceives it die away,
And fade into the light of common day.

In the three stanzas which were added when the ode
was taken up and finished in 1806, he asserts that the
richness of human experience makes up for what has
been lost; that nature, if no longer so exciting, has
become more deeply significant. Yet his real consolation, after all, is that there are times when wisdom is
unnecessary, times when the youthful mood comes back
in all its freshness.

Wordsworth was always to catch an occasional flicker
of the visionary gleam. The last stanza of a poem of
1818, *Composed upon an Evening of Extraordinary
Splendour and Beauty,* is pathetically reminiscent of
the *Immortality Ode.* The poet recognizes that the light
is fading, and no longer tries to find a philosophical
consolation for what he has lost:

Such hues from their celestial Urn
Were wont to stream before mine eye,
Whene'er it wandered in the morn
Of blissful infancy.
This glimpse of glory, why renewed?
Nay, rather speak with gratitude;
For if a vestige of those gleams
Survived, 'twas only in my dreams.
Dread Power! whom peace and calmness serve
No less than Nature's threatening voice,
If aught unworthy be my choice,
From THEE if I would swerve;
Oh, let thy grace remind me of the light
Full early lost, and fruitlessly deplored;
Which at this moment, on my waking sight
Appears to shine, by miracle restored;
My soul, though yet confined to earth,
Rejoices in a second birth!
—'Tis past, the visionary splendour fades,
And night approaches with her shades.

We have Crabb Robinson's authority for the statement
that although Wordsworth was not buried until 1850,
he died in 1814, the year of *The Excursion.* By 1806,
indeed, he had written most of his really great poems.
If we removed from Wordsworth's collected works the
hundreds of poems composed after about 1806, his
reputation as one of the four or five greatest English
poets would be undiminished; while if we removed
every poem written between 1797 and 1806, we should
have a versifier of ethical platitudes who sometimes
surprises us with a fine poem.

Wordsworth rapidly lost that sensuousness which is
the basis of all poetry; he lost the capacity to rejoice
in sensations of sight and sound and smell and touch
and taste for their own sake. His mind always had a
strong hortatory tendency; and an almost Miltonian
sense of the loftiness of his poetic mission gave him a
bardic self-consciousness, an impulse to take the reader by the buttonhole and impart a message. In the poems
of the great 1797-1806 period, his sensuousness and
his didacticism are harmonized in that union of feeling
and thinking which constitutes the best poetry. But the
equilibrium is of short duration: didacticism soon gets
the upper hand. The images in his later poems are
seldom derived from genuine sense impressions. The
objects of nature which he now writes *about* are not
enjoyed as real things, but are merely symbols consciously chosen to sugar-coat some ethical pill.

      They fade,
The mist and the river, the hill and the shade:
The stream will not flow, and the hill will not
  rise,
And the colours have all passed away from
  her eyes!

This means the death of poetry. In 1798, Wordsworth
had reproached Peter Bell because

A primrose by a river's brim
A yellow primrose was to him,
And it was nothing more.

Up to about 1806, Wordsworth wrote about real primroses that were also something more. After that his primroses continued to be something more, but they gradually ceased to be primroses.

Wordsworth knew what was happening to him better than anyone else. He wrote *To a Skylark* in 1805, when he was fully aware of the coming change. Up he soars with the lark; but soon, conscious of a different destiny, drops back to earth:

Up with me! up with me into the clouds!
    For thy song, lark, is strong!
Up with me, up with me, into the clouds!
    Singing, singing,
With clouds and sky about thee ringing,
    Lift me, guide me, till I find
The spot which seems so to thy mind!

. . . . .

Happy, happy liver,
With a heart as strong as a mountain river
Pouring out praise to the almighty Giver,
Joy and jollity be with us both!

Then observe how the metre changes with the mood:

Alas! my journey, rugged and uneven,
Through prickly moors or dusty ways must
    wind;
But hearing thee, or others of thy kind,
As full of gladness and as free of heaven,
I, with my fate contented, will plod on,
And hope for higher raptures, when life's day
    is done.

This recalls some verses by our own child poet, Hilda Conkling. One day she met a butterfly.

It said a small word, "Follow."
"I cannot follow," I told him;
"I have to go the opposite way."

Wordsworth knew that he had to go the opposite way from the skylark, as Hilda from the butterfly. His philosophy of nature is in part a compensation mechanism, a yearning bridge thrown out between what he has been and what he is to become. Surely he says this plainly enough in *The Prelude:*

Oh! mystery of man, from what a depth
Proceed thy honours. I am lost, but see
In simple childhood something of the base
On which thy greatness stands; but this I feel,

That from thyself it comes, that thou must
    give,
Else never canst receive. The days gone by
Return upon me almost from the dawn
Of life: the hiding-places of man's power
Open; I would approach them, but they close.
I see by glimpses now; when age comes on,
May scarcely see at all; and I would give,
While yet we may, as far as words can give,
Substance and life to what I see, enshrining,
Such is my hope, the spirit of the Past
For future restoration.

As "the hiding-places of man's power" recede further and further into the past, Wordsworth sometimes desperately feels that superstition would be preferable to insensibility. This familiar sonnet is a case in point:

The world is too much with us; late and soon,
Getting and spending, we lay waste our
    powers:
Little we see in Nature that is ours;
We have given our lives away, a sordid boon!
This Sea that bares her bosom to the moon;
The winds that will be howling at all ours,
And are up-gathered now like sleeping
    flowers;
For this, for everything, we are out of tune;
It moves us not.—Great God! I'd rather be
A pagan suckled in a creed outworn;
So might I, standing on this pleasant lea,
Have glimpses that would make me less
    forlorn;
Have sight of Proteus rising from the sea;
Or hear old Triton blow his wreathed horn.

And in *The Excursion* the Wanderer exclaims:

Life's autumn past, I stand on winter's verge;
And daily lose what I desire to keep;
Yet rather would I instantly decline
To the traditionary sympathies
Of a most rustic ignorance, and take
A fearful apprehension from the owl
Or death-watch: and as readily rejoice,
If two auspicious magpies crossed my way;—
To this would rather bend than see and hear
The repetitions wearisome of sense,
Where soul is dead, and feeling hath no place.

But of course no real remedy lies in this direction. Though romanticism may sometimes feel a lurking sympathy with superstition, it cannot recognize the full strength of the bond without surrendering the loftiness of its illusions.

The exact reasons for the decay of Wordsworth's poetic sensuousness are hidden from us. We can point, however, to factors which doubtless contributed to it.

Marriage to an estimable but not very exciting woman who bore him five children between 1803 and 1810 had a quieting effect, and blunted the old keen stimulus of association with his sister. For him who had spoken of poetry as "emotion recollected in tranquility," there was less and less emotion, and more and more tranquility—not the deep tranquility that lets us "see into the heart of life," but the insensitive tranquility of the world that "is too much with us." The disturbances which ruffled this uninspiring peace and quiet were not of the sort that would draw him closer to nature. In 1806, an estrangement arose between him and Coleridge, his partner in the creation of the naturalistic illusion. A personal tragedy played a still more important part: in 1804 his beloved brother John was drowned, and the blow crushed something within him.

Wordsworth's loss of the visionary gleam was accompanied by a growing conservatism. Though neither of these related developments was wholly the cause or the effect of the other, Wordsworth's illusioned view of nature was so closely bound up with an illusioned view of man that a cooling of his attitude toward man probably contributed to a cooling of his attitude toward nature. The growth of Wordsworth's conservatism also interfered with his spontaneous enjoyment of nature by encouraging his inherent didactic tendency. In a manner familiar to students of Victorian literature, he felt more and more the obligation to impart wholesome lessons to the public, forgetting that poetry instructs, if at all, through the contagion of beauty.

The change that came over Coleridge was somewhat different. He had always been more transcendental than Wordsworth. Actual things meant less to him: in his thought the creative imagination which gave significance to what it beheld was always more important than the objective world. As he becomes more and more deeply immersed in German philosophy, he recedes further and further from the concrete. By 1809, when he begins to publish *The Friend,* he is primarily a philosopher rather than a poet, and a philosopher to whom physical nature is not in itself particularly significant. Moreover, as we have seen, the religious conservatism which grows along with his transcendentalism makes him disapprove of nature worship. In a letter of August, 1820, he attacks Wordsworth's old idea of the benign influence of mountains upon mountaineers:

> Whether mountains have any particular effect on the native inhabitants by virtue of being mountains exclusively, and what that effect is, would be a difficult problem. At least the influence acts indirectly only, as far as the mountains are the *causa causae,* or occasion of a pastoral life instead of an agricultural. . . . I will not conceal from you that this inferred dependence of the human soul on accidents of birthplace and abode, together with the vague, misty, rather than Mystic, confusion of God with the world, and the accompanying nature-

worship of which the asserted dependence forms a part is the trait in Wordsworth's poetic works which I most dislike as unhealthy and denounce as contagious.

This is the man who had written *Frost at Midnight* and *This Lime-Tree Bower My Prison.* More will be said later about Coleridge's transcendentalism. At present it is enough to understand that his final philosophy implies the dominance of man's creative will over the material world. Since it now seems to him that the philosophy of nature subordinates mind to matter, he objects to any "inferred dependence of the human soul on accidents of birthplace and abode," even though the abode may be the Lake Country.

Unfortunately, by the time Coleridge came fully to believe in the dominance of man's creative will over the material world, his own creative will had temporarily lost its power to dominate anything, even the conduct of his own life. He had begun taking opium in the form of laudanum as early as 1797, and the habit grew on him until he was soon a slave of the drug. At first opium stimulated Coleridge's imagination, and some of the magical strangeness of *The Ancient Mariner, Kubla Khan,* and *Christabel* is traceable to it. Its ultimate effect, however, was to paralyze the creative faculty, and to leave the mind active but disorganized and sundered from the normal sources of its happiness in the external world.

The Pains of Sleep is a striking portrayal of the seamy side of opium taking, but the poem which shows most clearly how Coleridge becomes cut off from the inspiration of nature is *Dejection: an Ode.* The date of this poem, April 4, 1802, marks a definite stage in his career. What we now call the *reproductive* imagination—the ability to absorb sense impressions, retain them in the mind, and recall them to consciousness—was never displayed by Coleridge more strikingly than in this poem. Indeed, his perceptiveness, which can see the "peculiar tint of yellow green" in the sunset, is agonized and almost pathological in its intensity. But he feels himself losing that *inward* and *creative* imagination which alone can give meaning to his perceptions. In 1798 he had ended *France: an Ode* with the lines:

> Yes, while I stood and gazed, my temples bare,
> And shot my being through earth, sea, and air,
> Possessing all things with intensest love,
> O Liberty! my spirit felt thee there.

That power to shoot his being into nature and fill it with liberty and love has now decayed. Tragically, it has decayed just at the time when his philosophical studies have convinced him that this transcendental power is the most important thing in the world, for objective nature has no spiritual significance unless this power is brought to bear upon it:

A grief without a pang, void, dark, and drear,
  A stifled, drowsy, unimpassioned grief,
  Which finds no natural outlet, no relief,
    In word, or sigh, or tear—
O Lady! in this wan and heartless mood,
To other thoughts by yonder throstle wooed,
  All this long eve, so balmy and serene,
Have I been gazing on the western sky,
  And its peculiar tint of yellow green:
And still I gaze—and with how blank an eye!
And those thin clouds above, in flakes and
  bars,
That give away their motion to the stars;
Those stars, that glide behind them or
  between,
Now sparkling, now bedimmed, but always
  seen;
Yon crescent Moon, as fixed as if it grew
In its own cloudless, starless lake of blue;
I see them all, so excellently fair,
I see, not feel, how beautiful they are!
I may not hope from outward forms to win
The passion and the life, whose fountains are
  within.

O Lady! we receive but what we give,
And in our life alone does Nature live:
Ours is her wedding-garment, ours her shroud!
  And would we aught behold, of higher
  worth,
Than that inanimate cold world allowed
To the poor loveless ever-anxious crowd,
  Ah! from the soul itself must issue forth
A light, a glory, a fair luminous cloud
    Enveloping the Earth—
And from the soul itself must there be sent
  A sweet and potent voice, of its own birth,
Of all sweet sounds the life and element!

Nothing so interesting happened in the case of Robert Southey. He was a true-hearted, estimable gentleman and scholar, an accomplished writer of history and biography, a dependable editor and critic. Like many other bookish persons, he had creative hankerings and some creative ability as a youth. He grew up in stirring times, and he responded in poetry. But his excitement soon died down. All through his life he wrote reams of verse, much of it preserving an afterglow of the emotions that had moved him in earlier days. He was quite intelligent enough to know how poetry should sound, and quite skillful enough to manufacture a very fair imitation of the real thing. No one, however, would assert that after 1805 or thereabouts nature was to Southey more than a body of attractive material about which to make the proper romantic remarks. We need to remember that the romantic attitude can become quite as stereotyped and conventional as the pseudoclassic attitude. Indeed, one might make out a good case for saying that the "new poetry" of our own times is

partly a rebellion against conventionalized romanticism, just as romantic poetry was partly a rebellion against conventionalized classicism.

Along with the decay of naturalistic enthusiasm in the Lake poets appears a growing conservatism in political, social, and religious matters. You will remember that these poets return to nature after passing through two disillusioning stages of radicalism: the first, one of revolutionary ardor; the second, one combining eighteenth century sensibility with the abstract and theoretical rationalism of Godwin. During their period of nature worship, or at least until toward the end of that period, they have more temperately liberal opinions without being active reformers. They believe that reform as the world understands the term is impracticable, and that it is better for men to bring their souls into contact with nature than to clamor for their rights. This attitude, though not in itself conservative, easily slips into conservatism. Meanwhile our poets are rather glad to be sheltered from the turmoil of actual affairs. In 1797, John Thelwall, the old Jacobin, came down from Wales to visit Coleridge at Nether Stowey. "Citizen John," teased Coleridge, "this is a fine place to talk treason in." "Nay, Citizen Samuel," answered Thelwall, "it is rather a place to make a man forget that there is any necessity for treason." The poems of this group sometimes sound a note of almost selfish satisfaction at being withdrawn from the hubbub of the world. From his retreat in the Lake Country, Wordsworth looks out at all the strife and confusion, saying:

But list! a voice is near;
Great Pan himself, low-whispering through the
  reeds,
"Be thankful, thou; for if unholy deeds
Ravage the world, tranquillity is here!"

(Composed by the Side of Grasmere Lake)

But this Lucretian detachment gives place to a renewed interest in events—an interest which becomes distinctly conservative. As I said in commenting on Coleridge's *Fears in Solitude,* that very love of nature which Wordsworth and Coleridge had once associated with love of liberty now becomes associated with nationalism of a more or less fundamentalist sort.

The reversal of the opinions of the Lakists can be explained in various ways. First of all, they grew up. In 1805, to take a date by which their turn toward conservatism is clearly marked, Wordsworth is thirty-five, Coleridge is thirty-three, and Southey is thirty-one. Though far from being graybeards, they are a little too old for us to expect them to retain all the ardors of youth. Then, too, as men of their time, they shared in the general conservative reaction which followed the French Revolution. . . . England was scared into a distrust of all forms of liberalism—a panic like that in our own country after the Bolshevist revolution. From 1793 to the collapse of Napoleon in 1814, moreover, England was almost continuously at war with France, and we know what a strong conservative influence can be exerted by a really good war. Napoleon was responsible for the transformation of many a young English Jacobin into a stout Tory. After he became First Consul of the French Republic in 1799, and more especially after he was crowned Emperor of the French in 1804, there was no longer a revolutionary France for a liberal Englishman to sympathize with. Under the Corsican, France was a constant menace to England, and Pitt's rôle changed from that of Judas to that of the noble defender of his country.

In 1803, Dorothy Wordsworth writes of William to her friend Mrs. Clarkson:

> Surely there never was a more determined hater of the French, nor one more willing to do his utmost to destroy them if they really do come. . . . He wants all the people of England instructed in the use of arms.

In corroboration of this is a letter written to Sir George Beaumont in October of the same year by Wordsworth himself:

> They are sadly remiss at Keswick in putting themselves to trouble in defence of the country. . . . At Grasmere, we have turned out almost to a man. We are to go to Ambleside on Sunday, to be mustered, and to put on, for the first time, our military apparel.

Thanks to Napoleon, the old days of killing white butterflies have returned. How well one knows that pride in the filling of the local quota, that scornful glance at a less patriotic community, that thrill of putting on, "for the first time," the uniform of one's country! "O pleasant exercise of hope and joy!"

Beginning at about this time, Wordsworth writes a large number of poems which might cause a hasty reader to suppose that he is a devoted advocate of freedom. See especially the section in the collected works entitled *Poems Dedicated to National Independence and Liberty*. But upon more careful inspection it becomes evident that Wordsworth is merely championing the freedom of small nations which, if aroused, might make trouble for Napoleon. Once Napoleon falls, Wordsworth becomes a supporter of the Holy Alliance, in which the love of liberty is anything but a master passion. We need not impute conscious dishonesty to Wordsworth or to any of the Lakists. They were the sincere and well meaning victims of that self-deception which becomes a virtue during and just after a great war. At such times, there is no longer any truth to be spoken: there are only certain useful things that a patriot must

say. No one who did his bit to make the world safe for democracy should hasten to condemn these poets.

When I said that the Lakists grew up, I should have added that they became respectable. They were married and had families; they went into society and met nice rich powerful people. They ate better, dressed better, and learned to be polite to bores. The critics gradually ceased abusing them, so that by the time they had become almost wholly negligible as artists, they were generally admired and respected. This gave them a ruinous sense of responsibility to the nation, a feeling that they should be sound and wholesome in their sentiments. Southey became poet laureate in 1813, and Wordsworth succeeded him on his death in 1843. But long before this honor came to him Wordsworth had been a semi-official bard. He was appointed stamp distributor for Westmoreland in 1813, and received a state pension in 1842.

The factors contributing to Wordsworth's loss of poetic sensuousness contributed equally to his conservatism. The death of his brother is reflected in *Elegiac Stanzas Suggested by a Picture of Peele Castle* (1805). Since the painting includes a ship tossing in a storm, it naturally suggests to him the tragedy of the preceding year. In earlier days, he says, he could have painted in verse a beautiful picture of this scene:

> Ah! then, if mine had been the painter's hand,
> To express what then I saw; and add the gleam,
> The light that never was, on sea or land,
> The consecration, and the poet's dream;
>
> I would have painted thee, thou hoary pile,
> Amid a world how different from this!
> Beside a sea that would not cease to smile;
> On tranquil land, beneath a sky of bliss.
>
> . . . . .
>
> Such, in the fond illusion of my heart,
> Such picture would I at that time have made:
> And seen the soul of truth in every part,
> A steadfast peace that might not be betrayed.
>
> So once it would have been,—'tis now no more;
> I have submitted to a new control:
> A power is gone, which nothing can restore;
> A deep distress hath humanised my soul.
>
> Not for a moment could I now behold
> A smiling sea, and be what I have been:
> The feeling of my loss will ne'er be old;
> This, which I know, I speak with mind serene.

This poem resembles *Dejection* in the idea that the poet has lost the power to impose significance on what he beholds. It differs from Coleridge's ode, however, in an essential respect. Whereas Coleridge at present can see no remedy for the loss of his "shaping spirit of imagination," Wordsworth seems determined to make his sorrow a source of spiritual discipline. This "deep distress" has "humanised his soul"; his mind is "serene"; he has "submitted to a new control."

Wordsworth had never been a lover of outright wildness; he had always appreciated the importance of discipline and restraint. At the height of his naturalistic enthusiasm, however, he felt that nature herself had power to discipline the human spirit. In *Three years she grew,* Nature says of her relations with Lucy:

> Myself will to my darling be
> Both law and impulse; and with me
> The girl, in rock and plain,
> In earth and heaven, in glade and bower,
> Shall feel an overseeing power
> To kindle or restrain.

But Wordsworth gradually comes to believe that one looks to nature in vain for the necessary law and restraint. A poem of 1845, *The Westmoreland Girl,* shows how differently he feels in his old age. The Westmoreland girl bears all the earmarks of the Lucy type. The first part of the poem describes her rearing among the mountains and relates an incident in which she rescues a lamb from a flooded stream. But in the second part of the poem Wordsworth insists that so promising a child should not be

> Left among her native mountains
> With wild Nature to run wild.
>
>   . . . . .
>
> What then wants the child to temper,
> In her breast, unruly fire,
> To control the froward impulse,
> And restrain the vague desire?
> Easily a pious training
> And a steadfast outward power
> Would supplant the weeds, and cherish
> In their stead each opening flower.

So in the end Lucy is to be sent to Sunday School, for nature seems better at kindling than at restraining.

A symptom of this change is the sonnet beginning *Nuns fret not at their convent's narrow room.* It was published in 1807. We do not know when it was written, but Wordsworth began to cultivate the sonnet in 1802. One might guess that it was written in 1805, the year of the *Peele Castle* stanzas, for it uses the restrictions of the sonnet form to symbolize the "new control" to which Wordsworth has submitted:

> Nuns fret not at their convent's narrow room;
> And hermits are contented with their cells;
> And students with their pensive citadels;
> Maids at the wheel, the weaver at his loom,
> Sit blithe and happy; bees that soar for bloom,
> High as the highest peak of Furness-fells,
> Will murmur by the hour in foxglove bells;
> In truth, the prison unto which we doom
> Ourselves, no prison is; and hence for me,
> In sundry moods, 'twas pastime to be bound
> Within the sonnet's scanty plot of ground;
> Pleased if some souls (for such there needs
>   must be)
> Who have felt the weight of too much liberty,
> Should find brief solace there, as I have
>   found.

It should be noted that from about 1802 to about 1807, just when Wordsworth begins poignantly to feel that his joy in nature must pass away, he has an opportunity to become a great poet, not of the exuberance of nature, but of the discipline of moral and religious law. One sees clear hints of this possibility in the austere stoicism of *Michael* (1800), that most classical of romantic poems, in the sonnet *Nuns fret not,* and in *Character of the Happy Warrior* (1806). But the clearest explanation of what he means by saying in *Peele Castle* that he has "submitted to a new control" is the *Ode to Duty* (1805). This is the key passage:

> I, loving freedom and untried,
> No sport of every random gust,
> Yet being to myself a guide,
> Too blindly have reposed my trust:
> And oft, when in my heart was heard
> Thy timely mandate, I deferred
> The task, in smoother walks to stray;
> But thee I now would serve more strictly, if I
>   may.
>
> Through no disturbance of my soul,
> Or strong compunction in me wrought,
> I supplicate for thy control;
> But in the quietness of thought:
> Me this uncharted freedom tires;
> I feel the weight of chance desires:
> My hopes no more must change their name,
> I long for a repose that ever is the same.

The same note of triumphing over life by submitting to its laws is sounded at intervals as late as 1814, when—not to mention *The Excursion,* in which it is blurred by other themes—he speaks in *Laodamia* of "calm pleasures" and "majestic pains," and makes Protesilaus declare that

>   the Gods approve
> The depth, and not the tumult, of the soul.

Some students would trace this Matthew Arnold-like quality on into Wordsworth's later work. Where to draw the line between a nobly stoical philosophy of control and a reactionary and obscurantist conservatism depends on the temperament of the individual student. It seems to me that after about 1814 Wordsworth is definitely on the wrong side of that line. A brief but magnificent struggle to preserve a balance between romantic naturalism and a more or less stoically Christian humanism ends in his becoming soundly, stuffily, Anglican and Tory. He opposes the abolition of the Test and Corporation Acts, extension of the franchise, and most of the other liberal measures of his day. In 1821 he writes to Lord Lonsdale:

> When I was young . . . I thought it derogatory to human nature to set up property in preference to person, as a title to legislative power. That notion has now vanished. I now perceive many advantages in our present complex system of representation, which formerly eluded my observation.

He also perceived many advantages in placing on the freedom of the press heavy restrictions which had eluded his observation in the days when he wished to found a journal called *The Philanthropist.* . . . Professor Harper believes that [Wordsworth's] final acceptance of Anglican orthodoxy was motivated rather largely by the feeling that it was a civic duty to adhere to the Established Church. The parts of the *Ecclesiastical Sonnets* which relate to Henry VIII and the Reformation are certainly a tragic example of Wordsworth's downfall. An even more tragic example, however, occurs in his *Postscript* to the collected edition of 1835. Here he quotes the beautiful passage from the yet unpublished *Prelude* describing his intention to devote his verse to the lives of those who live close to nature, and solemnly says of it:

> The passage is extracted from my MSS. written above thirty years ago: it turns upon the individual dignity which humbleness of social condition does not preclude, but frequently promotes. It has no direct bearing upon clubs for the discussion of social affairs, nor upon political or trade-unions; but if a single workman—who, being a member of one of those clubs, runs the risk of becoming an agitator, or who, being enrolled in a union, must be left without a will of his own, and therefore a slave— should read these lines, and be touched by them, I should indeed rejoice, and little would I care for losing credit as a poet with intemperate critics who think differently from me upon political philosophy or public measures, if the sober-minded admit that, in general views, my affections have been moved, and my imagination exercised, under and *for* the guidance of reason.

Now that *The Prelude* has become a weapon against debating clubs and labor unions, we may glance more briefly at Coleridge. An important factor in his turn toward conservatism was his romantic love of tradition—the quality that we noticed in Edmund Burke. Coleridge had to an eminent degree the feeling that old customs are beautiful and worthy of being preserved, that old ideas are venerable and precious, that old superstitions probably contain much truth. When revolutionary enthusiasm had passed away and Napoleon was threatening to invade England, this Burkian romanticism was strongly stimulated. By 1802, Coleridge was a completely pro-Pitt and anti-Bonaparte patriot and a violent foe of English Jacobinism. This peril he saw everywhere: in 1809 he even opposed as a Jacobin measure a bill for the prevention of cruelty to animals. His fear of foes without and within the nation caused him to enlist his transcendental philosophy in the service of the Tory party and the Church of England, so that the British constitution became first cousin to the categorical imperative, and the Establishment first cousin to the absolute.

Coleridge's path to respectability was less straight and smooth than Wordsworth's. It was broken by the ups and downs of opium taking, his estrangement from his wife in 1804, his sojourn in Malta during the next two years, his journalistic ventures, and his lecturing. Although he had been on the side of the angels at least since 1802, it was not until 1816, when he went to live with the Gillmans at Highgate, that he could settle down in real peace and dignity as a prophet of transcendental Toryism. The details of the intervening years are complex, and I must ask you to dig them out for yourselves.

I shall, however, relate one incident illustrating the embarrassments which are likely to beset such a convert as Coleridge. In 1803, he attended a gathering of right thinking authors and gentlemen. On this occasion Sir Walter Scott recited from memory a poem whose sentiments he totally disapproved but whose vivid imagery and powerful rhythm he could not help admiring. The poem was entitled *Fire, Famine, and Slaughter,* and it breathed the most savage hatred of William Pitt. Of those present, only Sir Humphry Davy knew that Coleridge himself had written the poem seven years before. Coleridge knew that Davy knew. The other guests, less broad-minded than Scott, were shocked by this wild scream of radicalism, and abused it strongly. Davy, very uncomfortable, kept his secret. The much more uncomfortable author launched into a long, metaphysical, hypothetical defense of the anonymous poet, which curious document you may read in the *Apologetic Preface to "Fire, Famine and Slaughter"* (1817). But as the company still refused to forgive the unknown Jacobin, at last Coleridge exclaimed to Scott:

> I must now confess, sir! that I am the author of that poem. It was written some years ago. I do not attempt to justify my past self, young as I then was;

but as little as I would now write a similar poem, so far was I even then from imagining that the lines would be taken as more or less than a sport of fancy. At all events, if I know my own heart, there never was a moment in my existence in which I should have been more ready, had Mr. Pitt's person been in hazard, to interpose my own body, and defend his life at the risk of my own.

If you can credit this after reading *Fire, Famine and Slaughter* together with the bitter sonnet against Pitt which was quoted a few days ago, your credulity is greater than mine. I can manage to believe that Coleridge thought he was telling the truth in 1803, but I cannot believe that he did not loathe William Pitt in 1796. It is somewhat easier to believe that he would have confessed if Sir Humphry Davy had not been present.

Robert Southey was born to become conservative, and he simply went through the normal course of his development. Beginning in 1808, he was a regular contributor to the Tory *Quarterly Review*—writing, for example, against the freedom of the press and in favor of a seditious libel law. In 1813 the laurel crowned his brow. It is impossible to compare the fulsome loyalty of *A Vision of Judgment* with the radical ardor of an early work like *Joan of Arc* without feeling that Southey departed far indeed from the principles of his youth.

Students, however, have been too prone to regard the conservatism of these writers in the light of attacks made upon them by the younger generation of romantic radicals. The Lakists were not bribe-taking turncoats or unprincipled partisans of oppression. Factors in their personal lives and in their general environment caused them to turn from naturalistic romanticism to Burkian romanticism, with its almost mystical conception of the state as the sacred flower of an august tradition. They were as dissatisfied with present conditions as the most urgent of the reformers, but they saw in the reform movement a continuation of the eighteenth century radical spirit which they had come to detest. It was rationalistic, utilitarian, secular, and democratic; while their thought was anti-intellectualistic, idealistic, ecclesiastical, and feudal. Necessarily, therefore, Wordsworth, Coleridge, and Southey found themselves opposed to almost every change proposed by the liberal reformers, and were forced into an obstructionism which thwarted their earnest desire to benefit mankind. It must also be granted that they rather ignobly feared the ideas which they opposed, and too eagerly advocated their suppression by official methods.

They believed in a very close connection between church and state, and in as much education for the poor as would give them wholesome and loyal ideas. The division of society into ranks and classes seemed to them a part of the divinely constituted order of things. But hatred of the low for the high, and callous indifference of the high for the low, were alike sinful. The remedy was an abandonment of the evil spirit of competition engendered by democracy, and a return to the genial coöperative spirit of feudalism, in which everyone proudly knew his place and labored toward the ideal of a state that was a kind of *civitas Dei*. They advocated, therefore, an enlightened paternalism on the part of the upper classes, and a cheerful filial trust on the part of the lower.

The Lakists were so imperfectly understood by most of their contemporaries that they were never wholly comfortable even in the Tory camp, which was the only home they could find. But their thought, for better or worse, was not without influence. Their union of desire for social betterment with keen distrust of democracy, their preference of coöperation to competition, and their emphasis on emotional and imponderable factors in the social sciences enter deeply into Victorian thought. In varying proportions and combinations, their ideas are discernible in Carlyle and Ruskin, in the Oxford Movement, and in the Christian Socialism of F. D. Maurice. Recently, on reading *Coningsby* for the first time, I was struck by Disraeli's evident sympathy with this type of conservative thought. "I wish," declares the hero, "to see a people full of faith, and a government full of duty." "England," Sidonia observes, "is governed by Downing Street; once it was governed by Alfred and Elizabeth." Those remarks perfectly represent the spirit of Wordsworth, Coleridge and Southey after they became romantic Tories.

Since the Lakists inherited from their master, Burke, a distrust of abstract political and social theories, they were able to prick several *a priori* bubbles of reform in a shrewd and profitable way. But their realism was more limited than Burke's, and even more completely motivated by a very non-realistic desire to preserve certain traditional sentiments in the face of inevitable change. Hence they carried into political theory that mixture of hard fact and soft dream which is inherent in romanticism. The value of their contribution to the anti-utilitarian and anti-liberal strain in Victorian social thought must therefore depend upon our attitude toward romanticism, and cannot be stated in objective terms. . . .

Geoffrey Carnall

SOURCE: An introduction to *Robert Southey and His Age: The Development of a Conservative Mind*, Oxford at the Clarendon Press, 1960, pp. 1-11.

[*In the following essay, Carnall surveys the events that contributed to the conservative thinking of Southey and other early nineteenth-century figures.*]

In the years that followed Waterloo, few men were more obnoxious to radicals and democrats than Robert Southey. Not only was he a court hireling, an enemy to liberty, a man who wanted to punish seditious libel with transportation; but worse, he was an apostate. There was a time when he too had been loud in defence of liberty, and shared the generous enthusiasm of the French Revolution. It was unkindly supposed that he had been bribed into his Toryism: first by a pension, and then by the office of Poet Laureate. This explanation, however, is almost as unconvincing as Southey's own view that he had merely acquired greater wisdom with age and experience.

Southey's conversion, like that of his friends Wordsworth and Coleridge, has become a symbol. The Lake Poets are seen as Promethean heroes who grew degenerate and accepted pensions from Jove.

> Just for a handful of silver he left us,
> Just for a riband to stick in his coat.

Wordsworth's life squares with the myth particularly well, because his fall from grace was so conspicuously punished. The anticlimax of his later poetry is notorious. His apologists, indeed, find no difficulty in proving that the myth is in many ways a distortion. It nevertheless retains its vigour, because it expresses an anxiety which has increasingly disturbed people over the last two centuries: the feeling that society is crushing the individual. Richardson's Clarissa defying her family and her seducer, the Byronic hero protesting that he has not flattered the world's rank breath, John Stuart Mill arguing that the mere example of non-conformity is itself a service to human advancement, Mr. E. M. Forster hoping that he would betray his country rather than his friend: they are all in their various ways resisting Leviathan. Wordsworth and the rest are felt to have surrendered.

How far is this true? To answer the question, one needs to understand exactly what pressures they were subjected to, where they yielded and where they resisted. It is here that Southey's writings are of exceptional interest. He was a regular and copious contributor to newspapers, magazines, and reviews. In the very years in which he ceased to be a radical, he was writing the historical part of the *Edinburgh Annual Register,* where he had to record and analyse home and foreign politics at considerable length. Above all, he was a fluent and tireless correspondent. The letters that have been published are formidable in their bulk; but they are only a fraction of the surviving collections of his correspondence. Few men can have recorded the fluctuations and contradictions of their beliefs so fully, and to the extent that it ever is possible to understand the impulses that drive men to change their allegiance, it should be possible to understand what happened to Southey. . . .

Portrait of Robert Southey, from a water-color by Edward Nash.

Southey's development cannot be understood in isolation from the stresses of his time. His beliefs were a response to alarming political and social movements. It is not always easy for the modern reader to appreciate just how alarming those movements were, and it is tempting to ascribe panic fears and extreme depression to mere morbidity. When Shelley writes, in the preface to *The Revolt of Islam,* 'gloom and misanthropy have become the characteristics of the age in which we live', most of his readers will probably dismiss this as rhetoric, an affectation of romantic melancholy. The same readers may likewise discount the extravagances of Blake, the instability of Coleridge, the posturings of Byron, the bitter misanthropy of Hazlitt, and the feverish outpourings of Keats. And yet they ought not to do this without misgivings, for these writers are obstinately representative figures of their time, in a way which more sensible people like Scott, Peacock, or Jane Austen are not.

They are representative because they have clearly felt the shock of a great upheaval. It would be going beyond the scope of the present study to analyse in detail the relationship between the 'Industrial Revolution' and the romantic movement in literature. But the vast economic growth which set in as the eighteenth century came to an end produced at least one consequence which is reflected in the literature of the time. It increased feelings of insecurity, made people feel more uncertain of their relations with others, more isolated. Hence the cult of the solitary—'There is a pleasure in the pathless woods', 'I wandered lonely as a cloud', and (less pleasant)

> Alone, alone, all, all alone,
>   Alone on a wide wide sea.

Hence, too, an unusual interest in suicide. The popularity of *Werther* is notorious. How far the literary fascination is reflected in the suicide rate is hard to say, for there are no reliable statistics. But it is remarkable that between 1815 and 1822 three prominent British politicians committed suicide—Whitbread, Romilly, and Castlereagh. This must be a record in parliamentary history. One may observe, too, that the great economic crisis of 1810 was precipitated by the suicide of Abraham Goldsmid, a London banker. Those who did not go the length of suicide could sometimes be the victims of acute depression. Southey's friend John Rickman, secretary to the Speaker of the House of Commons, and a sturdy statistician, is a significantly unromantic example. He was convinced that England had never been so prosperous before in her history. The reign of George III, he said in 1820, had seen an unparalleled increase in the comforts of life. Nevertheless, he could not *feel* the new glories of his country, though he could argue himself into a juster frame of mind. Rickman explained this unreasonable reaction as the poisonous effect of the malignant opposition press. But Southey, who was not likely to feel any more goodwill than Rickman towards newspapers, seems nearer the mark in his assertion that the manufacturing system had increased enormously the activity and wealth of the nation; but it had also, in a far greater degree, 'diminished its happiness and lessened its security'.

The misery and insecurity were specially obvious among the working classes. It was, for example, the labouring man who bore the brunt of the great redistribution of population that took place as a result of the Industrial Revolution, with all the suffering necessarily involved in abandoning one's accustomed way of life. During the Napoleonic War, moreover, and for some years after it, high rents, high rates of interest, the system of taxation, the shortage of coin, and the difficulty of importing food, all worked together to worsen the economic status of labour. Among early nineteenth-century writers, perhaps the most sombrely eloquent of those who described the state of the poor was a medical man, Charles Hall, whose book, *The Effects of Civilization,* appeared in 1805. He lays great emphasis on the social irresponsibility of modern commerce. 'Trade knows no friends or kindred', he says, '—avarice no compassion—gain no bounds.' He is oppressed by an awareness of the 'regular, orderly,

silent' processes by which the poor are subdued. The power of the rich, he argues,

> is as strong and effective as that of the most absolute monarch that ever lived, as far as relates to the labour of the poor; indeed, probably more so, since it is doubtful whether any power ever existed, in any kind of government whatever, that could impose on the people what is imposed on them by the power of wealth. To condemn so many to the mines; to confine such numbers to such nauseous, irksome, unwholesome, destructive employments—is more than equal to any kingly power on earth. . . .

From the point of view of those who enjoyed this kindly power, such conditions could be exhilarating. As Mr. R. J. White has remarked in a recent study of the period, the will-to-power in man had a greater scope then than it has ever had. In industry there was no government interference, no effective trade unionism, no patents to prevent enterprising young men from picking any brains they chose. 'It was a matter of a large number of men letting loose the life within them into a new field of adventure.' 'Letting loose'—that is the clue to both the high and the low spirits of the time. It was exhilarating to feel identified with this power let loose, and intimidating to feel overwhelmed by it. Neither reaction was *social,* people responding to people.

The sense of insecurity produced in these conditions was expressed not so much by those, like the hand-loom weavers, who suffered slow extinction as a class, as by those who enjoyed enough privileges to fear losing them. Men who profited from the economic revolution might still feel threatened by the fate of the higher ranks of society in France. Hazlitt might speak of the 'grand whirling movements' of the French Revolution, of its 'tumultuous glow of rebellion' in head and heart. But to Burke these movements were terrifying. They seemed to portend the collapse of all social order. The spirit of the French Revolution, he said, in his second letter *On a Regicide Peace,* 'lies deep in the corruption of our common nature'. The rulers of France have found their resources in crimes. 'The discovery is dreadful: the mine exhaustless.' The doctrine of majority rule, put into practice by the French, loosens all old venerations and attachments, leaving society exposed to the untrammelled will of a succession of mob leaders.

Burke's fears belong to a region of experience unfamiliar, in England at least, before the eighteenth century. Shakespeare's Ulysses may express himself in terms which suggest such alarm:

> Then every thing includes itself in power,
> Power into will, will into appetite,
> And appetite, an universal wolf,
> So doubly seconded with will and power,

Must make perforce an universal prey,
And last, eat up himself.

But it is arguable that Shakespeare could not even imagine the intensity of panic that seized Burke. To Ulysses, disorder is only an episode. The heavens themselves, the planets and this centre observe degree, priority, and place; and however much the planets may wander in evil mixture to disorder, the glorious planet Sol remains enthroned and sphered in noble eminence. It is obvious that the orthodox doctrine of hierarchy, as stated by Ulysses, is put under a severe strain both in the play where it appears, and elsewhere in Shakespeare. But broadly speaking, although it sometimes looks as though humanity must perforce prey on itself, like monsters of the deep, the vile offences which are committed receive their punishment. Macbeth might be willing to let the frame of things disjoint, but his willingness is only a sign of the disorder which is within himself, by which he will soon be destroyed.

The disturbing novelty of the situation in the later eighteenth century can be appreciated if one compares Burke on the French Revolution with Clarendon on the Great Rebellion of the seventeenth century. To Burke, the revolutionaries were outlaws of the human race. Clarendon saw his opponents simply as factious and malicious men. The rebellion, he thought, arose from the interaction of infinitely various temperaments and qualities—

> the pride of this man, and the popularity of that; the levity of one, and the morosity of another; the excess of the court in the greatest want, and the parsimony and retention of the country in the greatest plenty; the spirit of craft and subtlety in some, and the rude and unpolished integrity of others, too much despising craft or art; like so many atoms contributing jointly to this mass of confusion now before us.

Clarendon here comments on a fact of political life in which Burke too was interested. The purposes of individuals may find issue in joint action that was far from any one man's intention. In his *Appeal from the New to the Old Whigs,* Burke describes how whole bodies of men may be hurried into schemes of politics through 'a careless and passive assent . . . a sort of activity of inertness', strengthened by 'the fear of differing with the authority of leaders on the one hand, and of contradicting the desires of the multitude on the other'. Burke feels himself hustled by the course of events. Clarendon, however, always makes one feel that matters could have been kept under control with a shrewder policy and a little more good fortune. If the Short Parliament had not been dissolved, if Sir Thomas Gardiner could have been Speaker in the Long Parliament, if the Earl of Bedford had not died so unseasonably, disaster might have been avoided. This underlying assurance is not to be found in Burke. He saw himself sinking under the attacks of atheists, and for him the only question was how he might arm himself against them before it was too late.

The sense of powerlessness in the face of events impressed many observers of the French Revolution. John Stuart Mill, for example, in his admirable review of Walter Scott's *Life of Napoleon,* described the revolution as a force independent of party interests, class interests, personal interests, depravity, virtue, or genius— these things appearing to influence the course of events only when they fell in with it and added force to the current, proving impotent when they found themselves thrust into opposition. Joseph de Maistre made the same observation, though from an entirely different standpoint. The more one examined the career of the leaders of the revolution, he said, the more passive and mechanical their activity appeared to be. They did not lead the revolution; they were mere tools of the revolution. Maistre saw proof in this that God used the revolution to punish the French for their irreligious presumption. But even those who were concerned to vindicate the revolution were obliged to acknowledge the part played in it by this terrifying force. Thus, James Mackintosh said that the burning of châteaux and other riotous acts of this kind were something that the National Assembly could not repress without either provoking a civil war or putting arms into the hands of their enemies. 'Placed in this *dilemma,* they were compelled to expect a slow remedy from the returning serenity of the Public mind. . . .' This is a reasonable defence, but of course a great deal might happen before the public mind returned to serenity. Thomas Paine, for one, was astonished that the National Assembly had been able to restrain so much of the confusion—'beyond the controul of all authority'. Paine argued, indeed, that the outrages committed by the Paris mob were no more the acts of the French people than the outrages of the London mob in the Gordon Riots of 1780 were the acts of the whole people of England. But the parallel could be used against Paine, for the Gordon Riots had shown, on a small scale, what could happen when normal loyalties broke down and the mob took control. Recalling the 'dreadful fermentation' of that time, Burke described how 'wild and savage insurrection quitted the woods, and prowled about our streets in the name of reform. Such was the distemper of the public mind, that there was no madman, in his maddest ideas, and maddest projects, who might not count upon numbers to support his principles and execute his designs.' Fortunately the cry of the mob had been 'No Popery!'— which was a little more favourable to the established order than 'The Rights of Man!' If it had been otherwise, Burke thought that England might have begun the democratic revolution instead of France.

Comparatively few people viewed the French Revolution with the desperate passion that possessed Burke. If he looked like a man who was going to defend himself against murderers, Fanny Burney, who tells us this, tells us also that she 'feared not with his fears', though tacitly assenting to his doctrines. This, however, does not make Burke unrepresentative, as is shown by the way he crystallized English opposition to France in 1792. What other people were haunted by as an occasional bad dream, was for him a habitual nightmare.

Southey, too, was subject to nightmares. They drove him from the radicalism of his earlier years into a fervent conservatism. In considering this change, it is useful to recall some wise words of his son Cuthbert. Some people, he said, might consider his father's apprehensions at the time of the Reform Bill of 1832 exaggerated and unfounded; but we should remember that 'we are often apt to think lightly of our own fears and those of others when the danger has passed by'. It is a salutary exercise to reconstruct the perspective in which Southey and his contemporaries saw the events of their time. It is easy for us, looking back on the evolution of British institutions in the nineteenth century, to feel superior to Southey's gloom and panic. His opposition to parliamentary reform and Catholic emancipation has, as the phrase goes, been proved wrong by 'history'. The citadel of the constitution was not taken by assault, as Southey believed it would be, and Lord Shaftesbury is remembered as a factory-reformer, not, as Southey further predicted, for his part in a counter-revolution. Even when Tory prophecies have come true, they seem less dreadful to us than to the original prophets. Many modern conservatives would agree with Rickman that universal suffrage has led to 'an organised Robbery of the Upper Classes'; but they seem to take this robbery philosophically enough. Still more striking is an accurate prediction in the *Courier,* at the time of Lord Grenville's election as Chancellor of the University of Oxford. Grenville was a leading advocate of Catholic emancipation, but he had none the less secured the votes of certain bishops. 'They have conspired', said the *Courier* with bitter sarcasm, 'to throw open the gates of the University to persons of every religious persuasion *whatever.*' The highest academic posts might well in future be given to Socinians and Catholics. This prophecy has been fulfilled to the letter. It would have been even more remarkable if the *Courier* had added atheists to the list, but doubtless it did not wish to exaggerate. It had appalled its readers enough already. Even today it should be possible to appreciate that the prospect conjured up must have appeared monstrous and intolerable. To the Duke of Wellington, the consequences of parliamentary reform seemed no less appalling. He preferred, he said, to fall in defence of the unreformed British Constitution rather than endure 'the lingering operation of a modern revolutionary system', such as would be established by the Reform Bill.

There is, in fact, nothing necessarily eccentric or unbalanced about Southey's reaction to the events of his

time. His state of mind was similar to those who nowadays wish to make a firm stand against communism, or Titoist revisionism, or the encroachments of the coloured races. The uncompromising resister of shifts in the balance of power may be wrong, but he is not abnormal.

FURTHER READING

Abrams, M. H., ed. *English Romantic Poets.* 1960. Reprint, London: Oxford University Press, 1968, 384 p.
> Collection of critical essays focusing on the major English poets of the Romantic period. Includes essays on Wordsworth and Coleridge.

Barfield, Owen. *What Coleridge Thought.* Middletown, Ct.: Wesleyan University Press, 1971, 285 p.

> Analysis of Coleridge's philosophy and beliefs regarding a variety of topics, including nature, imagination, science, and religion.

Barth, Robert J. *The Symbolic Imagination: Coleridge and the Romantic Tradition.* Princeton: Princeton University Press, 1977, 155 p.
> Examines many aspects of symbolism in the works of Coleridge and Wordsworth.

Brandl, Alois. *Samuel Taylor Coleridge and the English Romantic School.* London: John Murray, 1887, 392 p.
> Biographical account including a discussion of Coleridge's literary and personal relationships with Southey and Wordsworth.

Bush, Douglas. *Mythology and the Romantic Tradition in English Poetry.* New York: W. W. Norton & Company, 1937, 645 p.
> Explores the influence of mythology and the emphasis on myth and allegory in the works of the Romantic poets, including Coleridge and Wordsworth.

Byatt, A. S. *Wordsworth and Coleridge in Their Time.* London: Thomas Nelson and Sons, 1970, 287 p.
> Detailed study of society and politics that surrounded and influenced Wordsworth and Coleridge, including a discussion of the literary circle of the two poets.

Courthope, W. J. "The Lake School of English Poetry and the French Revolution." In *A History of English Poetry,* pp. 161-231. London: Macmillan, 1920.
> Analyzes the impact of the French Revolution on the poetical and political development of Coleridge, Southey, and Wordsworth.

Eilenberg, Susan. *Strange Power of Speech: Wordsworth, Coleridge, and Literary Possession.* New York: Oxford University Press, 1992, 296 p.

Intensive study of the various distinct poetic voices that can be discerned in the works of Coleridge and Wordsworth.

Greenberg, Martin. *The Hamlet Vocation of Coleridge and Wordsworth.* Iowa City: University of Iowa Press, 1986, 209 p.

Argues that Coleridge and Wordsworth were "called" much as Hamlet was "to a life of inwardness, introspection . . ." and examines the ways the two poets answered this calling.

Griggs, Earle Leslie, ed. *Wordsworth and Coleridge.* New York: Russell & Russell, 1962, 254 p.

A collection of essays examining various aspects of Wordsworth's and Coleridge's poetry and philosophy.

Harvey, Geoffrey. *The Romantic Tradition in Modern Poetry.* London: Macmillan, 1986, 112 p.

Traces the Romantic impulse, in several variations, through the works of Wordsworth, Thomas Hardy, John Betjeman, and Philip Larkin.

McFarland, Thomas. "The Symbiosis of Coleridge and Wordsworth." In *Romanticism and the Forms of Ruin: Wordsworth, Coleridge, and Modalities of Fragmentation,* pp. 56-103. Princeton: Princeton University Press, 1981.

Argues that the literary relationship between Coleridge and Wordsworth was one of mutual dependency.

Renwick, W. L. "The New Men." In *The Rise of the Romantics, 1789-1815: Wordsworth, Coleridge, and Jane Austen,* pp. 127-93. Oxford: Oxford University Press, 1963.

Detailed account of the development of the relationships between Coleridge, Wordsworth, and Southey and their influence on each other.

Robinson, Henry Crabb. *Blake, Coleridge, Wordsworth, Lamb, &c.,* edited by Edith J. Morley. Manchester University Press, 1932, 176 p.

Primarily biographical material pertaining to the association between Wordsworth, Coleridge, Southey, and their contemporaries, including Lamb, De Quincey, and Hazlitt.

Wordsworth, Jonathan, Michael C. Jaye, and Robert Woof. *William Wordsworth and the Age of English Romanticism.* New Brunswick: Rutgers University Press, 1987, 285 p.

Richly illustrated history of the Romantic period.

Additional coverage of the lives and careers of the individual Lake Poets is contained in the following sources published by Gale Research: Coleridge: *Nineteenth-Century Literature Criticism,* **Volume 9,** *Poetry Criticism,* **Volume 11, and** *Dictionary of Literary Biography,* **Volumes 93 and 107; Southey:** *Nineteenth-Century Literature Criticism,* **Volume 8, and** *Dictionary of Literary Biography,* **Volumes 93, 107, and 142; and Wordsworth:** *Nineteenth-Century Literature Criticism,* **Volumes 12 and 38,** *Poetry Criticism,* **Volume 4, and** *Dictionary of Literary Biography,* **Volumes 93 and 107.**

Polish Romanticism

INTRODUCTION

Influenced by the general spirit and main ideas of European Romanticism, the literature of Polish Romanticism is unique, as many scholars have pointed out, in having developed largely outside of Poland and in its emphatic focus upon the issue of Polish nationalism. Both of these characteristics stem from the fact that after 1815 Poland as such disappeared from the map of Europe, continuing to exist only as a concept in the minds of its population. The Vienna Congress of 1815, which represented an end to the era of Napoleon Bonaparte and to the political heritage of the French Revolution, orchestrated the division of Poland into two states—the Cracow Respublica, which became incorporated into Austria in 1848, and the Kingdom of Poland (or Congress Kingdom), which lost its constitutional independence to Russia following the failed November Rising of 1830, an attempt to overthrow Russian domination in Poland. The noted Polish literary critic Julian Krzyżanowski, stressing the significance of these historical events for Polish literature, has noted that, "The Kingdom of Poland, the small state which, theoretically, was constitutional and seemingly independent, and thus the natural centre of Polish cultural life, ceased to be such a centre, not only because its university and societies of learning were closed down and because all manifestations of independent thought and creative works were suppressed ruthlessly by police and military methods, but also because it lost a large part of its intellectuals, that is, the social group which created cultural life."

The Polish intelligentsia, along with leading members of its government, left Poland in the early 1830s, during what is referred to as the "Great Emigration," resettling in France, Germany, Great Britain, Turkey, and the United States. While the Polish émigrés were enthusiastically received in their new countries, they longed to return to Poland after what they hoped would be an all-European revolution that would restore the Romantic principles of liberty and individual as well as national rights. Since many foremost Polish emigrants relocated in Paris, that city emerged as the most important center for Polish Romantic literature in the period between 1830 and 1850. Characterized by its rich intellectual environment, the Polish émigré community carried on a lively political, philosophical, and literary tradition that nourished its writers and poets. Because these Polish artists could not conceive of a lost fatherland, their works were intensely patriotic, revolutionary, and enriched by elements from Polish history and folk tradition. As George Brandes has written, "It is as if the poets had felt that their mission was to give the people spiritual nourishment and a spiritual tonic to support them on their way." Adam Mickiewicz, with his expressive, nationalistic verse, emerged as the chief poetic voice of the Polish émigré community and exemplified the dominant traits of the movement. Besides his love for Poland, the other chief influences on his style were the spiritualism of the mystic Andrew Towiański and the notion of the poet as freedom fighter, at that time most closely identified with the English poet Lord Byron. Mickiewicz's *Ballady i romanse* (1822), a collection of ballads and romances, marked the beginning of Polish Romanticism; *Dziady* (1832; *Forefathers' Eve),* a celebration of the Polish past as well the most important work of the Polish theater, and *Pan Tadeusz; Czyli, ostatni zajazd na Litwie* (1834; *Master Thaddeus; or, The Last Foray in Lithuania)* reflect his devotion to and concern for the liberation of his homeland. In these and numerous other pieces Mickiewicz combined mystical, prophetic, folkloristic, and religious elements to convey his hope for the future of Poland. As literary historians point out, Mickiewicz's importance also lies in the fact that he popularized several new or long-unused genres— for example, the ballad, the satire, and the confessional autobiography—in addition to expanding the language of Polish literature to include biblical, regional, stylized, and archaic words, and stressing syntax and rhythm over traditional meter. A patriot above all else, he renounced his literary career while in its prime and devoted the last twenty years of his life to politics.

Zygmunt Krasiński, a friend of Mickiewicz, also wrote to inspire political and religious hope in his countrymen. Unlike his predecessors, who called for victory at whatever price in Poland's struggle against Russia, Krasiński emphasized Poland's spiritual role in its fight for independence, advocating an intellectual rather than a military superiority. His works best exemplify the Messianic movement in Poland: in two early dramas, *Nie-boska komedyia* (1835; *The Undivine Comedy)* and *Irydion* (1836; *Iridion),* as well as in the later *Psalmy przyszłości* (1845), he asserted that Poland, like Christ, was specifically chosen by God to carry the world's burdens, to suffer, and eventually to be resurrected. Deeply influenced by Mickiewicz's poetry, but, like his friend Krasiński, more mystical than political by nature, Juliusz Słowacki is also regarded as one of the greatest Polish Romantic poets and dramatists. In his best-known works, the poems *Anhelli* (1838) and *Król Duch* (1847) and the dramas *Ballad-*

yna (1862), *Kordian* (1899), and *Lilla Weneda* (1869), Słowacki explored the course of Polish history, particularly the nation's subjugation and partition by other European nations. Intended to offer solutions to Poland's political problems, Słowacki's works convey his belief that independence could be won only through the cooperation of the Polish people and their spiritual purity. Thus, his *Anhelli,* a symbolic poem about a group of exiles, exemplifies his apprehension about the squabbles that jeopardized the unity of the Polish émigreés, while *Beniowski* (1841), one of his most acclaimed poems, is a satire that ridicules the émigrés' ideas and plans to free Poland. While Mickiewicz, Krasiński, and Słowacki are generally considered the three leading bards of Polish Romanticism, the movement encompassed numerous other figures including philosophers, theologians, scientists, and critics. Literary historians have continued to write about the writers, works, and ideas of Polish Romanticism—as Czesław Miłosz has described it, "A jungle of criss-crossing currents, of madly daring ideas, of self-pity and national arrogance, and of unsurpassed brilliancy of poetic technique."

REPRESENTATIVE WORKS

Zygmunt Krasiński

> *Nie-boska komedyia* 1835
> > [*The Undivine Comedy*]
> *Irydion* 1836
> > [*Iridion*]
> *Psalmy przyszłości* 1845

Adam Mickiewicz

> **Poezje, I* 1822
> ***Poezje, II* 1823
> *Sonety* 1826
> > [*Sonnets*]
> *Oda do Młodości* 1827
> > [*Ode to Youth*]
> *Konrad Wallenrod* 1828
> > [*Conrad Wallenrod*]
> *Dziady, III* 1832
> > [*Forefathers' Eve*]
> *Księgi Narodu polskiego i Pielgrzymstwa
> > polskiego* 1832
> > > [*The Books of the Polish Nation and
> > > the Polish Pilgrimage*]
> *Pan Tadeusz; Czyli, ostatni zajazd na Litwie*
> > 1834
> > > [*Master Thaddeus; or, The Last Foray
> > > in Lithuania*]

Juliusz Słowacki

> *Anhelli* 1838
> *Beniowski* 1841
> *Król Duch* 1847
> *Mazepa* 1851
> *Balladyna* 1862
> *Marja Stuart* 1862
> > [*Mary Stuart*]
> *Fantazy* 1867
> *Lilla Weneda* 1869
> *Kordian* 1899

*This work includes *Ballady i romanse.*
**This work includes Parts II and IV of *Dziady.*

OVERVIEWS

George Brandes (essay date 1903)

SOURCE: "The Romantic Literature of Poland in the Nineteenth Century (1886)," in *Poland: A Study of the Land, People, and Literature,* William Heinemann, 1904, pp. 192-308.

[*Brandes, a Danish literary critic and biographer, was the principal leader of the intellectual movement that helped to bring an end to Scandinavian cultural isolation. He believed that literature reflects the spirit and problems of its time and that it must be understood within its social and aesthetic context. Brandes's major critical work,* Hovedstroomninger i det 19de aarhundredes litteratur *(1871;* Main Currents in Nineteenth Century Literature, *1872-90), won him admiration for his ability to view literary movements within the broader context of all of European literature. In the following excerpt from a work first published in 1903, he discusses some influences on Polish Romantic literature, comparing it with Romantic literature of other countries.*]

The period 1820-1850 was the richest and most important as regards poetry [of Polish Romanticism]. And in this period the three fundamental factors which determined the literature were evidently these: the national character, European romanticism, and the exceptional political situation.

The national character, as it had been developed down to this period, was specially adapted for the influences of romanticism. It was intelligent and magnanimous, splendour-loving and visionary, with a propensity to chivalrous virtues and religious aspirations. Then as now it lacked the ballast which the Germanic nations have in their native phlegm, and the Latin races in their native logic. It was akin to the French in its fickleness, different from it in the nature of its capriciousness; for the Frenchman is capricious when his native rationalism leads him to shatter his historic heritage, the Pole when temperament or enthusiasm carries him away. It was akin to the Italian in its idolatry and its vivacity, but differed from it in its want of shrewd political sense, and of that plastic tendency which has made the inhabitants of Italy pagans under all forms of religion.

When European Romanticism reached this nation, it did not fare as in Germany, where it was engendered in the non-political societies of provincial towns, and allied itself to the indefinite idealism, the want of social feeling, and the aversion to reality, which had laid hold of the minds of thinking men—nor as in England, where Romanticism found itself in direct antagonism with the ingrained bias of the people for the useful and the practical, and where it allied itself with the old Norse tendency to an indomitable independence and defiance in the free individual, even towards his fatherland—nor as in France or Italy, where a Latin and classical element, essentially foreign to Romanticism, prevented its conquest of the intellectual heart of the people, and limited it to a purely artistic intoxication of short duration.

In Poland, where the national character was peculiarly adapted to assimilate Romanticism, the common national misfortune had moreover given a romantic bias to minds. Romanticism, therefore, did not isolate souls either in egotism, as in Germany, or in wild independence, as in England, but bound them together in a visionary feeling of compatriotism. Neither was it contingent upon a dislike to reality, but upon the sense that the fatherland was already an unreality, something which must be believed in, and could not be seen with the bodily eye. Finally, the Latin element, even if stronger than in any other non-Latin country, was but an importation, and made no serious resistance.

Here, with far greater force than elsewhere, romantic enthusiasm swept away all barriers, spread out in far wider circles—because of the national character, which is not rational, but fantastically heroic—and harmonised far more thoroughly than elsewhere with existing times and conditions—because of the national fate, which occupies all thoughts, and round which all daydreams revolve.

We shall recognise this peculiarity most plainly if we turn our attention to countries and literatures where the political situation was akin to that of Poland. It is true that a counterpart is nowhere to be found, but there are analogies more or less strong.

Let us consider, for instance, the Flemish literature, which arose in Belgium about 1830. It resorts to great historical romance in the style of Walter Scott, in order to excite Flemish national feeling. Henry Con-

science's romance, *The Lion of Flanders,* is the leading work, a book of the same kind as Rzewuski's *Memoirs of Soplica*. This literature is strongest in the pure lyric. But it is the product of a peaceful nation, a nation not prone to exaltation. It is a literature of the common people, which clings to the earth, not like the Polish, a soaring and flaming poetry, which throws its light over the whole horizon, and loses itself in the clouds.

Or let us consider Finland, with her Runeberg, who has analogies with Mickiewicz. *Fanrick Stals Sägner,* which treats of the contest for Finland in the year 1810, is certainly the nearest European counterpart to *Pan Tadeusz.* The author describes the Finnish national character, as it appeared during the war, just as *Pan Tadeusz* presents the Polish national character of the same time. There is no national hatred in any of these poems. The only Russian officer who figures in the Finnish poetic cycle, Kulneff, is the type of a noble enemy, high-minded and gentle; the only Russian officer who figures in the Polish epic, Rykow, is an honourable man, incorruptible, faithful, and brave.

What is lacking in Runeberg is the lofty national self-criticism, which distinguishes Mickiewicz, and the poets of Poland as a whole. His Finns are heroes, heroes "in winter dress," heroes in tatters sometimes, but always heroes. They have almost no faults. In spite of all their glowing love for their countrymen, the poets of Poland are far more synthetic, painting the frail as well as the strong side of the inherited character of their nation. To be sure they have had a far richer material at their command; they were not an undeveloped people like the Finns, whose language even lacked all literary form and polish, but a people with the lights and shadows of a thousand years of civilisation.

The peculiar situation of Poland necessarily modifies the points of view from which we contrast Classicism and Romanticism elsewhere.

When we read Mickiewicz's poem, *Romanticism,* with its dogma that the superstitions of the people are worth more than classical rationalism, we note in this enthusiasm for a belief in ghosts, and this hatred for cold acumen, which observes through the microscope, something which is common to Romanticism in all countries, nay, something wearisomely romantic. The romanticists everywhere feel a satisfaction in leading the swelling currents of new emotion into spiritual beliefs and popular superstition. Everywhere also there is a connection between the advent of Romanticism in literature, and the great religious reaction of the nineteenth century against the indifference to all dogma of the eighteenth.

But there are two circumstances which nevertheless give Polish Romanticism a peculiar character. Firstly, the opposing catholic tendency had not the mediæval feudal stamp as elsewhere. Secondly, the double contrast of Classicism and Romanticism, Liberalism and Conservatism, did not obtain here as in so many other countries. In France, for instance, Romanticism from the beginning was suspected not only as hostile to enlightenment but as legitimist. Victor Hugo's first odes and ballads were both anti-Voltairean and loyal. The most distinguished opponent of the Romanticists was the celebrated liberal, Armand Carrel, the recognised leader of the French republicans. In Poland, on the contrary, the opponents of Romanticism (men like Sniadecki, Beku, Osinski) were usually officials, and conservative in their political convictions, while from the very first Romanticism was rightly regarded as oppositional.

As the recognised laureate of a whole nation in the first half of the nineteenth century Mickiewicz occupies a position, which finds a parallel in that of Oehlenschlæger and Tegnér. But apart from all other dissimilarities, there is this difference between Mickiewicz and the two Norse poets, that when the latter employed their talents to glorify their nation, they chose the material of its legendary world or worked out themes from its antiquity, its middle ages, or even a more distant past, substantially without ever describing the life they themselves had had the opportunity of observing, while Mickiewicz, especially where he is at his best (as in *Pan Tadeusz* and certain parts of *Dziady*) reproduces a life he has seen with his own eyes, or a life the memory of which still hovers in the air about him.

This is the secret of his superiority over a whole army of contemporary national poets; it is this which gives his Romanticism and that of several of his contemporaries in Poland a comparatively modern stamp. At that time they did not yet feel in Europe that the poet must be the offspring of his age as a rule; they were too strongly attracted by distant times or foreign countries. The results in their descriptions of mankind, oftener than not, were beings who never existed and never could exist, beings whose spiritual life was created by the subtraction of a great many qualities which only modern men can have, and by the mechanical addition of qualities which the poet's reading had taught him were found in the past. Not in consequence of a correct theory, but by virtue of a sound instinct, Mickiewicz resorted to an old subject or a distant period only when political considerations made it easier for him to express what he had at heart, when the fundamental thought concealed itself behind an allegory, as is the case in *Grazyna* and *Wallenrod*.

Throughout the romantic literature of Poland, we find here and there traits so realistic that they do not seem to belong to the period. In some of the poets the observance of reality is carried so far, that they even introduce living or recently deceased persons into their poems. But that which is peculiarly Polish, is that hand in hand with the hankering after reality and futurity there is an unconquerable tendency to abstraction, allegory, and superstition. They are at once realists and spiritualists.

Two circumstances united to make their poems abstract and allegorical: first, the propensity to mysticism which lay in the inmost recesses of their souls and which, after having slumbered for a while, was easily awakened in them all, since they had been educated as Catholics from the first; in the next place, the political oppression, the consideration of the censorship which compelled them to describe their thoughts by circumlocution, and etherealise the outlines of the beings whom they painted.

There were, in particular, two great persons, at that time recently deceased, who had set the forces of imagination in motion all over Europe, but who aroused greater enthusiasm here than in any other country outside of their native lands: Napoleon and Byron.

It was the period when the cult of Napoleon was spreading over Europe. The real being was forgotten; genuine historical research had not yet begun. Napoleon had become a legend, which had deeply affected Henry Beyle, of which Victor Hugo, Béranger, and Heinrich Heine, each in his own way, made themselves priests, and which Thiers unfolded as a great epopee, accessible to the crowd. However little cause the Poles had to thank Napoleon, they had attached such great hopes to him, that after the desolation of the last years of his life and his impressive death had cast a transfiguring light over his life, they continued to pay honour to his shade as their liberator and saviour.

As the years passed by after his fall, he became the superhuman, supernatural man to the popular fancy. To the Romanticists he became an enigma. In those days the eighteenth century was regarded as the time of frivolous exposition. Here was a phenomenon which could not be judged by ordinary standards of intellectual observation. This awakened anew the quality of admiration, which had been lost in the preceding century. They thought that the prosaic English hated him because he was incomprehensible to them. No human being had been able to strike him down, nor any general but General *Frost* and General *Hunger*. In the preface to *Dawn (Przedswit)* Krasiński dates a new epoch from Napoleon. He says:—

"The age of Cæsar has returned in that of Napoleon. And the Christian Cæsar, who is superior to his predecessor by the achievement of nineteen centuries, and who was perfectly clear as to himself and the object for which the divine spirit, which leads the course of history, had sent him—dying, said on his rock of exile:

'The beginning of a new period will be reckoned from me.' These words contain a complete revelation concerning him and the future." Mickiewicz in his mystic period reveres Napoleon as a demi-god. He was no Gaul, he had no *esprit,* no wit, he felt himself drawn to the East. "Like all the greatest men," says Mickiewicz with a turn which foreshadows Disraeli, "Napoleon felt himself mysteriously at home in the East." His life demonstrated to Mickiewicz the existence of the invisible and mystic world. He believed in omens, and acted on them; he had direct intuition. Therefore he is the man of the Slav race; for the Slavs are a people of intuition. And thus for Mickiewicz he becomes the source of everything which the Polish people of that time admire.

Again and again Mickiewicz contends that Napoleon created Byron, and that Byron's life and glory had awakened Pushkin, so that Napoleon had also indirectly engendered the latter.

Since poetry, according to Mickiewicz's definition, is action, Napoleon's life becomes the loftiest poetry. Nay, even more; his mission was to liberate nations and thereby the whole world. (Preface to *L'Église et le Messianisme.*) And while St. Helena comes near to being a place of suffering like Golgotha, a glimmer of the Passion of Christ falls over the life and death of Napoleon.

The same propensity to uncritical transports, the same enthusiasm for the dazzling, is brought to light in the relations of these Slav poets to Byron. Thus poets so diverse as Mickiewicz and Słowacki meet on common ground for years in their Byronism. As Washington had made no impression on them while Napoleon fascinated them, so not one of them cared for Shelley, while Byron was on everybody's lips. They believed in all seriousness that Byron was the greatest lyric poet of England.

To make Byron's intellectual descent from Napoleon more obvious, Mickiewicz, who had evidently no knowledge of Wordsworth, or Coleridge, or Keats, or Shelley, wrote: "I regard it as certain that the flash which kindled the fire of the English poet came from the soul of Napoleon. How could we otherwise explain this man's existence in the midst of the jejune English literature of his day, a survival of the former century? . . . Byron's English contemporaries, in spite of the example of his genius and the influence emanating therefrom, produced nothing which can be compared therewith; and after the death of the poet, English literature sank back to the level of that of the past century."

Every sentence here is a blunder. Every one of the contemporaries of Byron named above, so far as poetry is concerned, several times reached his level, and in some respects even excelled him. But undeniably no one of them was so dazzling as he; they were neither dandies and *poseurs* in youth, nor theatrically heroic as men. Even he who would by no means rob Byron of his undying honour as a poet, and of his never-to-be-forgotten services as a friend of freedom, must feel that in Poland he is estimated as much by his false prestige as by his real greatness.

Nevertheless Napoleon and Byron have this merit in common, that they drew the Poles out of their purely national absorption. Polish literature had been national in the sixteenth century, but it had lacked the stamp of common humanity which makes a literature accessible to Europe at large; in the eighteenth century it had been cosmopolitan, but in such a fashion that it ended in the French imitation of classical culture without the deeper national stamp, which makes a literature interesting to Europe. Sniadecki was a friend and admirer of Delille, Bogomolec imitated the plays of Molière in a conventional and foreign style. This literature had become petrified in its slavish reverence for rules. Now all barriers were broken down. A time of national wandering had returned. The material boundaries were no longer fixed, and the intellectual boundaries widened at the same time. The Poles fought under Napoleon in the most diverse countries, and Napoleon's hosts brought troops of the most diverse races through Poland. So, too, in the intellectual world, when the nations mingled intellectually, the Poles found in the poetry of Byron the common European despair and thirst for liberty, supplemented them with their national peculiarities, and introduced them after the manner of Byron to their countrymen.

Of the great poets whom the romantic school in Germany had first revealed to the romanticists in all countries, Shakespeare and Dante made the greatest impression in Poland. Słowacki especially appropriates Shakespeare's style and manner of treatment. Nevertheless what made the most impression in Shakespeare were the horrible events, the murders and mutilations, which appear in some of the historical plays and legendary tragedies. The Polish fancy was attracted by that side of Shakespeare which is most strikingly represented in his earlier drama, *Titus Andronicus,* with its accumulated horrors. Only rarely is this tempered by the influence of the Shakespearean comedies, as in *Ballandyna.*

But perhaps the kinship which the Polish authors of this time felt for the great exiled Italian, whose poem was separated from them by so many centuries, is most significant. They were unhappy and exiled as he was; like him, they looked on at the political destruction of a state by acts of violence, and sought, as he did, consolation in penal sentences and prophecies. Krasiński especially is under his influence, and through Krasiński, Słowacki. It is the influence of the *Inferno* which can be most plainly traced. Only rarely, as in some of Krasiński's poems, does a form like that of Beatrice point towards a regenerate world and a happy life.

Now just as the special fate of the nation determines its receptiveness of foreign influence, it modifies, as we have seen, the point of view in judging of opposing forces like classicalism and romanticism, reaction and progress. It acts on the character of the literature so strongly, because it first acts on that of the writers.

They have much in common. They are all of aristocratic birth, all educated in the Roman Catholic Church, all passionate patriots. But they have this in common especially, that they all left their country between twenty and thirty years of age, and never returned. Even those authors among them who had not taken part in the rebellion of 1830, went away to a foreign land in order to write freely. Therefore they all become emigrants and pilgrims, work as leaders who have no firm connection with their people, and are never sure of a following, and live in a state of hope constantly deferred as to a general revolution in European politics.

All this together evoked a political Romanticism of a special kind, very different from the reactionary German and the humanitarian French varieties.

But what especially interests us in these men is to note the influence of the emigrant's life on the emotional life of the author.

They are enthusiasts by nature, and as romanticists, enthusiasts by theory. The emigration gives their emotional life something morbid, impatient, meaninglessly restless, because it doubles its exaltation.

Let us see what forms an elemental emotion like love takes on with them.

Mickiewicz, who had long been in love with Eva Ankwiczova, had even been religiously affected by her childlike faith, nay, by her visions—she had seen him in white robes with a lamb in his arms—suddenly leaves Rome just as Eva's father is on the point of giving his consent to their union, which he had for some time forbidden, and never again seeks to see his loved one, the memory of whom nevertheless fills his chief work, *Pan Tadeusz.*

Krasiński, who had paid homage to his friend, Madam Delphine Potocka, in the most extravagant language as his soul's sister, his muse, &c., as a minor, abandons his loved one in obedience to his father, and marries another lady in accordance with his father's wish. But at the same time he writes to the deserted lady, whom he sings in his poem, *The Dawn*: "Pray for me, that my eternal love for thee may not drag me down to hell. Pray that I may sometime fight my way to God in heaven to meet thee again!"

Słowacki becomes acquainted with Maria Wodzinska, while in Madam Patteg's *pension* on the lake of Geneva. Both the two young people cherish a strong passion for each other, and Słowacki's delicate and intellectual poem, *In Switzerland,* survives as a memorial of the happy hours of this love in beautiful surroundings. But the middle-aged daughter of Madam Patteg, Eglantine, who is enamoured of Słowacki, languishes and raves in her jealousy, and makes scenes. This is enough to make the poet draw back from his beloved, and the Wodzinski family depart. Słowacki moves over to the other side of the lake of Geneva, writes a poem to Eglantine, *The Accursed,* and then returns to her again.

The passions, indeed, seem strong, but the characters are weak. These poets leave their loved ones, not to save themselves from the consequences of passion, nor from fear of ties (like Goethe), nor because they have ceased to love, or feel themselves drawn in another direction; they behave as if they had become a little unhinged.

As nomads or emigrants they are dependent, not lords of their fate, and far too fantastical to lay out a practical plan of life. They have no abiding place, no home. Their upheaval from their paternal soil affects their characters, makes them unstable, and increases their propensity to a mystic intellectual life.

When in the beginning of the forties, Towiański, a Polish nationalist visionary, a cross between Père Enfantin and Cagliostro, suddenly appears among them, most of them fall under his power. And even those who do not follow him, become none the less mystics, at least at some period in their life. They die young, worn out long before old age, either in monastic subjection, like the once indomitably defiant Słowacki, or, like Krasiński, in a mental condition of uninterrupted melancholy, to which he gave expression in the words: "Thy people has been given to other races to eat, for the renewal of their blood."

They were all religiously inclined or religiously educated. They expected that an object was to be accomplished directly or indirectly in every great event, consequently also in all that most nearly concerned them; they traced a divine plan in what they experienced in life. They did not understand that a nation could be annihilated, blotted out from the number of the living. When these Roman Catholics looked out over human life and history, they could not conceive that the bad and the hard-hearted, the cruel and the ruthless, should prosper so greatly, and that God should make no sign. They thought that the Almighty must have concealed a mysterious meaning in all things, so that at last everything must turn to good.

If they believed it possible to decipher this meaning they became preachers, seers, and prophets; when they despaired of finding this, they held their peace in disconsolate grief. But all their thoughts and dreams revolved about the mysterious significance of the great shipwreck their State had suffered.

There is something deeply romantic in this. The romantic intellect is . . . a kind of atavism. It questions, as men in remote superstitious times did. It asks for the significance of what happens, while the modern intellect asks for its cause. Thus these minds hardly ever seek the causes of Poland's fate, but they seek with anguish, with poetic frenzy, and the added passion of the religious visionary, to penetrate the darkness, to learn the significance of that fate, and phantasy, enthusiasm, and passion give the answer.

Generally they start from certain historical assertions as dogmas. In the past of their nation we note traits of character, peculiar and important, to be found in no other nation. These traits emanated from pre-historic Slav antiquity, and the future of the nation depended on loyalty to these primitive national institutions (the assemblies of the people, and the Slav communism in property, although the latter is more Russian than Polish). The misfortune of the nation was due to its defection from these. In other words, they fastened on a little group of cognate ideas and principles, which, as Spasovicz has expressed it, being inherent in the nation from its origin should indicate its *vocation*. The great and learned historian of that time, *Lelewel,* a writer somewhat earlier than the Romantic school, and one who in many respects had a very strong influence on their fundamental theories, formulated this theory, which for one or two generations was undisputed in Poland.

It might seem that the poets would have served their people better if they, with their greater insight into the powers which are effective in history, had presented the causes of the disappearance of the nation as a State; their readers would then have gained some insight into the means of withstanding the national decay, and of aiding in a resurrection. But, in reality, their poetry, by its very obscure and prophetic character, has had a greater bearing on the future of the nation than a lucid or even a logical and convincing poetry could have had. Their overexaltation which explained nothing, but which was in itself so explicable, inspired readers with an enthusiasm which, in the political conditions they were in, was very useful, nay, necessary. It inspired perseverance, self-reliance, firm faith in the future, and obstinate optimism, which were so much the more remarkable, as no country seemed likely to offer a more fruitful soil for pessimism.

It is as if the poets had felt that their mission was to give the people spiritual nourishment and a spiritual tonic to support them on their way, even if this should lead them on for some hundreds of years. Therefore in their works they concentrated all their thoughts upon their own nation, condensed and compressed patriotism, hope, hatred of treason and wrong, confidence in the final victory of the right, focussing these emotions round a common centre in a perfectly unique fashion. Hence they are not seekers of truth but soothsayers.

In this way their poetry acquired a peculiar stamp both religious and artistic. The idea of nationality which permeates everything with them, was embraced with a religious heartiness in its essence, and the contest for it was accepted as a duty of a religious nature.

Thus it came to pass that the Polish poetry of the Romantic period, which superficially gives such a defective picture of the condition of the country and of the people, taken as a whole constitutes a sort of modern Bible, an Old Testament with its books of the Judges and the Prophets, with patriarchal descriptions (as we find in Rzewuski or in *Pan Tadeusz*), with psalms (like Krasiński's), here and there with representations of a Judith, of a struggle of the Maccabees, or of a persecuted Job, and now and then with a hymn of love, more ethereal, but far weaker than that of old Palestine.

The whole may be regarded as a collection of national books of devotion.

The literature most distinctly assumes this character from the time (1830) when the Polish nation next conceives hopes, rises, and is crushed, and when its young generation is sent to Siberia, and its poets emigrate, so that we get three kinds of Polish literature—that of those who were transported, of those who emigrated, and of those who remained at home.

In the eyes of the Poles the cause of Poland, far from sinking from this moment, becomes for them the holy cause, the country the holy country, the people the martyr people, the people of freedom who suffer for the whole of humanity. The symbolic importance they had once given to Napoleon as the saviour of the nations, Poland itself now assumes, only the picture shines with still more glowing colours.

Stephen Garczynski writes thus during the cannonade of the redoubts of Warsaw:—

"O my nation! As the Saviour's wounded head for ever impressed its bloody image upon a veil, so wilt thou, my nation, stamp the bloody image of thy fate upon the whole of this generation. Thou wilt throw this generation into the face of Europe as were it Veronica's veil, and the history of thy suffering will be read thereupon. And the time will come, ye nations of Europe! when your eyes and thoughts will be fixed as if by enchantment on the bloody image of the crucified nation."

Thus also cries the Abbot in the second part of Mickiewicz's *Dziady* in the great vision scene, which symbolises the attitude of Russia, France, Prussia, and Austria towards Poland.

> He has risen, the tyrant—Herod! O Lord! see the whole of young Poland given over into the hands of Herod! what do I see? These white streaks are roads which cross one another, roads which are so long that they seem without end! Through deserts, through drifts of snow they all lead to the North. . . . See this multitude of sleighs, which drive away like clouds, which are driven by the wind, all in the same direction! O heavens, they are our children. . . .
>
> I see the whole of this troop of tyrants and executioners hastening to seize my fettered nation. The whole of Europe mocks at it: To judgment! The mob drags the innocent to judgment. Beings who are nothing but tongues, without hearts or arms, are their judges. And cries rise from all sides: 'Gallus, it is Gallus who shall judge this nation!— Gallus has not found it guilty, he washes his hands. But the kings shout: Sentence it, give it to its executioners, the blood be upon us and our children. Release Barabbas. Crucify the Son of Mary, crucify him! He has scoffed at Cæsar!'
>
> Gallus has delivered up my nation; it is already bound; see, they exhibit its innocent face, soiled with blood as it is, with a crown of thorns in derision about the forehead. And the people hurry and Gallus shrieks: 'See, this is the free, independent nation.'
>
> O Lord, already I see the cross. How long, how long time yet shall my nation endure it? Lord, have pity on thy servant, give him strength that he may not fall down and expire on the way. His cross has arms so long that they stretch out over the whole of Europe; it is made of three nations which are as dried up as three withered trees.
>
> They drag my nation away, there it is, there on the throne of sacrifice. The crucified one says: 'I thirst,' and *Ragusa* offers him vinegar, and *Borus* refreshes him with gall, and his mother, Freedom, who stands at the foot of the cross, lifts her head and weeps. . . . And see, the Muscovite soldier runs up and thrusts his spear into his side.

This is the picture which impresses itself most deeply on the memory, when one has studied the Polish poetry of the first half of the century; the pale profile of a martyred nation which consoles itself that its suffering is its honour, and that it suffers for the common cause of nations.

But the value of this romantic literature is not limited to its significance for the people of Poland. Even if European ignorance of the language in which it is written has made it impossible for it to have a wide influence, it yet has influenced the minds of other literatures (as Mickiewicz influenced Pushkin, and as his *Book of the Polish Pilgrims* was copied by Lamennais in *The Word of a Believer*); even now surprises and charms the foreigner by the intensity of its emotional life, by its love for the ideal, and, when it attains its highest level, by its vigorous pictures of nature in Poland, of the steppes of the Ukraine, of the forests of Lithuania, and of the human life in recent and distant times, for which these surroundings form the natural and indispensable background.

This group of poems showed to foreign countries the presence of a sum of life, whose strength people had begun to doubt, and which they did not know how to value. We must always, in the first instance, demonstrate that we are alive; for, as Schiller says, the living are right. In the next place, we must know how to show to friends and enemies that we are in no respect behind them, that we dare to measure ourselves against them, and that we have other rights besides the mere right to live, namely, the rights that pertain to culture and to intellectual superiority.

In both these respects the romantic poets of Poland have demonstrated what it was necessary for them to show to Europe.

Czesław Miłosz (essay date 1969)

SOURCE: "Romanticism," in *The History of Polish Literature,* 1969. Reprint, second edition, by University of California Press, 1983, pp. 195-280.

[*A celebrated Polish poet, essayist, and novelist, Miłosz was awarded the Nobel Prize for Literature in 1980. In the following excerpt from a work first published in 1969, he explores some of the main historical events that contributed to the character of Polish Romanticism, asserting that "Polish Romanticism was thoroughly imbued with historicism."*]

After the third partition [of Poland], the *Respublica* disappeared from the map of Europe, but it survived in the minds of its inhabitants. To keep the three areas of the previous Polish state apart, profoundly united as they were by a common language and tradition, was no easy task for the occupying powers. And it was not only in Polish minds that the *Respublica* remained alive: as late as 1848, Karl Marx called for a reconstruction of Poland based on the map of 1772, i.e., before the first partition. The fall of the Polish state coincided in time with the rise of Napoleon Bonaparte's star, and the hopes of the Poles went out toward this man. Indeed, so great was the impact of the Napoleonic legend upon the Polish mentality that it entitles us to include several decades of Polish history in this [essay].

In 1797, a Polish Napoleonic legion was created in Italy. Loyal to the French ruler, in spite of his callous treatment of Polish troops (out of several thousands of Polish soldiers who were sent to Haiti to put down the revolution of Toussaint L'Ouverture, only a few hundred returned), the commanders of the Polish Napoleonic troops saw their fidelity recompensed in 1806 when the Napoleonic army entered Warsaw (in Prussian hands since the third partition). Napoleon's victory over Prussia led to the creation (in the treaty of Tilsit) of a tiny Polish state called the Duchy of Warsaw. A constitution modeled upon France's was granted by Napoleon in 1807, and the Napoleonic Code was introduced. The constitution recognized the peasants as free and equal citizens, but did not give them ownership of the land. This should be stressed, as it explains the difference between the peasant's status in central Poland and his status in Russia and in the Grand Duchy of Lithuania. After the Napoleonic constitution went into effect, the peasant in central Poland was still obliged to work in the fields of his landlord, but he was not a serf.

The new Duchy of Warsaw was soon engaged in a successful war against Austria on the side of Napoleon and in this way was able to extend its boundaries to incorporate the territory taken from the Austrian-occupied provinces. Later on, in 1812, the Duchy supplied Napoleon with some troops for his invasion of Russia. In his army of over a half-million men, Poles accounted for about 100,000.

Napoleon's defeat and withdrawal took the faithful Polish units west again, and their commander, Marshal Józef Poniatowski, died on the battlefield near Leipzig. When the Holy Alliance of monarchs assembled at the Congress of Vienna to redraw the map of Europe, one of the most difficult problems, in view of the subterranean tensions between the victors, was the Polish question. The powers agreed, at last, to recognize the creation of a Kingdom of Poland (known later in history as the "Congress Kingdom") bound in a personal union to Russia. The Russian czar was to be crowned king of Poland, but was to pledge that his rule would respect local law and the parliament. Thus, an autocratic czar was to be a constitutional monarch in Poland. The paradox inherent in such an arrangement proved later to be the seed of failure. Russia, Prussia, and Austria retained large areas of the old *Respublica*'s territory. Unable to settle a troublesome dispute over Kraków, the Congress proclaimed it a free city under the international supervision of the three neighboring powers. It remained thus from 1815 to 1846.

The Kingdom of Poland, whose nominal head was Czar Alexander I (crowned the Polish king), possessed a strong army, trained mostly by former Napoleonic officers who were magnanimously forgiven their fighting against Russia. The army was the "pet" of the Czar's brother, Grand Duke Constantine, an unbalanced, if not half-insane man, who resided in Warsaw and behaved not unlike a boy playing with tin soldiers. Inhuman discipline in the army led to many desperate acts, including suicide, on the parts of both officers and subordinates. Grand Duke Constantine (who appears often in Polish literature) had, probably, a kind of passion for Poland. In any case, he cannot be held responsible for the proliferation of secret police "services"—of various kinds; these were fostered by Russian civil commissars such as the famous Novosiltsov. Steadily increasing friction weakened the already tenuous connection between the administration and the parliament, not to speak of public opinion, and reflected Alexander I's gradual abandonment of a liberal policy in Russia. Yet, for a decade and a half, the precarious order of things arranged at the Congress of Vienna gave the Poles, regardless of the province they inhabited, considerable opportunities for cultural and economic development. Much was done for the economy in the Kingdom by the minister of finance, Lubecki; while the network of schools created by the Commission for National Education freely continued its activity. A new university in Warsaw was founded in 1816. The University of Wilno (situated in the territory annexed to the Russian Empire) was considered the best institution of learning in all Russia, while an excellent new *lycée* was established in Krzemieniec in Volhynia. Kraków, of course, preserved its traditions as an ancient capital, and its university profited from the reforms introduced by the men of the Enlightenment. Generally speaking, in both the Kingdom of Poland and in the Russian-occupied provinces there were no attempts to curtail teaching or publishing in the Polish language.

Around 1820, a movement among the youth, the expression of which in literature came to be called Romanticism, spread through Poland, and it took on organizational forms similar to those of the revolutionary brotherhoods in Germany. Clandestine contacts were established with young Russians, who, after their attempt at seizing power in December of 1825, were to be known under the name of Decembrists. When the new czar, Nicholas I, unleashed his rule of unmitigated police terror upon the country, the revolutionary spark was ready to flare. In November 1830, a group of young officers of the Polish army revolted and, during a dramatic November night, succeeded in bringing Warsaw over to their side. The insurrection of 1830 amounted, in fact, to a war between Poland and Russia. The parliament voted an act which dethroned the Czar as king of Poland. Military activities lasted practically throughout the year of 1831, but Poland was at last defeated. During the so-called Great Emigration which followed, several thousands of officers and soldiers and a number of the most active intellectuals left the country, migrating first to Germany, then to France. Paris, for some two decades, became the center of Polish cultural and political life. The order upheld by the Holy Alliance of monarchs was looked upon by Polish writers and political leaders as a diabolical conspiracy against the peoples of Europe. Many of them placed their stakes, therefore, on revolutionary groups in Western Europe like the Italian *Carbonari* and the French Utopian Socialists. The Emigration was divided within itself: The conservatives grouped around the so-called "Hôtel Lambert" (a private residence in Paris). They were partisans of a constitutional monarchy for Poland and members of the aristocratic Establishment. The democrats, whose main organization was the Democratic Society, placed their hopes in a revolution of European peoples against the tyrants. Still further to the left were the Polish People's Communes (*Gromady Ludu Polskiego*), composed mostly of former rank-and-file soldiers residing on the mainland of England and on the island of Jersey. They advocated a revolution in Poland that would lead to a division of landed estates among the peasants in the spirit of Christian communism. The causes of the defeat of the 1830 revolution became the subject of infinite debates among the *émigrés*. According to radical democrats, the Poles could have won by proclaiming economic freedom for the peasants, arming them, and carrying their revolutionary fervor to the Russian masses. All Polish writings of the period abound in mystical appeals to the Napoleonic myth as a force which would abolish the reactionary order oppressing Europe.

The Kingdom of Poland, after the insurrection of 1830-1831, preserved but weak vestiges of autonomy. The University of Warsaw was closed down in 1831. The University of Wilno, regarded as a hot-bed of dangerous ideas, soon shared the same fate. The czarist government also began a campaign of persecution directed against the Greek Catholic Church in the former Grand Duchy of Lithuania, a church of Byelorussian peasants. The very existence of non-Orthodox Eastern Slavs was considered an offense to the principle of unity between the czarist throne and the Orthodox Church, a unity vital for the Russian monarchy.

The 1830s, in spite of the loss of the most energetic leaders, who had escaped to the West, witnessed some abortive conspiracies, which grew in force with the advent of the 1840s. A Roman Catholic priest from the neighborhood of Lublin, Father Piotr Ściegienny, succeeded in weaving a vast clandestine network among the peasants with a program of communist revolution. His propaganda booklet was conceived as a presumed letter from the Pope to the peasants, calling for banishment of the lords and for fraternity with the Russian peasant as a brother in the same fate. The participants

in that conspiracy were sent to hard-labor camps in Siberia. There, some of them became Dostoevsky's cell mates, and he mentions them in his *Notes from the House of the Dead*. The unrest in Poland increased with the approach of the fateful year of 1848, the "spring of nations." Edward Dembowski, a young philosopher of aristocratic origin, a brilliant writer in the spirit of the Hegelian Left, was one of the leaders of the short-lived revolution in the free city of Kraków in 1846, and he died in a clash of the crowd with the Austrian troops. He had tried in vain to avert an anti-revolutionary scheme of the Austrian authorities, namely, a peasant revolt in southern Poland. The peasants attacked the manors, massacring their owners (sometimes even sawing them in half). Their leader, Jakub Szela (a character who turns up often in the literature of the twentieth century), acted at the instigation of the Austrian officials, for whom a peasant revolt was a tool to drive a wedge into Polish solidarity based on patriotic aspirations—the gentry being frightened to death, after the peasant rebellion, of the "dark masses."

In 1848, an insurrection broke out in Prussian-occupied Poland, and, for a while, battles took place between Prussian troops and Polish volunteer detachments. The government of the Hapsburg Empire, pressured by revolutions in Vienna (and Lwów), granted Galician peasants the right to own land and freed them from obligatory duties to their lords. The revolution in Hungary attracted many Poles, among them a general of the artillery, Józef Bem, who became one of the chief commanders of the Hungarian revolutionary army and to this day has remained for the Hungarians a half-legendary figure, known as "Daddy Bem." In Italy, the leading Polish Romantic poet, Adam Mickiewicz, organized a small legion composed of artists and intellectuals that fought for the Italian cause against the Austrians in Lombardy, and then with Garibaldi in the defense of republican Rome. In 1849 Mickiewicz founded an international socialist newspaper in Paris, *La Tribune des Peuples*. The complete breakdown of the European revolutionary movement evoked despair and dejection among the Poles, but soon new hopes were born with the outbreak of the Crimean War, allying Turkey with France and England against Russia. A Polish legion was formed in Constantinople comprising Russian war prisoners of Polish descent. Adam Mickiewicz was active there, too, and together with his friend Armand Lévy, brought to short-lived fruition his idea of a Jewish legion, the first Jewish military unit in modern times. Russia's defeat in the Crimean War and the death of the "gendarme-czar," Nicholas I, released a movement of the liberal intelligentsia in Russia pressuring for decisive reforms. The emancipation of the peasants was proclaimed in 1861 (the czar's edict did not cover central Poland, where the situation of the peasant had been different ever since the Napoleonic constitution of 1807). Thwarted expectations of national autonomy in Poland resulted in increasing unrest among Warsaw's population, where a clandestine revolutionary committee had begun to act. It owed its organization primarily to a poet, Apollo Korzeniowski, father of the future English novelist, Joseph Conrad. Clashes between Warsaw crowds and Russian troops occurred more and more frequently. An unwise decision of Count Alexander Wielopolski, the civil governor of Poland and a most influential figure among the Polish conservatives, led to the outbreak of a new Polish insurrection in January 1863. Wielopolski had advised Russian military authorities to draft all young men suspected of political activity for some twenty years of service. The Provisional National Government, which grew out of the clandestine revolutionary committee, announced the economic emancipation of the peasants. The Russian troops fought throughout 1863—against detachments of guerrillas composed not only of Poles but also of some Russians, Germans, French, and Italians, followers of Garibaldi. A meeting of workers in London, organized by Karl Marx to express solidarity with the Poles, culminated in the creation of the First Socialist International. But the insurrection of 1863 was doomed in advance by lack of arms and by the nearly complete indifference of the peasants to the appeals of their compatriots. Guerrilla detachments included only the nobles, the petty gentry, artisans, and some workers of budding industrial enterprises. Only in Lithuania was peasant participation considerable. "Pacification" meant for Poland the gallows, deportations to Siberia, and ruinous taxation of landed estates. In its policy, the czarist government applied principles elaborated by certain Russian Pan-Slavists according to whom the upper layers of "Latinized" Polish society were traitors to the cause of Slavdom, as opposed to the "good" (i.e., truly Slavic) Polish peasants. The peasants were told that the insurrection was an intrigue of the nobles directed against the benevolent czar who had emancipated the peasantry. In fact, however, it had been the manifesto of the Provisional National Government that had forced the hand of the czarist authorities, who then granted Polish peasants economic emancipation with slightly better conditions than in Russia. The year 1863 closed a whole era, that of Romanticism in politics and in literature. A constant looking forward toward a mythical upheaval of European nations was to be superseded by a call for sober concentration upon small economic and cultural tasks.

Heroic insurrections, participation in revolutionary movements all over Europe, retaliative executions carried out by the occupying powers, and deportations to Siberia unavoidably shaped the Polish mentality. These crucial events came at a time when modern nationalism was crystallizing under the impact of the French Revolution and German philosophy. In the old *Respublica* the line between "Polishness" and "non-Polishness" had been a blurred one. Skarga's *Sermons,*

for instance, contained hints of a messianic vocation assigned to the Poles, but this idea can be interpreted as stemming from an attachment to the state's institutions, rather than from a worship, on Skarga's part, of the "nation" as a spiritual unit. But when Poland lost her independence, the concept of "Polishness" gradually emerged as an ethereal entity requiring loyalty and existing even without embodiment in a state. It is extremely difficult to make an impartial appraisal of the Polish mentality in the period we are dealing with. If the history of the country can be called "abnormal," its thought and literature were no less so. An old tendency to idealize "golden freedom," which had distinguished Poland from her neighbors, the autocratic monarchies, underwent a mutation: enormous talents for self-pity were displayed, and Poland was presented as an innocent victim suffering for the sins of humanity. This new version contained the additives of Napoleonic myth and Utopian Socialism. Hatred for the main occupying power, Russia, inclined the Poles to interpret the conflict between the two countries as a struggle between the forces of light (democracy), on the one hand, and those of darkness (tyranny), on the other. Russia was not "European"; it was "Asiatic," marked forever by the Tartar yoke. In all fairness we should add that such views were not the property of the Poles alone, as a leading revolutionary, Karl Marx, considered the Slavs as born slaves with the exception of two freedom-loving nations: the Poles and the Serbs.

To place Polish literature of this time in a proper perspective is a task that has never been brought to a conclusion. A jungle of criss-crossing currents, of madly daring ideas, of self-pity and national arrogance, and of unsurpassed brilliancy in poetic technique asks for constantly renewed explorations. If the term Romanticism is treacherous, denoting as it does different phenomena in each country, it would be doubly dangerous to apply its most widely accepted meaning to Polish literature. The struggle against the classical rules of good taste, which began in Poland (as in France) around 1820, concealed, from its inception, political undertones. Contrary to the brand of Romanticism which in many countries was identified with a withdrawal of the individual into his own interior world, Romanticism in Poland acquired an extremely activist character and was clearly a consequence of many ideas of the Enlightenment. Perhaps, after all, Prince Metternich, an archreactionary, an evil demon for the progressive intelligentsia of his time, gave the best definition of the new ferment in his secret memorandum written for Czar Alexander I in 1820:

> The progress of the human mind has been extremely rapid in the course of the last three centuries. This progress having been accelerated more rapidly than the growth of wisdom (the only counterpoise to passions and to errors), a revolution prepared by

the false systems, the fatal errors into which many of the most illustrious sovereigns of the last half of the eighteenth century fell, has at last broken out in a country [France] advanced in knowledge, and enervated by pleasure, in a country inhabited by people whom one can only regard as frivolous, from the facility with which they comprehend and the difficulty they experience in judging calmly.

In what, according to Prince Meternich, does the evil of modern time consist?

This evil may be described in one word—presumption; the natural effect of the rapid progression of the human mind toward the perfecting of so many things. This it is which at the present day leads so many individuals astray, for it has become an almost universal sentiment.

Religion, morality, legislation, economy, politics, administration, all have become common and accessible to everyone. Knowledge seems to come by *inspiration;* experience has no value for the presumptuous man; faith is nothing to him; he substitutes for it a pretended *individual conviction,* and to arrive at this conviction, dispenses with all inquiry and with all study; for these means appear too trivial to a mind which believes itself strong enough to embrace at one glance all questions and all facts. Laws have no values for him, because he has not contributed to make them, and it would be beneath a man of his parts to recognize the limits traced by rude and ignorant generations. Power resides in *himself;* why should he submit to that which was only useful for the man deprived of light and knowledge? That which, according to him, was required in an age of weakness cannot be suitable in an age of reason and vigor, amounting to universal perfection, which the German innovators designate *by the idea, absurd in itself, of the Emancipation of the People!* Morality itself he does not attack openly, for without it he could not be sure for a single moment of his own existence; but he interprets its essence after his own fashion, and allows every other person to do so likewise provided that other person neither kills nor robs him.

In thus tracing the character of the presumptuous man, we believe we have traced that of the society of the day, composed of like elements, if the denomination of society is applicable to an order of things which only tends in principle towards individualizing all the elements of which society is composed.

Presumption makes every man the guide of his own belief, the arbiter of laws according to which he is pleased to govern himself or to *allow* someone else to govern him and his neighbors; it makes him, in short, *the sole judge* of his own faith, his own action, and the principles according to which he guides them.

Metternich's memorandum could have been presented to the police for use as a miniature handbook on rebel psychology. But he gives more detailed advice too, being perspicacious enough to notice the multifaceted philosophical, literary, and political character of Romanticism:

> The real aim of the idealists of the party is *religious and political fusion,* and this being analyzed is nothing else but creating in favor of each individual an existence entirely independent of all authority, or any other will than his own, an idea absurd and contrary to the nature of man, and incompatible with the need of human society. . . . It is principally *the middle classes of society* which this moral gangrene has affected, and it is only among them that the real heads of the party are found.

If we keep in mind that the authority so praised by Metternich was, for the Polish rebels, a foreign authority, opposed to their patriotic feelings, we receive a portrait that delineates perfectly the nature of Romanticism in Poland.

A constant preoccupation with postulated political change explains the fondness Polish Romantics displayed for the philosophy of history. Their themes were elaborated sometimes in opposition to, sometimes in agreement with, Hegelian thought. In any case, Polish Romanticism was thoroughly imbued with historicism. One more observation should be made: though Shelley called the poet a lawgiver for humanity, few people in England, we may suspect, took that claim seriously. As a consequence of national misfortunes, the reading public in Poland gave literal acceptance to a similar claim on the part of their own poets. The poet was hailed as a charismatic leader, the incarnation of the collective strivings of the peoples; thus, his biography, not only his work, entered the legend. We may guess that a transference of the Napoleonic myth of a "providential man" into the realm of literature was at work here. Among foreign writers, no one more fully than Lord Byron, as a poet and a man of action, filled these deep emotional needs. Byron's fame in his native country was insignificant if we compare it with the near worship surrounding him in the Slavic countries. The three Polish Romantic poets, Adam Mickiewicz, Juliusz Słowacki, and Zygmunt Krasiński, were acclaimed as national bards, and these greatly magnified figures dominated several literary generations—a somewhat arbitrary triad, as they were not all writers of equal talent.

CLASSICISM AND PRE-ROMANTICISM

During the first two decades of the century, Warsaw dictated literary fashions. As in France, the classical principles of good taste were still the rule, not only in literature but also in theater and in the fine arts. There was a marked division into high-brow and low-brow genres. Poetry and versified drama (submitted to rigorous rules) belonged to the former class; while the sentimental novels and "bourgeois dramas" gradually invading the market were ranged in the latter. The bourgeois drama originated in Germany, and the most disparate works, starting with the so-called "horrible products of a sick imagination" like Schiller's *The Robbers* and ending with the prolific and shallow production of Kotzebue, were lumped together under this label. The Warsaw literati for a while successfully blocked the influx of such suspect novelties, which offended their rationalism and classical tastes. The classicists organized themselves into a "Society of X's" (*Towarzystwo Iksów*) and held gatherings where literary works and new plays staged in Warsaw were discussed. To exert pressure as a body, all of them signed their articles of criticism with an X. Perhaps the most important member of the X's was Kajetan Koźmian (1771-1856), a rich landowner, a senator, a poet, a translator, and a very active participant, as were all his colleagues, in the Society of the Friends of Learning. An excellent craftsman of late classical or, as it is sometimes called derogatorily, "pseudoclassical" Polish verse, Koźmian still makes pleasant reading, but his fate exemplifies the difficulties of writers who follow a moribund trend. For nearly twenty-five years, he worked on a long descriptive poem, *Polish Husbandry* (*Ziemiaństwo polskie*), comparable to Delille's imitations of Virgil's *Georgics* and composed in impeccable couplets; but by the time it was ready, works of that type were considered old-fashioned bores. Besides; Koźmian with his conservative and legitimist views and his extremely violent denunciations of Romanticism (much in the spirit of Metternich) made enemies for himself out of the young generation and was ridiculed by Mickiewicz as "an author of a thousand lines on planting peas."

Another luminary of the Society of X's was Ludwik Osiński (1775-1838), the author of graceful odes, a literary critic, for a while director of the Warsaw Theater, and a professor of literature at Warsaw University. More tolerant and open-minded than Koźmian, he acknowledged some literary value in the Germans of the *Sturm und Drang* period, commented favorably upon the brothers Schlegel, and even moderately praised Shakespeare. Franciszek Ksawery Dmochowski (1762-1808), . . . adapter of Boileau, translator of the *Iliad* and of Milton, died in Napoleonic Warsaw; but his son, Franciszek Salezy Dmochowski (1801-1871), became one of the most zealous defenders of the classical *status quo*. Stanisław Kostka Potocki (1752-1821) exemplifies another aspect of the period. The Warsaw literati, though accused by the young of undue respect for the established order, were, in fact, loyal inheritors of the Voltairian spirit. They directed their malice at superstitions, prejudices, and human folly much like their Enlightenment predecessors. They differed from them in renouncing larger political strivings. Potocki,

minister of education in the Congress Kingdom of Poland, a fervent Freemason, a supporter of the Society of the Friends of Learning, and one of the X's, wrote a kind of satirical novel which he had to publish anonymously, so violent was its attack on the clergy. The novel was entitled *A Journey to Dunceville* (*Podróż do Ciemnogrodu*, 1820*)*, and to our day *ciemnogród* in Polish has served to denote people of ultra-conservative views.

The Warsaw literati were particularly concerned with the theater. They dreamed of writing tragedies in verse (a genre also honored by Voltaire) and took for the greatest authorities such French codifiers of rules (for the neoclassical tragedy) as Jean François La Harpe (1739-1803). To understand what they were looking for in that genre, one may use the example of the most famous French painter of the Napoleonic era, Louis David. His was a painting of costume and gesture, where Frenchmen appeared as ancient Romans, or if specifically modern situations were celebrated (as, for example, in his large canvas, "The Death of Marat"), the characters were transformed into figures of an ancient tragedy. The Polish classicists believed that the fusion of contents taken from local history with rigorous, French-inspired form would result in a new literary genre, a national tragedy. For this reason they gave unreserved applause to Alojzy Feliński (1771-1820). A poet, a translator, a veteran of Kościuszko's uprising, and later on a professor of literature at the *lycée* of Krzemieniec, Feliński wrote a tragedy in verse, *Barbara Radziwiłł (Barbara Radziwiłłówna)*, performed in 1817 and even translated into French and German. The author's metrical inventiveness, without breaking out of thirteen-syllable rhymed couplets, proved itself within that framework. He used various combinations consisting either in parallelism between syntax and line or in anticlimaxes (for instance, a sentence broken by a caesura), etc. For his subject, Feliński chose a historical event of the sixteenth century. (As we have already remarked, the Poles turned toward their Golden Age as a kind of compensation.) The event, famous in its time and, for that reason, recorded copiously in literature, was not unlike the affair of Edward VIII and Mrs. Simpson in the twentieth century: the crown prince of Poland, son of King Sigismund I and the Italian princess, Bona Sforza, clandestinely married Barbara Radziwiłł, the daughter of a Lithuanian lord, but not of royal parentage. After the death of his father, when the prince was to ascend the throne as Sigismund August, violent opposition was voiced from the Senate—a demand was made that he either divorce his wife or abdicate. The leader of the anti-Radziwiłł faction was the queen mother, Bona. With great difficulty, the young king overcame innumerable intrigues, finally receiving the consent of the Diet to crown his wife, when suddenly, after a short illness, Barbara died. According to popular legend, since Bona was a vicious woman, skillful like all Renaissance Italians in the methods of poison and the dagger, she must have poisoned Barbara. This moving story of the royal love and despair of a king, who in his grief supposedly turned to a magician promising to show him the phantom of his beloved, acted powerfully upon popular imagination. Feliński studied historical documents, but to preserve the three unities he distilled a sort of extract, departing somewhat from facts and dates. He constructed a tragedy of conflict between passion and civic duty. As the action rises, the king is more and more cornered and at the climax finds three possibilities left to him: a civil war (his opponents are ready to attack the royal castle in Kraków), abdication (which for him would be a cowardly act), or divorce. He makes a very curious and very Polish decision: to avoid pressures from the lords in the Senate and to avert a civil war, he appeals to the Diet and promises to accept its verdict. But his victory in the Diet is turned to nothing when Barbara dies, poisoned. Throughout the five acts neither the passions of the king nor those of Barbara occupy the foreground, and the vicious Bona is perhaps the most vivid character. Contrasting figures of lords—one backs the king, another leads the rebels because of his anarchistic ambitions, still another is primarily concerned with the interests of the state as a whole—make us think of Kochanowski's *The Dismissal of the Grecian Envoys*.

The success of Feliński's play came at the time when Niemcewicz's *Historical Songs* (published in 1816) was at the peak of its popularity. The national past thus began its career as a legitimate subject for both poetry and drama. In Russia too, Kondraty Ryleyev, indebted in this respect to Niemcewicz, whom he translated, attempted between 1821 and 1823 to write a kind of lyrical history of Russia from the tenth century to the nineteenth century in a series of *dumy,* singing of such personalities as Oleg, Sviatoslav, Dimitry of the Don, Ivan Suzanin. He drew his themes from Karamzin's *History of Russia,* but made near rebels out of his heroes (for instance, the troops of Dimitry of the Don in the fourteenth century want to fight "for freedom, truth, and law").

The new Romantic fashions made their entrance slowly; at first they were visible only in low-brow genres, but some respected French writers also contributed to the opening of forbidden paths. Le Tourneur was the first to translate the collected works of Shakespeare into French (though he did it in prose), and in his preface he introduced the word *romantique:*

> Whoever will want to know him [Shakespeare] let him direct his gaze on the vast sea or fix it on the aerial and *romantique* landscape.

So what is the meaning of *romantique?* Paintings of Salvador Rosa, landscapes of the Alps, untrimmed English gardens, and Shakespeare—"everything which awakens in a moved soul tender affections and melan-

choly ideas." Next, Jean-François Ducis rewrote Le Tourneur's version in verse, diluting Shakespeare with a sentimentalist's melancholy sweetness and expurgating all "coarseness" and "nonsense" (there is no Iago in *Othello,* for instance, because the public could not have borne such a horror of villainy; and the names of characters are changed to add a Nordic flavor: Desdemona and Brabancio become Hedelmona and Odalbert). In Poland then, Shakespeare was played according to Ducis or according to a German translator, Schröder (in whose version of Hamlet, the protagonist does not die). But the Polish literary public soon discovered true Shakespeare through an excellent German translation by August Wilhelm Schlegel. In addition, Schlegel's Vienna lectures on "Dramatic Art and Literature," published in 1809-1811, served the innovators in Warsaw as their chief weapon against pseudoclassical views on drama. The theoretical principles of Romanticism were elaborated in Germany and spread all over Western Europe by Madame de Staël, whose book, *On Germany (De l'Allemagne),* had its first edition of 1810 completely destroyed at Napoleon's orders—Madame de Staël being his staunch enemy. By 1813, the year of its second edition, *On Germany* had won acclaim in Poland.

Among the writers on the border line of Classicism and Romanticism, we should place Julian Ursyn Niemcewicz, whose knowledge of English gave him direct access not only to the works of Pope and Samuel Johnson, but to those of Gray and Byron as well as to English and Scottish ballads. Another such transitional figure was Kazimierz Brodziński (1791-1835), a poet and a professor at Warsaw University. In 1818 he came out with a long treatise, *On Classicism and Romanticism (O klasyczności i romantyczności),* accompanied by an essay, "On the Spirit of Polish Poetry." Well-read in German philosophy, Brodziński took from Johann Gottfried Herder the idea of a specific national character expressing itself in every given literature. Moderate in his judgments, he tried to see advantages in both currents and to combine them in such a way as to remain true to what he called the "essence of Polish poetry." He came to the conclusion that the idyll is the truest expression of the Polish national character. In his poetic practice, he attempted to apply that principle, particularly in his idyll, *Wiesław* (1820), where he depicts somewhat too happy Polish peasants. Brodziński's moderation not only failed to satisfy the young, but provoked the anger of the classicists. It was against him that an eminent professor of the University of Wilno, Jan Śniadecki, a mathematician, an astronomer, and a rationalist, wrote his essay, *On Classical and Romantic Writings* (1819), in which he called Romanticism "a school of treason and plague," a danger for education and the purity of the language. Śniadecki was one of the brightest minds of his time, and his words should not be taken lightly. Yet he had to lose. Not only foreign imports, such as the poems of Ossian (treated as genuine Nordic songs) and sentimental novels, were promoting the change in sensibility. The novel form was already being imitated by Polish authors: the most successful of such works was *Malvina, or Intuitions of the Heart (Malwina czyli domyślność serca*, 1816*)*, by Princess Maria Wirtemberska, née Czartoryska. Perhaps the most important single phenomenon that determined the shift was the Napoleonic legend, releasing as it did new forces of feeling and imagination. Viewed in this light, Polish Romanticism came close to resembling that branch of French Romanticism which was represented by Stendhal. The poetry and prose produced by those who had served in the Napoleonic army was, thanks to their energy and broad vistas, far removed from the placid offerings of the Warsaw literati; this is apparent, for instance, in a poem by Cyprian Godebski, "To the Polish Legions in Italy" ("Wiersz do Legiów polskich," 1805). It is visible in a novel by the same author, *A Grenadier Philosopher (Grenadier filozof*, 1805*)*, where we have a story of Polish and French soldiers wandering from Italy through France, sharing a common disillusionment with the ideals which the French Revolution failed to bring to fruition. Besides, the conviction was growing that poetry is not just a matter of good taste as prescribed by the educated classes. While German theoreticians extolled the Nordic genius in opposition to the French classical genius, Polish writers began to realize the value of Slavic folklore. In this respect, the role of Zorjan Dołęga-Chodakowski (pen name of Adam Czarnocki—1784-1825) should be remembered. A self-taught ethnographer and archaeologist, he was responsible for collections of folk songs from Poland, Byelorussia, and the Ukraine.

Mickiewicz's "I Speak unto Myself"

I speak unto myself, say things inane;
My breathing halts, my wild heart seems to
   race;
Sparks blind my eyes and pallid grows my face,
While strangers ask aloud, 'Is he in pain?'

And others whisper, hint I am insane.
Daylong I am tortured, then would sleep
   embrace
To soothe my fevered mind, but in its place
My heart kindles strange fancies in my brain.

I run, I start, I murmur words that bite
With which to curse your cruelty untold,
Composed and lost before another night . . .
And once again when thee I may behold,
I am calm, as cool as flint at thy mere sight,
Only to burn again, be silent as of old.

Adam Mickiewicz, in Poems, *translated by various hands, edited by George Rapall Noyes, The Polish Institute of Arts and Sciences in America, 1944.*

Julian Krzyżanowski (essay date 1972)

SOURCE: "Polish Romantic Literature: Romanticism and Its Character," in *A History of Polish Literature,* translated by Doris Ronowicz, PWN-Polish Scientific Publishers, 1978, pp. 220-33.

[In the following excerpt from a work first published in Polish in 1972, Krzyżanowski surveys the historical, social, and cultural forces that shaped Polish Romantic literature.]

The powerful trend known as Romanticism, which emerged in the literature of all Europe and also of North America in the first half of the 19th century, had its source in the political and social relations prevailing generally because of the French Revolution and its consequences. True, the revolutionaries were not victorious anywhere, but their watchwords took deep root in the minds of social groups and classes and even in the consciousness of many peoples; they matured and gave forth shoots all through the 19th century, to produce their harvest in the first quarter of our century. The ferment they caused, systematically suppressed by the reactionary forces known as the Holy Alliance, which had gained predominance, erupted from time to time all through the first half of the 19th century. Then came what was almost an explosion with such movements as the Spring of Nations that brought the unification of Italy, the Hungarian revolution and, finally, the last belated romantic revolution, the Polish January Insurrection in 1863.

Literature was the universal and consistent spokesman of the revolutionary watchwords proclaimed by a large number of secret organizations of a national or—more rarely—international character, and the sowers of the seed were the poets, many of them soldiers, social leaders and patriots, large numbers of whom died on battlefields, while others spent hungry years in the casemates of fortresses and in the notorious political prisons of those times. Suffice it to recall the halo of heroism surrounding Lord Byron after his death while fighting for the liberation of Greece, Aleksander Petöfi's death on the battlefield in Hungary, or the execution of the Decembrist Konrad Ryleyev in Russia.

A detailed history of literature in the territory of the Russian empire will be full of dates of imprisonment, to mention the biographies of the Pole Mickiewicz, the Russian Pushkin, who lived under police supervision for many years, or the Ukrainian Shevchenko, sentenced to long years of military service. And the fate of Polish writers in the parts of the country under Austrian and Prussian domination was not much better, for in the biographies of Pol and Kaczkowski, Norwid and Berwiński prison sentences play no small part.

The revolutionary watchwords proclaimed by the Romantics concerned three basic fields, of varying importance, criss-crossing each other from time to time, a fact which lessens their clarity. They proclaimed the necessity to fight against political slavery, demanding the right of freedom for nations deprived of it, having been forcefully incorporated into powerful foreign state organisms, such as the Russian, Ottoman and Austrian empires, the Kingdom of Great Britain or Prussia. The political movement nourished by these watchwords gave forth a double harvest—part of the oppressed peoples had already at that time thrown off the yoke of slavery, particularly in the Balkans, or had won some kind of more or less permanent autonomy. Other peoples, whose liberation was to come much later, underwent profound inner transformations, they woke and prepared for freedom, and an infallible means of rebirth for these peoples was their national literature, which in many cases joined the all-European stream of literary life for the first time.

The second field, undoubtedly less important in that period, but which was proclaimed by romantic-revolutionary watchwords, was public life and the social struggle for the rights of the oppressed classes which were described as the "fourth estate", namely, the rights of the industrial workers and the peasants. In the industrialized countries of the West, where the working class had existed for some time, the champions of the cause demanding their rights were representatives of all kinds of utopian socialism, which only aroused a weak echo in central and eastern Europe, for there, if not the only problem, the most important one was that of the agricultural labourers, the peasants, most of whom were serfs. These problems too were dealt with by literature, and Polish writers, being exceptional in that they raised the question of the worker, were very energetic in fighting against the wrongs done to the peasant serfs.

The third watchword of the Romantics, of a different kind, and because of this linked in the most varied ways and sometimes actually artificially linked up with the other two fields, proclaimed the necessity to fight against social prejudices which cramped the freedom of the individual, particularly talented individuals who stood out from their environment. These prejudices were differences in birth, in estate and in social position, and also differences in political, social and even philosophical views, particularly in the field of religion. The Romantics placed a high value on exceptional or extraordinary individualism, attaining peaks generally inaccessible to ordinary people by heroism of thought or deed. And this was bound, sooner or later, to lead to unavoidable antinomy: the individual and the society, represented by the passive masses, the crowds, unable to reach the peaks upon which the exceptional individual lived. The solution to the difficulties emerging here was found in titanic heroism, in Titanism or Prometheus-like heroes, assuming that the exceptional individual is an outstanding man, of great social virtue, a man living not for himself alone but for his class, his nation, for all mankind. Titanism, understood in this way, in accord both with its ancient meaning and the historic notion, was the product of an epoch fighting for the realization of revolutionary watchwords, it was a symbol of rebellion against the dead principles hampering man, principles which had been evolved in the course of collective life in society, and this made it the third driving force of the Romantic movement.

The all-European, or rather the world ideology of the Romantic movement, from the moment it began to be assimilated into the Polish culture fell on very fertile soil due to the political and social situation of the country. The Vienna Congress (1815), which put an end to the Napoleonic epoch and thus the heritage of the French Revolution, was in fact a new, fourth partition of Poland. True, it did set up two little marionette lands, the tiny Cracow Respublica and the larger Kingdom of Poland, popularly known as the Congress Kingdom, but neither of these freakish creations had any chance of surviving. The former vanished in 1848, being incorporated into Austria, the latter ceased to exist even earlier, after the failure of the November Rising in 1831, when it lost its constitutional independence of Russia (though it had only been on paper).

These political relations had a very strange and significant influence on the literary life of Poland or, and this amounts to the same thing, on the development of its literature. Of particular importance here was the year 1831, which completely shattered the political illusions based on the paragraphs of the decisions of the Vienna Congress. The Kingdom of Poland, this small state which, theoretically, was constitutional and seemingly independent, and thus the natural centre of Polish cultural life, ceased to be such a centre, not only because its university and societies of learning were closed down and because all manifestations of independent thought and creative works were suppressed ruthlessly by police and military methods, but also because it lost a large part of its intellectuals, that is, the social group which created cultural life.

For the intelligentsia had left the country with the insurgent government and the army to settle in western Europe, mostly in France, although smaller groups settled in Germany, Great Britain, Turkey and even the United States. The members of what is usually referred to as the Great Emigration, these champions of freedom, received with enthusiasm in Germany and elsewhere, were convinced that a "universal war for the freedom of nations" would break out any moment and that they would be able to return to Poland. They did not foresee that the fate awaiting them was the typical lot of political émigrés, that they would waste away in an alien environment and that their ardent belief in the early outbreak of an all-European revolution was just an illusion.

From the point of view of the historian of literature, the Rising and the life of the émigrés has a varied and very significant meaning. In the course of twenty years (1830-1850) the most important centre of Polish literary life, a centre which produced masterpieces, was Paris. For it was in Paris that the most outstanding Polish writers settled, those who had already won recognition before 1830, and in addition, the capital of France attracted all those who did not want to or could not work in a country where they were liable to suffer from repression, or at least felt it would be impossible for them to work there.

The consequences of this situation were so strange that they go to make up a picture which is probably the only one of its kind in the history of world literature. It so happened that almost all the outstanding writers of that generation were among the émigrés, including two poets of genius—Mickiewicz and Słowacki. These writers quite naturally came under the pressure of the political atmosphere of émigré life, and as a result of this their works resounded with such strong political elements that they became incomprehensible to the foreign reader (though this view, already established then and still existing today, calls for far-reaching limitations and corrections). And added to this there was one more factor, a very important one. The literature of the émigré community came into being and developed uninfluenced by censorship, and this does not only mean without censorship by the partitioning powers, but no censorship at all. For the state censors of France, Britain or Germany were not interested in works published in the Polish language. Due to this situation the émigré writers could write things that would not have been allowed in any other language of the times and which later were to bring about many misunderstandings, not only in partitioned Poland, when these works began to appear there, but even after independence had been regained.

The flourishing development of Polish literature among the emigrants had in addition two aspects, opposite but inseparably linked with each other—its positive and negative sides. The positive side was constant contact with the rich cultural, philosophical, scientific, literary and theatrical life of France, a country which in those times was the most progressive in the true sense of the word and also held the leading position. For Paris was an important political centre of an international character. It was an ideological melting pot in which the most radical and most conservative tendencies were mixed and melted down, from Russian nihilism to all kinds and varieties of ultramontanism, that is, reactionary religious and political conservatism. All this had a very strong influence on the political and social ideas of the émigré community and on their literature, making it more profound and widening its horizons to an extent unprecedented in Poland either before or afterwards. This meant that the émigré community became the cradle of the most varied ideologies, from utopian socialism and a little later Marxism, to various rather odd kinds of systems and outlines of systems, melting down into religious and political mysticism.

Of all these systems, one which was seemingly uniform, or at least it was regarded as such, for it has not so far been thoroughly studied from the scientific point of view, gained undeserved fame, and gained it due to literature in which it was an ever present element—the system known as Polish Messianism. The thinkers of that time were clearly conscious of the fact that the European culture which had been shaken to its traditional foundations by the revolution was in a crisis situation and they tried to find a way out of this crisis. Their guide in seeking the way out were various systems of the philosophy of history, or in other words historiosophy, assuming that nations and groups of nations are called upon to play a certain definite role in the history of the world, a role enclosed within certain chronological limits. Of these systems, great popularity was gained by the views of the German philosopher Herder, which proclaimed that the old European culture had been built by the Romanic nations, whose strength had been completely exhausted by this work, and that their role was to fall to the Germanic nations building the present, and the builders of the future would be the Slavonic peoples. On the basis of ideas of this kind and the economic and political growth of large state organisms, nationalistic systems began to emerge, endeavouring to point to the development roads of history and its everyday tasks. This was the case in Germany, which intended to transform itself into a power, and in Russia, which made the mastery of the whole Slav world the aim of its policy as a power. And it was in this atmosphere that Polish Messianism was born.

It was a nebulous mixture of all kinds of views, so unorganized that a dispute even arose as to who was the man who had given it the name Messianism. The dispute was waged between Józef Hoene-Wroński, a philosopher and mathematician, who attributed the authorship of the name to himself, and Mickiewicz, who proclaimed the principles of Messianism in his university lectures on Slavonic literature, and to some extent he was right, for he had formulated these principles himself ten years earlier and, what is even more important, had managed to impose his views on many fraternal peoples. In actual fact, these principles were the programme of action of every nation deprived of freedom and striving to regain it. In waiting for the momentous time, when armed action was to bring liberty to the peoples deprived of it, the programme proclaimed the necessity for moral preparation and the attainment of exceptionally high moral standards as the guarantee of the proper utilization of the regained freedom. Poland, as the largest of the nations groaning under the burden of oppression, as a nation which had never been aggressive in the whole of its history, and as a people who had many times risen to fight for freedom, in the system of Messianism was given the role of the leader of the nations striving for liberation. These principles, simple and clear in the interpretation of various Messianists, were given various accessories and all kinds of ideas were added which blurred and darkened the original conception as a whole, bending it to suit the temporary needs of the moment. So whereas for some Messianism was a programme of an armed fight for liberation, for others it turned into a quietistic attitude, waiting for a miracle that would, without any effort on the part of man, bring freedom to the world, for slavery was in opposition to the notion of divine justice. Still others, taking the principles of Messianism as a basis, maintained that God had saved Poland from taking an active part in rotten political life which was based on the rule of force of the imperialist states, in order to resurrect her at the moment when these states had become just a part of the shameful past. As these ideas were coupled with biblical symbols in such formulations as: Poland, the Messiah of the nations; Poland—the Christ; Poland—Mary Magdalene, etc., the whole of this nebulous mixture gave and still gives the impression of religious and political speculation, to such an extent that it overshadows the original, simple and noble greatness of the principles, a greatness that was understood by those who, living outside Poland at that time, had read Mickiewicz's brochure, *Books of the Polish Nation,* which was a kind of national bible. These readers, residing in Germany, Italy, Ireland, the Ukraine and Hungary, saw in Polish Messianism a programme of action for liberation, lucid and well formulated revolutionary watchwords proclaimed by Romantic literature.

Manifestations of Messianism bordering on degeneracy resulted from the unfavourable fact that Polish Romanticism developed in the émigré milieu. The longer the emigrants remained in exile the farther their departure from the mother-tree, the life of the nation and its everyday language, in both the literal and metaphorical sense of the word. Literature gave an eloquent reflection of this phenomenon, for it was doomed to draw its life-blood from alien soil, and sank into various kinds of abstraction that could not be compared with the reality—regardless of whether these abstractions were mystic speculations as to the future or equally barren delving into the past. For both were an escape from the basic problems of the present, understanding of which became ever more blurred and about which the writers knew less and less. And the victims of this merciless process were not only the minor poets, but also such men of genius as Mickiewicz, who stopped writing,

and Słowacki, who got lost in a maze of mystic dreams.

The result of all these factors was that, although masterpieces of Romantic poetry were smuggled into Poland, where they were read in secret and aroused much enthusiasm, the literature being born in the country itself was of quite a different character. And this was not only because the censors everywhere, except in the Poznań region, were in hot pursuit of any literature that smacked of any political ideology sounding the call of liberation; works of this kind could be written and copies circulated by hand together with the writings of the authors in exile, which were distributed in this way. It was simply a matter of the reaction of writers in Poland to the multiple trends of the Romantic movement, for they chose, above all, elements that escaped the attention of the writers living abroad, namely, its social elements.

The social problems contained in Romantic literature—as has been pointed out—embraced problems of the workers and peasants, and in Poland, deprived of industry, only the problems of the latter were currently acute. So it was the social problems of the peasants that drew attention and were the subject of literary writings. And in all these writings one could find a voice of protest against the wrongs done to the peasants, but the fact that the writers were of gentry origin and had painful historical experience behind them demonstrating that the peasant masses had not yet acquired sufficient national consciousness, meant that these works only had the character of literary warcries. And it is a significant thing that these works usually dealt with the lot of the Byelorussian or Ukrainian peasants, for the peasants from the ethnically Polish territories, that is, from the regions of Mazowsze, Little Poland, Great Poland and Silesia were the subject not of literary works but of scientific ethnological studies, and only in time did they begin to appear in literary works.

This is not an indifferent matter, for the literature being born in Poland placed tremendous emphasis on its cognitive task, on the creative utilization of sociological and psychological studies (of course, these scientific terms were not then in use). In this field the writers fought for the right to Romantic individualism, demonstrating the conflict of the outstanding individual with his passive or hostile environment, but they paid a lot more attention to that environment and the great social processes taking place in the public life of their times. These processes included the problem of the peasant serfs, the emergence of the bourgeois class and the creation of the intelligentsia in Poland. And all this was viewed against the background of the economic and social processes taking place in the very differentiated mass of the former Polish gentry, processes that had so far not been scientifically investigated. It was noticed that in the gentry class as a whole there was a constant and systematic levelling out of the peaks represented by the old and new aristocratic families and in connection with this there was a gradual disappearance of the former huge estates known as latifundia, which were divided into medium sized estates. In addition, there was also a disappearance of the minor representatives of the gentry, living in the back-of-beyond, who either turned into peasants or went to the towns and townships to seek their bread, thus swelling the ranks of the bourgeois class. Finally, the moderately wealthy gentry produced representatives of the free professions, of which there were a growing number in the towns; so physicians, officials and military men originated from this strata of the gentry. These processes, which in the west provided material for the great novels of such writers as Balzac in France and Dickens in Britain, became a field of observation for their contemporaries in Poland and became the core of the literary ideas of writers living in Poland, such as Korzeniowski and Kraszewski, as well as a large group of lesser poets and prose writers.

This sociological interest of the Romantic movement in the surrounding life, in the current reality, was accompanied by similar endeavours to study the past, undertaken sometimes with the aim of finding out what traces of the past were present in the works of writers of their own epoch. However, in keeping with the general attitude of the Romantic writers, this fondness for the past was more frequently for the sake of the past itself, for its specific charm, revealed by archaeological excavations and old ruins, by old chronicles and old poetry. Prompted by an attitude known as Romantic historicism, writers living in Poland delved into the past, both bygone ages and more recent times, to relish the brilliant heroism and all the strange wonder they radiated. Following these paths, continuing the endeavours of the poets of before the November Rising, they found a point of contact with the émigré writers, complementing their work, particularly in one field. For they were able to draw on traditions that were still alive, getting material from oral accounts or from diaries dealing with the times of Stanisław Augustus, showing particular interest in the events connected with the Confederation of Bar. The turmoil of the Confederation was regarded as the first stage of the fight for liberation and the last manifestation of Baroque Sarmatism, fighting for God and their country against the Moslem world. Narrow local patriotism with its dislike of the culture of the Enlightenment period, blaming it for the downfall of the country, produced a rich literary harvest in the form of tales written in verse and prose. And it was a particularly interesting harvest because the source of these tales were offshoots of traditional stories passed down by word of mouth, above all by members of the gentry, but they were also seasoned with a large dose of folk elements, both Polish and Ukrainian.

The cradle of Romanticism was English literature; it was born of this literature, developed and began to spread all over Europe and America. On its way, it was greeted, as it was in Poland by Brodziński, with treatises endeavouring to grasp the character of the new trend and determine its place in the culture of that time. In the course of these deliberations it was given its name and its relation to known literary traditions was established—negative towards Classicism and positive towards other trends, particularly those of the Baroque period and the Middle Ages. Although the new trend energetically opposed the "serious" rationalism of the literature worshipped by the Classicists, of writers such as Virgil, Corneille and Racine, it could not of course exist without its own "serious" side, so it took as its patron the great Dante, author of *The Divine Comedy,* written not in Latin but in a Romanic language, Italian. Other later writers were soon to stand beside the mediaeval poet, sharing the patronage over the new movement with him. Above all, there were two representatives of Baroque drama, the Spanish writer Calderon de la Barca, and the English playwright Shakespeare, and the next was the great ironical and humorous Spanish writer Cervantes. And as classic philology at the end of the 18th century had promoted Homer to the rank of a folk poet, the bard who wrote *Iliad* also found himself in the company of the venerable patrons of Romantic poetry, next to two mythical "rhapsodists", the Celtic bard Ossian, known to all Europe, and Boyan the old Russian minstrel who sang the *Tale of Igor's Campaign.*

And due to this exceptional poetic areopagus, Romanticism gained a far-reaching and extensive literary tradition, extending from the ancient Greek rhapsodies of Homer, through the epics and ballads of the Middle Ages and Baroque drama, up to the folk poetry passed on by word of mouth, and still alive in the 19th century, particularly in Russia and Serbia, two Slav countries, and in Finland, whose people then decided to open up their treasure-trove of folk epic *Kalevala* to the amazed west European readers.

Thus armed, the Romantic movement went into action, proclaiming the already mentioned ideological watchwords, which all representatives of the new reactionary political order heard with a reluctant ear, but which were seized upon and taken up immediately by the oppositionists, particularly by the youth everywhere where freedom did not reign, which was practically all over Europe.

And this radical political and social ideology was accompanied by equally radical novelties of a purely literary nature, constituting a departure from the convictions and views of the Classicists, which had been made sacred by habit. For Romantic poetry broke the bonds of accepted "rules" and proclaimed such liberal principles that in some cases they bordered on anarchy.

So as regards subjects, class barriers and even questions of cast began to disappear, as did the convictions that the heroes of tragedies or epics could only be crowned heads or people very near to royalty. One half-hearted concession to tradition was that tragic heroes who were not of royal origin were usually presented against the background of court life. This did not apply, however, to the novel, which undoubtedly owed its flourishing development to the fact that traditional poetics had not been interested in this genre. Thus, Romanticism brought a more democratic choice of literary subjects, extending to the whole of literature what had previously been confined to the realm of comedies and satires.

This change was brought about by the different attitude taken by the Romantic poets towards basic aesthetic values and their functions, which the classicists had limited to certain literary genres, i.e. the tragic in tragedies and the comic in comedies. Being champions of realistic observation of life they demonstrated that situations of the tragic and comic kind are often inseparably linked up with each other, and as followers of the example set by Shakespeare who by his criss-crossing of the two elements attained exceptional artistic effects, the Romantic writers readily combined these two elements on the basis of either humour or irony. In fact they went even further, for they created new varieties of the traditional styles and kinds of literature, both the epic story and drama.

They also enriched the store of styles and genres by new ones, either by resurrecting old long forgotten forms or making ingenious combinations of existing forms. So they revived the mediaeval ballad, relics of which they found in folk poetry that was recognized as a leading item in the programme of the Romantic movement. They gave us the epic poem, generally constructed of lyric stanzas, and its ballad-like character was heightened by the repetition of refrains or couplets, that is, flourishes of a clearly lyrical character. As regards the kinds of literature obtained by the combination of existing forms, the ironical epic poem was particularly popular, and though it followed the old tradition of the humorous, ancient and Renaissance epics it had elements not met with in these older forms, such as autobiographical confessions, personal polemics and satirical attacks on the realities surrounding the writer. And in the field of drama the development was in the direction of spectacles untypical of the stage, often to the point of exaggeration, so that they became acted stories of a bookish type with a predominance of epic or lyrical elements, in other words, they were dramatic poems or "dramatic romances". It should also be added that the amorphism, the formlessness so typical of the compositional technique of the Romantic writers, was heightened by their mannerisms, bordering on the fragmentary, the deliberate construction of

works out of fractions so as to arouse the curiosity of the reader and amaze him with something unusual.

The artistic language of the Romantic writers was a radical departure from that of their predecessors, the Classicists. The scale of effects it could produce was greatly enlarged and there was a transition from the language which in its simplicity was somewhat reminiscent of colloquial speech, to ornamental, sophisticated language, which was a near approach to the Baroque with its ingenuous devices. Based, in principle, on the literary language, the Romantic language absorbed a large number of elements of dialect, and there were even cases, rare it is true, when it was actually based on dialect. It was further enriched by stylization. So in connection with the taste for historicity, archaic expressions were a common thing; the liking for oriental effects could be seen in the stylization of the language of the given work to give an impression of the life of the oriental peoples and was thus modelled on Persian, Arabian or Turkish poetry. Another frequently found feature was the biblical style, which led to the production of rhythmic prose, reminiscent in its melodiousness of the versicles of the Gospel. And apart from whole works stylized to a varying degree, it became a binding principle to use characteristic language both in novels and dramas, so that each character spoke in his own way within the bounds of the language obtained by introducing carefully selected idiomatic expressions, sayings and also elements taken from the specific language of certain professions, the language of the hunt, of the soldier, etc.

All these means of artistic expression, based on a careful observation of colloquial speech and special lexical studies and—in Poland—a great fondness for reading Linde's dictionary, went hand in hand with great care to bring variety into the rhyme forms, breaking away from the rigorous rules of Classicist poetry. The Romantic poets, even those who were most sensitive to the demands of meter, were at great pains to keep the rhythm without becoming "slaves to the meter" which might cramp their artistic style and the content of their works and create an impression of artificiality. They wanted their verse to sound natural, so natural as to be indetectable in conveying the content. So while observing a standard rhythmic model, they subordinated it to the demands of syntax, often resorting to content-links not only consisting of one or two lines. They even erased the separateness of stanzas. An example of this is the Devil's reproach in Mickiewicz's ballad *Mrs Twardowska (Pani Twardowska)*: "On ox-hide I've a pledge of thine Which thou didst sign and the demons Were to dance to thy tune and rhyme", in which the first two lines end one stanza and the line starting with the words "Were to dance" begins the next. This was a new Romantic principle giving syntax predominance over the meter while at the same time observing the demands of rhythm.

In Polish literature, preserving the traditional lyrical and epic, stichic and stanzaic meter, syllable patterns were used and also syllable and stress patterns were frequently found. As regards stanzas, the sonnet became a very widespread form and this was not because of a desire to follow the native Baroque tradition which had long been forgotten, but to go straight back to the original Italian source, Petrarch's *Canzoniere*. However, contrary to that tradition there was a certain tendency towards poetry with masculine rhymes, although there was no exaggeration in this respect. In any case, this was the style of the older representatives of the generation led by Mickiewicz, Słowacki, and Zaleski, who confined the use of masculine rhymes almost exclusively to small lyrical poems. It was only the later Romantic poets who were to go much farther in this respect, being very fond, or perhaps just persistent, in writing "iambic" verse with masculine rhymes.

Romantic liberalism, evident in the subjects dealt with by the literature of the times, which suited its poetic forms and other means of expression, was subordinated to the supreme principle recognized by the whole movement we know as Romanticism, although this was not always realized by its representatives and for this reason is not easy for the historian to distinguish. This principle was realism as a creative attitude, the specific realism of the Romantic writers, artistic realism. The difficulties encountered in this view of the Romantic art of writing arise from the basic feature of the movement, whose philosophy was idealistic, judging the world of things with criteria taken from the world of ideas and giving expression to the great ideals shaping the fate of the individual, the nation, mankind. To paraphrase the well known line from Mickiewicz's *Ode to Youth* "Reach up to realms beyond our sight" it can be regarded as the basic binding principle of the Romantic writers and as an equally good explanation of their general liking for the fantastic and—much more rarely—of staggering mystical speculations. But everything beyond the sight of man in the ideas and imagination of the poet, charmed up by chains of beautiful words, creating an image understandable to the reader, automatically had to enter the world of things, for the image had to take the form of phenomena that could be measured by human experience. Mickiewicz's ghost of the lover who bears his maiden away to the grave with him, behaves like an ordinary man would in the given situation; Słowacki's nymph of the Lake Gopło, Goplana, "a strange misty and gelatinous creature" is guided by purely human motives and—despite her powers—makes some very human mistakes; the absolutely idealistic speculations expressed by Krasiński, which are to explain the meaning and the causes of Poland's downfall, become the tirade of an apparition, of the 17th century warrior Czarniecki, who expresses himself by purely human reasoning, with which it is difficult to agree, and the errors of which can be easily detected. In a word, the world of fiction and the world of idealistic speculation are given the dimensions of the human world and are, of necessity, constructed in such a way as to make their message just as easy to understand as the world of things. In addition, they are closely connected with the world of things, human relations, which are the point of departure in entering the world of fiction and determine its function in a literary work. Added to all this—to a much greater extent than in allegorical or Baroque literature—the artistic stress in the works of the Romantic writers is usually placed more strongly on the realistic than the unrealistic phenomena, which, of course, heightens the realistic eloquence of a given work.

And it is precisely this realism that determines the uniform character of Romanticism, regardless of its different manifestations which depended on the individuality of the Romantic writers and on the cultural conditions in which Romanticism developed in various countries of Europe. This realism also determines the uniform character of Polish Romanticism, both of the writers working in exile and those in Poland, who during their development had several stages when the subjects or problems they wrote about differed to some extent, as did their creative dynamism, but not to such an extent that these differences should be regarded as basic ones of great importance.

This matter is worthy of attention because in Poland the forty years in which Romanticism developed is mechanically divided into certain sectors marked by the historical dates of 1830, the year of the outbreak of the November Rising, and 1848, the year of the Spring of Nations. The importance of the date 1830 is said to be due to the fact that, following the Rising, Polish literature was created in exile, where it assumed a definitely political tinge, which could not be introduced in the literature created in Poland. This approach would, in a way, be right if it corresponded to reality. The reality however, would rather indicate the borderline date as 1828, when the author of *Conrad Wallenrod (Konrad Wallenrod)* outlined his programme for the inclusion of political problems in Romantic literature, a programme he consistently carried out after the Rising as an émigré, and the peak phase of Romantic literature should be taken as the time of the death of Słowacki a year after the Spring of Nations (1849).

It is a much simpler matter to establish the initial date, namely, the year 1818, when Kazimierz Brodziński (1791-1835) published his treatise *On Classicism and Romanticism,* with an appendix *On the Spirit of Polish Poetry (O klasyczności i romantyczności, tudzież o duchu poezji polskiej).* The author, a poet very sensitive to literary phenomena, felt the near approach of a conflict between the new English and German trends and the classicist rules of the French literature, and sought an answer as to which way Polish literature should go. The answer was: Let us not imitate foreign models but walk our own paths. Brodziński was of the opinion that the idyll was the truest expression of the Polish national character, and supported this opinion with the argument that the old traditions of the Slavs showed that they did not want wars, but peace and songs. And for this reason he took a special interest in folk songs, which were a highly valued element in the programme principles and practical activity of the Romantic writers. Brodziński's views, though moderate, gave rise to lively discussion, which was joined in 1822 by Mickiewicz with his programme ballad *The Romantic (Romantyczność)*.

MAJOR FIGURES

M. Szyjkowski (essay date 1926)

SOURCE: "The Blossoming of Romantic Poetry of the Time of the Emigration," in *Polish Encyclopædia, Vol. I,* 1926. Reprint by Arno Press & The New York Times, 1972, pp. 384-408.

[*In the excerpt below, Szyjkowski presents an overview of the chief works of Słowacki and Krasiński.*]

Among the Polish emigrants, there was [besides Mickiewicz] yet another master of Polish romantic poetry: Julius Słowacki. Born in the year 1809, he was not yet 23 years old when the Emigration took place.

He was brought up under very different circumstances from those which had presided over Mickiewicz's education. He was an only son, early lost his father, who had been a dramatist and a professor at the University of Wilno. He was brought up by women, surrounded by luxury and refinement, growing rapidly like a plant in a hothouse. His mentality was a strong and manifold one, and he was wonderfully endowed especially for foreign languages, music and drawing.

His ambition to be a writer arose early, when, as a young boy, he is filled with enthusiasm for Mickiewicz's poems. He resolved also to attain to renown.

This craving for glory, were it even after death, is the great driving force of his life and during many years kept his spiritual faculties under its feverish strain. To rival Mickiewicz, a result of this wish, became one of the motives of the work of the ambitious youth hampering him in his evolution rather than helping him.

Besides Mickiewicz, other European writers exercised a noticeable influence on the imagination of the young poet, an imagination which was at the same time subtle and of extraordinary inspiration. He remained a long

time under this influence. Before the November Revolution, Byron was the Master of Słowacki. It is in taking Byron's poetical tales as models, that Słowacki wrote his first poems, which already showed absolute mastership of form.

He wrote two historical tragedies, one of them *Mindowe,* consecrated to a subject taken from the history of Lithuania; the other to the youth of Mary Stuart, the queen already immortalised by Schiller and Alfieri. These two pieces already show the great dramatic talent of their author, assuredly the greatest dramatic talent Polish tragedy has ever known. Above all *Maria Stuart,* written in Shakspearian mood, countains scenes which exhibit a passion as high as it is sincere.

Słowacki greeted the outbreak of the Revolution with many patriotic poems. Sent on a diplomatic mission to London, he could not come back to his country. Thus, then, the great artist begins his wandering life. This life was for him easier than for others, as he was free from material cares.

He stays some time in Paris, in order to prepare the publication of the works of his youth; they came out in two volumes which were unnoticed. The poet felt that he was at once misunderstood and wronged. His antagonism to Mickiewicz was only due to an absolute difference of their inner artistic organisation and motives. The indifference of his countrymen which he took for want of comprehension filled his soul with bitterness. These two feelings not only inspired his works for a long time, but they became the two main factors in the tragedy of his life.

Słowacki possessed a nervous, sensitive, frail organism, he was devoured by measureless ambition and social questions left him indifferent. His inner tendency to "Hamletism" was mingled in him with a certain disposition to melancholy. As an ardent patriot, he was full of desire to work for his country. As a poet, he possessed to a high degree the subtle sense of poetical form, a wonderful impressionability which he translated into picturesque words, full of colour, of music, of harmony.

Such are the characteristics of the creative genius of this great solitary.

His ardent craving for glory was only realised after death: posterity granted him a place among the greatest poets of the nation. Realising the words of a friend (Krasiński), he really shines as an eternal rainbow over Mickiewicz's granite statue! He really represents the necessary complement to the full expression of the Polish national genius.

Słowacki's talent shincs with all its radiance, when, after having left Paris, he lived for many years in

Switzerland on the borders of the lake of Geneva. It is there that he wrote his most beautiful lyrical poems, there, that under the spell of the beauties of the Swiss scenery, he conceived many artistic ideas, which he later expressed, such as the masterpiece: "In Switzerland". On the wonderfully harmonious background of lake and mountains, the golden thread of a love tale unrolls itself. He does not forsake dramatic works. This Polish Shakespeare worked in the most unfavourable conditions, far from his country, never seeing any of his works on the stage. But his conceptions were gigantic. Only an exceptional theatrical intuition could create works, which, today still live on the Polish stage, full of most palpitating interest. Excited by the reading of *Konrad Wallenrod* and of the *Ancestors,* Słowacki began an autobiographical trilogy but only finished the first part: This dramatic poem called: *Kordian,* notwithstanding many weaknesses, contains scenes of absolute beauty. Shakespeare's work tempted him to write a dramatic cycle, whose subject was inspired by the legends of Poland. He left two tragedies of this kind: *Balladyna* and the *Lilla Veneda.* He did not trouble much about historical truth, not even about the logical unfolding of facts, as he himself avowed. In writing his "dramatical chronicles" he relies on his own literary recollections and on the inexhaustible wealth of his fancy.

Master of the spoken word, and a born dramatist, he builds scenes full of genius, sounding, at will, the pathetic note, hastening or slackening the tone of the dialogue. In *Balladyna* appears a whole fairy-world, so subtle and ethereal that, even compared to the *Midsummer Night's Dream* it loses nothing. In the *Lilla Veneda* he revives the choruses and, in a most subtle way, introduces a lyrical element, personified by the magic harp, and brought to its apotheosis in the character of his heroine. The Polish *Antigone,* at the same time priestess and victim, is one of the most beautiful women-characters in all literature.

During his stay in Switzerland, Słowacki undertook many other dramatic works; he only completed a few and left the others unfinished. Let us, first of all, mention: *Mazeppa.* The historical period to which *Mazeppa* belongs does not appear clearly, though the characters of this tragedy belong to the history of Poland in the XVIIth century. The whole tragedy rests on complex love-problems, the character of the heroine reminds one of Desdemona.

From Switzerland, Słowacki went to Rome, where he met Sigismund Krasiński, the poet and thinker, with whom he became intimate. Although younger than Słowacki, Krasiński exercised a deep influence on his friend's mind. But it is, above all, thanks to his journeys to Greece, Egypt and Palestine, that Słowacki's spiritual life grows and expands.

Having returned from his travels, he stays at Florence. He brings back with him poems of unique beauty, amongst which a description of his journeys, under the form of a poem in "octaves".

Never before had this poetical form been used in Poland with such gorgeousness. We must also mention the masterpiece of elegiae poetry named: "The Father of the Plague-stricken" and other poems, to say nothing of sketches of vaster works.

These manifold conceptions gave birth to an important work, different from all the poet had yet produced. It was the outcome of long meditations in the solitary hermitage on Lebanon, meditations, thanks to which, the poet ripened inwardly and deeply examined what had up to that time, been his attitude towards national work.

It was for him of first rate importance to justify his attitude towards the nation. What benefits could the nation receive from the solitary efforts of his artistic creation? The nation needed action. Słowacki was not, like Mickiewicz, born for political action. He well understood that his work enriched the national treasure of Beauty—but this assurance no longer satisfied him. Like all great romantic writers, Słowacki was inclined towards mysticism, when still very young, he studied Swedenborg's theories and his books. He believed in presentiments and in premonitory dreams. Meditating on the road he had followed in his life, he discovered there a deep sense: silent and passive sacrifice for the good of his country. Sincerely and deeply he believed it, believed that such a sacrifice could be effective.

He expressed this idea in the form of a biblical poem, recalling, as to form, the "Books" of Mickiewicz. The subject of the poem, called: *Anhelli* has for its frame the ice-land of Siberia, where the banished Polish exiles live. In this land of cold and darkness, lighted only by the sinister dimness of the aurora borealis. Słowacki showed the sufferings and the dissensions of Polish emigrants. Each picture breathes of deep sadness, as do all the incidents in the lives of this handful of unhappy men.

The prose, in which this story is told, is wonderful. Never could its rhythm and the strength of its descriptions be sufficiently admired. Such melancholy is also found in some pages of the work of Dante. Even the final prophecy of delivery cannot attenuate this sadness, which shrouds in black veils the Siberian poem.

At the end of the year 1836, Słowacki establishes himself definitively in Paris. He begins then the rich literary production of recent years, which included not only the works of which we have just spoken, but shorter poems and less perfect works. At that time his fecundity was remarkable.

Juliusz Słowacki

Unceasingly, he composed new dramatic works and poems, which, generally, he does not complete. These fragments mostly published after his death, make one think of the heads of the statues of Phidias and are to be admired for the daring boldness of the chisel and the immaculate purity of the colouring. The unfinished poem *Beniowski* (the Polish *Don Juan*) shows a masterly artistic technique. Fragments of dramas such as "The Incorrigibles" and the "Golden Skull" show new characteristics in the dramatic talent of Słowacki. He read much in different languages. When at Florence, he was interested by the talent of Calderon, especially by the *El Principe Constante*. He reproduced this Spanish tragedy in wonderful poetry and transformed the subject according to his will. This transformation of a Spanish drama of the XVIIth century into a romantic Polish tragedy is really a unique work of its kind.

The author of *Anhelli,* the transformer of the *Indomitable Prince* could not escape Towiański's influence. He gets connected with the new teaching as closely as Mickiewicz.

He undergoes inner transformation, forsakes earthly ambition and gets reconciled with Mickiewicz. But he did not follow blindly the teaching of the "Master". He accepted what already existed potentially in the sphere of his own belief and of his own feelings. But he adds

much, not being in sympathy with the methods of activity of the "Towianists".

He began to act, he, who, till then, had been incapable of any lasting and systematical action. He gathers a small group of followers and does not cease writing. He even increased his literary activity, directing it entirely towards the solution of the ultimate mystery of human existence and of the destiny of his nation. He wrote propaganda, letters, philosophic controversies, ceaselessly creating, consumed by the fire of proselytism, also by the fever of increasing consumption. He believed himself to be the elected servant of God, the marvellous cup filled with grace whose contents were one day to be poured on the mistrustful and refractory masses of the people.

He staggered under the burden of this mission, but he followed with meekness and steadfastness this road to Golgotha, the unique road that was to lead to the freedom of Poland and of all humanity.

Under the unceasing strain of all his mental faculties, he wrote dramas, sketched new poems, and undertook the execution of gigantic conceptions. He was dying, but pen in hand, leaving fragments of a grand unfinished epic, called: *The King-Spirit*. The subject is gigantic. It would be difficult to find one akin to it, in the whole of universal literature. It was based on the idea of Reincarnation and described the successive incarnations of the Creative Spirit, the Leader of the Polish nation. He hoped to show in this poem the historiosophical mission of Poland. The poet was allowed to finish only the narration of the first incarnations. They are fragments of untold power, marvellous paintings, expressed in octave stanzas of wonderful perfection.

He died before reaching his fortieth year. Like Mickiewicz he sacrificed himself to the Polish cause; like his great colleague, he confounded this cause with that of humanity. He died early, broken by the ungrateful struggle to establish the Kingdom of God on earth. He was as he beautifully expressed it: "the pilot of a boat laden with spirits".

Particularities of his genius account for the fact, that, today, for modern Polish poets, it is Słowacki and not Mickiewicz, who is the adored Master and Model. But history, the "corrector of life", does not establish any comparison between these two lofty beings. It will set them both on the same level as two different expressions of Poland's national genius. And it will say of Słowacki, that he was, in the world's literature, one of the great Masters of the Word.

. . . . .

The third and youngest of the Polish "Trinity of poet prophets", was Count Sigismund Krasiński, the son of a general under Napoleon, born in Paris 1812. He was educated in the traditions of an aristocratic family.

He possessed a much more speculative spirit than his two colleagues and this spirit is the characteristic of his work.

Polish philosophy had taken a new life with romantic philosophy, and more especially that of Hegel, and Krasiński's mentality follows this lead. In Poland the philosophical movement inspired many interesting personalities, such as the genial universalist Joseph Hoehne-Wroński, author of French works ("Prolégomènes du Messianisme", "Prodrome du Messianisme" "Métapolitique messianique"), which, till today, have not been sufficiently studied. Ferdinand Trentowski, who for some time was privat-docent at the university of Freiburg (Grand-Duchy of Baden) and wrote in German ("Grundlage der universellen Philosophie", "Vorstudien zur Wissenschaft der Natur") and, finally, Augustus Cieszkowski, who wrote indifferently in Polish, French and German. We do not mention several other remarkable minds.

Krasiński was much interested in this movement. He was in intimate relation with many of these Polish thinkers. He possessed a deep knowledge of western philosophy, increased by incessant reading, by residing in the great European capitals, and by an active correspondence with many striking personalities of his time.

From childhood on, he was interested in social questions as well as in philosophy, but all was dominated by the problem of Poland, for all the efforts of Polish spirits aimed at its solution.

The expansion of Krasiński's mind was precocious, like that of Słowacki. Even more than for the author of the *King-Spirit,* his mental exceeded his physical strength. His organism was a feeble one, bent under the heavy inherited burden of consumption. A chronical weakness of the eyes obliged him to long seclusion in a dark room. This was the cause of a nervous depression, of a painful discord between his will to live and his physical possibilities. It is there we find the origin of the "Hamletism", which pervades his life and his work, of his ardent will for direct action and of the lack of strength of realisation. From another point of view, these same circumstances hastened the unfolding of his mental capacities of thought, of that vision "of the mind's eye" as Shakespeare calls it in *Hamlet.*

The circumstances of life rendered more acute the interior tragedy of life of this Polish magnate, who, in appearance, possessed all conditions to be the happiest of men. In reality, he had to fight unceasingly, against himself, against public opinion in his country, against

the democratic tendencies around him and against his own father, whom he deeply loved and who—in the Revolution of November—was not present amongst the best of Poland's sons. It was the "sorrow of sorrows" of the poet. After the year 1830, he went into voluntary exile, remaining alternately in Switzerland, in Italy, in Germany and in France, visiting from time to time the Russian capital and his hereditary estate in Poland, ever seeking physical health, which he never found, and that inner peace, which he rarely found and only for brief moments. With all his heart, he wished to serve the national cause, though far from the motherland and with but few links with most of the emigrants. He could not hope that his voice might be heard. But he relinquished all desire of personal glory; all his works were anonymous or signed by a friend's name.

He began to write very early (he was a mere youth), and adopted the form of the novel, attracted like so many of his contemporaries by the works of Byron and of Walter Scott. He wrote French as well as Polish. At Geneva, where he first stays, begins and ripens his inner transformation, and this, thanks to his personal contact with Mickiewicz. At Rome, where he goes later, he keeps up intimate relations with Mickiewicz.

The reading of the works of Cousin, Guizot, Ballanche and de Gérando formed, with the echoes of the events which unfolded themselves in his country, a most heterogeneous mass in the soul of the young man. He lays the foundations of different artistic conceptions and writes fragments, which later will become remarkable works. The social conflicts which already are becoming more acute in the West, incite him to deep meditation on the future of Europe, whose very foundations seemed shaken.

Then comes for him the painful necessity of spending five months in Petersburg, at the court of the Tsar. The soul of the poet goes through the fiery ordeal of temptation, he comes out victorious, having chosen between imperial favour and his duty as a patriot. And it is then, that Krasiński leaves aside universal, social questions, to undertake to unravel the national Polish problem.

This definite orientation of mind inspired the two great works of Krasiński, works which ripened together in his mind and took the form of two dramatic poems, written in wonderful rhythmical prose. They are the: *Infernal Comedy* and *Iridion.* The *Infernal Comedy* is one of the most powerful social dramas in the world. It sketches an appalling and thrilling picture of the ultimate struggle between the two opposite camps which divide humanity, aristocracy and democracy.

The Head of the first is Count Henry, a portrait of the author, which is far from being flattered. This Head of the aristocrats is a dreamer and a poet, of feeble will and lacking faith in the final victory of his cause. He not only sees the defects of his adversaries, but all those of his partisans. His adversaries besiege the castle of Count Henry, the Castle of the Holy Trinity, the last bulwark of the aristocrats. The besiegers are led by Pancrace. It is a character sketched with extraordinary relief and without the least tendency to caricature. Cold and impassible, he dominates the leader of the aristocrats by a mighty will-power but respects him and vainly seeks to convert him to his ideas. In this scene the dialogue is wonderful. At the moment of the supreme struggle, both adversaries fall and a Third, the Christ, triumphs. He appears in the Epilogue, crowned with thorns, the Symbol of love and sacrifice.

The concentration of the action of this dramatic poem cannot be sufficiently admired. The author, at that time, little more than twenty years old, undertakes an immense subject. He builds up his *Comedy* by utilising the bases of the problem of the earthly existence of Humanity. The Italian Master had formerly embraced in his "Divine" trilogy the immensity of super-earthly existence, outside time and space. For many years, the young poet had meditated on this subject. He exposes it in scenes and pictures, where the action unrolls itself quick as lightning, and, with this heroic action, he mingles lyrical fragments of matchless beauty.

The *Infernal Comedy* possessed for its author the value of a living document. In *Anhelli* Słowacki has expressed his attitude towards the Polish cause. In the *Infernal Comedy,* Krasiński examines his attitude towards the two main social contradictory ideas, which, both, are for him barren, when they are not redeemed by the fire of Christian love.

In this way Krasiński found again the peace of his conscience and calmed his ardent wish for action, a wish, always hampered by interior and external obstacles.

The second dramatic poem: *Iridion* gave, according to Krasiński, the solution of the national problem. The events of 1831 inspired him with the idea of this drama. It was entirely completed and printed only in the year 1836.

The action develops itself at the time of the decline of the Roman Empire in the III. century B.C. Helped by scientific researches and the reading of many books, Krasiński came to possess a deep knowledge of this historical period. The psychology of his hero testifies to the influence of *Konrad Wallenrod,* of the *Konrad* of the *Third Part of the Ancestors* and of *Kordian.* Iridion is, as they were, the avenger of the sufferings inflicted by Rome on Greece, his fatherland.

The son of a Greek and of a German, Iridion becomes a Christian in order to win to his scheme the followers of the new religion. He personifies the dements that helped to overthrow the Roman Empire, which seemed the omnipotent master of the world. But the idea of the triumph of revenge did not satisfy the poet. In this work, the real triumpher is the Christ-force, which frees the hero from the bonds of the impure spirit, Massinissa, the sinister "Old man of the wilderness".

In the Epilogue which follows the drama, Iridion goes to sleep, but, after centuries, awakes to a new life, to a new and different work. Without joy he sees the ruins of Rome. He no longer wishes to destroy, but he yearns to toil in the sweat of his brow and in a spirit of absolute sacrifice. A second test awaits him, he is sent to the far northern land "the land of crosses and tombs" where reigns the Evil he has to fight by love and sacrifice.

The publication of the *Iridion* was followed by years of labour, consecrated to the solution of the problem of Poland, to the study of her historical mission, of the causes of her fall and of the conditions necessary for her resurrection. This work fills the life of Krasiński. Slowly and with difficulty, he finds again his moral equilibrium, being engaged in a love affair which weighs on him and resisting his father's will to see him married, in order to secure the survival of their illustrious family.

Living in continual excitement, he never ceases working, using for his labour the favourite form of his prophetical dreams.

He writes his poems in prose, but is beginning to attempt versification. It is certainly Julius Słowacki, whose acquaintance he made in Italy, who incited him to write poetry. A sincere interchange of ideas unites these two exceptional men: soon they are bound by the close ties of mutual esteem and admiration. Unhappily, later, differences of social opinions were to separate them. At the beginning their union was beneficial for both. Słowacki immortalised it in the characters of the two brothers, riveted to the same chain and fighting for their motherland (*Lilla Weneda*). His most beautiful works were dedicated to the author of *Iridion.* In this way he showed his gratitude to Krasiński, who first recognised and appreciated at its due value the beauty of the poetry of the author of *Anhelli.*

Krasiński admired the verses of Słowacki so much the more, because he himself had great difficulty in conquering the mastery of verse, always hampered by his tendency to philosophical considerations and by a certain narrowness of vision. The poet found in his new friend a wonderful teacher, who taught him to face his difficulties. These difficulties were immediately surmounted by his first great love which took all his being and freed him from a painful self-analysis and from the hallucinations of a feverish imagination, which revelled in violent and exaggerated contrasts.

At this time, the speculative mentality of the poet attained the steadfast point he had yearned for. Thanks to the influence of the new-Hegelian school, modified by Cieszkowski, with whom the poet becomes intimate, Krasiński finds the solution of problems and the answer to questions which for so long had tortured him.

He delivered the message thus received in a fragmentary philosophical dissertation, recently published: "Of Divine and of human Trinity". This dissertation is a synthesis of all the meditations of the poet on the part played by Poland in general human evolution. According to Krasiński, this evolution has undergone two phases and is on the eve of a third one, where the chief part will be played by Slavonian nations, first of all by Poland, Poland being specially designed for this mission by her past glory and her present misery.

It is a glorious mission! This mission is not the conquest and domination of one nation on others; on the contrary, it entirely rests on universal love, on the fulfilment of a humanitarian ideal: the Freedom and Union of all Humanity.

The generous idealism of these Polish thinkers who wished to uplift the cause of their country to the height of an universal ideal, found a new life in the mind of the young romantic poet. Stronger than the natural feeling of resentment against injustices endured, this idealism had already conjured the thirst for revenge by the spirit of love and of sacrifice.

This conception of the historical mission of Poland was not an individual conception of Krasiński. The faith in this mission had for centuries been anchored in the Polish soul; it manifests itself in the literature and in the political history of the Poles. Historically speaking, their duty was to protect the open boundaries of their country against invasions of the West by the East. Poland sacrificed innumerable and bloody hecatombs of her sons for the defence of her soil which she considered as the most exposed bulwark of western Europe. She consecrates to her ideal her own political interests and, everywhere and always, she sympathised with all the movements which fought for human or national liberty.

It is not to be wondered at if Polish messianism was the natural offspring of such souls. The literary expression of this conception is already to be found in the "Psalmody" of Kochowski (XVIIth century), but its full expansion corresponds to the time of the Emigration, after the disaster of 1831.

These Polish poets and thinkers necessarily discovered in the Polish misfortune a superior, subtle, metaphysical sense, or else they would have cursed the destiny which had made them Poles. The idea of the sacrifice of a nation for all the nations, of the Redemption of the sins of the Universe by the sacrifice of a nation, this idea explained the ruin and decay of Poland, it calmed patriotic feeling, which, after 1831, was akin to despair. It allowed them to think that Poland—the Messiah of nations—would rise again as Christ Himself had risen from the dead, and that She would have a seat of honour in the meeting where all European nations would be reconciled.

No Polish poet expressed this idea more beautifully than Krasiński. After having perfected the form of his verse, in a series of lyrical poems, after having reached a philosophical synthesis, he began a new life under the guidance of his "Beatrice", his spiritual Beloved. He wrote "The Dawn", the most beautiful, the most loved of all his works (1843).

Everything contributed to the creation of this poem. The love-spell under which he was for the woman who became for the Polish poet what the "donna pietosa" was for Dante; the ideal scenery around the lake of Como, where both dreamt of future Poland and, above all, absolute, ardent faith in the realization of his dreams. The unperishable charm of this poem is due to the inner joy which radiates from it. This joy wins the soul of the reader, tired of seeing the triumph of evil, the preponderance of mediocrity, the brutality of blind, inhuman forces.

Few Poles still believe in the historiosophy of the "Dawn". Painful experiences have shattered these romantic dreams: today we know that tortured humanity is still very far away from the time of which the author of the "Dawn" was dreaming. But the unique charm of this poem and the melody of its rhythm cannot disappear, for they are everlasting, as are everlasting all Beauty's true manifestations in art.

The literary production of Krasiński does not go beyond the degree of perfection reached in the "Dawn". For a long while he remains at this high level, continuing to express in his five "Psalms of the Future" the ideas enunciated in "Dawn". He wrote them successively, beginning with the "Psalm of Faith", then came the "Psalm of Hope". He resumes in these writings the ideas of his philosophical dissertation on "Trinity" and of his poem "Dawn". Frightened by the extension in Poland of democratic currents which came from the Emigration, he wrote his "Psalm of Love", in which he condemned radicalism and warns people of its dangers. Słowacki answered him by a fiery and wonderful poem.— Krasiński replied by his "Psalm of Contrition", where he recalls the events of 1846, so tragic for Poland.

The deepest and most beautiful of these Psalms is the last one: the "Psalm of Good Will". The thesis of the real spiritual revival of the nation is given here in a most poetical and artistic form. The authority and the earnestness of a priest and a prophet penetrate this work through and through.

The "Psalm of Good Will" marks the term of the creative evolution of Krasiński. His other poems: "The Present Day", "The Last" and "Resurrecturis" contain partly the main idea of his work. He thought of composing a poem he never ended and which bears the name of "Unfinished Poem". It is a collection of fragments composed at different moments of his life, where may be found thoughts and pictures already published in other works of Krasiński, but reproduced here in more beautiful and more powerful variations.

In the last ten years of his life, Krasiński laid aside poetry and, with devotion, waited for the realisation of the prophecies contained in the "Dawn". He follows political events attentively, hoping that they would be the Herald of the important changes he expected. He writes French pamphlets, he sends open letters to different Statesmen, calling their attention to Poland. In 1848, he goes to Rome, where he had obtained an audience of Pope Pie IX. In the holy city he meets Mickiewicz, who had come there with the same object. Each followed a different road, but both served the same ideal: the freedom of Humanity.

Both considered Napoleon III as the man sent by Providence, and both saw in the Turkish war the beginning of great political changes. Krasiński undertakes political action: he sends the Emperor of the French a memoir on the Polish cause and twice discusses the subject with Napoleon in person.

He died in full activity at forty-seven years of age (1859) in Paris, where he was born. Death finds him at his post, bearing the banner on which he had written his high ideal for humanity indissolubly united to the vision of his liberated motherland.

Krasiński's "Psalm of Good Will" not only ends the ascending line of the poetical talent of the "Anonymous Poet", but it closes the series of the Polish masterpieces published in the first half of the XIXth century.

These masterpieces, due to the pen of the three masters of [Polish Romanticism], are entirely different and yet they mutually complete one another. Conceived on foreign soil, these works are the expression of a general human ideal, but also of the patriotic ideal and they unite, in a wonderful harmony, these two ideas.

Manfred Kridl (essay date 1956)

SOURCE: "Polish Romanticism before 1830," in *A Survey of Polish Literature and Culture,* translated by Olga Scherer-Virski, Mouton & Co., 1956, pp. 213-40.

[*In the following excerpt, Kridl comments on the career, works, style, and overall contribution of Mickiewicz to Polish Romanticism.*]

As a movement, romanticism affected not only literature but also certain other domains of intellectual and cultural life. . . . [In] different countries and among many writers of the same epoch and of the same general literary direction, the movement revealed a variety of facets. If we take such representative romantic poets and writers as Byron and Shelley in England, Novalis, the brothers Schlegel, Tieck, and Kleist in Germany, Victor Hugo, Lamartine, Musset, and Vigny in France, Manzoni in Italy, Mickiewicz and Słowacki in Poland, Lermontov in Russia, and so on, we notice that each of them represents a distinct creative individuality, a distinct creative style, although the problems they touch upon, and even their literary forms, may be the same or similar. Nevertheless, all of them appear to possess something in common, something which it is difficult to define and which is usually figuratively called the 'spirit of the epoch' or the spirit of a literary or cultural movement. One of these common traits is the claim to creative freedom, which had been propagated earlier and was by now considered basic. This freedom, of course, makes itself felt first of all in its relation to classicist poetics. Romanticism advocates the liberation of art from the chains and limitations imposed on it by classical poetics, especially the strict division between literary genres and the manner of their treatment. During romanticism literary genres do not so much cease to exist—certain general frames and requirements of the drama and lyric and epic poetry are and must be respected—as they begin to mingle together, to penetrate one another and form various new combinations which were unknown to or avoided by the classical poets. More than anything it is the lyric element that transforms the traditional forms. The lyric element appears even in the dramatic and epic genres; dramas were imbued with lyricism, while epic poems not only displayed strong lyric elements but abounded in long personal confessions, comments, opinions, invectives, accusations, and so on. Pure lyric poetry, which the classicist poets either neglected or cultivated rarely, now occupied a leading position; at the same time its basic character was altered to become more intensive, more tender, sometimes more explosive.

Creative freedom was rooted in a deeper, more general foundation; namely, that of individualism—the feeling and recognition of the rights of the individual, of the truth and holiness of his inner world, and of his opposition to all the limiting social demands. The individual was conceived not as a member of a certain collective, subject to its laws and duties, but rather as a value raised above the collective and distinct from it. The attitude toward the collective, towards the masses, was at best critical; most often it was negative, disdainful, inimical, mocking. By virtue of its structure, in which ordinary people, ordinary 'bread-eaters' (as Słowacki expressed it) compose the majority, the world can neither understand a higher individual nor grasp the tasks, aims, and destination of the poet. Hence pessimism, bitterness, and a fundamental discord with the world were the chief motifs of many romantic poets who led lonely and isolated spiritual lives. That same disharmony with the world found a different outlet among more vigorous individuals, those who felt the need for actively carrying out their ideals; rather than resorting to introversion or placing barriers between themselves and the world, they resolved to fight it, in an effort to refashion according to their own beliefs. One of the outstanding representatives of just this type of romantic personality was Adam Mickiewicz, 'the eternal revolutionary,' a destroyer of old forms and orders, always seeking a new, dreamed-of order in things, while keeping pace—especially in the last period of his life—with the most radical political and social movements.

The separation from classicism was accompanied by a complete rejection of rationalism. It is clear that the general attitude described above could not tolerate allegiance to 'reason' as the highest authority of control over the instincts and feelings of the human spirit. Quite to the contrary, the romanticists declared war on reason thus conceived. Sensing (perhaps subconsciously) that reason was their most dangerous foe, they waged war in all possible and impossible ways; they elaborated peculiar, fantastic theories and doctrines in order to win human minds and to push them in a new direction. What was that direction? The romanticists answered this question in various ways: frequently with splendid poems and at times with strange treatises in which they tried to combat reason with its own weapon— reasoning. On the whole, they tended to contrast 'feeling' and 'reason,' conceiving of the former in a very general and 'foggy' way; they also spoke of intuition as something apparently incompatible with reason. Furthermore, they introduced the domain of the 'infinite' which is the realm of inspiration, spiritual ecstasy, revelation—a domain allegedly unattainable to reason. The mysteries of the inner life of the soul as well as those of the world—not of the earthly, physical world, but the one beyond the earth, the supernatural, the one ungrasped by the senses, the world of eternity and the infinite—were the chief attraction for the romanticists. They searched for eternal matters, for the essence of things, the quintessence of life. Minor, ordinary, fleeting matters they disdained. This sent them back to the Middle Ages, to ancient beliefs, and folk superstitions. It led them into the world of magic and witches, ghosts and spirits, the world of the dead, and of the secluded cemeteries and chapels. It also frequently led them to mysticism and belief in the most fantastic and incredible faiths. They found a deeper meaning in all this; for them the most vulgar superstition could take on the shape of a symbol of some

hidden truth until then unknown; they saw mysterious emblems of those hidden truths everywhere, as they surrounded themselves with a world of premonitions, riddles, mysteries, and symbols.

The artistic embodiment of this spiritual world was of various kinds. Not only the minor poets but sometimes even the outstanding ones stooped to romantic mannerisms which, from the point of view of artistic effects, were not different from classical mannerisms. In such cases the magic, fantastic, or mystical world became a mere piece of stagecraft, a cheap decoration, which closely resembled the neoclassic personifications of ancient divinities. Ghosts, corpses, spirits, or the science of magic, expressed as little as did the personified Wars, Discords, and Loves.

Problems involved in romanticism are thus comparable to those of other literary movements. In its general character it undoubtedly expressed the spirit of the epoch—and it expressed it powerfully and profoundly or poorly and grotesquely, depending on its representatives in poetry. Its durable values lay where, overcoming a momentary, passing mood, it rose to universal and eternal problems, giving them a new and artistically forceful expression.

The romantic epoch of Polish literature begins with the year 1822. It is the date of the publication of the first small volume of poems by Mickiewicz in Wilno. The twenty-four-year old poet was at once accorded a position in the forefront of the Polish literary movement and remained there for many years to come. Nearly every new work of his was a milestone in the development of Polish literature. Mickiewicz was a poetical genius of such stature that he was able to raise Polish literature to its position as one of the first among the Slavic literatures and insure it a notable place in world literature.

The personal history of Mickiewicz is as interesting and moving as is his career as an artist. The story of his life reveals such a rich, many-sided, vital, and sparkling individuality—a splendid and profoundly human type of man—that it deserves detailed treatment. Both as man and poet, Mickiewicz was spokesman for the most essential values of Polish culture; his work was a magnificent testimony to its living power and imperishability. He was both the producer and product of that culture—a sculptor of the Polish soul for many generations to come.

Mickiewicz was a native of the territory of the former Grand Duchy of Lithuania, an area rich in age-old Polish culture, the cradle of many great Poles. The social class that gave him birth and upbringing was the middle gentry of the kind that could until recently be seen in those regions (there are still several Mickiewicz families). The place of his birth was probably Zaosie, a village situated at a small distance from Nowogródek, where his father, a lawyer at the Nowogródek court, owned a small piece of land. He was born on December 24, 1798, three years after the last partition of the Republic, already in captivity; the conditions and circumstances prevailing then, however, were quite similar to those of the last period of independence. . . . Russia had at first permitted some freedoms to the Poles living under its occupation and maintained a few of their former autonomous institutions. Thus at the time of Mickiewicz's youth there were still Polish courts, municipal and rural offices, and schools. According to the custom of the time, he was first educated at home; he later studied at the parochial school of the Dominican Brothers in Nowogródek. He preserved very pleasant memories of it. His parents spent most of the year in a house they owned in Nowogródek, both because of the official duties of the poet's father and the children's education.

Mickiewicz's 'idyllic and angelic' childhood—as he himself later called it—ended in the indelible impressions connected with the year 1812. The first was the march of Napoleon's armies, Polish divisions among them, on their way to Moscow through Nowogródek in the Spring of that year. This marked the beginning of a campaign which awoke great hope in the Polish nation and made a deep impression on the fourteen-year-old Mickiewicz. Too soon the joy was turned to sadness and despair, when in the winter of the same year, after the disaster in Russia, that same Nowogródek witnessed the return of the remains of Napoleon's once magnificent army. Its defeat was also the defeat of Polish hopes.

The second event to strike the poet was the death of his father, also in the year 1812. It greatly worsened the financial situation of the family and forced them to manage by themselves. There are testimonies that, as a student of the Nowogródek school, Mickiewicz helped his mother by giving private lessons.

In 1815 Mickiewicz entered the University of Wilno. We know that the University was then at its height and numbered many outstanding scholars among its faculties. Also, being the capital of a large province of Poland, Wilno was at the time a lively, busy city which sparkled with a worldly atmosphere and attracted the regional gentry. The intellectual movement was maintained not only by the University but also by scholarly and literary societies, and by excellent newspapers and periodicals to which outstanding authors contributed.

The young Mickiewicz thus found favorable conditions at the University for the development of his great innate talents. He studied under the faculty of the humanities, devoting himself particularly to Polish literature and the ancient languages and literatures as well as to history. His teachers were Leon Borowski,

a well-educated and conscientious scholar of Polish, Ernest Groddeck, of German origin, an outstanding expert in classical philology, and Joachim Lelewel, at the time an assistant professor of history, but eventually Poland's most distinguished historian of the nineteenth century. Mickiewicz's studies were serious, extensive, and deep. What he learned at the University of Wilno gave him a solid basis for further self-education. That these university studies were thorough is supported by the fact that twenty years after his graduation from the University, after the difficult and stormy period of his life when he had no time for systematic studies, Mickiewicz was invited by the University of Lausanne to teach Latin language and literature and fulfilled his task with excellent competence and great success; a year later he occupied the chair of Slavic literatures at the Collège de France.

However, other things absorbed the young Mickiewicz besides his studies. He manifested a social instinct and the need for social action quite early. In Wilno he found an opportunity for activity in the student organizations, in which he soon achieved a leading position. On the 1st of October, 1817, that is, two years after Mickiewicz's arrival in Wilno, a secret society was founded under the name of the Society of Philomats or friends of learning. It initially possessed a 'scholarly' character, or rather, the character of a 'self-educational' society, in that its purpose was mutual help in academic work in order to supplement the knowledge received at the University. Gradually, however, and especially thanks to Mickiewicz, the aims of the Society began to broaden, embracing the moral and patriotic education of the youth; eventually they were to widen still further by taking in even the older population, and establishing contact with the conspiratorial political organizations in the Congress Kingdom. This expansion of the aims of the initial 'self-educational circle' is quite characteristic for its founders and principal exponents, as well as for the general situation of the country, which seemed to impose an organization on a wider scale. In connection with this developed the organization of the Society. In this domain the Philomats, and particularly Mickiewicz, gave proof of an extraordinary sense of organization, of energy in carrying out their projects, and an ability for conspiratorial work as well as first-rate executive talent. The basis of the organization was simple, but very clever. The point was to maintain utter secrecy as to the existence of the Society of Philomats and at the same time subject the largest possible number of university youths to its influence. For this purpose the Society of Philomats admitted to the 'inner circle' only outstanding and trustworthy young men, united in friendship and devotion to the cause. For the others, the less experienced and less trustworthy youths, the Philomats founded separate societies, some secret, others open and legalized by the university authorities. The organization of those additional societies was not as strict; membership was not so restricted. These societies were to serve a double purpose: to furnish new members to the Society of Philomats, which was known only to the Philomats, and to organize youth according to the slogans and ideals of the Philomats. Thus were created the Circle of Friends, the Society of the Philarets or the Friends of Virtue, and others. These societies were informed neither about the existence of the Philomats nor even of the fact that they were directed by the Philomats; it was always one of the Philomats who founded a minor society, as a completely independent one, and it was he who acted either as its president or as a member of the administration. Sometimes several Philomats entered the executive board of a minor society. The advantages of such an organization were obvious. It kept the Society of Philomats from the danger of being 'discovered'; even in case of discovery by the authorities of one of the minor organizations, their kernel and principal power remained untouched.

Such is in brief the skeleton of the organization of the Wilno youth, planned and partly executed by a small group (nineteen) of outstanding young men, devoted to their cause and taking their work seriously, sometimes even excessively pedantic in matters of statutes and laws. On the other hand, they were healthy, gay boys who liked to have fun and to take a drink when there was an occasion; they frequently organized gay parties or excursions to the country, and so on. This entertainment did not disturb them in their intensive scholarly and social activity. The relations between the Philomats were warm and intimate, but without exaggeration or excessive sentimentalism. Among the outstanding Philomats we should mention Tomasz Zan, the leader of the Philarets, Józef Jeżowski, first president of the Society, Franciszek Malewski, son of the rector of the University, and Jan Czeczot, the closest friend of Mickiewicz in his youth.

It is in connection with the Society of Philomats that Mickiewicz's literary activity begins. As the chairman of the literary division of the Society he wrote and read aloud many literary treatises and reviews; it was also during the reunions of the division as well as at social gatherings of his colleagues that he presented his first poetic works. There are among them gay, carefree songs written on the occasion of birthdays—products of the moment; there are also more serious works, written in classical style, under the influence of Polish classical writers and of Voltaire. One of these works, the highly classical *Zima miejska* (City Winter), was printed in the *Tygodnik Wileński* (Wilno Weekly) in 1818. Others remained in manuscript form, though there were works among them much more worthy of printing, such as, for instance, an excellent adaptation (*Darczanka*) of one of the songs of *La Pucelle d'Orléans* by Voltaire, written in a racy, colorful language, in an easy, smooth verse.

Adam Mickiewicz

To all these experiences and adventures a new one was soon added: his first great love. In the summer of 1818 Mickiewicz met Maryla Wereszczakówna, daughter of an aristocratic and wealthy family; this acquaintance turned into love, unfortunately an unhappy love because of the excessive social difference between the poor student and an heiress to large estates who had been destined by her parents for a different matrimonial career. Much has been written about the history of this love; but most of it is based on Mickiewicz's poetic confessions rather than on facts. It is almost always disappointing to draw biographic conclusions from poetic confessions. We may, at any rate, conclude, basing ourselves on facts, that this feeling, which was not too absorbing at the beginning, intensified and strengthened at the moment when Maryla married, while the lonesome poet lived in Kowno, far from his beloved Society, his activity in it, and his friends.

Mickiewicz was educated in Wilno as a fellow of the University, in return for which he was obliged after his graduation to work for a few years as a teacher in a *gymnasium*. When he finished his studies in 1819, he secured a position as teacher in Kowno. Though life was difficult and lonely for him there, he fulfilled his task conscientiously, even attempting to introduce new methods of teaching. His stay in Kowno, however, was important chiefly from another point of view. Here the poet devoted himself to the study of the more recent English and German poetry; he went through periods of—as he expressed it himself—'Britannomania' and 'Germanomania'; he entered an entirely new poetic world, in connection with which his own creativeness began to undergo a transformation. As early as 1820 the *Oda do mlodości* (Ode to Youth) and *Romantyczność* (Romanticism) were written, the latter being a programmatic poem of the Polish romantic movement; then followed a series of poems which filled Mickiewicz's small volume published in 1822. Most of the space in it was devoted to ballads and romances, the character and significance of which are explained by the author in a preface. They prove how impressed he was with these new forms of West-European poetry and how eager to transplant them to the Polish poetic soil. The volume contained eleven ballads (among them a translation of Schiller's *Der Handschuh*) and two 'romances.' There was a kind of poetic introduction (*Primrose*), a poetical 'program' (*Romanticism*), three 'nixie-ballads,' three of a humorous character, one child-like tale and one folksong. It is true that even before the appearance of Mickiewicz, ballads of all kinds had been written in Poland (for instance, ballad-like *dumas* with lyric-reflective, historical, fantastic and folklore elements), but none of them, not even the best, could equal any of the ballads of Mickiewicz. Therein lies their principal significance. He at once placed this poetic genre in Poland on a high artistic level, which easily equalled that of the West-European masters of the ballad, Schiller and Goethe. It should be added that, far from imitating foreign models, these works, though conceived in a 'ballad' spirit, were quite original both in their motifs, their descriptions of nature, and their use of native folklore elements, not to speak of language and verse.

Let us, for instance, take, the following formulation of *Romanticism:*

> You delve among death truths, to men unknown,
> The world you see in dust and specks of light;
> But Truth you know not, miracles disown—
> Look in your heart, that still may see aright!

This simple, but condensed quatrain, addressed to the 'wise man,' contains profound problems of the relation of 'dead,' 'scientific' truths to 'live' truths of the sentiment—the relation of the world of thought to that of 'miracles.'

And how often, even in these earliest works of Mickiewicz, do we come upon first-rate beauties, extraordinary poetic formulations, and heart-tearing scenes of the native land.

One may also find in the ballads a considerable number of passages which are products purely of the epoch in which they were born, elements of a certain passing fashion in Polish and foreign literature. These are unavoidable phenomena in any older poetry. But even those elements—as we shall later see in *Dziady* (Forefathers' Eve)—gain a new, moving expression in Mickiewicz's work. This is true in *Forefathers' Eve* of certain beliefs and rituals of the peasants, which constitute merely an external decoration and are not yet taken seriously in the ballads. . . .

[*Ode to Youth*] is an extraordinary phenomenon in Polish poetry of the time. Since ancient times odes have been written all over the world; many were written in Poland, especially in the period of classicism. But against the background of the Polish acquest in this field the *Ode to Youth* rises as a young, powerful oak above the crowns of other trees. Conserving the general character of the classical ode—expressed in the 'sublime' subject, the weighty rhetorical elements shown in the formulation of slogans, in the invocations and exclamations, in the periphrases, the sophisticated epithets, and personifications—this ode yet represents a thoroughly new work. It is imbued with the new spirit, which shines not merely in its audacity and the revolutionary turn of concepts (the idea of humanity and of universal happiness, the cult of liberty, fraternity, and disdain for materialism), but primarily in the strength, the elan and the conciseness of poetic expression accorded these concepts. The uneven, broken rhythm, the lengthening and shortening of the rhythmic line, which sometimes contains only two words, the rejection of regular stanzas and their replacement by uneven parts of the poem, a free use of rhymes quite distant from one another, the sublime and pathetic but at the same time vivid and concrete language—all these taken together show the *Ode to Youth* to be a product of an already mature art.

Another mature work of this period is the poem *Żeglarz* (Sailor), an expression of strong individualism, of the idea that the individual is both the sole reality and represents a world in itself to which nobody, 'except God,' has access.

Forefathers' Eve, the two parts of which (designated as II and IV) appeared in Mickiewicz's next little volume of poetry, published in 1823, is a lyric-dramatic poem in the romantic style. The title is drawn from an ancient folk ritual, celebrated in White Russia on All Souls' Day for the purpose of honoring the memory of the dead forefathers. These rituals took place secretly and at night in abandoned chapels or cemeteries (since the clergy prohibited this semi-pagan custom) and involved 'evoking' the ghosts of the dead and serving them food and drink. According to testimonies, similar rituals, though in a somewhat different form from that presented in the poem, still took place in Lithuania at the time of Mickiewicz's youth. It is therefore probable that Mickiewicz could have witnessed such a ritual personally, as he summarily states in the preface to the poem. The poem is composed of three dramatized ballads: about children in Purgatory, a cruel landlord, and a proud, unapproachable shepherdess—all presented against the background of the ritual which takes place in an abandoned graveyard chapel. These ballads are thematically connected by the idea of the necessity of suffering on earth (more generally speaking, of 'a true and full human life'), which alone can open the road to better worlds. Thus the children cannot reach heaven because they have not suffered bitter fates on earth; the cruel landlord has to suffer tortures from the ghosts of the peasants he had mistreated; the ethereal virgin, who has rejected the homage of suitors and died without even knowing sorrow, is condemned to float eternally between heaven and earth. This idea itself would not possess any original quality, were it not presented in a new, impressive way. The poet achieves artistic suggestion by evoking an atmosphere of gravity, mystery, and horror in the presentation of the extraordinary ritual and by skillfully contrasting characters: first he introduces the suffering but innocent children, then the severe, pitiless village lord, finally the insensitive virgin and the ghost of a young suicide. He also achieves it through expressive symbolism, the rhythm of choirs (a connection with the operatic form), spersed among the utterings of the acting characters; in all this the language and verse are adapted to the general atmosphere.

Part IV of *Forefathers' Eve* conserves some external features of the ritual, but reaches farther in its visionary character and symbolism. Its principal character is probably the ghost of the young suicide, whom we have met toward the end of the preceding part, and the principal motif is the picture of a passionate, insane, typically romantic, erotic love, which is literarily related to *The New Heloïse* by Rousseau and *The Sufferings of Young Werther* by Goethe, but which is intensified and expressed with greater force of passion and the complete frenzy which fills the whole being and leads to insanity and suicide. The entire work has the character of a half-dream, half-vision; thus it artistically justifies all that which is unusual in the hero's monologues, appearance, and behavior; it also justifies the fantastic weirdness of certain scenes, the symbolism (not always clear) of others, and the mysterious connection between the character and the ritual of *Forefathers' Eve*. It may easily be said that this was the first time in Polish literature that the feeling of love was expressed with such force and artistic truth in such a tremendous scale of nuances, with such a passionate intensity, with such great, almost metaphysical loftiness, and at the same time with such deeply human accents.

Neither of these parts of *Forefathers' Eve* has, of course, anything to do with the traditional dramatic genre. If in the first one we can still find traces of some elements of drama, the second is completely deprived of them, at least as regards plot or dramatic conflict. The entire struggle is within the mind of the hero, Gustav; the whole work is one long monologue (monodrama), only from time to time interrupted by the utterances of a simple rural Uniat priest to whose house Gustav's ghost has come at night to confess his experiences.

Some fragments of the abandoned first part of this poem surpass even the fourth part by their mature and brilliant artistic values, their deep insight into human problems. This applies especially to the monologue of the 'Wizard', an impressive symphonic poem in which motifs of sadness, resignation, despondency, and hopelessness follow one another and express the vanity of human efforts.

The 'Lithuanian Tale,' *Grażyna*, also included in this volume, deviates from the two preceding poems both in atmosphere and in poetic devices. It belongs to the genre of tales or novels in verse, created by West-European romantics, but differs from them in its complete lack of any exoticism, fantasy, supernatural elements, and the like. It is rather preserved in the style of a semi-classical epic narrative about the Lithuanian prince, Litavor, his beautiful wife, Grażyna, his intentions of joining the Teutonic Knights against the odious Duke Witold, and the foiling of those intentions by the valorous and patriotic Grażyna. Dressed in her husband's armor, she leads the Lithuanian knights into battle against the Teutons instead of accepting their assistance against her compatriots. We see even from these few motifs of the subject that the 'tale' possesses a dramatic character; it is full of complications and a certain mystery (Grażyna's changing into the knight's clothes, the night scenery, the battle with the Teutonic Knights); its strong Lithuanian 'local' and historical elements, as well as the patriotic element in the fight against the Germans may also be noticed. Some of these elements descend from the spirit of romanticism; they put *Grażyna* in harmony with the spirit of the time. The poet himself did not attach any major importance to this work, confessing to his friends that he had written it 'invita Minerva,' that is, without inspiration.

Mickiewicz lived in Kowno for three years, with one interruption during the academic year 1821-22, which he spent in Wilno working on the publication of his poetry. At that time the sky above the Society of the Philomats and the subordinated organizations began to cloud. These organizations had grown so large that it was difficult to preserve absolute secrecy about them. The University authorities found out about the existence of certain student societies; they organized an official inquiry, but soon suspended the proceedings. This happened in 1822. Soon, however, a relatively minute event, which had no connection with the student organizations, provoked a renewed inquest, this time a more dangerous one, for it was not conducted by the authorities of the University but by the notorious Russian senator, Novosiltsov, a high official at the side of the Grand Duke Constantine in Warsaw. He arrived in Wilno with the definite intention of making a big political issue out of a little incident, the writing on the blackboard by a gymnasium student of the words: 'Long live the Constitution of the 3rd of May.' He was inspired by a desire to discredit the University and its authorities, and especially its curator, Prince Adam Czartoryski, whose ardent enemy Novosiltsov was. Mass arrests began among the youths; they were followed by long and fatiguing inquests, during which the existence of the Philomats was not discovered, but a trace of the Philarets was found. Since the Society of Philarets included some outstanding Philomats, they were also arrested and condemned; among others, there were Mickiewicz, Zan, Jeżowski, Malewski, and Czeczot. In relation to the gathered proof of 'guilt,' the verdict was very severe; it condemned a number of students, such as Zan and Czeczot, to prison in a fortress, and others, among them Mickiewicz, Jeżowski, Malewski, to deportation to Russia; this was officially called 'placing them at the disposal of the ministry of education' for the purpose of employing them as teachers in *gubernii* very distant from Poland. The general phrasing of the verdict was that the defendents were condemned to this punishment 'for spreading nonsensical Polish nationalism.'

On the 25th of October, 1824, after half a year spent in prison, Mickiewicz left for St. Petersburg, where his fate was to be further directed. He probably did not think then that he was leaving his native country forever.

Mickiewicz's stay in Russia lasted almost four years. One must not imagine this stay as one of a prisoner or a deportee in a concentration camp. His 'transgression' was not of a serious type, even in the eyes of the central Russian authorities. His deportation only meant isolation from his country; otherwise he was granted relative freedom.

After a few months in St. Petersburg he left for Odessa, where he was to become a teacher at the so-called Richelieu College. It did not come to that, however, because the Russian authorities again changed their plans for him. By the time his permission to reside in Moscow arrived, the poet had spent several months in Odessa, where—in his own words—'he lived like a pasha,' chiefly in the company of two beautiful Polish ladies, Sobańska and Zaleska, who had a deep interest and, as it is said, even deep feeling for him. The society in which he now moved had a worldly, cosmopolitan character, quite different from what he had known in his Wilno and Kowno life. No wonder then that he surrendered to the charm of this hitherto unknown way of living; he let himself be drawn into its

whirl and enjoyed life and love to the fullest. In the summer of 1825 he made a trip to the Crimea in the company of Mr. and Mrs. Sobański and the future novelist, Henryk Rzewuski. The fruit of his Odessian period was his volume of *Sonety* (Sonnets), published in Moscow in 1826 and composed of love sonnets and Crimean sonnets. They point to a basic change in the poet's creative work at least for a time. He turned away from the world of *Forefathers' Eve* (though, as we shall see, he did not break with it completely), the realm of obscure mystery, mystical moods, romantic witchery and ghosts, turning to the charms and beauty of the outer world, to the charm of earthly love, one which gives satisfaction and delight rather than despair and insanity. In the sonnets which he now wrote some traits, some aspects of his talent, already visible in his earlier works, appeared in their full glow and magnificence: great precision and expressiveness, an almost absolute control over poetic language, and infallibility in the choice of expressions and phrases. Hence, the unusual clarity of objects and intensity of colors and light. An 'oriental' tinge of style is provided by the use of foreign, Turkish and Tatarian names and words. To this he added mastery of the difficult form of the sonnet, a precise, compact structure, careful rhythm, and impressive final *pointes*. Almost every one of the Crimean sonnets is composed of two parts which are closely joined and constitute a compact whole. In the first part we usually have a description of the splendid Crimean landscape, traced in broad but forceful strokes; against this descriptive background in the final tercets appears the lyric element: feeling, memory, thought, discreetly but distinctly expressed. There is no trace here of characteristic romantic redundance, eloquence, or carelessness of structure, which, incidentally, are made impossible by the very form of the sonnet. Everything is compact, concentrated, single in its expression. These qualities characterize masterpieces, and the *Crimean Sonnets* undoubtedly are masterpieces—and not of Polish poetry alone. Polish verse had never before risen to [that] degree of originality and perfection. . . .

In November, 1825, Mickiewicz arrived in Moscow, where he was given a position as a minor employee in the office of the governor. But while official Russian circles destined the poet for only a lowly office, the intellectual and literary circles, as well as the highest Moscow society, accepted Mickiewicz with great cordiality and hospitality. As in the past and in the future, the Russian nation did not then know much of the conditions prevailing in Poland; the Russians were not aware of the policy of their government and, on the whole, treated the Polish residents in Russia very cordially and favorably, as if they were their own compatriots. We can well imagine how they must have received such a Pole as Mickiewicz, who was already an outstanding poet with an impressive education, a thorough knowledge of literature, history, art, and foreign languages. He soon became the favorite of the Moscow salons, and he also established close relations with distinguished Russians in Moscow and later in St. Petersburg, during his longer stay there. Among them were the poets Alexander Pushkin and Zhukovsky, some outstanding literati such as Prince Viazemski, Pogodin and Polevoy, and young Russian revolutionaries such as Ryleyev and Bestuzhev, the later 'Decembrists' (organizers of the unsuccessful revolution). He also became friendly with Princess Zeneyda Wolkonska, a sincere admirer of the poet, who was a patroness of literature and art and kept the most frequented literary salon in Moscow. Mickiewicz thus acquainted himself well with various groups in Russian society: the official, the literary, and the underground. He made definite conclusions about official Russia, which he later expresses in literary works and in action; but he found a great deal of value in unofficial Russia which he commended in, among others, the poem *Do przyjaciól Moskali* (To My Russian Friends). Furthermore, in Moscow he found a numerous Polish colony, which included the illustrious Polish pianist, Marja Szymanowska, and a group of his friends from Wilno, among them Jeżowski and Malewski. Life in both Russian capitals was thus interesting and rich in impressions.

The conception of his new work, *Konrad Wallenrod,* occurred during his stay in Moscow. It marks a return to the grim and despairing 'romantic' atmosphere, from which the poet had temporarily freed himself in the *Sonnets.* A tale in verse in the style of Byron, different in mood and style from *Grażyna,* more closely resembling its model in the looseness of its structure, the explosiveness of the lyricism, and the timely allusions and digressions, *Konrad Wallenrod* traces the history of a Lithuanian of the fourteenth century, who was forced by tragic fate to become a Teutonic Knight. Behind this mask, however, one detects the modern man with his internal conflicts, moral crises, spiritual storms, and hopelessness. Wallenrod's fate is tragic, in the essential meaning of the word. Kidnapped by the Teutonic Knights from his native Lithuania, he spends long years in captivity, thinking only of wreaking vengeance upon the enemies of his country. Once during a battle between the Teutonic Knights and the Lithuanians he flees to the Lithuanian side, where he is received by the Duke Kiejstut and marries his daughter, Aldona. But the Teutonic Knights attack Lithuania again and inflict a terrible defeat on the country. Wallenrod runs away, fights in different parts of Europe, and finally enters the Teutonic Order. He wins gradually higher positions until he finally becomes the grand master. He organizes a big campaign against Lithuania and conducts it deliberately in such a way that he causes a horrible defeat of the Teutonic Knights. His vengeance is fulfilled, but he himself, morally broken, dies by suicide. Such is, quite schematically, Wallenrod's problem. His tragedy consists of the fact that he is forced by circumstances, by the cruel fate of

his country, to perform deeds which are simultaneously good and evil; they are good in that they serve his country, but evil in that they are performed with the help of deceit and treason. In this originated Wallenrod's moral problem, which condemns him to eternal torture and from which there is no escape, for its contradiction cannot be solved. The only solution is death. Wallenrod therefore dies a suicide's death after performing his deed, fully conscious of the tragic, insoluble conflict.

The structure of the poem is loose; the plot does not follow traditional epic patterns either in chronology or in motivation. Such was the poet's intention, partly under Byron's influence, partly with the aim of concealing from Russian censorship the patriotic spirit of the poem. And it is an ardent, zealous patriotism, one which requires absolute sacrifice, a desperate and tragic patriotism that fills the entire work, especially its lyrical passages. . . .

At first the poet speaks about folk poetry, which is, as it were, an ark, the most holy collection of the thoughts and feelings of the common people, preserved from generation to generation. Gradually, however, this folk song grows into a symbol of poetry in general, the most durable and sublime fruit of the human spirit, which can be destroyed neither by fire nor war and which links the past with the present and the future. Intense patriotism bursts forth in the last stanza; though formally concealed under the words of the *wajdelota* (a Lithuanian priest) about the dead past, it was intelligible to every Pole of that time.

Konrad Wallenrod was published in St. Petersburg in 1828. In April of that year the poet appeared there personally and, as in Moscow, his charm, intellect, and poetic talent conquered the hearts of the Polish and Russian residents of the capital. There are authentic testimonies as to the profound impression made by his improvisations, recitations of poetic works, sometimes entire plays, on subjects suggested by those present at the gatherings. The historian, Mikołaj Malinowski, then a resident of St. Petersburg, who kept a careful diary of the events and experiences of his life, described the unforgettable moments when Mickiewicz, overcome by a passionate, almost superhuman inspiration, improvised magnificent poems with astonishing ease and facility.

It was also in St. Petersburg in the year 1828 that the poem *Faris* was written; it is the apotheosis of power and individual freedom, put into the image of an extravagant ride through the desert of an Arab horseman who conquers many of obstacles.

In spite of the general respect he enjoyed and the favorable, cordial atmosphere, Mickiewicz was drawn to see the farther and wider world; he had already dreamed of acquainting himself with Western European culture during his Wilno and Kowno days. In 1828, having collected some funds from his publishers, he decided to carry out his old plans. Thanks to the help of influential Russian friends, he secured permission to go abroad (which was not easy in Russia for anyone, even less so for a political deportee) and in May, 1829, he started out on his journey. He first visited Germany, where he attended lectures of Hegel, which, however, did not impress him; he also met the great German poet, Goethe. He went then to Bohemia, where he met with the Czech literati; finally through Switzerland he reached Italy. After visiting Milan, Venice, and Florence he settled in Rome for a prolonged stay. The Eternal City made a profound impression upon him. 'The cupola of St. Peter covers all other Italian monuments (with its body,)' he wrote in one of his letters. It was, however, not merely a question of artistic impressions. Slowly, under the influence of various factors, a religious crisis began to ferment in him; this crisis was to lay a sound basis for his faith for his whole life, to make it unshakable, though subject to various fluctuations and undergoing changes. Among the factors which caused this crisis, or rather this strengthening of faith, one should mention the company of Father Stanislaw Chołoniewski, priest and writer then residing in Rome, to whom Mickiewicz owed— as he himself confessed—'a new view of the world and of men.' It was probably through him that the poet became acquainted with the works of Father Lamennais, an excellent writer and apologist of catholicism, whose *Essai sur l'indifférence en matière de religion* was one of the most famous of the time. Also, among his companions in Rome, Mickiewicz had examples of deeply believing and devout persons. Rome, the capital of Catholicism, must have also influenced him.

This 'new view of the world and of men' expressed itself in poetic production by a series of religious lyric poems which belong among the masterpieces of Polish poetry and would probably occupy a high place in lyric poetry of the world if it were possible—as indeed it is with no poetry—to translate it with equivalency into other languages. These poems are characterized by a special attitude toward God, one which is not frequently found even in religious lyric poetry, but which seems to constitute the essence of true religiousness. It is the feeling of personal humility, insignificance, and nothingness in the face of the power and greatness of God, a feeling of boundless joy and gratitude for the mere fact that He is, that He exists, that man may feel His presence within himself, may 'receive Him as a guest in the little home of his soul.' Accusations, complaints, grief, revolt, or even personal claims to God, so numerous among the works of other poets, are absent here. The only complaint expressed in these poems is the complaint that man always keeps crucifying his God in his heart, that he always wounds Him and makes Him suffer because of his 'evil.' The only accusation, reproach, or revolt is the accusation, reproach, and revolt against himself, against the pretenses of human pride, and against the efforts of the human mind to embrace the Mystery.

It is easy to imagine that this sort of feeling and spiritual state could not be expressed by Mickiewicz in any other than the simplest, and at the same time most spiritualized, purest language and verse. This is indeed ideally 'pure' lyric poetry in the sense that its components are 'pure' feelings devoid of any intellectual conceptions; it requires hardly any elements taken from the external world. There are few poems of this type in world poetry. The religious lyric poems of Mickiewicz represent this type to perfection.

POLISH ROMANTIC DRAMA

Julian Krzyżanowski (essay date 1972)

SOURCE: "Polish Romantic Literature: The Romantic Theatre," in *A History of Polish Literature,* translated by Doris Ronowicz, PWN-Polish Scientific Publishers, 1978, pp. 307-18.

[*In the following excerpt from a work originally published in Polish in 1972, Krzyżanowski discusses Fredro and Korzeniowski as pioneers of Polish Romantic drama.*]

The leading representatives of Polish Romanticism— Mickiewicz, Słowacki, Krasiński and Norwid—all endeavoured to create modern Polish drama. The tragic historical events enacted in their times meant that none of them were destined to see their dramatic visions presented on the stage, that they were writing for the "grandson to come", for audiences of some undefined future time. But what was the actual situation as regards theatre repertoire in those times? The answer to this question is given by the names of two writers, almost of the same age, but representing radically differing stages in the development of European drama, namely Fredro and Korzeniowski.

Count Aleksander Fredro (1795-1876), as he was wont to sign himself (for his father, a landowner who had made a fortune, purchased the title of count in Vienna) was a man whose biography contained some exceptional and some very ordinary features. Barely out of his boyhood with only a smattering of education, he was swept into the stream of historical events, when in 1809 the troops of the Duchy of Warsaw entered Galicia and the sixteen-year-old youth, Fredro enlisted; after many military adventures he was only to leave the army after the fall of Napoleon. His memoirs of this period in his life are brilliantly presented in a volume called *Topsy-Turvy Talk (Trzy po trzy)* written about the year 1845, when the perspective of time had given his adventures the charm of days gone for ever. Back in Poland, this demobilized captain and adjutant of the emperor's general staff became a rustic gentleman, which did not mean that he had no literary or political aspirations. In Warsaw, his elder brother Maksymilian, former officer of Napoleon's army, aide-de-camp to Prince Józef Poniatowski and later of Tsar Alexander I, combined the duties of a general with literary work, winning laurels as a playwright (classicist tragedies and translations of Racine) and the young Fredro, not to be outdone, managed to get his play *Mr Moneyful (Pan Geldhab)* staged and this made him realize that his calling was to be a leading comedy writer of his times. He continued this literary activity for nearly fifteen years, during which more plays of his were put on in the theatre, until 1835, when he suddenly laid down his pen, considering himself gravely insulted by the vicious, critical attacks levelled against him almost simultaneously by the fierce political agitator and Romantic writer Seweryn Goszczyński and a man of his own milieu, the Galician Count Leszek Dunin Borkowski. Aleksander Fredro did, it is true, go back to his literary work after fifteen years, but these works were only brought to light after his death in 1876. This second period of literary activity was to bring quite a lot of political writings, particularly during the period of the Spring of Nations, when one of his works, regarded as *lèse-majesté* all but led to him being sentenced to a long term of imprisonment. Thus, in the middle of the 19th century, this "honest man" of Galicia was also to fall under the curse that hung over the lives of the generation "born in slavery, fettered at birth".

Fredro's theatrical debut was in 1821 and he fell silent as a comedy writer in 1835, two dates which coincide almost exactly with the dates of Mickiewicz's *Ballads and Romances* and his *Master Thaddeus,* that is, milestones in the history of Polish Romantic literature. Aleksander Fredro's attitude towards Romanticism is one of the controversial questions of Polish literature, which was settled "on principle" without taking certain facts into consideration, as a result of which the writer whose most intensive and prolific output coincided with the creative years of Adam Mickiewicz, was looked upon either as a precursor of Romanticism or as its opponent. The misunderstandings that arose because of this meant that the origin of Fredro's works was treated one-sidedly, for no consideration was given to the differences between the motives that led him to start his literary activity and the conditions in which his literary career developed. And it is precisely the interaction of these two factors that account for the specific and individual character of the works of this author.

As regards motive, his stay in Paris was behind his decision to write comedies, his imagination being stim-

ulated by his first contact with the theatre in that city, where strains of the swan-song of the classicist comedy originating from the works of Molière were already sounding. Going to the theatres of the Paris boulevards, Fredro, who as a boy had composed little comedies for entertainment in his own home, observed the traditional devices brought to perfection by several generations of Molière's imitators. But when he started writing his own comedies, he was living in quite different conditions, due to the emergence of the Romantic trend in Polish literature. The result of this duality was something quite unusual. The writer, who looked at life with the eyes of his generation, a generation of romantics, and expressed his observations in the form of comedies of classicist structure, put literary historians in a very difficult position, for they had become accustomed to classify literary phenomena according to certain accepted criteria. But his message had its eloquence and—like all classics—still has its eloquence for theatre-goers, who are not concerned with the criteria applied by the researcher and expect a literary work to provide them with entertainment, if nothing else.

And Fredro entertained his audiences from the very beginning to the end of his career, introducing ideas into his works which were intended not so much to strengthen or improve the morals of his audiences as to evoke laughter. In other words, true comedies in the strict sense of the word. And for this reason he did not reject farcical ideas, which did not find favour with the Romantic critics, although it was not this element of his works that they attacked. So in *Ladies and Hussars (Damy i huzary)* and *Good Lord! What the Devil is This! (Gwałtu, co się dzieje)* Fredro gave us two excellent farces, composed of an unending chain of comic situations. In the former, these situations were created by the belated love affairs of sworn bachelors well advanced in years, caused by the "invasion of ladies" who arrived in a remote locality where a typical small garrison was stationed. The hilarious piling up of comic situations does not, however, become so farcical as to hide the truth of life. An elderly major realizes that he was on the point of "making the same sort of fool of himself" when he hears from one of his companions of the same age that he intends to get married, following the example of their commander. The proverbial motif of the distorting mirror is replaced here by observation of the motives behind human behaviour. At the same time, through all the complications of the farce, one senses a situation which is far from comic. A girl who wins the affections of an elderly officer is in love with his young nephew, so the farce contains elements of conflict that are no laughing matter. It is only in *Good Lord! What the Devil is This!,* where the scene is set in the little town of Osiek, known for the proverbial stupidity of its populace, and the action is based on the motif of "the rule of the fair sex" that we have pure situational comedy of the circus type. The heroines of this farce are the garrulous wives of the town, who make their unfortunate husbands do all the housework and take their place in managing the affairs of the town, only to return to their kitchens when danger allegedly threatens. The artistic aim of the author is the same as that of comedy through the ages—to make people roar with laughter.

But these excursions into the realm of comedy for comedy's sake, though repeated later too, were just excursions, for the author of *Ladies and Hussars* was influenced by the literary tradition that made comedy an instrument of instructing the reader or audience, making fun of bad habits and customs, so these accents are usually to be found in Fredro's works, although they are never brought to the fore to overshadow the scenes from life that he paints. They were more evident in his earliest works, in *Mr Moneyful (Pan Geldhab, 1821)* and *Husband and Wife (Mąż i żona, 1822)*. The comedy of *Mr Moneyful,* a nouveau riche social climber, which was quite topical at the time it was written, for in the life of those days there were a number of people who had by their cunning amassed fortunes as suppliers to the army, tells of the very amusing adventures of the "swaggering fool" and his daughter in hot pursuit of a good match, a prince without a penny to his name. All through this comedy in verse we find mockery of the snobbery of the new rich, exemplified in the concluding couplet:

> Of princely estate didst think too much, the
>   prince of money only,
> You were left out in the cold, your daughter
>   jilted and lonely. . . .

In *Husband and Wife,* we have a comedy of four characters; apart from the husband and wife we have the friend of the family and the maid, and thus instead of the eternal triangle we have four persons and four love intrigues, making this play different from previous ones on the subject of marriage and betrayal. It is a comedy which could easily have been turned into a melodrama ending with murder or at the best a duel, or into a satire on the immorality of a world in which the Count deceives his wife and has a love affair with the maid and in turn is deceived by his wife who is also having a love affair, the whole thing ending in a compromise, the only victim being the maid, who is sent to a nunnery. But it is a calmly observed, objective picture of life. There was, from time to time some indignation at the amoral character of the comedy, and an attempt was even made to heighten its eloquent message by defence of the alleged victim of the whims of the highborn. The thing that makes *Husband and Wife* different from other comedies is the realistic approach to the whole problem, the new presentation of the soubrette originally created by Molière, as a participant in various intrigues on a par with her employers, or in other words, the use in comedy of the principle of realism, found rather in the romantic novels of the times than in plays.

This break-away from the conventions of the comedy determined the character of Fredro's next three works, which are generally regarded as his best. They are *Mr Jovial (Pan Jowialski), Maiden's Vows (Śluby panieńskie)* and *Revenge (Zemsta),* and a fourth, *Life Annuity (Dożywocie)* is usually included among Fredro's recognized masterpieces, which marked the close of the first period of Fredro's activity as a playwright. *Mr Jovial* is one of the most singular of his plays, for it is a complete departure from the first ones that had a simple one-thread plot and combines old and new motifs into a richly constructed whole. So we have the traditional story known from Baryka's little comedy *Peasant into King,* the only difference being that it is rather an upside-down version, for the poor man who is to be made a fool of for the amusement of the inhabitants of the manor house turns the tables on them when they discover that the "poor man" has played a trick on them. In Fredro's comedy the poor man is a writer called Ludmir who goes wandering in disguise searching for new experiences and is quite capable of making a dupe of his opponent, the squire's son, and what is more, when inside the manor where the inmates intend to amuse themselves at his cost, he finds his lost mother and wins the affections of the fiancée of the squire's son. So the old story is enriched by Fredro's ideas to such an extent that the comedy seems to be one with a multi-thread plot, a comedy showing Polish life, in which an artist wandering through the country in the summer was nothing uncommon in those days. Another thing increasing the impression of rich content is the large number of characteristic types going to make up the family of Mr Jovial, namely, the old gentleman himself, who loves telling anecdotes and quoting proverbs, his son, an idiot and the husband of a snobbish vixen, his daughter, a maiden lady whose head has been turned by reading romances. All of these characters live in a world of their own and each of them stands out distinctly against those surrounding them. Prominence is given to old Mr Jovial who has a proverb or a tale to tell on every occasion, a seemingly inexhaustible store of such entertaining anecdotes that they are enough to make a separate thread of the story by themselves. This comedy, which is one of the most amusing of Fredro's repertoire, in which laughter bubbles up constantly from beginning to end, is almost a farce, an effect heightened by the prosaic course of events, but it also contains certain satirical elements, and satire of a political nature. For there is undoubtedly some truth in the suggestion that *Mr Jovial* is a caricature of the systems prevailing in central and eastern Europe in the period of the Holy Alliance, though this side of the comedy should not be overestimated. However, Fredro's political poems and his later comedy *The Revolver (Rewolwer),* allow one to assume that the spectacle of the "Sultan" in *Mr Jovial* was aimed against the system of the Russian government that proclaimed it had originated from God.

The comedy of the salon, *Maidens' Vows or the Magnetism of the Heart (Śluby panieńskie czyli magnetyzm serca, 1833)* is quite different, the very title indicating that it is linked with the Polish sentimental novel genre, from which one of its characters, the tender lover, is taken. It also contains accents of the romantic-magnetic notions of the birth of love and what causes it to flower, notions that the reader will have already have found in *Forefathers' Eve*. But it is not the sentiments of the romantic novel that are brought to the fore, rather a subtle and penetrating analysis of the awakening of feelings of love, the tone being a far cry from the romantic stereotypes and more like the light comedies of the 18th century in which "a dandy goes acourting", or a genre scene from the life of Napoleonic officers, excellently described by Fredro in his *Topsy Turvy Talk*. The new dandy, bearing the name of Gustaw, which had its eloquence for readers of Mickiewicz's *Forefathers' Eve,* is trying to win the hand of one of the maidens, and succeeds by a simple artifice. Pretending to be wounded he asks her to write a letter on his behalf to his alleged lady love from whom he is parted. The maiden agrees and writes the letter, but while Gustaw is dictating it to her, she shows some confusion, betraying that her attitude towards him is far from indifferent, and so the comedy comes to its happy end. It is an unusual comedy, for contrary to *Mr Jovial*, it has very little action and the plot is built on an intrigue so thinly disguised that a few explanatory words would have sufficed to replace the letter which causes the "magnetic action" of the heart. And if the preceding and following comedies by Fredro could be called "epic" comedies, *Maidens' Vows* is more of a lyrical comedy, on condition that this term is not understood to mean the sombre and passionate Romantic lyric poetry, but the serene and elegant love poems of earlier times.

Revenge (1834) again is the epic type of comedy written at the same time as *Master Thaddeus* and, though this was unintentional, has some kinship with Mickiewicz's work, which was also based on a traditional motif known from the drama of earlier times: Shakespeare used this motif in his *Romeo and Juliet* and Zabłocki based a comedy on it *(Sarmatism),* or rather on the work of his French predecessor. It is the subject of stubborn antagonism between two neighbours, which is brought to an end by the marriage of their children. It is a motif not only taken from literature, for it reflects quite a frequent and typical situation in people's lives. Fredro might well have based his comedy on the story of the old castle of Odrzykoń, which his wife brought to him in her dowry, or on the tales told in the Lublin region, which were recorded by Koźmian, many years after the writing of *Revenge,* in his *Diaries*

(Pamiętniki). Wherever Fredro took the original plot from, he worked upon it in his own way, concentrating attention on two deadly enemies, neighbours who keep on picking quarrels with each other about very trifling matters. They are the tempestuous Mr Raptusiewicz, an old military man whose bark is worse than his bite, and the wily old lawyer Mr Milczek, out for gain, who bites without barking. These two men of completely opposite characters might be compared to the lion and the fox in the old fables. In creating these two characters the author was clearly aiming at preserving the "local colour". Among his papers a small dictionary of archaic words was found, compiled from Linde's dictionary. He makes such skilful and subtle use of these words in his octosyllabic verse that he obtains a specific atmosphere of the old times throughout the play, without any impression of artificiality. He links up his two antagonists very ingeniously with another character, Mr Papkin, a man who always pays visits at meal times, a liar, coward, humbug and braggart who brings into *Revenge* something of the atmosphere of the old folk comedies of Italy—the commedia dell'arte—or similar Polish comedies modelled on them. In comparison with these strongly drawn characters, the lovers appear rather insipid. Their marriage, the result of the unsuccessful "revenge" of Mr Raptusiewicz, is actually a mechanical device to bring the action to the desired end, the "action proper" being the plots and counter-plots of the two antagonistic neighbours, who are typical characters of the old Polish culture, brought to life in two highly individual dramatic creations.

Chronological considerations usually dictate the addition of a fourth of Fredro's comedies to the previous three, namely *Life Annuity (Dożywocie),* the story of an usurer trying to get his hands on what has remained of the estate of the young rake Mr Birbancki. This play, despite the excellently drawn character of Mr Łatka the usurer, does not come up to the level of the other three comedies as it contains an excess of farcical ideas.

Returning to his literary work after fifteen years, Fredro wrote nearly as many comedies as he did before 1834, but none of them attained the high artistic level of his earlier works and none of them won such great popularity as *Revenge* or *Maidens' Vows*. But there are among them some very good comedies, for instance, *The Revolver,* which is an excellent satire on the relations in a police state, which Fredro locates in distant Parma, although the action might just as well be set in Cracow or Lwów about the year 1861, when the play was written. It tells of the adventures of the cowardly Baron Mortara, residing in a town where the possession of firearms is a punishable offence, whom malicious fate presents with a cigar lighter in the shape of a revolver. This motif is built up into a satire with grotesque and farcical accents and a wealth of comic situations reminiscent of the times of *Mr Jovial*. Another play written about the same time *The Fosterling (Wychowanka)* is quite different in character, being a comedy of customs and manners, which did not please the great admirers of the playwright, for it lacked the hilarious scenes they had come to expect from this author. And indeed, the story of Zosia, a country girl, the alleged daughter of a forester Bajduła, brought up in a manor house under the guardianship of the Morderski family, is more like the "plays" of the end of the 19th century than the comedies usually written by Fredro, and even less like the plays in Molière's style. True, the finale is traditional—an unexpected change in the situation of the "fosterling" when it turns out that she is the daughter of a gentleman who fought in the Rising whom the forester had taken into his home—and brings the happy end of the comedy, but the life of the girl in the manor house of the Morderski family, the blackmail to which she is subjected by her alleged father, the eternal faultfinding of an ill-tempered vixen in the home of her guardian and the annoying attentions of the suitors for her hand, or rather for the dowry which her guardian, believing her to be his illegitimate daughter, intends to give her, all creates an atmosphere of gloom which audiences in later times were to know so well from the dramatic story of another fosterling, in T. Rittner's *James the Fool (Głupi Jakub)*. But *The Fosterling* was an unusual example of Fredro's realism, which was heightened by the bitter experiences of the author, who intended shortly to publish his *Notes of an Old Man (Zapiski starucha)*, a collection of pungent aphorisms on various afflictions of human life, published after the death of the author (1880) in the volume *Works (Dzieła)*, as were his memoirs *Topsy Turvy Talk*.

No particular difficulties are encountered in summing up the works of Aleksander Fredro and establishing his attitude towards the literary trends he came in contact with. Brought up in the traditions of the Enlightenment period, he reached artistic maturity at a time when Romanticism was flourishing and the end of his creative life coincided with the decline of Romantic literature. Although he allegedly turned his back on Romanticism, his works came very near to its realistic trend, which in Polish literature was only rarely found in epic and dramatic poetry, though it was fully evident in novels and comedies in prose. The attitude of the writer to the contemporary literary trends was a result of his particular kind of artistic talent, remarkable for his keen perception and observation of his surroundings, his great sense of the comic side of life and his predilection for a specific style of language. His comedies bring a rich gallery of pictures, large and small of the life of the landowner class, a wealth of details of customs and manners, which can equal the best novels of the times in which he lived, and his multitude of human characters, usually drawn with emphasis on their individuality mostly appear in comic situations which are treated with light humour, ironi-

cally or in the satirical vein. So we have resolute young girls, young rakes, old servants, contented old people—all of whom are characters the playwright was very fond of creating. His artistic language, both prose and verse, is enriched by a variety of excellent ideas, plenty of wit and generously seasoned with gnomic elements, proverbs and aphorisms penned with ease by the author, who liked to quote Andrzej Maksymilian Fredro, his predecessor of the 17th century, and in his old age, followed his example and wrote his own collection of maxims.

Fredro's great writing skill made all this possible. He had felt the urge to write from his early youth and his pen was never idle all through his life. He would write poems for himself and for his friends, very few of which were printed, but there are so many of them that they go to make up two large volumes of collected works. A thorough study of this "colloquial" poetry will one day show how the literary culture of the author developed and finally took shape, to find full expression in the verse and prose of his comedies, which were not written spontaneously but were altered and corrected many times, for the author spent a lot of time on them before his exacting requirements were fulfilled and the work was completed. And just how exacting he was towards himself is shown in his diary *Topsy Turvy Talk,* a seemingly chaotic and disorderly collection of stories about his childhood and youth and taking the reader up to the moment when as a young officer he gave up the military life and settled down to the life of a gentleman farmer. These colourful, pithy scenes, the boy's excursion in the Bieszczady Mountains, the adventures of the young officer in the army commanded by Prince Józef Poniatowski, his experience of the hardships of army life, crossing Europe on horseback, with episodes such as the march on Moscow and the battle of Leipzig, are all modelled on the method of composition used by Laurence Sterne, whose books *(The Life and Opinions of Tristram Shandy, Gentleman, A Sentimental Journey through France and Italy)* were greatly admired all over Europe due to their original structure and humour. *Topsy Turvy Talk* is the most outstanding example of "Sternism" in Polish prose.

Another pioneer of Polish drama, Józef Korzeniowski (1797-1863), a little younger than his fellow-countryman Fredro was just the opposite of the author of *Revenge* in every respect. A man with a very good education, who taught at the Krzemieniec Lyceum and who, towards the end of his life, became a high official organizing the educational system in Warsaw, including the Central Academy of Learning, was a serious scholar, the author of theoretical works on poetry, an untiring translator of dramas, including the works of Schiller and Shakespeare, and at the same time an unusually prolific writer. He published about fifty plays, that is, ten more than his eminent rival.

As a playwright, Korzeniowski worked hard, patiently and systematically carrying out a programme almost identical to that of Słowacki, with the aim of creating Poland's own national drama, and like the great, lone émigré writer, he carried out a large number of experiments before he found the path he wanted to take. And when he had achieved this he gained a position equal to that of Fredro's, or even higher up the scale, and managed to keep this position till the end of the 19th century, his plays being constantly included in the theatre repertoire and staged not only in public theatres, but also by amateur groups of players.

His experiments were aimed, first of all in the direction of historical tragedies, and his debut in this field was with *The Monk (Mnich,* 1830*),* the story of the crime and penance of the exiled king Bolesław the Bold, written in the ancient style. Other plays which won popularity were his dramatized version of Malczewski's *Maria,* which was staged in Lwów in 1831 and the play *Dmitri and Maria* (1843). Another play of this group was *Andrzej Batory* (1846), telling the tragic story of the efforts of the Bishop of Warmia and the king's nephew to win the throne of Transylvania. These first dramas show great mastery of the art of writing, but they lacked the vitality of real poetry. And it is rather amusing to note that Korzeniowski succeeded in putting this vitality into a play based on the life of the Huculs (highlanders of south-east Poland) with whom he came in contact during a holiday spent on the banks of the Czeremosz. He used the stories heard while he was there as the basis for his *Carpathian Highlanders (Karpaccy górale,* 1843*),* a classic example of the melodrama genre, which told of the adventures of a noble youth who was recruited to the army by artifice, his desertion and his colourful life as a robber, which ended with his death on the gallows. By some strange coincidence, Korzeniowski's drama was written almost at the same time as Kraszewski's *The Story of Sawka (Historia Sawki)* and Pol's *Scenes from Life and Travels (Obrazy z życia i podróży),* going to make up a triptych which introduced into Polish literature the subject of the wrongs done to the peasants and their love of freedom. One of the lyrical interludes of *Carpathian Highlanders,* the song of freedom "A sash of red, with weapon hid there" ("Czerwony pas, za pasem broń") has become an unfailingly popular song, though the author's name is not generally known.

Almost at the same time as *Carpathian Highlanders,* Korzeniowski published a long comedy of customs and manners *The Jews (Żydzi,* 1843*),* which was preceded by a few short pieces written to acquire proficiency in this field. *The Jews* gave a wide review of the prevailing customs and was an eloquent social satire, probably written under the influence of French drama, where the leading writer was Eugène Scribe, who was about the same age as the Polish writer. In this play Korzeniowski introduced problems which were earlier raised by the author of *Fantasius* and which were the subject of lively debate in the novels being written at the time, namely economic relations and their social consequences, the ruin of the estates of the magnates and the question of loans, in other words, problems which were to appear on the stages of Poland for many years to come. The gentlemen and the "semigents", as the upstarts on the make were called, the gentry, up to their eyes in debt and the Jewish bankers—this was a new world in which the Jews were not authentic adherents of the faith of Moses, but usurers bleeding the unfortunate debtors, that is, the titled landowners and the parvenues surrounding them.

The knife edge of his satire was aimed here at the privileged classes, not at the type of individual personified in Fredro's *Mr Moneyful,* but at a definite social group, which was also being attacked by Kraszewski in his novels, and who was to be aided in this by the author of *The Jews.*

Korzeniowski was nearer to Fredro in another field, namely in his comedy *Madam Maiden (Panna mężatka,* 1845*)* regarded—and rightly so—as the best of his dramatic works. It is based on the same motif as *Maidens' Vows,* that is, the artifice employed to compel a young lady firmly resolved to stay single into making a confession of love, and this story, written with the same subtlety was given such an original form that there can be no mention of it having been written under the influence of Fredro's earlier work. Other comedies by Korzeniowski deserving of mention are *The Old Husband (Stary Mąż,* 1842*)* and *The Authoress (Autorka,* 1849*)* based on the motif of Sappho, withdrawing from the life of a loved one who is in love with someone else. An elderly man who marries the young daughter of his friend, realises that he cannot make her happy; he chooses a young officer of the same name, contrives meetings to let their love grow and starts divorce proceedings to allow the young lovers to find fulfilment of their dreams. Korzeniowski, who had already provoked public opinion to charge him with philosemitism, threw down the gauntlet again with his play *The Old Husband,* which was a challenge to the current opinions of the power of love, showing this emotion in an unusually sublimated form, without any melodramatic effects such as are found in Słowacki's arch-romantic work *Horsztyński.*

In Korzeniowski's comedies, written also in Russia, where he worked for several years in lycea, and later in Warsaw, more individual features emerged in this writer's evolution, modern ideas which made him different from his predecessors. The playwright, who had left the world of the petty gentry and moved in the intellectual circles of the city, took the themes for his comedies from city life, introducing the townsfolk into the theatre, such characters as public officials and representatives of the theatrical world, and even (in his *Master and Apprentice—Majster i czeladnik,* 1847) found his characters among the artisans, thus bringing to the stage a side of life and its problems which had not so far caught the attention of playwrights.

All these new elements gradually led to a change in the old literary conventions but the process was slow, for the man who brought them into drama was a rather pedantic scholar and official, without the impetus of a real revolutionary, capable of overthrowing the old ideas, although he brought a lot of harsh criticism upon himself. However, he systematically introduced the principle of moderate realism in a field where he undoubtedly deserves the greatest credit, namely the theatre repertoire, which he produced in the course of thirty years, and which though not of the highest level, was good theatrical material. This continuator of Zabłocki, Bogusławski and of Fredro, who had then become silent, did not attain the peaks of drama, but he maintained the good level attained by his predecessors, added his own ideas and raised its rank, which in the conditions of those times not only had literary merit, but also social value. And it is in this light that one should look at Korzeniowski and his contribution to the Polish theatre. The example he set encouraged others to learn from him and strike out more boldly in the same direction, for instance, Stanisław Bogusławski—son of Wojciech—in Warsaw, the eminent historian Karol Szajnocha in Lwów and the poet Władysław Syrokomla in Wilno.

Harold B. Segel (essay date 1977)

SOURCE: An introduction to *Polish Romantic Drama: Three Plays in English Translation,* edited by Harold B. Segel, Cornell, 1977, pp. 21-71.

[*Below, Segel presents a detailed introduction to the dramatic works of Mickiewicz, Krasiński, and Słowacki.*]

In writing about a lesser-known literary culture, one is usually obliged, at the outset, to appeal to the sympathetic interest of the reader. The literature in question may not be familiar—so the plea goes—but its merits justify greater dissemination. The reader is asked to accept the argument on faith until proof is provided. For the most part, this proof takes the form of translations. If the translation is good, many of the qualities of the original penetrate the language barrier. If, on the other hand, the translation is weak, the reader is alienated. Even when the foreign literary work is available in good translation, the struggle for recognition is still not over. Differences in culture also erect barriers. If the foreign culture is appreciably different from that of the reader, the hurdles are sometimes impossible to clear. Where the work of art exhibits a strong parochial character—that is, it deals with events, personali-

ties, and issues of primarily local significance—the cultural gap is bridged only in rare instances. Here the motivation of the reader or unusual aesthetic qualities become decisive factors. Sometimes, however, the work of art of distinct national character succeeds in transcending parochial limitations and in achieving a sufficient degree of universality to attract the interest of, and even become meaningful to, the foreign public.

I should like now to suggest that Polish Romantic drama falls into the latter category. The plays . . . are among the most important in the history of the Polish theatre. Their importance, however, is determined not only by aesthetic criteria—within the context of Polish literary and theatrical tradition—but also by external cultural and political circumstances. These circumstances prevailed in the period when the plays were written and clearly leave their traces in the works themselves. To different degrees they impart to the plays an undeniable national character. Yet, at the same time, a remarkable concatenation of nation, spirit, and art spares these works an inhibiting parochialism and achieves the transcendence to which I previously referred. To appreciate this, some understanding of the elements out of which Polish Romantic drama was shaped is necessary.

By the conventional concept of "great powers," Poland was, historically, a great power. In political, economic, and military terms it was at its zenith in the sixteenth and seventeenth centuries. Although geographically a part of eastern Europe, its culture belongs to the West. This was virtually assured by its Roman Catholicism and its participation in European Latin civilization. Not surprisingly then, humanism, the Renaissance and Reformation, and the Enlightenment were well represented in Polish history. To regard this as merely the result of a vigorous policy of assimilation like that pursued, let us say, by Russia in the eighteenth century would be erroneous. Humanism, the Renaissance, and later stages in the development of Western civilization as we know it were not graftings in the case of Poland but organic phases of Polish cultural evolution.

Foreign wars, unwise policies, and domestic upheaval eroded Polish strength throughout the later seventeenth and eighteenth centuries. As the power of Poland steadily declined, that of its neighbors grew. By the later eighteenth century—despite vigorous efforts to reverse the downward spiral in the reign of the last sovereign Stanislas August Poniatowski (1732-1798; reigned 1764-1795)—Prussia, Austria, and Russia were powerful enough to intervene in Polish affairs. Emboldened by the sight of Polish political instability and uneasy over the democratic reform movement in the country which culminated in the Constitution of May 3, 1791, Poland's neighbors undertook its systematic dismemberment. The first partition came in 1772; the second in 1792; and the third in 1795. Once a great multinational and multiethnic commonwealth, Poland in 1795 no longer existed on the map of Europe. Independence was to come again only after World War I and the dissolution of the Austro-Hungarian, German, and Russian empires.

Throughout the long period of bondage, various attempts were made to restore Polish statehood. A few years after the third partition the Poles avidly supported Napoleon. By contributing soldiers to his campaigns they believed that they were working toward the ultimate goal of national independence. Napoleon lamented the plight of Poland and made promises in return for men. When the emperor's politics moved eastward, he seemed to be making good his promises and Polish support increased. Preparatory to his great campaign against Russia, Napoleon in 1807 created the miniature state of the Duchy of Warsaw out of captured territories. This action was not much more than a gesture, but it reaffirmed Polish faith in the French. In gratitude the Poles raised an army of nearly eighty thousand men to fight under Napoleon's banners in the invasion of Russia. They fought hard and well and even after the debacle many remained so loyal that they followed the emperor back to France and participated in all his later campaigns. The fall of Napoleon in 1815 brought an end to the Duchy of Warsaw and the Poles were back where they started. In one sense, their plight was worse. After Napoleon, there were no other "deliverers" in whom the Poles could invest their hopes for liberation. They had to fall back, therefore, on their own resources. On the threshold of the Romantic age this meant rebellion.

The Poles made two major attempts to regain independence by means of arms in the nineteenth century: in November 1830 (the so-called November Insurrection, Powstanie Listopadowe), and in January 1863 (the January Insurrection, Powstanie Styczniowe). Both insurrections erupted in the Russian-occupied part of the country; both failed.

For the study of Polish Romantic literature, and Polish Romantic drama in particular, the November Insurrection is the central historical event. Literary romanticism came to Poland in the early 1820's, that is, a few years after the dissolution of the Duchy of Warsaw. Inspired by Byron and German idealistic philosophy, the new Romantic literature marked a radical departure from the senescent classicism of the French-oriented Duchy. The traditional date for the appearance of romanticism in Polish literature is 1822, the year of publication of the first book of poetry by Poland's greatest poet, Adam Mickiewicz (1793-1855).

Between 1822 and the outbreak of the November Insurrection Polish literature showed every indication of conforming to dominant European trends. This is not to deny, of course, certain specific Polish features. The political reality gave a special relevance to the Romantic appeals for individuality and liberty. The Romantic interest in the folk brought to prominence two border areas from which Polish Romantic regionalism derived most of its material—Lithuania and the Ukraine, historically parts of the old Polish Commonwealth. Drawing on the history of the dynastic union of late medieval Poland and the Grand Duchy of Lithuania, the early Polish Romantics often used ancient Lithuanian settings for the plays and verse narratives they wrote in response to the Romantic medievalism of the West. The centuries-long domination of the Ukraine by Poland offered license to mine the rich folkloric treasures of the area in the elaboration of a Polish Romantic primitivism. In consonance with Western practice, the genres of the ballad and romance were enthusiastically cultivated. Mickiewicz's first volume of poetry in 1822 was, in fact, called *Ballady i romanse* ("Ballads and Romances"). His second volume, published in 1823, includes a two-part verse play entitled *Dziady (Forefathers' Eve)*, in which Mickiewciz appears to be endeavoring to create a new type of drama out of folk motifs. Neither of the two parts of *Forefathers' Eve* is independently suitable for theatrical production. Their importance lies instead in their reflection in this first stage of his career of Mickiewicz's closeness to early European romanticism and his desire to bring together common Romantic themes and techniques and Polish regional folklore—here the pagan ancestor celebration of the peasants of his own native Lithuania.

The November Insurrection and its aftermath transformed the nature of this early evolving Polish romanticism. Because of their participation in the revolt or their sympathy for it, thousands of Poles became exiles. Many of the luminaries of Polish political, intellectual, and cultural life joined their ranks. Refuge was sought primarily in the West, where the November Insurrection was followed closely and where public opinion strongly supported the Polish cause. Although there were important centers of Polish émigré life in London, Geneva, and Rome, the focus of the emigration was Paris. French enthusiasm for the Insurrection (never, to be sure, translated into concrete assistance) and Polish enthusiasm for the traditions of the Revolution of 1789 and for Napoleon made the French capital the obvious place of resettlement for the majority of the émigrés.

The Great Emigration, as it is known in Polish history, had a profound effect on literature. With few exceptions, all the prominent writers were part of the emigration. This meant that after 1831, when the Insurrection had been crushed and thousands of Poles had fled to the West, Polish literature—like Polish politics—would be dominated by the émigré community. In effect, a new Poland, that of the emigration, with its capital in Paris, was created by the failure of the Insurrection. The uncrowned head of state was Prince Adam Jerzy Czartoryski (1770-1861), former minister of foreign affairs under Tsar Alexander I and the most respected Polish political figure of the time. It was from Prince Czartoryski's headquarters at the Hotel Lambert in Paris that contacts were maintained with the émigré communities elsewhere in Europe and the Near East (Constantinople, for example), that missions were sent into occupied Poland, and that plans were formulated for the political cooperation of the great states of the West, England and France, in the liberation of Poland.

Paris now became the center of Polish cultural life. Polish schools were established, newspapers and journals launched, a library opened (it is still in existence), and serious publishing begun. With the leading writers in the emigration, it was understandable that their works would henceforth be printed in Paris and that Paris would be the hub of the post-Insurrection Polish literary world. This was also the perspective of Poles in the occupied country. Although literary activity—and cultural life in general—continued in Poland after the partitions, freedom of expression obviously was curtailed. The situation became bleaker after the November Insurrection, especially in the Russian area where the revolt had occurred. Anxious to avoid further outbreaks, the partitioning powers maintained a close watch over publications in Polish for the slightest sign of any encouragement of revolutionary sentiment. Writers were forced, therefore, to be circumspect; that they and the reading public in the occupied lands came to view Paris and the émigré literary community located there as a haven of the free Polish word was entirely natural. Helpless themselves to change their situation, people in partitioned Poland looked to the West, and to the emigration, for guidance, for political as well as spiritual leadership. The great figures of the emigration sought to provide that leadership.

This émigré period in Polish history had definite chronological boundaries. In the first decade of the emigration belief in the imminent rebirth of Polish independence was widespread. To hasten the day, a formidable variety of political enterprises—ranging from cooperative ventures with England, France, and the Ottoman Empire, to subversion and overt conflict—were undertaken. There was no single, unified émigré approach to politics. Rival factions sprang up, some supporting the diplomatic initiatives of the conservative Czartoryski, others contemptuous of diplomacy and eager for armed intervention of one sort or another. The failure of the revolutions of 1848, in which the Poles placed great hope, took much of the steam out of émigré politics. It was becoming all too clear that Polish independence could not be achieved quickly, that a long, hard road lay ahead. The inconclusive resolution of the Crimean War—the fact that the Russian Empire (or its grip on Poland) was not toppled—increased

frustration among the émigrés. In many cases, frustration gave way to despair. What finally ended the hegemony of the Great Emigration in nineteenth-century Polish political and cultural life was the disastrous January Insurrection of 1863. Encouraged both by émigré ideology and the failure of the emigration to regain national independence, Poles in Poland proper took matters into their own hands and tried for a second time in the nineteenth century to liberate their country by insurrection. Again the revolt broke out in the Russian partition. With suppression of the revolt came a sterner administration of the region, a more aggressive policy of Russification, tighter censorship, and a greater curtailment of Polish culture.

The Great Emigration as a prime source of political initiative, spiritual leadership, and literary direction also died in the fires of the January Insurrection. By 1863 many of the leading actors in the émigré drama had either left the stage of history or were too old to remain active on it. Its great writers were no more. The greatest of them, Mickiewicz, had died of cholera in Constantinople in 1855. It was also evident, in Poland and beyond, that the day of the emigration had passed, that henceforth it would be just another emigration, no longer Great. The political programs, enterprises, and undertakings of the émigrés had come to naught; thirty-three years after the November Insurrection a second uprising was launched and failed, and Poland was still partitioned. Among the émigrés, it was time to recognize that the foreign lands in which they had sought temporary refuge would have to be their permanent homes. In Poland, it was time to understand that nothing more was to be expected from the emigration, that insurrection would bear only more bitter fruit, and that some *modus vivendi* with the reality of indefinite partition had to be found. Further alienating the population in Poland from the émigrés was the common belief that much of the inspiration for the ill-fated January Insurrection came from the Romantic ideology of the emigration. Thus the emigration, which in one way or another had fostered the insurrection, had to bear the responsibility for its failure and for the subsequent repression visited on the occupied country.

With the passing of the dominant personalities of the emigration it became easy to dismiss any further initiatives by the émigrés as futile from the outset and to seek solutions henceforth within Poland proper and within the context of partition. A reaction against the Great Emigration and the Romantic politics and poets of the emigration welled up in Poland, stimulated greatly by the social and philosophical positivism that became predominant in Polish thought in the country itself after 1863.

Reference was made earlier to the view held widely in Poland after 1831 that because the masses of émigrés who sought shelter in the West were unaffected by the restraints operative in partitioned Poland, they enjoyed unlimited freedom of expression. But in fact restraints did exist within the émigré literary community. In Poland a rigorous censorship was imposed from above by the partitioning authorities. In the Great Emigration, the restraints originated in the very fact of the emigration. In other words, the emigration qua emigration imposed a burden on its writers because the community as a whole tended to look to them for spiritual guidance as a component of its solidarity.

For at least the first decade of the emigration most of the émigrés believed that their exile would be short-lived and that they soon would be able to return to a reborn Poland. In the light of such an attitude, which was the rule rather than the exception, the cohesion of the émigré community became an absolute necessity. The emigration saw itself as the instrument through which the rebirth of an independent Poland would be achieved. To function effectively in this capacity, therefore, unity in the ranks had to be maintained. Literature could play an enormously influential role in achieving this goal by combating divisiveness and keeping the grand purpose of the Great Emigration ever in view. There resulted a literary climate wherein the Polish cause and the emigration, regarded as its moving spirit, became the central preoccupations of writers. Aesthetic criteria did not diminish in importance because of this, but the popular success or failure of a literary work often rested on the degree of manifest commitment to the national struggle.

The special relationship of the literary community to the Polish émigré milieu as a whole becomes clearer if the prevailing romanticism is taken into account. The November Insurrection, like its immediate Decembrist predecessor in Russia in 1825, was a romantic act on the part of young revolutionary idealists. The Great Emigration which followed reached the West at a time when the Romantic movement was still vital. The writers who joined the emigration or later in one way or another became identified with it were the principal architects of Polish romanticism. The confluence of these various currents, this interaction of Romantic ethos and emigration, had so great an impact on the creative writing of the Polish exiles at the peak of the emigration between 1831 and 1848 that any serious study of the émigré literature and Polish Romantic drama has to reckon with it.

By the time of the November Insurrection the Polish writers who were to dominate the literary landscape of the emigration were already strongly oriented in the direction of European romanticism. If a Polish Romantic literature was initiated with the publication of Mickiewicz's first book of poetry in 1822, then, in the eight years from this major literary event to the major political event of the Insurrection of 1830, there was ample time for the dominant Anglo-German impulses to be absorbed and the clear outlines of a well-developed Polish romanticism adumbrated. Judging from the actual literature written between 1822 and 1830 we can say that this fledgling Polish Romantic movement gave every indication of adhering to the main patterns of Western romanticism. The literature was Polish yet very European at the same time.

With the outbreak of the November Insurrection, its suppression, and the subsequent Great Emigration, this early Polish romanticism was forced to alter course dramatically. Paradoxically, when the base of this literature was dislocated and resettled in the West, the literature itself lost much of its supranational and European character and became more parochial. The emigration, after all, was a Polish phenomenon; a literature born of it and reflecting its anxieties and aspirations could not avoid parochialism. Yet, despite this, something quite striking and unexpected began to occur. The more the émigré literature made itself the spirit of the emigration, the more it assumed the heavy burden of the national struggle, the more intense became its romanticism. Realizing tendencies latent or undeveloped elsewhere in European romanticism, the Polish émigré literature of the period 1831 to 1848 evolved into the foremost manifestation of the Romantic ethos itself. It is in this way, above all, that Polish romanticism transcends parochialism and achieves universal significance.

The European Romantic saw himself as a rebel, dissatisfied with existing social and political systems. His belief in the power of the human will to effect change was profound. The sense of alienation often accompanied or inspired an urge to revolt. Generally, however, domestic political conditions made the realization of this urge impossible. The result was usually idealistic abstraction or sublimation. In some cases an outlet was found in the assumption of an alien cause. When European romanticism was crystallizing in the second decade of the nineteenth century, the Greek liberation struggle became the quintessential Romantic political revolt. Byron's identification with it was a characteristic response of the Romantic artist as activist. For the Poles, however, no alien outlets were necessary. The November Insurrection offered ample opportunity for engagement either through actual combat or through relocation in the emigration that it spawned. The emigration itself, at its peak, can also be considered a concretization of the will to rebel and resistance to status quo.

Romantic primitivism, the sense of spiritual affinity with peoples invested with a romantic aura the greater their distance from European civilization, assumed more than mere literary significance among the writers of the Polish emigration. Because of their own dispersion, the Poles were able to relate directly to the themes of exile and wandering in pre-Mohammedan Bedouin poetry, for example; in the Polish instance, Romantic literary orientalism already took on another dimension.

Much the same can be said for the "Hebraicism" of European romanticism inspired by the Old Testament and Prophets. In searching for historical parallels to their own plight, the Polish émigrés quickly discovered how closely their own situation resembled the Diaspora of the Jews. In view of this "discovery," the appearance of Hebraic-Judaic motifs in Polish postinsurrectionary romanticism, which goes far beyond the conventional "Hebrew Melodies" poetry of the Western Romantics, should come as no great surprise. Again, literary mode fuses with existential experience.

The metaphysical propensities of romanticism offer a still more productive area of inquiry. Romantic cosmology and epistemology placed great emphasis on the supernatural and nonrational. Mystic vision, as in the case of Blake, was highly valued. If it came naturally, all the better. If not, there was the possibility of narcotic assistance, as with Coleridge and DeQuincey.

The actual literary reworking of mystic exploration was rare in European romanticism. But it was conspicuous among the Poles and again was something that came about, in the outstanding instances, through direct experience. A few of the leading Polish Romantics, above all Mickiewicz and Juliusz Słowacki, studied at the University of Wilno in Lithuania. For a long part of its history Wilno was a prominent center of Polish culture. It was also the greatest center of Orthodox Jewish culture in Europe during the nineteenth century and the home especially of Jewish mysticism when Mickiewicz, Słowacki, and other future Polish Romantic writers were students at the university there. Attracted to Romantic literature and Romantic supernaturalism—Rosicrucianism and Franz Mesmer's ideas on animal magnetism were much in vogue at the time—the Poles eventually came across Jewish mystic lore (the Cabala, above all) in Wilno. This was not, to be sure, their sole exposure to mysticism, but it had a twofold appeal. First, because it was Jewish and hence non-Christian it was exotic; and second, because to a great extent it was an "underground" activity frowned on by the ecclesiastical hierarchy of the Jewish community, it enjoyed the aura of the forbidden.

Another opportunity for direct contact with mystic activity was afforded by Russia and the capital city of St. Petersburg in particular toward the end of the reign of Tsar Alexander I. The emperor's personal inclinations in his late years encouraged a great deal of occultism both in the court and outside. Masonic lodges and Rosicrucian societies served as the principal outlets for such interests. But there were other generally smaller groups of more informal character devoted, in the main, to communal mystic experience. Poles exiled to Russia in the first half of the nineteenth century

occasionally found their way into such circles. The most striking case in the history of Polish romanticism involved a painter named Oleszkiewicz and Mickiewicz. Deported from November 1824 to May 1829 for alleged anti-Russian political activism during his student days in Wilno, Mickiewicz at some point encountered Oleszkiewicz, a former acquaintance and fellow exile, and was presumably introduced into mystic circles in Russia through him. The friendship with Oleszkiewicz, who played a considerable role in helping Mickiewicz shape a mystic vision of his own future, served to reinforce the young poet's earlier contacts with mysticism, both Christian and Jewish. Thus, when we find the poetic transmutation of the mystical in Mickiewicz's major dramatic work *Forefathers' Eve,* Part III, we must realize that we are dealing with more than literary pose or fashion.

Mysticism also reappeared as an important current in Polish émigré society and literature in Paris in the early 1840's. As the bleak reality of their status gradually but inexorably took hold of their consciousness, the émigrés turned from ever less fruitful stratagems for the reacquisition of Poland's independence by political or military means to sources of spiritual relief. For a frustrated people facing despair, the development was psychologically as well as emotionally understandable. Only by strengthening the spirit could the disasters of the recent past be understood and reconciled and the uncertain future that lay ahead be faced resolutely.

The role of the literary community in this turning inward to the spirit was central and decisive. As early as 1832, in his *Księgi narodu i pielgrzymstwa polskiego (The Books of the Polish Nation and Pilgrimage),* Mickiewicz had presented his fellow émigrés with a spiritual guidebook on how they were to interpret the Polish past and at the same time to conduct themselves in the period of their emigration. In short, the émigrés were called upon to regard the emigration as a pilgrimage, for they were indeed on a spiritual mission. What was their goal? Nothing less than the re-Christianization of a Christian Europe that had become so derelict in its faith that it could permit and even participate in the dismemberment of a sister Christian nation such as Poland. This restoration of Christianity in a lapsed Europe could be effected by the émigrés as the collective representation of the entire Polish nation which had been sacrificed, martyred as Christ had been in order to fulfill a higher, divine purpose. The partitions of Poland were viewed then as a political crucifixion which ultimately would bring about the redemption of Europe just as, in Christian thought, Christ's martyrdom was necessary for the redemption of man. Since the emigration was conceived of as the vanguard of the Polish nation, it was the émigrés' presence in the West that bore the burden of Poland's messianic destiny. In Mickiewicz's conception, the emigration represented both the spirit of Poland and the conscience of Europe. To be worthy of their truly noble role, the émigrés-pilgrims had to attain spiritual perfection. Once this was achieved, they would bring about a general revolution of the spirit that would return Europe to Christianity. The nations responsible for the perpetration of Poland's dismemberment would then perceive the sin into which they had fallen and would seek atonement in Poland's political resurrection.

Mickiewicz's Romantic messianism had a certain basis in history. In the seventeenth-century wars against the Ottoman Turks the Poles saw themselves as an instrument of divine will by serving as a bulwark against the infidel engulfment of European Christendom. Their sizable contribution to the lifting of the siege of Vienna in 1683, which ended for all time the Turkish threat to Central and Western Europe, easily lent itself to interpretation in messianic terms. That Poland was chosen (by God, of course) for this exalted role was attributed to the Poles' unswerving fidelity to the faith. Polish messianism thus may have lain dormant for nearly a century and a half after Vienna, but the partitions, the November Insurrection, and the Great Emigration were sufficiently powerful stimuli to reactivate it in the 1830's.

The messianic conception of Poland was amply elaborated by the Romantics. Mickiewicz may have been among the first to renew the tradition, but he was hardly the only one to do so. Much of Zygmunt Krasiński's poetry and philosophical writing developed along similar lines. But the most intriguing exponent of this ideology in the emigration was an enigmatic figure named Andrzej Towiański (1799-1878). Controversial to this day, Towiański (like Mickiewicz) was of Polish Lithuanian origin and appeared in 1840 to become a powerful voice among the émigrés. Some still insist that he was a tsarist agent assigned to Paris to sow discord among the Polish émigrés in order to render them ineffectual in influencing Western policy on Russia. Agent or mystic, Towiański was a magnetic speaker who quickly won the commitment of several leading figures of the emigration, above all, its poets. Preaching a messianic vision of Poland's destiny as a nation, Towiański appealed for a spiritual regeneration of the émigrés as a precondition to their assumption of the great mission ordained for them. The timing could not have been better. Towiański seemed like another Moses come to lead the chosen people out of the wilderness of their exile. Until he became an embarrassment to the French government and was duly banned from France in July 1842, he was the center of a Polish émigré cultism that counted such outstanding personalities as Mickiewicz and Słowacki among the faithful. To attain the inner perfection which Towiański called for, a Circle (Koło) of initiates was formed in June 1842 for the practice of spiritual exercises of marked mystic character. Although some members of the group (Słowacki, for example) defected after a year

or so, the appeal of Towiański's thought was so powerful that his "work" continued even after his expulsion from France. As the most steadfast of the apostles, Mickiewicz was the logical choice to assume the direction of the Circle in the absence of the "Master."

The emigration not only activated the latent proclivity of the Romantic writer toward the mystic, it also created an appropriate climate for the full realization of the poet as seer. To the Romantics, poetry was both the highest form of art and the privileged endowment of the very few, the select. By virtue of his gift the poet was, therefore, an extraordinary individual. Possessed of powers denied ordinary mortals, the poet could penetrate the mysteries of the universe. Through his art he could share with others glimpses of the higher realm, the greater reality. He could present fresh perspectives on the past and insights into the future. By uplifting his readers, by raising their spirits far above the mundane to higher levels of being and knowing, he could through the magic of poetic creation ultimately achieve a transformation of both man and society.

This exalted conception of the poet and poetry was universal among the Romantics throughout Europe. Few, however, were afforded an environment in which it could evolve into more than an abstract ideal. The Polish Romantics were among those few. Because of the nature of the emigration, leadership became an issue of vital concern. The longer the émigrés remained in the West, the more fragmented and disunited they became as a community. In the beginning, Prince Czartoryski was the acknowledged political leader. But as time went on and the various schemes and strategies for Polish independence proved fruitless, political dissension spread among the émigrés. Czartoryski's conservatism, which counseled against outright military action, was opposed by a revolutionary faction that saw military action as the only way to break the bonds of partition. When dissension and frustration gave rise to despair, others saw only religious devotion and spiritual self-perfection as the guarantors of Poland's resurrection. As political authority dissolved into strident factionalism, a crisis of leadership developed. The situation was now ripe for the poet.

In the absence of effective political guidance the poet would step in to fill the vacuum. Through his art he would supplant the crumbling political leadership with a spiritual one. And by means of this spiritual leadership factionalism and fragmentation would finally be overcome and a new sense of unity forged among the émigrés. Without this unity, it was rightly perceived that the emigration would indeed be rendered mute and ineffectual. Mickiewicz's major dramatic work, *Forefathers' Eve,* Part III (1832), must be interpreted, on one level, as a declaration by the foremost Polish Romantic poet of his intention to assume precisely that kind of spiritual leadership.

At the outset of his literary career in the early 1820's, Mickiewicz wrote two dramatic works in verse of unequal importance as Romantic poems and of slight value as drama. Both were based on the folklore of the poet's native region—the rural area around the town of Nowogródek in Polish Lithuania which contained a large number of Belorussian peasants of the Orthodox faith. Mickiewicz linked the two short plays together by calling them parts of a larger unfinished drama named simply *Dziady (Forefathers' Eve)*. The Polish title refers to the pre-Christian Belorussian rite of ancestor worship. Twice a year peasants would come together in cemeteries or chapels, summon the spirits of the dead, and regale them with food and drink to ease their life in the next world. Since it was pagan in origin, the ceremony was officially frowned on by the Church but was not totally suppressed because of the ease with which it could be related to the Christian celebration of the deceased on All Souls' Day. In its fusion of folklore, folk ritual, and a Wertherian tale of unrequited love culminating in madness and suicide *Forefathers' Eve* reads like a paradigm of romanticism.

The two short plays comprising *Forefathers' Eve* were published in Wilno in 1823 in Mickiewicz's second volume of poetry and were numbered Parts II and IV, respectively; a fragmentary first part, apparently written in the same period, was discovered and published only posthumously. Nine years later, Mickiewicz wrote another play which he designated *Forefathers' Eve, Part III (Dziady, Część III)*. Why he numbered the early parts of the play II and IV, instead of I and II, and the very different *Forefathers' Eve* of 1832 Part III remains a mystery. Also a mystery is the fact that Part III—complete in itself—states at the end that it is the "first act" of something longer. Although Mickiewicz thought of further work on the drama, to which he felt a deep personal attachment, no continuation was ever written nor have any important fragments of a sequel been discovered. The most plausible explanation for the eccentric numbering of *Forefathers' Eve* seems to be that the poet wanted to suggest a fragmentary structure for the drama as a whole in a literary mystification that was by no means untypical of the Pre-Romantics and Romantics—Sterne, Goethe, Coleridge, and Keats had already provided models of such mystification. Doubtless following Mickiewicz's example, Słowacki similarly subtitled his play *Kordian* (1834) the first part of a trilogy which never came into being.

Much had happened to Mickiewicz between the first two parts of *Forefather's Eve* and the third. He had been arrested, jailed, then exiled to Russia for four and a half years on unsubstantiated charges of membership in a Polish prorevolutionary society while a student at the University of Wilno. His fame as a poet, however, had preceded him to Russia where he was accepted and lionized in the most fashionable literary and polite

society; exile, in other words, was anything but hardship. After Russia, Mickiewicz traveled through Western Europe, finally settling in Rome, where he again moved freely in the best circles. It was in Rome that word reached him of the outbreak of the November Insurrection. Although he was expected, as the leading Polish writer of the day and one, moreover, who had been imprisoned and exiled for his Polish nationalism, to make his way posthaste to the battlefield, if only to serve as a symbol, he did not do so. He lingered awhile in Rome and then went to Paris, presumably to learn more about the uprising. Months later, when he had at last resolved to head for embattled Poland, he got as far as Poznań on the Prussian-Polish border only to discover that Warsaw was under siege and that no passage across the Russian frontier was possible.

Mickiewicz remained in the Poznań area until March 1832, thereafter proceeding to Dresden. He stayed here until June and in August was back in Paris. The long residence in Prussia and Saxony was spent mostly in socializing and hunting. This carefree life ended, however, when Mickiewicz began meeting remnants of the Polish army that had crossed into Prussia to lay down their arms and other exiles streaming after them on their way to safety in the West. Confronted thus with the reality of the Insurrection and his own ambivalence toward it, the poet fell into a state of agonizing self-scrutiny. It was at this time and in these circumstances that the new *Forefathers' Eve* was conceived.

While in Russia as an exile Mickiewicz had entry into Russian or Russo-Polish mystic circles, as we have already seen. His earlier interest in mysticism going back to his student days in Wilno had prepared him for such contacts. One result of these new experiences was the conviction that his place in Polish literature was destined to be that of a *wieszcz* (from the Latin *vates*), that is, a poet who is at the same time a seer. The opportunity to fulfill his destiny, as it were, was provided by the defeat of the November Insurrection. As Mickiewicz encountered the Poles fleeing westward after the suppression, he gradually saw himself serving them in the emigration as a spiritual leader. Without such direction, which he doubtless felt himself best able to offer, Mickiewicz feared that the emigration would soon sink into despair and be unable to assist the Polish cause in any meaningful way. If such thinking should seem to us an act of profound conceit, we have to remember that Mickiewicz was a Romantic imbued with the high sense of the poet's mission in the age of romanticism. But because of the Polish circumstances at the time, he could move from the realm of abstract ideals to deed.

Before becoming fully active as poet-seer, however, a major problem (at least in his own mind) had to be resolved and that was absence from the field of battle during the Insurrection. How could his fellow émigrés, after all, look to him for leadership of any kind if he bore a stigma of indifference or cowardice for his failure to throw himself headlong into the struggle of 1830? To clear this hurdle, Mickiewicz, once decided on his future course of action, composed the third part of *Forefathers' Eve* while in Dresden in a surge of creative energy. He took the completed work with him to Paris, where he established permanent residence among the Polish émigrés and where the drama was printed in December 1832 as the fourth volume of the Paris edition of his collected poems.

Apart from its many remarkable qualities as an innovative Romantic drama combining contemporary history and traditions of the medieval mystery play, *Forefathers' Eve,* Part III, also has to be read as a personal apologia. Mickiewicz had prepared such an apologia as early as 1828 in the most curious and ideologically revealing work he wrote during his Russian exile, the historical narrative poem *Konrad Wallenrod.* Clearly the most outstanding figure in the poem is the Lithuanian *wajdelota* or poet-seer Halban who refuses to join the "hero" (Konrad Wallenrod) in a suicide pact. A Lithuanian patriot, Wallenrod has finally succeeded in defeating the German Order of the Teutonic Knights— who have conquered and ravaged his native Lithuania—from within, after having become by subterfuge the Order's grand master. When Wallenrod's game is up at the end of the poem, he chooses suicide over certain execution and urges Halban, his lifelong companion and mentor, to join him. Halban refuses on the grounds that as a poet-seer he must live in order to immortalize Wallenrod. Through his art, in other words, Halban will pass on to future generations the courage and heroism of Wallenrod. He will transform his deeds into myth and as myth Wallenrod will live again to inspire Lithuanians from one generation to the next.

Despite the risk of reading too much into the text, it seems fair to assume that the figure of Halban in *Konrad Wallenrod* reflects a projection of Mickiewicz's own feelings at the time about the relationship of the poet, poetry, and history. His subsequent posture during the November Insurrection would appear to confirm this view. The link between *Konrad Wallenrod* and the third part of *Forefathers' Eve* offers additional evidence. In the Prologue to the play, the central character undergoes a transformation in his prison cell; under the impress of the dreadful events he experiences, Gustav becomes Konrad. The names are important here. From the earlier *Forefathers' Eve* we know that Gustav connotes the Romantic poet as ill-starred lover, Goethe's Werther. Konrad, of course, immediately evokes an association with Konrad Wallenrod, the avenger. In transforming his protagonist from Gustav to Konrad, Mickiewicz is showing, in effect, the spiritual metamorphosis of his hero from poet, Romantic lover, solitary singer, to *wieszcz,* or *vates,* the poet-seer who transcends personal feelings, identifies himself with his nation, makes its cause his own, and becomes its prophet.

In approaching *Forefathers' Eve,* Part III, as apologia the transformation of Gustav into Konrad can be applied directly to Mickiewicz himself. The play obviously traces Mickiewicz's own career from autumn 1823 to autumn 1824. Mickiewicz and several of his university friends were arrested and charged with belonging to an anti-Russian student political organization. They were detained for some six months in a monastery of the Basilian Fathers in Wilno that had been temporarily converted into a jail. In November 1824, Mickiewicz arrived in St. Petersburg to begin the Russian exile that was to last until spring 1829. What the later *Forefathers' Eve* depicts is the partial metamorphosis of Mickiewicz himself—in reaction to the events of 1823 and 1824—from the young Romantic poet of the first published poetry of 1822 and 1823 into the émigré poet ready to make his debut as *wieszcz* in 1832. I say "partial metamorphosis" because the process is incomplete in *Forefathers' Eve,* Part III; the play ends with the hero en route across the snows of Lithuania from Wilno to St. Petersburg. What lies ahead we already know: the lionization of Mickiewicz by the Russians as the greatest Polish poet of his age, his contacts with Pushkin and poets soon to take part in the Decembrist Revolt, his entry into Russian occultist circles, the mystic interpretation of his own destiny as an artist, and the projection of that destiny in *Konrad Wallenrod,* the major literary work of his Russian period (which, in fact, was published in St. Petersburg in 1828). But before Mickiewicz can become worthy of mystic revelation, of attaining the full prophetic power of the true *vates,* he must first be made to expiate the sin of pride through suffering. It is this process of spiritual maturation that the poet traces in the third part of *Forefathers' Eve.* The psychic predisposition to mystic experience of Gustav-become-Konrad or Mickiewicz-become-seer is definitely established in the drama in the hero's preference for nocturnal solitude, the "strangeness" of the songs he sings, and, above all, the so-called "little" and "great" improvisations in the play. The latter is especially noteworthy as a fine example of mystic ecstasy reconstituted as poetry.

The more transparent elements of apologia in *Forefathers' Eve,* Part III, appear in Mickiewicz's treatment of history. The play's subject is the jailing of the poet and his friends in Wilno in 1823 and 1824 and their subsequent exile to Russia. Since Mickiewicz must show that he had already become identified with the national cause and indeed had been made to suffer for it—despite his later behavior during the November Insurrection—it behooves him to portray his Wilno experiences as a national calamity. Yet the fact remains that however exaggerated the case against Mickiewicz and his friends and however brutal their arrest, imprisonment, and later dispersion throughout Russia might have been, the episode itself was of predominantly local significance. Broader humanitarian and political issues were involved, to be sure, but the Wilno events themselves simply did not represent a Polish national calamity, disaster, or anything of the sort. To place them on the same footing as the November Insurrection, which I believe Mickiewicz does by implication, may be poetic license but there is no mistaking the poet's intention. This is manifest, for example, in the play's geographic settings. The scene shifts from Wilno, in Lithuania, to Warsaw, in central Poland, and to Lwów, in the Ukraine. This simultaneity of events in disparate locations and the episodic structure of *Forefathers' Eve* situate the drama artistically in the forefront of avant-garde Romantic drama alongside the works of Christian Dietrich Grabbe and especially Büchner in Germany. But if Mickiewicz, in fact, surpasses a dramatist such as Büchner in the depth and range of his architechtonic conception, his motivation can be attributed to ideological as well as aesthetic considerations. By moving the action from Wilno, to Warsaw, and to Lwów, the poet suggests the national dimensions of the Wilno affair.

The treatment of Russian politics in the drama reflects the same ideological spirit. Mickiewicz and his friends were little more than pawns in a power struggle involving the Russian Senator Novosiltsev, who was in charge of the Wilno investigation, and the Polish Prince Czartoryski, then curator of the Wilno school district. The case against them was trumped up and their lives were indeed disrupted by the harsh sentences imposed on them. The facts speak for themselves. But whatever the harassment and dislocation suffered by the Wilno youths, the only way in which they can be viewed as the first victims of a Russian policy of *genocide* against the Poles—the undeniable accusation made by *Forefathers' Eve* not only in the prose Foreword to the play but in the long narrative passages in the first and seventh scenes—is in the metaphoric sense necessary to Mickiewicz's mythopoeic purposes in his drama.

Once we take notice of the political and psychic factors in the play's genesis, we can go on to appreciate those literary and dramatic qualities of *Forefathers' Eve* which establish it as one of the few unusual works of the European Romantic theatre of the first half of the nineteenth century.

Years after writing *Forefathers' Eve,* Part III, when he was lecturing as the first holder of a newly established chair of Slavic literature at the Collège de France in Paris, Mickiewicz expounded his views on the drama in his now famous sixteenth (or "theatrical") lecture of April 4, 1843. Anticipating Wagner's concept of a theatre of the future in which the dramatic, choreographic, auditory, and visual arts are brought together in an organic synthesis, Mickiewicz spoke of the need

for the new drama "to play all the most varied strings, to run up and down all the rungs of poetry from the simple song to the epos." This drama also had to be national in the sense of uniting all elements of a truly national poetic tradition.

Although these ideas were not developed enough to constitute a concrete program for a national theatre, they were imbued with a remarkable spirit of the visionary and monumental. It was in this spirit that Mickiewicz pleaded for a vibrant drama capable of striking responsive chords in the innermost beings of mass audiences and urged Slavic poets in particular to ignore the contemporary stage in their playwriting because of its physical limitations, opining that a great Slavic drama and theatre awaited new developments in architecture, painting, and lighting.

The principal sources for Mickiewicz's attempt to create a national drama in the *Forefathers' Eve* cycle—long before the articulation of his theoretical views in the Parisian lectures—were classical Greek tragedy, the Christian drama and theatre of the Middle Ages, the Catholic rites of confession, repentance, and sacrifice, and folklore. From classical antiquity the poet derived not so much specific techniques as the model of a great and universal Greek tragic drama developed integrally out of popular myth and ritual. The Belorussian folk rite of ancestor celebration was to serve as the same raw material for fashioning an exemplary new Polish and, indeed, Slavic drama.

The attraction of medieval drama was considerable. Its supernaturalism and looseness of form accorded with Romantic metaphysics and Romantic aesthetics. But Mickiewicz also saw medieval drama as especially relevant to his purpose in the third part of *Forefathers' Eve*. By welding medieval mystery form, Catholic rite, and actual events and people of his own time, he was, in effect, creating a modern Passion play celebrating the martyrdom of Poland as exemplified by the persecution of the Wilno youths. From Catholic tradition and the techniques of the mystery Mickiewicz derived the entire supernatural structure of *Forefathers' Eve*. This incorporates the conflict between Good and Evil—the axis on which the play turns—the inner spiritual drama of the central character Konrad, and such motifs as the Guardian Angel who keeps vigil over Gustav-Konrad, the good and bad spirits who urge Konrad in one direction or another (Heaven or Hell) as his high-soaring transport brings him ever closer to the damnation of blasphemy, the devils who fight among themselves on stage as they struggle to take possession of the soul of the exhausted Konrad, the exorcism of the chief devil by the pious and humble Father Peter who serves as Konrad's spiritual mentor in the play, Senator Novosiltsev's troubled dreams, and the divine retribution visited upon one of his henchmen.

The contribution of folklore to *Forefathers' Eve,* Part III, is minor. The twice-yearly rite of the graveyard banquet to which the souls of departed ancestory are invited serves as the setting of the earlier parts of the drama in which more extensive use of folk materials is made. In the later third part, the folk rite appears only in the ninth and last scene. The reintroduction of the folk motif at this point seems to have been motivated solely by Mickiewicz's desire to forge an obvious link between the play he wrote in 1832 and the *Forefathers' Eve* of 1823. The later play clearly is an entirely different work. If so, then why did the poet call it *Forefathers' Eve* and then designate it as the third part of a multipartite drama begun ten years earlier?

Romantic primitivism, the sense of spiritual affinity with peoples invested with a romantic aura the greater their distance from European civilization, assumed more than mere literary significance among the writers of the Polish emigration.

—Harold B. Segel

The answer to this question again touches on both the poet's personal drama and his literary ambitions. By designating the play of 1832 as the third part of a much earlier work and giving it the same general title as that work, Mickiewicz plainly signaled his intention to trace the spiritual evolution of Gustav and to suggest, moreover, that the metamorphosis of Gustav into Konrad is that of Mickiewicz himself. From the Romantic singer of Wertherian love in the second and fourth parts of *Forefathers' Eve,* Mickiewicz has become transformed by the personal and political events of the period from 1823 to 1832 into the poet-*vates* whose voice is now that of the entire Polish nation, whose very soul has become one with that of his people.

Mickiewicz's career after *Forefathers' Eve,* Part III, bears out this view. Following in rapid succession after the play were the last of the poet's major works, *The Books of the Polish Nation and Pilgrimage* and *Pan Tadeusz (Master Thaddeus,* 1834). Both lend themselves to interpretation as the creations of a poet-seer intent on serving a given community as its spiritual leader. The first, as we have seen earlier, is essentially a messianic reading of Polish history and a plea for the émigrés to perceive the Great Emigration as a Great Pilgrimage. The biblical prose style of *The Books* and the extensive use of parable leave no doubt concerning Mickiewicz's conception of the nature and significance of his own "holy" undertaking.

Master Thaddeus, on the other hand, is a superb evocation of a past Polish way of life. Its purpose was to enable the émigrés of the 1830's to understand that their common heritage should be a unifying factor in their lives and in the collective existence of the emigration as a whole, strong enough to hold them together as a community despite the divisive pull of dissension and frustration. Blending epic and pastoral, its style deceptively simple and even homey despite its classical epic meter, *Master Thaddeus* so transforms the everyday into the mythic that it deservedly ranks as one of the great books of world literature.

Although Mickiewicz's literary career virtually ended with *Master Thaddeus,* he tried in one way or another to fulfill himself as poet-seer and spiritual guide until his death in Constantinople in 1855. Even his appearance in Turkey was informed with the mystique of his reputation as poet and *wieszcz.* Polish volunteer forces had come to Turkey to fight with the Allies against the Russians during the Crimean War. By assisting the Allies, the Poles hoped to gain support for a restoration of even partial Polish independence following the anticipated defeat of the Russians. When divergent political attitudes brought rivalry and conflict to the different volunteer organizations and the entire operation seemed in jeopardy, Mickiewicz was prevailed upon because of his immense prestige to use his influence while in Turkey to restore harmony among them. At the very end of his life, Mickiewicz was still trying, as *wieszcz,* to maintain the unity of the emigration to which he so passionately and totally committed himself from the conception in 1832 of *Forefathers' Eve,* Part III, in Dresden.

While Mickiewicz's reputation as the foremost poet of the Polish language went unchallenged in his lifetime (and is still unquestioned today), his spiritual authority in the emigration did not. Much of the career of Poland's second greatest poet, Juliusz Słowacki, had the character of a contest for supremacy with Mickiewicz. Słowacki regarded himself as a superior poet, a "purer" talent, but convinced few of even his peer status until the end of the nineteenth century. His reputation since then has grown so rapidly that today he plays the Shelley to Mickiewicz's Byron.

Słowacki's resentment and even envy of Mickiewicz fed not only on the latter's preeminence as a poet but on his self-appointed role as a spiritual leader of the emigration. If Słowacki held himself to be the superior poetic talent, he also disagreed profoundly with Mickiewicz's views on the emigration and its future and, above all, on Mickiewicz's concept of the poet as seer and national leader. Through a series of works Słowacki conducted a running polemic with Mickiewicz about the poet and poetry, on the one hand, and the emigration and Polish destiny, on the other.

To Mickiewicz's belief in the emergence of a *wieszcz* who would conduct the émigrés from the hell of the emigration to the Promised Land of a resurrected Poland, Słowacki opposed the vision (especially in his biblical prose poem *Anhelli,* 1838) of an emigration fragmented by internal dissension and incapable of achieving anything positive in its own time. Mickiewicz's by no means uncritical but still warm embrace (in *Master Thaddeus,* for example) of the traditional Polish ruling class, the land-owning gentry (*szlachta*), was categorically rejected by Słowacki. The younger poet, anticipating a major current in later nineteenth-century Polish historiography, held the gentry's conservatism and narrow self-concern largely responsible for the disasters that had befallen Poland. Unlike Mickiewicz, Słowacki assigns the gentry virtually no role in the reestablishment of Polish independence. In a familiar Romantic gesture, he directs his gaze instead to the people, the folk or *lud* in Polish. It will be only in a general uprising of the people—everywhere— that Poland will be reborn in the context of a new European social order. Advocating social revolution as the only sure path to Polish emancipation, Słowacki repudiates the mysticomessianic philosophy of Mickiewicz. It follows, then, that if Mickiewicz's messianism and mysticism have little or no validity, the idea of the *wieszcz* or poet-seer as conceptualized by Mickiewicz in *Forefathers' Eve,* Part III, and embodied in a work such as *The Books of the Polish Nation and Pilgrimage* is equally invalid. In *Anhelli* and elsewhere Słowacki plays havoc with the very notion of a spiritual leader emerging from within the generation whose ineffectuality, according to the poet, was nowhere more apparent than in the failure of the November Insurrection. In an even stronger indictment, Słowacki lays the blame for the ineffectuality and even spiritual weakness of his own generation at the doorstep of romanticism itself. The generation of 1830 failed in its attempt to translate the poetry of abstract ideals into concrete action because it was a *Romantic* generation. The point is made unequivocally in Słowacki's best known dramatic work, *Kordian* (1834).

Słowacki's first major play and serious attempt at political drama, *Kordian,* was conceived as a direct response to Mickiewicz's *Forefathers' Eve,* Part III. The evidence for such an assertion is abundant, but suffice it to mention the title of the drama, which is the name of the "hero." Kordian is obviously an anagram of Konrad and the character represents a refutation of everything symbolized by the central figure of the third part of Mickiewicz's *Forefathers' Eve.*

Słowacki's Kordian is a dreamer, a Romantic dreamer, to be precise, who yearns to find meaning in life. The Polish cause seems to offer the best possibility for this, and accordingly he identifies with it by joining a conspiracy plotting to assassinate the Russian tsar during a state visit to Warsaw. Kordian personally assumes responsibility for the deed, already intoxicated with the image of himself as a national avenger and deliverer. But when the decisive moment comes and Kordian stands poised, bayonet in hand, above the sleeping body of the tsar he falters. Imagination and Fear, presented as actual characters in the play, take hold of him and he proves incapable of the assassination.

What Słowacki is trying to show through Kordian is the impossibility of a great avenger and deliverer, such as delineated on different levels by Mickiewicz in *Konrad Wallenrod* and the third part of *Forefathers' Eve,* appearing in his own time. And the reason for this—apart from an ethical tradition unequivocally opposed to violence, whatever the motivation—is the heavy burden of romanticism borne by his generation. Because of this burden, Słowacki sees his generation condemned to ineffectuality through its fondness for the (ill-conceived) Romantic gesture and for brilliant words and poetic images of no substance. In line with this attitude, Mickiewicz's conception of Konrad as *vates* and deliverer is nothing more than another example of Romantic image-making and self-delusion— worse in the case of Mickiewicz because his mysticomessianic vision is a projection of the poet himself.

An immature work in some respects, *Kordian* still delivers a forceful message. If it did not endear Słowacki to the many Polish émigrés who were happier with the palliatives proferred by Mickiewicz, it did establish the poet as a major dramatic talent. The play has since become a classic of the Polish theatre and is performed regularly. Before considering Słowacki's later and patently more satirical broadside against romanticism, *Fantazy,* let us turn our attention to the last member of the trinity of great Polish Romantic playwrights, Count Zygmunt Krasiński.

Krasiński's career followed very different lines than that of Mickiewicz and Słowacki and his reputation as a writer has fluctuated more than that of any other major figure of Polish literature. Although identified with the Great Emigration, Krasiński was no émigré like Mickiewicz or Słowacki and never lost physical contact with his homeland. Mickiewicz, we recall, left Russia after his exile in 1829, settled in the West, became a part of the emigration, and never returned to Poland. A graduate of the University of Wilno, like Mickiewicz, Słowacki left Poland not long before the suppression of the November Insurrection; after a sojourn in London, where he carried out an assignment as diplomatic courier for the revolutionary government in Warsaw, he, too, settled in Paris with the majority of the émigrés. Never entirely comfortable in the French capital, however—in part because of his sense of rivalry with Mickiewicz—he traveled a great deal, a journey to Greece and the Holy Land from 1836 to 1839 being of particular importance for his development as a writer. During the European uprisings of 1848,

Słowacki was able to make a short visit to Wroclaw, in Prussian Poland, where he was briefly reunited with his mother whom he had not seen in eighteen years.

Unlike Mickiewicz and Słowacki, Krasiński could come and go virtually as he chose. He was the son of a Polish general who had distinguished himself in Napoleon's service. When what remained of the Polish army that had fought for Napoleon was delivered over to the command of the Russian tsar after the French defeat, General Wincenty Krasiński, obedient soldier that he was, thereupon became a general in the imperial Russian army. This opened many doors in St. Petersburg but created deep psychological problems for young Zygmunt. To a great many Poles at the time, above all his school fellows, he was the son of a traitor—or of an opportunist. As a submissive son who worshiped as well as feared his father, Zygmunt was incapable of doing anything of which his father might disapprove. This meant that however strong his feelings for the cause of Polish independence, he could not make any display of them.

Because of his failing vision and the need for frequent medical treatment in the West, Krasiński spent much time outside Poland and Russia. Though circumstances prohibited his physical relocation in the emigration, he identified with it spriritually and turned to Polish national problems increasingly as his literary career developed. Desiring to become at least a spiritual émigré and to be heard by his fellow Poles in the West as a voice addressing their deepest aspirations, Krasiński published his works in Paris. But because of his sensitivity concerning his father and his own position, he insisted on publishing his works anonymously, for which he became known as the "anonymous poet."

Ambivalent feelings about Krasiński lingered long among the émigrés even when it was common knowledge that he was the "anonymous poet." His father's defection, the poet's subservience to him, his ease of movement in and out of Poland, and his family's wealth aroused resentment and envy. Yet Krasiński's dedication to Poland, his spiritual union with the Great Emigration were beyond dispute.

Despite sometimes acrimonious polemics with other Polish writers, notably Słowacki (who definitely had a penchant for acrimony and polemics), Krasiński was admired in his own time for his poetry and his philosophical writings. Much of his work was of a prophetically visionary and messianic character reminiscent of the ideology of Mickiewicz's *Books of the Polish Nation and Pilgrimage*.

When writers of the fin-de-siècle generation known as Young Poland (Młoda Polska) made their far-reaching reassessment of every aspect of the Romantic period, the reputations of the great Romantic trinity underwent extensive modification. Critical of Romantic mysticism and messianism, Young Poland insisted on the primacy of artistic values in literature as opposed to ideological engagement. Judged by these standards, Mickiewicz was faulted for so blatantly tendentious a piece of writing (or preachment) as *The Books* and looked upon with pity for the misfortune of his later involvement with Towiański and the futile efforts of the 1840's and 1850's to combine spiritual and political leadership. To the writers of Young Poland, the wasteland that was Mickiewicz's literary career after *Master Thaddeus* was the most grievous loss of all. But despite some reservations, they were generous in their recognition of Mickiewicz's genius in transforming national content into universal art in *Forefathers' Eve* and *Master Thaddeus*.

Because of his personal distaste for a "committed art," his aloofness from Polish Romantic émigré politics, and the sheer brilliance of his poetic gifts, Słowacki finally came into his own in the time of Young Poland. Not only was he the focus of new studies and appreciations, he was hailed by the poets of Young Poland as the most kindred spirit among the Romantics. So great was the admiration for him, and so extensive his influence, that Słowacki was considered by many not only the equal of Mickiewicz but indeed his superior. If he did not, finally, succeed in dislodging Mickiewicz

Zygmunt Krasiński

from his position as Poland's greatest poet, his reputation as second greatest is by now secure.

Krasiński's reputation suffered the most in the late nineteenth and early twentieth centuries. His poetry came to be regarded as little more than a pedestrian vehicle for an embarrassing messianism. Much of his other writing was neglected because of its reflection of Krasiński's extremely conservative social views and what came to be regarded as his amateur and shallow Romantic philosophizing. The only works of Krasiński that survived the general depreciation of his talent were his two plays, *Irydion* (begun in 1832, completed 1836) and *Nie-Boska komedia (The Un-Divine Comedy,* 1833).

With the establishment of a Communist regime after World War II, Krasiński was all but relegated to oblivion. His messianism, Catholicism, and social conservatism were totally repugnant to Poland's new leadership and for some years no new editions of his works could be published. The situation changed in the early 1960's owing to a more liberal cultural policy. Studies of the poet, supplemented by new editions of his works, started to appear after a long hiatus. As Krasiński came to be better known, a rehabilitation of his reputation as a writer ensued. The results are curious. The very early Romantic tales and most of his poetry are still considered weak, but his voluminous correspondence has at last been fully brought to light and reveals him as a superb prose stylist and easily the outstanding epistolary artist of Polish romanticism. Of his two dramatic works, *Irydion* attracts no great attention though it is staged from time to time. Apart from its markedly Christian ending, the play is yet another Romantic study in the psychology of vengeance much like Mickiewicz's *Konrad Wallenrod.* The main protagonist this time is a Greek burning with desire to avenge his native country for its subjugation by Rome. Like Konrad Wallenrod he enters the service of the enemy to destroy him from within. Despite their trappings of antique history, both *Konrad Wallenrod* and *Irydion* spoke directly to the Polish situation in relation to Russia in the nineteenth century and thus became irrelevant once Poland regained its independence after World War I. If *Konrad Wallenrod* is remembered more kindly than *Irydion,* this is only because of its pivotal importance in understanding Mickiewicz's later development as writer and *wieszcz* in the émigré period. *Irydion* has no such significance in any study of Krasiński's evolution and has less claim on our interest today.

The Un-Divine Comedy is an entirely different matter, however. The play has steadily gained prestige in the twentieth century and is widely regarded in contemporary Poland as one of the greatest dramatic works to emerge from the Romantic period. Enhancing its position in the history of modern Polish drama is the growing awareness of the play outside Poland. It has been successfully staged in other languages (including En-

glish) and enjoys the distinction of being the Polish Romantic drama to have attracted the most serious attention abroad thus far.

Setting *The Un-Divine Comedy* apart from most other Polish Romantic drama is its immediacy and its particular relevance for the twentieth century. The play deals with revolution, social upheaval, class war, political morality, and the historical process. The importance of such themes to the present century needs no commentary. Its composition in prose, albeit often a highly sylized prose, also helps its international career; it is easier to translate than the plays of Mickiewicz and especially Słowacki, almost all of which were written in verse. The play also demands no special initiation on the part of the foreign audience. Unlike the more obtrusive "Polishness" of Mickiewicz's *Forefathers' Eve,* Part III, or Słowacki's *Kordian* and *Fantazy,* its setting is indeterminate. Yet like these other masterworks of Polish Romantic drama, its genesis can be traced to the political predicament of Poland in the first half of the nineteenth century.

Krasiński reflected deeply on his age and on such specific Polish concerns as the partitions, the November Insurrection, the role of the emigration, and the future of the nation. His views conformed only partially to those of Mickiewicz and not at all to those of Słowacki. With Mickiewicz, he shared a mysticomessianic vision of Poland as the Christ of nations destined to be resurrected and, through its martyrdom and resurrection, to serve as the agency for the salvation of European Christendom. It was, however, in his social and political thought that Krasiński differed from his peers.

Mickiewicz accorded the gentry the political direction of a reborn Poland because of their heritage of leadership and their preservation of what were regarded in the emigration as the meaningful and authentically Polish traditions of the past. But the gentry Mickiewicz envisaged for the future was one firmly set on the path of a democratic evolution by the calamitous events of the period 1772 to 1831. A reconstitution of prepartition Poland was out of the question, as he suggests in *Master Thaddeus.* Mickiewicz was also very sympathetic throughout his life to the problems of the peasant and the minority group, especially the Jews, and fully appreciated that unless they were brought into the mainstream of Polish life as well as into the political process eventually, a newly independent Poland would have small hope for survival. His later participation in an international Socialist paper published in Paris only capped the development of his progressive social views.

Greatly influenced by Romantic providential and catastrophist philosophy (Ballanche, in particular), Krasiński could not accept Mickiewicz's vision of the future, and even less Słowacki's contempt for the gentry and his espousal of social revolution. To Krasiński—whatever his aristocratic biases—the political order of the past and the nobility who shaped that order were doomed to oblivion. Wherever he looked around him in the Europe of the 1830's Krasiński discerned the unmistakable signs of social unrest and political turmoil: the Russian Decembrist Revolt of 1825, the November Insurrection in Poland in 1830, the Belgian and French uprisings of the same year, the Lyons textile workers' riots of 1831, and so on. As a conservative, Krasiński recoiled in horror at the specter of revolution but resigned himself to what he regarded as the inevitable by interpreting the historical process in a curious mixture of Hegelian dialectical and Romantic providential terms.

It is this particular view of history that Krasiński propounds in *The Un-Divine Comedy,* which in its own way can be read as a refutation of ideas presented in both Mickiewicz's *Forefathers' Eve,* Part III, and Słowacki's *Kordian.* Working outward from the microcosm of the emigration with its internal stresses and divisions to the macrocosm of European civilization as a whole, Krasiński prophetically foresaw imminent social and political warfare. The great—and final—contest would pit the old order of the nobility and conservatives (represented in the play by Count Henry and the Holy Trinity Castle) against the revolutionary progressives (led by Pancras and Leonard) made up of all the disfranchised and oppressed. It was to be, essentially, a struggle to the death between master and servant, haves and have-nots. The outcome was a foregone conclusion: the old order was doomed; the handwriting was already on the wall of Europe.

Krasiński was hardly enthuasiastic about his conception of the future even though he could not intellectually reach any other conclusion about the direction of history. His animosity toward the social revolutionaries is manifest in the play. Their leader, Pancras, is portrayed as a cynic hungry for absolute power, to achieve which he is willing to sacrifice any principle. Lacking Mickiewicz's sympathy for Jews, Krasiński reveals an obvious bias in assigning baptized Jews an especially sinister role in Pancras' revolution. The Jews merely pretend to be Christians in order to identify themselves with the revolutionary camp. Secretly, however, they remain faithful to Judaism, like many of the converts in Inquisition Spain, and use the revolution of Pancras and his followers for their own purpose. Continuing Krasiński's line of thought—and without doing him injustice—the only conclusion possible is that in the poet's personal vision of the future the Jews would assist the social revolution until it became successful, whereupon they would subvert it from within to emerge finally as the dominant element. If Krasiński's play prophetically anticipates the Russian Revolution of 1917, as some critics have maintained (G. K. Chesterton, for example, in England), it also looks forward to the vicious anti-Semitism of a decade or so earlier in Russia, largely nourished by the "discovery" of the so-called *Protocols of the Elders of Zion.*

As a Hegelian, Krasiński could not have been expected to conclude *The Un-Divine Comedy* with the triumph of the revolution; otherwise how would the requisite synthesis be accommodated? Besides, if Krasiński's interpretation of history led him to the ascendancy of the new order over the old, his profound sense of Christian morality could not accept the triumph of godless materialism as definitive. Hence the ending of *The Un-Divine Comedy.*

In the play's final battlefield scene, as Pancras is about to exult in his decisive victory over Count Henry and the rest of the aristocracy collected together for the last scene in the Holy Trinity Castle, the sky darkens above him and in the clouds he beholds a vision so terrifying that he pales, becomes incoherent, falls into Leonard's arms, and expires. The vision is of the Day of Judgment. This is reinforced by the words Pancras utters as he breathes his last in Leonard's arms: "Galilaee, vicisti!" ("Galilean, Thou hast conquered"). The Galilean, of course, is Christ.

The play's conclusion is wholly consistent with Krasiński's world view: *Irydion* also concludes with the triumph of the Christian order even though Irydion's hatred of Rome and desire for vengeance were passionate enough to lead him into a pact with Satan. To Krasiński, it could not be otherwise. Human history, as he perceived it, whatever the mechanism operating it, was moving along a frightening path of disintegration and destruction. It was a path that led inevitably to chaos. If the old order with values and traditions dear to Krasiński was doomed to disappear, Krasiński may have been saddened by the thought but hardly blind to the contribution of the old order to its own demise. This is established clearly in *The Un-Divine Comedy.* Krasiński, however, was repelled by the forces emerging triumphant over the old order. He saw them only as those of darkness and evil. Anarchic, atheistic, amoral, and materialistic, they were capable only of destruction. In the end, nothing but chaos would remain. But precisely at this moment—the dissolution into chaos—Krasiński's vision turns optimistic. When human history runs its course and mankind has finally been brought to the very edge of the abyss, God's order will be established. A new era in the life of man on earth will dawn, an era founded on true Christian love and morality. Krasiński's Hegelianism thus acquires a Christian providential—and metaphysical—coloration. When antagonistic social forces (human history, the "un-divine comedy" of man) ultimately exhaust themselves in mortal combat, the void of chaos will be filled by the synthesis heralding the millennium, the coming of the divine order.

Krasiński's approach to the restoration of Polish independence was rooted in the same premises. If the destructive forces of human history could eliminate the once great Polish Commonwealth, then its reappearance would come only when the order of Christian love and morality was imposed. Had this order existed previously, had love and morality reigned supreme on earth, then no partitions, no rape of one Christian nation by another, could have been possible.

The first title of *The Un-Divine Comedy*—"Mąż" ("The Husband," or "The Man")—suggests the smaller dimensions of the original conception. In its final form, the play develops along two parallel lines which eventually merge. One is political, the drama of the revolution. The other is private, the drama of the family.

In what must have been the original nucleus of the play, the family drama, Krasiński approached Słowacki's perception of their own age. The domestic drama of *The Un-Divine Comedy*—the drama of Count Henry, his wife, and his son George—is a powerful indictment of what Krasiński regarded as the malady of "false" romanticism. Perhaps we may refer to it as the Kordian syndrome. If the indictment does not embrace, as indeed it might, the whole of romanticism, it does address itself to that aspect or dimension of the Romantic mind and world view that encourages a self-delusive intoxication with word and gesture. Instead of becoming the means through which man can be uplifted and society transformed, poetry (or art, in general), in a Romantic sense, becomes rather the narcotic from which the myth of the self is created. The greater the recognition of poetic endowment, the more ardent the elaboration of image for the sake of image and the making of gesture for the sake of gesture. As poetry creates an ever greater distance between art and life, vision becomes distorted and all that can be seen is self. Słowacki's Kordian is so beguiled by the image he constructs of himself as an avenging angel that he loses contact with reality. So overripe is his imagination that when at last he is able to act decisively, to translate into life the poetic image he has of himself, this imagination cripples his will and makes action impossible.

The ramifications of the syndrome are wider in *The Un-Divine Comedy*. In Słowacki's play Kordian destroys only himself in his failure to assassinate the tsar when he has the chance. The plan itself is hardly more than a romantic gesture, for how efficacious can the tsar's murder really be? Count Henry's romantic madness, in *The Un-Divine Comedy*, dooms not only his family but the social order which he represents and which he finally leads into a hopeless battle. Poetry so distorts Count Henry's perception that it functions only as a destructive force. In the play's domestic drama it is through poetry that Count Henry brings about the insanity and premature death of his wife and the mad-

ness of his son George. In the larger dimensions of the sociopolitical drama, Count Henry's poetic vision of the conflict and his personal role in it results in his own death and in the total destruction of the society he leads and struggles to preserve. Given the contiguity of Słowacki's and Krasiński's views in this area, the social drama could not have been resolved differently. The old order is doomed to disappear because it has proven itself incapable of change, of keeping pace with history; it has become an anachronism as surely as the world of Ranevskaya in Chekhov's *The Cherry Orchard*. Appropriately, in the play, this old order is ushered to defeat by a leader who is so blinded to surrounding reality by poetic romanticization that he becomes the perfect symbol for the order, and the age, that must perish.

If Count Henry represents an extreme form of Słowacki's Kordian, then his son George appears as truly a *reductio ad absurdum* of the type. George's world is only poetic vision. This is intensified by the boy's blindness, a probable autobiographical motif in view of Krasiński's own weak eyesight. Because he cannot see the outer world George lives only the inner life, which is composed exclusively of the poetic. In a grotesque distortion, he is the fulfillment of Count Henry's ambition that his son be a poet, but by his madness he becomes the means by which the count finally can glimpse the folly of his entire life.

After the grandiose historiophilosophical and Christian drama of *The Un-Divine Comedy*, with its interwoven themes of the human and divine and its "open," epico-lyrical structure, Słowacki's later debunking of romanticism, *Fantazy*, comes as a pleasant change of pace. As a realistic comedy and social satire, it is an unusual item in Słowacki's dramatic oeuvre and an altogether rare type of play for Polish émigré romanticism of the 1830's and 1840's.

Fantazy was among Słowacki's posthumously published works. It was discovered untitled and not quite finished among the poet's effects. For its first printing in 1866, its editor gave it the title *Niepoprawni* ("The Incorrrigible") with reference doubtless to the social types represented by Count and Countess Respekt, on the one hand, and the incurable Romantics Fantazy and Idalia, on the other. This title was later dropped in favor of *Nowa Dejanira* ("The New Deianira"), which alluded to the play's burlesque of a classical myth— the violation of Heracles' bride Deianira by the Centaur Nessus. The Słowacki revival in the late nineteenth and early twentieth centuries engendered voluminous new research on the poet which resulted, among other things, in still another change of title, from "The New Deianira" to *Fantazy*, after the name of the play's main character. Although some scholars have since argued that the comedy should have the double title *Fantazy, or The New Deianira* as conforming more to

Słowacki's intentions, and it has occasionally been published with this title, equally convincing arguments contend that such double titles were not the fashion in the 1840's when the work was written and that *Fantazy* is the best possible choice. The play is known today only by this title.

Establishing a precise chronology for the composition of *Fantazy* has also created controversy. The most reasonable opinion favors late 1843 or early 1844, not long after Słowacki had broken away from Towiański's influence. The departure from the Circle did not mark an end to the poet's interest in mysticism itself. Quite the contrary. In 1843, he began writing a series of works that one cannot comprehend fully without reference to mystic thought. The richest fruit of this period are the plays *Ksiądz Marek* ("Father Marek") and *Sen srebrny Salomei* ("The Silver Dream of Salome"), both of which deal with political events in the Polish Ukraine (the region in which Słowacki was born) during the eighteenth century, and *Ksiąze niezłomny* ("The Constant Prince"), a poetically brilliant adaptation of Calderón's play *El Principe Constante*. In a curious footnote to literary history, the Calderón adaptation began in 1842 as a project of the Towiański Circle; Towiański greatly esteemed the Spaniard's spiritual thought and initiated a group translation program of which Słowacki's contribution was the sole completed effort.

The plays of 1843 were followed by mysticomessianic and visionary poems of great scope, such as *Genezis z ducha* ("Genesis from the Spirit," written 1844) and the unfinished *Król-Duch* ("The King-Spirit," the first part of which was published in 1847). Here Słowacki examines the whole course of human history in terms of the metempsychic migration of several great spirits.

As a comedy, *Fantazy* may indeed seem an odd work for Słowacki to have written when he had only recently parted company with the Towiański Circle and was deep in mystic contemplation. When the play is viewed, however, as a reflection of the poet's new intellectual and spiritual values, it appears more natural for this strange period in his life.

Older studies of Słowacki used to make a strong point of *Fantazy's* putative autobiographical elements. In 1840 and 1841 the poet had a romantic liaison with Joanna Bobrowa (1807-1889), with whom Zygmunt Krasiński had once been in love. Słowacki's affair with the beauty was doomed to failure, but when the romance faded they remained good friends. Presumably, this did not prevent the poet, perhaps out of a kind of playful malice directed chiefly against Krasiński, from using her and Krasiński as the prototypes for the exaggeratedly Romantic lovers in *Fantazy*, Fantazy himself and the Countess Idalia. This biographical inter-

pretation still enjoys some currency but is of limited use in any serious analysis of the play.

Like *The Un-Divine Comedy, Fantazy* is a multifaceted work. In its combination of a domestic and political drama it recalls Krasiński's play. But *Fantazy* brings together the comic and tragic as well.

On the level of the comic, *Fantazy* mocks Romantic posturing and narcissism. By the 1840's, Słowacki's ironic disposition toward romanticism had so colored his vision that he could no longer approach it with the same intensity and seriousness as before. The Romantic fondness for the exalted word and gesture and the Romantic concept of ideal love now seemed so preposterous to him that he could treat them only as subjects for comedy. Anything even resembling the solemnity of *Kordian* was out of the question—hence the exuberant ridicule of *Fantazy*.

Interwoven with the comic satire of Fantazy and Idalia, two of the most absurd creations in Romantic literature, is the family drama, involving the Respekts, and the political drama centered on the Russian Major and the exiled Polish patriot and revolutionary Jan. For all the ludicrousness of their portrayal, the Respekts represent a very real socioeconomic condition of the time: the uprooting of Polish gentry families for political reasons and their subsequent impoverishment. To Słowacki, the situation has a moral dimension as well. So desperate is the financial plight of the Respekts that they are even prepared to barter their daughter Diana to Fantazy in exchange for a sizable cash settlement.

Through the Major and Jan the earlier Siberian exile of the Respekts is revealed and with it the whole political tragedy of postpartition revolutionary Poland. Even granting the contrived nature of Jan's reappearance just at the time Fantazy is negotiating his suit of Diana's hand and the play's resolution which reunites the former lovers Jan and Diana and provides them, moreover, with a handsome wedding present, Jan and the Major assume a highly important ideological role in the drama. The real world they represent is juxtaposed both to the unreality and absurdity of Fantazy and Idalia and to the moral hypocrisy of the Respekts for whom existence and appearance are one. What Słowacki implies unmistakably is that the real world of Jan and the Major, a world of courage, heroism, and self-sacrifice, constitutes true romanticism, in comparison to which the posturing and flirting with death of Fantazy and Idalia are mere sham. The play's marital intrigue itself is nothing more than conventional plot material—separated lovers, impoverished parents, a wealthy suitor, the *deus ex machina* acquisition of a fortune, the eventual reunion of the lovers—which Słowacki uses merely as a convenient structure within which to reexamine the entire Romantic ethos against the background of concrete social and political conditions.

The Major is perhaps Słowacki's most intriguing character in *Fantazy* and a significant point of contact with the poet's contemporary mysticism. If the character is viewed only in dramatic terms, he seems scarcely believable—a symbolic projection, an idealized version of a new order of Russo-Polish relations. In this sense, analogues to the type are to be found elsewhere in nineteenth-century and early twentieth-century Polish literature which often sought to draw a distinction between the Russian as an individual worthy of esteem and the Russian as an agent of imperial tsarist policy.

But the Major embodies far more importantly the ideas of Christian self-sacrifice and love that so strongly attracted Słowacki at the time to the plays of Calderón. What the Polish poet, dramatist, and mystic admired above all in *The Constant Prince,* in particular, is the noble figure of the Prince who staunchly refuses to compromise moral principle even when faced with death. The Prince's fidelity, devotion, suffering, and self-sacrifice ultimately gain him a spiritual triumph, and it was this triumph that Słowacki saw as the true salvation of mankind. By sacrificing himself out of love for Jan, the Major at the same time atones for his burdensome indecision during the Russian Decembrist Revolt of 1825. Faced with a second opportunity in his lifetime to act decisively for a cause dear to him, he does not fail. Through the Major's willingness to lay down his life so that Jan and Diana may find happiness, self-sacrifice for love becomes the supreme act of redemption.

INFLUENCES

Wacław Lednicki (essay date 1956)

SOURCE: "Goethe and the Russian and Polish Romantics," in *Bits of Table Talk on Pushkin, Mickiewicz, Goethe, Turgenev, and Sienkiewicz,* Martinus Nijhoff, 1956, pp. 198-219.

[*In the following excerpt, Lednicki explores the influence of Goethe on Mickiewicz and Krasiński, focusing on the reasons why Goethe's ideology was ultimately rejected by the Polish Romantics.*]

There exists in both Russia and Poland a rich literature on Goethe including innumerable special monographs and translations of *Werther,* the lyrics, *Wilhelm Meister,* and especially *Faust.* I may say without exaggeration that in Poland and Russia each generation down to the present has had its own Polish or Russian *Faust.*

On the seriousness and originality of Polish Romantic poetry:

> This literature, more than the existing literature of any people, deserves the attention of serious men; for this, above all other, bears upon itself the stamp of reality. It is serious, earnest, noble;—noble both by the spirit which inspires it, and the aim after which it strives. Every work is at the same time a deed. It is the life of the man himself that animates his book. What he has thought, has felt, reveals itself in the written word,—
>
> As joy in smiles; as sorrow in the tear.
>
> Thus speaks Mickiewicz—himself one of the most gifted of her sons—of the present literature of Poland. Nor can this praise, glowing as it is, be reproached with exaggeration. No one can open the books of the Polish writers of the [Romantic era], without feeling that he reads the words of men thoroughly in earnest; who write, not for the sake of book-making, not for popularity, not even for future fame; but because they feel they have that to say which the world should hear; or, as one of themselves has expressed it, "that they may declare the thought of God as it has rested upon them." At no period of the history of Poland has her literature been distinguished by a character so original . . . ; never before has it been so completely the exponent of the character and genius of the nation; never before animated by a spirit so truly Slavonian.
>
> *"Living Writers in Poland," in* North American Review, *April, 1848.*

. . . The first indications of some knowledge of and interest in Goethe appeared in both literatures almost simultaneously, in Poland in 1777 and in Russia in 1781, when the first Russian translation of *Werther* was made. The culmination of Goethe's vogue in Russia occurred between 1825 and 1845. Before and after this period Russian literature was rather under the influence of France or England. Actually Goethe never exercised any great influence on Russian literature and never attained the prestige of Byron, Sir Walter Scott, or Schiller. The greatest Russian writers remained beyond the radius of his influence. Pushkin, who laid the foundations of modern Russian literature, was unaffected by him, whereas his debt to the French classical writers, to Byron, Scott, Shakespeare, and even Mickiewicz, who provoked him ideologically, is considerable. Once Pushkin said: *"Shakespeare a saisi les passions, Goethe le costume."* Mickiewicz, who knew Pushkin very well, wrote in his article dedicated to the memory of the Russian poet: "He did not hold in high esteem those authors who were without a goal, without any direction. He disliked philosophical skepticism and the aesthetic coldness of Goethe." Lermontov's masters were Byron, Schiller, and the French romantics, and there is very little to say about his connections with Goethe. In fact, among important Russian literary figures, only Zhukovsky, Turgenev, Tyutchev, A. Tolstoy, and Fet came under Goethe's influence to any extent.

Some difference exists in this respect between Polish and Russian literatures, but it would be difficult to maintain that Goethe had a direct and widespread influence on Polish literature. The greatest Polish literary figure of the nineteenth century, the head of the Polish romantic school, Adam Mickiewicz, in many ways found himself in the atmosphere of Goethe's themes and literary genres, giving to Poland a Polish *Werther,* a Polish *Faust,* and a Polish *Hermann und Dorothea.* But all these Polish pendants to Goethe were in reality quite distant from him.

The same may be said for the other two members of the Polish romantic trinity, Słowacki and Krasiński. In other various works they show direct contacts with Goethe's *Faust,* but everywhere they maintain strong reservations.

My main subject, however, will not be an analysis of purely literary facts and problems. I shall discuss rather what I believe to be more important and more interesting, the ideological reactions of the Russians and Poles to Goethe.

Although I recognize the valuable achievements of the German, Russian, and Polish formalists, I do not believe that it is possible to place studies in literature under the same conditions as the sciences. Even within the framework of the liberal arts, one cannot apply the very same methods of investigation to all the arts. The efforts to detach literature from life are vain. There have been writers, like Tolstoy, who would never have accepted a purely formalistic approach to their creative work. To Tolstoy the pathos of his writings lay in their ideology. Naturally, I cannot here go into a discussion of methodological problems, but I would like to emphasize that, in considering that great phenomenon of modern European culture which is Goethe, I shall not separate the man from the artist. My guide in this approach is Walt Whitman: "Understand that you can have in your writing no qualities which you do not honestly entertain in yourself. Understand that you cannot keep out of your writing the indication of the evil or shallowness you entertain in yourself. If you love to have a servant stand behind your chair at dinner, it will appear in your writing; if you possess a vile opinion of women, or if you grudge anything, or doubt immortality, these will appear by what you leave unsaid more than by what you say. There is no trick or cunning, no art or recipe by which you can have in your writing that which you do not possess in yourself—that which is not in you cannot appear in your

writing. No rival of life—no sham for generation—no painting friendship or love by one who is neither friend or lover" [*Complete Writings of Walt Whitman* 1902].

Well known is Napoleon's greeting at his famous meeting with Goethe: *"Voilà un homme!"* This witty adaptation of *"Ecce homo!"* will be the leitmotif of my [essay].

All the Russians and Poles who went to see Goethe or discussed him in their writings or in private correspondence knew very well that modesty was not the outstanding quality of this Olympian. Goethe did not need to hear all the German and non-German panegyrics which for two hundred years have resounded in the world, or to examine the monuments erected by his admirers, in order to act with quite a sufficient estimation of his extraordinary greatness. And he attained this lucid and perspicacious judgment very early in his life. He wrote to Lavater in 1780: "The task with which I am charged and which becomes with each day easier and more difficult demands my attention day and night, my duty is constantly dearer to me and I would like to equal in it the greatest men. This ambition to raise as high as possible the pyramid of my existence, the foundation of which is now designed and laid, exceeds all else and leaves me hardly a moment of rest. I cannot wait. I am already advanced in years. Fate will, perhaps, break me in the middle of my work, and the Babylonian tower will remain crudely unfinished. At least let the people say it was daringly conceived, and if I live, let God preserve my forces to the end" [*Goethes Briefe,* 1902, Vol. II; quoted by Edouard Rod in *Essai sur Goethe,* 1898].

Perhaps Rod is just in saying that the "pyramid" and the "Babylonian tower" are not metaphors without some hyperbolism, particularly if one considers the real dimensions of the "foundation" laid for the "pyramid" and the "tower": "The administration of the duchy of Weimar, the direction of the Amateurs' Theater, the literary teas with the Dowager Duchess, manuscripts so readily abandoned, that even their author had difficulty in taking them seriously. Little enough indeed, a narrow foundation on which there stood the partly constructed walls, giving no promise of an imposing monument." . . .

There exists a short but excellent essay written by Mickiewicz in his early years, probably in 1826, when he was in Moscow. In this essay, entitled "Goethe and Byron," Mickiewicz gives a significant enumeration of what he considers the most important facts about Goethe: first, that Goethe was endowed with a genius equal to the demands of the epoch and under circumstances particularly favorable to its development; second, that Goethe was a child of parents of no particular political importance and that he was born in a free city whose citizens sided in turn with the French or the

Prussians, and was, therefore, free from any strong patriotic feelings; third, that his life was quiet and happy, his passions were lively but not violent, and his relationships never unduly upset him. In other words, Goethe never knew any great misfortunes or experienced any painful losses.

We are fortunate to have records of the meeting of Mickiewicz and Goethe in Weimar. The Polish record was written by Odyniec who accompanied Mickiewicz on the visit; the German record comes from the poet, Holtei, who was also present. In Mickiewicz, as it happens, there is only one reference to the entire episode.

Odyniec has described the visit in some fifty pages. They spent thirteen days in Weimar and had the opportunity of seeing Goethe on several occasions. One day Mickiewicz and Odyniec went to see *Faust* at the Weimar Theater. During their walk from the theater to Goethe's house, where they were to spend the evening at a big reception, Odyniec attempted to get some comment from Mickiewicz and was quite irritated with the poet's silence. Later, Goethe made similar inquiries, but Mickiewicz only praised some particulars, making no comment on the play in general.

The conclusion is obvious. The meeting with Goethe left Mickiewicz cold. It could not have been otherwise. The two men were so different, almost conflicting in the essence of their natures and ideologies. There was no common language between them. Goetheism, as Rod has justly defined it in his study on Goethe, is primarily intelligence, comprehension. This in itself would not have created an obstacle between Goethe and Mickiewicz, except that Goethe's intelligence and comprehension are confined to that which secures pleasure. It is a kind of dilettantism, and as such is hedonistic. Everything opposed to its concept of harmony is rejected. That is why Goethe rejected suffering, which he never comprehended. And though he began his *Faust* with the assertion, contrary to the Gospel, that first there was the deed and then the word, he himself was not a poet of action. Heine said of him: "His works are great, but they will never give birth to any deed."

From his earliest days Goethe firmly established a stronghold of egotism and never accepted anything which might disturb his personal existence or equilibrium. Let me quote some facts and some confessions. In 1830 he said to Chancellor von Müller: "When I see that people write to me for their own sake and desire something for themselves, I consider that it is not my concern. If, on the contrary, they write in my favor and address things to me that are of interest or give me an opportunity to progress, then I answer them."

Just as Goethe did not accept suffering, he did not accept heroism. He could see no advantage in struggling against obstacles. The struggle against obstacles, the suffering and heroism involved in this struggle, have always constituted essential elements of every philosophical system which is concerned with ethics and with the problem of the moral perfecting of the human personality. But for Goethe an obstacle was a nuisance, a senseless block, and heroism was foreign to his cult of personal comfort. His rejection of the redeeming beauty of the Cross went far. In his famous "Venetian Epigram" he stated: "I abhor like the venom of a serpent four things in the world: tobacco, bedbugs, garlic, and the Cross!" But he did not apply this abhorrence to any cross of decoration. "I confess that a small cross of honor on a suit is a pleasant object, but the horrible wooden cross of torment is the most hideous picture under the sun; a sensible man should not project its silhouette in the sky."

In contrast to Goethe, during his whole life Mickiewicz was devoted precisely to the three enumerated elements of moral philosophy—struggle, suffering, heroism. There are numerous illustrations, but I would like first to complete this list of moral conflicts between him and Goethe. Let us take, for instance, patriotism. When in 1771 J. von Sonnenfels published his book, *Über die Liebe des Vaterlands,* Goethe followed with an article in which he wrote: "If we find a place in the world where we and our belongings may rest, a field which will nourish us, a roof to shelter us, do we not have a fatherland there? Have not thousands and thousands of men these things in every state? Let God preserve us from Roman patriotism."

One may say, perhaps, that the fight for national independence immunized the Poles against bourgeois philistinism and secured to them a special conception of personal dignity which partially compensated for their national enslavement. It is possible to consider Goethe (and this is the way his admirers interpret him) as a personality so potent and rich that he does not require heterogeneous moral supports. From this point of view the men who worship the Cross and admire unredeemed heroism, who are ready to sacrifice themselves for some superior ideal, such as fatherland, are inferior beings. But the problem is more complicated, because we are not concerned here with average people, nor are we trying to distinguish between those who are strong enough to live by themselves and those who require external values to which they may anchor their own moral life. Here we are juxtaposing two great men, and it seems to me that Mickiewicz was endowed with such natural, organic elements of power, attractiveness, and personal prestige that it would have been exceedingly easy for him to follow a path of personal conquests and triumphs. But no! He bowed his head. He voluntarily adopted an attitude of humility, believing that this alone could dignify and enrich him. This attitude is not necessarily a Christian one, though it was in Mickiewicz's case. Disinterested sacrifice, readiness for heroism, love of obstacle, generosity, preference for giving rather than receiving—these are traits which characterize, above all, the aristocratic being, and it is by these traits that such individuals are distinguished from what we usually call bourgeois philistines. . . .

To Odyniec, Mickiewicz gave the following resumé of his impressions of the trip to Germany: "In Hamburg—beefsteak, in Bonn—potatoes, in Weimar—Goethe." This formula is certainly disconcerting, but one should not be too astonished by the coolness of Mickiewicz's feeling for Goethe. Though in his poetry he was more closely connected than Pushkin with Goethe, ideologically he was farther removed.

I have already mentioned the existence of a Polish *Werther,* a Polish *Faust,* and a Polish *Hermann und Dorothea.* But the Polish *Werther* lost its philosophic reflectiveness and became a cry of passion, the Polish *Faust* expressed the identification of the poet with the sufferings of millions, and the pale idyll of bourgeois life in *Hermann und Dorothea* became in *Pan Tadeusz* a colorful fresco of Polish nature and society, presented with Homeric scope.

The most important quality, however, which distinguishes Mickiewicz from Goethe is the resignation imposed by the poet upon himself. At the culmination in the development of his personality, Mickiewicz was prepared to reduce the universal possibilities of his art and his individual happiness for the sake of his nation. But through an act of polarization he attained a new universalism. The route to it was through solidarity with human suffering. There exists no greater opposition to Goethe than this. The author of *Konrad Wallenrod* and *Forefathers' Eve* had nothing in common with the Goethe who once (March 6, 1823) said to Chancellor von Müller: "I have not reached my present age to be busy with the history of the world, which is certainly the absurdest of all things. Whether a man die, or a nation succumb, I remain quite indifferent."

The pathos of solidarity with the suffering of the national collectivity found an issue precisely in the Cross in Poland, the Cross which Goethe had classified along with tobacco, bedbugs, and garlic. The Christian religion became a theodicy for Polish martyrdom, and the Messianic conception of Poland as the Christ of nations was not at all an expression of pretentious and ridiculous national ambition or glorification, but a genuine expression of grief and despair, of the search for a religious justification of sufferings which reason could neither explain nor accept.

It is exactly this road that was followed by Krasiński, the aristocrat and aristophile, who denied his aristocratic hero in *The Undivine Comedy* because of his lack of heart, and who led his other hero, Iridion, the

avenger of mutilated Greece, to resignation. Although in the character Masinissa in *Iridion* one may find reminiscences of Mephistopheles, Krasiński rejects Goethe too for lack of heart. This constitutes the poet's first refutation. The second is for the sake of will and deed. This is what he wrote to his mistress, Countess Delfina Potocka, about a poem he was considering, which was to be an addition to the *The Undivine Comedy:* "I recently read you an analysis of the second part of *Faust.* You observed that this poem embraces the history and fate of all of mankind, but in the form of an idea, in the form of the development of art. The Greek Helen and romantic poetry are the main actors there. The deeds of all centuries are expressed through the destiny of art. Mankind is literature there! My conception will be different. If this poem, the nucleus of which was born in my head in your honor, is ever realized, it will be a poem of will and deed, not art. In it will and deed will be transferred into the sphere of art, but this will not be art created out of art, as in Goethe."

No different were Słowacki's conceptions. To individual disharmony Słowacki opposed universal disharmony and showed that in the heart one might accept universal suffering and that infinite sorrow does not stem from a sick soul, as in Werther's case, but from the immensity of the real universal suffering. The consolation offered in *Anhelli* is based on the belief that human suffering and all sacrifice, though never rewarded, serve humanity as they enrich the spiritual content of the world. There is something in these dreams of Polish minds which makes me think of Dostoevsky's assertion that there is nothing more beautiful than an aristocrat in democracy, since such an aristocrat represents an act of voluntary sacrifice. . . .

In his memoirs of the famous Polish insurrectionist, Worcell, [Herzen] says: "Stanislaw Worcell was a saintly man. I have selected this word above all others because it expresses best the main quality of the man. His entire life was a heroic act of selflessness, of unlimited devotion. All that astounds us in the life of saints we find in him, only it is more humane, that is, full of greater love.

"Born in luxury and the brilliance of the highest Polish aristocracy, he died in poverty and a democrat. When his native land succumbed under the iron claw of Nicholas, he went into exile, leaving behind all his titles and wealth. I mention the latter fact only in passing, because there is no people on earth that sheds its wealth more readily than the Slavs. It seems to me the Poles have proved this sufficiently. Worcell did not leave Poland to seek a peaceful harbor, like those Romans of the first centuries who denied themselves worldly pleasures and withdrew into isolation so as not to observe the ruin of the world and to create out of their *far niente* a religion of despair. In alien lands his prolonged, tireless work first began—the formation and development of a democratic party of the Polish emigration . . ."

These tributes paid by a Russian to a Pole are deeply touching. But in addition Herzen comprehended the essence of the Polish outlook—let us use the excellent German word, *Weltanschauung*. A distinguished Polish scholar, Massonius, confirms Herzen's views in a study entitled "Dualism in Polish Thought." He writes: "While we [Poles] are indifferent to the questions: What exists? How it exists? and Why is it so? we react passionately to the questions: What is desirable? and What ought to be?" Massonius emphasizes that Poles have never been inclined to abstract speculation but have rather been attracted by practical philosophy. With them ontology has been replaced by ethics. This is a trait which appeared in Polish literature in the sixteenth century and has not disappeared. Massonius explains that the Polish conception of virtue does not permit recognition of any essential value that is or appears to be exclusively personal, that does not clearly tend toward the general good.

I believe that this explains why Goethe's ideology was not acceptable to the Poles of the romantic generation. . . . [The] same motives guided the Russian critics of Goethe. Their rejection of Goethe was essentially ethical, although they liked to philosophize more than the Poles did. On one side were Germans who erected a temple, worshipped an idol, and established a cult of certain principles of life in which they discovered the most beautiful expression of human thought and dignity. On the other side were Russians and Poles who saw in this cult, in this religion, and in this adoration an offense to the noblest human obligations, goals, and aspirations. And the more Goethe's worshippers attempted to impose him on others, insisting that he represented the final, the ultimate expression of human wisdom, the more unacceptable he became for the adversaries of this cult, who questioned with Whitman whether any "man or woman was invigorated, made cleaner, grander, sweeter, by his poems," or whether Goethe had "raised any strong voice for freedom and against tyrants." Yet for both sides Goethe became a symbol—a symbol of a philosophic interpretation of life.

For those who admired Schiller and Byron, to be reconciled with Goethe would mean to betray their very spiritual *raison d'être*. And this is why it seems to me that Goethe's irreconcilable critics were perhaps more human than Goethe and in a way closer to a universalistic conception of life, though this conception derived from anthropocentrism. And thus we return to *"Ecce homo!"*

It has often been said that Goethe was divine. But for this reason he was also nonhuman in the eyes of his adversaries. There is no doubt that in Goethe they found

the greatest opposition to Christianity; I do not have in mind the confessional or religious aspects of this faith, but its moral aspects—solidarity with human sufferings. Not to accept Goethe meant not to accept the world as it is. To accept Goethe meant to sublimate our own existence, to consider it to be more important than all else. To accept Goethe meant to accept our own happiness at the price of the sufferings of millions. Whether universal happiness is generally attainable is another question, but there is a difference between doubt and the mere acceptance of the present situation for the sake of our own comfort.

It has been said that Goethe was greater than Aeschylus, Sophocles, Dante, and Shakespeare because he was concerned with the impossible. To me the situation seems the reverse. I think that some part of humanity adores men like Schiller, Byron, Mickiewicz, and Tolstoy, although they may only have been modestly concerned with the possible. For who knows what constitutes the possible or the impossible?

Stefan Treugutt (essay date 1982)

SOURCE: "Byron and Napoleon in Polish Romantic Myth," in *Lord Byron and His Contemporaries: Essays from the Sixth International Byron Seminar,* edited by Charles E. Robinson, University of Delaware Press, 1982, pp. 130-43.

[*In the essay below, Treugutt comments on ways in which Byron, Napoleon, and the idea of the politically active artist were received and interpreted by the Polish Romantics.*]

While paying a visit in 1979 to the Institute of Russian Literature in Leningrad, I unexpectedly discovered a copy of *The Works of Lord Byron, Complete in One Volume,* published in Frankfurt am Main in 1826, and which came to the Institute from Pushkin's library. On the title page is this dedication in Polish: "Bajrona Puszkinowi poświęca wielbiciel obudwóch—A. Michiewicz" ("Here is Byron dedicated to Pushkin by an admirer of both of them—Adam Mickiewicz"). What impressed me was not the elegance of the dedication but the sign of a community transcending national boundaries: a volume of a great English author published in Germany had been presented to the foremost poet of Russia by a Polish poet in exile. This volume commemorates an internationalism of free spirits in which Byron's name, evoking an entire range of feelings and ideas, serves as the symbol of freedom.

"There was Byronism before Byron," says William Rose in his study on the origins and development of the notion of *Weltschmerz* in German literature [*From Goethe to Byron,* 1924], and he continues: "Weltschmerz was epidemic in German literature for the forty years or more which preceded the publication of *Childe Harold*. . . . There is no doubt equal scope for an enquiry into the symptoms of 'le mal du siècle' in France before Chateaubriand, while a study on the same lines of the precursors of Byron in England should yield fruitful results."

No doubt there was "Byronism before Byron" in Poland, whose artists also distrusted "reality" and lost confidence in the ideas of the Age of Reason. The Enlightenment was expected to bring the Poles a reform of their state, a constitution, democracy, and prosperity, but no such transformations occurred. Hopes ran high again during the Napoleonic wars, but the conqueror of Europe did not restore Poland. The feeling of bitterness, especially among young people, was even stronger than that of the preceding generation.

> Poland! o'er which the avenging angel pass'd,
> But left thee as he found thee, still a waste,
> Forgetting all thy still enduring claim,
> Thy lotted people and extinguish'd name,
> Thy sigh for freedom, thy long-flowing tear.

These words of Byron, dedicated to Poland after the fall of Napoleon and uttered with pathos in *The Age of Bronze* (ll. 161-65), were not known to Adam Mickiewicz as a young man. Yet the Polish poet found other reasons for admiring Byron when he wrote to a friend in 1822: "It is only Byron I am reading now. I push away books written in any other spirit, as I have no liking for lies." The point here is that for the young Polish poet, who was then affected by private grief, Byron was not a teacher of pessimism. What Mickiewicz found in his lines was the truth of his own feelings and a critique and condemnation of hypocrisy. There was surely Byronism before Byron, but for Mickiewicz and for the entire generation born as the eighteenth century succeeded to the nineteenth, the name of the English poet became a symbol, a token of an adopted attitude, a declaration of community.

We all know how great was Shakespeare's authority in Europe during the Romantic period. It is, consequently, very significant that the volume that proclaimed the triumph of Romanticism in Poland—the *Ballads and Romances* of Mickiewicz—contains in the discourse on Romantic poetry preceding the poems a rather unusual comparison: "In the descriptive genre and in the tale Byron is what Shakespeare was in the dramatic genre." What Mickiewicz has in mind is of course not prose fiction, but the Byronic poetic tale: perhaps the Turkish tales; or perhaps *Beppo* and the opening cantos of *Don Juan,* which the Polish author might have known at that time. According to Mickiewicz, Byron created "a new kind of poetry," a new and feeling expression of "the passionate soul." To some scholars, the equal footing conceded to Byron and to Shakespeare may seem extravagant, but Mickiewicz was right

in finding certain common elements in both poets, such as pathos side by side with raw realism, sublimity with irony, lofty ideals with the grotesque. Both writers told him truths about the nature of man, but of the two Byron stood for unrestrained individualism, for revolt, for cult of genius and worship of freedom. Besides, he was a contemporary, still living and working when Mickiewicz was placing him in the gallery of patron spirits of the new Romantic literature.

Searching for genealogies and adducing great examples from the past were characteristic of all the new literary trends until the twentieth century. The futurists and other radical avant-garde groups were the first to proclaim that they had neither ancestors nor family archives. But the Romantics, though in revolt against tradition and the classroom brand of classicism, were very anxious to have a good pedigree, and in this very respect they were legitimists. When Victor Hugo wanted to point to the ancient roots of Romantic poetry and attitudes, the names that appeared the most frequently in his manifesto were those of Homer, Dante, Cervantes, and Shakespeare, plus the Bible and—Byron. A comparative study of proclamations and manifestoes of the Romantic movement in Europe (from Italy to Scandinavia and from Madrid to Saint Petersburg) would reveal, undoubtedly, a similar and select assortment of the patrons of the new writing, with Byron's name among the predecessors and patrons of the new literature: he was the youngest, the closest to the new generation, and the most intelligible. He was also the most adaptable to the spiritual needs and experiences of differing societies, of various writers and their readers. H. G. Schenk says in *The Mind of the European Romantics:* "Although the enthusiasm for Byron's personality caught on all over Europe, the appeal of the poet whom Goethe hailed as the herald of world literature varied from nation to nation, in that each picked out that part of Byron's œuvre most congenial to itself." Byron's language became in an incredibly short time an international language of the generation in revolt, of the spiritual and social outcasts alienated from the conventional rules of living and thinking.

The practice of adducing literary patrons is as old as literature itself. For a number of centuries, the writers of ancient Greece and Rome played this part for most European artists. The eighteenth century chose the patronage of Voltaire, but Byron's impact was something of a different quality. Voltaire's influence was traditionally unifying: it raised the representatives of different traditions to the level of French intellectual culture. But Byron's individualism offered no ready-made doctrine and thus could become a stimulus within the bodies of various national literatures. Voltaire provided a national lesson to be learned; Byron provided an international inspiration that respected individuality. That is why the cult of Byron contributed in so many literatures, and quite certainly in Polish literature, to an increase of originality. It also stimulated literary invention and favored personal features in poetic expression. All this is valid, of course, only for a certain period: with the formation of clichés and rigid patterns, the poets whom literary history posthumously honors as leaders of their age outgrew the fashion of Byronism. It was then cultivated only by belated followers. Still, Byron's name, even more glorious after his death in Greece in 1824, continued to inspire and enthuse. This enthusiasm is eloquently documented in the Paris lectures on Slavonic literatures given by Adam Mickiewicz in Collège de France in 1840-44. According to Mickiewicz, Byron was a spokesman for collective feelings:

> Avec lord Byron commence l'époque nouvelle de la littérature, de la poésie. Cette littérature et cette poésie se rapprochent d'un côté de la philosophie, et d'un autre côté de la vie réelle. Personne n'a mieux que lui représenté les tourments de ces existences anormales qui ont marque le passage entre le XVIIIᵉ et le XIXᵉ siècle, ce voyage sans but, cette recherche des aventures extraordinaires, ces élans vers un avenir dont on n'avait encore aucune idée. Tout cela remplissait les âmes des jeunes gens de notre génération; tout cela a été représenté par lord Byron avec une grande fidélité. Sous ce point de vue, c'est un poëte de réalité.

Mickiewicz held Byron to be equally important as a harbinger of political ideas ("On connait aussi la hauteur et la sûreté de son coup d'oeil lorsqu'il jugeait les questions politiques") and as a metaphysical poet ("son désir incessant de sonder et de connaître les mystères de l'existence"). He ranked the English poet among the great who could express a whole age and at the same time point a way to the future:

> Ainsi, dans la politique, comme dans l'art, il y a toujours des individus qui conduisent les époques. . . . il faut suivre leurs traces, comme les navigateurs qui parcourent les mers sont obligés de suivre le chemin de ceux qui ont fait les premières découvertes, sauf ensuite à compléter leurs observations.

Yet, to follow such predecessors does not mean to imitate them, to counterfeit their literary form or their heroes. What should be followed is their spirit ("c'est s'inspirer de leurs esprit"). Mickiewicz's verdict is categorical:

> et nous sommes convaincu que ceux-là seulement qui ont saisi ce qu'il y avait de fort, de vrai, de sincère et de profond dans lord Byron, ont été appelés à prendre le devant dans la marche littéraire de notre siècle.

Mickiewicz further explains that many of his contemporaries did not see Byron's works but that they grasped a few lines, a few sounds that were sufficient to inspire them: "La force de cet homme était si grande qu'elle se faisait sentir même dans quelques paroles, et que ces paroles suffisaient pour remuer les âmes et leur faire découvrir le secret de leur propre existence." Byron, something much more than a distant literary authority, addressed his contemporaries without intermediaries and simply spoke their language.

Juliusz Słowacki, another Polish Romantic poet who antagonized and competed with Mickiewicz, still agreed with him on Byron's position in world literature when he wrote in April 1833:

> Dante wrote about Hell at a time when people believed in Hell; Voltaire was in agreement with a materialistic age; Byron while despairing about the future and its uncertainty opened the nineteenth century. These three people represent the epochs in which they lived, their spiritual countenances reflect the faces of their age. If one could put together one single monument of thought out of the thoughts of many people in those days, the statues on the monument would be those of Dante, Voltaire, and Byron. [*Dzieta Wszystkie*, ed. Juliusz Kleiner, 1954]

In short, Byron's contemporaries agreed that he was a personification of the spirit of the age, a voice of the Romantic Zeitgeist. He was, paradoxically, the leader of an international community of solitaries, of egocentrics, of individualists in revolt. Because of the universal appeal of the Byron cult, Romantic individualism did not mean the breaking of communication between people or an expression of doubt about such communication. Byron's language could be used for communication and mutual comprehension by all those who understood it, by those "Byronists before Byron" who experienced painfully the widening gap between their inner experience and the outer world. To them and on their behalf, the poet spoke a language of solitude and despair that at the same time was a language of pride and energy.

Because Byronism was a Continental more than a British phenomenon, the question arises why Byron's works, read in translation or in the original by people who were not native speakers of English, proved so much more interesting abroad than to his own countrymen. Perhaps the answer could be found in the quicker pace of literary developments in the British Isles, where Romanticism was no longer a revelation at the time of Byron's appearance upon the literary stage. In Germany, on the other hand, where the campaign for a national literature had already been successfully carried on by the Storm and Stress movement, where Byron's works could not inaugurate Romanticism, his prestige was very considerable, if not overwhelming as in Central or Southern Europe. Although Germany was as rich as Britain in Romantic inspirations of its own, the German peoples were fascinated with the personality of the English lord and poet. One could perhaps formulate the following principle: the further from Britain, from English literature, and from the actual biography of Byron, the stronger were the impact of the myth of his personality and the influence of his poetical works.

Slavonic literatures and the Polish writers in particular were indeed far away from Britain at that time, but they nevertheless recognized a kinship with Byron. The Polish Romantic artist discovered in him what he wished to be—a non-conformist, a solitary, and a man of magnanimity, a hero of freedom, an incarnation of creative genius. From the protean character and works of the man, Polish Romantics abstracted and formed their own ideal and pattern of an active poet who did not draw limits between literature and life, between his words and his deeds.

Byron's death in Greece played an important part in the shaping of his legend. For contemporary young enthusiasts of political freedom and of Romantic poetry, it was not an accident but the logical outcome of a certain attitude. Moreover, it refuted tales about the dissolute and perverted fiend. Continental poets exalted his death in a crusade for freedom, and Cyprian Norwid, the last of the great Polish poets bred in the Romantic tradition, concluded an evaluation of Byron as follows:

> How serious, indeed, is the poet's service and vocation! And yet this truth began to dawn only at the threshold of the present age upon which Byron lies with the lyre of Homer and the sword of Leonidas—a man who might have said about himself: *veni, cantavi, vici. [Wszystkie Pisma, 1938]*

Norwid's parallel, taken from ancient history, illustrates his conviction that Byron's death in a war for the sake of mankind confirms the truth of the poet's works, and that the two symbols of sword and lyre are the attributes of "serious" poetry. A poem is an actual deed, and there can be no boundary between poetry and action. This view is very characteristic for the Polish Romantics, especially after the failure of the uprising in 1830-31. The desperate national situation induced people to think of every possible means of struggle, both ideological and political. For creative artists, action and deed became a category that overshadowed the opposition of the spiritual and the real. One could speak here, perhaps, of a suppression and uplifting of the clash between the ideal and reality. Byron—the poet of freedom rushing to the battle of liberation—provided a sign: he prefigured the future role of poetry, that which would abolish the distinction between word and action.

In order to stress the importance of Byron's mission, Norwid identifies Byron's ancestors as the crusaders for the recovery of the Holy Land. Envisioning Byron's death as the beginning of a new era, Norwid writes about himself in his autobiography: "He saw the world . . . in the patrimonial estate a few miles away from Warsaw, at the time when Noel Byron was just dying in Greece." One could treat this reference as a simple stylistic ornament opening an autobiography, but Norwid actually postpones the date of his birth for three years (he was really born in 1821) in order to make it symbolically agree with the date of Byron's death. The beginning of his own life is to be connected with the end of the life of Byron.

Adam Mickiewicz, in his lectures at the Collège de France, best sums up the part Byron played in shaping the ideal of a poet both in Poland and in other Slavonic countries:

> Ce qui a élevé, ce qui a facilité la marche des poètes slaves, et ce qui en général pourra rendre plus claire l'idée qu'ils se font de la poésie, c'est la carrière politique de lord Byron. Lord Byron commence l'ère de la poésie nouvelle; lui, le premier, a fait sentir aux hommes tout le sérieux de la poésie; on a vu qu'il fallait vivre d'après ce qu'on écrit; que le désir, que la parole, ne suffisent pas; on a vu ce poëte riche et élevé dans un pays aristocratique quitter le parlement et sa patrie pour servir la cause des Grecs. Ce besoin profondément senti de rendre la vie poétique, de rapprocher ainsi l'idéal du réel, constitue tout le mérite poétique de Byron. Or, tous les grands poëtes slaves ont passé par là. Byron, c'est l'anneau mystérieux qui attache la grande littérature slave à celle de l'Occident.

It does not matter that Byron's biography has been simplified here. It is important to observe that this is how Mickiewicz wants to see, to interpret, and to understand Byron. He really saw in the English poet an example of the principle that "one should live according to what one is writing," proving that it is possible to bring an ideal close to reality. Such an interpretation was possible, and even natural, in the circumstances in which Polish literature had to operate in the period under discussion. The leading Romantics were involved in political activities; they were looking for effective ways and means of working for their nation. The art of beautiful speech consequently seemed unimportant and a secondary matter. Mickiewicz stopped his literary activities in the very middle of his dazzling career to become a politician, a prophet of a new religion, and finally a soldier. Juliusz Słowacki, the most Romantic of the Polish writers and a Byronist at the beginning of his career, suddenly at the age of thirty-three changed his views of poetry, stopped producing literature, and devoted himself to penetrating the mysteries of Nature and the ways of Creation. He went on writing feverishly, but his later works are visions put down in verse or prose, fragments of a mystical system of the Great Chain of Being and

Universal Evolution that would free Poland and all mankind. Like Byron and Mickiewicz, Słowacki finally hurried to the battlefield. At the end of his life he went to the German part of Poland, which was then caught by the fire of the revolution in 1848. He did not die in the campaign like the other two poets, but succumbed a few months later after his return to Paris.

The life of Juliusz Słowacki is an exemplary Romantic biography in the history of Polish literature. It began with solitude and alienation from the world and ended in the mystical communion with an all-embracing creative evolution. Słowacki is so typically Byronic that his period of Childe Haroldism, of the youthful cult of one's own personality, is followed at maturity by a phase of romantic irony and satire in which Byron served as master and example. Słowacki's *Podróz na Wschód (Journey to the East)* in six-line stanzas and the digressive poetic tale *Beniowski* in ottava rima are the best Polish equivalents of Byron's style in *Don Juan*.

Byron's pattern was followed by young Romantics, by young people searching for their own identity. But he still provided an example of how to render life poetic, how to bring about a close union between poetry and life, when the youthful solitaries grew up to become patriotic leaders, prophets, and spiritual commanders in the war "for our freedom and for yours." The years 1831 and 1863 were those of tragic Polish national uprisings, but were also the dates of the triumph and the end of great Romantic poetry in Poland. For the Polish Romantic poets who lived during these years, Byron was not a hero of the past. On the contrary, they looked upon him as their forerunner, a John the Baptist of the future, a prefiguration and a mythical impulse that was calling for fulfillment.

There is a striking parallel here with the myth of Napoleon: Byron died on his mission of a liberator, Napoleon did not accomplish his mission. The latter's genius had been tempted by egoism, which made him replace the sword of Europe's liberator and creator of a new order with the imperial crown of dynastic ambitions. In his case, as in that of Byron, the mission had to be taken up and the mystical impulse had to be brought to fruition. In the preface to his translation of *The Giaour,* Mickiewicz thus establishes a connection between the two geniuses as forerunners of the future: "The voice of the general has called Byron the Napoleon of the poets, while Napoleon has been acknowledged as the only poet of France." It is difficult to imagine a more striking declaration of unity between word and deed, between poetry and life. Byron himself had certain reservations about the subject when he treated the parallel between Napoleon and his own person with the irony of a grand seigneur:

> Even I—albeit I'm sure I did not know it,
> Nor sought of foolscap subjects to be king,—
> Was reckon'd, a considerable time,
> The grand Napoleon of the realms of rhyme.
> [*Don Juan* XI.1v]

For Mickiewicz and other Romantics, equating Byron and Napoleon was not a mere compliment paid to the poet. Mickiewicz was deeply convinced, and Byron and Napoleon served him as examples, that "il y a des signes de parenté entre toutes ces créations, malgré l'indépendance et l'originalité des créateurs." Characteristically, Mickiewicz stresses the affinity of poetry and practical action produced by a poet and a military leader, and not the links between different arts or between poetry and other kinds of intellectual creativeness. Also Norwid's praise of Byron (*"veni, cantavi, vici"*) paraphrases the famous words of Julius Caesar—a genius of poetry and a genius of energy and action are again put on the same level. The common denominator between Byron and Napoleon is their moral force that changes people and may shape life itself. This is exactly what, according to Mickiewicz, Byron saw and understood in Napoleon:

> C'est le seul des écrivains anglais qui ait compris quelque chose à Napoléon. Il est vrai qu'il l'a réduit aux proportions d'un corsaire. Il comprennait seulement la force que Napoléon exerçait sur ses semblables, force toute morale; il sentait aussi où elle résidait: Napoléon a dominé parce que son âme était toujours en travail; son sentiment ne pouvait dormir. *I suoi pensieri in lui dormir non ponno,* c'est la devise qu'a choisie lord Byron. Cette âme en travail dévelopait la force qui lui donnait le pouvoir sur ses semblables.

What is mentioned here is energy, but not energy for its own sake: energy must actively influence other people. Napoleon began the work of Europe's reconstruction and demonstrated man's creative scope and power; a poet should do likewise. Practical influence becomes the norm and canon of poetry. The anticlassical revolution had indeed come to its ultimate limit. By appealing to the memory of Napoleon as a poet of action and to Byron as the leader of souls of a generation, Polish Romantics raised poetry to such a high position that it stopped being what is called an art of language. In their view, poetry was a prediction, an expectation of the fulfillment of a prophecy—*"ut sermo . . . prophetae impleretur,"* as John 12:38 states. Poetry was no longer merely literary.

The historical explanation of this strangely utopian and anachronistic view of poetry is to be found in the situation of the Poles and in the situation of Europe on the eve of the revolution of 1848. The lack of real power made men's minds more heated and ecstatic. Words were plentiful and stood for the deeds and actions that were sadly lacking. Here are the sources of the phenomenon of heroizing poetry, of the cult of genius, of the posthumous career and activeness of the spirit of Napoleon. Here is also the explanation of the power of Byronism treated as a source of inspiration and energy. One must always keep in mind that, through Byronism, the poet's work and person were transformed into myth. Only in recent decades has critical examination of Byron's poetic work begun to prevail over biographical studies, over studies of the Byron legend and of the myth of a superman. The turning point was T. S. Eliot's essay on Byron's poetry in 1937. It is certainly important to strip Byron of the Byron mythology, to examine his poems in a critical way by using all the equipment of modern literary criticism. But one must not, in the process, overlook Byronism, a mythic force as real to nineteenth-century Europe as were Byron's poems.

Byronism is an important component of the history of ideas and of the history of literary consciousness. In Poland, the reading public actually acquaints itself with Byron's works through the tradition of Byronism. There is a very good translation of *Don Juan,* which was quite the rage with schoolboys of my generation. This translation was published in 1883 and is clearly modeled in its style upon Juliusz Słowacki's tale *Beniowski,* which, in turn, is a Polish replica of *Don Juan.* Byron's text in Polish was decisively influenced by Byronism as understood by an eminent Polish Romantic poet some forty years before the actual date of translation.

There are, however, reasons of much greater importance for this interest in Byronism and the Byron myth. The presence of Byronism in simple and naive forms—or in complicated and sophisticated shapes—is strong in the works of Polish Romantic literature, as well as in much contemporary literature. One may believe or not in the power of the word to change people's minds or to stir them to action, but in any case Polish readers expect poetry to offer more than linguistic delights or expressions of impotence. The ideal of effective poetry may be a utopia, and it is perhaps wrong to confuse poetry or literature in general with any sphere of activity. But poetry that abandons in advance its claim to the *energy* of despair and the *energy* of enthusiasm is not worth reading at all.

In any case, it is certainly worthwhile to continue research on Byronism as a community of the lonely, as a movement from narrow, personal truth to the larger truth of mankind. Sheer curiosity should be sufficient reason—a curiosity to learn something about the exceedingly high tasks that art undertook 150 years ago. By such research, one may observe an international exchange of ideas that still exert their influence on contemporary poetry and politics.

FURTHER READING

Csato, Edward. "Some History." In *The Polish Theatre,* pp. 12-41. Warsaw: Polonia Publishing House, 1965.
    Presents an overview of nineteenth-century Polish Romantic drama, which Csato describes as belonging to "an intermediary stage between the old travelling troupes and the modern permanent theatre."

Erlich, Victor. "The Cost of the Image: The Strange Case of Zygmunt Krasiński." In *The Double Image: Concepts of the Poet in Slavic Literatures,* pp. 38-67. Baltimore: The Johns Hopkins Press, 1964.
    Discusses Krasiński's *The Undivine Comedy* as a critique of the poet and a "warning against the moral pitfalls of poetry."

Krzyżanowski, Julian. *Polish Romantic Literature.* New York: E. P. Dutton and Co., 1931, 317 p.
    Detailed survey of the careers, works, and style of the major figures of Polish Romanticism, with chapters on predecessors, realism, and messianism.

Noyes, George Rapall. "Introduction." In *Poems,* by Adam Mickiewicz, edited by George Rapall Noyes, pp. 1-63. New York: The Polish Institute of Arts and Sciences in America, 1944.
    Survey of Mickiewicz's life and works, in the context of his role as the preeminent figure in Polish Romanticism.

Segel, Harold B. "Animal Magnetism in Polish Romantic Literature." In *The Polish Review* VII, No. 3 (Summer, 1962): 16-39.
    Explores the influence of Franz Mesmer's science of magnetism on Mickiewicz's *Forefathers' Eve,* Aleksander Fredro's *Śluby panieńskie (Maiden's Vows),* and the works of Tomasz Zan. Segel notes that "magnetism . . . travelled the full circle in Poland: from a major current of romantic mysticism it became a means of parodying this mysticism."

Nineteenth-Century Literature Criticism

Topics Volume
Cumulative Indexes

Volumes 1-52

How to Use This Index

The main references

Calvino, Italo
1923-1985.....CLC 5, 8, 11, 22, 33, 39,
73; SSC 3

list all author entries in the following Gale Literary Criticism series:

BLC = *Black Literature Criticism*
CLC = *Contemporary Literary Criticism*
CLR = *Children's Literature Review*
CMLC = *Classical and Medieval Literature Criticism*
DA = *DISCovering Authors*
DC = *Drama Criticism*
HLC = *Hispanic Literature Criticism*
LC = *Literature Criticism from 1400 to 1800*
NCLC = *Nineteenth-Century Literature Criticism*
PC = *Poetry Criticism*
SSC = *Short Story Criticism*
TCLC = *Twentieth-Century Literary Criticism*
WLC = *World Literature Criticism, 1500 to the Present*

The cross-references

See also CANR 23; CA 85-88;
obituary CA 116

list all author entries in the following Gale biographical and literary sources:

AAYA = *Authors & Artists for Young Adults*
AITN = *Authors in the News*
BEST = *Bestsellers*
BW = *Black Writers*
CA = *Contemporary Authors*
CAAS = *Contemporary Authors Autobiography Series*
CABS = *Contemporary Authors Bibliographical Series*
CANR = *Contemporary Authors New Revision Series*
CAP = *Contemporary Authors Permanent Series*
CDALB = *Concise Dictionary of American Literary Biography*
CDBLB = *Concise Dictionary of British Literary Biography*
DLB = *Dictionary of Literary Biography*
DLBD = *Dictionary of Literary Biography Documentary Series*
DLBY = *Dictionary of Literary Biography Yearbook*
HW = *Hispanic Writers*
JRDA = *Junior DISCovering Authors*
MAICYA = *Major Authors and Illustrators for Children and Young Adults*
MTCW = *Major 20th-Century Writers*
NNAL = *Native North American Literature*
SAAS = *Something about the Author Autobiography Series*
SATA = *Something about the Author*
YABC = *Yesterday's Authors of Books for Children*

Literary Criticism Series
Cumulative Author Index

Aldanov, Mark (Alexandrovich)
1886(?)-1957 . . . . TCLC 23
See also CA 118

Aldington, Richard 1892-1962 . . . . . . CLC 49
See also CA 85-88; CANR 45; DLB 20, 36,
100, 149

Aldiss, Brian W(ilson)
1925- . . . . CLC 5, 14, 40
See also CA 5-8R; CAAS 2; CANR 5, 28;
DLB 14; MTCW; SATA 34

Alegria, Claribel 1924- . . . . CLC 75
See also CA 131; CAAS 15; DLB 145; HW

Alegria, Fernando 1918- . . . . CLC 57
See also CA 9-12R; CANR 5, 32; HW

Aleichem, Sholom . . . . TCLC 1, 35
See also Rabinovitch, Sholem

Aleixandre, Vicente 1898-1984 . . . CLC 9, 36
See also CA 85-88; 114; CANR 26;
DLB 108; HW; MTCW

Alepoudelis, Odysseus
See Elytis, Odysseus

Aleshkovsky, Joseph 1929-
See Aleshkovsky, Yuz
See also CA 121; 128

Aleshkovsky, Yuz . . . . CLC 44
See also Aleshkovsky, Joseph

Alexander, Lloyd (Chudley) 1924- . . CLC 35
See also AAYA 1; CA 1-4R; CANR 1, 24,
38; CLR 1, 5; DLB 52; JRDA; MAICYA;
MTCW; SAAS 19; SATA 3, 49, 81

Alfau, Felipe 1902- . . . . CLC 66
See also CA 137

Alger, Horatio, Jr. 1832-1899 . . . . . NCLC 8
See also DLB 42; SATA 16

Algren, Nelson 1909-1981 . . . . CLC 4, 10, 33
See also CA 13-16R; 103; CANR 20;
CDALB 1941-1968; DLB 9; DLBY 81,
82; MTCW

Ali, Ahmed 1910- . . . . CLC 69
See also CA 25-28R; CANR 15, 34

Alighieri, Dante 1265-1321 . . . . CMLC 3

Allan, John B.
See Westlake, Donald E(dwin)

Allen, Edward 1948- . . . . CLC 59

Allen, Paula Gunn 1939- . . . . CLC 84
See also CA 112; 143; NNAL

Allen, Roland
See Ayckbourn, Alan

Allen, Sarah A.
See Hopkins, Pauline Elizabeth

Allen, Woody 1935- . . . . CLC 16, 52
See also AAYA 10; CA 33-36R; CANR 27,
38; DLB 44; MTCW

Allende, Isabel 1942- . . . . CLC 39, 57; HLC
See also CA 125; 130; DLB 145; HW;
MTCW

Alleyn, Ellen
See Rossetti, Christina (Georgina)

Allingham, Margery (Louise)
1904-1966 . . . . CLC 19
See also CA 5-8R; 25-28R; CANR 4;
DLB 77; MTCW

Allingham, William 1824-1889 . . . NCLC 25
See also DLB 35

Allison, Dorothy E. 1949- . . . . CLC 78
See also CA 140

Allston, Washington 1779-1843 . . . . NCLC 2
See also DLB 1

Almedingen, E. M. . . . . CLC 12
See also Almedingen, Martha Edith von
See also SATA 3

Almedingen, Martha Edith von 1898-1971
See Almedingen, E. M.
See also CA 1-4R; CANR 1

Almqvist, Carl Jonas Love
1793-1866 . . . . NCLC 42

Alonso, Damaso 1898-1990 . . . . CLC 14
See also CA 110; 131; 130; DLB 108; HW

Alov
See Gogol, Nikolai (Vasilyevich)

Alta 1942- . . . . CLC 19
See also CA 57-60

Alter, Robert B(ernard) 1935- . . . . . . CLC 34
See also CA 49-52; CANR 1, 47

Alther, Lisa 1944- . . . . CLC 7, 41
See also CA 65-68; CANR 12, 30; MTCW

Altman, Robert 1925- . . . . CLC 16
See also CA 73-76; CANR 43

Alvarez, A(lfred) 1929- . . . . CLC 5, 13
See also CA 1-4R; CANR 3, 33; DLB 14,
40

Alvarez, Alejandro Rodriguez 1903-1965
See Casona, Alejandro
See also CA 131; 93-96; HW

Alvaro, Corrado 1896-1956 . . . . TCLC 60

Amado, Jorge 1912- . . . . . . CLC 13, 40; HLC
See also CA 77-80; CANR 35; DLB 113;
MTCW

Ambler, Eric 1909- . . . . CLC 4, 6, 9
See also CA 9-12R; CANR 7, 38; DLB 77;
MTCW

Amichai, Yehuda 1924- . . . . . . CLC 9, 22, 57
See also CA 85-88; CANR 46; MTCW

Amiel, Henri Frederic 1821-1881 . . NCLC 4

Amis, Kingsley (William)
1922- . . . . . . CLC 1, 2, 3, 5, 8, 13, 40, 44;
DA; DAB
See also AITN 2; CA 9-12R; CANR 8, 28;
CDBLB 1945-1960; DLB 15, 27, 100, 139;
MTCW

Amis, Martin (Louis)
1949- . . . . CLC 4, 9, 38, 62
See also BEST 90:3; CA 65-68; CANR 8,
27; DLB 14

Ammons, A(rchie) R(andolph)
1926- . . . . . . CLC 2, 3, 5, 8, 9, 25, 57
See also AITN 1; CA 9-12R; CANR 6, 36;
DLB 5; MTCW

Amo, Tauraatua i
See Adams, Henry (Brooks)

Anand, Mulk Raj 1905- . . . . CLC 23
See also CA 65-68; CANR 32; MTCW

Anatol
See Schnitzler, Arthur

Anaya, Rudolfo A(lfonso)
1937- . . . . CLC 23; HLC
See also CA 45-48; CAAS 4; CANR 1, 32;
DLB 82; HW 1; MTCW

Andersen, Hans Christian
1805-1875 . . . . NCLC 7; DA; DAB;
SSC 6; WLC
See also CLR 6; MAICYA; YABC 1

Anderson, C. Farley
See Mencken, H(enry) L(ouis); Nathan,
George Jean

Anderson, Jessica (Margaret) Queale
. . . . CLC 37
See also CA 9-12R; CANR 4

Anderson, Jon (Victor) 1940- . . . . CLC 9
See also CA 25-28R; CANR 20

Anderson, Lindsay (Gordon)
1923-1994 . . . . CLC 20
See also CA 125; 128; 146

Anderson, Maxwell 1888-1959 . . . . . TCLC 2
See also CA 105; DLB 7

Anderson, Poul (William) 1926- . . . . CLC 15
See also AAYA 5; CA 1-4R; CAAS 2;
CANR 2, 15, 34; DLB 8; MTCW;
SATA-Brief 39

Anderson, Robert (Woodruff)
1917- . . . . CLC 23
See also AITN 1; CA 21-24R; CANR 32;
DLB 7

Anderson, Sherwood
1876-1941 . . . . TCLC 1, 10, 24; DA;
DAB; SSC 1; WLC
See also CA 104; 121; CDALB 1917-1929;
DLB 4, 9, 86; DLBD 1; MTCW

Andouard
See Giraudoux, (Hippolyte) Jean

Andrade, Carlos Drummond de . . . . . . CLC 18
See also Drummond de Andrade, Carlos

Andrade, Mario de 1893-1945 . . . . . TCLC 43

Andreas-Salome, Lou 1861-1937 . . . TCLC 56
See also DLB 66

Andrewes, Lancelot 1555-1626 . . . . LC 5
See also DLB 151

Andrews, Cicily Fairfield
See West, Rebecca

Andrews, Elton V.
See Pohl, Frederik

Andreyev, Leonid (Nikolaevich)
1871-1919 . . . . TCLC 3
See also CA 104

Andric, Ivo 1892-1975 . . . . CLC 8
See also CA 81-84; 57-60; CANR 43;
DLB 147; MTCW

Angelique, Pierre
See Bataille, Georges

Angell, Roger 1920- . . . . CLC 26
See also CA 57-60; CANR 13, 44

Angelou, Maya
1928- . . . . CLC 12, 35, 64, 77; BLC; DA;
DAB
See also AAYA 7; BW 2; CA 65-68;
CANR 19, 42; DLB 38; MTCW;
SATA 49

Annensky, Innokenty Fyodorovich
1856-1909 . . . . TCLC 14
See also CA 110

Anon, Charles Robert
See Pessoa, Fernando (Antonio Nogueira)

Author Index

Auden, W(ystan) H(ugh)
1907-1973 . . . . . **CLC 1, 2, 3, 4, 6, 9, 11,**
14, 43; DA; DAB; PC 1; WLC
See also CA 9-12R; 45-48; CANR 5;
CDBLB 1914-1945; DLB 10, 20; MTCW

Audiberti, Jacques 1900-1965 . . . . . . **CLC 38**
See also CA 25-28R

Audubon, John James
1785-1851 . . . . **NCLC 47**

Auel, Jean M(arie) 1936- . . . . **CLC 31**
See also AAYA 7; BEST 90:4; CA 103;
CANR 21

Auerbach, Erich 1892-1957 . . . . **TCLC 43**
See also CA 118

Augier, Emile 1820-1889 . . . . **NCLC 31**

August, John
See De Voto, Bernard (Augustine)

Augustine, St. 354-430 . . . . . **CMLC 6; DAB**

Aurelius
See Bourne, Randolph S(illiman)

Austen, Jane
1775-1817 . . . . . **NCLC 1, 13, 19, 33, 51;**
DA; DAB; WLC
See also CDBLB 1789-1832; DLB 116

Auster, Paul 1947- . . . . **CLC 47**
See also CA 69-72; CANR 23

Austin, Frank
See Faust, Frederick (Schiller)

Austin, Mary (Hunter)
1868-1934 . . . . **TCLC 25**
See also CA 109; DLB 9, 78

Autran Dourado, Waldomiro
See Dourado, (Waldomiro Freitas) Autran

Averroes 1126-1198 . . . . **CMLC 7**
See also DLB 115

Avicenna 980-1037 . . . . **CMLC 16**
See also DLB 115

Avison, Margaret 1918- . . . . **CLC 2, 4**
See also CA 17-20R; DLB 53; MTCW

Axton, David
See Koontz, Dean R(ay)

Ayckbourn, Alan
1939- . . . . **CLC 5, 8, 18, 33, 74; DAB**
See also CA 21-24R; CANR 31; DLB 13;
MTCW

Aydy, Catherine
See Tennant, Emma (Christina)

Ayme, Marcel (Andre) 1902-1967 . . . **CLC 11**
See also CA 89-92; CLR 25; DLB 72

Ayrton, Michael 1921-1975 . . . . **CLC 7**
See also CA 5-8R; 61-64; CANR 9, 21

Azorin . . . . **CLC 11**
See also Martinez Ruiz, Jose

Azuela, Mariano
1873-1952 . . . . **TCLC 3; HLC**
See also CA 104; 131; HW; MTCW

Baastad, Babbis Friis
See Friis-Baastad, Babbis Ellinor

Bab
See Gilbert, W(illiam) S(chwenck)

Babbis, Eleanor
See Friis-Baastad, Babbis Ellinor

Babel, Isaak (Emmanuilovich)
1894-1941(?) . . . . . . **TCLC 2, 13; SSC 16**
See also CA 104

Babits, Mihaly 1883-1941 . . . . **TCLC 14**
See also CA 114

Babur 1483-1530 . . . . **LC 18**

Bacchelli, Riccardo 1891-1985 . . . . . **CLC 19**
See also CA 29-32R; 117

Bach, Richard (David) 1936- . . . . **CLC 14**
See also AITN 1; BEST 89:2; CA 9-12R;
CANR 18; MTCW; SATA 13

Bachman, Richard
See King, Stephen (Edwin)

Bachmann, Ingeborg 1926-1973 . . . . . **CLC 69**
See also CA 93-96; 45-48; DLB 85

Bacon, Francis 1561-1626 . . . . **LC 18**
See also CDBLB Before 1660; DLB 151

Bacon, Roger 1214(?)-1292 . . . . . . **CMLC 14**
See also DLB 115

Bacovia, George . . . . **TCLC 24**
See also Vasiliu, Gheorghe

Badanes, Jerome 1937- . . . . **CLC 59**

Bagehot, Walter 1826-1877 . . . . . . **NCLC 10**
See also DLB 55

Bagnold, Enid 1889-1981 . . . . **CLC 25**
See also CA 5-8R; 103; CANR 5, 40;
DLB 13; MAICYA; SATA 1, 25

Bagritsky, Eduard 1895-1934 . . . . . **TCLC 60**

Bagrjana, Elisaveta
See Belcheva, Elisaveta

Bagryana, Elisaveta . . . . **CLC 10**
See also Belcheva, Elisaveta
See also DLB 147

Bailey, Paul 1937- . . . . **CLC 45**
See also CA 21-24R; CANR 16; DLB 14

Baillie, Joanna 1762-1851 . . . . **NCLC 2**
See also DLB 93

Bainbridge, Beryl (Margaret)
1933- . . . . **CLC 4, 5, 8, 10, 14, 18, 22, 62**
See also CA 21-24R; CANR 24; DLB 14;
MTCW

Baker, Elliott 1922- . . . . **CLC 8**
See also CA 45-48; CANR 2

Baker, Nicholson 1957- . . . . **CLC 61**
See also CA 135

Baker, Ray Stannard 1870-1946 . . . **TCLC 47**
See also CA 118

Baker, Russell (Wayne) 1925- . . . . . . **CLC 31**
See also BEST 89:4; CA 57-60; CANR 11,
41; MTCW

Bakhtin, M.
See Bakhtin, Mikhail Mikhailovich

Bakhtin, M. M.
See Bakhtin, Mikhail Mikhailovich

Bakhtin, Mikhail
See Bakhtin, Mikhail Mikhailovich

Bakhtin, Mikhail Mikhailovich
1895-1975 . . . . **CLC 83**
See also CA 128; 113

Bakshi, Ralph 1938(?)- . . . . **CLC 26**
See also CA 112; 138

Bakunin, Mikhail (Alexandrovich)
1814-1876 . . . . **NCLC 25**

Baldwin, James (Arthur)
1924-1987 . . . . . . **CLC 1, 2, 3, 4, 5, 8, 13,**
15, 17, 42, 50, 67, 90; BLC; DA; DAB;
DC 1; SSC 10; WLC
See also AAYA 4; BW 1; CA 1-4R; 124;
CABS 1; CANR 3, 24;
CDALB 1941-1968; DLB 2, 7, 33;
DLBY 87; MTCW; SATA 9;
SATA-Obit 54

Ballard, J(ames) G(raham)
1930- . . . . **CLC 3, 6, 14, 36; SSC 1**
See also AAYA 3; CA 5-8R; CANR 15, 39;
DLB 14; MTCW

Balmont, Konstantin (Dmitriyevich)
1867-1943 . . . . **TCLC 11**
See also CA 109

Balzac, Honore de
1799-1850 . . . . . **NCLC 5, 35; DA; DAB;**
SSC 5; WLC
See also DLB 119

Bambara, Toni Cade
1939- . . . . **CLC 19, 88; BLC; DA**
See also AAYA 5; BW 2; CA 29-32R;
CANR 24, 49; DLB 38; MTCW

Bamdad, A.
See Shamlu, Ahmad

Banat, D. R.
See Bradbury, Ray (Douglas)

Bancroft, Laura
See Baum, L(yman) Frank

Banim, John 1798-1842 . . . . **NCLC 13**
See also DLB 116

Banim, Michael 1796-1874 . . . . . . **NCLC 13**

Banks, Iain
See Banks, Iain M(enzies)

Banks, Iain M(enzies) 1954- . . . . **CLC 34**
See also CA 123; 128

Banks, Lynne Reid . . . . **CLC 23**
See also Reid Banks, Lynne
See also AAYA 6

Banks, Russell 1940- . . . . **CLC 37, 72**
See also CA 65-68; CAAS 15; CANR 19;
DLB 130

Banville, John 1945- . . . . **CLC 46**
See also CA 117; 128; DLB 14

Banville, Theodore (Faullain) de
1832-1891 . . . . **NCLC 9**

Baraka, Amiri
1934- . . . . **CLC 1, 2, 3, 5, 10, 14, 33;**
BLC; DA; PC 4
See also Jones, LeRoi
See also BW 2; CA 21-24R; CABS 3;
CANR 27, 38; CDALB 1941-1968;
DLB 5, 7, 16, 38; DLBD 8; MTCW

Barbauld, Anna Laetitia
1743-1825 . . . . **NCLC 50**
See also DLB 107, 109, 142

Barbellion, W. N. P. . . . . **TCLC 24**
See also Cummings, Bruce F(rederick)

Barbera, Jack (Vincent) 1945- . . . . . . **CLC 44**
See also CA 110; CANR 45

Barbey d'Aurevilly, Jules Amedee
1808-1889 . . . . **NCLC 1; SSC 17**
See also DLB 119

Barbusse, Henri 1873-1935 . . . . **TCLC 5**
See also CA 105; DLB 65

Barclay, Bill
See Moorcock, Michael (John)

Barclay, William Ewert
See Moorcock, Michael (John)

Barea, Arturo 1897-1957 . . . . **TCLC 14**
See also CA 111

Barfoot, Joan 1946- . . . . **CLC 18**
See also CA 105

Baring, Maurice 1874-1945 . . . . **TCLC 8**
See also CA 105; DLB 34

Barker, Clive 1952- . . . . **CLC 52**
See also AAYA 10; BEST 90:3; CA 121;
129; MTCW

Barker, George Granville
1913-1991 . . . . **CLC 8, 48**
See also CA 9-12R; 135; CANR 7, 38;
DLB 20; MTCW

Barker, Harley Granville
See Granville-Barker, Harley
See also DLB 10

Barker, Howard 1946- . . . . **CLC 37**
See also CA 102; DLB 13

Barker, Pat 1943- . . . . **CLC 32**
See also CA 117; 122

Barlow, Joel 1754-1812 . . . . **NCLC 23**
See also DLB 37

Barnard, Mary (Ethel) 1909- . . . . **CLC 48**
See also CA 21-22; CAP 2

Barnes, Djuna
1892-1982 . . . **CLC 3, 4, 8, 11, 29; SSC 3**
See also CA 9-12R; 107; CANR 16; DLB 4,
9, 45; MTCW

Barnes, Julian 1946- . . . . **CLC 42; DAB**
See also CA 102; CANR 19; DLBY 93

Barnes, Peter 1931- . . . . **CLC 5, 56**
See also CA 65-68; CAAS 12; CANR 33,
34; DLB 13; MTCW

Baroja (y Nessi), Pio
1872-1956 . . . . **TCLC 8; HLC**
See also CA 104

Baron, David
See Pinter, Harold

Baron Corvo
See Rolfe, Frederick (William Serafino
Austin Lewis Mary)

Barondess, Sue K(aufman)
1926-1977 . . . . **CLC 8**
See also Kaufman, Sue
See also CA 1-4R; 69-72; CANR 1

Baron de Teive
See Pessoa, Fernando (Antonio Nogueira)

Barres, Maurice 1862-1923 . . . . **TCLC 47**
See also DLB 123

Barreto, Afonso Henrique de Lima
See Lima Barreto, Afonso Henrique de

Barrett, (Roger) Syd 1946- . . . . **CLC 35**

Barrett, William (Christopher)
1913-1992 . . . . **CLC 27**
See also CA 13-16R; 139; CANR 11

Barrie, J(ames) M(atthew)
1860-1937 . . . . **TCLC 2; DAB**
See also CA 104; 136; CDBLB 1890-1914;
CLR 16; DLB 10, 141, 156; MAICYA;
YABC 1

Barrington, Michael
See Moorcock, Michael (John)

Barrol, Grady
See Bograd, Larry

Barry, Mike
See Malzberg, Barry N(athaniel)

Barry, Philip 1896-1949 . . . . **TCLC 11**
See also CA 109; DLB 7

Bart, Andre Schwarz
See Schwarz-Bart, Andre

Barth, John (Simmons)
1930- . . . . . . **CLC 1, 2, 3, 5, 7, 9, 10, 14,
27, 51, 89; SSC 10**
See also AITN 1, 2; CA 1-4R; CABS 1;
CANR 5, 23, 49; DLB 2; MTCW

Barthelme, Donald
1931-1989 . . . . . . **CLC 1, 2, 3, 5, 6, 8, 13,
23, 46, 59; SSC 2**
See also CA 21-24R; 129; CANR 20;
DLB 2; DLBY 80, 89; MTCW; SATA 7;
SATA-Obit 62

Barthelme, Frederick 1943- . . . . **CLC 36**
See also CA 114; 122; DLBY 85

Barthes, Roland (Gerard)
1915-1980 . . . . **CLC 24, 83**
See also CA 130; 97-100; MTCW

Barzun, Jacques (Martin) 1907- . . . . **CLC 51**
See also CA 61-64; CANR 22

Bashevis, Isaac
See Singer, Isaac Bashevis

Bashkirtseff, Marie 1859-1884 . . . **NCLC 27**

Basho
See Matsuo Basho

Bass, Kingsley B., Jr.
See Bullins, Ed

Bass, Rick 1958- . . . . **CLC 79**
See also CA 126

Bassani, Giorgio 1916- . . . . **CLC 9**
See also CA 65-68; CANR 33; DLB 128;
MTCW

Bastos, Augusto (Antonio) Roa
See Roa Bastos, Augusto (Antonio)

Bataille, Georges 1897-1962 . . . . **CLC 29**
See also CA 101; 89-92

Bates, H(erbert) E(rnest)
1905-1974 . . . . . . **CLC 46; DAB; SSC 10**
See also CA 93-96; 45-48; CANR 34;
MTCW

Bauchart
See Camus, Albert

Baudelaire, Charles
1821-1867 . . . . . **NCLC 6, 29; DA; DAB;
PC 1; SSC 18; WLC**

Baudrillard, Jean 1929- . . . . **CLC 60**

Baum, L(yman) Frank 1856-1919 . . . **TCLC 7**
See also CA 108; 133; CLR 15; DLB 22;
JRDA; MAICYA; MTCW; SATA 18

Baum, Louis F.
See Baum, L(yman) Frank

Baumbach, Jonathan 1933- . . . . . . **CLC 6, 23**
See also CA 13-16R; CAAS 5; CANR 12;
DLBY 80; MTCW

Bausch, Richard (Carl) 1945- . . . . . . **CLC 51**
See also CA 101; CAAS 14; CANR 43;
DLB 130

Baxter, Charles 1947- . . . . **CLC 45, 78**
See also CA 57-60; CANR 40; DLB 130

Baxter, George Owen
See Faust, Frederick (Schiller)

Baxter, James K(eir) 1926-1972 . . . . **CLC 14**
See also CA 77-80

Baxter, John
See Hunt, E(verette) Howard, (Jr.)

Bayer, Sylvia
See Glassco, John

Baynton, Barbara 1857-1929 . . . . . . **TCLC 57**

Beagle, Peter S(oyer) 1939- . . . . **CLC 7**
See also CA 9-12R; CANR 4; DLBY 80;
SATA 60

Bean, Normal
See Burroughs, Edgar Rice

Beard, Charles A(ustin)
1874-1948 . . . . **TCLC 15**
See also CA 115; DLB 17; SATA 18

Beardsley, Aubrey 1872-1898 . . . . . **NCLC 6**

Beattie, Ann
1947- . . . . **CLC 8, 13, 18, 40, 63; SSC 11**
See also BEST 90:2; CA 81-84; DLBY 82;
MTCW

Beattie, James 1735-1803 . . . . **NCLC 25**
See also DLB 109

Beauchamp, Kathleen Mansfield 1888-1923
See Mansfield, Katherine
See also CA 104; 134; DA

Beaumarchais, Pierre-Augustin Caron de
1732-1799 . . . . **DC 4**

**Beauvoir, Simone (Lucie Ernestine Marie
Bertrand) de**
1908-1986 . . . . **CLC 1, 2, 4, 8, 14, 31, 44,
50, 71; DA; DAB; WLC**
See also CA 9-12R; 118; CANR 28;
DLB 72; DLBY 86; MTCW

Becker, Jurek 1937- . . . . **CLC 7, 19**
See also CA 85-88; DLB 75

Becker, Walter 1950- . . . . **CLC 26**

Beckett, Samuel (Barclay)
1906-1989 . . . . . . **CLC 1, 2, 3, 4, 6, 9, 10,
11, 14, 18, 29, 57, 59, 83; DA; DAB;
SSC 16; WLC**
See also CA 5-8R; 130; CANR 33;
CDBLB 1945-1960; DLB 13, 15;
DLBY 90; MTCW

Beckford, William 1760-1844 . . . . **NCLC 16**
See also DLB 39

Beckman, Gunnel 1910- . . . . **CLC 26**
See also CA 33-36R; CANR 15; CLR 25;
MAICYA; SAAS 9; SATA 6

Becque, Henri 1837-1899 . . . . **NCLC 3**

Beddoes, Thomas Lovell
1803-1849 . . . . **NCLC 3**
See also DLB 96

Bedford, Donald F.
See Fearing, Kenneth (Flexner)

Beecher, Catharine Esther
1800-1878 . . . . NCLC 30
See also DLB 1

Beecher, John 1904-1980 . . . . CLC 6
See also AITN 1; CA 5-8R; 105; CANR 8

Beer, Johann 1655-1700 . . . . LC 5

Beer, Patricia 1924- . . . . CLC 58
See also CA 61-64; CANR 13, 46; DLB 40

Beerbohm, Henry Maximilian
1872-1956 . . . . TCLC 1, 24
See also CA 104; DLB 34, 100

Beerbohm, Max
See Beerbohm, Henry Maximilian

Beer-Hofmann, Richard
1866-1945 . . . . TCLC 60
See also DLB 81

Begiebing, Robert J(ohn) 1946- . . . . . CLC 70
See also CA 122; CANR 40

Behan, Brendan
1923-1964 . . . . CLC 1, 8, 11, 15, 79
See also CA 73-76; CANR 33;
CDBLB 1945-1960; DLB 13; MTCW

Behn, Aphra
1640(?)-1689 . . . . . . LC 1, 30; DA; DAB;
DC 4; PC 13; WLC
See also DLB 39, 80, 131

Behrman, S(amuel) N(athaniel)
1893-1973 . . . . CLC 40
See also CA 13-16; 45-48; CAP 1; DLB 7,
44

Belasco, David 1853-1931 . . . . TCLC 3
See also CA 104; DLB 7

Belcheva, Elisaveta 1893- . . . . CLC 10
See also Bagryana, Elisaveta

Beldone, Phil "Cheech"
See Ellison, Harlan (Jay)

Beleno
See Azuela, Mariano

Belinski, Vissarion Grigoryevich
1811-1848 . . . . NCLC 5

Belitt, Ben 1911- . . . . CLC 22
See also CA 13-16R; CAAS 4; CANR 7;
DLB 5

Bell, James Madison
1826-1902 . . . . TCLC 43; BLC
See also BW 1; CA 122; 124; DLB 50

Bell, Madison (Smartt) 1957- . . . . . . CLC 41
See also CA 111; CANR 28

Bell, Marvin (Hartley) 1937- . . . . . CLC 8, 31
See also CA 21-24R; CAAS 14; DLB 5;
MTCW

Bell, W. L. D.
See Mencken, H(enry) L(ouis)

Bellamy, Atwood C.
See Mencken, H(enry) L(ouis)

Bellamy, Edward 1850-1898 . . . . . . NCLC 4
See also DLB 12

Bellin, Edward J.
See Kuttner, Henry

Belloc, (Joseph) Hilaire (Pierre)
1870-1953 . . . . TCLC 7, 18
See also CA 106; DLB 19, 100, 141;
YABC 1

Belloc, Joseph Peter Rene Hilaire
See Belloc, (Joseph) Hilaire (Pierre)

Belloc, Joseph Pierre Hilaire
See Belloc, (Joseph) Hilaire (Pierre)

Belloc, M. A.
See Lowndes, Marie Adelaide (Belloc)

Bellow, Saul
1915- . . . . . . CLC 1, 2, 3, 6, 8, 10, 13, 15,
25, 33, 34, 63, 79; DA; DAB; SSC 14;
WLC
See also AITN 2; BEST 89:3; CA 5-8R;
CABS 1; CANR 29; CDALB 1941-1968;
DLB 2, 28; DLBD 3; DLBY 82; MTCW

Belser, Reimond Karel Maria de
See Ruyslinck, Ward

Bely, Andrey . . . . TCLC 7; PC 11
See also Bugayev, Boris Nikolayevich

Benary, Margot
See Benary-Isbert, Margot

Benary-Isbert, Margot 1889-1979 . . . CLC 12
See also CA 5-8R; 89-92; CANR 4;
CLR 12; MAICYA; SATA 2;
SATA-Obit 21

Benavente (y Martinez), Jacinto
1866-1954 . . . . TCLC 3
See also CA 106; 131; HW; MTCW

Benchley, Peter (Bradford)
1940- . . . . CLC 4, 8
See also AAYA 14; AITN 2; CA 17-20R;
CANR 12, 35; MTCW; SATA 3

Benchley, Robert (Charles)
1889-1945 . . . . TCLC 1, 55
See also CA 105; DLB 11

Benda, Julien 1867-1956 . . . . TCLC 60
See also CA 120

Benedict, Ruth 1887-1948 . . . . TCLC 60

Benedikt, Michael 1935- . . . . CLC 4, 14
See also CA 13-16R; CANR 7; DLB 5

Benet, Juan 1927- . . . . CLC 28
See also CA 143

Benet, Stephen Vincent
1898-1943 . . . . TCLC 7; SSC 10
See also CA 104; DLB 4, 48, 102; YABC 1

Benet, William Rose 1886-1950 . . . TCLC 28
See also CA 118; DLB 45

Benford, Gregory (Albert) 1941- . . . . CLC 52
See also CA 69-72; CANR 12, 24, 49;
DLBY 82

Bengtsson, Frans (Gunnar)
1894-1954 . . . . TCLC 48

Benjamin, David
See Slavitt, David R(ytman)

Benjamin, Lois
See Gould, Lois

Benjamin, Walter 1892-1940 . . . . . TCLC 39

Benn, Gottfried 1886-1956 . . . . TCLC 3
See also CA 106; DLB 56

Bennett, Alan 1934- . . . . . CLC 45, 77; DAB
See also CA 103; CANR 35; MTCW

Bennett, (Enoch) Arnold
1867-1931 . . . . TCLC 5, 20
See also CA 106; CDBLB 1890-1914;
DLB 10, 34, 98, 135

Bennett, Elizabeth
See Mitchell, Margaret (Munnerlyn)

Bennett, George Harold 1930-
See Bennett, Hal
See also BW 1; CA 97-100

Bennett, Hal . . . . CLC 5
See also Bennett, George Harold
See also DLB 33

Bennett, Jay 1912- . . . . CLC 35
See also AAYA 10; CA 69-72; CANR 11,
42; JRDA; SAAS 4; SATA 41;
SATA-Brief 27

Bennett, Louise (Simone)
1919- . . . . CLC 28; BLC
See also BW 2; DLB 117

Benson, E(dward) F(rederic)
1867-1940 . . . . TCLC 27
See also CA 114; DLB 135, 153

Benson, Jackson J. 1930- . . . . CLC 34
See also CA 25-28R; DLB 111

Benson, Sally 1900-1972 . . . . CLC 17
See also CA 19-20; 37-40R; CAP 1;
SATA 1, 35; SATA-Obit 27

Benson, Stella 1892-1933 . . . . TCLC 17
See also CA 117; DLB 36

Bentham, Jeremy 1748-1832 . . . . . NCLC 38
See also DLB 107

Bentley, E(dmund) C(lerihew)
1875-1956 . . . . TCLC 12
See also CA 108; DLB 70

Bentley, Eric (Russell) 1916- . . . . . CLC 24
See also CA 5-8R; CANR 6

Beranger, Pierre Jean de
1780-1857 . . . . NCLC 34

Berendt, John (Lawrence) 1939- . . . . CLC 86
See also CA 146

Berger, Colonel
See Malraux, (Georges-)Andre

Berger, John (Peter) 1926- . . . . . . CLC 2, 19
See also CA 81-84; DLB 14

Berger, Melvin H. 1927- . . . . CLC 12
See also CA 5-8R; CANR 4; CLR 32;
SAAS 2; SATA 5

Berger, Thomas (Louis)
1924- . . . . CLC 3, 5, 8, 11, 18, 38
See also CA 1-4R; CANR 5, 28; DLB 2;
DLBY 80; MTCW

Bergman, (Ernst) Ingmar
1918- . . . . CLC 16, 72
See also CA 81-84; CANR 33

Bergson, Henri 1859-1941 . . . . TCLC 32

Bergstein, Eleanor 1938- . . . . CLC 4
See also CA 53-56; CANR 5

Berkoff, Steven 1937- . . . . CLC 56
See also CA 104

Bermant, Chaim (Icyk) 1929- . . . . . . CLC 40
See also CA 57-60; CANR 6, 31

Bern, Victoria
See Fisher, M(ary) F(rances) K(ennedy)

Bernanos, (Paul Louis) Georges
1888-1948 . . . . TCLC 3
See also CA 104; 130; DLB 72

Bernard, April 1956- . . . . CLC 59
See also CA 131

Berne, Victoria
See Fisher, M(ary) F(rances) K(ennedy)

Bernhard, Thomas
1931-1989 .... **CLC 3, 32, 61**
See also CA 85-88; 127; CANR 32;
DLB 85, 124; MTCW

Berriault, Gina 1926-............. **CLC 54**
See also CA 116; 129; DLB 130

Berrigan, Daniel 1921-............ **CLC 4**
See also CA 33-36R; CAAS 1; CANR 11,
43; DLB 5

Berrigan, Edmund Joseph Michael, Jr.
1934-1983
See Berrigan, Ted
See also CA 61-64; 110; CANR 14

Berrigan, Ted.................... **CLC 37**
See also Berrigan, Edmund Joseph Michael,
Jr.
See also DLB 5

Berry, Charles Edward Anderson 1931-
See Berry, Chuck
See also CA 115

Berry, Chuck.................... **CLC 17**
See also Berry, Charles Edward Anderson

Berry, Jonas
See Ashbery, John (Lawrence)

Berry, Wendell (Erdman)
1934-............ **CLC 4, 6, 8, 27, 46**
See also AITN 1; CA 73-76; DLB 5, 6

Berryman, John
1914-1972 ...... **CLC 1, 2, 3, 4, 6, 8, 10,
13, 25, 62**
See also CA 13-16; 33-36R; CABS 2;
CANR 35; CAP 1; CDALB 1941-1968;
DLB 48; MTCW

Bertolucci, Bernardo 1940-........ **CLC 16**
See also CA 106

Bertrand, Aloysius 1807-1841 .... **NCLC 31**

Bertran de Born c. 1140-1215..... **CMLC 5**

Besant, Annie (Wood) 1847-1933 ... **TCLC 9**
See also CA 105

Bessie, Alvah 1904-1985........... **CLC 23**
See also CA 5-8R; 116; CANR 2; DLB 26

Bethlen, T. D.
See Silverberg, Robert

Beti, Mongo................. **CLC 27; BLC**
See also Biyidi, Alexandre

Betjeman, John
1906-1984 ... **CLC 2, 6, 10, 34, 43; DAB**
See also CA 9-12R; 112; CANR 33;
CDBLB 1945-1960; DLB 20; DLBY 84;
MTCW

Bettelheim, Bruno 1903-1990 ...... **CLC 79**
See also CA 81-84; 131; CANR 23; MTCW

Betti, Ugo 1892-1953............. **TCLC 5**
See also CA 104

Betts, Doris (Waugh) 1932-.... **CLC 3, 6, 28**
See also CA 13-16R; CANR 9; DLBY 82

Bevan, Alistair
See Roberts, Keith (John Kingston)

Bialik, Chaim Nachman
1873-1934 .... **TCLC 25**

Bickerstaff, Isaac
See Swift, Jonathan

Bidart, Frank 1939-.............. **CLC 33**
See also CA 140

Bienek, Horst 1930-........... **CLC 7, 11**
See also CA 73-76; DLB 75

Bierce, Ambrose (Gwinett)
1842-1914(?) .... **TCLC 1, 7, 44; DA;
SSC 9; WLC**
See also CA 104; 139; CDALB 1865-1917;
DLB 11, 12, 23, 71, 74

Billings, Josh
See Shaw, Henry Wheeler

Billington, (Lady) Rachel (Mary)
1942-........................ **CLC 43**
See also AITN 2; CA 33-36R; CANR 44

Binyon, T(imothy) J(ohn) 1936- .... **CLC 34**
See also CA 111; CANR 28

Bioy Casares, Adolfo
1914-... **CLC 4, 8, 13, 88; HLC; SSC 17**
See also CA 29-32R; CANR 19, 43;
DLB 113; HW; MTCW

Bird, Cordwainer
See Ellison, Harlan (Jay)

Bird, Robert Montgomery
1806-1854 .... **NCLC 1**

Birney, (Alfred) Earle
1904-.................. **CLC 1, 4, 6, 11**
See also CA 1-4R; CANR 5, 20; DLB 88;
MTCW

Bishop, Elizabeth
1911-1979 ...... **CLC 1, 4, 9, 13, 15, 32;
DA; PC 3**
See also CA 5-8R; 89-92; CABS 2;
CANR 26; CDALB 1968-1988; DLB 5;
MTCW; SATA-Obit 24

Bishop, John 1935-............... **CLC 10**
See also CA 105

Bissett, Bill 1939-................ **CLC 18**
See also CA 69-72; CAAS 19; CANR 15;
DLB 53; MTCW

Bitov, Andrei (Georgievich) 1937-... **CLC 57**
See also CA 142

Biyidi, Alexandre 1932-
See Beti, Mongo
See also BW 1; CA 114; 124; MTCW

Bjarme, Brynjolf
See Ibsen, Henrik (Johan)

Bjornson, Bjornstjerne (Martinius)
1832-1910 .... **TCLC 7, 37**
See also CA 104

Black, Robert
See Holdstock, Robert P.

Blackburn, Paul 1926-1971 ...... **CLC 9, 43**
See also CA 81-84; 33-36R; CANR 34;
DLB 16; DLBY 81

Black Elk 1863-1950 .... **TCLC 33**
See also CA 144; NNAL

Black Hobart
See Sanders, (James) Ed(ward)

Blacklin, Malcolm
See Chambers, Aidan

Blackmore, R(ichard) D(oddridge)
1825-1900 .... **TCLC 27**
See also CA 120; DLB 18

Blackmur, R(ichard) P(almer)
1904-1965 .... **CLC 2, 24**
See also CA 11-12; 25-28R; CAP 1; DLB 63

Black Tarantula, The
See Acker, Kathy

Blackwood, Algernon (Henry)
1869-1951 .... **TCLC 5**
See also CA 105; DLB 153, 156

Blackwood, Caroline 1931- .... **CLC 6, 9**
See also CA 85-88; CANR 32; DLB 14;
MTCW

Blade, Alexander
See Hamilton, Edmond; Silverberg, Robert

Blaga, Lucian 1895-1961 .... **CLC 75**

Blair, Eric (Arthur) 1903-1950
See Orwell, George
See also CA 104; 132; DA; DAB; MTCW;
SATA 29

Blais, Marie-Claire
1939-............. **CLC 2, 4, 6, 13, 22**
See also CA 21-24R; CAAS 4; CANR 38;
DLB 53; MTCW

Blaise, Clark 1940-............... **CLC 29**
See also AITN 2; CA 53-56; CAAS 3;
CANR 5; DLB 53

Blake, Nicholas
See Day Lewis, C(ecil)
See also DLB 77

Blake, William
1757-1827 .... **NCLC 13, 37; DA; DAB;
PC 12; WLC**
See also CDBLB 1789-1832; DLB 93;
MAICYA; SATA 30

Blake, William J(ames) 1894-1969 ... **PC 12**
See also CA 5-8R; 25-28R

Blasco Ibanez, Vicente
1867-1928 .... **TCLC 12**
See also CA 110; 131; HW; MTCW

Blatty, William Peter 1928-......... **CLC 2**
See also CA 5-8R; CANR 9

Bleeck, Oliver
See Thomas, Ross (Elmore)

Blessing, Lee 1949-.............. **CLC 54**

Blish, James (Benjamin)
1921-1975 .... **CLC 14**
See also CA 1-4R; 57-60; CANR 3; DLB 8;
MTCW; SATA 66

Bliss, Reginald
See Wells, H(erbert) G(eorge)

Blixen, Karen (Christentze Dinesen)
1885-1962
See Dinesen, Isak
See also CA 25-28; CANR 22; CAP 2;
MTCW; SATA 44

Bloch, Robert (Albert) 1917-1994... **CLC 33**
See also CA 5-8R; 146; CAAS 20; CANR 5;
DLB 44; SATA 12; SATA-Obit 82

Blok, Alexander (Alexandrovich)
1880-1921 .... **TCLC 5**
See also CA 104

Blom, Jan
See Breytenbach, Breyten

Bloom, Harold 1930-............. **CLC 24**
See also CA 13-16R; CANR 39; DLB 67

Bloomfield, Aurelius
See Bourne, Randolph S(illiman)

Blount, Roy (Alton), Jr. 1941- ..... **CLC 38**
See also CA 53-56; CANR 10, 28; MTCW

Bloy, Leon 1846-1917........... **TCLC 22**
See also CA 121; DLB 123

Blume, Judy (Sussman) 1938- ... **CLC 12, 30**
See also AAYA 3; CA 29-32R; CANR 13,
37; CLR 2, 15; DLB 52; JRDA;
MAICYA; MTCW; SATA 2, 31, 79

Blunden, Edmund (Charles)
1896-1974 .... **CLC 2, 56**
See also CA 17-18; 45-48; CAP 2; DLB 20,
100, 155; MTCW

Bly, Robert (Elwood)
1926- .... **CLC 1, 2, 5, 10, 15, 38**
See also CA 5-8R; CANR 41; DLB 5;
MTCW

Boas, Franz 1858-1942.......... **TCLC 56**
See also CA 115

Bobette
See Simenon, Georges (Jacques Christian)

Boccaccio, Giovanni
1313-1375 .... **CMLC 13; SSC 10**

Bochco, Steven 1943-............. **CLC 35**
See also AAYA 11; CA 124; 138

Bodenheim, Maxwell 1892-1954 ... **TCLC 44**
See also CA 110; DLB 9, 45

Bodker, Cecil 1927- .... **CLC 21**
See also CA 73-76; CANR 13, 44; CLR 23;
MAICYA; SATA 14

Boell, Heinrich (Theodor)
1917-1985 .... **CLC 2, 3, 6, 9, 11, 15, 27,
32, 72; DA; DAB; WLC**
See also CA 21-24R; 116; CANR 24;
DLB 69; DLBY 85; MTCW

Boerne, Alfred
See Doeblin, Alfred

Boethius 480(?)-524(?) .... **CMLC 15**
See also DLB 115

Bogan, Louise
1897-1970 .... **CLC 4, 39, 46; PC 12**
See also CA 73-76; 25-28R; CANR 33;
DLB 45; MTCW

Bogarde, Dirk .... **CLC 19**
See also Van Den Bogarde, Derek Jules
Gaspard Ulric Niven
See also DLB 14

Bogosian, Eric 1953- .... **CLC 45**
See also CA 138

Bograd, Larry 1953-.............. **CLC 35**
See also CA 93-96; SATA 33

Boiardo, Matteo Maria 1441-1494 .... **LC 6**

Boileau-Despreaux, Nicolas
1636-1711 .... **LC 3**

Boland, Eavan (Aisling) 1944-... **CLC 40, 67**
See also CA 143; DLB 40

Bolt, Lee
See Faust, Frederick (Schiller)

Bolt, Robert (Oxton) 1924-1995 .... **CLC 14**
See also CA 17-20R; 147; CANR 35;
DLB 13; MTCW

Bombet, Louis-Alexandre-Cesar
See Stendhal

Bomkauf
See Kaufman, Bob (Garnell)

Bonaventura................... **NCLC 35**
See also DLB 90

Bond, Edward 1934-....... **CLC 4, 6, 13, 23**
See also CA 25-28R; CANR 38; DLB 13;
MTCW

Bonham, Frank 1914-1989......... **CLC 12**
See also AAYA 1; CA 9-12R; CANR 4, 36;
JRDA; MAICYA; SAAS 3; SATA 1, 49;
SATA-Obit 62

Bonnefoy, Yves 1923-........ **CLC 9, 15, 58**
See also CA 85-88; CANR 33; MTCW

Bontemps, Arna(ud Wendell)
1902-1973 .... **CLC 1, 18; BLC**
See also BW 1; CA 1-4R; 41-44R; CANR 4,
35; CLR 6; DLB 48, 51; JRDA;
MAICYA; MTCW; SATA 2, 44;
SATA-Obit 24

Booth, Martin 1944-.............. **CLC 13**
See also CA 93-96; CAAS 2

Booth, Philip 1925-.............. **CLC 23**
See also CA 5-8R; CANR 5; DLBY 82

Booth, Wayne C(layson) 1921- ..... **CLC 24**
See also CA 1-4R; CAAS 5; CANR 3, 43;
DLB 67

Borchert, Wolfgang 1921-1947 ..... **TCLC 5**
See also CA 104; DLB 69, 124

Borel, Petrus 1809-1859........ **NCLC 41**

Borges, Jorge Luis
1899-1986 ... **CLC 1, 2, 3, 4, 6, 8, 9, 10,
13, 19, 44, 48, 83; DA; DAB; HLC;
SSC 4; WLC**
See also CA 21-24R; CANR 19, 33;
DLB 113; DLBY 86; HW; MTCW

Borowski, Tadeusz 1922-1951...... **TCLC 9**
See also CA 106

Borrow, George (Henry)
1803-1881 .... **NCLC 9**
See also DLB 21, 55

Bosman, Herman Charles
1905-1951 .... **TCLC 49**

Bosschere, Jean de 1878(?)-1953... **TCLC 19**
See also CA 115

Boswell, James
1740-1795 ...... **LC 4; DA; DAB; WLC**
See also CDBLB 1660-1789; DLB 104, 142

Bottoms, David 1949-............. **CLC 53**
See also CA 105; CANR 22; DLB 120;
DLBY 83

Boucicault, Dion 1820-1890...... **NCLC 41**

Boucolon, Maryse 1937-
See Conde, Maryse
See also CA 110; CANR 30

Bourget, Paul (Charles Joseph)
1852-1935 .... **TCLC 12**
See also CA 107; DLB 123

Bourjaily, Vance (Nye) 1922- .... **CLC 8, 62**
See also CA 1-4R; CAAS 1; CANR 2;
DLB 2, 143

Bourne, Randolph S(illiman)
1886-1918 .... **TCLC 16**
See also CA 117; DLB 63

Bova, Ben(jamin William) 1932-.... **CLC 45**
See also CA 5-8R; CAAS 18; CANR 11;
CLR 3; DLBY 81; MAICYA; MTCW;
SATA 6, 68

Bowen, Elizabeth (Dorothea Cole)
1899-1973 ...... **CLC 1, 3, 6, 11, 15, 22;
SSC 3**
See also CA 17-18; 41-44R; CANR 35;
CAP 2; CDBLB 1945-1960; DLB 15;
MTCW

Bowering, George 1935-........ **CLC 15, 47**
See also CA 21-24R; CAAS 16; CANR 10;
DLB 53

Bowering, Marilyn R(uthe) 1949-... **CLC 32**
See also CA 101; CANR 49

Bowers, Edgar 1924- .... **CLC 9**
See also CA 5-8R; CANR 24; DLB 5

Bowie, David .... **CLC 17**
See also Jones, David Robert

Bowles, Jane (Sydney)
1917-1973 .... **CLC 3, 68**
See also CA 19-20; 41-44R; CAP 2

Bowles, Paul (Frederick)
1910- .... **CLC 1, 2, 19, 53; SSC 3**
See also CA 1-4R; CAAS 1; CANR 1, 19;
DLB 5, 6; MTCW

Box, Edgar
See Vidal, Gore

Boyd, Nancy
See Millay, Edna St. Vincent

Boyd, William 1952-........ **CLC 28, 53, 70**
See also CA 114; 120

Boyle, Kay
1902-1992 ..... **CLC 1, 5, 19, 58; SSC 5**
See also CA 13-16R; 140; CAAS 1;
CANR 29; DLB 4, 9, 48, 86; DLBY 93;
MTCW

Boyle, Mark
See Kienzle, William X(avier)

Boyle, Patrick 1905-1982......... **CLC 19**
See also CA 127

Boyle, T. C. 1948-
See Boyle, T(homas) Coraghessan

Boyle, T(homas) Coraghessan
1948- .... **CLC 36, 55, 90; SSC 16**
See also BEST 90:4; CA 120; CANR 44;
DLBY 86

Boz
See Dickens, Charles (John Huffam)

Brackenridge, Hugh Henry
1748-1816 .... **NCLC 7**
See also DLB 11, 37

Bradbury, Edward P.
See Moorcock, Michael (John)

Bradbury, Malcolm (Stanley)
1932- .... **CLC 32, 61**
See also CA 1-4R; CANR 1, 33; DLB 14;
MTCW

Bradbury, Ray (Douglas)
1920- .... **CLC 1, 3, 10, 15, 42; DA;
DAB; WLC**
See also AAYA 15; AITN 1, 2; CA 1-4R;
CANR 2, 30; CDALB 1968-1988; DLB 2,
8; MTCW; SATA 11, 64

Bradford, Gamaliel 1863-1932..... **TCLC 36**
See also DLB 17

Bradley, David (Henry, Jr.)
1950-.................. **CLC 23; BLC**
See also BW 1; CA 104; CANR 26; DLB 33

Bradley, John Ed(mund, Jr.)
1958-...................... **CLC 55**
See also CA 139

Bradley, Marion Zimmer 1930-..... **CLC 30**
See also AAYA 9; CA 57-60; CAAS 10;
CANR 7, 31; DLB 8; MTCW

Bradstreet, Anne
1612(?)-1672 ...... **LC 4, 30; DA; PC 10**
See also CDALB 1640-1865; DLB 24

Brady, Joan 1939- .... **CLC 86**
See also CA 141

Bragg, Melvyn 1939- .... **CLC 10**
See also BEST 89:3; CA 57-60; CANR 10,
48; DLB 14

Braine, John (Gerard)
1922-1986 .... **CLC 1, 3, 41**
See also CA 1-4R; 120; CANR 1, 33;
CDBLB 1945-1960; DLB 15; DLBY 86;
MTCW

Brammer, William 1930(?)-1978 .... **CLC 31**
See also CA 77-80

Brancati, Vitaliano 1907-1954..... **TCLC 12**
See also CA 109

Brancato, Robin F(idler) 1936- ..... **CLC 35**
See also AAYA 9; CA 69-72; CANR 11,
45; CLR 32; JRDA; SAAS 9; SATA 23

Brand, Max
See Faust, Frederick (Schiller)

Brand, Millen 1906-1980 .... **CLC 7**
See also CA 21-24R; 97-100

Branden, Barbara .... **CLC 44**
See also CA 148

Brandes, Georg (Morris Cohen)
1842-1927 .... **TCLC 10**
See also CA 105

Brandys, Kazimierz 1916- .... **CLC 62**

Branley, Franklyn M(ansfield)
1915-...................... **CLC 21**
See also CA 33-36R; CANR 14, 39;
CLR 13; MAICYA; SAAS 16; SATA 4,
68

Brathwaite, Edward Kamau 1930-... **CLC 11**
See also BW 2; CA 25-28R; CANR 11, 26,
47; DLB 125

Brautigan, Richard (Gary)
1935-1984 .... **CLC 1, 3, 5, 9, 12, 34, 42**
See also CA 53-56; 113; CANR 34; DLB 2,
5; DLBY 80, 84; MTCW; SATA 56

Braverman, Kate 1950- .... **CLC 67**
See also CA 89-92

Brecht, Bertolt
1898-1956 ...... **TCLC 1, 6, 13, 35; DA;**
DAB; DC 3; WLC
See also CA 104; 133; DLB 56, 124; MTCW

Brecht, Eugen Berthold Friedrich
See Brecht, Bertolt

Bremer, Fredrika 1801-1865 ..... **NCLC 11**

Brennan, Christopher John
1870-1932 .... **TCLC 17**
See also CA 117

Brennan, Maeve 1917- .... **CLC 5**
See also CA 81-84

Brentano, Clemens (Maria)
1778-1842 .... **NCLC 1**
See also DLB 90

Brent of Bin Bin
See Franklin, (Stella Maraia Sarah) Miles

Brenton, Howard 1942- .... **CLC 31**
See also CA 69-72; CANR 33; DLB 13;
MTCW

Breslin, James 1930-
See Breslin, Jimmy
See also CA 73-76; CANR 31; MTCW

Breslin, Jimmy .... **CLC 4, 43**
See also Breslin, James
See also AITN 1

Bresson, Robert 1901- .... **CLC 16**
See also CA 110; CANR 49

Breton, Andre 1896-1966... **CLC 2, 9, 15, 54**
See also CA 19-20; 25-28R; CANR 40;
CAP 2; DLB 65; MTCW

Breytenbach, Breyten 1939(?)- .. **CLC 23, 37**
See also CA 113; 129

Bridgers, Sue Ellen 1942- .... **CLC 26**
See also AAYA 8; CA 65-68; CANR 11,
36; CLR 18; DLB 52; JRDA; MAICYA;
SAAS 1; SATA 22

Bridges, Robert (Seymour)
1844-1930 .... **TCLC 1**
See also CA 104; CDBLB 1890-1914;
DLB 19, 98

Bridie, James .... **TCLC 3**
See also Mavor, Osborne Henry
See also DLB 10

Brin, David 1950- .... **CLC 34**
See also CA 102; CANR 24; SATA 65

Brink, Andre (Philippus)
1935-...................... **CLC 18, 36**
See also CA 104; CANR 39; MTCW

Brinsmead, H(esba) F(ay) 1922- .... **CLC 21**
See also CA 21-24R; CANR 10; MAICYA;
SAAS 5; SATA 18, 78

Brittain, Vera (Mary)
1893(?)-1970 .... **CLC 23**
See also CA 13-16; 25-28R; CAP 1; MTCW

Broch, Hermann 1886-1951 .... **TCLC 20**
See also CA 117; DLB 85, 124

Brock, Rose
See Hansen, Joseph

Brodkey, Harold 1930- .... **CLC 56**
See also CA 111; DLB 130

Brodsky, Iosif Alexandrovich 1940-
See Brodsky, Joseph
See also AITN 1; CA 41-44R; CANR 37;
MTCW

Brodsky, Joseph .. **CLC 4, 6, 13, 36, 50; PC 9**
See also Brodsky, Iosif Alexandrovich

Brodsky, Michael Mark 1948- ..... **CLC 19**
See also CA 102; CANR 18, 41

Bromell, Henry 1947- .... **CLC 5**
See also CA 53-56; CANR 9

Bromfield, Louis (Brucker)
1896-1956 .... **TCLC 11**
See also CA 107; DLB 4, 9, 86

Broner, E(sther) M(asserman)
1930-...................... **CLC 19**
See also CA 17-20R; CANR 8, 25; DLB 28

Bronk, William 1918- .... **CLC 10**
See also CA 89-92; CANR 23

Bronstein, Lev Davidovich
See Trotsky, Leon

Bronte, Anne 1820-1849.......... **NCLC 4**
See also DLB 21

Bronte, Charlotte
1816-1855 .... **NCLC 3, 8, 33; DA;**
DAB; WLC
See also CDBLB 1832-1890; DLB 21

Bronte, Emily (Jane)
1818-1848 .... **NCLC 16, 35; DA; DAB;**
PC 8; WLC
See also CDBLB 1832-1890; DLB 21, 32

Brooke, Frances 1724-1789 .... **LC 6**
See also DLB 39, 99

Brooke, Henry 1703(?)-1783 .... **LC 1**
See also DLB 39

Brooke, Rupert (Chawner)
1887-1915 .... **TCLC 2, 7; DA; DAB;**
WLC
See also CA 104; 132; CDBLB 1914-1945;
DLB 19; MTCW

Brooke-Haven, P.
See Wodehouse, P(elham) G(renville)

Brooke-Rose, Christine 1926- ...... **CLC 40**
See also CA 13-16R; DLB 14

Brookner, Anita
1928- .... **CLC 32, 34, 51; DAB**
See also CA 114; 120; CANR 37; DLBY 87;
MTCW

Brooks, Cleanth 1906-1994 ..... **CLC 24, 86**
See also CA 17-20R; 145; CANR 33, 35;
DLB 63; DLBY 94; MTCW

Brooks, George
See Baum, L(yman) Frank

Brooks, Gwendolyn
1917- ...... **CLC 1, 2, 4, 5, 15, 49; BLC;**
DA; PC 7; WLC
See also AITN 1; BW 2; CA 1-4R;
CANR 1, 27; CDALB 1941-1968;
CLR 27; DLB 5, 76; MTCW; SATA 6

Brooks, Mel .... **CLC 12**
See also Kaminsky, Melvin
See also AAYA 13; DLB 26

Brooks, Peter 1938- .... **CLC 34**
See also CA 45-48; CANR 1

Brooks, Van Wyck 1886-1963 ...... **CLC 29**
See also CA 1-4R; CANR 6; DLB 45, 63,
103

Brophy, Brigid (Antonia)
1929-.................. **CLC 6, 11, 29**
See also CA 5-8R; CAAS 4; CANR 25;
DLB 14; MTCW

Brosman, Catharine Savage 1934-.... **CLC 9**
See also CA 61-64; CANR 21, 46

Brother Antoninus
See Everson, William (Oliver)

Broughton, T(homas) Alan 1936- ... **CLC 19**
See also CA 45-48; CANR 2, 23, 48

Broumas, Olga 1949- .... **CLC 10, 73**
See also CA 85-88; CANR 20

Brown, Charles Brockden
1771-1810 . . . . NCLC 22
See also CDALB 1640-1865; DLB 37, 59, 73

Brown, Christy 1932-1981 . . . . CLC 63
See also CA 105; 104; DLB 14

Brown, Claude 1937- . . . . CLC 30; BLC
See also AAYA 7; BW 1; CA 73-76

Brown, Dee (Alexander) 1908- . . CLC 18, 47
See also CA 13-16R; CAAS 6; CANR 11, 45; DLBY 80; MTCW; SATA 5

Brown, George
See Wertmueller, Lina

Brown, George Douglas
1869-1902 . . . . TCLC 28

Brown, George Mackay 1921- . . . . CLC 5, 48
See also CA 21-24R; CAAS 6; CANR 12, 37; DLB 14, 27, 139; MTCW; SATA 35

Brown, (William) Larry 1951- . . . . . . CLC 73
See also CA 130; 134

Brown, Moses
See Barrett, William (Christopher)

Brown, Rita Mae 1944- . . . . . CLC 18, 43, 79
See also CA 45-48; CANR 2, 11, 35; MTCW

Brown, Roderick (Langmere) Haig-
See Haig-Brown, Roderick (Langmere)

Brown, Rosellen 1939- . . . . CLC 32
See also CA 77-80; CAAS 10; CANR 14, 44

Brown, Sterling Allen
1901-1989 . . . . CLC 1, 23, 59; BLC
See also BW 1; CA 85-88; 127; CANR 26; DLB 48, 51, 63; MTCW

Brown, Will
See Ainsworth, William Harrison

Brown, William Wells
1813-1884 . . . . NCLC 2; BLC; DC 1
See also DLB 3, 50

Browne, (Clyde) Jackson 1948(?)- . . . CLC 21
See also CA 120

Browning, Elizabeth Barrett
1806-1861 . . . . . NCLC 1, 16; DA; DAB; PC 6; WLC
See also CDBLB 1832-1890; DLB 32

Browning, Robert
1812-1889 . . NCLC 19; DA; DAB; PC 2
See also CDBLB 1832-1890; DLB 32; YABC 1

Browning, Tod 1882-1962 . . . . CLC 16
See also CA 141; 117

Brownson, Orestes (Augustus)
1803-1876 . . . . NCLC 50

Bruccoli, Matthew J(oseph) 1931- . . CLC 34
See also CA 9-12R; CANR 7; DLB 103

Bruce, Lenny . . . . CLC 21
See also Schneider, Leonard Alfred

Bruin, John
See Brutus, Dennis

Brulard, Henri
See Stendhal

Brulls, Christian
See Simenon, Georges (Jacques Christian)

Brunner, John (Kilian Houston)
1934- . . . . CLC 8, 10
See also CA 1-4R; CAAS 8; CANR 2, 37; MTCW

Bruno, Giordano 1548-1600 . . . . LC 27

Brutus, Dennis 1924- . . . . CLC 43; BLC
See also BW 2; CA 49-52; CAAS 14; CANR 2, 27, 42; DLB 117

Bryan, C(ourtlandt) D(ixon) B(arnes)
1936- . . . . CLC 29
See also CA 73-76; CANR 13

Bryan, Michael
See Moore, Brian

Bryant, William Cullen
1794-1878 . . . . . . NCLC 6, 46; DA; DAB
See also CDALB 1640-1865; DLB 3, 43, 59

Bryusov, Valery Yakovlevich
1873-1924 . . . . TCLC 10
See also CA 107

Buchan, John 1875-1940 . . . TCLC 41; DAB
See also CA 108; 145; DLB 34, 70, 156; YABC 2

Buchanan, George 1506-1582 . . . . LC 4

Buchheim, Lothar-Guenther 1918- . . . CLC 6
See also CA 85-88

Buchner, (Karl) Georg
1813-1837 . . . . NCLC 26

Buchwald, Art(hur) 1925- . . . . CLC 33
See also AITN 1; CA 5-8R; CANR 21; MTCW; SATA 10

Buck, Pearl S(ydenstricker)
1892-1973 . . . . CLC 7, 11, 18; DA; DAB
See also AITN 1; CA 1-4R; 41-44R; CANR 1, 34; DLB 9, 102; MTCW; SATA 1, 25

Buckler, Ernest 1908-1984 . . . . CLC 13
See also CA 11-12; 114; CAP 1; DLB 68; SATA 47

Buckley, Vincent (Thomas)
1925-1988 . . . . CLC 57
See also CA 101

Buckley, William F(rank), Jr.
1925- . . . . CLC 7, 18, 37
See also AITN 1; CA 1-4R; CANR 1, 24; DLB 137; DLBY 80; MTCW

Buechner, (Carl) Frederick
1926- . . . . CLC 2, 4, 6, 9
See also CA 13-16R; CANR 11, 39; DLBY 80; MTCW

Buell, John (Edward) 1927- . . . . CLC 10
See also CA 1-4R; DLB 53

Buero Vallejo, Antonio 1916- . . . CLC 15, 46
See also CA 106; CANR 24, 49; HW; MTCW

Bufalino, Gesualdo 1920(?)- . . . . CLC 74

Bugayev, Boris Nikolayevich 1880-1934
See Bely, Andrey
See also CA 104

Bukowski, Charles
1920-1994 . . . . CLC 2, 5, 9, 41, 82
See also CA 17-20R; 144; CANR 40; DLB 5, 130; MTCW

Bulgakov, Mikhail (Afanas'evich)
1891-1940 . . . . TCLC 2, 16; SSC 18
See also CA 105

Bulgya, Alexander Alexandrovich
1901-1956 . . . . TCLC 53
See also Fadeyev, Alexander
See also CA 117

Bullins, Ed 1935- . . . . CLC 1, 5, 7; BLC
See also BW 2; CA 49-52; CAAS 16; CANR 24, 46; DLB 7, 38; MTCW

Bulwer-Lytton, Edward (George Earle Lytton)
1803-1873 . . . . NCLC 1, 45
See also DLB 21

Bunin, Ivan Alexeyevich
1870-1953 . . . . TCLC 6; SSC 5
See also CA 104

Bunting, Basil 1900-1985 . . . . CLC 10, 39, 47
See also CA 53-56; 115; CANR 7; DLB 20

Bunuel, Luis 1900-1983 . . CLC 16, 80; HLC
See also CA 101; 110; CANR 32; HW

Bunyan, John
1628-1688 . . . . . . LC 4; DA; DAB; WLC
See also CDBLB 1660-1789; DLB 39

Burckhardt, Jacob (Christoph)
1818-1897 . . . . NCLC 49

Burford, Eleanor
See Hibbert, Eleanor Alice Burford

Burgess, Anthony
. CLC 1, 2, 4, 5, 8, 10, 13, 15, 22, 40, 62, 81; DAB
See also Wilson, John (Anthony) Burgess
See also AITN 1; CDBLB 1960 to Present; DLB 14

Burke, Edmund
1729(?)-1797 . . . . LC 7; DA; DAB; WLC
See also DLB 104

Burke, Kenneth (Duva)
1897-1993 . . . . CLC 2, 24
See also CA 5-8R; 143; CANR 39; DLB 45, 63; MTCW

Burke, Leda
See Garnett, David

Burke, Ralph
See Silverberg, Robert

Burney, Fanny 1752-1840 . . . . NCLC 12
See also DLB 39

Burns, Robert 1759-1796 . . . . PC 6
See also CDBLB 1789-1832; DA; DAB; DLB 109; WLC

Burns, Tex
See L'Amour, Louis (Dearborn)

Burnshaw, Stanley 1906- . . . . . CLC 3, 13, 44
See also CA 9-12R; DLB 48

Burr, Anne 1937- . . . . CLC 6
See also CA 25-28R

Burroughs, Edgar Rice
1875-1950 . . . . TCLC 2, 32
See also AAYA 11; CA 104; 132; DLB 8; MTCW; SATA 41

Burroughs, William S(eward)
1914- . . . . CLC 1, 2, 5, 15, 22, 42, 75; DA; DAB; WLC
See also AITN 2; CA 9-12R; CANR 20; DLB 2, 8, 16, 152; DLBY 81; MTCW

Burton, Richard F. 1821-1890 . . . . NCLC 42
See also DLB 55

Busch, Frederick 1941- ... **CLC 7, 10, 18, 47**
See also CA 33-36R; CAAS 1; CANR 45;
DLB 6

Bush, Ronald 1946- .... **CLC 34**
See also CA 136

Bustos, F(rancisco)
See Borges, Jorge Luis

Bustos Domecq, H(onorio)
See Bioy Casares, Adolfo; Borges, Jorge
Luis

Butler, Octavia E(stelle) 1947- ..... **CLC 38**
See also BW 2; CA 73-76; CANR 12, 24,
38; DLB 33; MTCW

Butler, Robert Olen (Jr.) 1945-..... **CLC 81**
See also CA 112

Butler, Samuel 1612-1680 .... **LC 16**
See also DLB 101, 126

Butler, Samuel
1835-1902 ...... **TCLC 1, 33; DA; DAB;**
WLC
See also CA 143; CDBLB 1890-1914;
DLB 18, 57

Butler, Walter C.
See Faust, Frederick (Schiller)

Butor, Michel (Marie Francois)
1926- .... **CLC 1, 3, 8, 11, 15**
See also CA 9-12R; CANR 33; DLB 83;
MTCW

Buzo, Alexander (John) 1944-...... **CLC 61**
See also CA 97-100; CANR 17, 39

Buzzati, Dino 1906-1972 .... **CLC 36**
See also CA 33-36R

Byars, Betsy (Cromer) 1928-....... **CLC 35**
See also CA 33-36R; CANR 18, 36; CLR 1,
16; DLB 52; JRDA; MAICYA; MTCW;
SAAS 1; SATA 4, 46, 80

Byatt, A(ntonia) S(usan Drabble)
1936- .... **CLC 19, 65**
See also CA 13-16R; CANR 13, 33;
DLB 14; MTCW

Byrne, David 1952-............... **CLC 26**
See also CA 127

Byrne, John Keyes 1926-
See Leonard, Hugh
See also CA 102

Byron, George Gordon (Noel)
1788-1824 ..... **NCLC 2, 12; DA; DAB;**
WLC
See also CDBLB 1789-1832; DLB 96, 110

C. 3. 3.
See Wilde, Oscar (Fingal O'Flahertie Wills)

Caballero, Fernan 1796-1877..... **NCLC 10**

Cabell, James Branch 1879-1958 ... **TCLC 6**
See also CA 105; DLB 9, 78

Cable, George Washington
1844-1925 .... **TCLC 4; SSC 4**
See also CA 104; DLB 12, 74

Cabral de Melo Neto, Joao 1920-... **CLC 76**

Cabrera Infante, G(uillermo)
1929- .... **CLC 5, 25, 45; HLC**
See also CA 85-88; CANR 29; DLB 113;
HW; MTCW

Cade, Toni
See Bambara, Toni Cade

Cadmus and Harmonia
See Buchan, John

Caedmon fl. 658-680............. **CMLC 7**
See also DLB 146

Caeiro, Alberto
See Pessoa, Fernando (Antonio Nogueira)

Cage, John (Milton, Jr.) 1912- ..... **CLC 41**
See also CA 13-16R; CANR 9

Cain, G.
See Cabrera Infante, G(uillermo)

Cain, Guillermo
See Cabrera Infante, G(uillermo)

Cain, James M(allahan)
1892-1977 .... **CLC 3, 11, 28**
See also AITN 1; CA 17-20R; 73-76;
CANR 8, 34; MTCW

Caine, Mark
See Raphael, Frederic (Michael)

Calasso, Roberto 1941- .... **CLC 81**
See also CA 143

Calderon de la Barca, Pedro
1600-1681 .... **LC 23; DC 3**

Caldwell, Erskine (Preston)
1903-1987 .... **CLC 1, 8, 14, 50, 60;**
SSC 19
See also AITN 1; CA 1-4R; 121; CAAS 1;
CANR 2, 33; DLB 9, 86; MTCW

Caldwell, (Janet Miriam) Taylor (Holland)
1900-1985 .... **CLC 2, 28, 39**
See also CA 5-8R; 116; CANR 5

Calhoun, John Caldwell
1782-1850 .... **NCLC 15**
See also DLB 3

Calisher, Hortense
1911- .... **CLC 2, 4, 8, 38; SSC 15**
See also CA 1-4R; CANR 1, 22; DLB 2;
MTCW

Callaghan, Morley Edward
1903-1990 .... **CLC 3, 14, 41, 65**
See also CA 9-12R; 132; CANR 33;
DLB 68; MTCW

Calvino, Italo
1923-1985 ..... **CLC 5, 8, 11, 22, 33, 39,**
73; SSC 3
See also CA 85-88; 116; CANR 23; MTCW

Cameron, Carey 1952-............. **CLC 59**
See also CA 135

Cameron, Peter 1959-............. **CLC 44**
See also CA 125

Campana, Dino 1885-1932....... **TCLC 20**
See also CA 117; DLB 114

Campbell, John W(ood, Jr.)
1910-1971 .... **CLC 32**
See also CA 21-22; 29-32R; CANR 34;
CAP 2; DLB 8; MTCW

Campbell, Joseph 1904-1987 .... **CLC 69**
See also AAYA 3; BEST 89:2; CA 1-4R;
124; CANR 3, 28; MTCW

Campbell, Maria 1940-............. **CLC 85**
See also CA 102; NNAL

Campbell, (John) Ramsey
1946- .... **CLC 42; SSC 19**
See also CA 57-60; CANR 7

Campbell, (Ignatius) Roy (Dunnachie)
1901-1957 .... **TCLC 5**
See also CA 104; DLB 20

Campbell, Thomas 1777-1844 .... **NCLC 19**
See also DLB 93; 144

Campbell, Wilfred................ **TCLC 9**
See also Campbell, William

Campbell, William 1858(?)-1918
See Campbell, Wilfred
See also CA 106; DLB 92

Campos, Alvaro de
See Pessoa, Fernando (Antonio Nogueira)

Camus, Albert
1913-1960 .... **CLC 1, 2, 4, 9, 11, 14, 32,**
63, 69; DA; DAB; DC 2; SSC 9; WLC
See also CA 89-92; DLB 72; MTCW

Canby, Vincent 1924-............. **CLC 13**
See also CA 81-84

Cancale
See Desnos, Robert

Canetti, Elias
1905-1994 .... **CLC 3, 14, 25, 75, 86**
See also CA 21-24R; 146; CANR 23;
DLB 85, 124; MTCW

Canin, Ethan 1960-............... **CLC 55**
See also CA 131; 135

Cannon, Curt
See Hunter, Evan

Cape, Judith
See Page, P(atricia) K(athleen)

Capek, Karel
1890-1938 ...... **TCLC 6, 37; DA; DAB;**
DC 1; WLC
See also CA 104; 140

Capote, Truman
1924-1984 ...... **CLC 1, 3, 8, 13, 19, 34,**
38, 58; DA; DAB; SSC 2; WLC
See also CA 5-8R; 113; CANR 18;
CDALB 1941-1968; DLB 2; DLBY 80,
84; MTCW

Capra, Frank 1897-1991.......... **CLC 16**
See also CA 61-64; 135

Caputo, Philip 1941-.............. **CLC 32**
See also CA 73-76; CANR 40

Card, Orson Scott 1951- .... **CLC 44, 47, 50**
See also AAYA 11; CA 102; CANR 27, 47;
MTCW; SATA 83

Cardenal (Martinez), Ernesto
1925- .... **CLC 31; HLC**
See also CA 49-52; CANR 2, 32; HW;
MTCW

Carducci, Giosue 1835-1907....... **TCLC 32**

Carew, Thomas 1595(?)-1640........ **LC 13**
See also DLB 126

Carey, Ernestine Gilbreth 1908-.... **CLC 17**
See also CA 5-8R; SATA 2

Carey, Peter 1943-............. **CLC 40, 55**
See also CA 123; 127; MTCW

Carleton, William 1794-1869...... **NCLC 3**

Carlisle, Henry (Coffin) 1926-...... **CLC 33**
See also CA 13-16R; CANR 15

Carlsen, Chris
See Holdstock, Robert P.

Chandler, Raymond (Thornton)
1888-1959 . . . . TCLC **1, 7**
See also CA 104; 129; CDALB 1929-1941;
DLBD 6; MTCW

Chang, Jung 1952- . . . . CLC **71**
See also CA 142

Channing, William Ellery
1780-1842 . . . . NCLC **17**
See also DLB 1, 59

Chaplin, Charles Spencer
1889-1977 . . . . CLC **16**
See also Chaplin, Charlie
See also CA 81-84; 73-76

Chaplin, Charlie
See Chaplin, Charles Spencer
See also DLB 44

Chapman, George 1559(?)-1634 . . . . . . LC **22**
See also DLB 62, 121

Chapman, Graham 1941-1989 . . . . . . CLC **21**
See also Monty Python
See also CA 116; 129; CANR 35

Chapman, John Jay 1862-1933 . . . . . TCLC **7**
See also CA 104

Chapman, Walker
See Silverberg, Robert

Chappell, Fred (Davis) 1936- . . . . CLC **40, 78**
See also CA 5-8R; CAAS 4; CANR 8, 33;
DLB 6, 105

Char, Rene(-Emile)
1907-1988 . . . . CLC **9, 11, 14, 55**
See also CA 13-16R; 124; CANR 32;
MTCW

Charby, Jay
See Ellison, Harlan (Jay)

Chardin, Pierre Teilhard de
See Teilhard de Chardin, (Marie Joseph)
Pierre

Charles I 1600-1649 . . . . LC **13**

Charyn, Jerome 1937- . . . . CLC **5, 8, 18**
See also CA 5-8R; CAAS 1; CANR 7;
DLBY 83; MTCW

Chase, Mary (Coyle) 1907-1981 . . . . . . DC **1**
See also CA 77-80; 105; SATA 17;
SATA-Obit 29

Chase, Mary Ellen 1887-1973 . . . . CLC **2**
See also CA 13-16; 41-44R; CAP 1;
SATA 10

Chase, Nicholas
See Hyde, Anthony

Chateaubriand, Francois Rene de
1768-1848 . . . . NCLC **3**
See also DLB 119

Chatterje, Sarat Chandra 1876-1936(?)
See Chatterji, Saratchandra
See also CA 109

Chatterji, Bankim Chandra
1838-1894 . . . . NCLC **19**

Chatterji, Saratchandra . . . . TCLC **13**
See also Chatterje, Sarat Chandra

Chatterton, Thomas 1752-1770 . . . . LC **3**
See also DLB 109

Chatwin, (Charles) Bruce
1940-1989 . . . . CLC **28, 57, 59**
See also AAYA 4; BEST 90:1; CA 85-88;
127

Chaucer, Daniel
See Ford, Ford Madox

Chaucer, Geoffrey
1340(?)-1400 . . . . LC **17**; DA; DAB
See also CDBLB Before 1660; DLB 146

Chaviaras, Strates 1935-
See Haviaras, Stratis
See also CA 105

Chayefsky, Paddy . . . . CLC **23**
See also Chayefsky, Sidney
See also DLB 7, 44; DLBY 81

Chayefsky, Sidney 1923-1981
See Chayefsky, Paddy
See also CA 9-12R; 104; CANR 18

Chedid, Andree 1920- . . . . CLC **47**
See also CA 145

Cheever, John
1912-1982 . . . . . . CLC **3, 7, 8, 11, 15, 25,
64**; DA; DAB; SSC **1**; WLC
See also CA 5-8R; 106; CABS 1; CANR 5,
27; CDALB 1941-1968; DLB 2, 102;
DLBY 80, 82; MTCW

Cheever, Susan 1943- . . . . CLC **18, 48**
See also CA 103; CANR 27; DLBY 82

Chekhonte, Antosha
See Chekhov, Anton (Pavlovich)

Chekhov, Anton (Pavlovich)
1860-1904 . . . . . TCLC **3, 10, 31, 55**; DA;
DAB; SSC **2**; WLC
See also CA 104; 124

Chernyshevsky, Nikolay Gavrilovich
1828-1889 . . . . NCLC **1**

Cherry, Carolyn Janice 1942-
See Cherryh, C. J.
See also CA 65-68; CANR 10

Cherryh, C. J. . . . . CLC **35**
See also Cherry, Carolyn Janice
See also DLBY 80

Chesnutt, Charles W(addell)
1858-1932 . . . . TCLC **5, 39**; BLC; SSC **7**
See also BW 1; CA 106; 125; DLB 12, 50,
78; MTCW

Chester, Alfred 1929(?)-1971 . . . . CLC **49**
See also CA 33-36R; DLB 130

Chesterton, G(ilbert) K(eith)
1874-1936 . . . . TCLC **1, 6**; SSC **1**
See also CA 104; 132; CDBLB 1914-1945;
DLB 10, 19, 34, 70, 98, 149; MTCW;
SATA 27

Chiang Pin-chin 1904-1986
See Ding Ling
See also CA 118

Ch'ien Chung-shu 1910- . . . . CLC **22**
See also CA 130; MTCW

Child, L. Maria
See Child, Lydia Maria

Child, Lydia Maria 1802-1880 . . . . NCLC **6**
See also DLB 1, 74; SATA 67

Child, Mrs.
See Child, Lydia Maria

Child, Philip 1898-1978 . . . . CLC **19, 68**
See also CA 13-14; CAP 1; SATA 47

Childress, Alice
1920-1994 . . CLC **12, 15, 86**; BLC; DC **4**
See also AAYA 8; BW 2; CA 45-48; 146;
CANR 3, 27; CLR 14; DLB 7, 38; JRDA;
MAICYA; MTCW; SATA 7, 48, 81

Chislett, (Margaret) Anne 1943- . . . . CLC **34**

Chitty, Thomas Willes 1926- . . . . CLC **11**
See also Hinde, Thomas
See also CA 5-8R

Chivers, Thomas Holley
1809-1858 . . . . NCLC **49**
See also DLB 3

Chomette, Rene Lucien 1898-1981
See Clair, Rene
See also CA 103

Chopin, Kate
. . . . TCLC **5, 14**; DA; DAB; SSC **8**
See also Chopin, Katherine
See also CDALB 1865-1917; DLB 12, 78

Chopin, Katherine 1851-1904
See Chopin, Kate
See also CA 104; 122

Chretien de Troyes
c. 12th cent. - . . . . CMLC **10**

Christie
See Ichikawa, Kon

Christie, Agatha (Mary Clarissa)
1890-1976 . . . . . . CLC **1, 6, 8, 12, 39, 48**;
DAB
See also AAYA 9; AITN 1, 2; CA 17-20R;
61-64; CANR 10, 37; CDBLB 1914-1945;
DLB 13, 77; MTCW; SATA 36

Christie, (Ann) Philippa
See Pearce, Philippa
See also CA 5-8R; CANR 4

Christine de Pizan 1365(?)-1431(?) . . . . LC **9**

Chubb, Elmer
See Masters, Edgar Lee

Chulkov, Mikhail Dmitrievich
1743-1792 . . . . LC **2**
See also DLB 150

Churchill, Caryl 1938- . . . CLC **31, 55**; DC **5**
See also CA 102; CANR 22, 46; DLB 13;
MTCW

Churchill, Charles 1731-1764 . . . . LC **3**
See also DLB 109

Chute, Carolyn 1947- . . . . CLC **39**
See also CA 123

Ciardi, John (Anthony)
1916-1986 . . . . CLC **10, 40, 44**
See also CA 5-8R; 118; CAAS 2; CANR 5,
33; CLR 19; DLB 5; DLBY 86;
MAICYA; MTCW; SATA 1, 65;
SATA-Obit 46

Cicero, Marcus Tullius
106B.C.-43B.C. . . . . CMLC **3**

Cimino, Michael 1943- . . . . CLC **16**
See also CA 105

Cioran, E(mil) M. 1911- . . . . CLC **64**
See also CA 25-28R

Cisneros, Sandra 1954- . . . . . . CLC **69**; HLC
See also AAYA 9; CA 131; DLB 122, 152;
HW

Clair, Rene . . . . CLC **20**
See also Chomette, Rene Lucien

Clampitt, Amy 1920-1994 . . . . CLC 32
See also CA 110; 146; CANR 29; DLB 105

Clancy, Thomas L., Jr. 1947-
See Clancy, Tom
See also CA 125; 131; MTCW

Clancy, Tom . . . . CLC 45
See also Clancy, Thomas L., Jr.
See also AAYA 9; BEST 89:1, 90:1

Clare, John 1793-1864 . . . . . . NCLC 9; DAB
See also DLB 55, 96

Clarin
See Alas (y Urena), Leopoldo (Enrique Garcia)

Clark, Al C.
See Goines, Donald

Clark, (Robert) Brian 1932- . . . . CLC 29
See also CA 41-44R

Clark, Curt
See Westlake, Donald E(dwin)

Clark, Eleanor 1913- . . . . CLC 5, 19
See also CA 9-12R; CANR 41; DLB 6

Clark, J. P.
See Clark, John Pepper
See also DLB 117

Clark, John Pepper
1935- . . . . CLC 38; BLC; DC 5
See also Clark, J. P.
See also BW 1; CA 65-68; CANR 16

Clark, M. R.
See Clark, Mavis Thorpe

Clark, Mavis Thorpe 1909- . . . . CLC 12
See also CA 57-60; CANR 8, 37; CLR 30; MAICYA; SAAS 5; SATA 8, 74

Clark, Walter Van Tilburg
1909-1971 . . . . CLC 28
See also CA 9-12R; 33-36R; DLB 9; SATA 8

Clarke, Arthur C(harles)
1917- . . . . . . CLC 1, 4, 13, 18, 35; SSC 3
See also AAYA 4; CA 1-4R; CANR 2, 28; JRDA; MAICYA; MTCW; SATA 13, 70

Clarke, Austin 1896-1974 . . . . CLC 6, 9
See also CA 29-32; 49-52; CAP 2; DLB 10, 20

Clarke, Austin C(hesterfield)
1934- . . . . CLC 8, 53; BLC
See also BW 1; CA 25-28R; CAAS 16; CANR 14, 32; DLB 53, 125

Clarke, Gillian 1937- . . . . CLC 61
See also CA 106; DLB 40

Clarke, Marcus (Andrew Hislop)
1846-1881 . . . . NCLC 19

Clarke, Shirley 1925- . . . . CLC 16

Clash, The
See Headon, (Nicky) Topper; Jones, Mick; Simonon, Paul; Strummer, Joe

Claudel, Paul (Louis Charles Marie)
1868-1955 . . . . TCLC 2, 10
See also CA 104

Clavell, James (duMaresq)
1925-1994 . . . . CLC 6, 25, 87
See also CA 25-28R; 146; CANR 26, 48; MTCW

Cleaver, (Leroy) Eldridge
1935- . . . . CLC 30; BLC
See also BW 1; CA 21-24R; CANR 16

Cleese, John (Marwood) 1939- . . . . . CLC 21
See also Monty Python
See also CA 112; 116; CANR 35; MTCW

Cleishbotham, Jebediah
See Scott, Walter

Cleland, John 1710-1789 . . . . LC 2
See also DLB 39

Clemens, Samuel Langhorne 1835-1910
See Twain, Mark
See also CA 104; 135; CDALB 1865-1917; DA; DAB; DLB 11, 12, 23, 64, 74; JRDA; MAICYA; YABC 2

Cleophil
See Congreve, William

Clerihew, E.
See Bentley, E(dmund) C(lerihew)

Clerk, N. W.
See Lewis, C(live) S(taples)

Cliff, Jimmy . . . . CLC 21
See also Chambers, James

Clifton, (Thelma) Lucille
1936- . . . . CLC 19, 66; BLC
See also BW 2; CA 49-52; CANR 2, 24, 42; CLR 5; DLB 5, 41; MAICYA; MTCW; SATA 20, 69

Clinton, Dirk
See Silverberg, Robert

Clough, Arthur Hugh 1819-1861 . . NCLC 27
See also DLB 32

Clutha, Janet Paterson Frame 1924-
See Frame, Janet
See also CA 1-4R; CANR 2, 36; MTCW

Clyne, Terence
See Blatty, William Peter

Cobalt, Martin
See Mayne, William (James Carter)

Cobbett, William 1763-1835 . . . . . NCLC 49
See also DLB 43, 107

Coburn, D(onald) L(ee) 1938- . . . . . . CLC 10
See also CA 89-92

Cocteau, Jean (Maurice Eugene Clement)
1889-1963 . . . . CLC 1, 8, 15, 16, 43; DA; DAB; WLC
See also CA 25-28; CANR 40; CAP 2; DLB 65; MTCW

Codrescu, Andrei 1946- . . . . CLC 46
See also CA 33-36R; CAAS 19; CANR 13, 34

Coe, Max
See Bourne, Randolph S(illiman)

Coe, Tucker
See Westlake, Donald E(dwin)

Coetzee, J(ohn) M(ichael)
1940- . . . . CLC 23, 33, 66
See also CA 77-80; CANR 41; MTCW

Coffey, Brian
See Koontz, Dean R(ay)

Cohan, George M. 1878-1942 . . . . . TCLC 60

Cohen, Arthur A(llen)
1928-1986 . . . . CLC 7, 31
See also CA 1-4R; 120; CANR 1, 17, 42; DLB 28

Cohen, Leonard (Norman)
1934- . . . . CLC 3, 38
See also CA 21-24R; CANR 14; DLB 53; MTCW

Cohen, Matt 1942- . . . . CLC 19
See also CA 61-64; CAAS 18; CANR 40; DLB 53

Cohen-Solal, Annie 19(?)- . . . . CLC 50

Colegate, Isabel 1931- . . . . CLC 36
See also CA 17-20R; CANR 8, 22; DLB 14; MTCW

Coleman, Emmett
See Reed, Ishmael

Coleridge, Samuel Taylor
1772-1834 . . . . NCLC 9; DA; DAB; PC 11; WLC
See also CDBLB 1789-1832; DLB 93, 107

Coleridge, Sara 1802-1852 . . . . NCLC 31

Coles, Don 1928- . . . . CLC 46
See also CA 115; CANR 38

Colette, (Sidonie-Gabrielle)
1873-1954 . . . . . . TCLC 1, 5, 16; SSC 10
See also CA 104; 131; DLB 65; MTCW

Collett, (Jacobine) Camilla (Wergeland)
1813-1895 . . . . NCLC 22

Collier, Christopher 1930- . . . . CLC 30
See also AAYA 13; CA 33-36R; CANR 13, 33; JRDA; MAICYA; SATA 16, 70

Collier, James L(incoln) 1928- . . . . . CLC 30
See also AAYA 13; CA 9-12R; CANR 4, 33; CLR 3; JRDA; MAICYA; SATA 8, 70

Collier, Jeremy 1650-1726 . . . . LC 6

Collier, John 1901-1980 . . . . SSC 19
See also CA 65-68; 97-100; CANR 10; DLB 77

Collins, Hunt
See Hunter, Evan

Collins, Linda 1931- . . . . CLC 44
See also CA 125

Collins, (William) Wilkie
1824-1889 . . . . NCLC 1, 18
See also CDBLB 1832-1890; DLB 18, 70

Collins, William 1721-1759 . . . . LC 4
See also DLB 109

Colman, George
See Glassco, John

Colt, Winchester Remington
See Hubbard, L(afayette) Ron(ald)

Colter, Cyrus 1910- . . . . CLC 58
See also BW 1; CA 65-68; CANR 10; DLB 33

Colton, James
See Hansen, Joseph

Colum, Padraic 1881-1972 . . . . CLC 28
See also CA 73-76; 33-36R; CANR 35; CLR 36; MAICYA; MTCW; SATA 15

Colvin, James
See Moorcock, Michael (John)

Colwin, Laurie (E.)
1944-1992 . . . . **CLC 5, 13, 23, 84**
See also CA 89-92; 139; CANR 20, 46;
DLBY 80; MTCW

Comfort, Alex(ander) 1920- . . . . **CLC 7**
See also CA 1-4R; CANR 1, 45

Comfort, Montgomery
See Campbell, (John) Ramsey

Compton-Burnett, I(vy)
1884(?)-1969 . . . . . . **CLC 1, 3, 10, 15, 34**
See also CA 1-4R; 25-28R; CANR 4;
DLB 36; MTCW

Comstock, Anthony 1844-1915 . . . . **TCLC 13**
See also CA 110

Conan Doyle, Arthur
See Doyle, Arthur Conan

Conde, Maryse 1937- . . . . **CLC 52**
See also Boucolon, Maryse
See also BW 2

Condillac, Etienne Bonnot de
1714-1780 . . . . **LC 26**

Condon, Richard (Thomas)
1915- . . . . **CLC 4, 6, 8, 10, 45**
See also BEST 90:3; CA 1-4R; CAAS 1;
CANR 2, 23; MTCW

Congreve, William
1670-1729 . . . . **LC 5, 21; DA; DAB;
DC 2; WLC**
See also CDBLB 1660-1789; DLB 39, 84

Connell, Evan S(helby), Jr.
1924- . . . . **CLC 4, 6, 45**
See also AAYA 7; CA 1-4R; CAAS 2;
CANR 2, 39; DLB 2; DLBY 81; MTCW

Connelly, Marc(us Cook)
1890-1980 . . . . **CLC 7**
See also CA 85-88; 102; CANR 30; DLB 7;
DLBY 80; SATA-Obit 25

Connor, Ralph . . . . **TCLC 31**
See also Gordon, Charles William
See also DLB 92

Conrad, Joseph
1857-1924 . . . . **TCLC 1, 6, 13, 25, 43, 57;
DA; DAB; SSC 9; WLC**
See also CA 104; 131; CDBLB 1890-1914;
DLB 10, 34, 98, 156; MTCW; SATA 27

Conrad, Robert Arnold
See Hart, Moss

Conroy, Pat 1945- . . . . **CLC 30, 74**
See also AAYA 8; AITN 1; CA 85-88;
CANR 24; DLB 6; MTCW

Constant (de Rebecque), (Henri) Benjamin
1767-1830 . . . . **NCLC 6**
See also DLB 119

Conybeare, Charles Augustus
See Eliot, T(homas) S(tearns)

Cook, Michael 1933- . . . . **CLC 58**
See also CA 93-96; DLB 53

Cook, Robin 1940- . . . . **CLC 14**
See also BEST 90:2; CA 108; 111;
CANR 41

Cook, Roy
See Silverberg, Robert

Cooke, Elizabeth 1948- . . . . **CLC 55**
See also CA 129

Cooke, John Esten 1830-1886 . . . . . **NCLC 5**
See also DLB 3

Cooke, John Estes
See Baum, L(yman) Frank

Cooke, M. E.
See Creasey, John

Cooke, Margaret
See Creasey, John

Cooney, Ray . . . . **CLC 62**

Cooper, Douglas 1960- . . . . **CLC 86**

Cooper, Henry St. John
See Creasey, John

Cooper, J. California . . . . **CLC 56**
See also AAYA 12; BW 1; CA 125

Cooper, James Fenimore
1789-1851 . . . . **NCLC 1, 27**
See also CDALB 1640-1865; DLB 3;
SATA 19

Coover, Robert (Lowell)
1932- . . **CLC 3, 7, 15, 32, 46, 87; SSC 15**
See also CA 45-48; CANR 3, 37; DLB 2;
DLBY 81; MTCW

Copeland, Stewart (Armstrong)
1952- . . . . **CLC 26**

Coppard, A(lfred) E(dgar)
1878-1957 . . . . **TCLC 5; SSC 21**
See also CA 114; YABC 1

Coppee, Francois 1842-1908 . . . . . . **TCLC 25**

Coppola, Francis Ford 1939- . . . . **CLC 16**
See also CA 77-80; CANR 40; DLB 44

Corbiere, Tristan 1845-1875 . . . . . **NCLC 43**

Corcoran, Barbara 1911- . . . . **CLC 17**
See also AAYA 14; CA 21-24R; CAAS 2;
CANR 11, 28, 48; DLB 52; JRDA;
SAAS 20; SATA 3, 77

Cordelier, Maurice
See Giraudoux, (Hippolyte) Jean

Corelli, Marie 1855-1924 . . . . **TCLC 51**
See also Mackay, Mary
See also DLB 34, 156

Corman, Cid . . . . **CLC 9**
See also Corman, Sidney
See also CAAS 2; DLB 5

Corman, Sidney 1924-
See Corman, Cid
See also CA 85-88; CANR 44

Cormier, Robert (Edmund)
1925- . . . . **CLC 12, 30; DA; DAB**
See also AAYA 3; CA 1-4R; CANR 5, 23;
CDALB 1968-1988; CLR 12; DLB 52;
JRDA; MAICYA; MTCW; SATA 10, 45,
83

Corn, Alfred (DeWitt III) 1943- . . . . **CLC 33**
See also CA 104; CANR 44; DLB 120;
DLBY 80

Corneille, Pierre 1606-1684 . . . . **LC 28; DAB**

Cornwell, David (John Moore)
1931- . . . . **CLC 9, 15**
See also le Carre, John
See also CA 5-8R; CANR 13, 33; MTCW

Corso, (Nunzio) Gregory 1930- . . . **CLC 1, 11**
See also CA 5-8R; CANR 41; DLB 5, 16;
MTCW

Cortazar, Julio
1914-1984 . . . . . . **CLC 2, 3, 5, 10, 13, 15,
33, 34; HLC; SSC 7**
See also CA 21-24R; CANR 12, 32;
DLB 113; HW; MTCW

CORTES, HERNAN 1484-1547 . . . . . **LC 31**

Corwin, Cecil
See Kornbluth, C(yril) M.

Cosic, Dobrica 1921- . . . . **CLC 14**
See also CA 122; 138

Costain, Thomas B(ertram)
1885-1965 . . . . **CLC 30**
See also CA 5-8R; 25-28R; DLB 9

Costantini, Humberto
1924(?)-1987 . . . . **CLC 49**
See also CA 131; 122; HW

Costello, Elvis 1955- . . . . **CLC 21**

Cotter, Joseph Seamon Sr.
1861-1949 . . . . **TCLC 28; BLC**
See also BW 1; CA 124; DLB 50

Couch, Arthur Thomas Quiller
See Quiller-Couch, Arthur Thomas

Coulton, James
See Hansen, Joseph

Couperus, Louis (Marie Anne)
1863-1923 . . . . **TCLC 15**
See also CA 115

Coupland, Douglas 1961- . . . . **CLC 85**
See also CA 142

Court, Wesli
See Turco, Lewis (Putnam)

Courtenay, Bryce 1933- . . . . **CLC 59**
See also CA 138

Courtney, Robert
See Ellison, Harlan (Jay)

Cousteau, Jacques-Yves 1910- . . . . . . **CLC 30**
See also CA 65-68; CANR 15; MTCW;
SATA 38

Coward, Noel (Peirce)
1899-1973 . . . . **CLC 1, 9, 29, 51**
See also AITN 1; CA 17-18; 41-44R;
CANR 35; CAP 2; CDBLB 1914-1945;
DLB 10; MTCW

Cowley, Malcolm 1898-1989 . . . . **CLC 39**
See also CA 5-8R; 128; CANR 3; DLB 4,
48; DLBY 81, 89; MTCW

Cowper, William 1731-1800 . . . . **NCLC 8**
See also DLB 104, 109

Cox, William Trevor 1928- . . . **CLC 9, 14, 71**
See also Trevor, William
See also CA 9-12R; CANR 4, 37; DLB 14;
MTCW

Coyne, P. J.
See Masters, Hilary

Cozzens, James Gould
1903-1978 . . . . **CLC 1, 4, 11**
See also CA 9-12R; 81-84; CANR 19;
CDALB 1941-1968; DLB 9; DLBD 2;
DLBY 84; MTCW

Crabbe, George 1754-1832 . . . . **NCLC 26**
See also DLB 93

Craig, A. A.
See Anderson, Poul (William)

Craik, Dinah Maria (Mulock)
 1826-1887 .... NCLC 38
 See also DLB 35; MAICYA; SATA 34

Cram, Ralph Adams   1863-1942.... TCLC 45

Crane, (Harold) Hart
 1899-1932 .... TCLC 2, 5; DA; DAB;
 PC 3; WLC
 See also CA 104; 127; CDALB 1917-1929;
 DLB 4, 48; MTCW

Crane, R(onald) S(almon)
 1886-1967 .... CLC 27
 See also CA 85-88; DLB 63

Crane, Stephen (Townley)
 1871-1900 .... TCLC 11, 17, 32; DA;
 DAB; SSC 7; WLC
 See also CA 109; 140; CDALB 1865-1917;
 DLB 12, 54, 78; YABC 2

Crase, Douglas   1944- .... CLC 58
 See also CA 106

Crashaw, Richard   1612(?)-1649...... LC 24
 See also DLB 126

Craven, Margaret   1901-1980....... CLC 17
 See also CA 103

Crawford, F(rancis) Marion
 1854-1909 .... TCLC 10
 See also CA 107; DLB 71

Crawford, Isabella Valancy
 1850-1887 .... NCLC 12
 See also DLB 92

Crayon, Geoffrey
 See Irving, Washington

Creasey, John   1908-1973.......... CLC 11
 See also CA 5-8R; 41-44R; CANR 8;
 DLB 77; MTCW

Crebillon, Claude Prosper Jolyot de (fils)
 1707-1777 .... LC 28

Credo
 See Creasey, John

Creeley, Robert (White)
 1926- ..... CLC 1, 2, 4, 8, 11, 15, 36, 78
 See also CA 1-4R; CAAS 10; CANR 23, 43;
 DLB 5, 16; MTCW

Crews, Harry (Eugene)
 1935- .... CLC 6, 23, 49
 See also AITN 1; CA 25-28R; CANR 20;
 DLB 6, 143; MTCW

Crichton, (John) Michael
 1942- .... CLC 2, 6, 54, 90
 See also AAYA 10; AITN 2; CA 25-28R;
 CANR 13, 40; DLBY 81; JRDA;
 MTCW; SATA 9

Crispin, Edmund .... CLC 22
 See also Montgomery, (Robert) Bruce
 See also DLB 87

Cristofer, Michael   1945(?)- .... CLC 28
 See also CA 110; DLB 7

Croce, Benedetto   1866-1952 ...... TCLC 37
 See also CA 120

Crockett, David   1786-1836 .... NCLC 8
 See also DLB 3, 11

Crockett, Davy
 See Crockett, David

Crofts, Freeman Wills
 1879-1957 .... TCLC 55
 See also CA 115; DLB 77

Croker, John Wilson   1780-1857 .. NCLC 10
 See also DLB 110

Crommelynck, Fernand   1885-1970 .. CLC 75
 See also CA 89-92

Cronin, A(rchibald) J(oseph)
 1896-1981 .... CLC 32
 See also CA 1-4R; 102; CANR 5; SATA 47;
 SATA-Obit 25

Cross, Amanda
 See Heilbrun, Carolyn G(old)

Crothers, Rachel   1878(?)-1958..... TCLC 19
 See also CA 113; DLB 7

Croves, Hal
 See Traven, B.

Crowfield, Christopher
 See Stowe, Harriet (Elizabeth) Beecher

Crowley, Aleister.................. TCLC 7
 See also Crowley, Edward Alexander

Crowley, Edward Alexander   1875-1947
 See Crowley, Aleister
 See also CA 104

Crowley, John   1942-.............. CLC 57
 See also CA 61-64; CANR 43; DLBY 82;
 SATA 65

Crud
 See Crumb, R(obert)

Crumarums
 See Crumb, R(obert)

Crumb, R(obert)   1943-............ CLC 17
 See also CA 106

Crumbum
 See Crumb, R(obert)

Crumski
 See Crumb, R(obert)

Crum the Bum
 See Crumb, R(obert)

Crunk
 See Crumb, R(obert)

Crustt
 See Crumb, R(obert)

Cryer, Gretchen (Kiger)   1935-...... CLC 21
 See also CA 114; 123

Csath, Geza   1887-1919.......... TCLC 13
 See also CA 111

Cudlip, David   1933-.............. CLC 34

Cullen, Countee
 1903-1946 ...... TCLC 4, 37; BLC; DA
 See also BW 1; CA 108; 124;
 CDALB 1917-1929; DLB 4, 48, 51;
 MTCW; SATA 18

Cum, R.
 See Crumb, R(obert)

Cummings, Bruce F(rederick)   1889-1919
 See Barbellion, W. N. P.
 See also CA 123

Cummings, E(dward) E(stlin)
 1894-1962 ...... CLC 1, 3, 8, 12, 15, 68;
 DA; DAB; PC 5; WLC 2
 See also CA 73-76; CANR 31;
 CDALB 1929-1941; DLB 4, 48; MTCW

Cunha, Euclides (Rodrigues Pimenta) da
 1866-1909 .... TCLC 24
 See also CA 123

Cunningham, E. V.
 See Fast, Howard (Melvin)

Cunningham, J(ames) V(incent)
 1911-1985 .... CLC 3, 31
 See also CA 1-4R; 115; CANR 1; DLB 5

Cunningham, Julia (Woolfolk)
 1916- .... CLC 12
 See also CA 9-12R; CANR 4, 19, 36;
 JRDA; MAICYA; SAAS 2; SATA 1, 26

Cunningham, Michael   1952- ...... CLC 34
 See also CA 136

Cunninghame Graham, R(obert) B(ontine)
 1852-1936 .... TCLC 19
 See also Graham, R(obert) B(ontine)
 Cunninghame
 See also CA 119; DLB 98

Currie, Ellen   19(?)-.............. CLC 44

Curtin, Philip
 See Lowndes, Marie Adelaide (Belloc)

Curtis, Price
 See Ellison, Harlan (Jay)

Cutrate, Joe
 See Spiegelman, Art

Czaczkes, Shmuel Yosef
 See Agnon, S(hmuel) Y(osef Halevi)

Dabrowska, Maria (Szumska)
 1889-1965 .... CLC 15
 See also CA 106

Dabydeen, David   1955- .... CLC 34
 See also BW 1; CA 125

Dacey, Philip   1939- .... CLC 51
 See also CA 37-40R; CAAS 17; CANR 14,
 32; DLB 105

Dagerman, Stig (Halvard)
 1923-1954 .... TCLC 17
 See also CA 117

Dahl, Roald
 1916-1990 ...... CLC 1, 6, 18, 79; DAB
 See also AAYA 15; CA 1-4R; 133;
 CANR 6, 32, 37; CLR 1, 7; DLB 139;
 JRDA; MAICYA; MTCW; SATA 1, 26,
 73; SATA-Obit 65

Dahlberg, Edward   1900-1977... CLC 1, 7, 14
 See also CA 9-12R; 69-72; CANR 31;
 DLB 48; MTCW

Dale, Colin..................... TCLC 18
 See also Lawrence, T(homas) E(dward)

Dale, George E.
 See Asimov, Isaac

Daly, Elizabeth   1878-1967......... CLC 52
 See also CA 23-24; 25-28R; CAP 2

Daly, Maureen   1921-............. CLC 17
 See also AAYA 5; CANR 37; JRDA;
 MAICYA; SAAS 1; SATA 2

Damas, Leon-Gontran   1912-1978 ... CLC 84
 See also BW 1; CA 125; 73-76

Daniel, Samuel   1562(?)-1619........ LC 24
 See also DLB 62

Daniels, Brett
 See Adler, Renata

Dannay, Frederic   1905-1982 .... CLC 11
 See also Queen, Ellery
 See also CA 1-4R; 107; CANR 1, 39;
 DLB 137; MTCW

D'Annunzio, Gabriele
1863-1938 .... **TCLC 6, 40**
See also CA 104

d'Antibes, Germain
See Simenon, Georges (Jacques Christian)

Danvers, Dennis 1947- .... **CLC 70**

Danziger, Paula 1944- .... **CLC 21**
See also AAYA 4; CA 112; 115; CANR 37;
CLR 20; JRDA; MAICYA; SATA 36,
63; SATA-Brief 30

Da Ponte, Lorenzo 1749-1838 .... **NCLC 50**

Dario, Ruben 1867-1916 .... **TCLC 4; HLC**
See also CA 131; HW; MTCW

Darley, George 1795-1846 .... **NCLC 2**
See also DLB 96

Daryush, Elizabeth 1887-1977.... **CLC 6, 19**
See also CA 49-52; CANR 3; DLB 20

**Dashwood, Edmee Elizabeth Monica de la
Pasture** 1890-1943
See Delafield, E. M.
See also CA 119

Daudet, (Louis Marie) Alphonse
1840-1897 .... **NCLC 1**
See also DLB 123

Daumal, Rene 1908-1944 .... **TCLC 14**
See also CA 114

Davenport, Guy (Mattison, Jr.)
1927- .... **CLC 6, 14, 38; SSC 16**
See also CA 33-36R; CANR 23; DLB 130

Davidson, Avram 1923-
See Queen, Ellery
See also CA 101; CANR 26; DLB 8

Davidson, Donald (Grady)
1893-1968 .... **CLC 2, 13, 19**
See also CA 5-8R; 25-28R; CANR 4;
DLB 45

Davidson, Hugh
See Hamilton, Edmond

Davidson, John 1857-1909 .... **TCLC 24**
See also CA 118; DLB 19

Davidson, Sara 1943- .... **CLC 9**
See also CA 81-84; CANR 44

Davie, Donald (Alfred)
1922- .... **CLC 5, 8, 10, 31**
See also CA 1-4R; CAAS 3; CANR 1, 44;
DLB 27; MTCW

Davies, Ray(mond Douglas) 1944- .. **CLC 21**
See also CA 116; 146

Davies, Rhys 1903-1978 .... **CLC 23**
See also CA 9-12R; 81-84; CANR 4;
DLB 139

Davies, (William) Robertson
1913- ..... **CLC 2, 7, 13, 25, 42, 75; DA;
DAB; WLC**
See also BEST 89:2; CA 33-36R; CANR 17,
42; DLB 68; MTCW

Davies, W(illiam) H(enry)
1871-1940 .... **TCLC 5**
See also CA 104; DLB 19

Davies, Walter C.
See Kornbluth, C(yril) M.

Davis, Angela (Yvonne) 1944- ...... **CLC 77**
See also BW 2; CA 57-60; CANR 10

Davis, B. Lynch
See Bioy Casares, Adolfo; Borges, Jorge
Luis

Davis, Gordon
See Hunt, E(verette) Howard, (Jr.)

Davis, Harold Lenoir 1896-1960.... **CLC 49**
See also CA 89-92; DLB 9

Davis, Rebecca (Blaine) Harding
1831-1910 .... **TCLC 6**
See also CA 104; DLB 74

Davis, Richard Harding
1864-1916 .... **TCLC 24**
See also CA 114; DLB 12, 23, 78, 79

Davison, Frank Dalby 1893-1970 ... **CLC 15**
See also CA 116

Davison, Lawrence H.
See Lawrence, D(avid) H(erbert Richards)

Davison, Peter (Hubert) 1928- ..... **CLC 28**
See also CA 9-12R; CAAS 4; CANR 3, 43;
DLB 5

Davys, Mary 1674-1732 .... **LC 1**
See also DLB 39

Dawson, Fielding 1930- .... **CLC 6**
See also CA 85-88; DLB 130

Dawson, Peter
See Faust, Frederick (Schiller)

Day, Clarence (Shepard, Jr.)
1874-1935 .... **TCLC 25**
See also CA 108; DLB 11

Day, Thomas 1748-1789 .... **LC 1**
See also DLB 39; YABC 1

Day Lewis, C(ecil)
1904-1972 .... **CLC 1, 6, 10; PC 11**
See also Blake, Nicholas
See also CA 13-16; 33-36R; CANR 34;
CAP 1; DLB 15, 20; MTCW

Dazai, Osamu .... **TCLC 11**
See also Tsushima, Shuji

de Andrade, Carlos Drummond
See Drummond de Andrade, Carlos

Deane, Norman
See Creasey, John

**de Beauvoir, Simone (Lucie Ernestine Marie
Bertrand)**
See Beauvoir, Simone (Lucie Ernestine
Marie Bertrand) de

de Brissac, Malcolm
See Dickinson, Peter (Malcolm)

de Chardin, Pierre Teilhard
See Teilhard de Chardin, (Marie Joseph)
Pierre

Dee, John 1527-1608 .... **LC 20**

Deer, Sandra 1940- .... **CLC 45**

De Ferrari, Gabriella 1941- .... **CLC 65**
See also CA 146

Defoe, Daniel
1660(?)-1731 .... **LC 1; DA; DAB; WLC**
See also CDBLB 1660-1789; DLB 39, 95,
101; JRDA; MAICYA; SATA 22

de Gourmont, Remy
See Gourmont, Remy de

de Hartog, Jan 1914- .... **CLC 19**
See also CA 1-4R; CANR 1

de Hostos, E. M.
See Hostos (y Bonilla), Eugenio Maria de

de Hostos, Eugenio M.
See Hostos (y Bonilla), Eugenio Maria de

Deighton, Len .... **CLC 4, 7, 22, 46**
See also Deighton, Leonard Cyril
See also AAYA 6; BEST 89:2;
CDBLB 1960 to Present; DLB 87

Deighton, Leonard Cyril 1929-
See Deighton, Len
See also CA 9-12R; CANR 19, 33; MTCW

Dekker, Thomas 1572(?)-1632 .... **LC 22**
See also CDBLB Before 1660; DLB 62

Delafield, E. M. 1890-1943 .... **TCLC 61**
See also Dashwood, Edmee Elizabeth
Monica de la Pasture
See also DLB 34

de la Mare, Walter (John)
1873-1956 .... **TCLC 4, 53; DAB;
SSC 14; WLC**
See also CDBLB 1914-1945; CLR 23;
DLB 19, 153; SATA 16

Delaney, Franey
See O'Hara, John (Henry)

Delaney, Shelagh 1939- .... **CLC 29**
See also CA 17-20R; CANR 30;
CDBLB 1960 to Present; DLB 13;
MTCW

Delany, Mary (Granville Pendarves)
1700-1788 .... **LC 12**

Delany, Samuel R(ay, Jr.)
1942- .... **CLC 8, 14, 38; BLC**
See also BW 2; CA 81-84; CANR 27, 43;
DLB 8, 33; MTCW

De La Ramee, (Marie) Louise 1839-1908
See Ouida
See also SATA 20

de la Roche, Mazo 1879-1961 ...... **CLC 14**
See also CA 85-88; CANR 30; DLB 68;
SATA 64

Delbanco, Nicholas (Franklin)
1942- .... **CLC 6, 13**
See also CA 17-20R; CAAS 2; CANR 29;
DLB 6

del Castillo, Michel 1933- .... **CLC 38**
See also CA 109

Deledda, Grazia (Cosima)
1875(?)-1936 .... **TCLC 23**
See also CA 123

Delibes, Miguel .... **CLC 8, 18**
See also Delibes Setien, Miguel

Delibes Setien, Miguel 1920-
See Delibes, Miguel
See also CA 45-48; CANR 1, 32; HW;
MTCW

DeLillo, Don
1936- ..... **CLC 8, 10, 13, 27, 39, 54, 76**
See also BEST 89:1; CA 81-84; CANR 21;
DLB 6; MTCW

de Lisser, H. G.
See De Lisser, Herbert George
See also DLB 117

De Lisser, Herbert George
1878-1944 .... **TCLC 12**
See also de Lisser, H. G.
See also BW 2; CA 109

Deloria, Vine (Victor), Jr. 1933-.... **CLC 21**
See also CA 53-56; CANR 5, 20, 48;
MTCW; NNAL; SATA 21

Del Vecchio, John M(ichael)
1947-...................... **CLC 29**
See also CA 110; DLBD 9

de Man, Paul (Adolph Michel)
1919-1983 .... **CLC 55**
See also CA 128; 111; DLB 67; MTCW

De Marinis, Rick 1934-.......... **CLC 54**
See also CA 57-60; CANR 9, 25

Demby, William 1922-....... **CLC 53; BLC**
See also BW 1; CA 81-84; DLB 33

Demijohn, Thom
See Disch, Thomas M(ichael)

de Montherlant, Henry (Milon)
See Montherlant, Henry (Milon) de

Demosthenes 384B.C.-322B.C. ... **CMLC 13**

de Natale, Francine
See Malzberg, Barry N(athaniel)

Denby, Edwin (Orr) 1903-1983..... **CLC 48**
See also CA 138; 110

Denis, Julio
See Cortazar, Julio

Denmark, Harrison
See Zelazny, Roger (Joseph)

Dennis, John 1658-1734........... **LC 11**
See also DLB 101

Dennis, Nigel (Forbes) 1912-1989.... **CLC 8**
See also CA 25-28R; 129; DLB 13, 15;
MTCW

De Palma, Brian (Russell) 1940-.... **CLC 20**
See also CA 109

De Quincey, Thomas 1785-1859 ... **NCLC 4**
See also CDBLB 1789-1832; DLB 110; 144

Deren, Eleanora 1908(?)-1961
See Deren, Maya
See also CA 111

Deren, Maya .... **CLC 16**
See also Deren, Eleanora

Derleth, August (William)
1909-1971 .... **CLC 31**
See also CA 1-4R; 29-32R; CANR 4;
DLB 9; SATA 5

Der Nister 1884-1950............ **TCLC 56**

de Routisie, Albert
See Aragon, Louis

Derrida, Jacques 1930-......... **CLC 24, 87**
See also CA 124; 127

Derry Down Derry
See Lear, Edward

Dersonnes, Jacques
See Simenon, Georges (Jacques Christian)

Desai, Anita 1937-...... **CLC 19, 37; DAB**
See also CA 81-84; CANR 33; MTCW;
SATA 63

de Saint-Luc, Jean
See Glassco, John

de Saint Roman, Arnaud
See Aragon, Louis

Descartes, Rene 1596-1650 .... **LC 20**

De Sica, Vittorio 1901(?)-1974 ..... **CLC 20**
See also CA 117

Desnos, Robert 1900-1945....... **TCLC 22**
See also CA 121

Destouches, Louis-Ferdinand
1894-1961 .... **CLC 9, 15**
See also Celine, Louis-Ferdinand
See also CA 85-88; CANR 28; MTCW

Deutsch, Babette 1895-1982 .... **CLC 18**
See also CA 1-4R; 108; CANR 4; DLB 45;
SATA 1; SATA-Obit 33

Devenant, William 1606-1649 ...... **LC 13**

Devkota, Laxmiprasad
1909-1959 .... **TCLC 23**
See also CA 123

De Voto, Bernard (Augustine)
1897-1955 .... **TCLC 29**
See also CA 113; DLB 9

De Vries, Peter
1910-1993 .... **CLC 1, 2, 3, 7, 10, 28, 46**
See also CA 17-20R; 142; CANR 41;
DLB 6; DLBY 82; MTCW

Dexter, Martin
See Faust, Frederick (Schiller)

Dexter, Pete 1943-........... **CLC 34, 55**
See also BEST 89:2; CA 127; 131; MTCW

Diamano, Silmang
See Senghor, Leopold Sedar

Diamond, Neil 1941- .... **CLC 30**
See also CA 108

Diaz del Castillo, Bernal 1496-1584.. **LC 31**

di Bassetto, Corno
See Shaw, George Bernard

Dick, Philip K(indred)
1928-1982 .... **CLC 10, 30, 72**
See also CA 49-52; 106; CANR 2, 16;
DLB 8; MTCW

Dickens, Charles (John Huffam)
1812-1870 ...... **NCLC 3, 8, 18, 26, 37,
50; DA; DAB; SSC 17; WLC**
See also CDBLB 1832-1890; DLB 21, 55,
70; JRDA; MAICYA; SATA 15

Dickey, James (Lafayette)
1923- .... **CLC 1, 2, 4, 7, 10, 15, 47**
See also AITN 1, 2; CA 9-12R; CABS 2;
CANR 10, 48; CDALB 1968-1988;
DLB 5; DLBD 7; DLBY 82, 93; MTCW

Dickey, William 1928-1994 ..... **CLC 3, 28**
See also CA 9-12R; 145; CANR 24; DLB 5

Dickinson, Charles 1951-.......... **CLC 49**
See also CA 128

Dickinson, Emily (Elizabeth)
1830-1886 .... **NCLC 21; DA; DAB;
PC 1; WLC**
See also CDALB 1865-1917; DLB 1;
SATA 29

Dickinson, Peter (Malcolm)
1927-.................... **CLC 12, 35**
See also AAYA 9; CA 41-44R; CANR 31;
CLR 29; DLB 87; JRDA; MAICYA;
SATA 5, 62

Dickson, Carr
See Carr, John Dickson

Dickson, Carter
See Carr, John Dickson

Diderot, Denis 1713-1784 .... **LC 26**

Didion, Joan 1934-..... **CLC 1, 3, 8, 14, 32**
See also AITN 1; CA 5-8R; CANR 14;
CDALB 1968-1988; DLB 2; DLBY 81,
86; MTCW

Dietrich, Robert
See Hunt, E(verette) Howard, (Jr.)

Dillard, Annie 1945-............ **CLC 9, 60**
See also AAYA 6; CA 49-52; CANR 3, 43;
DLBY 80; MTCW; SATA 10

Dillard, R(ichard) H(enry) W(ilde)
1937-...................... **CLC 5**
See also CA 21-24R; CAAS 7; CANR 10;
DLB 5

Dillon, Eilis 1920-1994............ **CLC 17**
See also CA 9-12R; 147; CAAS 3; CANR 4,
38; CLR 26; MAICYA; SATA 2, 74;
SATA-Obit 83

Dimont, Penelope
See Mortimer, Penelope (Ruth)

Dinesen, Isak.......... **CLC 10, 29; SSC 7**
See also Blixen, Karen (Christentze
Dinesen)

Ding Ling....................... **CLC 68**
See also Chiang Pin-chin

Disch, Thomas M(ichael) 1940-... **CLC 7, 36**
See also CA 21-24R; CAAS 4; CANR 17,
36; CLR 18; DLB 8; MAICYA; MTCW;
SAAS 15; SATA 54

Disch, Tom
See Disch, Thomas M(ichael)

d'Isly, Georges
See Simenon, Georges (Jacques Christian)

Disraeli, Benjamin 1804-1881 .. **NCLC 2, 39**
See also DLB 21, 55

Ditcum, Steve
See Crumb, R(obert)

Dixon, Paige
See Corcoran, Barbara

Dixon, Stephen 1936-..... **CLC 52; SSC 16**
See also CA 89-92; CANR 17, 40; DLB 130

Dobell, Sydney Thompson
1824-1874 .... **NCLC 43**
See also DLB 32

Doblin, Alfred .... **TCLC 13**
See also Doeblin, Alfred

Dobrolyubov, Nikolai Alexandrovich
1836-1861 .... **NCLC 5**

Dobyns, Stephen 1941-............ **CLC 37**
See also CA 45-48; CANR 2, 18

Doctorow, E(dgar) L(aurence)
1931- ..... **CLC 6, 11, 15, 18, 37, 44, 65**
See also AITN 2; BEST 89:3; CA 45-48;
CANR 2, 33; CDALB 1968-1988; DLB 2,
28; DLBY 80; MTCW

Dodgson, Charles Lutwidge 1832-1898
See Carroll, Lewis
See also CLR 2; DA; DAB; MAICYA;
YABC 2

Dodson, Owen (Vincent)
1914-1983 .... **CLC 79; BLC**
See also BW 1; CA 65-68; 110; CANR 24;
DLB 76

Doeblin, Alfred 1878-1957........ **TCLC 13**
See also Doblin, Alfred
See also CA 110; 141; DLB 66

Doerr, Harriet   1910- .... **CLC 34**
See also CA 117; 122; CANR 47

Domecq, H(onorio) Bustos
See Bioy Casares, Adolfo; Borges, Jorge
Luis

Domini, Rey
See Lorde, Audre (Geraldine)

Dominique
See Proust, (Valentin-Louis-George-Eugene-)
Marcel

Don, A
See Stephen, Leslie

Donaldson, Stephen R.   1947-....... **CLC 46**
See also CA 89-92; CANR 13

Donleavy, J(ames) P(atrick)
1926- .... **CLC 1, 4, 6, 10, 45**
See also AITN 2; CA 9-12R; CANR 24, 49;
DLB 6; MTCW

Donne, John
1572-1631 .. **LC 10, 24; DA; DAB; PC 1**
See also CDBLB Before 1660; DLB 121,
151

Donnell, David   1939(?)-........... **CLC 34**

Donoghue, P. S.
See Hunt, E(verette) Howard, (Jr.)

Donoso (Yanez), Jose
1924- .... **CLC 4, 8, 11, 32; HLC**
See also CA 81-84; CANR 32; DLB 113;
HW; MTCW

Donovan, John   1928-1992 .... **CLC 35**
See also CA 97-100; 137; CLR 3;
MAICYA; SATA 72; SATA-Brief 29

Don Roberto
See Cunninghame Graham, R(obert)
B(ontine)

Doolittle, Hilda
1886-1961 ..... **CLC 3, 8, 14, 31, 34, 73;
DA; PC 5; WLC**
See also H. D.
See also CA 97-100; CANR 35; DLB 4, 45;
MTCW

Dorfman, Ariel   1942-.... **CLC 48, 77; HLC**
See also CA 124; 130; HW

Dorn, Edward (Merton)   1929-... **CLC 10, 18**
See also CA 93-96; CANR 42; DLB 5

Dorsan, Luc
See Simenon, Georges (Jacques Christian)

Dorsange, Jean
See Simenon, Georges (Jacques Christian)

Dos Passos, John (Roderigo)
1896-1970 ..... **CLC 1, 4, 8, 11, 15, 25,
34, 82; DA; DAB; WLC**
See also CA 1-4R; 29-32R; CANR 3;
CDALB 1929-1941; DLB 4, 9; DLBD 1;
MTCW

Dossage, Jean
See Simenon, Georges (Jacques Christian)

Dostoevsky, Fedor Mikhailovich
1821-1881 ...... **NCLC 2, 7, 21, 33, 43;
DA; DAB; SSC 2; WLC**

Doughty, Charles M(ontagu)
1843-1926 .... **TCLC 27**
See also CA 115; DLB 19, 57

Douglas, Ellen .... **CLC 73**
See also Haxton, Josephine Ayres;
Williamson, Ellen Douglas

Douglas, Gavin   1475(?)-1522........ **LC 20**

Douglas, Keith   1920-1944 .... **TCLC 40**
See also DLB 27

Douglas, Leonard
See Bradbury, Ray (Douglas)

Douglas, Michael
See Crichton, (John) Michael

Douglass, Frederick
1817(?)-1895 ...... **NCLC 7; BLC; DA;
WLC**
See also CDALB 1640-1865; DLB 1, 43, 50,
79; SATA 29

Dourado, (Waldomiro Freitas) Autran
1926- .... **CLC 23, 60**
See also CA 25-28R; CANR 34

Dourado, Waldomiro Autran
See Dourado, (Waldomiro Freitas) Autran

Dove, Rita (Frances)
1952- .... **CLC 50, 81; PC 6**
See also BW 2; CA 109; CAAS 19;
CANR 27, 42; DLB 120

Dowell, Coleman   1925-1985....... **CLC 60**
See also CA 25-28R; 117; CANR 10;
DLB 130

Dowson, Ernest Christopher
1867-1900 .... **TCLC 4**
See also CA 105; DLB 19, 135

Doyle, A. Conan
See Doyle, Arthur Conan

Doyle, Arthur Conan
1859-1930 .... **TCLC 7; DA; DAB;
SSC 12; WLC**
See also AAYA 14; CA 104; 122;
CDBLB 1890-1914; DLB 18, 70, 156;
MTCW; SATA 24

Doyle, Conan
See Doyle, Arthur Conan

Doyle, John
See Graves, Robert (von Ranke)

Doyle, Roddy   1958(?)-............ **CLC 81**
See also AAYA 14; CA 143

Doyle, Sir A. Conan
See Doyle, Arthur Conan

Doyle, Sir Arthur Conan
See Doyle, Arthur Conan

Dr. A
See Asimov, Isaac; Silverstein, Alvin

Drabble, Margaret
1939- ... **CLC 2, 3, 5, 8, 10, 22, 53; DAB**
See also CA 13-16R; CANR 18, 35;
CDBLB 1960 to Present; DLB 14, 155;
MTCW; SATA 48

Drapier, M. B.
See Swift, Jonathan

Drayham, James
See Mencken, H(enry) L(ouis)

Drayton, Michael   1563-1631........ **LC 8**

Dreadstone, Carl
See Campbell, (John) Ramsey

Dreiser, Theodore (Herman Albert)
1871-1945 .... **TCLC 10, 18, 35; DA;
WLC**
See also CA 106; 132; CDALB 1865-1917;
DLB 9, 12, 102, 137; DLBD 1; MTCW

Drexler, Rosalyn   1926- .... **CLC 2, 6**
See also CA 81-84

Dreyer, Carl Theodor   1889-1968.... **CLC 16**
See also CA 116

Drieu la Rochelle, Pierre(-Eugene)
1893-1945 .... **TCLC 21**
See also CA 117; DLB 72

Drinkwater, John   1882-1937...... **TCLC 57**
See also CA 109; DLB 10, 19, 149

Drop Shot
See Cable, George Washington

Droste-Hulshoff, Annette Freiin von
1797-1848 .... **NCLC 3**
See also DLB 133

Drummond, Walter
See Silverberg, Robert

Drummond, William Henry
1854-1907 .... **TCLC 25**
See also DLB 92

Drummond de Andrade, Carlos
1902-1987 .... **CLC 18**
See also Andrade, Carlos Drummond de
See also CA 132; 123

Drury, Allen (Stuart)   1918-........ **CLC 37**
See also CA 57-60; CANR 18

Dryden, John
1631-1700 .... **LC 3, 21; DA; DAB;
DC 3; WLC**
See also CDBLB 1660-1789; DLB 80, 101,
131

Duberman, Martin   1930-........... **CLC 8**
See also CA 1-4R; CANR 2

Dubie, Norman (Evans)   1945-...... **CLC 36**
See also CA 69-72; CANR 12; DLB 120

Du Bois, W(illiam) E(dward) B(urghardt)
1868-1963 ...... **CLC 1, 2, 13, 64; BLC;
DA; WLC**
See also BW 1; CA 85-88; CANR 34;
CDALB 1865-1917; DLB 47, 50, 91;
MTCW; SATA 42

Dubus, Andre   1936-... **CLC 13, 36; SSC 15**
See also CA 21-24R; CANR 17; DLB 130

Duca Minimo
See D'Annunzio, Gabriele

Ducharme, Rejean   1941-.......... **CLC 74**
See also DLB 60

Duclos, Charles Pinot   1704-1772 ..... **LC 1**

Dudek, Louis   1918- .... **CLC 11, 19**
See also CA 45-48; CAAS 14; CANR 1;
DLB 88

Duerrenmatt, Friedrich
1921-1990 ...... **CLC 1, 4, 8, 11, 15, 43**
See also CA 17-20R; CANR 33; DLB 69,
124; MTCW

Duffy, Bruce   (?)-................ **CLC 50**

Duffy, Maureen   1933- .... **CLC 37**
See also CA 25-28R; CANR 33; DLB 14;
MTCW

Dugan, Alan   1923- .... **CLC 2, 6**
See also CA 81-84; DLB 5

Author Index

Eiseley, Loren Corey 1907-1977 ..... **CLC 7**
See also AAYA 5; CA 1-4R; 73-76;
CANR 6

Eisenstadt, Jill 1963- .... **CLC 50**
See also CA 140

Eisenstein, Sergei (Mikhailovich)
1898-1948 .... **TCLC 57**
See also CA 114

Eisner, Simon
See Kornbluth, C(yril) M.

Ekeloef, (Bengt) Gunnar
1907-1968 .... **CLC 27**
See also CA 123; 25-28R

Ekelof, (Bengt) Gunnar
See Ekeloef, (Bengt) Gunnar

Ekwensi, C. O. D.
See Ekwensi, Cyprian (Odiatu Duaka)

Ekwensi, Cyprian (Odiatu Duaka)
1921- .... **CLC 4; BLC**
See also BW 2; CA 29-32R; CANR 18, 42;
DLB 117; MTCW; SATA 66

Elaine .... **TCLC 18**
See also Leverson, Ada

El Crummo
See Crumb, R(obert)

Elia
See Lamb, Charles

Eliade, Mircea 1907-1986 .... **CLC 19**
See also CA 65-68; 119; CANR 30; MTCW

Eliot, A. D.
See Jewett, (Theodora) Sarah Orne

Eliot, Alice
See Jewett, (Theodora) Sarah Orne

Eliot, Dan
See Silverberg, Robert

Eliot, George
1819-1880 ..... **NCLC 4, 13, 23, 41, 49;**
DA; DAB; WLC
See also CDBLB 1832-1890; DLB 21, 35, 55

Eliot, John 1604-1690 .... **LC 5**
See also DLB 24

Eliot, T(homas) S(tearns)
1888-1965 ..... **CLC 1, 2, 3, 6, 9, 10, 13,**
15, 24, 34, 41, 55, 57; DA; DAB; PC 5;
WLC 2
See also CA 5-8R; 25-28R; CANR 41;
CDALB 1929-1941; DLB 7, 10, 45, 63;
DLBY 88; MTCW

Elizabeth 1866-1941 .... **TCLC 41**

Elkin, Stanley L(awrence)
1930-1995 ...... **CLC 4, 6, 9, 14, 27, 51;**
SSC 12
See also CA 9-12R; 148; CANR 8, 46;
DLB 2, 28; DLBY 80; MTCW

Elledge, Scott .... **CLC 34**

Elliott, Don
See Silverberg, Robert

Elliott, George P(aul) 1918-1980 ..... **CLC 2**
See also CA 1-4R; 97-100; CANR 2

Elliott, Janice 1931- .... **CLC 47**
See also CA 13-16R; CANR 8, 29; DLB 14

Elliott, Sumner Locke 1917-1991 ... **CLC 38**
See also CA 5-8R; 134; CANR 2, 21

Elliott, William
See Bradbury, Ray (Douglas)

Ellis, A. E. .... **CLC 7**

Ellis, Alice Thomas .... **CLC 40**
See also Haycraft, Anna

Ellis, Bret Easton 1964- .... **CLC 39, 71**
See also AAYA 2; CA 118; 123

Ellis, (Henry) Havelock
1859-1939 .... **TCLC 14**
See also CA 109

Ellis, Landon
See Ellison, Harlan (Jay)

Ellis, Trey 1962- .... **CLC 55**
See also CA 146

Ellison, Harlan (Jay)
1934- .... **CLC 1, 13, 42; SSC 14**
See also CA 5-8R; CANR 5, 46; DLB 8;
MTCW

Ellison, Ralph (Waldo)
1914-1994 .... **CLC 1, 3, 11, 54, 86;**
BLC; DA; DAB; WLC
See also BW 1; CA 9-12R; 145; CANR 24;
CDALB 1941-1968; DLB 2, 76;
DLBY 94; MTCW

Ellmann, Lucy (Elizabeth) 1956- .... **CLC 61**
See also CA 128

Ellmann, Richard (David)
1918-1987 .... **CLC 50**
See also BEST 89:2; CA 1-4R; 122;
CANR 2, 28; DLB 103; DLBY 87;
MTCW

Elman, Richard 1934- .... **CLC 19**
See also CA 17-20R; CAAS 3; CANR 47

Elron
See Hubbard, L(afayette) Ron(ald)

Eluard, Paul .... **TCLC 7, 41**
See also Grindel, Eugene

Elyot, Sir Thomas 1490(?)-1546 ..... **LC 11**

Elytis, Odysseus 1911- .... **CLC 15, 49**
See also CA 102; MTCW

Emecheta, (Florence Onye) Buchi
1944- .... **CLC 14, 48; BLC**
See also BW 2; CA 81-84; CANR 27;
DLB 117; MTCW; SATA 66

Emerson, Ralph Waldo
1803-1882 ..... **NCLC 1, 38; DA; DAB;**
WLC
See also CDALB 1640-1865; DLB 1, 59, 73

Eminescu, Mihail 1850-1889 ..... **NCLC 33**

Empson, William
1906-1984 .... **CLC 3, 8, 19, 33, 34**
See also CA 17-20R; 112; CANR 31;
DLB 20; MTCW

Enchi Fumiko (Ueda) 1905-1986 .... **CLC 31**
See also CA 129; 121

Ende, Michael (Andreas Helmuth)
1929- .... **CLC 31**
See also CA 118; 124; CANR 36; CLR 14;
DLB 75; MAICYA; SATA 61;
SATA-Brief 42

Endo, Shusaku 1923- ..... **CLC 7, 14, 19, 54**
See also CA 29-32R; CANR 21; MTCW

Engel, Marian 1933-1985 .... **CLC 36**
See also CA 25-28R; CANR 12; DLB 53

Engelhardt, Frederick
See Hubbard, L(afayette) Ron(ald)

Enright, D(ennis) J(oseph)
1920- .... **CLC 4, 8, 31**
See also CA 1-4R; CANR 1, 42; DLB 27;
SATA 25

Enzensberger, Hans Magnus
1929- .... **CLC 43**
See also CA 116; 119

Ephron, Nora 1941- .... **CLC 17, 31**
See also AITN 2; CA 65-68; CANR 12, 39

Epsilon
See Betjeman, John

Epstein, Daniel Mark 1948- .... **CLC 7**
See also CA 49-52; CANR 2

Epstein, Jacob 1956- .... **CLC 19**
See also CA 114

Epstein, Joseph 1937- .... **CLC 39**
See also CA 112; 119

Epstein, Leslie 1938- .... **CLC 27**
See also CA 73-76; CAAS 12; CANR 23

Equiano, Olaudah
1745(?)-1797 .... **LC 16; BLC**
See also DLB 37, 50

Erasmus, Desiderius 1469(?)-1536.... **LC 16**

Erdman, Paul E(mil) 1932- .... **CLC 25**
See also AITN 1; CA 61-64; CANR 13, 43

Erdrich, Louise 1954- .... **CLC 39, 54**
See also AAYA 10; BEST 89:1; CA 114;
CANR 41; DLB 152; MTCW; NNAL

Erenburg, Ilya (Grigoryevich)
See Ehrenburg, Ilya (Grigoryevich)

Erickson, Stephen Michael 1950-
See Erickson, Steve
See also CA 129

Erickson, Steve .... **CLC 64**
See also Erickson, Stephen Michael

Ericson, Walter
See Fast, Howard (Melvin)

Eriksson, Buntel
See Bergman, (Ernst) Ingmar

Ernaux, Annie 1940- .... **CLC 88**
See also CA 147

Eschenbach, Wolfram von
See Wolfram von Eschenbach

Eseki, Bruno
See Mphahlele, Ezekiel

Esenin, Sergei (Alexandrovich)
1895-1925 .... **TCLC 4**
See also CA 104

Eshleman, Clayton 1935- .... **CLC 7**
See also CA 33-36R; CAAS 6; DLB 5

Espriella, Don Manuel Alvarez
See Southey, Robert

Espriu, Salvador 1913-1985 .... **CLC 9**
See also CA 115; DLB 134

Espronceda, Jose de 1808-1842 ... **NCLC 39**

Esse, James
See Stephens, James

Esterbrook, Tom
See Hubbard, L(afayette) Ron(ald)

Estleman, Loren D. 1952- .... **CLC 48**
See also CA 85-88; CANR 27; MTCW

Feydeau, Georges (Leon Jules Marie)
    1862-1921 . . . . **TCLC 22**
    See also CA 113

Ficino, Marsilio 1433-1499 . . . . **LC 12**

Fiedeler, Hans
    See Doeblin, Alfred

Fiedler, Leslie A(aron)
    1917- . . . . **CLC 4, 13, 24**
    See also CA 9-12R; CANR 7; DLB 28, 67;
    MTCW

Field, Andrew 1938- . . . . **CLC 44**
    See also CA 97-100; CANR 25

Field, Eugene 1850-1895 . . . . **NCLC 3**
    See also DLB 23, 42, 140; MAICYA;
    SATA 16

Field, Gans T.
    See Wellman, Manly Wade

Field, Michael . . . . **TCLC 43**

Field, Peter
    See Hobson, Laura Z(ametkin)

Fielding, Henry
    1707-1754 . . . . . . **LC 1; DA; DAB; WLC**
    See also CDBLB 1660-1789; DLB 39, 84,
    101

Fielding, Sarah 1710-1768 . . . . **LC 1**
    See also DLB 39

Fierstein, Harvey (Forbes) 1954- . . . **CLC 33**
    See also CA 123; 129

Figes, Eva 1932- . . . . **CLC 31**
    See also CA 53-56; CANR 4, 44; DLB 14

Finch, Robert (Duer Claydon)
    1900- . . . . **CLC 18**
    See also CA 57-60; CANR 9, 24, 49;
    DLB 88

Findley, Timothy 1930- . . . . **CLC 27**
    See also CA 25-28R; CANR 12, 42;
    DLB 53

Fink, William
    See Mencken, H(enry) L(ouis)

Firbank, Louis 1942-
    See Reed, Lou
    See also CA 117

Firbank, (Arthur Annesley) Ronald
    1886-1926 . . . . **TCLC 1**
    See also CA 104; DLB 36

Fisher, M(ary) F(rances) K(ennedy)
    1908-1992 . . . . **CLC 76, 87**
    See also CA 77-80; 138; CANR 44

Fisher, Roy 1930- . . . . **CLC 25**
    See also CA 81-84; CAAS 10; CANR 16;
    DLB 40

Fisher, Rudolph
    1897-1934 . . . . **TCLC 11; BLC**
    See also BW 1; CA 107; 124; DLB 51, 102

Fisher, Vardis (Alvero) 1895-1968 . . . . **CLC 7**
    See also CA 5-8R; 25-28R; DLB 9

Fiske, Tarleton
    See Bloch, Robert (Albert)

Fitch, Clarke
    See Sinclair, Upton (Beall)

Fitch, John IV
    See Cormier, Robert (Edmund)

Fitzgerald, Captain Hugh
    See Baum, L(yman) Frank

FitzGerald, Edward 1809-1883 . . . . **NCLC 9**
    See also DLB 32

Fitzgerald, F(rancis) Scott (Key)
    1896-1940 . . . . . . **TCLC 1, 6, 14, 28, 55;
                         DA; DAB; SSC 6; WLC**
    See also AITN 1; CA 110; 123;
    CDALB 1917-1929; DLB 4, 9, 86;
    DLBD 1; DLBY 81; MTCW

Fitzgerald, Penelope 1916- . . . **CLC 19, 51, 61**
    See also CA 85-88; CAAS 10; DLB 14

Fitzgerald, Robert (Stuart)
    1910-1985 . . . . **CLC 39**
    See also CA 1-4R; 114; CANR 1; DLBY 80

FitzGerald, Robert D(avid)
    1902-1987 . . . . **CLC 19**
    See also CA 17-20R

Fitzgerald, Zelda (Sayre)
    1900-1948 . . . . **TCLC 52**
    See also CA 117; 126; DLBY 84

Flanagan, Thomas (James Bonner)
    1923- . . . . **CLC 25, 52**
    See also CA 108; DLBY 80; MTCW

Flaubert, Gustave
    1821-1880 . . . . **NCLC 2, 10, 19; DA;
                            DAB; SSC 11; WLC**
    See also DLB 119

Flecker, (Herman) James Elroy
    1884-1915 . . . . **TCLC 43**
    See also CA 109; DLB 10, 19

Fleming, Ian (Lancaster)
    1908-1964 . . . . **CLC 3, 30**
    See also CA 5-8R; CDBLB 1945-1960;
    DLB 87; MTCW; SATA 9

Fleming, Thomas (James) 1927- . . . . **CLC 37**
    See also CA 5-8R; CANR 10; SATA 8

Fletcher, John Gould 1886-1950 . . . **TCLC 35**
    See also CA 107; DLB 4, 45

Fleur, Paul
    See Pohl, Frederik

Flooglebuckle, Al
    See Spiegelman, Art

Flying Officer X
    See Bates, H(erbert) E(rnest)

Fo, Dario 1926- . . . . **CLC 32**
    See also CA 116; 128; MTCW

Fogarty, Jonathan Titulescu Esq.
    See Farrell, James T(homas)

Folke, Will
    See Bloch, Robert (Albert)

Follett, Ken(neth Martin) 1949- . . . . **CLC 18**
    See also AAYA 6; BEST 89:4; CA 81-84;
    CANR 13, 33; DLB 87; DLBY 81;
    MTCW

Fontane, Theodor 1819-1898 . . . . . **NCLC 26**
    See also DLB 129

Foote, Horton 1916- . . . . **CLC 51**
    See also CA 73-76; CANR 34; DLB 26

Foote, Shelby 1916- . . . . **CLC 75**
    See also CA 5-8R; CANR 3, 45; DLB 2, 17

Forbes, Esther 1891-1967 . . . . **CLC 12**
    See also CA 13-14; 25-28R; CAP 1;
    CLR 27; DLB 22; JRDA; MAICYA;
    SATA 2

Forche, Carolyn (Louise)
    1950- . . . . **CLC 25, 83, 86; PC 10**
    See also CA 109; 117; DLB 5

Ford, Elbur
    See Hibbert, Eleanor Alice Burford

Ford, Ford Madox
    1873-1939 . . . . **TCLC 1, 15, 39, 57**
    See also CA 104; 132; CDBLB 1914-1945;
    DLB 34, 98; MTCW

Ford, John 1895-1973 . . . . **CLC 16**
    See also CA 45-48

Ford, Richard 1944- . . . . **CLC 46**
    See also CA 69-72; CANR 11, 47

Ford, Webster
    See Masters, Edgar Lee

Foreman, Richard 1937- . . . . **CLC 50**
    See also CA 65-68; CANR 32

Forester, C(ecil) S(cott)
    1899-1966 . . . . **CLC 35**
    See also CA 73-76; 25-28R; SATA 13

Forez
    See Mauriac, Francois (Charles)

Forman, James Douglas 1932- . . . . . . **CLC 21**
    See also CA 9-12R; CANR 4, 19, 42;
    JRDA; MAICYA; SATA 8, 70

Fornes, Maria Irene 1930- . . . . . . **CLC 39, 61**
    See also CA 25-28R; CANR 28; DLB 7;
    HW; MTCW

Forrest, Leon 1937- . . . . **CLC 4**
    See also BW 2; CA 89-92; CAAS 7;
    CANR 25; DLB 33

Forster, E(dward) M(organ)
    1879-1970 . . . . **CLC 1, 2, 3, 4, 9, 10, 13,
                       15, 22, 45, 77; DA; DAB; WLC**
    See also AAYA 2; CA 13-14; 25-28R;
    CANR 45; CAP 1; CDBLB 1914-1945;
    DLB 34, 98; DLBD 10; MTCW;
    SATA 57

Forster, John 1812-1876 . . . . **NCLC 11**
    See also DLB 144

Forsyth, Frederick 1938- . . . . . . **CLC 2, 5, 36**
    See also BEST 89:4; CA 85-88; CANR 38;
    DLB 87; MTCW

Forten, Charlotte L. . . . . **TCLC 16; BLC**
    See also Grimke, Charlotte L(ottie) Forten
    See also DLB 50

Foscolo, Ugo 1778-1827 . . . . **NCLC 8**

Fosse, Bob . . . . **CLC 20**
    See also Fosse, Robert Louis

Fosse, Robert Louis 1927-1987
    See Fosse, Bob
    See also CA 110; 123

Foster, Stephen Collins
    1826-1864 . . . . **NCLC 26**

Foucault, Michel
    1926-1984 . . . . **CLC 31, 34, 69**
    See also CA 105; 113; CANR 34; MTCW

Fouque, Friedrich (Heinrich Karl) de la Motte
    1777-1843 . . . . **NCLC 2**
    See also DLB 90

Fourier, Charles 1772-1837 . . . . . . **NCLC 51**

Fournier, Henri Alban 1886-1914
    See Alain-Fournier
    See also CA 104

Fournier, Pierre 1916-............ **CLC 11**
See also Gascar, Pierre
See also CA 89-92; CANR 16, 40

Fowles, John
1926-...... **CLC 1, 2, 3, 4, 6, 9, 10, 15,
33, 87; DAB**
See also CA 5-8R; CANR 25; CDBLB 1960
to Present; DLB 14, 139; MTCW;
SATA 22

Fox, Paula 1923-............... **CLC 2, 8**
See also AAYA 3; CA 73-76; CANR 20,
36; CLR 1; DLB 52; JRDA; MAICYA;
MTCW; SATA 17, 60

Fox, William Price (Jr.) 1926- ..... **CLC 22**
See also CA 17-20R; CAAS 19; CANR 11;
DLB 2; DLBY 81

Foxe, John 1516(?)-1587 .... **LC 14**

Frame, Janet .... **CLC 2, 3, 6, 22, 66**
See also Clutha, Janet Paterson Frame

France, Anatole .... **TCLC 9**
See also Thibault, Jacques Anatole Francois
See also DLB 123

Francis, Claude 19(?)- .... **CLC 50**

Francis, Dick 1920- .... **CLC 2, 22, 42**
See also AAYA 5; BEST 89:3; CA 5-8R;
CANR 9, 42; CDBLB 1960 to Present;
DLB 87; MTCW

Francis, Robert (Churchill)
1901-1987 .... **CLC 15**
See also CA 1-4R; 123; CANR 1

Frank, Anne(lies Marie)
1929-1945 .. **TCLC 17; DA; DAB; WLC**
See also AAYA 12; CA 113; 133; MTCW;
SATA-Brief 42

Frank, Elizabeth 1945-............ **CLC 39**
See also CA 121; 126

Franklin, Benjamin
See Hasek, Jaroslav (Matej Frantisek)

Franklin, Benjamin
1706-1790 .... **LC 25; DA; DAB**
See also CDALB 1640-1865; DLB 24, 43,
73

Franklin, (Stella Maraia Sarah) Miles
1879-1954 .... **TCLC 7**
See also CA 104

Fraser, (Lady) Antonia (Pakenham)
1932- .... **CLC 32**
See also CA 85-88; CANR 44; MTCW;
SATA-Brief 32

Fraser, George MacDonald 1925-.... **CLC 7**
See also CA 45-48; CANR 2, 48

Fraser, Sylvia 1935-.............. **CLC 64**
See also CA 45-48; CANR 1, 16

Frayn, Michael 1933-...... **CLC 3, 7, 31, 47**
See also CA 5-8R; CANR 30; DLB 13, 14;
MTCW

Fraze, Candida (Merrill) 1945-..... **CLC 50**
See also CA 126

Frazer, J(ames) G(eorge)
1854-1941 .... **TCLC 32**
See also CA 118

Frazer, Robert Caine
See Creasey, John

Frazer, Sir James George
See Frazer, J(ames) G(eorge)

Frazier, Ian 1951-................ **CLC 46**
See also CA 130

Frederic, Harold 1856-1898...... **NCLC 10**
See also DLB 12, 23

Frederick, John
See Faust, Frederick (Schiller)

Frederick the Great 1712-1786...... **LC 14**

Fredro, Aleksander 1793-1876..... **NCLC 8**

Freeling, Nicolas 1927- .... **CLC 38**
See also CA 49-52; CAAS 12; CANR 1, 17;
DLB 87

Freeman, Douglas Southall
1886-1953 .... **TCLC 11**
See also CA 109; DLB 17

Freeman, Judith 1946-............ **CLC 55**
See also CA 148

Freeman, Mary Eleanor Wilkins
1852-1930 .... **TCLC 9; SSC 1**
See also CA 106; DLB 12, 78

Freeman, R(ichard) Austin
1862-1943 .... **TCLC 21**
See also CA 113; DLB 70

French, Albert 1943- .... **CLC 86**

French, Marilyn 1929-...... **CLC 10, 18, 60**
See also CA 69-72; CANR 3, 31; MTCW

French, Paul
See Asimov, Isaac

Freneau, Philip Morin 1752-1832.. **NCLC 1**
See also DLB 37, 43

Freud, Sigmund 1856-1939 .... **TCLC 52**
See also CA 115; 133; MTCW

Friedan, Betty (Naomi) 1921-...... **CLC 74**
See also CA 65-68; CANR 18, 45; MTCW

Friedlaender, Saul 1932- .... **CLC 90**
See also CA 117; 130

Friedman, B(ernard) H(arper)
1926- .... **CLC 7**
See also CA 1-4R; CANR 3, 48

Friedman, Bruce Jay 1930-.... **CLC 3, 5, 56**
See also CA 9-12R; CANR 25; DLB 2, 28

Friel, Brian 1929-........... **CLC 5, 42, 59**
See also CA 21-24R; CANR 33; DLB 13;
MTCW

Friis-Baastad, Babbis Ellinor
1921-1970 .... **CLC 12**
See also CA 17-20R; 134; SATA 7

Frisch, Max (Rudolf)
1911-1991 ..... **CLC 3, 9, 14, 18, 32, 44**
See also CA 85-88; 134; CANR 32;
DLB 69, 124; MTCW

Fromentin, Eugene (Samuel Auguste)
1820-1876 .... **NCLC 10**
See also DLB 123

Frost, Frederick
See Faust, Frederick (Schiller)

Frost, Robert (Lee)
1874-1963 .... **CLC 1, 3, 4, 9, 10, 13, 15,
26, 34, 44; DA; DAB; PC 1; WLC**
See also CA 89-92; CANR 33;
CDALB 1917-1929; DLB 54; DLBD 7;
MTCW; SATA 14

Froude, James Anthony
1818-1894 .... **NCLC 43**
See also DLB 18, 57, 144

Froy, Herald
See Waterhouse, Keith (Spencer)

Fry, Christopher 1907-....... **CLC 2, 10, 14**
See also CA 17-20R; CANR 9, 30; DLB 13;
MTCW; SATA 66

Frye, (Herman) Northrop
1912-1991 .... **CLC 24, 70**
See also CA 5-8R; 133; CANR 8, 37;
DLB 67, 68; MTCW

Fuchs, Daniel 1909-1993 .... **CLC 8, 22**
See also CA 81-84; 142; CAAS 5;
CANR 40; DLB 9, 26, 28; DLBY 93

Fuchs, Daniel 1934-.............. **CLC 34**
See also CA 37-40R; CANR 14, 48

Fuentes, Carlos
1928-...... **CLC 3, 8, 10, 13, 22, 41, 60;
DA; DAB; HLC; WLC**
See also AAYA 4; AITN 2; CA 69-72;
CANR 10, 32; DLB 113; HW; MTCW

Fuentes, Gregorio Lopez y
See Lopez y Fuentes, Gregorio

Fugard, (Harold) Athol
1932- .... **CLC 5, 9, 14, 25, 40, 80; DC 3**
See also CA 85-88; CANR 32; MTCW

Fugard, Sheila 1932- .... **CLC 48**
See also CA 125

Fuller, Charles (H., Jr.)
1939-............. **CLC 25; BLC; DC 1**
See also BW 2; CA 108; 112; DLB 38;
MTCW

Fuller, John (Leopold) 1937-....... **CLC 62**
See also CA 21-24R; CANR 9, 44; DLB 40

Fuller, Margaret .... **NCLC 5, 50**
See also Ossoli, Sarah Margaret (Fuller
marchesa d')

Fuller, Roy (Broadbent)
1912-1991 .... **CLC 4, 28**
See also CA 5-8R; 135; CAAS 10; DLB 15,
20

Fulton, Alice 1952-................ **CLC 52**
See also CA 116

Furphy, Joseph 1843-1912........ **TCLC 25**

Fussell, Paul 1924-................ **CLC 74**
See also BEST 90:1; CA 17-20R; CANR 8,
21, 35; MTCW

Futabatei, Shimei 1864-1909...... **TCLC 44**

Futrelle, Jacques 1875-1912 ...... **TCLC 19**
See also CA 113

Gaboriau, Emile 1835-1873...... **NCLC 14**

Gadda, Carlo Emilio 1893-1973 .... **CLC 11**
See also CA 89-92

Gaddis, William
1922- ..... **CLC 1, 3, 6, 8, 10, 19, 43, 86**
See also CA 17-20R; CANR 21, 48; DLB 2;
MTCW

Gaines, Ernest J(ames)
1933-......... **CLC 3, 11, 18, 86; BLC**
See also AITN 1; BW 2; CA 9-12R;
CANR 6, 24, 42; CDALB 1968-1988;
DLB 2, 33, 152; DLBY 80; MTCW

Gaitskill, Mary 1954-............. **CLC 69**
See also CA 128

Galdos, Benito Perez
See Perez Galdos, Benito

Gale, Zona 1874-1938 . . . . **TCLC 7**
See also CA 105; DLB 9, 78

Galeano, Eduardo (Hughes) 1940-. . . **CLC 72**
See also CA 29-32R; CANR 13, 32; HW

Galiano, Juan Valera y Alcala
See Valera y Alcala-Galiano, Juan

Gallagher, Tess 1943-. . . . **CLC 18, 63; PC 9**
See also CA 106; DLB 120

Gallant, Mavis
1922- . . . . **CLC 7, 18, 38; SSC 5**
See also CA 69-72; CANR 29; DLB 53;
MTCW

Gallant, Roy A(rthur) 1924- . . . . **CLC 17**
See also CA 5-8R; CANR 4, 29; CLR 30;
MAICYA; SATA 4, 68

Gallico, Paul (William) 1897-1976 . . . **CLC 2**
See also AITN 1; CA 5-8R; 69-72;
CANR 23; DLB 9; MAICYA; SATA 13

Gallup, Ralph
See Whitemore, Hugh (John)

Galsworthy, John
1867-1933 . . . . . . **TCLC 1, 45; DA; DAB;
WLC 2**
See also CA 104; 141; CDBLB 1890-1914;
DLB 10, 34, 98

Galt, John 1779-1839. . . . . **NCLC 1**
See also DLB 99, 116

Galvin, James 1951-. . . . . **CLC 38**
See also CA 108; CANR 26

Gamboa, Federico 1864-1939. . . . . . **TCLC 36**

Gandhi, M. K.
See Gandhi, Mohandas Karamchand

Gandhi, Mahatma
See Gandhi, Mohandas Karamchand

Gandhi, Mohandas Karamchand
1869-1948 . . . . **TCLC 59**
See also CA 121; 132; MTCW

Gann, Ernest Kellogg 1910-1991. . . . **CLC 23**
See also AITN 1; CA 1-4R; 136; CANR 1

Garcia, Cristina 1958- . . . . **CLC 76**
See also CA 141

Garcia Lorca, Federico
1898-1936 . . . **TCLC 1, 7, 49; DA; DAB;
DC 2; HLC; PC 3; WLC**
See also CA 104; 131; DLB 108; HW;
MTCW

Garcia Marquez, Gabriel (Jose)
1928- . . . . **CLC 2, 3, 8, 10, 15, 27, 47, 55,
68; DA; DAB; HLC; SSC 8; WLC**
See also AAYA 3; BEST 89:1, 90:4;
CA 33-36R; CANR 10, 28; DLB 113;
HW; MTCW

Gard, Janice
See Latham, Jean Lee

Gard, Roger Martin du
See Martin du Gard, Roger

Gardam, Jane 1928-. . . . . **CLC 43**
See also CA 49-52; CANR 2, 18, 33;
CLR 12; DLB 14; MAICYA; MTCW;
SAAS 9; SATA 39, 76; SATA-Brief 28

Gardner, Herb. . . . . **CLC 44**

Gardner, John (Champlin), Jr.
1933-1982 . . . . . **CLC 2, 3, 5, 7, 8, 10, 18,
28, 34; SSC 7**
See also AITN 1; CA 65-68; 107;
CANR 33; DLB 2; DLBY 82; MTCW;
SATA 40; SATA-Obit 31

Gardner, John (Edmund) 1926-. . . . . **CLC 30**
See also CA 103; CANR 15; MTCW

Gardner, Noel
See Kuttner, Henry

Gardons, S. S.
See Snodgrass, W(illiam) D(e Witt)

Garfield, Leon 1921-. . . . . **CLC 12**
See also AAYA 8; CA 17-20R; CANR 38,
41; CLR 21; JRDA; MAICYA; SATA 1,
32, 76

Garland, (Hannibal) Hamlin
1860-1940 . . . . **TCLC 3; SSC 18**
See also CA 104; DLB 12, 71, 78

Garneau, (Hector de) Saint-Denys
1912-1943 . . . . **TCLC 13**
See also CA 111; DLB 88

Garner, Alan 1934-. . . . . **CLC 17; DAB**
See also CA 73-76; CANR 15; CLR 20;
MAICYA; MTCW; SATA 18, 69

Garner, Hugh 1913-1979 . . . . **CLC 13**
See also CA 69-72; CANR 31; DLB 68

Garnett, David 1892-1981 . . . . **CLC 3**
See also CA 5-8R; 103; CANR 17; DLB 34

Garos, Stephanie
See Katz, Steve

Garrett, George (Palmer)
1929- . . . . **CLC 3, 11, 51**
See also CA 1-4R; CAAS 5; CANR 1, 42;
DLB 2, 5, 130, 152; DLBY 83

Garrick, David 1717-1779 . . . . **LC 15**
See also DLB 84

Garrigue, Jean 1914-1972 . . . . **CLC 2, 8**
See also CA 5-8R; 37-40R; CANR 20

Garrison, Frederick
See Sinclair, Upton (Beall)

Garth, Will
See Hamilton, Edmond; Kuttner, Henry

Garvey, Marcus (Moziah, Jr.)
1887-1940 . . . . **TCLC 41; BLC**
See also BW 1; CA 120; 124

Gary, Romain . . . . **CLC 25**
See also Kacew, Romain
See also DLB 83

Gascar, Pierre. . . . . **CLC 11**
See also Fournier, Pierre

Gascoyne, David (Emery) 1916- . . . . **CLC 45**
See also CA 65-68; CANR 10, 28; DLB 20;
MTCW

Gaskell, Elizabeth Cleghorn
1810-1865 . . . . **NCLC 5; DAB**
See also CDBLB 1832-1890; DLB 21, 144

Gass, William H(oward)
1924- . . . **CLC 1, 2, 8, 11, 15, 39; SSC 12**
See also CA 17-20R; CANR 30; DLB 2;
MTCW

Gasset, Jose Ortega y
See Ortega y Gasset, Jose

Gates, Henry Louis, Jr. 1950-. . . . . . **CLC 65**
See also BW 2; CA 109; CANR 25; DLB 67

Gautier, Theophile
1811-1872 . . . . **NCLC 1; SSC 20**
See also DLB 119

Gawsworth, John
See Bates, H(erbert) E(rnest)

Gaye, Marvin (Penze) 1939-1984 . . . **CLC 26**
See also CA 112

Gebler, Carlo (Ernest) 1954-. . . . . . . **CLC 39**
See also CA 119; 133

Gee, Maggie (Mary) 1948-. . . . . **CLC 57**
See also CA 130

Gee, Maurice (Gough) 1931-. . . . . . . **CLC 29**
See also CA 97-100; SATA 46

Gelbart, Larry (Simon) 1923- . . . **CLC 21, 61**
See also CA 73-76; CANR 45

Gelber, Jack 1932-. . . . . **CLC 1, 6, 14, 79**
See also CA 1-4R; CANR 2; DLB 7

Gellhorn, Martha (Ellis) 1908- . . **CLC 14, 60**
See also CA 77-80; CANR 44; DLBY 82

Genet, Jean
1910-1986 . . . **CLC 1, 2, 5, 10, 14, 44, 46**
See also CA 13-16R; CANR 18; DLB 72;
DLBY 86; MTCW

Gent, Peter 1942-. . . . . **CLC 29**
See also AITN 1; CA 89-92; DLBY 82

Gentlewoman in New England, A
See Bradstreet, Anne

Gentlewoman in Those Parts, A
See Bradstreet, Anne

George, Jean Craighead 1919-. . . . . . **CLC 35**
See also AAYA 8; CA 5-8R; CANR 25;
CLR 1; DLB 52; JRDA; MAICYA;
SATA 2, 68

George, Stefan (Anton)
1868-1933 . . . . **TCLC 2, 14**
See also CA 104

Georges, Georges Martin
See Simenon, Georges (Jacques Christian)

Gerhardi, William Alexander
See Gerhardie, William Alexander

Gerhardie, William Alexander
1895-1977 . . . . **CLC 5**
See also CA 25-28R; 73-76; CANR 18;
DLB 36

Gerstler, Amy 1956-. . . . . **CLC 70**
See also CA 146

Gertler, T. . . . . **CLC 34**
See also CA 116; 121

Ghalib 1797-1869 . . . . **NCLC 39**

Ghelderode, Michel de
1898-1962 . . . . **CLC 6, 11**
See also CA 85-88; CANR 40

Ghiselin, Brewster 1903- . . . . **CLC 23**
See also CA 13-16R; CAAS 10; CANR 13

Ghose, Zulfikar 1935-. . . . . **CLC 42**
See also CA 65-68

Ghosh, Amitav 1956- . . . . **CLC 44**
See also CA 147

Giacosa, Giuseppe 1847-1906 . . . . . . **TCLC 7**
See also CA 104

Gibb, Lee
See Waterhouse, Keith (Spencer)

Gordimer, Nadine
        1923- .... CLC **3, 5, 7, 10, 18, 33, 51, 70;**
                DA; DAB; SSC 17
        See also CA 5-8R; CANR 3, 28; MTCW

Gordon, Adam Lindsay
        1833-1870 .... NCLC **21**

Gordon, Caroline
        1895-1981 ... CLC **6, 13, 29, 83; SSC 15**
        See also CA 11-12; 103; CANR 36; CAP 1;
        DLB 4, 9, 102; DLBY 81; MTCW

Gordon, Charles William 1860-1937
        See Connor, Ralph
        See also CA 109

Gordon, Mary (Catherine)
        1949- .... CLC **13, 22**
        See also CA 102; CANR 44; DLB 6;
        DLBY 81; MTCW

Gordon, Sol 1923-................ CLC **26**
        See also CA 53-56; CANR 4; SATA 11

Gordone, Charles 1925-.......... CLC **1, 4**
        See also BW 1; CA 93-96; DLB 7; MTCW

Gorenko, Anna Andreevna
        See Akhmatova, Anna

Gorky, Maxim........ TCLC **8; DAB; WLC**
        See also Peshkov, Alexei Maximovich

Goryan, Sirak
        See Saroyan, William

Gosse, Edmund (William)
        1849-1928 .... TCLC **28**
        See also CA 117; DLB 57, 144

Gotlieb, Phyllis Fay (Bloom)
        1926- .... CLC **18**
        See also CA 13-16R; CANR 7; DLB 88

Gottesman, S. D.
        See Kornbluth, C(yril) M.; Pohl, Frederik

Gottfried von Strassburg
        fl. c. 1210-................ CMLC **10**
        See also DLB 138

Gould, Lois .... CLC **4, 10**
        See also CA 77-80; CANR 29; MTCW

Gourmont, Remy de 1858-1915.... TCLC **17**
        See also CA 109

Govier, Katherine 1948-.......... CLC **51**
        See also CA 101; CANR 18, 40

Goyen, (Charles) William
        1915-1983 .... CLC **5, 8, 14, 40**
        See also AITN 2; CA 5-8R; 110; CANR 6;
        DLB 2; DLBY 83

Goytisolo, Juan
        1931- .... CLC **5, 10, 23; HLC**
        See also CA 85-88; CANR 32; HW; MTCW

Gozzano, Guido 1883-1916 .... PC **10**
        See also DLB 114

Gozzi, (Conte) Carlo 1720-1806 .. NCLC **23**

Grabbe, Christian Dietrich
        1801-1836 .... NCLC **2**
        See also DLB 133

Grace, Patricia 1937-............. CLC **56**

Gracian y Morales, Baltasar
        1601-1658 .... LC **15**

Gracq, Julien................... CLC **11, 48**
        See also Poirier, Louis
        See also DLB 83

Grade, Chaim 1910-1982 .... CLC **10**
        See also CA 93-96; 107

Graduate of Oxford, A
        See Ruskin, John

Graham, John
        See Phillips, David Graham

Graham, Jorie 1951-............. CLC **48**
        See also CA 111; DLB 120

Graham, R(obert) B(ontine) Cunninghame
        See Cunninghame Graham, R(obert)
        B(ontine)
        See also DLB 98, 135

Graham, Robert
        See Haldeman, Joe (William)

Graham, Tom
        See Lewis, (Harry) Sinclair

Graham, W(illiam) S(ydney)
        1918-1986 .... CLC **29**
        See also CA 73-76; 118; DLB 20

Graham, Winston (Mawdsley)
        1910- .... CLC **23**
        See also CA 49-52; CANR 2, 22, 45;
        DLB 77

Grant, Skeeter
        See Spiegelman, Art

Granville-Barker, Harley
        1877-1946 ....TCLC **2**
        See also Barker, Harley Granville
        See also CA 104

Grass, Guenter (Wilhelm)
        1927- ..... CLC **1, 2, 4, 6, 11, 15, 22, 32,**
                49, 88; DA; DAB; WLC
        See also CA 13-16R; CANR 20; DLB 75,
        124; MTCW

Gratton, Thomas
        See Hulme, T(homas) E(rnest)

Grau, Shirley Ann
        1929- .... CLC **4, 9; SSC 15**
        See also CA 89-92; CANR 22; DLB 2;
        MTCW

Gravel, Fern
        See Hall, James Norman

Graver, Elizabeth 1964-........... CLC **70**
        See also CA 135

Graves, Richard Perceval 1945- .... CLC **44**
        See also CA 65-68; CANR 9, 26

Graves, Robert (von Ranke)
        1895-1985 ...... CLC **1, 2, 6, 11, 39, 44,**
                45; DAB; PC 6
        See also CA 5-8R; 117; CANR 5, 36;
        CDBLB 1914-1945; DLB 20, 100;
        DLBY 85; MTCW; SATA 45

Gray, Alasdair (James) 1934- ...... CLC **41**
        See also CA 126; CANR 47; MTCW

Gray, Amlin 1946-............... CLC **29**
        See also CA 138

Gray, Francine du Plessix 1930-.... CLC **22**
        See also BEST 90:3; CA 61-64; CAAS 2;
        CANR 11, 33; MTCW

Gray, John (Henry) 1866-1934 .... TCLC **19**
        See also CA 119

Gray, Simon (James Holliday)
        1936- .... CLC **9, 14, 36**
        See also AITN 1; CA 21-24R; CAAS 3;
        CANR 32; DLB 13; MTCW

Gray, Spalding 1941-............. CLC **49**
        See also CA 128

Gray, Thomas
        1716-1771 ...... LC **4; DA; DAB; PC 2;**
                WLC
        See also CDBLB 1660-1789; DLB 109

Grayson, David
        See Baker, Ray Stannard

Grayson, Richard (A.) 1951-....... CLC **38**
        See also CA 85-88; CANR 14, 31

Greeley, Andrew M(oran) 1928-.... CLC **28**
        See also CA 5-8R; CAAS 7; CANR 7, 43;
        MTCW

Green, Brian
        See Card, Orson Scott

Green, Hannah
        See Greenberg, Joanne (Goldenberg)

Green, Hannah .... CLC **3**
        See also CA 73-76

Green, Henry.................. CLC **2, 13**
        See also Yorke, Henry Vincent
        See also DLB 15

Green, Julian (Hartridge) 1900-
        See Green, Julien
        See also CA 21-24R; CANR 33; DLB 4, 72;
        MTCW

Green, Julien................. CLC **3, 11, 77**
        See also Green, Julian (Hartridge)

Green, Paul (Eliot) 1894-1981...... CLC **25**
        See also AITN 1; CA 5-8R; 103; CANR 3;
        DLB 7, 9; DLBY 81

Greenberg, Ivan 1908-1973
        See Rahv, Philip
        See also CA 85-88

Greenberg, Joanne (Goldenberg)
        1932- .... CLC **7, 30**
        See also AAYA 12; CA 5-8R; CANR 14,
        32; SATA 25

Greenberg, Richard 1959(?)-....... CLC **57**
        See also CA 138

Greene, Bette 1934-.............. CLC **30**
        See also AAYA 7; CA 53-56; CANR 4;
        CLR 2; JRDA; MAICYA; SAAS 16;
        SATA 8

Greene, Gael .... CLC **8**
        See also CA 13-16R; CANR 10

Greene, Graham
        1904-1991 .... CLC **1, 3, 6, 9, 14, 18, 27,**
                37, 70, 72; DA; DAB; WLC
        See also AITN 2; CA 13-16R; 133;
        CANR 35; CDBLB 1945-1960; DLB 13,
        15, 77, 100; DLBY 91; MTCW; SATA 20

Greer, Richard
        See Silverberg, Robert

Gregor, Arthur 1923-.............. CLC **9**
        See also CA 25-28R; CAAS 10; CANR 11;
        SATA 36

Gregor, Lee
        See Pohl, Frederik

Gregory, Isabella Augusta (Persse)
        1852-1932 .... TCLC **1**
        See also CA 104; DLB 10

Gregory, J. Dennis
        See Williams, John A(lfred)

Grendon, Stephen
See Derleth, August (William)

Grenville, Kate 1950- .... **CLC 61**
See also CA 118

Grenville, Pelham
See Wodehouse, P(elham) G(renville)

Greve, Felix Paul (Berthold Friedrich)
1879-1948
See Grove, Frederick Philip
See also CA 104; 141

Grey, Zane 1872-1939 .... **TCLC 6**
See also CA 104; 132; DLB 9; MTCW

Grieg, (Johan) Nordahl (Brun)
1902-1943 .... **TCLC 10**
See also CA 107

Grieve, C(hristopher) M(urray)
1892-1978 .... **CLC 11, 19**
See also MacDiarmid, Hugh
See also CA 5-8R; 85-88; CANR 33;
MTCW

Griffin, Gerald 1803-1840 .... **NCLC 7**

Griffin, John Howard 1920-1980.... **CLC 68**
See also AITN 1; CA 1-4R; 101; CANR 2

Griffin, Peter 1942- .... **CLC 39**
See also CA 136

Griffiths, Trevor 1935- .... **CLC 13, 52**
See also CA 97-100; CANR 45; DLB 13

Grigson, Geoffrey (Edward Harvey)
1905-1985 .... **CLC 7, 39**
See also CA 25-28R; 118; CANR 20, 33;
DLB 27; MTCW

Grillparzer, Franz 1791-1872...... **NCLC 1**
See also DLB 133

Grimble, Reverend Charles James
See Eliot, T(homas) S(tearns)

Grimke, Charlotte L(ottie) Forten
1837(?)-1914
See Forten, Charlotte L.
See also BW 1; CA 117; 124

Grimm, Jacob Ludwig Karl
1785-1863 .... **NCLC 3**
See also DLB 90; MAICYA; SATA 22

Grimm, Wilhelm Karl 1786-1859 .. **NCLC 3**
See also DLB 90; MAICYA; SATA 22

Grimmelshausen, Johann Jakob Christoffel
von 1621-1676 .... **LC 6**

Grindel, Eugene 1895-1952
See Eluard, Paul
See also CA 104

Grisham, John 1955- .... **CLC 84**
See also AAYA 14; CA 138; CANR 47

Grossman, David 1954- .... **CLC 67**
See also CA 138

Grossman, Vasily (Semenovich)
1905-1964 .... **CLC 41**
See also CA 124; 130; MTCW

Grove, Frederick Philip .... **TCLC 4**
See also Greve, Felix Paul (Berthold
Friedrich)
See also DLB 92

Grubb
See Crumb, R(obert)

Grumbach, Doris (Isaac)
1918- .... **CLC 13, 22, 64**
See also CA 5-8R; CAAS 2; CANR 9, 42

Grundtvig, Nicolai Frederik Severin
1783-1872 .... **NCLC 1**

Grunge
See Crumb, R(obert)

Grunwald, Lisa 1959- .... **CLC 44**
See also CA 120

Guare, John 1938- .... **CLC 8, 14, 29, 67**
See also CA 73-76; CANR 21; DLB 7;
MTCW

Gudjonsson, Halldor Kiljan 1902-
See Laxness, Halldor
See also CA 103

Guenter, Erich
See Eich, Guenter

Guest, Barbara 1920- .... **CLC 34**
See also CA 25-28R; CANR 11, 44; DLB 5

Guest, Judith (Ann) 1936- .... **CLC 8, 30**
See also AAYA 7; CA 77-80; CANR 15;
MTCW

Guevara, Che .... **CLC 87; HLC**
See also Guevara (Serna), Ernesto

Guevara (Serna), Ernesto 1928-1967
See Guevara, Che
See also CA 127; 111; HW

Guild, Nicholas M. 1944- .... **CLC 33**
See also CA 93-96

Guillemin, Jacques
See Sartre, Jean-Paul

Guillen, Jorge 1893-1984.......... **CLC 11**
See also CA 89-92; 112; DLB 108; HW

Guillen (y Batista), Nicolas (Cristobal)
1902-1989 ..... **CLC 48, 79; BLC; HLC**
See also BW 2; CA 116; 125; 129; HW

Guillevic, (Eugene) 1907-.......... **CLC 33**
See also CA 93-96

Guillois
See Desnos, Robert

Guiney, Louise Imogen
1861-1920 .... **TCLC 41**
See also DLB 54

Guiraldes, Ricardo (Guillermo)
1886-1927 .... **TCLC 39**
See also CA 131; HW; MTCW

Gumilev, Nikolai Stephanovich
1886-1921 .... **TCLC 60**

Gunn, Bill .... **CLC 5**
See also Gunn, William Harrison
See also DLB 38

Gunn, Thom(son William)
1929- .... **CLC 3, 6, 18, 32, 81**
See also CA 17-20R; CANR 9, 33;
CDBLB 1960 to Present; DLB 27;
MTCW

Gunn, William Harrison 1934(?)-1989
See Gunn, Bill
See also AITN 1; BW 1; CA 13-16R; 128;
CANR 12, 25

Gunnars, Kristjana 1948-......... **CLC 69**
See also CA 113; DLB 60

Gurganus, Allan 1947- .... **CLC 70**
See also BEST 90:1; CA 135

Gurney, A(lbert) R(amsdell), Jr.
1930- .... **CLC 32, 50, 54**
See also CA 77-80; CANR 32

Gurney, Ivor (Bertie) 1890-1937... **TCLC 33**

Gurney, Peter
See Gurney, A(lbert) R(amsdell), Jr.

Guro, Elena 1877-1913.......... **TCLC 56**

Gustafson, Ralph (Barker) 1909-.... **CLC 36**
See also CA 21-24R; CANR 8, 45; DLB 88

Gut, Gom
See Simenon, Georges (Jacques Christian)

Guthrie, A(lfred) B(ertram), Jr.
1901-1991 .... **CLC 23**
See also CA 57-60; 134; CANR 24; DLB 6;
SATA 62; SATA-Obit 67

Guthrie, Isobel
See Grieve, C(hristopher) M(urray)

Guthrie, Woodrow Wilson 1912-1967
See Guthrie, Woody
See also CA 113; 93-96

Guthrie, Woody .... **CLC 35**
See also Guthrie, Woodrow Wilson

Guy, Rosa (Cuthbert) 1928-........ **CLC 26**
See also AAYA 4; BW 2; CA 17-20R;
CANR 14, 34; CLR 13; DLB 33; JRDA;
MAICYA; SATA 14, 62

Gwendolyn
See Bennett, (Enoch) Arnold

H. D. .... **CLC 3, 8, 14, 31, 34, 73; PC 5**
See also Doolittle, Hilda

H. de V.
See Buchan, John

Haavikko, Paavo Juhani
1931- .... **CLC 18, 34**
See also CA 106

Habbema, Koos
See Heijermans, Herman

Hacker, Marilyn 1942- .... **CLC 5, 9, 23, 72**
See also CA 77-80; DLB 120

Haggard, H(enry) Rider
1856-1925 .... **TCLC 11**
See also CA 108; 148; DLB 70, 156;
SATA 16

Hagiwara Sakutaro 1886-1942 .... **TCLC 60**

Haig, Fenil
See Ford, Ford Madox

Haig-Brown, Roderick (Langmere)
1908-1976 .... **CLC 21**
See also CA 5-8R; 69-72; CANR 4, 38;
CLR 31; DLB 88; MAICYA; SATA 12

Hailey, Arthur 1920- .... **CLC 5**
See also AITN 2; BEST 90:3; CA 1-4R;
CANR 2, 36; DLB 88; DLBY 82; MTCW

Hailey, Elizabeth Forsythe 1938-... **CLC 40**
See also CA 93-96; CAAS 1; CANR 15, 48

Haines, John (Meade) 1924-....... **CLC 58**
See also CA 17-20R; CANR 13, 34; DLB 5

Hakluyt, Richard 1552-1616....... **LC 31**

Haldeman, Joe (William) 1943-..... **CLC 61**
See also CA 53-56; CANR 6; DLB 8

Haley, Alex(ander Murray Palmer)
1921-1992 .... **CLC 8, 12, 76; BLC; DA;**
DAB
See also BW 2; CA 77-80; 136; DLB 38;
MTCW

Haliburton, Thomas Chandler
1796-1865 .... **NCLC 15**
See also DLB 11, 99

Hall, Donald (Andrew, Jr.)
1928- .... **CLC 1, 13, 37, 59**
See also CA 5-8R; CAAS 7; CANR 2, 44;
DLB 5; SATA 23

Hall, Frederic Sauser
See Sauser-Hall, Frederic

Hall, James
See Kuttner, Henry

Hall, James Norman   1887-1951 ... **TCLC 23**
See also CA 123; SATA 21

Hall, (Marguerite) Radclyffe
1886(?)-1943 .... **TCLC 12**
See also CA 110

Hall, Rodney   1935- .... **CLC 51**
See also CA 109

Halleck, Fitz-Greene   1790-1867 .. **NCLC 47**
See also DLB 3

Halliday, Michael
See Creasey, John

Halpern, Daniel   1945- .... **CLC 14**
See also CA 33-36R

Hamburger, Michael (Peter Leopold)
1924- .... **CLC 5, 14**
See also CA 5-8R; CAAS 4; CANR 2, 47;
DLB 27

Hamill, Pete   1935- .... **CLC 10**
See also CA 25-28R; CANR 18

Hamilton, Alexander
1755(?)-1804 .... **NCLC 49**
See also DLB 37

Hamilton, Clive
See Lewis, C(live) S(taples)

Hamilton, Edmond   1904-1977 .... **CLC 1**
See also CA 1-4R; CANR 3; DLB 8

Hamilton, Eugene (Jacob) Lee
See Lee-Hamilton, Eugene (Jacob)

Hamilton, Franklin
See Silverberg, Robert

Hamilton, Gail
See Corcoran, Barbara

Hamilton, Mollie
See Kaye, M(ary) M(argaret)

Hamilton, (Anthony Walter) Patrick
1904-1962 .... **CLC 51**
See also CA 113; DLB 10

Hamilton, Virginia   1936- .... **CLC 26**
See also AAYA 2; BW 2; CA 25-28R;
CANR 20, 37; CLR 1, 11; DLB 33, 52;
JRDA; MAICYA; MTCW; SATA 4, 56,
79

Hammett, (Samuel) Dashiell
1894-1961 .... **CLC 3, 5, 10, 19, 47;**
SSC 17
See also AITN 1; CA 81-84; CANR 42;
CDALB 1929-1941; DLBD 6; MTCW

Hammon, Jupiter
1711(?)-1800(?) .... **NCLC 5; BLC**
See also DLB 31, 50

Hammond, Keith
See Kuttner, Henry

Hamner, Earl (Henry), Jr.   1923- ... **CLC 12**
See also AITN 2; CA 73-76; DLB 6

Hampton, Christopher (James)
1946- .... **CLC 4**
See also CA 25-28R; DLB 13; MTCW

Hamsun, Knut .... **TCLC 2, 14, 49**
See also Pedersen, Knut

Handke, Peter   1942- .. **CLC 5, 8, 10, 15, 38**
See also CA 77-80; CANR 33; DLB 85,
124; MTCW

Hanley, James   1901-1985 ... **CLC 3, 5, 8, 13**
See also CA 73-76; 117; CANR 36; MTCW

Hannah, Barry   1942- .... **CLC 23, 38, 90**
See also CA 108; 110; CANR 43; DLB 6;
MTCW

Hannon, Ezra
See Hunter, Evan

Hansberry, Lorraine (Vivian)
1930-1965 ...... **CLC 17, 62; BLC; DA;**
DAB; DC 2
See also BW 1; CA 109; 25-28R; CABS 3;
CDALB 1941-1968; DLB 7, 38; MTCW

Hansen, Joseph   1923- .... **CLC 38**
See also CA 29-32R; CAAS 17; CANR 16,
44

Hansen, Martin A.   1909-1955 ..... **TCLC 32**

Hanson, Kenneth O(stlin)   1922- .... **CLC 13**
See also CA 53-56; CANR 7

Hardwick, Elizabeth   1916- .... **CLC 13**
See also CA 5-8R; CANR 3, 32; DLB 6;
MTCW

Hardy, Thomas
1840-1928 ...... **TCLC 4, 10, 18, 32, 48,**
53; DA; DAB; PC 8; SSC 2; WLC
See also CA 104; 123; CDBLB 1890-1914;
DLB 18, 19, 135; MTCW

Hare, David   1947- .... **CLC 29, 58**
See also CA 97-100; CANR 39; DLB 13;
MTCW

Harford, Henry
See Hudson, W(illiam) H(enry)

Hargrave, Leonie
See Disch, Thomas M(ichael)

Harjo, Joy   1951- .... **CLC 83**
See also CA 114; CANR 35; DLB 120;
NNAL

Harlan, Louis R(udolph)   1922- ..... **CLC 34**
See also CA 21-24R; CANR 25

Harling, Robert   1951(?)- .... **CLC 53**
See also CA 147

Harmon, William (Ruth)   1938- ..... **CLC 38**
See also CA 33-36R; CANR 14, 32, 35;
SATA 65

Harper, F. E. W.
See Harper, Frances Ellen Watkins

Harper, Frances E. W.
See Harper, Frances Ellen Watkins

Harper, Frances E. Watkins
See Harper, Frances Ellen Watkins

Harper, Frances Ellen
See Harper, Frances Ellen Watkins

Harper, Frances Ellen Watkins
1825-1911 .... **TCLC 14; BLC**
See also BW 1; CA 111; 125; DLB 50

Harper, Michael S(teven)   1938- .. **CLC 7, 22**
See also BW 1; CA 33-36R; CANR 24;
DLB 41

Harper, Mrs. F. E. W.
See Harper, Frances Ellen Watkins

Harris, Christie (Lucy) Irwin
1907- .... **CLC 12**
See also CA 5-8R; CANR 6; DLB 88;
JRDA; MAICYA; SAAS 10; SATA 6, 74

Harris, Frank   1856(?)-1931 .... **TCLC 24**
See also CA 109; DLB 156

Harris, George Washington
1814-1869 .... **NCLC 23**
See also DLB 3, 11

Harris, Joel Chandler
1848-1908 .... **TCLC 2; SSC 19**
See also CA 104; 137; DLB 11, 23, 42, 78,
91; MAICYA; YABC 1

Harris, John (Wyndham Parkes Lucas)
Beynon   1903-1969
See Wyndham, John
See also CA 102; 89-92

Harris, MacDonald .... **CLC 9**
See also Heiney, Donald (William)

Harris, Mark   1922- .... **CLC 19**
See also CA 5-8R; CAAS 3; CANR 2;
DLB 2; DLBY 80

Harris, (Theodore) Wilson   1921-.... **CLC 25**
See also BW 2; CA 65-68; CAAS 16;
CANR 11, 27; DLB 117; MTCW

Harrison, Elizabeth Cavanna   1909-
See Cavanna, Betty
See also CA 9-12R; CANR 6, 27

Harrison, Harry (Max)   1925- ...... **CLC 42**
See also CA 1-4R; CANR 5, 21; DLB 8;
SATA 4

Harrison, James (Thomas)
1937- .... **CLC 6, 14, 33, 66; SSC 19**
See also CA 13-16R; CANR 8; DLBY 82

Harrison, Jim
See Harrison, James (Thomas)

Harrison, Kathryn   1961- .... **CLC 70**
See also CA 144

Harrison, Tony   1937-............. **CLC 43**
See also CA 65-68; CANR 44; DLB 40;
MTCW

Harriss, Will(ard Irvin)   1922- ...... **CLC 34**
See also CA 111

Harson, Sley
See Ellison, Harlan (Jay)

Hart, Ellis
See Ellison, Harlan (Jay)

Hart, Josephine   1942(?)- .... **CLC 70**
See also CA 138

Hart, Moss   1904-1961 .... **CLC 66**
See also CA 109; 89-92; DLB 7

Harte, (Francis) Bret(t)
1836(?)-1902 . . . . TCLC 1, 25; DA;
SSC 8; WLC
See also CA 104; 140; CDALB 1865-1917;
DLB 12, 64, 74, 79; SATA 26

Hartley, L(eslie) P(oles)
1895-1972 . . . . CLC 2, 22
See also CA 45-48; 37-40R; CANR 33;
DLB 15, 139; MTCW

Hartman, Geoffrey H. 1929- . . . . CLC 27
See also CA 117; 125; DLB 67

Hartmann von Aue
c. 1160-c. 1205 . . . . CMLC 15
See also DLB 138

Haruf, Kent 19(?)- . . . . CLC 34

Harwood, Ronald 1934- . . . . CLC 32
See also CA 1-4R; CANR 4; DLB 13

Hasek, Jaroslav (Matej Frantisek)
1883-1923 . . . . TCLC 4
See also CA 104; 129; MTCW

Hass, Robert 1941- . . . . CLC 18, 39
See also CA 111; CANR 30; DLB 105

Hastings, Hudson
See Kuttner, Henry

Hastings, Selina. . . . . CLC 44

Hatteras, Amelia
See Mencken, H(enry) L(ouis)

Hatteras, Owen . . . . TCLC 18
See also Mencken, H(enry) L(ouis); Nathan,
George Jean

Hauptmann, Gerhart (Johann Robert)
1862-1946 . . . . TCLC 4
See also CA 104; DLB 66, 118

Havel, Vaclav 1936- . . . . CLC 25, 58, 65
See also CA 104; CANR 36; MTCW

Haviaras, Stratis . . . . CLC 33
See also Chaviaras, Strates

Hawes, Stephen 1475(?)-1523(?) . . . . . LC 17

Hawkes, John (Clendennin Burne, Jr.)
1925- . . . . . . CLC 1, 2, 3, 4, 7, 9, 14, 15,
27, 49
See also CA 1-4R; CANR 2, 47; DLB 2, 7;
DLBY 80; MTCW

Hawking, S. W.
See Hawking, Stephen W(illiam)

Hawking, Stephen W(illiam)
1942- . . . . CLC 63
See also AAYA 13; BEST 89:1; CA 126;
129; CANR 48

Hawthorne, Julian 1846-1934 . . . . . TCLC 25

Hawthorne, Nathaniel
1804-1864 . . . . NCLC 39; DA; DAB;
SSC 3; WLC
See also CDALB 1640-1865; DLB 1, 74;
YABC 2

Haxton, Josephine Ayres 1921-
See Douglas, Ellen
See also CA 115; CANR 41

Hayaseca y Eizaguirre, Jorge
See Echegaray (y Eizaguirre), Jose (Maria
Waldo)

Hayashi Fumiko 1904-1951 . . . . . . TCLC 27

Haycraft, Anna
See Ellis, Alice Thomas
See also CA 122

Hayden, Robert E(arl)
1913-1980 . . . . . . CLC 5, 9, 14, 37; BLC;
DA; PC 6
See also BW 1; CA 69-72; 97-100; CABS 2;
CANR 24; CDALB 1941-1968; DLB 5,
76; MTCW; SATA 19; SATA-Obit 26

Hayford, J(oseph) E(phraim) Casely
See Casely-Hayford, J(oseph) E(phraim)

Hayman, Ronald 1932- . . . . CLC 44
See also CA 25-28R; CANR 18; DLB 155

Haywood, Eliza (Fowler)
1693(?)-1756 . . . . LC 1

Hazlitt, William 1778-1830 . . . . . . NCLC 29
See also DLB 110

Hazzard, Shirley 1931- . . . . CLC 18
See also CA 9-12R; CANR 4; DLBY 82;
MTCW

Head, Bessie 1937-1986 . . . CLC 25, 67; BLC
See also BW 2; CA 29-32R; 119; CANR 25;
DLB 117; MTCW

Headon, (Nicky) Topper 1956(?)- . . . CLC 30

Heaney, Seamus (Justin)
1939- . . . . CLC 5, 7, 14, 25, 37, 74; DAB
See also CA 85-88; CANR 25, 48;
CDBLB 1960 to Present; DLB 40;
MTCW

Hearn, (Patricio) Lafcadio (Tessima Carlos)
1850-1904 . . . . TCLC 9
See also CA 105; DLB 12, 78

Hearne, Vicki 1946- . . . . CLC 56
See also CA 139

Hearon, Shelby 1931- . . . . CLC 63
See also AITN 2; CA 25-28R; CANR 18,
48

Heat-Moon, William Least. . . . . CLC 29
See also Trogdon, William (Lewis)
See also AAYA 9

Hebbel, Friedrich 1813-1863 . . . . . NCLC 43
See also DLB 129

Hebert, Anne 1916- . . . . CLC 4, 13, 29
See also CA 85-88; DLB 68; MTCW

Hecht, Anthony (Evan)
1923- . . . . CLC 8, 13, 19
See also CA 9-12R; CANR 6; DLB 5

Hecht, Ben 1894-1964 . . . . CLC 8
See also CA 85-88; DLB 7, 9, 25, 26, 28, 86

Hedayat, Sadeq 1903-1951 . . . . TCLC 21
See also CA 120

Hegel, Georg Wilhelm Friedrich
1770-1831 . . . . NCLC 46
See also DLB 90

Heidegger, Martin 1889-1976 . . . . . . CLC 24
See also CA 81-84; 65-68; CANR 34;
MTCW

Heidenstam, (Carl Gustaf) Verner von
1859-1940 . . . . TCLC 5
See also CA 104

Heifner, Jack 1946- . . . . CLC 11
See also CA 105; CANR 47

Heijermans, Herman 1864-1924 . . . TCLC 24
See also CA 123

Heilbrun, Carolyn G(old) 1926- . . . . . CLC 25
See also CA 45-48; CANR 1, 28

Heine, Heinrich 1797-1856 . . . . NCLC 4
See also DLB 90

Heinemann, Larry (Curtiss) 1944- . . CLC 50
See also CA 110; CAAS 21; CANR 31;
DLBD 9

Heiney, Donald (William) 1921-1993
See Harris, MacDonald
See also CA 1-4R; 142; CANR 3

Heinlein, Robert A(nson)
1907-1988 . . . . . . CLC 1, 3, 8, 14, 26, 55
See also CA 1-4R; 125; CANR 1, 20;
DLB 8; JRDA; MAICYA; MTCW;
SATA 9, 69; SATA-Obit 56

Helforth, John
See Doolittle, Hilda

Hellenhofferu, Vojtech Kapristian z
See Hasek, Jaroslav (Matej Frantisek)

Heller, Joseph
1923- . . . . CLC 1, 3, 5, 8, 11, 36, 63; DA;
DAB; WLC
See also AITN 1; CA 5-8R; CABS 1;
CANR 8, 42; DLB 2, 28; DLBY 80;
MTCW

Hellman, Lillian (Florence)
1906-1984 . . . . . . CLC 2, 4, 8, 14, 18, 34,
44, 52; DC 1
See also AITN 1, 2; CA 13-16R; 112;
CANR 33; DLB 7; DLBY 84; MTCW

Helprin, Mark 1947- . . . . . CLC 7, 10, 22, 32
See also CA 81-84; CANR 47; DLBY 85;
MTCW

Helvetius, Claude-Adrien
1715-1771 . . . . LC 26

Helyar, Jane Penelope Josephine 1933-
See Poole, Josephine
See also CA 21-24R; CANR 10, 26;
SATA 82

Hemans, Felicia 1793-1835 . . . . . . NCLC 29
See also DLB 96

Hemingway, Ernest (Miller)
1899-1961 . . . . CLC 1, 3, 6, 8, 10, 13, 19,
30, 34, 39, 41, 44, 50, 61, 80; DA; DAB;
SSC 1; WLC
See also CA 77-80; CANR 34;
CDALB 1917-1929; DLB 4, 9, 102;
DLBD 1; DLBY 81, 87; MTCW

Hempel, Amy 1951- . . . . CLC 39
See also CA 118; 137

Henderson, F. C.
See Mencken, H(enry) L(ouis)

Henderson, Sylvia
See Ashton-Warner, Sylvia (Constance)

Henley, Beth . . . . CLC 23
See also Henley, Elizabeth Becker
See also CABS 3; DLBY 86

Henley, Elizabeth Becker 1952-
See Henley, Beth
See also CA 107; CANR 32; MTCW

Henley, William Ernest
1849-1903 . . . . TCLC 8
See also CA 105; DLB 19

Hennissart, Martha
See Lathen, Emma
See also CA 85-88

Henry, O........ **TCLC 1, 19; SSC 5; WLC**
　See also Porter, William Sydney

Henry, Patrick　1736-1799 .... **LC 25**

Henryson, Robert　1430(?)-1506(?).... **LC 20**
　See also DLB 146

Henry VIII　1491-1547............. **LC 10**

Henschke, Alfred
　See Klabund

Hentoff, Nat(han Irving)　1925-..... **CLC 26**
　See also AAYA 4; CA 1-4R; CAAS 6;
　CANR 5, 25; CLR 1; JRDA; MAICYA;
　SATA 42, 69; SATA-Brief 27

Heppenstall, (John) Rayner
　1911-1981 .... **CLC 10**
　See also CA 1-4R; 103; CANR 29

Herbert, Frank (Patrick)
　1920-1986 ...... **CLC 12, 23, 35, 44, 85**
　See also CA 53-56; 118; CANR 5, 43;
　DLB 8; MTCW; SATA 9, 37;
　SATA-Obit 47

Herbert, George
　1593-1633 .... **LC 24; DAB; PC 4**
　See also CDBLB Before 1660; DLB 126

Herbert, Zbigniew　1924-........ **CLC 9, 43**
　See also CA 89-92; CANR 36; MTCW

Herbst, Josephine (Frey)
　1897-1969 .... **CLC 34**
　See also CA 5-8R; 25-28R; DLB 9

Hergesheimer, Joseph
　1880-1954 .... **TCLC 11**
　See also CA 109; DLB 102, 9

Herlihy, James Leo　1927-1993 ...... **CLC 6**
　See also CA 1-4R; 143; CANR 2

Hermogenes　fl. c. 175-........... **CMLC 6**

Hernandez, Jose　1834-1886...... **NCLC 17**

Herrick, Robert
　1591-1674 ..... **LC 13; DA; DAB; PC 9**
　See also DLB 126

Herring, Guilles
　See Somerville, Edith

Herriot, James　1916-1995 .... **CLC 12**
　See also Wight, James Alfred
　See also AAYA 1; CA 148; CANR 40

Herrmann, Dorothy　1941-......... **CLC 44**
　See also CA 107

Herrmann, Taffy
　See Herrmann, Dorothy

Hersey, John (Richard)
　1914-1993 .... **CLC 1, 2, 7, 9, 40, 81**
　See also CA 17-20R; 140; CANR 33;
　DLB 6; MTCW; SATA 25;
　SATA-Obit 76

Herzen, Aleksandr Ivanovich
　1812-1870 .... **NCLC 10**

Herzl, Theodor　1860-1904....... **TCLC 36**

Herzog, Werner　1942-........... **CLC 16**
　See also CA 89-92

Hesiod　c. 8th cent. B.C.-......... **CMLC 5**

Hesse, Hermann
　1877-1962 .... **CLC 1, 2, 3, 6, 11, 17, 25,
　　　　　　　　69; DA; DAB; SSC 9; WLC**
　See also CA 17-18; CAP 2; DLB 66;
　MTCW; SATA 50

Hewes, Cady
　See De Voto, Bernard (Augustine)

Heyen, William　1940- .... **CLC 13, 18**
　See also CA 33-36R; CAAS 9; DLB 5

Heyerdahl, Thor　1914-........... **CLC 26**
　See also CA 5-8R; CANR 5, 22; MTCW;
　SATA 2, 52

Heym, Georg (Theodor Franz Arthur)
　1887-1912 .... **TCLC 9**
　See also CA 106

Heym, Stefan　1913- .... **CLC 41**
　See also CA 9-12R; CANR 4; DLB 69

Heyse, Paul (Johann Ludwig von)
　1830-1914 .... **TCLC 8**
　See also CA 104; DLB 129

Heyward, (Edwin) DuBose
　1885-1940 .... **TCLC 59**
　See also CA 108; DLB 7, 9, 45; SATA 21

Hibbert, Eleanor Alice Burford
　1906-1993 .... **CLC 7**
　See also BEST 90:4; CA 17-20R; 140;
　CANR 9, 28; SATA 2; SATA-Obit 74

Higgins, George V(incent)
　1939- .... **CLC 4, 7, 10, 18**
　See also CA 77-80; CAAS 5; CANR 17;
　DLB 2; DLBY 81; MTCW

Higginson, Thomas Wentworth
　1823-1911 .... **TCLC 36**
　See also DLB 1, 64

Highet, Helen
　See MacInnes, Helen (Clark)

Highsmith, (Mary) Patricia
　1921-1995 .... **CLC 2, 4, 14, 42**
　See also CA 1-4R; 147; CANR 1, 20, 48;
　MTCW

Highwater, Jamake (Mamake)
　1942(?)- .... **CLC 12**
　See also AAYA 7; CA 65-68; CAAS 7;
　CANR 10, 34; CLR 17; DLB 52;
　DLBY 85; JRDA; MAICYA; SATA 32,
　69; SATA-Brief 30

Higuchi, Ichiyo　1872-1896....... **NCLC 49**

Hijuelos, Oscar　1951- ...... **CLC 65; HLC**
　See also BEST 90:1; CA 123; DLB 145; HW

Hikmet, Nazim　1902(?)-1963....... **CLC 40**
　See also CA 141; 93-96

Hildesheimer, Wolfgang
　1916-1991 .... **CLC 49**
　See also CA 101; 135; DLB 69, 124

Hill, Geoffrey (William)
　1932- .... **CLC 5, 8, 18, 45**
　See also CA 81-84; CANR 21;
　CDBLB 1960 to Present; DLB 40;
　MTCW

Hill, George Roy　1921-........... **CLC 26**
　See also CA 110; 122

Hill, John
　See Koontz, Dean R(ay)

Hill, Susan (Elizabeth)
　1942- .... **CLC 4; DAB**
　See also CA 33-36R; CANR 29; DLB 14,
　139; MTCW

Hillerman, Tony　1925-............ **CLC 62**
　See also AAYA 6; BEST 89:1; CA 29-32R;
　CANR 21, 42; SATA 6

Hillesum, Etty　1914-1943 .... **TCLC 49**
　See also CA 137

Hilliard, Noel (Harvey)　1929-...... **CLC 15**
　See also CA 9-12R; CANR 7

Hillis, Rick　1956-............... **CLC 66**
　See also CA 134

Hilton, James　1900-1954........ **TCLC 21**
　See also CA 108; DLB 34, 77; SATA 34

Himes, Chester (Bomar)
　1909-1984 .... **CLC 2, 4, 7, 18, 58; BLC**
　See also BW 2; CA 25-28R; 114; CANR 22;
　DLB 2, 76, 143; MTCW

Hinde, Thomas .... **CLC 6, 11**
　See also Chitty, Thomas Willes

Hindin, Nathan
　See Bloch, Robert (Albert)

Hine, (William) Daryl　1936-....... **CLC 15**
　See also CA 1-4R; CAAS 15; CANR 1, 20;
　DLB 60

Hinkson, Katharine Tynan
　See Tynan, Katharine

Hinton, S(usan) E(loise)
　1950- .... **CLC 30; DA; DAB**
　See also AAYA 2; CA 81-84; CANR 32;
　CLR 3, 23; JRDA; MAICYA; MTCW;
　SATA 19, 58

Hippius, Zinaida .... **TCLC 9**
　See also Gippius, Zinaida (Nikolayevna)

Hiraoka, Kimitake　1925-1970
　See Mishima, Yukio
　See also CA 97-100; 29-32R; MTCW

Hirsch, E(ric) D(onald), Jr.　1928-... **CLC 79**
　See also CA 25-28R; CANR 27; DLB 67;
　MTCW

Hirsch, Edward　1950- .... **CLC 31, 50**
　See also CA 104; CANR 20, 42; DLB 120

Hitchcock, Alfred (Joseph)
　1899-1980 .... **CLC 16**
　See also CA 97-100; SATA 27;
　SATA-Obit 24

Hitler, Adolf　1889-1945.......... **TCLC 53**
　See also CA 117; 147

Hoagland, Edward　1932-......... **CLC 28**
　See also CA 1-4R; CANR 2, 31; DLB 6;
　SATA 51

Hoban, Russell (Conwell)　1925- .. **CLC 7, 25**
　See also CA 5-8R; CANR 23, 37; CLR 3;
　DLB 52; MAICYA; MTCW; SATA 1,
　40, 78

Hobbs, Perry
　See Blackmur, R(ichard) P(almer)

Hobson, Laura Z(ametkin)
　1900-1986 .... **CLC 7, 25**
　See also CA 17-20R; 118; DLB 28;
　SATA 52

Hochhuth, Rolf　1931-........ **CLC 4, 11, 18**
　See also CA 5-8R; CANR 33; DLB 124;
　MTCW

Hochman, Sandra　1936-......... **CLC 3, 8**
　See also CA 5-8R; DLB 5

Hochwaelder, Fritz　1911-1986...... **CLC 36**
　See also CA 29-32R; 120; CANR 42;
　MTCW

Hochwalder, Fritz
　See Hochwaelder, Fritz

Howes, Barbara 1914- .... **CLC 15**
See also CA 9-12R; CAAS 3; SATA 5

Hrabal, Bohumil 1914-........ **CLC 13, 67**
See also CA 106; CAAS 12

Hsun, Lu
See Lu Hsun

Hubbard, L(afayette) Ron(ald)
1911-1986 .... **CLC 43**
See also CA 77-80; 118; CANR 22

Huch, Ricarda (Octavia)
1864-1947 .... **TCLC 13**
See also CA 111; DLB 66

Huddle, David 1942- .... **CLC 49**
See also CA 57-60; CAAS 20; DLB 130

Hudson, Jeffrey
See Crichton, (John) Michael

Hudson, W(illiam) H(enry)
1841-1922 .... **TCLC 29**
See also CA 115; DLB 98, 153; SATA 35

Hueffer, Ford Madox
See Ford, Ford Madox

Hughart, Barry 1934-............. **CLC 39**
See also CA 137

Hughes, Colin
See Creasey, John

Hughes, David (John) 1930- .... **CLC 48**
See also CA 116; 129; DLB 14

Hughes, (James) Langston
1902-1967 ..... **CLC 1, 5, 10, 15, 35, 44;**
BLC; DA; DAB; DC 3; PC 1; SSC 6;
WLC
See also AAYA 12; BW 1; CA 1-4R;
25-28R; CANR 1, 34; CDALB 1929-1941;
CLR 17; DLB 4, 7, 48, 51, 86; JRDA;
MAICYA; MTCW; SATA 4, 33

Hughes, Richard (Arthur Warren)
1900-1976 .... **CLC 1, 11**
See also CA 5-8R; 65-68; CANR 4;
DLB 15; MTCW; SATA 8;
SATA-Obit 25

Hughes, Ted
1930- ... **CLC 2, 4, 9, 14, 37; DAB; PC 7**
See also CA 1-4R; CANR 1, 33; CLR 3;
DLB 40; MAICYA; MTCW; SATA 49;
SATA-Brief 27

Hugo, Richard F(ranklin)
1923-1982 .... **CLC 6, 18, 32**
See also CA 49-52; 108; CANR 3; DLB 5

Hugo, Victor (Marie)
1802-1885 .... **NCLC 3, 10, 21; DA;**
DAB; WLC
See also DLB 119; SATA 47

Huidobro, Vicente
See Huidobro Fernandez, Vicente Garcia

Huidobro Fernandez, Vicente Garcia
1893-1948 .... **TCLC 31**
See also CA 131; HW

Hulme, Keri 1947- .... **CLC 39**
See also CA 125

Hulme, T(homas) E(rnest)
1883-1917 .... **TCLC 21**
See also CA 117; DLB 19

Hume, David 1711-1776............. **LC 7**
See also DLB 104

Humphrey, William 1924-......... **CLC 45**
See also CA 77-80; DLB 6

Humphreys, Emyr Owen 1919-..... **CLC 47**
See also CA 5-8R; CANR 3, 24; DLB 15

Humphreys, Josephine 1945-.... **CLC 34, 57**
See also CA 121; 127

Hungerford, Pixie
See Brinsmead, H(esba) F(ay)

Hunt, E(verette) Howard, (Jr.)
1918- .... **CLC 3**
See also AITN 1; CA 45-48; CANR 2, 47

Hunt, Kyle
See Creasey, John

Hunt, (James Henry) Leigh
1784-1859 .... **NCLC 1**

Hunt, Marsha 1946-.............. **CLC 70**
See also BW 2; CA 143

Hunt, Violet 1866-1942 .... **TCLC 53**

Hunter, E. Waldo
See Sturgeon, Theodore (Hamilton)

Hunter, Evan 1926- .... **CLC 11, 31**
See also CA 5-8R; CANR 5, 38; DLBY 82;
MTCW; SATA 25

Hunter, Kristin (Eggleston) 1931-... **CLC 35**
See also AITN 1; BW 1; CA 13-16R;
CANR 13; CLR 3; DLB 33; MAICYA;
SAAS 10; SATA 12

Hunter, Mollie 1922-............. **CLC 21**
See also McIlwraith, Maureen Mollie
Hunter
See also AAYA 13; CANR 37; CLR 25;
JRDA; MAICYA; SAAS 7; SATA 54

Hunter, Robert (?)-1734............. **LC 7**

Hurston, Zora Neale
1903-1960 .... **CLC 7, 30, 61; BLC; DA;**
SSC 4
See also AAYA 15; BW 1; CA 85-88;
DLB 51, 86; MTCW

Huston, John (Marcellus)
1906-1987 .... **CLC 20**
See also CA 73-76; 123; CANR 34; DLB 26

Hustvedt, Siri 1955-.............. **CLC 76**
See also CA 137

Hutten, Ulrich von 1488-1523....... **LC 16**

Huxley, Aldous (Leonard)
1894-1963 ..... **CLC 1, 3, 4, 5, 8, 11, 18,**
35, 79; DA; DAB; WLC
See also AAYA 11; CA 85-88; CANR 44;
CDBLB 1914-1945; DLB 36, 100;
MTCW; SATA 63

Huysmans, Charles Marie Georges
1848-1907
See Huysmans, Joris-Karl
See also CA 104

Huysmans, Joris-Karl.............. TCLC 7
See also Huysmans, Charles Marie Georges
See also DLB 123

Hwang, David Henry
1957- .... **CLC 55; DC 4**
See also CA 127; 132

Hyde, Anthony 1946-............. **CLC 42**
See also CA 136

Hyde, Margaret O(ldroyd) 1917- ... **CLC 21**
See also CA 1-4R; CANR 1, 36; CLR 23;
JRDA; MAICYA; SAAS 8; SATA 1, 42,
76

Hynes, James 1956(?)-............ **CLC 65**

Ian, Janis 1951- .... **CLC 21**
See also CA 105

Ibanez, Vicente Blasco
See Blasco Ibanez, Vicente

Ibarguengoitia, Jorge 1928-1983.... **CLC 37**
See also CA 124; 113; HW

Ibsen, Henrik (Johan)
1828-1906 .... **TCLC 2, 8, 16, 37, 52;**
DA; DAB; DC 2; WLC
See also CA 104; 141

Ibuse Masuji 1898-1993........... **CLC 22**
See also CA 127; 141

Ichikawa, Kon 1915-.............. **CLC 20**
See also CA 121

Idle, Eric 1943-.................. **CLC 21**
See also Monty Python
See also CA 116; CANR 35

Ignatow, David 1914-...... **CLC 4, 7, 14, 40**
See also CA 9-12R; CAAS 3; CANR 31;
DLB 5

Ihimaera, Witi 1944- .... **CLC 46**
See also CA 77-80

Ilf, Ilya.......................... TCLC 21
See also Fainzilberg, Ilya Arnoldovich

Immermann, Karl (Lebrecht)
1796-1840 .... **NCLC 4, 49**
See also DLB 133

Inclan, Ramon (Maria) del Valle
See Valle-Inclan, Ramon (Maria) del

Infante, G(uillermo) Cabrera
See Cabrera Infante, G(uillermo)

Ingalls, Rachel (Holmes) 1940-..... **CLC 42**
See also CA 123; 127

Ingamells, Rex 1913-1955 .... **TCLC 35**

Inge, William Motter
1913-1973 .... **CLC 1, 8, 19**
See also CA 9-12R; CDALB 1941-1968;
DLB 7; MTCW

Ingelow, Jean 1820-1897 .... **NCLC 39**
See also DLB 35; SATA 33

Ingram, Willis J.
See Harris, Mark

Innaurato, Albert (F.) 1948(?)- .. **CLC 21, 60**
See also CA 115; 122

Innes, Michael
See Stewart, J(ohn) I(nnes) M(ackintosh)

Ionesco, Eugene
1909-1994 .... **CLC 1, 4, 6, 9, 11, 15, 41,**
86; DA; DAB; WLC
See also CA 9-12R; 144; MTCW; SATA 7;
SATA-Obit 79

Iqbal, Muhammad 1873-1938 ..... **TCLC 28**

Ireland, Patrick
See O'Doherty, Brian

Iron, Ralph
See Schreiner, Olive (Emilie Albertina)

Irving, John (Winslow)
1942- . . . . **CLC 13, 23, 38**
See also AAYA 8; BEST 89:3; CA 25-28R;
CANR 28; DLB 6; DLBY 82; MTCW

Irving, Washington
1783-1859 . . . . . **NCLC 2, 19; DA; DAB;**
SSC 2; WLC
See also CDALB 1640-1865; DLB 3, 11, 30,
59, 73, 74; YABC 2

Irwin, P. K.
See Page, P(atricia) K(athleen)

Isaacs, Susan 1943- . . . . **CLC 32**
See also BEST 89:1; CA 89-92; CANR 20,
41; MTCW

Isherwood, Christopher (William Bradshaw)
1904-1986 . . . . **CLC 1, 9, 11, 14, 44**
See also CA 13-16R; 117; CANR 35;
DLB 15; DLBY 86; MTCW

Ishiguro, Kazuo 1954- . . . . . . **CLC 27, 56, 59**
See also BEST 90:2; CA 120; CANR 49;
MTCW

Ishikawa Takuboku
1886(?)-1912 . . . . **TCLC 15; PC 10**
See also CA 113

Iskander, Fazil 1929- . . . . **CLC 47**
See also CA 102

Ivan IV 1530-1584 . . . . **LC 17**

Ivanov, Vyacheslav Ivanovich
1866-1949 . . . . **TCLC 33**
See also CA 122

Ivask, Ivar Vidrik 1927-1992 . . . . . . **CLC 14**
See also CA 37-40R; 139; CANR 24

Jackson, Daniel
See Wingrove, David (John)

Jackson, Jesse 1908-1983 . . . . **CLC 12**
See also BW 1; CA 25-28R; 109; CANR 27;
CLR 28; MAICYA; SATA 2, 29;
SATA-Obit 48

Jackson, Laura (Riding) 1901-1991
See Riding, Laura
See also CA 65-68; 135; CANR 28; DLB 48

Jackson, Sam
See Trumbo, Dalton

Jackson, Sara
See Wingrove, David (John)

Jackson, Shirley
1919-1965 . . . . **CLC 11, 60, 87; DA;**
SSC 9; WLC
See also AAYA 9; CA 1-4R; 25-28R;
CANR 4; CDALB 1941-1968; DLB 6;
SATA 2

Jacob, (Cyprien-)Max 1876-1944 . . . **TCLC 6**
See also CA 104

Jacobs, Jim 1942- . . . . **CLC 12**
See also CA 97-100

Jacobs, W(illiam) W(ymark)
1863-1943 . . . . **TCLC 22**
See also CA 121; DLB 135

Jacobsen, Jens Peter 1847-1885 . . **NCLC 34**

Jacobsen, Josephine 1908- . . . . **CLC 48**
See also CA 33-36R; CAAS 18; CANR 23,
48

Jacobson, Dan 1929- . . . . **CLC 4, 14**
See also CA 1-4R; CANR 2, 25; DLB 14;
MTCW

Jacqueline
See Carpentier (y Valmont), Alejo

Jagger, Mick 1944- . . . . **CLC 17**

Jakes, John (William) 1932- . . . . **CLC 29**
See also BEST 89:4; CA 57-60; CANR 10,
43; DLBY 83; MTCW; SATA 62

James, Andrew
See Kirkup, James

James, C(yril) L(ionel) R(obert)
1901-1989 . . . . **CLC 33**
See also BW 2; CA 117; 125; 128; DLB 125;
MTCW

James, Daniel (Lewis) 1911-1988
See Santiago, Danny
See also CA 125

James, Dynely
See Mayne, William (James Carter)

James, Henry
1843-1916 . . . . . . **TCLC 2, 11, 24, 40, 47;**
DA; DAB; SSC 8; WLC
See also CA 104; 132; CDALB 1865-1917;
DLB 12, 71, 74; MTCW

James, M. R.
See James, Montague (Rhodes)
See also DLB 156

James, Montague (Rhodes)
1862-1936 . . . . **TCLC 6; SSC 16**
See also CA 104

James, P. D. . . . . **CLC 18, 46**
See also White, Phyllis Dorothy James
See also BEST 90:2; CDBLB 1960 to
Present; DLB 87

James, Philip
See Moorcock, Michael (John)

James, William 1842-1910 . . . . . **TCLC 15, 32**
See also CA 109

James I 1394-1437 . . . . **LC 20**

Jameson, Anna 1794-1860 . . . . **NCLC 43**
See also DLB 99

Jami, Nur al-Din 'Abd al-Rahman
1414-1492 . . . . **LC 9**

Jandl, Ernst 1925- . . . . **CLC 34**

Janowitz, Tama 1957- . . . . **CLC 43**
See also CA 106

Japrisot, Sebastien 1931- . . . . **CLC 90**

Jarrell, Randall
1914-1965 . . . . **CLC 1, 2, 6, 9, 13, 49**
See also CA 5-8R; 25-28R; CABS 2;
CANR 6, 34; CDALB 1941-1968; CLR 6;
DLB 48, 52; MAICYA; MTCW; SATA 7

Jarry, Alfred
1873-1907 . . . . **TCLC 2, 14; SSC 20**
See also CA 104

Jarvis, E. K.
See Bloch, Robert (Albert); Ellison, Harlan
(Jay); Silverberg, Robert

Jeake, Samuel, Jr.
See Aiken, Conrad (Potter)

Jean Paul 1763-1825 . . . . **NCLC 7**

Jefferies, (John) Richard
1848-1887 . . . . **NCLC 47**
See also DLB 98, 141; SATA 16

Jeffers, (John) Robinson
1887-1962 . . . . **CLC 2, 3, 11, 15, 54; DA;**
WLC
See also CA 85-88; CANR 35;
CDALB 1917-1929; DLB 45; MTCW

Jefferson, Janet
See Mencken, H(enry) L(ouis)

Jefferson, Thomas 1743-1826 . . . . **NCLC 11**
See also CDALB 1640-1865; DLB 31

Jeffrey, Francis 1773-1850 . . . . . . **NCLC 33**
See also DLB 107

Jelakowitch, Ivan
See Heijermans, Herman

Jellicoe, (Patricia) Ann 1927- . . . . . . **CLC 27**
See also CA 85-88; DLB 13

Jen, Gish . . . . **CLC 70**
See also Jen, Lillian

Jen, Lillian 1956(?)-
See Jen, Gish
See also CA 135

Jenkins, (John) Robin 1912- . . . . **CLC 52**
See also CA 1-4R; CANR 1; DLB 14

Jennings, Elizabeth (Joan)
1926- . . . . **CLC 5, 14**
See also CA 61-64; CAAS 5; CANR 8, 39;
DLB 27; MTCW; SATA 66

Jennings, Waylon 1937- . . . . **CLC 21**

Jensen, Johannes V. 1873-1950 . . . . **TCLC 41**

Jensen, Laura (Linnea) 1948- . . . . . . **CLC 37**
See also CA 103

Jerome, Jerome K(lapka)
1859-1927 . . . . **TCLC 23**
See also CA 119; DLB 10, 34, 135

Jerrold, Douglas William
1803-1857 . . . . **NCLC 2**

Jewett, (Theodora) Sarah Orne
1849-1909 . . . . **TCLC 1, 22; SSC 6**
See also CA 108; 127; DLB 12, 74;
SATA 15

Jewsbury, Geraldine (Endsor)
1812-1880 . . . . **NCLC 22**
See also DLB 21

Jhabvala, Ruth Prawer
1927- . . . . **CLC 4, 8, 29; DAB**
See also CA 1-4R; CANR 2, 29; DLB 139;
MTCW

Jiles, Paulette 1943- . . . . **CLC 13, 58**
See also CA 101

Jimenez (Mantecon), Juan Ramon
1881-1958 . . . . **TCLC 4; HLC; PC 7**
See also CA 104; 131; DLB 134; HW;
MTCW

Jimenez, Ramon
See Jimenez (Mantecon), Juan Ramon

Jimenez Mantecon, Juan
See Jimenez (Mantecon), Juan Ramon

Joel, Billy . . . . **CLC 26**
See also Joel, William Martin

Joel, William Martin 1949-
See Joel, Billy
See also CA 108

John of the Cross, St. 1542-1591 . . . . **LC 18**

Johnson, B(ryan) S(tanley William)
1933-1973 . . . . **CLC 6, 9**
See also CA 9-12R; 53-56; CANR 9;
DLB 14, 40

Johnson, Benj. F. of Boo
See Riley, James Whitcomb

Johnson, Benjamin F. of Boo
See Riley, James Whitcomb

Johnson, Charles (Richard)
1948- . . . . **CLC 7, 51, 65; BLC**
See also BW 2; CA 116; CAAS 18;
CANR 42; DLB 33

Johnson, Denis   1949- . . . . **CLC 52**
See also CA 117; 121; DLB 120

Johnson, Diane   1934- . . . . **CLC 5, 13, 48**
See also CA 41-44R; CANR 17, 40;
DLBY 80; MTCW

Johnson, Eyvind (Olof Verner)
1900-1976 . . . . **CLC 14**
See also CA 73-76; 69-72; CANR 34

Johnson, J. R.
See James, C(yril) L(ionel) R(obert)

Johnson, James Weldon
1871-1938 . . . . **TCLC 3, 19; BLC**
See also BW 1; CA 104; 125;
CDALB 1917-1929; CLR 32; DLB 51;
MTCW; SATA 31

Johnson, Joyce   1935- . . . . **CLC 58**
See also CA 125; 129

Johnson, Lionel (Pigot)
1867-1902 . . . . **TCLC 19**
See also CA 117, DLB 19

Johnson, Mel
See Malzberg, Barry N(athaniel)

Johnson, Pamela Hansford
1912-1981 . . . . **CLC 1, 7, 27**
See also CA 1-4R; 104; CANR 2, 28;
DLB 15; MTCW

Johnson, Samuel
1709-1784 . . . . . **LC 15; DA; DAB; WLC**
See also CDBLB 1660-1789; DLB 39, 95,
104, 142

Johnson, Uwe
1934-1984 . . . . **CLC 5, 10, 15, 40**
See also CA 1-4R; 112; CANR 1, 39;
DLB 75; MTCW

Johnston, George (Benson)   1913- . . . **CLC 51**
See also CA 1-4R; CANR 5, 20; DLB 88

Johnston, Jennifer   1930- . . . . **CLC 7**
See also CA 85-88; DLB 14

Jolley, (Monica) Elizabeth
1923- . . . . **CLC 46; SSC 19**
See also CA 127; CAAS 13

Jones, Arthur Llewellyn   1863-1947
See Machen, Arthur
See also CA 104

Jones, D(ouglas) G(ordon)   1929- . . . . **CLC 10**
See also CA 29-32R; CANR 13; DLB 53

Jones, David (Michael)
1895-1974 . . . . **CLC 2, 4, 7, 13, 42**
See also CA 9-12R; 53-56; CANR 28;
CDBLB 1945-1960; DLB 20, 100; MTCW

Jones, David Robert   1947-
See Bowie, David
See also CA 103

Jones, Diana Wynne   1934- . . . . **CLC 26**
See also AAYA 12; CA 49-52; CANR 4,
26; CLR 23; JRDA; MAICYA; SAAS 7;
SATA 9, 70

Jones, Edward P.   1950- . . . . **CLC 76**
See also BW 2; CA 142

Jones, Gayl   1949- . . . . **CLC 6, 9; BLC**
See also BW 2; CA 77-80; CANR 27;
DLB 33; MTCW

Jones, James   1921-1977 . . . . **CLC 1, 3, 10, 39**
See also AITN 1, 2; CA 1-4R; 69-72;
CANR 6; DLB 2, 143; MTCW

Jones, John J.
See Lovecraft, H(oward) P(hillips)

Jones, LeRoi . . . . **CLC 1, 2, 3, 5, 10, 14**
See also Baraka, Amiri

Jones, Louis B. . . . . **CLC 65**
See also CA 141

Jones, Madison (Percy, Jr.)   1925- . . . **CLC 4**
See also CA 13-16R; CAAS 11; CANR 7;
DLB 152

Jones, Mervyn   1922- . . . . **CLC 10, 52**
See also CA 45-48; CAAS 5; CANR 1;
MTCW

Jones, Mick   1956(?)- . . . . **CLC 30**

Jones, Nettie (Pearl)   1941- . . . . **CLC 34**
See also BW 2; CA 137; CAAS 20

Jones, Preston   1936-1979 . . . . **CLC 10**
See also CA 73-76; 89-92; DLB 7

Jones, Robert F(rancis)   1934- . . . . **CLC 7**
See also CA 49-52; CANR 2

Jones, Rod   1953- . . . . **CLC 50**
See also CA 128

Jones, Terence Graham Parry
1942- . . . . **CLC 21**
See also Jones, Terry; Monty Python
See also CA 112; 116; CANR 35

Jones, Terry
See Jones, Terence Graham Parry
See also SATA 67; SATA-Brief 51

Jones, Thom   1945(?)- . . . . **CLC 81**

Jong, Erica   1942- . . . . . . **CLC 4, 6, 8, 18, 83**
See also AITN 1; BEST 90:2; CA 73-76;
CANR 26; DLB 2, 5, 28, 152; MTCW

Jonson, Ben(jamin)
1572(?)-1637 . . . . **LC 6; DA; DAB; DC 4;
WLC**
See also CDBLB Before 1660; DLB 62, 121

Jordan, June   1936- . . . . **CLC 5, 11, 23**
See also AAYA 2; BW 2; CA 33-36R;
CANR 25; CLR 10; DLB 38; MAICYA;
MTCW; SATA 4

Jordan, Pat(rick M.)   1941- . . . . **CLC 37**
See also CA 33-36R

Jorgensen, Ivar
See Ellison, Harlan (Jay)

Jorgenson, Ivar
See Silverberg, Robert

Josephus, Flavius   c. 37-100 . . . . . . **CMLC 13**

Josipovici, Gabriel   1940- . . . . **CLC 6, 43**
See also CA 37-40R; CAAS 8; CANR 47;
DLB 14

Joubert, Joseph   1754-1824 . . . . **NCLC 9**

Jouve, Pierre Jean   1887-1976 . . . . . . **CLC 47**
See also CA 65-68

Joyce, James (Augustine Aloysius)
1882-1941 . . . . **TCLC 3, 8, 16, 35, 52;
DA; DAB; SSC 3; WLC**
See also CA 104; 126; CDBLB 1914-1945;
DLB 10, 19, 36; MTCW

Jozsef, Attila   1905-1937 . . . . **TCLC 22**
See also CA 116

Juana Ines de la Cruz   1651(?)-1695 . . . **LC 5**

Judd, Cyril
See Kornbluth, C(yril) M.; Pohl, Frederik

Julian of Norwich   1342(?)-1416(?) . . . . **LC 6**
See also DLB 146

Juniper, Alex
See Hospital, Janette Turner

Just, Ward (Swift)   1935- . . . . **CLC 4, 27**
See also CA 25-28R; CANR 32

Justice, Donald (Rodney)   1925- . . **CLC 6, 19**
See also CA 5-8R; CANR 26; DLBY 83

Juvenal   c. 55-c. 127 . . . . **CMLC 8**

Juvenis
See Bourne, Randolph S(illiman)

Kacew, Romain   1914-1980
See Gary, Romain
See also CA 108; 102

Kadare, Ismail   1936- . . . . **CLC 52**

Kadohata, Cynthia . . . . **CLC 59**
See also CA 140

Kafka, Franz
1883-1924 . . . . **TCLC 2, 6, 13, 29, 47, 53;
DA; DAB; SSC 5; WLC**
See also CA 105; 126; DLB 81; MTCW

Kahanovitsch, Pinkhes
See Der Nister

Kahn, Roger   1927- . . . . **CLC 30**
See also CA 25-28R; CANR 44; SATA 37

Kain, Saul
See Sassoon, Siegfried (Lorraine)

Kaiser, Georg   1878-1945 . . . . **TCLC 9**
See also CA 106; DLB 124

Kaletski, Alexander   1946- . . . . **CLC 39**
See also CA 118; 143

Kalidasa   fl. c. 400- . . . . **CMLC 9**

Kallman, Chester (Simon)
1921-1975 . . . . **CLC 2**
See also CA 45-48; 53-56; CANR 3

Kaminsky, Melvin   1926-
See Brooks, Mel
See also CA 65-68; CANR 16

Kaminsky, Stuart M(elvin)   1934- . . . **CLC 59**
See also CA 73-76; CANR 29

Kane, Paul
See Simon, Paul

Kane, Wilson
See Bloch, Robert (Albert)

Kanin, Garson   1912- . . . . **CLC 22**
See also AITN 1; CA 5-8R; CANR 7;
DLB 7

Kaniuk, Yoram   1930- . . . . **CLC 19**
See also CA 134

Kant, Immanuel   1724-1804 . . . . . . **NCLC 27**
See also DLB 94

Khlebnikov, Viktor Vladimirovich 1885-1922
See Khlebnikov, Velimir
See also CA 117

Khodasevich, Vladislav (Felitsianovich)
1886-1939 .... **TCLC 15**
See also CA 115

Kielland, Alexander Lange
1849-1906 .... **TCLC 5**
See also CA 104

Kiely, Benedict 1919-.......... **CLC 23, 43**
See also CA 1-4R; CANR 2; DLB 15

Kienzle, William X(avier) 1928- .... **CLC 25**
See also CA 93-96; CAAS 1; CANR 9, 31;
MTCW

Kierkegaard, Soren 1813-1855.... **NCLC 34**

Killens, John Oliver 1916-1987..... **CLC 10**
See also BW 2; CA 77-80; 123; CAAS 2;
CANR 26; DLB 33

Killigrew, Anne 1660-1685........... **LC 4**
See also DLB 131

Kim
See Simenon, Georges (Jacques Christian)

Kincaid, Jamaica 1949- ... **CLC 43, 68; BLC**
See also AAYA 13; BW 2; CA 125;
CANR 47

King, Francis (Henry) 1923-..... **CLC 8, 53**
See also CA 1-4R; CANR 1, 33; DLB 15,
139; MTCW

King, Martin Luther, Jr.
1929-1968 .... **CLC 83; BLC; DA; DAB**
See also BW 2; CA 25-28; CANR 27, 44;
CAP 2; MTCW; SATA 14

King, Stephen (Edwin)
1947- ...... **CLC 12, 26, 37, 61; SSC 17**
See also AAYA 1; BEST 90:1; CA 61-64;
CANR 1, 30; DLB 143; DLBY 80;
JRDA; MTCW; SATA 9, 55

King, Steve
See King, Stephen (Edwin)

King, Thomas 1943-.............. **CLC 89**
See also CA 144; NNAL

Kingman, Lee..................... **CLC 17**
See also Natti, (Mary) Lee
See also SAAS 3; SATA 1, 67

Kingsley, Charles 1819-1875..... **NCLC 35**
See also DLB 21, 32; YABC 2

Kingsley, Sidney 1906-1995....... **CLC 44**
See also CA 85-88; 147; DLB 7

Kingsolver, Barbara 1955-...... **CLC 55, 81**
See also AAYA 15; CA 129; 134

Kingston, Maxine (Ting Ting) Hong
1940- .... **CLC 12, 19, 58**
See also AAYA 8; CA 69-72; CANR 13,
38; DLBY 80; MTCW; SATA 53

Kinnell, Galway
1927- .... **CLC 1, 2, 3, 5, 13, 29**
See also CA 9-12R; CANR 10, 34; DLB 5;
DLBY 87; MTCW

Kinsella, Thomas 1928- .... **CLC 4, 19**
See also CA 17-20R; CANR 15; DLB 27;
MTCW

Kinsella, W(illiam) P(atrick)
1935- .... **CLC 27, 43**
See also AAYA 7; CA 97-100; CAAS 7;
CANR 21, 35; MTCW

Kipling, (Joseph) Rudyard
1865-1936 ...... **TCLC 8, 17; DA; DAB;
PC 3; SSC 5; WLC**
See also CA 105; 120; CANR 33;
CDBLB 1890-1914; CLR 39; DLB 19, 34,
141, 156; MAICYA; MTCW; YABC 2

Kirkup, James 1918- .... **CLC 1**
See also CA 1-4R; CAAS 4; CANR 2;
DLB 27; SATA 12

Kirkwood, James 1930(?)-1989 ...... **CLC 9**
See also AITN 2; CA 1-4R; 128; CANR 6,
40

Kirshner, Sidney
See Kingsley, Sidney

Kis, Danilo 1935-1989 .... **CLC 57**
See also CA 109; 118; 129; MTCW

Kivi, Aleksis 1834-1872......... **NCLC 30**

Kizer, Carolyn (Ashley)
1925-................... **CLC 15, 39, 80**
See also CA 65-68; CAAS 5; CANR 24;
DLB 5

Klabund 1890-1928.............. **TCLC 44**
See also DLB 66

Klappert, Peter 1942-............. **CLC 57**
See also CA 33-36R; DLB 5

Klein, A(braham) M(oses)
1909-1972................ **CLC 19; DAB**
See also CA 101; 37-40R; DLB 68

Klein, Norma 1938-1989 .... **CLC 30**
See also AAYA 2; CA 41-44R; 128;
CANR 15, 37; CLR 2, 19; JRDA;
MAICYA; SAAS 1; SATA 7, 57

Klein, T(heodore) E(ibon) D(onald)
1947-....................... **CLC 34**
See also CA 119; CANR 44

Kleist, Heinrich von
1777-1811 .... **NCLC 2, 37**
See also DLB 90

Klima, Ivan 1931-................ **CLC 56**
See also CA 25-28R; CANR 17

Klimentov, Andrei Platonovich 1899-1951
See Platonov, Andrei
See also CA 108

Klinger, Friedrich Maximilian von
1752-1831 .... **NCLC 1**
See also DLB 94

Klopstock, Friedrich Gottlieb
1724-1803 .... **NCLC 11**
See also DLB 97

Knebel, Fletcher 1911-1993........ **CLC 14**
See also AITN 1; CA 1-4R; 140; CAAS 3;
CANR 1, 36; SATA 36; SATA-Obit 75

Knickerbocker, Diedrich
See Irving, Washington

Knight, Etheridge
1931-1991 .... **CLC 40; BLC**
See also BW 1; CA 21-24R; 133; CANR 23;
DLB 41

Knight, Sarah Kemble 1666-1727 ..... **LC 7**
See also DLB 24

Knister, Raymond 1899-1932..... **TCLC 56**
See also DLB 68

Knowles, John
1926- .... **CLC 1, 4, 10, 26; DA**
See also AAYA 10; CA 17-20R; CANR 40;
CDALB 1968-1988; DLB 6; MTCW;
SATA 8

Knox, Calvin M.
See Silverberg, Robert

Knye, Cassandra
See Disch, Thomas M(ichael)

Koch, C(hristopher) J(ohn) 1932- ... **CLC 42**
See also CA 127

Koch, Christopher
See Koch, C(hristopher) J(ohn)

Koch, Kenneth 1925- .... **CLC 5, 8, 44**
See also CA 1-4R; CANR 6, 36; DLB 5;
SATA 65

Kochanowski, Jan 1530-1584........ **LC 10**

Kock, Charles Paul de
1794-1871 .... **NCLC 16**

Koda Shigeyuki 1867-1947
See Rohan, Koda
See also CA 121

Koestler, Arthur
1905-1983 .... **CLC 1, 3, 6, 8, 15, 33**
See also CA 1-4R; 109; CANR 1, 33;
CDBLB 1945-1960; DLBY 83; MTCW

Kogawa, Joy Nozomi 1935-........ **CLC 78**
See also CA 101; CANR 19

Kohout, Pavel 1928-.............. **CLC 13**
See also CA 45-48; CANR 3

Koizumi, Yakumo
See Hearn, (Patricio) Lafcadio (Tessima
Carlos)

Kolmar, Gertrud 1894-1943....... **TCLC 40**

Komunyakaa, Yusef 1947-......... **CLC 86**
See also CA 147; DLB 120

Konrad, George
See Konrad, Gyoergy

Konrad, Gyoergy 1933- ...... **CLC 4, 10, 73**
See also CA 85-88

Konwicki, Tadeusz 1926-..... **CLC 8, 28, 54**
See also CA 101; CAAS 9; CANR 39;
MTCW

Koontz, Dean R(ay) 1945-......... **CLC 78**
See also AAYA 9; BEST 89:3, 90:2;
CA 108; CANR 19, 36; MTCW

Kopit, Arthur (Lee) 1937- .... **CLC 1, 18, 33**
See also AITN 1; CA 81-84; CABS 3;
DLB 7; MTCW

Kops, Bernard 1926-.............. **CLC 4**
See also CA 5-8R; DLB 13

Kornbluth, C(yril) M. 1923-1958.... **TCLC 8**
See also CA 105; DLB 8

Korolenko, V. G.
See Korolenko, Vladimir Galaktionovich

Korolenko, Vladimir
See Korolenko, Vladimir Galaktionovich

Korolenko, Vladimir G.
See Korolenko, Vladimir Galaktionovich

Korolenko, Vladimir Galaktionovich
1853-1921 .... **TCLC 22**
See also CA 121

Landwirth, Heinz 1927-
See Lind, Jakov
See also CA 9-12R; CANR 7

Lane, Patrick 1939- .... **CLC 25**
See also CA 97-100; DLB 53

Lang, Andrew 1844-1912 .... **TCLC 16**
See also CA 114; 137; DLB 98, 141;
MAICYA; SATA 16

Lang, Fritz 1890-1976 .... **CLC 20**
See also CA 77-80; 69-72; CANR 30

Lange, John
See Crichton, (John) Michael

Langer, Elinor 1939- .... **CLC 34**
See also CA 121

Langland, William
1330(?)-1400(?) .... **LC 19; DA; DAB**
See also DLB 146

Langstaff, Launcelot
See Irving, Washington

Lanier, Sidney 1842-1881 .... **NCLC 6**
See also DLB 64; MAICYA; SATA 18

Lanyer, Aemilia 1569-1645 ..... **LC 10, 30**
See also DLB 121

Lao Tzu .... **CMLC 7**

Lapine, James (Elliot) 1949- .... **CLC 39**
See also CA 123; 130

Larbaud, Valery (Nicolas)
1881-1957 .... **TCLC 9**
See also CA 106

Lardner, Ring
See Lardner, Ring(gold) W(ilmer)

Lardner, Ring W., Jr.
See Lardner, Ring(gold) W(ilmer)

Lardner, Ring(gold) W(ilmer)
1885-1933 .... **TCLC 2, 14**
See also CA 104; 131; CDALB 1917-1929;
DLB 11, 25, 86; MTCW

Laredo, Betty
See Codrescu, Andrei

Larkin, Maia
See Wojciechowska, Maia (Teresa)

Larkin, Philip (Arthur)
1922-1985 .... **CLC 3, 5, 8, 9, 13, 18, 33,
39, 64; DAB**
See also CA 5-8R; 117; CANR 24;
CDBLB 1960 to Present; DLB 27;
MTCW

Larra (y Sanchez de Castro), Mariano Jose de
1809-1837 .... **NCLC 17**

Larsen, Eric 1941- .... **CLC 55**
See also CA 132

Larsen, Nella 1891-1964 ..... **CLC 37; BLC**
See also BW 1; CA 125; DLB 51

Larson, Charles R(aymond) 1938- ... **CLC 31**
See also CA 53-56; CANR 4

Las Casas, Bartolome de 1474-1566 .. **LC 31**

Lasker-Schueler, Else 1869-1945 .. **TCLC 57**
See also DLB 66, 124

Latham, Jean Lee 1902- .... **CLC 12**
See also AITN 1; CA 5-8R; CANR 7;
MAICYA; SATA 2, 68

Latham, Mavis
See Clark, Mavis Thorpe

Lathen, Emma .... **CLC 2**
See also Hennissart, Martha; Latsis, Mary
J(ane)

Lathrop, Francis
See Leiber, Fritz (Reuter, Jr.)

Latsis, Mary J(ane)
See Lathen, Emma
See also CA 85-88

Lattimore, Richmond (Alexander)
1906-1984 .... **CLC 3**
See also CA 1-4R; 112; CANR 1

Laughlin, James 1914- .... **CLC 49**
See also CA 21-24R; CAAS 22; CANR 9,
47; DLB 48

Laurence, (Jean) Margaret (Wemyss)
1926-1987 .. **CLC 3, 6, 13, 50, 62; SSC 7**
See also CA 5-8R; 121; CANR 33; DLB 53;
MTCW; SATA-Obit 50

Laurent, Antoine 1952- .... **CLC 50**

Lauscher, Hermann
See Hesse, Hermann

Lautreamont, Comte de
1846-1870 .... **NCLC 12; SSC 14**

Laverty, Donald
See Blish, James (Benjamin)

Lavin, Mary 1912- ...... **CLC 4, 18; SSC 4**
See also CA 9-12R; CANR 33; DLB 15;
MTCW

Lavond, Paul Dennis
See Kornbluth, C(yril) M.; Pohl, Frederik

Lawler, Raymond Evenor 1922 .... **CLC 58**
See also CA 103

Lawrence, D(avid) H(erbert Richards)
1885-1930 .... **TCLC 2, 9, 16, 33, 48, 61;
DA; DAB; SSC 4, 19; WLC**
See also CA 104; 121; CDBLB 1914-1945;
DLB 10, 19, 36, 98; MTCW

Lawrence, T(homas) E(dward)
1888-1935 .... **TCLC 18**
See also Dale, Colin
See also CA 115

Lawrence of Arabia
See Lawrence, T(homas) E(dward)

Lawson, Henry (Archibald Hertzberg)
1867-1922 .... **TCLC 27; SSC 18**
See also CA 120

Lawton, Dennis
See Faust, Frederick (Schiller)

Laxness, Halldor .... **CLC 25**
See also Gudjonsson, Halldor Kiljan

Layamon fl. c. 1200- .... **CMLC 10**
See also DLB 146

Laye, Camara 1928-1980 ... **CLC 4, 38; BLC**
See also BW 1; CA 85-88; 97-100;
CANR 25; MTCW

Layton, Irving (Peter) 1912- ..... **CLC 2, 15**
See also CA 1-4R; CANR 2, 33, 43;
DLB 88; MTCW

Lazarus, Emma 1849-1887 .... **NCLC 8**

Lazarus, Felix
See Cable, George Washington

Lazarus, Henry
See Slavitt, David R(ytman)

Lea, Joan
See Neufeld, John (Arthur)

Leacock, Stephen (Butler)
1869-1944 .... **TCLC 2**
See also CA 104; 141; DLB 92

Lear, Edward 1812-1888 .... **NCLC 3**
See also CLR 1; DLB 32; MAICYA;
SATA 18

Lear, Norman (Milton) 1922- ...... **CLC 12**
See also CA 73-76

Leavis, F(rank) R(aymond)
1895-1978 .... **CLC 24**
See also CA 21-24R; 77-80; CANR 44;
MTCW

Leavitt, David 1961- .... **CLC 34**
See also CA 116; 122; DLB 130

Leblanc, Maurice (Marie Emile)
1864-1941 .... **TCLC 49**
See also CA 110

Lebowitz, Fran(ces Ann)
1951(?)- .... **CLC 11, 36**
See also CA 81-84; CANR 14; MTCW

Lebrecht, Peter
See Tieck, (Johann) Ludwig

le Carre, John .... **CLC 3, 5, 9, 15, 28**
See also Cornwell, David (John Moore)
See also BEST 89:4; CDBLB 1960 to
Present; DLB 87

Le Clezio, J(ean) M(arie) G(ustave)
1940- .... **CLC 31**
See also CA 116; 128; DLB 83

Leconte de Lisle, Charles-Marie-Rene
1818-1894 .... **NCLC 29**

Le Coq, Monsieur
See Simenon, Georges (Jacques Christian)

Leduc, Violette 1907-1972 .... **CLC 22**
See also CA 13-14; 33-36R; CAP 1

Ledwidge, Francis 1887(?)-1917 ... **TCLC 23**
See also CA 123; DLB 20

Lee, Andrea 1953- .... **CLC 36; BLC**
See also BW 1; CA 125

Lee, Andrew
See Auchincloss, Louis (Stanton)

Lee, Don L. .... **CLC 2**
See also Madhubuti, Haki R.

Lee, George W(ashington)
1894-1976 .... **CLC 52; BLC**
See also BW 1; CA 125; DLB 51

Lee, (Nelle) Harper
1926- ..... **CLC 12, 60; DA; DAB; WLC**
See also AAYA 13; CA 13-16R;
CDALB 1941-1968; DLB 6; MTCW;
SATA 11

Lee, Helen Elaine 1959(?)- .... **CLC 86**
See also CA 148

Lee, Julian
See Latham, Jean Lee

Lee, Larry
See Lee, Lawrence

Lee, Laurie 1914- .... **CLC 90; DAB**
See also CA 77-80; CANR 33; DLB 27;
MTCW

Lee, Lawrence 1941-1990 .... **CLC 34**
See also CA 131; CANR 43

Lewisohn, Ludwig 1883-1955...... **TCLC 19**
See also CA 107; DLB 4, 9, 28, 102

Lezama Lima, Jose 1910-1976 ... **CLC 4, 10**
See also CA 77-80; DLB 113; HW

L'Heureux, John (Clarke) 1934-.... **CLC 52**
See also CA 13-16R; CANR 23, 45

Liddell, C. H.
See Kuttner, Henry

Lie, Jonas (Lauritz Idemil)
1833-1908(?) .... **TCLC 5**
See also CA 115

Lieber, Joel 1937-1971............. **CLC 6**
See also CA 73-76; 29-32R

Lieber, Stanley Martin
See Lee, Stan

Lieberman, Laurence (James)
1935- .... **CLC 4, 36**
See also CA 17-20R; CANR 8, 36

Lieksman, Anders
See Haavikko, Paavo Juhani

Li Fei-kan 1904-
See Pa Chin
See also CA 105

Lifton, Robert Jay 1926-........ **CLC 67**
See also CA 17-20R; CANR 27; SATA 66

Lightfoot, Gordon 1938-.......... **CLC 26**
See also CA 109

Lightman, Alan P. 1948- .... **CLC 81**
See also CA 141

Ligotti, Thomas (Robert)
1953- .... **CLC 44; SSC 16**
See also CA 123; CANR 49

Li Ho 791-817.................... **PC 13**

Liliencron, (Friedrich Adolf Axel) Detlev von
1844-1909 .... **TCLC 18**
See also CA 117

Lilly, William 1602-1681.......... **LC 27**

Lima, Jose Lezama
See Lezama Lima, Jose

Lima Barreto, Afonso Henrique de
1881-1922 .... **TCLC 23**
See also CA 117

Limonov, Edward 1944-.......... **CLC 67**
See also CA 137

Lin, Frank
See Atherton, Gertrude (Franklin Horn)

Lincoln, Abraham 1809-1865..... **NCLC 18**

Lind, Jakov .... **CLC 1, 2, 4, 27, 82**
See also Landwirth, Heinz
See also CAAS 4

Lindbergh, Anne (Spencer) Morrow
1906- .... **CLC 82**
See also CA 17-20R; CANR 16; MTCW;
SATA 33

Lindsay, David 1878-1945........ **TCLC 15**
See also CA 113

Lindsay, (Nicholas) Vachel
1879-1931 .... **TCLC 17; DA; WLC**
See also CA 114; 135; CDALB 1865-1917;
DLB 54; SATA 40

Linke-Poot
See Doeblin, Alfred

Linney, Romulus 1930- .... **CLC 51**
See also CA 1-4R; CANR 40, 44

Linton, Eliza Lynn 1822-1898.... **NCLC 41**
See also DLB 18

Li Po 701-763.................. **CMLC 2**

Lipsius, Justus 1547-1606 .... **LC 16**

Lipsyte, Robert (Michael)
1938- .... **CLC 21; DA**
See also AAYA 7; CA 17-20R; CANR 8;
CLR 23; JRDA; MAICYA; SATA 5, 68

Lish, Gordon (Jay) 1934-.. **CLC 45; SSC 18**
See also CA 113; 117; DLB 130

Lispector, Clarice 1925-1977....... **CLC 43**
See also CA 139; 116; DLB 113

Littell, Robert 1935(?)- .... **CLC 42**
See also CA 109; 112

Little, Malcolm 1925-1965
See Malcolm X
See also BW 1; CA 125; 111; DA; DAB;
MTCW

Littlewit, Humphrey Gent.
See Lovecraft, H(oward) P(hillips)

Litwos
See Sienkiewicz, Henryk (Adam Alexander
Pius)

Liu E 1857-1909................. **TCLC 15**
See also CA 115

Lively, Penelope (Margaret)
1933-.................... **CLC 32, 50**
See also CA 41-44R; CANR 29; CLR 7;
DLB 14; JRDA; MAICYA; MTCW;
SATA 7, 60

Livesay, Dorothy (Kathleen)
1909- .... **CLC 4, 15, 79**
See also AITN 2; CA 25-28R; CAAS 8;
CANR 36; DLB 68; MTCW

Livy c. 59B.C.-c. 17 .... **CMLC 11**

Lizardi, Jose Joaquin Fernandez de
1776-1827 .... **NCLC 30**

Llewellyn, Richard
See Llewellyn Lloyd, Richard Dafydd
Vivian
See also DLB 15

Llewellyn Lloyd, Richard Dafydd Vivian
1906-1983 .... **CLC 7, 80**
See also Llewellyn, Richard
See also CA 53-56; 111; CANR 7;
SATA 11; SATA-Obit 37

Llosa, (Jorge) Mario (Pedro) Vargas
See Vargas Llosa, (Jorge) Mario (Pedro)

Lloyd Webber, Andrew 1948-
See Webber, Andrew Lloyd
See also AAYA 1; CA 116; SATA 56

Llull, Ramon c. 1235-c. 1316..... **CMLC 12**

Locke, Alain (Le Roy)
1886-1954 .... **TCLC 43**
See also BW 1; CA 106; 124; DLB 51

Locke, John 1632-1704 .... **LC 7**
See also DLB 101

Locke-Elliott, Sumner
See Elliott, Sumner Locke

Lockhart, John Gibson
1794-1854 .... **NCLC 6**
See also DLB 110, 116, 144

Lodge, David (John) 1935-........ **CLC 36**
See also BEST 90:1; CA 17-20R; CANR 19;
DLB 14; MTCW

Loennbohm, Armas Eino Leopold 1878-1926
See Leino, Eino
See also CA 123

Loewinsohn, Ron(ald William)
1937- .... **CLC 52**
See also CA 25-28R

Logan, Jake
See Smith, Martin Cruz

Logan, John (Burton) 1923-1987..... **CLC 5**
See also CA 77-80; 124; CANR 45; DLB 5

Lo Kuan-chung 1330(?)-1400(?)...... **LC 12**

Lombard, Nap
See Johnson, Pamela Hansford

London, Jack.. **TCLC 9, 15, 39; SSC 4; WLC**
See also London, John Griffith
See also AAYA 13; AITN 2;
CDALB 1865-1917; DLB 8, 12, 78;
SATA 18

London, John Griffith 1876-1916
See London, Jack
See also CA 110; 119; DA; DAB; JRDA;
MAICYA; MTCW

Long, Emmett
See Leonard, Elmore (John, Jr.)

Longbaugh, Harry
See Goldman, William (W.)

Longfellow, Henry Wadsworth
1807-1882 ...... **NCLC 2, 45; DA; DAB**
See also CDALB 1640-1865; DLB 1, 59;
SATA 19

Longley, Michael 1939-........... **CLC 29**
See also CA 102; DLB 40

Longus fl. c. 2nd cent. - .... **CMLC 7**

Longway, A. Hugh
See Lang, Andrew

Lopate, Phillip 1943- .... **CLC 29**
See also CA 97-100; DLBY 80

Lopez Portillo (y Pacheco), Jose
1920- .... **CLC 46**
See also CA 129; HW

Lopez y Fuentes, Gregorio
1897(?)-1966 .... **CLC 32**
See also CA 131; HW

Lorca, Federico Garcia
See Garcia Lorca, Federico

Lord, Bette Bao 1938-............. **CLC 23**
See also BEST 90:3; CA 107; CANR 41;
SATA 58

Lord Auch
See Bataille, Georges

Lord Byron
See Byron, George Gordon (Noel)

Lorde, Audre (Geraldine)
1934-1992 .... **CLC 18, 71; BLC; PC 12**
See also BW 1; CA 25-28R; 142; CANR 16,
26, 46; DLB 41; MTCW

Lord Jeffrey
See Jeffrey, Francis

Lorenzo, Heberto Padilla
See Padilla (Lorenzo), Heberto

Loris
See Hofmannsthal, Hugo von

Loti, Pierre . . . . **TCLC 11**
See also Viaud, (Louis Marie) Julien
See also DLB 123

Louie, David Wong 1954- . . . . **CLC 70**
See also CA 139

Louis, Father M.
See Merton, Thomas

Lovecraft, H(oward) P(hillips)
1890-1937 . . . . **TCLC 4, 22; SSC 3**
See also AAYA 14; CA 104; 133; MTCW

Lovelace, Earl 1935- . . . . **CLC 51**
See also BW 2; CA 77-80; CANR 41;
DLB 125; MTCW

Lovelace, Richard 1618-1657 . . . . **LC 24**
See also DLB 131

Lowell, Amy 1874-1925 . . **TCLC 1, 8; PC 13**
See also CA 104; DLB 54, 140

Lowell, James Russell 1819-1891 . . **NCLC 2**
See also CDALB 1640-1865; DLB 1, 11, 64,
79

Lowell, Robert (Traill Spence, Jr.)
1917-1977 . . . **CLC 1, 2, 3, 4, 5, 8, 9, 11,
15, 37; DA; DAB; PC 3; WLC**
See also CA 9-12R; 73-76; CABS 2;
CANR 26; DLB 5; MTCW

Lowndes, Marie Adelaide (Belloc)
1868-1947 . . . . **TCLC 12**
See also CA 107; DLB 70

Lowry, (Clarence) Malcolm
1909-1957 . . . . **TCLC 6, 40**
See also CA 105; 131; CDBLB 1945-1960;
DLB 15; MTCW

Lowry, Mina Gertrude 1882-1966
See Loy, Mina
See also CA 113

Loxsmith, John
See Brunner, John (Kilian Houston)

Loy, Mina . . . . **CLC 28**
See also Lowry, Mina Gertrude
See also DLB 4, 54

Loyson-Bridet
See Schwob, (Mayer Andre) Marcel

Lucas, Craig 1951- . . . . **CLC 64**
See also CA 137

Lucas, George 1944- . . . . **CLC 16**
See also AAYA 1; CA 77-80; CANR 30;
SATA 56

Lucas, Hans
See Godard, Jean-Luc

Lucas, Victoria
See Plath, Sylvia

Ludlam, Charles 1943-1987 . . . . . **CLC 46, 50**
See also CA 85-88; 122

Ludlum, Robert 1927- . . . . **CLC 22, 43**
See also AAYA 10; BEST 89:1, 90:3;
CA 33-36R; CANR 25, 41; DLBY 82;
MTCW

Ludwig, Ken . . . . **CLC 60**

Ludwig, Otto 1813-1865 . . . . **NCLC 4**
See also DLB 129

Lugones, Leopoldo 1874-1938 . . . . . **TCLC 15**
See also CA 116; 131; HW

Lu Hsun 1881-1936 . . . . . . **TCLC 3; SSC 20**
See also Shu-Jen, Chou

Lukacs, George . . . . **CLC 24**
See also Lukacs, Gyorgy (Szegeny von)

Lukacs, Gyorgy (Szegeny von) 1885-1971
See Lukacs, George
See also CA 101; 29-32R

Luke, Peter (Ambrose Cyprian)
1919-1995 . . . . **CLC 38**
See also CA 81-84; 147; DLB 13

Lunar, Dennis
See Mungo, Raymond

Lurie, Alison 1926- . . . . **CLC 4, 5, 18, 39**
See also CA 1-4R; CANR 2, 17; DLB 2;
MTCW; SATA 46

Lustig, Arnost 1926- . . . . **CLC 56**
See also AAYA 3; CA 69-72; CANR 47;
SATA 56

Luther, Martin 1483-1546 . . . . **LC 9**

Luzi, Mario 1914- . . . . **CLC 13**
See also CA 61-64; CANR 9; DLB 128

Lynch, B. Suarez
See Bioy Casares, Adolfo; Borges, Jorge
Luis

Lynch, David (K.) 1946- . . . . **CLC 66**
See also CA 124; 129

Lynch, James
See Andreyev, Leonid (Nikolaevich)

Lynch Davis, B.
See Bioy Casares, Adolfo; Borges, Jorge
Luis

Lyndsay, Sir David 1490-1555 . . . . . . **LC 20**

Lynn, Kenneth S(chuyler) 1923- . . . . **CLC 50**
See also CA 1-4R; CANR 3, 27

Lynx
See West, Rebecca

Lyons, Marcus
See Blish, James (Benjamin)

Lyre, Pinchbeck
See Sassoon, Siegfried (Lorraine)

Lytle, Andrew (Nelson) 1902- . . . . . . **CLC 22**
See also CA 9-12R; DLB 6

Lyttelton, George 1709-1773 . . . . **LC 10**

Maas, Peter 1929- . . . . **CLC 29**
See also CA 93-96

Macaulay, Rose 1881-1958 . . . . . **TCLC 7, 44**
See also CA 104; DLB 36

Macaulay, Thomas Babington
1800-1859 . . . . **NCLC 42**
See also CDBLB 1832-1890; DLB 32, 55

MacBeth, George (Mann)
1932-1992 . . . . **CLC 2, 5, 9**
See also CA 25-28R; 136; DLB 40; MTCW;
SATA 4; SATA-Obit 70

MacCaig, Norman (Alexander)
1910- . . . . **CLC 36; DAB**
See also CA 9-12R; CANR 3, 34; DLB 27

MacCarthy, (Sir Charles Otto) Desmond
1877-1952 . . . . **TCLC 36**

MacDiarmid, Hugh
. . . . **CLC 2, 4, 11, 19, 63; PC 9**
See also Grieve, C(hristopher) M(urray)
See also CDBLB 1945-1960; DLB 20

MacDonald, Anson
See Heinlein, Robert A(nson)

Macdonald, Cynthia 1928- . . . . . . **CLC 13, 19**
See also CA 49-52; CANR 4, 44; DLB 105

MacDonald, George 1824-1905 . . . . . **TCLC 9**
See also CA 106; 137; DLB 18; MAICYA;
SATA 33

Macdonald, John
See Millar, Kenneth

MacDonald, John D(ann)
1916-1986 . . . . **CLC 3, 27, 44**
See also CA 1-4R; 121; CANR 1, 19;
DLB 8; DLBY 86; MTCW

Macdonald, John Ross
See Millar, Kenneth

Macdonald, Ross . . . . . **CLC 1, 2, 3, 14, 34, 41**
See also Millar, Kenneth
See also DLBD 6

MacDougal, John
See Blish, James (Benjamin)

MacEwen, Gwendolyn (Margaret)
1941-1987 . . . . **CLC 13, 55**
See also CA 9-12R; 124; CANR 7, 22;
DLB 53; SATA 50; SATA-Obit 55

Macha, Karel Hynek 1810-1846 . . **NCLC 46**

Machado (y Ruiz), Antonio
1875-1939 . . . . **TCLC 3**
See also CA 104; DLB 108

Machado de Assis, Joaquim Maria
1839-1908 . . . . **TCLC 10; BLC**
See also CA 107

Machen, Arthur . . . . **TCLC 4; SSC 20**
See also Jones, Arthur Llewellyn
See also DLB 36, 156

Machiavelli, Niccolo
1469-1527 . . . . **LC 8; DA; DAB**

MacInnes, Colin 1914-1976 . . . . . . **CLC 4, 23**
See also CA 69-72; 65-68; CANR 21;
DLB 14; MTCW

MacInnes, Helen (Clark)
1907-1985 . . . . **CLC 27, 39**
See also CA 1-4R; 117; CANR 1, 28;
DLB 87; MTCW; SATA 22;
SATA-Obit 44

Mackay, Mary 1855-1924
See Corelli, Marie
See also CA 118

Mackenzie, Compton (Edward Montague)
1883-1972 . . . . **CLC 18**
See also CA 21-22; 37-40R; CAP 2;
DLB 34, 100

Mackenzie, Henry 1745-1831 . . . . **NCLC 41**
See also DLB 39

Mackintosh, Elizabeth 1896(?)-1952
See Tey, Josephine
See also CA 110

MacLaren, James
See Grieve, C(hristopher) M(urray)

Mac Laverty, Bernard 1942- . . . . **CLC 31**
See also CA 116; 118; CANR 43

MacLean, Alistair (Stuart)
1922-1987 . . . . **CLC 3, 13, 50, 63**
See also CA 57-60; 121; CANR 28; MTCW;
SATA 23; SATA-Obit 50

Maclean, Norman (Fitzroy)
1902-1990 .... **CLC 78; SSC 13**
See also CA 102; 132; CANR 49

MacLeish, Archibald
1892-1982 .... **CLC 3, 8, 14, 68**
See also CA 9-12R; 106; CANR 33; DLB 4,
7, 45; DLBY 82; MTCW

MacLennan, (John) Hugh
1907-1990 .... **CLC 2, 14**
See also CA 5-8R; 142; CANR 33; DLB 68;
MTCW

MacLeod, Alistair 1936- .... **CLC 56**
See also CA 123; DLB 60

MacNeice, (Frederick) Louis
1907-1963 ...... **CLC 1, 4, 10, 53; DAB**
See also CA 85-88; DLB 10, 20; MTCW

MacNeill, Dand
See Fraser, George MacDonald

Macpherson, James 1736-1796 ...... **LC 29**
See also DLB 109

Macpherson, (Jean) Jay 1931- ...... **CLC 14**
See also CA 5-8R; DLB 53

MacShane, Frank 1927- .... **CLC 39**
See also CA 9-12R; CANR 3, 33; DLB 111

Macumber, Mari
See Sandoz, Mari(e Susette)

Madach, Imre 1823-1864 .... **NCLC 19**

Madden, (Jerry) David 1933- .... **CLC 5, 15**
See also CA 1-4R; CAAS 3; CANR 4, 45;
DLB 6; MTCW

Maddern, Al(an)
See Ellison, Harlan (Jay)

Madhubuti, Haki R.
1942- .... **CLC 6, 73; BLC; PC 5**
See also Lee, Don L.
See also BW 2; CA 73-76; CANR 24;
DLB 5, 41; DLBD 8

Maepenn, Hugh
See Kuttner, Henry

Maepenn, K. H.
See Kuttner, Henry

Maeterlinck, Maurice 1862-1949 ... **TCLC 3**
See also CA 104; 136; SATA 66

Maginn, William 1794-1842 ...... **NCLC 8**
See also DLB 110

Mahapatra, Jayanta 1928- .... **CLC 33**
See also CA 73-76; CAAS 9; CANR 15, 33

Mahfouz, Naguib (Abdel Aziz Al-Sabilgi)
1911(?)-
See Mahfuz, Najib
See also BEST 89:2; CA 128; MTCW

Mahfuz, Najib .... **CLC 52, 55**
See also Mahfouz, Naguib (Abdel Aziz
Al-Sabilgi)
See also DLBY 88

Mahon, Derek 1941- .... **CLC 27**
See also CA 113; 128; DLB 40

Mailer, Norman
1923- ...... **CLC 1, 2, 3, 4, 5, 8, 11, 14,
28, 39, 74; DA; DAB**
See also AITN 2; CA 9-12R; CABS 1;
CANR 28; CDALB 1968-1988; DLB 2,
16, 28; DLBD 3; DLBY 80, 83; MTCW

Maillet, Antonine 1929- .... **CLC 54**
See also CA 115; 120; CANR 46; DLB 60

Mais, Roger 1905-1955 .... **TCLC 8**
See also BW 1; CA 105; 124; DLB 125;
MTCW

Maistre, Joseph de 1753-1821 .... **NCLC 37**

Maitland, Sara (Louise) 1950- ...... **CLC 49**
See also CA 69-72; CANR 13

Major, Clarence
1936- .... **CLC 3, 19, 48; BLC**
See also BW 2; CA 21-24R; CAAS 6;
CANR 13, 25; DLB 33

Major, Kevin (Gerald) 1949- .... **CLC 26**
See also CA 97-100; CANR 21, 38;
CLR 11; DLB 60; JRDA; MAICYA;
SATA 32, 82

Maki, James
See Ozu, Yasujiro

Malabaila, Damiano
See Levi, Primo

Malamud, Bernard
1914-1986 ...... **CLC 1, 2, 3, 5, 8, 9, 11,
18, 27, 44, 78, 85; DA; DAB; SSC 15;
WLC**
See also CA 5-8R; 118; CABS 1; CANR 28;
CDALB 1941-1968; DLB 2, 28, 152;
DLBY 80, 86; MTCW

Malaparte, Curzio 1898-1957 ..... **TCLC 52**

Malcolm, Dan
See Silverberg, Robert

Malcolm X .... **CLC 82; BLC**
See also Little, Malcolm

Malherbe, Francois de 1555-1628 ..... **LC 5**

Mallarme, Stephane
1842-1898 .... **NCLC 4, 41; PC 4**

Mallet-Joris, Francoise 1930- ...... **CLC 11**
See also CA 65-68; CANR 17; DLB 83

Malley, Ern
See McAuley, James Phillip

Mallowan, Agatha Christie
See Christie, Agatha (Mary Clarissa)

Maloff, Saul 1922- .... **CLC 5**
See also CA 33-36R

Malone, Louis
See MacNeice, (Frederick) Louis

Malone, Michael (Christopher)
1942- .... **CLC 43**
See also CA 77-80; CANR 14, 32

Malory, (Sir) Thomas
1410(?)-1471(?) .... **LC 11; DA; DAB**
See also CDBLB Before 1660; DLB 146;
SATA 59; SATA-Brief 33

Malouf, (George Joseph) David
1934- .... **CLC 28, 86**
See also CA 124

Malraux, (Georges-)Andre
1901-1976 ...... **CLC 1, 4, 9, 13, 15, 57**
See also CA 21-22; 69-72; CANR 34;
CAP 2; DLB 72; MTCW

Malzberg, Barry N(athaniel) 1939- ... **CLC 7**
See also CA 61-64; CAAS 4; CANR 16;
DLB 8

Mamet, David (Alan)
1947- .... **CLC 9, 15, 34, 46; DC 4**
See also AAYA 3; CA 81-84; CABS 3;
CANR 15, 41; DLB 7; MTCW

Mamoulian, Rouben (Zachary)
1897-1987 .... **CLC 16**
See also CA 25-28R; 124

Mandelstam, Osip (Emilievich)
1891(?)-1938(?) .... **TCLC 2, 6**
See also CA 104

Mander, (Mary) Jane 1877-1949... **TCLC 31**

Mandiargues, Andre Pieyre de....... **CLC 41**
See also Pieyre de Mandiargues, Andre
See also DLB 83

Mandrake, Ethel Belle
See Thurman, Wallace (Henry)

Mangan, James Clarence
1803-1849 .... **NCLC 27**

Maniere, J.-E.
See Giraudoux, (Hippolyte) Jean

Manley, (Mary) Delariviere
1672(?)-1724 .... **LC 1**
See also DLB 39, 80

Mann, Abel
See Creasey, John

Mann, (Luiz) Heinrich 1871-1950... **TCLC 9**
See also CA 106; DLB 66

Mann, (Paul) Thomas
1875-1955 .... **TCLC 2, 8, 14, 21, 35, 44,
60; DA; DAB; SSC 5; WLC**
See also CA 104; 128; DLB 66; MTCW

Manning, David
See Faust, Frederick (Schiller)

Manning, Frederic 1887(?)-1935 ... **TCLC 25**
See also CA 124

Manning, Olivia 1915-1980...... **CLC 5, 19**
See also CA 5-8R; 101; CANR 29; MTCW

Mano, D. Keith 1942- .... **CLC 2, 10**
See also CA 25-28R; CAAS 6; CANR 26;
DLB 6

Mansfield, Katherine
..... **TCLC 2, 8, 39; DAB; SSC 9; WLC**
See also Beauchamp, Kathleen Mansfield

Manso, Peter 1940- .... **CLC 39**
See also CA 29-32R; CANR 44

Mantecon, Juan Jimenez
See Jimenez (Mantecon), Juan Ramon

Manton, Peter
See Creasey, John

Man Without a Spleen, A
See Chekhov, Anton (Pavlovich)

Manzoni, Alessandro 1785-1873 .. **NCLC 29**

Mapu, Abraham (ben Jekutiel)
1808-1867 .... **NCLC 18**

Mara, Sally
See Queneau, Raymond

Marat, Jean Paul 1743-1793........ **LC 10**

Marcel, Gabriel Honore
1889-1973 .... **CLC 15**
See also CA 102; 45-48; MTCW

Marchbanks, Samuel
See Davies, (William) Robertson

Marchi, Giacomo
See Bassani, Giorgio

Margulies, Donald................. **CLC 76**

Marie de France c. 12th cent. -.... **CMLC 8**

Marie de l'Incarnation 1599-1672.... **LC 10**

Mariner, Scott
See Pohl, Frederik

Marinetti, Filippo Tommaso
1876-1944 . . . . TCLC 10
See also CA 107; DLB 114

Marivaux, Pierre Carlet de Chamblain de
1688-1763 . . . . LC 4

Markandaya, Kamala . . . . CLC 8, 38
See also Taylor, Kamala (Purnaiya)

Markfield, Wallace 1926- . . . . CLC 8
See also CA 69-72; CAAS 3; DLB 2, 28

Markham, Edwin 1852-1940 . . . . . . TCLC 47
See also DLB 54

Markham, Robert
See Amis, Kingsley (William)

Marks, J
See Highwater, Jamake (Mamake)

Marks-Highwater, J
See Highwater, Jamake (Mamake)

Markson, David M(errill) 1927- . . . . CLC 67
See also CA 49-52; CANR 1

Marley, Bob . . . . CLC 17
See also Marley, Robert Nesta

Marley, Robert Nesta 1945-1981
See Marley, Bob
See also CA 107; 103

Marlowe, Christopher
1564-1593 . . . . . LC 22; DA; DAB; DC 1;
WLC
See also CDBLB Before 1660; DLB 62

Marmontel, Jean-Francois
1723-1799 . . . . LC 2

Marquand, John P(hillips)
1893-1960 . . . . CLC 2, 10
See also CA 85-88; DLB 9, 102

Marquez, Gabriel (Jose) Garcia
See Garcia Marquez, Gabriel (Jose)

Marquis, Don(ald Robert Perry)
1878-1937 . . . . TCLC 7
See also CA 104; DLB 11, 25

Marric, J. J.
See Creasey, John

Marrow, Bernard
See Moore, Brian

Marryat, Frederick 1792-1848 . . . . NCLC 3
See also DLB 21

Marsden, James
See Creasey, John

Marsh, (Edith) Ngaio
1899-1982 . . . . CLC 7, 53
See also CA 9-12R; CANR 6; DLB 77;
MTCW

Marshall, Garry 1934- . . . . CLC 17
See also AAYA 3; CA 111; SATA 60

Marshall, Paule
1929- . . . . CLC 27, 72; BLC; SSC 3
See also BW 2; CA 77-80; CANR 25;
DLB 33; MTCW

Marsten, Richard
See Hunter, Evan

Martha, Henry
See Harris, Mark

Martial c. 40-c. 104 . . . . PC 10

Martin, Ken
See Hubbard, L(afayette) Ron(ald)

Martin, Richard
See Creasey, John

Martin, Steve 1945- . . . . CLC 30
See also CA 97-100; CANR 30; MTCW

Martin, Valerie 1948- . . . . CLC 89
See also BEST 90:2; CA 85-88; CANR 49

Martin, Violet Florence
1862-1915 . . . . TCLC 51

Martin, Webber
See Silverberg, Robert

Martindale, Patrick Victor
See White, Patrick (Victor Martindale)

Martin du Gard, Roger
1881-1958 . . . . TCLC 24
See also CA 118; DLB 65

Martineau, Harriet 1802-1876 . . . . NCLC 26
See also DLB 21, 55; YABC 2

Martines, Julia
See O'Faolain, Julia

Martinez, Jacinto Benavente y
See Benavente (y Martinez), Jacinto

Martinez Ruiz, Jose 1873-1967
See Azorin; Ruiz, Jose Martinez
See also CA 93-96; HW

Martinez Sierra, Gregorio
1881-1947 . . . . TCLC 6
See also CA 115

Martinez Sierra, Maria (de la O'LeJarraga)
1874-1974 . . . . TCLC 6
See also CA 115

Martinsen, Martin
See Follett, Ken(neth Martin)

Martinson, Harry (Edmund)
1904-1978 . . . . CLC 14
See also CA 77-80; CANR 34

Marut, Ret
See Traven, B.

Marut, Robert
See Traven, B.

Marvell, Andrew
1621-1678 . . . . . LC 4; DA; DAB; PC 10;
WLC
See also CDBLB 1660-1789; DLB 131

Marx, Karl (Heinrich)
1818-1883 . . . . NCLC 17
See also DLB 129

Masaoka Shiki . . . . TCLC 18
See also Masaoka Tsunenori

Masaoka Tsunenori 1867-1902
See Masaoka Shiki
See also CA 117

Masefield, John (Edward)
1878-1967 . . . . CLC 11, 47
See also CA 19-20; 25-28R; CANR 33;
CAP 2; CDBLB 1890-1914; DLB 10, 19,
153; MTCW; SATA 19

Maso, Carole 19(?)- . . . . CLC 44

Mason, Bobbie Ann
1940- . . . . CLC 28, 43, 82; SSC 4
See also AAYA 5; CA 53-56; CANR 11,
31; DLBY 87; MTCW

Mason, Ernst
See Pohl, Frederik

Mason, Lee W.
See Malzberg, Barry N(athaniel)

Mason, Nick 1945- . . . . CLC 35

Mason, Tally
See Derleth, August (William)

Mass, William
See Gibson, William

Masters, Edgar Lee
1868-1950 . . . . . . TCLC 2, 25; DA; PC 1
See also CA 104; 133; CDALB 1865-1917;
DLB 54; MTCW

Masters, Hilary 1928- . . . . CLC 48
See also CA 25-28R; CANR 13, 47

Mastrosimone, William 19(?)- . . . . . . CLC 36

Mathe, Albert
See Camus, Albert

Matheson, Richard Burton 1926- . . . CLC 37
See also CA 97-100; DLB 8, 44

Mathews, Harry 1930- . . . . CLC 6, 52
See also CA 21-24R; CAAS 6; CANR 18,
40

Mathews, John Joseph 1894-1979 . . . CLC 84
See also CA 19-20; 142; CANR 45; CAP 2;
NNAL

Mathias, Roland (Glyn) 1915- . . . . . . CLC 45
See also CA 97-100; CANR 19, 41; DLB 27

Matsuo Basho 1644-1694 . . . . PC 3

Mattheson, Rodney
See Creasey, John

Matthews, Greg 1949- . . . . CLC 45
See also CA 135

Matthews, William 1942- . . . . CLC 40
See also CA 29-32R; CAAS 18; CANR 12;
DLB 5

Matthias, John (Edward) 1941- . . . . . . CLC 9
See also CA 33-36R

Matthiessen, Peter
1927- . . . . CLC 5, 7, 11, 32, 64
See also AAYA 6; BEST 90:4; CA 9-12R;
CANR 21; DLB 6; MTCW; SATA 27

Maturin, Charles Robert
1780(?)-1824 . . . . NCLC 6

Matute (Ausejo), Ana Maria
1925- . . . . CLC 11
See also CA 89-92; MTCW

Maugham, W. S.
See Maugham, W(illiam) Somerset

Maugham, W(illiam) Somerset
1874-1965 . . . . . . CLC 1, 11, 15, 67; DA;
DAB; SSC 8; WLC
See also CA 5-8R; 25-28R; CANR 40;
CDBLB 1914-1945; DLB 10, 36, 77, 100;
MTCW; SATA 54

Maugham, William Somerset
See Maugham, W(illiam) Somerset

Maupassant, (Henri Rene Albert) Guy de
1850-1893 . . . . . NCLC 1, 42; DA; DAB;
SSC 1; WLC
See also DLB 123

Maurhut, Richard
See Traven, B.

Mauriac, Claude 1914-............. **CLC 9**
See also CA 89-92; DLB 83

Mauriac, Francois (Charles)
1885-1970 .... **CLC 4, 9, 56**
See also CA 25-28; CAP 2; DLB 65;
MTCW

Mavor, Osborne Henry 1888-1951
See Bridie, James
See also CA 104

Maxwell, William (Keepers, Jr.)
1908- .... **CLC 19**
See also CA 93-96; DLBY 80

May, Elaine 1932- .... **CLC 16**
See also CA 124; 142; DLB 44

Mayakovski, Vladimir (Vladimirovich)
1893-1930 .... **TCLC 4, 18**
See also CA 104

Mayhew, Henry 1812-1887 ...... **NCLC 31**
See also DLB 18, 55

Mayle, Peter 1939(?)-............ **CLC 89**
See also CA 139

Maynard, Joyce 1953- .... **CLC 23**
See also CA 111; 129

Mayne, William (James Carter)
1928- .... **CLC 12**
See also CA 9-12R; CANR 37; CLR 25;
JRDA; MAICYA; SAAS 11; SATA 6, 68

Mayo, Jim
See L'Amour, Louis (Dearborn)

Maysles, Albert 1926- .... **CLC 16**
See also CA 29-32R

Maysles, David 1932-............. **CLC 16**

Mazer, Norma Fox 1931- .... **CLC 26**
See also AAYA 5; CA 69-72; CANR 12,
32; CLR 23; JRDA; MAICYA; SAAS 1;
SATA 24, 67

Mazzini, Guiseppe 1805-1872 .... **NCLC 34**

McAuley, James Phillip
1917-1976 .... **CLC 45**
See also CA 97-100

McBain, Ed
See Hunter, Evan

McBrien, William Augustine
1930- .... **CLC 44**
See also CA 107

McCaffrey, Anne (Inez) 1926-...... **CLC 17**
See also AAYA 6; AITN 2; BEST 89:2;
CA 25-28R; CANR 15, 35; DLB 8;
JRDA; MAICYA; MTCW; SAAS 11;
SATA 8, 70

McCall, Nathan 1955(?)-.......... **CLC 86**
See also CA 146

McCann, Arthur
See Campbell, John W(ood, Jr.)

McCann, Edson
See Pohl, Frederik

McCarthy, Charles, Jr. 1933-
See McCarthy, Cormac
See also CANR 42

McCarthy, Cormac 1933-..... **CLC 4, 57, 59**
See also McCarthy, Charles, Jr.
See also DLB 6, 143

McCarthy, Mary (Therese)
1912-1989 ... **CLC 1, 3, 5, 14, 24, 39, 59**
See also CA 5-8R; 129; CANR 16; DLB 2;
DLBY 81; MTCW

McCartney, (James) Paul
1942- .... **CLC 12, 35**
See also CA 146

McCauley, Stephen (D.) 1955- ..... **CLC 50**
See also CA 141

McClure, Michael (Thomas)
1932- .... **CLC 6, 10**
See also CA 21-24R; CANR 17, 46;
DLB 16

McCorkle, Jill (Collins) 1958-...... **CLC 51**
See also CA 121; DLBY 87

McCourt, James 1941-............. **CLC 5**
See also CA 57-60

McCoy, Horace (Stanley)
1897-1955 .... **TCLC 28**
See also CA 108; DLB 9

McCrae, John 1872-1918........ **TCLC 12**
See also CA 109; DLB 92

McCreigh, James
See Pohl, Frederik

McCullers, (Lula) Carson (Smith)
1917-1967 .... **CLC 1, 4, 10, 12, 48; DA;**
DAB; SSC 9; WLC
See also CA 5-8R; 25-28R; CABS 1, 3;
CANR 18; CDALB 1941-1968; DLB 2, 7;
MTCW; SATA 27

McCulloch, John Tyler
See Burroughs, Edgar Rice

McCullough, Colleen 1938(?)-...... **CLC 27**
See also CA 81-84; CANR 17, 46; MTCW

McDermott, Alice 1953- .... **CLC 90**
See also CA 109; CANR 40

McElroy, Joseph 1930- .... **CLC 5, 47**
See also CA 17-20R

McEwan, Ian (Russell) 1948- ... **CLC 13, 66**
See also BEST 90:4; CA 61-64; CANR 14,
41; DLB 14; MTCW

McFadden, David 1940-.......... **CLC 48**
See also CA 104; DLB 60

McFarland, Dennis 1950- .... **CLC 65**

McGahern, John
1934- .... **CLC 5, 9, 48; SSC 17**
See also CA 17-20R; CANR 29; DLB 14;
MTCW

McGinley, Patrick (Anthony)
1937- .... **CLC 41**
See also CA 120; 127

McGinley, Phyllis 1905-1978 ...... **CLC 14**
See also CA 9-12R; 77-80; CANR 19;
DLB 11, 48; SATA 2, 44; SATA-Obit 24

McGinniss, Joe 1942-............ **CLC 32**
See also AITN 2; BEST 89:2; CA 25-28R;
CANR 26

McGivern, Maureen Daly
See Daly, Maureen

McGrath, Patrick 1950-........... **CLC 55**
See also CA 136

McGrath, Thomas (Matthew)
1916-1990 .... **CLC 28, 59**
See also CA 9-12R; 132; CANR 6, 33;
MTCW; SATA 41; SATA-Obit 66

McGuane, Thomas (Francis III)
1939- .... **CLC 3, 7, 18, 45**
See also AITN 2; CA 49-52; CANR 5, 24,
49; DLB 2; DLBY 80; MTCW

McGuckian, Medbh 1950-......... **CLC 48**
See also CA 143; DLB 40

McHale, Tom 1942(?)-1982....... **CLC 3, 5**
See also AITN 1; CA 77-80; 106

McIlvanney, William 1936-........ **CLC 42**
See also CA 25-28R; DLB 14

McIlwraith, Maureen Mollie Hunter
See Hunter, Mollie
See also SATA 2

McInerney, Jay 1955- .... **CLC 34**
See also CA 116; 123; CANR 45

McIntyre, Vonda N(eel) 1948- ..... **CLC 18**
See also CA 81-84; CANR 17, 34; MTCW

McKay, Claude
.... **TCLC 7, 41; BLC; DAB; PC 2**
See also McKay, Festus Claudius
See also DLB 4, 45, 51, 117

McKay, Festus Claudius 1889-1948
See McKay, Claude
See also BW 1; CA 104; 124; DA; MTCW;
WLC

McKuen, Rod 1933-............. **CLC 1, 3**
See also AITN 1; CA 41-44R; CANR 40

McLoughlin, R. B.
See Mencken, H(enry) L(ouis)

McLuhan, (Herbert) Marshall
1911-1980 .... **CLC 37, 83**
See also CA 9-12R; 102; CANR 12, 34;
DLB 88; MTCW

McMillan, Terry (L.) 1951-..... **CLC 50, 61**
See also BW 2; CA 140

McMurtry, Larry (Jeff)
1936- .... **CLC 2, 3, 7, 11, 27, 44**
See also AAYA 15; AITN 2; BEST 89:2;
CA 5-8R; CANR 19, 43;
CDALB 1968-1988; DLB 2, 143;
DLBY 80, 87; MTCW

McNally, T. M. 1961- .... **CLC 82**

McNally, Terrence 1939-...... **CLC 4, 7, 41**
See also CA 45-48; CANR 2; DLB 7

McNamer, Deirdre 1950-.......... **CLC 70**

McNeile, Herman Cyril 1888-1937
See Sapper
See also DLB 77

McNickle, (William) D'Arcy
1904-1977 .... **CLC 89**
See also CA 9-12R; 85-88; CANR 5, 45;
NNAL; SATA-Obit 22

McPhee, John (Angus) 1931- ...... **CLC 36**
See also BEST 90:1; CA 65-68; CANR 20,
46; MTCW

McPherson, James Alan
1943- .... **CLC 19, 77**
See also BW 1; CA 25-28R; CAAS 17;
CANR 24; DLB 38; MTCW

McPherson, William (Alexander)
1933- .... **CLC 34**
See also CA 69-72; CANR 28

Mead, Margaret 1901-1978........ **CLC 37**
See also AITN 1; CA 1-4R; 81-84;
CANR 4; MTCW; SATA-Obit 20

Mori Ogai .... **TCLC 14**
See also Mori Rintaro

Mori Rintaro 1862-1922
See Mori Ogai
See also CA 110

Moritz, Karl Philipp 1756-1793 ...... **LC 2**
See also DLB 94

Morland, Peter Henry
See Faust, Frederick (Schiller)

Morren, Theophil
See Hofmannsthal, Hugo von

Morris, Bill 1952- .... **CLC 76**

Morris, Julian
See West, Morris L(anglo)

Morris, Steveland Judkins 1950(?)-
See Wonder, Stevie
See also CA 111

Morris, William 1834-1896 .... **NCLC 4**
See also CDBLB 1832-1890; DLB 18, 35,
57, 156

Morris, Wright 1910- ... **CLC 1, 3, 7, 18, 37**
See also CA 9-12R; CANR 21; DLB 2;
DLBY 81; MTCW

Morrison, Chloe Anthony Wofford
See Morrison, Toni

Morrison, James Douglas 1943-1971
See Morrison, Jim
See also CA 73-76; CANR 40

Morrison, Jim .... **CLC 17**
See also Morrison, James Douglas

Morrison, Toni
1931- .... **CLC 4, 10, 22, 55, 81, 87;
BLC; DA; DAB**
See also AAYA 1; BW 2; CA 29-32R;
CANR 27, 42; CDALB 1968-1988;
DLB 6, 33, 143; DLBY 81; MTCW;
SATA 57

Morrison, Van 1945- .... **CLC 21**
See also CA 116

Mortimer, John (Clifford)
1923- .... **CLC 28, 43**
See also CA 13-16R; CANR 21;
CDBLB 1960 to Present; DLB 13;
MTCW

Mortimer, Penelope (Ruth) 1918- .... **CLC 5**
See also CA 57-60; CANR 45

Morton, Anthony
See Creasey, John

Mosher, Howard Frank 1943- ...... **CLC 62**
See also CA 139

Mosley, Nicholas 1923- .... **CLC 43, 70**
See also CA 69-72; CANR 41; DLB 14

Moss, Howard
1922-1987 .... **CLC 7, 14, 45, 50**
See also CA 1-4R; 123; CANR 1, 44;
DLB 5

Mossgiel, Rab
See Burns, Robert

Motion, Andrew (Peter) 1952- ...... **CLC 47**
See also CA 146; DLB 40

Motley, Willard (Francis)
1909-1965 .... **CLC 18**
See also BW 1; CA 117; 106; DLB 76, 143

Motoori, Norinaga 1730-1801 .... **NCLC 45**

Mott, Michael (Charles Alston)
1930- .... **CLC 15, 34**
See also CA 5-8R; CAAS 7; CANR 7, 29

Moure, Erin 1955- .... **CLC 88**
See also CA 113; DLB 60

Mowat, Farley (McGill) 1921- ..... **CLC 26**
See also AAYA 1; CA 1-4R; CANR 4, 24,
42; CLR 20; DLB 68; JRDA; MAICYA;
MTCW; SATA 3, 55

Moyers, Bill 1934- .... **CLC 74**
See also AITN 2; CA 61-64; CANR 31

Mphahlele, Es'kia
See Mphahlele, Ezekiel
See also DLB 125

Mphahlele, Ezekiel 1919- ..... **CLC 25; BLC**
See also Mphahlele, Es'kia
See also BW 2; CA 81-84; CANR 26

Mqhayi, S(amuel) E(dward) K(rune Loliwe)
1875-1945 .... **TCLC 25; BLC**

Mr. Martin
See Burroughs, William S(eward)

Mrozek, Slawomir 1930- .... **CLC 3, 13**
See also CA 13-16R; CAAS 10; CANR 29;
MTCW

Mrs. Belloc-Lowndes
See Lowndes, Marie Adelaide (Belloc)

Mtwa, Percy (?)- .... **CLC 47**

Mueller, Lisel 1924- .... **CLC 13, 51**
See also CA 93-96; DLB 105

Muir, Edwin 1887-1959 .... **TCLC 2**
See also CA 104; DLB 20, 100

Muir, John 1838-1914 .... **TCLC 28**

Mujica Lainez, Manuel
1910-1984 .... **CLC 31**
See Lainez, Manuel Mujica
See also CA 81-84; 112; CANR 32; HW

Mukherjee, Bharati 1940- .... **CLC 53**
See also BEST 89:2; CA 107; CANR 45;
DLB 60; MTCW

Muldoon, Paul 1951- .... **CLC 32, 72**
See also CA 113; 129; DLB 40

Mulisch, Harry 1927- .... **CLC 42**
See also CA 9-12R; CANR 6, 26

Mull, Martin 1943- .... **CLC 17**
See also CA 105

Mulock, Dinah Maria
See Craik, Dinah Maria (Mulock)

Munford, Robert 1737(?)-1783 .... **LC 5**
See also DLB 31

Mungo, Raymond 1946- .... **CLC 72**
See also CA 49-52; CANR 2

Munro, Alice
1931- .... **CLC 6, 10, 19, 50; SSC 3**
See also AITN 2; CA 33-36R; CANR 33;
DLB 53; MTCW; SATA 29

Munro, H(ector) H(ugh) 1870-1916
See Saki
See also CA 104; 130; CDBLB 1890-1914;
DA; DAB; DLB 34; MTCW; WLC

Murasaki, Lady .... **CMLC 1**

Murdoch, (Jean) Iris
1919- ...... **CLC 1, 2, 3, 4, 6, 8, 11, 15,
22, 31, 51; DAB**
See also CA 13-16R; CANR 8, 43;
CDBLB 1960 to Present; DLB 14;
MTCW

Murnau, Friedrich Wilhelm
See Plumpe, Friedrich Wilhelm

Murphy, Richard 1927- .... **CLC 41**
See also CA 29-32R; DLB 40

Murphy, Sylvia 1937- .... **CLC 34**
See also CA 121

Murphy, Thomas (Bernard) 1935- ... **CLC 51**
See also CA 101

Murray, Albert L. 1916- .... **CLC 73**
See also BW 2; CA 49-52; CANR 26;
DLB 38

Murray, Les(lie) A(llan) 1938- ..... **CLC 40**
See also CA 21-24R; CANR 11, 27

Murry, J. Middleton
See Murry, John Middleton

Murry, John Middleton
1889-1957 .... **TCLC 16**
See also CA 118; DLB 149

Musgrave, Susan 1951- .... **CLC 13, 54**
See also CA 69-72; CANR 45

Musil, Robert (Edler von)
1880-1942 .... **TCLC 12; SSC 18**
See also CA 109; DLB 81, 124

Muske, Carol 1945- .... **CLC 90**
See also Muske-Dukes, Carol (Anne)

Muske-Dukes, Carol (Anne) 1945-
See Muske, Carol
See also CA 65-68; CANR 32

Musset, (Louis Charles) Alfred de
1810-1857 .... **NCLC 7**

My Brother's Brother
See Chekhov, Anton (Pavlovich)

Myers, L. H. 1881-1944 .... **TCLC 59**
See also DLB 15

Myers, Walter Dean 1937- ... **CLC 35; BLC**
See also AAYA 4; BW 2; CA 33-36R;
CANR 20, 42; CLR 4, 16, 35; DLB 33;
JRDA; MAICYA; SAAS 2; SATA 41, 71;
SATA-Brief 27

Myers, Walter M.
See Myers, Walter Dean

Myles, Symon
See Follett, Ken(neth Martin)

Nabokov, Vladimir (Vladimirovich)
1899-1977 ..... **CLC 1, 2, 3, 6, 8, 11, 15,
23, 44, 46, 64; DA; DAB; SSC 11; WLC**
See also CA 5-8R; 69-72; CANR 20;
CDALB 1941-1968; DLB 2; DLBD 3;
DLBY 80, 91; MTCW

Nagai Kafu .... **TCLC 51**
See also Nagai Sokichi

Nagai Sokichi 1879-1959
See Nagai Kafu
See also CA 117

Nagy, Laszlo 1925-1978 .... **CLC 7**
See also CA 129; 112

Naipaul, Shiva(dhar Srinivasa)
1945-1985 . . . . **CLC 32, 39**
See also CA 110; 112; 116; CANR 33;
DLBY 85; MTCW

Naipaul, V(idiadhar) S(urajprasad)
1932- . . . . . **CLC 4, 7, 9, 13, 18, 37; DAB**
See also CA 1-4R; CANR 1, 33;
CDBLB 1960 to Present; DLB 125;
DLBY 85; MTCW

Nakos, Lilika   1899(?)- . . . . **CLC 29**

Narayan, R(asipuram) K(rishnaswami)
1906- . . . . **CLC 7, 28, 47**
See also CA 81-84; CANR 33; MTCW;
SATA 62

Nash, (Frediric) Ogden   1902-1971 . . **CLC 23**
See also CA 13-14; 29-32R; CANR 34;
CAP 1; DLB 11; MAICYA; MTCW;
SATA 2, 46

Nathan, Daniel
See Dannay, Frederic

Nathan, George Jean   1882-1958 . . . **TCLC 18**
See also Hatteras, Owen
See also CA 114; DLB 137

Natsume, Kinnosuke   1867-1916
See Natsume, Soseki
See also CA 104

Natsume, Soseki . . . . **TCLC 2, 10**
See also Natsume, Kinnosuke

Natti, (Mary) Lee   1919-
See Kingman, Lee
See also CA 5-8R; CANR 2

Naylor, Gloria
1950- . . . . **CLC 28, 52; BLC; DA**
See also AAYA 6; BW 2; CA 107;
CANR 27; MTCW

Neihardt, John Gneisenau
1881-1973 . . . . **CLC 32**
See also CA 13-14; CAP 1; DLB 9, 54

Nekrasov, Nikolai Alekseevich
1821-1878 . . . . **NCLC 11**

Nelligan, Emile   1879-1941 . . . . **TCLC 14**
See also CA 114; DLB 92

Nelson, Willie   1933- . . . . **CLC 17**
See also CA 107

Nemerov, Howard (Stanley)
1920-1991 . . . . **CLC 2, 6, 9, 36**
See also CA 1-4R; 134; CABS 2; CANR 1,
27; DLB 5, 6; DLBY 83; MTCW

Neruda, Pablo
1904-1973 . . . . . **CLC 1, 2, 5, 7, 9, 28, 62;
DA; DAB; HLC; PC 4; WLC**
See also CA 19-20; 45-48; CAP 2; HW;
MTCW

Nerval, Gerard de
1808-1855 . . . . . **NCLC 1; PC 13; SSC 18**

Nervo, (Jose) Amado (Ruiz de)
1870-1919 . . . . **TCLC 11**
See also CA 109; 131; HW

Nessi, Pio Baroja y
See Baroja (y Nessi), Pio

Nestroy, Johann   1801-1862 . . . . . . **NCLC 42**
See also DLB 133

Neufeld, John (Arthur)   1938- . . . . . . **CLC 17**
See also AAYA 11; CA 25-28R; CANR 11,
37; MAICYA; SAAS 3; SATA 6, 81

Neville, Emily Cheney   1919- . . . . . . **CLC 12**
See also CA 5-8R; CANR 3, 37; JRDA;
MAICYA; SAAS 2; SATA 1

Newbound, Bernard Slade   1930-
See Slade, Bernard
See also CA 81-84; CANR 49

Newby, P(ercy) H(oward)
1918- . . . . **CLC 2, 13**
See also CA 5-8R; CANR 32; DLB 15;
MTCW

Newlove, Donald   1928- . . . . **CLC 6**
See also CA 29-32R; CANR 25

Newlove, John (Herbert)   1938- . . . . . **CLC 14**
See also CA 21-24R; CANR 9, 25

Newman, Charles   1938- . . . . **CLC 2, 8**
See also CA 21-24R

Newman, Edwin (Harold)   1919- . . . . **CLC 14**
See also AITN 1; CA 69-72; CANR 5

Newman, John Henry
1801-1890 . . . . **NCLC 38**
See also DLB 18, 32, 55

Newton, Suzanne   1936- . . . . **CLC 35**
See also CA 41-44R; CANR 14; JRDA;
SATA 5, 77

Nexo, Martin Andersen
1869-1954 . . . . **TCLC 43**

Nezval, Vitezslav   1900-1958 . . . . . . **TCLC 44**
See also CA 123

Ng, Fae Myenne   1957(?)- . . . . **CLC 81**
See also CA 146

Ngema, Mbongeni   1955- . . . . **CLC 57**
See also BW 2; CA 143

Ngugi, James T(hiong'o) . . . . **CLC 3, 7, 13**
See also Ngugi wa Thiong'o

Ngugi wa Thiong'o   1938- . . . . . **CLC 36; BLC**
See also Ngugi, James T(hiong'o)
See also BW 2; CA 81-84; CANR 27;
DLB 125; MTCW

Nichol, B(arrie) P(hillip)
1944-1988 . . . . **CLC 18**
See also CA 53-56; DLB 53; SATA 66

Nichols, John (Treadwell)   1940- . . . . **CLC 38**
See also CA 9-12R; CAAS 2; CANR 6;
DLBY 82

Nichols, Leigh
See Koontz, Dean R(ay)

Nichols, Peter (Richard)
1927- . . . . **CLC 5, 36, 65**
See also CA 104; CANR 33; DLB 13;
MTCW

Nicolas, F. R. E.
See Freeling, Nicolas

Niedecker, Lorine   1903-1970 . . . . **CLC 10, 42**
See also CA 25-28; CAP 2; DLB 48

Nietzsche, Friedrich (Wilhelm)
1844-1900 . . . . **TCLC 10, 18, 55**
See also CA 107; 121; DLB 129

Nievo, Ippolito   1831-1861 . . . . **NCLC 22**

Nightingale, Anne Redmon   1943-
See Redmon, Anne
See also CA 103

Nik. T. O.
See Annensky, Innokenty Fyodorovich

Nin, Anais
1903-1977 . . . . . . **CLC 1, 4, 8, 11, 14, 60;
SSC 10**
See also AITN 2; CA 13-16R; 69-72;
CANR 22; DLB 2, 4, 152; MTCW

Nissenson, Hugh   1933- . . . . **CLC 4, 9**
See also CA 17-20R; CANR 27; DLB 28

Niven, Larry . . . . **CLC 8**
See also Niven, Laurence Van Cott
See also DLB 8

Niven, Laurence Van Cott   1938-
See Niven, Larry
See also CA 21-24R; CAAS 12; CANR 14,
44; MTCW

Nixon, Agnes Eckhardt   1927- . . . . . . **CLC 21**
See also CA 110

Nizan, Paul   1905-1940 . . . . **TCLC 40**
See also DLB 72

Nkosi, Lewis   1936- . . . . **CLC 45; BLC**
See also BW 1; CA 65-68; CANR 27

Nodier, (Jean) Charles (Emmanuel)
1780-1844 . . . . **NCLC 19**
See also DLB 119

Nolan, Christopher   1965- . . . . **CLC 58**
See also CA 111

Norden, Charles
See Durrell, Lawrence (George)

Nordhoff, Charles (Bernard)
1887-1947 . . . . **TCLC 23**
See also CA 108; DLB 9; SATA 23

Norfolk, Lawrence   1963- . . . . **CLC 76**
See also CA 144

Norman, Marsha   1947- . . . . **CLC 28**
See also CA 105; CABS 3; CANR 41;
DLBY 84

Norris, Benjamin Franklin, Jr.
1870-1902 . . . . **TCLC 24**
See also Norris, Frank
See also CA 110

Norris, Frank
See Norris, Benjamin Franklin, Jr.
See also CDALB 1865-1917; DLB 12, 71

Norris, Leslie   1921- . . . . **CLC 14**
See also CA 11-12; CANR 14; CAP 1;
DLB 27

North, Andrew
See Norton, Andre

North, Anthony
See Koontz, Dean R(ay)

North, Captain George
See Stevenson, Robert Louis (Balfour)

North, Milou
See Erdrich, Louise

Northrup, B. A.
See Hubbard, L(afayette) Ron(ald)

North Staffs
See Hulme, T(homas) E(rnest)

Norton, Alice Mary
See Norton, Andre
See also MAICYA; SATA 1, 43

Norton, Andre   1912- . . . . **CLC 12**
See also Norton, Alice Mary
See also AAYA 14; CA 1-4R; CANR 2, 31;
DLB 8, 52; JRDA; MTCW

Orris
See Ingelow, Jean

Ortega y Gasset, Jose
1883-1955 . . . . **TCLC 9; HLC**
See also CA 106; 130; HW; MTCW

Ortese, Anna Maria 1914- . . . . **CLC 89**

Ortiz, Simon J(oseph) 1941- . . . . **CLC 45**
See also CA 134; DLB 120; NNAL

Orton, Joe . . . . **CLC 4, 13, 43; DC 3**
See also Orton, John Kingsley
See also CDBLB 1960 to Present; DLB 13

Orton, John Kingsley 1933-1967
See Orton, Joe
See also CA 85-88; CANR 35; MTCW

Orwell, George
. . . . . **TCLC 2, 6, 15, 31, 51; DAB; WLC**
See also Blair, Eric (Arthur)
See also CDBLB 1945-1960; DLB 15, 98

Osborne, David
See Silverberg, Robert

Osborne, George
See Silverberg, Robert

Osborne, John (James)
1929-1994 . . . . . **CLC 1, 2, 5, 11, 45; DA;**
DAB; WLC
See also CA 13-16R; 147; CANR 21;
CDBLB 1945-1960; DLB 13; MTCW

Osborne, Lawrence 1958- . . . . **CLC 50**

Oshima, Nagisa 1932- . . . . **CLC 20**
See also CA 116; 121

Oskison, John Milton
1874-1947 . . . . **TCLC 35**
See also CA 144; NNAL

Ossoli, Sarah Margaret (Fuller marchesa d')
1810-1850
See Fuller, Margaret
See also SATA 25

Ostrovsky, Alexander
1823-1886 . . . . **NCLC 30**

Otero, Blas de 1916-1979 . . . . **CLC 11**
See also CA 89-92; DLB 134

Otto, Whitney 1955- . . . . **CLC 70**
See also CA 140

Ouida . . . . **TCLC 43**
See also De La Ramee, (Marie) Louise
See also DLB 18, 156

Ousmane, Sembene 1923- . . . . **CLC 66; BLC**
See also BW 1; CA 117; 125; MTCW

Ovid 43B.C.-18(?) . . . . **CMLC 7; PC 2**

Owen, Hugh
See Faust, Frederick (Schiller)

Owen, Wilfred (Edward Salter)
1893-1918 . . . . . . **TCLC 5, 27; DA; DAB;**
WLC
See also CA 104; 141; CDBLB 1914-1945;
DLB 20

Owens, Rochelle 1936- . . . . **CLC 8**
See also CA 17-20R; CAAS 2; CANR 39

Oz, Amos 1939- . . . **CLC 5, 8, 11, 27, 33, 54**
See also CA 53-56; CANR 27, 47; MTCW

Ozick, Cynthia
1928- . . . . **CLC 3, 7, 28, 62; SSC 15**
See also BEST 90:1; CA 17-20R; CANR 23;
DLB 28, 152; DLBY 82; MTCW

Ozu, Yasujiro 1903-1963 . . . . **CLC 16**
See also CA 112

Pacheco, C.
See Pessoa, Fernando (Antonio Nogueira)

Pa Chin . . . . **CLC 18**
See also Li Fei-kan

Pack, Robert 1929- . . . . **CLC 13**
See also CA 1-4R; CANR 3, 44; DLB 5

Padgett, Lewis
See Kuttner, Henry

Padilla (Lorenzo), Heberto 1932- . . . **CLC 38**
See also AITN 1; CA 123; 131; HW

Page, Jimmy 1944- . . . . **CLC 12**

Page, Louise 1955- . . . . **CLC 40**
See also CA 140

Page, P(atricia) K(athleen)
1916- . . . . **CLC 7, 18; PC 12**
See also CA 53-56; CANR 4, 22; DLB 68;
MTCW

Paget, Violet 1856-1935
See Lee, Vernon
See also CA 104

Paget-Lowe, Henry
See Lovecraft, H(oward) P(hillips)

Paglia, Camille (Anna) 1947- . . . . **CLC 68**
See also CA 140

Paige, Richard
See Koontz, Dean R(ay)

Pakenham, Antonia
See Fraser, (Lady) Antonia (Pakenham)

Palamas, Kostes 1859-1943 . . . . **TCLC 5**
See also CA 105

Palazzeschi, Aldo 1885-1974 . . . . **CLC 11**
See also CA 89-92; 53-56; DLB 114

Paley, Grace 1922- . . . . **CLC 4, 6, 37; SSC 8**
See also CA 25-28R; CANR 13, 46;
DLB 28; MTCW

Palin, Michael (Edward) 1943- . . . . . **CLC 21**
See also Monty Python
See also CA 107; CANR 35; SATA 67

Palliser, Charles 1947- . . . . **CLC 65**
See also CA 136

Palma, Ricardo 1833-1919 . . . . **TCLC 29**

Pancake, Breece Dexter 1952-1979
See Pancake, Breece D'J
See also CA 123; 109

Pancake, Breece D'J . . . . **CLC 29**
See also Pancake, Breece Dexter
See also DLB 130

Panko, Rudy
See Gogol, Nikolai (Vasilyevich)

Papadiamantis, Alexandros
1851-1911 . . . . **TCLC 29**

Papadiamantopoulos, Johannes 1856-1910
See Moreas, Jean
See also CA 117

Papini, Giovanni 1881-1956 . . . . **TCLC 22**
See also CA 121

Paracelsus 1493-1541 . . . . **LC 14**

Parasol, Peter
See Stevens, Wallace

Parfenie, Maria
See Codrescu, Andrei

Parini, Jay (Lee) 1948- . . . . **CLC 54**
See also CA 97-100; CAAS 16; CANR 32

Park, Jordan
See Kornbluth, C(yril) M.; Pohl, Frederik

Parker, Bert
See Ellison, Harlan (Jay)

Parker, Dorothy (Rothschild)
1893-1967 . . . . **CLC 15, 68; SSC 2**
See also CA 19-20; 25-28R; CAP 2;
DLB 11, 45, 86; MTCW

Parker, Robert B(rown) 1932- . . . . . . **CLC 27**
See also BEST 89:4; CA 49-52; CANR 1,
26; MTCW

Parkin, Frank 1940- . . . . **CLC 43**
See also CA 147

Parkman, Francis, Jr.
1823-1893 . . . . **NCLC 12**
See also DLB 1, 30

Parks, Gordon (Alexander Buchanan)
1912- . . . . **CLC 1, 16; BLC**
See also AITN 2; BW 2; CA 41-44R;
CANR 26; DLB 33; SATA 8

Parnell, Thomas 1679-1718 . . . . **LC 3**
See also DLB 94

Parra, Nicanor 1914- . . . . **CLC 2; HLC**
See also CA 85-88; CANR 32; HW; MTCW

Parrish, Mary Frances
See Fisher, M(ary) F(rances) K(ennedy)

Parson
See Coleridge, Samuel Taylor

Parson Lot
See Kingsley, Charles

Partridge, Anthony
See Oppenheim, E(dward) Phillips

Pascoli, Giovanni 1855-1912 . . . . . . **TCLC 45**

Pasolini, Pier Paolo
1922-1975 . . . . **CLC 20, 37**
See also CA 93-96; 61-64; DLB 128;
MTCW

Pasquini
See Silone, Ignazio

Pastan, Linda (Olenik) 1932- . . . . **CLC 27**
See also CA 61-64; CANR 18, 40; DLB 5

Pasternak, Boris (Leonidovich)
1890-1960 . . . . . . **CLC 7, 10, 18, 63; DA;**
DAB; PC 6; WLC
See also CA 127; 116; MTCW

Patchen, Kenneth 1911-1972 . . . **CLC 1, 2, 18**
See also CA 1-4R; 33-36R; CANR 3, 35;
DLB 16, 48; MTCW

Pater, Walter (Horatio)
1839-1894 . . . . **NCLC 7**
See also CDBLB 1832-1890; DLB 57, 156

Paterson, A(ndrew) B(arton)
1864-1941 . . . . **TCLC 32**

Paterson, Katherine (Womeldorf)
1932- . . . . **CLC 12, 30**
See also AAYA 1; CA 21-24R; CANR 28;
CLR 7; DLB 52; JRDA; MAICYA;
MTCW; SATA 13, 53

Patmore, Coventry Kersey Dighton
1823-1896 . . . . **NCLC 9**
See also DLB 35, 98

Raleigh, Richard
See Lovecraft, H(oward) P(hillips)

Raleigh, Sir Walter 1554(?)-1618 .... **LC 31**
See also CDBLB Before 1660

Rallentando, H. P.
See Sayers, Dorothy L(eigh)

Ramal, Walter
See de la Mare, Walter (John)

Ramon, Juan
See Jimenez (Mantecon), Juan Ramon

Ramos, Graciliano 1892-1953 ..... **TCLC 32**

Rampersad, Arnold 1941-.......... **CLC 44**
See also BW 2; CA 127; 133; DLB 111

Rampling, Anne
See Rice, Anne

Ramsay, Allan 1684(?)-1758 .... **LC 29**
See also DLB 95

Ramuz, Charles-Ferdinand
1878-1947 .... **TCLC 33**

Rand, Ayn
1905-1982 ..... **CLC 3, 30, 44, 79; DA; WLC**
See also AAYA 10; CA 13-16R; 105;
CANR 27; MTCW

Randall, Dudley (Felker)
1914- .... **CLC 1; BLC**
See also BW 1; CA 25-28R; CANR 23;
DLB 41

Randall, Robert
See Silverberg, Robert

Ranger, Ken
See Creasey, John

Ransom, John Crowe
1888-1974 .... **CLC 2, 4, 5, 11, 24**
See also CA 5-8R; 49-52; CANR 6, 34;
DLB 45, 63; MTCW

Rao, Raja 1909- .... **CLC 25, 56**
See also CA 73-76; MTCW

Raphael, Frederic (Michael)
1931- .... **CLC 2, 14**
See also CA 1-4R; CANR 1; DLB 14

Ratcliffe, James P.
See Mencken, H(enry) L(ouis)

Rathbone, Julian 1935- .... **CLC 41**
See also CA 101; CANR 34

Rattigan, Terence (Mervyn)
1911-1977 .... **CLC 7**
See also CA 85-88; 73-76;
CDBLB 1945-1960; DLB 13; MTCW

Ratushinskaya, Irina 1954- .... **CLC 54**
See also CA 129

Raven, Simon (Arthur Noel)
1927- .... **CLC 14**
See also CA 81-84

Rawley, Callman 1903-
See Rakosi, Carl
See also CA 21-24R; CANR 12, 32

Rawlings, Marjorie Kinnan
1896-1953 .... **TCLC 4**
See also CA 104; 137; DLB 9, 22, 102;
JRDA; MAICYA; YABC 1

Ray, Satyajit 1921-1992....... **CLC 16, 76**
See also CA 114; 137

Read, Herbert Edward 1893-1968.... **CLC 4**
See also CA 85-88; 25-28R; DLB 20, 149

Read, Piers Paul 1941- ...... **CLC 4, 10, 25**
See also CA 21-24R; CANR 38; DLB 14;
SATA 21

Reade, Charles 1814-1884 .... **NCLC 2**
See also DLB 21

Reade, Hamish
See Gray, Simon (James Holliday)

Reading, Peter 1946- .... **CLC 47**
See also CA 103; CANR 46; DLB 40

Reaney, James 1926- .... **CLC 13**
See also CA 41-44R; CAAS 15; CANR 42;
DLB 68; SATA 43

Rebreanu, Liviu 1885-1944 .... **TCLC 28**

Rechy, John (Francisco)
1934- .... **CLC 1, 7, 14, 18; HLC**
See also CA 5-8R; CAAS 4; CANR 6, 32;
DLB 122; DLBY 82; HW

Redcam, Tom 1870-1933 .... **TCLC 25**

Reddin, Keith.................... **CLC 67**

Redgrove, Peter (William)
1932- .... **CLC 6, 41**
See also CA 1-4R; CANR 3, 39; DLB 40

Redmon, Anne................... **CLC 22**
See also Nightingale, Anne Redmon
See also DLBY 86

Reed, Eliot
See Ambler, Eric

Reed, Ishmael
1938- ... **CLC 2, 3, 5, 6, 13, 32, 60; BLC**
See also BW 2; CA 21-24R; CANR 25, 48;
DLB 2, 5, 33; DLBD 8; MTCW

Reed, John (Silas) 1887-1920 ..... **TCLC 9**
See also CA 106

Reed, Lou....................... **CLC 21**
See also Firbank, Louis

Reeve, Clara 1729-1807 .... **NCLC 19**
See also DLB 39

Reich, Wilhelm 1897-1957....... **TCLC 57**

Reid, Christopher (John) 1949-..... **CLC 33**
See also CA 140; DLB 40

Reid, Desmond
See Moorcock, Michael (John)

Reid Banks, Lynne 1929-
See Banks, Lynne Reid
See also CA 1-4R; CANR 6, 22, 38;
CLR 24; JRDA; MAICYA; SATA 22, 75

Reilly, William K.
See Creasey, John

Reiner, Max
See Caldwell, (Janet Miriam) Taylor
(Holland)

Reis, Ricardo
See Pessoa, Fernando (Antonio Nogueira)

Remarque, Erich Maria
1898-1970 .... **CLC 21; DA; DAB**
See also CA 77-80; 29-32R; DLB 56;
MTCW

Remizov, A.
See Remizov, Aleksei (Mikhailovich)

Remizov, A. M.
See Remizov, Aleksei (Mikhailovich)

Remizov, Aleksei (Mikhailovich)
1877-1957 .... **TCLC 27**
See also CA 125; 133

Renan, Joseph Ernest
1823-1892 .... **NCLC 26**

Renard, Jules 1864-1910 .... **TCLC 17**
See also CA 117

Renault, Mary.............. **CLC 3, 11, 17**
See also Challans, Mary
See also DLBY 83

Rendell, Ruth (Barbara) 1930- .. **CLC 28, 48**
See also Vine, Barbara
See also CA 109; CANR 32; DLB 87;
MTCW

Renoir, Jean 1894-1979 .... **CLC 20**
See also CA 129; 85-88

Resnais, Alain 1922-.............. **CLC 16**

Reverdy, Pierre 1889-1960 .... **CLC 53**
See also CA 97-100; 89-92

Rexroth, Kenneth
1905-1982 ...... **CLC 1, 2, 6, 11, 22, 49**
See also CA 5-8R; 107; CANR 14, 34;
CDALB 1941-1968; DLB 16, 48;
DLBY 82; MTCW

Reyes, Alfonso 1889-1959 .... **TCLC 33**
See also CA 131; HW

Reyes y Basoalto, Ricardo Eliecer Neftali
See Neruda, Pablo

Reymont, Wladyslaw (Stanislaw)
1868(?)-1925 .... **TCLC 5**
See also CA 104

Reynolds, Jonathan 1942-....... **CLC 6, 38**
See also CA 65-68; CANR 28

Reynolds, Joshua 1723-1792 .... **LC 15**
See also DLB 104

Reynolds, Michael Shane 1937- .... **CLC 44**
See also CA 65-68; CANR 9

Reznikoff, Charles 1894-1976 .... **CLC 9**
See also CA 33-36; 61-64; CAP 2; DLB 28,
45

Rezzori (d'Arezzo), Gregor von
1914- .... **CLC 25**
See also CA 122; 136

Rhine, Richard
See Silverstein, Alvin

Rhodes, Eugene Manlove
1869-1934 .... **TCLC 53**

R'hoone
See Balzac, Honore de

Rhys, Jean
1890(?)-1979 .... **CLC 2, 4, 6, 14, 19, 51; SSC 21**
See also CA 25-28R; 85-88; CANR 35;
CDBLB 1945-1960; DLB 36, 117; MTCW

Ribeiro, Darcy 1922-............. **CLC 34**
See also CA 33-36R

Ribeiro, Joao Ubaldo (Osorio Pimentel)
1941- .... **CLC 10, 67**
See also CA 81-84

Ribman, Ronald (Burt) 1932- .... **CLC 7**
See also CA 21-24R; CANR 46

Ricci, Nino 1959-................. **CLC 70**
See also CA 137

Rogers, Will(iam Penn Adair)
 1879-1935 . . . . **TCLC 8**
 See also CA 105; 144; DLB 11; NNAL

Rogin, Gilbert 1929- . . . . **CLC 18**
 See also CA 65-68; CANR 15

Rohan, Koda . . . . **TCLC 22**
 See also Koda Shigeyuki

Rohmer, Eric . . . . **CLC 16**
 See also Scherer, Jean-Marie Maurice

Rohmer, Sax . . . . **TCLC 28**
 See also Ward, Arthur Henry Sarsfield
 See also DLB 70

Roiphe, Anne (Richardson)
 1935- . . . . **CLC 3, 9**
 See also CA 89-92; CANR 45; DLBY 80

Rojas, Fernando de 1465-1541 . . . . . . **LC 23**

Rolfe, Frederick (William Serafino Austin
 Lewis Mary) 1860-1913 . . . . . . **TCLC 12**
 See also CA 107; DLB 34, 156

Rolland, Romain 1866-1944 . . . . **TCLC 23**
 See also CA 118; DLB 65

Rolvaag, O(le) E(dvart)
 See Roelvaag, O(le) E(dvart)

Romain Arnaud, Saint
 See Aragon, Louis

Romains, Jules 1885-1972 . . . . **CLC 7**
 See also CA 85-88; CANR 34; DLB 65;
 MTCW

Romero, Jose Ruben 1890-1952 . . . **TCLC 14**
 See also CA 114; 131; HW

Ronsard, Pierre de
 1524-1585 . . . . **LC 6; PC 11**

Rooke, Leon 1934- . . . . **CLC 25, 34**
 See also CA 25-28R; CANR 23

Roper, William 1498-1578 . . . . **LC 10**

Roquelaure, A. N.
 See Rice, Anne

Rosa, Joao Guimaraes 1908-1967 . . . **CLC 23**
 See also CA 89-92; DLB 113

Rose, Wendy 1948- . . . . **CLC 85; PC 13**
 See also CA 53-56; CANR 5; NNAL;
 SATA 12

Rosen, Richard (Dean) 1949- . . . . **CLC 39**
 See also CA 77-80

Rosenberg, Isaac 1890-1918 . . . . **TCLC 12**
 See also CA 107; DLB 20

Rosenblatt, Joe . . . . **CLC 15**
 See also Rosenblatt, Joseph

Rosenblatt, Joseph 1933-
 See Rosenblatt, Joe
 See also CA 89-92

Rosenfeld, Samuel 1896-1963
 See Tzara, Tristan
 See also CA 89-92

Rosenthal, M(acha) L(ouis) 1917- . . . **CLC 28**
 See also CA 1-4R; CAAS 6; CANR 4;
 DLB 5; SATA 59

Ross, Barnaby
 See Dannay, Frederic

Ross, Bernard L.
 See Follett, Ken(neth Martin)

Ross, J. H.
 See Lawrence, T(homas) E(dward)

Ross, Martin
 See Martin, Violet Florence
 See also DLB 135

Ross, (James) Sinclair 1908- . . . . **CLC 13**
 See also CA 73-76; DLB 88

Rossetti, Christina (Georgina)
 1830-1894 . . . . . **NCLC 2, 50; DA; DAB;
 PC 7; WLC**
 See also DLB 35; MAICYA; SATA 20

Rossetti, Dante Gabriel
 1828-1882 . . . **NCLC 4; DA; DAB; WLC**
 See also CDBLB 1832-1890; DLB 35

Rossner, Judith (Perelman)
 1935- . . . . **CLC 6, 9, 29**
 See also AITN 2; BEST 90:3; CA 17-20R;
 CANR 18; DLB 6; MTCW

Rostand, Edmond (Eugene Alexis)
 1868-1918 . . . . . . **TCLC 6, 37; DA; DAB**
 See also CA 104; 126; MTCW

Roth, Henry 1906- . . . . **CLC 2, 6, 11**
 See also CA 11-12; CANR 38; CAP 1;
 DLB 28; MTCW

Roth, Joseph 1894-1939 . . . . **TCLC 33**
 See also DLB 85

Roth, Philip (Milton)
 1933- . . . . . . **CLC 1, 2, 3, 4, 6, 9, 15, 22,
 31, 47, 66, 86; DA; DAB; WLC**
 See also BEST 90:3; CA 1-4R; CANR 1, 22,
 36; CDALB 1968-1988; DLB 2, 28;
 DLBY 82; MTCW

Rothenberg, Jerome 1931- . . . . **CLC 6, 57**
 See also CA 45-48; CANR 1; DLB 5

Roumain, Jacques (Jean Baptiste)
 1907-1944 . . . . **TCLC 19; BLC**
 See also BW 1; CA 117; 125

Rourke, Constance (Mayfield)
 1885-1941 . . . . **TCLC 12**
 See also CA 107; YABC 1

Rousseau, Jean-Baptiste 1671-1741 . . . **LC 9**

Rousseau, Jean-Jacques
 1712-1778 . . . . . **LC 14; DA; DAB; WLC**

Roussel, Raymond 1877-1933 . . . . . **TCLC 20**
 See also CA 117

Rovit, Earl (Herbert) 1927- . . . . **CLC 7**
 See also CA 5-8R; CANR 12

Rowe, Nicholas 1674-1718 . . . . **LC 8**
 See also DLB 84

Rowley, Ames Dorrance
 See Lovecraft, H(oward) P(hillips)

Rowson, Susanna Haswell
 1762(?)-1824 . . . . **NCLC 5**
 See also DLB 37

Roy, Gabrielle
 1909-1983 . . . . **CLC 10, 14; DAB**
 See also CA 53-56; 110; CANR 5; DLB 68;
 MTCW

Rozewicz, Tadeusz 1921- . . . . **CLC 9, 23**
 See also CA 108; CANR 36; MTCW

Ruark, Gibbons 1941- . . . . **CLC 3**
 See also CA 33-36R; CANR 14, 31;
 DLB 120

Rubens, Bernice (Ruth) 1923- . . . **CLC 19, 31**
 See also CA 25-28R; CANR 33; DLB 14;
 MTCW

Rudkin, (James) David 1936- . . . . . . **CLC 14**
 See also CA 89-92; DLB 13

Rudnik, Raphael 1933- . . . . **CLC 7**
 See also CA 29-32R

Ruffian, M.
 See Hasek, Jaroslav (Matej Frantisek)

Ruiz, Jose Martinez . . . . **CLC 11**
 See also Martinez Ruiz, Jose

Rukeyser, Muriel
 1913-1980 . . . . **CLC 6, 10, 15, 27; PC 12**
 See also CA 5-8R; 93-96; CANR 26;
 DLB 48; MTCW; SATA-Obit 22

Rule, Jane (Vance) 1931- . . . . **CLC 27**
 See also CA 25-28R; CAAS 18; CANR 12;
 DLB 60

Rulfo, Juan 1918-1986 . . . . **CLC 8, 80; HLC**
 See also CA 85-88; 118; CANR 26;
 DLB 113; HW; MTCW

Runeberg, Johan 1804-1877 . . . . . . **NCLC 41**

Runyon, (Alfred) Damon
 1884(?)-1946 . . . . **TCLC 10**
 See also CA 107; DLB 11, 86

Rush, Norman 1933- . . . . **CLC 44**
 See also CA 121; 126

Rushdie, (Ahmed) Salman
 1947- . . . . **CLC 23, 31, 55; DAB**
 See also BEST 89:3; CA 108; 111;
 CANR 33; MTCW

Rushforth, Peter (Scott) 1945- . . . . . **CLC 19**
 See also CA 101

Ruskin, John 1819-1900 . . . . **TCLC 20**
 See also CA 114; 129; CDBLB 1832-1890;
 DLB 55; SATA 24

Russ, Joanna 1937- . . . . **CLC 15**
 See also CA 25-28R; CANR 11, 31; DLB 8;
 MTCW

Russell, George William 1867-1935
 See A. E.
 See also CA 104; CDBLB 1890-1914

Russell, (Henry) Ken(neth Alfred)
 1927- . . . . **CLC 16**
 See also CA 105

Russell, Willy 1947- . . . . **CLC 60**

Rutherford, Mark . . . . **TCLC 25**
 See also White, William Hale
 See also DLB 18

Ruyslinck, Ward 1929- . . . . **CLC 14**
 See also Belser, Reimond Karel Maria de

Ryan, Cornelius (John) 1920-1974 . . . **CLC 7**
 See also CA 69-72; 53-56; CANR 38

Ryan, Michael 1946- . . . . **CLC 65**
 See also CA 49-52; DLBY 82

Rybakov, Anatoli (Naumovich)
 1911- . . . . **CLC 23, 53**
 See also CA 126; 135; SATA 79

Ryder, Jonathan
 See Ludlum, Robert

Ryga, George 1932-1987 . . . . **CLC 14**
 See also CA 101; 124; CANR 43; DLB 60

S. S.
 See Sassoon, Siegfried (Lorraine)

Saba, Umberto 1883-1957 . . . . **TCLC 33**
 See also CA 144; DLB 114

Sabatini, Rafael 1875-1950 . . . . **TCLC 47**

Sabato, Ernesto (R.)
1911- . . . . CLC 10, 23; HLC
See also CA 97-100; CANR 32; DLB 145;
HW; MTCW

Sacastru, Martin
See Bioy Casares, Adolfo

Sacher-Masoch, Leopold von
1836(?)-1895 . . . . NCLC 31

Sachs, Marilyn (Stickle) 1927- . . . . . CLC 35
See also AAYA 2; CA 17-20R; CANR 13,
47; CLR 2; JRDA; MAICYA; SAAS 2;
SATA 3, 68

Sachs, Nelly 1891-1970 . . . . CLC 14
See also CA 17-18; 25-28R; CAP 2

Sackler, Howard (Oliver)
1929-1982 . . . . CLC 14
See also CA 61-64; 108; CANR 30; DLB 7

Sacks, Oliver (Wolf) 1933- . . . . CLC 67
See also CA 53-56; CANR 28; MTCW

Sade, Donatien Alphonse Francois Comte
1740-1814 . . . . NCLC 47

Sadoff, Ira 1945- . . . . CLC 9
See also CA 53-56; CANR 5, 21; DLB 120

Saetone
See Camus, Albert

Safire, William 1929- . . . . CLC 10
See also CA 17-20R; CANR 31

Sagan, Carl (Edward) 1934- . . . . CLC 30
See also AAYA 2; CA 25-28R; CANR 11,
36; MTCW; SATA 58

Sagan, Francoise . . . . CLC 3, 6, 9, 17, 36
See also Quoirez, Francoise
See also DLB 83

Sahgal, Nayantara (Pandit) 1927- . . . CLC 41
See also CA 9-12R; CANR 11

Saint, H(arry) F. 1941- . . . . CLC 50
See also CA 127

St. Aubin de Teran, Lisa 1953-
See Teran, Lisa St. Aubin de
See also CA 118; 126

Sainte-Beuve, Charles Augustin
1804-1869 . . . . NCLC 5

Saint-Exupery, Antoine (Jean Baptiste Marie
Roger) de
1900-1944 . . . . TCLC 2, 56; WLC
See also CA 108; 132; CLR 10; DLB 72;
MAICYA; MTCW; SATA 20

St. John, David
See Hunt, E(verette) Howard, (Jr.)

Saint-John Perse
See Leger, (Marie-Rene Auguste) Alexis
Saint-Leger

Saintsbury, George (Edward Bateman)
1845-1933 . . . . TCLC 31
See also DLB 57, 149

Sait Faik . . . . TCLC 23
See also Abasiyanik, Sait Faik

Saki . . . . TCLC 3; SSC 12
See also Munro, H(ector) H(ugh)

Sala, George Augustus . . . . NCLC 46

Salama, Hannu 1936- . . . . CLC 18

Salamanca, J(ack) R(ichard)
1922- . . . . CLC 4, 15
See also CA 25-28R

Sale, J. Kirkpatrick
See Sale, Kirkpatrick

Sale, Kirkpatrick 1937- . . . . CLC 68
See also CA 13-16R; CANR 10

Salinas, Luis Omar 1937- . . . CLC 90; HLC
See also CA 131; DLB 82; HW

Salinas (y Serrano), Pedro
1891(?)-1951 . . . . TCLC 17
See also CA 117; DLB 134

Salinger, J(erome) D(avid)
1919- . . . . . . CLC 1, 3, 8, 12, 55, 56; DA;
DAB; SSC 2; WLC
See also AAYA 2; CA 5-8R; CANR 39;
CDALB 1941-1968; CLR 18; DLB 2, 102;
MAICYA; MTCW; SATA 67

Salisbury, John
See Caute, David

Salter, James 1925- . . . . CLC 7, 52, 59
See also CA 73-76; DLB 130

Saltus, Edgar (Everton)
1855-1921 . . . . TCLC 8
See also CA 105

Saltykov, Mikhail Evgrafovich
1826-1889 . . . . NCLC 16

Samarakis, Antonis 1919- . . . . CLC 5
See also CA 25-28R; CAAS 16; CANR 36

Sanchez, Florencio 1875-1910 . . . . . TCLC 37
See also HW

Sanchez, Luis Rafael 1936- . . . . CLC 23
See also CA 128; DLB 145; HW

Sanchez, Sonia 1934- . . . CLC 5; BLC; PC 9
See also BW 2; CA 33-36R; CANR 24, 49;
CLR 18; DLB 41; DLBD 8; MAICYA;
MTCW; SATA 22

Sand, George
1804-1876 . . . . . NCLC 2, 42; DA; DAB;
WLC
See also DLB 119

Sandburg, Carl (August)
1878-1967 . . . . CLC 1, 4, 10, 15, 35; DA;
DAB; PC 2; WLC
See also CA 5-8R; 25-28R; CANR 35;
CDALB 1865-1917; DLB 17, 54;
MAICYA; MTCW; SATA 8

Sandburg, Charles
See Sandburg, Carl (August)

Sandburg, Charles A.
See Sandburg, Carl (August)

Sanders, (James) Ed(ward) 1939- . . . CLC 53
See also CA 13-16R; CAAS 21; CANR 13,
44; DLB 16

Sanders, Lawrence 1920- . . . . CLC 41
See also BEST 89:4; CA 81-84; CANR 33;
MTCW

Sanders, Noah
See Blount, Roy (Alton), Jr.

Sanders, Winston P.
See Anderson, Poul (William)

Sandoz, Mari(e Susette)
1896-1966 . . . . CLC 28
See also CA 1-4R; 25-28R; CANR 17;
DLB 9; MTCW; SATA 5

Saner, Reg(inald Anthony) 1931- . . . . CLC 9
See also CA 65-68

Sannazaro, Jacopo 1456(?)-1530 . . . . . . LC 8

Sansom, William
1912-1976 . . . . CLC 2, 6; SSC 21
See also CA 5-8R; 65-68; CANR 42;
DLB 139; MTCW

Santayana, George 1863-1952 . . . . . TCLC 40
See also CA 115; DLB 54, 71

Santiago, Danny . . . . CLC 33
See also James, Daniel (Lewis)
See also DLB 122

Santmyer, Helen Hoover
1895-1986 . . . . CLC 33
See also CA 1-4R; 118; CANR 15, 33;
DLBY 84; MTCW

Santos, Bienvenido N(uqui) 1911- . . . CLC 22
See also CA 101; CANR 19, 46

Sapper . . . . TCLC 44
See also McNeile, Herman Cyril

Sappho fl. 6th cent. B.C.- . . . . CMLC 3; PC 5

Sarduy, Severo 1937-1993 . . . . CLC 6
See also CA 89-92; 142; DLB 113; HW

Sargeson, Frank 1903-1982 . . . . CLC 31
See also CA 25-28R; 106; CANR 38

Sarmiento, Felix Ruben Garcia
See Dario, Ruben

Saroyan, William
1908-1981 . . . . . CLC 1, 8, 10, 29, 34, 56;
DA; DAB; SSC 21; WLC
See also CA 5-8R; 103; CANR 30; DLB 7,
9, 86; DLBY 81; MTCW; SATA 23;
SATA-Obit 24

Sarraute, Nathalie
1900- . . . . CLC 1, 2, 4, 8, 10, 31, 80
See also CA 9-12R; CANR 23; DLB 83;
MTCW

Sarton, (Eleanor) May
1912- . . . . CLC 4, 14, 49
See also CA 1-4R; CANR 1, 34; DLB 48;
DLBY 81; MTCW; SATA 36

Sartre, Jean-Paul
1905-1980 . . . . CLC 1, 4, 7, 9, 13, 18, 24,
44, 50, 52; DA; DAB; DC 3; WLC
See also CA 9-12R; 97-100; CANR 21;
DLB 72; MTCW

Sassoon, Siegfried (Lorraine)
1886-1967 . . . . CLC 36; DAB; PC 12
See also CA 104; 25-28R; CANR 36;
DLB 20; MTCW

Satterfield, Charles
See Pohl, Frederik

Saul, John (W. III) 1942- . . . . CLC 46
See also AAYA 10; BEST 90:4; CA 81-84;
CANR 16, 40

Saunders, Caleb
See Heinlein, Robert A(nson)

Saura (Atares), Carlos 1932- . . . . CLC 20
See also CA 114; 131; HW

Sauser-Hall, Frederic 1887-1961 . . . . CLC 18
See also Cendrars, Blaise
See also CA 102; 93-96; CANR 36; MTCW

Saussure, Ferdinand de
1857-1913 . . . . TCLC 49

Savage, Catharine
See Brosman, Catharine Savage

Savage, Thomas 1915- . . . . CLC 40
See also CA 126; 132; CAAS 15

Savan, Glenn   19(?)- . . . . **CLC 50**

Sayers, Dorothy L(eigh)
   1893-1957 . . . . **TCLC 2, 15**
   See also CA 104; 119; CDBLB 1914-1945;
      DLB 10, 36, 77, 100; MTCW

Sayers, Valerie   1952- . . . . **CLC 50**
   See also CA 134

Sayles, John (Thomas)
   1950- . . . . **CLC 7, 10, 14**
   See also CA 57-60; CANR 41; DLB 44

Scammell, Michael . . . . **CLC 34**

Scannell, Vernon   1922- . . . . **CLC 49**
   See also CA 5-8R; CANR 8, 24; DLB 27;
      SATA 59

Scarlett, Susan
   See Streatfeild, (Mary) Noel

Schaeffer, Susan Fromberg
   1941- . . . . **CLC 6, 11, 22**
   See also CA 49-52; CANR 18; DLB 28;
      MTCW; SATA 22

Schary, Jill
   See Robinson, Jill

Schell, Jonathan   1943- . . . . **CLC 35**
   See also CA 73-76; CANR 12

Schelling, Friedrich Wilhelm Joseph von
   1775-1854 . . . . **NCLC 30**
   See also DLB 90

Schendel, Arthur van   1874-1946 . . . **TCLC 56**

Scherer, Jean-Marie Maurice   1920-
   See Rohmer, Eric
   See also CA 110

Schevill, James (Erwin)   1920- . . . . **CLC 7**
   See also CA 5-8R; CAAS 12

Schiller, Friedrich   1759-1805 . . . . **NCLC 39**
   See also DLB 94

Schisgal, Murray (Joseph)   1926- . . . . . **CLC 6**
   See also CA 21-24R; CANR 48

Schlee, Ann   1934- . . . . **CLC 35**
   See also CA 101; CANR 29; SATA 44;
      SATA-Brief 36

Schlegel, August Wilhelm von
   1767-1845 . . . . **NCLC 15**
   See also DLB 94

Schlegel, Friedrich   1772-1829 . . . . **NCLC 45**
   See also DLB 90

Schlegel, Johann Elias (von)
   1719(?)-1749 . . . . **LC 5**

Schlesinger, Arthur M(eier), Jr.
   1917- . . . . **CLC 84**
   See also AITN 1; CA 1-4R; CANR 1, 28;
      DLB 17; MTCW; SATA 61

Schmidt, Arno (Otto)   1914-1979 . . . . **CLC 56**
   See also CA 128; 109; DLB 69

Schmitz, Aron Hector   1861-1928
   See Svevo, Italo
   See also CA 104; 122; MTCW

Schnackenberg, Gjertrud   1953- . . . . . **CLC 40**
   See also CA 116; DLB 120

Schneider, Leonard Alfred   1925-1966
   See Bruce, Lenny
   See also CA 89-92

Schnitzler, Arthur
   1862-1931 . . . . **TCLC 4; SSC 15**
   See also CA 104; DLB 81, 118

Schopenhauer, Arthur
   1788-1860 . . . . **NCLC 51**
   See also DLB 90

Schor, Sandra (M.)   1932(?)-1990 . . . **CLC 65**
   See also CA 132

Schorer, Mark   1908-1977 . . . . **CLC 9**
   See also CA 5-8R; 73-76; CANR 7;
      DLB 103

Schrader, Paul (Joseph)   1946- . . . . . . **CLC 26**
   See also CA 37-40R; CANR 41; DLB 44

Schreiner, Olive (Emilie Albertina)
   1855-1920 . . . . **TCLC 9**
   See also CA 105; DLB 18, 156

Schulberg, Budd (Wilson)
   1914- . . . . **CLC 7, 48**
   See also CA 25-28R; CANR 19; DLB 6, 26,
      28; DLBY 81

Schulz, Bruno
   1892-1942 . . . . **TCLC 5, 51; SSC 13**
   See also CA 115; 123

Schulz, Charles M(onroe)   1922- . . . . **CLC 12**
   See also CA 9-12R; CANR 6; SATA 10

Schumacher, E(rnst) F(riedrich)
   1911-1977 . . . . **CLC 80**
   See also CA 81-84; 73-76; CANR 34

Schuyler, James Marcus
   1923-1991 . . . . **CLC 5, 23**
   See also CA 101; 134; DLB 5

Schwartz, Delmore (David)
   1913-1966 . . . **CLC 2, 4, 10, 45, 87; PC 8**
   See also CA 17-18; 25-28R; CANR 35;
      CAP 2; DLB 28, 48; MTCW

Schwartz, Ernst
   See Ozu, Yasujiro

Schwartz, John Burnham   1965- . . . . **CLC 59**
   See also CA 132

Schwartz, Lynne Sharon   1939- . . . . . **CLC 31**
   See also CA 103; CANR 44

Schwartz, Muriel A.
   See Eliot, T(homas) S(tearns)

Schwarz-Bart, Andre   1928- . . . . **CLC 2, 4**
   See also CA 89-92

Schwarz-Bart, Simone   1938- . . . . **CLC 7**
   See also BW 2; CA 97-100

Schwob, (Mayer Andre) Marcel
   1867-1905 . . . . **TCLC 20**
   See also CA 117; DLB 123

Sciascia, Leonardo
   1921-1989 . . . . **CLC 8, 9, 41**
   See also CA 85-88; 130; CANR 35; MTCW

Scoppettone, Sandra   1936- . . . . **CLC 26**
   See also AAYA 11; CA 5-8R; CANR 41;
      SATA 9

Scorsese, Martin   1942- . . . . **CLC 20, 89**
   See also CA 110; 114; CANR 46

Scotland, Jay
   See Jakes, John (William)

Scott, Duncan Campbell
   1862-1947 . . . . **TCLC 6**
   See also CA 104; DLB 92

Scott, Evelyn   1893-1963 . . . . **CLC 43**
   See also CA 104; 112; DLB 9, 48

Scott, F(rancis) R(eginald)
   1899-1985 . . . . **CLC 22**
   See also CA 101; 114; DLB 88

Scott, Frank
   See Scott, F(rancis) R(eginald)

Scott, Joanna   1960- . . . . **CLC 50**
   See also CA 126

Scott, Paul (Mark)   1920-1978 . . . . **CLC 9, 60**
   See also CA 81-84; 77-80; CANR 33;
      DLB 14; MTCW

Scott, Walter
   1771-1832 . . . . **NCLC 15; DA; DAB;
                                 PC 13; WLC**
   See also CDBLB 1789-1832; DLB 93, 107,
      116, 144; YABC 2

Scribe, (Augustin) Eugene
   1791-1861 . . . . **NCLC 16; DC 5**

Scrum, R.
   See Crumb, R(obert)

Scudery, Madeleine de   1607-1701 . . . . . **LC 2**

Scum
   See Crumb, R(obert)

Scumbag, Little Bobby
   See Crumb, R(obert)

Seabrook, John
   See Hubbard, L(afayette) Ron(ald)

Sealy, I. Allan   1951- . . . . **CLC 55**

Search, Alexander
   See Pessoa, Fernando (Antonio Nogueira)

Sebastian, Lee
   See Silverberg, Robert

Sebastian Owl
   See Thompson, Hunter S(tockton)

Sebestyen, Ouida   1924- . . . . **CLC 30**
   See also AAYA 8; CA 107; CANR 40;
      CLR 17; JRDA; MAICYA; SAAS 10;
      SATA 39

Secundus, H. Scriblerus
   See Fielding, Henry

Sedges, John
   See Buck, Pearl S(ydenstricker)

Sedgwick, Catharine Maria
   1789-1867 . . . . **NCLC 19**
   See also DLB 1, 74

Seelye, John   1931- . . . . **CLC 7**

Seferiades, Giorgos Stylianou   1900-1971
   See Seferis, George
   See also CA 5-8R; 33-36R; CANR 5, 36;
      MTCW

Seferis, George . . . . **CLC 5, 11**
   See also Seferiades, Giorgos Stylianou

Segal, Erich (Wolf)   1937- . . . . **CLC 3, 10**
   See also BEST 89:1; CA 25-28R; CANR 20,
      36; DLBY 86; MTCW

Seger, Bob   1945- . . . . **CLC 35**

Seghers, Anna . . . . **CLC 7**
   See also Radvanyi, Netty
   See also DLB 69

Seidel, Frederick (Lewis)   1936- . . . . . **CLC 18**
   See also CA 13-16R; CANR 8; DLBY 84

Seifert, Jaroslav   1901-1986 . . . . . **CLC 34, 44**
   See also CA 127; MTCW

Sei Shonagon   c. 966-1017(?) . . . . . . **CMLC 6**

Slaughter, Frank G(ill) 1908- ...... CLC 29
See also AITN 2; CA 5-8R; CANR 5

Slavitt, David R(ytman) 1935-.... CLC 5, 14
See also CA 21-24R; CAAS 3; CANR 41;
DLB 5, 6

Slesinger, Tess 1905-1945 .... TCLC 10
See also CA 107; DLB 102

Slessor, Kenneth 1901-1971....... CLC 14
See also CA 102; 89-92

Slowacki, Juliusz 1809-1849 ..... NCLC 15

Smart, Christopher
1722-1771 .... LC 3; PC 13
See also DLB 109

Smart, Elizabeth 1913-1986....... CLC 54
See also CA 81-84; 118; DLB 88

Smiley, Jane (Graves) 1949- .... CLC 53, 76
See also CA 104; CANR 30

Smith, A(rthur) J(ames) M(arshall)
1902-1980 .... CLC 15
See also CA 1-4R; 102; CANR 4; DLB 88

Smith, Anna Deavere 1950-........ CLC 86
See also CA 133

Smith, Betty (Wehner) 1896-1972... CLC 19
See also CA 5-8R; 33-36R; DLBY 82;
SATA 6

Smith, Charlotte (Turner)
1749-1806 .... NCLC 23
See also DLB 39, 109

Smith, Clark Ashton 1893-1961 .... CLC 43
See also CA 143

Smith, Dave.................. CLC 22, 42
See also Smith, David (Jeddie)
See also CAAS 7; DLB 5

Smith, David (Jeddie) 1942-
See Smith, Dave
See also CA 49-52; CANR 1

Smith, Florence Margaret 1902-1971
See Smith, Stevie
See also CA 17-18; 29-32R; CANR 35;
CAP 2; MTCW

Smith, Iain Crichton 1928- .... CLC 64
See also CA 21-24R; DLB 40, 139

Smith, John 1580(?)-1631 .... LC 9

Smith, Johnston
See Crane, Stephen (Townley)

Smith, Lee 1944-............. CLC 25, 73
See also CA 114; 119; CANR 46; DLB 143;
DLBY 83

Smith, Martin
See Smith, Martin Cruz

Smith, Martin Cruz 1942-........ CLC 25
See also BEST 89:4; CA 85-88; CANR 6,
23, 43; NNAL

Smith, Mary-Ann Tirone 1944-..... CLC 39
See also CA 118; 136

Smith, Patti 1946- .... CLC 12
See also CA 93-96

Smith, Pauline (Urmson)
1882-1959 .... TCLC 25

Smith, Rosamond
See Oates, Joyce Carol

Smith, Sheila Kaye
See Kaye-Smith, Sheila

Smith, Stevie .... CLC 3, 8, 25, 44; PC 12
See also Smith, Florence Margaret
See also DLB 20

Smith, Wilbur (Addison) 1933-..... CLC 33
See also CA 13-16R; CANR 7, 46; MTCW

Smith, William Jay 1918-.......... CLC 6
See also CA 5-8R; CANR 44; DLB 5;
MAICYA; SATA 2, 68

Smith, Woodrow Wilson
See Kuttner, Henry

Smolenskin, Peretz 1842-1885.... NCLC 30

Smollett, Tobias (George) 1721-1771 .. LC 2
See also CDBLB 1660-1789; DLB 39, 104

Snodgrass, W(illiam) D(e Witt)
1926- .... CLC 2, 6, 10, 18, 68
See also CA 1-4R; CANR 6, 36; DLB 5;
MTCW

Snow, C(harles) P(ercy)
1905-1980 .... CLC 1, 4, 6, 9, 13, 19
See also CA 5-8R; 101; CANR 28;
CDBLB 1945-1960; DLB 15, 77; MTCW

Snow, Frances Compton
See Adams, Henry (Brooks)

Snyder, Gary (Sherman)
1930- .... CLC 1, 2, 5, 9, 32
See also CA 17-20R; CANR 30; DLB 5, 16

Snyder, Zilpha Keatley 1927-...... CLC 17
See also AAYA 15; CA 9-12R; CANR 38;
CLR 31; JRDA; MAICYA; SAAS 2;
SATA 1, 28, 75

Soares, Bernardo
See Pessoa, Fernando (Antonio Nogueira)

Sobh, A.
See Shamlu, Ahmad

Sobol, Joshua.................... CLC 60

Soderberg, Hjalmar 1869-1941 .... TCLC 39

Sodergran, Edith (Irene)
See Soedergran, Edith (Irene)

Soedergran, Edith (Irene)
1892-1923 .... TCLC 31

Softly, Edgar
See Lovecraft, H(oward) P(hillips)

Softly, Edward
See Lovecraft, H(oward) P(hillips)

Sokolov, Raymond 1941-........... CLC 7
See also CA 85-88

Solo, Jay
See Ellison, Harlan (Jay)

Sologub, Fyodor .... TCLC 9
See also Teternikov, Fyodor Kuzmich

Solomons, Ikey Esquir
See Thackeray, William Makepeace

Solomos, Dionysios 1798-1857 ... NCLC 15

Solwoska, Mara
See French, Marilyn

Solzhenitsyn, Aleksandr I(sayevich)
1918- ...... CLC 1, 2, 4, 7, 9, 10, 18, 26,
34, 78; DA; DAB; WLC
See also AITN 1; CA 69-72; CANR 40;
MTCW

Somers, Jane
See Lessing, Doris (May)

Somerville, Edith 1858-1949 ..... TCLC 51
See also DLB 135

Somerville & Ross
See Martin, Violet Florence; Somerville,
Edith

Sommer, Scott 1951-.............. CLC 25
See also CA 106

Sondheim, Stephen (Joshua)
1930- .... CLC 30, 39
See also AAYA 11; CA 103; CANR 47

Sontag, Susan 1933-... CLC 1, 2, 10, 13, 31
See also CA 17-20R; CANR 25; DLB 2, 67;
MTCW

Sophocles
496(?)B.C.-406(?)B.C..... CMLC 2; DA;
DAB; DC 1

Sordello 1189-1269............. CMLC 15

Sorel, Julia
See Drexler, Rosalyn

Sorrentino, Gilbert
1929- .... CLC 3, 7, 14, 22, 40
See also CA 77-80; CANR 14, 33; DLB 5;
DLBY 80

Soto, Gary 1952-........ CLC 32, 80; HLC
See also AAYA 10; CA 119; 125; CLR 38;
DLB 82; HW; JRDA; SATA 80

Soupault, Philippe 1897-1990 ...... CLC 68
See also CA 116; 147; 131

Souster, (Holmes) Raymond
1921- .... CLC 5, 14
See also CA 13-16R; CAAS 14; CANR 13,
29; DLB 88; SATA 63

Southern, Terry 1926- .... CLC 7
See also CA 1-4R; CANR 1; DLB 2

Southey, Robert 1774-1843 .... NCLC 8
See also DLB 93, 107, 142; SATA 54

Southworth, Emma Dorothy Eliza Nevitte
1819-1899 .... NCLC 26

Souza, Ernest
See Scott, Evelyn

Soyinka, Wole
1934- .... CLC 3, 5, 14, 36, 44; BLC;
DA; DAB; DC 2; WLC
See also BW 2; CA 13-16R; CANR 27, 39;
DLB 125; MTCW

Spackman, W(illiam) M(ode)
1905-1990 .... CLC 46
See also CA 81-84; 132

Spacks, Barry 1931-.............. CLC 14
See also CA 29-32R; CANR 33; DLB 105

Spanidou, Irini 1946-............. CLC 44

Spark, Muriel (Sarah)
1918- .... CLC 2, 3, 5, 8, 13, 18, 40;
DAB; SSC 10
See also CA 5-8R; CANR 12, 36;
CDBLB 1945-1960; DLB 15, 139; MTCW

Spaulding, Douglas
See Bradbury, Ray (Douglas)

Spaulding, Leonard
See Bradbury, Ray (Douglas)

Spence, J. A. D.
See Eliot, T(homas) S(tearns)

Spencer, Elizabeth 1921- .... **CLC 22**
See also CA 13-16R; CANR 32; DLB 6;
MTCW; SATA 14

Spencer, Leonard G.
See Silverberg, Robert

Spencer, Scott 1945- .... **CLC 30**
See also CA 113; DLBY 86

Spender, Stephen (Harold)
1909- .... **CLC 1, 2, 5, 10, 41**
See also CA 9-12R; CANR 31;
CDBLB 1945-1960; DLB 20; MTCW

Spengler, Oswald (Arnold Gottfried)
1880-1936 .... **TCLC 25**
See also CA 118

Spenser, Edmund
1552(?)-1599 .... **LC 5; DA; DAB; PC 8;**
WLC
See also CDBLB Before 1660

Spicer, Jack 1925-1965 ...... **CLC 8, 18, 72**
See also CA 85-88; DLB 5, 16

Spiegelman, Art 1948- .... **CLC 76**
See also AAYA 10; CA 125; CANR 41

Spielberg, Peter 1929- .... **CLC 6**
See also CA 5-8R; CANR 4, 48; DLBY 81

Spielberg, Steven 1947- .... **CLC 20**
See also AAYA 8; CA 77-80; CANR 32;
SATA 32

Spillane, Frank Morrison 1918-
See Spillane, Mickey
See also CA 25-28R; CANR 28; MTCW;
SATA 66

Spillane, Mickey .... **CLC 3, 13**
See also Spillane, Frank Morrison

Spinoza, Benedictus de 1632-1677 .... **LC 9**

Spinrad, Norman (Richard) 1940-... **CLC 46**
See also CA 37-40R; CAAS 19; CANR 20;
DLB 8

Spitteler, Carl (Friedrich Georg)
1845-1924 .... **TCLC 12**
See also CA 109; DLB 129

Spivack, Kathleen (Romola Drucker)
1938- .... **CLC 6**
See also CA 49-52

Spoto, Donald 1941- .... **CLC 39**
See also CA 65-68; CANR 11

Springsteen, Bruce (F.) 1949- ...... **CLC 17**
See also CA 111

Spurling, Hilary 1940- .... **CLC 34**
See also CA 104; CANR 25

Spyker, John Howland
See Elman, Richard

Squires, (James) Radcliffe
1917-1993 .... **CLC 51**
See also CA 1-4R; 140; CANR 6, 21

Srivastava, Dhanpat Rai 1880(?)-1936
See Premchand
See also CA 118

Stacy, Donald
See Pohl, Frederik

Stael, Germaine de
See Stael-Holstein, Anne Louise Germaine
Necker Baronn
See also DLB 119

Stael-Holstein, Anne Louise Germaine Necker
Baronn 1766-1817 .... **NCLC 3**
See also Stael, Germaine de

Stafford, Jean 1915-1979... **CLC 4, 7, 19, 68**
See also CA 1-4R; 85-88; CANR 3; DLB 2;
MTCW; SATA-Obit 22

Stafford, William (Edgar)
1914-1993 .... **CLC 4, 7, 29**
See also CA 5-8R; 142; CAAS 3; CANR 5,
22; DLB 5

Staines, Trevor
See Brunner, John (Kilian Houston)

Stairs, Gordon
See Austin, Mary (Hunter)

Stannard, Martin 1947- .... **CLC 44**
See also CA 142; DLB 155

Stanton, Maura 1946- .... **CLC 9**
See also CA 89-92; CANR 15; DLB 120

Stanton, Schuyler
See Baum, L(yman) Frank

Stapledon, (William) Olaf
1886-1950 .... **TCLC 22**
See also CA 111; DLB 15

Starbuck, George (Edwin) 1931-.... **CLC 53**
See also CA 21-24R; CANR 23

Stark, Richard
See Westlake, Donald E(dwin)

Staunton, Schuyler
See Baum, L(yman) Frank

Stead, Christina (Ellen)
1902-1983 .... **CLC 2, 5, 8, 32, 80**
See also CA 13-16R; 109; CANR 33, 40;
MTCW

Stead, William Thomas
1849-1912 .... **TCLC 48**

Steele, Richard 1672-1729 .... **LC 18**
See also CDBLB 1660-1789; DLB 84, 101

Steele, Timothy (Reid) 1948-....... **CLC 45**
See also CA 93-96; CANR 16; DLB 120

Steffens, (Joseph) Lincoln
1866-1936 .... **TCLC 20**
See also CA 117

Stegner, Wallace (Earle)
1909-1993 .... **CLC 9, 49, 81**
See also AITN 1; BEST 90:3; CA 1-4R;
141; CAAS 9; CANR 1, 21, 46; DLB 9;
DLBY 93; MTCW

Stein, Gertrude
1874-1946 ..... **TCLC 1, 6, 28, 48; DA;**
DAB; WLC
See also CA 104; 132; CDALB 1917-1929;
DLB 4, 54, 86; MTCW

Steinbeck, John (Ernst)
1902-1968 ...... **CLC 1, 5, 9, 13, 21, 34,**
45, 75; DA; DAB; SSC 11; WLC
See also AAYA 12; CA 1-4R; 25-28R;
CANR 1, 35; CDALB 1929-1941; DLB 7,
9; DLBD 2; MTCW; SATA 9

Steinem, Gloria 1934-............. **CLC 63**
See also CA 53-56; CANR 28; MTCW

Steiner, George 1929-............. **CLC 24**
See also CA 73-76; CANR 31; DLB 67;
MTCW; SATA 62

Steiner, K. Leslie
See Delany, Samuel R(ay, Jr.)

Steiner, Rudolf 1861-1925 .... **TCLC 13**
See also CA 107

Stendhal
1783-1842 .... **NCLC 23, 46; DA; DAB;**
WLC
See also DLB 119

Stephen, Leslie 1832-1904 .... **TCLC 23**
See also CA 123; DLB 57, 144

Stephen, Sir Leslie
See Stephen, Leslie

Stephen, Virginia
See Woolf, (Adeline) Virginia

Stephens, James 1882(?)-1950...... **TCLC 4**
See also CA 104; DLB 19, 153

Stephens, Reed
See Donaldson, Stephen R.

Steptoe, Lydia
See Barnes, Djuna

Sterchi, Beat 1949-............... **CLC 65**

Sterling, Brett
See Bradbury, Ray (Douglas); Hamilton,
Edmond

Sterling, Bruce 1954-............. **CLC 72**
See also CA 119; CANR 44

Sterling, George 1869-1926 .... **TCLC 20**
See also CA 117; DLB 54

Stern, Gerald 1925- .... **CLC 40**
See also CA 81-84; CANR 28; DLB 105

Stern, Richard (Gustave) 1928-... **CLC 4, 39**
See also CA 1-4R; CANR 1, 25; DLBY 87

Sternberg, Josef von 1894-1969..... **CLC 20**
See also CA 81-84

Sterne, Laurence
1713-1768 ...... **LC 2; DA; DAB; WLC**
See also CDBLB 1660-1789; DLB 39

Sternheim, (William Adolf) Carl
1878-1942 .... **TCLC 8**
See also CA 105; DLB 56, 118

Stevens, Mark 1951- .... **CLC 34**
See also CA 122

Stevens, Wallace
1879-1955 .... **TCLC 3, 12, 45; DA;**
DAB; PC 6; WLC
See also CA 104; 124; CDALB 1929-1941;
DLB 54; MTCW

Stevenson, Anne (Katharine)
1933- .... **CLC 7, 33**
See also CA 17-20R; CAAS 9; CANR 9, 33;
DLB 40; MTCW

Stevenson, Robert Louis (Balfour)
1850-1894 ..... **NCLC 5, 14; DA; DAB;**
SSC 11; WLC
See also CDBLB 1890-1914; CLR 10, 11;
DLB 18, 57, 141, 156; JRDA; MAICYA;
YABC 2

Stewart, J(ohn) I(nnes) M(ackintosh)
1906-1994 .... **CLC 7, 14, 32**
See also CA 85-88; 147; CAAS 3;
CANR 47; MTCW

Stewart, Mary (Florence Elinor)
1916- .... **CLC 7, 35; DAB**
See also CA 1-4R; CANR 1; SATA 12

Stewart, Mary Rainbow
See Stewart, Mary (Florence Elinor)

Swenson, May
1919-1989 .... **CLC 4, 14, 61; DA; DAB**
See also CA 5-8R; 130; CANR 36; DLB 5;
MTCW; SATA 15

Swift, Augustus
See Lovecraft, H(oward) P(hillips)

Swift, Graham (Colin) 1949- .... **CLC 41, 88**
See also CA 117; 122; CANR 46

Swift, Jonathan
1667-1745 ...... **LC 1; DA; DAB; PC 9;**
WLC
See also CDBLB 1660-1789; DLB 39, 95,
101; SATA 19

Swinburne, Algernon Charles
1837-1909 ...... **TCLC 8, 36; DA; DAB;**
WLC
See also CA 105; 140; CDBLB 1832-1890;
DLB 35, 57

Swinfen, Ann .... **CLC 34**

Swinnerton, Frank Arthur
1884-1982 .... **CLC 31**
See also CA 108; DLB 34

Swithen, John
See King, Stephen (Edwin)

Sylvia
See Ashton-Warner, Sylvia (Constance)

Symmes, Robert Edward
See Duncan, Robert (Edward)

Symonds, John Addington
1840-1893 .... **NCLC 34**
See also DLB 57, 144

Symons, Arthur 1865-1945 .... **TCLC 11**
See also CA 107; DLB 19, 57, 149

Symons, Julian (Gustave)
1912-1994 .... **CLC 2, 14, 32**
See also CA 49-52; 147; CAAS 3; CANR 3,
33; DLB 87, 155; DLBY 92; MTCW

Synge, (Edmund) J(ohn) M(illington)
1871-1909 .... **TCLC 6, 37; DC 2**
See also CA 104; 141; CDBLB 1890-1914;
DLB 10, 19

Syruc, J.
See Milosz, Czeslaw

Szirtes, George 1948- .... **CLC 46**
See also CA 109; CANR 27

Tabori, George 1914- .... **CLC 19**
See also CA 49-52; CANR 4

Tagore, Rabindranath
1861-1941 .... **TCLC 3, 53; PC 8**
See also CA 104; 120; MTCW

Taine, Hippolyte Adolphe
1828-1893 .... **NCLC 15**

Talese, Gay 1932- .... **CLC 37**
See also AITN 1; CA 1-4R; CANR 9;
MTCW

Tallent, Elizabeth (Ann) 1954- ..... **CLC 45**
See also CA 117; DLB 130

Tally, Ted 1952- .... **CLC 42**
See also CA 120; 124

Tamayo y Baus, Manuel
1829-1898 .... **NCLC 1**

Tammsaare, A(nton) H(ansen)
1878-1940 .... **TCLC 27**

Tan, Amy 1952- .... **CLC 59**
See also AAYA 9; BEST 89:3; CA 136;
SATA 75

Tandem, Felix
See Spitteler, Carl (Friedrich Georg)

Tanizaki, Jun'ichiro
1886-1965 ...... **CLC 8, 14, 28; SSC 21**
See also CA 93-96; 25-28R

Tanner, William
See Amis, Kingsley (William)

Tao Lao
See Storni, Alfonsina

Tarassoff, Lev
See Troyat, Henri

Tarbell, Ida M(inerva)
1857-1944 .... **TCLC 40**
See also CA 122; DLB 47

Tarkington, (Newton) Booth
1869-1946 .... **TCLC 9**
See also CA 110; 143; DLB 9, 102;
SATA 17

Tarkovsky, Andrei (Arsenyevich)
1932-1986 .... **CLC 75**
See also CA 127

Tartt, Donna 1964(?)- .... **CLC 76**
See also CA 142

Tasso, Torquato 1544-1595 .... **LC 5**

Tate, (John Orley) Allen
1899-1979 .... **CLC 2, 4, 6, 9, 11, 14, 24**
See also CA 5-8R; 85-88; CANR 32;
DLB 4, 45, 63; MTCW

Tate, Ellalice
See Hibbert, Eleanor Alice Burford

Tate, James (Vincent) 1943- ... **CLC 2, 6, 25**
See also CA 21-24R; CANR 29; DLB 5

Tavel, Ronald 1940- .... **CLC 6**
See also CA 21-24R; CANR 33

Taylor, C(ecil) P(hilip) 1929-1981 ... **CLC 27**
See also CA 25-28R; 105; CANR 47

Taylor, Edward
1642(?)-1729 .... **LC 11; DA; DAB**
See also DLB 24

Taylor, Eleanor Ross 1920- .... **CLC 5**
See also CA 81-84

Taylor, Elizabeth 1912-1975 ... **CLC 2, 4, 29**
See also CA 13-16R; CANR 9; DLB 139;
MTCW; SATA 13

Taylor, Henry (Splawn) 1942- ...... **CLC 44**
See also CA 33-36R; CAAS 7; CANR 31;
DLB 5

Taylor, Kamala (Purnaiya) 1924-
See Markandaya, Kamala
See also CA 77-80

Taylor, Mildred D. .... **CLC 21**
See also AAYA 10; BW 1; CA 85-88;
CANR 25; CLR 9; DLB 52; JRDA;
MAICYA; SAAS 5; SATA 15, 70

Taylor, Peter (Hillsman)
1917-1994 ..... **CLC 1, 4, 18, 37, 44, 50,**
71; SSC 10
See also CA 13-16R; 147; CANR 9;
DLBY 81, 94; MTCW

Taylor, Robert Lewis 1912- .... **CLC 14**
See also CA 1-4R; CANR 3; SATA 10

Tchekhov, Anton
See Chekhov, Anton (Pavlovich)

Teasdale, Sara 1884-1933......... **TCLC 4**
See also CA 104; DLB 45; SATA 32

Tegner, Esaias 1782-1846........ **NCLC 2**

Teilhard de Chardin, (Marie Joseph) Pierre
1881-1955 .... **TCLC 9**
See also CA 105

Temple, Ann
See Mortimer, Penelope (Ruth)

Tennant, Emma (Christina)
1937- .... **CLC 13, 52**
See also CA 65-68; CAAS 9; CANR 10, 38;
DLB 14

Tenneshaw, S. M.
See Silverberg, Robert

Tennyson, Alfred
1809-1892 .... **NCLC 30; DA; DAB;**
PC 6; WLC
See also CDBLB 1832-1890; DLB 32

Teran, Lisa St. Aubin de .... **CLC 36**
See also St. Aubin de Teran, Lisa

Terence 195(?)B.C.-159B.C....... **CMLC 14**

Teresa de Jesus, St. 1515-1582 ...... **LC 18**

Terkel, Louis 1912-
See Terkel, Studs
See also CA 57-60; CANR 18, 45; MTCW

Terkel, Studs .... **CLC 38**
See also Terkel, Louis
See also AITN 1

Terry, C. V.
See Slaughter, Frank G(ill)

Terry, Megan 1932-............... **CLC 19**
See also CA 77-80; CABS 3; CANR 43;
DLB 7

Tertz, Abram
See Sinyavsky, Andrei (Donatevich)

Tesich, Steve 1943(?)-.......... **CLC 40, 69**
See also CA 105; DLBY 83

Teternikov, Fyodor Kuzmich 1863-1927
See Sologub, Fyodor
See also CA 104

Tevis, Walter 1928-1984 .... **CLC 42**
See also CA 113

Tey, Josephine................... **TCLC 14**
See also Mackintosh, Elizabeth
See also DLB 77

Thackeray, William Makepeace
1811-1863 .... **NCLC 5, 14, 22, 43; DA;**
DAB; WLC
See also CDBLB 1832-1890; DLB 21, 55;
SATA 23

Thakura, Ravindranatha
See Tagore, Rabindranath

Tharoor, Shashi 1956- .... **CLC 70**
See also CA 141

Thelwell, Michael Miles 1939- ..... **CLC 22**
See also BW 2; CA 101

Theobald, Lewis, Jr.
See Lovecraft, H(oward) P(hillips)

Theodorescu, Ion N. 1880-1967
See Arghezi, Tudor
See also CA 116

Townshend, Peter (Dennis Blandford)
1945- . . . . **CLC 17, 42**
See also CA 107

Tozzi, Federigo 1883-1920. . . . . . . **TCLC 31**

Traill, Catharine Parr
1802-1899 . . . . **NCLC 31**
See also DLB 99

Trakl, Georg 1887-1914. . . . . **TCLC 5**
See also CA 104

Transtroemer, Tomas (Goesta)
1931- . . . . **CLC 52, 65**
See also CA 117; 129; CAAS 17

Transtromer, Tomas Gosta
See Transtroemer, Tomas (Goesta)

Traven, B. (?)-1969. . . . . **CLC 8, 11**
See also CA 19-20; 25-28R; CAP 2; DLB 9,
56; MTCW

Treitel, Jonathan 1959- . . . . **CLC 70**

Tremain, Rose 1943-. . . . . **CLC 42**
See also CA 97-100; CANR 44; DLB 14

Tremblay, Michel 1942-. . . . . **CLC 29**
See also CA 116; 128; DLB 60; MTCW

Trevanian. **CLC 29**
See also Whitaker, Rod(ney)

Trevor, Glen
See Hilton, James

Trevor, William
1928- . . . . . **CLC 7, 9, 14, 25, 71; SSC 21**
See also Cox, William Trevor
See also DLB 14, 139

Trifonov, Yuri (Valentinovich)
1925-1981 . . . . **CLC 45**
See also CA 126; 103; MTCW

Trilling, Lionel 1905-1975 . . . . **CLC 9, 11, 24**
See also CA 9-12R; 61-64; CANR 10;
DLB 28, 63; MTCW

Trimball, W. H.
See Mencken, H(enry) L(ouis)

Tristan
See Gomez de la Serna, Ramon

Tristram
See Housman, A(lfred) E(dward)

Trogdon, William (Lewis) 1939-
See Heat-Moon, William Least
See also CA 115; 119; CANR 47

Trollope, Anthony
1815-1882 . . . . . **NCLC 6, 33; DA; DAB;
WLC**
See also CDBLB 1832-1890; DLB 21, 57;
SATA 22

Trollope, Frances 1779-1863 . . . . . **NCLC 30**
See also DLB 21

Trotsky, Leon 1879-1940. . . . . **TCLC 22**
See also CA 118

Trotter (Cockburn), Catharine
1679-1749 . . . . **LC 8**
See also DLB 84

Trout, Kilgore
See Farmer, Philip Jose

Trow, George W. S. 1943-. . . . . **CLC 52**
See also CA 126

Troyat, Henri 1911-. . . . . **CLC 23**
See also CA 45-48; CANR 2, 33; MTCW

Trudeau, G(arretson) B(eekman) 1948-
See Trudeau, Garry B.
See also CA 81-84; CANR 31; SATA 35

Trudeau, Garry B.. . . . . **CLC 12**
See also Trudeau, G(arretson) B(eekman)
See also AAYA 10; AITN 2

Truffaut, Francois 1932-1984. . . . . . **CLC 20**
See also CA 81-84; 113; CANR 34

Trumbo, Dalton 1905-1976 . . . . **CLC 19**
See also CA 21-24R; 69-72; CANR 10;
DLB 26

Trumbull, John 1750-1831 . . . . . . **NCLC 30**
See also DLB 31

Trundlett, Helen B.
See Eliot, T(homas) S(tearns)

Tryon, Thomas 1926-1991 . . . . **CLC 3, 11**
See also AITN 1; CA 29-32R; 135;
CANR 32; MTCW

Tryon, Tom
See Tryon, Thomas

Ts'ao Hsueh-ch'in 1715(?)-1763. . . . . . . **LC 1**

Tsushima, Shuji 1909-1948
See Dazai, Osamu
See also CA 107

Tsvetaeva (Efron), Marina (Ivanovna)
1892-1941 . . . . **TCLC 7, 35**
See also CA 104; 128; MTCW

Tuck, Lily 1938-. . . . . **CLC 70**
See also CA 139

Tu Fu 712-770. . . . . **PC 9**

Tunis, John R(oberts) 1889-1975 . . . **CLC 12**
See also CA 61-64; DLB 22; JRDA;
MAICYA; SATA 37; SATA-Brief 30

Tuohy, Frank. . . . . **CLC 37**
See also Tuohy, John Francis
See also DLB 14, 139

Tuohy, John Francis 1925-
See Tuohy, Frank
See also CA 5-8R; CANR 3, 47

Turco, Lewis (Putnam) 1934- . . . **CLC 11, 63**
See also CA 13-16R; CAAS 22; CANR 24;
DLBY 84

Turgenev, Ivan
1818-1883 . . . . **NCLC 21; DA; DAB;
SSC 7; WLC**

Turgot, Anne-Robert-Jacques
1727-1781 . . . . **LC 26**

Turner, Frederick 1943-. . . . . **CLC 48**
See also CA 73-76; CAAS 10; CANR 12,
30; DLB 40

Tutu, Desmond M(pilo)
1931- . . . . **CLC 80; BLC**
See also BW 1; CA 125

Tutuola, Amos 1920- . . . **CLC 5, 14, 29; BLC**
See also BW 2; CA 9-12R; CANR 27;
DLB 125; MTCW

Twain, Mark
. . . . . **TCLC 6, 12, 19, 36, 48, 59; SSC 6;
WLC**
See also Clemens, Samuel Langhorne
See also DLB 11, 12, 23, 64, 74

Tyler, Anne
1941- . . . . **CLC 7, 11, 18, 28, 44, 59**
See also BEST 89:1; CA 9-12R; CANR 11,
33; DLB 6, 143; DLBY 82; MTCW;
SATA 7

Tyler, Royall 1757-1826. . . . . **NCLC 3**
See also DLB 37

Tynan, Katharine 1861-1931 . . . . **TCLC 3**
See also CA 104; DLB 153

Tyutchev, Fyodor 1803-1873. . . . . **NCLC 34**

Tzara, Tristan . . . . **CLC 47**
See also Rosenfeld, Samuel

Uhry, Alfred 1936-. . . . . **CLC 55**
See also CA 127; 133

Ulf, Haerved
See Strindberg, (Johan) August

Ulf, Harved
See Strindberg, (Johan) August

Ulibarri, Sabine R(eyes) 1919- . . . . . **CLC 83**
See also CA 131; DLB 82; HW

Unamuno (y Jugo), Miguel de
1864-1936 . . . . **TCLC 2, 9; HLC; SSC 11**
See also CA 104; 131; DLB 108; HW;
MTCW

Undercliffe, Errol
See Campbell, (John) Ramsey

Underwood, Miles
See Glassco, John

Undset, Sigrid
1882-1949 . . . **TCLC 3; DA; DAB; WLC**
See also CA 104; 129; MTCW

Ungaretti, Giuseppe
1888-1970 . . . . **CLC 7, 11, 15**
See also CA 19-20; 25-28R; CAP 2;
DLB 114

Unger, Douglas 1952-. . . . . **CLC 34**
See also CA 130

Unsworth, Barry (Forster) 1930-. . . . **CLC 76**
See also CA 25-28R; CANR 30

Updike, John (Hoyer)
1932- . . . . . . **CLC 1, 2, 3, 5, 7, 9, 13, 15,
23, 34, 43, 70; DA; DAB; SSC 13; WLC**
See also CA 1-4R; CABS 1; CANR 4, 33;
CDALB 1968-1988; DLB 2, 5, 143;
DLBD 3; DLBY 80, 82; MTCW

Upshaw, Margaret Mitchell
See Mitchell, Margaret (Munnerlyn)

Upton, Mark
See Sanders, Lawrence

Urdang, Constance (Henriette)
1922- . . . . **CLC 47**
See also CA 21-24R; CANR 9, 24

Uriel, Henry
See Faust, Frederick (Schiller)

Uris, Leon (Marcus) 1924-. . . . . . . **CLC 7, 32**
See also AITN 1, 2; BEST 89:2; CA 1-4R;
CANR 1, 40; MTCW; SATA 49

Urmuz
See Codrescu, Andrei

Urquhart, Jane 1949-. . . . . **CLC 90**
See also CA 113; CANR 32

Ustinov, Peter (Alexander) 1921- . . . . **CLC 1**
See also AITN 1; CA 13-16R; CANR 25;
DLB 13

Vaculik, Ludvik 1926- .... CLC 7
See also CA 53-56

Valdez, Luis (Miguel)
1940- .... CLC 84; HLC
See also CA 101; CANR 32; DLB 122; HW

Valenzuela, Luisa 1938- ... CLC 31; SSC 14
See also CA 101; CANR 32; DLB 113; HW

Valera y Alcala-Galiano, Juan
1824-1905 .... TCLC 10
See also CA 106

Valery, (Ambroise) Paul (Toussaint Jules)
1871-1945 .... TCLC 4, 15; PC 9
See also CA 104; 122; MTCW

Valle-Inclan, Ramon (Maria) del
1866-1936 .... TCLC 5; HLC
See also CA 106; DLB 134

Vallejo, Antonio Buero
See Buero Vallejo, Antonio

Vallejo, Cesar (Abraham)
1892-1938 .... TCLC 3, 56; HLC
See also CA 105; HW

Valle Y Pena, Ramon del
See Valle-Inclan, Ramon (Maria) del

Van Ash, Cay 1918- .... CLC 34

Vanbrugh, Sir John 1664-1726 ...... LC 21
See also DLB 80

Van Campen, Karl
See Campbell, John W(ood, Jr.)

Vance, Gerald
See Silverberg, Robert

Vance, Jack .... CLC 35
See also Vance, John Holbrook
See also DLB 8

Vance, John Holbrook 1916-
See Queen, Ellery; Vance, Jack
See also CA 29-32R; CANR 17; MTCW

Van Den Bogarde, Derek Jules Gaspard Ulric
Niven 1921-
See Bogarde, Dirk
See also CA 77-80

Vandenburgh, Jane .... CLC 59

Vanderhaeghe, Guy 1951- .... CLC 41
See also CA 113

van der Post, Laurens (Jan) 1906- ... CLC 5
See also CA 5-8R; CANR 35

van de Wetering, Janwillem 1931- .. CLC 47
See also CA 49-52; CANR 4

Van Dine, S. S. .... TCLC 23
See also Wright, Willard Huntington

Van Doren, Carl (Clinton)
1885-1950 .... TCLC 18
See also CA 111

Van Doren, Mark 1894-1972..... CLC 6, 10
See also CA 1-4R; 37-40R; CANR 3;
DLB 45; MTCW

Van Druten, John (William)
1901-1957 .... TCLC 2
See also CA 104; DLB 10

Van Duyn, Mona (Jane)
1921- .... CLC 3, 7, 63
See also CA 9-12R; CANR 7, 38; DLB 5

Van Dyne, Edith
See Baum, L(yman) Frank

van Itallie, Jean-Claude 1936-....... CLC 3
See also CA 45-48; CAAS 2; CANR 1, 48;
DLB 7

van Ostaijen, Paul 1896-1928 ..... TCLC 33

Van Peebles, Melvin 1932- ...... CLC 2, 20
See also BW 2; CA 85-88; CANR 27

Vansittart, Peter 1920-............ CLC 42
See also CA 1-4R; CANR 3, 49

Van Vechten, Carl 1880-1964 ...... CLC 33
See also CA 89-92; DLB 4, 9, 51

Van Vogt, A(lfred) E(lton) 1912-..... CLC 1
See also CA 21-24R; CANR 28; DLB 8;
SATA 14

Varda, Agnes 1928- .... CLC 16
See also CA 116; 122

Vargas Llosa, (Jorge) Mario (Pedro)
1936- .... CLC 3, 6, 9, 10, 15, 31, 42, 85;
DA; DAB; HLC
See also CA 73-76; CANR 18, 32, 42;
DLB 145; HW; MTCW

Vasiliu, Gheorghe 1881-1957
See Bacovia, George
See also CA 123

Vassa, Gustavus
See Equiano, Olaudah

Vassilikos, Vassilis 1933-......... CLC 4, 8
See also CA 81-84

Vaughan, Henry 1621-1695 .... LC 27
See also DLB 131

Vaughn, Stephanie................ CLC 62

Vazov, Ivan (Minchov)
1850-1921 .... TCLC 25
See also CA 121; DLB 147

Veblen, Thorstein (Bunde)
1857-1929 .... TCLC 31
See also CA 115

Vega, Lope de 1562-1635........... LC 23

Venison, Alfred
See Pound, Ezra (Weston Loomis)

Verdi, Marie de
See Mencken, H(enry) L(ouis)

Verdu, Matilde
See Cela, Camilo Jose

Verga, Giovanni (Carmelo)
1840-1922 .... TCLC 3; SSC 21
See also CA 104; 123

Vergil
70B.C.-19B.C...... CMLC 9; DA; DAB;
PC 12

Verhaeren, Emile (Adolphe Gustave)
1855-1916 .... TCLC 12
See also CA 109

Verlaine, Paul (Marie)
1844-1896 .... NCLC 2, 51; PC 2

Verne, Jules (Gabriel)
1828-1905 .... TCLC 6, 52
See also CA 110; 131; DLB 123; JRDA;
MAICYA; SATA 21

Very, Jones 1813-1880........... NCLC 9
See also DLB 1

Vesaas, Tarjei 1897-1970......... CLC 48
See also CA 29-32R

Vialis, Gaston
See Simenon, Georges (Jacques Christian)

Vian, Boris 1920-1959 .... TCLC 9
See also CA 106; DLB 72

Viaud, (Louis Marie) Julien 1850-1923
See Loti, Pierre
See also CA 107

Vicar, Henry
See Felsen, Henry Gregor

Vicker, Angus
See Felsen, Henry Gregor

Vidal, Gore
1925- ..... CLC 2, 4, 6, 8, 10, 22, 33, 72
See also AITN 1; BEST 90:2; CA 5-8R;
CANR 13, 45; DLB 6, 152; MTCW

Viereck, Peter (Robert Edwin)
1916- .... CLC 4
See also CA 1-4R; CANR 1, 47; DLB 5

Vigny, Alfred (Victor) de
1797-1863 .... NCLC 7
See also DLB 119

Vilakazi, Benedict Wallet
1906-1947 .... TCLC 37

Villiers de l'Isle Adam, Jean Marie Mathias
Philippe Auguste Comte
1838-1889 .... NCLC 3; SSC 14
See also DLB 123

Villon, Francois 1431-1463(?) .... PC 13

Vinci, Leonardo da 1452-1519....... LC 12

Vine, Barbara .... CLC 50
See also Rendell, Ruth (Barbara)
See also BEST 90:4

Vinge, Joan D(ennison) 1948-...... CLC 30
See also CA 93-96; SATA 36

Violis, G.
See Simenon, Georges (Jacques Christian)

Visconti, Luchino 1906-1976....... CLC 16
See also CA 81-84; 65-68; CANR 39

Vittorini, Elio 1908-1966...... CLC 6, 9, 14
See also CA 133; 25-28R

Vizinczey, Stephen 1933-.......... CLC 40
See also CA 128

Vliet, R(ussell) G(ordon)
1929-1984 .... CLC 22
See also CA 37-40R; 112; CANR 18

Vogau, Boris Andreyevich 1894-1937(?)
See Pilnyak, Boris
See also CA 123

Vogel, Paula A(nne) 1951-........ CLC 76
See also CA 108

Voight, Ellen Bryant 1943- .... CLC 54
See also CA 69-72; CANR 11, 29; DLB 120

Voigt, Cynthia 1942- .... CLC 30
See also AAYA 3; CA 106; CANR 18, 37,
40; CLR 13; JRDA; MAICYA;
SATA 48, 79; SATA-Brief 33

Voinovich, Vladimir (Nikolaevich)
1932- .... CLC 10, 49
See also CA 81-84; CAAS 12; CANR 33;
MTCW

Vollmann, William T. 1959-........ CLC 89
See also CA 134

Voloshinov, V. N.
See Bakhtin, Mikhail Mikhailovich

Voltaire
1694-1778 . . . . LC 14; DA; DAB;
SSC 12; WLC

von Aue, Hartmann 1170-1210 . . . **CMLC 15**

von Daeniken, Erich 1935- . . . . **CLC 30**
See also AITN 1; CA 37-40R; CANR 17,
44

von Daniken, Erich
See von Daeniken, Erich

von Heidenstam, (Carl Gustaf) Verner
See Heidenstam, (Carl Gustaf) Verner von

von Heyse, Paul (Johann Ludwig)
See Heyse, Paul (Johann Ludwig von)

von Hofmannsthal, Hugo
See Hofmannsthal, Hugo von

von Horvath, Odon
See Horvath, Oedoen von

von Horvath, Oedoen
See Horvath, Oedoen von

von Liliencron, (Friedrich Adolf Axel) Detlev
See Liliencron, (Friedrich Adolf Axel)
Detlev von

Vonnegut, Kurt, Jr.
1922- . . . . . . CLC 1, 2, 3, 4, 5, 8, 12, 22,
40, 60; DA; DAB; SSC 8; WLC
See also AAYA 6; AITN 1; BEST 90:4;
CA 1-4R; CANR 1, 25, 49;
CDALB 1968-1988; DLB 2, 8, 152;
DLBD 3; DLBY 80; MTCW

Von Rachen, Kurt
See Hubbard, L(afayette) Ron(ald)

von Rezzori (d'Arezzo), Gregor
See Rezzori (d'Arezzo), Gregor von

von Sternberg, Josef
See Sternberg, Josef von

Vorster, Gordon 1924- . . . . **CLC 34**
See also CA 133

Vosce, Trudie
See Ozick, Cynthia

Voznesensky, Andrei (Andreievich)
1933- . . . . CLC 1, 15, 57
See also CA 89-92; CANR 37; MTCW

Waddington, Miriam 1917- . . . . **CLC 28**
See also CA 21-24R; CANR 12, 30;
DLB 68

Wagman, Fredrica 1937- . . . . **CLC 7**
See also CA 97-100

Wagner, Richard 1813-1883 . . . . **NCLC 9**
See also DLB 129

Wagner-Martin, Linda 1936- . . . . **CLC 50**

Wagoner, David (Russell)
1926- . . . . CLC 3, 5, 15
See also CA 1-4R; CAAS 3; CANR 2;
DLB 5; SATA 14

Wah, Fred(erick James) 1939- . . . . . . **CLC 44**
See also CA 107; 141; DLB 60

Wahloo, Per 1926-1975 . . . . **CLC 7**
See also CA 61-64

Wahloo, Peter
See Wahloo, Per

Wain, John (Barrington)
1925-1994 . . . . CLC 2, 11, 15, 46
See also CA 5-8R; 145; CAAS 4; CANR 23;
CDBLB 1960 to Present; DLB 15, 27,
139, 155; MTCW

Wajda, Andrzej 1926- . . . . **CLC 16**
See also CA 102

Wakefield, Dan 1932- . . . . **CLC 7**
See also CA 21-24R; CAAS 7

Wakoski, Diane
1937- . . . . CLC 2, 4, 7, 9, 11, 40
See also CA 13-16R; CAAS 1; CANR 9;
DLB 5

Wakoski-Sherbell, Diane
See Wakoski, Diane

Walcott, Derek (Alton)
1930- . . . . CLC 2, 4, 9, 14, 25, 42, 67, 76;
BLC; DAB
See also BW 2; CA 89-92; CANR 26, 47;
DLB 117; DLBY 81; MTCW

Waldman, Anne 1945- . . . . **CLC 7**
See also CA 37-40R; CAAS 17; CANR 34;
DLB 16

Waldo, E. Hunter
See Sturgeon, Theodore (Hamilton)

Waldo, Edward Hamilton
See Sturgeon, Theodore (Hamilton)

Walker, Alice (Malsenior)
1944- . . . . CLC 5, 6, 9, 19, 27, 46, 58;
BLC; DA; DAB; SSC 5
See also AAYA 3; BEST 89:4; BW 2;
CA 37-40R; CANR 9, 27, 49;
CDALB 1968-1988; DLB 6, 33, 143;
MTCW; SATA 31

Walker, David Harry 1911-1992 . . . . **CLC 14**
See also CA 1-4R; 137; CANR 1; SATA 8;
SATA-Obit 71

Walker, Edward Joseph 1934-
See Walker, Ted
See also CA 21-24R; CANR 12, 28

Walker, George F.
1947- . . . . CLC 44, 61; DAB
See also CA 103; CANR 21, 43; DLB 60

Walker, Joseph A. 1935- . . . . **CLC 19**
See also BW 1; CA 89-92; CANR 26;
DLB 38

Walker, Margaret (Abigail)
1915- . . . . CLC 1, 6; BLC
See also BW 2; CA 73-76; CANR 26;
DLB 76, 152; MTCW

Walker, Ted . . . . **CLC 13**
See also Walker, Edward Joseph
See also DLB 40

Wallace, David Foster 1962- . . . . **CLC 50**
See also CA 132

Wallace, Dexter
See Masters, Edgar Lee

Wallace, (Richard Horatio) Edgar
1875-1932 . . . . **TCLC 57**
See also CA 115; DLB 70

Wallace, Irving 1916-1990 . . . . . . **CLC 7, 13**
See also AITN 1; CA 1-4R; 132; CAAS 1;
CANR 1, 27; MTCW

Wallant, Edward Lewis
1926-1962 . . . . CLC 5, 10
See also CA 1-4R; CANR 22; DLB 2, 28,
143; MTCW

Walley, Byron
See Card, Orson Scott

Walpole, Horace 1717-1797 . . . . **LC 2**
See also DLB 39, 104

Walpole, Hugh (Seymour)
1884-1941 . . . . **TCLC 5**
See also CA 104; DLB 34

Walser, Martin 1927- . . . . **CLC 27**
See also CA 57-60; CANR 8, 46; DLB 75,
124

Walser, Robert
1878-1956 . . . . TCLC 18; SSC 20
See also CA 118; DLB 66

Walsh, Jill Paton . . . . **CLC 35**
See also Paton Walsh, Gillian
See also AAYA 11; CLR 2; SAAS 3

Walter, Villiam Christian
See Andersen, Hans Christian

Wambaugh, Joseph (Aloysius, Jr.)
1937- . . . . CLC 3, 18
See also AITN 1; BEST 89:3; CA 33-36R;
CANR 42; DLB 6; DLBY 83; MTCW

Ward, Arthur Henry Sarsfield 1883-1959
See Rohmer, Sax
See also CA 108

Ward, Douglas Turner 1930- . . . . **CLC 19**
See also BW 1; CA 81-84; CANR 27;
DLB 7, 38

Ward, Mary Augusta
See Ward, Mrs. Humphry

Ward, Mrs. Humphry
1851-1920 . . . . **TCLC 55**
See also DLB 18

Ward, Peter
See Faust, Frederick (Schiller)

Warhol, Andy 1928(?)-1987 . . . . **CLC 20**
See also AAYA 12; BEST 89:4; CA 89-92;
121; CANR 34

Warner, Francis (Robert le Plastrier)
1937- . . . . **CLC 14**
See also CA 53-56; CANR 11

Warner, Marina 1946- . . . . **CLC 59**
See also CA 65-68; CANR 21

Warner, Rex (Ernest) 1905-1986 . . . . **CLC 45**
See also CA 89-92; 119; DLB 15

Warner, Susan (Bogert)
1819-1885 . . . . **NCLC 31**
See also DLB 3, 42

Warner, Sylvia (Constance) Ashton
See Ashton-Warner, Sylvia (Constance)

Warner, Sylvia Townsend
1893-1978 . . . . CLC 7, 19
See also CA 61-64; 77-80; CANR 16;
DLB 34, 139; MTCW

Warren, Mercy Otis 1728-1814 . . . **NCLC 13**
See also DLB 31

Warren, Robert Penn
1905-1989 .... CLC 1, 4, 6, 8, 10, 13, 18,
39, 53, 59; DA; DAB; SSC 4; WLC
See also AITN 1; CA 13-16R; 129;
CANR 10, 47; CDALB 1968-1988;
DLB 2, 48, 152; DLBY 80, 89; MTCW;
SATA 46; SATA-Obit 63

Warshofsky, Isaac
See Singer, Isaac Bashevis

Warton, Thomas 1728-1790 .... LC 15
See also DLB 104, 109

Waruk, Kona
See Harris, (Theodore) Wilson

Warung, Price 1855-1911 .... TCLC 45

Warwick, Jarvis
See Garner, Hugh

Washington, Alex
See Harris, Mark

Washington, Booker T(aliaferro)
1856-1915 .... TCLC 10; BLC
See also BW 1; CA 114; 125; SATA 28

Washington, George 1732-1799 ...... LC 25
See also DLB 31

Wassermann, (Karl) Jakob
1873-1934 .... TCLC 6
See also CA 104; DLB 66

Wasserstein, Wendy
1950- .... CLC 32, 59, 90; DC 4
See also CA 121; 129; CABS 3

Waterhouse, Keith (Spencer)
1929- .... CLC 47
See also CA 5-8R; CANR 38; DLB 13, 15;
MTCW

Waters, Frank (Joseph) 1902- ...... CLC 88
See also CA 5-8R; CAAS 13; CANR 3, 18;
DLBY 86

Waters, Roger 1944- .... CLC 35

Watkins, Frances Ellen
See Harper, Frances Ellen Watkins

Watkins, Gerrold
See Malzberg, Barry N(athaniel)

Watkins, Paul 1964- .... CLC 55
See also CA 132

Watkins, Vernon Phillips
1906-1967 .... CLC 43
See also CA 9-10; 25-28R; CAP 1; DLB 20

Watson, Irving S.
See Mencken, H(enry) L(ouis)

Watson, John H.
See Farmer, Philip Jose

Watson, Richard F.
See Silverberg, Robert

Waugh, Auberon (Alexander) 1939- .. CLC 7
See also CA 45-48; CANR 6, 22; DLB 14

Waugh, Evelyn (Arthur St. John)
1903-1966 ...... CLC 1, 3, 8, 13, 19, 27,
44; DA; DAB; WLC
See also CA 85-88; 25-28R; CANR 22;
CDBLB 1914-1945; DLB 15; MTCW

Waugh, Harriet 1944- .... CLC 6
See also CA 85-88; CANR 22

Ways, C. R.
See Blount, Roy (Alton), Jr.

Waystaff, Simon
See Swift, Jonathan

Webb, (Martha) Beatrice (Potter)
1858-1943 .... TCLC 22
See also Potter, Beatrice
See also CA 117

Webb, Charles (Richard) 1939- ...... CLC 7
See also CA 25-28R

Webb, James H(enry), Jr. 1946- .... CLC 22
See also CA 81-84

Webb, Mary (Gladys Meredith)
1881-1927 .... TCLC 24
See also CA 123; DLB 34

Webb, Mrs. Sidney
See Webb, (Martha) Beatrice (Potter)

Webb, Phyllis 1927- .... CLC 18
See also CA 104; CANR 23; DLB 53

Webb, Sidney (James)
1859-1947 .... TCLC 22
See also CA 117

Webber, Andrew Lloyd .... CLC 21
See also Lloyd Webber, Andrew

Weber, Lenora Mattingly
1895-1971 .... CLC 12
See also CA 19-20; 29-32R; CAP 1;
SATA 2; SATA-Obit 26

Webster, John 1579(?)-1634(?) .... DC 2
See also CDBLB Before 1660; DA; DAB;
DLB 58; WLC

Webster, Noah 1758-1843 .... NCLC 30

Wedekind, (Benjamin) Frank(lin)
1864-1918 .... TCLC 7
See also CA 104; DLB 118

Weidman, Jerome 1913- .... CLC 7
See also AITN 2; CA 1-4R; CANR 1;
DLB 28

Weil, Simone (Adolphine)
1909-1943 .... TCLC 23
See also CA 117

Weinstein, Nathan
See West, Nathanael

Weinstein, Nathan von Wallenstein
See West, Nathanael

Weir, Peter (Lindsay) 1944- .... CLC 20
See also CA 113; 123

Weiss, Peter (Ulrich)
1916-1982 .... CLC 3, 15, 51
See also CA 45-48; 106; CANR 3; DLB 69,
124

Weiss, Theodore (Russell)
1916- .... CLC 3, 8, 14
See also CA 9-12R; CAAS 2; CANR 46;
DLB 5

Welch, (Maurice) Denton
1915-1948 .... TCLC 22
See also CA 121; 148

Welch, James 1940- .... CLC 6, 14, 52
See also CA 85-88; CANR 42; NNAL

Weldon, Fay
1933- .... CLC 6, 9, 11, 19, 36, 59
See also CA 21-24R; CANR 16, 46;
CDBLB 1960 to Present; DLB 14;
MTCW

Wellek, Rene 1903- .... CLC 28
See also CA 5-8R; CAAS 7; CANR 8;
DLB 63

Weller, Michael 1942- .... CLC 10, 53
See also CA 85-88

Weller, Paul 1958- .... CLC 26

Wellershoff, Dieter 1925- .... CLC 46
See also CA 89-92; CANR 16, 37

Welles, (George) Orson
1915-1985 .... CLC 20, 80
See also CA 93-96; 117

Wellman, Mac 1945- .... CLC 65

Wellman, Manly Wade 1903-1986 .. CLC 49
See also CA 1-4R; 118; CANR 6, 16, 44;
SATA 6; SATA-Obit 47

Wells, Carolyn 1869(?)-1942 ...... TCLC 35
See also CA 113; DLB 11

Wells, H(erbert) G(eorge)
1866-1946 .... TCLC 6, 12, 19; DA;
DAB; SSC 6; WLC
See also CA 110; 121; CDBLB 1914-1945;
DLB 34, 70, 156; MTCW; SATA 20

Wells, Rosemary 1943- .... CLC 12
See also AAYA 13; CA 85-88; CANR 48;
CLR 16; MAICYA; SAAS 1; SATA 18,
69

Welty, Eudora
1909- ...... CLC 1, 2, 5, 14, 22, 33; DA;
DAB; SSC 1; WLC
See also CA 9-12R; CABS 1; CANR 32;
CDALB 1941-1968; DLB 2, 102, 143;
DLBD 12; DLBY 87; MTCW

Wen I-to 1899-1946 .... TCLC 28

Wentworth, Robert
See Hamilton, Edmond

Werfel, Franz (V.) 1890-1945 ...... TCLC 8
See also CA 104; DLB 81, 124

Wergeland, Henrik Arnold
1808-1845 .... NCLC 5

Wersba, Barbara 1932- .... CLC 30
See also AAYA 2; CA 29-32R; CANR 16,
38; CLR 3; DLB 52; JRDA; MAICYA;
SAAS 2; SATA 1, 58

Wertmueller, Lina 1928- .... CLC 16
See also CA 97-100; CANR 39

Wescott, Glenway 1901-1987 .... CLC 13
See also CA 13-16R; 121; CANR 23;
DLB 4, 9, 102

Wesker, Arnold 1932- .. CLC 3, 5, 42; DAB
See also CA 1-4R; CAAS 7; CANR 1, 33;
CDBLB 1960 to Present; DLB 13;
MTCW

Wesley, Richard (Errol) 1945- .... CLC 7
See also BW 1; CA 57-60; CANR 27;
DLB 38

Wessel, Johan Herman 1742-1785 .... LC 7

West, Anthony (Panther)
1914-1987 .... CLC 50
See also CA 45-48; 124; CANR 3, 19;
DLB 15

West, C. P.
See Wodehouse, P(elham) G(renville)

West, (Mary) Jessamyn
    1902-1984 .... CLC 7, 17
    See also CA 9-12R; 112; CANR 27; DLB 6;
    DLBY 84; MTCW; SATA-Obit 37

West, Morris L(anglo) 1916-..... CLC 6, 33
    See also CA 5-8R; CANR 24, 49; MTCW

West, Nathanael
    1903-1940 ..... TCLC 1, 14, 44; SSC 16
    See also CA 104; 125; CDALB 1929-1941;
    DLB 4, 9, 28; MTCW

West, Owen
    See Koontz, Dean R(ay)

West, Paul 1930- .... CLC 7, 14
    See also CA 13-16R; CAAS 7; CANR 22;
    DLB 14

West, Rebecca 1892-1983 .. CLC 7, 9, 31, 50
    See also CA 5-8R; 109; CANR 19; DLB 36;
    DLBY 83; MTCW

Westall, Robert (Atkinson)
    1929-1993 .... CLC 17
    See also AAYA 12; CA 69-72; 141;
    CANR 18; CLR 13; JRDA; MAICYA;
    SAAS 2; SATA 23, 69; SATA-Obit 75

Westlake, Donald E(dwin)
    1933- .... CLC 7, 33
    See also CA 17-20R; CAAS 13; CANR 16,
    44

Westmacott, Mary
    See Christie, Agatha (Mary Clarissa)

Weston, Allen
    See Norton, Andre

Wetcheek, J. L.
    See Feuchtwanger, Lion

Wetering, Janwillem van de
    See van de Wetering, Janwillem

Wetherell, Elizabeth
    See Warner, Susan (Bogert)

Whalen, Philip 1923- .... CLC 6, 29
    See also CA 9-12R; CANR 5, 39; DLB 16

Wharton, Edith (Newbold Jones)
    1862-1937 ...... TCLC 3, 9, 27, 53; DA;
                          DAB; SSC 6; WLC
    See also CA 104; 132; CDALB 1865-1917;
    DLB 4, 9, 12, 78; MTCW

Wharton, James
    See Mencken, H(enry) L(ouis)

Wharton, William (a pseudonym)
    .... CLC 18, 37
    See also CA 93-96; DLBY 80

Wheatley (Peters), Phillis
    1754(?)-1784 .... LC 3; BLC; DA; PC 3;
                                            WLC
    See also CDALB 1640-1865; DLB 31, 50

Wheelock, John Hall 1886-1978 .... CLC 14
    See also CA 13-16R; 77-80; CANR 14;
    DLB 45

White, E(lwyn) B(rooks)
    1899-1985 .... CLC 10, 34, 39
    See also AITN 2; CA 13-16R; 116;
    CANR 16, 37; CLR 1, 21; DLB 11, 22;
    MAICYA; MTCW; SATA 2, 29;
    SATA-Obit 44

White, Edmund (Valentine III)
    1940- .... CLC 27
    See also AAYA 7; CA 45-48; CANR 3, 19,
    36; MTCW

White, Patrick (Victor Martindale)
    1912-1990 .. CLC 3, 4, 5, 7, 9, 18, 65, 69
    See also CA 81-84; 132; CANR 43; MTCW

White, Phyllis Dorothy James 1920-
    See James, P. D.
    See also CA 21-24R; CANR 17, 43; MTCW

White, T(erence) H(anbury)
    1906-1964 .... CLC 30
    See also CA 73-76; CANR 37; JRDA;
    MAICYA; SATA 12

White, Terence de Vere
    1912-1994 .... CLC 49
    See also CA 49-52; 145; CANR 3

White, Walter F(rancis)
    1893-1955 .... TCLC 15
    See also White, Walter
    See also BW 1; CA 115; 124; DLB 51

White, William Hale 1831-1913
    See Rutherford, Mark
    See also CA 121

Whitehead, E(dward) A(nthony)
    1933- .... CLC 5
    See also CA 65-68

Whitemore, Hugh (John) 1936-..... CLC 37
    See also CA 132

Whitman, Sarah Helen (Power)
    1803-1878 .... NCLC 19
    See also DLB 1

Whitman, Walt(er)
    1819-1892 ..... NCLC 4, 31; DA; DAB;
                                    PC 3; WLC
    See also CDALB 1640-1865; DLB 3, 64;
    SATA 20

Whitney, Phyllis A(yame) 1903-.... CLC 42
    See also AITN 2; BEST 90:3; CA 1-4R;
    CANR 3, 25, 38; JRDA; MAICYA;
    SATA 1, 30

Whittemore, (Edward) Reed (Jr.)
    1919- .... CLC 4
    See also CA 9-12R; CAAS 8; CANR 4;
    DLB 5

Whittier, John Greenleaf
    1807-1892 .... NCLC 8
    See also CDALB 1640-1865; DLB 1

Whittlebot, Hernia
    See Coward, Noel (Peirce)

Wicker, Thomas Grey 1926-
    See Wicker, Tom
    See also CA 65-68; CANR 21, 46

Wicker, Tom .... CLC 7
    See also Wicker, Thomas Grey

Wideman, John Edgar
    1941- ..... CLC 5, 34, 36, 67; BLC
    See also BW 2; CA 85-88; CANR 14, 42;
    DLB 33, 143

Wiebe, Rudy (Henry) 1934-... CLC 6, 11, 14
    See also CA 37-40R; CANR 42; DLB 60

Wieland, Christoph Martin
    1733-1813 .... NCLC 17
    See also DLB 97

Wiene, Robert 1881-1938........ TCLC 56

Wieners, John 1934-.............. CLC 7
    See also CA 13-16R; DLB 16

Wiesel, Elie(zer)
    1928- ...... CLC 3, 5, 11, 37; DA; DAB
    See also AAYA 7; AITN 1; CA 5-8R;
    CAAS 4; CANR 8, 40; DLB 83;
    DLBY 87; MTCW; SATA 56

Wiggins, Marianne 1947-......... CLC 57
    See also BEST 89:3; CA 130

Wight, James Alfred 1916-
    See Herriot, James
    See also CA 77-80; SATA 55;
    SATA-Brief 44

Wilbur, Richard (Purdy)
    1921- .... CLC 3, 6, 9, 14, 53; DA; DAB
    See also CA 1-4R; CABS 2; CANR 2, 29;
    DLB 5; MTCW; SATA 9

Wild, Peter 1940-................ CLC 14
    See also CA 37-40R; DLB 5

Wilde, Oscar (Fingal O'Flahertie Wills)
    1854(?)-1900 .... TCLC 1, 8, 23, 41; DA;
                          DAB; SSC 11; WLC
    See also CA 104; 119; CDBLB 1890-1914;
    DLB 10, 19, 34, 57, 141, 156; SATA 24

Wilder, Billy .... CLC 20
    See also Wilder, Samuel
    See also DLB 26

Wilder, Samuel 1906-
    See Wilder, Billy
    See also CA 89-92

Wilder, Thornton (Niven)
    1897-1975 ...... CLC 1, 5, 6, 10, 15, 35,
                          82; DA; DAB; DC 1; WLC
    See also AITN 2; CA 13-16R; 61-64;
    CANR 40; DLB 4, 7, 9, MTCW

Wilding, Michael 1942-........... CLC 73
    See also CA 104; CANR 24, 49

Wiley, Richard 1944-............. CLC 44
    See also CA 121; 129

Wilhelm, Kate .... CLC 7
    See also Wilhelm, Katie Gertrude
    See also CAAS 5; DLB 8

Wilhelm, Katie Gertrude 1928-
    See Wilhelm, Kate
    See also CA 37-40R; CANR 17, 36; MTCW

Wilkins, Mary
    See Freeman, Mary E(leanor) Wilkins

Willard, Nancy 1936-........... CLC 7, 37
    See also CA 89-92; CANR 10, 39; CLR 5;
    DLB 5, 52; MAICYA; MTCW;
    SATA 37, 71; SATA-Brief 30

Williams, C(harles) K(enneth)
    1936- .... CLC 33, 56
    See also CA 37-40R; DLB 5

Williams, Charles
    See Collier, James L(incoln)

Williams, Charles (Walter Stansby)
    1886-1945 .... TCLC 1, 11
    See also CA 104; DLB 100, 153

Williams, (George) Emlyn
    1905-1987 .... CLC 15
    See also CA 104; 123; CANR 36; DLB 10,
    77; MTCW

Williams, Hugo 1942-............. CLC 42
    See also CA 17-20R; CANR 45; DLB 40

Williams, J. Walker
    See Wodehouse, P(elham) G(renville)

Williams, John A(lfred)
1925- .... **CLC 5, 13; BLC**
See also BW 2; CA 53-56; CAAS 3;
CANR 6, 26; DLB 2, 33

Williams, Jonathan (Chamberlain)
1929- .... **CLC 13**
See also CA 9-12R; CAAS 12; CANR 8;
DLB 5

Williams, Joy 1944- .... **CLC 31**
See also CA 41-44R; CANR 22, 48

Williams, Norman 1952- .... **CLC 39**
See also CA 118

Williams, Sherley Anne
1944- .... **CLC 89; BLC**
See also BW 2; CA 73-76; CANR 25;
DLB 41; SATA 78

Williams, Shirley
See Williams, Sherley Anne

Williams, Tennessee
1911-1983 ..... **CLC 1, 2, 5, 7, 8, 11, 15,
19, 30, 39, 45, 71; DA; DAB; DC 4; WLC**
See also AITN 1, 2; CA 5-8R; 108;
CABS 3; CANR 31; CDALB 1941-1968;
DLB 7; DLBD 4; DLBY 83; MTCW

Williams, Thomas (Alonzo)
1926-1990 .... **CLC 14**
See also CA 1-4R; 132; CANR 2

Williams, William C.
See Williams, William Carlos

Williams, William Carlos
1883-1963 .... **CLC 1, 2, 5, 9, 13, 22, 42,
67; DA; DAB; PC 7**
See also CA 89-92; CANR 34;
CDALB 1917-1929; DLB 4, 16, 54, 86;
MTCW

Williamson, David (Keith) 1942- .... **CLC 56**
See also CA 103; CANR 41

Williamson, Ellen Douglas 1905-1984
See Douglas, Ellen
See also CA 17-20R; 114; CANR 39

Williamson, Jack................. **CLC 29**
See also Williamson, John Stewart
See also CAAS 8; DLB 8

Williamson, John Stewart 1908-
See Williamson, Jack
See also CA 17-20R; CANR 23

Willie, Frederick
See Lovecraft, H(oward) P(hillips)

Willingham, Calder (Baynard, Jr.)
1922-1995 .... **CLC 5, 51**
See also CA 5-8R; 147; CANR 3; DLB 2,
44; MTCW

Willis, Charles
See Clarke, Arthur C(harles)

Willy
See Colette, (Sidonie-Gabrielle)

Willy, Colette
See Colette, (Sidonie-Gabrielle)

Wilson, A(ndrew) N(orman) 1950- .. **CLC 33**
See also CA 112; 122; DLB 14, 155

Wilson, Angus (Frank Johnstone)
1913-1991 .. **CLC 2, 3, 5, 25, 34; SSC 21**
See also CA 5-8R; 134; CANR 21; DLB 15,
139, 155; MTCW

Wilson, August
1945- ...... **CLC 39, 50, 63; BLC; DA;
DAB; DC 2**
See also BW 2; CA 115; 122; CANR 42;
MTCW

Wilson, Brian 1942- .... **CLC 12**

Wilson, Colin 1931- .... **CLC 3, 14**
See also CA 1-4R; CAAS 5; CANR 1, 22,
33; DLB 14; MTCW

Wilson, Dirk
See Pohl, Frederik

Wilson, Edmund
1895-1972 .... **CLC 1, 2, 3, 8, 24**
See also CA 1-4R; 37-40R; CANR 1, 46;
DLB 63; MTCW

Wilson, Ethel Davis (Bryant)
1888(?)-1980 .... **CLC 13**
See also CA 102; DLB 68; MTCW

Wilson, John 1785-1854......... **NCLC 5**

Wilson, John (Anthony) Burgess 1917-1993
See Burgess, Anthony
See also CA 1-4R; 143; CANR 2, 46;
MTCW

Wilson, Lanford 1937-....... **CLC 7, 14, 36**
See also CA 17-20R; CABS 3; CANR 45;
DLB 7

Wilson, Robert M. 1944-........ **CLC 7, 9**
See also CA 49-52; CANR 2, 41; MTCW

Wilson, Robert McLiam 1964- ..... **CLC 59**
See also CA 132

Wilson, Sloan 1920- .... **CLC 32**
See also CA 1-4R; CANR 1, 44

Wilson, Snoo 1948-............... **CLC 33**
See also CA 69-72

Wilson, William S(mith) 1932- ..... **CLC 49**
See also CA 81-84

Winchilsea, Anne (Kingsmill) Finch Counte
1661-1720 .... **LC 3**

Windham, Basil
See Wodehouse, P(elham) G(renville)

Wingrove, David (John) 1954-...... **CLC 68**
See also CA 133

Winters, Janet Lewis .... **CLC 41**
See also Lewis, Janet
See also DLBY 87

Winters, (Arthur) Yvor
1900-1968 .... **CLC 4, 8, 32**
See also CA 11-12; 25-28R; CAP 1;
DLB 48; MTCW

Winterson, Jeanette 1959-........ **CLC 64**
See also CA 136

Winthrop, John 1588-1649......... **LC 31**
See also DLB 24, 30

Wiseman, Frederick 1930-........ **CLC 20**

Wister, Owen 1860-1938 .... **TCLC 21**
See also CA 108; DLB 9, 78; SATA 62

Witkacy
See Witkiewicz, Stanislaw Ignacy

Witkiewicz, Stanislaw Ignacy
1885-1939 .... **TCLC 8**
See also CA 105

Wittgenstein, Ludwig (Josef Johann)
1889-1951 .... **TCLC 59**
See also CA 113

Wittig, Monique 1935(?)-......... **CLC 22**
See also CA 116; 135; DLB 83

Wittlin, Jozef 1896-1976 .... **CLC 25**
See also CA 49-52; 65-68; CANR 3

Wodehouse, P(elham) G(renville)
1881-1975 ... **CLC 1, 2, 5, 10, 22; DAB;
SSC 2**
See also AITN 2; CA 45-48; 57-60;
CANR 3, 33; CDBLB 1914-1945;
DLB 34; MTCW; SATA 22

Woiwode, L.
See Woiwode, Larry (Alfred)

Woiwode, Larry (Alfred) 1941-... **CLC 6, 10**
See also CA 73-76; CANR 16; DLB 6

Wojciechowska, Maia (Teresa)
1927- .... **CLC 26**
See also AAYA 8; CA 9-12R; CANR 4, 41;
CLR 1; JRDA; MAICYA; SAAS 1;
SATA 1, 28, 83

Wolf, Christa 1929- .... **CLC 14, 29, 58**
See also CA 85-88; CANR 45; DLB 75;
MTCW

Wolfe, Gene (Rodman) 1931-...... **CLC 25**
See also CA 57-60; CAAS 9; CANR 6, 32;
DLB 8

Wolfe, George C. 1954- .... **CLC 49**

Wolfe, Thomas (Clayton)
1900-1938 ..... **TCLC 4, 13, 29, 61; DA;
DAB; WLC**
See also CA 104; 132; CDALB 1929-1941;
DLB 9, 102; DLBD 2; DLBY 85; MTCW

Wolfe, Thomas Kennerly, Jr. 1931-
See Wolfe, Tom
See also CA 13-16R; CANR 9, 33; MTCW

Wolfe, Tom .... **CLC 1, 2, 9, 15, 35, 51**
See also Wolfe, Thomas Kennerly, Jr.
See also AAYA 8; AITN 2; BEST 89:1;
DLB 152

Wolff, Geoffrey (Ansell) 1937- ..... **CLC 41**
See also CA 29-32R; CANR 29, 43

Wolff, Sonia
See Levitin, Sonia (Wolff)

Wolff, Tobias (Jonathan Ansell)
1945- .... **CLC 39, 64**
See also BEST 90:2; CA 114; 117;
CAAS 22; DLB 130

Wolfram von Eschenbach
c. 1170-c. 1220 .... **CMLC 5**
See also DLB 138

Wolitzer, Hilma 1930-............. **CLC 17**
See also CA 65-68; CANR 18, 40; SATA 31

Wollstonecraft, Mary 1759-1797...... **LC 5**
See also CDBLB 1789-1832; DLB 39, 104

Wonder, Stevie .... **CLC 12**
See also Morris, Steveland Judkins

Wong, Jade Snow 1922-........... **CLC 17**
See also CA 109

Woodcott, Keith
See Brunner, John (Kilian Houston)

Woodruff, Robert W.
See Mencken, H(enry) L(ouis)

Woolf, (Adeline) Virginia
1882-1941 . . . . **TCLC 1, 5, 20, 43, 56;**
DA; DAB; SSC 7; WLC
See also CA 104; 130; CDBLB 1914-1945;
DLB 36, 100; DLBD 10; MTCW

Woollcott, Alexander (Humphreys)
1887-1943 . . . . **TCLC 5**
See also CA 105; DLB 29

Woolrich, Cornell 1903-1968 . . . . . . **CLC 77**
See also Hopley-Woolrich, Cornell George

Wordsworth, Dorothy
1771-1855 . . . . **NCLC 25**
See also DLB 107

Wordsworth, William
1770-1850 . . . . **NCLC 12, 38; DA; DAB;**
PC 4; WLC
See also CDBLB 1789-1832; DLB 93, 107

Wouk, Herman 1915- . . . . **CLC 1, 9, 38**
See also CA 5-8R; CANR 6, 33; DLBY 82;
MTCW

Wright, Charles (Penzel, Jr.)
1935- . . . . **CLC 6, 13, 28**
See also CA 29-32R; CAAS 7; CANR 23,
36; DLBY 82; MTCW

Wright, Charles Stevenson
1932- . . . . **CLC 49; BLC 3**
See also BW 1; CA 9-12R; CANR 26;
DLB 33

Wright, Jack R.
See Harris, Mark

Wright, James (Arlington)
1927-1980 . . . . **CLC 3, 5, 10, 28**
See also AITN 2; CA 49-52; 97-100;
CANR 4, 34; DLB 5; MTCW

Wright, Judith (Arandell)
1915- . . . . **CLC 11, 53**
See also CA 13-16R; CANR 31; MTCW;
SATA 14

Wright, L(aurali) R. 1939- . . . . **CLC 44**
See also CA 138

Wright, Richard (Nathaniel)
1908-1960 . . . . **CLC 1, 3, 4, 9, 14, 21, 48,**
74; BLC; DA; DAB; SSC 2; WLC
See also AAYA 5; BW 1; CA 108;
CDALB 1929-1941; DLB 76, 102;
DLBD 2; MTCW

Wright, Richard B(ruce) 1937- . . . . . . **CLC 6**
See also CA 85-88; DLB 53

Wright, Rick 1945- . . . . **CLC 35**

Wright, Rowland
See Wells, Carolyn

Wright, Stephen Caldwell 1946- . . . . **CLC 33**
See also BW 2

Wright, Willard Huntington 1888-1939
See Van Dine, S. S.
See also CA 115

Wright, William 1930- . . . . **CLC 44**
See also CA 53-56; CANR 7, 23

Wroth, LadyMary 1587-1653(?) . . . . . **LC 30**
See also DLB 121

Wu Ch'eng-en 1500(?)-1582(?) . . . . **LC 7**

Wu Ching-tzu 1701-1754 . . . . **LC 2**

Wurlitzer, Rudolph 1938(?)- . . . **CLC 2, 4, 15**
See also CA 85-88

Wycherley, William 1641-1715 . . . . **LC 8, 21**
See also CDBLB 1660-1789; DLB 80

Wylie, Elinor (Morton Hoyt)
1885-1928 . . . . **TCLC 8**
See also CA 105; DLB 9, 45

Wylie, Philip (Gordon) 1902-1971 . . . **CLC 43**
See also CA 21-22; 33-36R; CAP 2; DLB 9

Wyndham, John . . . . **CLC 19**
See also Harris, John (Wyndham Parkes
Lucas) Beynon

Wyss, Johann David Von
1743-1818 . . . . **NCLC 10**
See also JRDA; MAICYA; SATA 29;
SATA-Brief 27

Yakumo Koizumi
See Hearn, (Patricio) Lafcadio (Tessima
Carlos)

Yanez, Jose Donoso
See Donoso (Yanez), Jose

Yanovsky, Basile S.
See Yanovsky, V(assily) S(emenovich)

Yanovsky, V(assily) S(emenovich)
1906-1989 . . . . **CLC 2, 18**
See also CA 97-100; 129

Yates, Richard 1926-1992 . . . . . **CLC 7, 8, 23**
See also CA 5-8R; 139; CANR 10, 43;
DLB 2; DLBY 81, 92

Yeats, W. B.
See Yeats, William Butler

Yeats, William Butler
1865-1939 . . . . . **TCLC 1, 11, 18, 31; DA;**
DAB; WLC
See also CA 104; 127; CANR 45;
CDBLB 1890-1914; DLB 10, 19, 98, 156;
MTCW

Yehoshua, A(braham) B.
1936- . . . . **CLC 13, 31**
See also CA 33-36R; CANR 43

Yep, Laurence Michael 1948- . . . . . . **CLC 35**
See also AAYA 5; CA 49-52; CANR 1, 46;
CLR 3, 17; DLB 52; JRDA; MAICYA;
SATA 7, 69

Yerby, Frank G(arvin)
1916-1991 . . . . **CLC 1, 7, 22; BLC**
See also BW 1; CA 9-12R; 136; CANR 16;
DLB 76; MTCW

Yesenin, Sergei Alexandrovich
See Esenin, Sergei (Alexandrovich)

Yevtushenko, Yevgeny (Alexandrovich)
1933- . . . . **CLC 1, 3, 13, 26, 51**
See also CA 81-84; CANR 33; MTCW

Yezierska, Anzia 1885(?)-1970 . . . . . **CLC 46**
See also CA 126; 89-92; DLB 28; MTCW

Yglesias, Helen 1915- . . . . **CLC 7, 22**
See also CA 37-40R; CAAS 20; CANR 15;
MTCW

Yokomitsu Riichi 1898-1947 . . . . . . **TCLC 47**

Yonge, Charlotte (Mary)
1823-1901 . . . . **TCLC 48**
See also CA 109; DLB 18; SATA 17

York, Jeremy
See Creasey, John

York, Simon
See Heinlein, Robert A(nson)

Yorke, Henry Vincent 1905-1974 . . . **CLC 13**
See also Green, Henry
See also CA 85-88; 49-52

Yosano Akiko 1878-1942 . . **TCLC 59; PC 11**

Yoshimoto, Banana . . . . **CLC 84**
See also Yoshimoto, Mahoko

Yoshimoto, Mahoko 1964-
See Yoshimoto, Banana
See also CA 144

Young, Al(bert James)
1939- . . . . **CLC 19; BLC**
See also BW 2; CA 29-32R; CANR 26;
DLB 33

Young, Andrew (John) 1885-1971 . . . . **CLC 5**
See also CA 5-8R; CANR 7, 29

Young, Collier
See Bloch, Robert (Albert)

Young, Edward 1683-1765 . . . . **LC 3**
See also DLB 95

Young, Marguerite 1909- . . . . **CLC 82**
See also CA 13-16; CAP 1

Young, Neil 1945- . . . . **CLC 17**
See also CA 110

Yourcenar, Marguerite
1903-1987 . . . . **CLC 19, 38, 50, 87**
See also CA 69-72; CANR 23; DLB 72;
DLBY 88; MTCW

Yurick, Sol 1925- . . . . **CLC 6**
See also CA 13-16R; CANR 25

Zabolotskii, Nikolai Alekseevich
1903-1958 . . . . **TCLC 52**
See also CA 116

Zamiatin, Yevgenii
See Zamyatin, Evgeny Ivanovich

Zamora, Bernice (B. Ortiz)
1938- . . . . **CLC 89; HLC**
See also DLB 82; HW

Zamyatin, Evgeny Ivanovich
1884-1937 . . . . **TCLC 8, 37**
See also CA 105

Zangwill, Israel 1864-1926 . . . . **TCLC 16**
See also CA 109; DLB 10, 135

Zappa, Francis Vincent, Jr. 1940-1993
See Zappa, Frank
See also CA 108; 143

Zappa, Frank . . . . **CLC 17**
See also Zappa, Francis Vincent, Jr.

Zaturenska, Marya 1902-1982 . . . . **CLC 6, 11**
See also CA 13-16R; 105; CANR 22

Zelazny, Roger (Joseph)
1937-1995 . . . . **CLC 21**
See also AAYA 7; CA 21-24R; 148;
CANR 26; DLB 8; MTCW; SATA 57;
SATA-Brief 39

Zhdanov, Andrei A(lexandrovich)
1896-1948 . . . . **TCLC 18**
See also CA 117

Zhukovsky, Vasily 1783-1852 . . . . **NCLC 35**

Ziegenhagen, Eric . . . . **CLC 55**

Zimmer, Jill Schary
See Robinson, Jill

Zimmerman, Robert
See Dylan, Bob

Literary Criticism Series
Cumulative Topic Index

This index lists all topic entries in Gale's *Classical and Medieval Literature Criticism, Contemporary Literary Criticism, Literature Criticism from 1400 to 1800, Nineteenth-Century Literature Criticism,* and *Twentieth-Century Literary Criticism.*

Topic Index

Yellow Journalism NCLC 36: 383-456
 overviews, 384-96
 major figures, 396-413

Young Playwrights Festival
 1988–CLC 55: 376-81
 1989–CLC 59: 398-403
 1990–CLC 65: 444-48

Topic Index

NCLC Cumulative Nationality Index

IRISH
- Allingham, William **25**
- Banim, John **13**
- Banim, Michael **13**
- Boucicault, Dion **41**
- Carleton, William **3**
- Croker, John Wilson **10**
- Darley, George **2**
- Edgeworth, Maria **1, 51**
- Ferguson, Samuel **33**
- Griffin, Gerald **7**
- Jameson, Anna **43**
- Le Fanu, Joseph Sheridan **9**
- Lever, Charles (James) **23**
- Maginn, William **8**
- Mangan, James Clarence **27**
- Maturin, Charles Robert **6**
- Moore, Thomas **6**
- Morgan, Lady **29**
- O'Brien, Fitz-James **21**

ITALIAN
- Da Ponte, Lorenzo **50**
- Foscolo, Ugo **8**
- Gozzi, (Conte) Carlo **23**
- Leopardi, (Conte) Giacomo **22**
- Manzoni, Alessandro **29**
- Mazzini, Guiseppe **34**
- Nievo, Ippolito **22**

JAPANESE
- Higuchi Ichiyo **49**
- Motoori, Norinaga **45**

LITHUANIAN
- Mapu, Abraham (ben Jekutiel) **18**

MEXICAN
- Lizardi, Jose Joaquin Fernandez de **30**

NORWEGIAN
- Collett, (Jacobine) Camilla (Wergeland) **22**
- Wergeland, Henrik Arnold **5**

POLISH
- Fredro, Aleksander **8**
- Krasicki, Ignacy **8**
- Krasinski, Zygmunt **4**
- Mickiewicz, Adam **3**
- Norwid, Cyprian Kamil **17**
- Slowacki, Juliusz **15**

ROMANIAN
- Eminescu, Mihail **33**

RUSSIAN
- Aksakov, Sergei Timofeyvich **2**
- Bakunin, Mikhail (Alexandrovich) **25**
- Bashkirtseff, Marie **27**
- Belinski, Vissarion Grigoryevich **5**
- Chernyshevsky, Nikolay Gavrilovich **1**
- Dobrolyubov, Nikolai Alexandrovich **5**
- Dostoevsky, Fedor Mikhailovich **2, 7, 21, 33, 43**
- Gogol, Nikolai (Vasilyevich) **5, 15, 31**
- Goncharov, Ivan Alexandrovich **1**
- Herzen, Aleksandr Ivanovich **10**
- Karamzin, Nikolai Mikhailovich **3**
- Krylov, Ivan Andreevich **1**
- Lermontov, Mikhail Yuryevich **5**
- Leskov, Nikolai (Semyonovich) **25**
- Nekrasov, Nikolai Alekseevich **11**
- Ostrovsky, Alexander **30**
- Pisarev, Dmitry Ivanovich **25**
- Pushkin, Alexander (Sergeyevich) **3, 27**
- Saltykov, Mikhail Evgrafovich **16**
- Smolenskin, Peretz **30**
- Turgenev, Ivan **21**
- Tyutchev, Fyodor **34**
- Zhukovsky, Vasily **35**

SCOTTISH
- Baillie, Joanna **2**
- Beattie, James **25**
- Campbell, Thomas **19**
- Ferrier, Susan (Edmonstone) **8**
- Galt, John **1**
- Hogg, James **4**
- Jeffrey, Francis **33**
- Lockhart, John Gibson **6**
- Mackenzie, Henry **41**
- Oliphant, Margaret (Oliphant Wilson) **11**
- Scott, Walter **15**
- Stevenson, Robert Louis (Balfour) **5, 14**
- Thomson, James, **18**
- Wilson, John **5**

SPANISH
- Alarcon, Pedro Antonio de **1**
- Caballero, Fernan **10**
- Castro, Rosalia de **3**
- Espronceda, Jose de **39**
- Larra (y Sanchez de Castro), Mariano Jose de **17**
- Tamayo y Baus, Manuel **1**
- Zorrilla y Moral, Jose **6**

SWEDISH
- Almqvist, Carl Jonas Love **42**
- Bremer, Fredrika **11**
- Tegner, Esaias **2**

SWISS
- Amiel, Henri Frederic **4**
- Burckhardt, Jacob **49**
- Keller, Gottfried **2**
- Wyss, Johann David Von **10**

Nationality Index